The Watkins
dictionary *of*
RELIGIONS
AND SECULAR FAITHS

Gerald Benedict graduated in Divinity from the University of London, and has a postgraduate diploma from the School of Ecumenical Studies, University of Geneva, and a PhD from the Open Univeristy. His main academic interest is comparative religious philosophy, and after teaching religious studies and philosophy in colleges and universities in Britain, he moved to France. He has won awards for a novel, several short stories, and radio drama for the BBC World Service.

The Watkins
dictionary *of*
RELIGIONS
AND SECULAR FAITHS

Gerald Benedict

WATKINS PUBLISHING
LONDON

Distributed in the USA and Canada by Sterling Publishing Co., Inc.
387 Park Avenue South, New York, NY 10016

This edition first published in the UK and USA 2008 by
Watkins Publishing, Sixth Floor, Castle House,
75–76 Wells Street, London W1T 3QH

1 3 5 7 9 10 8 6 4 2

Designed by Jerry Goldie
Typeset by Dorchester Typesetting Group

Printed and bound in Great Britain

Library of Congress Cataloging-in-Publication Data Available

ISBN 13: 978-1-905857-52-4
ISBN 10: 1-905857-52-7

www.watkinspublishing.co.uk

For information about custom editions, special sales, premium and
corporate purchases, please contact Sterling Special Sales
Department at 800-805-5489 or specialsales@sterlingpub.com.

For

Ralph Biddiscombe
1928–2006

'A great architect is not made by way of a brain, nearly so much as he is made by way of a cultivated, enriched heart.' (Frank Lloyd Wright)

'Architecture of all the arts, is the one that acts most slowly, but most surely, on the soul.' (Ernest Dimnet)

and

Wendy Podmore
1932–2006

'So laugh with me, hold my hand, let us say goodbye,
Say goodbye to meet again.
We meet today, we will meet tomorrow, we meet at the source in every moment,
We meet each other in all forms of life.' (Thich Nhat Hanh)

Contents

Acknowledgements

Thanks are due to …
My editor, Michael, whose unlimited patience, wisdom and encouragement has ensured that the job was completed; Mario Reading who helped hatch the plot, and who, having walked a similar, lexicographic path, steered me in the right direction; Dr David Loy of Xavier University, Cincinnati, whose friendship has never failed to support, and by whose writings I've never failed to be illuminated; Caroline Mann for being so willing to provide the entries on 'Meditation for Children', and 'Visualization for Children'; Penny Stopa for her unrelenting help with the nuts and bolts which, somehow, I always manage to misplace; Barbara Vesey, whose copy-editing gently turned the text into a style acceptable to my publisher; Gillian Holmes, for the comforting and necessary support of her proofreading; Michael D. Jacobson, whose reference library and passion to 'find out', is testimony to his unquenchable thirst for knowledge; Peter Smith, of Masclat-Micros, whose genius with computers has ensured that the impossible took no time at all.

I am grateful to Dr Ramses Seleem, for guidance on Egyptian themes; Dr James Anglin for his insights into the Baha'i; Wim van den Dungen for his translation of the papyrus quoted in the entry on, 'Funerary Practices'.

Particular thanks are offered to the following, for permission to use illustrations, etc.:

K Vipkin for, 'Aum', under the entry 'Om'. **http://www.exoticindia art.com**

Dr Raymond Pfister, for the Fish Profile under the entry, 'Ichthus'. **http://www.icthus.ws**

Kerry Godsall, for her drawing for the entry, 'Lotus'. **http://www. allaboutdrawings.com**

Louré and Johann van Schalkwyk for, 'Ox Herding'. **http://www. emoyeni-retreat.com**

Andrew Woolman, for translations from Latin and Greek texts.

The Open University for the use of their course, AD208, *Man's Religious Quest*.

The support, thoughout, of my wife, Nadège, has been indispensable; her patience in checking ever-changing lists of entries, chronological dates and bibliographic names has made a shared pleasure out of what might have been irksome. I owe a huge debt of gratitude to my daughters, Noémie and Amélie, for letting me try out ideas on them, but also an apology for subjecting them to my enthusiasms for so many 'Eureka' discoveries.

Abbreviations Used in the Text

Religions

A African Religions
AE Ancient European
AME Ancient Middle
East
Ami Amerindian
Az Aztec
B Buddhism
C Chinese
CA Central American
Cel Celtic
Con Confucianism
E Egyptian Religion
G Greek
H Hinduism
I Islam
J Judaism
Ja Jainism
Jap Japanese
Religions
Mes Mesopotamian
Nor Norse
P Pacific Religions
R Roman
S Sikhism
Shin Shintoism
T Taoism
X Christianity
Z Zen
Zo Zoroastrianism

Languages

Amh. Amharic
Arab. Arabic
Aram. Aramaic
Chin. Chinese
Ger. German
Gk. Greek
Heb. Hebrew
Hin. Hindi
Jap. Japanese
Kor. Korean
Lat. Latin
N. Norse
Pal. Pali
Per. Persian
Pun. Punjabi
Skt. Sanskrit
Tib. Tibetan

Others

boldface Indicates
cross-reference
b. Born
BCE Before the
Christian Era
Bibl. biblical
c. *circa*
CE Christian Era
d. Died
K. Koran
KVG. King James
Version of the Bible
NEB. New English
Bible
N.T. New Testament
O.T. Old Testament
RSV. Revised
Standard Version of
the Bible
Tan. Tanakh

Notes
1. Authors and their works referred to in the text are listed alphabetically in the Bibliography.
2. Old Testament quotations are from the Tanakh, the Hebrew Bible. New Testament quotations are from the New English Bible.
3. Quotations from the Koran are from Arthur J. Arberry's translation, Oxford University Press, 1964.

INTRODUCTION

The debate between religion and secularism amounts to one question: Is this life the only one we have? Do we live our lives in the knowledge that death is the final end of consciousness or 'in the hope of a glory to come'?[1] Religion does not, of course, deny death; it denies that death is the *end* of being and affirms that, despite our physical demise, some form of conscious existence continues. For Secularism, death is the sting in the nettle grasped when recognizing our span of life is the measure of our personal existence. According to Dietrich Bonhoeffer, religion celebrates death as 'the supreme festival on the road to freedom'.[2] Secularism, as a Roman epitaph recorded, takes death to be the final state of non-being – *Non fui, fui, non sum, non curo*: 'I was not. I was. I am not. I care not.' The difference is both stark and ultimate.

'Religion' is notoriously difficult to define. Not only does every religious tradition have a different understanding of what the word means, but so also do the different disciplines that study it, be it history, sociology, psychology or philosophy. Wittgenstein's perceptive advice may help to some extent, 'Don't ask what the word means, ask how it is used'[3] The word 'religion' is covered in the Dictionary entry; for the present we can say that it refers to a system of belief in a god or gods or other spiritual beings and to the institutions, rites and practices that are considered indispensable to the fulfilment of their declared goals. Some forms of religion can only be fully developed when every aspect of society is an expression of it; Islam, for example, requires theocracy, while such systems as some African tribal religions, Polynesian and aboriginal religions seem to exist, quite happily, for themselves.

The meaning of the 'secular' is also discussed under its Dictionary entry. Here we can take 'secular' to mean those aspects of thought and society that have been entirely liberated from religious control and influence. Secularism has been a determining part of culture and as such is woven into the fabric of our lives as an attitude which takes no account of transcendental perceptions or values. These attitudes, of course, have hardened into political policies responsible for the secularization of education and health-care and the enforcement of philosophies such as Communism and Nazism.

A developed secular philosophy has been significant in Western culture only relatively recently, but it has always co-existed with religion. Throughout its history, religious institutions have distinguished between the sacred and the secular, not only to identify the different functions of the clergy, but also to distinguish between religious and secular music, courts and governments. In the latter sense, secularism is similar to the French concept of *laïcité*, referring to secular education and the separation of State and Church. The opposing views have resulted in wars and the fiercest political debates in which religious adherents and atheists have confronted each other over every aspect of society and its government.

Religion has always struggled to defend the status quo against secularism's constant demand for radical social, political and ethical change. And yet, neither the philosophy of secularism, nor the process of secularization has any interest in persecuting or displacing religion. A truly secular society simply passes religion by on its way to a different destination.

The ferment of debate generated by these seemingly irreconcilable views has given rise to rich and creative thinking. Religion has made lasting and positive responses to the implications of secularism, reworking its language and doctrines in the search for authentic religious meaning relevant to contemporary society. Secularism, on the other hand, has had to consider that metaphysics is not necessarily incompatible with the knowledge science discloses. Having abandoned the agendas of traditional religion, the secular society has had to come up with alternative perceptions of humanity, the purpose of life, of individual and social potential.

Having, thus, withdrawn from metaphysics, what is secularism left with? The answer is scientific rationalism. This, of course, defines the universe, human beings and their culture, in wholly materialist terms. Theories such as Darwinism and the 'Big Bang' have provided new accounts of the origins of the universe and the human species that dispense with the doctrine of a creator God; humanism provides for millions of people a perfectly adequate ideology from which to live a purposeful and moral life; Socialism and Nationalism have proved to be powerful cohesive forces capable of raising the concept of the State to that of a God. Anthropology reinterpreted religion, its myths and miracles, as a form of social functionalism. Atomic and sub-atomic physics, relativity and quantum theory have considerably advanced our comprehension of space and time. Euclid's view that geometry is inherent in nature and was therefore a part of God's revelation, dominated Western philosophy and science until Einstein told us that geometry, far from being inherent, is an invention of human intellect. However, as already intimated, religion and its secular alternatives are not, necessarily, mutually exclusive.

The abandonment of belief in life continuing after death leaves the secularist with the uncompromising reality of death's democracy. Far from offering conscious survival, anyone, as Hamlet pointed out, could end up as a bung for a hole: 'Alexander died, Alexander was buried, Alexander returneth into dust; the dust is the earth; of earth we make loam and why of that loam, whereto he was converted, might they not stop a beer-barrel.'[4] Given such scientific 'truths', what does secularism do with them? At base, it determines that if our present life is all we have, we must set about making the very best of it. The evolutionary anthropologist Sir Arthur Keith drew up what amounts to a secularist manifesto: 'If men believe, as I do, that this present earth is the only heaven, they will strive all the more to make heaven of it.'[5] In the making of this earthly heaven, the secular society is concerned for morality, ethics, compassion and the quest for a just and stable society, founded on the respect human beings have for each other, without recourse to the idea that we are the bearer of a divine spark or the image of a creator-god, marred by sin and in need of redemption. Samuel Johnson had it that 'All of life is but keeping away the thought of death,'[6] a preoccupation which secularism has exposed. And yet, people are still reaching for something beyond scientific rationalism, because it fails to satisfy their sense of lack and incompleteness. For this reason, the advocates of religion argue that secularism is just another attempt by man to 'save' himself.

For Christianity, the doctrine of incarnation implies that the supposed difference between the sacred and the secular is a misconception, God having secularized himself by 'becoming flesh'. In his attempt to secularize Christianity, Dietrich Bonhoeffer spoke of the need for man '*to come of age*'. In its adolescence, mankind needed the authoritative framework of traditional biblical religion. To 'come of age' means to let the support go, to mature is to be free of dependent relationships and influences and to be able to accept the responsibility of that freedom. Bertrand Russell expressed a similar idea. 'In spite of Death, the mark and seal of the parental control, Man is yet free, during his brief years, to examine, to criticize, to know and in imagination to create. To him alone, in the world with which he is acquainted, this freedom belongs; and in this lies his superiority to the resistless forces that control his outward life.'[7]

Central to all of this is the nature of religious language, by far the most significant part of our Western cultural inheritance. In this respect secularism's challenge to religion is to abandon the language in which its concepts were first recorded; if there is truth in the perceptions of biblical religion, then it cannot be confined to the literal world-view of the Old and New Testaments or of the Koran. All religious language began as technical language, the words used were intended to describe, define, explain and witness. The redactors of the biblical texts were able to assume that the words and phrases used would be understood by their contemporaries and because the texts were understood, they had authority. This is no longer true. Words have different meanings according to context, period and even location. This is especially the case when meaning travels down the generations in the form of oral tradition or across languages in the process of translation. The meaning of words change and sometimes they change so much that their original use fails to communicate their original intention. This is what a Chinese scholar meant when he remarked to Wei Wu Wei that, 'Buddhism in China is another language'.[8] If the religion-secularism debate focuses on whether or not there is a form of survival after death, then the entire problem of religious language focuses on how the term 'God' is used. In April, 1944, awaiting execution in his prison cell, Bonhoeffer wrote a letter to one of his friends: 'We are proceeding toward a time of no religion at all … How do we speak of God without religion … How do we speak in a secular fashion of God?'[9] Theologians and philosophers have responded creatively to this question. Rudolph Bultmann (1884–1976) demythologized the New Testament;[10] Paul Tillich (1886–1965) a Protestant theological philosopher, proposed that God was 'being itself'; he developed a theology of culture in which 'faith need not be unacceptable to contemporary culture and contemporary culture need not be unacceptable to faith.'[11] The Jewish philosopher Martin Buber

(1878–1965) placed humanity's spiritual quest in the context of persons in relationship, wherein both the personal and eternal 'Thou' can be addressed in true mutuality.[12]

These concepts are not, of course, confined to Western biblical religions and the cultures evolved from them. Hinduism and Buddhism are religions of inwardness, tolerant of secularism and seem not to be threatened by it other than when secularization, as materialism, threatens the principles that have formed their communities. The responses of the major religions to secularism are given under their separated entries; here, we can say broadly that Eastern religions, together with the entire world, are distracted by secularism in the form of consumerism and the market. While for millions these have become, the 'ground of their being', they are not religions and it is misleading to call them so, but they are certainly secular alternatives to religion, offering their own way to satisfy people's innate and gnawing sense of deficiency. It would seem, however, that consumerism offers only temporary satisfaction and is, in any case, an entirely illusory solution to humanity's deepest needs. David Loy sums it up thus: 'According to Buddhism, any truly satisfactory resolution of this situation must address the root problem, my lack of self. This can lead to an awakening that transforms my lack from such festering anxiety into an 'empty' (*sunya*) source of creativity. The self's sense of separation from the world motivates me to try to secure myself within it, but the only authentic solution is the essentially religious realization that I am not other than it.'[13]

Paul Tillich suggested[14] that the major world faiths are challenged by what he called 'quasi-religions', broadly classed as Nationalism, Communism and Humanism. These huge energies and movements have bred numerous secular alternatives to religion. They include, for example, the Positivism of Auguste Comte, the dialectic materialism of Marx and Lenin and the psychoanalytic systems of Freud and Jung. History has shown, however, that conceptual idealism, as with consumerist materialism, offers no permanent solution to either an individual or collective sense of deficiency. The same is true of what David Loy calls 'individualistic secular religions', based on money, fame or romantic love,[15] each of which implies the quest for a secular salvation.

It is important to clarify that when something is described as a secular alternative to religion, it in no way implies that the alternative is 'religious'. If that were true, then anything which passionately centred and nourished individual and community life would be a 'religion'. To call Communism or consumerism a religion is to entirely misuse the word or to use it metaphorically. A religion, in whatever form it takes, will connect the individual with something essentially beyond himself; it will have a metaphysical agenda. But even this assertion needs qualification, since the hard edges between religion and secularism begin to dissolve when seemingly secular ideas and movements become the means by which individuals pursue the spiritual quest to find the ground of their being.

* * *

The Dictionary offers an exploration of religious and secular traditions and their philosophies. All the major belief systems are described, as are many of the denominations, cults and sects that have stemmed from them. Cross-references lead to the words most frequently found in the vocabularies of these systems, indicating how the word is used and understood. In addition, there are many dozens of 'stand-alone' words and phrases that contribute to the mosaic of the whole picture. Clearly, no one author can be an authority on such wide-ranging themes and I have been dependent on sources, either acknowledged in the text or referred to in the selected Bibliography. For whatever misunderstandings and misinterpretations occur I must accept responsibility, even as I acknowledge under the appropriate heading the indispensable help and advice that has guided me.

Notes
1. Colossians 1:27
2. Bonhoeffer, *Letters and Papers from Prison* (Fontana, 1959)
3. L. Wittgenstein, *Philosophical Investigations* (trans. G. E. M. Anscombe; Oxford: Blackwell, 1976)
4. Shakespeare, *Hamlet* V.i
5. Sir Arthur Keith, *Concerning Man's Origins* (Presidential Address to the British Association, 1927)
6. James Boswell, *Life of Johnson* (Oxford University Press, 1982)
7. Bertrand Russell, *A Free Man's Worship* (George Allen & Unwin, Unwin Paperbacks, 1976)
8. Wei Wu Wei, *The Open Secret* (Boulder, CO: Sentient Publications Ltd., 2004)
9. Bonhoeffer, op cit
10. Rudolph Bultmann, *Religion without Myth* (co-authored with Karl Jaspers; NY: Noonday Press, 1958)
11. Paul Tillich, *A Theology of Culture* (Oxford University Press, 1959)
12. Martin Buber, *I and Thou* (Edinburgh: T & T Clark, 1958)
13. David R. Loy, 'The Spiritual Roots of Modernity: Buddhist reflections on the idolatry of the nation-state, corporate capitalism and mechanistic science', in Sulak Sivaraksa (ed), *Socially Engaged Buddhism for the New Millennium* (Bangkok: Sathirakoses-Nagapradipa Foundation, 1999): 86-113
14. Tillich, op cit
15. David R. Loy, 'Trying to Become Real, A Buddhist Critique of some Secular Heresies', *International Philosophical Quarterly* 32.4 (December, 1992): 403-25

A

Aaronic Order A splinter group of the Church of Jesus Christ of the Latter Day Saints (see **Mormons**). It was founded in 1942 by Maurice Glendenning who had been excommunicated by the Mormons for receiving and publishing 'revelations' known as *The Levitical Writings*.

Abbasid Caliphate *I*. The Islamic Sunni dynastic house that overthrew the Umayyads in 750 CE. Almost from the beginning the Abbasids found themselves in conflict with various sects and schisms. They were supportive of the *mawali*, the non-Arab Muslims who remained outside the kinship-linked Arab culture and who were branded as second-class citizens under the **Umayyad** rule. Aided by the Persians in their fight against the Umayyads, the empire's capital was moved from Damascus to Baghdad. While this strengthened Persian–Arab integration, it alienated other groups, including some of those who had fought for the Abbasid cause. Because of their family connection through a cousin of the Prophet, the Abbasids adopted **Sunni** Islam, implicitly distancing themselves from Shiite belief. In 786 there was a bloody revolt in Mecca and many of the Shiite fled to the western Maghreb, where they established the first Arab dynasty, the **Idrisids**, ruling from 788 to 985 CE. They can be considered the originators of an independent Morocco. There were other conflicts, most notably with the Byzantine Empire in Syria and Anatolia, which resulted in more Abbasid splinter groups. The threatened dynasty was held together by Al-Ma'mun who seized the Caliphate from his brother in 813 CE. Under his leadership the course of Islamic culture and history was changed irrevocably. The first innovation was the creation of a slave army, the **Mamluks**, loyal only to their Caliphate, which displaced the armies of both Persia and Arabia and which brought a new ethnic group into the Islamic world which, ironically, would play a huge part in the decline of the Abbasids. More importantly, Al-Ma'mun established a university to promote the translation of Hellenistic and Indian works and to incorporate Greek philosophy into medieval Islamic culture, with the result that such philosophers as **Plato** and **Aristotle** became part of the curriculum of Islamic centres of learning. The Abbasids are thus responsible for cultural and political division within the Islamic world and the consequent decentralization of both secular power and religious authority. The dynasty thrived for two centuries before being overrun by the **Mongols** in 1258. See **Islamic Dynasties**

Abhidharma *B*. Skt. Pal. 'Special Teaching' or higher doctrine based on scholastic analysis and commentaries on the sacred texts. The result is a systematic presentation of the earliest philosophical, psychological and spiritual discourses. The term also refers to the *Abhidharma-pitaka*, the third part of the Buddhist canon, known as the **Tripitaka**. See **Theravada**

Aborigines Used generally to refer to an indigenous group that have always inhabited a region – that is, they are believed to be the original human settlers. Similar in use to the term 'native', as in Native Americans. See **Australian Aboriginal Religion**

Abraham *J.* The first patriarch of Israel. Born in Ur in **Chaldea**. Sometime during c.2000–1500 BCE, he migrated to **Canaan**. (See **Palestine**) Through a process of progressive revelation, God eventually established a covenant with him, promising innumerable descendents (a nation) and their settlement in the **Promised Land**. Through his son, **Isaac**, Abraham is the ancestor of the Jewish people. The historicity of Abraham has been questioned by some scholars who read the Genesis accounts as the story of a tribe.

Absolutism The notion that in any particular genre of thought, a statement is absolutely true or absolutely false. Its application to religion mostly concerns statements (see **Creeds**) which define absolute or orthodox truth. In Ethics, Moral Absolutism assumes that there are finite standards against which moral questions can be judged, with the result that they are either good or evil regardless of context or motive. Enlightenment absolutism was a philosophical response to the liberalizing consequences of the **Reformation**, which attempted to justify the security and benefits of absolute power – as, for example, the Divine Right of Kings. See **Divine Kingship**

Academy of Athens *G.* Effectively the first university. It was established by **Plato** c.385 BCE. The Lyceum was **Aristotle**'s school and, following his death, his pupil Theophrastus founded in 317 BCE the Peripatetic School to continue the teaching of his master. The Academy grew into the Second Academy of Hellenistic Platonists associated with various philosophies that included the **Stoics**, Cynics and Sceptics. The Academy continued until the 6th century CE. See **Hellenism, Scepticism, Socrates**

Activism Usually, the organized religious involvement in politics. The extent and nature of this involvement is the subject of continuous debate and the cause of fundamental divisions across all religious traditions. The extremes are represented by those who believe that it is not the function of religion to be involved with politics or the state and those who believe that their religion should be the basis on which the state is founded and governed, as with the theocratic principles of Islam. The middle ground is held by those who believe their religious values should be evident, for example, in the highest standards of social morality and justice.

Actualism In philosophy, the assertion that only the 'actual' world exists. Originally, for **Aristotle**, anything that has form exists, in contrast to something that only has the possibility of form. Thus form verifies existence. 'Possibilists' would claim there are alternatives to the actual world, that it is 'possible', for example, for another world to exist inhabited by other life-forms. Actualism's response is to analyze such a claim to see if it has the verifiable attribute of form. Its conclusion would be that another world with other life-forms exists only in the sense that it is possible, but not actual. The German philosopher Husserl proposed that actuality is existence in both space and time. Actualism therefore implies just one mode of existence, whereas Possibilism allows various notions of existence. The term 'Actualism' has spun off to include cultic insights such as Star Path which offers accelerated spiritual growth based on an awareness of the individual's 'actual' Self. Also, a **New Age** tendency based on Panentheism, the belief that God is actually 'in' everything. Philosophically, such assertions are entirely subjective.

Adam *J. X.* Heb. 'man'. The first man of the Genesis myth, who was made by God out of earth, in his own image. **Eve**, the first woman, was created from one of Adam's ribs. After their expulsion from the Garden of Eden (see **Paradise**) they had three sons: Cain, Abel and Seth. In New Testament theology Jesus is understood as the second Adam, the 'New Creation', the means offered by God for creating a new people made righteous by faith in Jesus the Christ. See **Adam Kadmon**

Adam Kadmon *J.* In the Kabbalistic mysticism, the first or original man, the spiritual prototype of Adam, the first man in the Genesis creation myth who is also the spiritual substance of the universe. The idea was first used by the Alexandrian Jewish philosopher **Philo**, who contrasted the dust-made physical Adam with the spiritual Adam 'made in the image of God'. Adam Kadmon is also the **Logos**, the Word of God. In the **Zohar**, the central book of the Kabbalah, he is the 'highest man' in whom are embodied the *Sephiroth*, the ten attributes or radiances of God. The concept was finally developed by Izaac Luria (1534–72) in his Lurianic **Kabbalah**. See **Universal Man**

Adat see **Urf**

Adhan *I.* The familiar ritual call to prayer sung by a **muezzin** or sounded from a mosque's minaret through loud-speakers. Tradition has it that Muhammad chose the Adhan in place of bells. It opens with three repetitions of 'God is the greatest'. This is followed by two repetitions of 'I testify that there is no God but God'. then two repetitions each of 'I testify that Muhammad is the messenger [or, Prophet] of God'. 'Come to Prayer', 'Come to Prosperity', 'God is the Greatest'. It closes with repetitions of 'There is no God but God.' On hearing the Adhan, a Muslim will repeat it, adding the phrase, 'There is no strength nor power but in God'.

Adidam A religious movement founded in 1939 in New York by Adi Da Samraj, born Franklin Albert Jones. Known also as the 'Way of the Heart', it has strong affinities with **Hinduism** and **Buddhism**. Based on the founder's conviction of his own divine incarnation, the basic objective is the realization of God in every present moment, 'this moment', in which everything resides and which contains the seeds of full spiritual potential.

Adi Granth *Sik*. Pun. One of the names for the Sikh scriptures. See **Guru Granth Sahib**

Adonai *J*. Heb. 'Lord' or 'ruler'. One of several names for God in Judaism. *Adonai* is the plural form of *Adon*, and there are various explanations as to why the plural is used. Hebrew uses abstract plurals as, for example, with the '-*im*' ending of *chayyim*, 'life'. The meaning of *Adonai* is thus not syntactic but probably carries the respectful 'Lord of Lords'. Historically, the plural form charts the development of Hebrew monotheism, the concept of God as all-inclusive and overcoming the many gods, both of the Hebrews' ancestors and of the nations among which they eventually settled. In English the use of 'we', in reference to 'one', as in the 'Royal we', is perhaps the nearest we can get. The term contains the Hebrew possessive form which might be rendered 'My Lord' but which has no more grammatical significance than the possessive in the name 'Madonna'. More importantly the vowel sounds of *Adonai* are used in the Divine name of the **Tetragrammaton**, and its required substitute. Out of reverence this is never pronounced and the Jew will use *Adonai* in its place. The four Hebrew letters of the unspoken Divine name are transliterated as YWEH, which is usually translated 'Lord'. In Hebrew scriptures the vowels of the name *Adonai* are inserted into the four letters YWEH, thus YeHoWaH. To read this as 'Jehovah' is mistaken. Traditionally, on the Day of **Atonement** only the High Priest pronounced God's name in the **Holy of Holies**. *Adonai* is also the origin of the Greek **Adonis**. See **Elohim, El Shaddai, Yahweh**

Adonis *G*. His name discloses his origins, being from the Semitic title *Adoni*, 'Lord'. He was the offspring of the union between Cinyras, King of Cyprus and his daughter Myrrha who, as punishment for her incest, was turned into a myrrh tree, the myrrh secreted from bark being her tears. This metamorphosis occurred before Adonis was born and his issuing from the tree confirmed him as a god of vegetation. When grown to handsome manhood, **Aphrodite** fell in love with him and in one of several variant myths he was killed while hunting and she commemorated her loss by drawing an anemone from his blood. Various, more ancient, forms of the myth exist which suggest **Canaanite** and **Phoenician** origins in the form of Anat and **Astarte**, and **Ishtar** and **Tamuz** of Mesopotamia. The cult of Adonis, with that of Aphrodite, probably made its way to Greece via Cyprus, to be celebrated annually throughout the country. His story is the subject of Ovid's *Metamorphoses*.

Advaita *H*. Skt. 'non-duality'. Uniquely, an attribute of God or the Absolute and the state aspired to by all Hindus and Buddhists. The experience or knowledge of *advaita* requires **enlightenment,** without which it is not possible for humans to step out of the subject–object relationship. Thus, *advaitananda* (Skt.) is that state of bliss acquired by an experience of the Absolute. See **Advaita-Vedanta, Dualism and Non-Dualism, Dvaita-Vedanta, Maya**

Advaita-Vedanta *H*. Skt. One of the three core **Vedanta** philosophies, principally developed by **Shankara** (788–820). His philosophy is non-dualistic in that *atman*, the soul and *Brahma*, God, together with the entire universe, are identical. The mind is subject to *maya*, the illusory existence of a world of multiplicity which covers the single, non-plural, non-dual reality, *Brahman*. Maya is not hallucinatory, it causes the world to be seen falsely, like the snake in the corner of the room which is actually a coiled rope. What we see as separately existing, ever-changing shapes is but a mirage, an image we take to be real but which obscures the reality behind it. Shankara's **monism** is extreme in the sense that it leaves an impersonal universe in which relationships cannot exist, since there can be no relationship between things or beings that are absolutely identical. It follows that in Shankara's form of non-duality, love, devotion to God or any sense of conscious relationship between God and an individual is made redundant. **Ramanuja**'s philosophy was an attempt to overcome this by reconciling the message of the **Upanishads** (that *atman* is to be equated with *Brahman*) with the doctrine of *bhakti*, devotion, as a means of gaining *moksha*, liberation. See **Dvaita-Vedanta, Madhva**

Advent *X*. From the Latin *Adventus Redemptoris*, the 'coming of the Saviour'. The period beginning the Sunday nearest the 30th November, continuing to Christmas Eve. It is a holy season for the Christian Church which prepares for the celebration of Christ's nativity.

Adventism *X*. A widespread inter-denominational movement that began with William Miller's prediction that Jesus' return would take place in 1843. Perhaps inevitably, it was immediately followed by the 'Great Disappointment', but many people in the movement continued to believe, revising the chronology and dates. Others believed the event had taken place, but in heaven and thus, invisible. See also **Armstrongism, Branch Dravidians, Millerite Movement, Second Coming, Seventh Day Adventism**

Aeons In belief systems influenced by **Gnosticism**, aeons are divine emanations. They are sent to redeem spirit from its material state or captivity. They reside in the **pleroma**, the very centre or fullness of Divinity. See **Merkabah Mysticism**

Aesir *AE*. The principal pantheon of Norse mythology which includes **Odin, Frigg, Thor, Balder** and **Tyr**. They lived on the plane of Asgard and, under the leadership of father Odin, governed the lives of mortals. A second, rival clan of gods, the **Vanir**, is also featured and some of the gods appear to be members of both, an oddity that illustrates the way the Aesir and Vanir interact, for example by taking hostages and counting them among their own pantheon. See **Anglo-Saxon Religion**, **Germanic Religion**

Aesthetic Realism Foundation A pseudo-religious energy based on the notion that happiness can be achieved through the harmony of opposites, for example through realizing and accepting that the world is both a beautiful and horrific place. (See **Taoism**) It was founded in New York in 1941 by Eli Siegel, a poet and critic. He suggested that in art beauty was realized by the balancing of order and freedom, logic and passion, strength and grace. One's attitude to the world determines how we see things. Siegel taught that it is every person's 'greatest, deepest desire to like the world on an honest or accurate basis'. But there is another desire opposing this – the need to have contempt for the world. Such contempt, while enhancing the importance of the self and self-esteem, can only be unjust. The movement was criticized when high school teachers in the USA tried to introduce the philosophy into the Biology and Art curriculum.

Aetherius Society Founded by George King (1919–97) who was born in Shropshire, England. He was a taxi driver, fascinated by yogic meditation which he practised for many hours a day, channelling his psychic ability into healing. In 1954 he claimed to receive telepathic communications from extraterrestrials. He gave up his job to found the Society, through which he could communicate the messages he received. See **Chen Tao**, **UFO Cults**

African Religions *A*. The African continent has the greatest diversity of religious forms and practices in the world. From 100 CE to 600 CE Christianity dominated the northern African territories, to be swept aside by Islam from 700 CE onwards; only the **Coptic** church in Egypt and Ethiopia survived. Since the early 19th century missionary societies have re-established Christianity in Africa. It has been estimated that there are in excess of 6,000 tribes, each with their own religion. Despite Islamic and Christian missions, the 19th-century 'scramble for Africa' by European colonizing powers and the technical and social changes that must have touched even the most isolated areas, tribal religions continue to have authority and influence.

A brief summary cannot do justice to the diversity and plurality of African tribal religions. They have been described as 'primitive', 'traditional', 'indigenous' and '**pagan**', but each of these requires qualification. 'Traditional' implies a religious practice and structure that has remained unchanged, but it is unlikely that any local group has entirely resisted outside influence. Even without the effects of introduced religion, culture and politics, local beliefs have almost certainly changed because of the natural development of their own social structure. More research needs to be done before we can understand, for example, what effect the slave trade might have had on these religions, together with the influence of feedback from the new religious forms developed by the slaves in the countries of their captivity. In addition to the effects of change, is the lack of literature and language. There are no written sources, no histories or accounts of these religions provided by the people themselves. For this reason it is extremely difficult to ascertain anything of the origin and development of their belief systems. Field anthropologists, working to compile grammars and dictionaries of local languages, have not always been able to step outside their own culturally conditioned perceptions and provide an objective interpretation of the indigenous concepts. When such projects have been undertaken by missionaries of whatever faith, the results have inevitably been influenced by the imposed religion.

Allowing for these provisos, a general description can be attempted. Being non-literate, the tribal religions have not produced the kind of philosophers and philosophical movements familiar to the West. Oral tradition, however, has its own forms of philosophy. While in the West philosophy is based on the concept of 'being', in tribal religion it is based on the concept of 'force' or 'power'. In general, the belief systems share the concept of a powerful High God, an inaccessible, impersonal cosmic activity. Some tribes understand this God to be 'Father' or a named Sky or Earth god. For others it remains a power above and beyond human beings, which by means of pragmatic ritual is made accessible through **ancestor worship** and the mediation of lesser spirits. The worship and deference given to the High God through these lower forms is life-affirming. There is no tradition of world denial and the vitality and dynamism of life are expressed in polygamy, the healing shrines, erotic dance, phallic symbolism and the concept of 'power'. This dynamism has its root in **animism**, the notion that the whole universe is throbbing with spirit-life. This cosmic dynamism resides within every human being and if there is one word that expresses a general characteristic of African tribal religion, it is the word already referred to: 'power'. The aim of life is to tap into this power and fill one's life with it; the more an individual's power is increased, the greater his prestige.

The African world is, therefore, full of spirits, potent natural phenomena and dead ancestors, all of which suggest that there is no sense of permanent death. Allowing for local variations, every tribe subscribes to a belief in an active after-life with the possibility of reincarnation. Religious ceremony is led by medicine-men, witch-doctors and rain-makers, practising both **black magic** and **white magic**; frequently the tribe is associated with a cultic animal, such as a snake or alligator. The rituals include the use of **fetishes**, **ju-jus**, **charms** and **oracles**. Membership of adult tribal society is by **initiation**, and the social structure includes secret initiatory societies. Tribal government is based on an ethical system which judges the quality of a person's behaviour by the extent to which his actions help or hinder human power. African tribal religion is generally tolerant and conservative, more concerned to protect the status quo than to evangelize.

FINAL WORD: 'More central is the concept of "power", or potent life ... "vital force" ... or "dynamism". It is the importance of power, its increase or diminution, which is a constant concern in prayers and invocation, in spells and magic. All beings have their own power and the most fortunate are those who have the greatest amount, whereas misfortune, disease and witchcraft are held to diminish power. Fundamental to the notion of power is the dynamic nature of the universe and human life.' Parrinder

Afterlife The concept of some form of life continuing after death. See **Eschatology**, **Immortality**, **Resurrection**

Agama *H. B.* Skt. 'Source of the Teaching'. The term has various meanings. In **Hinduism** it is a reference to sacred literature, for example a **Tantra** concerned with the mysticism associated with **Shiva** and **Shakti**. In **Mahayana** Buddhism four Agama collections form part of the Sanskrit canon and include the core teachings of **Hinayana**, given by the Buddha in his first discourse, namely the **Four Noble Truths** and the **Eightfold Path**.

Agams *Ja.* The Jain scriptures (see **Jainism**). They are classified in two groups: the original scriptures written in Prakrit and the commentaries and explanations of the Agam literature compiled by nuns, monks and scholars. These are written in many different languages, depending on the nationality of the commentators. In Jain tradition there is no one sacred book, like the Bible or Koran, but several written by different people at different times. The first scriptures were derived from oral tradition and written from about 500 CE, approximately 1,000 years after the death of **Mahavira**, the last of the Jain 'Ford-Makers' or teachers.

Agape *X.* Gk. 'wide open'. A love feast held by early Christians and associated with the **Eucharist**. The term also connotes spiritual, asexual love and charity. The Platonic sense carried the notion of universal love, as in a love of truth or humanity. Agape is always volitional and unconditional. Perhaps it is best understood as an intentional promotion of well-being in response to that which causes ill-being. In biblical usage, agape returns good for evil.

Agapemonites *X.* A messianic sect that followed the teachings of German mystics. Known also as the **Community of the Son of Man**, it existed from 1846–1956. It was founded by the Rev. Henry James Prince, a medical doctor and curate of the church of Charlinch, in Somerset, of which he had sole charge due to the illness of the Rector. The sect's primary object was to spiritualize the matrimonial state, that is 'marrying' the soul to God. Prince believed his first 'spiritual' marriage had made him the visible embodiment of the Holy Spirit, a notion confirmed when the Rector, Samuel Starkey, was cured from persistent illness by reading one of his curate's sermons. Prince, Starkey and others left the church to found their own brotherhood, Prince at Adullam Chapel, Brighton and Starkey at Weymouth, where Prince soon joined him. Eventually they established a form of 'all things in common' community based in Spaxton, Somerset, known as 'The Abode of Love'. Despite 'spiritualizing' marriage, there were scandals involving children, custody cases at law, bigamy and a controversial mixture of immorality and blasphemy that proved insupportable for the genuinely faithful. When Prince died in 1899, his messianic status was transferred to the Rev. J. H. Smyth-Pigott but, following Smyth-Pigott's death in 1927, the sect declined, its last member dying in 1956.

Agiary *Zo*. A Fire Temple, the place of worship for Zoroastrians. The sacred heart of the temple is the room or hall, that houses the sacred fire. The Laity bring offerings to the fire, while the priests use it as a focus for rituals. Fire is revered as the son of **Asura Mazda**, and is considered to be the purest of all the elements. There are three grades of fire: the Atash Dadgah, the fire of the hearth, is the lowliest, being the fire of the house-holder class; the Atash Adaran, literally 'the fire of fires', is associated with the warrior class and burns constantly in the Agiary and is made up from the ashes contributed by many different classes of people, thus symbolizing social unity; and the Atash Behram, the 'fire of victory', also called the 'Cathedral Fire', the fire of kings and royalty, which triumphs over evil and darkness.

The sacred fire is constructed by means of complicated holy rituals, which can take a year to work through, since it requires the ashes of a thousand and one fires to complete. Each contribution must come from a different strata of society represented by every trade, craft and profession. The ritual requires that the fire should be started by lightning and that the officiating priests pass through numerous purifying rituals. Laymen and women bathe copiously before entering the sacred hall with the fire, demonstrating the belief that 'cleanliness is next to godliness'. See **Fire, Sacred**

Agni *H*. A Hindu god of fire associated primarily with the sacred fire used in **Vedic** rituals. The fire has three emanations: the sun, lightning and earthly fire – the implication being that Agni operates at various levels of reality and through sacrifice by fire, as a mediator between gods and humans. See **Deva, Trans-polytheistic Theism**

Agnosticism Philosophy's challenge to **metaphysics** and **fideism**. The seeds of modern agnosticism were sewn very early in the **scepticism** of pre-Socratic philosophy and by the philosophers of the **Hellenistic Academy**. The term 'agnosticism' has its root in the Greek *agnosis*, 'without knowledge'; it implies we cannot know anything outside our experience of natural phenomena, a perception that supports open-mindedness to concepts about which we can never be sure. How to be certain about what we know is a major theme running through the history of philosophy (see **Epistemology**) and the enquiry has always concentrated on ways of validating the knowledge we claim to have. Both atheists and theists profess confidence in the views they represent, agnosticism holds the middle ground of healthy scepticism.

Blaise Pascal [1623–62] was in despair about a person's inability to accept certain levels of experience on the basis of faith; 'Humble yourself, weak reason; be silent, foolish nature; learn that man infinitely transcends man and learn from your Master what is your true condition, of which you are ignorant. Hear God.' Pascal recognized we must always remain 'cosmically ignorant, reason can decide nothing here'. Because we have to make the agnostic assumption that we cannot be sure about anything, he suggested his famous wager: We should bet our eternal lives on Roman Catholicism. If it turns out to be true, then we win an eternity of bliss; if it turns out to be false and there is actually nothing at all beyond death, what has been lost? 'And so our contention is of infinite force, when there is the finite to stake in a game in which the chances of winning and of losing are equal and there is the infinite to gain.'

David Hume (1711–76) criticized metaphysics from the point of view of scepticism and **empiricism**. On picking up a book in a library Hume asked, 'Does it contain any abstract reasoning concerning quantity of number? No. Does it contain any experimental reasoning concerning matter of fact and existence? No. Commit it then to the flames: for it can contain nothing but sophistry and illusion.' [2004] Hume's argument is that the only meaningful terms and ideas that we can have are either sense impressions or mathematical concepts. Knowledge comes basically from perception. When an idea or an event seems to have its origin beyond human experience, it is wiser to suppose the report is false as, for example, with Jesus of Nazareth's miracles. Hume's philosophy was in tune with the new scientific method of the **Enlightenment**.

Kant (1724–1804) challenged religious claims in general and his arguments are taken further than Hume's. He agrees with the empiricists that knowledge is founded on experience but, 'although all our knowledge begins with experience it does not follow that it arises from experience.' [1996] He allows for a kind of knowledge that is both universal and necessary, but is independent of experience. He called this *a priori* knowledge and wanted to discover if there was such a thing as *a priori* metaphysical knowledge. Kant's arguments, which have been hugely influential, led him to conclude that the metaphysical project was destined to fail.

As a consequence of Hume, Kant and many of the philosophers that have followed them, it has been generally accepted that the kind of knowledge sought by metaphysicians is not attainable. Either they have developed Hume's criticism into the **Positivism** of, for example, Auguste **Comte**, or they have followed Kant, accepting that what we know about anything cannot transcend the categories or 'forms of intuition' that we use to organize our experience. T. H. Huxley, who coined the word 'agnostic', tells us 'It is wrong for a man to say that he is certain of the objective truth of any proposition unless he can produce evidence which logically justifies that certainty.' [1946]

Agnosticism has kept company with the long and contentious debate between faith and knowledge or reason. Faith is promoted as a special or refined faculty which in the Judeo–Christian–Islamic tradition is understood as a gift from God. Not everyone is a recipient of this gift. Modern religious philosophy suggests that insoluble problems arise when statements of belief, creeds for example, are treated as if they were scientific assertions. They cannot, of themselves, be said to make statements about the nature of reality but they do presuppose other levels of reality which are subjective and of a different order. The functions of these belief statements serve an entirely different purpose.

Agnosticism requires the suspension of judgement on issues for which there is not sufficient evidence to reach a conclusion. The New Testament definition of faith as 'the assurance of things hoped for, the conviction of things not seen' (Hebrews 11.1) is an agnostic statement because it implies that the final ground for a person's belief lies beyond present evidence and experience. Huxley's agnosticism is more radical because it was intended to invalidate precisely these hoped for, unseen things. In the debate between science and theology Huxley questioned specific subjects such as the Mosaic authorship of the **Pentateuch**, and the credibility of the miracle stories of the New Testament. Gradually the word 'agnostic' took flight beyond the immediate religion-versus-science controversy. It went beyond the agnosticism of Huxley into the broader search for philosophical verification principles as, for example, with **Logical Positivism**'s refusal to speculate about 'ultimate' questions. The agnostic debate made a formative contribution to the development of **secularism**. See **Freethinkers**

FINAL WORD: 'Every variety of philosophical and theological opinion was represented there [the Metaphysical Society] and expressed itself with entire openness; most of my colleagues were "…ists" of one sort or another; and, however kind and friendly they might be, I, the man without a rag of a label to cover himself with, could not fail to have some of the uneasy feelings … So I took thought and invented what I conceived to be the appropriate title of "agnostic".' T. H. Huxley [1977]

Agon Shu Buddhism *B*. A Buddhist sect founded by **Seiyu Kiriyama**, based on the wisdom of the *Agama Sutras*. Also known as 'original Buddhism', it was established in Japan in 1978 by Kiriyama Kancho, as a modern, democratic Buddhist organization dedicated to carrying higher wisdom to the world. The movement encourages everyone to embrace the path of liberation and truth as taught by the **Buddha**. It has a demanding social programme which includes funding hospitals and AIDS hospices, education, the care of the elderly and ecology and disaster relief.

Agyeman, Jaramogi Abebe See **Pan African Orthodox Christian Church**.

Ahimas *H*. An attribute of the soul or core personality. Perhaps better, our sense of our true selves made sensitive by conscience and evident by a person's disposition. Ahimas follows from the notion of **Brahma** as an all-pervading universal divinity, engendering reverence and compassion for everything existing.

Ahimsa *H*. Skt. Absolute 'non-hurtfulness'. A principle which according to **Gandhi** is 'to be practised by everybody in all affairs of life. If it cannot be practised in all departments, it has no practical value.' See **Caste**, **Jainism**

Ahmadiyyah Movement *I*. Islamic sect founded by Mirza Ghulam Ahmad (1839–1908), an Indian Muslim who claimed to be the **Messiah**. Most followers in the USA are black, Indian or Pakistani.

Ahriman *Zo*. An alternative name for **Angra Mainyu**, 'The Hostile Spirit' of **Zoroastrianism**.

Ahura Mazda *Zo*. The Supreme Being of **Zoroastrianism**. *Mazda* means 'Great Creator', from *maz*, 'great' + *da*, 'to create' and *Ahura*, 'divinity', thus 'The Great Creator Lord'. An alternative reading gives 'The Wise Lord' or 'Lord Wisdom'. **Zoroaster** usually reversed the phrase, 'Mazda Ahura' and frequently used 'Mazda' by itself. In the **Pahlavi literature** the two words are combined to form the name **Ohrmazd**. Zoroaster's teachings about Ahura Mazda are to be found in the **Gathas**, the verses he wrote which are part of the **Avesta**, the Zoroastrian scriptures. These verses affirm that Ahura Mazda is the one God, creator of everything including the human body and mind; he is both seen and unseen, the spirit of the sun, the eternal and only truth, wholly good and the only God worthy of worship. Adherents are expected to offer him total devotion in the way they live their lives and in the symbolic actions in their worship, bowing, praying and making offerings. Ahura Mazda is opposed by a devil or 'The Hostile Spirit', **Angra Mainyu**, over which he has no control. Both have existed from the beginning, but in the end Ahura Mazda will triumph. The **Parsees** of modern Zoroastrianism do not regard the traditional source of evil as a being but as an evil tendency in man. Ohrmazd remains wholly good, but not all powerful. See **Daevayasnians**, **Mazdayasnian**

Aiyetoro Community A Nigerian sect that broke away from Christian revivalist religion to establish a community on the coast based on communist principles of administration and production. Their village, Aiyetoro (Yoruba for 'Happy City'), about 35km south of Igbokoda, numbers 3,000 to 4,000 inhabitants. Centred on fishing, their business was so successful that they turned over a considerable profit. They abandoned their plain, uniform dress for individual attire and enjoy a standard of living far in excess of most Nigerians, continuing to operate collective services within a community structure. Under the leadership of the Holy Apostles the community is an experiment in utopian Christianity. See **Utopia**

Ajivaka Buddhism *B*. 'Followers of the Way of Life'. An ascetic order founded by Makkhali Gosala during the lifetime of the Buddha and continuing until the 14th century. Its texts have not survived but some of them were inserted into **Jain** literature. The philosophy is about *niyati*, **fate**, destiny and **determinism**. Against fundamental fate there is nothing a human being can do but to accept it, thus the doctrine of **karma** is superfluous. **Nirvana** was reached only after uncountable numbers of lives. Gosala structured his philosophy around six inescapable factors of life: gain and loss, joy and sorrow, life and death.

Akal Purakh *S*. 'The Being Beyond Time' or the 'timeless being that never dies'. Sikhism's principal theological name for God, implying his transcendence, immanence and omnipresence. See **Sikhism, Waheguru**

Akan *A*. A West African matrilineal people that include the Ashanti, Fanti and Nzema of Ghana and the Ivory Coast. Their mythologies are in the form of collections of stories called *Anansasem*, which might mean 'traveller's tales' and **Nyankomsem**, 'words of a sky-god'. Many of the stories have at their centre a trickster spider-spirit, Kwaku Ananse, one of the most important of the West African gods. The Akan's highest god is Brekyirihunuade, 'he who knows and sees everything'. See **African Religions**

Akh *E*. The 'shiner' or a kind of ghost, being one of the five constituent parts that make up the Egyptian concept of the soul. See **Soul, Egyptian**

Akhenaten (c.1352–c.1336 BCE) *E*. The Pharaoh, Amenhotep IV, whose principal wife was Nefertiti. He was something of a religious revolutionary and heretic, in that he attempted to eradicate the state cult of **Atum-Ra** in favour of **Aten**, the solar creator-god. Some commentators see this more positively as an attempt to displace the **syncretism** by proclaiming the visible sun to be the sole deity, thus introducing to Egypt a true monotheism and opening the way to a personal relationship to god. Akhenaton's reforms have also been interpreted as a means of centralizing power by undermining the authority of the traditional priesthood. His personal faith is recorded in the 'Great Hymn to Aten' (c.1360 BCE) thought to be the indirect inspiration of Psalm 104. After his death the cult was obliterated.

Akkadians *AME*. A Semitic people living on the Arabian Peninsula during the period of the expansion of the Sumerian city-states, c.2400 BCE. As they migrated north they came increasingly into conflict with the Sumerians. In 2340 BCE, under Sargon, they conquered Sumer and established an empire based at Akkad in northern Mesopotamia, on the left bank of the Euphrates. (Present Iraq and c.50km southwest of Baghdad.)

Their short-lived empire extended to the Lebanon but in 2125 BCE the empire fell before a revolt of the city of Ur. Little is known of Akkadian culture. Akkad was the Semitic language of **Mesopotamia**, also known as Assyrian. Their religion was subsumed, with only slight, local variations, into that of the **Sumerians**.

Albigensians *X*. A heretical sect named from the town of Albi, in southern France, flourishing in the 12th and 13th centuries as an off-shoot of the Cathars. They held that Jesus Christ was not a substantial, physical being but an angel with a phantom-like body, who consequently neither suffered on the cross nor was resurrected, thus his salvatory work is based exclusively on his teachings. Believing all matter to be evil, the efficacy of the sacraments was rejected. Their lives were characterized by an extreme moral code which included the condemnation of marriage and the use of any products of animal origin. In 1233, the **Dominican** Order was charged by Pope Gregory IX with the work of eradicating the heresy, a task completed by the end of the 14th century. See **Cathars**

Alchemy A proto-scientific and philosophical discipline originating some 2,500 years ago, probably in Egypt. But it is also known to have been practised in India and China. The 'science' comprised of theories and experiments involving the transmutation of base metals to form gold using chemical and supernatural processes. In fact, alchemy was multi-disciplinary, combining chemistry, metallurgy, physics, medicine, **astrology**, **semiotics** and **mysticism**. From the Middle Ages, European alchemists searched for the 'philosopher's stone', a mythical substance believed to be indispensable for curing diseases and prolonging life. It spread widely in the West during the Renaissance, being developed by Kabbalists (see **Kabbalah**), **Rosicrucians**, astrologers and occultists. On a spiritual level, alchemists worked to purify themselves by eliminating the 'base' material of the self and achieving the 'gold' of enlightenment. Secular scholars now read both the aims and records of alchemy in allegorical terms, but most scientists agree that modern chemistry evolved naturally from the ancient discipline.

Aleph *Jap*. A new name, adopted in January 2000, by the Japanese doomsday cult **Aum Shinri Kyo**.

Aletheia Psycho-Physical Foundation A group offering **New Age** seminars on the inner self, paraconsciousness, **meditation** and **visualization**. The Greek *aletheia* means 'truth', *logos* 'discourse' and thus the science or doctrine of truth and the branch of logic that deals with truth. Based on the teachings of Jack Schwartz, the Foundation teaches the science of Autogenics, a form of self-regulation discipline using relaxation and attention-focusing techniques and is combined with the study of brainwaves. In 1969 Schwartz invented an instrument, the I.S.I.S., that 'photodrives' the subject to different brain-wave states.

FINAL WORD: 'I am fond of telling people to love each other. L.O.V.E. that is, Life. Omnipotently. Victoriously. Expressed. And I also recommend that people practise nonverbal adaptation to each other's needs. Serve each other. Be grateful for that ability.' Jack Schwartz

Alexander the Great (c.356–323 BCE) The Greek King of Macedonia who conquered Persia, then continued to create an empire that expanded across most of the then-known world. His life and wars are copiously researched and documented, see for example Roisman and Lane Fox. His career was not only a turning-point for Greek history but also for the history and culture of the entire Near and Middle East. Before Alexander, Greek civilization developed through the unification of city-states but remained independent and somewhat isolated. After Alexander, **Hellenism** carried every aspect of Greek culture across the world to encounter Eastern traditions, mingle with them and carry them back to make their own contribution to the Near East and to Europe. Alexander's campaigns opened up huge territories, with the result that previously nomadic tribes settled to build towns and cities and to establish networks of communication over both land and sea. The resulting expansion of trade led to commercial and economic reforms. More importantly, perhaps, Alexander, who had been tutored by **Aristotle**, was driven by a vision of universal religious tolerance, believing his military initiatives would bring peace and the realization of the brotherhood of mankind. This ideal was only partially realized, as Alexander died young. The illness which ended his life at the age of 33 remains a mystery. His successors, known as the *Diadochi*, were rivals and their internecine wars fractured the empire.

Algonquin *Ami*. Algonquin is actually the language used by the most populous and widespread of the North American Native American groups and it gives them their recorded name. However, they call themselves the *Anishnabe*, the 'Original People', *Anishnabe* being a sub-language within the same linguistic group. Initially semi-nomadic, the nine 'nations' settled in the Quebec and Ontario regions of Canada. Their religion and its belief-structure is based on **Shamanism**, communication with a great spirit and with lesser spirits that control the elements. Evil spirits bring disaster and illness, good spirits success and good health. The Shaman is also an interpreter of dreams, a significant practice for the Algonquians. They believe in an afterlife where the spirits of dead men will chase the spirits of dead animals. The hunt goes on.

Ali Ibn Abi Talib *I*. A cousin of **Muhammad** and his son-in-law by virtue of his marriage to Fatima, Muhammad's daughter. He was the second convert to Islam (Muhammad's wife Khadija having been converted before him) and the fourth Caliph of the **Sunni** Muslims. His rule deteriorated into civil war as a result of his Caliphate being contested by the **Kharijites**, and the rival claim of Muawiya, the governor of Damascus. The **Shiite** believed Ali was appointed by Muhammad as his successor, that he is imamate, divinely inspired and blessed; they place him at the centre of their religious life. The **Sunni** recognize him only as the fourth Caliph. In 660 CE, Ali was murdered while praying in a mosque. His life has served as a model for political activism in the face of injustice and his writings, in the form of sermons, commentaries and letters, provide the Shiite rule for Islamic government. See **Imamis, Isma'ilis**

Allah *I*. Arab. 'God'. The 'Great Name' for God. The name equally applies to the **God** of the other major monotheisms, Judaism and Christianity. Allah revealed himself to **Muhammad** by *tanzil*, the sending down of the **Koran**, showing himself to be the omnipotent, omniscient creator and the judge of all mankind. 'There is nothing in heaven or earth beyond the power of Allah … Mighty is He and all knowing' (Koran 35). He is the God of history, working through his prophets Abraham, Moses, Jesus and Muhammad by means of whom he established the Islamic communities, the *ahl al-kitab*, the People of the Book. Allah must not be represented by any form of image, nor can he be associated with any other god; to do so is to commit the sin of *shirk*.

Alliance for Jewish Renewal *J*. Known also as *Aleph*. Concerned to rein-vigorate **Judaism** through mystical, Hasidic, musical and meditative practices. It was founded during the 1960s by Schachter-Shalomi, an orthodox Rabbi in Winnipeg (later based in Philadelphia) and known then as the *B'nai Or*, 'Sons' or 'Children of Light', later changed to *P'nai Or*, 'Faces of Light' and eventually, to broaden its focus, to the heading title. Schachter-Shalomi was influenced by both **Sufism** and **Buddhism**. See **Chasidism, Jewish Renewal**

All-One-God Faith A group founded by Emanuel H. Bronner, a third-generation master soap-maker, born in 1908 to an orthodox Jewish family in Germany. His philosophy was a response to the fate of his family in the Holocaust. Taking a notion from **Process Theology**, the sect teaches that God is continually recreating himself, wanting all nations and religions to unite in an 'all-one-God' faith. This ecumenism will be achieved by following and applying the 13 precepts and 20 directives revealed by God to Dr Bronner. His philosophy was passionately committed to ecology and to saving planet Earth, 'our Spaceship Earth'. His Magic Soap Company and the pure-castile liquid soaps it produces are said to clean both the body and the soul and are widely available in health stores.

Al-Rahman *I*. Arab. 'The Compassionate One' is one of the 99 **Beautiful Names** for God listed in the **Koran**. *Al-Rahman* represents the over-abundance of God's mercy, suggesting that God, who sustains the universe, cares enough for mankind to 'send down' (Arab. *tanzil*) his revelation in the form of the Koran that was received by **Muhammad**. The significance of *Al-Rahman* as a name for God is indicated by its use in all but one of the phrases heading the *surahs* or chapters of the Koran:

'In the Name of Allah (Al-Rahamn) the Compassionate, the Merciful'. The implication is that the revelation that follows is a measure of God's compassion for mankind.

Al-Rajin *I*. 'The stoned one', 'the accursed'. The Islamic devil.

Altar Originally any construction on which sacrifices or other offerings were made to God or the gods. The first altar recorded in the **Old Testament** was constructed by Noah (Gen. 8:20), with others erected by Abraham, Isaac, Jacob and Moses and there are references to altars of burned offerings, brazen altars and the 'table of the Lord'. From these early days most places of worship have been equipped with an altar, be it the simplest of tables or a huge, dominating baroque structure. Altars usually form a focus point within the architecture of the building, from which the rites are practised and the liturgy of the services conducted.

Alvar Saints *H*. A group of 12 mystic saints who practised *bhakti*, Skt. 'devotion' and recorded their experience in the *Divya-prabandha* or Divine Hymns, a collection of Tamil verses. The Saints were born at different times in various parts of south India during the period 500–800 CE, but an orthodox tradition places them BCE. The hymns draw on philosophical and religious subjects from the **Upanishads**, **Ramayana** and **Mahabharata**.

Ambrosia *G*. In Greek mythology the food of the gods, usually taken with the drink **nectar**. Scholars have never agreed which actual substance, eaten by mortals, might be behind the mythological food but the most likely is honey in some form, perhaps as a honey-cake or cone. In the mythologies Ambrosia was more than just a food, it was also used as a balm, perhaps in a different form to what was eaten. In this usage it conferred grace, even immortality and as a cosmetic could endow beauty. In the Homeric Hymn, Aphrodite was anointed by the Graces with an oil of ambrosia in preparation for a seduction; in the *Iliad*, a sea-nymph, Thetis, uses a preparation of ambrosia to embalm the body of Patroclus. See **Fountain of Youth**, **Sacred Plants**

Amerindian Religion *Ami*. The religious beliefs, practices and rituals which are the treasured inheritance of modern Native Americans. The origins of 'Red' Indians, frequently the subject of American and European fiction and film, are obscure. They developed from people migrating into North America across the land bridge of the Bering Strait, over 25,000 years ago. There are evidences of Neolithic culture, of wood-built village settlements based on an agricultural economy. The types of indigenous religion range widely from the **Peyote Cults** and the hunting and war-making cults of the southern plains Indians, to the **Shamanism** of the Alaskan Eskimo-Aleut. In more recent times, syncretistic forms of Indian religion have developed as a result of contact with Christianity. In reaction to this there has been a renaissance of the older traditions led by the **Revitalization Movement**, Pan-Indianism and the **Red Power Movement**. The original religious diversity and its renewal makes it hard to talk of just one religion, but some of the sharper differences have been eroded through long contact with American whites.

Despite the diversity there are common religious concepts characterized by **animism** and **spiritism**, and an overarching belief in a Great Spirit. These beliefs, whether formally expressed in traditional terms or lived in a secular context, hold to a sense of the sacredness of nature and the environment. Natural objects are imbued with a spirit presence that inspires awe and the rituals associated with them are designed to ensure the continued interrelatedness of human beings with their habitat, for the benefit of both. Amerindian religion understands nature as theophany and no distinction is made between the enactment of a ritual and the mythology inspiring it. The individual, who is a combination of a body, a 'free' soul and a 'life' soul, strives for perfection through key relationships with the immediate family and the tribal group. Mythologies provide an explanation of both the divine origins and the ecological condition of the territory, the world and the universe; they also give authority to the values and ethical codes of the society. Most traditions affirm the existence of a supreme power in either a personal or impersonal form. The principal deities are usually associated with the sky, for example the wide-ranging Pueblo regard the sun as the most important deity, but sky gods are not organized into a hierarchy. There is a general feeling that the 'being' or essence of things is good and there is a belief in postmortem survival.

The most important myths are dramatized at events marked in the ceremonial calendar. The Pueblo act out stories which describe their origins in the underworld and which illustrate the teachings of the ancestors about the correct way to live. Among the plains Indians, the **Sun Dance** exemplifies a passionately felt tribal unity and ensures the continuance of the fertility of man and nature on which tribal survival is dependent. Across the tribes, songs and dances tell of the pristine character of the tribe at the time of its inception, when everything would have been paradisial. For some, the stars are windows into another world above this one, for others, they are the campfires of celestial tribes living in a world where no hunting is necessary and where human beings and animals can live together without the need to kill. It is a compelling image of the original state of innocence and perfection.

Survival was dependent on the skill of the hunter and hunting dominated Indian culture, as signified in animal cults and their associated ceremonies, in the Male supreme being, in shamanistic practices, in the annual cycle of regeneration and the need to migrate seasonally with the hunted animals. The concept of an afterlife was of one in which no hunting would be necessary. Religious practices fall into regional patterns which are influenced by the landscape and the flora and fauna it supports. These will determine the type of spirits indwelling the natural phenomena. Ceremony and ritual aim to make contact with the supernatural world, so that the individual may acquire spiritual power for his own ends. This process, known as **Vision Quest**, is usually embarked on through a rigorous form of initiation, during which the initiate hopes to secure a guardian spirit. There is a price to pay for this, usually in the form of physical and mental suffering. Hastings recorded the testimony of Igjugarjuk, an Eskimo Caribou, 'I chose suffering through the two things that are most dangerous to us humans, suffering through hunger and suffering through cold.' Through initiatory visions, individuals, even when quite young, bond with the power of the guardian spirits (sometimes those of ancestors) who show themselves in the form of birds or animals: 'Suddenly, I felt an overwhelming presence. Down there, with me in my cramped hole was a big bird. The pit was only as wide as myself and I was a skinny boy, but that huge bird was flying around me as if he had the whole sky to himself. I could hear his cries ... I felt the feathers. This feeling was so overwhelming that it was too much for me. I trembled and my bones turned to ice.' (Lame Deer, in Hastings)

Gradually, settlement and agriculture displaced the hunting culture and gave rise to rain and fertility ceremonies, priestly rituals, medicine cults. Because agriculture required permanent settlement, there were permanent shrines, temples and holy sites. Tribes are often identified with a specific spirit-image with which they have a special association; these are represented in sculptured forms and totem poles. (See **Totemism**) The official religious leaders, priests or shamans secure their power from several guardian spirits. The Central Algonquian tribes organize the shamans into lodges where, by progressing through various degrees, they may graduate to priest. Religious leaders direct calendric rites which follow the rhythms of nature, such as the migrations of animals and birds, celestial and seasonal variations. Aspects of the seasons, the calmness or severity of the weather, are sometimes revealed through ecstatic vision. It is necessary for hunting tribes to know about the migration, for example, of buffalo and salmon. Forewarned, the tribes are able to prepare traps and snares and build up the supply of arrows and spears. The more settled agricultural tribes hold their ceremonies in sacred houses accessible only to initiates. The Pueblo used *kivas*, underground chambers, decorated with images of gods and spirits. The Iroquois built long houses made of elm bark, reserved for tribal elders. See **Handsome Lake Religion**

The deep connection Native Americans feel between people and animals confirms their belief that everything in nature is a manifestation of the spirit world; tribes are identified with the totem of their particular animal, such as deer, elk, otters, eagles. What once was considered to be totem worship, a kind of idolatry, is now understood to be an expression of Indian cosmology and the inextricable relationship humans have with every natural phenomena. Today, Amerindian religious perceptions have been mingled with Christian beliefs (see **Native American Church**), with **New Age** obsessions and with the opportunism of charlatans, the result being that the traditional Amerindian beliefs have slipped into the background, causing controversy and concern. See **Calumet**, **Iroquois**, **Navaho**, **Peyote Cults**, **Sioux**, **Sweat Lodge**, **Wakan Tanka**

FINAL WORD: 'In the philosophy of the true Indian people, Indian is an attitude, a state of mind; Indian is a state of being, the place of the heart. To allow the heart to be the distributor of energy on the planet; to allow your heart, your feelings, your emotions to distribute your vital energy; to pull that energy from the earth, from the sky; to pull it down and distribute it from your heart, the very centre of your being – that is our purpose.' Brooke Medicine Eagle, quoted in Hastings

Amesha Spentas or **Amahraspand** *Zo*. See **Bounteous Immortals**

Amida *B & Z*. Jap. 'Boundless Light'. An important and popular **Mahayana** Buddha, symbolizing wisdom and compassion. He is the principal object of devotion in various schools of Chinese and Japanese **Pure Land Buddhism**. Unknown in early Buddhism, Amitabha is understood as the ruler of the 'western paradise', not a geographical location but the term for a particular state of consciousness. Amitabha represents mercy and wisdom and is the focus of the spiritual practice of Pure Land Buddhism. See **Amidism**

Amidism *B*. Centred on the Buddha **Amida**, Amidism was an important development in **Buddhism**, a new 'way' to salvation that does not lead through endless rebirths but elicits the external help of a Buddha. Amidism really amounts to a Buddhist attempt at a theism in a religion that is non-theistic and there are those who believe that Amidism, with its faith in what amounts to the messianic role of Amida, is only Buddhist in terms of its roots. Ling records that Karl **Barth**, in his *Church Dogmatics*, 'noted a striking resemblance between this development in Japanese religion and evangelical Christian piety'. Ling goes on to suggest that, 'Amidism is about as much an authentic form of Buddhism as the sect of **Jehovah's Witnesses** is an authentic form of Christianity.' However, 'Amidism' is properly used to refer generally to all schools of Chinese and Japanese Buddhism that make Amitabha the focus of their teaching. See **Tariki**

Amish *X*. A denomination of **Anabaptists** predominantly of Swiss-German origin, found now mostly in the USA and Canada. They do not proselytize or accept converts, remaining a tight-knit quasi-communistic community noted for the simplicity of a way of life unencumbered by modern facilities. There are numerous and sometimes conflicting communities each governed by their own *Ordnung*, their rules for living. Believing they are 'in the world but not of it', they do not vote, undertake military service or subscribe to or draw from social security. They are pacifist, refusing to defend themselves if attacked physically or legally. See **Hutterian Brethren**, **Mennonites**

Amitabha *B*. *Z*. Skt. *Amida*, Jap. 'Boundless Light'. See *Amida*

Amritdhari *S*. Pun. The initiated members of the Sikh community, access to which is gained by **amritsankar**, the rite of initiation. Members are visibly distinguished by their dress and the enforcement of the *panja kakke*, the **Five Ks**.

Amrite *S*. Pun. *Amrit*, literally 'nectar', is holy water into which sugar crystals have been stirred with a double-edged sword. Used in the **Amritsankar**, the Sikh initiation ceremony, it is prepared during the singing of the liturgical hymns, then is brought to the kneeling initiate who drinks the water in his cupped hands. The candidate recites the Mul Mantra, making a commitment to keep the vows. See **Sahaj-dhari**, **Sikhism**

Amritsankar *Sik*. Pun. The initiation rite of a Sikh man or woman, wishing to be a member of the **Khalsa**. It is also known as *amrit pahul* or *khande de pahul*, 'tempered with steel'. The initiation includes a form of baptism and an oath to accept the *kurahit*, the Khalsa code of discipline. See **Amrite**, **Initiation**, **Sikhism**

Amulet An object believed to have magical properties that can protect against ill-luck, witchcraft, evil spirits and their influences. See **Charms**, **Mana**, **Superstition**, **Talisman**

Amun *E*. One of the forms of the Egyptian creator god who was first worshipped at Thebes as a local god. After being elevated (c.1550 BCE) to the position of King of Gods he was established as the state god. He became linked with Re, the sun god in the new cult of Amun-Re, whose principal temple was at Karnak where he was worshipped with his consort, **Mut**. The priesthood (see **Mansion of the Gods**) threatened the Pharaoh's sovereignty with Amun-Re gathering so much authority as the cult of a supreme god, that Egypt became something of a monotheistic theocracy. This set the stage for **Akhenaton**'s radical reforms.

Anabaptists *X*. Meaning 're-baptizers', a movement among the pre- and post-**Reformation** churches affirming that baptism should be given to mature believers only and that those who had been baptized as infants should be re-baptized. They repudiated the **Trinity** and were opposed to any relationship between Church and state; many were pacifists who refused to take part in forms of secular government. They believed that after death the soul slept until the day of resurrection. Their object was to establish a 'pure' Church of baptized and regenerated saints. Despite their pacifism some Anabaptist groups were notoriously violent and claims of personal visions and revelations led to all manner of schisms. In America, the **Mennonites** are founded on the Anabaptist tradition. See also **Amish**, **Baptism**, **Baptist**, **Christianity**, **Hutterian Brethren**

Ananda Church of Self-Realization *H*. A worldwide movement based on the teaching of **Yogananda** Paramhansa, founded in 1968 by one of his disciples, Swami Kriyananda, in Nevada. Originally he worked with Yogananda at the Washington HQ of the **Self-Realization Fellowship**, then went to India to spread the guru's teachings. On his return to the USA he was effectively dismissed from the SRF, since it was felt his teaching promoted separatism. He continued to teach the message of Yogananda, gradually establishing the Ananda Church. Today it is thought to have about 5,000 members.

Ananda Marga A yoga society founded at Jamalpur, Bihar, India in 1955 by Marga Guru Shri Anandamurti, 'He who attracts others as the embodiment of bliss'. His birth name is Prabhat Ranjan **Sarkar** and he is also known as *Ba'ba*, 'father'. The devotional practice follows a form of **Tantric** Yoga but the teaching is based on the **Progressive Utilization Theory** (PROUT), a social and economic system concerned to establish worldwide justice. The group holds to a universalist ideology and has a strong commitment to aid the progress of all sentient beings by serving those who suffer. To this end the Ananda Marga Universal Relief Team (AMURT) was created in 1965 to help victims of the numerous floods in India, since when its services have been carried to 80 countries. In 1967 Anandamurti founded a sister organization which provides medical care for pregnant and nursing mothers, helps educate women in home industries such as tailoring, handicraft and commercial food production and promotes effective birth control. Today, Ananda Marga is a worldwide organization with centres in over 160 countries, including the USA. See **Neo-Humanism**

Anapanasati *B*. Pal. 'wakefulness' or '**mindfulness**' through breathing. It is a basic exercise in developing *Dhyana*, 'absorption', as a meditation practice. One technique is to count inhalations and exhalations in the process of calming the mind. *Anapanasati* forms part of the instructions given by the Buddha in the *Satipathana* sutra. See **Meditation, Mindfulness, Samatha, Smriti, Vipassana**

Anarchism The term, with the noun 'anarchy', is from the Greek *anarxia*, 'without rulers'. It is not meant to imply chaos or anomy, but a form of social organization based on egalitarianism, intentionally established and maintained. Anarchists advocate the abolition of all forms of imposed or involuntary authority, social hierarchies, governments and coercive powers. They would replace authoritarian society with one based on voluntary co-operation and mutual aid, all forms of government being totally open and accountable. Anarchism's central doctrine is based on individual freedom and the right to oppose the state if that freedom is threatened. Thus everyone would be given their say in proportion to the degree to which the issues raised personally affected them. There is no agreement about how this egalitarian society should be achieved or what forms of relationship should prevail. The system appears to have a built-in contradiction in that, if a true anarchist society could be established, no form of government would be given the authority to maintain or protect it. Even so, the fundamental values of anarchism, balanced between freedom and responsibility, are attractive to any established society. The more laws a society needs the less secure it is; conversely, a society that thrives with a minimum number of laws could be said to have 'come of age' and to have achieved a considerable degree of maturity. Because there is no real consensus as to how the doctrine should be applied, it cannot be said to be a unified ideology. On its own, it does not provide a world view other than to represent the principle that imposed authority of any kind is undesirable and unnecessary. The term has encompassed a variety of political philosophies and ideologies. The founders of modern anarchism were **Proudhon** (1809–65), who advocated peaceful change and Blanqui (1805–81), who sanctioned the seizure of power by violence. **Bakunin** (1814–76), a later follower of Blanqui, considered 'the father of modern anarchism', clashed with Marx and in 1876 broke up the 1st Internationale. Proudhon set out the basic theories of Anarcho-Syndicalism which were in evidence in the Russian and Spanish Civil Wars and, more recently, in the activities of *les gauchistes* during the 'May Events' of 1968 in France.

FINAL WORD: 'Things fall apart; the centre cannot hold;
Mere anarchy is loosed upon the world,
The blood-dimmed tide is loosed and everywhere
The ceremony of innocence is drowned;
The best lack all conviction, while the worst
Are full of passionate intensity.'
W. B. Yeats, 'The Second Coming'

Anat see **Astarte**

Anatman *B*. Skt. Pali, *anatta,* 'non-self'. The central Buddhist concept of the absence of any kind of personal essence that is unchanging or eternal. One of the **Trilaksana**, the three characteristic marks of all existing phenomena. What we understand as the 'ego' has, in Buddhism, no permanent existence or reality, both in terms of personality and of everything that arises conditionally. In **Mahayana** this absence of self is a form of freedom known as 'emptiness'. See **Anitya**, **Dukkha**

Anatta *B*. 'no-self'. The key Buddhist doctrine affirming there is no such thing as an enduring self, it being made up of five *khandhas* or impermanent elements. The same principle applies to all objects in that they have no enduring or unchangeable attributes. See **Five Aggregates**

Ancestor Worship The widespread practice of worshipping the spirits of dead relatives in order to appease them or to seek their guidance. It is based on the belief that the dead continue to live and can affect the life of later individuals and communities. The worship becomes the focus of cultic ritual, involving prayer and in some cases the making of offerings and sacrifice. Examples of such practices can be found in Japanese and Chinese religions. (See **Shinto** and **Confucianism**) In **African Religion**

a variant, better-termed Ancestor Veneration plays a major part, echoing the fundamental importance of kinship. Ancestors are said to be the guardians of tradition who punish, by sickness or misfortune, those who break with it; they are venerated as elders in much the same way as living leaders of the tribe, but with an added mysticism, necessary ritual procedures and, in some cases, new names. A careful distinction is maintained between venerating ancestors and worshipping gods. In the **Benin** and **Ibo** of West Africa, veneration reflects a belief in the reincarnation of the ancestor in a descendent. See **Australian Aboriginal Religion**, **Fijian Religion**, **Yoruba Religion**

Anchorite *X*. From the Gk. *anakhorein*, 'to retire' or 'withdraw'. Originally a Christian who abandoned human company, but generally anyone who retires in seclusion for religious reasons. See **Hermit**

Ancient Mystic Order of Melchizedek (AMOM) Also known as **Nuwaubians** or the Nubian Nation of Moors. Founded in 1993 by Dwight York in Georgia, USA, the group originally followed traditional Islamic beliefs and dressed accordingly. Centred on an estate in Putnam County, around 400 followers, believing themselves to be descendents of Egyptians who migrated before the continents drifted apart, attempted to become a sovereign state. The group, who have no settled religious practice, set out to live at peace with 'Mother Nature'. They have moved from the original Islamic base to a broad, even vague interest in wanting to know the factual basis and truths of the world. For many Nuwaubians such truths include the existence of **UFOs**. Their leader claims to be from the 19th galaxy, named *Illyuwn*. One such craft was prophesied by York to arrive in 2003 from Illyuwn, to transport the elected 144,000 faithful to the planet Rizk where, through rebirth, they would live eternally. A 1993 FBI report stated that the group is 'a front for a wide range of criminal activity, including arson, welfare fraud and extortion'. York's group has operated under several names, including the Nubian Islamic Hebrew Mission and the Ansaaru Allah Community, which is an Islamic sect similar to **Nation of Islam**.

Ancient Mystical Order Rosae Crucis (AMORC) A non-sectarian group concerned with the study and practical application of natural and spiritual laws. 'Our purpose is to further the evolution of humanity through the development of the full potential of each individual.' They have no structured belief system, dogma or creed and their teachings draw on metaphysics, mysticism, psychology, parapsychology and science. The order, now spread to over 100 countries, is divided by languages into administrative regions called Grand Lodges. The teachings are presented in a series of nine degrees, on the conclusion of which the subject becomes a member of the Order. There is a preliminary Neophyte Degree which offers an overview of the nine degrees.

Angel Gk. *angelos* and L. *angelus*, 'a messenger'. An ethereal being found in many religions whose task is to assist God or the gods. In the **Tanakh**, the Hebrew word for angel, *mal'ach*, is given further significance by attachment to God's name, 'angel of the Lord' or 'angel of God'. They can appear as humans of extraordinary beauty, they can fly, they may appear in vast numbers or alone or be invisible; sacrifices touched by them immediately catch fire. They are portrayed as dreadful and powerful, like the 'avenging angel' and have complete knowledge of human affairs. Holy and just, they are in the service of God. There are evil angels such as Beelzebub and Satan and archangels, superior angels of a higher rank, like Gabriel and Michael. Angels are central to **Islam**, the **Koran** having been dictated to **Muhammad** by an angel. In **Zoroastrianism**, the **Amesha Spentas** are regarded as angels. A mystical tradition suggests that the soul grows in steps from minerals, plants and animals to humans; when the body dies the soul might evolve further to become an angel. The Christian mystic **Swedenborg** believed that the soul of a man and woman united by marriage in heaven becomes an angel. See **Spirit**

Anglicanism or **Anglican Communion** *X*. The name given to a group of churches known as, or associated with, the Church of England and in communion with the See of Canterbury. Since the expansion of the Church through 19th-century colonialism, the group includes several overseas dioceses. The theological standard for Anglicanism is the Bible, together with the Nicene Creed (see **Creeds**); its bishops claim to be in apostolic succession through the 16th-century English episcopate. Anglican **liturgy** is based on the Book of Common Prayer. For the greater part of the Communion, worship is in the language of the countries in which it has been founded.

Anglo-Saxon Religion *AE*. Anglo-Saxons, comprising the Angles, Saxons and Jutes, came to Britain from Germany, Scandinavia and the Netherlands from the mid-5th century CE. The gods and their mythologies are virtually the same as those of Germany and Scandinavia. Largely an illiterate society, its myths were transmitted orally in verse and dispersed among the tribes by the *scops*, travelling poets and minstrels. They believed in *Wyrd*, a cognate of 'weird' usually translated as 'fate' and in dwarves and giants who brought harm to people. There are no written records and scholars are not confident in ascribing to Anglo-Saxon gods the qualities or activities ascribed to Norse gods. The religion was polytheistic, the many gods being worshipped in sacred places associated with woods, rocks, rivers and other natural features. Idols of the gods were housed in temples and displayed on altars. Pope Gregory (c.540–604) instructed Augustine to destroy the idols but to use the temples as Christian places of worship. The major gods may be identified with the English weekday names, for example, Tiw with *Tiwesdæg*, Tuesday and Frige with *Frigedæg*, Friday. The 'Osses' correspond to the **Aesir**, the Norse pantheon and the 'Wones' with the **Vanir**, the fertility gods. Christianity, both Celtic and Roman, displaced the religion during the 8th and 9th centuries. The **Synod of Whitby**, held in 664, settled for Roman Christianity. See **Celtic Christianity**, **Germanic Religion**, **Norse Mythology**

Angra Mainyu or **Ahriman** *Zo*. 'The Hostile Spirit' of Zoroastrianism, central to its conception of evil. In the **Gathas**, **Zoroaster** taught that at the beginning of time there were twin Sprits or energies, one holy, the other evil. Virtually nothing is said in the **Avesta** about the origin of the evil spirit except that like its opposite virtuous form, **Ahura Mazda**, it was independent and free to act as it wished. The implication is that the evil spirit was free to choose and that its choice for evil was irrevocable. Thus, two separate spirits are responsible for everything in the universe and are set in ultimate opposition to each other. In one sense this is a paradigm for human responsibility, that as individuals we are free, like the Spirits themselves, to choose the direction we will take, either for Good or for Evil, 'Truth' or 'Lie', thereby setting Zoroastrianism in the form of a classical **dualism**. Angra Mainyu uses the **daevas**, gods associated with earlier Indo-Iranian religions, to disseminate the 'lie' or evil among human beings. Ahura Mazda has no control over evil, which exists like a parasite in human consciousness. The truth will eventually triumph in a final victory, the **Frashokereti**, but what will bring this about is the responsibility of human beings worked out by the choices people make between good and evil. Human strength of will, the choices made each day, can bring about the impotence of Angra Mainyu and the omnipotence of Ahura Mazda.

Animal Cults The ritual burial of animals in graves furnished with provisions, provides evidence of Egyptian animal cults dating back to the 4th millennium BCE. The earliest examples are of tribal animal deities that proliferated before the two Kingdoms of Egypt were united. Groups, sometimes those of a specific city, deified and anthropomorphized these animals and as the cults became assimilated into the developing pharaohnic religion they were worshipped not as gods, but as manifestations of gods. The animal statues, a feature of Egyptian art, could be made alive if the gods chose to inhabit them. The concept was represented, for example, by statues of **Anubis** in the form of a jackal and **Horus** in the form of a falcon. Notable bull cults were associated with Memphis and Heliopolis; other animals included cats, crocodiles and ibises, who were thought to be custodians of a deity's power and were revered during their lives and mummified at death. Across the world many other forms of animal cults developed, including those identified with the Totemism of **Amerindian religion**, the Eskimos and African Tribal religions. See **African Religion**, **Egyptian Religion**, **Mummification**, **Totem**

Animatism The attribution of consciousness and personality to all natural phenomena, such as wind, thunder and plants, and to inanimate objects like rocks and mountains. More generally, the belief that everything is infused with an impersonal life force, such as **mana**. It is less specific than **animism** which endows phenomena with more personal spirits or supernatural beings, rather than with a common and omnipresent energy. The term was coined by the British ethnologist and social anthropologist R. R. Marett (1866–1943).

Animism *L. animus* or *anima*, 'mind' or 'soul'. A widely used term with various meanings originally referring to the doctrine of spiritual beings. It was extended to include the belief that ordinary 'inanimate' objects as well as animate subjects were, or could be, inhabited by supernatural beings endowed with reason, intelligence and volition. This became the basis for **pantheism** and **animatism**. Another layer of meaning refers to the notion that the world is a community of living beings, only some of whom are human. Today, Animism is identified both with theories of the origin of religion and with numerous Animist societies across the world that follow animistic practices such as **Neopaganism** and the **Eco-Pagans**. See **African Religion**, **Native American Religion**, **Shamanism**

Anitya *H. B.* Skt. Pali. *annica*, 'impermanence'. In **Hinduism**, everything is seen to be in flux and passing away. This transitoriness is one of the three marks of everything existing. The fundamental property of all conditioned things. See **Anatman**, **Dukkha**, **Three Marks of Existence**

Anointing Also known as 'unction'. A rite during which oil or something like it, is applied to the subject. The substance is sometimes called 'chrism'. It is usually practised as a ceremony of initiation or consecration, setting aside the subject for a special office or function. The anointment is a sign of the intervention of God or the gods, having chosen the person to fulfil the designated task. In biblical tradition the Israelites anointed their Kings and their High Priests together with their vestments and sacred vessels (Exodus 29:29 and Lev. 4:3, for example). Anointing remains part of the coronation service of English monarchs, for which a special anointing robe is worn. Anointing may be used in the rite of exorcism and, as part of Catholicism's office of Extreme Unction, offered to the terminally ill. Here 'extreme' means last and 'unction' anointing. Catholics are also anointed with oil at Baptism, Confirmation and Holy Orders. There are secular usages of the practice derived, as though by superstition, from the religious precedent. Queequeg anointing his boat in Melville's *Moby Dick* is one of many examples from literature.

Anselm *X.* (1033–1109) A native of Aosta in Lombardy. First a pupil of Lanfranc, then following him in 1063 as Prior of the Abbey of Bec in Normandy. Because his relationships with Rufus and Henry I were strained, he was driven into exile. Anselm opposed Rufus' feudal dues and refused to compromise the spiritual rights of the Church or to consecrate bishops invested by Henry I. In 1093 he was elected Archbishop of Canterbury, a post he held for 15 years until his death. During this time he completely reorganized the structure of the Church through reforming synods, discipline and clerical celibacy. Apart from being a talented administrator, he was a brilliant philosopher and theologian. More than half of his written work was done in the decade following his election to Canterbury. Two of his major works developed the **ontological argument** for the existence of God and in *Cur deus homo?* he presented a classical theology of the Atonement. His concern was to establish the nature and meaning of a secure faith. See **Arguments for the Existence of God, En Realissimum**

FINAL WORD: 'I do not seek to understand so that I may believe; but I believe so that I may understand. For I believe this also, that "unless I believe, I shall not understand."' Anselm

Antaratman *H*. Skt. 'inner self' or 'Higher Self'. The divine spark, amounting to the presence in everyone of God or the Absolute as inborn and eradicable. It is what, within us, interprets our experiences and the energy driving our spiritual development. It is the real self hidden inside us but layered over with ignorance and misconceptions. The goal of **Hinduism** is to disperse these confusing layers so as to reveal *antaratman* as a divine effulgence. Such a breakthrough is the purpose of Hindu self-realization. Ghandi chose the word *antaratman* for the inner voice of conscience, synonymous for him with God or the true self. '... so long as I have not directly experienced this truth, till then that which my inner self (*antaratman*) counts as true, that which is only conceived by me as true, will be counted by me as my support, my beacon, as the foundation for the course of my life.' (Mahatma Ghandi)

Antaryamin *H*. Skt. 'inner leader' or 'inner control'. A subtly differentiated variation of *antaratman*, the 'inner self', representing an awareness of our divine spark as an 'inner witness' or super-consciousness, sensitive to everything we think and do. It is this watchful or mindful faculty that acts as our guide. See **Atman**

Anthropomancy A method of divination using the entrails of dead or dying men and women; frequently use was made of young, virgin females in the process of sacrifice. Sometimes called splanchomancy, divination by examining the entrails of sacrificial victims. The ancient Egyptians and the Roman Emperor Varius Avitus Bassanius (205–221 CE) were known to have practised anthropomancy and Julian the Apostate (331–363 CE) sacrificed countless children for his nocturnal divinations. A more acceptable form is **augury**, in which birds are used. See **Auspicia, Bibliomancy, Mantike**

Anthropomorphism A form of personification in which human or animal qualities are ascribed to inanimate objects or more generally the attribution of human qualities and characteristics to non-human beings, animals, objects and natural phenomena. The device is widely used in all religions to render intelligible what otherwise would be ineffable. This is particularly true of the perception of God in biblical religions, where he is frequently referred to as, 'Father' and having human form, parts, qualities and emotions. Thus, God has a face and eyes, he has arms and feet, he is capable of mercy, anger, jealousy and love. Behind this literal anthropomorphism is the authority of Gen. 1:27. 'And God created man in his image, in the image of God created he him; male and female he created them.' Anthropomorphism is, to some extent, found in all religions as, for example, in the descriptions of the Hindu **Avatars** and the Greek and Roman gods. See **Theomorphism**

Anthroposophy X. A movement started by Rudolph Steiner (1861–1925) who, in 1912, resigned from being the head of the German Theosophists to form the Anthroposophical Society. His move away from **Theosophy** seemed an abandonment of divine wisdom in favour of human wisdom, but his main reason for leaving the theosophists was that the place they accorded to Jesus and to Christianity was not, in his view, sufficiently central. His philosophy, however, was somewhat syncretistic and together with his Christian convictions, he held a belief in **karma** and **reincarnation**. By 1922 Steiner had established the Christian Community complete with liturgy and rituals. Anthroposophy and the Christian Community continue today, but as separate movements. At the age of about 40 Steiner added the occult to his long list of interests, which already included agriculture, architecture, art, chemistry, drama, literature, maths and medicine.

Steiner retained two central doctrines of Theosophy: that there is a form of spiritual consciousness that offers access to higher spiritual truths; and that human spiritual evolution is hindered by being over-involved in the material world. On this base he developed his Anthroposophy into what he called a 'spiritual science' which asserted that the spiritual was the only true reality. Humans must learn to understand the spiritual dimension through letting go of their attachments to the material world and Steiner developed a programme of education specifically to achieve this end. It is for his philosophy of education that Steiner is, perhaps, best known. Steiner schools do not actually teach religion, leaving this to the parents. One of the most challenging concepts of Steiner's views on education is seen in his attempts to teach the physically and mentally handicapped. Because it is the spirit that comprehends and drives our existence, that spirit is the same in everyone having the same potential without regard to mental or physical limitations.

In 1913 Steiner built his Goetheanum, a 'school of spiritual science' at Dornach near Basel, Switzerland. From this centre developed the famous Steiner or Waldorf schools. The first American Waldorf school opened in New York in 1928; there are now thought to be about 125 schools educating children in the USA, with over 600 school across 32 other countries, teaching something like 120,000 students.

FINAL WORD: 'Anthroposophy is a path of knowledge, to guide the Spiritual in the human being to the Spiritual in the universe.'
Steiner [1973]

Antichrist *X*. In **eschatology** this has come to mean a person or another entity that is the embodiment of evil and utterly opposed to truth. The word does not appear in the New Testament's apocalyptic or eschatological literature and each of its five appearances is to be found in the Apostle John's two letters, where it refers to any false teacher or corrupter of the faith. The idea, however, has been carried over in popular usage to refer to 'the man' or 'son of perdition' of 2 Thessalonians 2 and to include **Revelation**'s notions of the Dragon, the Beast, the Whore of Babylon, etc. These have been interpreted either as institutions, such as an evil form of government or as an individual political or religious leader who, as the incarnation of **Satan**, inspires false worship or veneration. The Christian doctrine of the 'last things' has the Antichrist ushering in an age when evil will dominate, causing 'trials and tribulations'. Finally he will be thrown into the lake of fire by a triumphant Christ.

Islam has its antichrist, known in the **Hadith** and **Koran** as Dajjal. In **Shiite** belief the Imam Mahdi is expected to rule the world for seven years and provoke a global battle between good and evil, prior to the final judgement. The tradition is similar to the biblical account of the Antichrist and Armageddon.

Throughout history various people have been identified as the Antichrist; early contenders were Nero and Vespasian; others included, for the **Old Believers**, the Czar Peter the Great; for Protestants, various Popes; for Christians, Muhammad as a false prophet who placed himself above Jesus and forcibly converted Christians, Jews and others; for Jews, Hitler and Nazism. Contemporary contenders are too numerous to list, but include kings, politicians and American presidents. What or who the Antichrist is and when he, she or it will come, remains a mystery wrapped in an enigma.

FINAL WORD: 'Here is the key. Let him that hath understanding count the number of the beast: for it is the number of a man; and his number is Six hundred threescore and six.' (Revelation 13:18)

Anti-Cult Movement A loose association of various groups concerned to draw public attention to sects, cults and movements considered to be threatening and dangerous. Such movements are believed to be coercive, manipulative and in extreme cases to employ mind-control methods. The majority of such cults are religious, placing an emphasis on doomsday predictions of the end of the world; the record shows that in some cults preparation for the event has led to mass suicide. Exposure has discredited many of these cults in the USA, but they are still influential in China, Japan and parts of Western Europe. See **Aum Shinri Kyo**, **Branch Dravidians**, **Heaven's Gate**, **Order of the Solar Temple**, **People's Temple**

Antifoundationalism The philosophical position that all standards of judgement are historically and culturally provisional and never universally applicable or value-free. Applying this concept is thought to sharpen the use of language in the process of helping people to arrive at decisions in situations in which absolute standards or certain knowledge cannot be used. Exponents include Karl **Popper**, **Lyotard** and **Derrida**. See **Postmodernism**

Anti-Semitism *J*. See **Semitic**

Antra *H*. The concept of chaos in Indo-Iranian religion originated with the Vedas, with reference to the chaos that existed before and in the process of cosmic creation. In Zoroastrianism the chaos resides in the dualistic conflict between **Ahura Mazda**, the Wise Lord and **Angra Mainyu**, the Hostile Spirit. See **Indo-Iranian Religion, Rta, Zoroastrianism**

Anu *AME*. The sky god of the Sumerians, associated with Babylonian-Assyrian cults. He formed the supreme triad of the pantheon with the earth god Enlil and the water god Ea. See **Mesopotamian Religion**

Anubis *E*. An animal cult associated with the 17th Upper Egypt nome (administrative district) known as the Jackal Nome because it was represented by the image of a man with the head of a jackal. Originally, Anubis was the god of the dead before this role was assumed by **Osiris**; he presided over the ritual of mummification, guided the souls of the dead through the underworld and supervised the judging of the heart when it was placed on the scales of justice. Prayers to Anubis were found carved on most ancient tombs. The cult's centre was Cynopolis. See **Animal Cults, Egyptian Religion**

Anussati *B*. Pal. 'recollection'. A group of subjects, usually set as six or ten, used for contemplation. The complete set of ten are i) The **Buddha**, ii) the **dharma**, iii) the **sangha**, iv) **Sila** (morality), v) Dana (generosity), vi) **Deva** (gods), vii) death, viii) the body, ix) **Prana** (the breath), and x) peace. By meditating on these subjects the three roots of evil – greed, hatred and delusion – can be destroyed.

Aphrodite *G*. The sea-foam born Aphrodite was the goddess of love, beauty and fertility. Her cult was widespread throughout the Greek world and she became known to the Romans as **Venus**. An extensive mythology developed centred on her principal sanctuaries which included Corinth, the island of Cythera, Paphos and Amathus in Cyprus from where she originated, probably as a mother-goddess. Long before Aphrodite came on the scene, the Greeks, as part of their creation mythology, made a god out of sexual potency in the form of **Eros**. Hesiod made use of this by associating Aphrodite with Eros and describing creation as the result of sexual union between cosmic forces. By the time of the *Iliad* and the *Odyssey*, Aphrodite was one of the Olympian gods and the daughter of **Zeus** and Dione. But the mythology is multi-layered and alternative forms preserve her eastern origins, which account for her association with **Adonis,** with whom she fell passionately in love. The myth of her birth from the foam of the ocean is famously depicted in Botticelli's *The Birth of Venus*. See **Atarte, Syria**

Apocalypse The biblical 'Book of Revelation' and the name for numerous Jewish and Christian texts written between the 2nd century BCE and the 2nd century CE, which contained prophetic visions of impending disaster such as the end of the world and the final judgement of God. Several mythologies and religions hold to a tradition that anticipates an apocalypse before the end of time, for example the Germanic and Norse **Ragnarok**. See **Eschatology**

Apocatastasis See **Universalism**

Apocrypha Gk. *apocruptien*, 'to hide away'. Traditionally the term is used of both religious and non-religious texts as a standard by which to identify doubtful sources. Thus, 'apocryphal' applies to something highly questionable. In religious usage it refers to texts that are not canonical but are approximately similar in age and style to the accepted sources. There are, inevitably, differences between Jews, Catholics, the Orthodox and Protestant churches as to what are considered apocrypha texts or authorized texts. There are apocryphal books associated with both the **Old Testament** and **New Testament**, the *Book of Jubilees* being an example of the former and *The Gospel of Thomas* of the latter. It is not possible to form any classification that will not, somewhere, meet with objection and questions are still raised about the canonicity of some of the generally acceptable books, such as the Epistle of James, on the grounds that the authorship is not secure. The different criteria of canonization for each community determines what 'orthodox' authority accepts as the biblical canon.

Apollo *G. R.* The son of Zeus and Leto, Apollo is the archetypal all-rounder. The mythology presents him as the radiant sun god, the god of music, archery, poetry, painting, prophecy, plagues, healing, animal welfare and those are only part of it. Each of his titles represents a different function, over 300 of which have survived in ancient literature and on stone inscriptions, indicating his universal popularity. He can be understood as the god or embodiment of Greek civilization, idealized in art as a young man with virile beauty. His origins may lie in a pre-historic non-Greek deity, perhaps the Hittite Apulunas, but his most important shrine was at Delphi, 'beneath snowy Parnassus', where as a child he killed a dragoness with his bow, the first of many great exploits. In later mythology the dragon became a python, the derivation of Apollo's title, Pythian, in which connection he is associated with the Delphic oracle. The ruins of his temple and the *omphalos*, the stone believed to be the centre of the earth, can still be visited. The Romans retained his name and adopted him as a healing god and as patron of oracles and prophecy. The oldest record we have of him in Rome is in a prayer offered by Vestals (see **Vestal Virgins**) when because of a pestilence he was addressed as

Physician and Healer. His cult flourished until it was deemed pagan and ousted by Christianity.

Apostle Gk. *apostolos*, 'one who is sent out', a missionary or emissary commissioned to spread the teachings of a master. The term is most familiarly associated with the 12 Apostles of Jesus Christ: 'He called unto him his disciples and of them he chose 12, whom also he named apostles' (Luke 6:13). See **Disciple**

Apostolic Churches *X*. Any group of churches founded on the teachings of the **Apostles**. Historically these were the churches of Rome, Alexandria, Antioch and Jerusalem. By tradition, the term is used broadly of the greater part of the Roman Catholic orthodox and Protestant churches. The contemporary Apostolic Church is a branch of **Pentecostalism** which includes both various denominations and independent churches bearing the name 'Apostolic', such as the Apostolic Church of Pentecost of Canada. Many of the Apostolic Churches adhere to **Oneness Pentecostalism**, also known as 'Jesus Only Theology', a movement that denies the doctrine of the **Trinity** and teaches a strict monotheism. They constitute the fastest growing of the churches. See **Branhamism** and **Modalism**

Apotheosis Gk. *apotheoun*, 'to deify'. Glorification, usually to a divine level and the recognition of a human being as a god, for example the apotheosis of the Kings of Egypt, Peru, China, Japan (see **Japanese Religion**, **Shintoism**). Most familiar is the deification of Roman Emperors. See **Emperor Worship**, **Divine Kingship**

Appalachia Presbyterianism *X*. A form of **Bible Belt** Christianity drawn from the Church of Scotland and established in the USA during the colonial settlement of the southern States. See **Tidewater Anglicanism**

Aquarian Age Teaching See **New Age Religion**

Aquarian Church of Universal Service One of the organizations that represent the concept of Celestial Awareness of a universal force or celestial consciousness that manifests itself in ultra-high levels of frequency. Its force is given in the form of symbols and impressions to those who attune themselves to those frequencies. These impressions are translated by a channeler. Founded in 1969 by Paul Shockley in the USA, the movement is concerned with cosmic awareness but has no specific doctrines. Similar to **Unitarian-Universalists**.

Aquinas, Thomas (1225–74) known as 'Doctor Angelicus' and 'Doctor Universalis', Aquinas was an Italian Catholic philosopher and theologian in the tradition of **Scholasticism**. He instigated the Thomist school of philosophy and is considered by the Catholic Church to be its greatest theologian. Aquinas left a considerable amount of writing, most notably the *Summa contra Gentiles* and the *Summa theologica*, which was never completed. His systematic theology was influenced by the rediscovered philosophy of Aristotle and is based on **Natural Theology**. This asserts that God's existence and attributes may be ascertained by natural reason on the basis of logical argument. For example, one of the classical arguments for the existence of God is the **cosmological argument**, stating that reality must have 'a necessary ground' or 'first cause' which is to be identified as God. There are other truths, dependent on revelation, to which reason has no access, but these truths are not fundamental to belief. Since man participates in God's being, the rules of reason are as binding as a biblical commandment; they have their source in God's eternal law by which he regulates all creation. Natural law bears the imprint of eternal law. Aquinas' work covered the whole field of theology and biblical exegesis. He was canonized in 1323, but not until the 16th century did his theology become the dominant view of the Catholic Church. In 1880 he was declared the patron saint of all Catholic educational establishments. See **Thomism** and, for an opposing view, **Calvinism**

Arahant or **Arhat** *B. Z.* Pal. Skt. a 'worthy one' who, in the **Hinayana** tradition, has achieved enlightenment or **bodhi**. The Arhat is not a Buddha, but one who has achieved liberation by following the teachings of another and who, in this process, concentrates on his own self-realization. In contradistinction the bodhisattva of the **Mahayana** tradition is concerned for the liberation of all sentient beings. The Buddha was an Arhat and is given this epithet. He is invoked in Pali texts as 'Worthy One, the Perfectly Awakened One'. However, the Buddha achieved nirvana as a result of his own effort in meditation and without a teacher. The term has various shades of meaning across different Buddhist traditions. See **Bodhisattva**, **Types of Buddha**

Aranyakas *H.* Skt. 'belonging to the woods'. Vedic texts supplementary to the **Brahmanas**, intended for forest hermits and older people of the priestly class. In the **Rig-Veda**, Aranyani is the goddess of the woods and forests. The texts are mystical in style and ascetic in emphasis and represent a movement away from the priest-centred religion of the time, focused on the sacrificial cult which was the *raison d'être* of the **Rig-Veda** hymns. For purposes of meditation, aspects of the sacrificial rituals were reduced to symbolism; as **Hinduism** developed the meditation practices gradually replaced the orthodox sacrificial cult. This and the rituals of the priests were finally rejected by Hindu heterodoxy, by **Jainism** and by Buddhism. As such the Aranyakas constitute a theological and philosophical bridge to the **Upanishads**. See **Vedas**

Arcadia *G.* A province of ancient Greece traditionally associated with the Peloponnesus. Somewhat isolated from the rest of the world by mountains, the people lived an uncomplicated pastoral life. Greek mythology made Arcadia the home of the god Pan and a type of paradise in Greek and Roman poetry, a concept that re-emerged in Renaissance literature. Its inhabitants inspired **Rousseau**'s Noble Savage, the ideal of a people who live close to nature.

Archetypes Jung's term for the innate and usually universal concepts populating the **collective unconscious**. They are inherited patterns of thought sometimes expressed as symbolic images representing past collective experiences drawn from both human ancestry and pre-human animal existence.

Ares *G*. From the Greek *ares*, 'battle' or 'strife'. Probably a Thracian sun-god by origin, he was worshipped before battles. Important in poetry, he was rarely the centre of a cult, exceptions being at Sparta and in the early mythology of Thebes. Apart from the sacrifices made to him by field commanders, he was mostly worshipped in conjunction with other gods – for example he shared his cult with **Aphrodite** in the temple at Thebes. The Romans identified Ares with **Mars**, the god of war, a much more important cult.

Arguments for the Existence of God Numerous arguments for the existence of God have been suggested by philosophers and theologians. The problem of proof lies in the tension between belief or faith and knowledge. Because something is believed in, it does not imply that it is 'known'. To use belief as a proof of the existence of God is entirely subjective and beyond rational validation. The classical arguments for God's existence fall into two categories: **Metaphysical** and Empirical (see **Empiricism**). Metaphysics offers the cosmological argument or the argument from **First Cause**, the mathematical argument that defines God as the 'absolute infinite', the **Ontological** argument and the pantheistic argument (see **Pantheism** and **Panentheism**). The Empirical arguments include the **Teleological** argument (the argument from design) and the moral argument which suggests that because objective morality exists, so must God. There are several other arguments, as well as many that set out to prove that God does not exist. It is also suggested that arguments, valid or otherwise, for the existence of God miss the point entirely. **Wittgenstein** would encourage us to consider how the 'word is used' and the point has been put that 'God' used by philosophers is a concept wholly determined by our culture, whereas 'God' used by believers is a radically different concept identified in a variety of terms, for example Yahweh, Vishnu, Allah and Zeus or any other deity that is the subject of religion. So which 'God' are we concerned with? **Pascal** picked up this point exactly in his *Pensées*: 'The God of Abraham, Isaac and Jacob – not the God of the philosophers!' See **Agnosticism, Anselm, Atheism, Deism, Descartes, En Realissimum, Fideism**

Arianism *X*. A Christian heresy based on a doctrine of Arius of Alexandria (c.250 CE–c.336 CE), the substance of which was that while God was supremely immanent in Jesus Christ, he was not the same as God and therefore essentially less than God. Technically, Jesus was not of 'one substance' with God and therefore was a being created by 'God the Father', an intermediate being between God and the world. The heresy was rejected by the Church, specifically by Athanasius (296–373), the Bishop of Alexandria. See **Christianity, Creeds**

Aristotle (384–322 BCE) A Greek philosopher, student of **Plato** and teacher of **Alexander the Great**. A polymath, he wrote books on philosophy, physics, poetry, zoology, logic, rhetoric, government and biology. Beyond the subjects of his books he studied every subject discipline he came across and is one of the few thinkers in history to have an almost totally comprehensive knowledge of what constituted, at the time, the scope of human knowledge. Along with Plato and Socrates he is considered to be among the most influential of the ancient Greek philosophers on Western thought. His importance for religion stems from his writings on metaphysics and ethics. His metaphysics is founded on what he termed the four 'causes', not as we understand the word 'cause' as in 'cause and effect', but as four different ways of explaining the world. They are i) The Material Cause, 'That from which it comes'; ii) The Formal Cause, 'That which it is'; iii) The Efficient Cause, 'That which moves it'; and iv) The Final Cause, 'That of which its purpose is'. An example of an artefact that has all four causes would be a table, which has material causes (wood and nails), a formal cause (the blueprint or a generally agreed idea of what tables are), an efficient cause (the carpenter) and a final cause (using it to dine on). Aristotle's *Nichomachean Ethics*, one of three ethical treatises, is considered to be one of his greatest works. Put simply, his ethical system was based on the study of virtues, but in order to understand a virtue the individual must not just study what it *is*, but understand how it works in practice. Not only should 'justice' be practised and applied, but the individual should *become* 'just'. The *Nichomachean Ethics* concentrates on an ontology of ethics, of giving 'being' to virtue, not just practising it as an expediency or as a good thing to do. Thus, rather than undertaking specific 'good' actions, the individual should strive to develop virtue by continually behaving virtuously that is, to become a good man one must behave like a good man. Only by this means is it possible to discover what goodness is. Thus, for Aristotle, ethics is the means or art of making that discovery. He believed that 'happiness' was the end of life and that so long as a person was striving for goodness, good deeds will result, thus making the person happy.

FINAL WORD: 'Men acquire a particular quality by constantly acting in a particular way ... you become just by performing just actions, temperate by performing temperate actions.' Aristotle

Ark of the Covenant *J*. A wooden chest constructed by Bezalel (Exod.25: 10–22 and Deut.10: 1–5). The chest was first placed in the tabernacle that accompanied the Israelites in the wilderness and served as a symbol of the presence of God. It was the focus of worship from where the High

Priest presided over the expiation of the people's sin on **Yom Kippur**, and it went into battle with the Israelite forces. Eventually it was placed in the **Holy of Holies** in Solomon's Temple in Jerusalem, but references to the Ark do not appear after the Temple's destruction in 70 CE. The **Synagogue** Ark or Ark of the Law, houses the sacred **Torah** scrolls. The veil or curtain of the Ark hangs either in front of or behind the doors, depending on the tradition of the synagogue.

Armageddonists A variant of **Millennialism** that interprets aspects of international relations as signs heralding the final battle, Armageddon, that will bring this era of the world and human civilization to an end. An example of these 'signs' is the proliferation of nuclear weapons and the tensions caused by the international agencies set up to limit it, such as the International Atomic Energy Agency. A more telling sign is the long-running Middle East crisis focused on the Israeli-Palestinian conflict which is wrapped around by resurgent fundamentalist Islam supported by terrorist agencies like, Al-Qu'ida, the attack of 9/11 and the USA intervention in Iraq. Many of the illustrations drawn from contemporary events are thought to be valid interpretations of the apocalyptic vision of John recorded in **Revelation**, the book terminating the New Testament. FINAL WORD: 'Armageddon-style terrorism will be recognizable by a global network that enables events to be directed with relative anonymity. Its goal will be terrorism as a form of war or the creation of a 'brave new world' from the ashes of what it seeks to destroy. Rather than intermittent attacks in retaliation for perceived injustices, the war paradigm of Armageddon will mean an almost unceasing threat for the duration of the conflict.' Lynn Lynch, *Terror-Vision* website

Arminianism *X*. A modification of **Calvinist** doctrines offered by the Dutch theologian, Jacobus Arminius (1560–1609). Arminius was particularly concerned with the doctrine of **predestination**, and modified Calvin's hard-edged account of it to allow for man's free will in matters of **salvation**. Arminius argued that the salvatory efficacy of Jesus' death and the grace of God, were for all humanity and not for an exclusive 'elected' group. At the council of Dordrecht in Holland (1618–19), Calvin's doctrines were ratified and codified and Arminianism condemned. Eventually, both in Holland and England, Arminius moved towards Unitarianism but he questioned the substitutionary theory of **Atonement**, the doctrine that Jesus Christ died 'in our place'. By the middle of the 18th century, the Methodists and Anglicans had established a Protestant orthodoxy on matters of the Atonement and the doctrine of predestination was rejected.

Armstrongism *X*. The doctrines and religious movement founded by Herbert Armstrong (1892–1986) who established the Worldwide Church of God (WCG). He rejected some of the basic doctrines of orthodox Christianity such as the **Trinity**, the divinity of **Jesus** and the personality of the Holy Spirit. His theme was British Israelism (see **British**

Israelites) and the belief that any morally sound person could 'become God as God is God'. Salvation is by works, to be demonstrated by **Sabbatarianism,** by tithing one's income at 20–30 per cent, by keeping the **Old Testament** feast days and observing the dietary laws. Under the leadership of Armstrong's successors, Joseph Tkach and his son Joe, the doctrines of the WCG were radically revised with the result that numerous splinter groups were formed such as the Global Church of God and the United Church of God, which continue to maintain various forms of Armstrongism.

Artemis *G.* 'Lady of wild thing'. She was **Apollo**'s twin sister and the virgin moon-goddess of the hunt and wild animals. One tradition has her identified as Hecate, the primal pre-Olympian feral goddess. She was worshipped less in Greece than in Asia Minor where she was a principal deity. The cult may have been of Cretan origin and in different forms was established at Sparta and most famously at Ephesus, whose metal smiths felt threatened by St Paul's preaching (Acts 19:23–30). The cult was later conflated with the Roman **Diana**. Festivals of Artemis were the *Brauronia*, held in Brauron and that of Artemis Orthia, held at Sparta.

Aryan Skt. 'noble'. The term has various meanings. It can refer to the group of languages also known as Indo-European or Indo-Germanic. The group includes Sanskrit, Zend, Greek, Latin, Celtic, Teutonic and Slavonic. Thus, 'Aryan' is used to refer to the Asian forms of these languages or to the original language. Beyond reference to the linguistic group, the term applies to tribes thought to have migrated from central Asia from the beginning of the 2nd millennium BCE. Some authorities put the date at least a thousand years earlier. The migration was widespread and included Iran, the name of which is derived from 'Aryan'. It is also thought the name 'Arya' is echoed in the name 'Eire' which, if true, demonstrates the spread of a language with the same root. Tradition has it that the migration through the Indus valley, into what is now known as the Punjab was, in effect, an invasion by a martial people who brought with them their own religion, to which was added features of the indigenous religion of the **Indus Valley Civilization.** As a result of this invasion the native **Dravidians** were totally subjugated. There is controversy concerning the Aryan invasion theory. The alternative model is one that combines Aryan migration (possibly beginning as early as 3500 BCE) with a long process of settlement and assimilation in which there was cross-fertilization between Aryan and Dravidian culture. It seems, however, that Aryan culture and religion dominated. Certainly the Aryans brought with them a priestly caste that had talent for writing hymns that accompanied a sacrificial cult and the pressing of *avestan haoma* or **soma**, for its inebriating juice. Other religious features included the mother-goddess, the yogic god, the sacred tree, a phallic emblem, a pantheon of divine beings and an emphasis on domestic observance. Each of these, to a greater or lesser extent, became features of early Hinduism. Most importantly, the hymns composed by the priests became

Hinduism's earliest scriptures, the **Vedas** (specifically the **Rig-Veda**), written in **Sanskrit**. The term 'Arya' has survived in **Buddhism** as, for example, in *Arya-pudgala*, 'noble one', designating someone who is at any stage of the Nobel Path.

The adoption of the term 'Aryan' by the National Socialist Party in Germany in the 1930s, to depict the concept of racial purity, has meant the word has little useful modern currency.

Aryan Nations Church An American neo-Nazi paramilitary organization which is part of the **Christian Identity Movement**. It preaches against all non-Caucasian groups. In 1984 a splinter group, the Order, killed Alan Berg, a Jewish radio personality. They attracted international attention when, in 1992, the wife of a member, Randy Weaver, was killed when the FBI raided their compound.

Asa *Zo.* The 'Right' or 'Good', being the positive side of the Zoroastrian dualism and associated with **Ahura Mazda**. As with **Druj**, the evil or negative aspect of the dualism, the forces are so strong that the Avesta sometimes gives the impression that they take on the status of gods or spirits. In effect, Asa and Druj are more akin to an attitude or inclination towards the 'good' or the 'evil' respectively. Critically, in this clearly defined conflict human beings do have a choice to be disposed towards one or the other. See **Dualism and Non-Dualism**, **Fravarane**, **Zoroastrianism**

Asatru *Nor.* 'belief in the gods'. Emerging in Iceland in the 1960s and 1970s, it is a new religion concerned with rehabilitating Norse paganism as represented by the pre-Christian Eddas. It is officially recognized by the governments of Iceland, Norway and Denmark; groups have also been formed in the USA. See **Germanic Religion**, **Norse Mythology**

Ascended Masters A **New Age** cult based on belief in a company of teachers or masters who live on an astral plane as non-physical entities, beyond time and space. They communicate spiritual truth to human beings through 'channelling' or other occult methods. Members of this group of super-teachers include **Buddha**, **Jesus** and St Germain (see **I AM movement**). They are also known as the Great White Brotherhood.

Ascension Day *X.* The Christian doctrine of ascension holds that **Jesus Christ** bodily ascended to heaven after his resurrection. The belief is affirmed in the Apostles' and Nicene **creeds**. It is observed annually as one the great feasts of the Christian calendar, celebrated on a Thursday, the fortieth day following **Easter**.

Asclepius, the **god** *G.* A Greek healing god of medicine, said to be a direct ancestor of the physician **Hippocrates** (460–377 BCE). The legend has it that he killed a snake and watched as another snake revived it with herbs. In this fashion he learned about the medical power of plants. Probably founded on this legend is the symbol of the medical profession, a caduceus, a staff entwined with serpents. As his skills developed he learned to revive the dead, with the result that **Hades**, god of the underworld, believing his role was threatened, persuaded his brother **Zeus** to kill him with a thunderbolt and to decree that all mortals should die.

Asclepius, the **text** *G*. One of the longer and most influential of the **Hermetica**. It is preserved in a Latin translation of c.3rd century CE, which was known and cited by **Augustine**. It is this text that determined the character of the Hermetica in the Middle Ages and during the **Renaissance**. Magic, perhaps, comes closest to philosophy in the famous 'god-making' passages of the Asclepius (23–4, 37–8) which describe how material objects can be manipulated to invoke a god to inhabit a statue and thus endow it with a soul.

Asha *Zo*. The term, usually translated 'righteousness', inevitably carried the notion of 'truth' with it. It is an empowering force stemming directly from the Zoroastrian God, **Ahura Mazda**. The difference between order and chaos is, for Zoroastrians, not just a philosophical distinction but one founded on ethics. Because *asha* comes directly from Ahura Mazda, it is not dependent on the mediatory role of the priests or their rituals. Perhaps the closest we can get to understanding *asha* is to compare it with the Christian concept of the **Holy Spirit**, but entirely free of the doctrine of the **Trinity**.

Ashari, **Abu-Al-Hasan** *I*. An Isma'li philosopher (c.873–935 CE) who founded the school of orthodox Islamic theology. He was born in Basra at a time when the city was the centre of intellectual activity in Iraq and thus of the Muslim world. He is said to have seen **Muhammad** in a vision during the month of Ramadan, calling him to strict adherence to the original Islamic tradition. Early in his career he joined the philosophical school of the **Mu'tazila**, and until he was 39 years old remained one of its principal disciples. During this period he wrote the *Maqalat al-Islamiyin*, 'Theological Opinions of the Muslims', which was a synthesis of the varying opinions of Muslim scholars. When Ashari was 40 he abandoned what he believed had become a rational manipulation of the reality of God, converting to a more traditional or orthodox theology. He became an opponent of Mu'tazila theological dogmatism, but retained its method of *kalam*, rational argument. He openly proclaimed his new faith and wrote the *Kitab al-Luma*, 'The Luminous Book', which marks his break with the Mu'tazila. In 915 he moved to Baghdad, gathering about him his first disciples and putting down the foundation of a new school of philosophical theology, the Asharite school. Ashari eventually ordered and systematized his philosophy in the form of a treatise, *Statement of the Principles of Religion*, which has become the standard for Islamic orthodoxy.

Ashkenazim *J*. Heb. The biblical name for the descendents of Ashkenazi, the eldest son of Gomer (Gen.10:3), and identified by the **Talmud** as a people from the Roman province of Asia. The Ashkenazim ('German' in medieval Hebrew) can ultimately be traced back to Jews who migrated from Israel to Italy in the 1st and 2nd centuries and from Italy to southern Germany in the 7th–8th centuries, spreading thereafter to central and Eastern Europe. From the mid-16th century the name has been applied to Eastern European Jewry, in contradistinction to the **Sephardim**, a Western European and specifically Spanish group originally from Islamic Mediterranean countries. The two represent the main cultural division in world Jewry, even to the point where, in Israel, they have their own chief Rabbis. The Ashkenazim have their own distinct liturgy and pronunciation of Hebrew and comprise around 90 per cent of all Jews. The Chasidim, also from Eastern Europe but with a Sephardic allegiance, use the term 'Ashkenazim' for Jews who are not Chasidic (see **Chasidism**).

Ashram *H*. Skt. 'domicile'. A centre for religious teaching and training. There is no official direction as to the kind of place that might be used – it could be the poorest home or an aristocrat's villa, it could be a hermitage or monastery, a forest glade or mountain side. It usually focuses around a particular guru or teacher.

Ashrama *H*. Skt. The Vedic precept of the **Four Stages of Life**. See **Sacred Thread Ceremony**

Ashtart See **Astarte**

Ashoret See **Astarte**

Ashur See **Assur**

Ash Wednesday *X*. The first day of **Lent**. It is calculated as 40 days before **Easter**, not counting the Sundays. Because Easter is a moveable feast, its date is also variable. Some Christian traditions use the day to remember their mortality, 'Remember that you are dust and to dust you will return.' Some uphold the ancient symbolic act of throwing ashes over their head, obtained from burning the palms from the **Palm Sunday** of the previous year. The ashes are fixed with oil, then spread on the body. Some traditions observe the day with a fast.

Asoka *B*. A Buddhist layman who ruled the Magadhan empire from around 270–232 BCE. He is known for being the patron of Buddhism and is celebrated for 33 edicts carved on rocks around his kingdom which provide information about the nature and development of the religion. He attempted to apply Buddhist social principles, which included tolerance of other religions such as Brahmanism. He was not concerned just with the **Sangha** and the training of monks, but with everyone within his administration. The Third Buddhist Council, which was called during his reign, decided the contents of the **Pali canon** and established the need to send Buddhist missionaries throughout the empire, including what was then Ceylon.

Assemblies of God *X*. The world's largest Pentecostal Protestant Christian Denomination, with approximately 15 million members worldwide. They hold to a conservative Protestant theology set out in their 'Statement of Fundamental Truths' that include **baptism**, **speaking in tongues** and faith-healing. Their congregations are independent and autonomous, but only the HQ has the authority to ordain ministers. See **Pentecostalism**

Assimilationism An attitude or policy that promotes religious and cultural integration. It forms an uneasy and contested boundary between religion and secularism. Assimilationism results in the gradual erosion of the religious, racial and cultural character of a minority group, to the point of their being absorbed into the melting pot of society. Such a policy has been aggressively adopted by various governments, such as Australian administrations in order to assimilate Aboriginal communities. (See **Australian Aboriginal Religion**) In Western Europe and America the ethnicity of Jews has been similarly threatened. Such a policy is a negative response to multiculturalism. It has to be said, however, that people of racial and religious minorities have frequently severed themselves from their roots in order to be 'assimilated', thus less noticeable. In contradistinction there are minority groups who not only resist the assimilationist pressure, but do everything they can to remain distinct and separate, so as to preserve their religious and cultural identities, as for example the **Amish** in America and Hasidic or Yeshiva Jews throughout history. A current example of assimilationist policy is the pressure put on Muslim women in Britain to abandon the veil.

Association for Research and Enlightenment Founded in 1931 to promote the work of Edward Cayce (1877–1945), thought to be one of the most comprehensively documented psychics. ARE is a community of people whose lives have been transformed in various ways by reading Cayce's work.

Assur *AME*. A variant of Ashur. The principal god of the Assyrian pantheon, its name given to the traditional capital of ancient Assyria (3rd millennium BCE) located on the River Tigris. He became the principal god of Mesopotamia, displacing **Marduk**, a usurpation that figures the military defeat of Babylon by the Assyrians. Perhaps for this reason he was primarily the god of military prowess. See **Assyrian Religion**, **Mesopotamian Religion**

Assyrian Church of the East *X*. A Christian community of Parthia, western Iraq and Iran originally founded by converts made by St Thomas and established under the See of Babylon. They are associated with **Nestorianism**, but while they protected Nestorius after his heresy was condemned by the Council of Ephesus in 431 CE they did not teach Nestorius' dualism, but a similar Christological doctrine developed by Babai the Great (551–628), the head of their Church. Following the Muslim invasion of the Middle East, the community survived in the Kurdistan mountains and in the Middle Ages were the first Christian representatives to reach China. In 1885 Benson, the Archbishop of Canterbury, sent a mission to help them with educational projects. The extent of their martyrdom was greater than any other Church, for which reason Pope John Paul II proclaimed them as 'The Martyrs Church'. They were driven out of Kurdistan during the 20th century and communities now exist in Syria, Iraq, Lebanon and the USA. In India the community is known as the Chaldean Syrian Church.

Assyrian Religion and Empire *AME*. Assyrian civilization developed in northern **Mesopotamia**, c.1900–c.612 BCE. Its name is derived from its capital Ashur. When the Assyrian empire was established by Tiglath-Pilesar I, c.1120 BCE, it included the northern half of Mesopotamia, the southern part of which was **Babylonia**. The Assyrian Empire flourished from c.8th–6th centuries BCE, expanding to cover the whole of Mesopotamia, Babylon, Syria, Palestine, Cyprus, northern Arabia and northeastern Egypt. It was not, in the usual sense, an empire unified by a single government, but a free association or confederacy of city-states. There are important references in Old Testament history (See 2 Kings and Isaiah 10) when, for example, Hezekiah, King of Judah, formed an alliance with Egypt against Assyria. The account records the decimation of Sennacherib's army, not through military victory but because of some form of plague which Herodotus ascribes to field mice. Their polytheistic religion had much in common with Babylon, but Ashur, the eponymous and patron god of the city, is found only among the Assyrians. His consort was Ishtar, a goddess of fertility and war. Assyrians have kept their identity as a distinct ethnic group, mainly in northern Iraq where they are distinguished by their Christian religion and Aramaic dialect. See also **Harranian Religion**

FINAL WORD: 'Assyrians: Remnants of the people of the ancient Mesopotamia, succeeding the Sumero-Akkadians and the Babylonians as one continuous civilization. They are among the first nations who accepted Christianity.' Agnes G. Korbani

Astarte A widely adopted **Semitic** goddess. She was known to the Egyptians as Ashtart, the war goddess, to the **Phoenicians** as the daughter of Sky and Earth and the sister of the god, **El**. In Judea the Hebrews knew her as Ashtoret, the principal goddess of the Phoenicians and in Jewish mythology she is a female demon of lust. Her cult was one of the main challenges to Hebrew monotheism. She appears in a 4th millennium BCE **Syrian** fertility cult as the Virgin Anat and as Ashtart was accepted by the Greeks as **Aphrodite**, goddess of fertility, sexuality and war. See **Ishtar**

Astika *H*. Skt. 'orthodox' or ' true to the Veda'. Thus, one who believes or affirms the truth. Also an alternative name for the six philosophical schools of Hinduism. See **Darshanas**, **Nastika**

Astral Body In **occult** and **New Age** thought, a subtle body existing alongside the physical body as a vehicle for the soul or consciousness. In Neoplatonism it is associated with the soul, which might dissolve after death or be immortal or 'starry' – that is, astral. In **Theosophy** 'astral' was used by **Blavatsky** to refer to the lowest but one of the seven principles, but later became associated with 'desire' or 'emotion', the fourth principle, eventually designated as the 'emotional body'. It is thought of as a psychic body or aura composed of emotions in the same way that the physical body is composed of matter and exists on the 'astral' plane independently of individual consciousness.

Astrology 'We are born at a given moment, in a given place and, like vintage wine, we have the qualities of the year and of the season in which we are born. Astrology does not lay claim to anything more.' (C. G. Jung [1933])

Astrology may be considered a secular alternative to religion. It does not deal in God as such, nor has it a creed or any proselytizing purpose. Its aim is to provide the individual with a system of self-knowledge that might give insight to the nature and purpose of a life influenced, if not governed, by the planetary forces of our solar system. In this respect it fulfils, for many, the role others look for in traditional religions, raising questions that have always fascinated and concerned the questing mind. Central to these is the vexed problem of determinism and the extent to which we human beings have free will. Its system is allegedly based on an art or, as some would claim, a science that interprets the significance of the interrelated positions of the planets in conjunction with the date and place of a person's birth. That established, a kind of life-trend is interpreted, but qualified each year around the anniversary of the subject's birth and each month in association with lunar and other cycles. Specific analysis enables the astrologer to predict a person's or a group's future or at least to indicated trends.

Astrology has a long history. Astral omens were charted in Mesopotamia 2,000 years BCE. From there it can be followed to Greece, thence to Egypt by which time it had developed into the system of depicting individual fate. By around 100 CE Rome had developed astrology into a high art which continued to be refined throughout the Middle Ages and up to the time of the **Renaissance**. The discovery of new planets led to modern refinements. In France and England of the 1890s and in Germany a little later, the system was supported by a burgeoning interest in the **occult**, **magic**, **Kabbalah** and H. P. Blavatsky's **Theosophy**. Throughout this long history, India and China developed their own forms of astrology.

Astrology's principal method of determining information is the horoscope, the authority of which is authenticated by the system itself and the reputation of the astrologer who casts it. The horoscope is, at base, a scientific document that records observable and attestable astronomical data. Laid over this objective analysis is the so-called influence of the 12 'Houses', which represent phases of life or aspects of daily existence. For example, the First House is concerned with the development of personality, environment, childhood, the physical body and constitution; the Fifth House with procreation, sexuality, pleasure and speculation; the Tenth House with vocation, profession and public life. The aspiring astrologer will first learn the 12 signs of the zodiac and the traditional attributes given to each of them. For instance, Aries is associated with courage, impetuosity and energy; Cancer with inspiration, sensitivity, creativity and evasiveness; Sagittarius is linked with justice, propriety and sophistry; and Pisces with compassion, tolerance and indolence. The date when the sun 'enters' each sign is very significant. It rises ('ascends') in the East, reaches its zenith at noon and sets in the evening. The ascending and descending axes determine the angles of the horoscope to be cast. In broad terms, a new zodiacal sign is on the ascendant every two hours. With the exact date and time of a person's birth and the precise co-ordinates of the place of birth, the horoscope can be cast. From this information, by means of an ephemeris and complicated mathematical calculations (all now available in published tables) the astrologer can calculate the auspicious and interrelated zodiacal positions of the planets and sun at the place and moment of birth. The further division of the horoscope into 12 Houses is entirely speculative and subject to the application of complicated spherical geometry. Most astrologers are happy to use the available tables and accept the inconsistencies to be found in them. From a combination of all these factors, a person's character can be deduced, together with the kind of life-journey that might be expected. Everything depends on the 'art' of interpreting the data of the horoscope. For example, the subject might be born under the sign of Virgo, thus having the characteristics of reason, logic, exactitude and pedantry; at the time and place of the subject's birth, the planetary associations may have coincided with the Third House, the life aspects of which are family relationships and communication. It is the astrologer's task to consider the significance of the conjunction of these factors and to offer the prediction suggested by them. The best predictions are not given by someone dependent on the data alone, but by the astrologer who has an intuitive knowledge of astrological symbolism which, in broad terms, can produce a well-pointed account of the subject's psychological make-up.

The desire to predict and the hunger for prediction is universal. In its mystical antiquity, China produced the *I Ching*; in Nigeria, the Yoruba have their renowned **Ifa Oracle**. In the late Middle Ages, northern Italy came up with the **Tarot**, and every market or fairground across the world has its palm readers and crystal ball gazers. Today, hundreds of millions search the newspaper columns or Internet for their daily horoscope, as if knowing their fate will give them control over it.

FINAL WORD: 'The only way to predict the future is to have the power to shape the future.' Eric Hoffer

Atavism A term used to account for the reappearance in an individual of ancestral characteristics after several generations of absence. The concept has been in vogue in the period between the acceptance of Darwin's theory of evolution and our understanding of modern genetics. In a cultural context, **Resurgent Atavism** refers to the reversion of people today to attitudes and beliefs of a former time; one example is the quest for simplicity and the 'good life', another is the new interest in primitive religions, **animism**, nature gods and **neo-paganism**. See also **New Age Religion, Wicca**

Aten *E*. The familiar sun-disk god of Egyptian mythology. He was known long before **Akhenaten**'s reign, but it was he who elevated the god to an unprecedented status in Egypt, when the deity became the one god and the source of all life. It was this monotheistic cult that established the specific relationship between *the* god and a **Pharaoh** (king) leading to a similar association between divinity and monarchy, the influence of which has been evident throughout subsequent Western history.

Atharvaveda *H*. Skt. The fourth of the **Vedas** which, according to Dowson, 'is of comparatively recent origin'. A section of this Veda comprising 731 hymns is derived from the **Rig-Veda**. Its origin can be traced back to an ancient priest, Atharvan, who with others is thought to have written or 'seered' the Atharvaveda. Much of its content is apocryphal (see **Apocrypha**), being texts added by later schools of Hinduism. It preserves traditional folk customs and beliefs, curses, magical spells, atonement rites and hymns used for the rites of passage.

Atheism Generally the absence of belief, for any reason, in the existence of deities. Several variant ideas are associated with the term so as to include, for example, **Ignosticism, Nontheism, Agnosticism** and some traditions of **Buddhism** and **Taoism**. Atheists look for empirical evidence of the existence of God based on the scientific method. Some atheists may well be religious or spiritual, but without recourse to a belief in a form of **theism**. It has been said that Atheism requires as much an act of faith as theism, since as it cannot be known that God does *not* exist, the position is held without empirical evidence and thus as an act of faith. 'Weak' atheism or soft, neutral or negative atheism, is the absence of belief in deities without asserting that they don't exist. Such atheism is implicit in the belief held. 'Strong' atheism or hard or positive atheism, is the categorical belief that deities do not exist. Such atheism is explicit. **Wittgenstein**, perhaps, represents the view of the former, 'Whereof one cannot speak therefore one must remain silent.' Noam **Chomsky** speaks for the stronger view: 'How do I define God? I don't ...That's why you haven't found my thoughts on this [for your] critical question. I have none, because I see no need for them.' See **Freethinkers, Scepticism**

FINAL WORD: 'I am a born-again atheist.' Gore Vidal
'I don't know if atheists should be considered citizens, nor should they be considered patriots. This is one nation under God.' President George Bush, August 27th 1988

Athena or **Athene** *G.* She is the personification of wisdom and war, the bringer of victory and the mother of crafts; she was pre-eminently the city goddess of Athens. Shown attended by an owl and wearing a goat-skin breastplate, she was a warrior goddess and a virgin (*parthenos*) whose most celebrated shrine is the Parthenon in Athens, her eponymous city. Plato traced the etymology of her name as *E-theo-noa*, 'the mind of God'. In the Olympian mythology (see **Olympus**) Athena is shown as the favourite daughter of **Zeus**, born from his forehead, an image clearly suggestive of an intellectual origin. She was also the patron of the art of weaving and other crafts; in her function as a warrior goddess, her talents lay in strategy and tactics. She took the side of Greece in the war against Troy and assisted Odysseus in his journey home.

Atherius Society Founded by Sir George King in 1954, who claimed to have received transmissions from Cosmic Masters. The record of these, *The Twelve Blessings* and *The Nine Freedoms*, are the group's 'sacred' literature, parts of which are read during Sunday services. A central belief is that because we exist in our own consciousness we shall continue to live after the demise of our body when it moves to an astral plane awaiting reincarnation. Service and Mission are the keys to salvation, with missions such as Operation Sunbeam, Spacepower, Starlight and Blue Water empowered by a 'large intergalactic spacecraft'. See **Heaven's Gate**, **Raelianism**, **UFO Cults**

Atman *H. B.* Skt. In Hinduism, the true immortal self, one's essence or unchanging eternal core. Perhaps the closest Western term is '**soul**', except that this carries the notion of a consciously surviving self or ego. When an individual achieves absolute consciousness, transcending all aspects of duality, atman becomes identical to **Brahman**, and takes on the aspects characteristic of Brahman, the eternal, absolute being. **Buddhism** denies the existence of an atman (see **Anatman**), asserting that there is no independent, self-conscious or imperishable entity within the human being. However, modern scholarship has suggested that the Buddha denied only the existence of the lower, ignorant, ego and each individual is endowed with Buddha nature, realization of which leads to **nirvana**. See **Self-Realization**

Atomism Gk. *atomos*, 'that which cannot be cut into smaller pieces'. A theory in natural philosophy that everything existing in the universe is made up of very small, indestructible elements or building blocks. Philosophical interest was first expressed by the Greeks. Lucretius' universe contained nothing but variously shaped atoms moving through space; Epicurus and Democritus held that everything could be accounted for in terms of two notions, matter and movement. From this beginning there developed various perceptions of existence, such as determinism and indeterminism, fatalism and optimism. The philosophy of atomism can be applied to society, religion, a moral system, thought and language and to 'being' itself. It was Bertrand **Russell**'s **logical atomism** that sought to identify the atoms of thought, the pieces of thought that cannot be divided into smaller pieces of thought, thus having in the conceptual and intellectual world the same fundamental place as elements do in the physical world. (See **Wittgenstein**) Eastern philosophy was also taken up with atomism; Hinduism's **Vaiseshika** school (6th–3rd century BCE) known also as the Atomic School and Jaina philosophy (see **Jainism**) dating back to the 1st century CE, were similar to the classical exposition except that 'souls' were exempt from the theory of atomic agglomerations. According to early Buddhist atomism, which emerged c.4th century CE, atoms have basic functions and characteristics, such as causing and maintaining growth. In Islamic **Kalam** philosophy, atoms are the only perpetual, material things in existence. The story continued in the West through the Medieval and Renaissance periods with thinkers such as **Galileo**, Francis **Bacon**, Thomas **Hobbes**, **Descartes** and so on. See **Semiotics**, **Structuralism**

FINAL WORD: 'Everything is vague to a degree you do not realize until you have tried to make it precise.' Bertrand Russell

Atonement *J. & X.* The central doctrine of Christianity from which all others are derived. It concerns the reconciliation with God of those who have sinned against him which, in effect, is everyone. The doctrine sets out to explain why the sinless Jesus, who as God the Son (the second Person of the **Trinity**) willingly submitted to death by crucifixion. Dominant in Western Christianity is 'substitutionary atonement', the notion that Christ died 'in our place' as a 'fitting sacrifice'; this is understood to be a propitiation for our sins to the point of 'satisfying' God's sense of justice. The doctrine was first propounded by **Anselm**, then adapted by subsequent theologians such as Abelard, **Aquinas** and Calvin (see **Calvinism**). Eastern Orthodoxy has an alternative soteriology which is usually cited as the main theological difference between the Churches. For Eastern Orthodoxy, salvation is a matter of being released from the consequences of our separation from God, thus the ultimate goal of life is a theosis, a union with God expressed thus: 'God became man so that man might become God.' The whole process is more mystical and understated than in the Western tradition. In Judaism the notion of atonement is focused on **Yom Kippur**, the Day of Atonement. Reconciliation is effected in terms of the **covenant**, by repentance and the conscientious observance of **halakah**, the Law. The original Hebraic practice of animal sacrifice fell away, but it is on this practice and precedent as an Old Testament 'type' that the sacrifice of Jesus is interpreted by Christians.

Atum and **Atum-Re** *E.* A central god of Egyptian creation mythology and associated with Ra, as Ra-Atum, the principal pairing of the **Ennead** of

Heliopolis. Born as a serpent from the waters of **Nun**, he is depicted in art as a man wearing the double crown of Upper and Lower Egypt. He is also associated with **Ptah**, acting as his heart and tongue. His name means the 'complete one' or the 'Great he-she', a reference to his hermaphrodism. He created 'with his semen and fingers' by taking his semen into his mouth and spitting out **Shu** and **Tefnut**.

Augury See **Auspicia, Divination**

Augustine of Canterbury *X.* Commissioned by Pope Gregory I, Augustine arrived in England in 597 as the evangelizer of the Anglo-Saxons. He rebuilt and re-consecrated an old church at Canterbury, making it his cathedral and establishing a monastery. See **Celtic Christianity, Synod of Whitby**

Augustine, St and **Augustinianism** *X.* St Augustine of Hippo (354–430 CE), the first significant Christian philosopher who, being influenced by **Plato**, determined the classically formulated doctrines that dominated Christianity until the 13th century. Augustine rejected Plato's notion of the pre-existence of the soul, but accepted that the soul governs and takes precedence over the body, since it is endowed with the divine 'Ideas of God' that illuminate the soul, as the eye illuminates the body. The ability to see truth by means of the soul's illumination is a natural faculty shared by all humanity, enabling us to perceive the 'realities' (the Ideas and Forms of Plato) and the interconnecting natural laws that regulate and govern them. God's illumination of the soul is indispensable for our perception of truth, beauty and goodness. It is unlikely that Aristotelian philosophy was accessible to Augustine; he thus differs from **Aquinas**, who maintained the distinction between natural and revealed theology (see **Natural Theology**). For Augustine there was no way to the Truth except by God's revelation (illumination in the soul) of it. In maintaining that God was the only and unique creator, he opposed the **Manicheans**. In emphasizing that it was the committed purpose or will of the adherent and not their character, that made the Church holy, he opposed the Donatists. His conservative doctrine of the **fall**, **original sin** and **predestination** were developed as a correction to **Pelagian** heresy. Civil authority served God only in so far as its administration was just. His theology apart, Augustine was also a Bishop and pastor to his people, totally involved in everyday, mundane life and all the controversies of his time. In his passion to lead and protect his flock, his extrovert African character caused him, at times, to be impetuous and to exaggerate his views. But his influence continued to spread, first to St **Anselm** and the Middle Ages, thence to Thomas **Aquinas** and the Reformers who looked to him for guidance on essential principles of faith, particularly with regard to the relationship between faith and reason. In this latter respect he has influenced modern theologians such as John Baillie and Reinhold **Niebuhr**. See **Scholasticism**

Aum *H. B.* Skt. See **Om**

Aum Shinri Kyo *Jap.* From 'Aum', and *Shinri Kyo*, 'Supreme Truth'. An apocalyptic Doom's Day cult formed in 1986 and suspected, in 1995, of attacking the Japanese underground system with nerve gas. Stockpiles of ingredients for biological warfare were discovered during a police raid on their compound. Their leader, Chizuo Matsumoto (known also as Asahara Shoko) predicted the end of the world in 1997 and again in 2000. He claimed to be a disciple of the Dalai Lama, who has refuted this. The sect is hugely wealthy, with upwards of $29 million in assets. There are approximately 10,000 disciples in Japan with a further 30,000 in Russia and a presence in other countries such as Australia and the USA. In 2000 the cult changed its name to 'Aleph'.

Aurelius, Marcus (121–180 CE) Roman Emperor from 161 until his death. Known as the last of the 'Five Good Emperors'. That apart, Aurelius was a significant stoic philosopher (see **Stoics**) and the author of 12 volumes of 'Meditations'. A central theme of his philosophy was a cyclic theory of history cast in cosmic terms: everything recurs and the entire universe will be consumed by fire but, Phoenix-like, will renew itself. As with everything else in life, death should be faced with stoic calm. Despite his Stoic philosophy and being a committed devotee of Roman religion, Aurelius was a cruel persecutor of Christians. It is likely that he knew very little about Christian belief and regarded them as fanatics. 'How lovely the soul that is prepared – when its hour comes to slough off this flesh, for extinctions, dispersion or survival! But this readiness should result from a personal decision, not from sheer contrariness like the Christians ...'

FINAL WORD: 'Constantly regard the universe as one living being, having one substance and one soul; and observe how all things have reference to one perception, the perception of this one living being; and how all things act with one movement; and how all things are the co-operating causes of all things which exist; observe too the continuous spinning of the thread and the contexture of the web.' Aurelius

Aurobindo, Ghose, Sri (1872–1950) *H.* An Indian spiritual leader and author of many works on **yoga** and the **Bhagavad Gita**, among the principal of which are *The Divine Life* and *The Synthesis of Yoga*. The world famous **Matrimandir** ashram was established to realize Aurobindo's work and his techniques of yoga. Believing that established systems of yoga were too elite and rarefied, he devised and taught the system of **Purna** or Integral Yoga. Having been educated in England in a secular, humanist context, he became a leading interpreter to the West of Eastern religious thought and spirituality. On the death of his father in 1893, he returned from England to India to take up a teaching career, eventually to become the director of the National College. He also worked for Indian independence against the British authorities and was imprisoned for a year, during which period he had his first real spiritual experiences. On his release he abandoned his career and political activity to devote himself to yoga. Threatened once more with imprisonment he fled to the French enclave of Pondicherry where he spent the rest of his life. There he met Mira Alfassa (1878–1973), who became his life-long companion. Known as 'the Mother', it was her initiative and energy that established the Aurobindo ashram, as well as her own at 'Auroville'.

FINAL WORD: 'Men have tried to reach the divine by raising themselves up to it; what was not attained was a method to integrate it into one's life.' Sri Aurobindo

Auspicia *R.* L. *auspicium*, 'bird-watching'. In Rome, it was a religious and civic responsibility to take and interpret signs from nature; such signs, it was believed, were given to human beings by the gods. Augury was not a form of divination, it was not concerned with what will happen, but with the course of action to be taken when, for example, planning a wedding, erecting a public building or planning war. If the gods looked upon the project with favour the time was 'auspicious'. It is not to be confused with Haruspicy ('men who look at guts'), the art of interpreting the entrails of sacrificial animals; Auspicia was exclusively concerned with noting bird-flight and song. It was not the auger or priest who read the signs, but the Roman magistrate; the auger would be present at the ceremony and probably advised the magistrate, who would specify the project for which he wanted the gods' opinion, mark out the *templum* – the ritually designated observation site from which to observe celestial activity – then watch and note the flight and calls of birds. Virtually every political decision in Rome was preceded by taking the auspices. See **Anthropomancy**, **Bibliomancy**, **Fortune Telling**, **Divination**, **Mantike**, **Sibyllene Books**, **Syrian Religion**

Australian Aboriginal Religion The Aborigines of Australia are said to have the oldest sustained culture in the world. The myths that generate the belief systems were created from the landscapes, events and people encountered by the earliest migrants. The time when the Aborigines first appeared on the continent is debated, but consensus suggests that they began to settle between 40,000 and 35,000 BCE. They are believed to have migrated from southeast Asia when there was a land-bridge between the Asian archipelago and northern Australia. Gradually, as a result of population increase and the need for groups to find food and water-places that could sustain them, they spread throughout the continent. From 1788 CE, when the first Europeans settled in Australia, the population was estimated at a million with over 200 languages spoken. The influence of European immigration was devastating for the Aborigines; something approaching 96 per cent of those living in southeastern Australia were wiped out by disease, slave-labour or genocide. Eventually, the evangelical Christianity of Wesleyan missionaries displaced much of the indigenous religion.

The heart of Aboriginal mythology is referred to as 'Dreamtime'. This is thought of as their 'time before time' when they and all forms of life were first created by powerful beings or totemic ancestor spirits. These spirit-groups had their own language and were linked with particular tracts of land, their food-gathering country. A spirit-group was thought of as a large family, made up of a man and his brothers, their children and grandchildren. Their sisters married into other local groups from which their own wives were taken. They remained near their water-place or some other natural feature, such as a mountain or forest, until they entered their mother's womb to be born or reincarnated. At death they returned to their spirit homes. Some of these ancestor spirits are regarded as heroes charged with immense power. Striking mountains with ritual staffs or boomerangs hurled at them, created gaps through which the later migrating groups could pass. In a similar way paths were beaten through the forests and laid across the deserts. The ancestral spirits could take on human or animal form, the latter creating totemic associations. Once their work of creation was completed, the ancestor spirits changed into animals, stars, hills and other natural phenomena.

Dreamtime is ever existing and will always remain so. The ancestor spirits are continuously present in the form they assumed at the end of the Dreamtime period. Stories handed down orally throughout their history, 'Songlines' as they are called, are an innate part of a person's 'Dreaming'. The Ngintaka Songline is the central creation story of the Angatja region, which is traversed by the tracks of several Creation Beings such as the lizard, the carpet snake, dingo, emu and honey-ant. Other stories tell of 'Earth dying – Earth Reborn', of how the sun was made and of how light was preserved for the world. Creation stories do not always tell of a perfect state of things, but also of perfection thwarted by death: 'The swamp oak trees sighed incessantly, the gum trees shed tears of blood.' (Roland Robinson)

'Dreaming' refers to the more local mythology of an individual's or group's belief structure. Stemming from this, an aboriginal might experience Kangaroo Dreaming, Shark Dreaming or Honey-Ant Dreaming arising out of the animal-form his totemic ancestor assumed at the end of their Dreamtime. Or he could experience a combination of these relevant to the fauna of his own territory. An Aboriginal who says he is a 'wallaby' understands himself and the wallaby species to be of one flesh; the wallaby's and his own human forebears have the same origin since the spirit-ancestor took wallaby form at the end of Dreamtime. This genealogical relationship is created by the mother who, passing by a spirit centre, will have, for example, the wallaby, bandicoot, pigeon or plum tree enter her body in the form of a spirit child. When she conceives her husband will tell her she has walked 'the incarnation road' and which of the animal or plant spirits will be incarnated in their child.

Ritual and ceremony are usually led by a shaman or 'clever man' or 'man of high degree'. He will recount 'celestial ascents' in order to meet with sky gods such as Biral, Goin or Budjil. Their descriptions of ascents, ritual initiation, death and rising again and the phrase 'men of high degree' mysteriously parallel accounts of the so-called UFO abductions. Other recurring aspects of shamanic tradition include the ritual removal or rearrangement of body parts, symbolic disembowelment, journeys into other realms, alien initiation and enlightenment.

In summary, we can say that Aboriginal mythology is not concerned with ultimate or absolute truths, but exists to explain the origin of the Australian landscape and its natural phenomena and how people came to inhabit and settle it. It amounts to a vast collection of racial memory that has remained, for the most part, unaltered for tens of thousands of years. Jennifer Isaacs has shown that the myths have scientific validity, in that they recall massive geological changes, the rising sea-level which submerged the land-bridge with southeast Asia, the movements from lush, tropical vegetation and fauna to arid desert, the eruption of volcanoes and earthquakes and the migration of the first human beings to populate the continent.

FINAL WORD: 'The more you know, the less you need.' Australian Aboriginal Proverb

Authoritarianism The process of enforcing oppressive ideas and measures on an individual, group or state without their consent. In political terms, examples of such impositions are to be found throughout history, from the Roman Emperors to Franco's Spain, the regime of the Nazis and Stalin's Russia. In religious terms, Authoritarianism is the rigorous imposition of a **creed** and ethic of the kind seen in the Spanish Inquisition and Calvin's Geneva. Currently, it is a form of Neo-conservatism that breeds religious **fundamentalism** of which a refusal, in the USA, to teach Darwinian theories of evolution is an example. Its protagonists argue for the positive imposition of conservative ideas and orthodoxy and that this is religion's responsible defence against liberalism and free-thinking and the means of maintaining religious and social discipline. Psychologically, Authoritarianism exhibits a need for a dogmatic and rigid framework of thought set in a clearly structured hierarchy. Authoritarianism stands in contradistinction to **Anarchism**.

FINAL WORD: 'We are at heart so profoundly anarchistic that the only form of state we can imagine living in is Utopian; and so cynical that the only Utopia we can believe in is authoritarian.' Lionel Trilling

Avalokitesvara *B. Z.* Skt. An important **bodhisattvas** of the **Mahayana** Buddhism. The name translates as 'The Lord who Looks Down' or 'He Who Hears the Cries of the World'. He represents two fundamental characteristics of Buddhahood: compassion and wisdom. In the **Pure Land School**, Avalokitesvara is the energy of the Buddha Amitabha or **Amida**, where his limitless compassion is available to help everyone at times of great danger. In Tebetan Buddhism, the **Dalai Lama** lineage is derived, by means of reincarnation from Avalokitesvara. There are 33 different iconographic forms. Usually he is shown with 1,000 arms and eyes and 11 faces, depicting his all-embracing compassion.

Avatar *H.* Skt. 'descent'. An **incarnation** or manifestation of divine consciousness on earth, born not as a result of **karma** but free will, to offer new paths for religious realization, relevant to the time in which it occurs. The god **Rama** is understood to be an *avatar* of Vishnu. Interestingly, Hinduism also understands Jesus to be an *avatar*. Others believed to be avatars in their respective traditions include **Abraham**, the **Buddha**, **Jesus**, **Krishna**, **Meher Baba**, **Muhammad**, Noah, **Rama** and **Zoroaster**. It is the function of the avatar to 'awaken' everyone to their true identity with God. He lives a human life which provides a model for compassion in thought, word and deed. Although he lives within the –constraints of a human body, he is omnipotent and omniscient. Calling on the '4th plane of consciousness' may allow him to work miracles as it did for Jesus.

Avesta *Zo*. The Zoroastrian scriptures (see **Zoroastrianism**), the content of which was first transmitted orally in the Avestan language. The Avesta is sacred, spoken and used only for ritual purposes. When the tradition came to be collected, much of it was written in Middle Persian (**Pahlavi literature**) probably during the **Sassanian** period c.226–651 CE. The Avesta is made up of many separate books such as the apocalyptic *Bundahishn* and *Dinkard* and the expository the **Yasna**, **Vispered** and the **Gathas**. The *Yasna* is thought to be the oldest and is quoted in the others. In addition to the three books there is a collection of 24 **Yashts**, or hymns, which take the form of invocations of individual deities. For example, the Yashat of Mihir is an invocation to a Mithra or **Mithras**, and the Yashat of Fravadean is an invocation to the **Bounteous Immortals**, or guardian angels. The *Gathas* make up the oldest part of the Yasna. The Avesta is the only source we have for Zoroastrianism and its organization into sections concerned with ritual provides little hint as to their chronology. Some of the texts, for example the hymn to Mithra, are pre-Zoroastrian, while the *Gathas* were written by **Zoroaster** himself. Other strands of tradition are believed to have appeared immediately after the prophet's death, while some were written centuries later when the Avesta was finally committed to writing. Zoroastrians believe the Avesta to be a miracle brought by Zoroaster from God. There is a kind leitmotiv formula to the opening of many of the hymns, '**Ahura Mazda** said to Zoroaster …' As such they are understood as revelations carried to human beings by the prophet to whom they were given. The Avesta contains no lies, offers a full scheme of salvation and is the embodiment of supreme wisdom. As oral tradition was considered more sacred than written forms of revelation, the priests were expected to commit the Avesta to memory. During the process which established Zoroastrianism as the official religion of the kings of the Achaemenid (early Persian), **Parthian** and **Sassanian** empires, little changed in the traditions of the Avesta, testimony to the belief that it was the pure word of God.

Avidya *H. B. Z.* Skt. Literally, 'ignorance'. In Hinduism, **Shiva**, the third member of the Hindu trinity, is the destroyer of ignorance. In Buddhism it concerns ignorance of the basic teachings about non-duality (see **Dualism**), **karma**, the **Four Noble Truths** and the **Three Jewels**, and is the cause of our continued cycling through **samsara** and suffering. In practice it is the attitude that refuses to understand that what we take to be reality is an illusion. We settle for the world of senses and appearance without seeing the false and transitory nature of these; we feed our cravings and appetites without realizing that, ultimately, they can never be satisfied. See **Maya**

Ayatollah *I.* Arab. 'miraculous sign from God'. An honorary title in the **Shiite** hierarchy given to **Mujtahids**, outstanding legal scholars of Iranian origin. In more recent times, particularly in the latter part of the 20th century, the title has been earned by those with a certain cast of personality or charisma, who although grounded in traditions of Islamic law, assume a political role. Since the Iranian revolution the title has become familiar through Ayatollah Khomeini, who in the 1960s became the main opponent of the Shah of Iran.

Ayer, A. J. (1910–89) A British philosopher known for his innovative work in **Logical Positivism**, the manifesto of which was his book *Language, Truth and Logic*, published when he was only 26 years old and still a student. He was a committed atheist, vehemently criticizing religious language as being unverifiable and therefore nonsense. In the year of his death he was reported as having had a 'near-death experience', about which he said 'it weakened my conviction that death would be the end of me, though I continue to hope it will be.' See **Logical Positivism, Metaphysics**

Azhi Dahaka Zo. The serpent or dragon god of **Zoroastrian** mythology, whose story is told in the **Avesta**. The demon has three heads and six eyes but is never just an animal, having human qualities as well. The god symbolizes the Babylonian occupation of Iran. See **Vritra**

Aztecs A people of central Mexico with an established civilization from the 14th to the 16th centuries. Their capital, Tenochtitlan, was named after their legendary founder Tenoch and built on raised islets on Lake Texcoco, the site of Mexico City. The Aztecs have a rich mythology centred on their sun god, Huitzilopochtli, who directed them to build their city on a site where an eagle would land while eating a snake. This legend is depicted on the coat of arms of Mexico. The Aztec earth is called *Cemanahuac* and is given a form of divine status, being the abode of the pantheon of gods headed by Itzamna and his son, **Hunab-Ku**. The Aztec empire differed from our usual conception of unified or centralized rule in that it was a group of city-states bound by tribute and in that one respect Toynbee [1948] likened it to the **Assyrian** empire. Their society had two classes, the peasants and the nobility, but there were also slaves whose commitment was personal, not hereditary, their children being free. A slave could own slaves and buy his freedom. The children of the nobility were educated at special schools called the **Calmecac**. Their religion was based on nature and its cycles, its power and destructiveness impressing them particularly, thus many of their rituals were designed to mitigate its force. The cycles were recorded on the famous Calendar or Sun Stone, which measured not just days and months but also cosmic cycles. Its use demonstrates the development of sophisticated mathematics and knowledge of astronomy. Its intricate carving and imagery took 52 years to complete (1427–79). Originally the stone was placed above the great temple of Tenochtitlan. The Aztec month is made up of 20 days, the year of 18 months; the five 'floating' days making up the standard 365 are called *Nemontemi* and were used for sacrificial rituals. The Aztec calendar has clear similarities with that of the **Maya**. The cosmos was divided into time and space and they believed themselves to be living in the fifth and last era, at the conclusion of which the earth would be destroyed and time would end. Complicated calendars guided them through the seasons and the space-time continuum of the earth, which, being flat, was divided into five directions – each point of the compass plus the centre where they believed their city to be. Their gods were related to the creation of the cosmos, to fertility, regeneration, death, war and to the sacrificial nourishment of the sun god, Huitzilopochitli. A second principal god was Tatloc, the rain and fertility god. Rich and complicated rituals were practised daily, ceremonies being held in temples that were round or pyramidal. Human sacrifice was practised on an extensive scale. See **Mexican Religions**

B

Ba *E*. A concept in Egyptian religion close to the idea of a soul. *Ba* is one of the five constituent parts of the soul, being the unique aspect of an individual. See **Soul, Egyptian**

Baal *AME*. Literally meaning 'lord', was a god of the Syrian-Canaanite pantheon whose myths, recorded on the **Ugaritic** Ras Shamra tablets, described him as the god of rain, thunder and lightning. He was the son of **El**, a deity the Hebrews associated with the Phoenicians. His cohort was **Astarte** known to the Greeks as **Aphrodite**. In the Bible, Baal is called **Beelzebub** or Baalzebub; during the time of Moses he was worshipped by the Moabites and Midinites and was a constant threat to Jewish monotheism. He survives in Christian demonology. See **Canaan, Syria**

Babism *I*. A 19th-century Shiite Muslim sect and a precursor of the **Baha'i**. Sayyid Ali Muhammad of Shirazi (1819–50) proclaimed himself to be the *Bab*, 'the gateway' to the mysteries of the **'Hidden Imam'**, an occultation that inspired Babism's messianic vision and turned it into a militant movement for radical religious and social change. Ali Muhammad spoke of an alternative prophetic cycle; his own message revoked that of the **Koran** and the prescriptions of **Shariah**, the Islamic law. There was an attempt to seize power in Persia but the Bab was executed in 1850 and his movement suppressed. A large collection of writings survived him, believed by many of his followers to be divinely inspired and which became the basis for the Baha'i movement under the leadership of **Baha'ullah**.

Babur *I*. Zahir al-Din Muhammad Babur (1483–1530), the first **Mughal** ruler of India. He was a descendent of the **Mongol** conqueror Timur (Tamerlane) and the founder of the Mughal dynasty in India. He spent the last years of his life organizing an administration for his new empire and collecting its revenues. In 1530 his son, Humayun, contracted a serious illness and the court physicians told Babur that he had no chance of surviving. Babur was deeply distressed and began to pray, walking round and round his son as he did so. In his prayers Babur asked that the disease should pass from Humayun to himself and that he should die in his son's place. His prayers were answered and, as Humayun recovered, Babur became ill and died, aged 47. He was succeeded by the son his prayers had saved. In accordance with his wishes he was buried at Kabul, Afghanistan.

Babylon *AME*. The ancient city of Mesopotamia with references dating from c.2300 BCE. From 612 BCE Babylon was the seat of the Neo-Babylonian Empire, its most famous leader being King Nebuchadnezzar II, 605–562 BCE. His reconstruction of Babylon made it a wonder of the ancient world. It is made familiar through biblical references (2 Kings) to the conquering of the Hebrew Kingdom of Judah in 586 BCE. The Jews were taken to Babylon, where they remained until freed by the Persians in 539 BCE. The period is known as the Babylonian exile, during which the Babylonian **Talmud** was redacted. Chaldea is the Hellenistic term for the region of Babylon referred to in the KJV of the Bible, where the people are identified as the Chaldeans. See **Mesopotamian Religion**

Babylonian Religion *AME*. The indigenous polytheistic religion is very similar to that of the **Assyrians** but **Mamluk**, one of their principal gods, is exclusively the patron-god of Babylon. As the political and military power ranged between the opposed States, the supremacy of the various gods shifted; for example, by 1000 BCE, when Assyria was in the ascendant, their northern gods, especially the warlike Ashur, gained greater prominence. See **Assyrian Religion**, **Harranian Religion**, **Mesopotamian Religion**

Bacchanalia *G*. In Greek and Roman mythology, the rites associated with the cult of **Dionysus**, honouring **Bacchus**, the god of wine. They took place three times a year in the grove of Simila near the Aventine Hill and were confined to women. Eventually men were able to take part and the rites were celebrated five times a month. Originally it was a festival similar to the Liberalia, a rustic rejoicing and merrymaking at which Roman youths first assumed the toga. The festival eventually deteriorated into one of drunkenness and promiscuity. It was banned in Rome in 186 BCE, but reintroduced in the 1st century CE.

Bacchantes or **Maenads** *G*. Female worshippers of **Dionysus**, whose name translates as 'the raving ones', whose abandoned dancing was a figure of union with primal nature. They were wild, insane women wandering the forests and mountains in a state of entrancement, driven in their worship to ecstatic excesses of violence, bloodletting, sex, intoxication and mutilation. They were depicted wearing crowns, fawn skins and carrying the *thrysus*, large staffs covered in ivy vines and topped with pine cones.

Bacchus *G*. The Roman god of wine and intoxication identified with the cult of **Dionysus**, the Greek God of fertility whose worshippers were called Bacchae or **Bacchantes**. The worship of Bacchus is graphically depicted in Euripides' play *The Bacchae*.

Bacon, Francis (1561–1626) A true polymath: lawyer, statesman, essayist, philosopher and advocate of science. In developing his passion for the advancement of learning, he aimed to eradicate the received intellectual traditions of **humanism**, **scholasticism** and natural magic. His new system, designed to be entirely inductive and empirical (see **Empiricism**), would be developed by new arts and scientific invention. They would provide a practical and utilitarian service to humanity (see

Utilitarianism). Bacon was knighted in 1603 and through assuming successive offices of State became Lord Chancellor in 1618, but was forced to retire when charged with bribery. He then devoted himself to philosophy, literature and science. His writing was prolific. In summary, it can be said that Bacon was concerned for the future betterment of society almost in apocalyptic terms; he broadly accepted Christian doctrine but his references to them were ironic and weighted towards reason as against revelation. Only religion founded on reason could properly benefit mankind and ensure the utopian vision to be realized by science and technology. His inductive philosophy set in motion an energy that was to culminate in J. S. **Mill**'s *System of Logic* and his re-categorization of the subjects of knowledge was adopted by the French compilers of the *Encylopédie*. In *Novum Organum*, his discussion of the '**idols of the mind**', the attitudes that inhibit objective knowledge, was the first systematized description of the psychological motives lying behind philosophy.

FINAL WORD: 'The world is a bubble and the Life of man less than a span.' Bacon, 'Life', a poem

Baganda *A*. The largest traditional kingdom in present day Uganda. See **Ganda Religion**

Baha'i A religious movement having its origins in Islamic **Babism** in Persia during the 19th century. Its founder, Baha Allah (or **Baha'ullah**) the Iranian Mirza Husayn Ali Nuri (1817–92) had been a Babi who, after the execution of his leader Sayyid Ali Muhammad, the **Bab**, went into exile where he became convinced he was the new Prophet about whom Sayyid had preached. Baha'ism developed from being a Shiite sect to a form of humanitarian universalism which taught that revelation was progressive. While the Baha'i acknowledged that Muhammad was the last temporal prophet, they argued that Allah never left his people without guidance and leadership and that divine manifestations would continue. Thus, for the Baha'i, the Islamic tradition is not fixed or final but an ongoing revelation addressed to the changing needs of the day. The core of the Baha'i message is the oneness of God, humanity and all religions. 'Baha'ullah taught that Religion is the chief foundation of Love and Unity and the cause of Oneness. If a religion becomes the cause of hatred and disharmony, it would be better that it should not exist. To be without such a religion is better than to be with it.' (Abdul Baha, son of Baha'ullah). The Baha'i is an undogmatic faith that holds all people to be equal and that there is an underlying harmony to be found in religion and science that provides a spiritual basis for society. Even as Baha'ullah taught that Prophecy did not end with Muhammed, so also it does not end with him. Revelation is progressive and the progression will continue under the supervision of the Baha'i central administration, The Universal House of Justice in Haifa, Israel, so named from Baha'ullah's affirmation 'The essence of all that We have revealed for thee, is Justice.' The faith has no authoritative scripture, no priesthood, no public ritual;

communities of believers meet together for informal devotions and are loosely bound by a governing administration. However, this informal structure contains a clear hierarchy working out of its centre in Haifa. Remarkably, this structure has made Baha'i one of the most unified of the world's religions, despite one or two schismatic groups like the 'Orthodox Baha'i', based in Arizona and the Azali Babis, a quasi-secret community who are descendents of the original Babis still surviving in Iran. It has always been important for the Baha'i to carry their message to others and the movement spread to Europe, America and Africa. Currently 7,600,000 adherents are posted, with the largest community being in India (Adherents.com). Islam considers the Baha'i to be heretical.

FINAL WORD: 'All the teaching of the Prophets is one; one faith; one Divine light shining throughout the world. Now, under the banner of the oneness of humanity all people of all creeds should turn away from prejudice and become friends and believers in all the Prophets. As Christians believe in Moses, so the Jews should believe in Jesus. As the Mohammadans believe in Christ and Moses, so likewise the Jews and the Christians should believe in Muhammad. Then all disputes would disappear, all then would be united. Baha'u'llah came for this purpose.' Abdul Baha

Baha'ullah (1817–92) 'Glory of God'. The Persian founder and prophet of the **Baha'i** faith, born Mirza Husayn-Ali. He claimed to be the fulfilment of the prophecy of the Bab (see **Babism**), 'He whom God shall make manifest', but he carried this further, believing himself to be the supreme manifestation of God, the last of a line of prophets from Adam, the Abrahamic religions, Zoroastrianism and the religions of dharma. Baha'i is, therefore, a highly syncretistic faith and Baha'ullah saw himself as the founder of a new, distinct religion in much the same way as were Jesus and Muhammad. He called for radical change in all human relationships, both between human beings and between themselves and the natural world. This combination of social and religious teaching redefined religion as the transformation of civilization. In this sense he was the originator of a new cycle in human history, as was Adam. Exiled from Persia, he took refuge in Palestine where he died and was buried. He left a copious literature comprising mysticism, ethical and social teachings, law and ordinances.

FINAL WORD: '... is not the object of every Revelation to effect a transformation in the whole character of mankind, a transformation that shall manifest itself both outwardly and inwardly, that shall affect both its inner life and external conditions? For if the character of mankind be not changed, the futility of God's universal Manifestations would be apparent.' Baha'ullah

Bakunin, Mikhail (1814–76) One of the intellectual founding fathers of **anarchism**, he was Karl Marx's rival, opposing him at the 1st Internationale. Marx advocated a state-run socialism, but Bakunin the

abolishment of the State as a constitutional entity. Only this would, ultimately, guarantee freedom. See **Marxism, Proudhon**
FINAL WORD: 'Freedom without Socialism is privilege and injustice ... Socialism without freedom is slavery and brutality ... I am truly free when all the men and women about me are equally free. Far from being a limitation or a denial of my liberty, the liberty of another is its necessary condition and confirmation.' Attributed to Bakunin

Balder *Nor.* In Norse mythology the god of innocence, beauty, joy, purity and peace. He is **Odin**'s second son. His ship, *Hringhorni*, was the largest ever built. He is known primarily for the myth describing his death which was seen as the first in a chain of events that would lead to the destruction of the gods at **Ragnarok** ('fate of the gods'), the battle at the end of the world. Balder would be reborn in the new world. When he died he was ceremonially burned on his ship which was pushed out to sea by the giantess, Hyrrokin. See **Germanic Religion, Norse Mythology**

Balinese Religion Outside of India, Bali has the largest Hindu following in the world. Its two major sites are the Besakih temple complex and the sacred mountain of Agung, thought to be the naval of the world and identified with Mt **Meru**. Vestiges of the original Malayo-Polynesian culture survive in the form of the ancient god Twalen, who in the famous shadow-puppet theatres is made to be the servant of the Hindu gods. The Malayo-Polynesian religion and Hinduism combine in the *Agama Tirtha*, the Religion of the Holy Water associated with a network of Water Temples, as well as village and caste temples. There are five related cycles of rituals, the *dewa yajna*, sacrifice rituals with their origins in the original Vedic literatures. A clear Tantric influence is to be seen in the belief in demonic powers.

Ball Court *CA.* A form of Mayan sports stadium for playing *Juego de Pelota*, from which the Basque game is certainly derived. The walls enclosing the terrain contained temples which suggests that the sacred game·was more than a sport. Decorations on the walls show that players were subjected to beheading in the centre of the area and it was thought that the losers would die at the end of the game, but this interpretation has now been revised. The divine twins of the Mayan creation story played the game for their lives against the lords of the underworld. See **Popol Vuh**

Bantu *A.* A widespread people of central and southern Africa, who are linguistically related through over 100 languages which include Swahili, Kirundi, Zulu and Xhosa. As to be expected of such a hugely diverse group spread across vast territories, their various religious practices have certain features in common, such as a dominating belief in **magic**, and cults wrapped around **ancestor worship** founded on the belief that the body and spirit separate after death. Aspects of these practices were transported through the slave trade and the **Quimbanda** of Brazil is an example of contemporary Bantu religion and spirituality. See **Santeria, Shona Religion**

Baptism *X*. A Christian sacrament that initiates the subject into the Church. The practice of the Early Church was modelled on **John the Baptist**'s baptism of Jesus, setting the precedent for the sacrament to be conferred on adults. Baptism was by total submersion, the action of being taken down under the water and being raised up symbolic of dying and resurrection. 'Have you forgotten that when we were baptized into union with Christ Jesus we were baptized into his death? By baptism we were buried with him and lay dead, in order that, as Christ was raised from the dead in the splendour of the Father, so also we might set our feet upon the new path of life' (Romans 6:3–4). The baptism of infants by affusion has been practised from the 3rd century to the Reformation. The **Anabaptists** and later the **Baptists** denied infant baptism, affirming that the sacramental was only for confessed believers. Infant baptism, however, has been retained by the Roman Catholic Church and many of the Protestant confessions, including the Anglican, Lutheran and Presbyterian churches. The debate between the two theologies continues.

Baptists *X*. At one time nicknamed '**Anabaptists**', this Christian denomination has its origins with John Smyth (c.1554–1612), who used the baptism of believers as a condition of church membership. In 1612 Thomas Helwys founded, in London, the church of the General (Arminian) Baptists, to be followed in Southwark by the Particular (**Calvinist**) Baptists. In 1644 they issued a joint confession, but not until 1891 were these two groups united as the Baptist Union of Great Britain and Ireland. The revivalist element stemming from the Particular Baptists gave rise to a worldwide missionary movement. Through their tradition of preaching, the Baptists became established in the USA, the British Commonwealth and, eventually, in most parts of the world. The Baptist World Alliance was formed in 1905, with its headquarters in Washington, DC. There are many Baptist churches that are in no way affiliated to any official body, which makes their practices and theologies diverse.

Bardos *B*. Tib. 'in-between state'. The processes connecting a person's death with the following rebirth. The concept was systematized by the **Vajrayana** School of **Tibetan Buddhism,** differentiating six connecting states being the bardos of birth, dream, meditation, the moment of death, supreme reality and becoming. The first three represent 'suspended states' while the last three involve the 49-day process of death and rebirth.
FINAL WORD: 'I have found that the easiest way to understand what is happening during the process of dying, with its outer and inner dissolution, is as a gradual development and dawning of ever more subtle levels of consciousness … the process moves gradually toward the revelation of the very subtlest consciousness of all: the Ground Luminosity of Clear Light.' Sogyal Rinpoche

Bar Mitzvah *J*. Heb. 'The Son of the Commandment'. The Jewish rite of passage that initiates a boy into adulthood in terms of synagogue practice and ritual. Bar mitzvah qualifies the boy to make up a *Minyan*, the minimum number of ten male Jews needed to form a congregation. Originally the term was applied to all adult Israelites, but from c.14th century it was used exclusively for a boy attaining his 13th birthday. Usually, in the synagogue on the Sabbath following his birthday, the boy gets an *aliyah* ('calling up') to read a portion of the law and to recite the *Haftarah*, a section of the Prophets. It is an occasion of great joy for the boy and his family and is frequently extravagantly celebrated. The rite of *Bat Mitzvah*, 'The Daughter of the Commandment', is a feature of modern Judaism. First introduced in the **Reconstructionist Judaism** of Mordecai Kaplan in 1922, the rite is now more widely practised.

Barth, Karl (1886–1968) *X*. Born in Basle, Switzerland, Barth was the most influential Reform theologian since **Calvin**, and one of the leading thinkers in the Neo-Orthodox movement. Pope Pius XII considered him to be of equal importance to Thomas **Aquinas**. His theology is contained in his huge opus the *Church Dogmatics*, which he worked on from 1932 until he died. It is thought by many to be one of the most important theological treatises ever written. His fundamentalist interpretation of scripture kept the person of Jesus Christ central and he reinterpreted the entire corpus of Christian theology around this pivotal point of God incarnate. In 1934 he was principally responsible for the Barmen Declaration which opposed Nazi influence on German Christianity. Refusing to swear an oath to Hitler, he resigned his post at the University of Bonn and returned to Basle. See **Neo-Orthodoxy**

Basmala *I*. Arab. see **Bismillah**

Batak Religion *P*. The religion of the Bataks of northern Sumatra is characteristically functional, focused on rice-growing and kinship relationships. The *marga*, the patrilineal clans, provide the all-important kinship lineages sustained by complex marriage ceremonies involving a hierarchy of major and minor wives. Ritual oratory is a central part of these ceremonies. The Batak universe is conceived on three levels. Gods inhabit *Banua Ginjang*, an upper world; human beings populate *Banua Tonga*, the middle world; dragons, demons and spirits occupy *Banua Toru*, the lower world. Their myths are cast in simple dualisms of life and death, male and female, village and forest, war and agriculture. It was once thought that these were all one and rituals exist that attempt to unify the opposites since 'power' is derived from the centre. In a similar way cosmic harmony is realized by unifying or balancing the three levels or worlds. Concepts of an independent soul are complex; if a person is frightened the soul can escape from the head and rituals conducted by a *datu*, a sorcerer, are used to reunite the soul with the body. Today Batak religion is mingled with **Christianity** and Islam, resulting in a rich **syncretism**.

Beatific Vision *X*. In **Roman Catholic** theology an immediate perception and knowledge of God which the saints and souls of the just will experience in heaven, imparting supreme blessedness. 'How great will your glory and happiness be, to be allowed to see God, to be honoured with sharing the joy of salvation and eternal light with your Christ your Lord and God' (St Cyprian, Epistle 58).

Beatitudes *X*. The declarations of who will be blessed as given by Jesus in his **Sermon on the Mount**. Eight are given in Matthew's version (Matt. 5:3–10) and four in Luke's (6:20–22). Matthew's account is considered by scholars to give the complete list of those particularly blessed: the poor, the sorrowful, the gentle of spirit, the righteous, the merciful, the pure in heart, the peacemakers and the persecuted.

Beautiful Names *I*. For Muslims 'Allah' is 'The Great Name' for God, but the Koran lists 99 alternatives. These are known as 'The Beautiful Names'. Each offers insight into a different attribute or function of Allah. A few examples will illustrate how the names are used: *Al-Fattah*, 'The Opener', is God in the act of opening everything that would otherwise be closed, from kingdoms (to be conquered) to hidden or mystical truths to be revealed. *Ar-Rahim*, 'The All-Merciful'; *Al-Malik*, 'The Absolute Ruler'; *Al-Quddus*, 'The Pure One'; *As-Salam*, 'The Source of Peace; and *Al-Mu-min*, 'The Inspirer of Faith'. See **Islam**, **Salaam**

Beelzebub *AME*. With many variants of the name, Beelzebub was a deity worshipped by the **Philistines** in Ekron. There seems to have been little distinction made between him and the Semitic god **Ba'al**. In Christian writings either form may appear as an alternative for Satan or the Devil. Beelzebub may be translated as 'Lord of the Flies'.

Behemoth *J*. Heb. Probably derived from the plural form of the Hebrew word *bahemah*, 'beasts' or 'animals'. The Old Testament reference is from Job 40:15ff (Tan. and KJV). In the NEB the word is translated 'chief of beasts' or 'crocodile'. In Jewish tradition, just as the **Leviathan** is the dominant beast of the sea, so Behemoth is the dominant beast of the land. Its meaning, metaphorically or mythologically, is unclear but the reference serves to illustrate both the range of God's creation and the human being's place among living things. The Behemoth is supreme in all creation, it is neither preyed on nor threatened by any other living creature and, compared to it, man is puny. It is a figurative way of presenting the almighty power of God, since it was God who created the Behemoth.

Behmenists See **Bohme**

Bektashis *I*. A Sufi dervish order founded by Hajj Bektash Veli in 13th-century Anatolia, Turkey, where it remained powerful until early in the 20th century. The order is deeply influenced by Shiite thought.

Characteristically, the function of the spiritual teacher is central, his authority derived from the tradition of the 12 Imams (see **Twelvers**) and **Ali Ibn Abi Talib**, a cousin of **Muhammad**; they were believed to be the revealers of the mystical truth of the **Koran**. As mediator, the spiritual teacher may be called on to intercede in prayer and blessing. Muhammad and Ali are regarded as a single person sharing the unity of the revelation. The Sunnis regard the Bektashis as heretical, even though they are known to be followers of Shi'ah Islamic law. Anatolia became their centre when Ataturk abolished the Sufis from the Turkish republic in 1925. See **Dervish, Dervish Groups, Murid, Shi'ism, Sufism, Tariqah**

Benedictines X. A monastic order founded by St Benedict (c.480–c.550) of Nursia. Members may be either Roman Catholic or of one of the churches of the Anglican Communion. In about the year 500, disillusioned with the immorality of Roman life, Benedict decided to live as a hermit and withdrew to a cave at Subiaco. Gradually a community developed around him and he established 12 small monasteries, each comprising 12 monks under an Abbot. In about 525 he and a small following moved to Monte Cassino where, during the 11th century, the community reached a peak of prosperity. The Norman church was consecrated in 1071, when the monastery became famous for its scriptorium. The order is famous for the 'Rule of St Benedict' which since the 7th century has also been adopted by communities of women. Over its 1,500 years of use the Rule has become the leading guide for Western monastic communities. The motto of the Benedictines, *Pax ora et labora*, 'Pray and work', successfully balances the demands of individual religious devotion with the necessities of community living. There is no evidence that Benedict intended to found a religious order and it is not until the Middle Ages that there is mention of the 'Order of St Benedict'. Even so, St Benedict is sometimes referred to as the Patriarch of Western Monasticism. Though spoken of as an order there is no central authority and each monastery is self-governing.

Benin A. West Africa. Formally the monarchy of Dahomey, the Republic of Benin's spiritualist-animist religious tradition is thought to be the origin of **voodoo**, carried by slaves to Brazil and the Caribbean. **Vodun**, the indigenous religion, is still practised by something like 65 per cent of the population and was recognized in 1996 as Benin's official religion, with Christianity 20 per cent and Islam 15 per cent respectively of the population representing the other major groups. See **African Religion, Yoruba**

Bentham, Jeremy (1748–1832) English philosopher and law reformer, he was a leading utilitarian (see **Utilitarianism**). Asserting that life is cast between pain and pleasure, he argued that all actions should be judged to be morally right or wrong to the degree they maximized pleasure (or happiness) and minimized pain. He wrote against 'orthodox' religion because he believed it conflicted with enlightened self-interest and because, in Parliament, the clergy always voted with the 'Oppressionists', the name Bentham gave to one of the two current political parties alternating power. He criticized the Oppressionists for hating the mass of the people so much as to refrain from doing anything to help the poor. The other more liberal party, he dubbed the 'Depredationists' who encouraged improving the conditions of the poor so long as they would profit by it. Religion centred on **Anglicanism** was a puritan subjugation of all forms of freedom and Bentham believed that the best could be achieved if people were educated to think for themselves; the proper foundation of life should be free choice, of which adherence to a religion might be one. To this end he left his entire estate to University College, London, one of the provisos being that it became the first college in England to drop courses in religion from the curriculum. In his will Bentham requested that his body be preserved and placed in a cabinet at University College. He wanted it known as 'Auto-Icon' and brought out for Council meetings, the roll of which marks him 'present but not voting'. The exhibited head is a replica; having been the object of student rags, the original is locked away.

Berbers *I*. Also called *Imazighen* (sing. *Amazigh*), 'free men'. They are an ethnic group indigenous to northwest Africa, spreading through Morocco, Algeria and southwards across the mountains into the Sahara. Berber groups are not only separated by deserts and mountains but also by dialects, all of which contrived to prevent them becoming a unified nation. Predominantly **Sunni** Muslims, they are significant for the history of Islam, but some converted to **Judaism**, or to Christianity as **Donatists**. Others maintained an indigenous polytheism. Berbers first converted to Islam during the 8th century CE after strongly resisting the Muslim armies bent on expanding the Islamic Empire. They experienced further Arabization through the **Fatimids**, who sought to punish them for abandoning Shiite beliefs. From the 11th and 12th centuries CE two separate Berber groups, the Almoravids and the Almohads, carried Islam further into Africa and to Spain, establishing their own dynasties and combining to produce a rich Moorish-Iberian culture. See also **Islamic Dynasties, Umayyad Caliphate**

Bhagavad-Gita *H*. Skt. 'Song of the Exalted One', a philosophic poem that has been called the gospel of Hinduism. It was included in the **Mahabharata** (c.5th century BCE) as its sixth book. The Bhagavad-Gita affirms that the only foundation for true faith is spiritual experience and that this must never contradict reason. The spiritual path requires the absence of desire leading to freedom from our attachment to things. Our love and devotion must be given not to what is temporary and subject to change, but to what is eternal and changeless. 'In the battle of the Bhagavad-Gita there is a great symbol of hope: that he who has a good will and strives is never lost and that in the battle for eternal life there can never be defeat unless we run away from the battle' (Juan Mascaro).

Bhagavan *H*. Skt. Pali. 'noble', 'holy', 'the exalted one'. The term is an epithet for God. Saints and holy figures are addressed by their followers as *Bhagavan*. In Buddhism it is a title for the Buddha used in the **Sutras**, and translated in different ways as 'Lord', 'Master', 'Blessed One'.

Bhagwan Shree Rajneesh *H*. 1931–90. An Indian guru known also as Osho, who lived in India and the USA and who founded the **Osho-Rajneesh Movement**. He claimed that the greatest values in life are love, meditation and laughter. He is sometimes called the 'sex guru' because of a collection of lectures entitled 'From Sex to Superconsciousness', according to which 'everything is holy, nothing is unholy.' For Osho meditation was not something to be done but something to be; it was a state of thoughtlessness that can just happen, not something we can do. He devised preliminary techniques, 'Dynamic Meditation', to help bring about altered breathing, talking gibberish, laughing or crying so as to release repressions. Once achieved the state can be maintained through ordinary activities. His followers lived frugally, but Osho lived in luxury. It is said he owned 27 Rolls Royces. See **Rajneesh Meditation**

Bhajan *H*. *S*. Hindu and Sikh devotional songs deeply rooted in Indian culture. They are a form of worship and prayer. Known to Hindus also as *Kirtans*, their origins are in ancient Vedic tradition, known to have evolved from the singing worship of seers such as Narsinh Mehta and Mirabai. They were transmitted over centuries by oral tradition until the communities and their worship liturgies became established. *Bhajans* are songs, which for Sikhs constitute a central path of devotion, since they are the Sacred Hymns of the **Guru Granth Sahib**. It is expected of the committed Sikh that they will sing the songs as frequently as possible. In some traditions of yoga such as Shabd Yoga, the focus is listening to an inner sound. The two basic or classical forms are the *ragas* and the *talas*.

Bhakti *H*. Skt. 'love of God', 'devotion'. There are various forms of *bhakti*. For example, *guru-bhakti* is total compliance to the guru; *vaidhi-bhakti* is a preliminary stage of teaching by the guru and *raga-bhakti* a level at which the pupil on the yogic path is focused exclusively on God, which leads to *para-bhakti*, conscious unity with God. See **Yoga**

Bhakti Yoga *H*. Skt. The way of love and devotion. One of the principal yogic paths. See **Yoga**

Bhava-chakra *H*. Skt. see **Wheel of Life**

Bhikkhu *B*. Skt. Pali. 'sharesman' or 'almsman'. A mendicant monk and fully ordained member of the **Sangha**. A Bhikkhu owns nothing, but is equipped with practical essentials such as his robe, a razor, needle and thread, toothbrush, a staff and a begging bowl with which he begs for his food. In early Buddhism the Bhikkhus formed the principal community, since it was taught that only by total renunciation of the world could nirvana be achieved. They were originally wanderers but eventually became members of monastic communities. In some of the schools of Tibetan and Japanese Buddhism Bhikkhus may marry and have families. Monks have a symbiotic relationship with the lay community, mutually dependent for practical support and spiritual guidance. In some Therevadan communities a layman might be expected to become a bhikkhu for a period of time. The same general principles of poverty and renunciation also apply to *bhikkhuni*, the fully ordained female members of the sangha. See **Mendicants**

Bible *J. X.* Usually the canonical scriptures of the Church comprising two parts, known to Christians as the Old and New Testaments. The collection of writings found in the **Old Testament** (also part of the sacred literature of Jews and Muslims) was written mostly in Hebrew and is arranged in three sections: Law, Prophets and Writing. The Law is known as the **Pentateuch**, being the first five books. The canonical status of the Old Testament books was debated between 400 and 200 BCE, but there is no clear indication as to when the canon was finally decided. There is also a collection of intertestamental literature known as the **Apocrypha** which is not found in the Hebrew Bible. Much of it, however, is found in the **Septuagint**, a Greek translation of the Hebrew Bible. This was started in Alexandria in the 3rd century BCE, intended for use by the Greek-speaking Jewish community of the city. Practice and beliefs vary between the Churches in the acceptance and use of the Apocrypha as canonical literature. The **New Testament** is a collection of 27 texts all written in the 100 years following the death of Jesus Christ and contains a cross-section of the teaching and preaching of the early Church. The canon was finalized sometime in the 4th century CE. Christian understanding of the New Testament is greatly influenced by the way in which the Old Testament is interpreted, but generally the New Testament's central assertion of the messiahship of Jesus and the covenantal relationship between God and Christians, is seen to be a fulfilment of Old Testament prophecy.

The Bible has always held a central place in Christian worship and literature and for most of the main Christian denominations the form of service is structured around readings from the Bible and preaching based on it. Its authority on matters of faith has given rise to a theology of scripture which accounts for its origins as the 'Word' of God. Not only are rules of interpretation set out, but also criteria as to who has the authority to offer such interpretations. The conflict between the authority of the Bible and extra-biblical tradition continues to be debated. In **Roman Catholicism** and the **Orthodox Churches**, the validity of scriptural revelation has to reside within the traditions of the church, whereas in some **Free Church** Protestant traditions believers are able, subjectively, to interpret the Bible for themselves without regard to tradition.

Throughout Christian history there have been innumerable versions of the Bible such as the Septuagint, translations of which were made into Syriac, Coptic and Latin. Jerome's translation, commissioned in 382 CE by Pope Damasus, was the first reliable Latin text. His later translation, made directly from the Hebrew Masoretic text (the Hebrew text of the **Tanakh**), became the basis for the Vulgate Latin version. The English, King James Version of the Bible, commissioned at the request of James I, appeared in 1611 and, although never sanctioned by the Church, became known as the Authorized Version. It had a huge influence on the liturgies of the Protestant churches and on future translations into English. There are simply too many versions of the Bible to survey in this article, but the sources for doing so are easily accessible. It is worth mentioning the most important translations to have appeared in the 20th century. They include the American Revised Standard Version of 1901, a Catholic translation, the Jerusalem Bible, which first appeared in English in 1966 and the New English Bible, which appeared between 1961 and 1970.

Modern attitudes and responses to the Bible, together with its status and authority, have been greatly influenced by biblical criticism, arising from increased knowledge of the Bible's original languages and discoveries such as the **Dead Sea Scrolls**. The outcome is that the Bible has been subjected to the same kinds of analysis as other ancient literatures in order to ascertain the original wording and authorship of the texts and the nature of the oral tradition on which they were based. In addition '**form criticism**' aimed to understand the syntax and structures the texts given when the oral tradition came to be written, whilst verifying the validity of their historical content against extra-biblical information. Research has aimed to cast light on the subjective attitudes of the authors on the received oral tradition and the extent to which, in the process of being written, it was subject to interpretation rather than just being recorded.

For many the Bible remains a gift of God, a revelation of huge proportions and import that only faith can illuminate. For many others the Bible represents a remarkable source of ancient literature and history. See **Wycliffe**

FINAL WORD: 'The Bible is literature, not dogma.' Santayana

'It was subtle of God to learn Greek when he wanted to become an author – and not to learn it better.' Nietzsche [1988]

Bible Belt X. An area of the USA covering Midwestern and Southern states, where fundamentalist Protestant Christianity is a dominant and pervasive influence. The name derives from the overriding importance of the Bible in evangelical Christian practice. See **Tidewater Anglicanism**

Bibliomancy Known also as Stichomancy (divination from lines) or Libromancy, a form of **divination** that seeks to know the future from randomly selected, usually sacred texts, by no means always the Bible. Virgil's *Aeneid* was used in the Middle Ages and the Koran by Muslims. Some practitioners use dice or other randomizers to determine page numbers. This form of practice is formalized in, for example, the use of yarrow sticks or coins in the consultation of the *I Ching*. See **Anthropomancy, Auspicia, Mantike**

Bismillah or **Basmala** *I*. Arab. 'invocation', of the divine name. Usually the invocation is in the form of the words that head all but one of the **surahs**, the chapters of the **Koran**, 'In the Name of Allah, the Compassionate, the Merciful'. The *Bismillah* is used to consecrate ritual prayer or any form of solemn act performed in daily life and in this sense is similar to the Hebrew *brocheh* or blessing. The written *Bismillah* is frequently found in forms of Islamic calligraphic art. See **Fatihah**

Black Friars *X*. A nickname for the **Dominicans**, used because of the black mantel worn over their white habit.

Black Jews *J*. A term applying to several distinct religious groups which gathered momentum in the USA from 1886, with the preaching of William Saunders Crowdy. From the start of the Black Nationalist movements, Christianity as the religion of the slave owners was rejected and a new religion adopted. Judaism was held to be the most appropriate since its people had been enslaved, then emancipated, yet were still constantly persecuted and repressed. There was also a new public awareness of Israel as the Jewish homeland with the Ethiopian Jews, the '**Falashas**', being received in Israel with full civil (but not religious) rights. Many black Jews claimed to be descended from the Falashas and the growth of **Rastafarianism** added energy to the whole cause. Generally Black Jewish sects have held to the **Old Testament** in English translation – similar, for example, to the Old Testament of the Protestant Bible. Some hold that God is black, others that colour cannot be an attribute of God. In general, such groups have endeavoured to maintain much of the Jewish ritual calendar, celebrating the major and minor festivals, but especially **Pesach** (the Passover) as a remembrance of emancipation from slavery. There is running debate as to whether these sects are legitimately Jewish; they are not recognized as such by the world Jewish community, although positive relationships have been established with some of them. One such group, the Hebrew Israelites, left the USA to live in Israel, where they have been allowed to stay; another, The Kingdom of God, founded in Chicago in the 1960s by Ben Ammi Carter, are also now settled in Israel. See **British Israelites, Nation of Yahweh, Pan African Orthodox Christian Church**

Black Magic The magic associated with the **Left-Handed Path** or **Satanism**. See **Magic, Path Symbolism**

Black Mass A ritual in **Satanism** that attempts to negate or profane the Catholic Mass. The rite includes the **Lord's Prayer** recited backwards, the cross inverted, the use of black candles and the defilement of the **Eucharistic** elements, substituted by a combination of matter and flesh. The latter is associated with sexual rites but the celebration of the black mass on the body of a naked woman is a latter addition. Allegedly the communion is sometimes performed using human blood and flesh.

Black Muslims *I*. An African-American religious and political movement that broke away from the **Nation of Islam** in 1964. Its most famous minister was El-Haji Malik El-Shabazz (1925–65) known also as, Malcolm Little or, more famously, as **Malcolm X**. The Black Muslims aimed at a radical improvement in the quality of life for a minority of blacks living in a white, Caucasian culture. Malcolm X was converted in 1948, having discovered Islam while serving a prison sentence for burglary; he became minister of the Harlem-based Temple 7, from 1954. After being actively involved in various educational, social and political projects supporting black liberation, he distanced himself from the Nation of Islam, repudiating their extremism. In 1964, he converted to **Sunni** Islam and performed the *hajj*. He was assassinated on 21st February 1965 by members of the Nation of Islam. There has alwas been a popular confusion between the Black Muslims and the Nation of Islam, but the majority of Black Muslims are not members of the Nation, preferring to identify themselves with local or regional organizations and leaders.

Black Stone *I*. An actual stone set in a corner of the **Ka'bah**, the pivotal point of the Mosque at Mecca. See **Hajar al-Aswad**

Blavatsky, Helena (1831–91) The founder of the Theosophical Society. See **Theosophy, Possession, Spiritism, Spiritualism**

Bloch, Ernst (1885–1977) A Jewish-Marxist philosopher and atheist theologian, born in Germany into an assimilated Jewish family. Returning to Germany from the USA in 1949, he took up the Chair of Philosophy at Leipzig, moving to the university of Tübingen in 1961. Influenced by expressionist art, Marxism and his friendship with Brecht and Lukacs, his utopian philosophy envisaged a world free of exploitation and oppression. His work influenced two important socio-political energies, one being the student 'revolution' of 1968, the other, **Liberation Theology**. He is not to be confused with the Swiss-born American musician and composer of the same name. See **Marxism**
FINAL WORD: 'In capitalist society health is the capability to earn, among the Greeks it was the capability to enjoy and in the Middle Ages the capability to believe.' Bloch

Blue Cliff Record *Z*. A collection of koans of the Chinese Zen master. See **Koan**

B'nai Noah *J*. A Jewish sect founded on the concept of the 'Dual Covenant', being the covenant God made with Noah after the flood, in addition to that made with Abraham (see Gen. 9: 1–17). The Noachide Covenant is also thought to be binding on gentiles. Members of the sect are not Messianic Jews, neither are they Christians; they keep the oldest religious tradition known, being the faith of Adam, Able, Enoch, etc. Put simply, the sect's faith is a belief in the single Creator God to whom they related personally without any form of mediation and to whom they are directly responsible. They live by the moral code derived from the seven laws of the Noachide Covenant, the reminder of which is always present in its sign, the rainbow. See **Flood**

B'nai Or *J*. Heb. 'Sons' or 'Children of Light'. See **Alliance for Jewish Renewal**

Bodhi *H. B. Z*. Skt. Pal. 'perfect knowledge' or 'awakened'. Bodhi is attained by overcoming **avidya**, ignorance and by the realization of The **Four Noble Truths** and the end of suffering. In the **Hinayana** tradition Bodhi is related to the perfection of insight, in **Mahayana** to wisdom based on perceiving the unity of **nirvana** and **samsara**. See **Saddha**

Bodhidharma *B*. Tradition offers two dates, either 440–528 CE or 470–543 CE, for the founder of the Chinese Buddhist school of **Ch'an** and the first school of **Shao-Lin**, an expansion of the **Yogachara** or the '**Mind Only**' School of Buddhism. Bodhidharma was, thus, first patriarch of the **Zen** Buddhist lineage. His teachings were based on the Lankavatara Sutra used for 'sealing the mind'. The **dharma**, or **enlightenment**, is to be discovered by a combination of study and practice combined with meditation; study leads to an understanding of one's personal Buddha nature which remains confused and unclear because of ignorance, attachment, appetite, aggression and passion. Practice, meaning living in the Buddhist way according to the **precepts**, enables the individual to realize that his personal Buddha nature is co-existent and equal to that of the Buddha. Bodhidharma's distinctive and critical emphasis is on an intuitive grasp of the nature of true mind, rather than on ritual and the formalization of practice. A holistic combination of intellectual, spiritual and physical skills are the conditions for experiencing enlightenment. When Ch'an was carried to Japan in the 9th century, it had an instant appeal for the **Samurai,** who adopted it as their way of life and code.

Bodhisattva *B & Z*. Skt. 'Enlightenment Being'. In Mahayana Buddhism the *bodhisattva* is a person who seeks buddahood by achieving an exemplary moral life through the perfecting of the **paramitas**, the ten qualities or virtues. Having done so, he forgoes **nirvana** until all sentient beings are saved. To achieve this the bodhisattva is prepared to take on the sufferings of others, transmitting his positive **karma** to help others overcome their negative *karma*. In Mahayana the bodhisattva ideal replaces the Hinayana notion of the **arhat** who, concerned for his own liberation, was thought to be self-interested. The bodhisattva ideal represents one of the highest spiritual aspirations to be found in any religion. In Tibet the concept of kingship took on the bodhisattva principle. The ruler was conceived as a person who would want to create the best possible conditions so as to ensure the welfare of his people and the flourishing of Buddhism within his realm. The king in Tibet *had* to be a bodhisattva, thus after his death it was necessary to discover in which Tibetan infant or child, the king had been reborn, thence to prepare him to rule. This was the accepted notion of succession and on this principle the heads of the four Tibetan schools of Buddhism attest their bodhisattva lineage, as is illustrated by the succession of Dalai Lamas. In much the same way, several great contemporary Buddhist scholars and teachers are believed to be the reincarnation of previous saint-teachers, ensuring that the transmission of their teachings is uncorrupted. See **Precepts, Tibetan Buddhism**

Bogomils X. A dualistic **Gnostic** sect flourishing in Bulgaria from 950–1396 CE as a reaction to state and clerical oppression. Bogumil, who was a priest, may have given the sect its name or he may have assumed it afterwards. The heresy was syncretistic, drawing on **Docetism** and **Manicheanism**. They denied the divine birth of Jesus, the personal coexistence of the members of the **trinity**, and the validity of the sacraments. Christ's miracles were analogies, **baptism** was for adults only and the use of icons, the cross and the veneration of saints was idolatry. As agents disseminating these ideas both in Russia and throughout Europe, the Bogomils were an important connecting link between Eastern and Western heresy. Their doctrines were most apparent in Europe in the 12th and 13th centuries, influencing the beliefs of the **Albigensians, Cathars, Waldenses** and **Anabaptists**. Their name has survived pejoratively, as 'bugger', in English and in Italy, Germany and Hungary in various cognate forms synonymous with sodomy.

Bohme, Jakob (1575–1624) A German Lutheran mystic and shoemaker. His vision in 1600 was the culmination of several received during his youth. The spiritual structure of the world was revealed to him in a beam of light, as was the relationship between good and evil. In 1610, after another vision, he decided to 'go public' and wrote his *Aurora*, but his other more major writings were considered heretical. His mysticism concerned the nature of sin, evil and redemption. Where he departed from accepted tradition was in his conception of the **fall** as a necessary stage in the evolution of the universe. He believed it was necessary for humanity to depart from God and from all original unities so as to experience the 'differentiations', desires and conflicts known to such as Satan and Adam and Eve and suffered as a result of acquiring the knowledge of good and evil. This, for Bohme, was not so much a 'fall' as a learning curve. On this model of spiritual evolution, creation continues in a series of new states of 'differentiation' and reconciliation, until arriving at a state even more perfect than the original Eden. Creation was both part of and distinct from God, whose self-awareness would be enriched by interacting with a creation constantly improving. In this whole process a person's most important faculty is free will, which allows the individual to seek grace by choice. Bohme was influenced by Neoplatonism and the alchemy of **Paracelsus**. His importance rests on the influence he has had on anti-authoritarian and mystical movements such as the Religious

Society of Friends (see **Quakers**), the **Philadelphians, theosophy** and, not least, on German romanticism and the philosophy of **Hegel**.

Bolshevism The policy adopted by the Russian Bolshevik party between 1903 and 1917 with a view to seizing state power and establishing a dictatorship of the proletariat. In effect, Soviet Communism based on **Marxism** and **Leninism**.

Bon Tib. 'invocation' or 'recitation'. The name for the autochthonous religion of Tibet, before the introduction of Buddhism. The doctrines were transmitted in three cycles by its founder, **Tonpa Shenrab Miwoche**, the final cycle being divided into **Sutra, Tantra** and **Dzogchen**. These and other aspects of Bon are to be found within the tradition of **Tibetan Buddhism**. There is a positive white Bon and a negative black Bon. Both were concerned with ancestral deities, divination and rituals for protection against evil spirits; the black tradition concentrated on black magic to bring about disaster or evil. Hostile to Buddhism, Bon developed its own canon, but under Buddhist influence established a monastic order which still survives.

Bonhoeffer, Dietrich (1906–45) *X*. A pastor, teacher and theologian who, through his association with the German Confessional Churches, protested against the Nazi State. He was the author of several important books, but it was his *Letters and Papers from Prison*, published posthumously, which brought him to the attention of the wider public. The book is a collection of fragments written while he was in prison and aimed at a non-religious interpretation of biblical ideas which was formative in the '**religionless Christianity**' movement. Accused of being involved in the plot to assassinate Hitler, he was arrested in 1943 and executed at Flossenburgh in 1945. His work became even more widely known in 1963 through J. A. T. Robinson's book *Honest to God*. See also **Barth, Crisis Theology**

Book of Changes See **I Ching**

Bounteous Immortals *Zo*. Or 'Beneficent Immortals', called *Amahraspand* in the **Pahlavi literature**. A group of high spiritual beings created by **Ahura Mazda**. They are heavenly beings, sometimes referred to as 'archangels'. Traditionally they numbered seven, but the Pahlavi texts disagree about who should be included in the list. If Ahura Mazda is included there are eight. Each Immortal is responsible for protecting an aspect of the Good Creation, thus, for example, Ameretat (later called Amurdad and given the English name 'Immortality') protects plants; Asha (later called Ardvahist, with the English name 'Righteousness') protects Fire; and Vohu Manah (later called Bahman, English name 'Good Purpose') protects cattle. In the **Avesta**, the sacred literature, they are either male or female and are represented symbolically. It is Vohu Manah who meets the righteous on the **Chinvat Bridge** and accompanies them to heaven. The Immortals represent qualities of the Supreme Being's nature; by living righteous and ethically sound lives the Immortals become indwelling, sharing their qualities with human beings.

Brahma *H*. Skt. The first god of the Hindu trinity, together with **Vishnu** and **Shiva**. The aspect of God represented by Brahma is that of creator. In modern Hinduism, **Brahmanism** no longer dominates and the great forms of Hindu worship to have survived are **Vaishnavism**, **Shaivism** and **Shaktism**. In Hindu iconography Brahma is often shown with four faces and four arms, holding symbols such as a rosary or the scriptures. The term 'Brahman' is also used to refer to the impersonal, ultimate divinity or absolute reality. Brahman is recognized in Buddhism but holds no significant position.

Brahmacharya *H*. Skt. 'continence' or 'chastity'. For the Hindu, the period of youth and adolescence, being the first of the **Four Stages of Life**. See **Ashrama**, **Sacred Thread Ceremony**

Brahman *H*. Skt. A member of the priestly class, the highest **caste**, or *varna*, rendered in English as, brahmin. The term is also used to refer to a genre of Hindu scripture (see **Brahmana**). Accepted as the 'revealed word' they are appendices to the **Vedas**, compiled c.800 BCE. They take the form of instruction manuals used for sacrificial rituals and explanatory, philosophical texts speculating about the nature and origin of the universe. Another use of the word is in reference to the absolute, the ultimate, unchanging reality. There is no similar concept in the religions of duality. See **Manu**

Brahmana *H*. Compiled 900–700 BCE. A manual of instruction constituting a section of each **Veda** that includes commentaries and explanations of the texts developed as philosophies. They were compiled towards the end of the Vedic period and are known as **Vedanta**, 'end of the Veda'.

Brahmanirvana *H*. Skt. Absorption and release in Brahma. In the Vedanta it is achieved at the highest, transcendent state of consciousness, the point at which the adherent is able to say, 'I am one with Brahma.' It is the actual experience of what, until the moment of realization, has been only an idea in the mind.

Brahmanism *H*. Most familiarly, a general Western term for orthodox Hinduism. For Hindus however, Brahmanism is the worship of Brahma as the creator god (see **Brahma**) but the notion of god as creator takes less of a central place than in the West. In Hinduism, the worship of a creator god is a later development. The **Rig-Veda**, probably the oldest of the Hindu scriptures, makes the somewhat startling assertion that god appeared after the creation. Only with the emergence of the Hindu trinity was Brahma worshipped as creator.

Brahma Sutra *H*. Also known as the Vedanta-Sutra, it is thought to have been written between 400 and 200 BCE. It provides insights into the relationship between **brahman** and **atman**, of the kind found in the **Upanishads**, and its philosophy is the basis of the **Vedanta**.

Branch Dravidians *X*. One of a series of splinter groups originating with the Seventh Day Adventist Church (see **Mormons**). They were led by Vernon Howell who went to Palestine, Texas where, in 1990, he changed his name to David Koresh, thus associating himself with the biblical Kings David and Cyrus. The group was apocalyptic, believing themselves to be living at a time when Christian predictions of a final judgement were coming to pass. Koresh's authority was a detailed analysis and exposition of scripture, particularly the Book of Revelation. Koresh was known to have been polygamous and the father of several children whose mothers were still young girls. In February 1993, the campus at Mt Carmel was raided and four Federal Agents and five Dravidians were killed. The ensuing siege resulted in the compound being set alight and the deaths of 75 men, women and children, including Koresh. Koresh's remaining followers still have access to the property and hold services in the church and a new chapel has been built. Visitors can see memorials to the Dravidian victims and to the Federal Agents who lost their lives.

Branhamism A sect founded by William Branham (1906–65) a Pentecostal prophet who claimed to have been hearing voices since he was a child and to have been commissioned by an **angel** of God to be a forerunner of the Second Coming of Christ. He received the gift of healing and the 'word' of knowledge. His followers believed that he was a prophet and that we live in the Age of Laodicea, the final church age. Branham denied the doctrine of the **Trinity**, claiming that none of the existing Churches represented the full or final revelation of Christ. The sect holds to the doctrine of the **Serpent Seed** which is based on the notion that Eve had intercourse with the Serpent in Eden, thus bringing about the **Fall** of man. Branham's credibility came from his power of healing and the visions he received. There is a temple of Branhamism in Indiana, USA. See also **Charismatic Movement**, **Latter Rain Movement**, **Modalism**, **Pentecostalism**

Breath See **Prana**

Brigit *AE*. In Irish mythology she is the daughter of Dagda, the Celtic equivalent of the Greek **Athena** and the Roman **Minerva**. The history of her name associates her with arts and crafts, poetry and prophecy. She was the patron goddess of the **Druids** and the 'Sacred Flame' of Kildare. She owned an apple orchard in the Other World to which bees travelled to collect magical nectar. The orchard had an association with Avalon and Brigit may be the Lady of the Lake in the Arthurian Legend. See **Celtic Religions**

Brihadaranyaka-Upanishad *H*. Skt. A long and profound **Upanishad**, famous for the teaching on the Self. The work develops a concept formative for Hindu philosophy, that of the absolute identity of **Ataman** and **Brahman**.

British Israelites A sect based on the belief that the true location and identity of modern Israel (that is, the ten **Lost Tribes**) is Britain and, in some cases, the British colonies, especially America. An extreme form of the sect has Israel identified with a specific race, usually of Anglo-Saxon, Germanic or Scandinavian origin. It is suggested that the Celtic names *Hibernia* and *Iberia* are derived from the term *Habiru*, 'Hebrews' and that these races have their origins in an area southeast of the Black Sea, from which they migrated. There are opposing versions that claim the Black races are God's Chosen People. These theories are usually held by British Protestant Christians claiming descent back to the **Chosen People**. In the USA, one branch of the sect became the **Christian Identity Movement**. Another group, The Kingdom of God, was founded in Chicago in the 1960s. See **Black Jews, Nation of Yahweh**

Brudherhof Community *X*. Ger. 'place of brothers'. A Christian community with bases in the USA, Britain, Germany and Australia. They have also been known as the Society of Brothers and associated with the **Hutterian Brethren**. The community is based on the 16th-century Moravian Anabaptist sect of Jacob Hutter, which was part of the **Radical Reformation** and, therefore, Protestant and biblically-based in character. Their articles of faith are cast in terms similar to the Apostles' Creed and the Didache (the Sermon on the Mount) which serves as its life-model. The church follows the principles of the first church in Jerusalem, whose members were of one mind, one heart and had all things in common. Membership today is thought to be in the region of 2,500, but internal conflicts have led to ex-members denouncing an authoritarian leadership, resulting in splinter groups. Regarded by mainstream Christianity as heretical, the Community resorts to the law and the courts to silence their critics; among themselves they practise 'shunning' and various forms of spiritual disciplines.

Buber, Martin (1878–1965) Buber's work is probably best known from his book *I and Thou*, in which he established a dialogical philosophy encapsulated in the word-pairs 'I-Thou' and 'I-It', which carry, potentially, a possible encounter with the 'Eternal Thou'. Buber developed this dialogic to include the whole range of relationships in which a human being is involved, applying it to a search for meaning in an existence fraught with problems. He therefore belongs to a philosophical tradition which starts from a study of persons in relationship and by focusing his philosophy in the individual, problematic man is set at the centre of a philosophical anthropology. The prevailing philosophic atmosphere in which Buber developed his dialogical philosophy was determined, for the most part, by the ideas of the neo-Kantian schools (see **Kant**). It is in the context of his critical discussion of Kant's answer to the question 'What is Man?' that Buber provides his fullest account of philosophical anthropology. 'A legitimate philosophical anthropology must know that there is not merely a human species, but also peoples, not merely a human soul, but also types and characters, not merely human life, but also stages in life, so as to provide a clear and comprehensive vision of humanity's unity and wholeness.' He is not simply concerned with comprehensive self-knowledge, but also to penetrate into the very sanctuary of the other's knowledge of himself. In the process of enquiry this involves, Buber understands philosophical anthropology to be concerned solely with knowing man himself. This is not to reduce the scope of philosophy to human existence, but to make that existence the proper point of departure for an enquiry into such matters as the nature of the cosmos, the meaning of life and the existence of God. In short, philosophical anthropology places man firmly at the centre of all enquiries, including that of metaphysics. Buber's influence on Christian Protestant theology (see **Protestantism**), contemporary philosophy and **existentialism** is comprehensively documented. (See the Bibliography for Tillich, Friedman, Paton)

FINAL WORD: 'All real living is meeting.' Buber [1959]

'The great question which is more and more deeply agitating our age is this: How can I act?' Buber [1946]

Buchmanism An alternative name for the **Moral Rearmament Movement**, founded by the Rev Frank Buchman.

Buddha *B*. Skt. Pa. 'The Enlightened' or 'Awakened One'. Not a name, but a title given to anyone who has achieved enlightenment and release from the birth-death-rebirth cycle of existence. The title is mostly associated with Siddhartha Gautama, who became *the* Buddha and founder of **Buddhism**. He lived in India during the 6th–5th century BCE and is sometimes referred to as **Shakyamuni**, a name used for the historical Buddha or as Gotama (Skt. *Gautama*) which is also a clan name. Siddhartha is the Buddha's personal name. He is also known by the title **Tathagata**, the 'thus-gone, thus-come, thus-perfect one', referring to his attainment of supreme enlightenment; in the Benares sermon, given as he started his teaching ministry, he used this title of himself. Shakyamuni Buddha is thought to be one of a long and continuous line of Buddhas; the future Buddha is known as **Maitreya**. See **Types of Buddhas**

Buddhadharma *B*. Skt. The doctrines or teachings of the Buddha or the Buddha law. Usually this refers to the teachings of the historical **Shakyamuni** Buddha, which have their origin in his **enlightenment** and which show the way that leads to it. In the West, Buddhadharma is a synonym for Buddhism. **Zen** offers an important qualification of this in as much as the term does not apply to conceptual teachings or the written or oral forms through which they are transmitted, but to the truth which was the core of the Buddha's enlightenment and which, because it is beyond reach conceptually, can only be experienced in the moment of realization.

Buddhism The religion was founded on the teachings of Siddhartha **Gautama** who, following his enlightenment, became the first Buddha. (See **Types of Buddhas**) The term 'Buddhism', which appeared in the West only in the 19th century, has no equivalent in the original languages Sanskrit and Pali. These sources use various terms which include **dharma** and **Buddhadharma**. At its inception Buddhism was an off-shoot of **Hinduism**, appearing during a period of intense religious activity in India as a reaction to the highly formalized, ritualistic practices of the **Brahman** priests. The **Upanishads**, written between c.600 and 500 BCE, provided a philosophical bridge between the old Vedic religion (see **Vedas**) and Buddhism; they suggested that behind the pantheon of gods lay one, single reality. Instead of practising complicated ritual acts, liberation could be achieved by union with this one reality. In its earliest form Buddhism was one of many protests against the prevailing formalism of the received tradition but its perceptions were entirely new, both ethically and philosophically.

Buddhism is non-theistic, there is no doctrine of a personal, creator-saviour God. What Buddhism affirms is the possibility for an individual to achieve ultimate wisdom and compassion. It denies there is any immortal soul but testifies to personal continuity through cycles of rebirths until the liberating attainment of **nirvana** is realized. In his first sermon in Benares (c.530 BCE) the Buddha assured his audience that there was an answer to **samsara**, the relentless cycle of birth-death-rebirth and to *dukkha*, the suffering characteristic of this. Suffering is brought about by craving and ignorance. The one binds you to the inconsequential, transient aspects of life, the other prevents you from seeing the truth of this. Nirvana is to be found by overcoming craving and ignorance. To this end the Buddha spoke of the **Four Noble Truths**, the last of which was expanded as the **Eightfold Path**. These represent a Middle Way between the extremes of asceticism and self-indulgence. In the Indian philosophy of the time it was axiomatic that you became what you desired or what you thought. 'We are what we think. All that we are arises with our thoughts. With our thoughts we make the world' (*The Dhammapada*). Thus, following the Way requires the 'three trainings' in morality, **meditation** and wisdom. Morality means observing the **Five Precepts**, the emphasis being to avoid, in any way, harming human or animal life. In practice, it is the recognition that all living, sentient beings are the interconnected members of one family. Meditation concerns training in **dhyana**, the Four Abodes of Mindfulness, characterized by single-minded or one-pointed concentration until, free of all aspects of duality, union with the absolute is experienced. Morality is the foundation of meditation which, in turn, supports wisdom. The Buddha rejected the Upanishadic tradition of Brahman, the world soul and of **atman**, an individual 'real' self that plays host to the ever-changing and transient characteristics we refer to as 'I'. The interaction of cause and effect is not a change or modification of substances, but a process of **Dependent Origination**, a fundamental doctrine of Buddhism. The Middle Way, living life between the extremes, sets up the creative tension of constant mindful, moral choices that might lead the individual to nirvana, the cessation of all thought and feeling, the final liberation from the cycle of *samsara*. Rebirth includes the transmission of consciousness made up of the residue of **karma**, good and evil deeds acted out during this and previous lives. The familiar, illustrative image of this transmission is of a flame being passed from one candle to another. Recognizing the three characteristic marks of existence, that life is impermanent, without essence and subject to suffering, is the beginning of the Buddhist path. A person becomes a Buddhist by vowing to take refuge in the **Three Jewels**, the **Buddha**, the **dharma** and the **sangha**.

There are four discernable phases in the development of Buddhism. The first stage was from the 6th–5th century BCE when the Shakyamuni, the historical Buddha, expounded his teachings. At his death he left a large community of followers, the sangha. He appointed no successor other than the dharma, the teachings, which were disseminated by his disciples orally. In this early stage, the forms of Buddhism known as **Hinayana** were established. It was also the period of the first Buddhist councils that agreed the canonical scriptures. The second long phase from 4th century BCE to 1st century CE, saw the division of the community into different sects and schools as a result of variant interpretations and emphases of the teachings. The latter part of this period coincident with beginning of the Christian era, sees the emergence of the **Mahayana** school and its ideal of the **Bodhisattva**. During this period, the Emperor **Asoka** (c.270–232 BCE) gave Buddhism a huge impetus by adopting a policy of conquest by Dharma, rather than the sword and by sending missionaries throughout his realms. As a result of Asoka's initiative, Buddhism spread beyond India, adapting to new national cultures and philosophies. During the third period, 1st–7th century CE, the Mahayana school continued to develop through its two main expressions, **Madhyamaka** (the Middle Way School), which avowed to be faithful to the Buddha's original teachings and **Yogachara**, the practice of **Yoga** (the Way of Consciousness). The fourth stage, from the 7th century, saw the emergence in Tibet of **Tantra** and **Vajrayana**, the 'Diamond Vehicle'. From the 13th century Buddhism became almost extinct in India, but in recent times it has begun to rediscover its Buddhist heritage. Of the 18 schools of Hinayana, **Theravada** is the only one to have survived and it is the principal tradition of Buddhism in Sri Lanka, Burma, Thailand, Laos and Cambodia. Mahayana is to be found in China, Japan, Vietnam and Korea, Vajrayana in Tibet, Mongolia and Japan. In more recent times there has been an extraordinary flowering of Buddhism in the West.

The collective name for the Buddhist canon is the **Tripitaka**, a threefold arrangement of sacred texts of the older schools. As with many religions, the scriptures compiled purported to record the exact words of the founder's teachings. To these original scriptures were added analyses, commentaries and additional philosophical texts contributed by scholar-monks. Buddhists do not consider the teachings to be divinely inspired as, for example, do adherents of biblical religions. The canon of scriptures was arranged in its present form only after the original community began to split up into various sects and schools. Each of these has made their own collections which reflect the cultural influences of the countries into which Buddhism spread. Only one complete Indian language collection survives, the Canon of the School of Elders (**Theravada**) written in Pali, agreed at the first Council of Rajagrha in the year of the Buddha's death, c.483 BCE. It is accepted as the authoritative scriptural source in Sri Lanka, Burma, Thailand, Laos and Cambodia. Other canons written in Sanskrit have survived only in fragments, but due to the oral transmission of the teachings through widely spread monastic communities they show considerable differences from the Pali canon. Once they were preserved in their written from they spelled out the traditional differences that exist between the various schools of Buddhism. Mahayana schools left their canon open, accepting later writings considered to be inspired teachings. These texts are called **sutras**. The whole considerable collection, which includes vast Chinese and Tibetan canons, chart the long and complex development of the various Buddhist traditions.

FINAL WORD: 'So the nature of Dharma always exists for the weald of
the world,
And it refreshes by this Dharma the entire world.
And then, refreshed, just like the plants,
The world will burst forth into blossoms.'
Saddharmapunadrika V, v. 38 trans. Edward Conze

Buddhism and Secularism *B*. Being a non-theistic religion, Buddhism presents a very different notion of secularism, since the Buddhist path cannot be followed if the adherent clings to the 'God-idea'. In one sense, because of its avowal of **advaita**, non-dualism (see **Dualism**), the terms sacred and secular or religion and secularism, are also abandoned. What challenges Buddhism is when life is distracted by materialistic, intellectual and scientific perceptions that displace the **dharma**. Assuming the conventions of the perceived world of our senses to be reality is a secularization of the concept of **maya**, illusion; it is the 'dust in the eyes' of humankind that, at first, made the Buddha reluctant to impart his message. See **Buddhist Humanism, Humanism, Komeito, Religious Humanism, Secularism, Soka Gakkai**

Buddhist Humanism *B*. There is much in Buddhist philosophy that suggests affinity with some forms of Western Humanism and rationalism. Its metaphysics is grounded in nature, in understanding the appearance of everything for the illusion it is, with remorseless flux and change evidence of the endless process of cause and effect. Its philosophy also denies the transcendental, determinism and any kind of fatalism. Such terms, however, are used so variously in both Western and Eastern philosophy that only a broad generalization is possible here. A Buddhist-humanist perception is not the same as Western post-Renaissance humanism or the secular-humanism that influenced, for example, Marxism. Buddhist humanism is an affirmation of the human over-against the Divine (as all humanism must be) and of human potential and responsibility grounded in **empiricism** and reason. This is centred on the individual and not in any form of religious or social collectivism. More importantly, Buddhist humanism is not subject to doctrinal authority, there is no party line, in fact the opposite is nearer the truth, in that the individual is encouraged to find out for himself whether or not what the Buddha teaches is 'right' (see **Kalama Sutra**). The **dharma** affirms that of all forms of existence only that of the human being offers the opportunity to be released from *dukkha*. This doctrine heightens the wonder of human life and perfectly expresses the true meaning of Buddhist humanism. See **Buddhism and Secularism**, **Humanism**, **Komeito**, **Religious Humanism**, **Soka Gakkai**

Bultmann, Rudolf (1884–1976) *X*. A German scholar and systematic theologian whose **demythologizing** of the New Testament made him one of the most influential thinkers of the 20th century. See **Bonhoeffer**, **Existentialism**, **Reductionism**, **Tillich**

Burning Man Festival An annual festival held at Black Rock, Nevada. The name refers to the culmination of the festival when a wooden man with outstretched arms (resembling crucifixion) is burned by the crowd. The impact of taking part has been so impressive that a culture, if not to say a cult, has been formed around it. It takes the form of a community, gathered for one week, during which the participants are encouraged to live in a way not normally experienced. Everyone is expected to make a contribution which is frequently a form of conceptual, preformed or exhibited art designed to express whatever the given theme is for the year. The art theme is perpetuated through the Black Rock Arts Foundation. The Burning Man Festival is a syncretistic celebration of **Satanism**, **Neo-paganism**, New Earth Paganism, **Gaia**, the **occult**, Mystery cults, self-expression, self-indulgence, a combination of some of these, all of these or none of these. One of the numerous Burning Man websites says that, 'trying to explain what Burning Man is to someone who has never been to the event is a bit like trying to explain what a particular colour is like to someone who is blind.'

Bushmen A general term for people who live and travel in the wilderness or 'bush'. The term is familiarly associated with the nomadic hunters of the Kalahari Desert in South Africa. They were made famous by Laurence van der Post's book, *The Lost World of the Kalahari*. Their central deity is Kaggen, a trickster god who can assume the form of several animals, reptiles and birds, but who otherwise lives like one of the Bushmen. The eland is the most sacred animal and it figures in the four central rituals: i) a boy's first kill; ii) a girl's puberty; iii) marriage; and iv) trance dance. In some communities there is a belief in two gods, one from the East, the other from the West. The communities are served and protected by the 'Medicine People' or Shamans. The term 'Bushmen' is also associated with Australian aborigines (see **Australian Aboriginal Religion**).

Byzantine Empire (306–1453 CE) A term used since the 19th century to describe the Greek-speaking Roman Empire during the Middle Ages, centred on its capital, Constantinople. The dates for the start of the Empire are debated but consensus falls on the end of the reign of Theodosius (379–395 CE) when the Western and Eastern halves of the Roman Empire diverged. Its golden age is held to be from the 9th to the 11th century when Byzantine art and architecture flourished and the territory spread from Azerbaijan and Armenia in the east, to southern Italy in the west. For Christianity the 11th century was momentous; the deteriorating relations between the Greek-speaking Eastern Church and the Latin-speaking Western Church led, finally, to the **Great Schism**, the consequence of centuries of gradual separation. It was from this divergence that the Eastern Orthodox and Roman Catholic Churches developed. In the East the Church survived the overthrow of the Empire by the **Abbasid Caliphate**, marked by the fall of Constantinople in 1204. The Eastern empire left Europe a priceless legacy which included the widespread adoption of Christianity through the so-called 'Byzantine commonwealth', which carried the faith to the Slavic peoples where it still flourishes throughout Russia, the Ukraine, Serbia, Bulgaria, Macedonia and Greece. The greatness of Byzantium lay in what Robert Byron called 'the Triple Fusion, that of a Roman body, a Greek mind and an oriental, mystical soul'.

C

Cabbala *J.* See **Kabbalah**

Caer Avalon *AE.* Originating in Wales, Caer Avalon has become a Pan-Celtic pagan tradition associated with the sacred Tree, Well and Fire. The seasons and equinoxes provide the focus for celebration and worship with offerings made to sacred rivers and groves, where it is believed the 'Old Ones' whisper their messages on the wind. Drawing on poetry, history, mythology and archaeology it is, in effect, a neo-pagan cult within which adherents are free to find and follow their own path. See **Celtic Religion, Neo-Paganism**

Calendar Stone *Az.* The Calendar or Sun Stone, by which the Aztecs calculated their cycles of time. See **Aztecs**

Caliph *I.* Arab. *khalifa*, 'deputy' or 'representative'. A term used for the lieutenant, firstly of the Prophet Muhammad then, when he died in 632 CE, for the Muslims' political-military leader. The first four Caliphs were chosen by consensus after which the position became hereditary, ruling through two notable Islamic dynasties, the **Umayyad** Caliphs (661–750 CE) and the **Abbasid** Caliphs (750–1517). From 1258, however, the **Mameluke** sultans held the real power and the Abbasid Caliph was merely titular. From 1517 the leadership was taken over by the Turkish Ottoman sultans, secular leaders displaced in 1924 by Kemal-Ataturk, who abolished the office of Caliph. The **Sunnis** regarded the Caliphate merely as a practical necessity, but the **Shiite** believed the office to be *imamate* (**Imam**) or inspired, a difference that impeded Islamic unity. See **Islamic Dynasties**

Calmecac *Az.* A kind of Aztec Public School where the children of the nobility were educated. They were single-sex schools where priests taught their pupils practical wisdom and good judgement and the rudiments of history, mathematics, astronomy, literacy, poetry and the codes of the Elders. The pupils were expected to inflict pain on themselves by piercing their genitals with pins. This was thought to instil courage. They were also expected to carry out some religious duties. The *Macehualtin*, or workers' children, were educated at the *telpochcalli* where they were taught practical crafts and skill and the arts of war. A bright student could graduate to the *Calmecac*.

Calumet *Ami.* The French term for the 'reed pipe' found among the Miami and Illinois Indians in North America. The term now applies to all ceremonial smoking appliances of the Amerindians. It is made from a long stem, usually with a bowl attached for the tobacco. The design and decoration, which varies between tribes, are symbolic, the whole pipe being a symbol of the universe: the stone bowl being the earth, the stem the vegetation and the carvings representative of animals and birds. Smoking the pipe is an acted parable of the interconnectedness of the whole cosmos, but also a symbol of the positive relationships between those who share the pipe and smoke together. It was used to signify the signing of a peace treaty, hence the epithet 'Peace Pipe'. To refuse to smoke the offered peace pipe was a gross insult. See **Peyote Cults**

Calvinism X. A Christian denomination broadly associated with those churches influenced by John Calvin (1509–1564), one of the leaders of the **Reformation**. In Geneva, Calvin established a partial theocracy based on his work *The Institutes of the Christian Religion*, in which he set out a specific form of **soteriology**, asserting that humans can do nothing to contribute to their own salvation, which is given by God through grace alone. Even a person's faith and the decision to follow Christ are initiated by God. Thus, Calvin repudiated **natural theology,** which claimed that God is revealed in creation. He insisted that such knowledge is initiated exclusively through scripture but, once 'the eye of reason' has been opened, the created world can be read as a supplement to the 'spectacles' of scripture. Central to Calvin's system is the doctrine of election or **predestination**, that affirms the absolute sovereignty of God in determining every detail of a person's life; God's sovereignty must be realized on earth through church and civil government. These doctrines were definitively formulated at the Synod of Dordrecht (1618–19). Calvin's passionate biblical fundamentalism, sometimes referred to as Reformed **Protestantism**, had wide-ranging influence and is what is thought of as 'Calvinism'. The doctrines were spread by John Knox, founder of the **Presbyterian** Church, John Bunyan, the English **Baptist**, Jonathan Edwards, an American Revivalist theologian and through the work of the neo-orthodox theologian Karl **Barth**. See **Camisards**

Cambrian Episcopal Church of the Grail An evangelical foundation that teaches the Christianity of the major creeds but which focuses on the characteristics of the Church up to the middle of the 2nd century CE. The Cambrian church believes that later orthodoxy and **institutionalization** led to the discouragement and eventual annihilation of original escoteric doctrines which survive only because they are veiled in symbolic or secret language. It traces its history, beliefs and practices through **Celtic Christianity**, and to the *desposyni*, Jesus' blood relatives. This is significant, in that they believe Christianity is intended to be a family-centred religion and that the true Body of Christ is manifested in the family and not in the institutionalized Church. Thus its episcope is given to fathers as priests. See **Grail Religion**

Camisards X. Occitan *camisa*, 'smock' or 'shirtsleeves'. A group who revolted against the Revocation of the Edict of Nantes, issued by Louis XIV in 1685, which ordered the destruction of **Huguenot** churches and the closure of Protestant schools. They were mostly made up of Calvinist peasants (see **Calvinism**) in the region of the Cévennes and Bas-Languedoc, the traditional heartland of religious heterodoxy (see **Cathars**). The Catholic Dragonades, 'missionaries in boots', enforced conversions and terrorized the Protestant communities, but were met by fierce and effective guerrilla tactics that overcame superior forces in several battles. Sporadic fighting continued until 1710 and, after the death of Louis XIV in 1715, Protestantism was restored in the region. The Camisards' faith was millenarian and they believed the Last Judgement was imminent; their worship was characterized by 'ecstatic enthusiasm' and young children were trained as propagandists. Their spiritual orientation influenced the philosophy of Jean-Jacques Rousseau and of Ann Lee, the founder of the **Shaker** movement. Many Huguenot Camisards fled from the Cévennes and settled in England and America.

Canaan *J*. 'Low Land'. The country that was defined by the river Jordan in the east, the Mediterranean in the west, the Lebanon hills in the north and the Sinai wilderness in the south. It was originally populated by the Canaanites who were 'vomited out' (Lev. 18:25) by the Israelites to whom the land had been promised by God. The Israelite army was led by Joshua and at the time of the conquest there were numerous other tribes living in Canaan, such as the Amorites, **Hittites** and Jebusites. It is doubtful that the 'conquest' was achieved quickly, it being more likely that the Israelites subdued the land over a long period of time (1200–1025 BCE). Tradition says nine-and-a-half of the 12 tribes of Israel settled in Canaan, the other two-and-a-half settling east of the River Jordan. Canaan is refereed to as 'the Promised Land' or 'the **Holy Land**'. The name **Palestine** was given to the territory by the Romans and is probably derived from *Philistia*, the territory occupied by the Philistines. Canaanite religion was a ritual polytheism and its practice, based on a fertility cult, was particularly sensual and lewd. It proved to be more influential than any other religion in the ancient Near East. The Canaanite language was predominantly Ugaritic and its principal deities were **El** and his son **Ba'al**. 'El' is used in the **Old Testament** in epithets for God, for example *El Elyon*, 'the most high God' and *Elohim*, 'the God of Israel'. **Philo** describes El as a merciless tyrant whose three wives were also his sisters, terrifying the other gods, usurping his father, beheading his daughter and murdering one of his sons. He was succeeded by **Ba'al**, the god of rain and storms and thus of fertility. God's promise of the land of Canaan to Abraham and his successors was not based on their holiness or righteousness, but on the need to have the pagan gods of Canaan – and the people who worshipped them – exterminated. See **Israel**, **Judea**, **Ugaritic**

Candomblé A Brazilian Afro-American religion known also as **Macumba**. See also **Quimbanda**, **Umbanda**

Cantor *J*. & *X*. An official in charge of music and chants. In Judaism the *Chazzan* leads the **synagogue** liturgy and congregational prayers. In small synagogues the role sometimes doubles with that of the Rabbi; in large synagogues it is a professional and ordained post that combines leading the music with the religious education of the young. In medieval Christianity, the Cantor presided over cathedral music and the training of the choir. The term is sometimes used for the head of a college of church music.

Cao Dai Vietnamese for 'high place', the abbreviated name for God. A relatively new syncretism that was established in 1926 in Tay Ninh, a southern province of Vietnam. Its full name translates as 'Great Religion of the Third Period of Revelation and Salvation'. Before God existed there was **Tao**, the nameless source of the *Tao-Te Ching*. God represented Yang, creating Yin out of himself, thus forming the raw materials for creation and the basis for the worship of both God the Father and the Mother Goddess. Caodeism offers three levels of spiritual attainment based on the teachings of the Saints, the Sages and the Buddha. There are three periods of salvation and revelation, the first being that of the Buddha, Sages and Saints; the second that of the Buddha **Shakyamuni**, **Lao-Tzu**, **Confucius** and **Jesus**; the third the rule of God. Cao Dai worship enables direct communication with the transcendental world through institutionalized séances. Administration is tripartite on the American pattern of a Legislative, Executive and Judicial tier. The Tay Ninh Holy See, the hierarchy of the clergy, is similar to that of the Catholic Church, the leader being a 'pope'. Cao Dai asserts that all religions are one, a claim substantiated by combining elements from all the major faiths. It is the third largest religion in Vietnam, with over eight million adherents.

Capuchins *X*. From the French *capuche*, the pointed cowl worn by monks of an order founded by Matteo dei Bassi of Urbino, who died in 1552. Originally a friar of the **Franciscan** Order, he broke away from them to return to what he believed to be the primitive simplicity of the order based on poverty and austerity. The Rule was drawn up in 1529, since when the Capuchins have been the most severe order of the Franciscan group.

Cargo Cults Developed in the 1880s around Fiji and among the native peoples of Melanesia and West Africa, these cults were based on the notion that manufactured Western goods (cargoes) were created by ancestral spirits, but that their distribution had been unfairly monopolized by white people. The cults set out to break that monopoly and assume ownership of the consumer goods by rituals imitative of white practice and behaviour. The most famous instances of this included building harbours, airstrips and airports out of coconut and straw, believing the structures would attract ships and transport planes complete with their cargoes. Some cults have prophetic leaders who claim to have millenarian-type visions of imminent doom, redemption and a utopian future. See **John Frum**

Carmelite Order *X*. Full name the 'Order of Our Lady of Mount Carmel', founded in 1154 in Palestine by St Berthold but originating in a community of hermits on Mt Carmel. Its rule of extreme asceticism was laid down in 1209. An order of Carmelite Sisters was founded in 1452, but the rule became relaxed until the 16th century when St **Teresa** restored the original 'Primitive Rule'. St **John of the Cross** did the same for the friars. Carmelite spirituality is characterized by distrust of physical comforts, a passion for spiritual development and insight into mystical experience.

Carthage An ancient north African city on the shore of the Bay of Tunis. Like Rome, it lends its name to both a place and a culture. Founded by the trading and colonializing Phoenicians in the 9th century BCE, it became a commercial and political rival of Rome who eventually destroyed the city during the 2nd Punic Wars (218–201 BCE) defeating their most famous general, Hannibal. Carthaginian religion was virtually the same as **Phoenician** religion, which focused on the power, seasons and processes of nature. The primary fertility couple were Tanit and Ba'al Hammon, with the goddess **Astarte** favoured during the earlier years of the city's life. During the years of its greatest powers **Carthage** played host to many of the gods of the states with which it came in contact, such as the Etruscans, Egyptians and the Greeks. Archaeology has identified the goddess Tanit with a sacred Temple location called 'Tophet', translated as 'place of burning', implying sacrifice. Punic texts indicate a sophisticated system of priesthood and acolytes; the horror of child sacrifice is recorded by Plutarch (c.46–127 CE). Carthage was Christianized and Cyprian called several Church Councils, the first of which was in 251 CE, and continued until 419 under Aurelius, when the Carthaginian Church resisted the jurisdiction of Rome.

Caste *H*. Skt. *Varna*, 'colour'. Originally four class structures were assimilated from the **Aryans**. Tradition claims that the priests of the Aryan sacrificial cult and writers of the early hymns that were the basis of the **Rig-Veda**, formed the embryo of the highest class that became the **Brahmans**. As well as priests this group included scholars, philosophers and religious teachers. The other three castes originated with the **Dravidians**, the indigenous Indian population. These were the *Kshatriya* (the warriors, generals, politicians and civil authorities), the *Vaishyas* ('providers', being traders and farmers), and the lowest social level, the *Shudras* (servants and workers). The *pariahs* and *harijans*, 'untouchables' or 'outcasts', have no part in the caste system. Beyond this classical social hierarchy are literally thousands of castes, sub-castes and kindred groups or *jati* (Skt. 'birth' or 'race'). The hierarchy and its sociology is complicated but, in broad terms, each caste was defined precisely so that the entire population understood the terms of reference. Sub-castes served the same functions throughout the different regions, while kindred groups served the locality or village. Caste, therefore, was associated with a social function that proliferated into every form of occupation. The functional demarcation is further complicated by the existence of castes that are non-functional, that is those having tribal, ethnic and sectarian definitions. Caste members were expected to follow their traditional occupations and remain within their cultural group, but as society developed and changed some skills were in more demand than others, requiring caste members to seek alternative occupations. This process of change eventually influenced the entire caste structure. The strength and universalism of the Indian caste system was founded on divinely sanctioned notions of purity and impurity believed to be the ideal pattern for society. For this reason caste is thought by some to be a 'social' religion. In practice, from the top levels of Indian society to the grass-roots Hinduism of the villages, what mattered and what happened depended on how the balance was struck between the ideal and the actual.

The caste system, despite its tradition and divine sanction, has always been in a state of flux and change and there have been those like Mahatma **Gandhi**, who did much to mitigate its worst abuses. Modern Indian society is subject to the influences of **secularism**, and the caste and sub-caste system is under threat, but generalizations about the caste system are dangerous. It is probable that there has never been a time in Indian history when there were those who believed the caste system was on the point of breaking down. See **Hinduism**

Catacombs X. A subterranean location for the burial of the dead, some-times a crude cave but usually constructed with galleries and recesses for tombs. There are catacombs under several cities, among them **Carthage**, Alexandria, Susah in North Africa and in Asia Minor. The Roman cata-combs are ancient Jewish and Christian burial places, excavated on a large scale in the 2nd century CE. Christian use was determined by belief in the resurrection of the body, thus cremation was not an option. There are 40 known Roman catacombs, but an ordinance prohibiting burial within the city required their location outside its boundaries. The Paris catacombs are a network of galleries constructed in what were Roman-era limestone quarries; they were converted into a mass tomb towards the end of the 18th century. Catacombs were also used as a refuge from per-secution, as shrines for saints and for funerary feasts.

Catechism X. A summary or exposition of doctrine traditionally used by Christians for teaching. They usually take the form of manuals with a question and answer structure, the answers to be learned by heart. The method of instruction is usually oral and given by a priest, a nun, a pastor or parent. The forms of catechism were influenced by Rabbinic and Socratic methods of teaching and Christian catechetical schools were established early, such as that of Mark the Evangelist in Alexandria, c.61–68 CE. The 1556 Roman Catechism is untypical, as it was written for the instruction of priests rather than children and converts. Until the 1960s, the Baltimore Catechism was the standard in America, since when this form of teaching has declined. Catechisms such as Luther's were used by **Protestants** from the beginning of the Reformation; Calvin's finally revised catechism appeared in 1545. There are numerous other catechisms associated with different **creeds** such as the Westminster Catechism. Modern catechisms of the Orthodox and Catholic Churches are not meant to be learned by heart or to be used didactically, but are massive compendia of doctrine and teaching. In a secular context, a similar structure is used in multiple-choice examinations.

Cathars *X*. A Christian sect associated with the **Albigensians** that sprang up in the 12th and 13th centuries. The name 'Cathar' has its roots in the Greek word *katharizein*, 'to purify', suggesting a connection with Greek-speaking Eastern Orthodoxy. Catharism is also considered to be a Western off-shoot of the **Bogomils**, a Christian sect founded in Bulgaria in the 10th century. The Cathars believed themselves to be the only true Christians, custodians of an earlier original Christianity which the Roman Catholic Church had usurped by its authority and sacraments. The 'purified' expression of the faith was seen both in their forms of government and ritual and in their practice of piety, chastity and poverty. The teachings had their origins in **Gnosticism** and **Manichaeism**. Cathar philosophy was based on a heretical **dualism**. Two opposed powers, one Good the other for Evil, dominated the universe. Most Cathars regarded the evil principle as being less real or weaker than the good. But the good principle, God, was not all-powerful. He had to suffer the opposition of an evil power sometimes known as 'the Monster of Chaos'. The evil principle, although manifest in various forms such as man, fish, bird, beast, Lucifer and Satan, had the attribute of spirit. Cathar theology taught that Satan created flesh and matter and God created celestial and eternal things. It was incumbent on believers to emancipate the spirit from its material captivity. Only the effects of the evil principle were eternal; evil itself would eventually be destroyed. Christ's appearance was illusory; his task was to teach the doctrine of salvation as explained in the **gospels**, and to carry a warning that the God of the Old Testament was the demon who had created the material world. The Cathars rejected the cult of the cross, Christ's death in this world being a fiction, his true mission accomplished in 'superior worlds'. They claimed the wood of the cross was taken from the tree of the knowledge of good and evil in the Garden of Eden and rejected the doctrine of the Virgin birth and the resurrection of the body. The Cathars were structured into two groups, the Perfecti, *les bonshommes* or 'ancients' who constituted the hierarchy of the Church, and the 'believers' who were the rank and file. The Perfecti undertook long and rigorous initiation, culminating in the *consolamentum*, a ceremony combining the equivalent of baptism, confirmation and the ordination of a priest. Training prepared them to endure torture rather than betray their faith and many of them went willingly to appalling deaths.

Remarkable as it may seem, the Cathars became so established that the Roman Catholic churches were empty. The Cathars had become a Church in their own right. Efficiently organized and with zealously trained missionaries, they attracted many converts and were a serious threat to the established Church and by 1149 they had consecrated their first Bishop in northern France. From the mid-12th century Catharism spread throughout southern France and into northern Italy and by the end of the century 11 Cathar Bishops had been consecrated: five in France, six in Italy. The Cathars had also spread to Germany, centred around Cologne. In 1162 a German-led Cathar mission to England was expelled, each member being branded on the forehead. Gradually schisms and differences arose within the movement itself – a sure sign, some would say, of its mature establishment. By 1208 Rome's toleration ended and Pope Innocent III declared the Cathars 'worse than the very Saracen' and what became known as the 'Albigensian Crusade' was mounted. The crusade became confused with the ambitions of its leaders, particularly those of Simon de Montfort, who sought to be Count of Toulouse. It took a century of war, persecutions and massacres to put down the Cathar heresy, but its influence has survived in later religious movements. As late as the Second World War, there was a neo-Cathar sect in Toulouse. FINAL WORD: 'Show mercy, neither to order, nor age, nor sex … Cathar or Catholic, kill them all, God will know his own.' (Papal Legate, at the siege of Beziers, 1209)

Catholic *X*. Gk. *katholikos*, 'universal' or 'general'. The term may apply to the 'whole orthodox Christian Church' (*Webster's Dictionary*) or to the doctrines and faith of the Catholic Church as governed by the Bishop of Rome and the bishops in communion with him. Most Christian denominations affirm faith in the creedal statement, 'One Holy Catholic and Apostolic Church'. However, the Oriental and Eastern Orthodox Churches (see **Orthodox Church**), the Anglican Communion (see **Anglicanism**) and others hold themselves to be non-Roman branches of the same Episcopal and apostolic tradition. Neo-Lutheranism argues that it is a Protestant reform movement within the Catholic Church. See **Roman Catholicism**

Catholicism *X*. See **Roman Catholicism**

Celibacy The term may refer to being unmarried or to sexual abstinence. An oath of celibacy may be a prerequisite for ordination or vows taken, for example, by ordinands and nuns. In Western Catholic and Eastern Orthodox Churches, married men can be ordained deacons or priests, but not bishops; marriage is prohibited after ordination. The vow and practice of celibacy was one of the issues debated by the **Reformation** theologians who argued that requiring an oath of celibacy was contrary to biblical teaching (see for example 1 Tim. 4: 1–5 and Heb. 13:4); it dishonoured the sacrament of marriage and was the reason behind widespread clerical misconduct. The matter is still strongly debated, mostly on the same grounds. In certain traditions of Buddhism, monks and nuns are expected to refrain from sexual relationships; Judaism has no tradition of celibacy for rabbis or priests and some community functions are occupied only by married men. Celibacy was not part of the original practice of **Islam**, and even among the **Sufi** it is rare.

Celtic Christianity *X*. From 597 CE, Augustine of Canterbury evangelized England. Christianity was later taken to Ireland by St Patrick, who is credited with establishing the Celtic church. Celtic Christianity was allied to Roman Catholicism and influenced by it, but despite this, vestiges of polytheistic traditions survived through their emphasis on natural religion. Gradually the papacy asserted authority and the differences between the Celtic church and Rome, as well as those between the Celtic Churches, were eradicated during the Middle Ages. Modern attempts to revive Celtic Christianity draw on a mixture of Catholicism and Protestantism and the scene is further confused by neo-pagan interest in the ancient religion.

Celtic Religion The Celtic tribes were widely spread across Europe early in the first millennium CE, but are usually associated with Britain. Because of their contact with Rome the mythologies of the Gauls and Celtiberians have not survived (see **Celtic Christianity**). Other tribes, like the Gaels, guarded their political and linguistic identity and their mythologies, transmitted by oral tradition, were recorded in the Middle Ages. The gods were clustered under various mythological traditions such as those of the ancient Celts, the Irish and the Welsh. The name **Dagda**, the supreme god of the Celtic pantheon, means 'Good God' not in a moral sense, but 'good at everything' and thus, powerful. He was a father-figure and protector of the tribes and as such his tradition runs into Irish mythology where his consort was Morrigan, the 'Great Queen' of both earth and heaven. As the goddess of Sovereignty she is associated with war and battlefields, somewhat like Badb, the carrion-crow battle-goddess of **neo-paganism**. Morrigan is also associated with the cauldron of rebirth which Dagda protects. Although widespread, the cult of Lug (whose name survives in those of the cities of Lyon, France and Leiden, in southern Holland) is a late-comer to the pantheon. He was known to be skilled with a spear and a sling. There were numerous other gods, but little more than their names survive. Despite the tradition that worship was held outside in sacred groves, there is evidence of temples throughout the Celtic world. Trees such as the yew and holly were held to be sacred and human sacrifice was practised. Celtic Christianity is known by other names such as the Old British Church and the Culdes Church. See **Caer Avalon**, **Druids**, **Synod of Whitby**

Cemanahuac *Az*. The Aztec name for the Earth. See **Aztecs**

Cerberus *G*. Greek mythology's guardian of the entrance to **Hades**, who took the form of a three-headed dog. Cerberus, who had the giant Typhon for a father and a monstrous mother called Echidna, half-woman, half-snake, craftily allowed spirits to enter Hades, but not to leave. **Orpheus** famously deceived him, having learned that he could be put to sleep by music, notably of the lyre.

Ceres *R*. In Roman mythology the goddess of growing plants (especially 'cereals', a word derived from her name) and of motherly love. She was adopted by the Romans in 496 BCE, when the first temple was dedicated to her. It was a time of devastating famine and the **Sibylline Books** advised the adoption of the associated Greek goddess, **Demeter**. She was personified and celebrated by women in secrete rituals; from the 3rd century BCE her main festival was the *Cerealia* held annually in April, at which she was mostly worshipped by the plebeians, who monopolized the corn trade. The strange ritual of tying lighted brands to the tails of foxes and letting them loose in the Circus Maximus is one of the few recorded customs associated with her cult. The odd story of Samson torching the tails of 300 foxes, then turning them loose among the 'standing grain of the Philistines' (Judges 15: 4–5), suggests a more ancient origin of the ritual.

Ch'an *B & Z*. The Chinese form of the Sanskrit word *dhyana*, meditative absorption. It is the name of a major **Mahayana** school of Chinese Buddhism, the Meditation School which abandoned all forms of textual, ritualistic and ethical practices in favour of techniques that led to direct realization or **enlightenment** by immediate perception. Ch'an Buddhism was brought to China from India by **Bodhidharma** in the late 5th or early 6th century CE. Ch'an first appeared as a formal practice in Japan in the 9th century, where it is known as **Zen**. See **Dhyana, Ox Herding Pictures**

Chakras *H. B.* Skt. *cakram*, 'wheel', 'circle'. The simplest meaning for Hindus is a circle of worshippers, but beyond that lies a complex and esoteric system of relationships between centres of body energy which do not always have identical correspondences with actual body parts. In Indian Kundalini-yoga there are seven chakras, six of which are dispersed along the spinal column, with the seventh located above the crown of the head. The spine is the main conduit for subtle energy through which rises the *kundalini*, the spiritual force that lies coiled, snake-like, at the base of the spine. Awakened by yoga practice, the rising kundalini activates each chakra in turn, resulting in mystical visions and spiritual knowledge. Each of the chakras has different names in other cultures and each has a symbolic shape, its own colour, seed syllable, animal symbol and a divinity association. The first or lowest chakra is located between the genitals and the anus where the kundalini rests; when this is activated it rises through the other chakras, located at the root of the genitals, the navel, the heart, the lower throat, between the eyebrows and above the head, which is the dwelling place of the god **Shiva**. Chakras have their place in Buddhism, especially in **Tantra**. Where the system is similar to that of **Hinduism** but the symbolism is different, being taken from classical Buddhist iconography in which the chakras are symbolized by the **lotus** flower. The meditation practice is also markedly different from kundalini-yoga. Full expositions of these practices are given by Woodroffe and Govinda. See **Yoga**

Chaldea The Hellenistic term for the region of **Babylon** referred to as such in the KJV of the Bible. The people are referred to as the Chaldeans.

Chaldean Syrian Church See **Assyrian Church of the East**

Chant See **Gregorian Chant**

Chanukah *J*. Heb. 'Dedication'. A very popular family festival, sometimes known as the 'festival of lights' celebrated for eight days from the 25th of the Hebrew month of *Kislev* (November-December). The festival rehearses the revolt, in 168 BCE, of Judas Maccabeus and his followers over the Syrians, who wanted Judaism to be assimilated into the pagan practices of **Hellenism**. Having recaptured Jerusalem, Judas rekindled the light in the Temple, signifying the presence of God. The cruse of oil charged with one day's supply miraculously lasted for eight days. Using a **menorah**, an eight-branched candelabra, one candle is lit the first night, two on the second night and so on until all eight are lit from a ninth which is housed separately. During Chanukah it is customary for gifts to be exchanged and for the family to play games together.

Chaos Magic A recent form of ritual and empty-handed magic that has its origin in the theories of Austin Osman Spare and Peter Carroll's influential book *Liber Null*. The system uses models or paradigms on the principle that 'nothing is true and everything is permitted', understood to mean that there is no such thing as objective truth, but only what we perceive as being true. The 'magic' concerns the power of belief to transform existing paradigms into new experiences of perception and consciousness, especially the 'gnostic' state claimed to be in the tradition of the Buddhist, *samadhi*. In effect, Chaos Magic is a war-game waged against all received religious traditions and aims to question and displace the mind's status quo. What is central is the fact of the energy of belief rather than its content. It is anarchic, thus chaotic, refuting the notion that there is any form of order or meaning in the universe which is in constant flux and of such complexity that only subverting rationality can bring about the state of mind that would conform to the will of the magician. FINAL WORD: 'I tell you, one must have chaos in one, to give birth to a dancing star. I tell you, you shall have chaos in you.' (Nietzsche [1964])

Charismatic *X*. Gk. *charis*, 'grace' or 'gift'. In biblical theology, a reference to supernatural experiences. See I Cor. 12–14 where St Paul speaks of 'the gifts of the Spirit', meaning the 'Holy Spirit'. The key 'signs' of charismatic manifestation are **glossolalia**, healing, prophecy and miracles, all of which have been in evidence throughout Christian history, but more so, perhaps, in its earlier phases of development. Irenaeus, **Tertullian**, Origen, Eusebius and other early **Church Fathers** all recorded evidence of these signs.

Charismatic Movement *X*. Gathering momentum from the 1950s, the movement drew on central **Pentecostal** beliefs and practices referred to as the 'biblical charismas'. It is not synonymous with, but is inspired by, Pentecostalism, differing from it in some important ways. It does not give the same importance to speaking in tongues (**glossolalia**) and cuts horizontally across all the main vertical divisions of the church, so that we can talk of Anglican, Roman Catholic, Baptist, Methodist charismatics and so on. Clearly Pentecostalism and the Charismatic Movement have much in common and can be distinguished only by the styles of worship, preaching and ministry of the denominations with which they are associated. The movement is thought to have started with Dennis Bennett, an American Episcopalian Rector who in 1960 told his congregation in Van Nuys, California that he had received an outpouring of the Holy Spirit. He moved to Vancouver where he led seminars on the work of the Holy Spirit which eventually influenced large numbers of Anglicans worldwide and stimulated a renewal movement in the Roman Catholic and Orthodox Churches. In some cases the charismatics left their mother churches to form new associations such as the **House Church** movement in the UK and the Vineyard Churches in the USA. Generally, critics have branded the Movement as being 'other worldly', without any real interest in the mundane things of everyday life. See also **Branhamism, Latter Rain Movement**

Charms In a religious context, charms are small objects presumed to have intrinsic or ascribed magical power. They are worn to ward off evil, to ensure good luck and to protect from bad luck. A charm may also be a verbal formula or action believed to have magical power and influence and may include in their usage phrases, chants and incantations. Charms of both kinds have been in use from the first human responses to nature and the environment and are to be found in inexhaustible variety in virtually every religion, cult and sect throughout the world. They may be made of the simplest, natural material or formed from existing objects such as a stone or piece of wood, a bone, a tooth or a nail paring, which are held to be sacred and protected by **taboos**. Or they may be made of the most precious metals and jewels and worn as jewellery or insignia. 'Amulet' is an alternative name. See **Mana, Superstition, Talisman**

Chasidism *J*. Heb. A mystical and pietistic Jewish movement that gathered momentum in the 18th century in Eastern Europe. Its founder was Israel ben Eliezer (1700–60) later known as the Baal Shem Tov or Besht, who began as a faith-healer travelling around the Ukraine and southern Poland. Eliezer drew on already existing mystical doctrines that had become part of the **Torah**, but emphasized the joy of faith and the importance of an attitude of devotion in religious practice, rather than its more disheartening aspects. Doctrinally, Chasidism is founded on the concept that in every created being there is a 'holy spark' or divine particle. It is a form of **panentheism**. Each divine particle awaits reunification with God, something realized when Jews serve God with the right kind of mindfulness and in accordance with *Haskalah*. Before any prayer or action the Chasid will say he is doing this 'for the sake of the unification of the Holy One, blessed be he and his **Shekhinah** in the world'. In an important sense, Chasidism was a challenge to traditional Rabbinic Judaism. Because God is everywhere and *in* everything, the Besht affirmed a subjective devotion to God as a means of union with him, over against the objective observation of *mitzvoth*, the commandments. What matters is a person's sincerity, his *devekut* or devotion. The movement thus developed not around the rabbis but the **Zaddiks**, the 'great-souled' or holy men, often remarkable mystics who had the power to lead and inspire and to perform miracles. Somewhat in the manner of **Kabbalah**, Chasidism had a formative influence and significance in the development of Judaism. Zaddiks, being anti-intellectual, used the short story and mystical fairy tales as a way of teaching; music and dance also made a significant contribution. Others encouraged withdrawal in order to practise forms of meditation. Eventually, towards the end of the 18th century, Chasidism was deemed heretical and some of the Zaddiks, even the Besht himself, were imprisoned for a time. Remarkably, as the movement became institutionalized and the established tradition of the Ukrainian, Galician and Polish Jews, the heretical sect was absorbed back into Jewish orthodoxy. As a result of immigration from Eastern Europe from the late 19th century and of the aftermath of both World Wars and the **Holocaust**, the Chasidic tradition is now worldwide and has been made accessible, and to some extent popular, by the work of the German-Jewish philosopher Martin **Buber**. See **Yiddish**

FINAL WORD: 'The core of Hasidic teaching is the concept of a life of fervour, of exalted joy. ... The Hasidic movement did not weaken the hope of a Messiah, but it kindled both its simple and intellectual followers to joy in the world as it is, in life as it is, in every hour of life in this world, as that hour is.' (Martin Buber [1975])
'In the world to come I shall not be asked why I was not you, Abraham, Jacob or Moses; I shall be asked why I was not Zusya.' (Rabbi Zusya, Chasidic Master, 18th-century Poland)

Chen Tao The 'right or true way', also known as 'The Soul of Light Resurgence Association'. An apocalyptic Taiwanese UFO sect founded by Hon-Ming Chen, which emigrated from Taiwan to establish their HQ in Garland, Texas in 1993. Hon-Ming Chen drew international attention to the group when he predicted that God would descend on their compound in a flying saucer on 31st March 1998 and be reincarnated in his body. When his prophecy failed he stated he had never claimed to be a prophet. Little or nothing has been heard of the group since 1999. See **Heaven's Gate**, **Raelianism**, **UFO Cults**

Chen-Yen *B*. The Tantric Buddhist 'School of Secrets'. See **Mi-tsung**

Cherubim *J*. The Hebrew plural form of 'cherub'. A type of supernatural creature mentioned several times in the **Tanakh** (the Hebrew Bible) and in the Book of **Revelation**. Medieval Catholic theology held them to be the highest rank in the hierarchy of **angels**. The Bible describes them as winged creatures armed with flaming swords, combining human and animal features and as having specific functions such as guarding the way to the Tree of Life and the gates of Eden. They guarded the **Ark** of the Covenant and when Yahweh was still making physical appearances, they formed his living chariot (2 Sam. 22:11). Through their iconography in art, they have become associated with children or babies or baby angels perhaps.

Chi *T*. Chin. Translated in various ways such as 'air', 'vapour', 'breath' and 'temperament', 'energy', 'strength'. A concept important to **Taoism** and Chinese medicine. Taoism understands *chi* to be a quintessential life-energy or vital essence which sustains life in all of its myriad forms, from the micro-cosmos of the nucleus to the macro-cosmos of the universe. It is not a uniquely human energy; everything that lives and is sentient throbs with this life-force. Chinese medicine is based on an understanding of the patterns of *chi* within the human body and it is on the basis of this knowledge that methods of healing have developed that include herbal remedies, acupuncture and the series of physical exercises, among which are **Tai Chi Chuan** and **Chi Kung**, now so familiar in the West. There are also **meditation** breathing techniques like *nie-tan* (Chin) 'inner chamber' or 'Inner Alchemy' which are concerned with purifying and directing the *chi* so as to achieve specific objectives. A distinction is made between the inner *chi*, the essential life energy, and the air we breathe. **Confucianism** has its own perception of *chi* that distinguishes between material or outward qualities and their inner aspects. See **Feng-Shui**
FINAL WORD: 'The source of life, of birth and change is chi; everything under heaven and earth obeys this law. Chi in the periphery envelops the cosmos; chi in the interior activates all.' (Nei Jing, quoted by Wong Kiew Kit)

Chih *Con*. 'wisdom' or 'insight'. One of the cardinal virtues of **Confucianism**, the source of which is our knowledge of right and wrong with, presumably, the 'wisdom' to tell the difference. Such knowledge, it is argued, is drawn from our own minds and the concepts of right and wrong are therefore innate (see **Innate Ideas**). The idea was introduced into Confucianism by the Chinese philosopher **Mencius**. See **Ju**

Chi-Kung *C*. A system of meditational exercises, based on deep breathing, for promoting spiritual and physical well-being. It is a form of developed and focused energy that claims to be able to maintain health and vitality, inner strength and clarity of mind. See **Chi**, **Kung-fu**, **Shao-Lin**

Children of God *X*. Also known as the Family of Love or the Family International. The cult grew out of the **Jesus Movement** in the late 1960s, attracting the 'hippies'. It was one of the groups at the centre of the cult controversy in the 1970s and 1980s, giving rise to the anticult group Free the Children of God. The cult's main tenets were **millenarian** and Salvationist, which combined to initiate a 'spiritual' revolution against society in general, which the Children of God dubbed 'the System'. **'Flirty Fishing'**, a form of evangelism that uses sexual practices to the point of religious **prostitution**, was a means of witnessing to the love of God, a practice discontinued after 1987. After the death of its founder David Berg, the cult was led by his widow Karen Zerby. Somewhat incongruously the group is generally classified as fundamentalist, rooted in the divine inspiration of the Bible and the commission laid on every Christian to evangelize. They believe that the tenet 'to love one another' supersedes all other biblical laws and that sexuality is a God-given means of expressing this love. Sex with minors is strictly prohibited, but otherwise sexual relationships are to be openly 'shared' with anyone in need. No one is forced to have a sexual relationship against their will, but unwillingness may be considered to be 'unloving'. See **Salvationism**

Chinese Religions Until the collapse of the Ch'ing dynasty in 1912, ancient Chinese religions such as **Taoism** and **Confucianism**, and **Buddhism**, continued to flourish as did **ancestor worship**, a tradition of ancient China. **Christianity** was brought to China by the **Nestorians** in the 7th century; **Islam** followed in the 8th century and, although to a different extent, each of these religions continue to have a presence. The constitution of the People's Republic, established in 1949, affirmed the freedom of religious belief, but public rituals and worship were discouraged. During the 1950s, so as to ensure they conformed to the prevalent political orthodoxy, the Bureau of Religious Affairs authorized the founding of official associations for Taoism, Buddhism and Islam. The communist authorities in China were hostile to the more visible aspects of Taoism, interpreting its magic, divination and superstitions as being counter-revolutionary. Confucianism, with its ideology wrapped around a kernel of social codes, has survived under the Nationalist administration and provides an intellectual structure for educated Chinese who adhered to no particular religion. Its emphasis on family life, however, has been eroded by the Communist shift of priorities from the family to service to the State. Both in its **Tibetan** and **Therevadan** forms, Chinese Buddhism was identified with minority groups against which the authorities moved only gradually. The result has been a drastic cutting back of the importance of the monasteries in the every day life of Buddhists. As part of a land-reform programme, monastic estates were seized and shared among peasants and temples and shrines were transformed into recreation centres. The far larger Muslim communities have suffered a similar fate. Because the communist regime identified it with Western imperialist capitalism, Christianity was treated harshly even though it represented a minority of less than one per cent of the Chinese population. A form of Roman Catholicism, without any ties to the Vatican, has continued to function under the supervision of the Communist authorities. See **Pure Land Buddhism**

Chinvat Bridge *Zo*. A metaphor from **Zoroastrian** eschatology. The *Cinvaotperetu* is sometimes translated as 'The Bridge of the Separator' or the 'Account-Keeper's Bridge'. According to the tradition, the soul of a dead person lingers near the body for three days before facing judgement on the Bridge. Judgement takes the form of weighing the good and evil deeds of the deceased. The Bridge crosses to paradise, arching over hell as it does so. Should the good deeds outweigh the evil deeds the soul will be encouraged to cross, if not, it will fall off the Bridge into hell. FINAL WORD: 'O Mazda Ahura, whosoever, man or woman, gives me those things which you know are the best of existence: reward for truth and power through good thought and whom I stimulate to glorify those such as you, with all those I will cross over the Account-keeper's Bridge.' (Yasna 46.10)

Chishti *I*. Full name, Chishti Qadhiri. A popular order of the Sufi tariqah, founded in the 10th century by Khawaja Abu Ishaq Shami, nicknamed 'the Syrian'. Known as the *Chishtiyya* they spread throughout Indian, Pakistan and Bangladesh. The Chishti tariqah is renowned for its openness, tolerance and its emphasis on love and mystical ecstasy. The way of life is directed by nine principles that include obedience to the leader or master, poverty, distancing oneself from temporal power, devout prayer and fasting, reliance on offerings, service and respect for other Islamic traditions. To this is added the *Sama* or *Kawali*, an assembly at which music is played; this is not a form of worship but a devotional means of contemplating Allah. Eventually, the principle of having nothing to do with temporal power was relaxed and the Mogul Emperor Akbar became an ally of the Chishti. See **Dervish**, **Dervish Groups**, **Murid**, **Sufism**, **Tariqah**

Chosen People *J*. An epithet for the Jewish people based on the **covenant** of God made with Abraham. (Gen. 15v18) The concept of being chosen, or 'elect', was absorbed by Christianity. Modern Judaism is uncomfortable with the concept, and has made adjustments to their liturgies. See **Augustinianism** amd **Predestination**

Christ *X*. Gk. *christos*, 'anointed'. The use of the word in this spelling stems from the 18th century when, as a consequence of the **Enlightenment**, it became the vogue to transliterate certain words to fit their Greek and Latin originals. It became the descriptive title of **Jesus**, the given name of God's anointed **Messiah**.

Christadelphians *X*. A Christian denomination at variance with mainstream Christianity. Their name is derived from the Greek, meaning 'Brothers in Christ', a title coined by John Thomas whose book, *Elpis Israel*, written in 1848–9, outlined what he considered to be the main doctrines of the **Bible**. Loosely associated groups of Christadelphians developed from the mid-19th century, meeting under various names until the American Civil War required a church affiliation that enabled an adherent to register as a conscientious objector. The group trace their biblically-based beliefs back to Apostolic times. God is the creator of all things and his son is a separate and independent being; the **Holy Spirit** is not a distinct person but simply the power or energy of God in action as seen in creation and salvation. This is effected through Jesus, the Messiah prophesied by the **Old Testament**. Jesus is wholly the 'son of man' since from his mother he inherited the sinful aspects of human nature. He is wholly the son of God as a result of his miraculous conception. In addition to rejecting the doctrine of the Trinity, Christadelphians deny the pre-existence of Christ, the immortality of the soul and belief in the Devil or Satan. Where these terms are used in the Bible they do not refer to a power in opposition to God, but are symbolic of the inherent evil or sin in mankind. Various divisions have occurred among the group concerning the inspiration of the Bible (some believing it was only partially inspired), conscientious objection and divorce and remarriage. The group is mostly found among English-speaking people, predominantly in America and England.

Christ-consciousness *X*. An appropriation of the name 'Christ', that has both Christian and non-Christian associations. For example, Paramahansa **Yogananda** writes about 'Christ-consciousness' interchangeably with '**Krishna**-consciousness'. In **New Age** or postmodern terms it refers to a psychic force or quality developed by an individual through what **Thomas à Kempis** called 'The Imitation of Christ'. Through forms of devotional practice, whether by prayer or meditation, the subject endeavours to live life as Christ lived it, that is to be conscious of Christ-like perceptions, attitudes and values. Theologically it is a combination of the Pauline notion of *en Christos*, of being 'in' Christ and of the Christ within, the indwelling Christ as synonymous with the Holy Spirit.

Christian Existentialism *X*. See **Religious Existentialism, Tillich, Bonhoeffer**

Christian Expansion and Denominations *X*. Over two millennia Christianity has spawned an extraordinary variety of churches, denominations and innumerable sects. All the significant subgroups are discussed under their own entries; there is space here for only a brief overview of the complex and worldwide expansion of the Church.

After the spread of the early Church, mostly under the leadership of St Paul, Christianity became distinguishable from Judaism and no longer enjoyed the status of legitimacy under Roman rule. It suffered a succession of violent persecutions, for example under the Emperor Nero (see **Emperor Worship**), who in 64 CE used the Christian community as a scapegoat for the burning of Rome. The early Church survived these persecutions to have its existence legitimized by Constantine's Milan edict of 313 CE. In a series of decrees from 389 CE, Theodosius established Christianity as the state religion of the Roman Empire, but with a marked division between its Western and Eastern halves, the latter developing as the **Byzantine Empire**. In 476 CE the Western Empire collapsed before the barbarian invaders; Byzantine Christianity continued until 1453 CE, when it was overrun by Islam. By the end of the 11th century Christianity had consolidated its Western and Eastern affiliations. In the West it was traditionally linked with the Latin-speaking Church of the western provinces of the Roman Empire, developing as **Roman Catholicism** which, after the decline of Rome, resided under the leadership of the Bishop of Rome or the **papacy**. The Eastern **Orthodox Church**, so named because of its roots in the Greek-speaking Christianity of the eastern provinces of the Roman Empire, constitutes numerous Eastern European and North African national Churches. Throughout the medieval period the dominance of Western Christianity was consolidated under the Papacy, but many national, social, economic and philosophical influences threatened the seemingly inviolable unity of the Church. It faced increasing internal conflict in the from of **heresy**, and external threat as Church and State opposed each other in the struggle to rule (see the **Conciliar Movement**). The unity of Western Christendom finally gave way in the 16th century to the **Reformation** and **counter-Reformation**, both of which, by the polarization of **Protestantism** and **Catholicism**, set radical new directions. The Roman Catholic Church remained the largest Christian body, but in the ensuing years in northern Europe the Reformation led to the flowering of numerous Protestant subdivisions such as the **Lutheran**, **Calvinists** and **Anglican** Churches. The Church of England, resulting from Henry VIII seceding from Rome, occupies its own unique place in Christian history, developing into the worldwide Anglican Communion under the Archbishop of Canterbury. In the 17th and 18th centuries English Protestantism produced a new family of non-conformist or 'Free' Churches such as the **Congregationalists**, **Baptists**, **Presbyterians** and **Methodists**. Smaller church groupings, for example the **Anabaptists**, were to have considerable influence on the development of Protestantism. Through **mission** and colonialism, most forms of Christianity were carried to every continent. Other important groups to emerge were the **Quakers**, the **Unitarians**, the **Mormons**, **Christian Scientists**, the **Salvation Army** and the **Pentecostalists**. In more recent times, influenced by the **Ecumenical Movement**, some of these churches have combined, for example the Congregationalists and some Presbyterians have formed the United Reform Church.

Throughout its history Christianity has claimed the authority of absolute and exclusive truth, and during the expansion of the British Empire its 'exportation of the Union Jack and the Cross' coloured and reformed the indigenous religions and cultures of all the countries in which it took root. See **Free Churches**

FINAL WORD: 'The contrast between the forces working against Christianity and the vitality inherent in the faith had not appeared for the first time in the 19th century, nor was it to end with that century. It had been present from the beginning and was most vividly seen in the seeming triumph of the opposition in the crucifixion, followed as that was by the resurrection of Christ and the birth of the Church ... After 1914 ... many declared that mankind was entering the post-Christian era ... yet the 20th century was one of the greatest days in the history of Christianity and if the world was viewed as whole, never before had Christ been as influential in the affairs of the human race.' (Kenneth Scott LaTourette).

Christian Humanism *X*. A view that individuals and culture contribute positively to the Christian life. The idea, lost during the medieval period, was recovered by the **Renaissance** which restated Thomas **Aquinas'** focus on the human being and 'man's discovery of himself in the world'. A proper understanding of the **incarnation** implies that our worldly existence has intrinsic worth, an emphasis that led to a through-going **secularism**. Christian Humanism was an attempt to pull this back towards metaphysical terms of reference, a movement initiated by French Roman Catholic philosopher Jacques Maritain (1882–1973), who reinterpreted Aquinas for the 20th century. He wrote, 'If the philosophy of Aristotle, as revived and enriched by St Thomas and his school, may rightly be called the Christian philosophy ... it is not proposed here for the reader's acceptance because it is Christian, but because it is demonstrably true.' Among the many proponents of Christian Humanism are **Erasmus**, Thomas More and **Kierkegaard**. See **Humanism**

Christiania Started in 1970, Freedom Christiania is an independent community located in the Christianshavn district of Copenhagen. It began as occupation of land owned by the Ministry of Defence and has grown to be an established community of around 800 associated with all forms of art, but neither the art nor the studios and homes built by members are owned by anyone. The community is governed by a form of consensus democracy providing daycare centres for both young children and infirm old people. The name implies an addition of various forms of Christianity, loosely governed by a Citizens' Council; there are no laws, just a few prohibitions such as no hard drugs, no weapons, no violence and no trading of buildings or residential areas. The community is currently under threat from Government plans to privatize all houses and apartments. As no one owns the property at Christiania, it is theoretically possible for anyone to move in and take over. (Source: Christiania website)

Christian Identity Movement *X*. A loosely applied term for sects and churches that have a racial theology. Usually they promote a Caucasian and Euro-centric form of Christianity. One energy behind such movements is **British Israelism** centred on the belief that Europeans are descended from the ten (lost) tribes of Israel. The CIM teaches that modern Christian churches are based on heresy in that they deny their true identity as the spiritual people of 'Israel'. There is an anti-Semitic tradition based on the **Serpent Seed** doctrine which teaches that Jews are the descendents of Eve's sexual relations with the serpent (Gen. 3) and are therefore not fully human. It is estimated that there are about 350,000 adherents in the USA, Canada and the British Commonwealth. See **Aryan Nations Movement, Lost Tribes of Israel**

Christianity *X*. Christianity is a religion of salvation teaching that humanity is alienated from God by **original sin**, and that salvation is available through faith in **Jesus Christ** and/or through the **sacraments**. It has always been a matter of great urgency that every human being should be 'saved' and it is with this conviction that Christian missionaries have travelled to every part of the world.

Because of the 'Fall' of Adam and Eve, the first human beings, all humanity was brought under the judgement of God. The consequence of this original sin is a problematic life, ending with physical death; traditionally the surviving **soul** will endure eternity either in Heaven or Hell, according to the quality of the life of faith lived by the individual. A religion of salvation, however, is a religion of hope. Hope enables the Christian believer to trust in the mercy of God for personal survival and an eternity in his presence. Christianity adopted the body–soul duality of Greek philosophy in the form of a flesh–spirit antithesis. This dualistic conflict is resolved in Christianity by a belief in the resurrection of the body and the salvation of the soul, thus the 'whole' person survives. In **Roman Catholic** belief the deceased's soul may not be in a state of readiness for heaven and might need 'purgation after death'. The transition from **purgatory** to heaven can be facilitated by the prayers of saints and other Christians and by the saying of the **mass**.

Salvation is through Jesus Christ, the **Messiah** for whom the Jews are still waiting. Jesus' death by crucifixion, together with his resurrection, is the climax of his mission to save humanity. Throughout the history of Christianity (see **Christian Expansion**) there have been traditions teaching divine election and **predestination**, and the indispensability of the sacraments of baptism and the **Eucharist** confirming a believer's status within the Church. For some traditions, according to the maxim *extra ecclesiam nulla salus*, there is 'no salvation outside of the Church'. This has set up fundamental theological conflicts. On the one hand there is the efficacy of the sacraments and the authority of the priesthood; on the other the efficacy of personal faith and the authority of subjective religious experience. Faith was not always thought to be the most important, indispensable criterion for salvation; that has, at times, been accorded to the **sacrament** of baptism, a ritual that initiated the adherent irrevocably into the Church, the 'body' of Christ. Traditionally baptism was for infants, but Christian denominations such as the **Baptists** hold to the baptism of believers only and, thus, of adults.

Whether the path to salvation is by personal faith, sacrament or a combination of both, the believer does not merit salvation; this is available only because of the mercy of God and the gift of his **grace**. There are different views as to how the individual survives death and in what form a future life will be experienced. The views range from belief in a literal, physical resurrection to a vague notion of the soul's survival in an indefinable heaven or paradise. Christian **fundamentalism** maintains that the surviving soul will be given a new and uncorrupted body and that in this form, beyond death, people will recognize and enjoy the fellowship of deceased friends and relatives. A long tradition of Christian mysticism, in parallel with a relatively modern **demythologized** Christian theology, no longer holds to the survival of the body in any form and looks instead to the hope of spiritual union with God. The Christian perception of God is formed from the way it has interpreted its own sacred history, of which the **Old Testament** record is an indispensable part. It therefore conforms to a Hebraic monotheism illuminated by the life and teaching of Jesus of Nazareth and by the subsequent councils that formed the **creeds**. The doctrine of what Kipling called 'tangled Trinities' (see **Trinity**) – the triad of God the Father, Jesus the Son and the **Holy Spirit** – proved at times to be too problematic and gave rise to heresies such as 3rd-century **Arianism**, modern **Unitarianism** and to new philosophical systems like '**Process Theology**'. Jesus Christ, believed to be God incarnate, is at the same time the founder of the religion and the 'Way' that must be followed by disciples. The **gospel** accounts of the life and ministry of Jesus carry the message of self-sacrifice and self-abandonment as the way of salvation. Jesus 'showed' the way by paying the ultimate price of salvation himself, thus exemplifying unconditional love. 'For there is no greater love, than that a man should lay down his life for his friends' (John 15:13). It is the heart of the Christian message that Jesus went one step further and gave his life for his enemies. In making this ultimate sacrifice Jesus revealed the Christian God as a God of love and grace. Thus, to a considerable extent the Christian understanding of God is derived from Jesus himself. This is especially associated with his messianic mission. The concept of Messiah is derived from Old Testament 'types' or models filled out by prophecies, most familiarly those of Isaiah, who spoke of the suffering servant 'despised and rejected of Men' (Isaiah Ch. 53). To this must be added the 'model' of animal sacrifice carried out by the Temple priests as an expiation for sins and that of the **scapegoat**, driven outside the walls of the town, burdened with the community's sins. Such types and images were originally taken to be a figure of the role of Israel in world history, but became identified with Jesus himself. The title most frequently used of Jesus is 'Son of God'. This is understood to be a substantive relationship – that is, Jesus is the actual son of God. When the compilers of the New Testament referred to the 'Son of God', they would have understood that the true and faithful 'second Adam', progenitor of a new Israel, had come among them.

Christian cosmology is founded on a belief in a creator-God whose work is recorded in the Genesis myths of the Old Testament. The entire universe, our home planet and everything that populates it, is understood to be part of God's self-revelation. Space and time, as aspects of this creation, witness the grandeur and majesty of the Creation and an eternity in paradise is the reward for those who recognize and accept the revelation and its redemptive message. Blake's poetic vision affirms that we can 'hold infinity in the palm of our hand and eternity in an hour'. It speaks of the tension between **immanence** and transcendence. References to space in a dimensional sense have had to be revised. There are believing Christians who are no longer inspired by the idea of a God 'up there' who has 'sent' his Son to earth 'down here' or by a hell of any kind, wherever it is located. The Christian understands the second coming of Christ as an event that will take place 'in time' and herald the end of time. The **last judgement** will result in a relocation of the righteous in an afterlife. An understanding of the notion of eternal life has also had to be recast. Present life is experienced as having a beginning and an end, but Christianity teaches that eternal life means life, as we know it, continuing beyond death, the difference being that it is without suffering and unending. These familiar and comforting beliefs have never fully given way to the idea of eternity being something which is timeless and which therefore implies a wholly different mode of being.

The metaphorical and anthropomorphic God-language of Christianity has been challenged by many philosophers and theologians such as **Bultmann** and **Tillich**. There are those for whom these attempts at a new language are threatening, being a watering-down of the essential, fundamental notion of a personal God who is always caringly involved in human existence. In the face of **Darwinism**, science and **secularism**, some Christian apologists have responded by reverting to biblical **fundamentalism**. In contrast, liberal and philosophical thinkers have not felt threatened by the inevitable questioning of traditional language and concepts and have received the results of scientific discovery as an enlightenment, even as a further revelation. Rather than regarding this as a threat, they have taken the opportunity to re-interpret the Christian message in terms more compatible with a scientific world-view. Bultmann explained that, 'there is nothing specifically Christian in the mythical view of the world as such. It is simply the cosmology of a pre-scientific age.'

FINAL WORD: 'The Christian religion was not only at first attended with miracles, but even at this day cannot be believed by any reasonable person without one.' (David Hume)

'The Christian ideal has not been tried and found wanting; it has been found difficult and left untried.' (G. K. Chesterton)

Christianity and Secularism X. Logic suggests that the Christian doctrine of **incarnation** abolishes the concept of secularism since God, assuming human form, has consecrated all matter. Hans Hoekendijk suggested that, 'the coming of Jesus Christ in this world is a secular event.' Everything to the eye of faith is thus sacred. However, the rigorous dualism of Christianity has maintained the distinction between the sacred and the secular, as it has between spirit and matter and good and evil. In general, orthodox Christianity opposes the process of secularization as the delivery of man from religious and metaphysical bondage. It presents the faith in terms of a conflict between God and the Devil for the individual's **soul**, and in terms of the hope of eternal life through salvation. Other, more liberal, forms of Christianity regard secularism as an opportunity to look for new religious meaning and language (see **Bonhoeffer, Bultmann, Tillich**), understanding it to be a consequence of religious revelation rather than the enemy of it. See **Christian Humanism, Secularism**

Christian Kabbalah *X*. A contradiction in terms. The sources for a 'Christian' Kabbalah are various and mostly found in the writings of Spanish Jews forcibly converted to Christianity during the 13th–15th century. Their object was not to Christianize the Kabbalah, but to preserve texts threatened by the **Inquisition**. Some of these compilers, for example Abner de Burgos and Paul de Heredia, closely imitated the style of the principal Kabbalahist source, the *Zohar*, which appeared in Spain during the 13th century. A second, primary source of Christian Kabbalah are the writings of Christian mystics, for example the early Church fathers who drew on their knowledge of Kabbalah so as to inform and heighten their religious experience, believing that in the Kabbalah hidden secrets of 'original' Christianity were to be found. A further tradition is associated with the Platonic Academy of the Florentine Medicis and the work of Giovanni Pico della Mirandola (1463–94), the Italian **Renaissance** humanist philosopher who used Latin translations of the Hebrew texts. Typical of Christian interpretations of Kabbalah is to read the sixth of the ten *Sephiroth*, the *Tifereth*, as a symbolic association with Jesus Christ. The *Tifereth* or 'Divine Force', sacrifices itself as a transmutation of energy and matter, thus providing the raw material of creation even as God the Son sacrificed himself to become the spiritual raw material of the 'new creation'. The Church's response to Christian Kabbalah has varied from that of extreme suspicion and accusations of heresy to a broad acceptance by the post-Reformation Churches of Germany, Italy and France, who are probably better understood as being Christian Neoplatonists than Christian Kabbalahists. Being a blend of Platonism, **Neoplatonism**, Aristotelianism and Hermeticism, Christian Kabbalah is too eclectic and syncretistic to have claim to be a close relation to the original Jewish mystical tradition. See **Kabbalah**
FINAL WORD: 'No science can better convince us of the divinity of Jesus Christ than magic and the Kabbalah.' (Pico della Mirandola)

Christian Marxism A loose reference to the views of those who espouse Marxist principles of communality with notions of theocratic utopianism. They work for a future that will establish the kind of divine **Communism** hinted at in Acts 2:44, 'All whose faith had drawn them together held everything in common; they would sell their property and possessions and make a general distribution as the need of each required.' See **Christian Humanism**

Christian Reconstruction Put simply, a movement working to establish a world order on Christianity's terms. Christians are spiritually and morally obliged to recapture every part of life and every institution and organization that has been lost to secularism and atheism. Jesus is King and

Christian Reconstruction proclaims his 'crown rights'. The authority lies in the Genesis covenants renewed by God's incarnation and Jesus' salvatory work. The movement is confined to Protestant Christianity and has no relationship to, for example, **Jewish Reconstructionism** or any of the other Reconstructionist energies. It is a form of Theonomy (Gk. *theos*, 'god' + *nomos*, 'law'), the rule of God's law based on **Old Testament** and **New Testament** precedents of moral and case law intended to govern nations, the Church and the family. Some sociologists of religion refer to it as 'Dominionism'. Its beginnings are to be traced to the colonial government of New England and unsurprisingly its founders were all Calvinists (see **Calvinism**) nostalgic for the **Reformation** heydays of Calvin's Geneva.

Christian Scientists *X*. Founded by Mary Baker Eddy (1821–1910) of New Hampshire, USA. Her system of healing developed from the perennial debate concerning the relationship between mind and matter. Mrs Eddy held that mind was the only true reality and that matter was a necessary illusion so that mind could grasp organize and codify experience and phenomena. God is divine Mind (synonymous with spirit), Life, Truth, Love and Principle, and the divine Mind's expression of itself is humanity, created in the image of God. Thus the right mind or attitude can prevail over whatever problems have their source in matter such as sin, death and illness. Like the matter from which they stem, they are an illusion. On this assumption she interpreted the healing miracles of Jesus and developed the system explained in her book *Science and Health with a Key to the Scriptures* (1875). While healing is a religious function the object of Christian Scientism is not simply to heal, but to spiritually regenerate humanity. In 1879 the Church of Christ the Scientist was founded in Boston, which remains the headquarters. The movement, which has spread widely through the English-speaking world, publishes the newspaper *The Christian Science Monitor*. See **Divine Science**

Christmas *X*. Officially a one-day holiday held on 25th December to celebrate the birth of Jesus of Nazareth. The Eastern Orthodox Church, using the Julian calendar, holds the feast on the 7th January. 'Christmas' is derived from middle and old English words that gave 'Christ's mass'. Despite the many sincere observers the holiday, which always lasts for more than its official day, is now thoroughly secularized and celebrated by the exchanging of gifts and an overindulgence in food and drink. The gifts, by tradition, are distributed by Father Christmas, otherwise known as St Nicholas or Santa Claus, the part played in the home by the father and in public places by someone hired to do the job. In secular terms the holiday has positive value, since it is one of the few occasions in the year when it is traditional for the dispersed and extended family to be together.

Christ's Church of the Golden Rule See **Mankind United**

Christ the Saviour Brotherhood See **Holy Order of MANS**

Chronos *G.* See **Cronos**

Chthonic Religion Gk. *khthonios*, of or relating to the underworld. The term designates gods associated with the underworld, especially in Greek mythology (see **Greek Religion**). Generally, the term suggests devotion to gods of earth as against those of the sky. In chthonic cults animal sacrifices were made in a pit, but in the Olympian cults the animal was sacrificed on a raised altar. Chthonic deities preferred black to white victims and their offerings were burned whole then buried instead of being cooked and eaten by the worshippers.

Chuang-tzu *T.* The eponymous author of *The Book of the Master Chuang*, reputedly the second most important Taoist text after the **Tao-te Ching** of **Lao-Tzu**. There is some doubt as to whether Lao-Tzu actually lived, but the historicity of Chuang-tzu seems secure. Little is known of him beyond his personal name, Chou, and that he lived sometime in the 4th century BCE, in a village called Meng, possibly in Honan to the south of the Yellow River. The book is written in 33 chapters but only the first seven are thought to have been written by Chuang-tzu. While there are similarities to the *Tao-te Ching*, the author makes no reference to it and his philosophy is markedly different, offering a more personal and idiosyncratic form of mysticism. Like all abiding philosophy the book goes directly to the heart of the matter, discussing the nature of knowledge and reality in terms of *tzu jan*, naturalness, and *wu wei*, non-doing (see **Taoism**). Burton Watson identifies the theme of the book as 'freedom'. The problem addressed is how do we live meaningfully in a seemingly absurd, chaotic world. Chuang-tzu's response was that of the mystic, the way to freedom is to get free of all seeming opposites, to abandon discriminatory thought, to achieve emptiness by means of *hsin chai*, 'fasting the mind' and to accommodate change. The style of writing is enigmatic, cast in the form of pithy anecdotes and sayings, the meaning of which is sometimes obscure. This highly abstract philosophy does not lie easily with the magical, alchemical and superstitious aspects of developed Taoism and Thomas Merton makes the beguiling suggestion that, 'the true inheritors of the thought and spirit of Chuang-tzu are the Chinese Zen Buddhists of the T'ang period.'

Chun-tzu *Con.* Chin. 'ruler's son' or 'nobleman'. **Confucius'** term for the ideal person in contradistinction to the term *Hsiao jen*, 'little man' or 'plebeian'. For Confucius the *chun-tzu* has all the qualities of the properly educated gentry and is thus someone fit to rule. Such people, in fact, do not acquire the qualities to rule by virtue of birth, but by virtue of their demeanour, conduct and their sense of the fitness of things. The closest English word is 'gentleman'. It was not the hereditary rulers who were the true aristocrats, but the 'gentlemen' who exhibited the necessary qualities to rule. In some ways Confucius' *chun-tzu* is similar to Plato's Philosopher King.

Church *X*. The Greek word *ecclesia* is translated in the **Septuagint** as both Church and **Synagogue**, and both terms are found in the New Testament. During the 1st century CE, from the beginning of the emergence of the Early Church, 'synagogue' has been used for the place of worship of the Jewish community and 'church' for that of the Christian community. In general use, however, 'church' has a far wider connotation than a physical place of worship. Broadly, it can refer to the community of Christians in a town or city, as for example in St Paul's use of the term in his letters to the 'Churches' of Rome, Corinth and Ephesus. It can also refer to the worldwide community of Christian believers regardless of denominational affiliation, expressed in such terms as the holy, catholic (universal) and apostolic (by descent) Church; theologically, the universal Church is also understood as being the 'body' of Christ. Most understand the Church 'visible' as being an imperfect expression of the ideal 'invisible' Church comprising the dead who have been 'saved' (see **Salvation**). The Church is sometimes referred to as the 'communion of saints', being the community of those bound together *en Christos*, 'in Christ'. The 'Church militant' refers to the community of Christians on earth, while the 'Church triumphant' to the community in **heaven**. In all the various denominations of the Church, measures have been taken to define the nature and conditions of Church membership which, for **Roman Catholicism**, resides in the administration of the **sacraments**; this is underwritten by morality applied through canon law established over the years by the great Councils called by bishops and Popes. The canons of **Anglicanism** were set out during the Medieval period, the most recent of subsequent revisions being in 1969. Many of these Churches authorize the administration of canon law through ecclesiastical courts and resort to **excommunication** in matters of heresy or immorality. All the orders of Christian **monasticism** have their own disciplines or Rules established by their founders.

Roman Catholicism, Anglicanism and some forms of Protestantism consider themselves to be the true custodians of Christianity, but throughout its history the theology and constitution of the Church have been subjected to fundamental reform and Church doctrine has been constantly revised. From the beginning of the 19th century the role, structure and doctrine of the Church has been brought under constant scrutiny as a result of **secularism**, and a new theology emerging from modern biblical criticism (see **Bible**). Other major changes have been wrought by the **Ecumenical Movement**, the **Liturgical Movement** and a reconsideration of the relationship between the 'established' Church and the State. See **Christian Expansion and Denominations**

Church Fathers *X*. The early theologians and philosophers of the Church, usually those of the first five centuries CE. They are not necessarily saints, but writers and teachers; the authors of the books of the New Testament are not included. They are broadly disposed in two groups, the Latin and Greek Fathers, according to the language in which they wrote. The earliest of the Fathers, those writing during the first two centuries CE, are known as the Apostolic Fathers, St Clement of Rome being the best known. Later, in response to persecution, came the Apologetic Fathers among them, St Justin Martyr, Anthenagoras and Turtullian. Famous Latin Fathers included St **Augustine**, St Ambrose and St Jerome, the translator of the Vulgate (see **Bible**). Another group centred on Egypt and called the Desert Fathers were monastic, among them St Anthony the Great. Their collection of sayings and teachings is compiled in the *Apophthegmata Patrum*. The study of the works of the Church Fathers is know as Patristics. See **Greek Fathers, Latin Fathers**

Church of England *X*. See **Anglicanism**

Church of Jesus Christ of the Latter Day Saints *X*. See **Mormonism**

Church of Satan Anton LaVey, author of the *Satanic Bible*, founded the church in 1966. It is said he was a lion-tamer, church organist, hypnotist, artist and photographer. LaVey did not believe in a personal, literal devil, but used the cult, culture and imagery of Satanic magic to express his disenchantment with Christianity. The religion of Satanism is pre-Christian originating in traditions of pagan power, sexual virility and sensuality. The concept of Satan is radically different from that given in the scriptures and art of established religions, he is not a fallen angel or a quasi-demi-god of evil, but a force of nature. Thus, the Church of Satan does not worship a deity, power is invested in each individual Satanist and not in a god or goddess; everyone is their own redeemer and responsible for their own potential and children and animals are taken as the purest forms of the life force and are held to be sacred. The Church operates as an umbrella organization for numerous, similar cults and a distinction must be made between the Church of Satan and other forms and expressions of Satanism. See **Satan, Satanism, Church of Set**

Church of Scientology See **Scientology**

Church of Set or **Temple of Set** A cult founded in 1975 by Michael Aquino as a breakaway group from the **Church of Satan**, concerned with the veneration of the Egyptian god **Set**. It emphasizes the Setian aspect of Chaos, perusing the irresistible quest for wisdom that drove Adam and Eve to eat the forbidden fruit of the tree of knowledge. The Church claims to be one of the world's most influential **Left-Handed Path** religions, teaching the magic and philosophy of Set which heightens 'the worship of individualism'.

Church of the Nazarene *X*. A Protestant denomination broadly allied to Methodism. Their name comes from a reference in Acts 20:5 in which **St Paul** is described as 'a fomenter of discord among the Jews all over the world, a ring leader of the sect of the Nazarenes'. The Church was founded in 1895 in Los Angeles by a group wanting to further American holiness. They were soon joined by other established churches such as the Association of Pentecostal Churches of America. Nazarene doctrine includes belief in one self-existing, eternal God manifest in the **Trinity**, the divinity of Jesus, baptism, the Lord's Supper (see **Eucharist**) administered for believers only, and the return of Christ who will raise the dead. Their activities focus in mission and higher education through their eight American universities and several in other countries. Kansas City, Missouri is the administrative centre for approximately 1,300,000 adherents in over 13,000 churches spread across the world.

Circumcision *J*. In Judaism the rite *berit milah* initiates the male child into the community of the Abrahamic covenant. The prescription is *Halakhic*, that is, a matter of law, requiring the removal of the foreskin on the baby's eighth day. The rite is performed by the *mohel*, a professional who need not be a doctor. During the operation the child lies across the knees of the *sandek*, a relative or family friend who may well serve as godfather. Usually circumcision takes place in the home of the child's parents and a celebratory meal will follow.

The appropriateness of the rite has long been debated. Circumcision for reasons of hygiene date back to **Philo** (20 BCE–40 CE); the Jewish philosopher **Maimonides** (1135–1204 CE) associated its symbolism with the notion of sexual restraint, but no such rationalizations are sought by orthodox Jews. There are contemporary Jewish communities that have dispensed with circumcision and still regard themselves as Jews. On the other hand the significance of the rite has so influenced Jewish culture that even non-practising parents and couples where one or the other is not Jewish, may have their sons circumcized.

In Islam, circumcision (Arab. *tahara*) is practised on male candidates and excision on female candidates, but neither of these are prescribed by the Koran. The *sunna*, the Islamic code of custom, regards circumcision as an initiation and as a rite of passage of the male into adulthood. The operation is usually performed before the age of puberty and in modern practice a local anaesthetic is allowed. Male converts to Islam of any age will usually be expected to undergo circumcision and in Europe and the USA this is done in hospital both for adults and for Muslim children at birth. Circumcision is a part of initiatory rites in Australian aboriginal religion and in African tribal religion such as that of the **Dogon** in West Africa and the Nilotic Nandi (see **Nilotic Religion**). Circumcision is also practised for medical and therapeutic purposes.

Cittamatra *B*. Skt. 'mere mind' or 'mind only'. A misapplied term for the Mind Only School of **Buddhism**, but an important concept for the **Mahayana** school of **Yogachara**. *Cittamatra* is a term derived from the Lankavatara Sutra, the main reference for **Bodhidharma**, who carried Buddhism from India to China in the late 5th or early 6th century CE.

City of God *X*. An influential book written by St **Augustine**, which he began c.410 CE after Alaric and the Vandals sacked Rome. Many blamed this catastrophe on the Roman Empire's conversion to Christianity and

Augustine's book is an apologia for the **Church**. He conceived Earth and Heaven as two cities. The earthly city holds the damned whom God has chosen not to save, while the heavenly city is populated by those 'repaired' by God's grace. God's city is not geographically located in heaven but here on earth, not as an actual city but as an association of righteous people whose society is founded on a spiritual charter. The book influenced various themes running through Christian theological history, such as predestination and election and the Church as a theocracy.

Clairvoyance Defined as a form of extra-sensory perception that enables the adept to see distant objects, people or events. This may include the gift of 'seeing' through opaque materials and the perception of energies not usually discernible, such as radio waves. Clairvoyant practice is a feature of most religions, usually associated with their mystical traditions and disciplines. In Hinduism, for example, clairvoyance is one of the *siddhis*, skills, that can be acquired through meditational practice and personal discipline. More usually it is a 'gift' accorded to psychics and is a subject on the agenda of The Society for Psychical Research and the Edinburgh College of Parapsychology. See **Extra-sensory Perception**, **Séance**

Coenobitic *X*. A form of monastic community in which everything is shared: shelter, food, work and prayer. In Eastern and Russian orthodoxy an Episcopally-appointed supervisor, the archimandrite, guides the community who are bound by the rules of a *typicon*, a document that determines every aspect of monastic life and the recitation of Divine Office. The founder of coenobitic monasticism is thought to have been Pachomius (b.292 CE) who established his first monastery in 323 CE at Tabennae, an island in the Nile. He was the leader of some 3,000 monks and remained the Father of the Coenobites for 40 years, finally dying of plague. His typicon, translated into Latin by St Jerome, is the basis of the **Benedictine** rule.

Cokelers *X*. Also known as the Society of Dependents, a strict Puritanical sect founded in 1850 in London by a shoemaker, John Sirgood, and which still has a following today. The sect is exclusive to West Sussex and parts of southwest Surrey. The sect did not advocate marriage; adherents could marry but not under the aegis of the Cokelers since their object was to mortify the flesh by sexual abstinence. It seems that despite their doctrine of 'married' celibacy the sect prospered but, perhaps inevitably, did not grow. A few of their meeting houses remain but they are attended only by remnant members of the group. Visitors are welcome to the meetings during which, after prayer and the singing of hymns (without accompaniment), members can stand up and testify to God's grace.

Collective Unconscious **Jung**'s term for a deeper and more significant level of consciousness. At this level reside what he termed 'archetypes' – innate, unconscious and universal concepts, usually manifested as symbols. Incorporating **Darwin**'s theory of evolution, Jung described the collective unconscious as 'a storehouse of latent memory traces inherited from man's ancestral past, a past that not only includes the racial history of man as a separate species, but his pre-human animal ancestry as well.' (Jung [1969]) He believed the collective unconscious to be the foundational structure of the personal conscious and thus of human personality, in which religion, as myth, has its indispensable place.

Communalism See **Sectarianism**

Communion *X*. See **Eucharist**

Communism A political philosophy concerned to establish a classless society based on the common ownership of the means of production. Clustered under this philosophy are numerous political movements that have the principles of communism as their goal. Despite the huge influence of Marxism and Leninism on 20th century history, the ideal communist state is still a utopia to be realized. The leitmotiv of communism is 'class struggle', the ideological conflict being between the capitalist class (the owners of capital) and the working class. For the working class to assume the administration of society, Marx suggested that an interim revolutionary dictatorship of the proletariat would be necessary. The philosophy has never been fully applied and the term 'Communism' refers to political regimes dominated by a communist party. The philosophical rift has been typically polarized by Russia, perhaps the archetypal communist country, and the USA, the archetypal representative of capitalism, which has a history of virulent anti-communism. A rift developed when the 'Eurocommunism' of Eastern Europe became independent of the authoritarian and orthodox communism of the Soviet Union. Marxist ideology prophesied that religion would disappear when its economic basis was destroyed, but it was in Eastern Europe that Communism met deeply-rooted traditions such as Polish Catholicism and Bulgarian Orthodoxy which had determined the cultures of those countries and provided the values for and the foundation of their societies. For these reasons the communist regimes developed an uneasy co-existence between religion and secularism, Albania being the one country that actually prohibited religious assembly and practice. Political communist parties have made a fairly strong showing in France and Italy, but with the demise of Eastern European Communism from the late 1980s and the fracturing of the Soviet Union in 1991, the presence of communism in Europe has declined. Even so, something like a quarter of the world's population continues to be governed by communism, the largest being China. See **Leninism**, **Marxism**, **Stalinism**, **Trotskyism**
FINAL WORD: 'Under capitalism, man exploits man. Under communism, it's just the opposite.' (J. K. Galbraith)

Communistic Religious Movements Socialist and Christian Socialist historians have argued that the Early Church practised a form of communism. The notion is based on texts such as Acts 2:44, 'All whose faith had drawn them together held everything in common; they would sell their property and possessions and make general distribution as the need of each required,' and on passages in the Letters of St Paul which express concern about the inequality of the local churches, slavery, the rift between rich and poor and problems with the administrative hierarchy. However, it is likely that the Jewish sect, the **Essenes**, represented a more thoroughgoing communist society than did the early Church. Generally it can be argued that most orders of monks, friars and nuns in both Christianity and Buddhism exemplified some principles of communism; they differ from the political ideology in that they are communities of only one sex, live under a hierarchical authority and emphasize the virtue of poverty rather than a communism of possessions. More properly communistic are those religious groups that apply the principles of communism as a means of establishing an independent community. In such cases communism is adopted as an expedient rather than a principle. Examples of communities that have endeavoured to established a form of utopian communism are the **Amish**, the **Mennonites**, the **Hutterian Brethren**, the Russian **Doukhobors** and the African **Aiyetoro Community**.

Community for German Beliefs A secret society, membership of which required that the applicant had no Aryan blood. A vow was taken to preserve, by marriage, the purity of the blood. See **Germanen, Order of**

Community of the Son of Man See **Agapemonites**

Compatibilism The thesis that free will is compatible with determinism. It is an attempt to solve the enigma of 'free will' – that is, the extent to which the individual is free to determine his own course through life. The territory has long been fought over by religion and secularism, religion claiming that it is in the destiny of humanity to ascertain and the obey the will of God. Biblical religions are all about obedience; in **Judaism** it is to the Law, in **Christianity** to the will of God, while submission to the will of Allah is the foundation of **Islam**. An extreme form of determinism is the fatalism represented by the predestinationists (see **Predestination**), who argue that every aspect of our lives has been preordained by God before we were born, indeed even the fact of our birth and that we are not in any respect free. Secularists balance freedom of will against the inexorable influence of our genetic make-up that predetermines our disposition to act and live in a certain way, allied to the influence of our upbringing, education and environment. Traditionally, in both religious and secular philosophy free will and **determinism** are defined in such a way that one explicitly excludes the other. However, the majority of Western philosophers who wrote on this theme were compatibilists, notably **Hobbes**, Leibniz, **Locke** and **Hume**. The argument rests on the notion of 'action'. Even the person who acts under compulsion, whether of an authority or of conditioning, remains an agent, whereas the person subject to some ultimate main force is not. Although many human actions may be attributed to a cause, not all of them are. Hume, the leading champion of compatibilism, argues that free acts are not uncaused or self-caused, as **Kant** would have it. What we do freely, we do because of our desire and disposition. In other circumstances we may have acted differently, thus our determinism, like our freedom, is relative. Eastern philosophy is wrapped around the concept of **Karma**, the present consequences of previous deeds, even those of a previous life. Here volition rather than action is the pivotal issue and what we do 'wilfully' we do as a link in the endless chain of cause and effect. (For a full and balanced discussion, see Daniel Dennett. For the Buddhist view see **Dependent Origination**.) FINAL WORD: 'We think in terms of doing something or refraining from doing something with the intention that a subsequent event may or may not occur. This view is based on the misconception that the future depends on our volitional actions today. It is this false premise of autonomy and the retribution or reward, which are the basis of volitional ethics, that make the chains of our supposed bondage.' (Ramesh Balsekar)

Conciliar Movement *X*. A 14th- and 15th-century reform movement of the **Roman Catholic Church**, which determined that the final authority in all things spiritual was, or should be, held by a General Church Council and not by the pope. One of the central issues was the problem of authority as between scripture on the one hand and the government of the **Church** (the Vatican or papacy) on the other, when they seemed to be in conflict. The movement developed into the schism of the papacy between the Vatican, Rome and Avignon, France, that led to the Council of Constance, 1414–18. The authority of the institute of the papacy in Rome was finally confirmed and Conciliarism condemned at the Fifth Lateran Council, 1512–17. The doctrine of Papal Infallibility, however, was not established until the first Vatican Council of 1870.

Confession *X*. See **Creeds**

Confirmation *X*. One of the three forms of Christian initiation that incorporates the individual into the Church, the other two being **Baptism** and the **Eucharist**. Confirmation is more usually associated with those traditions that practise infant baptism, following which at the age of 12 or 13 the subject affirms the faith implicit in the earlier sacrament. In traditions practising the baptism of believers only there is no additional Confirmation. Originally called 'bishoping', the act of Confirmation is believed to bestow God's special grace which will support the individual in living the Christian faith. See **Baptism, Baptist, Bar Mitzvah, Sacrament**

Confucianism *C*. A Western term for the teachings of **Confucius**, which are a complex mixture of moral, social, political and religious teachings concerning the nature of government and personal relationships. Its influence, for example on the cultures of China, Japan, Korea and Vietnam, began virtually from its inception, c.5th–4th century BCE and has been sustained to the 20th century CE. Its adherents to do not use the name Confucian to refer to themselves. If asked, they would say they are the followers of the way of *Ju* and the ancient sages. Confucius was the last of these sages and he drew on a tradition of wisdom the Chinese believe to have been in existence since the beginning of history. He did not regard himself as an original, nor was he regarded as such; he made no claim to the authority of divine revelation or to being a prophet or representative of any god. His teachings do not draw on any metaphysical terms of reference or concern themselves with previous existences, death or an afterlife. Confucianism is essentially a secular disposition, an attitude to this world based on ethical principles that are entirely pragmatic. The fundamental virtue of Confucianism is *Jen*, in one sense a general, all-inclusive form of philanthropy, in another a more personal expression of love for one's fellow human beings. If *Jen* is the overarching principle, *Ju*, the four basic virtues, is the ethical principle that energizes it. Put simply, *Jen* is the way we should live, *Ju* is the means to do so.

In formulating his social ethics, Confucius drew on a body of ancient literature known as the 'Classic Texts'; only in the broadest sense should they be thought of as scriptures. Originally there were six collections of texts: the *Classics of Songs*, an anthology of early poems; the *Classics of History*, a collection of documents, speeches and records of the councils of rulers and ministers; the *Classics of Rites*, a manual of rituals; the *Classics of Music*, sadly, now lost; the *Classics of Changes*, the well-known *I Ching*, a manual of divination with philosophical commentaries; and the *Spring and Autumn Annals*, a chronicle of the state of Lu. Apart from these ancient original literatures, the canon of Confucianism includes four additional books: the *Analects of Confucius*, the *Doctrine of the Mean*, the *Great Learning* and the *Meng Tzu* of **Mencius**. That these books became the official canon by Imperial decree underlines the secularism of Confucius' moral code. The *Classics* enshrine the concept that the natural world is a model of society as it should be. Everything that happens on earth ('earth' being China) happens because it is decreed so by Heaven. There is a visible order: the seasons follow each other, night follows day; this rhythm is the 'way of Heaven'. What is true of the order seen in the natural world, which provides the context in which human beings form society, should also be true of the way in which that society functions. A father should be followed by a son in harmonious and natural relationship, a ruler will be served by his ministers as the seasons are served by the weather; the same principle applies to all relationships – husbands and wives, teachers and pupils, the old and the young, friend with friend. The whole vibrant, relational structure abides under the beneficent rule of the Emperor, the 'Son of Heaven', whose power and authority are derived from the same 'decree of Heaven' that orders the natural world. Taken to its ideal conclusion, the Emperors did not need to govern. The moral energy which emanated from them was sufficient to bring about and sustain peace and posterity. 'Was not Shun one who ruled without action? For what action did he take. He did nothing but sit reverently facing due South' (Confucius, *Analects* 14.4). Confucius reasoned that if the ruler was righteous and honest, so would be his subjects. Any reforms must begin at the top.

Confucianism, as we know it today, was developed during the Sung dynasty (960–1279 CE) from the school of Neo-Confucianism which combined **Taoist** and **Buddhist** ideas with existing Confucian concepts in order to create a more developed metaphysics. In this process, Confucianism absorbed the Taoist concepts of **Yin and Yang**, and the ancient Chinese theory of the Five Elements: earth, wood, metal, fire and water, the basic elements of the universe. Two schools of Neo-Confucianism developed: the School of Principle and the School of Mind. Both schools revolved around the central Confucian concept of **Li**, the rites, customs and ethics of human relationships and how they should be conducted. The Confucian State Cult promoted traditional worship of Heaven, the sacred mountain, rivers and the ancestors, but it was not thought of as a religious cult; its application was entirely secular. Confucianism prevailed until the collapse of the Ch'ing dynasty in 1912, which was followed by the establishment of the People's Republic of China in 1949.

Whether Confucianism is a religion has been much debated and it is probably correct to say that it is a secular alternative to religion. There is ancestor-worship and sacrifice to ancestral spirits and celestial deities and there is the deification of ancient kings, even of Confucius himself, but these practices can be traced back to ancient Chinese beliefs established in pre-Confucian times. The teachings comfort and guide, they make life fuller and more complete, they address suffering, explain the world and understand human nature. While in these respects Confucianism fulfils the *functions* of religion, it is not generally considered as such by the Chinese, nor the Asian people it influenced. See **Chinese Religions**

FINAL WORD: 'To govern by virtue, let us compare it to the North star: it stays in place while the myriad stars wait upon it.' (Confucius, *Analects* 2:1)

'Respectfulness, without the Rites, becomes laborious bustle; carefulness, without the Rites, becomes timidity; boldness, without the Rites, becomes insubordination; straightforwardness, without the Rites, becomes rudeness.' (*Analects* 8:2)

Confucius *Con. T.* K'ung-tzu or K'ung-fu-tzu. 551–479 BCE. The dates are traditional but approximately correct. He was the founder of the Chinese Wisdom school, known in the West as **Confucianism**. The available sources for Confucius' life were written later and idealized when his social ethics were made the official State Cult in 136 BCE. Sima Qian (145–c.85 BCE), the Han dynasty's court historian, in his *Records of the Grand Historian*, identifies Confucius' ancestors as members of the Royal State of Song, which suggests that his grandparents may have been aristocrats, even of royal blood. The genealogy, however, is obscure and nothing certain can be said of the social status of his ancestors. We do know that Confucius was born in Lu, a small provincial town near Qufu in southeastern Shantung and that whatever his background, he experienced an impoverished childhood. It is clear that while supporting himself with work such as accounting, storekeeping and land-management, he managed to get an education, either by teaching himself or from tutors or a combination of these. The tradition records that he studied ritual with a Taoist master, Lao Dan, music with Chang Hong and the lute with the music master Xiang. Probably on his own initiative he studied, then taught, the traditional ancient philosophies, drawing to him a group of students. When he was about 50 he was appointed a minister of public works, then a minister of justice, but political rivalry drove him into exile. The standard accounts have Confucius returning to Lu in c.484 BCE where he spent the rest of his life teaching and editing the collection of literature known as the *Classics*. Sima Qian records that in these later years he became preoccupied with the *Yi*, the Book of Changes, a divination manual popular to this day in both China and the West. His own teachings are preserved in the *Analects* and they form the basis of Chinese notions of government and education, of the way people should conduct themselves with respect both to society and to each other. Fung Yu-lan, a contemporary authority on the history of Chinese philosophy, has suggested that Confucius' influence on the development of Chinese ideas is similar to that of **Socrates** in the West.

FINAL WORD: '[Confucius] believed that in the long run the people in general would be able to distinguish the good official from the bad. He trusted the human race.' (H .G. Creel)

Congregationalism *X*. A denominational movement in English **Protestantism** that governed the Church through officers elected by the congregation. Congregationalism put into practice theories of union published by Robert Browne in 1592. Its much earlier beginnings can be traced to John **Wycliffe** (c.1320–1384) and the **Lollards**. Together with this principle of democracy went the independence of each local church, loosely bound by an overall administration. This belief in the autonomy of the congregation is thought to emulate the practice of 1st-century Christianity. In 1658 the Savoy Declaration gave tentative structure to Congregationalist principles of faith and church government. From 1691 Congregationalists and **Presbyterians** shared the rites of ministerial ordination and in 1972 they merged as the United Reformed Church. Congregationalism was originally Calvinist in doctrine and through the **Pilgrim Fathers** strongly influenced New England Christianity, since when it has maintained an important presence in the USA.

Conservative Zoroastrianism See **Zoroastrianism, Traditional**

Contagious Magic A form of magic based on the principle that things or persons once in contact can afterwards influence each other and that there is a permanent relationship between an individual and any part of his or her body. Practitioners make use of things like hair, fingernail cuttings, teeth, clothes and faeces. Anyone obtaining these objects could perform magic with them that would cause the original owner to be affected. See **Magic, Sympathetic Magic**

Convent A community of nuns bound by vows to a religious life under the leadership of a Superior, often in partial or complete seclusion. Also the buildings in which such a community is housed. The tradition is to be found in several major religions, such as Buddhism and Christianity.

Conversion The adoption of a religious belief that differs from the subject's previously held beliefs. **Christianity** and **Islam** are mandated to convert as many people as possible – indeed, the entire world – while other religions such as **Judaism** do not actively proselytize. Conversion to Judaism implies joining an ethnic group as well as assuming its belief system. The UN has constituted conversion as a 'right': 'Everyone has the right to freedom of thought, conscience and religion; this right includes the freedom to change his religious belief' (Article 18).

Convulsionnaires X. French millennial prophets, 1720–70. See **Shakers**

Coonyites X. A 19th-century Christian sect. See **Two by Twos**

Coptic Church X. According to tradition the Apostle Mark established Coptic Orthodox Christianity in Egypt in c.42 CE. The Church is part of Oriental Orthodoxy under the See of Alexandria, which since the **Council of Chalcedon** in 451 CE has been a distinct Church with its own Pope, currently Shenouda III. After the Arabic conquest of Egypt in 641 CE, Christians, being 'People of the Book', were allowed to practise their faith, but under the restriction of Islamic **Shariah** law. The language of the Church gradually changed from Coptic to Arabic. Something like 95 per cent of Egyptian Christians are members of the Coptic Church, with Christmas celebrated on 7th January as a national holiday.

Cosmological Argument One of the classical arguments for the existence of God. See **Arguments for the Existence of God, First Cause**

Council of Chalcedon X. 451 CE. Held at Chalcedon, now part of Istanbul, it was the fourth of the first seven Ecumenical Councils of Christianity. Its definitions of dogma are accepted as infallible by the **Roman Catholic** and Eastern Orthodox (see **Orthodoxy**) churches. The creed agreed by the Council accepts both the full humanity and full divinity of Jesus. See **Coptic Church**

Council of Trent X. (1545–63) See **Counter-Reformation**

Counterculture The concept is generally associated with young people who are anti-establishment and who assume a lifestyle that is opposed to mainstream values, of which the 'hippie' movement of the 1960s is a clear example. Sociologists interpret countercultural movements as a reaction to the ethical and political conservatism of the 1950s, the Cold War and the Vietnam War; the movement embraces both religion and atheism. **Neo-paganism** and **New Age** religions developed a theology of counterculture that defined a new perception of and relationship to nature, **pantheism** and liberal politics. Beginning in San Francisco and New York, the counterculture erupted in Europe in the general strike in France and the Paris riots and 'Prague Spring' of 1968. It gave rise to the phrase 'drop out' and created the milieu for countless underground news-papers, 'Flower Power', the Beatnik café, feminism, uninhibited sexual relationships, experiments with psychedelic drugs and the Beatles' song in praise of LSD, 'Lucy in the Sky with Diamonds'. The bio-conservationist ideas of counterculture were disseminated by the *Whole Earth Catalogue*; designed to provide people with resource information about the environment and its protection, it was published twice yearly from 1968 to 1972, then intermittently until 1998. Inevitably, as the first-wave counterculture generation aged its energy was absorbed into the mainstream community, influencing every aspect of American and European politics and culture.

Counter-Reformation *X*. Usually dated as starting from the **Council of Trent** (1545–63) and continuing to the Thirty Years War (1618–48). It is commonly thought of as Roman Catholicism's reaction to the **reformation**, but the counter-reformation had far wider and more radical implications. The doctrinal reforms of the Catholic Church were the subject of the Council of Trent which, intermittently, over an 18-year period, produced the basis for a new advance of the Church. One such document, which appeared in 1564, was Cardinal Carlo Borromeo's Catechism of Trent. New energy was given to the Church by a flowering of mysticism, notably in Spain through St **Teresa** of Avila (1512–82), St **John of the Cross** (1542–91) and Ignatius **Loyola** (c.1491–1556), the founding father of the **Jesuits**. Tribunals in Rome and Spain rigorously suppressed heresy through the **inquisitions** and the Index, a list of prohibited books produced by Pope Paul III (1534–49), the first of a series of reforming popes who recovered some of the papacy's lost prestige and authority. They encouraged the foundation of new monastic orders of which the **Jesuits**, known also as the Society of Jesus, were foremost in initiating worldwide missions. The reinvigoration of the papacy and Catholic doctrine was finally established by the latter stages of the Council of Trent. See **Free Churches**

Covenant *J*. A term usually applied to the solemn, mutually binding agreement between the Israelites and **Yahweh**, concerning creation and man's relationship with nature, history and God. Technically the first covenant was between God and Noah which, following the flood, established the importance and permanence of 'nature' (Gen.8:21–9:7). More significant for Israel was the covenant between God and Abraham (Gen.15:18 and 17: 7–14), in which God assigned the land of **Canaan** to

Israel in exchange for obedience, devotion and faithfulness. It is the Abrahamic covenant that established **circumcision** as one of its signs. The third covenant was with Moses (c.1200 BCE) and is thought to be a consolidation and extension of the first. It was formed on Mt Sinai, where God gave Moses the **Decalogue**, the Ten Commandments (Exod.20: 1–14). These defined the core of Israel's obligations that were expanded by many other prescriptions recorded in the following chapters of Exodus. As **Torah** they form a constitution for the people of Israel and include, for example, the observation of the Sabbath as a sign of the covenant (Exod.31: 16–17). Around 587 BCE, through the Prophet Jeremiah God spoke to the 'House of Israel' about an entirely new kind of covenant (Jer.31: 31–4), cast not in terms of law and commandment, but of indwelling truth. 'I will put My Teachings into their inmost being and inscribe it upon their hearts.' Both the **Essenes** and the Christian Church have regarded themselves to be people of this new covenant, but for orthodox Jews the observation of *mitzvoth* (see **Mitzvah**) has remained the binding condition.

Covenanters *X*. Radical groups known also as the 'godly band', which both in Scotland and England supported the **Reformation** and who, against overwhelming odds, struggled to establish Scottish **Presbyterianism**. The first such band was formed in December 1557, but John Craig's covenant of 1581 is more significant in face of the efforts of the Roman Catholic Church to regain control of Scotland. Craig's group was called the King's Confession or the National Covenant. The Confession, which totally denounces the Pope and the doctrines of the Catholic Church, was adopted by the General Assembly, signed by King James VI and his household and universally decreed. It was ratified in 1590 and 1596. The Covenanters were finally established when, in 1638, in Greyfriars Church, Edinburgh, the National Covenant was ratified both as a protest against Charles I's prayer book and as an affirmation of Presbyterianism. As with other Reformation-inspired movements, the Covenanters stood for freedom of conscience and religious liberty. Their persecution drove many to emigrate to America, but their persistence finally brought to an end 500 years of French Catholicism's domination of Scotland. Their stand for Presbyterianism led to the Protestant King, William of Orange, assuming the English throne in 1690 and to the Political Act of Union between England and Scotland in 1707.

Cow, sacred *H*. See **Sacred Cow**

Creationism A broad term given various meanings according to the vested interests of the user. Generally it is an anti-Darwin, thus anti-evolution attitude, holding to the belief that God or some form of ultimate being, created the universe. There are the biblically literal creationists who assert the Genesis account of the origin of the earth and the universe, indeed the origin of everything, including the creation of man and woman in the form of **Adam** and **Eve** and of the earth remaining flat. Such literalism poses perennial problems when it comes to enquiring into the origins, for example, of suffering and evil. We might term such a position 'Christian Creationism', but among both Jews and Muslims are those who hold to a similar and rigid fundamentalism. For such, the earth is young, merely 6,000 to 10,000 years old. Another view, suggested by the English naturalist Philip Henry Gosse in 1857, which he called the Omphalos argument, suggests that the earth is young but is given the 'appearance' of being old. A variation allows that the earth is indeed ancient, but that life was created as testified by Genesis. The prevailing view is that held by the Progressive Creationists which accepts, in part, scientific insights including the 'Big Bang' theory, but which rejects aspects of modern biology in favour of the notion that God created sequentially rather than evolutionally, in the order suggested by fossil remains. Creationism also includes a kind of science-fiction world view such as the **Raelian** belief that the earth was created by scientists from another planet. More plausible, perhaps, is the view of Panspermia, that bacteria and other microbes were carried to earth from distant star systems. Other examples of creationist theories are described in the literatures of Vedic Hinduism, Native American mythology, Finnish mythology and in the 'Spoken Word' myth of the Quiche Maya. See **First Cause**, **Plotinus**

FINAL WORD: 'Our duty, as men and women, is to proceed as if limits to our ability did not exist. We are collaborators in creation.' (Teilhard de Chardin)

'A subject for a great poet would be God's boredom after the seventh day of creation.' (Nietzsche)

Creation Myths All the world's religions have in common some form of creation mythology. These describe creation as a 'premeditated' act by a supreme being, the creator. In secular terms, theories of the origin of the universe based on philosophical or scientific assumptions may also amount to a myth, with acceptance being given to those theories that seem to be the most plausible. One such example is Panspermia, the theory that the seeds of life are dispersed universally and may have been delivered to earth. Exogenesis is a related theory that suggests, more reasonably, that life on earth may have originated elsewhere. Perhaps the current, most generally accepted account of the origin of the universe is the 'Big Bang' theory. Common characteristics of religious creation mythology include the world's emergence from primordial chaos or of it being 'parented' by **earth mother** and **sky father** gods or accounts of the land arising from a limitless ocean. The interface between religious and scientific theories has given rise to a fierce and long-running debate termed the Creation-Evolution Conflict, prevalent in the USA in the on-going war between the two cultures, science and religion. See **Creationism**

Creeds X. Brief, summary statements of Christian belief. Christianity began as a Jewish sect and its converts needed little instruction in matters of faith. As the sect spread into the Greek world the conversion of pagans to Christianity required a statement of belief that served both as a curriculum of instruction and a confession of faith. The open permissiveness of the Hellenistic world meant that answers were needed to resolve disputes in matters of faith and practice, thus the earliest creeds probably identified baptism as the indispensable means of Christian initiation. One of the early formulations is the Apostles' Creed, accepted in the West for use in sacramental liturgies and in general worship. As the early church spread and matured, creeds emerged from ecumenical councils both to establish a Christian orthodoxy and to refute heresy. They were a corporate expression of faith and began with the formula, 'We believe ...' The most famous of these is the Nicene Creed based on the findings of the Council of Nicaea (325 CE) and intended to answer the heresy of **Arianism**. It was developed and confirmed by the Council of Constantinople in 381 CE and became the standard Creed used for the **Mass** (or **Eucharist**). It included the *Filio-que* clause which stated that the Holy Spirit proceeds from the Father and the Son, a doctrine rejected by the **Orthodox** Church. The so-called Anathasian Creed (which has nothing to do with Athanasius or the Athanasian Creed) was composed in Latin. Its anathemas or 'damnation clauses' threatening formal excommunication from the Church for heresy have made it less ecumenical and while it has been used by the Roman, Lutheran and Anglican communions, it is now used with less regularity. Following the Reformation numerous Confessions of Faith were produced such as the Augsburg Confession of the **Lutherans** and the Westminster Confession of the **Presbyterians**. Luther's 39 Articles have also been used as a confession for Anglicanism.

Crisis Theology *X*. A theological response made to the First World War and sometimes known as dialectical theology or neo-orthodoxy. Its instigator was the Swiss theologian Karl **Barth** (1886–1968), who was followed by a succession of other significant theologians such as Emil Brunner, Nikolay Berdyayaev, Reinhold **Niebuhr** and Paul **Tillich**. The term 'crisis' refers both to the state of *fin de siècle* Christian theology which lacked the intellectual vigour and optimism of liberal theology and to the social and political conditions created by world war. Barth, especially, gave theological weight to the word 'crisis' (Greek *krisis*) meaning judgement, that is, the judgement of God falling severely on all human endeavours, plans and policies, whether social, moral or religious. To these theologians of crisis the carnage of the First World War was the final proof of the extent to which human society had failed to realize its potential for good, justice and compassion. Each of these theologians responded in their different ways, but by endeavouring to reconstruct a theology for their 'times', found that the language of post-**Reformation Protestantism** was a useful vehicle. In terms of the **Bible** being the 'Word' of God and of Jesus as the 'Word' incarnate, they addressed the whole range of Christian theology, endeavouring to interpret anew the doctrines of Creation, the **Trinity**, the **Fall** of man and **original sin**, each in relationship to the salvatory work of Jesus Christ. The term 'neo-orthodoxy' was applied to their work, but rejected by them as they disavowed biblical literalism. In America criticism of contemporary culture and its political and economic institutions focused a new theological emphasis on human responsibility in every aspect of life. Niebuhr, especially, developed a theology that required all aspects and structures of human society to be seen and understood as a whole, rather than in its separate entities of religion, morality, economics and politics. Tillich developed a theology of culture as the foundation on which a Christian society should be built. Crisis theology thus became welded to the driving issues of the day such as race relations, nuclear weapons and medical ethics. From the end of the Second World War onwards, the direct influence of crisis theology declined. One of the most abiding influences came from Dietrich **Bonhoeffer** who was executed by the Nazis in 1945. The seminal influence of his *Letters and Papers from Prison* can only be fully understood and appreciated when read in the context of crisis theology.

Cronos or **Chronos** *Gk*. The leader and youngest of the first generation of Titans, the divine descendents of **Gaia**, the earth, and **Uranus**, the sky, whom he overthrew. He reigned during the Golden Age until displaced by his own son, **Zeus**. In Roman mythology he was identified with the god **Saturn**; for the Greeks, Cronos became the god of human time, that is of calendars and seasons. He is depicted as an old man with a long grey beard and is not to be confused with the Titan **Cronos**.

Crucifix *X*. Usually a cross bearing a representation of the body of Jesus Christ. It is the characteristic symbol of Christianity used mostly by Roman Catholics, Lutherans and Anglicans. Some crucifixes have a skull and crossbones beneath the corpus, illustrating the myth that the cross was planted on the burial place of Adam. Protestant denominations are more likely to use an empty cross symbolic of the resurrected Christ. In continental Europe crucifixes are placed at the boundaries of towns and villages. The symbol is frequently worn as a necklace or is attached to a rosary. They are made in innumerable styles, from many kinds of materials.

Crusades *X*. A long series of violent military campaigns, usually undertaken on the authority of the papacy, during the 11th–13th centuries CE. They began as a Roman Catholic initiative to recapture the **Holy Land** and Jerusalem from Muslim occupation, but some crusades had other targets, for example Constantinople (the 4th crusade, 1202–04) and the **Albigensian** crusade of 1209, designed to eliminate the **Cathars** of southwestern France. The so-called Northern Crusades were sent against the 'still heathen' population of northeast Europe, in the region of the Baltic. Beyond its military use the term 'crusade' has many applications, usually associated with any righteous initiative to root out evil or heresy or to fight for a just cause of any kind, religious or secular. In the latter sense we have become familiar with the 'crusade' against adult illiteracy and the crusade for women's rights.

Cult A usually small group, religious or secular, which – at least to begin with – gathers around a charismatic leader. Usually they live in a colony in some degree of isolation, holding to unorthodox beliefs and practices. Sometimes when the leader dies or moves on the cult will collapse, but not always. Cults are usually not conversionist, that is, while their self-definition may be cast in terms that distinguish them from others, they exist for themselves so as to achieve their spiritual or secular goals. The meaning is clearer when the movement in question is focused on a particular figure such as the 'Cult of Mary', a reference to the specific tradition within Roman Catholicism of worshipping the Virgin (see **Mary and Mariology**). In general the term 'cult' may be applied to the separation and heightening of one aspect of the original religious 'culture' which became the principal focus for its adherents. A secular example is the **First Preslyterian Church of Elvis the Divine**. The term, however, is so loosely used as to defy clear definition. See **Anti-Cult Movement**

Cupid See **Eros**

Cybele *Gk. R.* The great goddess of fertility and nature who originated with the Phrygians in the 13th century BCE, spreading to Greece by the 5th century BCE and brought to Rome in 204 BCE. Readings of the **Sibylline Books** by Roman priests recommended them to worship Cybele and they dedicated a temple to her on the Palatine Hills. She was always in the company of her lover or son, Attis. The mythology has her as the daughter of **Gaia** and **Uranus**, and married to **Cronos**. In the Greek and Roman world the cult was known for its noise and frenzy and its ecstatic rites and ceremonies of purification which included a ritual bath in the blood of a sacrificed bull. The cult was psychologically similar to that of **Dionysus**.

D

Daemons G. A Hellenized or Latinized spelling to distinguish between the 'daemons' of Greek mythology and the Judeo-Christian concept of 'demon' as a malignant spirit. The Greek daemons were supernatural beings somewhere between mortals and gods, lesser divinities or ghosts of dead **heroes**. They were divided into good or evil categories, the former called Eudaemons, being something like the Old Testament concept of guardian angels. They were important to neoplatonic philosophy which carried the concept into Christianity as angels. Towards the end of the 4th century CE, Cyprian incited the destruction of the statues of the gods believing malevolent daemons to be 'lurking under' them. The face, being the identifying feature, was destroyed – that is the statues were 'defaced'. But Christianity, while believing in the reality of daemons, remained confused as to what they were, deriving its belief from ancient apocryphal, even heretical literature, as well as from canonical tradition. Daemons have been made familiar by Philip Pullman's trilogy *His Dark Materials*, in which many of his characters have visible daemon-companions that are inseparable from their 'essential' selves. See **Demonology, Demons**

Daevas *Zo*. 'False gods'. Usually associated with the original gods of **Indo-Iranian** religions who were strongly rejected by **Zoroastrianism** because of those, such as **Indra** for example, who were thought to be violent and amoral. Daevas are also known as 'the deceitful ones'. It is the duty of a righteous person to keep away from them and to guard against their influence. Through the daevas, **Angra Mainyu** threatens the lives of those who are righteous. See **Ahura Mazda, Asa, Druj, Fravashi**

Daevayasnians *Zo*. Worshippers of the evil spirit manifested as **Daevas**. They are understood to be the obverse of the **Mazdayasnians**, who worship the true god Mazda. See **Ahura Mazda, Angra Mainyu, Zoroastrianism**

Dagda *AE*. Celtic 'Good god', the father of all. See **Celtic Religion**

Dakhma or **Dokhma** *Zo*. The Zoroastrian '**Towers of Silence**' on top of which corpses were placed so that they could be consumed by vultures rather than buried or cremated, thus polluting the elements of earth and fire. See **Zoroastrianism**

Dalai Lama *B*. Tib. 'teacher whose wisdom is as great as the ocean'. An honorific title first given to the third head of the **Gelugpa** school of **Tibetan Buddhism** by the Mongolian prince Altan Khan in 1578. Eventually the title was applied to the ruler of Tibet. The Dalai Lama is thus a head of state, the religious leader believed to be the reincarnation of his predecessor and in terms of lineage the incarnation of

Avalokitesvara. The Panchen Lama is the Dalai Lama's representative, a spiritual aid and until the 20th century without political responsibility. The current incumbent is Tensin Gyatso; born in 1935, he is the 14th Dalai Lama. Since the Chinese invasion of Tibet in 1950, he and the Tibetan Buddhist community have been exiles, based at **Dharamsala** in northwest India.

Dar al-Harb *I*. Arab. 'Territory of War' or 'War Zone', thought of as 'the Household of non-Islam'. Originally the term referred to the territories that bordered the Islamic empire, the *Dar al-Islam* or 'Household of Islam'. Such a territory is designated by the observation and sovereignty of Islamic law. The 'War' refers to the obligation to convert the neighbouring, non-Islamic nations and all too frequently this implied actual war. In practice it only affects those nations not having a treaty of non-aggression with Islam. If such a treaty exists, then the nation is referred to as *Dar al-sulh*, 'Territory of Treaty'. In this case the agreement is to protect Muslims, for which service a tax or tribute is paid. It has to be remembered that, ideally, any state under Islamic rule should aspire to be a true **theocracy** (see **Islam**). As the Islamic empire expanded, Islamic law debated the status of the colonized territories. In India, for example, it was decided that because it was technically British territory it was *Dar al-Harb*, a Territory of War, and the same designation was given to Algeria while under French rule. In such circumstances Islamic scholars debated the obligation of such Muslims to emigrate to *Dar al-Islam*, the Household or Territory of Islam.

Dar al-Islam *I*. Arab. 'the Household of Islam'. See **Dar al-Harb**

Darbar Sahib *Sik*. Pun. 'Divine Court'. The principal hall within a Sikh *gurdwara* or temple, where the **Guru Granth Sahib** is placed. Darbar Sahib is also the Sikhs' preferred name for the Harmandir Sahib, popularly known as the **Golden Temple** in Amritsar, the central Sikh shrine and place of pilgrimage.

Darshana *H. B.* Skt. Pal. *dassana*, 'demonstration' or 'system'. In Hinduism *darshana* is i) to pay respect to a holy place or person so as to receive blessings and purifications (all such meetings are *darshana*); ii) the six classical schools of Hindu philosophy: **Nyaya**, **Purva-mimansa** (see **Mimamsa**), **Sankhya**, **Vaiseshika**, **Vedanta**, **Yoga**. All six schools are to be found in the **Bhagavad-Gita**, and all have the same object of unifying **atman** with **Brahman** by freeing the spirit from the birth-death-rebirth cycle. In Buddhism *darshana* is closely allied to the first of the Hindu philosophical schools, *Nyaya*, the school of logical analysis and reason which trains the mind not to rely on emotions, misconceptions, doubt or outward forms of religious practice. *Darshana* moves the practitioner from blind trust to clear-sighted understanding. The dates of the establishment of these schools is unclear, but the consensus is that they developed later than the 5th century BCE. There is an interesting spin-off, since the later the date of the schools the more likely it is that their teachings were influenced by Greek philosophy, thus 'the Hindus were in this instance the teachers, not the learners' (Dowson, quoting Colebrook).

Darwinism As a philosophical concept, Darwinism is a term loosely and variously used for a theory of evolution by natural selection. The term is less used by scientists than by Darwin's detractors who are usually defending a religious, mostly Christian, **creationism**. 'Survival of the fittest' (not Darwin's phrase, but Herbert **Spencer**'s1820–1903) and the notion of 'descent' are terms that have caused huge problems for those religions whose doctrines are founded on a belief in a creator God. To biological Darwinism has to be added Spencer's Social Darwinism which applied the principles of biological evolution to sociology and philosophy, arguing that only those social institutions that are most suited to humanity's well-being will survive. The teaching of Darwinian theories of evolution is still contested by schools in America's **Bible Belt**.
FINAL WORD: 'The theory of evolution is a theory, not a fact' (a sticker put on the textbooks of a school in Georgia, 2002).

David *J.* 2nd King of Israel and successor to Saul. He reigned for 40 years from c.1005–965 BCE, conquering the Jebusite city of Jerusalem c.1000. Regarded as the most righteous of Israel's ancient kings, as well as being a warrior, musician and poet and traditionally credited with being the author of many of the Psalms. Judaism holds that the **Messiah** will be a direct descendent of King David and Christians trace the lineage of Jesus back to him. The question of his actual historicity has not been settled, but in 2005 Eilat Mazar, an Israeli archaeologist, discovered in East Jerusalem what he claims to be the Palace of David. See **Soloman**

Day of Atonement *J.* Jewish festival see **Yom Kippur**

Dayak Religion *P.* Dayak is a general, non-ethnic term for certain non-Muslim inhabitants of Borneo. Mostly a riverine people, they live in longhouse communities. Despite Islamic and Christian mission their indigenous religion survives as *Kaharingan*, a combination of complex animistic and shamanistic beliefs and ritual practices. Among the Melanau group, there are a few who practise *Liko*, thought to be the earliest surviving form of *Kaharingan*. Intertribal warfare and head-hunting persists.

Dead Sea Scrolls *J.* From 1947 to 1956, in the Wadi Qumran on the northwest shore of the Dead Sea, approximately 850 documents were discovered in 11 caves. They included texts from the Hebrew Bible dating from before 100 CE. They comprised of fragments from the Hebrew Bible, non-canonical but traditional Hebrew texts, biblical commentaries, manuals of discipline and rules of war. The view generally held is that they were written and hidden by the **Zealot/Essene** community that was destroyed by Romans during the 'Great Rebellion' of the Jews in 66–70 CE. An alternative, well-supported view is that the scrolls belonged to a community of **Sadducees**. It has further been suggested that the scrolls were the scriptures of an early Christian community, more fundamentalist than those of the New Testament. Conspiracy theories abound, notably that the Vatican kept several important scrolls under wraps for decades in order to suppress controversial theories about early Christian history. See **Essenes**

Death of God Theology *X*. Since the end of the 2nd century theologies have been put forward suggesting and accounting for the death of God. For example, Praxeas, known to us only because of **Tertullian**'s *Adversus Praxean*, taught that the Godhead was entirely emptied into the person of Jesus Christ, thus God died of incarnation. It was, therefore the Father, born as the Son, who suffered and died again on the cross. Jean Paul Richter's (1763–1825) 'Speech by the dead Christ … that there is no God' was a description of what it would be like to be an atheist, a speculation noticed by **Hegel** in 1802, who claimed that at Easter the Good Friday awareness of Christ's death was characteristic of a general religious consciousness. The 'what if God did not exist?' notion was taken up by the Romantic imagination of the 19th century and lead to philosophies that contributed to the death of God theology, creating a vacuum filled by a kind of aesthetic romanticism. Since the end of the 19th century, 'Death of God' has become a slogan derived from **Nietzsche**'s story of the madman who runs through the streets crying, 'I'm looking for God, I'm looking for God.' 'Where has God gone?' … 'I shall tell you. We have killed him – you and I. We are all his murderers.' Nietzsche's conclusion was that since human beings were responsible for God's death, they must make themselves gods or supermen; they must take charge of their history, be determinate over their affairs. **Feuerbach** and **Marx**, following Nietzsche, ascribe all the attributes once accorded to God, to human beings. Theology has thus metamorphosed into anthropology. These philosophers were, of course, influenced by the gathering momentum of **rationalism** and **secularism** and contributed to them.

Decalogue *J*. The Greek term refers to the Ten Commandments reputed to have been given by God to **Moses** on Mt Sinai (Exod.20:1–14 and Deut.5:6–21). Tradition has it that God spoke, then carved the words on two tablets of stone which Moses later broke on finding the Israelites worshipping a golden calf. The commandments spell out the conditions of the **covenant** between God and the Israelites and they cover the entire code guiding relationships, both with God and with people. Eventually, the Decalogue was expanded post-biblically by rabbinic commentators to 365 prohibitions, deliberately matching the number of days in the year and 248 mandates thought to correspond with the number of bones in the human body. There are differences in the order and wording of the Ten Commandments; the Talmudic or biblical order is followed by the Greek Orthodox church and, except for Lutherans, by **Protestants**. The **Roman Catholic** church follows the order set out by **Augustine**.

Deconstructionism A term coined by the French philosopher Jacques **Derrida** to identify a philosophical theory applied to language and literary criticism, which questions the assumptions traditionally made about certainty, identity and truth. It applies especially to metaphysical assumptions used to argue that an idea or presumed fact, is objectively true or valid. While **epistemology** concerns theories of knowledge, deconstruction concerns theories of meaning and the way meaning is constructed by writers, the texts they write and the readers who read them. The suggestion is that a text only contains such meaning as the mind of the reader gives to it. Derrida's agenda was to criticize the entire tradition of Western philosophy's attempt to define the structure of knowledge and reality in the face of the limitations of human thought. Interestingly, Derrida identifies the problems of doing this as a series of dualisms such as subject/object, being/non-being, reality/appearance, male/female. For a deconstructionist account of meaning, what is *not* written – that is, what the text excludes or silences – is of equal importance as the evident text. The result has frequently been to show that a definitive interpretation of any text is impossible or that deep-seated contradictions exist below the textual surface. Although the movement has lost some of the energy gathered in the 1960s and 1970s, it has had considerable influence on numerous disciplines including religion, history, sociology, educational theory, linguistics, art and architecture. Its influence on the reading and interpretation of religious texts has led to most of the contemporary attempts to find new, relevant meanings, making the quest for a new religious language urgent. See **Demythology**, **Postmodernism**, **Wittgenstein**

Deism An alternative term for 'natural religion', that is, religion without revelation. In the 17th and 18th centuries Deism was influential on writers such as **Rousseau** and Voltaire in France and Benjamin Franklin and Thomas Jefferson in the USA (both of whom were ministers to France). It was believed that the study of Nature and the use of reason were a better means of understanding the existence of God than were the scriptures, creeds and the received tradition of the Church. Deists believe that all the major religions are essentially concerned with the same message and that priests, formal religious observance and ritual are irrelevant. See **Hume**, **Natural Theology**, **Theism**

Delphi *G.* The most influential oracle of the ancient world, located at the temple of **Apollo** on Mt Parnassus, Greece. Apollo spoke through an old woman of unimpeachable character, chosen from the local peasantry. As a sibyl or priestess, she took the name Pythia and seated herself on a tripod over a fissure in the earth. Fumes from the decomposing Python, slain by Apollo, caused the sibyl to fall into a trance allowing Apollo to take possession of and speak through her. Contemporary geological research suggested that Pythia's trance may have been the result of ethylene gas. Unsurprisingly, then, she spoke in riddles that were interpreted by temple priests. The oracle was consulted on all manner of personal, public and state affairs. See **Medium**, **Oracle**, **Séance**

Dema-deity *P*. Mythological gods or goddesses who transferred to humans their land, crops, general farming skills and totems. They also transmitted their crafts such as spear, bow and canoe-making, together with instructions for performing rituals and dances. Some groups believe that the origins of the different tribes and the lands they inhabit are the divided and scattered body of the deity. Among root-crop cultivators the belief is held that the Dema-deity was killed, then cut up and that from these body-parts grew the crops that sustain humanity. This may well be a mythology that reflects cannibalism. The cult is especially associated with the Marind-Anim of New Guinea. See **Melanesian Religion**

Demeter *G*. The Greek goddess of corn, agriculture, fertility, the preserver of marriage and sacred law, invoked in the Homeric hymn as the bringer of seasons. Her cult was an important civilizing influence, drawing people to a settled life based on the home and agriculture. She pre-dates the Olympian gods and with her daughter **Persephone** was the focus of the **Eleusinian Mysteries**, the origins of which were associated with the goddess-cults of Minoan Crete. She was assimilated into the Roman cult as **Ceres**, from which the word 'cereal' is derived.

Democratic Transhumanism A term coined by James Hughes in 2002 to identify a movement concerned with liberal, social and radical democratic politics, the features of biopolitics. Maurizio Lazzaroti suggests 'that life and living beings, that the species and its productive requirements have moved to the heart of political struggle is something that is radically new in human history.' The philosophy promotes the thesis that human happiness and wellbeing are dependent on people controlling the rational and social forces that affect their lives. Greater faith in science and democracy was shown from the 17th–19th centuries than today, when a resurgent Biopo-luddite attitude and its accompanying bio-conservatism frustrate research and development. See **Institute of Noetic Sciences, Posthumanism, Secular Humanism, Transhumanism**
FINAL WORD: 'For millennia, man remained what he was for Aristotle: a living animal with the additional capacity for a political existence; modern man is an animal whose politics places his existence as a living being in question.' (Michel Foucault)

Demonology In Christianity, the systematic study of demons is a legitimate branch of theology based on catalogues that name and arrange in a hierarchy lists of malevolent spirits such as Heinrich Kramer's 1487 *Malleus Maleficarum*. Demons are believed to be fallen angels and those wishing to invoke them used **grimoires**. **Judaism** and **Islam** also have traditions of demonology, the former probably derived from **Zoroastrianism**. Hindu mythology has extensive accounts of warfare between the gods and their opponents, such as that between **Indra** and **Vritra**, and some branches of Buddhism (see **Mara**) believe in demons that attempt to frustrate the achievement of enlightenment. Demonology is also a feature of **witchcraft, paganism, Satanism** and the **occult**.

Many fundamentalist Christians believe UFOs and aliens to be demons in disguise, bent on distracting the faithful from the true path during what they believe to be the 'last days'. See **Daemons, New Age Religion, UFO Cults**

Demons From the Greek *dàimon*. A supernatural spirit generally thought to be malevolent. It may be conjured as a force and partly controlled. Demons form a part of the mythologies of most of the world's major religions. See **Daemons, Demonology, Possession**

Demythology *X*. A method of interpreting the **New Testament** (see **Bible**) first proposed by the German theologian Rudolph **Bultmann** (1884–1976) who proposed that the foundation of Christian truth was the Christ of faith, not the Jesus of history. The process extrapolates what is considered to be the mythological content of the texts so as to arrive at the original agenda or intention of the authors. Thus, freed from the actual record of Jesus' life, the focus of faith turned to the living, resurrected Christ; this in turn enabled a 'translation' of the mythological aspects of the New Testament into the language of contemporary human existence. The true function of theology is to comprehend and describe human existence as it is confronted by God in the present. The process of demythologizing is, therefore, an examination of religious language and an attempt to find new terms that are more appropriate for contemporary culture. Bultmann argued that the language of the New Testament was cast in the perceptions and cosmology of the age of its authors and that these were not shared by modern man. Familiar examples of this include the biblical image of the three-storeyed universe of **heaven** and **hell** with earth in the middle and the accounts of the miracles including the **Virgin Birth** and the **resurrection**. Bultmann believed these presented a view of reality that was totally beyond the grasp of the modern mind and that what we need is a reinterpretation that provides an acceptable conceptuality. In brief, what we are concerned with is the problem of an outmoded religious language and that the construction of a new language is possible. To develop this, Bultmann looked to **Heidegger**'s **existentialism**. Bultmann's demythologizing programme has had a profound influence on contemporary theology and religious perception; it has been taken up by other influential philosophical theologians, including **Tillich** and **Bonhoeffer**. In March 1963 the concept of demythologizing the Bible became the subject of controversy and public debate when J. A. T. Robinson published his book *Honest to God*.

Dependent Origination *B*. Skt. *Pratitya Samutpada*. *Pratitya*, 'because of' or 'dependent on', *Samutpada*, 'arising' or 'origination' – thus 'conditioned arising' or 'dependent arising'. It is a formative philosophy unique to Buddhism suggesting that all psychological and physical phenomena which make up our individual existence condition each other and are completely interdependent. The classical and simplest Pali formulation translates as:

'When there is this, that is.
With the arising of this, that arises.
When this is not, neither is that.
With the cessation of this, that ceases.'
(The Buddha, *Samyutta-Nikaya* ii:28)

It is important to understand that the doctrine is concerned only with **samsara**, the birth-death-rebirth cycle. It is not a creation theory and makes no attempt to account for the origin of the universe or for evolution. It represents a kind of causal logic supporting the notion that for every cause there is an effect, except that in this case the effect may also condition the cause. Substances or phenomena are not ultimately real because they have no independent existence, thus no self-existing essence. Such reality that phenomena have resides in their causal relationship to what preceded and what will succeed them; all that is real are relations. That everything exists because something else pre-existed it does not deny its relative reality, but affirms that reality is dependent on something else having taken place. Put together with the **anatman**, 'no self' doctrine, the theory of Dependent Origination forms the core of all Buddhist teaching and **enlightenment** depends on our understanding its implications. 'Whoever sees Dependent Origination, sees the Dharma; whoever sees the Dharma sees Dependent Origination' (The Buddha, *Majjhima-Nikaya*).

The sequence of Dependent Origination forms a series of 12 links grouped in accordance with the three modes of time – past, present and future:

In time past:
Ignorance gives rise to karmic activity.
Karmic activity gives rise to consciousness.
In the present:
Consciousness gives rise to names and forms.
Names and forms give rise to the six sense organs.
The six sense organs give rise to contact.
Contact gives rise to feeling.
Feeling gives rise to emotional love or craving.
Emotional love or craving gives rise to grasping.
Grasping gives rise to existing.
Existing gives rise to birth.
In the future:
Birth gives rise to old age and death.
Old age and death give rise to ignorance.

Thus, like a round-song, the cycle starts again. The cycle begins and ends with 'ignorance', in Sanskrit **avidya**, with the better translation 'delusion'.

The secret, it seems, is to see the truth and implications of Dependent Origination. The Buddha, however, cautioned his followers, 'Monks, the thought arose in me, thus: This truth which I have realized is profound, difficult to see abstruse, calming, subtle, not attainable by sophisticated logic.' And yet Buddhism affirms that we can overcome this ignorance and in so doing stop the whole chain of events, link by link, here and now, through **meditation**.

Dereligionizing An aspect of **Secularization** that includes, for example, the disestablishment of State religions and the withdrawal of religious education from school curricula. As with the process of secularism, all religions have had to adapt to the implications of dereligionizing.

Derrida, Jacques (1930–2004) French philosopher and literary critic and founder of the philosophical movement **Deconstructionism**. See **Postmodernism**

Dervish *I*. Per. *darwish*, 'poor', 'religious mendicant'. The name is used generally to identify groups of ascetic **Sufi** Muslims, characterized by their poverty and austerity, a way of life indicated by their wearing plain woollen clothing. In this respect they can be compared with Western mendicant friars. The term is also used of anyone who is non-acquisitive and indifferent to the material aspects of life. Dervishes may be lay members of the community, solitary wanderers or, as happens most frequently, take a vow of poverty and join one of the Sufi *tariqah* or orders, living in monasteries not dissimilar to those of Christian monks. The Turkish **Mevlevi** Order practise the whirling dance for which they are well known. The dance is a technique used to achieve the state of *majdhb* or ecstasy, which will carry them into communion with Allah. The **Rifa'is** are 'howling' Dervishes, who have figured in documentary films showing them cutting or piercing themselves with knives, needles or metal spikes, walking or lying on red-hot coals and handling venomous snakes. Many of the more extreme Dervish practices have unfortunately become tourist attractions and some groups 'perform' only for that purpose. However, most of the Sufi orders of Southern Asia are true mystics, dedicated to prayer, fasting and mind-calming meditation. See **Bektashis, Chishti, Fakir, Murid, Rumi, Silsilah, Tariqah**

Dervish Groups *I*. See **Bektashis, Chishti, Dervish, Mevlevi, Murid, Rifa'is, Rumi, Silsilah, Tariqah**

Descartes (1596–1615) Descartes' philosophy is a complete structure from which it is necessary to extrapolate his influence on religion and secularism. Descartes' metaphysics is built on three universal components he called substances: God, Mind and Matter. Everything is either an example or a modification of one of these. Thus, the universe is a vast machine made up of an infinite variety of smaller machines such as animals, all operating according to mechanical principles. Mind, however, is not part of this machine, since it works by mental rather than mechanical principles. Descartes' philosophy begins with doubt and the first step to sure knowledge concerns the existence of self: 'I am, I exist, is necessarily true …' a proposition famously formed as, 'I think, therefore I am'. Descartes built on this to offer theories of knowledge that took him, broadly, in two directions. The first was to consider the existence of God as the highest, most perfect class or quality of 'idea'; Descartes argued that he could be the originator of all ideas save one, the idea of God. Since his mind was finite and less than perfect, the idea of an infinite and perfect being like God is not one that he could have conceived. In *Discourse Part IV* he concludes 'that the mere fact that I exist and have within me an idea of a most perfect being ... provides a very clear proof that God indeed exists.' He also drew on other arguments for God's existence (see **Arguments for the Existence of God**).

The second direction led Descartes to consider the possibility of all truth resting on a firm foundation which had no need of metaphysics. The same premise, 'I think, therefore I am' led him to argue that human reason was, in itself, a perfectly valid basis for sure knowledge. The very fact that human beings were uniquely capable of thought was a basic truth upon which all others could be constructed. There was no necessity to assume that God's existence was the starting point for 'Truth'. Descartes thus settled for a concept of God that was relative rather than absolute; we can only understand God to the extent that we are capable and in that process everyone has different aptitudes. Hence the variety of religious expression and experience. In summary, it can be said that Descartes provided a philosophical basis for a scientific and **secular** world view, used and developed first by his contemporary Newton. It has been suggested that Descartes was an atheist (see **Atheism**) and that his arguments for the existence of God were little more than a cosmetic ornamentation of the metaphysical mystery so much a part of his own culture. On the other hand, both in his private letters and his published work there are frequent references and appeals to God. Perhaps he was anxious to keep his 'thinking' mind as open as possible or maybe he was hedging his philosophical bets. See **Spinoza**

FINAL WORD: 'It's not enough to have a good mind. The main thing is to use it well.' (Descartes)
'If you would be a real seeker after truth, you must at least once in your life doubt, as far as possible, all things.' (Descartes)

Despachos Ritual 'contests' carried out at a crossroads, with the offering of food, candles, cigarettes and cigars. The cult is identified with **Umbanda** federations in Rio and Sao Paulo, but has spread throughout Brazil and is officially constituted as a religion. There are two major traditions, one of which is African. The other is based on **Kardecism**, founded on the teachings of Allan Kardec, a 19th-century French spiritualist. See **Ancestor Worship**, **Macumba**, **Quimbanda**

Determinism Generally, the philosophical proposition that every happening, including human cognition and actions, are causally determined, thus eliminating 'mysterious' or random events. It does not follow that everything is predetermined and that what is going to happen is inevitable. Such a view concerns a somewhat different concept, **fatalism**. One of the consequences of determinist philosophy is that the notion of free will becomes an illusion. In the debate, 'Determinism' and 'Free Will' are usually shown to be mutually exclusive, but **compatibilism** is a fair attempt at a middle way, pointing to a balanced reconciliation of the two views (see **Hume**). In terms of Western religion the debate is cast in the tension between the sovereign will of God and the free will of humanity. Some religious philosophies allow that humans are free to choose whether or not to accept what God wills, to avoid the implications of a doctrine of **predestination**. In the West, the old Greek atomists like Democritus (see **Atomism**), together with Newton's 'billiard ball' hypothesis, have done much to promote determinism as the mechanistic process of the interplay of atoms. Once the balls have been placed on the table and set in motion, they will move according to law and produce predictable results.

Hinduism's notion of determinism is illustrated by the story of **Indra's Net**, and **Buddhism**'s by that of **Dependent Origination**. In Buddhism the purpose of examining the implications of determinism is more a question of heightening the significance of everything being interdependent, than of examining the notion of free will. See **Voluntarism**

Devas *H. B.* Skt & Pal. 'bright', 'shining'. A god, deity or supernatural being, somewhat mythological and perhaps akin to the Christian **angel**. In Hinduism the term has various connotations such as Brahman in the aspect of a personal God or the name for beings who inhabit a higher realm, like a heaven, but who remain mortal. They are also the gods who maintain heaven and the elements, like **Agni**, **Varuna** and **Surya**, the gods of fire, water and the sun respectively. *Deva* is also an epithet for someone who has achieved enlightenment. In Buddhism a *deva* is a celestial being or god and part of the pantheon of gods inherited from Hinduism. In Buddhist mythology they are blessed with long, happy lives and live in one of the 28 divine realms, a reward for previous meritorious lives. They are still bound up with *samsara*, and are reborn when their positive **karma** is used.

Devi *H.* Skt. 'goddess'. The term may be used in reference to any female divinity, sometimes being added to the name, for example Lakshmi-Devi. See **Durga**, **Lakshmi**

Devil In biblical religions the angel who endeavoured to usurp the sovereignty of God and was cast out of heaven, thus forming the traditional good versus evil, God versus **Satan** dualism. Throughout the mythologies of all religions, devils or their equivalents are manifestations of evils such as temptations, disease and all forms of human suffering.

Dhammapada *B.* Pal. Probably the best-known scripture of Theravada Buddhism, consisting of an anthology of 423 verses spoken by the Buddha traditionally in response questions put to him on different occasions. The Dhammapada is therefore regarded as a kind of compendium of his teaching and the Buddha clearly stated that anyone who reads it and practises the teachings will experience the joy of 'awakening'. It has been translated from Pali into many languages.

Dhanb *I*. Arab. 'sin'. For Muslims there are two categories of sin: i) *Dhanb*, inadvertent sin; and ii) *Ithm*, intentional sin. A sin is any action or thought that distracts a person from the 'true path' human beings should follow, revealed by God in the Koran. Islamic tradition says that *Ithm* was not inherent in creation but became a part of human existence when Cain slew Abel. *Dhanb* can be corrected at will by a person's decision to change his behaviour. *Ithm*, by contrast, requires *tawba*, true repentance shown by remorse, pleading for God's forgiveness and the resolve never to sin in that way again. A sinner should make amends for all sins committed against another person. If a sinner is truly repentant there is no sin so grave as to be beyond the forgiveness of God.

For **Islam**, as for other biblical religions, the question of sin impinges on the nature of God's oneness and sovereignty. Put simply, if God is entirely sovereign and has predetermined everything in creation, where has evil or the recalcitrance of human will come from? In answer the **Mu'tazila**, a school of Islamic speculative philosophy, argued that God had bestowed free will on human beings with the result that people have both the power and the responsibility to choose how they act. This proposition is similar to that asserted by **Judaism** and **Christianity**, though the latter's solution to sin is radically different to that of Islam which, as with the Jews, disavowed any form of mediatory saviour. The notion of partnership with God, together with compromising the Lord's sovereignty, is anathema to orthodox Muslims and the Mu'tazila were suppressed. The Koran is not consistent in the way it presents this problem; there are texts asserting that God has both decreed and will judge wrong-doing, while other texts state clearly people's responsibility for their actions. Despite attempts to offer rationalized interpretations of Qur'anic texts dealing with predestination (an entire *Surah* is given up to the theme), **Ashari** theology, which represents Muslim orthodoxy, has the Koran on its side; a person's fate is sealed before birth, everything is predestined. See **Fatalism, Predestination, Sin**

Dharam Yudh *Sik*. Pun. The Sikh concept of the just war. War is permissible on five conditions: i) that it is a last resort; ii) that you are not the aggressor or fight for reasons of revenge; iii) conquered territory or property should not be annexed and appropriated but should be returned when peace is made; iv) that the soldiers should themselves be in accord with the justice of the war (thus there is no use of mercenaries) and soldiers should not drink, smoke or sexually abuse women; and v) that the war is fought with the minimum of force necessary to gain its objective. See **Jihad**

Dharamsala *H. B.* Skt. 'rest house'. A charitable hospice or temporary accommodation for travellers and pilgrims. The town so named is now famously associated with the exiled Tibetan community and the residence of the **Dalai Lama**. Dharamsala is situated in the northern Indian state of Himachal Pradesh and is divided into two parts, Lower and Upper Dharamsala. Today, Tibetan refugees from all over the world come to Dharamsala to receive the blessings and teachings from His Holiness, the Dalai Lama. Tourists and scholars from all over the world visit this reconstituted ancient civilization of Tibet at Dharamsala. See **Tibetan Buddhism**

Dharana *H*. Skt. 'binding' or 'concentration'. The 6th and 8th stages of **Yoga** in **Patanjali**'s system. See **Meditation**

Dharma *H. B. Z*. Skt. From the root *dhr*, meaning 'to support' or 'to hold'. Dharma has wide-ranging meanings. For **Hinduism** it represents what determines our true nature, the foundation of morality, ethics and religion and the overarching law of the universe. Perhaps the variant 'dharam' can simply be expressed as 'absolute truth'. Hindus use dharma to refer to lifestyle or conduct, which will vary according to **caste** and in association with the four goals of life, being the attainment of wealth, virtue, the satisfaction of sensuality and liberation. Each of these have to be pursued with regard to the right moral precepts. For Buddhists, 'dharam' represents each of these concepts, together with the law of **karma** and the teachings of the Buddha as universal truth. Dharma has its own being, it existed before the birth of the Buddha who embodied it as a result of his enlightenment. Once realized, dharma becomes the expression of reality, of things 'as they are' and of all the components of existence, both phenomena and **noumena**, the ideas or reflection of phenomena in the human mind.

Dhikr *I*. Arab. 'remembering' or 'reminding'. The term refers to the recitation of the Koran by memory. In general use, *Dhikr* helps Muslims to be mindful, at all times, of the Koran and its teachings. It is based on Qur'anic instructions such as 'O, you who believe, remember Allah with frequent dhikr' (Surah 33:41). *Dhikr* is also a technical term for the ritual recitations and services of the **Sufis** and **Dervishes**, usually in a group, although *dhikr* may be used for individual devotion. Remembrance is a religious activity that binds Muslims to their origins in the divine inspiration of Muhammad, sustained by revelation in the Koran.

Dhyana *H. B. Z*. Skt. 'meditation' or 'absorption'. Various nuances of meaning and practice are attached to this concept, but generally it refers to a deep level of **meditation** leading to lucid awareness and the elimination of all forms of duality. It is part of **Patanjali**'s system of **yoga** practice, in which an unbroken stream of attention is focused on a physical or mental object of concentration, as a means to attaining *samadhi*. In certain formalized practices *Dhyana Yoga* represents four stages of absorption or the Four Abodes of Mindfulness, beginning with the elimination of desire which brings a sense of joy and well-being. The second stage sees the quietening of the ever-restless process of thought, leading to a deep inner calm or 'one-pointedness'. In the third stage the sense of joy is replaced by peaceful equanimity, one remains aware and the sense of well-being is sustained. Finally, everything slips from consciousness, all forms of duality cease to register, the meditator and the object of meditation are one, only equanimity and a sense of bright wakefulness remain.

Dialectic Materialism A term given to Marxist philosophy by Communists and Communist parties. The dialectic principle tries to resolve conflict by rational discussion, a method that goes back to **Socrates**. For Marx (see **Marxism**) and **Engels**, however, it was **Hegel's** influence that dominated. The multi-layered philosophy as applied to the dialectic of **Capitalism** and **Communism** is accessible in copious litera-ture. Here it should be noted that the philosophy has been at odds with religion in all of its manifestations, emerging as a strong secular alterna-tive to religious commitment. Marx believed capitalist society to be seri-ously out of joint, in which people were 'alienated' from the product of their work and from society itself. Famously, religion was defined by Marx and Engels as 'the opiate of the masses', since in the face of alien-ation and suffering it supported what was only illusory happiness and comfort. To that extent, it served a necessary and beneficial social func-tion. Religion also provided the Marxist philosophy with a powerful simile: 'Unless a grain of wheat falls into the earth and dies, it remains alone; but if it dies, it bears much fruit' (John 12:24). In Marxist terms, 'each' must sacrifice himself to 'all' so that he in turn may be enriched and nourished. The principle is written into the Communist Manifesto: '... we shall have an association in which the free development of each is the condition for the free development of all.' It is not difficult to understand why the energy of dialectic materialist philosophy provides all the necessary conditions for Communism to offer an alternative to religion. See **Communistic Religious Movements**

Diana *R*. Sometimes referred to as 'Diana the Huntress', the cult was Rome's adoption of the Greek **Artemis**. She was the perpetual virgin and goddess of the hunt, animals, the forests and the moon. Her oak groves were particularly sacred. With Egeria the water nymph and Virbius the woodland god, she constituted a triad of goddesses. She was worshipped on the Aventine Hill and at Ephesus (see Acts 19:35) and was particularly revered by people of the lower classes and by slaves. She holds her place in modern mythology, for example, in Dianic **Wicca**.

Dianic Wicca *AE*. An alternative name for Feminist Dianic Witchcraft, a coven exclusively concerned with the goddess **Diana**, who is worshipped as the source and sustainer of life. While there are mixed-sex groups, many Dianics practise in women-only covens, the movement being vehe-mently feminist. Because its specific interest is in celebrating women and femininity, there is little interaction with other pagan groups. See **Neo-Paganism, New Age Religion, Wicca**

Diaspora *J*. The term is most familiarly associated with the Jewish community outside of Palestine and since 1948 outside the **State of Israel**. Jewish history makes a distinction between Diaspora and *galut*, exile, since Jews can be of the Diaspora without the sense of compulsion exile implies. The Diaspora has been a feature of Jewish history almost from the beginning and there are many excellent historical overviews that describe the different periods of migration, emigration and settlement (see for example Bright and Seltzer). The attitudes of dispersed Jews towards the 'homeland' vary and are complex. For the greater part of history, however well established their communities might have been, Jews thought of themselves as homeless, knowing that the homes they had were temporary and vulnerable and their future insecure. They prayed constantly for the biblical territory of Palestine to be restored to the Jewish people and for the coming of the Messiah which would bring about a similar result. The hope of the restoration of **Zion** took on powerful religious and political dimensions (see **Zionism**). Both before and after the establishment of the State of Israel, Jews who had settled across the world had become fully integrated with the cultures of their 'hosts' and there are Jews today who would regard Israel as a foreign country. Conversely there are others who are, in every way, staunch supporters of Israel and visit regularly, sometimes as a form of pilgrimage. Both in Israel and in the Diaspora every tradition of Judaism is to be found, including Jews who are entirely secular, but who would still unequivocally count themselves to be Jews and, where appropriate, Israeli. See **Judaism; Judaism, Ethnic Divisions of; Synagogue**

Dietary Law Most religions have dietary laws prohibiting certain kinds of foods or imposing a partial prohibition for specific fasts and periods. In Judaism, biblical law prohibits some kinds of food. The Bible prohibits consuming blood, since it is believed to carry the essence of life, 'For the life of all flesh – its blood is its life. Therefore I say to the Israelite people: You shall not partake of the blood of any flesh, for the life of all flesh is its blood. Anyone who partakes of blood shall be cut off' (Lev. 17:14). The range and detail of Jewish dietary law is vast and complex and based on criteria that determines whether or not a food is kosher, 'clean'. Certain kinds of 'clean' foods cannot be mixed, thus milk (including milk-based dairy produce) and meat are forcibly prohibited. During the observation of **Lent**, Christians may chose to abstain from meat. **Mormons** abstain from alcohol and coffee. The Muslim *halal* lists among its prohibited foods pork and birds of prey, while alcohol and other stimulants are avoided by the devout. Hindus do not eat beef because the cow (see **Sacred Cow**) is held to be a sacred animal, but products from cows – milk, ghee (clarified butter) and yoghurt – are considered innately pure and beneficial to the purity of body, mind and spirit. The practice of *ahimsa*, the principle of non-violence, is applied by Hindus and Buddhist to animals, many are therefore lacto-ovo-vegetarians. Such practices will vary according to the traditions of the countries and regions in which adherents live.

Din *I*. Arab. 'religion'. The term is used to denote a general way of life. *Din* is the addition of the **Five Pillars of Islam**, a combination of religious belief and religious duty manifest in the way Muslims live their lives based on law, action, duty, conduct and obligation. The purpose of *Din* is to be committed to Truth and to embody it in the social order in the process of creating a new world made in the image of that Truth. Thus, *Din* 'is a system of life that prepares man to play this role and provides him with guidelines for the development of a new personality and a new society.' (Islamic Foundation, Leicester, 1976)

Dinka *A*. Nilotic people of southern Sudan, neighbours of the **Nuer** and **Shilluk**. Ethnically they are black Africans differing markedly from the Arab tribes. A pastoral lifestyle characterizes their religion, which is **animistic**. Their god, Nhialic (the sky) is associated with rain, thunder and lightning and is encountered by means of *jok*, powerful spirits that communicate by temporary possession. A central rite is the sacrifice of oxen undertaken by a priestly clan, the 'Masters of the Fishing Spear'. Initiation is the most important rite of passage during which young men are marked on the forehead. Their religion has been subjected to violent repression by the Sudanese Islamic government based in Khartoum. See **African Religion**

Dionysus *G*. The god of mystery religion rites, such as those of **Demeter** and **Persephone** at Eleusis near Athens. His own rites, the Dionysian Mysteries, were the most secretive of all (see **Bacchantes**) and in the Thracian form of the cult Dionysus wore a *basseris*, a fox skin as the symbol of new life. He is thought by Herodotus (2:146) to have arrived later in Greece than the Olympian pantheon and was equated with both **Bacchus** and the Liberalia, 'the free ones' (see **Bacchanalia**). In the mythology one account of his birth gives him a mortal mother, Semele and a god, **Zeus**, as his father; in another version he is the son of Zeus and Persephone, the queen of the Underworld. Both accounts of his birth and those of his life are involved and convoluted, as with most mythologies concerning the Greek gods. See **Greek Religion, Satyr**

Disciple *L. Discipulus*, 'a pupil'. Someone who has learned and believes the truths of a teacher and has become an adherent. Although familiarly associated with the followers of Jesus of Nazareth, there can be 'disciples' of any teacher, religious or secular, for example **Plato** or **Marx**. Even though the 12 disciples of Jesus became the 12 **Apostles**, the terms should not be confused and it should be noted that the Apostles called together a meeting of their own disciples (Acts 6:17). The term 'discipleship' defines the commitment to become a follower of a teacher.

Discordianism A modern chaos-based religion founded in the late 1950s which has been described as 'a religion disguised as a joke disguised as a religion', and has been called 'Zen for "roundeyes"', a disparaging term for English-speaking Asians. Traditional religion puts value on notions such as the 'order' and 'harmony' of the universe, while Discordianism claims that chaos and disharmony are equally valid principles. The Greek goddess Eris (Gk. 'strife'), known to the Romans as Discordia, is the mother deity of Discordianism. The scripture or foundational document, is the *Principia Discordia*, written by Malaclypse the Younger, an alias, perhaps, for Greg Hill. In the introduction to the 5th edition, Kerry Thornley writes, 'If organized religion is the opium of the masses, then disorganized religion is the marijuana of the lunatic fringe.' The movement is organized on the basis of the Five Degrees of POEE (a manifestation of Discordianism) and its main doctrine is The Law of Fives. To know more it is necessary to read the *Principia* in all 'five' of its editions. *Bon courage*!

Discursive Meditation *Lectio Divina*, a form of **meditation** that combines reading, prayer, meditation and contemplation. It is a 'thinking' form of meditation that centres, for example, on a verse from the Bible or other literature, which one 'thinks through' rationally, expounding it and applying it to oneself. It is a mental and interiorized practice that requires imagination and visualization. Probably the best-known examples are the *Spiritual Exercises* of Ignatius **Loyola**. The discursive nature of the method seems in stark contrast to, for example, **Zen** Buddhist meditation which endeavours to be 'one-pointed', focused and formless.

Divination A magical and supernatural method of accessing information which is unobtainable by other means. Such information includes knowledge of future events, the recovery of lost objects, insight into hidden character-traits, etc. It is to be distinguished from fortune-telling or prophecy in that the methods are usually employed in a social context, associated with religious beliefs and rituals. Thought by sceptics to be the spurious practice of charlatans, it remains a current feature of many of the world's established religions. Examples include the **Ifa Oracle** of the Yoruba, the *I Ching* of **Taoism**, the consultation of Oracle or Dragon Bones practised in China from 1350 BCE and dream interpretation (see **Dreams**). Whatever the view of sceptics, the 'need' for divination has not abated as the worldwide use of **astrology**, the **Tarot**, **palmistry**, **phrenology** and the Ouija board attests. The **Etruscans** practised a form of divination known as hepatoscopy, an examination of the liver, a method that was brought to Rome. See **Anthropomancy**, **Auspicia**, **Bibliomancy**, **Mantike**, **Oracles**

Divine Kingship A religio-political concept that understands rulers to be the incarnation, manifestation, mediator or agent of God or gods. The first established examples were the dynasties of Egyptian **Pharaohs**, closely followed by the Roman Emperors (see **Emperor Worship**). In Europe the concept took the form of the Divine Right of Kings as authority for political **absolutism**, founded on a belief in God-given Royal rights ritually expressed in Coronation and **anointing**. Early in the reign of Louis XIV (1638–1715), Bossuet (bishop, theologian and court preacher), drawing on the **Old Testament** precedent, asserted that kings were God's anointed representatives on earth. The English Stuarts, however, were not able to persuade Parliament of their divinity. See **Apotheosis**

FINAL WORD: 'Kings are justly called Gods, for that they exercise a manner or resemblance of divine power on earth: for if you consider the attributes of God, you will see how they agree in the person of the King.' (James I, *Works*)

Divine Life Society Founded by Swami Sivananda Saraswati in India in 1936. Its philosophy is based on spiritual and intellectual development leading to **realization** and to making known 'the inherent divinity in all human beings'. The Swami's intention was to offer ways by which people could express in their lives the characteristics of Ultimate Reality. The process is not simply other-worldly, but includes the active expression of social and personal ethical values, learned and applied by austere discipline. The Society is heavily involved worldwide in promoting its own educational and spiritual programme and in charitable work that provides relief to lepers and to any who suffer from poverty, disease and ignorance. While its headquarters remain at Utteranchal, in India, it has major branches throughout the world. See **Kriya, Yoga**

Divine Light Mission *H*. A Hindu-based New Age sect, know also as 'Elan Vital', founded by Sri Hans Ji Maharaji in northern India in1960, focused on the realization of the 'God within'. On his father's death in 1966 the Maharaji's fourth son, Prem Rawat, assumed the leadership, bringing the Mission to the USA in 1971. The Mission's practice of inner peace was sustained by *satsang*, association with higher truth through a guru and by service and meditation, which amounted to what Prem Rawat called 'Knowledge', that is *Kriyas*, techniques within a yoga discipline. (See **Kriya, Yoga**). Members meditated formally twice a day and attended Knowledge discourses. Vegetarianism was encouraged. After the Houston Astrodome gathering in 1973, the Mission became the butt of the **anti-cult movement**; that and the criticisms of deprogrammed ex-members, brought the Mission into disrepute. Allegations were made to the effect that Rawat and his company laid claims to personal divinity for personal gain and that he exploited the 'premies', the students, in order to create a luxurious lifestyle for himself. The original success and spread of the Mission was remarkable, at one time amounting to 480 centres in 38 countries, with an estimated six million members in India alone. The Mission eventually foundered on accumulated debts and internal conflict, particularly those of Rawat's family. By 1990 the worldwide membership had dwindled to just over one million.

Divine Mother *H*. For Hindus, the function and attribute of God that is responsible for creation as *Shakti*, the force or female energy traditionally associated with **Shiva**. See **Astarte, Earth Mother, Mariology, Mother goddess, Shaktism**

Divine Plan of the Ages A concept held by various religious traditions that God, like an architect, has laid down plans outlining human destiny from the covenantal promise made to Abraham, until such time as his ultimate purpose for the world is fulfilled. It is also the title of several books by various authors, which set out the biblical agenda and the curriculum for the progress of this plan. Several religions, for example the **Baha'i**, have a concept of sacred history comprising universal cycles and dispensations that stretch over millions of years. Hindus and Buddhists believe in a cycle of creation and destruction in epochs that last for hundreds of thousands of years. Since the 19th century, **Pyramidology** has contributed to the notion of a divine plan. C. T. Russell, among others, provided a historical-eschatological interpretation of the Great Pyramid based on Nelson Barbour's system of biblical chronology. His conclusion was that the Great Pyramid is the 'divine plan of the ages' in stone and part of that plan was that it should be encoded long before the Bible was written. FINAL WORD: '… if we ignore or neglect the Pyramid in these perilous days at the close of this Age we will miss something valuable which God has specially provided for us in this day and generation. The Great Pyramid displays the Christian religion upon a scientific basis in response to the scientific appeal of our age.' (Adam Rutherford)

Divine Principles See **Unification Church**

Divine Right See **Apotheosis, Divine Kingship**

Divine Science A religious group founded in 1887 in Denver, Colorado, by Nora Brooks and Fannie James. It was one of several churches that sprung up under the impetus of the **New Thought Movement**. The group eventually established churches throughout the United States. The Church believes in the omnipresence and benevolence of God, but does not teach the dualism of God being opposed by Satan. Divine Science asserts that every living being is indwelt by God and that human nature is made up of God's nature. Nothing a person can do can separate them from the source from which sprung both their physical life and spiritual potential. Our essence is spiritual and the purpose is to let go of the physical aspects of life until, gradually, the spiritual dominates. Practice is thought-based, since the mind is the Temple of God; if the mind is truly spiritual, the word and action will follow. Its emphasis is on spiritual healing modelled on Jesus Christ's healing ministry. See **Christian Scientists**

Diwali *H*. The Hindu festival of lights. See **Hindu Festivals and Feasts, Hinduism**

Docetism *X*. The heretical belief that Jesus did not have a physical body and that bodily appearance was an illusion, as was his crucifixion. The belief is generally attributed to **Gnostics**, who asserted that all matter was evil and that therefore God would never incarnate himself. The concept of illusion is similar to that of the Hindu-Buddhist concept that everything temporary is but the illusion of reality (see **Maya**). Docetism was rejected by ecumenical councils that established Christian orthodoxy. It re-emerged with the **Cathars**, but the **Albigensian** massacres finally eliminated the doctrine. See **Bogomils, Manicheanism**

Dogmatics *X*. The systematic study of dogma, especially that of the Christian Churches. The subject matter of Dogmatics are religious truths given by revelation, defined by the Councils of the various Churches and summarized as **creeds**. The Bible is accepted as the source book of Christian truth but it does not organize or systematize the truths in any way, thus the task was taken up by theologians starting, perhaps, with Origen (185–254 CE). Another term used is Systematic Theology. The development of critical-historical techniques of biblical study, backed by archaeology and a securer knowledge of biblical languages, led to new methods of interpretation (see **Demythology**). The dogmaticians as defenders of Christian orthodoxy produced vast works such as for example, Karl **Barth**'s *Church Dogmatics*. See **Greek Fathers, Latin Fathers, Scepticism**

Dogon Religion *A*. The Dogon are a group of people living on the central plateau region of Mali. They are known for their mythology, mask dances, wooden sculptures and architecture. Although significant numbers have been converted to Islam and Christianity, their indigenous religion flourishes. It is animistic in character with Nommo, the entire universe and Amma the creator god, forming a central male-female dualism. Yuruga, the trickster who impeded the orderly development of the universe, represents the unpredictable aspect of life. Order was restored by Lebe, the first man, who was sacrificed. The star Sirius, which they call *Po Tolo*, is the seed of the Milky Way and the navel of the universe. Dogon ancestry is traced by the patrilineal method, the original ancestors being four pairs of twins, making eight the sacred number. Each village has a headman, the *hogon* and the entire social and agricultural life is arranged so as to symbolize their cosmology and intricate numerology. Their knowledge of stars, especially that of Sirius B, which is invisible without a telescope, inspired Robert Temple's book *The Sirius Mystery* (1975), which suggested that the Dogon had ancestral astronauts. This beguiling notion has since been refuted by more recent scholarship.

Dokhma *Zo*. See **Dakma**

Dominionism See **Christian Reconstruction**

Dominicans *X*. A Roman Catholic Order known also as Friars Preachers or, in England, by their nickname, **Black Friars**. The order was founded and constituted by St Dominic at two General Councils gathered at Bologna in 1220 and 1221. Originally, Dominic was a **Franciscan**, but went to Rome to obtain the permission of Pope Honorius III to found an order to win back the **Albigensian** heretics of Languedoc, in southern France. At first they practised individual and community poverty, living by begging. In 1475 Pope Sixtus IV revoked their law of poverty and the order was allowed to own property. It eventually became known for its preaching and scholarship and during the Medieval period provided many of the leaders of European thought, including Albertus Magnus (1200–80) and his pupil Thomas Aquinas (1225–74). A succession of Popes used the Dominicans for preaching crusades, for the Inquisitions and to accompany Portuguese and Spanish explorers. There is a Second Order of enclosed nuns and a Third Order of Sisters who live an active life freer of confinement.

Donatists X. A schismatic group of the African church which occurred in the 4th and 5th centuries CE. It sprung from a refusal to accept Caecilian as Bishop of **Carthage** because he had been consecrated (311 CE) by a defector from Diocletian's persecution of Christians. In opposition, Numidian bishops consecrated Majorinus who was succeeded by Donatus, after whom the schism was named. They drew heavily on the Numidian jealousy of Carthage and regional economic problems and being theologically conservative they believed they alone constituted the true church. A commission in Rome decided against the Donatists and from 316–321 CE, the State intervened to suppress the schism by force, but they survived until the 7th–8th century when the church in Africa was virtually destroyed.

Doukhobors X. A Christian sect established in Russia during the 16th–17th centuries. The name, meaning 'Spirit Wrestler', was coined derogatively by priests of the Russian Orthodox Church. The sect rejected the formalism and ritual of Russian orthodoxy, together with secular government, the authority of the Bible and the divinity of Jesus. Committed pacifists, they refused military service and were harshly suppressed and subjected to torture and exile. Tolstoy and other sympathizers, with the help of the Society of Friends (see **Quakers**) in England, petitioned Nicholas II to allow the sect to emigrate and in 1899 the first group settled in Canada. The radical wing, the 'Freedomites' or 'Sons of Freedom' used subversive action, mass nudity and arson, in an attempt to make the Canadian Government deport them back to Russia. It is estimated that around 30,000 Doukhobors live in Canada, with a similar number still living in Russia.

Dravidians The early inhabitants of India and ancestors of the Tamils. They were thought to be the original settlers of the Indus valley, but by process of migration continued on to India and Ceylon as early as 4000 BCE. Traditionally, it was understood they were subject to 'invasion' by the **Aryans**, but the invasion theory is now in question. Certainly, the Aryans followed the same migratory routes into India and the two cultures assimilated to a considerable degree. The Dravidians established a settled village agriculture centred on the cult of the *gramadevata*, Skt. 'village deity'. Being female, the goddess reflected the earth-mother perceptions of communities dependent on farming crops and grazing cattle. What has survived of this early Dravidian culture into modern Indian Hinduism, is both the village agricultural pattern and the inclination to think of the sacred in terms of motherhood. Gilbert Slater, suggests that the dominant and formative law of **karma**, is also thought to have had its origins in Dravidian religion. See **Indus Valley Civilization**

Dreams The act of dreaming and the content of dreams remains one of the unexplained enigmas of human experience. Egyptian texts record some of the dreams of kings in which gods figured; probably the most notable example is the dream of Thothmes IV (1425–08 BCE) recorded on a stele of pink granite set between the paws of the great Sphinx. In ancient Greek and Roman society dreams were regarded as one of the chief means whereby the gods communicated with humans. **Divination** through dreams was an established science in the ancient world. The **Old Testament** recounts Joseph's interpretation of Pharaoh's dreams as a warning of seven years of plenty followed by seven years of famine. In the West, the use of dreams for divination was associated with witchcraft, but they were also the inspiration of great vocations, for example those of **St Francis of Assisi**, and St Dominic. For **Jung** (1875–1961) 'dreams were a kind of impartial photography of unconscious life', the 'voice of the other'; he regarded them to be a part of what he called 'the collective unconscious', a notion Freud denied. For his part, Freud (1856–1939) understood dreams to be neurotic phenomena populated by 'manifest' and 'latent' content, the one being the memory of the dream, the other its meaning discernible through analysis. See **Symbolism**, **Visions**
FINAL WORD: [That dreams] 'may be situated in the most primitive part of the brain and not in the cerebral cortex also confirms the ancestral, hereditary and collective basis of the dream.' (Raymond de Becker)

Druids *AE*. The name of a priestly class in Celtic society, widely spread through pre-Roman Western Europe and Britain. The name 'Druid' may be derived from a word meaning oak and there is an association with the mistletoe that was cut from it. A lack of primary sources makes it difficult to discern the Druid practices that were distinct from other forms of pagan animism, such as that of the pre-Christian Irish Celts (see **Celtic Religion**). What seems clear is that Druids were custodians of ancient lore and wisdom, of astronomical and calendric knowledge and given to prophecy, law-making and the almost holocaustic sacrifice of both animals and humans bound up in the huge wicker constructions described by Strabo and Caesar. Aspects of the lore survives in the celebration of Halloween, the making of corn-dollies and other harvest rituals, in the myths of Puck, woodwoses, the Green Man and in superstitions associated with luck and with unlucky plants and animals. Modern Druidism has both a cultural and religious strand, the one associated with the poetry, literature and music of the Eisteddfods, the other with the Order of the Bards, Ovates and Druids and the solstice ceremonies held at places like Stonehenge, Tower Hill, Primrose Hill and other locations. But it is not always possible to distinguish between the two strands. The assumption, made by the antiquary John Aubrey, that the megalithic sites were Druid temples, is probably mistaken. William Blake, in *Jerusalem*, makes it clear that he did not like them, 'The Building is Natural Religion, & its Altars Natural Morality; A building of eternal death, whose proportions are eternal despair …'

Druj *Zo.* The Kingdom of the Lie, populated by the evil **Daevas**, the spirits that were originally Indo-Iranian gods. Druj represents the evil side of the Zoroastrian dualism, a manifestation of **Angra Mainyu**. In some texts of the **Avesta** the follower of the Lie is a thieving nomad, a spirit that undermines well-regulated agriculture and animal husbandry. In the Avesta *Druj* is found constantly opposed to *Asa*, the Right or Good, aspect of the dualism known as **Ahura Mazda**. Human beings are held in the tension of these polarities, with the responsibility to choose. See **Dualism and Non-Dualism, Fravarane, Zoroastrianism**

Druze *I.* A religious community spread through the Lebanon, Israel, Syria, Turkey and Jordan with small expatriate groups living in the USA, Canada, Latin America, Australia and Europe. They appeared in the 11th century as an off-shoot of **Isma'ili Shi'ism**, believing in the Imamate (see **Imam**) – that is, the divine authority and inspiration of the Fatimid Caliph, al-Hakim be-Amr al-Lah. The movement developed under the direction of a Persian missionary, Hamzah Ali who proclaimed al-Hakim to be the incarnation of God and 'Ruler in the Name of God', who would eventually 'disappear', only to return again at the 'end of days'. During his lifetime Hakim was opposed by orthodox Muslims for his apostasy and extreme violence, especially towards religious minorities. In 1009, he destroyed the Church of the Holy Sepulchre in Jerusalem.

The Druze do not practise the **Five Pillars of Islam** like orthodox Muslims do and they are better understood as a separate religion rather than as an Islamic sect. Since the death of Hakim in 1021, they have been violently persecuted by orthodox Muslims and have survived by means of what, in Islam, is called *taqiyya*, dissimulation, keeping their true beliefs secret and discouraging both converts to Druze and Druze conversion to other religions. For this reason what they actually believe and how they practice is wrapped in an aura of secrecy. There are two Druze groups the *Uqqal*, 'Knowledgeable Initiates', and the *Juhhal*, 'the Ignorant'. The *Uqqal*, who make up about ten per cent of the community, shave their heads and grow moustaches, wear dark clothes and white turbans and form the military and political leadership. The *Juhhal* do not have access to the *Hikma*, the Book of Wisdom, one of the Druze sacred and secret holy texts, nor do they receive formal religious education.

At its inception Druze thought was syncretistic, drawing on many influences that included Greek philosophy, **Gnosticism** and

Christianity. In summary, we can say the Druze are committed monotheists, their name for themselves being, 'The People of Monotheism'. The basis of their belief is that God continually interacts with the world through various forms of emanation; in addition there will be periodical *makam*, manifestations of God veiled in human form that disguises the divine nature. The Druze believe in **reincarnation**, thus the veiled human manifestations may be a reincarnation of an earlier leader or prophet. Al-Hakim was the last of the incarnations from whom emanated the Five Cosmic Principles that form the core of Druze philosophy. These five principles are represented by a complex colour symbolism: i) green represents intelligence and symbolizes the farmer and life with the soil; ii) red, the soul and symbolizes the heart and love of humanity; iii) yellow, the word and symbolizes the sun and wheat; iv) blue, precedents and symbolizes faith and the sky; and v) white, immanence and symbolizes purity and the air. The colour symbolism can also be represented by a series of numbers and as a five pointed star. The five colours also combine to form the Druze flag, but it has no international status. In the Lebanon, Syria and Israel, the Druze are recognized as an independent religious community with its own administrative and court system, but these are subsumed by the constitution and legal systems of the host States.

Dualism and Non-Dualism The debate concerning dualism and non-dualism is threaded through the history of Eastern and Western philosophy. Western tradition has mostly assumed the dualistic framework while in the East, as both Hindu and Buddhist philosophy developed, non-dualism became the accepted view. In Western philosophy dualism concerns the basic categories into which substances can be divided. They are either material or mental and neither can be part of the other. In general, dualism is a world-view that the 'real' or 'ultimate' is of two kinds or vested in two controlling absolute powers, usually cast in opposition to each other. We are familiar with such conflicting categories as spirit and matter, good and evil and with the way they are represented by the culturally established archetypes such as sinner and saint, God and the Devil. This entrenched dichotomy carries over into a Western view of man as having two irreconcilable substances, the physical (flesh, the body) and the mental or spiritual (mind, soul, spirit). In religious terms this perception involves the individual in a state of spiritual warfare in which ultimate powers make battle for the soul.

Monism stands in opposition to both dualism and **Pluralism**. The latter holds that the world consists of many kinds of substances and that these cannot be reduced to one, as in Monism or two, as in Dualism. Monistic philosophy represented, for example, by **Spinoza** and **Hegel**, takes the view that reality is of one kind and it does not matter which view a monist might take if he stays with the one reality. For example, a monist may hold the view that everything is spirit (**Idealism**), another that everything is matter (**Materialism**). As a view of man, monism rejects any body/mind or flesh/spirit duality. The neutral monism of William **James**, and Bertrand **Russell**'s **logical atomism**, holds the view that these seeming oppositions are only different aspects of the one being or substance. 'The material of which the world is constructed is neither mind nor matter, but something anterior to both' (Russell). All these views have their variations and qualifications. For example, the Irish philosopher George Berkley (1685–1753) asserts the existence of a plurality of substances, but remains a monist since he says they are all mental substances and thus of the same kind.

Generally, Western non-dualistic philosophy has made little inroad into the prevailing religious traditions of **Judaism**, **Christianity** and **Islam**, each of which were in this respect, influenced by **Zoroastrianism**. In Eastern religious philosophy the debate focuses on the relationship between the individual and the absolute or ultimate reality, rather than on the constituent elements and substances of the universe. Hinduism developed philosophies that moved between the extremes of non-dualism and dualism. The view of non-dualism is put by **Shankara** (788–820 CE), the representative of **Advaita-Vedanta**, a philosophy that led to the renewal of Hinduism at a time when it had been somewhat displaced by Buddhism. He affirmed that the soul (**atman**) and God (**Brahma**) together with the entire universe, are identical. What we see as separately existing, ever changing things and shapes is like a mirage, an image we take to be real, but obscuring the reality behind it. Visible creation, the soul and God are identical. An illustration sometimes used from particle physics, shows matter to consist of continually moving fields of energy; in much the same way the *rishis*, the writers of the **Vedanta**, recognized that reality consists of energy in the form of consciousness and that we human beings, because of our identification with the ego-limited body, perceive the universe as material by means of our natural senses. That which is real and unchanging is overlaid in the mind by our perception of an ever-changing manifest world of names and forms. Shankara's own, well known, illustration is the piece of rope that is taken in the dark, to be a snake. All the emotions we have, of anxiety, repugnance and fear are induced by a snake that was never born, will never die and which has no existence except in the mind. Once the rope is recognized as rope, it can never turn back into the idea of a snake. The initial error involves not only nescience of what it is, but also the superimposition of a notion that has nothing to do with what is. *Advaita* teaches that we, in our ignorance, continually superimpose the idea 'snake' (the manifest world) on the 'rope' (Brahman). Shankara wrote, 'May this one sentence proclaim the essence of a thousand books: *Brahman* alone is real, the world is appearance, the Self is nothing but *Brahman*.'

Ramanuja (b. c.mid-11th century CE) reacted to what he felt was the impersonal abstraction of Shankara and developed a philosophy of *vishishtadvaita-Vedenta*, Skt. 'qualified non-dualism'. In this he offers a view of the world founded on a spiritual principle (Brahman) from which the individual soul and inanimate nature are essentially distinct. Ramanuja's focus is the relationship between God and world; God is real and independent, whereas individual souls and the world are equally real, but not independent, since their reality is fully dependent on God. Personal values are subordinate to the impersonal supreme reality, but a person who loves God, truth, beauty and goodness, possesses a reality that cannot be reconciled with the abstraction of *advaita* – non-dualism.

Of interest to Westerners, is the Indian 13th-century philosopher **Madhva**, who moved Ramanuja's qualified non-dualism, into a pure dualism. The basic qualities of the universe and of our lives, of God, the soul and all phenomena are and remain completely distinct. Thus salvation or enlightenment has nothing to do with union with God. Rather than transcend the subject-object relationship, it must be maintained so that one can draw as close to God as possible and dwell in his salvatory grace. There are more than just echoes here of Jewish and Christian salvation theology and it is possible that even as early as the 13th century a Christian influence has touched this aspect of Hinduism.

It is the term **advaita**, which represents in Buddhism a non-duality, that is, perhaps, its purest and most developed form. It is expressed in the term '**Mind-Only**'.'Our Essence of Mind is intrinsically pure. All things are only its manifestation and good deeds and evil deeds are only the result of good thoughts and evil thoughts respectively.' (The Sutra of Wei Lang) And, 'All that we are is the result of what we have thought; it is founded on our thoughts, it is made up of our thoughts.' (The Dhammapada, Primary sources: Buddhism). Buddhist philosophy takes the notion of non-duality to its logical conclusion in making the point that even the relationship between the thinker and thought, must be transcended. Non-duality does not allow the mind to exist on the one hand and its thoughts or experiences on the other. The mind, free from subject-object relationship, is no longer divided against itself. The experience of this in meditation is *samadhi*, a state of profound peace.

FINAL WORD: 'When you live in the wisdom home, you'll no longer find a barrier between "I" and "you", "this" and "that", "inside" and "outside"; you'll have come, finally, to your true home, the state of non-duality.' (Sogyal Rinpoche)

Dukkha *B*. Pali. Suffering, a central concept of **Buddhism** and the theme of the **Four Noble Truths**. 'Suffering' is the nearest word in English, but it is too strong, casting a negative and misunderstood haze over Buddhism. Dukkha does include the standard notion of suffering, but its truth lies deeper and has to do with a feeling of inadequacy, a sense of lack brought about by the impermanence and transitoriness of life. See **Anatman, Anitya**

Dunkers or **Dunkard Brethren** *X*. A Christian sect that emigrated from Germany to Pennsylvania in the 18th century to escape persecution. Their name comes from, 'dunking', a reference to **baptism** by total emersion, available only to adults since it was given on confession of faith. They try to emulate the life of the early Christians, holding an *agape*, 'love feast', biannually. Through missionary initiative, the sect has grown in recent years and is known as, the Dunkard Brethren.

Durga or **Devi** *H*. Skt. 'The unfathomable One', 'Inaccessible' or 'The Great Goddess'. As the consort and female energy of Shiva, she has two aspects, calm and fierce, but she is most frequently worshipped as Durga, her terrible form. She wields huge power and her iconography depicts this, showing her ten-armed body standing on the back of a lion. She can either punish human beings or endow them with grace. She is the destroyer of the demons of ignorance, but feeds the poor and guides those seeking realization. In Bengal she is celebrated in an annual festival, the *Durga-Puja*.

Durkheim, Emile (1858–1917) French sociologist, thought to be the father of modern sociology, who made a formative contribution to the sociology of religion. Religion is one of the elements of society that helps maintain cohesion and balance, thus for Durkheim it was part of a functionalist social theory. Religion divides the world into what is sacred and what is profane, a distinction that has its inception in the origins of religion. Durkheim suggested that religion is made up of 'elementary forms' evident in the earliest characteristics common to all religions. In broad terms these elementary forms are suggested in his definition of religion: 'A religion is a unified system of beliefs and practices relative to sacred things, that is to say, things set apart and forbidden, beliefs and practices which unite into one single moral community called a Church, all those who adhere to them. The second element which thus finds a place in our definition is no less essential than the first; for by showing that the idea of religion is inseparable from that of the Church; it makes it clear that religion should be an eminently collective thing.' (Durkheim) From this, we can extrapolate such elementary forms as, i) a unified system of belief; ii) the idea of the 'sacred'; iii) beliefs and practices that have a unifying effect on a moral community, such as the Church; and, iv) religion as a collective entity. One of Durkheim's running themes was Totemism (see **Totem**) which he took to be an elementary form since it perfectly defines the sacred-profane dividing line, together with the function it fulfils in unifying the clan or society. See **Introversionism**
FINAL WORD: 'For a society is not made up merely of the mass of individuals who compose it, the ground which they occupy, the things which they use and the movements which they perform, but above all is the idea which it forms of itself.' (Durkheim)

Dvaita-Vedanta *H*. Skt. *dvaita*, 'duality'. One of the philosophical schools of Hindu **Vedanta**. It was developed by the philosopher **Madhva**, to contradict the non-dualism of **Shankara**'s **Advaita-Vedanta**. Dvaita-Vedanta argues that the individual soul and God are eternally separated and that the world is not *maya*, illusion, but reality. See **Dualism and Non-Dualism**, **Ramanuja**

Dzogchen *B*. Tib. 'great perfection', also known as *ati-yoga* or extraordinary yoga. It forms the principal teaching of the **Nyingmapa** school of **Tibetan Buddhism**. Dzogchen is considered to be the definitive, yet most secret teaching of **Shakyamuni Buddha**. Put simply, the teaching focuses on a concept of purity of mind that is believed to be present in all human beings and only needs to be realized or recognized as such. The tradition was carried from India to Tibet by **Padmasambhava** and Vimilamitra in the 8th century, but it was not until the 14th century that **Longchenpa** brought various aspects of the teaching together to form a system. The heart of this system is the axiom that our minds are a self-existing intelligence, pure and uncontaminated by nature. Because we do not recognize this, we remain caught up in the cycles of **samsara**. The practice of *dzogchen* opens the door to primordial knowledge, which itself is the unity of emptiness with clarity. That is, we come to see clearly and without obstruction, the true nature of our mind that has been hidden under layers of misconception. We need to practise without any thought of aims or success, simply practising will lead us to the realization of the 'rainbow body', that is, the dissolution of the physical body into pure light. Sogyal Rinpoche tells us that, 'dzogchen is a state, the state, the primordial state, that state of total awakening that is the heart-essence of all the buddhas and all spiritual paths, the summit of an individual's spiritual evolution.' Training in *dzogchen* should be carried out under the supervision of an accredited master. At its simplest it is divided into View, **Meditation**, and Action. 'View' is seeing things as they actually are, realizing that the true nature of our minds is actually the true nature of everything. The absolute nature of our minds is 'emptiness', every other view is merely relative. 'Meditation' is the practice of concentrating on the View, resting in it, letting everything else go, to the point of abandoning mental concepts, but without effort or without thought to the result. 'Action', is better understood as awareness or mindfulness. Having glimpsed the View and being able to sustain that in meditation, we must always be aware of our thoughts in everyday life, mindfully watching the way we live. It is very hard to rest in meditation without the distraction of discursive thought and it is hard to self-liberate the thoughts and emotions as they arise. Dzogchen assures us that we are capable of doing it.

FINAL WORD: 'Masters of Dzogchen tradition have stressed again and again that without being thoroughly and deeply acquainted with the essence and method of self-liberation through long practice, meditation only furthers the path of delusion. This may seem harsh, but it is the case, because only self-liberation of thoughts can really end the reign of delusion …' (Sogyal Rinpoche)

E

Earth Mother The Earth Mother, **Mother Goddess** or Great Goddess, has prehistoric origins transmitted in myths identifying the earth as a female who mates with the male **Sky Father** to produce the universe. The concept is universal. In Greek mythology her name was **Gaia**, 'land', the goddess of the earth and she is present in Icelandic, Norse, Lithuanian and Germanic mythology. She is known under many names, for example in Pacific culture, as Maori and in ancient Mexican traditions as Tonantzin Tlalli, 'Revered Mother Earth'. In the Andes the cult of Pachamama is still followed and in Indian religions, she is 'Gayatri'. Gaia is currently worshipped by many neo-pagan cults, some of which understand her actually to be the earth or a spiritual embodiment of the earth. Others believe Gaia to be the goddess of all creation, the Mother Goddess in whom all other gods originate. The mythology has been taken up by the scientific theory, the Gaia Hypothesis, which suggests the planet Earth is a single, highly complex organism. See **Environmentalism, Navajo, Rhea**

Easter *X*. A 'moveable' feast and the most significant festival of the Christian year, celebrated between March 22nd and April 25th. The festival starts on Good Friday when **Jesus Christ's crucifixion** is traditionally remembered, with the climax on Easter Sunday, the day of his resurrection. There are considerable variations within both Western and Eastern observance as well as between them. Easter, like **Christmas** and other festivals, is nowadays celebrated as a non-religious event of huge commercial importance, with statutory national holidays. The chocolate Easter egg and Easter 'bunny' are, for children, the most familiar images of the holiday. Like all ancient religious festivals Easter was subjected to pagan influences. The Venerable Bede records that the word 'Easter' is derived from *Eostremonat* and thus from the so-called goddess of the Anglo-Saxons, Eostre. Others have suggested an association between Eostre and the Sumerian goddess **Ishtar** (**Astarte**) and that the Good Friday tradition of hot cross buns and the Easter Sunday custom of painting and rolling hard-boiled eggs, were features of Chaldean rites (see **Chaldea**). Easter is closely linked with the Jewish festival of **Passover**.

Eastern Orthodoxy See **Orthodox Church**

Ebionites From the Hebrew *ebionim*, 'the poor ones'. A Judean Jewish-Christian sect associated with **John the Baptist** and Jesus' brother, James. Because they were led by a relative of Jesus some scholars (e.g. Hyam Maccoby, Robert Graves [1953] and H. J. Schonfield) maintain that their views may well be more authentic than those formulated as Pauline Christianity. Others suggest that the Ebionites were not 'real' Christians since some of them believed that Jesus was simply a virtuous man, born of the Virgin Mary, but having no pre-existence. The modern Ebionite Jewish Community affirms Yahwism (see **Yahweh**), the belief that Jesus was a Jewish prophet and not the Messiah of Christianity. They are strict monotheists (to the point of denying the dualism represented by **Satan**) actively concerned with social justice based on the **Tanakh**, and they campaign against Christian proselytizing.

Ecclesia Gnostica A Gnostic church founded in the USA in 1959 under its full title, the Pre-Nicene Gnostic Catholic Church. It was founded to promote studies in Gnosticism in association with its sister organization, The Gnostic Society.

Eckankar The Religion of the Light and Sound of God, a **New Age** move-ment. Its beliefs focus on the soul which is the individual's true identity and which, since the moment it was born of God's love, embarked on a journey towards God and **Self-Realization**. This may be accelerated by conscious contact with the divine spirit *Eck*, by means of spiritual exer-cises. The spiritual world can be explored through Soul Travel and Spiritual Dreams. The living *Eck* Master is called the Mahanta, currently Sri Harold Klemp.

Eco-Paganism A branch of **neo-paganism** particularly concerned with the environment and conservation. Eco-Paganists are environmental activists who regard nature or aspects of nature as an embodiment of spir-ituality and being associated with gods and goddesses. The sacredness of nature and the 'feeling' of interconnectedness with the whole planet, is the inspiration for political action. The tenets of Eco-Paganism are rooted in Eco-Philosophy (such as that of the various Green Parties), 'Deep Ecology', and Eco-Feminism. There are associations with **Wicca**, modern **Druidism** and **Chaos Magic**. The UK Eco-Pagan Dragon Environmental Network, was founded in 1990. See **Druids**, **Gaia**, **Earth Mother**

Ecumenical Movement *X*. Gk. *oikumene*, 'the inhabited earth'. In the **New Testament** it refers to the 'world', the people of the world or to the whole known world being at the time, the Roman Empire. In the modern period it has been used mainly by Protestants, to denote the unity of all things in Christ and implicitly, the unity of the Church. The first formal attempt to promote unity was mooted in 1910 at the International Missionary Conference in Edinburgh, which led to the establishment of the **World Council of Churches** (WCC) in 1948. All major branches of Christianity have become affiliated to the WCC, which is synonymous with the Ecumenical Movement. There are, however, churches not affil-iated to the WCC whose members work for Christian unity. Despite endless conferences, consultations, study papers and the reassurances that unity does not imply or require uniformity, the merging of churches has not been achieved. Presbyterians and Congregationalists united in 1972 to form the **United Reformed Church**, but an attempt in the same year to unite English Anglicanism with Methodism failed. The original hope of establishing a single, doctrinally united Church has given way to a broader theological understanding, to greater tolerance of fundamental differences such as those existing between Episcopal and non-Episcopal churches and to various forms of practical co-operation. Many Protestant churches now allow worshippers of other traditions to participate in their sacraments and there is reciprocal, but discretionary, sharing between Anglicans and Roman Catholics. What the Ecumenical Movement has achieved is a re-arrangement of the ancient divisions; rather than being divided vertically by sharp differences of theology, horizontal differences cut across the original traditions to show that almost all Christian churches have their share of both conservative and radical thinkers.

Edda *Nor*. The title is given to two collections of Norse mythological literature. It was once believed that the term meant 'great grandmother', but this has been discarded by scholars in favour of 'poetics'. The 'Poetical' or 'Younger Edda' was compiled by the Icelandic historian Sturluson (1178–1241) and its most important text is the 'Upsala Codex' (c.1300). The 'Elder Edda' is a collection of songs written in Old Icelandic and recorded in the 'Codex Regius', found in Iceland in 1643. They celebrate the mythology and heroic saga that includes the *Voluspa*, the prophecy of the sibyl, the most important of the sources of Norse cosmology. See **Germanic Religion, Norse Mythology**

Eddy, Mary Baker Founder of the First Church of Christ the Scientist. See **Christian Scientists**

Egotheism Self-deification. One of the implications is **atheism**, in that believing there is no God the need is felt to fill the vacuum with oneself. Some see it as promoting faith in oneself regardless of an atheistic or **agnostic** world view. Christian tradition holds that the usurpation of God brought about by self-deification, amounts to the 'unforgivable sin'. Throughout religious history there is a theme of worshipping 'the god within', which may take the form of an external absolute or relative deity that is indwelling. Mykultura, as it is sometimes known, promotes a form of **monotheism**, the one existing god being the self whose divinity is the source of all meaning and purpose; it is a solipsism which by definition denies omnipotence and omniscience, since the self is divine only relative to itself. It can be understood, therefore, as a religion without metaphysics.

Egyptian Religion, Ancient *E*. Two natural features, the Nile and the sun, have formed and dominated the major themes of Egyptian religion. Because of the deposits left by the flooding of the Nile, the Egyptians called their country *Kemet*, 'Black Land'. The Pharaoh **Akhenaten** (c.1352–c.36 BCE) attempted to focus religion exclusively on a solar creator god. During the Thinite Period (c.3200–c.2780 BCE), the two Kingdoms of Upper and Lower Egypt (the Mediterranean Egypt of the Nile delta and the African Egypt of the Nile valley) were united under pharaohnic rule. This enabled the centralized control of the navigable Nile, the irrigation of adjoining land and a systematized method of agriculture. The Old Kingdom or **Pyramid** Age (c.2686–c.2181 BCE) saw the development of civilization and the establishment of Egyptian religion as we know it. Before the unification of the two kingdoms, religion clustered around tribal gods consisting of a pantheon of cosmic deities and the local gods of each settlement. These were housed in a temple or **Mansion of the Gods**. In parallel, most people also worshipped their own household gods at dedicated shrines. Each local display of power was understood as a manifestation of a separate god, but this particularism was gradually rationalized by the priests. They grouped the gods into 'families' such as the **Great and Little Enneads** of Heliopolis, whose chief deity was **Atum**, and the **Ogdoad** of Hermopolis, whose chief deity was **Ra**. A further rationalization established divine triads, for example **Amun**, **Osiris** and **Seth**, which eventually developed into a form of **universalism**, with the separate manifestations of power understood as emanating from the one source. Egyptian religion was thus forged in the tension between polytheism and monotheism with the one overarching power irresistibly evident in three forms: the sun as creation, animal life as procreation, and earth as annual 'resurrection'. The **Pharaoh** became the focus of these sources of power, and consequently the Egyptian concept of deity became one of an ultimate potentate-creator who sustained a territory that was both habitable and productive and upon whose will the quality of people's lives depended. It was within this process that the great Egyptian myths developed to account for the life-death-rebirth cycle of natural phenomena, mirrored in human existence.

We have it from Herodotus that 'the names of all the gods have been known in Egypt from the beginning of time …' (Herodotus 2.50.2). Even so, Egyptian mythology was never a fixed canon, but constantly changed and adapted to the requirements of the leaders of successive dynasties. An example of this syncretism occurred during the New Kingdom (c.1550–c.1069 BCE), when Ra and Amun merged as one god, Amun-Ra. Deities also played different and, sometimes, conflicting roles, as when the lioness Sekhmet was dispatched by Ra to eat human beings for rebelling against him. Later, she became the fierce protectress of life, the kingdom and the sick.

The major myths and gods are described under their own entries and only a brief overview of Egyptian cosmology is given here. At the outset of creation the entire universe was a chaos of dark water. **Atum-Ra**, the principal pairing of the **Ennead** of Heliopolis, appeared from the water as Egypt itself reappears each year from the Nile floods. When Ra-Atum spat out the water, the gods **Shu** (air) and **Tefnut** (moisture) were created and gave birth to **Nut** and **Geb**, gods of sky and earth. Humans were created when Shu and Tefnut, lost in the 'dark wastes', were found by Atum-Ra's eye (the sun). His tears of joy became human beings. Ra had two sons, Osiris was the king of Egypt and Seth the evil urge. After murdering his brother to become king, Seth divided Osiris' body into innumerable parts and scattered them, but **Isis** reassembled most of the pieces and buried them beneath a temple. Osiris' son **Horus** successfully challenged Seth's usurpation of his father and he was banished to the desert where he became the god of violent storms. After his body had been mummified by **Anubis**, Osiris became god of the Underworld. Horus became king and all the pharaohs were descended from him. With the Sumerians (see **Sumerian Religion**), the Egyptians were the first to create 'visible speech', a form of writing that was as expressive as the spoken word. Its development was celebrated in the cult of **Thoth**, god of language, writing and wisdom.

Egyptian religion, the most enduring of all the world's faiths, had a formative influence on the religions of **Greece** and **Rome**. The ancient religion, together with its arts and traditions, is still practised in Egypt.

FINAL WORD: 'You make the Nile in the Other World and bring it whither
you wish,
In order to sustain the people, even as you have made them.
For you are Lord of them all, who weary yourself on their behalf,
The lord of every land, who arises for them,
O, Aten of the day, great of majesty!'
Hymn to Aten, the sun's disk. (Joseph Kaster)

Eightfold Path *B*. The path that leads to liberation and the end of *dukkha*, suffering, is developed as the last of the **Four Noble Truths**. In most Western translations, each of the eight prescriptions opens with the word 'Right ...', a translation of the Skt. *samyak* or Pal. *samma* meaning 'complete', which is perhaps better rendered 'perfect'. The eight prescriptions are: i) Perfect View, an acceptance of the essential Buddhist teachings; ii) Perfect Resolve, a positive outlook with a mind unhindered by ill-will or any kind of craving; iii) Perfect Speech, using speech in positive and creative ways rather than in anger or criticism or in any way that might cause harm; iv) Perfect Action, observing of the **Five Precepts**; v) Perfect Livelihood, avoiding professions or a form of work that will cause harm to others; vi) Perfect Effort, keeping the mind wholesome and directing it towards spiritual goals; vii) Perfect Mindfulness, being constantly aware of what one is doing and thinking; viii) Perfect Meditation, training the mind in focused, one-pointed attention in order to achieve deeper levels of meditation. The Path is not linear, something to be followed from 'A' to 'Z'. Rather the eight prescriptions should be practised together as a way of life. Usually, they are grouped progressively, 3–5, which are concerned with morality; 6–8, which are concerned with meditation; and 1–2 which are concerned with insight. In training and practice, 3–5 are the first to be cultivated since morality, as so often in **Buddhism**, provides the foundation for the others. The emphasis of **Mahayana** is different, finding the **Hinayana** presentation of the Path over-concerned with personal enlightenment. According to its own doctrines, suffering is the result of ignorance, *avidya*, thus liberation is to be achieved by the removal of the root causes of ignorance and not only through right conduct.

Eight Precepts *B*. A condensed form of Buddhist ethics. See **Precepts**

Ein Sof *J*. The Kabbalistic term for God, the endless, boundless one, a being both incomprehensible and ineffable. He is known to exists only through the manifestations of ten attributes, symbolically represented in Kabbalistic mysticism by the **Sephiroth**. See **Kabbalah**

El *AME*. The chief of the **Canaanite** and **Phoenician** gods, the name means 'god' but sometimes expanded as the 'father of mankind' or 'creator of the creation'. In his Canaanite form he is the major creator god of the pantheon and head of the council of gods; in his Phoenician aspect he is the father of Cronos, known to them as Elus. The name is found in **Ugaritic** inscriptions, at the head of various lists of gods and has numerous manifestations. His wife Asherah, called **Astarte** by the Greeks, was the great **Mother Goddess**. The **Old Testament** uses the name to form epithets for God, such as **Elohim** and **El Shaddai**; in Christian patristic theology 'El' was the primary Hebrew name for God.

Elamites *AME*. A black-skinned people Herodotus referred to as 'Asiatic Ethiopians' who lived in what today is the Iranian province of Khuzestan. **Sumerian** and **Akkadian** texts record a pantheon of over 200 gods, but over half of them are unknown in Elamite texts, their changing status exactly reflecting that of the current ruler and the political situation. Elam assimilated gods, cosmology and rituals, by conquest and expansion and it is difficult to extrapolate specific Elamite elements. The role of the gods was to give and preserve life, then to take it back, accompanying the dead to the 'other' world. Death and how to deal with it, seems to have been the dominant Elamite concern; religious buildings, like the great ziggurat of Chogha Zanbil were centres of a cult of the dead. Elamite dynasties lasted from 2700 BCE to c.540 BCE. See **Mesopotamian Religion**

Elan Vital An international educational trust founded to advance the teachings of Prem Rawat. See **Divine Light Mission**

Election See **Predestination, Augustinianism**

Eleusian Mysteries *G*. They were celebrated annually in honour of **Demeter** and **Persephone** at Eleusis near Athens, one of Demeter's principal temple sites. Initiates were promised increased well-being and prosperity before death and a good life after it. The rites drew on a wide public since everyone who could speak Greek had access. What form they took remains, unsurprisingly perhaps, a mystery and only scant information has been gleaned from Roman mosaics. The Lesser Mysteries were preparatory and included a procession from Athens to Eleusis, a purification ceremony and a fast, broken by a drink of barley water flavoured with pennyroyal. The ritual of the Great Mysteries had three stages, the Initiation, the Perfection and the Beholding. Their prestige was enhanced by an account in Herodotus describing how the Eleusian deities assisted the victory at the battle of Salamis in 480 BCE. A cloud of dust like that put up by the procession, and a cry like that made during the procession seems to have confounded the enemy. The importance of the Mystery was sustained through the Roman period until, in 395 BCE, the sanctuary was destroyed by Alaric. See **Mystery Religions**

Elijah Muhammad See **Muhammad, Elijah**; **Black Muslims**

Elixir of Life Alchemists were not just concerned with their quest for the **philosopher's stone**, said to turn ordinary metals into gold, but also with arresting the process of ageing and prolonging life indefinitely. This universal panacea was known as the Elixir of Life, which it was believed could also create life. For the alchemists, the quest was not simply a matter of living forever as an end in itself, but a means to the end of being able to practise the sacred art of alchemy seemingly indefinitely. See **Fountain of Youth**

Elohim *J*. Heb. 'God'. One of several Jewish names for **God** which, like *Adonai*, is a plural form. It is the most frequently used term for the God of the Israelites but is also employed for pagan gods. Some scholars have taken the plural form to be a *pluralis majestatis* or *excellentiae*, an expression of God's majesty and excellence and it can be rendered, 'Divinity'. In various periods, Christian theologians have attempted to interpret the plural *Elohim* as evidence of a proto-Trinitarian doctrine, but modern scholars now dismiss this as exegetically fallacious. The singular form, *Eloah*, is rarely used in the **Old Testament**, and is probably close to an Arabic word for God, *Ilah*, which is used in the Old Testament for heathen deities (Daniel 11: 37, 38). Its root meaning is obscure but may suggest bewilderment or fear or 'to hide' because of fear, suggesting that *Elohim* may be translated 'He of whom one is afraid' or 'He with whom one hides because of fear'. See **El Shaddai**, **Tetragrammaton**

El Shaddai *J*. Heb. 'God Almighty'. One of the Jewish names for God. It is also the name of a charismatic Catholic movement based in the Philippines. See **Adonai**, **Elohim**, **Tetragrammaton**

Elvis Presley See **First Preslyterian Church of Elvis the Divine**

Elysian Fields In Greek mythology, the final resting place of the souls of the heroes and the virtuous. The concept is based on Homeric passages in the *Iliad* and the *Odyssey*. The Fields lay on the western margin of the earth, near Oceanus, the encircling steams. In Hesiod and Pindar the Fields are located on the Isles of the Blessed. The concept of **Elysium** has remerged in **New Age** cults of **Neo-paganism**, where it is understood as a multilayered paradise or Heaven, beyond which lies the Golden City. See **Land of Youth**, **New Jerusalem**, **Paradise**

Elysium *G.* In Greek mythology, an ideal place where a person or spirit can reside in perfect happiness (see **Elysian Fields**). A similar concept is to be found in many religions, for example in Celtic mythology. See **Land of Youth, Mag Mell**

Emin Originally called the 'Way', Emin evokes the ancient meaning 'faithful'. The association was started in 1971 by a small group of friends, through a chance meeting with Richard Armin, known to them as Leo. It is a loose association of like-minded people seeking a better understanding of the meaning and purpose of life. Broadly nature-based, they are concerned to realize a human potential that is far greater than our experience of life suggests and 'to reclaim our lives to their natural purpose'. Its tenets include the concept of a continually evolving creation in which human beings are participating. The full life is the one lived in harmony with the laws that ordered creation and which are the source of all knowledge. The ultimate human responsibility is to be creative and to live creatively. Richard Armin died in 2002, but Emin continues, 'forming a shared endeavour in an open spirit of search, research and discovery and creating an ecology of mutual support for each individual's self-chosen and self-directed personal development' (from the Emin website).

Emperor Worship In Roman tradition, an Imperial cult in which an emperor was worshipped as a god. The cult started in 44 BCE with Julius Caesar, who allowed a statue of himself to be inscribed, 'to the unconquered god'. Augustus Caesar, the adopted son of Julius, built a temple dedicated to Divus Julius, 'deified Julius'. Augustus was already titled 'the son of a god' and inscriptions to this effect appeared on temples such as that at Myrna, 'Divine Augustus Caesar, son of God, imperator of land and sea …' Tiberius, Caligula and Claudius also had temples dedicated to them, although Caligula's was razed after his death. Most Roman emperors resisted deification during their lives, even though there were those who thought refusal was a sign of weakness. There were others, like Seneca, who ridiculed the cult and sarcastically satirized the anticipated deification of Claudius. Vespasian allegedly remarked on his deathbed, 'I think I'm turning into a god.' The power of the emperor became absolute after Hadrian and subsequent emperors could claim divinity during their lifetimes. This was one of the reasons for the persecution of Christians, who believed the cult to be idolatrous. Citizens were required to make sacrifices to the *genius* or titular spirits of the emperor and received a certificate for doing so.

Until the Second World War, the Japanese emperor made similar claims to deity and the concept of *Arahitogami*, 'a god who is a human being', applied to Emperor Hirohito. On New Year's day, 1946, the Emperor formally disavowed his claim to divinity in accordance with the values of **Shintoism**. The Caribbean cult of **Rastafarianism** claimed the Ethiopian Emperor Haile Selassie, to be a manifestation of Jah, but this was not direct Emperor worship, in that he was believed to be an earthly aspect of the same God as worshipped by Christians. See **Divine Kingship**

Empiricism A theory of knowledge opposed to **Rationalism**. Believing reason to be fallible, philosophers searched for a theory that was consistent with ordinary human behaviour. Rationalism seeks absolute knowledge about a world presumed to be real, empiricists try to discover how we acquire our knowledge and how reliable it is. Instead of rejecting the data accumulated by the senses, empiricists examined our sense experience as though it was the only source of what we know; equipped with this data they tried to construct a theory of knowledge based on it. The relationship between knowledge and experience is dependent on the various ways 'experience' may be defined. An 'experience' of a dog, for example, is a mind-dependent experience of, perhaps, having one in our home; such an experience gives us a certain kind of knowledge. Empiricists would argue that a dream, picture or story of a dog is also a valid experience of 'dog', but being somewhat of different order of experience it affords a different kind of knowledge. Empiricism denies the Platonic-Rationalist **idealist** thesis that when we first engage with the world our mind is already equipped with innate ideas or concepts that owe nothing to experience. The philosopher, John Locke (1632–1704) said that at birth the mind is a 'white paper, void of all characters' and that only experience will mark it with ideas. Empiricists explored every aspect of experience: reflection, intuition, scientific description and the various kinds of knowledge derived from it. Two aspects of Empiricism are important for religion. Firstly, the philosophy has developed in a practical and worldly context. For example, in England, the context was the commercial, industrial and scientific expansion of the 17th century, when the perennial search for the absolute knowledge of the Rationalists was abandoned. In the face of the new sciences all that could be attempted was a probable hypothesis of the immediate world. The innovative thinkers were not professional philosophers, but men like Francis **Bacon** (1561–1626), Lord Chancellor under James I and John **Locke**, a doctor. Secondly, empiricism led religion into subjectivity and opened the way for an inner experience of God, which although not 'rational' was held to be valid. Since the 17th century the polemics have continued and the faith-reason, faith-experience debate has had to take into consideration not only the philosophies of people like **Russell** and **Wittgenstein**, but the philosophical theologies of, for example, **Bultmann**, **Tillich** and **Bonhoeffer**. To this must be added the insights of both gestalt and behaviourist psychology.

FINAL WORD: 'A person with an experience is never at the mercy of a person with an argument.' (Rebecca Benedict, in a letter to the author)

Emptiness A concept found in the mystical heart of several religions, most formally, perhaps, in **Mahayana** Buddhism. It is based on the doctrine *anatta*, of no-self (see **Five Aggregates**). Rather than being a negative concept suggesting that something is lacking, it lies at the heart of the end of suffering, *dukkha*, and the realization of **nirvana**. A similar concept is applied to forms of advance **meditation**, such as Zen *shikantaza*, which requires the development of 'no-mind' or 'empty mind'. In Christian and Sufi mysticism, emptiness refers to the loss of a preoccupation with the self and the potential for the realization of something greater, the state of pure consciousness. In secular philosophy the concept 'emptiness' is expressed by **nihilism**, the notion that life is a meaningless void, without point or purpose. Perhaps this is better put as the 'emptiness of nihilism'.

Energumen Someone thought to be possessed by the devil, usually showing strength in excess of what is normal for a human being. The synoptic Gospels give an account of the man possessed with 'an unclean spirit' whose strength enabled him to break the chains with which he had been secured. The term is also used of someone who is in a frantic or hysterical state of the kind deliberately induced by certain kinds of trance. See **Possession**

Engels, Frederick (1820–95) 19th-century German political philosopher who, with Karl **Marx**, co-authored *The Communist Manifesto* of 1848 and was an active participant in the Revolution of the same year. After Marx's death in 1883, he devoted his time to editing and translating Marx's work. He was a committed Hegelian, impressed by **Hegel**'s assertion that, 'the whole world, natural, historical, intellectual, is for the first time represented as a process, i.e., as in constant motion, change, transformation, development.' See **Marxism**

Engrams See **Scientology**

Enlightenment *B. Z.* In **Buddhism**, 'enlightenment' is the familiar translation of the Skt. term *bodhi* which, more literally, means 'awakening'. In many ways the latter is a more useful rendering, since it carries with it the notion of the radical difference between sleep and wakefulness. It also avoids a confusion with the concepts attached to, *the* '**Enlightenment**' as an aspect of Western cultural history. But in Western literature, 'enlightenment' is far too established to be jettisoned in favour of an alternative. The concept refers to the goal of the Buddhist path and its model is the Buddha's own enlightenment gained as a result of his meditation. The experience of enlightenment is always the same but there are various degrees of it and its achievement is more usually progressive, but it can be given in a flash of sudden and complete insight. It is a Western misconception to think of enlightenment as the observation or perception of a separate world, different from the world of phenomena, with an observer and an object to be perceived or experienced. This sustains precisely the duality that enlightenment overcomes. There are not two or more distinct worlds, only the one. Experiencing this unity is the consequence of enlightenment. In **Zen**, the term for enlightenment is *Satori* or *Kensho*. See **Haskalah**

FINAL WORD: 'There are many paths to enlightenment, be sure to take one that has a heart.' (**Lao-tzu**)

Enlightenment, The An 18th-century movement, also known as the 'Age of Reason', generated by liberal reformist ideas that, in France, led to the Revolution. The movement was greatly influential on Western philosophy. Put briefly, the energy came from an addition of new scientific knowledge which stimulated **empiricist**, **naturalist** and **materialist** theories vehemently opposed to clericalism. The received traditions of religion inhibited enquiry and free thinking and the general trend was to abandon religious belief and the authority of the Church as a ground for sure knowledge. Instead, thinkers looked to a deeper understanding of the natural world and animal and human behaviour. All truth resides in natural phenomena, which includes reason as a mental processes. Reason determines what is necessary and useful, both for the individual and society. Once determined, what is necessary should be addressed not on the whim of rulers, but by democratic politics. The English Enlightenment had an early start during the 1680s as a reaction to the Civil War, the execution of Charles I and the restoration of the monarch. The end result was the English Bill of Rights, that underpinned both parliamentary authority and personal liberties. A more open society developed that enabled science, the arts and philosophy to flourish. Both the philosophers **Hobbes** and **Locke** developed systems that responded to these radical changes. See **Freethinkers**, **Rationalism**, **Secularism**, **Voltaire**

Ennead *E*. From Gk. *enneas*, 'nine'. In Egyptian mythology the Enneads are a group or family of nine deities. Numerous enneads are referred to in the **Pyramid Texts** such as the Great Ennead, the Little Ennead, the dual and plural enneads. Some Pharaohs, for example Seti I, created enneads that included themselves. The Great Ennead or the Ennead of Heliopolis, was the most important, comprising **Atum** and his children **Seth** and **Tefnut** and their children **Geb**, **Nut**, **Osiris**, **Isis**, **Set** and **Nephthys**. The Great Ennead is associated with the creation myths of Egypt. See **Egyptian Religion**

En Realissimum L. 'the most real being'. The idea of a 'super reality' lies behind the ontological argument for the existence of God. The idea that God is greater than anything of which we can conceive was developed by **Anselm**, but derived from **Plato** by way of **Plotinus** and **Augustine** (see **Ontological Argument**). The concept is not confined to the God of biblical religions and the notion of the inconceivable (and ineffable) supreme being is also to be found in **Hinduism** and **Buddhism**.

Environmentalism Concern for the well-being of our planet and increasing interest in Green Party politics, has brought 'Environmentalism' close to being an animistic religion. This concern and the urgency for conservationist action endows the 'earth' with a quality akin to sacredness and draws people whose passions are no less powerful than those inspired by religious conviction. The spoliation and pollution of the earth and its atmosphere is due to 'evil' man who, for reasons of commercially vested interest is, to say the least, reluctant to make adjustments to industrial processes or compromise his use of fossil fuels. The apostles of Environmentalism conscientiously adopt 'rituals' such as vegetarianism and the eating of organic foods and have an established hierarchy of concern, furry animals being more protected than ants, dolphins more than sardines, pine martins more than mice and so it goes on, with campaigns against chlorine, nuclear energy, genetic modification, etc. This is not to decry these concerns, but to illustrate how, for its secular adherents, the movement replaces religion. See **Earth Mother**, **Gaia** FINAL WORD: 'If you look carefully, you see that environmentalism is in fact a perfect 21st-century remapping of traditional Judeo-Christian beliefs and myths … So it's time to abandon the religion of environmentalism and return to the science of environmentalism and base our public policy decisions firmly on that.' (Michael Crichton)

Epiphany X. From the Greek meaning an 'appearance' or 'manifestation'. In Greek philosophy it refers to the appearance of the Divine or Eternal in all physical things, a concept underlying natural **theology**. It is better known as the Church festival (January 6th) celebrating the birth of Jesus as the manifestation of God incarnate. The festival which originated in the East to honour Jesus' **baptism**, was introduced in the West in the 4th century CE and the reference to baptism fell away, leaving the focus on the 'presentation' of Christ to the gentiles, specifically to the **Magi**. Traditionally they were the first gentiles to see the child, however there is no reason why they could not have been Jews of the **diaspora**. In terms of biblical theology the only complete Epiphany of Christ will be the 'end of time'. See **Eschatology**

Episcopalians X. In general any church, usually of the Anglican communion, ruled by Bishops; the Protestant Episcopal Church of the USA, for example, is in communion with the see of Canterbury. Prior to the War of Independence, Anglican churches founded in America (the first at Jamestown, Virginia in 1607) were under the administration of the Bishop of London. After the war the Protestant Episcopal Church became autonomous. In 1789, a General Convention produced a constitution, a canon and a revised Prayer Book. Since the Civil War the church has expanded and initiated missions to many parts of the world. Its constitution is more democratic than the Anglican model, with bishops being elected by both the clerics and laity of diocesan synods.

Epistemology That branch of philosophy concerned with the nature of knowledge, with what we know, how we know it and how such knowledge may be validated. It has been a central theme in philosophy since the 17th century, when the received theories of knowledge were challenged by the developing sciences. There emerged the **Rationalist**

philosophers such as **Pascal**, **Descartes**, Leibnitz and **Spinoza**, all of whom argued for the existence of innate ideas (*a priori*) underwritten by experience (*a posteriori*). Opposing them were the **Empiricists**, who totally refuted the existence of innate ideas. Among the Empiricists are to be found **Locke**, **Hume** and John Stuart **Mill**. Other theories of knowledge have emerged, for example **Pragmatism** and 'Causality', the notion that there are intermediaries between the object and the perception of it, such as the nervous system. Despite these more modern theories, the validity of religious knowledge has usually been debated in the tension between the Rationalists and Empiricists.

Erasmus, Desiderius (1469–1536) Humanist philosopher, whose *Praise of Folly* (1509) is a bitter satire on the monasticism and the corruption of the Church. In 1524, he contributed to **Reformation** polemics by contradicting Luther's concept of free will. He produced a Greek New Testament and his publications of the texts of the **Church Fathers**, confirmed him as one of the principal scholars of his period. His satires helped to prepare the way for the Reformation and it is said that, 'Erasmus laid the egg and Luther hatched it.'

Eros *G*. The god of love was not always the attractive, chubby, boy-archer depicted on Victorian Valentine cards, rococo art and by the famous statue in Piccadilly Circus. Long before the cult of **Aphrodite** was established, Eros was a god of fertility, charged with sexual potency. The myths have numerous versions of his birth, from that of hatching as a monster from a silver egg, to him being the son of Aphrodite, with **Zeus**, **Ares** and **Hermes** contending paternity. Originally, as a cosmic principle, he was both a creative and destructive agent and his assortment of imputed fathers represented his different functions. From Hermes, he got the cunning and the sexual potency that saw him worshipped with phallic symbols; from Ares, the warrior's attraction for women; from the incestuous union of Zeus and Aphrodite, stemmed the notion that erotic love crosses established boundaries with impunity. There was also something of the Peter Pan about Eros, a god who never grew up, remaining perpetually youthful. Sappho described his contradictory qualities as 'bitter sweet'. He was known to the Romans as Cupid, from *cupido*, 'desire', where he appeared less as a god and more as a mischievous child, referred to by Shakespeare in *A Midsummer Night's Dream* as, the 'knavish lad … this wimpled, whining, purblind, wayward boy', and by Ovid, because of the misuse of his arrows, as having 'savage spite'. His most familiar story tells of his love for **Psyche**, who lost him when she gazed at his face. Psyche is Cupid's *alter ego*, the personification of the human soul. In Platonic philosophy love is the most refined and elevated of the senses and from the 4th century BCE, Psyche and the god of love are shown together in art and sculpture as an allegorically idealized union.

Eschatology Gk. *Eschaton*, 'doctrine of the last things'. In all religions this is the science of the last four states: existence, death, judgement, heaven and hell. Such theologies speculate about the ultimate fate of human beings and of the world, about what death actually is and about the last judgement which determines the final outcome. Hindus, for example, believe that the individual 'soul' is taken up into the realm of the Divine Beings but, on the basis that practice makes perfect, only after innumerable reincarnations. Buddhism, also through innumerable incarnations, looks for freedom from *dukkha*, suffering. Judaism longs for the Messiah, Islam hangs everything on resurrection and a judgement on which depends an eternity in torment or paradise. Christian apocalyptic writing affirms that the end of the world will be marked by the second coming of **Jesus Christ**, who will overthrow the **Antichrist** and after presiding over the **Last Judgement**, will usher in an age of peace and justice. See **Epiphany**

FINAL WORD: 'I shall tell you a great secret my friend. Do not wait for the last judgement – it takes place every day.' (Camus)

Eskimos Eskimo-Aleut religion is influenced by their hunting and fishing lifestyle and the extreme environment in which they live. Radical changes of harsh weather accounts for the theme of fear in their mythology which is populated by capricious ghosts, spirits and sorcerers. They believe in an **anthropomorphized** universal power, *inua* (also *yua* or *tayaruu*), who among the Alaskan Eskimos takes the form of Guardian Spirits, the 'owners' of animals. Other groups see guardian spirits in ordinary, everyday objects such as cooking pots, which like all other spirits have to be appeased so as to function properly. A central feature of Eskimo culture is the *angakok* or shaman (see **Shamanism**) who uses **charms** to communicate with the spirits he is called upon to placate. When the sun begins to move southwards, a form of string-art ritual is enacted, rather like the Western cat's cradle, so as to trap the sun and delay the arrival of the long, remorseless winter. Beliefs and rituals indicate a harmonious or neutral cosmos and only human negligence or disobedience will result in disaster. As with all animistic religious systems, the sky, the sea and land, are associated respectively with a masculine and feminine power. Spirits move and can be separated from the objects, animals or humans in which they reside. It is one of the functions of a shaman to direct the spirit back to its residence and thus alleviate the suffering the separation has caused. In the case of permanent separation, 'loose' spirits will be returned to the kingdom of the dead.

Essenes *J.* Heb. but probably from the Aramaic, meaning 'pious'. They referred to themselves as the 'Sons of Light'. The Essenes were an ascetic Jewish sect that flourished from the 2nd century BCE to the 1st century CE. For most of this time they occupied the Qumran plateau in the Judean desert near the Dead Sea. Their origin is obscure and has been linked to a group who opposed the 'illegal' purchase of the High Priesthood by Jason from Antiochus Epiphanes IV in 175 BCE or to the followers of Shammai and Hillel, two famous Rabbis who flourished in Jerusalem during the decades preceding the Christian era. The Essenes founded monasteries with communities which, in some ways, might well have been a model for the modern Israeli kibbutz, working the land, holding all property in common and eating together in strict silence. They bathed every morning in fresh spring water and observed the Sabbath with rigorous orthodoxy. They denounced the Temple and its sacrificial cult, instead laying great importance on charity to the poor, the sick, the weak and the aged. The **Dead Sea Scrolls**, discovered at Qumran in 1947, are accepted as being the library of the Essene community. During the 'Great Rebellion', the Jewish uprising against the Romans (66–70 CE) many of the Essenes joined the **Zealots**, believing they were engaged in the 'last' battle that would usher in the messianic age. A large number of them perished, by ritual suicide at Masada. See **Qumran Community**

E.s.t Or, 'est', Erhard Seminars Training, was a controversial **New Age** training programme, started in San Francisco in 1971 by Werner Erhard, born, John Paul Rosenberg. They claim **Heidegger** as an 'ancestor' of the organization and Erhard also cites **Zen** as a major influence. The founding principle of Est is that we created the universe ourselves and then amnesia, as a practical joke. Other acknowledged influences are Gestalt Therapy and **Scientology** which accused Erhard of 'borrowing' the concept of 'being at cause', the notion of being at the cause of an event or 'in on' the cause. See also **Human Potential Movement, Life Spring**
FINAL WORD: 'Erhard Seminars Training, [Est] is a pricey, psycho-babbling series of long and demeaning behaviour-modification sessions that preached the virtue of selfishness.' (Hunter S. Thomson)

Eternal Life In Christianity, the belief that through faith in Jesus Christ the individual will survive death and live for ever. There is some debate about the form this everlasting life will take. Much depends on a belief in the resurrection of the body, regardless of the natural processes of decay or cremation. Eternal life is more usually accredited to the **soul**, which in spirit form will 'enjoy' the presence of God. Accessed in some-what different ways, both Judaism and Islam carry the same hope. In Eastern Religion, notably Hinduism and Buddhism, the concept of endless reincarnation alters the perception of eternal life since, through **enlightenment**, the individual gains freedom from *samsara*, the per-petual cycle of birth-death-rebirth and enters **nirvana**. The term, 'eternal life' is sometimes wrongly associated with 'immortality'. An immortal being is one that is not subject to death and has thus little need for either reincarnation or enlightenment. (See **Greek and Roman religions, Olympian Pantheon**). Religion apart, there is a perennial quest for eternal or, at least, an infinitely prolonged life. This is currently in vogue through the science of cryonics, the deep freezing of corpses against the day when solutions to the causes of death might be found and resuscita-tion will be possible. A BBC science news item (October 2003) told of a round worm that had had some of its genes tweaked by scientists at the University of California, with the effect that its life was prolonged to the human equivalent of 500 years, 'the longest life-span ever achieved by scientists'. It was asserted that the same might be done for mammals. So much for the biblically ascribed, 'three-score and ten' years.

FINAL WORD: 'O Death, where is thy sting-a-ling-a-ling,
O Grave, thy victoree?
The bells of Hell go ting-a-ling-a-ling
For you but not for me.'
(Anon. First World War British Army song)

Eternal Return A myth originating in Egypt with subsequent variations by Pythagoras and various religious traditions. The concept suggests that time is not infinite, but subject to the physical limitations of the universe, thus all actions and events recur cyclically, again and again. In this process the universe, which will have no final state, is held a cycle of the changes of time and matter. The theory is an alternative to the rectilinear concept of time suggested by Aristotle and hence, the perception of time in biblical religion. In the Renaissance, the Ouroborus, the image of the snake devouring its own tail, became the symbol of eternal return. The idea is contained within the *dharmic* (see **dharma**) patterns of **Hinduism** and **Buddhism**, and in their image of the 'Wheel of Life'. For **Tibetan Buddhism**, *Kalachakra* is the doctrine of the 'Wheel of Time'. **Nietzsche** uses the term 'eternal recurrence', an idea he thought 'horrifying and paralyzing'; only an *Amor Fati*, a love of fate, might make endurable the recurrence of all the suffering and pain.

Ethical Dualism The concept that human beings are faced (all of the time) with moral choices polarized by the absolutes of 'good' and 'evil'. **Zoroastrianism** is probably the clearest expression of this concept. In **Christianity**, the idea is expressed in the 4th Gospel, 'Here lies the test: the light has come into the world, but men preferred darkness to light because their deeds were evil.' (John 3:19) The implication of ethical dualism is that thoughts and actions are either right or wrong and that there is little place for ethical relativism. See **Dualism**

Ethical Egoism A theory that individual action should be based on self-interest. It is the basis for several **New Age** cults, especially those of an anarchic nature (see **Anarchism**). But it carries with it its own built-in problem, that it might not be in *anyone's* self-interest to have everyone else acting in their own interest. The system does not necessarily imply that one disregards the concerns of other people, so long as it remains in one's self-interest to do so. Thus ethical egoism can be an absolute or a relative doctrine depending on the moral sensibility of the individual. In terms of what is best for society, individuals need to compromise some of their self-interested aims, but to achieve the kind of society they want, this might be no hardship. What we are concerned with is a post Judeo-Christian notion of morality and it is easily forgotten that classical Greek culture did not base its moral system on altruism. Both secular and religious moralists end by condemning ethical egoism, the one because it is not expedient for the common good, the other because it exposes a lack of true spirituality.

Ethical Monotheism A concept devolved from the notion of Judaism's radical **monotheism**. While the duality of good and evil (see **Ethical Dualism** and **Dualism**) is the context for the moral choices to be made in everyday life, ethical monotheism emphasizes the absolute sovereignty of God and the individual's submission to God's will. In Jewish terms God's will is manifested in *mitzvoth*, the law and keeping it implies honouring the terms of the **Covenant**. The imperative to do God's will is carried through in Christianity and Islam, as an indicator both of individual and collective spirituality. Thus ethical monotheism is derived from a biblical world view, it has no other source. Western secular society is governed by laws which have various origins, but which nevertheless enshrine the ethical values of the **Ten Commandments** and the **Sermon on the Mount**.

Ethic of Reciprocity See **Golden Rule**

Ethike Gk. 'ethics'. Originally meaning the study of habit, manner, spirit or attitude, the term is the etymological ancestor of the English 'ethics'. In Aristotle's philosophy *ethike* and practical politics are associated but treated separately, opposing Plato's identification of both fields as one. The debate set the pattern for what is 'good' or 'best', both in terms of individual human behaviour, social behaviour and practical government. It pointed the way to movements such as **Functionalism** and **Utilitarianism**.

Ethiopian Religion The 1955 constitution states that, 'The Ethiopian Orthodox Church, founded in the fourth century on the doctrines of St Mark, is the established church of the Empire and is, as such, supported by the State.' The Ethiopian Orthodox Church (see **Orthodox Church**) is closely related to the **Coptic Church** of Egypt. The Government tolerates other religions for example, Islam, which represents about 45 per cent of the population, but while respecting Islamic courts, has taken over Muslim schools and discourages the teaching of Arabic. In southern parts of the country indigenous animistic religions survive. The Beta Israel or **Falashas**, a Jewish community in Ethiopia, are now citizens of Israel.

Etruscans An ancient Italian civilization of unknown pre-historic origins, which was eventually assimilated into the Roman Republic. Sources of our knowledge are archaeological, such as evidence from tombs, inscriptions on clay tablets, texts found on the bindings of an Egyptian mummy and what can be derived from the remnants of remarkable wall-paintings. Translation of the texts is frustrated by an incomplete knowledge of their language. Traditionally, the Etruscans are thought to be 'mysterious', wrapped about with a somewhat frightening and daunting religion that dwells on hell, damnation and sacrificial rites. A priestly group, the *Haruspices* practised hepatoscopy, a form of **divination** which examined the livers of sacrificed animals. The belief system was an animistic polytheism, all phenomena were thought to be endowed with a spirit, regarded as being a manifestation of the one, divine power. The numerous deities were ordered in a complicated hierarchy, the upper echelon of which was similar to the gods of the Indo-European system. Thus they had Tin or Tinia, the sky, Uni his wife (who may have become known as Juno) and Cel, the earth goddess. Some of these Greek gods evolved and travelled to become **Artemis**, **Minerva** and **Bacchus**. Tombs, called *muni*, were the dwelling place of the *mani*, ancestral spirits (see **Manes**). The current view of scholars is that Rome was founded by the Etruscans, in which case what has usually been described as the Etruscan influence on Rome, is in fact Rome's cultural heritage.

Eucharist *X*. The central sacrament of the Christian Church, known also as the **Mass**, Holy Communion or **Lord's Supper**. It has its origin in the 'last supper' taken by Jesus with his disciples before his arrest, trial and execution. The meal is thought to have been a celebration of the **Passover**, with Jesus' blessing of bread and wine being a self-identification with the slaughtered Pascal Lamb. Whether or not the 'last supper' was a Passover meal or a meal to inaugurate the Sabbath, Jesus identified the bread as his body and the wine as his blood. The theology of the Eucharist takes markedly different forms across the denominations. The Catholic doctrine of transubstantiation affirms that at the moment of consecration the 'substance', or inner reality of the bread and wine actually become the body and blood of Christ. **Anglicanism** and the **Orthodox** churches attest to a change, but do not attempt to define it, reading it symbolically rather than literally. The doctrine of Consubstantiation, the coexistence of the elements with the Body of Christ, is held by **Lutherans**, while **Calvinists** and some Anglicans deny that any change takes place, but that a spiritual power or blessing, is transmitted to the worshipper. Others, rejecting entirely the notion of sacrifice, understand the sacrament simply as a memorial. The liturgies of the different traditions vary considerably, from the elaborate Masses of the Catholics, to the simplicity of the 'Breaking of Bread' of the **Baptists** and **Plymouth Brethren**. The **Ecumenical Movement** has rationalized some of the doctrinal and liturgical variations between denominations so as to enable Christians of different traditions to celebrate the sacrament together.

European Religion, Ancient See **Celtic Religion, Druids, Germanic Religion, Norse Religion**

Evangelism Familiarly, the preaching of the Christian gospel, but by reference the proselytizing by any group so as to win converts. It is closely related to **Revivalism**, specifically 19th-century American revivalism which was followed in the 20th century by the mass rallies of evangelists such as Billy Graham. Evangelism of all forms is associated with biblical **fundamentalism**, terms the belief in the Bible as the literal Word of God, which gives a mandate of absolute authority to the evangelist. Evangelism is always edged with urgency because of the possibility of sudden death and its association with **millennialism**.

Evil A varied concept which, in one form or another, is found throughout history in all forms of religion and secularism. It can refer to anything that is morally bad or corrupt, consciously inhuman or wicked. In ancient paganism and animism, the concept of evil was not associated with human beings, but with spirits and malign 'forces' believed to have the power to bring about individual or collective catastrophe. In established religious traditions such as **Zoroastrianism** and the biblical religions, the world and the individual **soul** is understood as a battle ground where the forces of good and evil engage. In **Judaism**, **Christianity** and **Islam**, the term evil is associated with the concept of 'sin', construed as disobedience to God's will. In Eastern religion, evil is less associated with human disposition than with the capricious nature of gods and **demons**. The **eschatology** of most religions offers the hope that, finally, evil will be overcome in one fashion or another. **Buddhism** understands evil to be the many forms of suffering, which because of *avidya*, ignorance, is illusory and mitigated by **enlightenment**. See **Kakon**

Exclusive Brethren *X*. An authoritarian, non-democratic religious sect, believing the Bible to be the inspired and literal word of God, that salvation is by faith through Jesus Christ and that the second coming is imminent. Worship is inspired by the Holy Spirit and there is no ritual liturgy or set form; women may not preach or pray aloud. The Brethren have no clergy and the 'priesthood' includes all believers; worship is directed by the leader, who has overall power and is known as, 'The Man of God', or the 'Elected Vessel'. See **Plymouth Brethren**

Exclusivity The notion found in some religions that the form in which they were founded and the doctrines which they developed, make them the exclusive means of achieving salvation. **Judaism**, by virtue of its election as the 'chosen people' of God, is fenced about by conditions that determine the 'Jewishness' of its adherents, one of which is circumcision, another that a person must be born of a Jewish mother, a third, that the subject is *halakhic*, that is, he observes both the letter and spirit of the law. Judaism is not, naturally, a proselytizing religion, but will accept converts. Christianity affirms that Church membership, whether by **baptism** or confession of faith, is indispensable to salvation – *Extra Ecclesiam nulla salus*, 'outside the Church, no salvation'. This is made uncompromising by those denominations that subscribe to a doctrine of **election** and **predestination**, some of which, like the **Jehovah's Witnesses** actually limit the number of the saved. **Islam** also restricts access to salvation to those who 'submit' to the will of Allah, to certain ethical and theocratic conditions. Such exclusivity is characteristic of religions of revelation that are based on the absolute authority of the revealed truths of God. Eastern religions, such as Hinduism and Buddhism, being traditions of realization, enlightenment or awakening, are more universalistic. Biblical religions endeavour to hold exclusivity in balance with a kind of **universalism** by affirming that the means of salvation is potentially open to anyone who cares to avail themselves of it.

Existence of God See **Arguments for the Existence of God**, **First Cause**, **Ontological Argument**, **Teleological Argument**

Existentialism A term applying to different philosophical trends that seek to address the broad questions we ask about human existence, such as does it have meaning, value or purpose? Existentialism denies that the universe is an ordered, stable or determined system, it is thus opposed to **rationalism** and **empiricism**. Thus, questions about knowledge, whether based on reason or experience, are less important than questions about being; moreover, since each individual is a unique presence in a hostile and ever-changing world, being cannot be the subject of objective enquiry. We can only understand existence in terms of our own experience of ourselves as a feeling, thinking, joyful, suffering, changing being, with a will that requires and enables us to make our own choices. Even though Existentialism concludes that we are caught up in a meaningless world, we have to cope with existence and to make 'sense' of it and in this process we have firstly to experience what **Sartre** called the 'nausea of existence' and our 'dreadful freedom'. **Kierkegaard**, usually thought to be the originator of existentialism, offered a solution to its problems in terms of an act of the will to believe in God, a decision to accept, on faith, that life does have meaning. Sartre took **Nietzsche**'s message, 'God is dead' to heart, thus denying Kierkegaard's solution and throwing humanity back on its own resources. For Sartre, our only resource is our freedom to choose both our world-view and our way of living in the world; this burden of free choice is made harder because there are no guidelines for the choices we are compelled to make and for which we must accept responsibility. It is this situation that causes us to live in a state of anxiety. By our choices we may arrive at either 'authentic' or 'inauthentic' existence, the former being a strong sense of our personal identity in consideration of the freedom of others and our ability to communicate with them; the latter, a kind of individual and collective anonymity, which consigns humanity to being the plaything of circumstance and capricious fate. The implications of Existentialism for religion is clear, but see **Religious Existentialism**.

FINAL WORD: 'I see it all perfectly; there are two possible situations – one can either do this or that. My honest opinion and my friendly advice is this; do it or do it not – you will regret both.' (Kierkegaard)

'Man is nothing else but what he makes of himself. Such is the first principle of existentialism.' (Sartre [1974])

Exit Counselling Also known as, 'Thought Reform Consulting', it is a service offered to ex-members of harmful or dangerous cults who are trying to extricate themselves from their influence. Techniques of education and counselling are offered over a two- or three-day period attended voluntarily and frequently under the supervision of a qualified mental health professional familiar with cult dynamics. The therapy places an emphasis on personal and religious freedom by endeavouring to put the authoritarian nature of the cult into a reasoned perspective so as reduce the level of fear or guilt.

Exodus *J*. The second book of the **Pentateuch** which tells the story of the Hebrew people's emancipation from slavery in Egypt under the leadership of **Moses**, of their years of wandering in the wilderness which took them to Mt Sinai, of the giving of the Ten Commandments to Moses and the establishment of the Mosaic **covenant**. The festival of **Passover**, one of the most important of the Jewish liturgical year, is a commemoration of this flight from Egypt and the ensuing journey.

Extra-Sensory Perception (ESP) The alleged knowledge or experience or a response to an external event, that is acquired apart from the five senses. This may take place in either a conscious or dreaming state. See **Clairvoyance**, **Medium**, **Parapsychology**, **Séance**

Extropianism See **Transhumanism**

Eye of the Spirit See **Third Eye**

F

Faith The absolute certainty in the correctness or trustworthiness of an idea, a system of ideas or in a person or group representing them. Usually, the use of the word implies a transpersonal relationship with a god, God or a Higher Power. It can also be used to specify a belief system, such as the faith of Islam, Judaism or the Baha'i. In creedal religions (see **Creeds**) the term implies an implicit trust in the doctrinal structure of the faith, in non-creedal traditions faith implies a loyalty to a community like the Buddhist **Sangha**. Being an entirely subjective response, faith is no guarantee of the validity of its object and the concept has been challenged by philosophies such as **rationalism** and **empiricism**. From the point of view of religion it is sometimes argued that religious knowledge ought not to be based on rational or natural information, but only on faith. See **Fideism**

FINAL WORD: 'To one who has faith, no explanation is necessary. To one without faith, no explanation is possible.' (Aquinas)

Fakir *I*. Arab. *faqir*, 'poor'. Someone who has adopted a mendicant lifestyle or who is in need of God. It is also a general, alternative term for a **Dervish**, or anyone living as a **Sufi** and practising Sufi rituals. Originally, the name was accorded to a Muslim who had carried out missionary work, thus aiding the spread of Islam. The tradition is based on a saying of Muhammad's, '*Al-fakr fakhri*', 'poverty is my pride.' In Islamic tradition there are two kinds of fakir, the *ba shiar*, those within the law and the *be shiar*, those without the law. The difference is simply one of Muslim orthodoxy, the former practising within the terms of Islamic doctrine, the latter although claiming to be Muslims, freer and more open in their associations. The two groups founded fraternities from c.770 CE. Frequently these fraternities were formed from secular occupations, like fishermen and camel-drivers. The *be shiar* fraternities practised extreme asceticism, even self-mortification. The concept and practices are by no means limited to Islam and have parallels, both with the medieval Christian **friars**, and with Indians who practise extravagant forms of asceticism, like walking on red hot coals, lying on a bed of nails or remaining immersed in water for long periods of time. Others reputedly remain in one place until birds nest in their hair or creepers grow around their limbs. As with all such groups the object is to gain spiritual merit by a renunciation of the world.

Falashas *J*. Amh. 'exiles'. Also know as *Beta Israel, House of Israel*. A Jewish ethnic group that began to emigrate to Israel from Ethiopia in 1975. Their Judaism is based on the **Bible** and certain books of the **Apocrypha**. Tradition has it that their progenitors were the Queen of Sheba and Jews returning with her to Ethiopia after she visited Solomon (I Kings 10). Falashas who converted to Christianity were known as the Falash Mura; many have now reverted to Judaism. Their religious authority remains the **Torah** which is handwritten and bound in book-form rather than rolled in a scroll as in traditional Judaism. Life centres around the *mesgid*, the synagogue which has two halls, one of which houses the Torah in a form of **Holy of Holies**, and an outside altar for the Passover sacrifice. Because of its long contact with Christianity there is a form of syncretism in which a priesthood in the line of Aaron, exists alongside communities of nuns and monks who maintain a monastic tradition. They also share the indigenous Ethiopian belief in nature spirits and the use of **charms**, and **amulets** to appease or oppose them. The debate as to the authenticity of Falashic Judaism continues in Israel, but the community has achieved an economic viability. See **Black Jews**

Fall of Man *X*. The Christian doctrine of man is developed from the biblical account of creation and the events in the Garden of Eden described in Genesis 1–3. The myth establishes that Adam, archetypal man, was created out of dust and in the image of God. God asked him and the first woman Eve, to tend the garden and to give everything names, but prohibited them from eating the fruit of the tree of 'knowledge of good and evil'. This prohibition established man's fee will and the act of disobedience that followed is known as 'The Fall'. Man's quest for knowledge is understood as a prideful attempt at 'knowing good and evil', thus to be like God. The myth sets the agenda for the Christian and Islamic doctrine of man who, originally good and endowed with freedom and responsibility, becomes guilty of originating sin (see **Original Sin**). The character of human existence and society is established and sin escalates to the point where people become the perpetrators of all manner of evil. The biblical story, continuing to the conclusion of the **New Testament**, teaches that to regain **paradise** on Christian terms humanity must accept the redemptive achievement of Christ's life. The fruits of redemption may be known in this life, but not entirely. Even though forgiven human beings remain sinners; they may realize only a limited potential of their regenerated lives, the final and full regeneration is for another world. See **Eschatology**, **Sin**

Falsafah *I*. Arab. 'philosophy'. The term is a neologism for the Greek, 'philosophy' but in the Islamic system it usually has a somewhat narrow meaning, referring to an enquiry into the physical or natural world. The term **Hikma** is used of those forms of philosophy that are concerned with theology, mysticism and theosophy. See **Islamic philosophy**

False Prophecy *J. X*. Generally any teaching by a prophet that is judged to be not true. Specifically and historically, a pronouncement or prediction made by an individual or group that claims to speak with God's or a Divine authority of a specific event that falls within the time-frame stipulated. In the **Old Testament** warnings were given that such prophecies would distract from the worship of Yahweh (Deut. 13:1–5 and 18: 21–22). False Prophets have sometimes claimed Messianic status. See **Messiah**, **Prophecy**

Falun Gong *C*. Chin. 'Practice of the Wheel of Dharma'. The movement was founded by Li Hongzhi, in 1992. The central practice is a set of five exercises called *Falun Dafa*, designed to cultivate body, mind and spirit; three exercises are controlled physical movements, the other two involve being still for long periods of time. The object is to tune oneself to the truths of human life and achieve higher levels of existence which require the practice of three virtues, *Zhen-Shan-Ren* ('Truthfulness, Compassion, Forbearance') historically **Confucian**, **Taoist** and **Buddhist** virtues. While Falun Gong does not oppose or preclude faith, its members claim that it is not a religion but the cultivation of a disciplined practice. Currently Falun Gong is being persecuted by the Chinese Government which, for reasons that are not clear, feel the size and popularity of the movement to be a threat.

FINAL WORD: 'Followers are frustrated and feel misunderstood, claiming that they are not interested in political power, just in being recognized as a legitimate religious entity permitted to practise their beliefs. These beliefs, they say, include morality, marital fidelity and physical exercise, as well as the overriding principles of truth, compassion and forbearance. Such things can only be good for a society, contend Falun Gong adherents' ('China's Falun Gong. The World Is Watching & Joining.' Website statement).

Familiar Spirit A spirit that can allegedly communicate with humans, often through a form of possession of a medium, channeler or psychic. The term is also used of a particular kind of **demon** that may impersonate the deceased during an attempt to communicate with the dead. See **Necromancy**, **Séance**

Family International See **Children of God**

Family of Love See **Children of God**

Fascism Its beginnings are to be found in Italy with the Fascist Movement formed by Mussolini in 1919, which he led as the elected leader from 1922–45. The term is derived from the *fasces*, the bundle of rods and projecting axe carried before the Roman consuls as an insignia of their authority. The movement, which fed on the widespread social and economic crisis that gathered momentum following the First World War, is also identified with Nazi Germany, the Falange of Franco's Spain, the Iron Guard of Rumania and the British Union of Fascists under Sir Oswald Mosley. These disparate fascist parties shared a passion for **nationalism**, were violently anti-communist, suspicious of anything liberal, democratic and the traditional forms of parliamentary government. Very quickly they assumed a Para-military character, adopted tactics of mass propaganda, promoted terrorism and used the cutting edge of ruthlessly efficient secret police. Fascist anti-Semitism (see **Semitic**) which led to the **Holocaust**, was the darkest side of a policy of racism designed, in Germany, to assert the myth of neo-Aryanism. Not all religious groups disassociated themselves with the policies of Hitler and Mussolini but needless to say, although the churches and chapels remained open, religion in general had little part to play in the culture of a fascist society, except in terms of protest. (See **Barth, Bonhoeffer**) Indeed, the passion and commitment shown to the 'Party' (as with **Communism**) filled for many the void created in society by a religion-less regime. The adoration shown to fascist leaders was not less than the adoration given to God by the Church and other religions.

Fast The practice of abstention from food for a given period of time, either as a form of aestheticism or in celebration, is common to most established religious traditions. Examples include the one day fast observed by Jews on **Yom Kippur**, the 19-day fast stipulated by **Baha'ullah** observed immediately before the **Baha'i** New Year, and the Muslim fast of **Ramadan**. There are innumerable variations of the practice, with Catholics fasting for an hour before Mass and abstaining from meat on important holy days; Hindus will fast on new moon days and Mormons on the first Sunday of each month.
FINAL WORD: 'The goal of fasting is inner unity … Fasting of the heart empties the faculties, frees you from limitations and from preoccupations.' (Chuang Tzu, trans. Thomas Merton)

Fatalism For religion, the acceptance that 'what will be will be', since all past, present and future events are predetermined by Divine will. The concept is akin to the doctrine of **Predestination**, the sombre belief that our eternal fate is fixed before we are born, however virtuous and spiritual our lives may be. Fatalism is the negation of human free will, the belief that the course of our life is governed by a portentous, impersonal power. In secular terms, who we are and the disposition to do what we do is determined by the interplay of genetics, the environment and DNA. See **Fate**

Fate A word interchangeable with 'destiny', designating the outcome of an event, a series of events or a lifetime. The notion is mostly used in the context of **fatalism**, the inevitability of something that may or may not be determined by a god, God or a Divine will. The human need to know one's fate whether in the course of a short period of time or in the long term, is the energy behind all forms of prophecy and divination. It may be that the course set is inevitable and nothing can be done to avert it, such was the general belief in ancient Greece and Rome, when human life was thought to be in the capricious control of the gods or the Fates. (See **Moirae**) Alternatively, knowledge of one's fate may afford the chance to alter it, by following certain ritual prescriptions, by making sacrifice or simply by a change in behaviour, habit or disposition. See **Determinism, Divination**
FINAL WORD: 'This whole act's immutably decreed. 'Twas rehearsed by thee and me a billion years before this ocean rolled. Fool! I am the Fates' lieutenant; I act under orders.' (Herman Melville)

Fates, The Of Greek mythology, see **Moirae**

Father Divine (1880–1965) See **Peace Mission Movement**

Fatihah *I*. Arab. 'the Opener', the first **Surah** of the **Koran**. It is said that the whole of the Koran is contained in this opening chapter and the whole chapter within the *Bismillah*, the invocation of the divine name. The tradition goes on to say that the whole of the *Bismillah*, lies within the '*bi*', the invoking preposition. In Arabic there is a point, below the 'B', of *Bismillah*, suggesting a mystical sense in which Muslims are the 'People of the Point', since their whole religion is contained within it.

Fatimah Zahra (606/614–32 CE) *I*. The earlier date for her birth is the Sunni tradition; the later date the Shiite. One of **Muhammad**'s and Khadijah's four daughters and the wife of Muhammad's cousin, **Ali Ibn Abi Talib**, the fourth Caliph of **Sunni** Islam. There are two views of the role of Fatima in Islamic tradition and they are radically opposed. **Shiite** Muslims claim she was Muhammad's only daughter and that the existence of other daughters were rumours spread by their Sunni opponents. They promote her as a dutiful daughter close to her father and a model wife who loved her children. Her husband Ali, was Muhammad's closest lieutenant but his assumption of the Caliphate was controversial and the cause of internecine violence. Fatima, who was pregnant, died as a result of a Sunni raid on Ali's house led by Umar, a rival claimant to the Caliphate. She was buried secretly by night. Fatima is known to the Shiite as the 'Mother of the Imams', because of their belief that only someone descended directly from Muhammad by Fatimah could be an **imam**. In opposition, the Sunni historians asserted that Fatima was the youngest of four daughters whose mother was Muhammad's first wife, Khadija. According to the Sunni account, Fatima died of natural causes and not from injuries sustained by the raid. They hold her to be a model daughter and wife, a true Muslim and an example to all Muslim women. For them she is Al-Zahra, the Lady of Light. The *Khamsa*, an amulet used in Maghreb, is thought to protect against evil and symbolizes the Hand of Fatima. It is not possible to decide which view of Fatima's history is the more authentic, since the only sources available are oral traditions that were not committed to writing until at least 100 years after the events described. Islam has always lived with the two traditions but in some respects, they have been formative of the sharp divisions between the Shiite and the Sunni. The Egypt-based **Fatimid Caliphate**, 909–1171 CE, was named after Fatima and authenticated by virtue of their claiming the direct line of dissent.

Islam and **Catholicism** appear to meet in the cult of **Mary** whose name is mentioned 30 times in the Koran, describing her as *Virgin, ever Virgin*. Fatima is not mentioned once. This suggests that either there is a special relationship in Islam with the Christian cult of Mary or that the traditions surrounding Fatima have been strongly influenced by it.

Fatimid Caliphate *I*. A dynasty of **caliphs** of the **Isma'ili Shiite** empire based in Egypt, 909–1171 CE. They were named after Muhammad's daughter **Fatima**, claiming to be descended from her. The Shiite sect originally from the Yemen, was considered to be heretical, rejecting the **Abbasids** as usurpers. As Abbasid power declined the Shiite, believing themselves to be by right of descent the true custodians of the faith, conquered Egypt in 969. Their object was not territorial dominance but to found a new caliphate that would replace the Abbasids. They built and made Cairo their capital and extended their empire throughout North Africa, Sicily, Syria and western Arabia. The cycle of decline and fall of successive Caliphates continued and the Fatimid power declined from c.1100 CE until, in 1171, Sulah ad-Din (Saladin) the military leader who fought against the Christian crusaders, returned the Fatimid territories to **Sunni** Islam. See **Islamic Dynasties**

Fatwa, pl. **Fatawa** *I*. Arab. 'legal pronouncement' or 'opinion', offered on a point of law by a **Mufti**, a canon lawyer. It is usually issued by a specialist whose 'opinion' is requested by a judge. Contrary to what is believed by many non-Muslims and even by the majority of Muslims, a *fatwa* is not binding on all persons professing the Muslim faith. The only ones who are obliged to obey any specific *fatwa* are the mufti who issued it and his followers. Since there is no centralized priestly hierarchy in Islam there is much argument as to who has the right to issue a *fatwa* and there are Islamic scholars who feel that too many are issued by those not qualified to do so. The most well known *fatawa* are those associated with Osama bin Laden, who in 1996 issued a *fatwa* against the USA with the title, 'Declaration of War against the Americans Occupying the Land of the Two Holy Places'. Ben Laden was opposing the American occupation of military bases in Syria. His second *fatwa*, issued with other muftis in 1998, specified three objections: i) USA occupation of the Arabian Peninsula; ii) USA aggression against the Iraqi people; and iii) USA support of Israel. Bin Laden concluded the *fatwa* thus, 'The International Islamic Front for Jihad against the USA and Israel has issued a crystal-clear *fatwa* calling on the Islamic nation to carry on jihad aimed at liberating holy sites. The nation of Muhammad has responded to this appeal.' It is believed the attack on the World Trade Center on 11th September 2001, was a response to this *fatwa*. The overwhelming majority of *fatawa* are issued on ordinary, everyday matters. Those declaring war or pronouncing death sentences on an individual, as was issued in 1989 by the Iranian Ayatollah Ruhollah Khomeini against Salman Rushdie for the authorship of *The Satanic Verses*, are not at all representative, despite the attention they attract in the media. See **Jihad**

Fellowship of Isis An international sect dedicated to honouring the goddess **Isis**. It was founded in 1976 at its centre Clonegal Castle, in Ireland. Isis is believed to be the Divine Mother of all sentient beings and the fellowship has attracted adherents from across the world. The manifesto states that, 'The Fellowship reverences all manifestations of Life.

The God also is venerated. The Rites exclude any form of sacrifice, whether actual or symbolic. Nature is revered and conserved. The work of the Noble Order of Tara is for the conservation of Nature.'

Feminist Dianic Witchcraft See **Dianic Wicca**

Feng-Shui A religious 'science' applied to balance **Yin and Yang** in the environment. It has its origin 3,000 years ago in **Taoism**, when the practice was used by farmers. The universe is charged with a flowing energy *Chi*, which in this world passes through lines called channels or meridians. For optimum health and quality of life one must be aligned with these meridians. How we position furniture, for example, affects the flow of *Chi* and our ability to harmonize with it. The whole internal and external environment is arranged by practitioners so as to be properly aligned with *Chi*. Nature's balance will thereby be improved for everyone's benefit.

Festival Usually calendric celebrations through the religious year marking significant events in the lives of the gods, goddesses, God or in the history of the religion. They have been a feature of religious life since early antiquity and are countless in number. Examples are given under most of the entries for each religion or god.

Fetish An object believed to have magical and spiritual powers, usually associated with **animism** and **shamanism**. It can have symbolic significance in that the object may substitute for the person or concept it represents. Fetishism is the practice of using fetishes and is in use to a greater or lesser extent in all religions. The term also has secular applications; for example 'commodity fetishism' is the **Marxist** notion of inauthentic relationships based on the commodity being the medium for the relationship. Binet and **Freud** introduced the concept of sexual fetishism where an inanimate object or a part of a person's body is the focus of affection and probably indispensable to true sexual arousal.

Feuerbach, Ludwig (1804–72) A German philosopher who rebelled against the arid academic philosophies of the 19th century. He was a leader of the radical 'Young Hegelians' (see **Hegel**). His philosophy is based on a repudiation of religion and **Idealism**, arguing that culture and civilization can only be advanced by their negation. As an alternative, he advocated materialistic **humanism** and social ethics, creating a link between Hegel and **Marx**. Modern scholarship has reinstated Feuerbach's system in its own right.

Fideism A reaction in the philosophy of religion to what was considered to be the inadequacy of **proofs** for the existence of God. Fideism asserts that our religious knowledge is not properly founded if it relies on rational or natural information and that faith alone is the only valid authority, since religious experience is beyond the limits and comprehension of human reason. To use reason is evidence of impiety and arrogance, since the finite mind and imagination of man cannot begin to grasp the infinite and unimaginable. However, fideism has been turned in on itself since agnostics and non-believers have used the principle of 'faith alone' as the clearest way to state their doubts. If reason and **natural religion** are excluded, what then is the basis of faith? It is founded on subjective experience, how is that to be validated? To start with doubt and then accept the validity of faith, is to reject rational evidence for religious knowledge, but it was on this platform that **Pascal** and **Kierkegaard**, for example, constructed their religious philosophy. Faith, they submit, is a gamble but one well worth taking. On the same platform, but arguing differently, secular thinkers like **Hume** and **Voltaire** built their systems. See **Agnosticism**

Fijian Religion *P*. The original religion was an animistic polytheism associated with nature spirits, with gods of sea and sky and of hunting, fishing and war. These were centred on a form of Totemism (see **Totem**) and **ancestor worship**, a tradition permeating every facet of life. Tribal leaders descended from ancestor heroes were accorded almost priestly status some of whom, aspiring to divinity, delegated a brother to manage the secular administration. Female descent is figured in hereditary land-ownership made sacred by taboos protecting flora and fauna. Missionary activity displaced the indigenous beliefs, 79 per cent of the population now being associated with various Christian denominations, markedly Catholic and Methodist. Other religions include Hinduism, Sikhism and Islam.

Fiqh *I*. The concept of a person's or group's effort to interpret and apply **Shari'a**, the divine law. In contrast to the perfect and absolute nature of Shari'a, Fiqh is fallible and inconsistent, as any mere interpretation has to be. Interpreting the divine law is a process entirely dependent on understanding the divine will. See **Ijma**, **Ijtihad**, **Sunni**, **Ulema**, **Urf**

Fire Giants *AE*. In Germanic and Norse mythology, the Fire Giants were in at the beginning of creation, dwelling in Muspell, the region of fire, reminiscent of the original chaotic, molten form of the world. The light was as fearful as the fire and only the Fire Giants could live there. The border of Muspell was guarded by Surt, their leader, who carried a flaming sword. As the world began, so it will end with Giants destroying the world of the gods with fire. The role of the Fire Giants will be to set the world ablaze during the final battle of **Ragnarok**. See **Frost Giants**

Fire, Sacred Fire was worshipped in antiquity and a cult of sacred fire has been a feature of various religious beliefs and rituals. Greek mythology records how **Prometheus** stole fire from **Zeus** and brought it down to earth as a gift for mankind. The Romans honoured the sacred fire burning in the temple of **Vesta** as a symbol of her presence and tended by the **Vestal Virgins**. In **Hinduism** sacrifice to the fire god **Agni**, was one of the first acts of morning devotion Zoroastrians (**Parsis**) believe fire to be the purest element on earth and worship it as the son of **Ahura Mazda** the spirit of the sun. There are three grades of fire housed in an **Agiary**, or Fire Temple, the Atash Behram, the Fire Cathedral, being the highest. Agiary are to be found throughout India, southern Asia, Iran and America. See **Goma Fire Ritual**, **Shingon School**, **Zoroastrianism, Traditional**

First Cause A classical argument for the existence of God, also known as the cosmological or prime mover argument. One of the first and most influential versions of the argument was offered by **Aquinas** on his reading of **Aristotle**. It is simply stated: i) Everything has a cause; ii) nothing can cause itself; iii) everything is caused by another thing; iv) a causal chain cannot be of infinite length; v) there must be a first cause; vi) God is the first cause. In terms of cause and effect the entire universe is considered, hence the syllogism: whatever begins to exist has a cause, the universe began to exist, therefore the universe had a cause, i.e. God. The debate continues for even the 'Big Bang' must have been caused, thus prior to that, something must have existed, therefore ...etc. Stephen Hawking suggests that the 'Big Bang' was the beginning of both space and time, thus to ask what was before the 'Big Bang' is like asking what is north of the North Pole. However, creationist religions point out that Hawking's contribution is to cosmology, not to theology. See **Arguments for the Existence of God**, **Creationism**, **Onotological Argument**, **Teleological Argument**

First Church of Christ the Scientist The movement founded by Mary Baker Eddy in the 19th century. See **Christian Scientists**

First Preslyterian Church of Elvis the Divine Founded in Bethlehem, PA, USA in 1988 by Farndu and Karl Edwards. It was set up as a spoof religion designed to be a marketing ploy focused on the 'worship' of Elvis Presley. Weekly services were held on the Internet and in the campus chapel of Lehigh University. It hoped to put the 'fun' back into **fundamentalism**, and votes are taken on whether or not Presley was divine and/or a messenger of God. There are branches of the church in several countries. Numerous, more serious, testimonies of visions of Elvis have been recorded, associated with healing, near-death experiences and by those in the presence of people dying.

Fitnah *I.* Arab. 'trial', 'testing' or 'temptation'. A central concept in Islamic tradition, *fitnah* refers, firstly, to the opposition to Islam experienced by early Muslims and secondly, threats to the security and well-being of the *umma*, the community. These terms are extended to include any form of disorder or persecution perpetrated against the individual or the community so as to unsettle or distract from the faith. Historically the term is often used for the First Islamic civil war in 656–661 CE, being a prolonged struggle for the **caliphate** after the 656 CE assassination of Caliph Uthman Ibn Affan. The Second Fitnah or Second Islamic civil war, is usually identified as the 683–685 CE conflict among the **Umayyads** for control of the caliphate. There is a *hadith* stating that the greatest *fitnah* for men, is women.

Five Aggregates *B. Z.* Skt. *skandhas*, meaning 'group', 'aggregate' or 'heap'. They represent an important aspects of the Buddhist perception of 'personality'. The five aspects of personality are i) *Rupa*, corporate reality or form; ii) *Vedana*, sensation; iii) *Sanna*, perception; iv) *Samskara*, mental formations; and v) *Vijnana*, consciousness. Together, through craving and desire, they bind us to this world and its cycles of birth, old age, death and change, in short, to everything associated with *dukkha*, suffering. However, seen for what they are, they have no essence (*anatman*) are impermanent (*anitya*) and empty (*shunya*). As with all other qualities and characteristics, Buddhism sees personality as an illusion since neither separately nor together do the aggregates constitute an abiding self.

Five Elements School See **Sanna**

Five Ks or **Panja kakke** *Sik.* Pun. The distinguishing marks given to Sikhs initiated by the rite of *amritsankar* into the **Khalsa**. The five marks or signs are: i) uncut hair; ii) the comb; iii) the dagger or short sword; iv) the bangle; and v) breeches that must not go below the knee.

Five Pillars of Islam See **Pillars of Islam**

Five Precepts *B.* Skt. and Pal. *Panca-sila.* The basic ethical code by which a Buddhist should live. See **Precepts**

Flamen *R.* Sacrificial Priest of Ancient Rome. There were 15, each serving a particular God. For example, the flamen Dialis, Martialis and Quirinalis were the most important, being priests of **Jupiter**, **Mars** and **Quirinus**, respectively. A fourth major flamen was added in 44 BCE, dedicated to Julius Caesar. The major flamen were patricians, the others drawn from the plebeians. The 15 flamens formed part of the Pontifical College responsible for the administration of the state-sponsored religion of Rome. See **Roman Religion**

Flirty Fishing A form of Christian evangelism that uses sexual practice and rituals to witness to the love of God. See **Children of God**

Flood *J.* Hebrew, *mabal.* The biblical flood was a divine judgement against the wickedness of humanity inflicted at the time of Noah (see Gen. 6:5ff). Noah and his family were the only survivors, together with representatives of 'every bird, beast and creeping things'. The Bible shares the myth of a great flood with other ancient religious cultures, notably the **Assyrian** and **Babylonian**. Archaeology has established the likelihood that an actual flood did occur but that it was probably a local, rather than global, event the destruction of the entire world being a reference to the then known world. In Jewish tradition the whole human race stems from the offspring of Noah's sons, Shem, Ham and Japheth. See **B'nai Noah**

Folklore The traditional beliefs, myths, tales and customs of people that have been transmitted orally, also the comparative study of these. Folklore is usually thought to be unfounded, its sources lost in ancient antiquity. Many superstitions are part of a folklore culture. Although it is the oral tradition that distinguishes folklore, it is now an exhaustively researched subject with an extensive bibliography. See **Legend**, **Myth**, **Superstition**

Fon Religion A. The Fon are a major ethnic and religious group found in **Benin**, Dahomey and southern Nigeria. Their religion is very varied and it is not possible to provide a simple overview. The belief system is polytheistic but with a supreme but not omnipotent god called, Nana Buluku. The Benin national religion is Vodun, more familiarly known as the much-travelled **Voodoo**, a monotheistic and magical form of animism. Dahomey mythology centres on an entire pantheon of thunder gods whose head is Sogbo. Their creator deities are Liza (male) and Mawu (female). The pantheon includes gods of smallpox, war, the moon, hunters, the wilderness and gods of various crafts. As a result of the slave trade many Fon descendents live in the USA and together with the **Yoruba** and **Bantu**, they merged with French, Portuguese and Spanish culture, producing distinct religions such as Voodoo, **Candomblé** and **Santeria**. See **Snakes**, **Snake Deities**

Form Criticism A critical method used by scholars to identify the literary forms of the **Bible**, so as to place them in their original historical, sociological and cultural setting. It aims to distinguish between, for example, different literary styles and vocabulary, various forms of Psalms, lamentation, thanksgiving or adoration and the varied features of the **Gospels**, such as parables, miracle stories, events and geography. Both similarities and differences in the texts aid in interpretation and liberal Christianity has concluded that many of the forms are legendary or mythical, rather than being a historical record of actual events. See **Higher Criticism**, **Redaction Criticism**, **Source Criticism**

Fortune Telling An ancient but popular form of **divination** that attempts to predict the future of an individual by means of objects such as crystal balls, cards and palms (see **Palmistry**), using the paranormal powers that the practitioners are presumed to have. Most fortune-tellers are professional and their craft is akin to **astrology**. See **Auspicia**

Foundation of Human Understanding Originally called the Institute of Hypnosis, it was founded in 1961 by Roy Masters in Los Angeles, USA. Having been a stage hypnotist, then working with witch doctors in South

Africa, the better to understand the workings of the mind, Masters concluded that we are all under a form of hypnosis caused by the stress and anxieties with which we live. In 1968 he published *Your Mind Can Keep You Healthy* and started a radio show. Having been recognized, after a law suit, as a religion the Foundation moved to Oregon where Masters set about teaching the world psychocatalysis, a form of meditation technique. Many who attended remained to form a community. It is believed that some three million people tune in to the radio station.

Four Awakenings of Mindfulness See **Satipathana**

Fountain of Youth In mythology, magical waters which have the property of transforming old age into youth and thus of prolonging life indefinitely. See **Ambrosia, Elixir of Life, Nectar**

Four Noble Truths *B*. The foundational doctrines of **Buddhism**, given by the Buddha in his first discourse at Sarnath, near Benares. They are: i) *Dukkha*, the truth of suffering; ii) *Samudaya*, the truth of the origin of suffering; iii) *Nirodha*, the truth of the cessation of suffering; and iv) the truth of the **Eightfold Path** that leads to the cessation of suffering. The realization of these truths amounted to the Buddha's **enlightenment**. The standard text is found in the **Pali Canon**.

Four Stages of Life *H*. Skt. *Ashram*. The four classical stages of a Hindu's life according to the principles of the **Vedas** and through which the three castes of the twice-born Hindu should pass. The four stages are: i) *Brahmacharya* (Skt. 'continence', 'chastity') – the youth receives religious and secular instruction from parents and teachers, he develops his intellect and the virtues that lead to the spiritual life and to investiture with the sacred thread, symbolic of his second birth (see **Sacred Thread Ceremony**); ii) *Grihastha* (Skt. 'householder'), based on marriage and family – marriage is a spiritual exercise which expands consciousness and teaches self-control, and almost all Hindu gods are represented as married (according to the Vedic prescription, this stage ends when the householder is aware 'that wrinkles are beginning to appear and that his hair is growing grey and when his sons are themselves fathers of sons'); iii) *Vanaprastha* (Skt. 'forest abode') – having fulfilled the duties of a householder and served the community, a man withdraws into the forest, maybe with his wife, to devote himself to the study of philosophy and the scriptures, to practise meditation and to discipline the body in preparation for iv) the *Sannyasin*: *H*. (Skt. 'renunciation') – the Hindu has discharged his three duties and now endeavours to slough off everything that holds him to this world and to give up all selfish interests. His efforts are focused on obtaining *moksha*, liberation and union with God. Together with the original four castes, this four-stage passage through life was intended to provide the structure within which Hindu society could operate effectively. See **Ashrama, Hinduism, Sacred Thread Ceremony**

Francis of Assisi, St (c.1181–1226 CE**)** *X*. Founder of the Franciscan Order or 'Friars Minor' and patron saint of animals, merchants and the environment. The legends and stories establishing his special relationship with nature are recorded in the *Fioretti*, 'Little Flowers', the most famous of which include the story of him preaching to his 'little sisters', a tree full of birds and taming a 'brother' wolf that had killed people. His order was founded in 1209 with the approval of Pope Innocent III, but only after the Pope had had a dream in which he saw the Church falling apart, but held together by St Francis. See **Franciscans, Waldenses**

Franciscans *X*. The Order of Friars Minor was founded in 1209 by Francis of Assisi (1181–1226), the son of a rich merchant family who, while making a pilgrimage to Rome, met and exchanged clothes with a beggar. Disowned by his father, he set about repairing a ruined church. In 1208 he responded to Christ's call to discipleship (Matt. 10:7–19) and, quickly attracting a following, wrote a simple Rule for them, the *Regula Primitiva*, which was approved by Pope Innocent III and finally recast and confirmed by Pope Honorius III in a Bull of 1223. The main feature of the Rule was complete poverty, both for individuals and for the community. From 1219 St Francis travelled and preached in Egypt and Eastern Europe, after which he never attempted to resume the leadership of the Franciscan Order. St Francis founded the 'Tertiaries' in 1221, a form of friar community who lived by the Rule while continuing a normal way of life. In 1224, he received the **stigmata**. The Order became divided between those who interpreted the Rule literally, the 'Spirituals' and those who sought to modify it, the 'Observants'. The matter was decided in 1317 by Pope John XXII who pronounced the Spirituals' literalism heretical and allowed the modifying party to consolidate the Order and to own property. Further reforms led, in 1529, to the creation of the **Capuchins**, and in the 17th and 18th centuries to other reform parties. In 1897 a reunification of the disparate groups gave the Order a new momentum. There is a Second Order of contemplative nuns and a Third Order of women who, devoted to charity, are not strictly enclosed. In 1921 a Church of England Order of Franciscans was established at Cerne Abbey in Dorset, ministering to the unemployed. They were established as a full religious community in 1931.

Frashokereti *Zo*. Per. 'making wonderful'. The renovation or restoration of the universe according to the teachings of **Zoroastrianism**. The rehabilitation of the universe is the ultimate goal of **Ahura Mazda**, and any of his followers who choose to live by the Truth, rather than the Lie, contribute to achieving this goal. The **Yasna** ritual is also a means of aiding cosmic renewal.

Fravarane *Zo*. 'I declare …' The **Zoroastrian** creed or confession of faith. A summary of the main tenets are: i) 'I declare myself a Mazda-worshipper, a supporter of **Zarathustra**, hostile to the **Daevas**, fond of Ahura's teaching, a praiser of the **Amesha Spentas**, a worshipper of the Amesha Spentas'; ii) 'I choose the good Spenta Armaiti [one of the **Bounteous Immortals**, the spirit of Piety and Devotion] for myself; let her be mine'; iii) 'I reject the authority of the Daevas, the wicked, no-good, lawless, evil-knowing, the most druj-like of beings, [**druj** is the 'lie', the name for everything that is wrong] the foulest of beings, the most damaging of being'; iv) 'I profess myself a Mazda-worshipper, a Zoroastrian, having vowed it and professed it. I pledge myself to the well-thought thought, I pledge myself to the well-spoken word, I pledge myself to the well-done action'; v) 'I pledge myself to the **Mazdayasnian** religion, which causes the attack to be put off and weapons put down ... which of all religions that exist or shall be, is the greatest, the best and the most beautiful. I ascribe all good to Ahura Mazda.' (Yasna 12. Avesta. trans. J. H. Peterson)

Fravashi *Zo.* The **Zoroastrian** concept of a power, spirit or energy, inherent in all substances. The word has two roots, *Fra*, which may be translated 'to progress', 'to go forward' and *vashi*, from a root meaning 'to grow'. *Fravashi* can then be interpreted as 'moving forward', 'growing' or 'making progress'. The **Avesta** explains that *Fravashi* is what aids the development of all animate and inanimate aspects of Nature. In another sense it is the real, abiding essence of things, the spiritual core of everything **Ahura Mazda**, the Zoroastrian Supreme Being, created. One of the Avesta hymns, the *Fravadin Yasht*, records that Ahura Mazda created the Fravashi before he created anything else, suggesting everything created has its own spiritual agency watching over it, 'moving it forward', to perfection. The whole universe is therefore evolving and growing towards the ultimate goal of *Frashokereti*, the renovation or restoration of the cosmos. A myth tells how the Fravashis of human beings were consulted as to whether they wanted a physical manifestation which would involve them in the conflict between Good and Evil. They chose to take on human physical form. Behind this lies a central doctrine of Zoroastrianism, the critical importance of free will. See **Asa, Daevas, Druj**

Freak Scene The so-called 'freak scene' first developed in the 1960s and 1970s, as a drop out sub-culture that has rejected religion. 'Freak' is a reference to biological distortions and mutations that produced unique and sometimes hideous human forms. The term is now loosely applied to anything or anyone thought to be markedly different, extreme or eccentric and in a religious context the terms 'Jesus Freak' and 'Mind Freak', have been coined. The 'Scene' is akin to Punk culture with its ritual of piercing and the presentation of 'Freak Shows'. Although disassociated with traditional religion those who identify themselves with the Freak Scene may well have their own, effective ways of developing their spirituality.

Free Churches *X.* Churches of any denomination that are entirely free from government control as opposed to Established Churches or those governed by some form of theocracy. Historically, the Christian church was a Free Church until Theodosius adopted Christianity as the State religion of the Roman Empire. The status of being 'free' was not achieved until after the **Reformation**, when certain radical groups like the **Anabaptists** wrested government to themselves. Two extremes are in evidence, one that seeks to destroy the church by secularization, the other, which by theocracy (**Calvin**'s Geneva, for example) endeavours to bring all matters of secular government within the control of the church. The relationship between Church and state is a long debated theological and political issue. Separation is part of the American Constitution, but in the absence of a constitution the 'established' status of the Church of England is underwritten by law. In the United Kingdom there are two state 'approved' churches, the Church of Scotland, which is **Presbyterian** and a national church guaranteed by law to be separate from the state, and the Church of England, which is **Anglican** and state-established. In both cases the King or Queen is legally obliged to uphold the rites of these churches and in England the Sovereign is Supreme Governor of the Church, holding the title 'Defender of the Faith'. In the United Kingdom, the Free Churches have their origin in nonconformism having, in 1662, dissented from the Act of Uniformity which imposed the use of the creeds, prayers, sacraments and ceremonials of the Book of Common Prayer, also of 1662. They include Presbyterians, **Congregationalists**, **Baptists** and, later, **Methodists**, **Quakers** and the **Salvation Army**. Thus, the Free Churches in the United Kingdom are those independent of the Church of England or the Scottish Presbyterian Church. See **Christian Expansion and Denominations, Counter-Reformation**

Freedomites *X*. See **Doukhobors**

Freemasonry Originally a fraternal order associated with guilds of 'operative' masons or stonecutters. Freemasonry or 'speculative' masons, sought to give philosophical, moral and spiritual meaning to the Lodge, tools and oaths of the medieval stonecutters' guilds. All Freemasonry in existence today can be traced back to the Grand Lodge of England formed in 1717. In 1723 Dr James Anderson, minister of the Church of Scotland, published the Anderson Constitutions, comprising 39 General Articles which formalized the government of the Craft. Following the formal constitution of Freemasonry in the 18th century, there was rapid expansion, firstly within the British Isles and then beyond them. An English Lodge was founded in Paris in 1732 and within three years the Craft had reached Portugal, Holland and Sweden, with the first German Lodge constituted in Hamburg in 1737. Today, Freemasonry flourishes throughout the world, together with various splinter groups that, for historical or philosophical reasons, have severed their Grand Lodge connection. Varied rites are followed but most expressions of the Craft honour their constituted commitment to aid charitable and educational foundations and a huge amount of benefit has been derived from this. The outsider is inevitably perplexed by the movement's status as an initiatory society, the secrets of which are closely guarded. However, almost everything there is to be known about Freemasonry is accessible through available literature, which is copious. The so-called secrets of Freemasonry were once indispensable for preserving the quality of the craft of itinerate operative masons, especially from the Middle Ages onwards. By means of questions, passwords and signs, the master of a working lodge could discover if a stonecutter looking for work was an apprentice or Master Mason, a true master of his craft and worthy of being employed or even of teaching his fellow craftsmen. The 'secrets' of Freemasonry refer to these questions, passwords and signs, by which means one Mason might recognize the status of another, and they are therefore symbolic and have no other significance or purpose beyond their representational value within the rite of the Lodge and none at all beyond it.

Even though many clergy and adherents of all the major world religions have become Freemasons, the Craft's relationship with religion has always been controversial, at times to the point of persecution. Currently, the movement is banned in Communist countries, Roman Catholic Spain and Portugal, but not in Italy. It is also opposed by most forms of fundamentalist religion. The reasons for this are complicated and have to do with theology, with the religious and political authorities feeling threatened and the fear that although Freemasons do not proselytize, the movement might distract men from religious commitment. Freemasonry is not a closed order and any man, so long as he is of good repute, is eligible to become a Freemason, regardless of his social, political or religious affiliations. Thus, in any one Lodge might be found Jews, Christians, Muslims, Buddhists, Hindus, as well as those without any commitment to a received religious tradition. All that is asked is that a candidate is able to confess a belief in a higher power termed, 'the Grand Architect of the Universe', which might just as easily be the **Yahweh** of the **Old Testament**, the Christ of the **New Testament**, **Allah**, **Ahura Mazda** or the enlightened or realized 'self'. The question as to whether or not Freemasonry is a religion continues to be debated. Freemasons would claim that the Craft is not a religion, but like a flying buttress supports all religions from the outside. It depends, of course, on how 'religion' is defined, but by the usually accepted functional, rather than theological definitions, Freemasonry would qualify. A further important question asks if Freemasonry is an alternative to religion and judged by the role the movement plays in the lives of its adherents, it would certainly seem to offer that possibility.

FINAL WORD: 'Freemasonry harmonizes all the spiritual, moral, social, cultural and mystical elements of human nature and good men, to their surprise, have found delight and fulfilment in it over many centuries.' (John Acaster)

Freethinkers Those who have rejected the authority and dogma of a received tradition, especially religious, in favour of rational enquiry and speculation. Although there have always been people sceptical and critical of the religions and philosophical culture of their time, free thinking as we know it is a child (become sturdy adult) of the **Enlightenment** and of **rationalist** philosophers not all of whom disavowed religion, but who undoubtedly set us free to think about it on any terms we choose. See **Agnosticism, Atheism, Illuminati**

Freud, Sigmund (1856–1939) Psychologists have asked if religion is a response to a necessary psychological drive, rather than to the existence of God. Freud, a non-believing Jew nervous of the power of Catholicism, offered several theories concerning the origin and nature of religion and our experience of it. Mostly these were based on his thesis that religion was a childhood neurosis caused by our having been a helpless baby absolutely dependent on our parents. The infant relates to the parents as all-powerful beings who love, guide, correct and satisfy its necessary needs. Freud argued that this pattern is sustained throughout life and is identical to the way people regard their God. A child's feelings for its parents, itself and the world are very complicated, and religious beliefs and rituals offer a satisfying way of working these relationships out.
FINAL WORD: 'Religion is an illusion that derives its strength from the fact that it falls in with our instinctual desires.' (Freud [1965])
    'In the long run nothing can withstand reason and experience and the contradiction religion offers to both is palpable.' (Freud [1989])

Freyr, Freyja & Frigg *Nor. AE.* In **Norse mythology** Freyr and Freyja were members of the **Vanir**, one of the groups of Nordic gods. Freyr was the god of peace, prosperity and fruitfulness and Freyja, Freyr's twin sister, the goddess of the earth and sexuality. Frigg was a member of the **Aesir**, another group of gods, the wife of **Odin**, goddess of marriage, motherhood and fertility and, in this respect, shows similarities to Freyja. See **Germanic Religion, Nordic Mythology**

Friars Preachers *X.* See **Dominicans**

Frost-Giants *Nor. AE.* In Nordic mythology a mythical race of giants with super-human strength who were adversaries of the gods although they mingled with and sometimes married them. They represent cold, chaos and sterility, with a reputation for a hideous appearance, having claws, fangs, disfigured faces and bodies, sometimes with many heads and non-humanoid shapes. Their ugliness comes with poor intellect and the **Eddas** depict them as bad-tempered children. In Scandinavia they are commonly known as trolls. See **Fire Giants**

Functionalism A definition of something based on what it does, achieves or affects. Religion has been defined functionally as that which provides social cohesion and solidarity, thus contributing to society's culture and survival. A functionalist analysis of religion will want to know if specific religious institutions meet individual or social needs, help bind society together, create a sense of belonging, focus common values, priorities and beliefs or explain the inexplicable. If a religion achieves these objectives it is 'socially' valid. Thus religious beliefs, hopes, practices are of secondary importance to the creation and maintenance of a harmonious society. The theory would seem to have application to a society with an established theocracy, such as the Islam of Iran or Saudi Arabia, but would be more difficult to apply to a society that is religiously pluralistic like Great Britain. For **Marx** and **Engels** religion was the opium of the masses, it gave temporary and illusory relief to anxiety and suffering and in that sense was 'useful'. See **Marxism**, **Pragmatism**, **Utilitarianism**

Fundamentalism A concept usually applied to biblical religions, cults, sects and their literature, identifying a belief in the absolute and infallible truth of whatever authority they rest on. If it is the Bible, their fundamentalism will be derived from the belief that every word is the given and inviolable 'word' of God. The concept was originally inspired by a series of tracts, *The Fundamentals*, distributed in the USA in 1909, that defended the basic doctrine of Christian faith against **Form** and **Source Criticism**, and the 'new' theologies of, for example, **Bultmann**, **Tillich** and **Bonhoeffer**. However, although Christian apologetics might have been the origin of fundamentalism, its mind-set is not confined to Christianity. There are vehement Jewish fundamentalists calling for a more rigorous and literal observation of Law and similar, militant movements within Islam, to the point where the principle of fundamentalism has become a dominant feature of Western religious and political culture.

Fundamental Rule See **Golden Rule**

Funerary Practices *E*. It could be argued that the Egyptians were obsessed with death; it can also be argued that they were so much in love with life that the wealthy took whatever measures they could to ensure its continuation in the 'afterlife'. The range of funerary goods included everything from the viscera contained in canopic jars, jewellery and furniture, to toilet equipment, food and drink. Models were made of brewers, bakers and butchers to ensure the supply of food. The deceased were accompanied by mummified animals and *ushabtis*, figures in the shape of mummies representing a labour force who, in a later period were equipped with the tools of their respective trades and crafts. A deep belief in the power led to the **Pyramid Texts** being carved on any available surface of the tomb; other funerary inscriptions, know as Coffin Texts, were carved into the sides of the sarcophagi. The celebrated 'Book of the Dead', contained spells and guidance for the deceased intended to facilitate access to the afterlife by means of a favourable judgement which took the form of weighing the heart in a pair of scales. The best-known funerary practice was that of **mummification**, a method of preserving the body so that the soul could return to it with food offerings. See **Soul, Egyptian concept of**

FINAL WORD: 'Osiris, the scribe Ani, said : "O my heart which I had from my mother! O my heart which I had from mother! O my heart of my different ages! May there be nothing to resist me at the judgement. May there be no opposition to me from the assessors. May there be no parting of You from me in the presence of him who keeps the scales! You are my Ka within my body, which formed and strengthened my limbs. May You come forth to the place of happiness where to I advance. May the entourage not cause my name to stink and may no lies be spoken against me in the presence of the god! It is indeed well that You should hear!'" (Papyrus of Ani: XXVIII Dynasty: Translated by Dungen, van den, Wim)

Futurism One of the initiatives contributing to the ideology was F. T. Marinetti's *Futurist Manifesto* published in the French newspaper *Le Figaro* on 20th February 1909. Entirely literary in its reference it was quickly taken up by other arts, to become assimilated in the ideology of **fascism**. A brief summary would include in its agenda the notion of 'dynamism', the cult of speed, the glories of the machine, a total rejection of the past, the super-value of patriotism and the efficacy of war in transforming society. Each of the arts responded to these aspects of the manifesto, throwing up, for example, Apollinaire's poetry, English and American Vorticism and, by influence, German Expressionism, and eventually spawning brutist architecture, concrete poetry, concrete music and kinetic art. Since the Second World War the fascist association has fallen away and futurism has become identified with a resurgent optimism, the belief that the true salvation of humanity will be measured by our continual and technological progress, as well as our intellectual development and maturation. This view has been put forward by well-known science fiction writers including Frederick Pohl, Ben Bova and Isaac Asimov. It is for each us to judge the extent to which this optimism is being realized or remains a fiction.

G

Gaia *G*. Originally the Greek goddess of the earth and wife to **Uranus**. The mythology has currently moved across to scientific theory, for example the 'Gaia Hypothesis' of James Lovelock, and Lynn Margulis, which proposes that the earth is an entire super organism, with its own vital and self-regulated functions. The concept is of the earth as one living organism made up of numerous symbiotic and interconnecting parts. The theory has led to the formation of what amounts to religious cults sometimes associated with **Druidism** and **Wicca**. The nameis also linked with the 'whole earth' policy of conservation and with politically active groups like Green Peace. See **Earth Mother**, **Environmentalism**, **Rhea**

Galileo Galilei (1564–1642) Italian scientist, mathematician, astronomer and philosopher and founder of modern mechanics. Galileo argued for the Copernican principle of the heliocentricity of the universe – the solar system. His theories of mechanics were set out in *Dialogue on the Two Chief Systems of the World* (1632), which purported to be an objective debate between the Copernican and Ptolemaic system. The argument is between two characters, one of which poses the Aristotelian orthodox natural philosophy that held to the geo-centricity of the universe, only to have it ridiculed by the other. This brought Galileo into conflict with the religious authorities and he lost favour with the Church. In 1633 he was forced to recant his Copernican views and was placed under house arrest, to be a prisoner of the **Inquisition** for the remainder of his life. Galileo pleaded for theological and scientific issues to be kept apart, since each discipline demanded a different expertise; the truths of one could never conflict with the truths of the other. The religious authorities failed to realize that his demand for the autonomy of science was, by default, also a demand for the autonomy of theology – a failure which has shadowed the religion v science debate ever since.

FINAL WORD: 'No one's virtue is complete:
  Great Galileo likes to eat.
  You will not resent, we hope,
  The truth about his telescope.'
  (From *The Life of Galileo*, Bertolt Brecht)

Ganapati *H*. See **Ganesha**

Ganda Religion *A*. The root word for Buganda, a kingdom of 52 tribes of the Baganda people, the largest of present-day Uganda's traditional kingdoms. Originally the culture was authoritarian and much of the mythology is supportive of the concept of Kingship, serving a social and political purpose as well as individual and family needs. Among the tribal and linguistic groups there are several varieties of religious belief and practice. Broadly they have in common the veneration of **ancestors**, belief in a creator God (like the southern-Ugandan **Bantu** god, *Ntu* or *Muntu*) and the use of prayer and sacrifice. In western Uganda, the Mbandwa mediators, acting on behalf of the people, use hypnosis, prayer and sacrifice to appease both the spirit world and the *Chwezi*, ancestor spirits which are believed to be the original, mythical rulers. The theme of supporting political and social life runs through the religious mythologies and practices of all the tribes and in Ganda religion it has the almost secular function of reinforcing the institution of kingship, thus in many areas of life religion overlaps with politics, a pattern that tends towards stability.

Gandhi, Mahatma (1869–1948) An Indian political and spiritual leader, famously active in the Indian Independence movement. He was responsible for the principle of *satyagraha*, resisting authority by civil disobedience and of *ahimsa*, absolute non-violence. His work to alleviate the sufferings of the poor, the emancipation of women, and the promotion of brotherhood across religious and racial boundaries did much to redress the worst abuses of the **caste** system. The title, Mahatma, is Sanskrit and means 'Great Soul'. He was sometimes called 'Bapu', 'Father'.

Ganesha *H*. The Lord god of the *Ganas*, groups of inferior deities. He was known also as Ganapati, the son of **Shiva** and **Parvati**. He is the god of wisdom and the destroyer of obstacles, invoked at the outset of an important project and at the inception of writing a book. Ganesha undertakes to succeed on the secular as well as the spiritual level. Depicted as yellow, small and squat, with a big belly and the head of a single tusked elephant, he is sometimes shown riding on a rat. His cult has numerous temples.

Ganges *H*. *Ganga*, the Indian name for the river. It rises in the Himalayas and flows into the Bay of Bengal. The river is sacred to Hindus in much the same way as is the Jordan for Christians. The **Rig-Veda** tells of the Ganges springing up from **Vishnu**'s foot. Whenever possible water from the Ganges is used in every **Puja** (religious ceremony) and drops of it are given to a person on the point of the death.

Gassho *B. Z.* Jap. Meaning 'to bring the palms together'. It is used as a gesture of respect. In **Zen Buddhism** it is the term for the ancient gesture of greeting, gratitude and veneration and is similar to the Indian salutation, *anjali*, used between priests and as a salutation in worship. Chinese Buddhism uses the term, *ho-chang*. Bringing the palms together is an action symbolic of the unity of opposites and the mind of non-duality.

Gateless Gate *Z*. A collection of **Zen** koans published in 1229. See **Koan**

Gathas *Zo*. The only section of the **Avesta**, the sacred **Zoroastrian** scriptures, believed to have been written by Zoroaster himself. It comprises 17 verses written in a particular poetic style with specific metrical rules, found in both Iranian and Indian literature. The Gathas are allegorical and esoteric. Peter Clark says that, 'the technique required for composing this kind of poetry was learnt over many years of study and it presupposes an educated and privileged studentship drawn from the priestly class.' As with the other sections of the Avesta the tradition was transmitted orally by priests, over a very long period of time until they came to be written down, probably during the **Sassanian** period, c.226–651 CE.

Gautama or **Gotama** or **Satananda** *H*. founder of the **Nyaya** school of Hindu philosophy, sometime between the 6th and 3rd centuries BCE. He was the author of the *Dharma-sastra*, a book of laws or civil codes, but the 12 volumes also discuss creation, transmigration, liberation and copious instructions for the obligations of the various social classes. *Nyaya*, Skt. 'correct', 'logic' or 'propriety', is one of Hinduism's six classical philosophical systems or *Darshanas*. It contributes largely to Hindu epistemology, being a crucial test of what we can know, using logical proofs.

Gayatri Mantra *H*. A **mantra** which is one of the most sacred texts of the **Rig-Veda**. It is given to a boy at the close of the *Upanayana*, the initiation ceremony that makes him a 'twice born'. (See **Sacred Thread Ceremony**) One of the frequently used translations of the text reads, 'Let us meditate on the brilliant light of that one who is worthy of worship and who has created all the worlds! May he direct our minds to the truth!' The boy will then be expected to recite the text three times a day, on rising, at noon and before sleeping.

Geb *E*. An Egyptian god of the earth, consort to **Nut** and a member of the **Ennead** of Heliopolis. Thought to represent the earth, he is depicted lying under the sky goddess Nut. Sometimes represented as a goose he is also known as the 'Great Cackler', laying the egg from which the sun was hatched. In his manifestation as a god of vegetation he has green patches painted on his body. In repose, he leans on an elbow with one knee bent upwards, thus representing the valleys and mountains of the earth. See **Egyptian Religion**, **Shu**, **Tefnut**

Gelugpa *B*. Tib. 'school of the virtuous'. The last of the **Tibetan Buddhist** schools to be founded. It concerned itself with the observation of monastic rules and a detailed study of the relevant texts. It follows that the school's spiritual practice is concerned with the development of concentration (*samadhi*). The school's founder, Tsongkhapa, left clear guidance that *samadhi* is to be realized through the combination of calm abiding, *samatha*, and special insight, *vipassana*. The school also relies on the teachings of the **Tantras**. Since the 16th century and until the Communist invasion, the school controlled Tibet and it is from this school that the **Dalai Lama** and **Panchen Lama** are chosen. See **Kagyupa**, **Nyingmapa**, **Sakyapa**, **Tibetan Buddhism**

Gentile Someone who is not of the Jewish faith. The **Old Testament** word *goy* (plural, *goyim*) is translated as 'the nations' or 'people' and as *gentilis* in Latin translations such as the **Vulgate Bible**. Thus 'gentile' is synonymous with those who are not of the Jewish faith or race. In the King James version of the Bible 'gentile' is taken to mean someone who historically is not an Israelite, thus having political rather than religious relationship with Israel. **Mormonism** uses the word 'gentile' for those who are not members of their Church.

Geometry, Sacred See **Sacred Geometry**

Germanen, Order of Also called the Teutonic Order, founded in Berlin in 1912, by Fritsch, Pohl and Stauff, as a secret society off-shoot of the Community for German Beliefs. With its incongruous interest in the **Edda**, and German mystics such as Meister Eckart and Jacob Boehme, there was a loose association with **Theosophist** and **Anthroposophist** groups. These, however, were internationalist in outlook and admitted Jews. The Order of Germanen became Nazi-orientated, representing German nationalism and ant-Semitism in its most virulent and psychopathic form. It was probably the inner core of the so-called Hammer League (*Hammerbund*) concerned with disseminating anti-Semitic propaganda.

Germanic Religion Referring to the pagan religion of Germany prior to Christianization. Sources include Julius Caesar, Tacitus and other Latin writers, together with 10th- and 11th-century accounts of **Norse mythology** and the substantial literature of the **Eddas** and **Sagas** of Iceland. The majority of sources were probably destroyed or suppressed by **Christianity** as it gained political power, both in Germany and Scandinavia. Broadly the religion was polytheistic and similar to other European and West-Asian traditions, like Baltic, Finnish, Slavic and **Vedic** paganism. The principal gods are well known by their English names **Balder**, **Odin**, **Thor** and **Tyr**. There are considerable overlaps between the beliefs and practices of these pagan systems, made complicated by the same gods re-appearing under different names. The cults have in common an elaborate system of nine-worlds of men and other beings, all connected to the **Yggdrasil**, the World Tree, doomed to destruction at **Ragnarok**, the doom or twilight of the gods. Other features include excessive human sacrifice, the use of powerful religious symbols such as the horse, wolf, eagle, raven, ship, spear and hammer and mead or beer as the inspirational drink of the gods. Regional variations among the Franks, Anglo-Saxons, Saxons, Frisians, Scandinavians and Icelanders, are too numerous to outline and the mythologies change in emphasis through the Viking and Medieval periods, a constant pagan presence lurking beneath the façade of Christianity. See also **Celtic Religion, Troth**

Ghost Dance Religion A movement that started among Amerindian tribes in the late 1880s to revitalize their culture in reaction to poverty, hunger, disease and the influence of encroaching Christianity and government authority. The inspiration for Ghost Dance was a vision given to the shaman (see **Shamanism**) Wovoka during an eclipse of the sun; he saw the second coming of Christ and warnings of the evil of the white man. Word of Wovoka's vision spread and delegations from across the tribal communities came to visit him in Nevada some, like Good Thunder, Short Bull and Kicking Bear, becoming leaders of the new religion. The name 'Ghost Dance' was given to the movement by whites because of its association with **resurrection** and reunion with the dead. Salvation would be granted when the Indians purged themselves of the evils infected by the whites. Before dancing the participants would purify themselves in a **sweat lodge**, then, their bodies painted with red pigment, they dressed in sacred cotton muslin decorated with feathers and the painted symbols the wearer had seen in a vision. Only the Lakota believed the ghost shirt was bullet-proof. Members danced in a circle to the accompaniment of their own singing and chanting, holding hands as the tempo gradually increased. The dance could last for days, provoking mass hysteria or trance-like states, eventually collapsing as if in death. Because of rumours of renewed Indian warfare, the settlers panicked and the government responded by outlawing the cult and its practices. At the Wounded Knee Massacre, of 29th December 1890, upwards of 300 men, women and children of the Ghost Dance Religion, all of them Hunkpapa Sioux (Lakota) were killed, together with their charismatic leader, Sitting Bull.

Gideons Gideons International were founded in 1899 by John Nicholson, Samuel Hill and William Knights, to be an association of Christian business men serving as an evangelical missionary arm of the Church. Their purpose 'is to win men, women, boys and girls to a saving knowledge of the Lord Jesus Christ' (from the G.I. website). They are named after the Gideon of Judges 6–7, a humble, faithful and obedient servant of God and known, worldwide, for placing a copy of the Bible in hotel bedrooms and other locations. Many of the early Gideons were commercial travellers and salesmen and it seemed natural that they should leave a copy of the Bible as a 'silent witness' in the rooms of the hotels they used.

Gilgamesh, Epic of *AME.* Originating in Sumeria, the epic poem is thought to be the most ancient story every written. Carved on 12 tablets in cuneiform script, its theme is the travels and adventures of a real person, the King of Uruk, mythologized as the hero-king Gilgamesh, whose friendship with a half-wild man, Enkidu, is a central theme. The tale is set between 2750 and 2500 BCE. The poem had wide-ranging influence on subsequent literature, for example, there are striking, evident parallels with the Genesis story of the flood in the Bible. Other influences have been seen in Homer's, *Odyssey and* in ancient Indian literature.

Girlingites *X*. The late 19th-century followers of Mary Anne Girling (1827–86) who styled herself 'Bride of Christ'. She refused the title 'English Shakers' for her group preferring 'Bible Christians', or 'Children of God'. They believed that if they remained celibate they would never die. Their worship, held under a converted railway arch in Walworth, was ecstatic, the worshippers falling into trances and collapsing. They danced and jumped up and down, for which reason they were dubbed the 'Walworth Jumpers'. Mary Girling asserted she was the reincarnation of Jesus and more important than the Holy Spirit. Before she died she assumed the name, God-Mother.

Global Church of God See **Armstrongism**

Glossolalia 'Speaking in Tongues', a characteristic practice of the Pentecostal Movement. See **Pentecostalism, Vineyard Churches, Xenoglossolalia**

Gnosticism From the Greek *gnosis*, 'knowledge' or 'wisdom'. A term referring to systems of belief based on a secret knowledge of God, access to which initiation is required. Traditions of secret knowledge occur in many religions for example in **Brahmanism, Buddhism, Taoism**, in later **Babylonian** and Persian religions, in the **Egyptian** myths of **Isis** and **Osiris**, and in Pythagorean and **Platonist** philosophy. In the **Old Testament**, the *maskilim* are the 'initiated' whose secret knowledge re-emerges in the Rule of the **Essenes** at Qumran and later in **Kabbalah** and **Merkabah** mysticism. Gnostics claimed a unique insight into Christ's message, believing other forms of Christianity to be misrepresentations. The influence of Gnosticism on the **New Testament** can be seen, for example, in the *logos* prologue of St John's Gospel and the letters of Paul to the Corinthians; he refutes the power derived from *gnosis*, the system's ascetic tendencies and its denial of a physical resurrection. Gnostics believe in the 'Supreme God of Truth' who is remote and unknowable to the senses. He created *Aeons*, supernatural, finite beings such as Sophia, a virgin who gave birth to a defective Demiurge, known as *Jaldabaoth* (Arabic, 'the begetter of the Heavens') who is the **Jehovah** of the Old Testament, an evil, jealous, uncompassionate God, guilty of genocide. The 'Earthly Cosmos' is made up of our world and the underworld; the coiled snake, **Leviathan**, devours its tail beyond the spheres of the planets among which live the *Archons*, demonic beings and beyond them **Paradise** with the 'Tree of Knowledge of Good and Evil' (see **Fall of Man**). Beyond Paradise lie the fixed stars of the 12 signs of the zodiac (see **Astrology**). As well as the **Kingdom of God**, there is the Intermediate Kingdom of Sophia. One of the most influential Gnostic beliefs is the **dualism** of spirit and body, the former being divine in origin, the latter earthly and evil. The writings of the Gnostics were considerable and included works by Simon Magus (possibly the Simon of Acts 8:9); Marcion (85–160 CE), author of the apocryphal Gospel of Marcion; Valentius (c.100–c.153) founder of the Gnostic School of

Rome; and non-canonical apostolic writing, such as the *Gospel According to Thomas*, *The Gospel of Philip* and the *Apocryphon of John*. No Gnostic canon was established. It is likely that many Gnostics were solitary practitioners while others were members of established Christian congregations, like that in Corinth. New religious forms in the West have adopted Gnostic beliefs, such as the **Mormon** church and the Apostolic Gnostic Church in America. See **Aeons, Pleroma**

Gnostic Order of Christ Founded in 1988 by members of the Order of the **Rosy Cross** (see **Rosicrucians**) to provide a spiritual structure for those called to the Western tradition of priesthood within the **Ancient Mystic Order of Melchizedek**. The Gnostic Order is spiritual, lacking any form of institutional structure, its members being all the religions of the world, hence the concept of universal priesthood. It has two principles: first to love God and secondly to love God by loving others as ourselves. Its spiritual ideal lies in the very earliest form of Christianity before the formation of institutional communities, during the time when John the Baptist and Jesus were teachers. The Order is committed to the universalism of that proto-message which called people to know God for themselves and to express that knowledge in the moral quality of their lives. Apart from asserting that Jesus was a Universalist (see **Universalism**) they have no dogma. The tradition of the Melchizedek priesthood and the Order's lineage was recorded by St Paul (see Heb. 6:20 and 7:1ff) and the succession was received by Father Paul Blighton in a revelation during the mid-1960's. Father Paul Blighton and 11 others, one of whom was Sufi Murshid Samuel Lewis, together with some who were already ordained, continued the tradition, primarily through The **Holy Order of MANS** founded in 1968.

God A term with innumerable connotations and associations. In biblical religions the name represents a perfect being, omnipotent, omnipresent and omniscient, the absolute ruler-creator of the Universe and of all life. Usually conceived as being a male deity, the revealed terms on which he has established relationships with human beings require that he is to be worshipped and obeyed. The forms given to God vary hugely, he can be the absolute 'one' God of monotheistic traditions such as Judaism, or be understood as 'One' yet given a Trinitarian interpretation as the Father, Son and Holy Spirit of the Christian **Trinity**, itself understood differently by the many Christian denominations. The attributes of God also vary, he can be just, angry, punishing, merciful and loving. He can be wholly transcendent, wholly immanent or both. He is invisible, ineffable and inconceivable and yet can be the subject of the most intimate personal experience and visions. In ancient polytheism, there were innumerable gods (see **Greek and Roman Religion**) not given to personal relationships, but endowed by their mythologies with attributes that seemed to mirror human characteristics and human failings. In ancient Paganism (see **Icelandic** and **German Mythologies**) the gods were feared as much as they were revered, inhabiting their own worlds, conducting their own affairs and making incursions into human life in direct relation to the rituals associated with their cults. In animistic religions such as those of the Amerindians and tribal Africans, 'god' is manifest in all the powers of nature to which humans are subject.

Especially today, the word 'God', perhaps more than any other word, illustrates the problem of religious language. God has been called **Brahman** by Hindus, **Dharma** by Buddhists, but is too sacred to be named by Jews; he is called 'Love' by Christians, while Muslims use 100 **'Beautiful Names'**, of which 'Allah' is the 'Great Name'. He has been pronounced dead by **Nietzsche**, described as a childhood neurosis by **Freud**, and called the 'ground of our being' by **Tillich**. The Jewish philosopher Martin **Buber** in his poignantly titled book *The Eclipse of God*, writes about a conversation with an old man who asked him, 'How can you bring yourself to say "God" time after time? How can you expect your reader will take the word in the sense in which you wish it to be taken?' In reply Buber said, 'We cannot cleanse the word "God" and we cannot make it whole; but defiled and mutilated as it is, we can raise it from the ground and set it over an hour of great care.'

FINAL WORD: 'Theist and Atheist: The fight between them is as to whether God shall be called God or shall have some other name.' (Samuel Butler)

Goddess In ancient **Roman and Greek religion**, **paganism**, **animism** and **neo-paganism**, 'goddess' is a term affirming either the feminine aspect of the divine or an actual female divinity. Broadly all goddess cults have three features in common: i) they revere an **Earth Mother**, or Mother Nature or the earth as divine (see **Gaia**); ii) they worship a particular female deity, such as the Greek goddess **Aphrodite**, which may be carried through to a pagan cult like **Wicca**; iii) the search, by women themselves, for the 'divine spark' of the goddess within them, as found in some expressions of occult and **New Age** feminism and **Egotheism**.

Godhead *J. X.* The essential, divine nature of God, the abstract 'essence' of being, usually biblical religion. In Judaism, God Almighty or Jehovah, expressed as an absolute monotheism, a doctrine shared with **Islam**; for Christianity the godhead is in Trinitarian, Binitarian or Unitarian form.

Goetheanum Steiner's school of spiritual sciences. See **Anthroposophy**

Gog and Magog Variously presented as supernatural beings, **demons** or giants derived from a somewhat cryptic reference in the apocalyptic prophesy of Ezekiel. (38:2ff) But the tradition is ambiguous, maybe corrupt and the names could refer to nations or territories, as they do in Marco Polo's *Travels*, across the great plane of Tenduk in Mongolia. One of the problems is due to the differences in the Hebrew of the **Tanakh** and its translation in the **Septuagint**. References also occur in the Koran, as well as in folklore and various mythologies such as those of Ireland. The Gog and Magog hills, south of Cambridge in the UK, are said to be the metamorphosis of the giants after rejection by the nymph, Granta. Godmagog is referred to in Monmouth's 12th-century *Historia Regum Britanniae*, as having been slain by Corin, the eponymous Cornish hero. Somehow they became the traditional guardians of the City of London and representations of the giants are paraded in the Lord Mayor's Show procession.

Golden Dawn See **Hermetic Order of the Golden Dawn**

Golden Ratio or **Golden Section** See **Sacred Geometry**

Golden Rule Based on the 'ethic of **reciprocity**', the Golden or Fundamental Rule is to be found in one form or another in most of the established religious traditions. This is not a rule of revenge, the 'eye for an eye' principle, it is entirely about treating other people with the same kind of values and respect with which one would wish to be treated. Most religions represent, in some form, the classical formulation of the rule. Judaism has it as, 'What is hateful to you do not do to your fellowmen. This is the entire Law, all the rest is commentary' (Talmud, Shabbat, 3id). Matthew 7:12, echoes this for Christianity in a positive form, 'Always treat others as you would like them to treat you: that is the law and the prophets.' Taoism, in a key text on ethics, calls on adherents to 'regard your neighbours gain as your gain and your neighbours loss as your own loss.' (Carus and Suzuki) The principle is that we should treat all people in this manner, not just our family and our 'in group'. There is a problem, however. If the Golden Rule is interpreted consequentially, that is so long as the end is good, anything is permissible, we have the end justifying the means. The converse view is that however praiseworthy the goal an immoral action in achieving it is impermissible. Any of these propositions can be applied in secular terms, there is no requirement for a belief in a God or a commitment to a religious system in order for the Golden Rule to be valid.

FINAL WORD: 'The golden rule is that there are no golden rules.' (Attributed to George Bernard Shaw)

Golden Temple *Sik.* A non-Sikh name for the **Darbar Sahib**, the 'Divine Court', the central shrine of **Sikhism** at Amritsar, also called the Temple of God. The site, said to be a place where Guru Nanak meditated, is located in Amritsar standing in the centre of a man-made lake, with access by a causeway. It is architecturally impressive, constructed in marble with a gold leaf dome. There are four entrances symbolizing unrestricted access regardless of **caste**. Work began on the Temple in 1577 and was completed in 1601. It has been the site of many conflicts, the most notorious being the 1919 massacre perpetrated by British troops commanded by Brigadier General Dyer. The massacre was one of the events that gave rise to Gandhi's *satyagraha* movement of non-violent disobedience.

Goma Fire Ritual *B*. The Japanese name for the **Vedic** fire ritual still practised by the **Shingon school**, a form of Japanese Tantrism. (See **Tantra**) The ritual involves the lighting and maintaining of a sacred fire, with symbolic sexual associations. The training of a Shingon priest requires him to set the fire, understood as a male force, while visualizing himself between the spread thighs of the goddess contemplating her **yoni**. (Payne.) See **Fire, Sacred**

Gomorrah One of the infamous 'cities of the plain' mentioned in Genesis 19. See **Sodom and Gomorrah**

Good Friday Probably the most solemn of holy days celebrated by Christians, it being the day when the **crucifixion** of **Jesus** is commemorated. It is the occasion for special prayers and Masses and in some cases the following of the seven stages of the cross, a symbolic re-enactment of Jesus' progress to Calvary. Christians regard Jesus' execution as a voluntary and vicarious act which, coupled to his resurrection on **Easter Sunday**, is the final and absolute conquering of death. Because of differences in both calendar and tradition, the day is celebrated on different dates by the different Churches. The consensus as to the most probable date is 3rd April, 33 CE. In some traditions the day is observed with a fast.

Good Shepherd A sobriquet for Jesus Christ based primarily on John 10:14, 'I am the good shepherd; I know my sheep and my sheep know me. But there are other sheep of my mine, not belonging to this fold, whom I must bring in …' Thus, the good shepherd offers his service both to his own flock and to others outside it. On this principle the name has been applied to all manner of institutions such as hospitals, schools, hostels and shelters, with the intent to care and not, necessarily, to proselytize.

Gosala *B*. See **Ajivaka Buddhism**

Gospel *X*. The word is from the Anglo-Saxon *godspell*, 'God-story' and is the English translation of the Greek *evengelion*, 'good tidings', also used in the **Septuagint**, for example Isaiah 61:1, 'The Spirit of the Lord is upon me … to bring good news to the humble.' In the **New Testament** the gospel is the 'good news' of the Kingdom of God as proclaimed by Jesus and for the subsequent apostolic 'good news' of his resurrection. The term is familiarly used in the titles of the opening four books of the New Testament, 'The Gospel According to Matthew', being the first, followed by that of Mark, Luke and John.

Gouranga *H*. Full name, Shri Krishna Caitanya Mahaprabhu, accepted as being the founding father of the **Hare Krishna** movement. He was born in west Bengal in 1486 and became a sage and saint, regarded as an incarnation of Lord **Krishna**. When he was 24 he was ordained monk, taught the philosophy of **Vaishnavism**, and worshipped Krishna as the supreme being, instructing his pupils to repeat the name, mantra-like. Members of the sect have two perpendicular white stripes of sandalwood paste drawn from the forehead, converging at the bridge of the nose and wear a three-stringed necklace of tulasi beads. 'Gouranga' originally meant 'golden limbed', thought to be a reference to Shri Krishna's skin tones. In popular **New Age** culture 'Gouranga' is taken to mean 'be happy', and is painted on motorway and railway bridges in England and Scotland suggesting the ideal destination, perhaps, for travellers. Members of the cult can be seen in the streets and at festivals such as Glastonbury, handing out tracts. See **Haranath**

Grace X. From the Latin *gratia*, and Greek *charis*, meaning a favour freely shown by a higher authority on a lesser being. In its Greek use it means a divine gift or favour, a quality given by the gods that could be exhibited by mortals. In Christian theology the word has acquired a special meaning to describe an aspect of man's relationship to God. In the biblical view everything that God does is gracious since, by virtue of **original sin**, humanity does not merit his favour. God's ultimate, freely given act of grace is the incarnate life and redemptive death of his son, 'God loved the world so much that he gave his only Son …' (John 3:16) Essential to the theological implication of grace is the willingness and freedom in which it is given. As St **Augustine** put it, 'grace is not grace unless it is *gratis*.' Across Christian denominations there are variations in the theology of grace. **Protestantism** understands it as the means by which sin is forgiven and the subject 'justified' or restored to favour with God. Only faith can make grace available to the sinner. Catholicism's emphasis is on the sacraments as the means by which grace is implanted in the soul, uniting it with Christ. **Augustine** and later **Calvin** put forward the extreme view that even if grace produced faith, it would be no guarantee of salvation unless the subject was also among the elect, that is, **predestined** to eternal life. The assertion that only by God's gift of grace can the believer live a moral life has set up conflicts in Christian theology, since it raises the question of humanity's freedom and moral responsibility. The argument is that as God bestows grace freely, man's response must also be freely made, since coercion would make it worthless. God, willing mercy to mankind, must be met by man's willing morality. The issue is thrown into clear relief by the secularization of morality which has demonstrated that human beings are fully capable of living a moral life independently of God's grace. The debate continues. See **Salvation by Grace**

Grail Religion Grail Religion is a 1st-century syncretism of **Judaism**, **Christianity** and **Paganism**. It claims to be Jewish by recognizing Jesus as the Messiah of Israel by right of kinship, that is through his blood-line and by accepting the early Church's interpretation of Mosaic law since the Church was led by James, the brother of Jesus. It is Christian because it is in accord with orthodox Christianity and the Ecumenical **creeds** of the Church. It is pagan in following **Natural Religion**, based on God's self-revelation in nature. Grail Religion understands Christianity as a paganism adjusted by special revelation and accepts as 'natural' human sensuality as an expression of the spiritual life-force. The salient points of its creed are: the doctrine of the Holy Spirit as the feminine principle of deity; the fundamental unit is the Grail Family; Jesus had to be married in order to be the Messiah; and modern civilization is out of kilter with the created order. The established church of Grail Christianity is the **Cambrian Episcopal Church of the Grail** (*Cambrian* referring to the **Celtic** tradition of pre-medieval Wales) described as 'a completed Body in liturgy, doctrine and government' offering support to a home-based practice. It has a regular publication, the *Cambrian Pesher*. Grail religion is part of the wider Grail Movement that is thought to have in the region of 17,000 adherents worldwide. See **Celtic Religion**, **Holy Grail**, **Natural Theology**

Great Rebellion *J*. The Jewish uprising against the Romans, 66–70 CE, which ended with the sacking of Jerusalem and the destruction of the **Temple of Solomon**. See **Essenes**, **Zealots**

Great White Brotherhood See **Ascended Masters**

Greek Fathers The Greek contributors to the mission and writings of the **Church Fathers**. They included Origen (185–c.254), whose extensive writings were among the earliest intellectual explanations of the Christian faith; Athanasius (296–373), the inspirer of St **Augustine** and apologist for the theology of Word Incarnation (see **Logos**); St Basil (330–379 CE), concerned for orthodoxy and church unity and the organizer of charity in the face of famine; his brother St Gregory of Nyssa; St John Chrysostom, the most prolific of the Greeks known also as 'Golden Mouth', famous for his 'Baptismal Homilies, Priesthood, Baptism and Virginity.' See **Dogmatics**, **Latin Fathers**

Greek Gods See **Pantheon, Greek**

Greek Religion Herodotus claimed that, 'The names of nearly all the gods came to Greece from Egypt.' 'Names' is understood to mean 'the gods themselves or at any rate the concept or idea of them' (Cartledge). Whatever its origin, it is not possible to speak of Greek religion as a unified system of belief and practice. The religion of the Greek city-states was characterized by the range of its polytheism and the variety of local forms. Different cities worshipped different deities; Athens had **Athena**; Sparta, **Artemis**; Corinth, **Aphrodite**; Delphi and Delos had **Apollo**; Olympia had **Zeus**; and smaller towns had their own gods. The worship of a deity with the same name did not guarantee the same cult; the virgin-huntress Artemis worshipped at Sparta, was strikingly different from the multi-breasted Artemis worshipped at Ephesus. Moreover the worship of major deities spread from one locality to another and some cities had temples to several gods. Homer's *Iliad* indicates that the **pantheon** of Olympian gods was well established, he makes no mention

of **Dionysus** which suggests his cult developed later to become sufficiently important for him to join the Olympian deities, ousting **Hestia** in
the process. The Greek system developed from the Minoan-Mycenaean
age (c.2500–c.1050 BCE) to the end of the Hellenistic period (c.31 BCE).

Classical Greek religion had no sacred texts, no official creeds and was
not troubled by heresy. The temple locations of the major gods were sup-
plemented by local cults of tutelary spirits associated with sacred groves,
crossroads and altars erected outside the temples. The **heroes** were
demigods, thought of as god-like humans who became part of local folk-
history, each with their own cults, sometimes in the form of **oracles**.
There was a balanced reciprocity in the relationship between gods and
mortals; gods, majestic (*sebastos*) and sublime (*semnos*) merited respect,
an important virtue of Greek religion and it followed that if in the event
of local conflict a sacred site was destroyed, retaliation in the name of the
god(s) was justified. Religion was a collective affair, expressed in public
rituals and festivals, with an emphasis on the here and now rather than on
the hope of an idealized state to be realized in the future. In summary,
Greek religion was a traditional orthopraxy concerned with cultural self-
definition and formulating a concept of existence (*kosmos*) that provided
a unified context for the otherwise disparate aspects of life. What was
achieved was a coherence vested with ultimate significance.

Temples were not used for public acts of worship but for housing the
cult idol and the accumulated results of votive giving, the principle of
which was expressed by the Roman formula *do ut des*, 'I give that you
may give.' The altars were placed in the *temenos* or sacred enclosure,
where most public acts of worship included sacrifice. When a myth tells
us that horses are sacred to Poseidon or roosters to Hermes, they are
saying that these were the sacrificial animals. Behind animal sacrifice
lurked the earlier, abandoned practice of human sacrifice, recorded in the
mythology of heroes like Tantalus and Pelops or Agamemnon and
Iphigenia. There was little coherent theology but the *Homeric Hymns*
have something to say about belief and worship and the poet Hesiod's,
Theogony, includes a creation myth based on a deification of abstractions
like, Night and Time. **Socrates** and others were accused of **atheism** when
they pointed out that the lack of systematization made it difficult to
accept traditional beliefs because they were so disparate and sometimes
contradictory. Eventually the more abstract notions of Socrates survived,
of remote, genteel gods who sustained private and public morality. The
exception to the collective and public veneration of the gods were the
Mystery Religions that provided personal experience and satisfaction in
terms of consolation, mystical revelation, doctrine and fellowship. They
led eventually to the more exotic mysteries of **Osiris** and Mithras (see
Mithraism), which during the Roman Empire were widespread. Greek
mythology is so vast that even a brief summary is not possible, but
aspects of it are covered under specific entries. The lives and relationships of all the Greek gods are involved and convoluted, but copiously
recorded. See for example, Graves, Grant and Rose. See **Hellenism**

FINAL WORD: 'There is one race of men one race of gods,
both have breath of life from a single mother.
But sundered power holds us divided so that one is nothing,
while for the other the brazen sky is established their sure
citadel for ever.
Yet we have some likeness in great intelligence or strength,
to the immortals, though we know not what the day may
bring, what course after nightfall destiny has written we
must run to the end.' (Pindar)

Gregorian Chant Also known as 'plainchant' or 'plainsong', a form of
monophonic unaccompanied singing which was developed in the
Catholic Church, between 800–1000 CE. It is named for Pope St Gregory
the Great, who brought the formative of the Byzantine chant back from
the East. Traditionally, the music is sung by monks during religious services. Unlike other musical forms, there is no beat or accent in the singing
and the time is kept free so the text rather than the note can be accented.
Neither is the pitch fixed, which allows the chant to be sung over any
range so long as the intervals between notes are respected. Even after the
advent of polyphony and accompaniment, Gregorian Chant remained the
official music for the liturgy of the Roman Catholic Church.

Grey Friars *X*. A name given to Friars of the **Franciscan** Order due to the
colour of their habit. The name sticks, even though no, the habit is brown.

Grihastha *H*. Skt. 'householder'. For Hindus the second of the **Four
Stages of Life**. See **Ashrama, Sacred Thread Ceremony**

Grimoire Broadly, a manual or text book for the practising of European
traditions of witchcraft. Instructions are given for invoking spirits and
demons by means of ceremonies, rituals and spells usually dating from
the Middle Ages. Instructions are also included for making **charms**, and
talismans. Famous Grimoires include *The Key of Solomon the King*,
based on 16th-century texts from much older sources; *The Sworn Book of
Honorius*, 13th century; *and The Book of Shadows*, of which there are
many, each coven probably having their own copy. (See **Wicca,
Witchcraft**)

Guna *H*. Skt. 'basic quality'. The term indicates a well-pointed Hindu
view of the nature of reality and human consciousness, in that everything
is made up of three fundamental multi-layered aspects or qualities of
maya, 'illusion'. They are: i) *Sattva*, the quality of being pure and
abstract, for example, light or sound; ii) *Rajas*, the quality of movement
or action, like the flow of a river or an earthquake; iii) *Tamas*, the quality
of solidity and weight, like a mountain and also that of ignorance and
inactivity. Each of these qualities are dependent on **Brahman** but being
aspects of *maya*, obscure Brahman's true, unchanging reality. In terms of
the spiritual development of the individual, *sattva* takes the aspect of

what it is we must 'realize', or be enlightened to; *tamas* take the aspect of the barriers to **enlightenment**, and *rajas*, the power to overcome the barriers. Another level of meaning concerns qualities of human consciousness, with *sattva* embodying calm, *rajas* restlessness and passion and *tamas* indolence and ignorance.

Gurdjieff, George (1866–1949) He is considered by some to have been the greatest mystical teacher of all time. Born in Armenia, he spent many years in Tibet and Central Asia before teaching in Russia. He was unconventional, using idiosyncratic language and methods to convey ideas that were a synthesis of psychic, occult, Buddhist and Kabbalhistic ideas. In 1922, he founded at Fontainebleau in France, the **Institute for the Harmonious Development of Man**. He taught that ordinary people are 'asleep', conditioned by habit and set patterns of thought we act mechanically, governed by three brain centres, Thinking, Feeling and Moving, which are uncoordinated. The solution is conscious effort and deliberate suffering caused by exercises designed to develop our self-awareness and to free trapped energies. His teachings have had considerable influence on both religious and secular thought and adapted versions of them are taught by American and European institutions founded by his followers. Some of these are under the auspices of the Gurdjieff Foundations in New York, London and Paris.

FINAL WORD: 'Religion is doing; a man does not merely think his religion or feel it, he lives his religion as much as he is able, otherwise it is not religion but fantasy or philosophy.' (Gurdjieff)

Gurdwara *Sik.* Pun. 'the Guru's door'. A Sikh place of worship. Originally this took the form of any suitable place for singing the hymns that make up the *Adi Granth*, the scriptures. Such a place might well have been just a room known as the *dharmasala*, but as **Sikhism** developed and the interests and responsibilities of the *panth* became more demanding and complicated, more suitable premises were necessary. The meeting place or temple focused the spiritual, social and political concerns of the community. The most famous of these is the **Golden Temple** at Amritsar, known to Sikhs by their preferred name, **Darbar Sahib**.

Guru *H. B.* Skt. *gu*, 'darkness', *ru*, 'that which dispels'. So, the 'dispeller of darkness', a spiritual master who knows the way and acts as a guide along the path. Eventually, with practice and wisdom, one can become one's own guru, the informed mind and a refined intuition assumes the guiding principle *Antaryamin* (Skt.), 'inner leader'. In Tibetan Buddhism a meditation technique enables the pupil to identify his guru with the essence of all Buddhas. Through guru **yoga**, he visualizes himself as being of the same essence and participating in the same root emptiness or *sunyata*. By means of guru yoga, the qualities of the Buddha can be transmitted to the pupil. 'Guru' in **Sikhism** has markedly different connotations and functions. See **Guru in Sikhism**

FINAL WORD: 'To tune in to the guru's consciousness, visualize him in the spiritual eye. Mentally call to him there. Imagine his eyes, especially, gazing at you. Invite his consciousness to inspire your own.' (Paramhansa Yogananda [2000])

Guru Granth Sahib *Sik. Granth* (Pun) 'book'; *Sahib* (Hin.) 'master'. The central scriptures of Sikhism comprising written collections of hymns compiled firstly by Angad, 1539–52, the second of the ten Sikh Gurus. Further hymns, not always written by Sikhs, were added up to the time of Guru Arjan, 1581–1606. This was called the **Adi Granth**, the first collection, by which the canon is still sometimes known. After the death, in 1708, of the last guru, Gobind Sing, the collected scriptures took on a new authority. Both the content and the physical embodiment of the scriptures came to be regarded as a **guru**, that is a manifestation of the human guru's power, and as spirituality or divine infilling and inspiration. For this reason the scriptures hold a central place in every *gurdwara*, the Sikh place of worship.

Guru in Sikhism For the Sikhs a guru is far more than a teacher, he is a Divine Preceptor. God is the original Guru, who by means of revelation makes his *hukam*, or will, known. The concept of the Guru is similar to that of the Old Testament **prophet** who has received the revealed 'word' of God together with the vocation, inspiration and authority to deliver it. The Sikh concept takes this an important step further, in that while the prophet spoke *for* God, the Guru is understood as being God actually speaking, that is the word of God is manifest in the person of the Guru. But the Sikh Guru is emphatically not an incarnation. Nanak said, 'Burnt be the tongue that sayeth, "God falleth into the womb".' The Sikh scriptures are also believed to embody exactly this notion of both the presence of God and his word and are placed in the centre of the *Gurdwara*, the Sikh place of worship. See **Guru Yoga**

FINAL WORD: 'Almost all the great religions of the world emphasise the need of a preceptor or Guru or holy man for the attainment of salvation … Even Guru Nanak emphasises that bliss can be obtained only through the grace of the Guru … The real Guru is one who knows the Supreme Being. What is important is not the person but the *word* – "The word is the Guru. The Guru is the word."' (Gobind Singh Mansukhani)

Guru Nanak (1469–1539) *Sik.* The founder of **Sikhism** and its first **Guru**. Nanak was born in Talwandi, a village in what was then the Punjab, now Pakistan. At that time India was dominated by the Moguls and relatively little is known of him beyond the record left of his teachings. His story is told in the *janam-sakhis*, hagiographic narratives that do not really constitute a historical biography. It is known that he travelled, maybe beyond India, possibly making pilgrimages to various places sacred to Hindus. Finally, he settled at Kartarpur, a village near Lahore. Tradition has it that following his morning bath in the river Ravi, he disappeared and remained missing for three days. Whether this number is symbolic or actual is not discussed. On his return he remained silent, we do not know for how long, but when he did speak he is reputed to have said, 'There is neither Hindu nor Muslim so whose path shall I follow? I shall follow God's path. God is neither Hindu nor Muslim and the path which I follow is God's.' In Kartarpur, c.1521, Guru Nanak established the first Sikh *Panth*, or community where his followers met daily to listen to his teachings, but it is unlikely that he had any intention of founding a new religion. In wanting to dissolve the major differences between Hinduism and Islam, his vision seems to have been ecumenical. Nanak taught that the truth could not be encapsulated or monopolized by any one religion, since it was greater than all of them. He was critical of religious institutionalism, dogma and ritual, claiming that such things obscured the very truth for which people were seeking.

Guru Yoga *H. B.* A spiritual relationship between guru and disciple found in **Hinduism** and **Buddhism**, centred around teaching and the transmission of spiritual power. In Hinduism, the guru is understood as a guide in exactly the sense of someone able to direct a person around a place of which he has neither knowledge nor experience. The guru is a native of spirituality, he has the realm mapped. There should be no sense of obligation; if the subject wants to know the way and to be guided along the path, the trust shown should be freely given and implies commitment and perseverance. In times of separation, special meditation practices can keep the pupil in touch with the mind of the guru. Eventually, the time may come when a person can be their own guru, by developing the *antaryamin*, the 'inner leader'. In Tibetan **Buddhism** guru yoga is a devotional meditative practice, in which one's root guru is identified with the essence of all Buddhas. The pupil forms an identification with the guru by meditating on his own and his guru's **'emptiness'**, imagining himself to be of the same basic nature. It is believed that by this method, all the attributes of a Buddha can be transmitted to the pupil through his guru. See **Zaddik**

Gypsies and Religion See **Roma**

H

Ha *E*. The god of the Western Egyptian deserts, associated with the underworld, who busies himself with protecting Egypt from invading enemies like the Libyans and creating oases. Also one of the five constituent parts of the Egyptian concept of the soul. See **Soul, Egyptian**

Hades *Gk. Haides*, 'unseen'. The Greek term for both the abode of the dead and the god of the underworld or, 'House of Hades'. The corresponding Roman god was **Pluto**. In Christian terminology an alternative for **hell**.

Hadith *I*. Arab. 'a statement'. An important tradition and authority in Islam, second only to the Koran and based on the reported deeds and words of **Muhammad** and his family. *Hadith* is the foundation of Islamic culture or custom and for two centuries after Muhammad's death in 632 CE, it remained an oral tradition. Gradually, the *Hadith* was recorded and arranged and there are various collections only six of which are considered to be truly authoritative and based on recognized transmissions. The Shiite accept as fully authoritative *hadith* derived through the line of Muhammad's family, Ali and Fatimah. Ideally the chain of transmission is traced back to Muhammad himself and is believed to embody his *Sunnah*, his own habits, customs and example.

Hafidha *I*. Arab. 'memory'. One of the five inner senses of Islamic philosophy and a central concept of its system of belief. It is derived from the root *hafadha*, meaning to protect or to keep safe. The implication is that anything committed to memory is stored and kept secure from any kind of corruption. Memory works by what Muslims understand as 'pictures of attributed meaning', and are deposited in the mind as if in a bank vault. The term is directly associated with *dhikr*, a devotional act of remembrance and with *Hifz al-Koran*, 'having the Koran by heart'. 'The memory stores the pictures of attributed meanings in the same way that the imagination stores the pictures of the unifying sense [see **Inner Senses of Islam**] as well as its own inner pictures of imagination. 'The faculty of memory can bring back any picture of the past that it wants, provided that the picture has not been erased.' (Sheikh Fadhlalla Haeri)

Hafiz *I*. Arab. A term given to someone who is able to recite the whole of the Koran by heart. See *Hifz al-Koran*

Haggadah *J*. Heb. 'narration' or 'discourse'. A type of Rabbinical literature that is not concerned with law, but concerned to teach and illuminate. In the **Torah** and the **Talmud** law, prophecy and narrative exist together. *Haggadah* shows the Rabbis wearing their hats as preachers and teachers, the subject matter is always didactic. Theology, philosophy and ethics are presented in a way that is accessible to the ordinary people and stories, fables, parables and legends are used to this end. The content and method of *Haggadah* has reached beyond Jewish circles and its influence can be seen, for example, in the Koran and other Islamic literature, as well as in European literature generally. There is no binding authority in *Haggadah*, it makes no demands on a person's beliefs, no claim for any kind of ultimate authority. The main period of *haggadic* compilation was during the first six centuries CE, when the material was arranged in separate collections, for example as sets of sermons. Another form of *Haggadah*, the narrative, is used in the liturgies celebrating Jewish festivals. The most familiar of these is the **Passover** Haggadah, used for the *Seder*, the banquet held in Jewish homes on the eve of the Passover festival celebrating the emancipation of the Hebrew slaves from Egypt. See **Halakhah, Judaism**

Hagiography Collections of writings concerning the lives of the **saints**.

Hajar al-Aswad *I*. 'Black Stone'. The stone is built into the southeast corner of the **Ka'bah**, about four feet off the ground. The stone does not belong to the region's geology, but it is part of the original construction of the Ka'bah. Tradition has it that it was placed there by the prophet Abraham and his son Ismail (Ishmael) and reinstalled after flood damage, by Muhammad himself. During his own last or farewell **Hajj**, Muhammad is said to have touched and kissed the Hajar al-Aswad. For this reason, a pilgrim doing the same is considered *sunnah*, that is, a follower of the example of the Prophet. Kissing or touching the stone is believed to absolve the pilgrim from sin.

Hajj *I*. Arab. 'pilgrimage'. The 5th of the **Pillars of Islam**. See **Pilgrimage**

Halakhah *J*. Heb. 'Guidance' or 'usage'. The legal content of Jewish religious literature, in contrast to the non-legal *Haggadah*. In general use the term refers to the entire Jewish law which offers detailed prescriptions for every aspect of life. Originally an oral tradition, a structured and organized form of *Halakhah* probably existed before the destruction of Solomon's Temple in 586 BCE; the first systematic collection was put together by Rabbi Akiba, c.50–135 CE. This formed the basis for subsequent emendations, additions and collections that were finally collated by Rabbi Judah ha-Nasi, c.200 CE as the philosophical law code known as the **Mishnah**. The complete Jew is a 'halakhic man, ... is, indeed, a free man. He creates an ideal world, renews his own being and transforms himself into a man of God.' (Soloveitchik)

Halal *I*. Arab. 'permissible'. A term used in the Koran for what is lawful. Halal is best known for indicating dietary restrictions. *Haram* refers to prohibited food that includes, pork, blood, alcoholic drinks and any scavenging animal. All *halal* meat has to be ritually slaughtered and the name of God pronounced over it in blessing. See **Kosher**

Halloween X. The term originally referred to 'All-Hallow's Eve', a Catholic observance of the night preceding All Saint's Day. However, in its modern form it has become a holiday based on **pagan**, **occult**, **Celtic** and **Druid** beliefs and rituals observed as a holy day by those practising witchcraft (see **Wicca**) and **Satanism**. It is celebrated on October 31st and the evening has been taken over by groups of children dressed in ghost and ghoul costumes, who knock on people's doors demanding sweets and chocolates against the penalty of mischief if none is given, a tradition known as 'Trick or Treat'.

Hammerbund A German anti-Semitic organization. See **Germanen, Order of**

Hammurabi From an Amorite root meaning, 'The Kinsman is a Healer'. He was the sixth king of **Babylon**, and after conquests over Sumer and Akkad (see **Sumerians** and **Akkadians**) became the first king of the Babylonian Empire which he ruled (according to one chronology) from c.1728–c.1686 BCE. He is famous for his laws, the *Code of Hammurabi* carved onto a stela and placed where the public could see it, whether or not they could read. It is now in the Louvre museum. The code and his improved systems of irrigation are thought to have advanced Babylonian settlement and civilization. 'Innocent until proved guilty' is a surviving principle of the code, although it masks what today would be considered severe penalties for those found guilty. The Hammurabic period is something of a divide in the religions of Mesopotamia. See **Mesopotamian Religion**

Handsome Lake Religion *Ami.* A **Seneca** (Iroquois) religious cult alternatively named Longhouse Religion or *Gui'wiio*, 'Good Message'. Its prophet founder, Ganioda'yo Handsome Lake (1735–1815), received instruction given to him in visions in 1799. His syncretistic teaching combined traditional religion and rituals, **Quakerism**, a Puritan ethic (see **Puritanism**) and a programme aimed at adapting to reservation life. He travelled with a delegation of Indians to Washington to meet President Thomas Jefferson, whose endorsement of the teachings gave authority to the movement which then spread through the Iroquois. Quakers living among the tribes encouraged farming and an agricultural economy. Eventually Handsome Lake fell out with his half-brother Complanter, a senior Seneca leader, and with the Quakers. Handsome Lake was incorporated into Longhouse Religion and still guides some thousands of adherents in Upper New York, Ontario and Quebec.

Hanif *I.* Arab. 'pure' or a 'non-idolater'. Historically the term *hanif* was used of people who were pious, paragons of religious virtues before the Islamic revelation. Abraham, whose monotheism was pure, whose heart was sincere, whose will was totally submitted to that of God, was a *Hanif*. Muslims believe that these qualities are inherent in the way human beings were created and that it is incumbent on all believers to maintain a pure monotheism and to guard against its adulteration by polytheism or sectarianism.

Hanuman or **Hanumat** *H.* Skt. 'The one with big jaws'. A mythological monkey king of divine origin possessing super-human powers including the ability to fly, jumping from Indian to Ceylon in one leap. He figures importantly in the epic war story, the **Ramayana**, in which he and his monkey associates supported Rama. He is described as 'as vast as a mountain and as tall as a gigantic tower. His complexion is yellow and glowing like molten gold. His face is as red as the brightest ruby; while his enormous tail spreads out in an interminable length' (Dowson). It also speaks of Hanuman's perfection, the extent of his scholarship and knowledge and of his unequalled interpretation of sacred texts. The Monkey King symbolizes the necessary attitude of one who loves God, the devotion and loyalty of a servant to his master.

Haoma *AME.* The sacred plant of **Indo-Iranian** religion, being the **soma** of the **Vedas**.

Haqiqah *I.* Truth or reality, conceived in ultimate terms. It is a vision of divine power experienced through a mystical union with God. Both Shiites and Sufis follow the path of *Shari'a*, law and *Tawhid*, in their quest for *haqiqah*.

Hara *AME.* The mythological mountain range that rims the earth in **Indo-Iranian** religion.

Haranath, Sri *H.* There are many thousands of modern Hindus who believe Sri Haranath was the reincarnation of **Gouranga**, a 16th-century saint and embodiment of **Krishna**. He was born on 1st July, 1865 in Western Bengal. His father was a **Brahman**. Haranath's disciples believed he was born to continue Gouranga's unfulfilled mission to spread *Krishna prem*, divine love, as widely as possible by chanting Krishna's name. Such chanting has been made familiar by robed, bell-ringing youths who wander the streets chanting '**Hare Krishna**'. The tradition records that Haranath had exceptional, even superhuman powers and was given to ecstatic trances. There are recorded cases of his converting the worst criminals into saints, the most vicious animals into docile pets. At one level his life seemed normal enough, he earned his living as a civil servant, married and raised a family in accordance with the Hindu obligation to be a householder. But at another level his life was extraordinary. He was gifted with exceptional powers of healing and clairvoyance, heard spirit voices warning of disasters and travelled out of his physical body to the astral plane in order to prevent them. He never claimed these powers to be his own, but gifts from Krishna. Through the love and compassion he had for people his immediate family became extended to include many tens of thousands of people. Of those he helped he asked only that they should chant 'any divine name that melted their hearts'. Those he healed or led to enlightenment, usually chanted his name, Kusuma Haranath, as do hundreds of thousands today. He died in May, 1927. See **ISKCON**

Hare Krishna *H*. The Maha Mantra, the 'Great Mantra' of Hinduism. It is composed of 16 words used to invoke or praise **Vishnu**. The mantra may be repeated out loud or softly to oneself or internally within the mind. The full form of the Mantra is, 'Hare Krishna, Hare Krishna, Krishna Krishna, Hare Hare Hare, Rama Hare Rama, Rama Rama, Hare Hare.' The mantra's invocation of the gods is an affirmation of 'He who is all-attractive', 'He who is the source of all pleasure', and 'He who is the energy of God'. The mantra has been popularized by robed youths known as 'Hari Krishnas', chanting the mantra in the streets as witnesses to 'Krishna Consciousness', for which there is an International Society, **ISKON**. See **Gouranga**, **Haranath**, **Krishna**

Hari-Hara *H*. Skt. Hari, is an epithet for **Vishnu**, Hara, for **Shiva**. Their combination underlies the unity of the two divinities so as to affirm *advaita*, the philosophy of non-duality. See **Dualism**

Harijan *H*. A member of the Indian order of untouchables. See **Caste**

Harmonic Convergence A New Age syncretism that combines social, environmental and personal transformation. It was founded by Jose Arguelles in the 1980s based on alleged **Mayan** prophecies and European and Asian astrological predictions of an imminent 'new age'. In August 1987 he organized assemblies of New Age believers on the earth's vortexes all over the world believed to be the centres of psychic powers. There they meditated and chanted so as to invoke a cosmic transformation. The event put before the world the New Age culture, the mystical efficacy of quartz crystals, the concept of channelling and the possibilities of reincarnation and extraterrestrial life. A future culmi-nating event is anticipated in 2012. See **New Age Religion**

Harranian Religion *AME*. Named from the city of Harran in northwest Mesopotamia, the centre of a mysterious religion that involved the worship of the planets. There is controversy about both its origins and beliefs since the little information available mostly comes from hostile sources. A cautious overview includes polytheism and the cult of the mood god Sin, established also at Ur, with the two centres connected by **Abraham** who, with his family, moved from Ur to Harran. (Gen 11:31) In Mesopotamian mythology Sin was associated with Shamash the sun god and Ishtar the goddess of fertility. Harran was the site of the temple of Sin, patronized by Assyrian Kings and later by the Roman Emperors, Caracalla (211–217 CE) and Julian (331/2–363 CE). Muslim accounts associated the Harranian cult with the **Sabians** whose existence the Koran legitimizes. The Sabians worshipped a supreme creator-deity who, remaining aloof, gave governance of the universe to the planets. It was the demons of these planets the Sabians/Harranians worshipped, by means of mystery rites which included human sacrifice. See **Mesopotamian Religion**

Harris Movement The largest mass Christian movement in West Africa. Founded by William Wade Harris (1850–1929) a catechist at a Christian mission in Liberia. From 1913 to 1915 he led some 120,000 people from Liberia to the Ivory Coast and Ghana in an abandonment of traditional tribal religion. About 100,000 are still believed to worship in Harris Churches which are closely aligned to **Methodism**.

Harrowing of Hell *X*. A traditional English term in Christian theology for Jesus' descent into **hell**, or **Hades**, as mentioned in the Apostles' Creed. The harrying or despoiling of the underworld is a theme in Greek mythology, effected by such heroes as **Hercules**, **Theseus** and **Orpheus** who 'descended' and returned. King Arthur is also thought to have raided hell. The symbolism of the journey is clear, it illustrates the triumph of death. Christ harrowed hell between his crucifixion and **resurrection**, celebrated at **Easter**, respectively on **Good Friday** and **Easter Sunday**.

Hasidism A mystical and pietistic Jewish movement that gathered momentum in 18th century in Eastern Europe. See **Chasidism**.

Haskalah *J*. The Jewish counterpart of the **Enlightenment**. It was influenced, for example, by the rational philosophy of Moses **Mendelssohn** and led to the **Scientific Study of Judaism** (*Wissenschaft des Judentums*). It threw up central issues such as the relationship between being an observant Jew and the secular citizenship of the country of residence; the relationship between those polarities and the implications of being a member of the Jewish nation, racially and nationally. Thus *Haskalah* challenged the *halakhic* (see **Halakah**) or biblical and legal definitions of Jewish identity.

Hatha Yoga Sanskrit *Ha*, 'the breath of the sun', with *Tha*, 'the breath of the moon'. A basic form of Hindu **yoga** being originally one of the techniques of raja-yoga, designed to unite the two 'breaths' as the means of overcoming duality. See **Dualism and Non-Dualism**

Haus Tambaran *P*. Specifically, the ancestor **Spirit House** of the Tambaran cult of the Sepik area of northern New Guinea, but also used generally for the sacred Male Cult houses throughout Melanesia. See **Male Cults, Melanesian Religion**

Hawaiki *P*. A mythical homeland in tropical Polynesia believed to be the place of origin of the Maoris and other Polynesian groups. The legend tells how they migrated in open canoes from their legendary home across the Pacific, eventually beaching on the islands of the archipelagos. 'Hawaiki' is cognate with Hawaii, with *sauali'I*, 'spirits', in Samoan and *hou' eiki*, 'chiefs' in Tongan. Hawaiki is the place to which people's spirits return after death. See **Polynesian Religion**

Healing The 'gift' of healing is one of the familiar indications of religious or magical efficacy, practised in numerous and varied ways by pagan and religious cults since recorded history. The most famous healing god of classical antiquity was **Asclepios**, whose cures, the *Iamata*, were recorded on tablets set in the walls of his temple at Epidaurus. The Hellenistic-Egyptian god **Serapis**, healed through dreams and visions; his temple at Memphis was shared with **Imhotep**, a historical person who was deified by the Egyptians. Ancient practices of Japanese healing show strong similarities with the techniques used in Egypt, Greece and Rome, including that of 'incubation', what today would be termed 'isolation' or quarantine. All religions have their healing tradition and the ability to heal, especially by faith, was taken as a mark of the spirituality of the healer. Christ's healing miracles were one of the signs of his Messiahship and of his followers' Apostleship. Healing has always figured in pagan religion and witchcraft where, apart from spells, herbs are used based on knowledge derived from ancient lore and apothecary practice. Today much is made of psychosomatics, the healing power of the mind imposed either by an agent or by oneself. No recourse to a belief in gods, God or a spirit world is necessary and there are many who practice healing without relying on the notion of 'faith' – they simply have the 'power' to heal. To this must be added that current research into how healing actually works in the mass evangelical rallies or in a one-to-one contact with a faith-healer, has shown the healing to be a placebo combination of the healer's confidence and the subjects desire to be healed.

FINAL WORD: 'Although the world is full of suffering, it's also full of the overcoming of it.' (Helen Keller)

Heathen The term was generally used of someone who does not acknowledge the biblical creator-God of Judaism, Christianity and Islam. More generally, a term used pejoratively of someone who is irreligious or uncivilized.

Heathenry In some uses the term is an alternative to **Paganism**, but it is also a specific reference to the revival of ancient German paganism. It defines the modern re-creation of the old religion from literary and archaeological sources that are thought not to be the same as those of paganism. Adherents would claim that Heathenry is a modern reconstruction of **Anglo-Saxon** religion and **Norse** mythology. The distinction is made between the ancient German-Nordic religions and, for example, the 'paganism' of **Amerindians** or **African** (tribal) religions. See **Neo-Paganism**

Heaven An afterlife concept found in most religions, spiritual movements and cults. In Western mythology it has amounted to a geographical association with the sky, just as '**Hell**' is traditionally located below the earth, as an 'underworld'. In Christian theology it is the place to which Jesus ascended after his resurrection. Whatever form of belief is attached to the word it is considered to be the final destination of the righteous soul and the place where it will survive eternally in the presence of God. Heaven is a destination available to people who have fulfilled various conditions within the belief system of their committed faith. Biblical religions share similar concepts of heaven. In Catholicism it is the physical realm of God, Mary, Angels and the Saints, for Protestant Christianity and Eastern Orthodoxy it is considered to be the Kingdom of God. For Muslims its association is with Eden, for the Baha'i, life on earth is akin to being in one's mother's womb and heaven is a new birth. Judaism understands heaven to be the 'world to come', or the 'new earth', but there is little speculation about it except in Jewish Kabbalahist mysticism that speaks of 'seven heavens'. Eastern religious traditions aspire to '*Moksha*', a liberation of the soul from the birth-death-rebirth cycle. Pagan cults and witchcraft speak of astral projections and planes. Other terms found in the various mythologies include, Elysium, Limbo, **Mag Mell** and **Valhalla**. See **Elysian Fields**

FINAL WORD: 'The inventor of their heaven empties into it all the nations of the earth, in one common jumble ... they have to mix together, pray together, harp together, hosanna together – whites, niggers, Jews, everybody – there's no distinction. Here in the earth all nations hate each other and every one of them hates the Jew. Yet every pious person adores that heaven and wants to get into it. ... And he thinks that if he were only there he would take all the populace to his heart and hug and hug and hug!' (Mark Twain)

Heaven's Gate A secretive **New Age** cult, dubbed 'the UFO cult'. It was led by Marshal Applewhite and subsequently, until her death, by Bonnie Nettles. The cult terminated, literally, in 1997 with the appearance of the comet Hale-Bopp, at which auspicious time Applewhite persuaded 39 of his followers to 'exit their human vehicles' by committing suicide. It was hoped their souls would take a ride on a spaceship believed to be hidden by the comet. The level of commitment to the cult was in some cases total, the adherents selling their homes and everything they had so as to be free from earthly ties and connections. The group lived for many years in isolation in the western USA, their community in some ways resembling a medieval monastic order. Some male members accepted voluntary castration. See **Atherius Society**, **Chen Tao**, **Raelianism**, **UFO Cults**

Hebrew The ancient classical language of the Jewish people and the official language of the **State of Israel**. Hebrew belongs to the Semitic group of languages that include Phoenician and Moabite and may have become the language of the Hebrews when they settled in Canaan, where it had been in use from c.1400 BCE. Small sections of Jewish literature were written in Aramaic, a closely related language, for example parts of Daniel and Ezra, otherwise the whole of Jewish literature to the present day, is written in Hebrew. The Hebrew alphabet consist only of consonants and the vowels pointed below them in certain texts were added later to make reading easier. There is a distinct difference of pronunciation between the **Ashkenazim** and **Sephardim**, but it is the former that remains the standard used in the synagogues of Western Jewry.

The word 'Hebrew' was sometimes used for ancient Israelites, designating individuals or the people as being 'Hebrew' (e.g. Deut. 15:12 and Gen. 40:15). The word has also been used of modern Jews. Seltzer discusses the similarity between the words *Habiru* (or *Apiru*) and Hebrew. 'Mentioned in many documents from different areas and ranging from the late third millennium down to the 12th century BCE, the Habiru were a social stratum living on the fringes of settled society … The patriarchal clans may have been part of this *Habiru* element in Canaan.'

Hegel, George (1770–1831) A German **idealist** philosopher and professor of philosophy in Berlin from 1818 until his death. His main influences came from **Spinoza, Kant, Rousseau** and Goethe. Among those he influenced were **Kierkegaard, Feuerbach, Marx, Engels, Heidegger** and **Sartre**. After his philosophy was banned by the Prussian right-wing, his influence re-emerged in the British idealism of philosophers like Bradley, Moore and **Russell**. Hegel's philosophy is extensive, his writing obscure; one of his major works, *The Phenomenology of Mind*, is also the most difficult. He set out to develop as comprehensive a system as possible aiming to give an account of reality as a whole. For Hegel, the Absolute or Absolute Spirit, is everything that exists and his system endeavours to describe the Absolute's rational structure, the way it is manifest in nature and history, together with its purpose and direction, that is, its **teleology**. Since the 'Absolute' is everything, he tried to resolve the contradictions and tensions of a series of dualistic oppositions such as the subject/object of knowledge, mind and nature, self and the other, freedom and authority, knowledge and faith, Enlightenment and Romanticism. He explored these oppositions by a method known as 'dialectic', that is, by setting up a kind of 'dialogue' between propositions and counter propositions, working to resolve the conflicts by resorting to the 'absolute idea' or 'absolute knowledge', a form of ultimate unifying principle. For this reason Hegel is an **idealist**, mind is everything. Hegel's philosophy focuses on history, religion, art and philosophy itself. Like art, religion is a way of apprehending reality, it is a means of evoking and expressing feelings, it is a species of thought. But religion works through *Vorstellung*, a form of pictorial thinking (imagination, perhaps) which is less than the highest form, that being philosophy, because it is less pure and lacks that ultimate degree of abstraction. Hegel's concept of religion pivots around this same kind of abstraction and absolutism. He defines religion as, 'the consciousness of God, of God the absolute object.' (Hegel [1988]) For Hegel, mind and consciousness are virtually synonymous, thus God as object conceived by consciousness, is an abstraction of the entire universe. God is everything, 'the whole; hence he is universal power, the substance of all existence.' Religion is therefore the content of our consciousness of God as this power and substance. Hegel's philosophy of religion runs close to **Panentheism**, yet the content of our religious consciousness must remain rational and Hegel's philosophy can be seen as a paean for rationality. See **Panlogism**

FINAL WORD: 'The real is rational, the rational is real.' (Hegel)

Heidegger, Martin (1889–1976) Although he did not consider himself to be an **existentialist** Heidegger's influence by **Kierkegaard**, and his analysis of what he termed 'authentic living', set his work in this category. Within this tradition his philosophy is about the meaning of 'being', what it means 'to be'. Everything depends on the extent to which we are 'open to being', and the essence of our humanity resides in sustaining this openness. It is a matter of acceptance without judgement, facing the existential truth of every given situation. The quality of being open is opposed to the 'will to power', which causes us to subordinate others to our own ends rather than simply let them be what they are. In his later work, Heidegger saw poetry as the fullest expression of this openness because it reveals the play of absence and presence, which is being itself. Heidegger's 'openness' takes the form of 'dread', perhaps better understood as 'awe', not before God, but before, 'nothingness', a central theme that influenced **Sartre**. The 'Self' is the centre of everything, but it is in the nature of 'self' to abide in specific 'situations'. These situations are full of 'care', 'sorrow', 'indebtedness' and 'guilt', all theme words in Heidegger's system. In whatever situation we find ourselves, 'to live authentically' is to face the dominating dread of human life, our mortality. In response, Heidegger's ideal person does not seek to escape in religion, pietism or solitude, but is a person of action, totally committed to and involved in life. Authentic living requires a kind of pragmatism, where each situation is a tool to be used, something to be worked with despite the inevitability of it frustrating the objective. Heidegger does not consider the moral values of mutual help, since authentic living takes no account of human relationships, either personal or social and submission to Hitler's regime was not in conflict with his philosophy, but just another 'situation' in which 'the journey through dread' had to be worked out. Heidegger stripped our confrontation with life of all its comforts, cushions and rationalizations since life's commitment is to, 'a fundamental, knowing resolve toward the essence of being.' He used this phrase in his Rectorial Address given in 1933 when he was made Rector of Freiburg University. In the same address, he professed his 'conversion' to Hitler's **National Socialism**, and he distanced himself from his former Jewish teacher, Husserl.

FINAL WORD: 'It is only that the nothing is revealed to us in the very foundation of our human-reality that the utter strangeness of the existent can assail us. It is only on the condition that its strangeness oppresses us that the existent can awaken and compel our wonder.' (Heidegger)

Hel *Nor.* In Scandinavian mythology the underworld or realm of the dead, sometimes called Niflheim. Derived from early **Germanic mythology**,

Hel is also the name of the goddess ruling it, who was the daughter of **Loki**. In Christian mythology it became **Hell**, a place of punishment.

Hell The term as Western religious tradition uses it comes from the old English form, 'Hel'. It is the place ruled by **Satan**, where condemned souls reside eternally after the final judgement. (See **Eschatology**) As such, it is the equivalent of the Hebrew **She'ol** and the Greek **Hades**. While in some traditions of Eastern religion there are devils and evil spirits, there is no equivalent of the biblical notion of hell. Rather, the unending cycle of birth-death-rebirth is something from which to break free by a process of progressive spiritual evolution through many incarnations.

Hell Fire Club An English club that met between 1746 and 1763 at Medmenham Abbey on the River Thames. The club, founded by Sir Francis Dashwood, had something of a notorious reputation of orgiastic and satanic meetings. Like that of more dedicated Satanists, their motto, taken from Rabelais, was 'Do What Thou Wilt', and was adopted by the English occultist Aleister Crowley. (See **Occult**) The name 'Hell Fire Club' has since been used by other groups, many of whom were just tearaways and swingers. See **Medmenham Monks**, **Satanism**

Hellenism *G*. Greek, *Hellas*, 'Greece'. The culture and philosophy of the Hellenistic period in Greek history, roughly between c.323 BCE with the death of Alexander the Great, to c.31 BCE when the Hellenistic empire succumbed to Rome. Characteristic of the period was the exportation of all things Greek to the then known world, a form of globalization of Greek culture. As later philosophers became more preoccupied with religion, Hellenistic philosophy had a considerable influence on the development of Christian doctrine, especially the Neoplatonism of **Plotinus** and his successors. Hellenism also made a distinct and abiding contribution to Jewish philosophy; Jews occupied one of the five wards of Alexandria and there were large settlements in Cyrenaica, Antioch, Phrygia, Greece and Italy. The philosophy of Hellenistic Judaism was more open and universalistic than that of Palestinian Judaism. The hugely influential **Philo** (20 BCE–50 CE) produced a synthesis of Greek and Jewish thought that would be determinative of aspects of Christianity theology. For example, Philo's **Logos** theology was formally adopted by the Church as its Christology, most famously expressed in the first verse of the prologue of John's Gospel: 'When all things began, the Word [Gk. *logos*] already was. The Word dwelt with God and what God was, the Word was.' See **Academy of Athens**

Henotheism A belief in a god without denying the existence of others. The term was coined by the 19th-century sociologist of religion Max Muller, who described henotheism as 'monotheism in principle but polytheistic in fact.' The term is to be distinguished from **Kathenotheism**, 'one god at a time' and **Monolatry**, the worship of only one god within the pantheon. Examples of henotheism are to be found in Greek and Roman religion, as witnessed by Maximus Tyrius (2nd century CE) '... there is one God, the King and Father of all things and many Gods, sons of God, ruling together with him.' Further examples can be seen in Hinduism, in early Israelite beliefs and in Christianity, where God the Father is the principal actor.

Hephaestus *G*. The divine smith of Greek mythology and as the lame god of elemental fire, patron of metal workers. Because he was born ugly his mother, **Hera**, threw him into the sea, but he was found and raised by two nereids (sea nymphs). When his reputation as a craftsman spread the gods summoned him to his rightful place in heaven and gave him a smithy at Olympus. His story is told by Homer in the *Iliad* and *Odyssey* and an account of his birth is offered by Hesiod in the *Theogony*. In the 6th century BCE, when the Greeks colonized parts of Italy, Hephaestus' presence in the volcanoes of Italy and Sicily appeared in the writings of Aeschylus and Pindar. His cult was originally centred at Lycia, but the vents of ignited gas throughout the Aegean were believed to be the chimneys of his underground forge. He was known in Athens but also had 50 shrines dotted around Asia Minor. His Roman name was **Vulcan**.

Hera *G*. The wife and sister of **Zeus** and the presiding goddess of marriages. Her cult is almost certainly derived from a pre-Greek faction, perhaps from a goddess of the Minoan pantheon. Her sanctuaries were established somewhere between the city-states of Argos and Mycenae, also at Samos, where emblems of the goddess, ivory votive pomegranates and poppy capsules were found. Her temples were at Olympia, Corinth, the island of Delos and elsewhere. Most typically the mythologies show her to be a goddess of women, but there is a tradition of her being a cow-goddess, unflatteringly referred to by Homer as *boopis*, 'cow-eyed' or 'cow-faced'. There is also an association with birds originally the cuckoo and later in Hellenistic imagery her wagon was pulled by peacocks, a bird not known to Greece pre-Alexander. The peacock iconography was revived in the Renaissance, an image that unified Hera with Juno, by which name she was known to the Romans.

Heracles G. In Greek mythology the divine hero, the demigod son of **Zeus** and a mortal woman, Alcmene. Famous for his superhuman strength, he was probably the greatest of the mythical heroes, his most celebrated feats recorded as, *The Twelve Labours of Heracles*. There are numerous and overlapping stories of Heracles' origins. One account explains that since he was the progeny of one of Zeus' many illicit affairs, Heracles was detested by **Hera** who constantly threatened his life. Another tells of Zeus tricking Hera into suckling the infant and when she discovered who he was she pulled her breast away, the spilt milk forming the Milky Way. He married three times and had innumerable affairs with both men and women, fathering a great many children, the Heracleidae. That he was a prodigious sexual Olympian is illustrated by the story of his stop-over at the palace of the King of Thespios who, admiring his physique, encouraged him to make love to all 50 of his daughters which, even in pre-Viagra days, the hero obliged to do in one night. Heracles died a voluntary death on a pyre, suffering from a poison-infected shirt. After his death the gods immortalized him and in this form he married Hebe. His cult was identified by the Romans as **Hercules**.

Hercules The name given by the Romans to their adoption of the Greek cult of **Heracles**. A full litany of his exploits is provided by Virgil in the *Aeneid*. Inevitably there were Roman additions to the Greek tradition, such as the account of his killing the monster Cacus who had driven cattle to its cave in the Aventine Hill. Hercules' suffering and death described by Ovid and Seneca, make it clear that the cremation only burned off his mortal remains, thus establishing his divine nature. In later philosophical and religious literature his cult continued to grow in prestige. His human characteristics of physical strength, his courage and his outbursts of temper, made him a peculiarly human hero and it was for this reason that he was used by **Zeus** and **Jupiter** as an intermediary when dealing with human beings.

Heresy A contravention of Christian belief judged and defined by a Church authority. It is the denial of defined doctrine in which, as sometimes happens, the heretic accuses the orthodox view of being heretical. In **Roman Catholicism** a 'formal heresy' is the wilful belief to an error by a baptized person. It is a serious sin that may lead to excommunication or worse. 'Material heresy' is the adherence to false doctrine 'in good faith' and is not considered a sin. See **Albigensians**, **Cathars**, **Gnosticism**, **Manicheanism**, **Pelagianism**

Hermeneutics Theories and methods of interpretation, usually of religious texts, so as to disclose the intentions and truths of the original authors and later compilers. See **Redaction Criticism**

Hermes *G*. Greek mythology had Hermes as a jack-of-all-trades god. He was associated with boundaries, travellers, shepherds, cowherds orators, literature and poets, with athletics, weights and measures, invention, commerce and cunning thieves. He was also the messenger of the gods, familiarly depicted wearing winged sandals and a helmet. As a *hermaion*, an interpreter or translator, he has given us the term 'hermeneutics'. An alternative tradition identified Hermes with a cairn (Gk. *hermaion*) or heap of stones, presumably associated with boundaries and travellers. In true manner, the Greeks created a myth to account for this; it seems that when tried for killing the monster Argus, the gods acquitted him casting their voting stones at his feet, thus the cairn grew around him. Superstitious travellers still add a stone to a cairn for good luck, but it is also responsible maintenance. Among his inventions was the lyre, made from a turtle shell and sheep's intestines. His cult was assimilated into the Roman cult of **Mercury**.

Hermes Trismegistus *G*. Gk. 'Thrice-Greatest-Hermes'. A powerfully influential syncretism formed by the cult of **Hermes**, with the Egyptian god, **Thoth**. As gods of writing and magic, the duo's beguiling combination of communication and escoteric wisdom or the communication *of* esoteric wisdom travelled down the years to appear in the traditions of **Hermetica**, **Hermeticism** and Renaissance Kabbalism. Together Hermes and Thoth have made available, albeit by secret means, the arts of magic, alchemy and astrology.

FINAL WORD: 'He [Hermes] carried an emerald, upon which was recorded all of philosophy and the caduceus, the symbol of mystical illumination. Hermes Trismegistus vanquished Typhon, the dragon of ignorance and mental, moral and physical perversion.' (From: Guiley, Rosemary Ellen)

Hermetica A collection of Hellenistic mystical philosophy compiled during the 2nd and 3rd centuries CE. They were named after **Hermes Trismegistus**, identified with the Egyptian god **Thoth**. Tradition has it that Hermes revealed these mysteries so as to provide mortals with the wisdom necessary for life. Some of the texts take the form of letters, others of Socratic dialogue. Its Greek sources are Platonic and Stoic and its cosmology is drawn from the **Septuagint**. The Hermetic texts were gathered together at an unknown date in a collection called the *Corpus Hermetica*, which still exists. Also preserved is another collection made in the 5th century CE, by John Stobaeus. There are two other texts that stand alone, the **Asclepius**, and the *Kore Kosmou*.

Hermeticism An ancient spiritual and magical tradition, taking its names from the Greek god, **Hermes Trismegistus**. The teachings drew on astrology and alchemy, influencing the occult lore of Europe. Interest in Hermeticism flowered in the 19th century through groups such as the **Hermetic Order of the Golden Dawn**. The philosophies of the **Hermetica** have been compared to that of **Gnosticism**, and the similarities touch on our knowledge of God, the world, the **soul**, and their interrelationships. What the two systems share is there origin within the same period (1st–3rd centuries CE) and the idea that only by accessing privileged knowledge, the *gnosis*, can the soul escape being in bondage to matter. Beyond that, the similarities must not be too closely drawn. Hermeticism developed the notion that man combines a godlike and a mortal nature, he is therefore superior to lesser gods who are only immortal and to other creatures who are only mortal. The **Asclepius**, one of the most influential Hermetic texts, assures us we can create gods by endowing statues with the souls of demons and angels, thus empowering them to cause good and evil. We can do this by the use of 'holy and godly mysteries'. The first Asclepius (the god) and the first **Hermes** were among the gods created this way. As a mortal, man is subject to **Fate**, but as an immortal he is the master of all things. In this tension the human being must look for knowledge in order to hold the contradictions in balance. Furthermore, while all beings were originally androgynous, the male and female aspects gradually separated, creating another dualism. In order to reach 'surpassing goodness' it is necessary for a man (or woman) to know himself as 'original' man. The alternative is to remain enmeshed in matter and in the love of the body which results in the loss of that part of human nature that is a god and therefore in the loss of immortality. The Hermetica tell us there is only one virtue, the disposition to know and understand God, the world and man. The 'one virtue' amounts to a totally comprehensive agenda.

Hermetic Order of the Golden Dawn Also known as Stella Matutina, it was founded by three members of the Rosicrucian Society in 1887, who had discovered in 1880, coded manuscripts believed to be a unique Western repository of magical knowledge. All three men were Masons and they combined the degree structure and initiation rites of **Freemasonry** with Christian, Egyptian and Rosicrucian symbolism. The order became the most influential magical order of modern times, establishing temples in London, Paris and Edinburgh. Its members undertook extensive studies of esoteric subjects, including **Astrology**, **Kabbalah**, **Tarot** and forms of meditation and ritual magic. Of the three founders, S. L. MacGregor Mathers (1854–1918) emerged as the somewhat autocratic leader, attracting resentment and opposition which resulted in the fracturing of the Order. Some of these splinter groups still meet and practice. Among its influential members were W. B. Yeats, Aleister Crowley and Algernon Blackwood, the author of ghost stories.

Hermit From the Greek *eremos*, signifying 'desert' or 'uninhabited'. Generally, a reference to Christian monks or nuns who choose to live alone, although there are parallels in Hinduism, Buddhism, Sufism and other religions. In principle the term may apply to anyone withdrawn from society for religious reasons. Famous Christian hermits include, St Anthony of Egypt and St Simeon Stylites. (See **Stylites**) Some, like the ancient desert-dwelling anchorites were walled up with only a small window left to admit light; in medieval Europe the cell was usually attached to a church. Their solitude is often compromised by people seeking advice and instruction, sometimes to the point of having so many disciples that they have no solitude at all and develop communities as did St Anthony and the Buddha. The Carthusian Roman Catholic order of monks and nuns is a variant in that they are communities of hermits each equipped with their own cells comprising a sleeping area, a study and workshop. They meet only in church for worship. See **Monasticism**

Hero In folklore, legend and mythology, a man, sometimes of divine ancestry, who is endowed with great courage and strength. The qualities of a hero are usually brought to light by having to perform dangerous exploits. Dissatisfied with the limitations of human existence, the hero undertook a trial, in order to overcome them. His adventures or 'heroic deeds' were a figure of a spiritual quest that blazed a trail for others to follow. The Greek poet Pindar described heroes as the offspring of gods and mortals, thus they were Demi-gods each with cults of their own and a distinct feature of Greek religion. Roman heroes, such as the cults of the Emperors, differed in that at death they did not ascend to Olympus or gain divinity, but remained under the earth with only local power. Every religion and culture has thrown up its heroes, who are the subjects of some of the earliest and most famous mythologies and literatures. One of the oldest accounts, believed to originate in the 3rd millennium BCE, is *The Epic of Gilgamesh;* Homeric heroes inspired the *Iliad* and *Odyssey*, Germanic heroes inspired *Beowulf* and the *Nibelungenlied* and the **Eddas** of Norse mythology. In India heroes populated the *Ramayana* and *Mahabharata*. The English King Arthur, the Irish Cu Chulainn and Finn, the Icelandic Sigmund, the French Roland and the early Russian heroes of Kiev and Novgorod, are other examples of heroes whose legends have produced extensive literatures. The Jews, during their struggle to establish themselves in the 'Promised Land', were led by heroic leaders such as Gideon, Samson and David who slew Goliath and whose subsequent story is a saga of heroic proportions. Heroes, even though they have brief lives and untimely tragic ends, like Achilles, are accorded lasting glory; they are leaders with faithful followers, like Alexander the Great and Charlemagne; they are identified with pioneering settlers like Davy Crockett; with the struggles of the poor and oppressed, like Robin Hood and the Mexican revolutionary, Zapata or the Argentinian-born Cuban, Che Guevara. The classical accounts of the heroes are not escapist, fairy tales, but have a serious core which is best read as a source of enduring wisdom. In general use, a hero is someone who has shown great courage, possibly at risk to his own life and for a noble purpose. The term is now gender free and applies equally to women.

Hero *G*. The tragic priestess of the cult of **Aphrodite**, who was bound by a vow of celibacy. Because of her great beauty, her parents willed that she lived in a high tower on the sea near Sestus, perhaps the 'Tower of Hero', that was in ruins by the time of Alexander. She took a lover, Leander, who lived at Abydus on the Asian side of the Hellespont and by lighting a candle to guide him to her, she turned the tower into a lighthouse. Every night Leander swam the 1,300 metres across the Hellespont to meet her. During one of these trysts he drowned in the contrary currents and the grief-stricken Hero killed herself by jumping from the tower into the sea. Because the currents favour the swimmer, it is said that swimming from Sestus to Abydus is easier. This was proved in 1810 when Lord Byron, without the incentive of a priestess of Aphrodite waiting for him, swam the distance in one hour and ten minutes.

Hestia *G*. The goddess of the hearth, domesticity and family, the virgin daughter of **Cronos** and **Rhea**. She had no public cult, but was one of the three great goddesses of the first Olympian generation, renouncing her seat among the 12 Olympian gods in favour of **Dionysus**. She has no developed mythology, meriting only five lines in the Homeric *Hymn to Hestia*. Probably because of her withdrawal from Olympus, the hymn identifies her with Delphi, the central Hellenic 'hearth'. Her Roman counterpart was **Vesta**, whose sacred flame was maintained by the **Vestal Virgins**.

Hesychasm *G*. Gk. 'stillness', 'quiet' or 'rest'. An ermetic practice of prayer in Eastern Orthodoxy. No one seems to know the origin of the term, but it appears as early as the 4th century in the writings of St John Chrysostom and other sources. By the 14th century, at Mt Athos, the practice had become more formalized and amounted to methods of mental ascesis, the use of the Jesus Prayer and, although this is denied by adherents of Hesychasm, psychophysical techniques akin to the yogic practices of Hinduism, Buddhism and Sufism. The aim is to acquire deep inner stillness, ignoring physical sensations so as to have an experiential knowledge of God. Hesychasm eventually gave rise to theological controversy concerning the distinction made between the 'energies' or operations of God and the 'essence' of God and it has never been accepted by the Roman Catholic Church.

Hidden Imam *I*. Arab. A belief based on the lineage of the **Twelvers**, that the twelfth descendent of the Prophet Muhammad did not die in the normal way but was occulted. It carries a messianic implication in that he will return as a **Mahdi** to establish a just and peaceful society. A modern interpretation of the concept was given by the Iranian, Ayatollah Ruhollah Khomeini (1900–89) who suggested the most learned jurist should be the representative of the Hidden Imam and assume the rulership of the state. See **Shi'ism**

Hierarchy Gk. from *hieros*, 'sacred' and *arkho*, 'rule'. A system of ranking or organizing things, ideas or people, where each part is subordinate to another element. In religion the concept is applied to just about everything, to the religious establishment, be it church, synagogue or mosque, to the clergy, rites, ritual and sacraments, to the authority given to different lay echelons of administration and where there is a polytheistic tradition, to the standing and order of the gods. Wherever there is a group of people bound together by some kind of common idea or cause, there will be a hierarchy. Abraham Maslow suggested a hierarchy of needs, a psychological theory suggesting that as we meet our 'basic needs' we need or seek, to satisfy 'higher needs'. In religious history, questioning the nature of the authority behind established hierarchies has led to the emergence of major denominational divisions in most religions.

Hieroglyphs *E*. The race to decipher Egyptian hieroglyphics was one of the most dramatic intellectual events of the 19th century. Proto-hieroglyphs, together with phonograms and ideograms, were already developed by c.3200 BCE, as a method of writing. They were used for over 3000 years as a way of inscribing tombs, temples and religious artefacts. Eventually a cursive script, hieratic, was developed by priests compiling parchments and for writing secular texts. A demotic form (the people's writing) developed from c.700 BCE and was used in the Greco-Roman period. The most ancient body of religious writing is the **Pyramid Texts**. More than 2,000 hieroglyphs are in use each one representing a common object in the form of either its sound or its idea or both. Coptic, written in Greek, followed the sentence structure of the Egyptian language and was the key to the translation of the **Rosetta Stone**.

Hifz al-Koran *I*. Arab. 'having the **Koran** by heart'. It is related to the concept of *dhikr*, 'remembrance', which is a devotional obligation for Muslims. Not every adherent gets to the point of being able to recite the whole of the Koran by heart, but it is an aspiration most would share. The Koran is itself a constant and divine reminder to man of the merciful revelation of Allah to Muhammad and the responsible believer will commit to memory as much of the text as he can so that it is for ever on his heart and tongue. Someone who can recite the whole of the Koran by heart is known as a *hafiz* and to achieve this is a prerequisite for traditional Muslim education. Memorizing the Koran will condition the mind to think in certain ways; the process is not primarily one of reason but of emotion, the feeling, passion and truth of the text impregnates the mind as dye will impregnate a cloth. For much the same reason many Arabic buildings, especially mosques, have walls lined with tiled calligraphy of verses from the Koran so as to create the Koran's particular ambiance for that space.

Higher Criticism In general literary use the critical and analytical study of texts so as to examine the sources and methods of the authors. Since the early 19th century Higher Criticism has been associated with a critical examination of the Bible one aspect of which, linguistic analysis, has disclosed the various sources used, for example, by the compilers of the Pentateuch and the Gospels. In the latter case the technique exposed the 'Synoptic Problem', a combination of sources shared by two or more of the first three gospels and the sources unique to each of them. The process of critical examination of sacred literature is not confined to Judeo-Christian texts. See **Form Criticism**, **Redaction Criticism**, **Source Criticism**, **Textual Criticism**

Hijrah *I*. Arab. *hegira*, 'emigration', 'withdrawal'. The term applied particularly to the breaking of the kinship tie required by new religious faith. In Islamic tradition *hijrah* refers to Muhammad's migration from Mecca to Medina in 622 CE, it was not, as is sometimes translated, a 'flight', but a planned withdrawal or 'emigration'. The term thus symbolizes a willingness to suffer for one's faith and in the face of opposition to maintain it with hopefulness. The migration was a formative event in Islamic history and the only time-date reference point to be found in the Koran. The act of *hijrah* established irrevocably the political-military dimension of Islam and 622 CE was fixed as the year marking the new Islamic era.

Hikma *I*. Arab. 'wisdom' or 'truth'. It refers to both mundane knowledge of the kind derived from science, and to the truth as revealed by Allah through Muhammad. The **Koran** is revealed *Hikma*. A distinction is made between the exoteric knowledge of the nature and origin of the world and the esoteric truth derived from Koranic revelation. It is on the latter form of wisdom that Islamic philosophy was founded and developed. *Hikma* has much broader terms of reference than the natural philosophy of *Falsafah*, extending the enquiry to include theology, mysticism and theosophy, which makes it akin to the terms of reference of Western metaphysics.

Hilal *I*. Arab. 'crescent' or 'new moon'. Hilal was the moon god of pre-Islamic Arabia. Also an Islamic symbol used, for example, by the Red Crescent Society.

Hinayana *B. Z.* Skt. The smaller or lesser vehicle referring to the earlier original schools of Buddhism. Adherents of Hinayana called their tradition **Theravada**, the teachings of the elders, and claimed it to be the original teaching of the Buddha as recorded in the *sutras*. Theravada was one of 18 Hinayana schools (although there is textual evidence that there were many more) established during the period between the death of the Buddha (c.483 BCE) and the end of the 1st century BCE. It is the only school to have survived and is the traditional Buddhism of Sri Lanka, Thailand, Burma, Cambodia and Laos. Hinayana doctrine focuses on the Buddha's teachings concerning the truth of *dukkha*, suffering, as outlined in the **Four Noble Truths** and the way to liberation or **nirvana** as described in the **Eightfold Path**. It is a realistic, 'looking life in the face' approach to truth that analyzes the nature of human existence and presents what, in modern terms, amounts to a psychological understanding of our individual make-up. Hinayana eschews philosophy and speculation about the goals of the spiritual journey, putting its emphasis on enlightenment as an experience attained by one's own efforts to renounce the world and whatever attaches us to it. The monk or nun must make a full-time commitment and there is little offered to the layperson. In Hinayana teaching the Buddha is not a transcendent, other-worldly being, but a historical person and teacher. From the point of view of **Mahayana**, Hinayana wrongly concentrates on personal liberation rather than that of all sentient beings. In this respect the earlier doctrine is thought to be the foundation on which the Buddha went on to construct a more complete system, the greater vehicle of Mahayana.

Hindu Festivals and Feasts *H*. Beyond the Hindu's patterns of daily life and worship, are the calendric celebrations of festivals, feasts and fasts, the abundance of which is a feature of Hinduism. As with worship, the festivals are associated with specific deities and as in most countries, the major festivals are nationally observed as occasions for public holidays. Aside from the festivals associated with the major gods, are other innumerable celebrations of which only a few examples can be given. Perhaps the most well-known is, *Diwali*, the 'festival of lights', when oil lamps and candles are placed around the home, courtyard and garden. It celebrates different things to different regions, from the homecoming and coronation of **Rama**, to the honouring of the goddesses **Kali** and **Lakshmi**. The festival of *Ganapati* is in honour of the elephant-headed god, **Ganesha**, whose image is usually the centrepiece of a procession to a *mandap*, a pavilion where songs and dances are performed. This festival became associated with the movement for Indian independence. *Raksha Bandhan*, 'protective bond', celebrates the inviolable ties between brothers and sisters, involving a thread-tying ceremony and the exchange of gifts. See **Hinduism**

Hindu Initiation *H*. See **Sacred Thread Ceremony, Initiation**

Hinduism *H. Sanatana-Dharma*. Skt. *Sanatana*, 'imperishable', 'eternal', with *Dharma*, 'teaching', or 'truth', thus the eternal religion or eternal truth. Hinduism is unique among the major world religions in that it has no founder. Neither is there a single body of beliefs that might constitute a creed. Rather it is a family of faiths which despite diversity, are bound together by their similarities. Hinduism's foundation is a body of literature, the **Vedas** ('wisdom' or 'knowledge') and its origins derive from the earliest writings, which are included in the **Rig-Veda**. They are thought to have been written by **Aryan** priests between 1500–1000 BCE, who carried the oral tradition of the Vedas and their sacrificial cult into India by way of the Indus valley, possibly as early as 3500 BCE. The theory of Aryan 'invasion' has given way to one of more gradual migration and the Aryans' assimilation of the indigenous **Dravidian** culture. Early Hinduism incorporated the imported cult of offering sacrifice to a plurality of gods, such as Indra and Varuna, invoking them to endow humans with prosperity, large families and victory in war: 'For sustained sacrifice the gods will give you the food of your desires' (**Bhagavad Gita**). To this was added the Dravidian belief in reincarnation that became a corner-stone for Hinduism, Buddhism and **Jainism**. As Hindu doctrine developed, the efficacy of sacrifice was demoted, its emphasis moving from the outward and visible forms of religious practice, to the inward and invisible challenges of the spiritual life. As the inspired sages gradually made this adjustment, Vedic philosophy reached its zenith with the new perceptions of the **Aranyakas** and **Upanishads**. (Primary Sources: Hinduism)

What were these new perceptions? The Hindu mind seems to be naturally disposed to metaphysics and to pondering abstract perennial questions such as who or what is it that sustains the world and the universe around it? Is there something within the individual that constitutes the essence of our personal existence, that is not subjected to the vicissitudes of mood, emotion or the process of aging and dying? Is there a single unchanging, unmoving reality behind every visible and changing phenomenon? The answers to these questions explored the use of basic concepts such as 'breath', 'mind', the ability to 'accept' and to 'understand'.

But of themselves, they offered no lasting satisfaction. It was the philosophy of the **Upanishads** that offered more substantial solutions, introducing Hinduism to the idea that our individual essence, atman, and the cosmic reality **Brahman**, are identical. Words were inadequate to express the truth of this solution and the whole purpose of life and of the spiritual journey, was to 'realize', through experience what is sometimes described as, 'cosmic consciousness'. Those who have realized the unity of atman with Brahman speak of knowing the cosmos to be immaterial, absolutely spiritual in nature and rippling with the kind of life that consigns even death to the realms of illusion. 'Those who see all beings in the Self and the Self in all beings, will never shrink from it.' Such is the mind-set of the Upanishads.

For some these philosophies were too abstract and impersonal and a parallel, theistic movement developed. The problem was that the individual's search for the union of atman and Brahman undermined the experience we all have of ourselves as an independently existing being, among other independent beings, thus denying the individual's need for relationship. It was a psychological perception that did not match the available metaphysical template. Even in the Upanishads (for example, the Svetasvatara Upanishad) and in the Bhagavad-Gita, there is sometimes more than a hint of Brahman being a personal God. In the former, God is Rudra-Shiva, in the latter, **Vishnu** as an incarnation of **Krishna**. These gods did not figure largely in early Hindu literature and it is significant that they later appear as 'God' in the orthodox Hindu trinity Brahma, Vishnu and Shiva. As with the Christian **trinity**, the three are to be understood as aspects or qualities of the one. The image used is of a wheel, the same wheel that figures in the centre of the Indian flag. God is both the hub and rim, our individual selves being the spokes that hold the two together. We have now reached the stage in Hindu thought where we are inseparable from God, without being identical to him. It is a critically important turning point in the development of Hindu philosophy and what takes this development further, is the **Bhagavad-Gita** (Primary Sources: Hinduism) which is not part of the Vedas and technically stands outside the Hindu canon. Nevertheless the Gita has always been considered to be of supreme importance by both philosophers and ordinary, village-dwelling Hindus. The reason is not difficult to understand since it introduces to Hinduism the quality of love. In his incarnation as Krishna, Vishnu is a God of love and the model now becomes one of intimate relationship with this God. In this relationship, the individual learns of his dependence on God and it is this that engenders a deep love of and an indispensable communion with, the divine. In this pattern the supreme Vishnu-Krishna is the 'base supporting Brahman, immortal Brahman which knows no change – supporting too the eternal law of righteousness and absolute beatitude.' This is the message of the Bhagavad-Gita, that the personal God is raised above Brahman, who becomes the quality of eternity, leaving the personal God to share with you the quality of 'being', yet remaining separate as both the giver and receiver of love. Additional information on the nature and roles of Krishna, Vishnu, **Shiva** and **Shakti**, are given under their separate entries. Around these gods, powerful and popular splinter groups developed, **Vaishnavism**, **Shaivism** and **Shaktism**. From c.800 CE, when Hinduism was under threat from Buddhism, the Hindu saint **Shankara** developed his non-dualistic philosophy (see **Dualism**) which proved to be a unifying and rejuvenating force.

The daily life and practice of a Hindu is played out against the background of these characteristic, introspective, philosophies and the majority will not engage in them over much. Hinduism's practical face is a from of socio-spirituality which touches every aspect of a person's daily life, from birth, to the **Sacred Thread Ceremony**, to death and rebirth. All Hindus will be conscious of *samsara*, this endless round of birth-death-rebirth from which only 'realization' can assure escape. Throughout the cycles of the **transmigration** of the soul, a person might be reborn as a human being or, depending on **karma**, as an animal or a bird. More pertinently, only the law of karma can explain why, on rebirth, people are distributed among the various **castes**.

From its earliest beginnings Hinduism has been a domestic religion with its grass-roots in villages sustained by an agricultural economy. For the average Hindu villager, religious practice follows the pattern of the **Four Stages of Life**, from youth with all its potential, to old age and *sannyasa*, the renunciation of the world. These life-stages follow a Vedic prescription, but socially the Hindu's life is also conditioned by the rigorous hierarchy of caste. These are the circumstances in which Hindus pursue their quest to identify with the eternal self, Brahman, uniting with it by means of *jnana*, knowledge, *karma*, service and *bhakti* devotion. Each of these have specialized **yoga** practices. Within the daily life of the village the Hindu is consciously concerned with three aspects this religious quest: i) for survival and betterment in this life; ii) for the acquisition of merit so as to assure a good rebirth; and iii) for liberation from the confines of *samsara*. The whole of daily life is ritualized. 'The kitchen lies at the heart of the sacred geography of the household. The family shrine … is also important. It is sometimes located in the kitchen for the simple reason that this is the place of guaranteed purity.' (L. A. Babb) Individual and communal worship takes place in the home, around village shrines, at temples and at any other suitable place. Once the worshippers have ensured their ritual purity, the object of their worship will vary. It can be directed towards the gods of family shrines represented by a variety of sculptures and images or towards any of the major gods, such as Krishna, **Rama**, **Ganesha**, Vishnu, Shiva, in any of their many forms of incarnation.

In summary, it can be said that *Sanatana-Dharma*, 'eternal truth', is a fitting epithet for Hinduism and its central teaching, derived from the Bhagavad-Gita. There are many paths to the Truth, probably as many as there are those seeking it. Although Hinduism allows philosophies that indicate alternative paths, it would affirm that it is more advantageous to pursue the faith into which one is born, rather than to convert to another.

See **Hindu Festivals and Feasts, Hinduism and Secularism, Sacred Thread Ceremony, Trans-polytheistic Theism**
FINAL WORD: 'He who knows both the transcendent and the immanent, with the immanent overcomes death and with the transcendent reaches immortality.' (Isa Upanishad)

Hinduism and Secularism *H*. Of all major religions, Hinduism expresses the most positive attitude to secularism. Traditionally, Hindus have always believed it is a matter for each individual to decide which **dharma** should be followed, but that once chosen, it should be nurtured and sustained by loyal, unwavering commitment. Hinduism is inward-looking, self-examining and tolerant of other faiths and philosophies even when these are non-theistic or atheistic. This built-in freedom of choice and the lack of pressure to proselytize is, for Hindus, true secularism. Only in a secular context, where religion is a personal matter standing without any official authority or status, can all forms of reason co-exist and progress. Secularism is thus, 'the great emancipator' and in general, Hinduism is wholly supportive of India's secular state.
See **Hinduism**
FINAL WORD: 'The fundamental mistake of Indian secularism is that Hinduism is put in the same category as Islam and Christianity. Islam and Christianity's intrinsic irrationality and hostility to independent critical thought warranted secularism as a kind of containment policy. By contrast, Hinduism recognizes freedom of thought and does not need to be contained by secularism.' (Koenraad Elst)

Hippocrates (460–377 BCE) A Greek physician who came to be regarded as the father of medicine. Convinced that illness had rational and physical causes he rejected the superstitious beliefs that it was the result of spirit-possession or the disfavour of the gods. His medical knowledge was founded on observation and research of the human body which should be treated holistically and not as a collection of separate parts. His 'Oath of Medical Ethics' is still taken by practitioners today.
See **Asclepius**

Hittite Religion The Hittite Empire, c.1460–1190 BCE, was equal in power and influence to that of the **Egyptian, Babylonian** and **Assyrian**. Isolated city communities were unified in the office and person of the King who ruled from the capital city, Hattusas, but local religious autonomy was preserved. Through the familiar process of syncretism the state and the office of kingship was set under protection of national deities who were accorded rituals or festivals. The state's patron was a sun goddess, the Queen of Heaven and Earth and the sun god, the 'King of Gods', was lord of righteousness and justice. Hatti, the consort of the sun-goddess was a weather god. The mythology shows the character of the gods to be taken from natural phenomena, so there were the usual storm gods, wind gods and gods of other elemental forces. The gods were enlisted as witnesses to, and guardians of, contracts and peace treaties drawn up with foreign powers, such as Egypt. The cults were centred in city temples which were also places of administration. See **Hurrian Religion, Mesopotamian Religion**

Hobbes, Thomas (1588–1679) A British rationalist, philosopher and political scientist. His philosophy was given in *Leviathan*, his master-piece, in which he developed the notion that the key to success was to discover and follow the right method. For Hobbes, the famous image is the watch, the mechanism of which cannot be understood unless it is taken apart. Thus it is necessary to discover by analysis what, for example, people are really like, especially what they would be like if unconditioned and free of the controls of law and society. From the indi-vidual, Hobbes carries the thesis to society and the state which must be examined as if society was free of its controlling and defining traditional structures. In such a case, Hobbes claims, there would be, 'a war of every man against everyman, … No arts; no letters; no society and which is worst of all, continual fear and danger of violent death; and the life of man, solitary, poor, nasty, brutish and short.' Just over a century later **Rousseau**'s (1712–78) solution would be the 'social contract', but for Hobbes it was a necessary covenant, cast in the speculative form of what would happen 'if' and what would happen 'unless'. His confidence was placed in just one person or a collection of people holding power, a form of beneficent oligarchy, although his preference was for beneficent monarchy, a Platonic 'philosopher king'. Like examining the parts of a watch so as to understand its function, it is necessary to ascertain the various and separate parts and capacities of the state, so as to understand how it may properly perform its function. Hobbes' view is thus, ratio-nalist and materialistic (see **Rationalim** and **Materialism**). He holds a compatibilists (see **Compatibilism**) view of free will and determinism and a functional view of language, particularly religious language. He reasoned that religious doctrines were not necessarily false, but merely incoherent.

FINAL WORD: 'The "value" or "worth" of a man is, as of all other things, his price; that is to say, so much as would be given for the use of his power.' (Hobbes)

Holiness Movement *X.* An association of people who believe that the 'carnal nature' of man can be cleansed and mitigated by faith in the power of the Holy Spirit. This is conditional on having been 'justified', that is, having one's sins forgiven by faith in the salvatory work of Jesus Christ. The faithful will receive the gifts of 'spiritual power' and of a pure heart, since, 'blessed are those whose hearts are pure; they shall see God' (Mat. 5:8). This doctrine is known as, 'entire satisfaction' or 'Christian perfection'. The origins of the Movement lie in aspects of **Reformation** theology that were advanced through **Puritanism**, **Pietism** and **Quietism**. In the 18th and 19th centuries the incentive of 'Christian per-fection' inspired the evangelists of the two 'Great Awakenings' in America, and through the 20th century provided the spiritual energy for the mass-meeting evangelical campaigns such as those of Dr Billy Graham. The Holiness Movement led to the formation of several dedicated church denominations that include the Wesleyan Church, the Salvation Army and the World Gospel Mission. See **Introversionism**

Holocaust *J*. Literally, from the Greek, 'a sacrifice wholly consumed by fire', the term came to be used for a great slaughter or massacre. In the 20th century it became associated with the extreme anti-Semitism of Nazi Germany, whose policy was to annihilate world Jewry. Between 1933 and 1945, something like six million Jewish men, women and children died in extermination camps, together with those of minority groups such as gypsies, the mentally ill, the physically handicapped and political opponents of the Nazi regime. What was called by the Nazis 'the final solution' to the Jewish problem, was driven by the concept of a pure race based on a misconceived anthropological **Aryan** model. There is now a huge archive in every media recording the Holocaust, much of which is housed in dedicated libraries. In a creatively positive response, modern Jews now speak of 'the Holocaust and the Redemption of Judaism', in that the establishment of the **State of Israel** represents a phoenix-like rebirth of European Jewry out of the fires that consumed the murdered millions. The redemptive movement did not happen immediately on the establishment of the Israeli state, but poignantly as a response to the Six Day War of 1967. The Arab threat to annihilate the State of Israel was powerfully evocative of the Holocaust and the near miraculous victory of the Israeli army, together with the expansion of territory that went with it, was the source of a galvanizing energy that enabled world Jewry to rethink and to re-establish its ethnicity. The holocaust threatened Jewish belief in the God of history and the question, 'Where is God now?' was constantly on the lips of those interned in the extermination camps. Answers were sought from every point of view, from the radical Jewish atheism of Richard Rubenstein to the re-affirmation of the 'hidden' God of history proposed by Eliezer Berkovits. Steven Katz provides a summary of the ways in which Jews have responded to the Holocaust in terms of religion and philosophy, while Dow Marmur is concerned to discuss the future of Judaism against the implications of the holocaust. FINAL WORD: 'I have mixed feelings. Some can forgive and some cannot. I can forgive, but with a cold heart.' (Greek Holocaust survivor, Benjamin Capon)

Holy, Concept of The state of being holy, that is, set apart for the worship or service of gods or God. Ascribed mostly to people, it can also be applied to objects and places. It is a concept found throughout religious history, but most frequently in those that have a formally established and structured theology. In **Protestantism** holiness is not just an acquired state, but a process of remaking the person who has died to self and 'come alive' to Jesus Christ (Romans 6:19–22). In Catholicism, it is a state achieved sacramentally and maintained in association with holy objects like, rosaries, crucifixes and statues. In Judaism the term *tzadik* is used meaning 'righteous', a quality accrued by keeping the *Halakhah*, the Law. A Tzadik, is a righteous or holy man.

Holy Grail *X*. Despite the many confident assertions, interpretations and commentaries, what the Holy Grail actually is remains a mystery. The idea of it has passed from myth and legend into everyday speech and is as much part of our own culture as it has been of any other. In Christian mythology it was the dish, plate or cup used by Jesus at the **Last Supper**. Some versions of the legend say that Joseph of Arimathea collected some of Christ's blood in the cup while interring him in the tomb, then carried it to Britain where a line of guardians have secretly protected it. Grail romances have their origins in France, from where they were translated into other European languages. Earlier accounts of the legend were associated with Percival and threaded into the fabric of the Arthurian legend. The quest to find the Grail has inspired Tennyson's, *Idylls of the King*, Wagner's *Parsifal*, Rossetti's painting *The Holy Grail* and numerous films. In some accounts the Grail is not a cup, but the earthly remains of Mary Magdalene cast as the wife of Jesus. The term has become a metaphor for the unattainable or indiscoverable; the search for an anti-gravity device, artificial consciousness, a proto-world language, a cure for all forms of cancer or a theory of everything have become the 'holy grails' of modern science. See **Grail Religion**

Holy Land *J*. The biblical **Canaan**. It was later called Palestine by the Romans, who intended the name to be a secular replacement for the 'Land of Israel', with its religious associations. It remained Palestine until November 1947, when the United Nations voted to divide the territory between the *yishuv*, the Palestinian Jews and the indigenous Arabs. In May 1948, Israel became an independent state and 'Palestine' is now limited to Gaza. The country is equally holy for Jews, Christians and Muslims, for each of whom the land holds deeply religious significance. See **Israel**

Holy of Holies *J*. The innermost sanctuary of the Temple in Jerusalem. It could only be entered by the High Priest on **Yom Kippur**, the Day of Atonement. There, he would sprinkle the blood of a sacrificed animal and burn incense as atonement for his own sin and his priestly colleagues. It was also the shrine of the Ark of the **Covenant**, or **Torah**. A form of ark has always been a feature of the **synagogue**.

Holy Order of MANS A **New Age** monastic order founded in 1968 by Earl W. Blighton, an engineer, and 11 others, one of whom was Sufi Murshid Samuel Lewis. The Order practised an esoteric mystical religion, blending biblical and occult themes with concepts such as reincarnation. 'MANS' was an acronym for a phrase given only to initiates and men advancing through the Order could reach the status of Brown Brother of the Holy Light and for women the Immaculate Sister of Mary. After Blighton's death the group was radically altered and the majority, somewhat incongruously, converted to Orthodoxy, resulting in the loss of members. In its new orthodox manifestation and under the auspices of the autocephalous Archdiocese of Queens, New York, it settled for the name, Christ the Saviour Brotherhood. Further splinter groups included the **Gnostic Order of Christ** and the Science of Man.

Holy Rollers A derisory American term to describe members of the **Pentecostal Church**. It is based on the belief that those speaking with tongues (see **Glossolalia**) end up in a trance-like state, rolling around the floor. William Branham (1909–65), the Pentecostal healer and prophet, reclaimed the idea, 'And what the world calls today holy-roller, that's the way I worship Jesus Christ.'

Holy Roman Empire *X*. Established in the West on Christmas Day, 800 CE, after the coronation of Charlemagne (c.742–814 CE) as Emperor in Rome, by Pope Leo III. He was the first Emperor of the Holy Roman Empire, a title the fell into abeyance in 924, but which was reinstated in 962 when Otto I of Germany was crowned Emperor by Pope John XII. The office continued through the Hapsburg dynasty until 1806, but Charles V was the last to be crowned Emperor.

Holy Spirit *J*. *X*. In the **Old Testament** God's creative power is his spirit or 'breath' and he speaks audibly to prophets. In the **New Testament** the spirit of God has new significance, being the power given to Jesus that enables him to fulfil his mission. After his death and resurrection, his followers are given the same Spirit at the feast of **Pentecost** (Acts 2:1–4) This the third member of the **Trinity** is Jesus' *alter ego*, his constant 'presence'. By means of this indwelling Spirit, Christians are empowered to be Jesus' representatives. In the Fourth Gospel the term 'Paraclete' is used for the Holy Spirit (see for example, John 14: 16 and 26). It is translated 'Advocate', implying one who will defend. Some translations have it as 'comforter', or 'helper', but 'advocate' is better. In 16th and 17th century England, the term Holy Ghost is used, from the Anglo-Saxon *gast* (similar to the German, *Geist*) meaning 'spirit'. At the time 'ghost' had none of the spooky connotations it has now and was used in traditional forms of liturgical worship, as in the 1662 *The Book of Common Prayer*. In modern use the term 'spirit' is preferred.

Holy Week *X*. The name given to the week in the Christian calendar, between **Palm Sunday** and Easter Saturday, its climax being the **Good Friday Passion** of Christ, leaving **Easter Sunday** for a celebration of his resurrection. See **Easter**

Hopi *Ami*. From *hopituh shi-nu-mu*, 'the peaceful people'. A part of the Pueblo Indian group of North America, who inhabit areas within **Navajo** reservations. After the migrations of their ancestors through four underground worlds, the Hopi settled on the Black Mesa of the Colorado plain. Their mythology is based on a dualism of space and time and a reciprocal relationship between the lower and upper worlds. It is the harmonic balance of these two worlds that ensures health, the supply of food and social stability. Important divinities include the sky god, Sotuqnangu and an earth-death god, Masua. There is also a sun god, twin war gods, a spider-woman, as well as gods associated with animal life and vegetation. Ceremonies include an initiation rite, a winter solstice rite and a bean dance. The origins of the clans and secret societies important to Hopi rituals are recorded in their mythologies.

Horoscope An interpretation of a person's character and fate calculated from the positions of planets and stars. See **Astrology**

Horus *E*. In established Egyptian mythology, a member of the **Ennead** of Heliopolis as the dutiful son of **Osiris** and **Isis**, and the avenger of his father's murder by **Seth**. His name means 'face' and in more primitive worship he had two eyes, the sun and the moon. In this early form he was known as Horus the Elder, the god of light. On nights when there was no moon he had no eyes and was venerated as the god of the blind. His most common representation is the falcon-headed man, an image perhaps of the power of his two-eyed vision, but he is also depicted as a falcon-headed lion or **sphinx**. See **Egyptian Religion**

Hospitallers *X*. The Knights Hospitallers began as a Benedictine nursing order in Jerusalem, following the first **crusade**, 1096–99. It developed into a Christian military order with its own charter, commissioned to protect pilgrims to the Holy Land. With the loss of influence there, it made Rhodes and later Malta its base, from which the alternative names, Knights of Rhodes and Knights of Malta derive. Ejection from Malta by Napoleon brought the medieval Maltese Order to an end. After their English priories were taken over by Henry VIII, they fell into decline, but were revived in 1888, as the Knights Hospitallers when they were awarded a Royal Charter by Queen Victoria. Since then they have taken on various guises and names, the most familiar of which is St John Ambulance. They are also known as Cavaliers of Malta and the Order of St John of Jerusalem, with the motto 'Defence of the Faith and Assistance to the Poor'. Their full, current title is Sovereign Military Hospitaller Order of St John of Jerusalem of Rhodes and of Malta.

House Church Movement *X*. The house church is thought to be the original biblical church, one of which is greeted by St Paul in a letter he wrote to the Corinthians: 'Many greetings in the Lord from Aquila and Prisca and the congregation at their house.' (1 Corinthians 16:19) The HCM believes that all of the churches in the New Testament era were small assemblies of this kind, meeting in homes. While setting up institutional forms of the Church may or may not be a way to honour God, the movement toward institutionalization and the human authority that tends to accompany hierarchical institutional structures are not theologically neutral. Groups of this kind believe themselves to be the ultimate, the ideal 'free' church, allowing complete independence in terms of forms of worship, democratic government and the priesthood of all believers. It is thought to be the most authentic expression of the form of Christian fellowship envisaged by Jesus.

Huguenots *X*. French members of **Calvin**'s Reformed Church, established in 1550. The origin of the name is obscure, but was probably a pejorative nickname. On 29th January 1536, an Edict was issued encouraging the extermination of Huguenots and on March 1st 1562, 1,200 were killed at Vassy, France. On 23/24th August of the same year, 8,000 were killed in Paris, in what became known as the St Bartholomew's Eve massacre. The event ignited the War of Religions which was brought to an end in 1598 by Henry IV's, Edict of Nantes. The Edict created 20 'free' cities in which the Huguenots were allowed to practise their 'reformed' faith and for a decade France was united and in peace. After Henry's murder the persecution of Huguenots was led by Cardinal Richelieu and the last free city, La Rochelle, fell in 1629. Louis XIV continued in the same vein ('one faith, one law, one King'), introducing the infamous *Dragonnades*, the billeting of dragoons in Huguenot households. Their churches, houses and bibles were burned, as were many of the Huguenots themselves. Those who did not die were made galley-slaves and forced to work in French ships or were sold to Turks to suffer the same fate. Emigration was made illegal. A quarter of a million managed to flee to Switzerland, Germany, Holland, England and Poland, with some going to America or South Africa; a similar number died in France. American Huguenots from Wallonia, in southern Belgium are known as the Walloons. Huguenots had to wait a century for the Edict of Toleration (1787) to see a partial restoration of their civil and religious rights.

Huitzilopochtli *Az*. The sun god and principal divinity in **Aztec** religion.

Hukam *S*. Arab. 'divine order', or will. It refers to the Sikh notion of the will of God to which the adherent must submit in order to follow the path. In a broader sense 'divine order' is a quality of creation of which the human being is a part. The term is used in contradistinction to the idea of *haumai*, self-will. Whether a person follows *hukam* or *haumai*, is in their control by choice. The need to submit to the will of God is fundamental Islamic doctrine. **Guru Nanak**, founder of Sikhism, absorbed *hukam* in his teachings.

Human Potential Movement Developed out of the social culture of the 1960s in the belief that the extraordinary potential residing in each person has never been fully realized. If this huge human resource is realized, not only will it enhance the life of the individual but society also will benefit in terms of positive social change. The movement had its origins in both **existentialism** and **humanism**, and in the self-actualization theories of Abraham Maslow (1908–70) founder of the school of humanistic psychology. Maslow's psychology is concerned to help individuals to understand themselves so as to develop their talents and capacities in balance with a realistic appraisal of their limitations. Sometimes associated with New Age ideology, the HPM would make a clear distinction between the latter's occult-spiritualist interests and its own concern with a person's secular capabilities. In broader terms, it is the originator of modern self-help and personal growth movements that have virtually become an industry. The movement has its critics; there are those who dismiss it as pseudoscience, the effects of which can be explained by placebo. The second criticism is that its psychology is too self-focused and too subjective, giving rise in some cases to narcissistic attitudes that concentrate on what inhibits potential, rather than on realizing it. See **Est**, **Life Spring**, **Transpersonal Psychology**

Humanism The term has a variety of meanings. Generally, it is used to refer to a theory or doctrine primarily concerned with man, having its origin in the European Renaissance when those interested in the classical cultures of Greece and Rome were know as 'Humanists'. The emphasis was placed on the potential of being human without calling on metaphysical resources or speculations. It was a recalling of the aphorism inscribed in golden letters on the gateway of the Temple of Apollo at Delphi, 'Know Thyself'. Alexander Pope took up the theme in his couplet which became a Humanist manifesto: 'Know then thyself, presume not God to scan, the proper study of mankind is man.' Even so, humanism is not incompatible with religion, **Theism**, **Deism** or **Supernaturalism**, but it does deny the importance of these over humanistic methods of understanding and ordering life. Religious humanism allows a philosophy of self-fulfilment within the framework of the principles of each religion. It makes religion a personal affair and a personal responsibility. The term 'humanist' identifies those who entirely reject religious belief and actively seek to exclude religious influence from all aspects of life, especially education and welfare. Humanism has become the atheistic face of secularism and the energy behind formative and influential philosophers such as **Sartre**, **Russell**, **Wittgenstein**, **Ayer** and **Popper**. See **Evolutionary Humanism**, **Pragmatism**, **Religious Humanism**, **Secularism**, **Selcular Alternatives to Religion**, **Secular Humanism**
FINAL WORLD: 'Man is the measure of all things.' (Protagoras, *Fragments* I)

Humanism and Buddhism See **Buddhist Humanism**

Humanism and Christianity See **Christian Humanism**

Humanism and Judaism See **Jewish Humanism**

Humanism and Religion See **Religious Humanism**

Hume, David (1711–76) Born in Edinburgh, Hume was a philosopher and historian concerned with an **empiricist** criticism of metaphysics. He argued that meaningful experience and language is based on either sense impressions or mathematical concepts. He advocated a 'book burning' crusade; 'if we take in our hand any volume ... let us ask, does it contain any abstract reasoning concerning quantity or number? No. Does it contain any experimental reason concerning matter of fact and existence? No. Commit it then to the flames: for it can contain nothing but sophistry and illusion.' Hume's philosophy is a trenchant scepticism with an important element of **naturalism**. During his period, criticism of religion was a dangerous undertaking and for this reason Hume and other empiricists, developed their arguments somewhat obliquely; he did not acknowledge authorship of *A Treatise of Human Nature* until the last year of his life and other important works such as his *Dialogues Concerning Natural Religion* were published posthumously. Hume's scepticism goes beyond the empiricist-rationalist debate, to focus on the dispute between Christian defenders of their faith and their atheist opponents. Hume's philosophical goal was to examine the groundlessness of religious doctrine and institutions and to unmask the repressive influence they had on human life and thought. The balanced and humane way in which Hume achieved this influenced **Kant**, **Bentham** (see **Utilitarianism**), **Darwin**, **Russell** and numerous other secularist philosophers.

FINAL WORD: 'The Christian religion not only was first attended by miracles, but even at this day cannot be believed by any reasonable person without one.' (Hume)

Hunab-Ku *Az. CA.* The ancestor god of the **Mayan** and **Aztec** pantheons. The gods lived on Cemanahuac, the Aztec name for the Earth where Hunab-Ku was eventually replaced by his son, Itzamna, whose own son, Hunhu-Ahpu, ruled over the realms of the underground where its god, Mitnal lived. It seems the Aztec gods, led by Tezcatlipoca, frequently made war on the Mayan gods, some of whom were members of both the Aztec and Mayan pantheons.

Hurrian Religion An ancient near-eastern people who lived in northern **Mesopotamia**, from c.2500 BCE. The largest and most influential Hurrian group was the Kingdom of Mitanni, dominated by a ruling caste of Indo-Aryans. They had an important influence on the Hittite Empire through both their language and religion. By a process of syncretism the old Hittite and Hurrian religions were gradually merged and in various forms this defined the religious culture of the entire ancient near East, with the exception of Egypt and southern Mesopotamia. Their considerable pantheon included: Teshub, the supremely powerful weather god; Shaushka, the counterpart of the Assyrian **Ishtar**; Shimegi, the sun god; Kushu, the moon god; and each had their own consorts and progeny. They did not have their 'home' temples, but there were important cult centres like that of Shimegi at Harran and Shaushka at Nineveh. See **Hittite Religion**, **Mesopotamian Religion**, **Mitra**

Hutchinsonism *X*. Followers of the Yorkshire-born John Hutchinson (1674–1737), an English theologian who served as steward to several influential families. He was the author of numerous books on subjects as diverse as Newtonian physics, the history of the earth, mineralogy and the 'religion' of Satan. He held that the Hebrew Scriptures contained the elements of all rational philosophy, natural history and true religion. Hebrew, he contested, should be read without points (vowels) and his interpretation of the scriptures was based on a somewhat fanciful symbolism. His followers included Bishop George Home of Norwich.

Hutterian Brethren An amorphous and widespread group of dissenters, stemming from the **Anabaptists** of the early 16th century. The Hutterites emerged as a distinct religious group in the late 1520s in the Austrian province of Tyrol, later migrating to Transylvania, Ukraine and Slovakia. To escape Russian military service many Hutterites emigrated to the USA during the 19th century where, during the First World War, their pacifism led to their persecution. Of the 18 settlements, 17 left the USA for Canada. There is a Japanese Hutterite community of ethnic Japanese who have assumed the same way of life. They practise a total community of goods and all property is owned by the Church; members and their families are provided for out of common resources. The communities are called 'colonies', which consist of 10 to 20 families, dependent on an agricultural economy. Once a colony is thought to be spiritually and economically viable, approximately half, chosen by lot, are sectioned off to start a new colony. They are similar in belief and culture to the **Amish** and **Mennonites**. See **Brudherhof Community**

Hymn A song of praise or thanksgiving to a god or deity. The process of singing a hymn is called 'hymnody', the term also being used for a collection of hymns, for example, the 19th-century 'Methodist hymnody' for which the hymnologist Charles Wesley was responsible. In Christian tradition hymns are directed to God, but in **Roman Catholicism** they may be sung in praise of **Mary**. Usually, but not always, hymns are accompanied by an organ and sung congregationally, sometimes led by a choir. Hymns have an ancient origin; the *Great Hymn to Aten* was composed by the Pharaoh **Akhenaton**; **Hinduism** has collections of hymns called **Vedas**. The Western tradition begins with the Homeric hymns the earliest of which were written during the 7th century BCE in praise of the gods of Greek mythology. African-Americans have developed a tradition of hymns known as 'spirituals', that has become an influential musical genre. In the modern period, the established collections of hymns have given way to new writing and many churches employ both the instruments and styles of rock music. Today the term 'hymn' is used in a secular context for a song in praise, for example, of political leaders such as Stalin and Chairman Mao. Others have become the hymns or anthems of political movements such as the Red Flag of Jim Connell sung to the tune of the German carol, *O, Tannenbaum* and of the British Labour Party at a time when socialism was still an apparent doctrine.

I

Iblis *I*. A devil mentioned in the Koran. (See **Satan, Shaytan**)

Ibo or **Igbo** *A*. One of the largest ethnicities in Africa, mostly based in southeast Nigeria where they constitute 18 per cent of the population. The group extends to Cameroon and Equatorial Guinea. Some Ibo clans trace their ancestry to the Kingdom of **Benin**. In their tribal mythology the Ibo supreme god is Chukwu, 'great spirit', a solar deity who created the world and who is associated with rain, trees and other plants. Ala, the goddess of fertility and death, relates to him as both wife and daughter. The concept of Ofo and Ogu represents the law of retributive justice which vindicates anyone who is innocent of the crimes with which they are charged. Only the innocent can invoke the principle of 'Ogu-na-Ofo', otherwise a person doing so will be subject to the wrath of Amadioha, the god of thunder and lightning. The pantheon includes a sky and forest god, a god of fortune and industry, a god of divination and healing and a god of medicine and yams. The Ibo believe everyone has their own personal god, *Chi*, who is a personification of individual fate and responsible for a person's good luck or misfortune. A failed *coup d'etat* by Nigerian army officers in 1966 led to the secession from Nigeria of the Ibo eastern regions and in May 1967 they constituted their own State of Biafra, causing civil war. After a vicious starvation campaign by the Nigerian army in January 1970, the Ibo state collapsed and the people reverted to Nigeria. Chinua Achebe's distinguished novel *Things Fall Apart*, is an account of the clash between British influences and the traditional life of the Ibo.

Icelandic Mythology See **Germanic Religion, Norse Mythology**

I Ching *T. Con.* Chin. *I*, 'change', with *Ching*, 'seed' in the sense of semen or 'seed essence', or 'source of life'. The book so named is probably the oldest in existence it's tradition dates being c.2852–2738 BCE. Familiarly called the *Book of Changes*, it was used 3000 years ago, but its origins are far more ancient. The text is complicated, esoteric and fraught with problems for the translator and interpreter. The most successful translations include those of Richard Wilhelm, John Blofeld, and Ritsema and Sabbadini.

The *I Ching* is an oracle, a method of divination based on Confucian philosophy (see **Confucianism**) but with clear **Taoist** associations. At its core are the polar energies of **Yin-Yang**, whose active interrelationship brought everything into existence. This creative symbiosis brings about change, *I*, in the form of directed movement which the *I Ching* understands as the *Tao*. It is this idea of change through directed movement that lies at the heart of the book and it can be argued that the *I Ching* is based on a philosophy of change. It is a notion particularly difficult for the Western mind to grasp, since the history of science in the West has conditioned us to think in terms of natural law, which in turn gives rise to an ordered, mechanistic world view and the assumption that we understand how things work. Any deviation from this order is thought to be 'unnatural' or exceptional, rationalized as, 'the exception that proves the rule'. The minds behind the *I Ching*, however, perceived the world differently. It is precisely the deviations from natural law that interested its creators who considered the possibility that there was significance and meaning to be found in chance, in arbitrary and inexplicable events and in what in the West is dismissed as coincidence. The *I Ching* confronts us with a movement away from the cause and effect view of the world, to that of synchronicity.

It is not possible here to offer a full explanation of how the *I Ching* works and the way to consult it. The translations mentioned above provide the most comprehensive accounts available in English. Briefly, there are three ways to consult the *I Ching*. The first is by casting a bundle of 50 sticks (originally yarrow stalks), secondly by the tossing of three coins, thirdly by the use of six specially prepared and marked wands. Originally, when oracles were first consulted in China, the answer given was in the simple form of 'yes' or 'no'. This was shown by either an unbroken line — or a broken line — — —, but the complexity of life and the questions posed to the oracle required a more comprehensive system and eventually a series of trigrams and hexagrams were designed, consisting of unbroken and broken lines. There are 8 trigrams and 64 hexagrams, each of which can offer a range of answers and are the subject of extensive commentaries (see *Figure 1*).

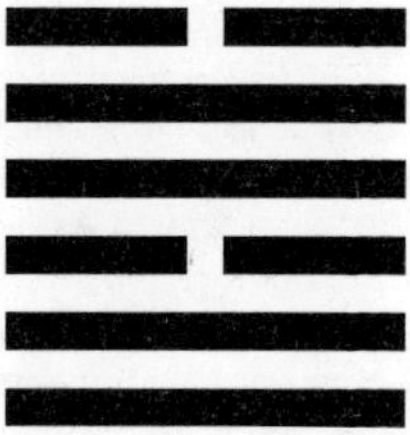

Figure 1 The Hexagram of Joy

The person casting the yarrow stalks or the three coins will hold in mind the questions he wants to pose to the oracle. According to the result of the cast, he will be directed to a hexagram or sometimes to two and even to a specific line in the hexagram. Once the hexagrams have been established, three series of texts are consulted so as to interpret them, *The Judgement*, *The Commentary* (also called the *Ten Wings*) and *The Image*.

FINAL WORD: 'The *I Ching* insists upon self-knowledge throughout. The method by which this is to be achieved is open to every kind of misuse and is therefore not for the frivolous-minded and immature; nor is it for intellectualists and rationalists. It is appropriate only for thoughtful and reflective people who like to think about what they do and what happens to them.' (C. G. Jung [1989])

Ichthus X. Gk. *ixthus*, 'fish'

A sign used by the early church based on the acrostic of Greek words for, 'Jesus', 'Christ', 'Son', 'God', 'Saviour'. The initial letters of the Greek words form the word *ixthus*. The extreme persecution to which the early Christians were subjected necessitated secrecy and the sign was used in

Figure 2 Fish Profile

various ways to mark a place of meeting. It can still be seen, for example, in the rear windows of cars (see *Figure 2*).

Icon Gk. *eikon*, 'image', 'picture' or 'likeness'. In Christianity, a representation or picture of a sacred or sanctified person. Their most traditional use is by the Eastern Orthodox Church. (See **Orthodox Church**) In more general use, an enduring symbol or someone who is the centre of public attention and admiration, similar to that of an idol.

Iconography Judaism and Islam, for fear of idolatry, prohibited images of God, otherwise all religions have represented their gods in many forms of painting and sculpture. Christianity is rich in visual representation and as the iconographic tradition developed images of Christ, the Virgin Mary and the saints became the objects of devotion and reverence, particularly in the **Orthodox Church** and **Roman Catholic** traditions. Some icons have become associated with miraculous happenings or were accredited with the power to perform miracles. For example, the Byzantine icon of 'Our Lady of Victory' in St Mark's, Venice, was believed to have the power to bring about military triumph. In a largely illiterate culture icons were considered to be the 'Bible of the poor'. Icons are also a feature of pagan religion; examples include the well-endowed, 'Venuses', such as the Venus of Willendorf, a statue-icon that focused on maternal features and the notion of fecundity, as the power to create new life. In early Buddhist art the presence of the Buddha was signified by his footprint, an empty throne, the wheel of *samsara*, or a riderless horse. The sun disk featured as an image of the Babylonian sun god, Shamash and is also a familiar Egyptian icon. Secular society makes icons of famous people from all walks of life who are venerated as ideals of success. See **Idolatry**

FINAL WORD: 'Don't call me an icon, I'm just a mother trying to help.' (Diana, Princess of Wales)

Idealism Idealist philosophy addresses those systems of thought that affirm mind and spirit as the most significant elements in our attempts to understand the nature of reality. The fullest expression of this philosophy came from an Irish Anglican Bishop, George Berkeley (1685–1753). He insisted that all we can know about objects is not ascertained from its substance (matter) but from the ideas we have about them. These ideas appear to us as the objects themselves which have no existence outside the sensations and perceptions we have of them. It becomes an argument for the existence of God, since we exist only because God perceives us as existing. For Berkeley there are only minds and ideas, 'the proper objects of vision constitute a universal language of the Author of nature …' (George Berkeley)

FINAL WORD: There was a young woman who said, God
Must think it exceedingly odd
If he finds that this tree
Continues to be
When there's no one about in the Quad.'
Reply:
Dear Sir:
Your astonishment's odd:
I am always about in the Quad.
And that's why this tree
Will continue to be,
Since observed by
Yours faithfully,
GOD.
(Ronald Knox)

Ideology Originally from the French philosopher de Tracey, the term denoted the 'science of ideas', an objective analysis of the sources of human bias and prejudice in the tradition of English **empiricism**. It is Marx's use of the term that nudged it towards its current meaning, with the publication in 1932 (written with **Engels**) of *German Ideology*. The term is used to denote a system of ideas and beliefs, a *weltanschauungen*, a philosophy of life, be it religious, secular or political. Sometimes, when the term is applied to a system, it is thought to be a distortion of reality, 'ideology' being an expression of an unattainable ideal. Thus, Marx qualified his use of the term, preferring 'true consciousness'.

FINAL WORD: 'When we conceive things thus, as they really are and happen, every profound philosophical problem is solved.' (Marx [1932])

Idolatry The worship of an image, idea or object, in place of or as representing a divine being. It is vehemently forbidden by the Abrahamic religions and the term is used pejoratively to describe the worship practices of other religions. The Bible is unclear as to whether the worship of idols implied a belief in the image actually being a god or spirit or if it was simply a representation of these. This applies also to the Israelites' worship of the Golden Calf (Exodus 32). While Judaism and Islam are absolutely clear about idolatry, the matter is somewhat ambiguous in Christianity, since the adoration of icons and statues seems to come very close to idolatry. (See **Iconography**) The tradition of Hinduism's early polytheism has left the religion with an extensive imagery of its many gods, but it can generally be assumed that these are representations of the gods and spirits. Buddhists do not venerate objects, but the meaning and symbolism of some objects are held to be useful aids in practices of meditation and visualization. Pagan polytheism does not necessarily imply idolatry since the images used, whether they are cave drawings, figures or masks, are understood to be representations of the gods and spirits and they do not hold any supernatural powers of themselves. Secularism has its own forms of idolatry, as the acceptance of an idea, object, occupation or institution taken to have ultimate meaning for life. Huge sacrifices are made in order to gain social status, possessions, reputation, even education. Acquisitiveness, **Materialism**, the drive for success and power combine to form an idolatrous culture, as does the need for the public to create and venerate their **idols** as role models and images of the ideal, probably unattainable life. See **Henotheism**, **Iconography**

FINAL WORD: 'Science can purify religion for idolatry and superstition. Religion can purify science from idolatry and false absolutes.' (Pope John Paul II)

Idols of the Mind The false assumptions and illusions described in Francis **Bacon**'s *Novum Organum* Book 1. (1620) They are the four errors or impediments inhibiting the mind's search for truth: i) tribal idols, 'inherent in human nature … for man's sense is falsely asserted to be the standard of things.'; ii) the idols of the 'cave', being individual and personal; iii) the idols of the market-place, derived from our rubbing shoulders with others, the received tradition based on 'bad and unapt formation of words'; and iv) the idols of the theatre, acquired from false philosophies. In Bacon's philosophy these four 'idols' inhibit the mind's ability to perceive the truth. See **Empiricism**, **Utilitarianism**

Idrisids *I*. The first Arab dynasty, established in the Maghreb and ruling from 788–985, etc. See **Abbasid Caliphate**

Ifa Oracle *A*. A **Yoruba** system of divination. See **Oracles**

Igbo *A*. See **Ibo**

Iglesia Ni Cristo *X*. Filipino for Church of Christ, a religious organization founded in the Philippines by Felix Manalo in 1914. It claims to be the reestablishment of the church founded by Jesus and rejects both his divinity and the **Trinity**. The Church is thought to be the second largest (after Catholicism) Christian denomination in the Philippines. Its missionary activities extend to a television programme, *The Message*, transmitted to the San Francisco Bay Area in the USA and an official magazine, *God's Message*, that has worldwide distribution. Membership requires a six month period of teaching and training, followed by baptism at a minimum age of 12. Manalo teaches that the Church is elected to be 'the nation of God', as were the Israelites. The movement is strongly political. See **Philippine Religion**

Ignosticism The secularist view that the question of the existence of God is without point, since it is a proposition without verifiable arguments, a view consistent with scientific method. The term was coined by Rabbi Sherwin Wine, the founder for the Society of Humanistic Judaism. (See

Jewish Humanism) Ignosticism is consistent with rationalist philosophies such as **Logical Positivism** that argue the word 'God' is meaningless because theism is incoherent. Thus, to engage an ignostic in argument the word 'God' must be given a coherent definition, but an important corrective is that 'God' may still have emotional, ethical and aesthetic significance. The problem arises when the notion of 'a being' is applied to the word.

FINAL WORD: It is 'very important not to mistake hemlock for parsley, but to believe or not to believe in God is not important at all.' (Denis Diderot)

Ijma *I*. Arab. 'consensus', or 'agreement'. One of the four recognized authorities or proofs of **Sunni** law and its application based on *taqlid* or precedent. There are two kinds of consensus, *Ijma Shari'a* which are explicitly expressed and *Ijma al Sukuti, ijma* by silence (where silence is taken to be consent) but in the view of most scholars the latter is not a working proof and for an *ijma* to be authoritative it must be established textually. In modern practice, what has been established as valid law by consensus, refers exclusively to precedents and is of little use in the application and formulation of new law. An alternative is *Maslaha*, which permits or prohibits something according to whether it may benefit or harm public interest. The principle behind this is an important **hadith** in which Muhammad said, 'My community will never agree on error.' An individual's opinion may be wrong, because it is personal and subjective, but because Muslims are ideally Koran conscious, corporate decision based on consensus has a built-in guarantee of being right since the Islamic common mind will not be in error. Only in the event of consensus not being reached, can legal experts invoke the practice of *ijtihad*, independent reasoning based on analogy or syllogism. Such decisions may only be reached by those with absolute knowledge and experience of law and theology and must not contradict the Koran. Sunnis do not allow *ijtihad*, since they argue that by this means more than one interpretation can be reached and thus, no decision can be definitive. The name given to those who practice *ijtihad*, is, Mujtahids. See **Fiqh, Ijtihad, Shari'a, Urf**

Ijtihad *I*. 'Authority'. In Islamic law it has two meanings: i) Universal authority – the ability to offer an opinion based on the established principles of **Shari'a**; ii) Partial authority – the ability to offer an opinion on only some of the principles of Shari'a. The practice of both is offered by scholars who have been proved through examination and experience. See **Fiqh, Ijma, Ulema, Urf**

Illuminati, Order of Founded 1776, it took its name from Latin meaning, 'the enlightened ones'. The order was originally founded in Bavaria by a group of **freethinkers**. Their members, including **Freemasons**, were arranged in a hierarchy of three orders, Nursery, Masons and Mysteries; each of these orders was sub-divided into other, ascending orders through which it was possible to advance by following certain rites. Within ten years of its foundation there were branches throughout Europe and the order numbered between 3,000 and 4,000 members attracting men like Goethe, Herder and the reigning dukes of Gotha and Weimar. In 1784 an edict of the Bavarian government banned all secret societies and the Illuminati declined. Its aims were to combat ignorance, superstition, religious restraint and tyranny. It was thought by some to be a prototype secret society, paving the way for the French Revolution on its way to a political domination of Europe. But there is little truth in the conspiracy theories put about by the Order's detractors. In the USA Thomas Jefferson believed the Illuminati were concerned to spread information and the principles of true morality, understanding their secrecy to be a necessary response to despotic opposition and 'the tyranny of priests'. It is suggested that the founding fathers of the USA, some of whom were Freemasons, might also have included members of the Illuminati and that the eyed pyramid symbol in the Great Seal of the USA, may have derived from them. In 1995 de Rojas founded an Illuminati Order in Barcelona, which elaborated the rites of its Bavarian antecedent and incorporated the higher degrees of the Scottish rite of 33 degrees. Despite the decline of the original Order it has remained a mysterious presence and currently, 'Illuminati' is a name taken by several groups, actual and fictional and the subject of conspiracy theories that have spawned best-selling novels.

Illuminism A form of Illuminist philosophy is associated with the Apocryphal gospels, particularly that of Thomas and with the gnostic tradition generally. In broadly Christian terms, Illuminism had to do with a perception and acquisition of wisdom, understanding and knowledge, as the basis for a way of life and an unimpeachable morality. In the gospel 'The Kingdom of Light' is a metaphor for the quintessence of everything, 'The Living Father' a metaphor for the underlying power or energy of the universe. The Illuminists suffered with Jews and Muslims during the Spanish Inquisition which began in 1478.

More significantly, for modern thought, Illuminism is a philosophy based on the use of reason and logic rather than on opinion and belief. It had its inception with the English Enlightenment in the 1680s, gathering momentum towards and influencing the French Revolution. It was heralded in England by **Locke**'s deductive reasoning and in France by **Descartes**' 'good sense'. From an empiricist (see **Empiricism**) and atheistic base, it attacked religion and metaphysics, its fullest expression in England being the rationalist philosophy of Thomas **Hobbes**. In France, Illuminism had a slightly different emphasis; La Mettrie and Paul Holbach (German born but French educated) were atheists, while Diderot, **Voltaire** and **Rousseau** advocated **Deism**, a form of '**natural religion**', a perception succinctly summed up by Voltaire, 'If God did not exist, it would be necessary to invent Him. But all nature proclaims that He exists.' The philosophy of Illuminism is inevitably associated with the **Illuminati**, but few philosophers would count themselves as a member of that illustrious group.

Imam *I*. Arab. 'leader' in the broad sense of 'one who stands in front'. The term was used for the leader of congregational prayers in the **mosque**, then for the spiritual head of a community and finally for a Muslim leader. In this context the term is interchangeable with 'Caliph', the political head of **Sunni** Muslims who also use the title for their most prominent jurists. Underlying the status of the Imam in Sunni Islam is the belief that in every age there was an infallible Imam to whom God had entrusted the leadership of Muslims. The concept of Imamate gradually crystallized into a clear theological formula in which the Imam is a recipient of the Divine Light given to certain Prophets since the time of Adam. Some Shiites regarded **Ali**, Muhammad's son-in-law and successive Imams, as incarnations of God. Faithful Muslims were called to believe in all Imams, but especially in the Imam of their own period. So important was this to the Sunni that they exalted the belief into an additional **Pillar of Islam**. In fact, the Imam was a spiritual displacement of the temporal powers, authorities and functions of the Caliph. He is the divinely inspired ruler in the line of the Prophet himself and possesses superhuman powers derived from Adam, the first man, but transmitted by Muhammad. Sunni lore has it that the Imam's body casts no shadow and that he is physically invulnerable. Following the Iranian revolution of 1979, Khomeini was accorded the title Imam. See **Hidden Imam**, **Islam**, **Twelvers**

Imamis *I*. Known also as the *Ithna Asharis* and the **Twelvers**. They recognize a succession of 12 imams since **Ali Ibn Abi Talib**, believed by the Shiites to have been appointed by Muhammad. They are the largest group within Shiite Islam. See **Islam**, **Isma'lis**, **Shi'ism**

Iman *I*. Arab. 'faith' or 'belief'. Islamic faith is founded on the belief in the unity of God, his revelation in the Koran transmitted to Muhammad his prophet, in angels, an afterlife and in judgement and punishment. The Koran spells out the close connection between faith and practice, thus real faith is evident in right actions. The nub of it all is submission and obedience to the will of God, which is precisely what the term 'Islam' means. (See **Islam**) Muslim faith seems to be austere, a committed belief expressed by a code of conduct, but within this basic formula there is much passion, true devotion and a longing for the heart's union with God. These latter characteristics are perhaps more in evidence in Islamic mysticism. 'In Islam there is no faith without action; to live up to Iman, calls for a certain quality or presence, in the mind and the heart. This is called taqwa which implies a God-fearing, God-heeding, God-loving, God-knowing frame of being.' The 'Five Pillars of Faith serve to promote this quality' (Mona Abul-Fadl). See **Shiite**, **Sufi**, **Sunni**

Imhotep *E*. Doctor, architect, High Priest, Scribe and Vizier to King Djoser who reigned c.2630–c.2611. As architect, he was responsible for building the first great stone building, the Step Pyramid at Saqqara. In the Late Period, c.600 BCE, he was deified and worshipped at his temple in Memphis as the god of medicine. Tradition has it that he extracted medicines from plants to treat diseases such as appendicitis, gout and arthritis. After the Greek conquest he was identified with **Asclepios** and his shrine at Saqqara became known as the Asclepieion where both Egyptians and Greeks sought miraculous cures. His tomb has never been found, but he is believed to have worked under four kings. The Greeks continued to build temples to him and his reputation lasted until the Arab invasion of North Africa in the 7th century CE. See **Healing**

Imitative Magic A form of magic based on the principle that 'like produces like'. See **Magic, Sympathetic Magic**

Immaculate Conception *X*. In Roman Catholic theology the doctrine asserting the sinlessness of the **Virgin Mary**. This is thought, by some, to refer to the conception of Jesus, in that he was God's son and not that of her husband Joseph. Thus she conceived 'immaculately'. It is more proper, however, to term her pregnancy the 'miraculous conception', leaving 'immaculate' for her own conception. Since other doctrines state that we are born with sin (see **Original Sin**) presumably because of the carnal processes by which humans are conceived, the conception of Mary was of a different order. Further to which, from the moment of her birth she was preserved from the slightest taint of sin in order to be the immaculate vehicle for her son's birth. The Immaculate Conception was made an article of faith by Papal Bull in 1854. The feast of the Immaculate Conception is celebrated on December 8th, being the date of the Bull and, if tradition is to be accepted, clearly not the date of the conception of Jesus.

Immanent Meaning 'indwelling'. The term is used by pantheists (see **Pantheism**) to refer to God's 'indwelling' omnipresence. Strict usage however, would term this belief Panenthiesm, the notion that God is *within* everything, a somewhat different concept to the belief that God actually *is* everything (the whole of reality being divine) as denoted by Pantheism. See **Transcendent**

Immortality It was Plato's proposition that if we survive in some form in the future, may we not also have had an existence in the past? Both possibilities have beguiled the human spirit and imagination and have provided a central theme for most major world religions. In biblical religion the question of previous existence is not developed, all the emphasis being on the future life and how, by means of the conditions represented by dogma, we can ensure our future survival. The terms on which survival is made available from the core doctrines of these traditions. For Judaism it resides in the ethical implications of obedience to the Law, while Christianity focuses either on the efficacy of Church sacraments or on justification by faith alone. Islam's emphasis is on submission to the will of Allah. In Eastern traditions the concept of **nirvana** replaces that of immortality, nirvana being the sublime state in which the individual has finally become free of the cycle of **samsara**, birth, death and rebirth.

In proper usage 'immortality' is a concept best kept for the gods of Greek and Roman religion, since the strength of its meaning lies in the notion that the subject is at no risk of death. What Western religions think of as immortality, is life beyond mortality – a contradiction in terms. Plato's question about the possibility of previous existence has been made currently familiar by documented accounts of past life memories. See **Reincarnation**

FINAL WORD: 'Our birth is but a sleep and a forgetting,
The soul that arises within us, our life's Star,
Hath elsewhere its setting,
And cometh from afar.' (Ode, 'Intimations of Immortality', William Wordsworth)

Incantation Verbal formulas or phrases believed to have magical and supplicatory properties. In pagan religion and witchcraft, language or the 'word', is believed to be one of the most powerful mediums of magic. Incantations can cure diseases, inflict harm and summon spirits. Incantations are not confined to **grimoires**, but were used in Egyptian, Greek and Roman religious rites and are also found in the prayers of Western religions, in Hindu and Buddhist mantras and in the spinning prayer wheels of Tibet. However, there is a difference between an incantation and a prayer; the former has the character of command, the latter of request. But the mind does not always order things so neatly and in practice there are overlaps and many of the grimoires have sincere prayers beseeching God to come to the magician's aid. Nor are prayers free of magical associations; some in the form of formulas, imply that their efficacy is dependent on the exact words being spoken in their precise order. See **Magic**, **Mantra**

Incarnation L. *in carne*, 'in flesh'. A doctrine of several major religious traditions asserting the divinity's manifestation in actual human form. Egyptians believed the Pharaoh was the incarnation of the sun; Hinduism has many *avatars*, with its most notable example in the cult of Vishnu who is reincarnated in every age, 'for the rescue of the pious and for the destruction of the evil-doers'. In Buddhism the concept of incarnation is associated with the **Bodhisattva** ideal, while in Christianity the doctrine is of the incarnate son of God, the second person of the **Trinity**, is the foundation of the religion.

Incas It took four centuries for the Incas to expand from being rulers of parts of a small town, to a tribe led by the semi-divine Sapa Inca, that ruled a huge empire, *Tawantin Suyu* or Four United Regions. It was located in what is now Peru and lasted from c.1438 until the arrival of the Spanish in c.1533, when the last Inca Emperor, Atahualpa was killed on the order of Fransico Pizarro. The expansion of the empire absorbed the greater part of western South America, with its centre in the Andes, its most celebrated archaeological site being the remains of the city of Machu Pichu. Their religion was pantheistic, the polytheism including a sun god, earth god and corn god. The sun god, Inti, was supreme and so long as his sovereignty was not compromised the worship of ancestor spirits was permissible. Contact between the upper and lower classes was ritualized in ceremonies that could last from sunrise to sunset. They built numerous temples, such as the Sun Temple at Cusco which housed a huge image of the sun. Huacas, sacred sites widespread around the empire, were the locations of deities believed to reside in natural objects such as rivers, mountains, boulders and streams. Priests lived in the sacred temples and at the most important Huacas and practised a form of divination and sacrifice that included, at times of disaster or on important occasions, human beings.

Incubus See **Succubus**

Indians See **Amerindian Religion, North American Indians**

Indian Shaker Church An interesting syncretism drawing together **Amerindian**, **Catholic** and **Protestant** beliefs. It was founded in 1881 by John Slocum, a **shaman** and **prophet** and a member of the Squaxin Island Tribe, in Washington. They have no connection with either the **Shakers** of New England or with the **Native American Church**. Presumed to have died, Slocum 'recovered' during the wake held for him and reported his visit to heaven and his mandate to start a new religion. When he fell ill, his wife Mary shook uncontrollably while praying and the shaking, believed to have healing powers, became a feature of congregational worship together with the ringing of hand bells. The religion met with considerable opposition and legal attempts to suppress it. In the 1960s a split occurred between those who rejected scriptures, such as the Bible and those who wanted to use them. Indian shakers continue to practise throughout the northwest coast states of the USA.
FINAL WORD: 'The following regulations have been observed, 1st, keep windows or a door open at all meetings, 2nd, use only one bell to give signals, not continuous ringing, 3rd, do not admit school children at night meetings. It has been reported ... that there are some women who are violating the Rules ... they shake at all hours of the day and night. ... If they do not stop you will lock them up until they agree to stop.' (From a notice posted by the USA Indian Service, at Quileute Reservation)

Indo-European Religion The term 'Indo-European' (India + Europe) is properly used by scholars to refer to a vast and complex group of languages. The original parent group can be traced through similarities in languages such as Greek, Latin and Sanskrit. By extension, it became a collective name for the cultures and religions associated with these languages, the origins of which are to be found among the **Aryans**, whose migration from what was probably central Asia began c.3500 BCE. These migratory groups are sometimes referred to as Indo-Aryans or Proto-Indo-Europeans. Some of these groups settled in Iran. (See **Indo-Iranian**

Religion) The nomads brought with them an extensive oral tradition eventually preserved in the oldest of the Hindu **Vedas**, the **Rig-Veda**, and in the **Avesta**, the scriptures of **Zoroastrianism**. The range of Aryan settlement is extensive and stretches from Greece and Italy to Scandinavia. The sub-cultures of these groups share common religious notions and practices, such as the veneration of fire, a basic nature-worship that perceived natural phenomena like the sun, the sky and water in the form of rivers, to be gods. Vestiges of these early religions can be found, for example, in **Norse, Icelandic** and German mythology, and in the religion of the **Druids, Celts** and **Anglo-Saxons**.

Indo-Iranian Religion The term 'Indo-Iranian' (India + Iran) refers properly to a complex group of languages now spoken by the millions of people living across territories that include Iran, Afghanistan, Pakistan and parts of central Asia. The oldest forms of the Iranian languages are Old Persian and Avestan, the latter being the language of the **Avesta**, the religious texts of **Zoroastrianism**. The term may also be used in reference to the culture of the **Aryans**, whose migration c.3500 BCE–1000 BCE (dubiously referred to as 'invasion') from central Asia and the southern-Russian steppes occurred in several phases. It is among these nomadic Aryans that Indo-Iranian ancestry is to be found, together with a proto-Zoroastrian religion in the form of nature worship. This was not merely an anthropomorphism of natural forces but involved complex rituals, a rigorous morality and sophisticated abstract concepts. A hierarchy of beneficient gods were opposed to powers that threatened every aspect of human life, their appeasement effected by animal sacrifice. Gods are described in human terms, they live in houses, ride horses, travel in chariots, wear clothes and their affairs and relationships, both between themselves and with humans, are described by images of war and conflict. In effect, these gods and demons are metaphorical expressions of all the forces and energies humans experience, controlling everything from crops to animal husbandry, from safe childbirth and health, to longevity. The characteristics of the indigenous religion can be reconstructed from the **Vedas** and the Avesta, and may be summarized as: i) serving a nomadic lifestyle; ii) the conflict between good and evil powers; iii) an ordered universe threatened by chaos; iv) the goal of reaffirming order on earth by strengthening the gods; v) the anthropomorphism of abstract concepts, such as Anger, Contract or Covenant and Victory; vi) the world originated by means of divine ritual sacrifice and sustained by priestly offerings; vii) the hope of material blessing by conscientious religious practice; and viii) a paradise that can only be reached by special knowledge. The cosmology shows a world derived from a succession of creations, sky, water, earth, plants, animals, man and fire. The sky was a sphere of rock crystal in which floated the earth, round and flat like a plate. Around the earth are the *Hara*, a rim of mountains from which a river flows before cascading over the edge into the cosmic ocean, *Vourukasa*. A tree of all seeds grows in this ocean and their fruits are transported to earth by the rains. The sun and moon cycle around the highest peak of *Hara*, from which the bridge of judgement reaches to the world's edge. It is across this bridge that people move after death, to meet whatever fate awaits them. (See **Chinvat Bridge**) Religious practices honoured the gods, the main rite being *yasna*, the consecration of the *haoma* plant, the *soma* of the Vedas. Rituals were centred around the sacred fire, the earthly aspect of the cosmic fire which sustains all of life. Sacrifices were made and bits of the sacrificial victim (a cow or bull) were fed to the fire as an offering. The rituals were an acted parable of what Zaehner [1962] calls the 'interpenetration of the human and the divine'. All Indo-Iranian beliefs and practices were held together by *rta*, harmony or balance, an order visible in the movements of the sun and moon and the cycle of seasons on earth. The purpose of the religion was to reflect this order socially, maintaining *rta* and overcoming *anrta*, chaos.

Indra *H*. For Hinduism the god of weather and war, the Lord of Heaven, the atmosphere personified. He is the supreme deity of the **Vedas** but, having parents, he is not an uncreated original divinity. The texts describe him as being golden in colour with very long arms, but the mythology shows him to have innumerable forms and names, indeed he can take any form he wishes. The **Rig-Veda** says, 'He under whose supreme control are horses, all chariots and the villages and cattle; he who gave being to the Sun and the Morning, who leads the waters, He, O, me, is Indra.' He is an important God to the Hindus and the subject of numerous stories and epics such as the **Ramayana** and **Mahabharata**, in which he leads the **Daevas**, the gods who maintain heaven and the elements. In the timeless battle between good and evil, he fights against the demons of the underworld and against all who oppose morality and **dharma**. With such a crowded agenda, one can quite understand why he was very fond of the intoxicating drink made from **soma**.

Indra's Net Indra's mythology includes the image of Indra's net which hangs in his palace in Heaven. It extends infinitely in all directions and at each node of the net there is a clear gem, so arranged as to reflect all the other gems in the net. The net is an allegory of the interdependence of everything. As the threads of Indra's net bind the gems, so our bodies bind our minds; through the interconnectedness of the net we reach each other, passing information across the intervening spaces. As each gem of Indra's net reflects every other one, so are we reflected by everything in the universe and everything in the universe is reflected by us.

Indus Valley Civilization From c.1500 BCE, when the **Aryans** migrated into the northwest of the Indian subcontinent and until 1920, only the Vedic texts yielded information about India's earliest civilization. Since the 1920s the excavation of the sites of two large cities, Mohenjo-Daro and Harappa, have disclosed a civilization similar to those of Babylon and Egypt. The civilization predates the Aryans by at least a thousand years. There is considerable literature now available describing in detail, the cities' structure, economy and culture. (See Wheeler and Piggott) The excavations were important for the insight they gave to the religion of the indigenous people. Various kinds of images, seals and terra-cotta statuettes indicate, a mother-goddess cult the figures of which are in the cross-legged Indian yogic position of meditation, the idolization of phallic symbols and a sacred tree. These religious characteristics are similar to those of early **Hinduism**, and Trevor Ling has suggested that the 'Hindu cults of the post-Buddhist period do not constitute a new development, but something which in essence is to be found at least two thousand years earlier.'

Initiation An African youth who submits to the painful process of cicatrization, a medieval squire who keeps an all-night vigil in a church, a man submitting to a rearrangement of his clothing and to being led blindfold around an obstacle course, a barrel-making apprentice allowing himself to be rolled around in a tar barrel, a young girl submitting to artificially induced vaginal bleeding, all have in common that they are in the process of being initiated. All initiation ceremonies as a rite of passage involve the idea of new birth as an image of passing from one form of life to another. The equally important parallel theme of death is also acted out ritually in the sense that the new life cannot be embraced until the old life has been disposed of. Among the Loango of the Congo, young boys are given a drink that makes them lose consciousness; in their 'dead' state they are circumcized, 'buried' in the fetish house, then painted white as a symbol of their being ghosts of their former existence. (See M. Eliade [1958]) Trials of strength and endurance are also characteristic features of initiation rites that associate the subject with ancestor heroes and preparing the way for the kinds of trials to be experienced and surmounted by brave and resolute adults. Melanesian initiates are subjected to the noise of the bull-roarer or to being beaten with stinging nettles; in East Africa, Naudi novices have their bodies exposed to hornets. Established forms of initiation include the anointing and coronation of kings and queens, the ordination of priests, the consecration of bishops, the installation of national presidents and the 'tests' imposed on new members of male fraternities or female sororities. See **Amritsankar, Anointing, Baptism, Bar Mitzvah, Confirmation, Sacred Thread Ceremony**

Innate Ideas In rationalist philosophy, they are ideas or knowledge, present in the mind independent of sense experience. Empiricists use the concept to propose that at birth, the mind is not a *tabula rasa* on which sense experience makes the first marks, but that certain ideas are already etched on the pristine mind and carried into life when we are born. These ideas are recollected by memory and brought to light by reason. Examples include mathematical truths $1 + 1 = 2$, the ideas of God, space, time and the concept of causality. **Plato**'s 'Forms', are derived from innate ideas as are, according to **Descartes**, the principles of science and the existence of the self. The innate idea of 'God' is discoverable by reason through **Natural Theology**. Innate ideas are similar to *a priori* knowledge, concepts that appear to be true before or regardless of experience. If it can be shown they have always existed, *a priori* concepts may also be innate. Noam **Chomsky** has argued that language learning is based on inborn imprinting of certain linguistic principles. The concept of innate ideas has been rigorously opposed by, for example, **Locke**, who argued that at birth the mind is a complete *tabula rasa*. The debate continues. See **Empiricism**, **Rationalism**

Inner Senses of Islam *I*. Sometimes thought of as inner faculties that parallel the outer senses. Islam recognizes five inner senses which are represented and interpreted differently by the various Islamic traditions and sometimes given in technical psycho-philosophical terms. The names here are given by Sheikh Fadhlalla Haeri: i) common sense; ii) imagination; iii) the faculty of co-ordination, which enables us to give value to forms or attributes; iv) the faculty of memory; v) the faculty of thinking or cognition. The Islamic philosophies of the 'self' teach that the five outer senses (sight, hearing, smell, taste and touch) together with the five inner senses, serve the 'heart', by which is meant the divine element or spark carried by each individual and which survives the demise of the body. See *Hafidha*

Inquisition It refers principally to four major retributive movements initiated by the Roman Catholic Church to suppress **heresy**. They were: i) the Medieval and Episcopal Inquisitions of 1184 and 1230, set against the **Cathars**. ii) The Spanish Inquisition founded in 1478, set against Muslims Jews and **Illuminists**. It went on to include the Peruvian and Mexican Inquisitions. It was abolished in 1834. iii) The Roman Inquisition established in 1542 by Pope Paul III, was a permanent body called the Congregation of the Holy Office, staffed by cardinals and others to protect the faith from false doctrine and error. Part of the Roman Curia, it is the supervisory body of local Inquisitions. iv) The Portuguese Inquisition, established in 1536 by Joao III, King of Portugal, as a parallel to the Spanish Inquisition. In general, secular usage, because of the negative connotations of the term 'inquisition' it is used pejoratively and to express disapproval; the USA Senate investigations are sometimes labelled 'inquisitions', as was the 'Red Scare', the anti-communist purge of the 1940s and 1950s.

Institute for the Harmonious Development of Man Fleeing the Russian Revolution with his family and many friends, Georges Ivanovich **Gurdjieff** settled in France in 1922 and established the Institute at the Château Le Prieuré at Fontainebleau-Avon. The school was dedicated to work on oneself as a means of spiritual self-perfection and self-observation, being a focused affirmation of the classical 'Know thyself' philosophy. Clifford Sharpe comments, 'All the teaching is strictly practical ... The student may, if he likes, believe all he is told, but he is always reminded that belief is not knowledge and can be of no value to him until he has verified it by direct self-observation; and he is continuously discouraged from discussing ideas or even using words, of which he cannot offer concrete illustrations drawn from his own experience.' The Institute continued the work of the society founded in 1895 called, 'Seekers After Truth', a group of people from various backgrounds and professions who travelled the world, before returning to Russia in 1913. The Institute operated until 1934.

Institute of Noetic Sciences Located in northern California, the Institute is concerned with research into the powers of consciousness. Their website lists their interests as 'perception, belief, attention, intention and intuition', researching phenomena that do not fit scientific paradigms. The Institute has no religious association. 'Noetic' refers to a form of 'inner knowledge', and three primary areas of research are pursued: i) Extended Human Capacities; ii) Integral Health and Healing; iii) Emerging Worldviews. The current 'distant healing programme', integrates all three areas. See **Democratic Transhumanism**, **Transhumanism**

Institutionalization The process by which an *ad hoc* situation is transformed into a movement, school, cult, party or religion, through the imposition of a formal organizing structure. Characteristically, institutionalized groups had established patterns of belief and behaviour, themselves governed by doctrines, rules and laws. 'Established' religions such as **Roman Catholicism**, **Anglicanism** and the United Hebrew Congregation of the Commonwealth are examples of the institutionalization of religion. The argument for the process is that it makes it easier to maintain orthodoxy and stability and provides a necessary sense of moral, philosophical or theological security for the adherents. Against this view is the belief that institutionalization frustrates the innovative, creative ideas that founded the religion or movement in the first place and which maintain the elusive sense of a living, exuberant and relevant commitment. The process tends to neutralize and tame the charismatic, to the point where such energies need to break out and express themselves as happened, for example, with the **Reformation**. Striking the balance between control and freedom is a notoriously difficult ideal to achieve in any institutionalized system.

Integral Yoga *H*. See **Aurobindo**, **Yoga**

International Chivalric Organization of the Solar Tradition See **Order of the Solar Temple**

Intertestamental Period From, c.400 BCE, after which no further writings were added to the Jewish Bible, to roughly the end of the 1st century CE, when the writing that would become the Christian Bible had begun to be written. A body of biblically related literature was written during this period known as Intertestamental Literature, collected as the

Apocrypha, sometimes referred to as the Pseudoepigraphia, providing considerable insight into the cultural and religious milieu out of which Christianity developed.

Introversionism A term used by sociologists of religion to refer to the tendency in some sects not only to separate from orthodoxy, but also from the wider society in which they live. Known as 'Introversionists', their strength and authority is centred in their religious community to the point of absolute spiritual self-sufficiency. In Christian fundamentalist terms this is focused in the 'saving power of Christ', and the fellowship shared with other likeminded people. The community takes on the character of being holy and becomes the object of adoration as the visible manifestation of the living Christ. The French sociologist Emile **Durkheim** suggested that what people really worship when they worship God, is the society itself. Introversionism has powerful secular parallels as can be seen in the passion with which people embrace a political philosophy or party or give their absolute support to a football team, finding in the 'Supporter's Club', a *raison d'être* little different from that of a religious community. See **Holiness Movement, Sport**

Ioskeha The 'good' twin of **Iroquois** Indian cosmology, being the principle of good in their dualistic creation myth. See **Tawiscara**

Iroquois *Ami*. A group of five North American Indian tribes of the Hokan-Siouan linguistic group whose constitution, 'The Great Law of Peace' was established before contact with Europeans, probably sometime in the period 14th to 16th century, but Iroquois oral tradition suggests a date as early as 1100 CE. The peace message was brought by two prophets, Hiawatha and the Great Peace Maker. The cosmology recounts the birth of twin brothers, Ioskeha and Tawiscara, the principles of good and evil respectively. Their mother was the daughter of the sky-woman. Ioskeha created human beings, dividing them into tribal groupings. The 'False Face' are a group of masked medicine-men representing benevolent spirits, who aid in the protection against illness and its cure. The Iroquois are led by the *Haudenosaunee*, the 'People Building a Long House', symbolic of the idea that people should live together in peace as one family. Traditionally the **Seneca** were guardians of the western door and the Mohawk of the eastern door. Their aboriginal religion was revived by the Seneca prophet Handsome Lake. See **Handsome Lake Religion**

Isaac *J*. The second of the three biblical patriarchs, with **Abraham** and **Jacob**. As a child he was brought to the point of being sacrificed by Abraham as a test of his father's faith, but spared by God who provided a ram to take the boy's place. Isaac and his wife Rebecca, had twin sons, Jacob and Esau.

Ishtar The fertility goddess of **Harranian religion** and **Assyrian religion**. Ishtar is cognate with the Semitic **Astarte** (Heb. Ashtoret). In

Babylonian astro-mythology Ishtar is related to **Venus** and as such she travelled to the Greeks as **Hera**, or **Aphrodite**. See also **Mesopotamian Religion**

Ishvara *H*. Skt. 'Lord of the universe'. See **Iswara**

Isis *E*. One of the earliest and principal goddesses of Egyptian mythology, associated with the **Ennead** of Heliopolis. She was the wife of **Horus** and, at a later time, the wife of **Osiris** and mother of Horus. She is the feminine counterpart of Osiris, an archetype of creation and a goddess of fertility. She is one of the most enduring of Egyptian deities and although her cult was never centralized, it eventually spread throughout the ancient world of the Middle East and Europe to be identified as Isis-**Aphrodite**. As a winged goddess she may have represented the wind and in the Osiris myth she is described as wailing and moaning like the wind. She is also familiar as a great enchantress, a goddess of magic. The hieroglyphic symbol of her name is a throne and she is depicted wearing one on her head as an alternative to horns and a solar disk.

ISKCON *H*. 'International Society for Krishna Consciousness', also known as '**Hare Krishna**', was founded in 1966 by an elderly Indian monk, Swami Prabhupada. Some see ISKON as a new religious movement but in fact, it has antecedents in ancient texts like the **Bhagavad-Gita**. The Society helped to spread the practice of **Bhakti** Yoga, the yoga of devotion, focused on **Krishna** the Supreme Lord together with his consort **Radha**, and on other incarnations of Krishna such as **Sita** and **Rama**. Central to their philosophy is the belief that the individual soul is an eternal, personal identity which does not ultimately become absorbed into a void, as is believed by the monastic interpretations of **Hinduism** and the texts. The aims of the Society include the spreading of spiritual knowledge and techniques, to develop Krishna consciousness, to help members of the Society to draw nearer to Krishna and to encourage a simpler, more natural way of life. Sadly the Society has not been without its scandals and controversies that include charges of murder, kidnapping, fraud and the obstruction of justice. In 1969 the Beatles made a hit single out of the Hare Krishna chant, which was performed by George Harrison and adherents of the Radha-Krishna Temple in London. It made Hare Krishna a household name. See **Haranath**, **Yoga**

Islam *I*. Arab. from the root *s-l-m* meaning, 'submission' or 'peace'. A **Muslim** is, therefore, one who submits himself to God, **Allah**. For Muslims Allah is, 'The Great Name' for God, but tradition lists 99 other names, 'The **Beautiful Names**', each of which offers a different insight into an attribute or function of Allah. Those who submit to the will of Allah are at peace with him, with their fellows and with themselves. Every aspect of life is to be submitted to Allah's will, including the state and its government, to the end of establishing every Islamic nation as a true theocracy. Territories were given different designations dependent on whether or not they were governed by Islamic rule, thus, *Dar al-Harb*, 'Territory of War' or *Dar al-Islam*, the 'Territory of Islam', or 'Household of Islam'.

Islam claims to offer the final and definitive answer to the basic religious questions and to be the religion of which God himself approves. Like Judaism and Christianity, its revelation is also its authority. But Islam is distinguished by it's name, it being the only name for a religion that actually describes the basic attitude and quality on which that religion is founded. After Christianity, it is the most widely distributed religion, adherents numbering well in excess of one billion. While its geographical focus is **Mecca**, the Arab countries do not have the largest Islamic population; these exist in Indonesia, Bangladesh, Pakistan, India, Central Asia and Africa, as well as a considerable presence in Europe and the USA. Because of Islam's worldwide distribution, Muslims sometimes refer to themselves as 'The People of the Point', the focus being the *Qiblah*, a 'point' of direction marked in every **mosque** by the *mihrab*, the niche which indicates the direction of Mecca, towards which worshippers must face when praying. Both *Salat*, their ritual prayer and their mental attitude, focuses Muslims on the place where the Prophet **Muhammad** was born and where the **Koran**, the sacred scripture of Islam, was first revealed to him.

What is known of the life of Muhammad is derived mostly from oral tradition, which when written in 8th and 9th centuries recorded his birth in Mecca c.570 CE. In mid-life he turned towards religion, spending long periods in meditation. He was 39 when in the face of prevalent polytheism and idol-worship, he received his vocation to prophethood and to proclaim Allah as the only true God.

Although Muhammad's perception of Allah was influenced by Judaism and Christianity, his message is unique, embodying a faith that deliberately drew away from the earlier traditions. Islam became free of the controls of Jewish law, teaching that Judaism had misinterpreted the scriptures and the Abrahamic religion; it accused Christianity of compromising a radical **monotheism** by worshipping Jesus as God, together with its doctrine of the **Trinity**, and believed Christianity to be weakened by deep internal divisions. Muhammad passionately understood Islam to be the original, pre-Christian, pre-Jewish religion of pure monotheism. The religious concepts that Muhammad first developed in Mecca do not represent the entire Islamic belief-system. As with all religions this continued to be refined, defined and systematized after the founder's death. Koranic **sutras** can be identified as either Meccan or Medinan. The earlier, Meccan tradition is based on Muhammad's vision of Allah. In the Koran, Allah is depicted as wrapped in overawing mystery, sharing many of the characteristics of the Judeo-Christian God; he is creator and judge, providential and merciful, but his unity and majesty are absolute and must never be compromised. The Koran declares that Allah has dominion over the universe and that everything created belongs to him, 'His throne extends over the Heavens and the Earth ... all things in the Heavens and on the Earth are His.' As the judge of the unfaithful he is terrible and terrifying, but to the pious who experience him as loving and compassionate, his glory is overwhelming. Allah is the 'One Lord Alone' to whom total loyalty must be given, the sharp focus for the individual, the community and the nation. His devotees are the servants of one unique master and they can appeal only to the One source of guidance throughout life.

It is interesting to notice that there is little here that is different from Judaism and Christianity, the other monotheisms present in Mecca at the time. That the people of Mecca disavowed both as a solution to their problems was for political and not theological reasons. Mecca was concerned to safeguard its neutrality. Trevor Ling explains that 'for Meccans to have turned in large numbers to the Jewish faith would have meant becoming associated with the strong Jewish element in Persia; on the other hand, if Meccans had turned to the Christian faith they would immediately have identified themselves with Christian Byzantium.' Mecca could not have risked being drawn into the conflict between Persia and Byzantium. The key-element Muhammad drew from the existing traditions was the concept of ethical monotheism and it was from this base that Muhammad preached against the irreligious character of a Meccan culture controlled by the individual power and wealth of merchant princes. His prophetic message had a hard, ethical core and was aimed to turn the lives of the people away from the power of wealth to the omnipotence of God, from individual self-indulgence to submission to God's will. Muhammad did not oppose wealth or individuality, but he wanted to place both, 'firmly within a theocratic instead of materialistic context' (Ling).

Muhammad was not unopposed in Mecca and in 622 CE he and his followers undertook the *hijra*, the migration, to Medina. The date marks the beginning of the Islamic era. The outcome of the migration was the establishment of the *umma*, an Islamic theocracy. In summary, after Muhammad's death in c.632 CE, the religious ideas that were consolidated by the Median **caliphate** can be summarized as: i) *Tawhid*, the defining doctrine of Islam, being the omnipotence and unity of God; ii) the establishment of *shirk*, the sin of representing the divine in human form or image; iii) the concept of *jihad*, the passionate striving to establish the *dar-al-Islam*, those areas of government and society that have been surrendered to God; iv) *Shariah*, the divine and immutable will of God expressed in the Koran and Muhammad's *Sunnah*, as law. The *Arkan al-Islam*, the Five Pillars of Islam (see **Pillars of Islam**) support the practice of the faith and are obligatory for all Muslims.

The Koran is clear about death stating that everyone should be aware of the need to be prepared for the 'Last Assize'. After death, the soul's destiny in either Heaven or Hell is determined by the quality of a person's life on earth, that is, their righteousness or otherwise. Man is not to be understood as a fallen being needing a saviour to effect salvation for him; Muhammad is not a Christ. People have the intelligence to understand the responsibility of being made in God's image and endowed with a will that can choose the path that will lead to **Paradise**. In Islam, intelligence and will are inextricably related, in the same way as are Truth and Law. Truth is understood by intelligence, the Law is obeyed by the will, but *Dhanb*, sin, corrupts both. What is necessary for the soul to survive death is piety, the fear of God and faithful observation of ritual obligations. The Koran stresses God's mercy and forgiveness, but also the imminence of the Day of Judgement, when he will assign people either to Heaven or to Hell. From this fundamental, almost logical basis, various other views of death and the afterlife have developed. The **Kharijites** taught that a Believer who had sinned without repenting becomes an apostate and is judged accordingly. The **Murji'a** held the view that the dividing line between the believer and unbeliever is known only to God. Various other positions are taken up in the debate about the relative importance of faith and works in meriting God's pleasure. Koranic images of heaven and hell are rich and allow a range of interpretation. There is a tradition in Islam suggesting that in order to discover the meaning of the life we live now, we must discover and experience death within ourselves. This practice of a voluntary death, of 'dying before we die', is a way of experiencing something of the nature of death while we are still in the prime of life. Traditional Islamic **eschatology** rests on the belief in the resurrection of the body and the individual's future survival, but there are those who believe only the soul will survive and that true happiness in Paradise is intellectual. Others believe in the 'torment of the grave', that people's souls will be interrogated in the tomb and rewarded, accordingly, with either misery or pleasure until summoned on the Day of Judgement. Alternatively, it is suggested that such language is not to be interpreted literally, but is figurative, describing in metaphorical terms the experience of the soul after death.

Muhammad's first and urgent task after his move to Medina was to consolidate his community of followers. Once this was achieved, Islam began its characteristic military progress with a battle against his old adversaries in Mecca. This was the beginning of *jihad*, the concept of the holy war, the duty to fight all unbelievers.

FINAL WORD: 'Allahu Akbar! God is Great!' (The takbir, part of the call to prayer)

'Truly religion, with God, is Islam.' (Koran: Surah 3:19)

'There is no god but God and Muhammad is the messenger of God.' (From the *Shahadah*, the Islamic creed.)

Islam and Secularism *1.* Islam's response to secularism is probably the clearest of all major religions. It takes secularism to be a denial of the existence of God and the refutation of all forms of faith and worship; it regards the process of secularization as the abandonment of any dialogue with religion and a prohibition of any form of religious education. Thus, secularism is contrary to *Shariah*, the immutable revealed will of Allah and his sacred rule, which touches every aspect of human life and relationships. For Muslims, the philosophy of secularism is an embodiment of the ultimate, unforgivable sin of *kufr*, unbelief and a denial of the implications of the *Shariah* ideal of life, the implementation of which requires a **theocracy**. For these reasons, in an Islamic state secularism is both abhorrent and irrelevant. See **Islamic Humanism**, **Islamic Modernism**, **Secularism**, **Ulema**

Islamic Brotherhood *I*. 'The Believers are but a single Brotherhood' (Koran. Surah: Al-Hujurat 49:10). See **Muslim Brotherhood**.

Islamic Dynasties and Empires The rapid and orderly expansion of Islam from a localized sect to the established religion of a considerable empire, is exhaustively documented and only the briefest summary can be provided here. From the time of Muhammad's death in 632 CE and until 661 CE the Islamic community was administered by a succession of **Caliphs** known as 'the Rightly Guided' or 'the Orthodox' of Medina. To subdue Arab tribesmen rebelling against the payment of the alms tax and established treaties, the Caliphs' military campaigns spread through all points of the compass. Within six years of Muhammad's death the whole of Syria and Iraq was subject to Medina. Four years later, Egypt became a part of the growing empire. These earlier conquests marked the first stage of what became an even greater expansion that included Morocco, Spain and France and which swept to Constantinople and across central Asia to the Indus valley. These first Caliphs were followed by the **Umayyads** (661–750 CE) who established Damascus as their centre. Umayyad power collapsed in the face of the disaffection of non-Arab subjects and civil war between Arab tribes. The leadership was taken up by the **Abbasids** (750–1258) who, having transferred the Empire's capital to Baghdad, turned their attention to strengthening the inner cohesion of the Islamic nations and to enriching its commerce and culture. In all of this they were brilliantly successful. Muslim passage into Europe had been by way of the islands of Rhodes and Cyprus and in the 9th century the Arabs added Sicily to their occupied territories. Except for the north, Spain was conquered and held for Islam from 8th to the 15th century CE. During the 10th and 11th centuries CE, the power of the Abbasids waned and was followed by political disintegration, as a result of which the Empire succumbed to the Turkish Sultanates who carried Islam eastwards, while the **Berbers** carried it into Negro Africa. Having defeated the Byzantines at Manzikert in 1017 the **Seljuks**, forerunners of the Ottomans, established a considerable empire governed by a dynasty that lasted until the 13th century. It made possible the settlement of Turkic-speaking people in Anatolia, an event that led, by way of the Ottomans, to the founding of the Turkish Republic in the 20th century. The **Fatimid** Caliphate (969–1171) were left to rule Cairo as vassals, with the **Mamluk** Sultanate retaining power. There followed the devastating invasions by the Mongols of Genghis Khan, who between 1220 and 1225 crushed the northern and eastern provinces and who, a short while later, overthrew Persia and Iraq, terminating the Baghdad Caliphate in 1258.

In 1517, the Mongols were overrun by the **Ottoman** Turks, since when their empire dominated Syria, Egypt and most of Arabia. They celebrated the fifth centenary of their capture of Constantinople in 1953. Concurrent with Ottoman expansion was the establishment from 1526, of the **Mughal** Empire on the Indian subcontinent and from 1501 the founding of the **Safavid** dynasty in Persia. This frenetic and complicated history is well summarized by Guillaume, Zaehner, Ling, Gibb and comprehensively covered by Holt, Lambton and Beckingham, editors of *The Cambridge History of Islam.*

FINAL WORD: 'The expansion of the Ottoman Empire in Asia and North Africa and the establishment of the Mughal Empire in India in the 16th century brought the greater part of the Muslim world once more under the government of powerful and highly centralized civil State. A marked feature of both Empires was the strong emphasis laid on Muslim orthodoxy and the Sacred Law [the **Shariah**]; Church and state were not indeed unified, since the military and higher civil polity was constructed on independent non-Islamic lines, but buttressed one another by a sort of concordat that endured into the 19th century.' (Gibb)

Islamic Humanism *I.* It is to be expected that Islam would reject the basic premise of **Humanism**, that man is the measure of all things. Its culture was barely touched by the **Renaissance** or **Reformation** and its encounter with Catholic Inquisitions had the effect of hardening its orthodoxy. This refers, of course, to secular humanism, and Islam does not admit even a secular dimension to the societies over which it has control, since those societies are theocracies, thus every aspect of them is brought under the rule of Islamic religious law. Having said that, Islamic secular humanism does have its eloquent protagonists that include Edward Said and Noam **Chomsky**. However, even orthodox forms of modern Islam would want to represent those aspects of humanism that suggest the highest standards of personal relationship, compassion, service and individual freedom, although a true democracy might not be an expression of this.

FINAL WORD: 'Progressive Muslims are likely to combine a Koranic call for serving as "witness to God in justice" (Koran 42:15) with an Edward Said-ian call to speak truth to the powers.' (Omid Safid)

Islamic Modernism *I.* What passes for modernism in Islam is mostly the result of influence from Western intellectualism and **materialism**. Muhammad Abduh (1849–1905), the rector of Al-Azhar, the famous Cairo-based educational institution of **Sunni** Muslims, reformed the classical theological curriculum by introducing the study of Western languages and science; his disciple, Rashid Rida (1865–1935) made the journal *al-Manar*, a channel for a reformism that appealed to an earlier, pristine Islam, inspiring the movement of **Muslim Brotherhood** that encourages social change and adaptation. Its political activism has been the cause for concern of several Islamic governments. Modern Islam is caught in the tensions of new technologies, oil revenues, population pressures, economic imbalance, secular influences and with the violence propagated by resurgent **fundamentalism**. Islamic modernism is guided by three interpenetrating attitudes: 'conserve', 'adapt' and 'renew'. See **Islamic Humanism**

Islamic Mysticism *I*. See Sufism

Islamic Philosophy *I*. *Falsafah*, 'philosophy'. Since its inception, Islamic philosophy endeavoured to find a balance, if not harmony, between faith and reason – that is, between the intuitive and the rational. The issue is more clearly defined than in any other biblical religion, since faith requires total submission to the revealed will of Allah and philosophical enquiry into its concepts could infringe the religious principles on which Islam is founded. It is argued by some devout Muslims that you cannot be both a true adherent of Islam and a philosopher, since the two 'ways' are divergent. As the history of Western philosophy illustrates, a revealed religion cannot, satisfactorily, be synthesized with rational analysis. Others disagreed, believing such a synthesis was not only possible but informative and illuminating. To use philosophy to demonstrate that one's religious presuppositions are correct is a resource used by both Jewish and Christian philosophers, but the more objective enquirers would claim that that was not true philosophy, since the goal at which one wants to arrive is determined before the enquiry is undertaken. Islam is not open to the Cartesian form of doubt (see **Descartes**) – that is, the abandonment of every held proposition so as to enquire objectively, as to whether any statement or assertion is true. The truths of Islam are inviolable, beyond question or contradiction and thus philosophy, if it is to be active at all, must serve the purpose of those truths. Nevertheless, down the centuries, attempts at philosophical analysis and synthesis have been made and a copious literature exists. Philosophers grappled (see **Kalam**) with the same familiar themes such as whether or not the Koran was created or eternal; whether evil was created by God; the relationship between predestination and free will; and whether God's attributes in the Koran were to be interpreted allegorically or literally. Perhaps, inevitably, philosophy was driven from the schools by fundamentalist orthodoxy and to the Jews was given the honour of carrying Islamic thought into the Christian world. Since the Muslim withdrawal from Spain and Portugal in the 15th and 16th centuries, Islamic philosophy disappeared from Western Europe, but in the East it was developed by Ottoman philosophers and by the teaching of logic in Muslim seminaries. What we are left with are two very important traditions of philosophy still strongly active in the modern world, represented by Shi'ite (see **Shi'ism**) and **Sunni** thought. Running alongside these is also the philosophy of the **Sufi** mystics. See **Hikma**, **Mu'tazila**

FINAL WORD: 'Knowledge is a Way to Action, to Love, to Truth. But since it is not the kind of knowledge that people hold it to be, they do not benefit from it. It is everywhere, but they cannot see it and call out for it while it is besides them all the time.' (Rauf Mazari, *Niazi*. Quoted by Idries Shah)

Island of Creation *E*. A feature of Egyptian creation mythology. The Island is said to have emerged from the primeval, chaotic waters to become the home of the first god or a mound on which the god could stand. By the time of the establishment of the Old Kingdom (c.2686 BCE) the priests of Heliopolis, Memphis and Hermopolis asserted their own god as having the definitive role in creation and each of these centres developed their own creation myths, believing the temple of the locals gods were the actual location of the original island. At Heliopolis the creation myth is centred on Ra-Atum, at Memphis on **Ptah**, at Hermopolis **Thoth** was the main contender. During the later period of the New Kingdom (1550–1069 BCE) the tradition of Thebes was added to the creation mythologies centred around **Amun**. See **Atum**, **Ra**

Isma'ilis *I*. A major offshoot of the Islamic **Shiite** sect, named after Ismail who, in opposition to all other Shiites, is believed to be the seventh **Imam**. Their familiar name, the Seveners, derives from this assertion (see **Twelvers**). The succession, however, was confused and controversial. What is important is that the Isma'ilis became the most extreme group of Shiite Islam, represented in the Middle Ages by a revolutionary sect, the 'Carmathians' (or Qarmatis), the Fatimid **Caliphate** in Egypt (969–1171) and the infamous 'Assassins', who, drugged with hashish, killed all those who opposed them. The man who led them against the Crusaders was known to them as 'The Old Man of the Mountains', a term comfortably settled in Anglophone vocabulary. The Medieval sects were virtually obliterated by the Mongols since when the Isma'ilis have splintered and for the most part ceased to be fanatical and war-mongering. The reason for their success has to take into account that Isma'ilism was exploited by its leaders to their own advantage. Its popular appeal, however, lay in the recognition that the laws were written by rulers to contain and control the poorer, least advantaged orders of society. In that process it was highly syncretistic, converts from other religions could bring with them values and ideas they believed to be indispensable. Guillaume described the basis of their faith as **Neoplatonic**, a belief in a world or cosmic intelligence which since Adam has been continuously manifested by divine incarnations, each of which contributes to their received tradition. Offshoots of the Isma'ilis exist today in Lebanon, India and East Africa and one such sect, the Nizari Isma'ilis, hold the Aga Khan to be a direct, lineal descendent of the first Shiite imam, Ali.

Israel *J*. Heb. *Yisra'el*, from *sara*, 'he fought' or 'he contended' together with *El*, 'God'. Thus, 'He that fought with God' or 'may God strive'. The name first appears in Gen. 32:28, when it was given to Jacob after he had wrestled with the divine messenger and subsequently to all of Jacob's natural descendents (the Children of Israel) or to anyone, who by choice, enters into the covenantal relationship with God. The accepted collective name for the Jewish people is therefore, 'Israel'. In the Bible, for example in the Books of Chronicles, Samuel and Kings, there are references to 'the Land of Israel' as the territory promised by God to the 'Chosen People'. The name was also given to the northern Kingdom of Israel (c.933–721 BCE) which after the death of Solomon and under the leadership of Jeroboam, seceded from the southern Kingdom of **Judah**

which was ruled by Solomon's son and successor, Rehoboam. Rabbinical theological writing gave great importance to the fact that the name 'Israel' combined the two concepts, 'land' and 'people'. It was argued that the concept 'Israel' was indispensable to the actualization of **Torah** in creation and that for this reason the land was in God's mind before his work of creation began. Israel is 'made' to exist in order to be the recipient of Torah and in this respect is unique among the peoples of the world. In November, 1947 the United Nations voted to partition Palestine, according to the Jews their own territory. When the British withdrew in May, 1948 the leaders of the Jewish State assembled in Tel Aviv to announce the independence of the State of Israel. The political formation of the State was opposed by fundamentalist orthodox Judaism which holds that a New Israel will be established by messianic divine intervention. See **Jew**, **Judaism**, **Judaism orthodox**

Iswara *H*. Skt. 'Lord of the universe'. The supreme personal God of Hinduism, taken as the creator of the world. In relation to the phenomenal world **Brahman** is Ishvara and as such the object of worship. With characteristic psychological insight Hinduism understood, early in its development, that the mind is incapable of conceiving divinity unless it is cast as form. Hence the identification of Iswara with all phenomena. As Brahman, Iswara oversees the activities of the universe. He is the true Self to be realized and once the illusion of individuality is abandoned he ceases to exist. For Hindus, Ishvara represents a kind of universalism, since their developing mythology identified him with the biblical God. Ishvara is also a title given to **Siva**. See **Atman**, **Dualism**
FINAL WORD: 'Ishvara is the supreme interpretation of the Absolute (brahman) by human thought.' (Swami Vivekananda)

Ithm *I*. Arab. An 'intentional' or 'conscious sin' associated with dereliction of duty. The Christian doctrine of '**original sin**', has no place in Islam, leaving the field open to either intentional sin or *dhanb*, inadvertent sin. A sin is anything that impedes or distracts from Allah's divine intention for human behaviour. Ithm, requires, *tawba*, remorse, penance and forgiveness and if possible the making of restitution to those sinned against. A Muslim may have confidence that if forgiveness is sought, it will be accorded so long as the repentance is sincere. 'So long as you call upon me and hope in me, I forgive you all that originates from you; and I will not heed, O son of man, should your sins reach the horizon of the heavens and then you asked My pardon and I would pardon you.' (Hadith Qudsi).

Itmi'nan *I*. In Islam, the concept of tranquillity and serenity. It is the state of being fully satisfied and completely at rest, a spiritual state beyond serenity. If serenity is the beginning of being free of theoretical knowledge and on the threshold of being awakened to the truth, peacefulness is the final point or conclusion. *Itmi'nan* is very close to the concept of *Sakina*.

J

Jacob *J*. The third of the biblical patriarchs, with **Abraham** and **Isaac**. He obtained his twin brother's birthright for a bowl of lentil soup. (Gen:27) After wrestling with an angel (Gen:32) his name was changed to **Israel**, meaning 'he that fought with God' or 'may God strive'. During the first six centuries CE, rabbinical writings took Jacob's life to be symbolic of historical events, with 'Israel' representing the nation and his brother Esau the antagonism of Rome.

Jainism *H*. Skt. *Jaina*. An ancient religion that has its origins in the **Sankhya** philosophy of **Hinduism**, with its sublime perception that the universe is created by the union of nature with consciousness. They are also thought to have originated with the ancient *Jinas* (see **Jina**). Because of its rejection of the authority of the **Vedas** and its radical atheism, it has been regarded as unorthodox. Jain tradition is based on 24 teachers or *Tirthankaras* ('ford-makers'), the last of which, Mahavira (6th–5th BCE) formed Jainism into a religious community. In the 3rd century BCE the community migrated to Gujarat and Rajasthan. The teachings of the *Tirthankaras*, especially those of Mahavira, were transmitted by oral tradition. Approximately a thousand years after Mahavira's death they were written and compiled to form the Jain scriptures, the *Agams*. Jains believe that divinity lives within every individual soul and that 'perfect' souls should be worshipped as the Supreme Spirit. There is no place, therefore, for a conventional belief in God and the most that can be said is that the Supreme Spirit is an addition of all the perfected souls. The spiritual quest is focused in *moksha*, liberation, which is gained by right belief, right knowledge, right action and by forms of asceticism. Differences of opinion about the extent to which asceticism should be carried caused divisions. There were those known as the 'Sky-clad', who believed it was wrong to wear clothes, those who dressed were known as 'White-clad', because of their plain white garments. The modern 'Sky-clad' wear clothes in public. Each group developed its own literature which was principally concerned with commentaries on the concept of **karma**. The Jains are probably best known for taking the doctrine of *Ahimsa*, 'non-violence', to an extreme form. **Ghandi** was influenced by the way they practised *Ahimsa*. Jain practice includes strict vegetarianism, but also requires everyone to go to extreme lengths to prevent even the accidental killing of the smallest of creatures, such as flies and mosquitoes or the harming of atoms in wind and water. Monks wear a mask over the mouth to avert the possibility of damaging the atoms of the air or of inhaling insects, they carry a broom, sweeping the ground in front of them to avoid walking on an insect inadvertently. Such rigorous care is not confined to monks. Lay people will not drink water after dark in case an insect is swallowed. Rich Jains employ people to lie on their beds to attract whatever bed bugs may be there, before they themselves sleep. *Ahimsa*, therefore, prohibits some kinds of livelihood, such as agriculture, since ploughing or tending the soil is contrary to Jain ethics. They are therefore mostly merchants and traders or in commerce of different kinds. The collective wealth of a community is used to build impressive temples and to raise huge rock-cut images like the 10th century statue at Sravana Belgola at Mysore, of a standing, naked, male figure. In everyday life a Jain will endeavour to live by the highest standards of conduct, exercising disciplined self-control and restraint. Anger, conceit, deceit, lies and greed are cardinal sins and the first step in purging them is the purification of the mind through meditation. In summary, Jainism represents an extremely fundamentalist form of the doctrine of universal piety and a respect for all forms of life. It is estimated that there are 4.2 million Jains in communities across the world. FINAL WORD: The Jain World Website's statement of mission and objectives includes, 'Educate world masses about the fact that Jainism is the oldest living religion, a very scientific, most environment friendly, ecology protecting and independent religion with built-in respect and equality for all living beings (human, animals, creatures, birds, insects, etc) and provision for the highest level of enlightenment for all. Make the world understand how Jainism is relevant to today's age. The permanent solutions it offers to the gigantic problems facing mankind. To create a global identity for Jainism as an independent, unique religion and for its great value system.'

James, **William (1842–1910)** American psychologist and philosopher and brother to the novelist, Henry James. His range of interests covered the science of psychology, the philosophy of history, pragmatism and the psychology of religious and mystical experience. His philosophy of religion emphasized religious experience as the most important aspect of the study of religions and not religious history, institutions or doctrine, since it is the religious experience that is the source of each of these. Understanding intense and sometimes pathological experiences (not just those of religion) is the role of the psychologist, since by that science alone can the mind be examined. Religious experience is a form of 'over-belief' which magnifies our more common experiences; the validity of such experiences cannot be proved empirically, but they can enrich our lives. In his examination of mysticism James experimented with certain chemicals such as chloral hydrate and amyl nitrate and with drugs including, in 1896, peyote (see **Peyote Cults**). He concluded that while the revelations of the mystics were valid, they were true only for the mystics themselves; for others, they were simply ideas that should be considered, but unless the experience was made personal, the truth of them remained inaccessible. See **Pragmatism**

Jansenism X. A movement within **Roman Catholicism**, that laid the emphasis on predestination and human depravity due to **original sin**, thus heightening the need for the grace of God. The movement was named after its founder Cornelius Otto Jansen (1585–1638) bishop of Ghent and Ypres. He promoted St **Augustine**'s extreme form of '**Irresistible Grace**' coupled with an austere morality. In this he opposed **Jesuit** casuistry and in 1653 and 1713, Jansenism was condemned by the Papacy. When the nuns of the Convent of Port-Royale (near Paris) refused to accept the papal decision the philosopher **Pascal**, whose sister was a nun of the convent, wrote his *Provincial Letters* in support of the Jansenists. Persecuted in France, they fled to Holland and in 1723 consecrated their own Bishop in Utrecht. This schism is the origin of the **Old Catholics**.

Janus In Roman mythology (see **Roman Religion**) Janus was the god of doorways, gates, beginnings and endings. He is familiarly depicted as Janus Geminus (twin Janus) with two faces looking in opposite directions originally one bearded, the other clean-shaven. Sometimes he is shown as Janus Quadrifrons, with four faces. Early associations understood the two faces to be those of the sun and moon. As the god of transitions, change and progress from the past to the future, he was worshipped at the time of planting and harvest, at births, marriages and deaths; he ruled over the middle ground between, barbarity and civilization, rural and urban life, youth and adulthood. It has been suggested that the Italian city, Genoa, was named after him, as is the first month of the year, January. There are also 'Janus words' or self-antonyms, such as the word 'fast' which can qualify a movement, 'running fast' or can mean not moving at all, 'stuck fast'.

Japanese Religions According to the reports of the Japanese education department, in the latter part of the 20th century, Shinto, **Buddhism** and what are termed New Religious Cults, numbered more members than the total population of the country. This illustrates the plurality and pattern of religious affiliation among the Japanese, who are happy to offer worship to Shinto and Buddhist gods, as well as those of other cults with which they may be associated. The earliest Japanese religion was similar to the **Shamanism** of northeastern Asia and included polytheistic nature worship. From these early beginnings Japanese religion has been concerned with defilement and purification rather than with the notion of sin characteristic of religions with a built-in ethical system. The common taboos were physical contact with the dead and with blood, from which contamination purification was effected by exorcism, cleansing rituals and forms of abstention. The origin of **Shintoism**, the 'Way of the Gods', is to be found in these practices. Buddhism was brought to Japan in c.9th century CE, but it did not begin to gather momentum until the monk Eisai Zenji founded the first **Rinzai** Zen monastery, in 1187 CE. Other major Buddhist schools included **Shingon** and **Tendai**. In 1868 Shintoism, with its characteristic ancestor worship, was made the official state religion and the Emperor was worshipped as a direct descendent of the sun-goddess. The same constitution guaranteed religious freedom: 'Japanese subjects shall, within the limits not prejudicial to peace and order and not antagonistic to their duties as subjects, enjoy freedom of religious belief' (Meije Constitution, Article 28). Thus emancipated, Christian groups, mostly Roman Catholic who had been practising secretly since the mid-17th century, came out of hiding. Eventually, most Christian denominations established a presence in Japan but were required by the government to form a united group, the *Nihon Kirisuto Kyodan* (the United Church of Christ in Japan). This pluralism and the Japanese tendency to belong to more than one group, wove the characteristic religious fabric.

Following the defeat of Japan at the end of the Second World War, Shintoism lost its position as the state religion and the Emperor renounced his divine lineage. However, a syncretistic Shinto sect, **Konkokyo**, founded in 1859, remains active. Religious activity in present day Japan is mostly associated with new religious sects, but only their formulation is new since they draw on classical and traditional teachings, attracting most of their followers from the lower social classes. There are many dozens of these new sects and the largest have a decidedly secular front, providing their adherents with facilities for sport, music and art. Many of these are Buddhist, others are syncretistic pulled together from Buddhist, Shinto and Christian sources. **Tenry-Kyo** is a typical example, given government approval as early as 1908 with full recognition as a Shinto sect. Probably the best-known of these mass Buddhist movements is **Soka Gakkai**, the 'Scientific Society for the Creation of Values'. Associated with **Nichiren** Buddhism or the 'New Lotus School', it has attracted around 14 million followers across 190 countries, including the USA and Brazil. In 1964, its president Daisaku Ikeda established the political party **Komeito**, the 'Party for Cleanliness', a Buddhist-based democracy based on a form of social humanism and dedicated to purifying society, eradicating corruption and to world peace. Rish'o Koseikai, the 'Society for the Establishment of Justice and Community for the Right', is another example of the proliferation of modern sects. The 'Right', better translated as 'perfect', refers to the Buddha principle, prefixing each element of the 'Eightfold Path' ('Perfect View, Perfect Resolve, etc.). Founded in 1938 by Mrs Naganuma Myoko and Niwano Nikkyo, it is based on devotion to the *Lotus Sutra* and belief that salvation can be achieved through chanting it. Adherents are expected to follow the **bodhisattva** ideal developed through discussion groups offering the chance of self-expression, similar to the Christian notion of confession. Practice retains the daily veneration of ancestors. The society is a lay organization, without monks or nuns and runs institutions that provide social aid and education.

Despite the intense religious affiliations to be found in some of the new cults, there has been no religious revival in Japan. It appears that the nation is moving away from religious terms of reference and is looking to solve its problems and plan its future entirely on secular terms. The old values prevail for their own sake and because they are worthwhile. Ultimate value is placed on, for example, fidelity to one's commitments, thrift, hard work, the struggle to succeed even if the odds are stacked against you and self-improvement in terms of both skills and ethics. They all point to what provides Japanese society with its central energy, the drive to achieve. Edward Norbeck makes the point that this virtue is close

to what the West knows as, the 'Protestant ethic', but with far less motivation derived from religion.

FINAL WORD: 'Japanese culture has no conception of a God existing
abstractly, completely separate from the human world. In the ultimate
analysis, the Japanese consciousness of the object of religious devotion
grows out of direct-contact relations between individuals ... Even the
Emperor, with his ancestors, is conceptualized as the ultimate figure of
successive lineal extensions of such actual links common to all Japanese
through their respective ancestors: he is not a sacred figure divorced
from his people.' (Chie Nakane)

Japji *Sik*. Pun. The revealed word of God in the form of a long poem
written by Guru Nanak and forming the opening and most important
section of the **Guru Granth Sahib**, the Sikh scriptures.

Jati *H*. Skt. 'birth'. The sub-castes of the four major **castes** of Hindu
society. They are groups associated with various types of work and professions, for example, *Ghandi jati* is an association or guild of greengro-
cers. Some *jati* are related to religious beliefs, for example,
Vaishnavism.

Javanese Religion Behind the complex religious and cultural pluralism of
Java, is an indigenous animism centred on ancestral spirits, a guardian
spirit who is the twin of an individual's soul and guardian spirits of
sacred places such as wells, banyan trees and caves. There was a belief
in ghosts, giants, fairies and dwarfs set against a culture of magic that
could empower people, parts of the body, plants and certain animals and
objects. Java is now more than 90 per cent Islam blended with a syncretism of Hindu and Buddhist practices. *Agami Jawi*, 'Javanese
Religion', is the most popular form of Islam, while *Agami Islam Santri*
(Santri Islam Religion) is more orthodox and puritanical. **Sufism** has also
made an important contribution. Islam's assimilation of original, mystical pantheistic perceptions is described in the 19th-century classical
work, the *Serat Centhini* and the magico-mystical books of the Suluk, an
ethnic group originally from the Philippine island of Sulu.

Jehovah *Heb*. A reconstruction of the ancient Hebrew name for God,
transliterated as Yahweh from the Hebrew consonants and transliterated
without the vowels as, YHWH (see **Tetragrammaton**). 'Yahweh' is mis-
takenly translated as 'Jehovah' in Christian translations of the **Old
Testament**. For Jews, the name of God is ineffable and never pronounced; instead the four Hebrew consonants, YHWH are replaced by
Adonai, usually translated as 'Lord'. See **Elohim**, **El Shaddai**

Jehovah's Witnesses *X*. A Christian sect founded c.1879 by Charles
Russell, in Pittsburgh, USA originally as the 'International Bible
Students'. They are also known as The Watch Tower Bible and Tract
Society and as the 'Millenarians', who believed in the immanence of the

thousand years of Christ's rule on earth. They interpret the Bible literally, reject the doctrine of the Trinity and hold to the belief that Jesus Christ was not identical to God (see **Arianism**). The Christ-ruled Millennium will end with Armageddon, the last battle, after which the Witnesses will rule with Christ. Only those who are Witnesses, the 'elect' of Jehovah, will share the Messianic Kingdom.

Jen *Con. T*. Chin. 'humanity', 'love of fellow man'. The basic virtue of **Confucianism**. Before Confucius' time, *jen* was the kindness and benevolence of rulers to their subjects. Confucius used the term to mean a perfect individual or 'perfect virtue', as a person's distinguishing characteristic. During the Tang and Ming dynasties, influenced by Buddhism's universal compassion, Neo-Confucianism extended the meaning of *jen* to the notion of 'forming one body with Heaven, Earth and all things.' In 17th- and 18th-century China the emphasis moved yet again to the social and active aspects of *jen*, that of people living together harmoniously. 'To apply one's own wishes and desires as a yardstick by which to judge one's behaviour towards others is the true way of *jen*' (Confucius, *Analects* 6.28). When he was asked what he thought the essence of *jen* was Confucius replied, 'To love your fellow men.' It is necessary to understand that the motivating energy behind this is entirely secular, there are no religious presuppositions behind Confucius's ethics. It is founded on the simple pragmatic notion of the ideal behaviour of one person towards another. See **Yi**

Jenoi *H*. The sacred thread given to Hindu boys at their *Upanayana*, initiation. See **Sacred Thread Ceremony**

Jesuits *X*. Members of the Society of Jesus, a **Roman Catholic** monastic order founded by Ignatius **Loyola**, Francis **Xavier** and others, on August 13th 1534, taking the vow of poverty and chastity. Pope Paul III gave his approval in 1540. As a reaction to the **Reformation**, it spearheaded reforms within the Catholic Church and took the missionary initiative, especially in newly discovered parts of the world. The Order was at the pope's disposal and its members, who wore no distinguishing habit, were exempt from the Offices of public prayer. Gradually, the work of the Jesuits became focused in teaching and supervising catechisms. Loyola's Manresa treatise, better known as the 'Spiritual Exercises', is a compilation of meditations and rules designed to help adherents overcome all the obstacles met in giving themselves entirely to God. Missions were established worldwide. In the 17th century the casuistry of the Jesuits was opposed by the **Jansenists** and others and eventually in the mid-18th century they were expelled from Portugal, Spain and France. In 1773, Clement XIV suppressed the Society. In 1814 it was formally restored by Pius VII, since when it has continued to function across the world.
FINAL WORD: 'I do further declare that the doctrine of the churches of England and Scotland, of the Calvinists, Huguenots and others of the name Protestants or Liberals to be damnable and they themselves

damned who will not forsake the same. I do further declare, that I will help, assist and advise all or any of his Holiness' agents in any place wherever I shall be … and do my uttermost to extirpate the heretical Protestants or Liberals' doctrines and to destroy all their pretended powers, regal or otherwise.' (From the Jesuit Oath of Induction)

Jesus Christ *X.* The founder of Christianity, born in Bethlehem, c.5 BCE and who lived in Nazareth in Galilee until c.27 CE. Tradition records his presence in the Temple, aged about 12, but nothing is known about the intervening years during which he disappeared from view, re-emerging when he started his public ministry, marked with his **baptism** by **John the Baptist**. Much of his teaching was offered as the fulfilment of **Old Testament** prophecy in which tradition he presented his message. He preached about a God who is pre-eminently the Father and of the immanence of his **Kingdom**. Jesus' mission was to the Jewish people and like the prophets that preceded him, he was concerned to revitalize a spirituality lost in the casuistry of law and ritual. Although the Jews recognized in him an authority equal to that of Moses, his messianic language presented the Jewish establishment with a challenge they resisted. At what might have been the celebration of the **Passover**, Jesus interpreted his anticipated death as an acted parable, using the bread and wine as symbols of his body and blood, thus initiating what became the **Eucharist**. Following his betrayal by Judas and his trial by the Sanhedrin, the Jewish court, he was found guilty of blasphemy and handed over to Pontius Pilate for crucifixion. The date of his death has been variously suggested as 29, 30 or 33 CE. Three days after being interned in a cave tomb, Jesus revealed himself to his disciples in a recognizable form. The **resurrection**, together with the doctrine of the Virgin birth and the miracles performed by him, combine to make a rich mythology, capable of profound spiritual and theological interpretation.

Apart from brief references in **Josephus**, Tacitus, Suetonius and the **Talmud**, the main sources available for Jesus' life are the four **Gospels**. Vast libraries of books have been written to expound the Bible in terms of Jesus fulfilling the Old Testament prophecies and to develop the theologies, philosophies, doctrines and creeds that appear like milestones down the centuries of Church History. Alongside these interpretative traditions has been the search for the Jesus of history, since clearly the Christ, the Jesus of the Church, is a Jesus defined by the subjectivity of belief statements. *The Quest of the Historical Jesus* (the title of Albert Schweitzer's classical account) began with the criticism of Christianity first prompted by the **Enlightenment**, and subsequently by 19th-century **Source** and **Form** criticism, techniques brought to bear on the analysis of biblical texts and the influence of **Bultmann**'s process of **demythologizing**.

Jesus Movement *X.* A general term referring to groups of evangelical Christians that sprung up in the 1960s, spreading over the next decade throughout North America and Europe. The movement was partly a reaction to the liberal **counterculture** of the 1960s and its adherents were sometimes dubbed 'Jesus freaks'. They were energetic in their 'rediscovery' of Jesus, using all forms of media to communicate their message, including poster campaigns, Jesus bumper stickers and 'Jesus Loves Me' sweatshirts. Some branches of the movement remained within recognizable affiliations like **Pentecostalism**, but other, independent groups like the Christian World Liberation Front, were thought to be heretical or concerned with political lobbying. The movement influenced the formation of heterodox groups, such as the Catholic Charismatic Renewal and Jews for Jesus which, unsurprisingly, has caused orthodox Jewry some concern. See **Children of God**

Jesus Revolution Army *X*. Their website reads 'for the salvation of the Youth of Europe'. The interdenominational movement was founded in Norway in 1997 by Stephen and Anne Christiansen, its aim is to convert young people to Christianity through concerts and road shows, with follow-ups by teams from each locality. It is not in opposition to any existing church and welcomes co-operation. Those who wish can train in Oslo to work as missionaries and with the concert tours; there are currently about 180 young people involved. Their beliefs reflect a biblical fundamentalism which aims to influence spiritual life throughout Europe; personal commitment to Jesus as the 'living Lord' is more important than a specific church affiliation. See **Jesus Movement**

Jew *J*. Heb. *Yehudi* via the Latin *Judaeus* and the Greek *Ioudaios*. For the Greeks and Romans, Jews were the people of Judea, the southernmost of the two kingdoms of biblical history. Thus originally, the name 'Jew' referred to a member of just a small section of the early Israelites. Broadly a Jew is anyone who is an adherent of **Judaism**, but because the term's ethnic associations are combined with religious commitment and national affiliation, the definition has become complicated. Thus the name has two distinct meanings: a member of the Jewish race and someone who believes in Jewish religious dogma. The meanings may or may not coincide. In an Israeli census a person may declare themselves to be a Jew and at the same time, an atheist. Alternatively, a non-Jew may convert to the Jewish religion, but for Jewish Orthodoxy this will not make him 'a Jew' since Jewish racial law deems a person to be 'a Jew' only if the mother is Jewish. **Liberal** and **Reconstructionist** Judaism allow a Jewish father as a criterion. The **State of Israel** which is constitutionally **secular**, is made up of a comprehensive cross-section of most religions and races. Generally speaking, for Jews of every nationality, ethnicity probably takes precedence over theology. See **Jewish Humanism**

Jewish Humanism *J*. A movement within Judaism for which Jewish history and culture are a more significant criteria of Jewish identity than religion, which may or may not be adhered to by its members. The Society for Humanistic Judaism affirms that a Jew is someone who identifies with the history, culture and future of the Jewish people and that Jewish identity is best preserved in a free, pluralistic environment. Judaism is the historic culture of the Jewish people, who possess the power and responsibility to shape their own lives independent of supernatural authority. See **Scientific Study of Judaism**

FINAL WORD: 'We are humanistic Jews. We believe in the value of our secular identity while cherishing the values of our Jewish identity. … Our humanism and our Judaism are intimately intertwined.' (From a service created for the 13th Annual Meeting of the Society for Humanistic Judaism: Quoted in *Humanistic Judaism*, Spring 1983, Vol. XI, No.1)

Jewish Renewal Broadly, a diverse movement concerned with the reinvigoration of Judaism by means of Hasidic, meditative and musical practices. In this sense, it is to be found throughout the various Jewish denominations. The worldwide 'Jewish Renewal Movement' claims 'to be grounded in Judaism's prophetic and mystical traditions'. It brings together **Kabbalistic** and Hasidic practice within an non-Orthodox but egalitarian framework and addresses contemporary issues such as pacifism, drugs, feminism and environmentalism. The Movement is clearly syncretistic, borrowing from **Buddhism**, **Sufism** and **Amerindian** religion, as well as from other faiths. For this reason Jewish **Orthodoxy** regards the Movement as being outside the religious prescriptions of the Jewish faith. See **Alliance for Jewish Renewal**; **Chasidism**; **Jewish Humanism**; **Judaism**; **Judaism, Reconstructionist**

Jewish Zen *J. Z.* Mostly an attitude and a disposition to a certain kind of humour. The Jewish ability to turn the direst situation into a joke, coexists easily with the Zen notion of emptiness which when practised takes the heat and tension out of any situation. The jokes, of course, hide real anxiety and suffering which become evident when the humour is peeled away. The parody of the famous Zen koan, 'What is the sound of one God clapping?' disguises what Jews throughout history have suffered in sustaining their monotheism.

FINAL WORD: 'The Torah says, "Love thy neighbour as thyself." The Buddha says there is no "self". So, maybe you are off the hook.' (Source unknown)

Jihad *I.* Arab. from the root 'to strive' or 'to fight'. Originally the duty incumbent on all Muslims to fight unbelievers. In practice it has various shades of meaning. The term may be applied to a struggle with oneself to overcome evil and sin or generally to fight to improve standards of morality and the quality of faith of the Islamic community as a whole. The most familiar use of the term is concerned with the effort made to convert unbelievers and when this is collective, it is understood to be a 'holy war'. (See *Dar al-Harb*, 'Territory of War', or 'War Zone') The Koran (2:186ff) exhorts Muslims to 'Fight in the way of God with those who fight with you, but aggress not: God loves not the aggressors. And slay them wherever you come across them and expel them from where they expelled you; … Fight them, till there is no persecution and the religion is God's; then if they give over, there shall be no enmity save for evildoers.' These and other Koranic verses clearly refer to the original Islamic community and specifically to Muhammad's war against Mecca. While other texts make a distinction between *Jihad* against Jews and Christians, the original call to *Jihad* always referred to an inter-Arabic conflict on Arabian territory. World media is constantly focusing on the threat of *Jihad* beyond the nations now governed by Muslims. The terrorist attacks in New York, London and elsewhere and the struggle for Palestinian autonomy are examples of *jihad*. Koranic fundamentalism holds that *jihad* is to be fought until the opponent pays tribute money. (See **Zakat**, alms, one of the five obligatory **Pillars of Islam**). In short, *jihad* can only be carried to another community of Muslims, whether that be a city or a nation. Thus in Islamic law, *jihad* against a Western power is not possible, it has no Koranic sanction and Muslims know this to be true. See **Fatwa, Wahhabis**

Jina *Ja*. In Jain religion (see **Jainism**), a 'victorious one', a sage who having achieved omniscience purifies the law where it has been corrupted by people. There are thought to have been 24 Jina, who appeared in succession over very long intervals. Some scholars regard jinas as gods because they are venerated as such by the Jains; others understand them to be archetypes of the perfect existence of an individual soul, a model to which a Jain can aspire. Jina are pure souls, omniscient, happy and eternal. Everyone has the potential to become an ideal soul and thus a god.

Jinn *I*. Arab. Creatures of air and fire that have conscious intelligence. In the folklore and mythologies of Islam which have their origin in pre-Islamic polytheistic religions. They are similar to **nymphs** and **satyrs**. In the Koran they are described as being parallel to human beings but made from fire rather than clay. Islamic folk religion recounts how jinns can be invoked to perform magic (Aladdin's genie of the lamp) or healing. See **Satan, Shaytan**

Jiriki *B. Z*. Jap. 'One's own power', referring to the personal efforts to actualize **enlightenment** and achieve **nirvana** as, for example, in **Zazen**. The term is used in contradistinction to *tariki*, 'the power of the other'. At another level however, **Zen** teaches that no one can actually go it alone. The path of *jiriki* becomes a manifestation of the 'other' in the process of passing beyond duality. See **Dualism**

Jivan mukti *H. S*. Pun. *Jivan*, 'life', with *mukti*, 'liberation'. A belief held by Hindus and Sikhs that an individual can attain liberation during the course of the present lifetime and it is not just something to be hoped for at death. For Hindus, the belief is contained within **Advaita** philosophy which teaches that the adherent must undertake rigorous ethical practice together with the worship of the Personal God (see **Ishvara**), so as to purify the mind in preparation for intense meditation on the impersonal Divine reality. This leads to the transcendence of dualism and to the realization that the individual's body and the rest of the phenomenal world are illusory. For Sikhism, *Jivan mukti* is the highest spiritual state to which the individual can aspire, combining being in tune with the Ultimate and at peace with society. See **Moksha**

FINAL WORD: 'He alone is liberated while still living Who is cleansed of the ego inside.' (Guru Granth: 1010).

Jnana *H. B.* Skt. From the root *jna*, 'to know'. In **Hinduism** the term refers to both general and spiritual knowledge or wisdom. It is the apprehension of the ultimate reality of **Brahman** and **Ataman** being one. It is a purely intellectual path leading to knowledge of the divine and, hopefully, free of the distortions of emotion and reason. As such it is thought to be the most abstract and difficult path to follow. In **Buddhism**, the Pali form of the word, *nana*, is an integral part of wisdom, the intellectual knowledge about the real nature of phenomena and natural law. **Mahayana** regards *nana* as the mastery of the rational aspects of the Buddha's teaching. The concept is similar to the Greek *gnosis*, knowledge or direct perception, that has influenced the doctrines and theology of Western religion. See **Gnosticism**

Jnana-yoga *H.* Skt. The 'way of knowledge'. One of the four principal yogic paths. See **Yoga**

John Frum *P.* A legendary person associated with the **Cargo Cults** of the south Pacific island nation of Vanuatu. A native, Mancheri, posed as the god 'Kerapenmun' and, under the alias Jon Frum, promised to provide from the delivered cargos, housing, clothing, food and transport. The followers believe Frum will one day return on the 15th February, which is celebrated as John Frum day. The Duke of Edinburgh who is revered as the head of the cargo suppliers, is also worshipped by the cult. John Frum is still politically active, led by Song Keaspai. Mancheri's alias is presumed to have been taken from American GIs introducing themselves, as 'John from America'.

John of the Cross, **St** (1542–91) *X.* A Spanish Carmelite friar, notable for his partnership with St **Theresa** of Avila in reforming the **Carmelite** order. He is also celebrated for his poetry and his writings on the growth of the soul as it progresses from detachment to 'creatures and materialism', to its attachment to God. His works are thought to be the high peak of Spanish mystical writing and have influenced many other writers and philosophers throughout history. In recent times these include T. S. Eliot, Thomas Merton and the French Catholic philosopher Jacques Maritain.

John the Baptist *X*. Known as the 'forerunner of Christ', his birth was foretold to his father Zacharias by the angel Gabriel. Tradition, according to Luke, gives his birth to be about six months before that of Jesus, hence the Catholic feast of John the Baptist held on the 24th June. John proclaimed a message of repentance and baptism and Jesus of Nazareth was among his candidates. His denunciation of King Herod led to his death (See Matt.14:1–12) but his continued influence is attested by Acts18:25 and there is an extra-biblical reference to him in **Josephus**. The importance of his cult is indicated by his place in the traditional Canon of the **Mass**, and that he is acknowledged as a prophet by the biblical religions, Islam and the Baha'i Faith.

Jombola Cult A mystical cult, made up of several hundred men and women. The group came to light in the war-torn southern regions of Sierra Leone. It surfaced in November 1996 after the signing of the peace treaty between the government and the rebel Revolutionary United Front. The cult created mayhem in the regions through which it moved, murdering and destroying property. There are clear signs of the practice of magic and witchcraft and it is believed members have the power to turn themselves into various kinds of animals such as cats, bats and dogs. A captured cult member admitted that, 'Our objective is to overthrow the government and the Kamajors, the local hunters' militia and we are doing this not only by force of arms, but through the power of the dark.'

Josephus, Flavius (c.37 BCE–c.100 CE) *J*. Born into a priestly family with royal ancestry, he became a historian and apologist of Judaism. As a young man he was one of the original leaders of the **Zealots'** 'Great Rebellion' and among the last defenders of **Masada**. He avoided the suicide pact and, surrendering to Vespasian, became a Roman citizen and successful historian. His account of the events of Masada is the only one to have survived. His writings are an important source of information about Judaism and Jewish history.

Jotun *AE*. The giants of Norse mythology, a race of superhuman beings who although mingled with the gods by marriage, were opposed to them. They are clearly mythological but the tradition exists that they may have been descended from an ancient Scandinavian people who became 'writ large' in the accounts of the myths. The land they inhabited was known as Jotunheim with its capital, Utgard. See **Fire Giants**, **Frost Giants**

Ju *Con*. The ethical philosophy of Confucianism with four basic virtues: *Chih*, insight or wisdom; *Jen*, the compassion that enables one to identify with the joys and troubles of others; *Li*, the correct understanding and practice of ritual together with the rules by which human relationships are conducted; *Yi*, righteousness or the sense of justice, responsibility, duty, one's obligation to others.

Juche Kor. 'self-reliance'. A secular ideology which is, in effect, the North Korean form of Marxist Communism (see **Marxism**). It is known also as 'Kimilsungism', named from its founder, Kim Il-sung. Gathering momentum since the 1950s, it is the only government-authorized ideology, all other religions being excluded. The ideology is a syncretism derived from **Neo-Confucianism**, Soviet **Stalinism** and **Maoism**, its core principle being that 'man is the master of his own destiny.' It is promoted as a secular, ethical philosophy, but as a sub-set of Communism Juche can be read as a secular alternative to religion. However its adherents, virtually the total population, assert its independence of Communism. The ideology requires total loyalty to the party and to its current leader, Kim Jong-Il. Ceausescu, the luckless President of Romania visited North Korea and Juche probably influenced his policy of systematization.

Judaism The origins of Judaism and the Jewish people are unclear, the only source being the biblical narratives written by **Hebrews** from orally transmitted tradition. In an important sense, Judaism is founded in its history and its God is the God of history. The narrative and purpose of God's history is focused on the '**Chosen People**', who by virtue of a **covenant** were elected to fulfil a specific role, namely to be a witness to the one God. The historical tradition establishes **Abraham** as the first and most significant **patriarch** of the Hebrew people, but his religion is markedly different from that formed after the **Exodus** from Egypt, the **revelation** to **Moses** on Sinai and the subsequent return to **Canaan**. The religion of the Jewish people, as we know it today, developed from the period following the destruction of the second Temple in 70 CE and the councils of Yavneh, 70–132 CE and Usha, from 140 CE. These councils effected a radical shift from the priest-driven, sacrificial cult of biblical Judaism, to a religion of the home and the **synagogue**. Judaism became almost entirely a lay religion, its communities led by a **Rabbi**, an authority on *Halakhah*.

At the heart of Jewish faith is its **monotheism**, a belief in the one God who will send a **Messiah** to inaugurate **redemption**, and judge the actions of each individual, rewarding or punishing accordingly. The core of Jewish belief is perfectly expressed by the *Shema*, the central prayer of Jewish liturgy which opens, 'Hear O, Israel, the Lord thy God, the Lord is One.' It is on this rigorous monotheism that all Jewish theology is founded. The one God is the absolute sovereign, both transcendent and immanent, an eternal and incorporeal Divinity and it is abhorrent to the Jew to conceive of God's unity being in any way compromised. For this reason Judaism has always been at odds with the Christian doctrine of Trinity. Judaism requires absolute faith in God whose existence is not demonstrable by reason and Jewish sacred literature does not attempt to explain an existence that is presumed. Hebrew offers several names for the one God, the most important being the **Tetragrammaton**, *Adonai* and *Elohim*. Other names are used to express attributes of the one God, for example *El Shaddai*, 'God Almighty', *El `Elyon*, 'The Most High

God', *El `Olam*, 'Everlasting God', *El Hai*, 'Living God' and *El, Elohe Israel*, 'God, the God of Israel'. In response to his request for a name, Moses got the reply, *Ehyeh asher ehyeh*, 'I am that I am' (Exod. 3.14). All the variant translations imply what is embedded in the Hebrew and established by Jewish theology, that God is beyond expression or definition. God's reply to Moses turns us to the nature of his 'being' and the belief that we are formed in his image. On this basis Jews hold to God as the ineffable ground of their own being.

Second only to God in Jewish life is the place of **Torah**, **Talmud** and **Mishnah**. Each of these is covered under their own entries thus, briefly: the Mishnah is a vast collection of Jewish legislative writing, the Babylonian and Jerusalem versions of the Talmud are commentaries on the Mishnah and *the* Torah refers to the **Pentateuch**, the first five books of the **Old Testament** ascribed, by tradition, to Moses and specifically to the handwritten scrolls that are housed in the **Ark** of the **synagogue**. More broadly, Torah is used for the entire revelation from God both in oral and written form and concerns both practical and speculative teaching on just about every aspect of Jewish daily life and thought. What is of uttermost importance is the reverence given to these writings and to the study of them. It is claimed that 'the scholar is greater than the King,' and the Jews approach to study, especially the study of Torah, confirms this ideal. The learned Rabbi or sage is believed to embody Torah, he is so immersed in it that every tiny thought and action of his life is a living expression of it. At the heart of Torah is wisdom, which is said to have existed before the creation of the world. The Book of Proverbs affirms that 'the Lord founded the world by wisdom', and that wisdom is itself a partner with God in creation, 'when he appointed the foundations of the earth, I was with him as a confident' (Prov. 3:19 & 8:30). However, study, knowledge and wisdom are not enough of themselves; the only true expression of Torah is to be found in the way the Jew observes *mitzvah*, the code of law that guides every aspect of Jewish custom, ritual and daily life. Throughout Jewish history, it has been the observation of *mitzvoth* that has defined a Jew and made Judaism culturally distinctive The observation of the 613 *mitzvah* is the visible evidence of a Jew's orthodoxy and of his obedience to the Divine will. For this reason orthopraxy is probably a better way of describing traditional Judaism than orthodoxy. Obedience, however, is not just an outward sign of a Jew's fidelity, it is also a means of nurturing a close fellowship with God. Both **Chasidism** and **Kabbalism** practice a mystical interpretation of *mitzvoth*, believing each act of obedience has universal significance that concerns the coalescence of all things with the essential unity of God. Alan Unterman quotes a Chasidic meditative prayer used before the benediction of a *mitzvah*, 'For the sake of the unification of the Holy One, blessed be He [the divine masculine principle] and His Shekhinah [the divine feminine principle], in awe and devotion I am prepared and ready to perform mitzvah, X or Y, to fulfil the command of my creator.' Many Jews, less devout, will observe *mitzvoth* on the grounds of moral principle, others select those considered to be relevant to a postmodern society, still others regard *mitzvoth* as an aspect of culture or symbolic of Jewish history. Orthopraxy thus enshrines the essential point of *mitzvoth*, in that life lived in obedience to them is *imitatio dei*. This has important implications for an understanding of Judaism. The first is that human beings are not automata, they have a choice about the way they live and the freedom to choose is axiomatic to Judaism. The second is that for the perfection of both individual and community the combined effort of God and man is required; the concept of God as not being self-sufficient and needing man, is the unique perception that underlies Kabbalistic mysticism.

Although throughout its history, attempts have been made to find a concise and formal expression of doctrine, Judaism is a faith without a formal **creed**. The most significant of these summaries are the '13 Principles of Faith' of Moses **Maimonides** (1135–1204). These are cast as a hymn, the *Yigdal*, used in Jewish liturgy with the creedal formula, 'I believe with perfect faith …' The *Yigdal* is not however a creed because it is thought to lack the logic and philosophical weight that would protect it from contradictory interpretation. There are sound, practical reasons for putting the emphasis on orthopraxy. A code of practice based on obligations to the Law is more easily understood and controlled than systems of belief presented as philosophy or theology. A unified code of practice provides an observable and accountable bond that has held Jews together during centuries of **Diaspora**. Thus a 'good' Jew is likely to be a 'Halakhic' Jew (see **Halakhah**) that is, for example, 'one who keeps the **Sabbath**, and 'one who supports charity'. It has to be said, however, that observance of the law is ineffectual unless born out of a love of God. Behind this code of practice lies an extensive theology, both implicit and explicit, regarding the nature of God and the world, the nature of man and the complex relationships between these. Judaism has no saints, nor does it glorify its own heroes. The **Haggadah**, the liturgical book that tells the story of the Exodus and which is used for the celebration of the **Passover**, makes no mention of Moses. The world in which the Jew lives is understood to be basically good, but not perfect. It can be improved, even perfected through man's partnership with God. God needs man as much as man needs God. This mystical aspiration of mutual dependence, is mirrored in life by the belief that a Jew's duty is to use his own potential to serve God and his fellow human beings. But the individual is free to choose whether he follows the path of Torah or not. He has the ability and responsibility to mould his own life. Kabbalah teaches that the soul is a spark of the **Godhead**, an element of the divine within man, it is therefore immortal. However, doctrines about the after-life and the future of the **soul**, remain unclear, one should serve God without thought of reward. Redemption is more readily understood as the salvation of society, than of the individual. The Jew rarely prays in the first person singular, he sees himself as he believes God sees him, as a member of the Jewish people, the people of the covenant.

The hub of this attachment is the family. The Sabbath, and all the major festivals of the Jewish year are celebrated in both the synagogue and the home. The cohesiveness of the family is undoubtedly one of the reasons why Judaism has survived millennia of persecution and dispersal; these two, family and synagogue, hold the Jewish faith in creative tension, the latter being a meeting place for 'a family of families'. The liturgical calendar guides Jews through the observation of the major festivals. Sabbaths and festivals begin with sunset, ending with nightfall marked by the appearance of the first star. In addition to the weekly Sabbath, the principal festivals are **Chanukah** (the festival of lights), *Pesach* (the **Passover**), *Purim*, *Shavuot* (**Pentecost**), *Sukkoth* (Tabernacles), *Rosh Ha-Shanah* (New Year) and *Yom Kippur* (the Day of Atonement). There are numerous minor festivals associated with special Sabbaths such as *Rosh Chodesh* (the new moon) and fast days in commemoration of events in Jewish history, for example, the destruction of the Temple, Nebuchadnezzar's siege of Jerusalem and Moses' descent from Sinai with the tablets of the law.

Judaism is the only major religion which combines the concepts of 'a people' and a faith that may or may not interconnect. Without Jews there would be no Judaism, but Jews who do not profess their faith or any kind of religious belief would, nevertheless, staunchly regard themselves as Jews with an inalienable attachment to the Jewish community anywhere in the world. The 19th century saw the beginnings of movements that questioned traditional **orthodoxy**, and which aimed at modifying beliefs and practices. These movements have evolved into **Conservative**, **Reform** and **Reconstructionist** Judaism, as distinct and separated denominations. Attitudes towards the significance and centrality of *halakhah*, the Law, is the main distinguishing feature between these denominations. Modern Judaism has been irrevocably influenced by the **Holocaust**, and redefined by the establishment of the State of **Israel**. See **Bar Mitzvah**; **Covenant**; **Jew**; **Jewish Renewal**; **Judaism, Conservative**; **Judaism, Ethnic Divisions of**; **Judaism, Orthodoxy**; **Judaism, Reconstructionist**; **Judaism, Reform**

FINAL WORD: 'How odd,
> Of God to choose
> The Jews,' mused W. N. Ewer.
> To which a Jew might reply,
> 'It is not odd.
> The Jews chose God.'

Judaism and Secularism *J*. Judaism's responses to secularism is complicated by the question of Jewish identity and the extent to which this is defined by the observance of *Halakhah*, and ethnic or national (Israeli) identity. Israel is a secular state and makes a clear distinction between constitutional citizenship and the religious status of individuals, which is decided by religious law. Given that a person is a practising Jew, secularism is simply understood as the natural milieu in which life is to be lived. The Bible has no word for either 'religion' or 'secularism', since every aspect of human existence is God's rightful domain or 'kingdom'. Everything is therefore the concern of religion. The Jew regards secularization in Western culture to be a consequence of the dualism imposed on society by Christianity's distinction between the **Church** and the world, the sacred and the secular. Only such dualism can conceive of areas of life that are not sacred and of a way of life without God. Such perceptions are anathema to the Jew committed to orthodoxy and orthopraxy. Thus, for the Jew, secularism is but one of many scenes set on the stage of life against which Halakhic Man plays out his distinctive role. Many positive responses to secularism have been by Jewish thinkers (see **Scientific Study of Judaism**). One such recasting is offered by the philosophical anthropology of Martin **Buber**, which interprets the principles of *Halakah* in terms of interpersonal relationships. See **Humanism**; **Jewish Humanism; Judaism, Ethnic Divisions of**

Judaism, Conservative A movement in modern Judaism that occupies the middle ground between Orthodoxy and Reform. It continues to insist on the revelatory authority of *Halakhah*, the Law, but argues that since its interpretation has always changed through history, it is not a fixed tradition. This philosophy of change legitimizes a creative reinterpretation of Law. The Conservative Jew thus has it both ways; in line with orthodoxy, the Law is obligatory and remains central, but is malleable and adaptable to the socio-cultural needs of a changing society.

Judaism, Ethnic Divisions of *J*. Several ethnic communities have come to light since the founding of the **State of Israel** in 1947. The **Ashkenazim** and **Sephardim** make up 90–95 per cent of the world's Jewish population, but among the minority are small Jewish communities settled in and sometimes assimilated by other cultures. It is possible only to give a brief selection of these.

Africa: The Beta Israel from Ethiopia, well known as the **Falasha**, were brought to Israel in their tens of thousands by Israeli initiatives such as Operation Moses and Operation Solomon, effecting the Law of Return, the right of a Jew anywhere, to become an Israeli citizen. The related group, the Falasha Mura, were Ethiopian Jews who had converted to Christianity, but who have since reclaimed their original faith. The 'House of Israel' comprises several hundred of the Sefwi tribe from Ghana and there is an emergent Jewish community of some 30,000 among the Ibo of Nigeria and a variety of smaller communities scattered around other regions of Africa.

The Americas: *Iglesia Israelita* are found among Amerindians in Chile. Believing themselves to be Jewish they observe some of the laws and festivals. Inca Jews from the Andes, north of Lima, Peru, are converts to Judaism. Some of them are of Amerindian descent, others *mestizo*, mixed Spanish and Amerindian. Many of these have made the *aliyah*, the 'ascent', the term used for Jewish immigration to Israel and have undergone orthodox Jewish conversion.

India and China: The Bene Israel, are Jews of Mumbai, India, many of whom now live in Israel. Bhaghdadi Jews came to India in the 18th century, from Iraq, Iran, Afghanistan and Arab countries. Bnei Manashe, who live in northeast India, claim to be the descendents of the biblical tribe Menasseh. The most prominent of Chinese Jews are the Kaifeng, descendents of merchants living in China from the era of the Tang Dynasty (c.618–c.907 CE). Many of their descendents are currently redis-covering their heritage.

Many other minority Jewish ethnic groups are to be found throughout the Middle East and Central Asia, as well as in Europe and the Caucasus. The whole pattern does much to substantiate in history the myth of the 'Wandering Jew'. There is no doubt that they wandered, but the intriguing anthropological question is, how many of these tiny groups are the vestiges of the **Lost Tribes**? See **Twelve Tribes of Israel**

Judaism, Orthodox Orthodox Judaism insists on an uncompromised belief in the divine revelation and authority of **Torah** and its laws, both in its written and oral forms. In addition, Rabbinical writing throughout Jewish history, is also both divinely inspired and immutable. The *Shulhan Arukh*, the 16th-century codification of law compiled by Joseph Caro, together with subsequent commentaries and emendations, provides the final definition of orthopraxy and since Judaism revolves around practice, this may be a better term than orthodoxy. An example of modern Jewish orthodoxy or Neo-orthodoxy as it was called, was that of Rabbi Hirsch (1804–88). The leitmotiv of his movement was 'Excellent is the study of Torah together with a practical livelihood.' Like many leading intellectual German Jews, Hirsch was influenced by the humanitarian idealism of, for example, the poet Friedrich Schiller. Hirsch coined the phrase 'Israel-Man' to define the Jew who is both orthodox and cultured, but because of a demand for a Judaism that allowed more integration with the non-Jewish world, Hirsch's fundamentalism faltered. Nevertheless orthodoxy remains a strong energy in the various currents of Jewish thought. It opposed the establishment of the State of **Israel**, on the grounds that this would be achieved by divine intervention at the outset of the messianic age.

Judaism, Reconstructionist An American Jewish movement founded by the Lithuanian, Mordecai Kaplan (1881–1983) who was ordained as an Orthodox Rabbi, a tradition he left in 1922 to form the Society for the Advancement of Judaism. Kaplan's reconstruction of Judaism might well be understood as socio-cultural rather than theological. He started by examining different aspects of American Judaism, concluding that **Reform** was right in accepting the imperative to change and that **Orthodoxy**'s commitment to the immutability of Law and the orthopraxy that went with it, made the religion static and lifeless. Kaplan accepted the **conservative** commitment to *Wissenschaft des Judentums*, the **Science of Judaism** and its history, but considered it held too tradition-ally to the role of *halakhah* (the Law 'has a vote but not a veto'), and lacked the will to respond to rapidly changing social conditions. Kaplan's philosophy is crystallized in the question that was ever before him, 'What shall man believe and do in order to experience that life, despite the evil and suffering that mar it, is extremely worthwhile?' He defined 'worth-while' in terms of salvation, 'When religion speaks of salvation it means in essence the experience of the worthwhileness of life,' an experience that combines moral responsibility with loyalty, love and service, which in turn leads to self-fulfilment. In practice this involves 'reciprocity with others'. Kaplan's concept of reciprocity was inherent in the 'organic' nature of Jewish communities which he hoped to establish as a world-wide network. His philosophy concerns the tension between the religious and the secular, a conjunction ever present in the history of Judaism.

Judaism, Reform A modern movement in Judaism that does not neces-sarily believe that *halakhah* was part of God's revelation and for that reason is not binding. Reform Judaism, sometimes thought of as being post-*halakhic*, was influenced by the philosopher Franz Rosenzweig (1886–1929) who said that a modern Jew might find some of the Laws relevant and useful to his circumstances and that using these meaning-fully engendered both a personal piety and a personal freedom. In Reform synagogues men and women sit together following a liturgy that combines Hebrew with their natural language. The Reform perception of **diaspora** was not as an exile caused by the vicissitudes of history, but as a God-given mission to carry the message of ethical monotheism to the world. See **Pittsburgh Platform**

Judea *J.* A Greek and Roman reading of the name of the territory Judah, the southernmost of the two kingdoms that made up biblical Palestine, **Israel** being the northern kingdom. Judah was the fourth son of Jacob and Leah and the eponymous ancestor of the tribe and country of Judah. The biblical history of Judea (c.933–568 BCE) is complex and can be traced through the relevant books of the **Tanakh**, the Hebrew scriptures. In terms of Judaism's spiritual history, that the Kingdom of Judea lasted over 150 years longer than the northern Kingdom of Israel, is significant. Judea had the inestimable advantage of the single and uninterrupted Davidic dynasty, with a people whose character was disposed to monotheism and social justice. Of equal importance was the Hebrew prophetic movement which although originating in Israel, nevertheless took root and had far greater influence in the southern kingdom.

Judgement of the Dead Most religions share, in one form or another, the idea that a person's final destination in a future life depends on the quality of the life lived in this world. That final place could be the kind of hell depicted by Virgil, a place of retribution where demons and writhing snakes inflict continual misery on sinners or it could be a place of bliss, of the kind suggested by **Paradise**, a garden of joy and peace. A person's fate is determined by a post-mortem judgement, the earliest account of which was inscribed on Egyptian **Pyramid Texts**, c.2400 BCE. Egyptian sources also provide us with the concept of a future destination being held in the balance, as the heart is placed on scales and weighed against Truth. This has carried into Western thought via **Coptic**

Christianity, as a *psychostasis*, a weighing of the souls. Medieval concepts of the judgement maintain the Paradise-Hell dualism; Dante's *Inferno*, describes ten divisions of hell which allow the punishment to be suited to the crime. Neither Greek nor Roman religion offered a clear hope of an afterlife, thus there was no defined concept of judgement. The influence of the cult of Orpheus and Neo-Pythagoreanism, led to the belief that the fate of the dead turned on whether or not the subject had been initiated into the Mysteries (see **Mystery Religions**). **Zoroastrianism** proposed the **Chinvat Bridge**, the Bridge of the Separator, the crossing of which is a post-mortem ordeal; the wicked will fall off into the abyss, the good will reach the 'paradise' of the other side. Christianity (see, for example, Matt. 25:31–3) portrays the Last Judgement both as an Assize of Nations and as a trial of individuals. The Revelation account (20:11–13) adds the **Apocalyptic** tradition that the judgement will include the resurrection of the dead, summoned by the **Last Trump**. Islam teaches the post-mortem judgement tradition of Judeo-Christianity. Buddhism has no concept of judgement, but pending a person's full 'awakening', the law of **karma**, and the **transmigration** of souls determines whether or not the individual is to be liberated from the birth-death-rebirth cycle of *samsara*. See **Eschatology**

FINAL WORD: 'And the pit of torment shall appear and over against it shall be the place of rest: and the furnace of hell shall be showed and over against it the paradise of delight.' (IV Esdras, Ch.6)

Juggernaut *H.* Skt, *Jagannatha*, 'Lord of the Universe'. It is one of the many names for **Krishna**, together with that of the Temple of Jagannatha at Puri in Orissa. An annual ceremony, the Ratha Yatra, takes the form of a procession of chariots bearing statues of *Jagannatha*. The chariots were huge in size and height and frenzied adherents were sometimes crushed under the wheels. Doubtless, through British colonialism, the term 'juggernaut' came to mean any outsized vehicle or an inexorable force that crushes everything in its way. Since 1968, the festival has been seen in the West through the activities of the **Hare Krishna** movement.

Juju *A.* The term is Hausa originating in Nigeria. A juju is an object used as a **fetish**, **charm** or amulet, characteristic of West African tribal ritual and magic. The term may also be applied to the spirit power ascribed to the object. The practice of using jujus is still widespread.

Jung, C. G. (1875–1961) Carl Gustav Jung was one of the 20th century's most influential psychiatrists. A disciple of **Freud**'s, he went on to criticize his mentor for being too focused on repressed sexual tendencies as an explanation for nervous disorders and his book, *The Psychology of the Unconscious* (1912), included further radical criticism that led to the permanent rupture of their friendship. Jung painted on a wider canvas; his concept of the 'libido', for example, went beyond that of Freud's 'energy of the sexual instincts', to a more general drive that certainly took account of sex, but included the energies of fear, anger and the emotions.

Jung abandoned Freud's term 'psychoanalysis' and adopted 'analytical psychology' to describe his own theories and therapeutic methods. His system was much concerned with the integration of opposites, such as masculine and feminine (the unconscious animus and anima) thinking and feeling, science and religion. In seeking integration he turned from experimental natural sciences, preferring to study the world of dreams, myth and psychopathology, on the way to a deeper understanding of the unconscious. In this, he was influenced by William **James** who believed the only valid basis for the analysis of the mind, was experience. The aim of Jung's work was to reconcile the individual with the world of supra-personal archetypes; this is a life-long process that he called 'Individuation' and is both subjective, in that a person becomes a whole, integrated, indivisible unity, and objective in that it, necessarily, involves relationships. In developing his theory, Jung proposed the formative concept of a 'collective unconscious', the idea that all human beings have a common psychological make-up, in the same way that they have a similar physical form. The 'collective unconscious' has been called the DNA of the human psyche and is indispensably related to Jung's concept of archetypes and his discovery of the shared, but uninfluenced, symbolism existing across all cultures. It was in this context that Jung examined religion, understanding it to be mythological, not real in essence, but having a real effect on human personality. In contradistinction to Freud, who believed religion to be a neurosis, Jung understood religions to be 'indispensable spiritual supports' (Thomas Szasz). Jung's later studies were concerned with alchemy, astrology, spiritualism and folklore, which in addition to his theories of psychiatry created the system inevitably dubbed, 'Jungianism'. There are those for whom Jungianism has become a 'religion', or at least a satisfying substitute for it, in that it offers a perception of life that has a meaning, indeed of a life the meaning of which is accessible through Jung's work. It allows the traditional religious focus in a god or the Divine as an absolute expression of, for example, the archetypal father-figure; it also allows for the abandonment of metaphysics, substituting for it a concept of the psyche that can be wholly secular. See **Psychology of Religion**, **Transpersonal Psychology**
FINAL WORD: 'All esoteric teachings seek to apprehend the unseen happenings in the psyche and all claim supreme authority for themselves. What is true of primitive lore is true in even higher degree of the ruling world religions. They contain a revealed knowledge that was originally hidden and they set forth the secrets of the soul in glorious images.' (Jung [1969])

Juno *R*. Identified by the Romans with **Hera**, she was worshipped as the queen of heaven and the protectress of females, as **Jupiter** was of males. Juno was responsible for watching over women from birth to death and the month of June, named for her, was considered to be the best month for marriages. She is associated with the cult of **Hercules** and the 'Herculean Knot' that bound the bride's marriage girdle, that could only be untied by her husband. See **Roman Religion**

Jupiter *R*. The **Zeus** of the Greek **pantheon**, Jupiter became the patron deity of the Roman state, otherwise his mythology is the same as that of Zeus. In the Roman cult his name was adopted for the planet and more apparently from the French *Jeudi* (Jovis) for the English 'Thursday'. His credentials are comprehensive, with epithets associating him with heaven, light, lightning, rain and thunder, victorious armies and with the lover of the gods. Plutarch's and Livy's history of early Rome tells of his power and sovereignty in the tale of Romulus invoking Jupiter to terrify Rome's enemies. As the cult became established, Jupiter became the head of the Archaic Triad, with Mars and Quirinus. They combined, through their respective function, to be the symbol of Roman society. Jupiter assumed the augural role of the priests or **Flamens**; Mars' agricultural and warlike functions represented the powers of leaders to bring prosperity and victory; Quirinus, 'men together', symbolized the combined strength of the Roman people. During the Imperial period, emperors such as Julian, Claudius and Domitian, had their portraiture styled on characteristics of Jupiter so as to represent their absolute and universal authority. Jupiter's principal temple was on the Capitoline Hill, where he was worshipped with the two other members of the Capitoline Triad, **Juno** and **Minerva**. There was a period when Jupiter was associated with justice and, in the Roman courts of law, people swore on oath to Jove, leaving us with the expression, 'by Jove', a phrase less used now than it once was. See **Roman Religion**

K

Ka *E*. The 'life force', the distinguishing element between the living and the dead. See **Soul, Egyptian concept of**

Ka'bah *I*. Arab. 'Cube-shaped'. 'House of God', or 'shrine', specifically the large construction that is the pivotal point of the mosque in **Mecca**. It is the focus of the **Hajj** pilgrimage, the seven times circumambulation by the pilgrims, a ritual re-enactment of the angels walking around the throne of God in heaven. One corner of the Ka'bah contains the Black Stone (see **Hajar al-Aswad**) which the faithful try to touch or kiss in the belief that doing so will absolve them of all sin. The Ka'bah is covered with the *kiswah*, black draping embroidered with verses of the Koran. Each Mosque is furnished with an architectural feature, the *Mihrab*, which indicates the direction of Mecca towards which Muslims must face when they pray and prostrate themselves. In this way the Ka'bah becomes the 'point' that focuses Islam both as a religion and as a community.

FINAL WORD: 'Thus, the Ka'bah which is historically the symbol of the Unity of Religion and the consecration of the Unity and Oneness of the Only True God, comes to symbolise and consecrate the Unity, Equality and brotherhood of those who bow themselves in willing submission to Him Alone and are committed to the Guidance and the Way He has chosen for them.' (Abul-Fadl)

Kabbalah *J*. Heb. 'reception' or 'received', in reference to knowledge. An esoteric and complex Jewish mysticism that emerged in Provence, southern France in 12th century CE, in the form of a book called the *Bahir*, 'Brightness'. Its authorship is not known but it was modelled on the **Midrash** and influenced by **Neoplatonism**. In the 13th century Kabbalah spread to Spain, where Gerona became the centre of an important Kabbalistic school. The **Zohar** (*The Book of Splendour, Radiance, Enlightenment*) the principal Kabbalist text, was written or compiled in Spain in the 1280s CE, partly in Hebrew and partly in Aramaic. Its principal author was Moses de Lyon. He adopted the literary device of creating a 2nd-century CE context for the book, using the voice of Rabbi Simeon ben Yochai, but the Zohar as we know it was probably not finally completed until the 16th century, when it was printed. The book is an anthology of texts concerned with the hidden meaning of the Jewish scriptures, particularly the **Pentateuch** and its account of creation and the cosmos. Medieval Jewish philosophy perceived God as 'one' and totally transcendent. In the Zohar, Kabbalists spoke of two aspects of God, the *Ein Sof*, the 'infinite', and the **Shekhinah**, a feminine emanation of God that could be directly experienced. These two polarities, transcendence and immanence, are connected by ten *sefiroth*, a matrix of spiritual realities which constitute a path the individual can follow to the point of union with the divine. The *sefiroth* are represented by a system of symbols that have distinct mythological associations, the most familiar being a tree, sometime referred to as the **Tree of Life**. Another image is of *Adam Kadmon*, Primal Man, an archetypal human being. 'Sin' nourishes the forces of evil or impurity, while virtue earned by faithful and literal observation of the law, keeps evil under control and maintains the harmony of the cosmos. In that they have responsibility to observe the *halakhah*, the Law, human beings are in control of both personal and collective destiny. There are two important implications of this; the first is that human beings have a choice about the way they live and the freedom to choose is axiomatic to **Judaism**. The second is that for the perfection of both individual and community the combined effort of God and man is required; that God is not self-sufficient and that he needs man, is the uniquely Jewish perception that underlies Kabbalistic mysticism. Kabbalah is thus, a symbolic blending of mythology, **Gnosticism** and **dualism**, all of which are in conflict with mainstream non-mystical Judaism.

In the 16th century Kabbalistic mysticism was further developed by Isaac Luria (1534–72) known as 'the Holy Lion', who addressed the problem of how God could create a world 'outside' of himself since he was, himself, everything. Luria's answer introduced the concept of *tzimtzum*, God's self-contraction; the *Ein Sof* withdrew from a central point creating a spiritual vacuum within which God created the world. From this premise, Luria developed a complex account of how, in creation, evil became entrapped and how through a process of **reincarnation** or **metempsychosis** the human soul will be reborn countless times until it succeeds in being perfected. The whole involved structure of Luria's mysticism is known as, the Lurianic Kabbalah.

Kabbalah has had considerable influence on Judaism's exegetical and theological thinking and since the middle ages on Christianity (see **Christian Kabbalah**). There are today numerous non-Jewish forms of Kabbalistic practice, such as the **Hermetic Order of the Golden Dawn** that has its origin in 19th-century syncretism. In this form the ten *sefiroth* are combined with Greek and Egyptian deities and systems of **magic**. More familiar perhaps, is the revival of Kabbalah through Philip Berg and his Los Angeles Kabbalah Centre, established in 1984. Aided by his sons Yehuda and Michael Berg, he has opened branches across the world. It has become something of a **New Age** cult, attracting celebrities such as Madonna, Demi Moore, Mick Jagger and Britney Spears. Unsurprisingly, it has been subjected to searching criticism by orthodox Jewish groups.

Kaddish *J*. Aram. 'holy'. A Jewish prayer most frequently associated with mourning for the dead, recited at funerals and at the graveside. In an orthodox home the son will recite the Kaddish every day for 11 months after the death of a parent. However, Kaddish is not only a mourner's prayer since variations are recited on occasions other than bereavement. It is used as praise and adulation in face of the wonder and magnificence of God, when the prayer is a link between various sections of the synagogue liturgy.

Kaffir *I*. Arab. An infidel or unbeliever. Tradition has it that the term was applied to the Meccans who refused to submit to Islam but more generally, a kaffir is anyone who rejects divine revelation. Modern Islam uses the term to identify other Muslims who refuse to live by a fundamentalist interpretation of the Koran. European settlers in South Africa called the Xhosa, kaffirs and the name became derogatively applied to all black South Africans. The Kaffirs of Sri Lanka are an ethnic people descended partly from 16th-century Portuguese traders and settled African slaves, their name is probably derived from an early period of trading between Portugal and Arabia. See **Kufr**

Kagyupa *B*. Tib. 'Oral transmission lineage'. One of the four main schools of Tibetan Buddhism. One of the main principles of the school is the importance of direct teaching or the transmission of instruction from teacher to disciple. The original teachings known as **mahamudra**, the 'great seal', were carried to Tibet by Marpa, a translator in the 11th century and after considerable ascetic discipline were mastered by his pupil, **Milarepa**. It was Milarepa's student Gampopa, who organized the teaching into a school. The principal emphasis is the direct transmission of the teachings from teacher to disciple. See **Gelugpa**, **Nyingmapa**, **Sakyapa**, **Tibetan Buddhism**

Kaharingan *P*. See **Dayak Religion**

Kakon *G*. The word Plato used in *The Republic* for 'evil', or what has been dubiously translated as 'evil'. In fact the meaning of **evil** does not have the same content before, as after the Christian Era. For Plato, an ominous intuition of evil was associated with privation, that is with a sense of the lack of something essential to being. Thus, *kakon* threatened non-being. Put simply, it is the absence of good, rather than a force that seeks to undermine it. Evil, as we think of it, exists for Plato only in the lives of people, that is when the absence of good is made manifest. Such an absence would have been a fundamental flaw in the nature of being, since it is axiomatic to his philosophy that human beings have an inborn or natural disposition to the good.

Kalam *I*. Arab. 'speech', 'reason'. It is one of the 'religious sciences' of Islam, developed by means of a dialectic process. Kalam begins with the received, revealed tradition and uses reason and logic to try and resolve ambiguities and seeming contradictions. It is concerned with the object of faith in three ways: i) to define its content, ii) to show that neither the faculty of faith nor its content contradicts logic or experience, iii) to provide the individual with personal reasons to be convinced of the content of faith. Kalam has been a feature of Islam theology since the 9th century. See **Islamic Philosophy**

Kalama Sutra *B*. A significant discourse of the **Pali Canon**, which the Buddha delivered to the Kalamas, a clan of noblemen. It is much quoted, since it includes the Buddha's critical teaching about not accepting something to be true simply on his or any other religious teacher's authority. Whether something is true can only be verified by trying it. The acid test of truth, the Buddha assures, is *prajna*, intuitive insight (see citation on page vi).

Kali *H*. Skt. 'black'. It has various associations such as the personification of evil, the 'snake-eyes' cast in a game of dice and most importantly, the terrifying aspect of the Earth Mother, Durga, the black-faced, vampire-fanged consort of **Siva**. Kali is usually represented as dancing with or in sexual union with, Siva. The symbol of division and destruction, her cult is centred on Bengal where she is celebrated in an annual autumn festival lasting for five or six days. Even into modern times travellers in isolated places could be set on and ritually strangled in Kali's honour.

Kalimah or **Shahadah** *I*. Arab. 'word of witness'. See the **Pillars of Islam**.

Kama or **Kamadeva** *H*. The Hindu god of love and the subject of the Kama Sutra, the text that describes the art or science of love. Kama is the son of **Lakshmi**, depicted as a good-looking, winged young man, sporting a bow and arrow made from sugar cane and honeybees; all the decorative accompaniments of his images are symbols of spring. There is a clear association with Cupid and **Eros**. Being touched by his arrows arouses the five senses, creating in the mind visions of beauty. Since he is identified with the desire that entraps us in **samsara**, Kama is not worshipped. In Buddhism he is known as **Mara**, a demon who is the enemy of enlightenment.

Kant, Emanuel (1724–1804) One of the most influential of European philosophers, developing a profound and complex system that combined the two most important philosophical movements of his time, the **rationalism** of **Descartes** and Leibniz, and the empiricism of **Locke**, Berkeley and **Hume**. He was the last philosopher of the **Enlightenment**. His most important works are his three *Critiques*, that *of Pure Reason* (1781), *of Practical Reason* (1788) and *of Judgement* (1790). By means of a critical examination of reason and metaphysics, Kant hoped to make advances in philosophy comparable to those made in science; he was an admirer of Newton. Kant's understanding of what 'critique' is amounted to an examination of what the mind can legitimately know. In terms of morality, for example, the purpose of 'knowing' is to enable us to judge whether an action is right or wrong. The test of the legitimacy of such knowledge is that it must have universal validity, that is, the criteria of moral judgement must be capable of being a universal law of nature. What is legitimately knowable in metaphysics is less clear but religious experience or an assertion based on it, must conform to the same criterion, that is, it needs to have features common to all such cases, so as to constitute a universal law of nature. Prior to Kant, making conclusions about the nature of the universe, God or the soul, was based on logical thought, on what seemed 'reasonable'. Kant's problem was that for every philosopher who asserted that God or the universe, must be like this or that, there was another who claimed the opposite to be true. For Kant, this was a state of affairs that debased both the human mind and the philosophies it gave rise to. Kant's radical break from traditional modes of thinking requires that we confine ourselves to the somewhat narrow limits of 'pure reason', which may draw only on the sciences and sense perception. Metaphysics was therefore 'doomed to failure', in that its claims were about concepts that could not be based on either science or the senses. Some schools of thought such as German Idealism and philosophers like **Heidegger** with a theological agenda, have refused to accept the limited terms of Kant's system and have attempted to arrive at a new metaphysical system that address such notions as the 'Absolute', 'God' or 'Being'. Generally, however, Kant's legacy has left the Western world with a rigorous rationalism that has deeply influenced the humanities and social sciences. The claim that it is possible to have an ordered and comprehensible world-view, with a secure epistemology has been taken up by many subsequent philosophers. In broader terms, Kant is to be seen in **Marx**'s social theories, in Freud's notion of the ego producing a principle of reality, in **Chomsky**'s transformational grammar and in modern humanities and social sciences that call on the 'social construction of reality'.

FINAL WORD: 'Live your life as though your every act were to become a universal law.' (Kant)

'Experience without a theory is blind, but a theory without experience is mere intellectual play.' (Attributed, Kant)

'Two things fill the mind with ever new and increasing wonder and awe – the starry heavens above me and the moral law within me.' (Kant)

Karapans *Zo*. The villains of the **Gathas**, the **Zoroastrian** sacred scriptures, who were a clan of priests against whom Zarathustra fought. He rejected their beliefs and rituals. See **Kavis**

Kardecism or **Kardecist Spiritism** A religious and philosophic doctrine originated in 19th-century France by Allan Kardec, a pseudonym for Hippolyte Leon Denizard Rivail. An academic with an accomplished scientific background, he became interested in the new vogues of mesmerism and spirit-tapping and set about doing his own research. The result was a series of influential books, the first, *The Spirits Book*, comprising 1,018 questions about spirits, the spirit world and its relationship to the material world. He used the pseudonym when told by a medium, that in a previous life he had been a Druid named, Allan Kardec. See **Spiritism, Swedenborg**

Karma *H. B. Z.* Skt. 'deed' or 'action'. A term carrying a wide and complex range of meanings central to Hindu and Buddhist teachings. In summary: i) karma involves mental or physical action, ii) the

consequences of these, iii) the accumulated consequences of these in an individual's present and previous lives and, iv) the knock-on consequences of the way we respond to an ethical code. A person's karma is created by their disposition or inborn tendencies, which themselves will be determined by a previous existence. It is a form of behavioural potential directing the motives that lead someone to act in a particular way. Karma will thus bear its own joyful or sorrowful fruit according to the seeds planted in a previous life. This should not be understood as a form of determinism or **predestination**. Whatever a person's karma is, they retain the freedom to determine how they live in each moment; they can choose to resist the negative tendencies or to cultivate the positive ones. This is the freedom of a person's inner consciousness. The most significant aspect of karmic law is this dependence on volitional actions for which a person can be consciously responsible. The second most important aspect of karmic law is that a person's karma is not, necessarily, determined by the nature of the action itself, but by the *intention* or motive behind it. Thus, if one hurts another person unwittingly no negative karma will accrue; but if one sets out to hurt a person, whether it be mentally or physically, then the result will be negative karma. Negative or positive karma will also accrue from an intention that cannot be carried out. What counts ultimately is what is the attitude of mind, whether or not, in any given moment, a person has the disposition to good or evil. Over countless lifetimes the accumulation of negative or positive karma become ingrained and will be apparent in a person's temperament or disposition. It is important to understand, however, that while karma can determine the manner or type of a person's rebirth, it cannot determine the way that person will live in moral terms. That remains within the control of everyone's free choice. See **Samsara**
FINAL WORD: 'If you want to know your past life, look at what your life is like now. If you want to know of your future life, look at what you do now.' (Padmasambhava)

Karmapa *B*. The title of the head of the **Nyingmapa** School of **Tibetan Buddhism**. The current incumbent is Holiness Gyalwang Karmapa, exiled from Tibet and living in northwest India.

Karma-Yoga Skt. One of the four principal yogic paths. See **Yoga**

Karmi no Michi *Shin*. 'The Way of the Gods'. See **Shintoism**

Kashatriya *H*. Skt. The second **caste** into which Hindu society was organized. They were the warrior and ruler class, whose function was to safeguard the community.

Kashrut *J*. The Jewish **dietary law**. See **Kosher**

Kasinas B. Visualized objects used to support **meditation** practice. The Pali Canon lists ten, earth, water, fire, wind, blue, yellow, red, white, space and consciousness. Sometimes, for example, a coloured disc was set up and used as a preliminary image. The practitioner concentrates on this until the external physical object becomes a mental or acquired image. Further concentration leads to a counter-image which when held steadily induces *dhyana*, total absorption or trance. See **Visualization**

Kathenotheism A term coined by the philologist and orientalist Max Muller (1823–1900) to describe a system of religious practice centred on the worship of one god at a time. In a polytheistic culture, the supreme god may change and the focus of worship will change with it. Muller put it this way; 'a monolatrist worships one god throughout life (that is, if they do not convert); they accept that other gods exist, but they do not worship them. A kathenotheist may worship many gods throughout life, but only one at a time. Kathenotheism is a sub-type of **henotheism**.'

Kavis *Zo.* In early **Zoroastrianism** Kavis were a wealthy, but corrupt ruling class opposed by Zoroaster. Their priests, the **Karapans**, practised black magic. **Yasna** 46.11 tells us that 'By their dominion the Karapans and the Kavis accustomed mankind to evil actions, to destroy Life. Their own soul and their own self shall torment them when they come where the Bridge of the Separator is.' See **Chinvat Bridge**

Kensho *Z.* Jap. 'Seeing nature'. The **Zen** term for **enlightenment**. 'Seeing nature' is understood to refer to one's own true nature, thus *kensho* is sometimes translated 'self-realization' (see *satori*).

Khafre *E.* Egyptian King (2520–2494 BCE) The builder of the Great **Pyramid** and the massive complex that includes the **Sphinx**. See **Egyptian Religion**

Khalsa *Sik.* Pun. The community of *amritdhari*, comprising Sikhs initiated by the *amritsankar* rite. The community was founded in 1699 by Guru Gobind Singh, the tenth and last of the Sikh **Guru** Preceptors. While there were political reasons for forming the Khalsa community, there were spiritual associations as the Guru believed himself to be manifest in the Khalsa. 'The Khalsa is my other self, in it I live and move and have my being. So long as the Khalsa remains distinct I will confer glory on it' (**Guru Granth Sahib**). Perhaps to ensure the Khalsa remained distinctive, the Guru provided its members with five distinguishing characteristics, the **Five Ks**, together with the **Khalsa Code**, a code of conduct which set the group apart from the rest of society. See **Amritsankar, Sikhism**

Khalsa Code *Sik.* Pun. *kurahit*, 'prohibitions'. Sikhs initiated into the **Khalsa** are required to abstain from, removing body hair, tobacco, meat killed in the Muslim tradition, adultery and sexual intercourse with Muslim women. Men were required to add Singh to their names and women, Kaur. See **Amrite, Amritsankar, Sikhism**

Khandhas or **Skandhas** *B. Z.* Skt. 'group' or 'aggregate'. See **Five Aggregates**.

Kharijites *I.* Arab. 'those who seceded'. A general term for a variety of Islamic sects which rejected the Caliphate of **Ali**, the cousin and son-in-law of **Muhammad** and the fourth Caliph of the **Sunni** Muslims. The Kharijites were neither Sunni nor **Shiite** but a sect apart and their belief that Ali's caliphate was invalid was the cause of the first Islamic civil war. Like all civil wars it was a struggle for power, in this case for supremacy over the Muslim community. In 656 CE, the third Caliph, Uthamn ibn Affan, was murdered and Ali was involved in a conflict for the succession with Muawiya, governor of Damascus. The ensuing battle was stopped when Muawiya commanded his troops to hoist copies of the Koran on their lances, a signal that he wanted the conflict to go to arbitration rather than to fight over it. Ali agreed and some 12,000 members of his army thought they had been betrayed and stood down. These were later to be known as the Kharijites, meaning 'those who seceded'. Arbitration, they argued, belonged to God alone and that God's decision would be ratified by the result of the battle. They actually opposed both sides, Ali for submitting to arbitration and Muawiya for his original rebellion against Ali's caliphate. Their belief was based on Surah 49:9 of the Koran, which asserts the right to fight if peace is not possible and if one party transgresses 'beyond bounds against the other'. The outcome was that Ali defeated the rebellion in 658 but was himself murdered by the Kharijites in 661, while praying in a mosque.

Kharijite belief is founded on radical fundamentalism and the absolute equality of the faithful. Extreme and violent in their practice of *jihad*, holy war, they advanced the cause of anti-authoritarianism. Only the most pious should be a Caliph, elected by the entire community of believers. They were severe in all their relationships, imposing *takfir*, a denial of Muslim status and a form of excommunication, on those deemed to be less than orthodox. Many such were killed. New recruits had to submit to *imtihan*, a 'test of sincerity' which entailed cutting the throat of a prisoner or *isti rad*, 'demonstration', which took the form of the 'religious' murder of men together with their wives and children. The territory occupied by other Muslims was deemed **Dar al-Kufr**, the 'house of unbelief (see **Dar al-Harb**, the 'Territory of War' or 'War Zone') as Muhammad had called Mecca at the time of his 'emigration' to Medina. During the years 690 to 730 CE they made Basra a centre of Islamic theology which provided the *raison d'être* for rebellion against the Sunni Caliphate.

The Kharijites have survived into the present day through the Ibadis, although they reject the original name. They constitute a substantial part of the population of Oman, where they first settled in 686 CE. Other, smaller communities can be found in Algeria, Tunisia, Libya and Zanzibar. See **Umayyad Caliphate**

Khlysty An orgiastic flagellant sect who believed in overcoming sin with sin, primarily through group sex. See **Skoptsy**

Kiddush or **Kiddish** *J*. Heb. 'sanctification'. The traditional ceremonial blessing and prayer made over the wine, the symbol of joy, and bread the symbol of plenty, at the start of the Jewish Sabbath on Friday evenings. The Kiddush is similarly used for other festivals. There are other forms of Kiddush, one recited before the morning meal on the Sabbath and festivals and the prayers recited in the synagogue at the conclusion of evening prayers on the Sabbath and festivals. The Kiddush Lebanah, is the Blessing of the New Moon. See **Judaism**

Kierkegaard, **Soren (1813–55)** Danish philosopher and theologian, who set himself against **rationalism**. His philosophy emphasizes the primary importance of the 'existing individual' and analysing aspects of religious consciousness such as faith, choice, despair and dread. In so doing he provided the underlying theories that gave rise to **existentialism**. The central questions of his enquiry were, 'What is the point of a man's life?' 'What sense is there to be made out of human existence?' 'What is the purpose of human events?' His writing gives a sombre picture of human life as anguished, absurd, frightening and meaningless. He was influenced by Plato's *Meno*, which sets out his theory that learning anything new is a 'recollection' of something already residing within us (see **Innate Ideas**), otherwise we would have no standard and would not be able to recognize it as 'truth'. Kierkegaard built on this notion, but reasoned that we don't actually carry *all* knowledge within us. That being so, something additional to recollection is needed; his solution is one of the most important concepts of his thought. What is needed is 'the leap of faith', which amounts to an enlightenment. This presupposes an 'enlightener' who for Kierkegaard is God. But in the process of being enlightened by our leap of faith we have changed, we are not the same person as we were before the leap of faith was taken. Of themselves, human beings are not capable of knowing anything with certainty, thus something in the order of a miracle is required. Kierkegaard's 'miracle' is this radical 'change', an individual transformation, but it is something we must desire and once experienced must accept without judgement or qualification. The relationship between ignorance and knowledge is exactly parallel to that between doubt and faith. Doubt is an aspect of faith and for Kierkegaard, to have without ever having doubted, is a poor kind of faith; for a person's faith in God to mean anything, it can only be founded on doubt. The 'self's' relationship to the world is subjective, grounded on introspection and reflection. 'Subjectivity is truth. And truth is subjectivity.' It amounts to 'self' being the ultimate discerner of what life is and what life means.

Kierkegaard had no interest in establishing a unified all-explaining system that accounted for absolutely everything. According to the trend of his time he wrote pseudonymously under several names, but also because he wanted to express the view that the self has many faces and it is for this reason that his philosophy reflects the multifaceted and fragmentary nature of the self. His influence was so considerable, that it is impossible to survey it here other than to say it touched the arts and existential psychology, philosophers as diverse as Jaspers and **Wittgenstein**, theologians as opposed as **Tillich** and **Barth**, and novelists as varied as Camus and Updike.

Kimbanguist Church X. Its full name is, L'Église de Jésus Christ par le Prophète Simon Kimbangu. It was founded in the Lower Congo in 1921 by Kimbangu who was a **Baptist** mission catechist. By means of his miraculous healings and biblical teaching he set in motion a mass movement that provoked the suspicion of the Belgian authorities. Kimbangu was arrested for sedition and spent the greater part of his life in prison where he died. The Church is based on a puritan ethic and avoids politics, violence, polygamy, alcohol, tobacco, dancing, witchcraft and magic. In 1959, the Church was recognized formally and is thought to have three million adherents in Zaire and neighbouring countries. It is a member of the **World Council of Churches**.

Kimilsungism North Korean form of Marxist communism. See **Juche**.

Kingdom of God X. For Judaism this meant a visible manifestation of the just rule and sovereign power of God, not at present actualized, but will be so on the 'Day of the Lord'. It is this Jewish eschatological understanding that lies behind Jesus' teaching about the Kingdom. It emerged, however, that as Jesus proclaimed it the Kingdom was not to be political or social, but the revelation of God's saving power, spiritually realized. There are two emphases found in the realization of the Kingdom, one being that it can be established now, in this life, within the individual, by faith or by the sacraments; 'The Kingdom of God is among you,' or 'within you' or, 'within your grasp', being the variant translations of Luke 17: 20–21. The other emphasis is the future, eschatological hope, concerning the end of time and the post-judgement Kingdom of righteousness that will be governed by Christ in Majesty. There is a third interpretation which understands the Kingdom of God to be the Christian Church developed in history, a point of view associated with the Jesus of history (see **Jesus Christ**) which regards the cataclysm of judgement and the prophesied apocalyptic conclusion to time, as the dispensable, mythological context which obstructs a clear perception of the Jesus of history. The term 'Kingdom of Heaven' is also used, but specific religious qualities and ethical standards are to be met before a person can be received into 'the Kingdom', whatever its designation. The eschatological hope of the 'coming' Kingdom is inextricably linked in Christian theology with the Second Coming of Christ, Eternal Life and the resurrection of the body. The name, 'The Kingdom of God', is also given to a black Jewish community founded in the 1960s, in Chicago, by Ben Ammi Carter. The group are now based in Israel. See **Black Jews, Eschatology**

Kirtans *H. S.* Devotional songs. See **Bhajan**

Kitawala *A.* A radical synthesis of African and Christian religion, first appearing in the Katanga (now Shaba) region of the Congo (Zaire) in the 1920s. It stemmed from South Africa, where black American missionaries of the **Watchtower Bible and Tract Society** (see **Jehovah's Witnesses**) converted miners. The movement, which spread into the copper mining regions of Katanga, was anti-colonial but had no effective political or revolutionary strategy. They practised radical equality, believed in the immanence of God's kingdom on earth and the taking back of Africa for the Africans. As with the Kimbanguists (see **Kimbanguist Church**), the State attempted to repress the movement by a process of rural isolation which had the effect of strengthening the cause, as exiled members converted their new rural neighbours. Eventually, because the anti-colonial message became so strong, the Watchtower sect renounced it. In 1979, Kitawala caused riots and deaths and has suffered strong repression. Many have now moved deep into forest areas so as to avoid all contact with civil authorities.

Knights of Columbus *X.* A Roman Catholic fraternity named in honour of Christopher Columbus. Its membership is open to 'practical [practising] Catholics', in union with the Holy See and over the age of 18. The Order's agenda includes charity, fraternity, patriotism and unity. Pope John Paul II called them 'the strong right arm of the Church'. It was founded by Father McGivney in 1882, in New Haven, Connecticut, spreading rapidly through the USA and abroad. The object was to provide a fraternity for Catholics too frequently excluded from Unions and other men's organizations and to offer a Catholic alternative to **Freemasonry**. The reference to Columbus was a statement against Anglo-Saxon Protestantism which, marginalized Catholic immigrants. Their organization is hierarchical, with the Supreme Knight represented by State Deputies and Councils. They have ceremonial uniforms and closed rituals. The term 'Knight' is purely fraternal and has no sovereign status. Today, the Movement is a multi-million-dollar, non-profit-making, charitable organization.

Knight's Hospitallers See **Hospitallers**

Knights Templar There is no clear evidence connecting the medieval **Order of Knights Templar**, with its modern manifestation as a branch of **Freemasonry**, an international templar organization concerned with philanthropy. Membership is restricted to Master Masons of the Mark Master Degree and the Holy Royal Arch Degree. A candidate must be of sound moral character and reputation and believe in a Supreme Being (however generally this is cast). See **Masonic Knights Templar**

Koan *Z.* Chin. *kung-an*, 'a legal case offering a precedent' or 'Public notice'. Sometimes wrongly referred to as riddles, koans are brief stories, sayings or snatches of dialogue taken from various sutras and other sources that present a paradox or a question, that might seem absurd. A famous example is the koan called 'Mu'. A monk asked the **Zen** master, Chao-chou, if a dog really has buddha-nature or not? In response, Chao-chou said, *Mu*. It is the task of the Zen student, while practising **Zazen**, to go beyond intellect and come to an immediate experience. The *Mu* koan is a *hosshin-koan*, one that is suitable to help a student make a breakthrough and therefore given early in training. The *Mu* is to be experienced and when the student has succeeded in doing so, he is said to know 'the world of *Mu*'. The answer cannot be arrived at by reason (thus a koan is not a riddle) but lies beyond thinking, logic and conceptualization. Zen masters have used koan training since the 10th century. Working progressively through koans enables the student to break down the rational habits of the mind and discover the limits of thought, thus to arrive at the point where thought itself is transcended. In this way, the student is able to offer the master his own solution to the problem in the form of a *wato*, the word or words in which the koan is resolved. Koan training is associated mostly with the **Rinzai** school of Zen, but is also used in the **Soto** school. Rinzai identifies five types of koan, each aiming to train the student in differing ways. There are numerous collection of koans, but two anthologies are particularly well established. *The Blue Cliff Record* is a translation of the *Pi Yen Lu*, a collection of 100 koans accompanied by commentaries and verses from the teachings of Chinese Zen masters. First compiled in the 11th century and completed in the 12th it is considered one of the great treasures of Zen literature and an essential study manual for students of Zen. *The Gateless Gate* was compiled towards the end of the 12th century and finally published in 1229. These collections are compilations of classical koans, but the tradition continues with modern masters composing their own.

Komeito *Jap.* A Japanese political party made up of Buddhist laity, an off-shoot of **Soka Gakkai**, sometimes known as the 'New Clean Government Party'. Its manifesto declared the Party's mission to pioneer, 'people-centred politics, a politics based on a humanitarianism that treats human life with the utmost respect and care.' It is a working example of Buddhist **humanism**, appealing to the poorer classes who are not members of the labour unions or 'salarymen', thus lacking the security of lifetime employment. It has its own universities, schools and press. A candidate will join the church of the person who has introduced them to the cult, hence it cuts across local and family affiliations. Like Soka Gakkai, Komeito appears to have overtly secular interests. Chie Nakane, explains how its horizontal associations will have interests in banks, insurance companies, industrial plants, export and import business and shipping companies. It is obvious how these links might combine in commercial projects such as real estate and land development. See **Japanese Religions**

Konkokyo *Jap.* A Japanese **Shinto** sect, founded in 1859 by Bunjiro Kawate. Its religion is syncretistic, **henotheistic** and **pantheistic**. God is worshipped under the name of Golden God of Heaven and Earth or the Parent God. Everything is believed to be in interrelationship with everything else, thus the Parent God is not remote but an integrated part of the whole. Suffering is the consequence of individual disregard for the intricate network of human and spiritual relationships. Konkokyo aims to make the world a better place by prayer, mutual help, apology and gratitude. By this means being linked with God, each person can become *Ikigami*, a living God and at death will return to the Parent God. The deceased remain in this world as part of the Golden God. Most adherents believe Konkokyo to be an independent religion regardless of its official status as a Shinto sect. There are something like 1,700 churches in Japan, with close on half a million adherents. Through missionary work, the sect has been carried to several countries.

Koran Arab. 'recitation'. The sacred scriptures of Islam comprising God's revelation to **Muhammad**. Muhammad received the Koran by revelation *Tanzil*, being the sending down from God. The transmitting agency or mediator between God and the Prophet is described in the Koran as the 'Holy Spirit' and the 'faithful spirit'. God tells Muhammad, 'We have revealed to thee a spirit of our word.' What is meant by 'spirit' is unclear, but Muslim tradition associates 'faithful spirit' with the archangel Gabriel. Islam affirms that the Koran is the last and final scripture or the last 'edition of the divine will'. Surah 85.22 tells of a 'preserved tablet' on which the text was inscribed, that it existed in heaven before the creation of the world. Thus the Koran was not created, but is eternal. The revelation was given gradually, starting in 610 CE and to begin with only the first five verses of Surah 96 were transmitted. Muhammad had to wait two years for more when he was given the assurance that what he was receiving came from Allah and not from the devil. From that point onwards the revelation was given until his death in 632 CE. It was the third Caliph, Uthman, who 20 years after Muhammad's death put together what is considered to be the definitive version, comprising 114 Surahs or chapters of varying length. The basic message of the Koran is summarized by the term *Tawhid*, the defining doctrine of Islam founded on absolute monotheism. It is the final authority on all questions of religious faith and practice and on ethical, social, economic and political principles.

All major religions based on revealed truths fixed in sacred literature, have been faced with the question of the relative value of the knowledge so received, compared to the knowledge derived from independent human reasoning. Since sacred literature exists as a guide to the mysteries of the origins of life and to the complexities of living, it is inevitably subject to interpretation. Islam, as is apparent, is not exempt from the conflicts caused by variant readings, some of which are literal and conformed to what orthodoxy believed to be an unchallengeable authority, while others are flexible, with an eye on the needs of a world radically different to the age in which the revelation was first given.

FINAL WORD: 'The Koran was assembled from a variety of prior Hagarene texts (hence the contradictions *re* Jesus' death) in order to provide the Moses-like Muhammad with a Torah of his own ...' (Robert M. Price)
'This Book is not to be doubted ...' (Koran 2:2)

Koran Alone Muslims *I*. An orthodox tradition in Islam that rejects the **Hadith** or any other literary or oral additions to the Koran. They hold to its exclusive authority and build their belief and practice on it. See **Mohammedans**

Kore Kosmou One of the longer, stand-alone **Hermetic** texts. Its odd name may mean 'daughter of the world' or 'pupil of the world' or 'virgin of the cosmos'. It has connections with the earlier mythologies of Egypt and the god Thoth, with whom Hermes was later identified. John Stobaeus' 5th-century collection of texts, *The Corpus Hermetica*, includes extracts from it. In one of these it is asserted that, 'no prophet about to raise his hands to the gods has ever ignored any of the things that are, so that philosophy and magic may nourish the soul and medicine heal the body.' It implies that all knowledge – magical, medical and any other – contributes to the quest for Gnostic salvation.

Kosher *J*. Heb. 'fit' or 'proper'. The term is used with reference to anything that according to Jewish law may be used without risk of contact with impurity. It is most frequently used in the context of food and the laws controlling diet. See **Dietary Laws**, **Judaism**, **Taboo**

Krewes Clubs founded specifically to organize participation in **Mardi Gras** celebrations. They may or may not have religious affiliation. Some of their affiliations may be with ancient Egyptian or Greek cults, but whatever their identity, their mandate is to ensure exuberant, costumed celebration. Membership may be hereditary and family orientated. They are famously associated with the New Orleans Mardi Gras.

Krishna *H*. Skt. 'black' or 'dark blue', a colour symbol of infinite space. There is a tradition that suggests Krishna was based on an actual historical figure; as such, he first appears in the Chandogya-Upanishad. His mythological evolution takes him from babyhood, through youth, to becoming a hero of the **Mahabharata**. When presented as a god he is the most important figure of Hindu mythology and considered to be the eighth incarnation of **Vishnu**. In the **Bhagavad-Gita** he is the 'Divine One' the teacher of Arjuna, who regarded him as ultimate universal consciousness. The life-story of Krishna, in the form of a collection of myths, legends and fairy tales is recorded in the *Bhagavad-Purana*, reputed to have been compiled in the 10th century CE. He has many human characteristics and is revered as the source of sacred and profane love, inspired by his affair with Radha. The **Radha-Krishna** theme was central to the cult of Krishnaism, developed from **Vaishnavism** in the

15th century. It was an early attempt to make Hinduism more appealing to ordinary people. The veneration of Krishna has become familiar in the west through the **Hare Krishna** movement, known also as the International Society for Krishna Consciousness (**ISKCON**) founded in the USA by Swami Prabhupada, who was its leader until his death in 1977. See **Haranath**

Krishna Consciousness See **Hare Krishna, ISKON**

Kriya *H. B.* Skt. *kri*, 'to do', 'to act', 'to react'. The term *kriya* conveys the notion of action, but not activity or effort at any cost. As an ancient and somewhat esoteric **yoga** technique, it claims to accelerate the subject's spiritual growth. The practice requires the controlling of the kriya so that a physiological balance is maintained. Its efficacy is based on dealing directly with the source of growth, a spiritual energy deep within our spines (see **Kundalini**), an energy with which all yoga techniques work, but indirectly. The claim for kriya is that the practitioner works directly with this energy, controlling the force by mentally drawing it up and down the spine. According to **Yogananda**'s teaching, one kriya, which takes about 30 seconds, is the equivalent of a year of normal spiritual growth. The implication is that the more kriyas one works, the greater the acceleration of a person's spiritual evolution. The technique of working a kriya is accessible only through initiation by a Kriyaban, a kriya yogi. It is called the 'science' of kriya yoga, because of the psychochemical and psychophysiological decarbonization of blood which is recharged with oxygen. The additional atoms derived from this are transmuted into the life-current rejuvenating the brain and spinal cords, transforming the cells into pure energy. As with all yoga disciplines much depends on the use and control of the breath. In kriya, the outgoing breath is subsumed by the inhalation and the incoming breath by the exhalation. The technique is similar to the circular breathing aboriginals use in playing the didgeridoo so as to sustain an unbroken stream of sound. Patanjali, Hinduism's foremost exponent of yoga, put it like this, 'Liberation can be accomplished by that **pranayama** which is attained by disjoining the course of inspiration and expiration.' The kriya technique, however, does not stand alone and is accompanied by other disciplines such as Energization Exercises, the Hong-Sau technique of concentration and the Aum technique of **meditation**. All of this has to be held within the tradition of discipleship, accepting the lineage of Kriya masters as one's spiritual guides and **Gurus**. Kriya is also a term used to categorize one of the four forms of **Tantra** in Tibetan Buddhism, that focus on external, object-based techniques of meditation and rituals.

Kufr *I.* Arab. 'disbelief'. A central concept in Islam with the word or its derivatives appearing in the Koran nearly 500 times. In its early use the term was used of anyone who denied the unity of God. Thus Jews, with their radical monotheism, were never dubbed *kufr*, while due to the doctrine of **Trinity**, Christians were. To believe in anything but the inviolable unity of God constitutes *shirk*, idolatry. There is some ambiguity within Islam as to whether some **Sufi** mystical perceptions and practices edge towards *kufr*, not as 'disbelief' but as a form of pluralism. See **Kaffir**

Kumarajiva *B*. 3rd–4th century CE. A Kuchean Buddhist monk who eventually became a **Mahayana** adherent. He is important to Chinese Buddhism for the prolific translations of Buddhist texts from Sanskrit into Chinese that included the Diamond, Amitabha, Heart and Lotus Sutras. He was more concerned to convey the message of the texts, than with their literal meaning and his style is characterized by a poetic smoothness. For this reason his work remains the preferred texts to later, more precise translations.

Kundalini *B*. A mysterious and esoteric form of Tantric yoga (see **Tantrism**) designed to rouse the dormant snake said to exist at the base of the spine. This is the lowest **chakra** in the human body, one of several centres of subtle energy. The snake is symbolic of unrealized spiritual knowledge and power and once aroused, it will rise through the chakras until reaching the highest which is above the crown of the head, stimulating mystical experiences and visions that lead the practitioner to **nirvana**. Such practices must be followed only under the supervision of an experienced teacher, without whom the yoga is considered to be dangerous. See **Kriya**

Kung-fu *C. Z*. A general term referring to a variety of Chinese martial arts which apply sharp blows and jabs to the body's pressure points. It applies to the principles of both judo and karate and has been popularized through the Hong-Kong kung-fu film genre, featuring Bruce Lee and also the eponymous television series. Originally, kung-fu was a form of Chinese boxing. **Shao-Lin** kung-fu is the form developed in the Shao-Lin temples. However, the term is used to denote the process of training and the developing of skills that are not necessarily martial, but concerned with strengthening both body and mind. Such kung-fu can be applied to cooking, painting, calligraphy or the tea ceremony. The Zen equivalent of kung-fu is *kufu*, which Suzuki [1970] describes as, 'one of the most significant words used in connection with Zen and also in the field of mental and spiritual discipline.' It means 'to seek the way out of a dilemma'. Both the intellect and the will can be used, but these are superficial and one must go deeper. It is this going deeper, this finding out the 'how' for oneself that is *kufu*. Suzuki affirms 'this is where spirituality lies and it is *kufu* that finally wakes us to our spirituality, distinguishing us from mere animality as well as mere mechanicality.' See **Chi**, **Chi-Kung**

Kurdish Religion The Kurds regard themselves as being indigenous to a region known as Kurdistan which includes areas of Iran, Iraq, Syria and Turkey. In recent times communities have established themselves in Europe and the USA. Throughout history they have struggled for independence, fighting against the Sumerians, Assyrians (see **Assyrian Religion**, **Sumerian Religion**), **Persia**, the **Mongols**, Turks and the **Crusaders**. Today they are thought to be upwards of 30 million Kurds which makes them the largest ethnic group in the world without their own nation-state. The majority speak Kurmanji. Their religious history is varied and complex having drawn on ancient traditions such as Yardanism, the 'Cult of Angels', three branches of which have survived and are still observed by a small percentage of the population. Yardanism holds to a belief in an omniscient Universal Spirit, *Haq* originally manifested as an **Avatar** who created the material world. There are also minority communities of Kurdish Jews, Christians and Baha'i. In recent years the Jews have emigrated to Israel. By far the greater majority of Kurds are followers of the Shafi'i School of Sunni Muslims as distinct from more dominant Hanafi. There is also a considerable following of Sufi mysticism.

L

Labbaika *I*. Arab. 'Here I am, here I am, present before you.' The phrase with which the Muslim pilgrim greets the *Ka'bah*, on arriving at Mecca for the obligatory pilgrimage. See *Hajj*

Labyrinth Gk. *laburinthos* or possibly *labrys*, 'double-axe'. The dynasty of King Minos was known as the House of the Double Axe and the architectural complexity of his palace compound at Knossos may have been the origin of the myth of the labyrinth. A labyrinth is an intricate structure of interconnecting passages in which it is difficult to find one's way. Some authorities make a distinction with the maze, which has blocked passages arranged in any form, while the passages of a labyrinth are all open and usually circular in form. In Greek Mythology, the labyrinth was designed and constructed by Daedalus as a place in which to hide the **Minotaur**.

The Cathedral of Chartres has one of the best-known Western labyrinths (see *Figure 3*). It is has been given various names: The 'Daedalus' from the Greek myth; the 'League', being the distance one might walk in an hour, the time it took pilgrims to work the labyrinth on their knees; the 'Road to Jerusalem' since walking the labyrinth was a substitute pilgrimage; and the 'Road to Heaven' since the faithful could rehearse their lives from birth (the entrance) to death, the 'Divine' centre. The way out symbolized purgatory and resurrection.

A labyrinth is a non-verbal, **numerological** and geometric image of multidimensional but invisible patterns that contributed to **sacred geometry**, the concrete representation of cosmic order and various levels of consciousness. Drawing, constructing or walking a labyrinth can be a ritual of self-integration, an enactment of the spiralling journey into and out of various incarnations (see **Samsara**), the physical body born at the entrance, metamorphosing to pure spirit on arrival at the 'Divine' centre.

The image and its symbolism is widespread through many cultures. The seven circuits of the classical labyrinth have been associated with Hinduism's seven primary **chakras** of the body ('chakra' meaning 'wheel of light') and with the form of Buddhist **mandalas**. The labyrinth is to found in **Amerindian**, **Celtic**, **Norse** and Medieval art.

There are also musical patterns for labyrinths constructed by an arrangement of notes (see *Figure 4*). Modern composers interested in composing

Figure 3 Chartres Cathedral labyrinth

Publisher:
Ahsha Studios

Labyrinth

Figure 4 Musical labyrinth

for the labyrinth form include Harrison Birtwistle and the Hungarian, Gyorgy Kurtag.

Lakshmi *H*. Skt. 'Fortune'. Also known as *Shri*, a personified goddess who brings both fortune and misfortune as the consort of **Vishnu** and the mother of **Kama**. She is worshipped as a goddess of happiness and plenty, for which reason her shrines are probably never neglected. Her iconography depicts her with four arms, but as she is also associated with beauty, she is more frequently shown with two, one of which enfolds a lotus flower.

Lama *B*. From the Tibetan *bla-ma*, 'none above'. A term for a religious teacher or guru, especially revered by his students because he is believed to be an emanation or embodiment of the Buddha's teachings. In **Vajrayana**, the Lama will not simply teach but conduct ritual and may be the head of monastery. The **Dalai Lama** stands at the head of **Tibetan Buddhism**. See **Panchen Lama**

Lamaism *B*. An alternative name for **Tibetan Buddhism**, a term also found in China and Mongolia and since the Chinese occupation of Tibet, in many centres throughout the world.

Lamb of God *X*. A name for Jesus Christ as the sacrifice made by God in order to redeem the world. It is based on **Old Testament** types or models of sacrifice and the belief that the blood of an animal had to be shed in order to propitiate sin. Leviticus 17:14 records that, '… the life of every creature is the blood of it'. It was in lamb's blood that the mark had to made on the doorposts of the houses of the Hebrews, so that when the Egyptians were afflicted with the killing of the first male born of every family, the Angel of Death knew to, 'pass over' that house. (Ex. 12) **John the Baptist** recognized Jesus as the Lamb of God (John 1:29) and, consistent with the New Testament's use of Old Testament types and parallels, the Messianic prophecies had to be fulfilled ' … with the precious blood of Christ, like that of a lamb without blemish or spot'. The symbolism was established in the sacrament of the **Eucharist**, 'for this is my blood, the blood of the Covenant, shed for many for the forgiveness of sins' (Matt. 26:27–28).

Land of Youth *AE*. In **Wicca**, the heavenly state in which the individual resides when no longer reincarnated. Wicca teaches post-death rebirth through many cycles until everything needing to be learned has been received and understood. In the Land of Youth, the spirit will be reunited with those with whom it had close personal relationships in previous lives. In Celtic mythology, the Land of Youth is one of the names for **Elysium**. See **Celtic Religion, Elysian Fields, Mag Mell, Reincarnation**

Landscape Symbolism Landscape, in all its forms, has provided religion with powerful symbolism, the most familiar being the concept of Heaven as being a garden paradise. Eden was a place set apart, where nature was 'tamed' and only beauty cultivated and where nothing needed to die in order to sustain another life. St **Anselm** thought it was spiritually dangerous to sit in a garden because it was too pleasant for the senses. A garden symbolizes the feminine, the secret source of life (the **Tree of Life**) or the golden apples of immortality that grew in the garden of the Hesperides at the end of the world. In contrast to the peaceful order of the garden, is the forest. In modern psychology (see **Freud** and **Jung**) the garden is sometimes taken to be a symbol of the conscious mind. By contrast the forest, with its strange noises and shadows and tangled undergrowth, represents the unconscious. The mountain is where a person may ascend to receive revelation or reach a higher spiritual realm, it was the home of the Greek gods and where God spoke to Moses. The desert or wilderness, outside the normal human environment, is a place of trial and temptation, where one's spiritual metal is tested and mystical visions are given. The Celestial City of Bunyan's *Pilgrim's Progress*, is set on a high hill, an image of the new Jerusalem of Revelation (Ch. 21) Other well used images are the valley of death, the city of God, the tower of strength, the slough of despond, the 'green pastures' or **Elysian Fields** of Greek mythology and still, silent, lakes, with their sinister and mysterious depths. The river is both Time that carries us all along and life, flowing from its source (birth) to its mouth (death) or the absorption of the one into the whole. See **Path Symbolism**

FINAL WORD: 'A garden locked is my own, my bride,
> A fountain locked, a sealed-up spring.
> Your limbs are an orchard of pomegranates
> And of all luscious fruits …
> You are a garden spring,
> A well of fresh water,
> A rill of Lebanon.'
> (The Song of Songs Ch.4)

Lao-Tzu *T*. Chin. 'Old Master'. Tradition holds him to be the author of the *Tao-te Ching*, and a contemporary of **Confucius** which places him in the 6th century BCE. Despite references in the official *Historical Records*, written 3rd–2nd century BCE, there is some doubt as to whether Lao-Tzu is a historical person and his reputation rests on tradition and legend. It is unlikely that he wrote or even contributed to the *Tao-te Ching* which is believed to have been written between 500–300 BCE. When Taoism became an established religion, Lao-Tzu was elevated to the status of a *Tao-te t'ien-tsun*, a god, a Celestial Noble of the Tao and Te and was revered as the founder of Taoism. Confucius is reputed to have told his students that, 'roaming animals may be caught in a pit or cage, fish with a rod and birds can be shot down with an arrow. The dragon however cannot be caught by such cleverness. It wings towards Heaven on wind and clouds. Today I have seen Lao-Tzu. He is like a dragon!' (Max Kaltenmark)

Lapp Religion *AE*. The Lapps are a nomadic, reindeer-herding people spread across northern Scandinavia, a vast territory known as Sapmi and the people as the Sami. These are the preferred names since 'Lapp', originally introduced into the Norse languages, is used pejoratively. The indigenous religion was practised until the 18th century until it was subjected to Catholic and Lutheran mission. It resembled that of the **Eskimos**, and was influenced by **Norse** mythology, with which it has elements in common, and later by Christianity. As might be expected, Sami gods represent aspects of the environment, natural phenomena and forces, with the sun god, Pieve, as the primordial cosmic being. Pieve has supporting gods of thunder, wind and moon. As with the Eskimos the dominant Sami cult is that of the *noaide*, the **shaman**, who uses the magic rune drum and the *fadno*, a flute-like instrument, to induce a trance in which his spirit leaves his body to journey to the 'other' world. The drum, made from fir, pine or birch, cut from a tree that is never touched by the sun, is hung with fetishes and charms made of brass or bone or with bits of animals such as a bear's claw or penis. The bear, a sacred animal, is given names like Woolly One, Grandfather and Honey Paws and is the subject of a ritual hunt. Without a country of their own, the Lapps extend over an area that stretches from Atlantic Norway to the Kola peninsula in Russia; their pluralistic political dependence has caused many problems which historically are reflected in the *Stallo*, a cycle of traditional legends. Across their territories are cult-sites sometimes associated with impressive natural features. The Lapps have reverence for all forms of nature and a deep sense of unity and interdependence with the landscape and everything that inhabits it.

Last Judgement Several religions have a doctrine of the Last Judgement, which take various forms and offer different emphases, the biblical doctrine being probably the most clearly developed. For Christianity the final reckoning is heralded by the **Last Trump**. It is usually a reference to the 'assize of the nations' and is to be distinguished from the post-mortem individual judgement. In Judaism, the Day of Yahweh, when he will punish the oppressors and persecutors of his people, became a final judgement at the end of the world. See **Eschatology**

Last Supper *X*. The last meal taken by Jesus with his disciples. It was followed by his betrayal by Judas, his arrest, trial and crucifixion. The meal, regarded by some scholars as a celebration of the **Passover**, is also the occasion when Jesus instituted the Communion. Paul provides an account of it in 1 Cor. 11:23ff. See **Eucharist**

Last Trump *J. X.* A general term for a blast on a trumpet. A reference in Judaism to the blowing of the *Shofar*, the Ram's Horn, in the synagogue at **Rosh Hashanah**, New Year. This begins the ritual period of God's judgement and its emotive sound calls the congregation to remorsefully reflect on their sins. The *Shofar* is also blown to conclude **Yom Kippur**, the Day of Atonement. In the **Old Testament** the *Shofar* was also blown to herald revelation (Ex. 29:16, 19) a national jubilee (Lev. 25:9) the advent of the Sabbath, festivals and the new moon (Num.10:10). The way the *Shofar* is played is itself symbolic, in that it is blown several times, the first notes being short and plaintive, while the last are long and triumphant. This Old Testament 'type' has become a New Testament symbol for the heralding of Jesus Christ's second coming and the resurrection of the dead: '...because at the word of command, at the sound of the archangel's voice and God's trumpet-call, the Lord himself will descend from heaven; first the Christian dead will rise ...' (1 Thes. 4:16). There is no way of knowing when the Last Trump may be sounded, 'In a moment, in the twinkling of an eye, at the last trump: for the trumpet shall sound and the dead shall be raised incorruptible and we shall be changed' (1 Cor. 15:52).

Latihan The central spiritual exercise of the Javanese cult of **Subud,** being a trance-like state that can give rise to ecstatic experiences or total calm. See **Javanese Religion**

Latin Fathers The Latin contributors to the mission and writings of the **Church Fathers**. They included, St Ambrose (340–397 CE) who introduced hymn-singing; St Jerome (347–420 CE) famous for The Vulgate, his Latin translation of the Hebrew and Aramaic scriptures (see Bible) and for his biblical commentaries; St **Augustine** (354–430 CE), pastor, teacher and bishop of the Church in North Africa, celebrated for his books *Confessions* and *The City of God*. See **Dogmatics**, **Greek Fathers**

Latter Rain Movement A movement that gathered momentum in Saskatchewan, Canada, between 1947 and the 1960s. Its energy was a revivalist initiative by the Pentecostal Church, which went on to have considerable widespread influence spawning numerous cults. The name 'Latter Rain' is drawn from the Old Testament that describes the final downpouring of God's Spirit on earth, a '**baptism**' of the **Holy Spirit**, heralding the end of time. The Movement was carried across Canada and the USA on the high tide of evangelism, led by the evangelist Billy Graham and others. Its adherents taught that in the 'last days', the various Christian denominations would dissolve and that the true Christians within each of them, would come together to form city-states under the leadership of apostles and prophets. During this period a select group of 'overcomers' would emerge from the Church to receive the 'spiritual bodies', described by St Paul (1 Cor. 15:44–49). These are the 'Manifest Sons of God', they will be immortal and endowed with divine gifts enabling them to change their shapes, to teleport to wherever they wish and to perform miracles. They will spread the Gospel across the world, thus preparing for the millennial reign of Christ. See also **Branhamism**, **Pentecostalism**

Left-Handed Path A term identifying religious and superstitious practices that focuses on individualism, freedom, self-indulgence and self-centredness. Opinions vary as to its origin, accrediting it to Madam **Blavatsky** and the **theosophists**, to **shamanism** or **Satanism**, which was associated with the left-handed path by Aleister Crowley. In many cultures the left hand has connotations of evil, of being threatening, *sinister* (L. 'left' and 'unlucky') and antipathy to traditional religion. In the **Old Testament** it is the right hand of the Lord that is 'exalted;' in the **New Testament** accounts of the **Last Judgement** (e.g. Matthew 25:31–46) the sheep are set on the right hand of the **Son of Man**, the goats on the left. The sheep are blessed, the goats cursed. Similar distinctions are made in Hindu and Buddhist **Tantra**, where right-handed practices include traditional asceticism and meditation, whereas the left-handed path practices sexual rites, the use of stimulants and animal sacrifice. The left and right paths have innocuous associations with the **Yin and Yang**, where the emphasis is on finding the balance between the two or on ways to overcome the implied dualism. Left-handed path religions include **Chaos Magic**, **Church of Satan**, Demonolatry (see **Demonology**), the **Temple of Set** and **Quimbanda**. See **Right-handed Path**

Legalism It has various shades of meaning, but generally, in religion, it describes any system that makes God's love, mercy and forgiveness conditional on obedience to laws and rules. In religious history legalism makes salvation a reward for performance, it hardens the edges of 'faith' and 'works' as opposing means of winning God's grace. Furthermore, in the interpretation of sacred literature it heightens the conflict between the 'spirit' and the 'letter', and is akin to **fundamentalism**. Legalism is used as a device used by religious institutionalism to establish and maintain its authority and the orthodoxy of its beliefs. In a secular context it presumes the law and political dogma to have absolute validity and as with religion, it protects against heterodoxy and obstructs freedom of conscience, speech and belief, as basic qualities of life.

Legend L. *legenda*, 'for reading', 'to be read'. A traditional, unverified story believed to be historical. It may have been handed down by oral tradition before being written. The term is also used of a body or collection of such stories. A legend may describe a romanticized modern story that has been popularized or a person whose reputation, for what ever reason, has assumed larger-than-life proportions. They are loosely distinguished from myths in that these are prehistorical, explanatory and not believable, whereas a legend can be read as a historical event that is believable, but not necessarily believed. Legends that break the boundaries of realism, become fables. Examples of legends would include, the city of Atlantis, King Arthur and the Knights of the Round Table, The Holy Grail, Vlad the Impaler, Robin Hood, the Wandering Jew and the Bermuda Triangle and what are termed, 'modern urban legends'. Whether religious stories, like parting of the Red Sea, the feeding of the 5,000, Muhammad's night journey or Shamanic transportations, are myths, fables, parables or legends, depends entirely on the belief system that such 'events' serve. See **Folklore**

Legio Maria The 'Legion of Mary', a worldwide organization of Catholic men and women who offer their lay services to a priest to aid him in his spiritual work in the parish. They place themselves under the 'banner' of Mary, so as to gain greater holiness in their own lives and encourage deeper devotion in others. Legio Maria was founded in Dublin, Ireland in 1921 and there are now, in the region of three million active members worldwide, with a further ten million auxiliaries. See **Maria Legio**

Leibnitz, Gottfried Wilhelm (1646–1716) A German **pluralist** philosopher who argued that the world was comprised of many substances that were created and whose existence is maintained by God. He argued that because the world was created by God, it is the best of all possible worlds. What Leibnitz meant by a 'substance' was a unit, so basic that it could not be broken down. He called this a 'monad'. Substance is not necessarily material, thus a soul or a spirit, is a monad. Leibnitz's substances were entirely independent, they in no way impinged on each other; what we call interaction between 'things' is the harmony of substances as God created them. The divine order of the universe is reflected in each of its parts, that is to say, each substance is created in such a way as to 'express' or reflect or represent all the others. Thus, in each substance the whole universe is to be seen. This proposition led to what is called 'Leibnitz's law', the concept that if one thing is identical to the other then anything that is true of one must also be true of the other. This seems obvious, but its simplicity occludes logical fallacy. Leibnitz tried to establish a philosophical theology as the basis for dialogue between Catholicism and Protestantism. This eclecticism included a committed interest in **alchemy** which contributed a level of **mysticism** to his writings that some have suggested indicates a **Kabbalistic** view of reality. Leibnitz, who was also a distinguished mathematician, invented a calculating machine and developed the basis for what today we know as differential and integral calculus. That this is 'the best of all possible worlds' has led to Leibnitz to being dubbed an optimist and it was his optimism that Voltaire satirized in, *Candide*. George I called Leibnitz a 'walking encyclopaedia'.

FINAL WORD: '… if we were able to understand sufficiently well the order of the universe, we should find that it surpasses all the desires of the wisest of us and that it is impossible to render it better than it is, not only for all in general, but also for each one of us in particular.' (Leibnitz)

Leninism A political and economic theory which developed the central ideas of **Marxism**. As with Marx, Lenin's theories were influenced by **Hegel** whom he studied while in exile from 1914–1916. Taking as a starting point Marx's concept of **communism** (the transfer of power and production to the proletariat), Leninism provided a doctrinal authority for **Bolshevism**, and a justification of revolutionary activism in undeveloped countries. He shifted Marxism from an economic determinism to a political **voluntarism** or a 'willed' determinism, proposing that 'there can be no revolutionary action without revolutionary theories'. Lenin argued that only a Communist Party, as a revolutionary vanguard, could lead the proletariat to successful revolution. These theories justified for Lenin the seizure of power by the Bolshevik party, both in non-Marxist Russia and elsewhere, since the concept of imperialism is the last decaying strategy of 'monopoly capitalism'. Thus, Leninism provided the theoretical basis for the long ensuing struggle between imperialism and socialism and for a ruthless, uncompromising secularism. Leninist theories were always controversial across the whole political spectrum, including the Mensheviks, the moderate wing of his own party. Trotsky was his most vehement political opponent. The theories have since polarized between Marxist-Leninism and **Trotskyism**.

Lenin, Vladimir (1870–1924) A Russian Communist revolutionary, leader of the Bolshevik Party and the first Premier of the Soviet Union. He described his social and political theories (**Leninism**) as an adaptation of **Marxism** to 'the age of imperialism'. His embalmed body is on permanent display in the Lenin Mausoleum in Moscow. See **Communism**

Lent X. The 40-day **Fast** that precedes **Easter**. Originally a true fast with only one vegetarian meal a day allowed, but this rigour has been entirely relaxed by Protestantism. In 1966 the *Paenitemini*, an Apostolic Constitution convened to revise Roman Catholic penitential observance and to set the obligatory Lenten fasts for the first day, **Ash Wednesday**, and for **Good Friday**. It prescribed the observation of a proper Mass for each day of the period. Generally, the Fast is now observed as a time for reflection and quietude, with abstention from normal forms of pleasure, rich foods, alcohol etc. and by almsgiving. Some churches cover up their art work and those who wish practise special spiritual disciplines. See **Ramadan, Yom Kippur**

Leviathan From the Hebrew meaning, 'twisted', 'coiled'. A biblical sea monster referred to in the Old Testament, for example, '... it was you ... who crushed the heads of the Leviathan' (Ps. 74:14) and 'In that day the Lord will punish ... Leviathan the Elusive Serpent – Leviathan the Twisting Serpent' (Isaiah 27: 1). The legend of the beast probably evolved from Canaanite Ba'al mythology and/or Babylonian creation myths. The Leviathan may be interpreted as the sea itself or in the opinion of some scholars as a reference to sea-faring invaders that threatened the Kingdom of Israel. In Christian terminology, it is a demon or monster associated with Satan. Other biblical scholars interpret the Leviathan as the primordial state of chaos and God's destruction of it, as a figure of creation. In the Satanic Bible (see **Satan**) the Leviathan is one of the 'Four Crowned Princes' who has the number 3, the colour blue, the element water and who represents our carnal nature and chaos. There are parallels in eastern religions, for example with the seven-headed *Naga* of Indian and southeast Asian mythology. Its secular application is most famously given in Thomas **Hobbes**' formative work *Leviathan*, a telling image of everything that has to be destroyed, tamed and controlled on the way to creating a just social contract and an ideal State in the form of a Commonwealth.

Li *Con.* Chin. 'rites of propriety', made up of the two parts of the Chinese character *Li*, meaning 'spirit' and 'sacrifice'. Originally the term referred to the officially observed rites of State and domestic religion, but more importantly to the rules of suitable conduct, the behaviour fitting to specific circumstances and generally, to the best means of conducting all human relationships. The concept is central to **Confucius**' philosophy of social and personal ethics. The detailed guide to the application of *Li* is to be found in the *Classic of Rites*, one of the six parts of the canon of **Confucianism**.

Liberal Catholic Church *X*. The denomination originated with the Dutch Catholic Church (see **Old Catholics**) when it broke from Rome, having given refuge to the heretical Jansenists in the early 18th century (see **Jansenism**). The Church considers itself 'liberal' because it enjoys freedom of thought and 'catholic' because its message is universal. It has existed as an independent Church since 1917–1918, when the Old Catholics were reorganized.

Liberal Protestantism *X*. A term referring to a movement beginning in 19th-century Protestantism that adopted a critical attitude to biblical fundamentalism and the dogmatism characteristic of it. More positively, it set out to present the Christian message in contemporary terms, the authority for which was the individual's spiritual experience. Albrecht Ritschl (1822–89) set the theological agenda, that an understanding of Jesus Christ and his message must take into account historical research into his life and that a person's reconciliation to God must be reflected in the moral quality his life. Adolf Harnack (1815–1930) provided what became the standard expression of Liberal Protestantism, interpreting Christianity in terms of the Fatherhood of God, the brotherhood of man and all believers and the command given by Jesus that we should love one another.

Liberation Theology *X*. An initiative in contemporary Catholic theology which gathered momentum in the 1960s, aimed at interpreting the Christian message in terms of urgent social and political needs by focusing on human rights and political activism. Its programme addressed issues such as the problem of the economic exploitation of Third World countries, discrimination against and the sexual exploitation of women, racial discrimination and political tyranny. Social analysis was based on Marxist theories and applied to Jesus' identification with the poor and oppressed. It is Jesus the 'liberator' that gives the movement its name and its mandate to emancipate people from poverty, injustice, laws and governments that restrict development and progress. Spiritually it fostered liberation from all forms of sin, especially attitudes and practices that impede relationship with God and other people. The Latin American Episcopal Conference, created in Rio de Janeiro in 1955, successfully lobbied the 2nd Vatican Council (1962–1965) to take up a more active response to these issues. Liberation Theology arose out of this initiative and became established with the publication in 1972 of Gustavo Gutiérrez's essay, 'A Theology of Liberation: History, Politics and Salvation', which formally introduced the socio-catholic theme and confronted the Church with it. The movement has been condemned by the Vatican for being based on Marxist materialism. Interestingly, Cardinal Ratzinger praised the movement for rejecting violence and for 'stressing the responsibility which Christians necessarily bear for the poor and the oppressed'.

Life Spring Broadly linked with **Est** and the **Human Potential Movement**. In 1974, in association with the Gestalt Institute, John Hanley founded a seminar-based group concerned with the 'manipulation of reality' and introspection. Hanley's aim was that participants should understand the control they could have over their own lives. The starting point is to realize that 'truth' is relative and capable of being variously perceived, but that its 'core' resides in every human soul, together with love and self-identity. This core has to be seen, then realized in the way each person lives their everyday life. Members of a seminar are paired off into 'dyads' so as to explore similarities and confrontations, by which process the individual is 'broken down', or has the disguising layers peeled away to reveal the 'core' truth. Once that is revealed additional training actualizes it. Life Spring is believed to have around 300,000 members.

Lila *H*. Skt. 'play'. The play of the divine in the manifest world. **Vaishnavism** describes creation as God's *lila*, his play. The term is also used in Hindu philosophy to refer to the relative or impermanent state, as opposed to *nitya*, the Absolute or permanent state. See **Anitya, Shankara**

Linga or **Lingam** *H*. Skt. The male organ or phallus. Frequently shown as a stone pillar, it is the symbol by which **Siva** is usually worshipped. Not mentioned in the **Vedas**, it features in the **Mahabharata** where, as an 'emblem – a plain column of stone, sometimes a cone of mud – suggests no offensive idea. The people call it Siva or Maha-deva and there's an end.' Shiva, once known as the god of destruction, has become the object of veneration in a form symbolic of generative power. Such are the reversals to be found in the history of religions. In conjunction with the **yoni**, the female organ, it is venerated also by the worshippers of **Shakti**.

Lion and Lamb Ministries A Messianic Jewish sect founded in 1980 by Monte Judah, as a non-denominational, independent ministry. It teaches that Jesus is the biblical Messiah and that his return is imminent. The ongoing energy of the Ministries comes from Judah's correlation of current events and natural disasters (such as 9/11 and Hurricane Katrina) to biblical prophecy. Judah prophesied that the 'Abomination of Desolation', would happen in March 1997 and subsequently apologized for the false prophecy. The movement is said to have legalistic tendencies, practises **Sabbatarianism**, and observes Jewish holy days. Its website outlines its Ministry: 'Our mission is to present the Messiah Yeshua, as the King of Israel and ourselves as Bondservants; to provide prophetic insight and understanding concerning the return of Yeshua the Messiah to the Earth; to prepare the saints of God both Jew and non-Jew for the events of the Great Tribulation and the last years of this age; to teach the Torah and strengthen our faith and obedience in the God of Abraham, Isaac and Jacob.'

(*NB:* The movement should not be confused with the Texas-based Lamb and Lion Ministries, a reputable Christian organization led by David Reagan.)

Literalism (i) Interpretation of scripture according to the letter, usually based on a fundamentalist belief in the divine origin of the text. (ii) A way of explaining a ritual by the effect it is supposed to create, e.g. the practice of dancing because of the belief that spirits can be induced to give rain, i.e. a 'literal' relationship between cause and effect.

Liturgical Movement It began in the early 20th century by the **Roman Catholic Church** as means of encouraging the laity's closer participation in the **Mass**. The results of the reforms include a greater number of Eucharistic celebrations, simplified forms of worship and the availability of the Mass in the languages of the congregations. The influence of the movement is not confined to the Roman Church and since 1935 similar reforms have made the language, forms and orders of service more accessible to Anglicans. The Solemn Eucharist, at which only the celebrant communicated, has been replaced by a 'Parish Eucharist', at which all present may receive communion. In some parishes, the Eucharist is followed by a breakfast, a counterpart of the original **Agape** meal. With the exception of the Eastern Orthodox Churches, most Churches have revised their forms of worship, not just to accommodate modern language, but to find ways of making the liturgical forms and the sacraments relevant to modern society and its needs. As frequently happens with such movements, the reformers and theologians tend to move more quickly than the clergy or laity would wish and in some cases the reforms have been controversial.

Liturgical Year Most established religions have a calendar of feasts and festivals which mark the sequence of worship in a given year. The terms 'liturgy' and 'liturgical', however, are associated mostly with Christianity and the special form of worship given to the main festivals that follow the salient events of Jesus' life. **Advent**, the celebration of his birth and **Epiphany**, his 'showing' to the gentiles. **Ash Wednesday** marks the start of **Lent**, and **Good Friday** commemorates Jesus' death, **Easter** Sunday his resurrection and Ascension Day his reception in heaven. **Pentecost**, or Whit Sunday, recalls the gift or descent of the **Holy Spirit**, and a week later the Trinity is honoured. Not all of these are 'fixed' feasts and there are variations in the year of the **Orthodox** Churches, with -additional festivals celebrated by Catholicism. In a similar manner, other religions follow a yearly liturgy following the major events in their histories and in the lives of their founders or gods. For Jews, Christians and Muslims, the year is also pegged out by the observation of the **Sabbath** (the *Shabbat*, of the Jews) observed on different days according to the religion's tradition. See **Hindu Festivals and Feasts, Islam, Judaism**

Liturgy X. From the Greek *leitourgia*, 'a public work'. Used in the narrow sense for the **Eucharist** as the Church's central corporate act of worship. In general use, the term refers to all forms of congregational worship in contradistinction to the less formal worship of loosely associated groups or an individual's private worship. The established, formal worship of most major Church traditions have a fixed order or form as set out, for example, in the 1549 **Anglican** *Book of Common Prayer*. Orthodox Jewish liturgy follows the Authorized Daily Book of the United Hebrew Congregation; Islamic liturgy is typified in the ritual of *Salat*. See **Pillars of Islam**

Living Stream Ministry See **Local Church**

Local Church, The A controversial movement begun in China in the 1920s by Ni To-Sheng, otherwise known as Watchman Nee. Its second leader, Witness Lee, moved to America in 1962 and founded a sect called the 'Living Stream Ministry'. One of its controversial doctrines concerns the use of the word 'mingling' to describe the Jesus-like human/divine character of its adherents. Other criticisms claim that the Church compromises an orthodox doctrine of the **Trinity**. Denominationalism is believed to be derived from the Devil and Lee insists that each city should have only one Church as an embodiment of the body of Christ. Hence the name 'Local' Church. Any Church outside this body, that is, the other churches in that city are outside the will of God. The doctrine is an application of Paul's guidelines (1 Cor. 6:1–8) which argue that all disputes be they doctrinal or business, should be settled within the one 'local' community.

Locke, John (1632–1704) A medical doctor and probably the most significant and influential English philosopher. Arguing that all knowledge is based on sense experience, his thought was the foundation of both **empiricism**, and liberal democracy. In one of his major works, *Essay Concerning Human Understanding*, he argues that what we know is not based on innate **ideas**, but entirely on an addition and interreaction of different kinds of experience. In this way we build up a simple concept of, for example, 'blue', but also the most complex concepts such as a 'city' or 'state'. He believed the mind of the newly born child was like 'a white paper', a total blank which is marked by the very first sensations received. However, in addition to experience there is reflection on what the mind has received, enabling us to order those experiences, explaining them firstly to ourselves and then to others. We also make relationships between associated experiences, thus deepening our knowledge of any one subject. There are, therefore, simple and complex ideas, the one being of a single element, the other being of several elements. For example, we experience the whiteness of a lily, then its smell, the appearance of ice, then its coldness, thus our senses provide a gradually changing, but accumulating knowledge through different experiences of the same thing. Locke deals with the relationship of reason to faith. He argues that religion makes use of reason so far as it can, but when reason fails, it recourses to faith, claiming that what was revealed is above reason; but Locke makes the point that in order to do this, there must be clear boundaries between the two. Locke defines reason as the use of the natural faculties of sense experience and reflection and the fruits of reason as, 'the discovery or certainty or probability of such propositions or truths, which the mind arrives at by deduction'. Faith, on the other hand, is an assent to any proposition based, 'on the credit of the proposer, as coming from God in some extraordinary way of communication'. So we have faith in what is disclosed by revelation and which cannot be discovered by reason. The influence of the breadth and liberality of Locke's ideas are extensive; he virtually provided the American revolutionaries with their mandate and with some of the most important principles in the Declaration of Independence and the Constitution.

Logical Atomism A philosophy developed by Bertrand **Russell** (1872–1970) and Ludwig **Wittgenstein** (1889–1951) that offered a contemporary perception of the basic functions of philosophy itself, namely an enquiry into the nature of the world, how we access that knowledge and how by observation and experiment, we describe it. Logical Atomism asserts that the only form of knowledge in which we can have confidence is derived from the scientific method which is, in effect, mathematical logic applied to language. In the physical world, everything is made up of elements or atoms that once analysed and understood, can explain the nature and function of everything. Human beings are part of that physical world, but wholly dependent on language for accessing the truth. Thus language must also subscribe to the same kind of analysis, being composed of small pieces which are beyond divisibility. Once isolated and defined, these elements or 'atoms' apply to the conceptual and intellectual world, in the same way as they apply to the elements of the physical world. In making that application, certain conditions must prevail before it can be said that a sentence has definite meaning, namely that molecular sentences or propositions, have to be made up of atomic, fundamental units of meaning. These 'atomic facts' must be related directly to references in the non-linguistic world. An atomic fact is one that is basic and unanalysable whether, as Russell asserts, it is derived from experience (sense data) or whether, according to Wittgenstein, it is unspecified. Although both philosophers eventually abandoned this mode of enquiry, it was the precursor of **logical positivism** and, as such, formatively influential on all succeeding philosophy. Logical Atomism is an uncompromising secular enquiry, characteristic of Russell's uncompromising atheism. However, Bernard Linsky allows that, 'the right way to analyse certain expressions into a logical language would seem to follow from a correct metaphysical analysis of facts rather than leading to it.'

Logical Positivism The name given to a range of ideas typical of the **Vienna Circle** of philosophers in the 1920s and 1930s. It was influenced by **empiricism**, particularly that of **Hume**. It is said that it was given a kick-start by **Wittgenstein**'s comment in the *Tractus*, that 'philosophy is not a theory but an activity'. It was this view that the Vienna group elaborated. They argued that philosophy does not produce propositions which are true or false, it simply clarifies the meaning of statements by showing their terms of reference – some are mathematical, some scientific, some nonsensical. Logical Positivism is, therefore, an analysis of language using conceptual equipment derived from mathematical and logical theories, especially those of **Russell** and **Wittgenstein**. Put simply, logical positivism regards every statement either as one of formal logic (including mathematical statements) or of science. The latter type would include all statements concerning physical law, but also singular statements like, 'this is blue'. Other statements might be regarded as being poetic, emotive, pictorial, motivational, but not cognitive. There are also, 'analytic' and 'synthetic' propositions. Both are true, but they differ in the *way* they are true. For example, take the statements, 'all children have heads', and 'all children are young'. The first is true of every child, a child without a head is simply not to be seen anywhere. The second statement is true as a matter of fact, but it is also impossible to imagine any situation in which a child is not young. The meaning of the word 'child' carries with it, necessarily, the fact of their being young. To ensure the first statement is true we would need, empirically, to examine every single child; however, we can assume the second statement to be true without making an such survey. The first kind of truth, the one requiring investigation is 'synthetic', the second kind of truth, the one that follows from the meaning of the words, is 'analytic'. But what about the kind of statement that someone *claims* to be true, like, 'God exists', – how can such an assertion be found to be true? Logical positivists developed what was called the 'Verification Principal', which came in a variety of ways depending on the philosopher proposing it. A. J. Ayer made out his case for such principle by asserting that 'a sentence is factually significant to any given person, if and only if, he knows how to verify the proposition which it purports to express – that is, if he knows what observations would lead him, under certain conditions to ascertain whether the proposition was true or reject it as being false'. There are, of course, problems. It has been suggested that the verification principle itself is not verifiable. Further to this, logical positivism cannot seriously entertain either ethics or aesthetics since propositions offered by either are not empirically verifiable; it follows that logical positivism radically limits the scope of philosophical enquiry. In its demand for an analysis of language, it has had a considerable influence on religion. Its challenge has been one of the energies (another being **secularism**) that has driven some thinkers to look at religious language in an entirely new way and to ask in what sense a statement of belief or a statement of doctrine, as set out in a **creed** for example, can be accepted as being analytically, synthetically or significantly true. The result has thrown up serious quests for a new religious language that is conceptually a part of modern culture.

FINAL WORD: 'Our charge against the metaphysician is not that he attempts to employ the understanding in a field where it cannot profitably venture, but that he produces sentences which fail to conform to the conditions under which alone a sentence can be literally significant.' (A. J. Ayer)

Logos Gk. 'Word'. This is its usually translation into English, but it has other connotations such as thought, reason, principle, standard or logic. Heraclitus offered a *logos* doctrine in which it represented a form of non-human intelligence that unifies disparate elements into a whole. The **Sophists** used the term to refer to an argument or part of an argument. For the **Stoics**, the logos was an aspect of God identified with Universal sources of rationality. The concept is most familiar to Western thinkers through the Prologue of St John's Gospel where the logos is identified with the medium of creation. The philosophical influence on John is clearly Greek, specifically that of the Stoics. The logos concept (not doctrine) has its parallel in Eastern religions with the Tao of **Taoism**, the **dharma** of Buddhism and the **Aum** of Hindu cosmology.

FINAL WORD: 'From the beginning, Christianity has understood itself to be the religion of the Logos, as the religion according to reason … In the so necessary dialogue between secularists and Catholics, we Christians must be very careful to remain faithful to this fundamental line: to live a faith that comes from this Logos, from creative reason.' (Pope Benedict XVI, April 2005)

Loka-Samgraha *H*. Skt. 'Work for the benefit of the world'. An aspect of Karma-**yoga** that aims to be free of all selfish motives while continuing to live in the world fulfilling one's social duties and obligations. With **realization** comes the understanding that we are not actually the agents of what we do and that there is no longer need to act in any particular way. Thus there is no need to be withdrawn from the world. The liberated working for the benefit of the world is an ideal represented in the **Bhagavad-Gita**, 'If I should cease to work these worlds would fall in ruin and I should be the creator of disordered life and destroy these people' (3:24). Without the sense of personal agency, the realized or liberated person can act in freedom. See **Bodhisattva**

Loki Full name Loki Laufeyjarson, one of the chief deities of **Norse** mythology. He is a son of Farbauti and Laufey and the god of mischief, the 'contriver of all fraud'. But, 'the figure of Loki remains obscure; there is no trace of a cult and the name does not appear in place-names' (*Encyclopaedia Britannica*, 1971). He was not thoroughly bad, more a loveable rogue, somewhat like Cayote, the trickster god of **Amerindian** mythology. He could change his shape, transmogrifying to a horse, salmon, bird or flea; versatile enough to change his sex, he is not only the father of several children, creatures and monsters, but in one instance, the mother. He was the slayer of **Balder**, and despite his mischief, a friend to man with tales told of how he protected people from trolls.

Lollards *X*. The followers of John **Wycliffe** (1320–84). Gathering momentum during the 1350s, the Lollard movement gained academic respectability through Wycliffe's base at Oxford where he was Master of Balliol college and official recognition by the court of Edward III. As the movement grew it became increasingly unpopular, mostly because of its anti-clericalism. The Lollards travelled the country, preaching and teaching Wycliffe's reformed theology based on the English Bible he had translated. They advocated personal faith, Divine election and the equality of the sexes, encouraging women preachers. They criticized the Church on the grounds that it was concerned more with form than substance. Although his thought was the energy behind the Lollard movement, the extent of Wycliffe's personal involvement is still debated. The Lollards were eventually viciously persecuted and the movement went underground. While it can be said that Wycliffe and the Lollards were ahead of their time, the question as to how long the movement lasted is answered by the English Reformation, which 200 years later picked up on many of Wycliffe's ideas.

FINAL WORD: 'Very severe laws were now enacted against the Lollards … In 1401 a terrible statute, *De Heretico Comburendo*, condemned relapsed heretics to be burnt alive and left the judgement solely to the Church, requiring sheriffs to execute it without allowing an appeal to the Crown. Thus did orthodoxy and property make common cause and march together.' (Churchill)

Longchenpa (1308–64) *B*. A Tibetan **Buddhist** philosopher and teacher, responsible for organizing the teachings of **Padmasambhava** into the philosophy and practice of **Dzogchen**, the supreme teaching of the **Nyingmapa** school. So great were his teachings considered to be that he was accorded the title of the 'Second Buddha', an honour usually associated with Padmasambhava. He also carried the title Kunkhyen, 'All-knowing'. He left a considerable literature, in excess of 250 treatises and books, the greatest of which is thought to be his *Seven Treasures*, Dzogchen Tantras that brought together the previous 600 years of Buddhist teaching in Tibet. He was abbot of Samye, one of Tibet's principal monasteries, gathering a huge following around him. But he remained a simple monk, often a hermit living in caves when he was not travelling and teaching. Solitude in nature, he believed, was a source of spiritual awakening.

Longhouse Religion See **Handsome Lake Religion**

Lord's Day Observance Society A pressure group founded in the United Kingdom in 1831 to protect the **Sabbath** in the form of its original institution as a day of rest. The authority is the 4th of the Ten Commandments, 'Remember the Sabbath day and keep it holy. Six days you shall labour and do all your work, but the seventh is a Sabbath of the Lord your God: you shall not do any work ...' (Ex. 20:8–10). Since 1831 every kind of incursion has been made into the traditional religious Sunday, the use of which has been debated to the present moment with issues over Sunday trading, sport and the opening hours of pubs. The matter is not confined to Great Britain and in the USA the 'Blue Laws', first mentioned in 1781, have endeavoured to impose restrictions so as to preserve the original Puritan observation of the Sabbath in the New World. The ubiquitous 'weekend' has all but absorbed the concept of the Sabbath, be it Jewish, Christian or Muslim. The Sabbath is now observed according to the rites and practices of these religions without them impinging on the freedom of non-adherents to do pretty much as they wish. See also **Sabbatarianism**

Lord's Prayer X. The prayer Jesus offered to his disciples as a model for intercession, recorded, for example, in Mat. 6:9, beginning, 'Our Father in heaven, Thy name be hallowed ...' See **Prayer**

Lord's Supper See **Eucharist**

Lost Tribes of Israel The ancient tribes of **Israel** that 'disappeared' from the biblical account after the destruction of the northern Kingdom of Israel by the Assyrians (see **Assyrian Religion**). The greater part of the population was taken into captivity and innumerable legends and theories have arisen to account for the fate of the descendents of the captives. It seems that according to Esdras II, the exiles resumed their wandering for upwards of two years before settling again; from this juncture two theories have been suggested. One traces their wanderings eastwards, identifying the tribes with the Tartars, the Japanese or even the Amerindians, since it is pointed out that at the time of these migrations the continents of Asia and North America were still physically joined. The alternative theory has the wanderers turning west to settle in Europe, including the

British Isles. (For advocates of this theory, see **British Israelites**.) It is suggested that some of these tribes are to be traced in European nomenclature, thus the tribe of Dan settled in Denmark, while the Saxons were sons of Isaac. In medieval Jewish literature there are numerous references by travellers claiming to come from communities derived from the missing, but assimilated tribes. From all of these legends, there are but two serious claims, those of the Afghans and Nestorians. The former are also known as the Beni Israel (Sons of Israel) whose name has favourable references in the **Koran**. In the 13th century, based on the writings of Marco Polo, they were known to have practices similar to the Hindus, except that they circumcised their boys on the 8th day and observed the Sabbath and other Jewish festivals. Many thousands of them have settled in Israel since 1948. The **Nestorians** are thought by some authorities, to have derived from Jewish communities settled by Shalmaneser III, after his subjugation of Israel. American missionaries in the mid-19th century have recorded that their language was similar to Aramaic, that they offered sacrifices and 'first fruits', observed dietary restrictions, prepared for the Sabbath the preceding evening and had Jewish names and features. See **Twelve Tribes of Israel**

Lotus *H. B.* Skt. *padma*. A member of the water-lily family. In Hinduism it is a symbol of the **chakras**, the different centres of consciousness, with its petal a symbol of non-attachment. It being in the water, yet remaining dry, is a figure of the spiritual aspiration to be in the world but not influenced by it. In Hindu iconography the flower is a symbol of purity and beauty (see *Figure 5*).

In Buddhism the lotus symbolizes our true Buddha-nature and our original pure mind in that we are not sullied by the muddy waters of *samsara*, the cycles of life and by *avidya*, ignorance. In Buddhist iconography the lotus forms the seat of the Buddha. There are numerous Buddhist variations of lotus symbolism.

Figure 5 Lotus Flower

Lotus Position See **Padmasana**

Lotus School See **T'ien-t'ai**

Lovedu Religion *A.* Transvaal sect whose religion pivots around Mujaji, divine queens and ancestral spirits. They are a matriarchal society whose descent is patrilineal. Women to women marriages prevail and close kinsmen are required to impregnate them. No ancestor spirit is more powerful than a mother's mother. The Mujaji are rain queens who although they send drought to their enemies, also cause rain to fall on them. There was a proto-Mujaji, sometimes called, Mujaji I, both wise and immortal, who mated with her father, Mugodo and gave birth to Mujaji II, who succeeded her mother as queen. It was during her reign and that of Mujaji III, that the homeland was invaded by Europeans. Rain is a symbol of life at its best, cool, fruitful, with social stability; the heat and drought symbolize evil, sorcery, passion and social upheaval. There is no developed cosmology and the role of Khuzwane, the creator god, is vague. He is not prayed to, nor do the ancestors act as mediators. The wellbeing of their society depends on the health and emotional happiness of their actual queen who is the political and religious head. She draws on her inner divine power and is sustained by rain-medicines and the royal ancestor spirits. She remains secluded and at her death by her own hands, a period of social unrest and confusion ensues.

Loyola, Ignatius (1491–1556) *X*. The founder of the Society of Jesus, familiarly known as the **Jesuits**. A man of noble birth who, when wounded as a professional soldier in 1521, assumed another form of military service as a soldier of Christ. During a year spent in Manresa (1522–23) he wrote his *Spiritual Exercises*, then went on to study in Spain and Paris. In 1534 he and his companions made a vow of poverty and chastity, dedicating themselves to a life devoted to Jesus. In 1550 the Society was formally ratified by Paul III and Ignatius became its first General. The Order was put at the service of the pope.

Lubavitch *J*. Full name Chabad-Lubavitch, from an acronym of three Hebrew words meaning 'wisdom', 'knowledge' and 'understanding' together with the Russian meaning 'town of brotherly love'. The Lubavitch movement was founded by the mystic philosopher Rabbi Shneur Zalman, in the late 1700s. It had its origins in **Chasidism**, and today forms the largest branch of Chasidism and the largest worldwide orthodox Jewish community, with a considerable presence in the USA. They follow the teachings of Chasidism's founder, the Baal Shem Tov, which are based on the Kabbalistic writings of Rabbi Isaac Luria (see **Kabbalah**). As with all Hasidic groups the relationship between the leader, the *Tzadik*, and his followers, is very special, somewhat like that of the eastern **guru** with his pupil (see **Guru Yoga**). Controversy arose when in some groups, the *Tzadik* was accorded qualities that came very close to divinity, a concept abhorrent to Jewish orthodoxy. The problem became centred on the Seventh Chabad-Lubavitch Chief Rabbi, Menachem Schneerson (1902–94) whose teachings, some claimed, came close to presenting himself as the Messiah. As recently as 2001 Rabbi Dr David Berger published his criticisms of the Lubavitch Messianic teachings; others have published responses to his criticism. And so the debate about Messiahship runs and runs.

FINAL WORD: 'In sum, this generation has presided over a historic transformation of the Jewish religion. We now live in a world in which Judaism affirms the possibility of the Second Coming of the Messiah – and perhaps even of his divinity – as a fully acceptable belief … we will continue to acquiesce in the ongoing Christianization of the Jewish faith' (Rabbi Dr David Berger)

Lucifer From, L. *lux*, 'light' and Gk. *fero*, 'to bear' or 'bring', thus the 'bringer of light'. In Greek mythology he is the 'Dawn Bringer' and the Morning Star. In Christian tradition Lucifer was God's second in command, the highest archangel in heaven. Motivated by pride and greed he rebelled against God and was cast out of heaven together with a third of heaven's host. Eventually he became identified with **Satan**. He is the key protagonist in Milton's *Paradise Lost* and in his war against God he is aided by **Mammon** and **Beelzebub**.

Lupercalia *R*. An annual Roman festival, the origins of which are older than the founding of Rome. It was held near the cave of Lupercal on the Palatine Hill and celebrated annually on February 15th in honour of Faunus, the god of forests and fertility. The rituals enacted were to purify the new life of spring. The rite was directed by the Luperci, 'brothers of the wolf', the priests of Faunus dressed in goatskin. A dog and two male goats were sacrificed. The full agenda of the rite is complicated and uses symbolic action. Shakespeare's play *Julius Caesar*, opens with the Lupercalia. See **Saturnalia**

Luther, Martin (1483–1546) While a professor at Wittenberg, Luther went through a period of spiritual introspection and anxiety concerning his salvation. He was 'saved' by his reading of St Paul's doctrine of justification by faith, which Luther developed in his lectures on the Letter to the Romans, given in 1516–17. The controversy that led to the **Reformation** began when he set faith over against other mediatory methods of salvation such as the selling of indulgences, that claimed to forgive sin and to impart the **grace** of God. Luther went on to challenge scholastic theology (see **Scholasticism**) against which he preached, producing a considerable number of published treatises, the most famous of which were written between May and November of 1520. It was the treatise against indulgences that Luther nailed to the door of the church in Wittenberg. The treatises provoked a general revolution against the papacy and would eventually provided most of the material for the Augsburg Confession of 1530. On the 15th June 1520, the famous Bull issued by Pope Leo X, cited and condemned 41 propositions taken from Luther's books. Assured of safe-conduct, he appeared before the Diet of the German Empire held at Worms in 1521, where he was given a further opportunity to recant, an offer he graciously and courageously rejected. 'Unless therefore I am convinced by the testimony of scripture or by the clearest reasoning, – unless I am persuaded by means of the passages I have quoted, – and unless they thus render my conscience bound by the Word of God, I cannot and will not retract, for it is unsafe for a Christian to speak against his conscience. Here I stand, I can do no other; may God help me! Amen!' Much of Luther's time was given over to the translation and interpretation of the **Bible**, so as to make it available to the laity.

Known as the Father of the German Reformation, his life and work is copiously recorded and examined. See Bainton, Green, and Hillerbrand. See **Soul**, **Traducianism**, **Wycliffe**
FINAL WORD: 'Afterwards they allowed Dr Martin to stay until Wednesday after St George and dealt no further with him.' (From a newspaper account of the Diet. Hillerbrand)

Lutheranism *X*. That the followers of Martin **Luther** came to be called 'Lutherans' was contrary to their leader's expressed wishes. The term came to designate those churches founded on Lutheran doctrine and authority, established by the Augsburg Confession of 1530, which has become the standard Lutheran confession of faith. Its main points of doctrine were established in the five treatises Luther wrote in 1520 and can be summarized as: i) justification by faith which is to be expressed in good works; ii) the Church is not an administrative hierarchy, but a spiritual community, the leaders of which are responsible for reform through councils. Obedience to popes and bishops is not required when they are disobedient to the Word of God; iii) the sacraments take their meaning and efficacy from the **New Testament** and not the papacy. The doctrine of **transubstantiation** is abandoned, as also is the concept of the 'spiritual presence of Christ's absent body'; iv) belief in the priesthood of all believers of which the true Church consists; and v) the concept of the freedom of the individual within the bond of faith. In these doctrines, Luther set the agenda for all future Protestantism.

Lyotard, Jean-François (1924–98) French philosopher, particularly noted for carrying a Postmodernist influence to literary theory, aesthetics, knowledge and communication, to philosophy itself and to the human condition in general. He coined the term, 'differand' and used it to identify conflict without the possibility of solution, a poignant term that would seem to have increasing application in today's world. It also resonates with those philosophies that focus on the nature and function of language, in as much as conflict is due to a failure in communication and to the misuse and abuse of language. The differand can apply not just to opinion, but also to 'phrases in dispute', and to those moments and events in history when the victims of injustice are not only victims but rendered 'wordless' and 'voiceless', because there are no means of redress or appeal. To be able to accept a problem as unsolvable and to accommodate it to a world-view, is in itself, positive. Lyotard also used 'differand' to identify a situation in which unsolvable problems offer creative opportunity since, 'to stifle the differand is to stifle the ways we think and act'. Lyotard is indebted to **Wittgenstein**. See **Postmodernism**
FINAL WORD: We must not say: 'That of which we cannot speak, we must condemn to silence.' We can speak of everything … And what one has to do (what one 'must' do), is not to limit the capacity of sentences in presented universes, but to extend it. Not only can one speak of everything, but one must.' (Lyotard [1983])

M

Maat *E*. Egyptian goddess of truth and justice. Daughter of **Ra**. Her symbol was a feather, against which the heart of the deceased was weighed and if found to be *maa kheru*, 'true of voice', was admitted to the kingdom of **Osiris**. See **Egyptian Religion**, **Funerary Practices**

Mabinogion *AE*. A collection of Celtic lore and legend which includes some the earliest known accounts of the Arthurian stories. The 'Four Branches', the oldest part of the collection, appeared in the 11th century, inspiring and influencing European medieval secular literature. Despite the elegance of the prose the descriptions of the ancient culture reveals a barbarous mythological tradition. The collection is in two parts, the *White Book of Rhydderch* and the *Red Book of Hergest*. It is probable that many of the stories existed as an oral tradition and were told by peripatetic bards before being written down. The story-teller was highly regarded in Celtic history. See **Celtic Religion**

Macrocosm and Microcosm The early 3rd-century Christian theologian Origen (see **Dogmatics**, **Greek Fathers**) said, 'Know that you are another world in miniature and that in you there is a sun, a moon and star too.' Seeing the cosmic whole in the human part is a dramatic form of **anthropomorphism**. The macrocosm (Gk. *makros kosmos*, 'great world') is conceived as a human organism on a huge scale of which each person is a minute copy or model. (Gk. *mikros kosmos*, 'little world'). Thus, every human being has a counterpart in the universe. In biblical tradition man is made in the image of God, thus God is the addition of the whole universe, plus man and man is a tiny replica of both. The theory has proved of great importance to magic; it is reasoned that if man is in miniature both the whole universe *and* God, he is capable from his own resources of exercising power over everything. Robert Fludd (1574–1637) made diagrams to show the connections between the 'great world' and man. Such parallels are also to be seen in the **Adam Kadmon** of the Lurianic **Kabbalah**. The theory is basic to **alchemy** as expressed in its motto 'As Above so Below' and axiomatic to **astrology**.

Macumba *A*. A Bantu word with various meanings which include the name for a musical instrument, a central African deity and 'magic'. In the 19th century, among the Afro-Brazilians of Rio de Janeiro it was the name coined for various Bantu-originating religious practices. These have subsequently been reorganized into what are now called **Umbanda**, **Quimbanda** and Omoloko. Macumba practice is syncretistic, combining a European tradition of witchcraft, with African voodoo, chanting, dancing and trance-induced spirit healing. In some regions it is called **Candomblé**, but the latter's practices are distinguished by its worship of spirits derived from **African religion**. The sect also flourishes in the USA where the name 'Macumba', is retained as a slang pejorative reference to anything of African origin.

Madhva (1199–1278) *H*. The principal Hindu philosopher of *Dvaita-Vedenta*, dualism (see **Advaita-Vedenta**). It is one of three principal schools of **Vedenta** philosophy. Madhva identified five dualistic distinctions: i) between God and the individual soul; ii) between God and matter; iii) between the individual soul and matter; iv) between individual souls; and v) between individual elements and matter. God, the soul and the world are the eternally existing substances. Madhva opposed non-duality and his philosophy turned **Ramanuja**'s qualified non-dualism into a pure dualism.

Madhyamaka *B*. Skt. '*madhyama*', 'the middle'. A school of **Mahayana** Buddhism established by Nagarjuna (c.150–250 CE) and developed by his disciple Aryadeva. An adherent of the school is known as a *Madhyamika*. The 'middle way' taken by the school refers to charting a path between opposing notions of whether or not things exist. Madhyamakan philosophy was developed further by the **Yogachara** School with its advanced methods of logic. During the 11th century CE, Madhyamaka was carried from India to Tibet where later, blended with Yogachara philosophies, it and had a determining influence on **Tibetan Buddhism**. Because of nihilistic implications in the philosophy, Madhyamaka was strongly criticized by both Buddhists and non-Buddhists. Its literature is to be found in the Siddhanta texts, anthologies of the various schools of Indian philosophy. See **Buddhism**

Maenads *G*. See **Bacchantes**

Mag Mell *AE*. Celtic 'Plain of Joy'. The paradise of Celtic mythology where the deceased live under the rule of giant god, King Tethra. It is described in the mythologies either as a beautiful island or an undersea realm. Access is for those who have died gloriously and thus, probably a heaven for heroes. An alternative tradition has the ruler as the sea god, Mannanan mac Lir. Mag Mell is also known at the **Land of Youth**. The myth passes into the Christian era, maintained by the early monks who were intrepid seamen and who probably took courage from the old stories of a heaven beneath the ocean. See **Celtic Religion**, **Elysium**

Magadha *B*. A northern Indian kingdom at the time of the Buddha Shakyamuni, the historical **Buddha**. The region lay south of the Ganges and includes most of what today is Bihar. At first, its capital was Rajagriha then later, Pataliputra. It is the region where Buddhism had its beginnings and from whence, after the third Buddhist council and under the direction of **Asoka**, it spread to other parts of India. There is a direct relationship between the languages, Magadha, Magadhi and **Pali**. Magadhi is thought to be the language spoken by the Buddha Shakyamuni.

Magi *AME*. There are several ideas associated with this term which has a complicated and ancient etymology. The Greek form of the word, transliterated in English as *magus*, is a direct borrowing from Old Persian, itself derived from an Indo-Iranian root *magauuan* suggesting the idea of 'sacrifice', while the Indo-European root carries the idea of 'power' or 'ability'. For the Median priests, who were called Magi, there is more than a hint of 'power'. Herodotus, in the context of pre-Zoroastrian Persian religion, makes reference to the Magi as the sacred caste of the **Medes**, specifically those priests who could interpret dreams. Because their power had been limited by the Persian emperor Cyrus, they led a revolt against his son Cambyses, in an attempt to set their own man, Smerdis, on the throne but were defeated by Darius I. Despite this the Magi survived in Persia, some migrating to Greece and Italy (555 BCE–330 CE) It is probable that they took **Mithraism** with them. The Magi adopted **Zoroastrianism** as it spread throughout Iran and the term *mobed* or magus, is given to the Zoroastrian priests who preside over the **Yasna** ritual. In modern practice, the office of priest is hereditary, passing from father to son. The Old Testament Jewish prophet Daniel, is thought to have been a *rab mag*, a 'chief magus' who was given a Messianic vision. More generally the term has been used to refer to an enchanter, a wizard or magician or to a wise man. The three Magi of Matthew 2:1 Kaspar, Melchior and Balthasar, who brought gifts to the infant Jesus and who are celebrated in the Christian festival of **Epiphany**, were more likely to have been 'wise' men than kings. See **Magic, Medes, Zurvanism**

Magic A system of interrelated and sometimes complex rituals designed to produce certain results that bypass accepted physical causes and their laws. Magic, in one form or another, touches on every religious tradition, either in the form of the simple folk-magic or more complex psycho-metaphysical systems. Whatever the form, magic is always founded on a belief in correspondences between different orders of being. (See **Macrocosm and Microcosm**) Thus, symbolic ritual practices enacted in one realm will have complementary effects in another. **Sympathetic magic** is based on the principle that 'like produces like', that is, the effect will resemble the cause. Thus, hunting dances that climax in the mimed killing of the prey, will prefigure the actual hunt. It is sometimes called 'Imitative Magic' associated with the concept or law of 'contagion' (see **Contagious Magic**), the belief that things or people that have been in contact with them, will continue to interact long after they have been separated or disconnected. For magic to have effect, forces deep within the practitioner's being must be liberated; the ultimate goal is omnipotence, the ability to control 'the all encompassing divine power which religion reserves for God but which magic reserves for man' (Eliphas Lévi). The magician uses his will to effect a change in the reality around him and others, but he will know that it may take the lifetimes of several reincarnations to achieve this degree of power. Magic is wrapped around with secrecy which is the reason for the obscurity of so much of the subject's literature. It is a combination of imperspicuously acquired esoteric

knowledge and an act of the will, thus if you are the custodian of secret knowledge you will guard it jealously, because to share it will diminish its power. But the better reason for secrecy is that magic is an art to be learned, but which may not be taught. Thus, cults or schools of magic have a strict hierarchy, usually of ten degrees, through which the initiates must work their way to qualify, receiving guidance in ever more complex and mysterious systems. This notion of ascent is also symbolic of the soul's journey as it rises through the spheres (the **sephiroth** of the **Kabbalah**) first in this life, then after death. Magic is amoral, its theory and practice making no real distinction between black or evil magic and white or good magic. For magicians, good and evil do not exist except as opposite aspects of a reality that is greater than either and which unites them. If the goal is to be a master of all things, then all things must be experienced, harnessed and reconciled. Magic is not always distinct from religious ritual, in which symbolism is used to evoke feelings and attitudes. In Western magical tradition symbolic correspondences, for example those believed to exist between the macrocosm and microcosm, have been employed to fit the adept to be God's or the 'power's' pure and conscious channel. Magic appeals to the non-rational and creative aspects of the human mind and as such has made formative contributions to religion, psychotherapy and art. See **Magi**
FINAL WORD: 'Magic is the traditional science of the secrets of Nature which has been transmitted to us from the magi. By means of this science the adept becomes invested with a species of relative omnipotence and can operate superhumanly – that is, after the manner which transcends the normal possibility of men.' (Eliphas Lévi)

Mahabharata *H*. Skt. 'the Great Epic', and after the **Ramayana** the second monumental epic of Hindu literature. It tells of the battle of descendants of Bharata, the saintly king and progenitor of the Bharata clan. The poem is probably one of the longest in existence, divided into 18 books of 106,000 verses with something like, 220,000 lines. Tradition says the poem is of divine origin, its author reputed to be the mythical sage Krishna Dwaipayana, the compiler of the **Vedas**. The date of the poem remains uncertain, but it is likely that between the 5th and 3rd centuries BCE, many compilers worked on the text which became a compendium of India's favourite myths and legends. The **Bhagavad-Gita** forms the sixth book consisting of **Krishna**'s instructions to Arjuna, as he prepares for the 18-day battle which is the central theme of the poem. Helmut Hoffman suggests that, 'the key to understanding this immense work is seen by Indians to lie in its moral intention to portray the triumph of virtue and the subjugation of vice … No other work except the Bible has had such influence on the moral education of a culture.' See **Hinduism**

Mahamudra *B*. Skt. 'the great seal'. An important and influential form of teaching and Tantric yoga practice within Tibetan *Vajrayana*. Having been transmitted to Tibet through various agencies, the teaching was finally given to **Milarepa**, thence to Gampopa under whose direction it became one of the main doctrines of the **Kagyupa** School. Sometimes called the 'Tibetan Zen', the philosophy is concerned with the relationship between 'compassion', 'insight' and the nature of 'emptiness'. The yoga practices are designed to enable the meditator to experience these relationships, ultimately to achieve a realization of emptiness which effects spiritual freedom and the end of *samsara*, the birth-death-rebirth cycle. There are two levels of practice. The 'ordinary' practice is concerned to train the mind to 'dwell in peace' (*Samatha*) which results in 'clear seeing' and the transformation of all experience; the 'extraordinary' practice' (**Vipassana**) is an intensive extension of this. See **Tibetan Buddhism**

FINAL WORD: 'The ground of purification is the mind itself, indivisible luminosity and emptiness. The means of purification is the great vajra yoga of mahamudra. What are to be purified are the transitory contaminations of confusion. The untainted pure fruit is the dharmakaya [the true nature of the Buddha] – may I realize this.' (The Karmapa Rangjung Rigpe Dorje. 1924–81)

Mahavira *H. Ja*. Skt. 'great hero'. In Hinduism, the monkey king, Mahavira Hanuman, 'the one with the great jaws' (see **Hanuman**). Also, Mahavira Tirthankara (6th–5th century BCE), the founder of **Jainism**. He was roughly contemporary with the **Buddha**, and lived in eastern India in what is today Bihar.

Mahayana *B. Z*. Skt. 'Great Vehicle', signifying a major movement in the development of **Buddhism** and comprised of many schools. It emerged during the 1st century CE and is dubbed, the greater vehicle because of its concern for the liberation of all sentient beings. It is to be distinguished from **Hinayana**, the 'lesser vehicle', but like Hinayana it is founded on the basic teachings of the Buddha. Mahayana makes its own application of the earlier doctrines in respect of Buddha's transcendence, the notion of emptiness and of its broader, almost universalistic concern for everyone's liberation (see **Universalism**). This ultimate compassion has its ideal expression in the **bodhisattva**. The tradition places less emphasis on monasticism, teaching that the layman can also achieve enlightenment. In this process a person is not alone, but may call on the help of Buddhas and bodhisattvas. In Mahayana the tradition of Shakyamuni, the historical Buddha gives way to the principle of Buddha-nature indwelling all beings. Thus, nirvana is not just a question of release from the birth-death-rebirth cycle, but the realization that because everyone shares in the Buddha-nature, the natural state of things is to be at one with the absolute. As Mahayana developed, it spread from India to Tibet, China, Korea and Japan. The doctrine is to be found in the Mahayana sutras and in the *shastras* that expand and interpret the philosophy. They represent some of the most sublime and profound writings in Buddhism.

Mahdi *I*. Arab. 'the rightly guided one'. The concept of an Islamic redeemer. The failure of an early Islamic political and social revolt, led by Muhammad al-Hanfiya, a son of **Ali**'s, had an important spin off. It was given out that the Prophet Muhammad was not dead but in 'concealment' in the mountains around Mecca. A second coming of the Prophet was to be looked for by the faithful, which would restore peace and justice to the Arab world and created the ideal Islamic society, a task the Mahdi would share with the Prophet Jesus.This piece of eschatological propaganda is the source of the Mahdi myth and as with all messianic movements gave rise to numerous pretenders. The title was actually applied to Muhammad and the first four Caliphs as an honorific. See **Sunni**

Maimonides (1135–1204) *J*. A Spanish Jewish writer and philosopher who has had a formative influence on both Jewish and non-Jewish thought. A physician by profession, he studied science and metaphysics from Jewish and Arabic sources. Forced to flee Spain in 1148, he and his family went first to Fez in Morocco, then to Acre and Jerusalem. Finally in 1165, settling in Old Cairo, he eventually became court physician to the Caliph, but refused an invitation to serve Richard I who was crusading in Palestine. Something of a polymath, his work on *Halakhah*, Jewish law and ethics met with opposition during his lifetime. Posthumously, he came to be regarded as one of Judaism's greatest rabbinical authorities and his works have survived to be the standard of Jewish Orthodoxy.

Maitreya *B. Z.* Skt. Jap. *Miroku*, 'The Loving One', an epithet for the future Buddha, the embodiment of all-embracing love. The cult of Maitreya emerged early in both the **Hinayana** and **Mahayana** schools and may have been influenced by an Iranian saviour-cult associated with someone called **Mitra**. It is well established in **Tibetan Buddhism**, where Maitreya's heaven is known as **Pure Land**. In the Tibetan tradition, he is expected to come in about 30,000 years.

Malcolm X (1925–65) *I*. Born Malcolm Little, but known under several other names, he was a spokesman for the **Nation of Islam** and a black nationalist leader. He considered 'Little' to be a slave-name and used 'X' to signify his lost African tribal name. He advocated black pride, black economic self-reliance and black identity politics, rising to become a world-renowned human rites activist and founder of Muslim Mosque Inc. He was assassinated in New York on February 21st 1965, it being the first day of National Brotherhood Week. See **Black Muslims**
FINAL WORD: 'Human rights are something you are born with. Human rights are your God-given rights.' (Malcolm X. From a speech given in Cleveland, Ohio, April 3, 1964)

Male Cults A term with various applications. Among the most established religious examples are the public Melanesian initiation rites which are accompanied by secret initiations into male cults. The rites themselves are physically demanding, requiring circumcision, blood-letting and tattooing. The object is to purify the young male of 'contagion' from contact with their mothers and other women during the period of early childhood. Initiation also includes teaching novices tribal lore and secret rituals. The object is to appease ancestral spirits who live with the men in the *Haus Tambaran*, the sacred cult house. Within the general tribal cult are sub-cults for bachelors and sorcerers, as well as other groupings. The concept of male cult is also found in the Old Testament's prohibition of homosexuality, 'Do not lie with a male, as one lies with a woman; it is an abhorrence' (Lev. 18:22). Here, the cult was identified with that of the pagan god **Molech** and ritual practice by male prostitutes. It is important to understand this in the context the Hebrew abhorrence of idolatry and that homosexuality was seen as sexual idolatry and the infringement of the laws of ritual cleanliness. The Hebrew word, *toevah*, translated in the **Tanakh** as 'abhorrence', is more concerned with something that is ritually taboo than with something inherently evil. It is precisely this issue that is currently represented in the Gay Pride demonstrations in Israel. Male cults were to be found also among the Greek and Roman mystery religions and are still very much in evidence in university and military fraternities, Freemasonry and similar organizations. See **Aum Shinri Kyo**

Mamluk *I*. Arab. *Mamluk*, 'owned' or 'possessed'. In Muslim countries, 'a slave'. The Mamluks were a military regime of Circassian slave soldiers who were used by Muslim **Caliphs** and Ottoman Turks, but who sometimes seized power for themselves. The Mamluk army was first recruited from non-Muslim slaves by the **Abbasid** Caliphs in the 9th century in Baghdad. They were drawn from a wide area that included Eastern Europe, the Steppes of Volgograd, the Caucasus and what is now modern Turkey. The Mamluk army had no links with the established power structures, thus enlisting them had the advantage of avoiding Muslims fighting each other. Gradually the Mamluks were converted to Islam and were rigorously trained as cavalry soldiers. Technically, once recruited they were no longer slaves but still owed total allegiance to the **Sultan**. Many Mamluks achieved high rank both in military and civil posts throughout the Islamic Empire. The most celebrated of Mamluks were those who, in 1254, seized power in Egypt undermining the Fatimid Caliphs, who remained in place with only titular authority. The Mamluk flag flew over Cairo until c.1375. The two Mamluk dynasties that ruled Egypt were instrumental in defeating the **Mongols**, and the Mamluk Sultan, Baybars (c.1260–77) fought against the Crusaders in Syria-Palestine. In 1340, large numbers of Mamluks in Egypt and Syria were killed off in the Black Death. In 1517, the **Ottomans** overran the Mongols, absorbing Egypt into the Empire. The Mamluks, however, retained authority over the State with a considerable degree of independence from Constantinople. Their influence is still apparent in the architecture of the mosques, the schools and libraries, in the style of bridges, fountains and other public buildings.

The Mamluks were defeated when Napoleon invaded Egypt in 1798. When the Emperor left in 1801, they continued their struggle for independence. Muhammad Ali was appointed governor of Egypt in March 1806 and knowing he would have to contend with the Mamluks and their feudal ownership of the land and for the sources of wealth, he succeeded in splitting them and settling half of them in the Sudan. In 1811, having invited all remaining Mamluk soldiers to his palace on the pretext of celebrating the declaration of war against the Arabs, Muhammad set an ambush and six or seven hundred soldiers were killed. There followed a massacre of Mamluks throughout Egypt. A minor irony of history is that Napoleon, early in the 19th century, formed his own Mamluk corps, sections of which served in his Imperial Guard. After the Battle of Austerlitz in 1805, they won their own regimental flag. Napoleon's famous personal bodyguard, Roustan, was an Egyptian Mamluk.

Mamluk history is colourful, even romantic and during Islam's medieval period the Mamluk's 'finest hour' lasted for two and a half centuries during which the old Arabic Muslim civilization prospered and was culturally enriched by their architecture, the geometric detail and intricacy of their decorative arts and by the extraordinary range and quality of their metalwork. See **Mawali**

Mammon. *X*. A word of Aramaic and/or Hebrew origin, meaning 'riches' or 'treasure' used in the Bible to refer to material wealth or avarice, for example, 'You cannot serve God and Mammon' (Mat.6:24). The New English Bible translates, 'mammon' as 'money', and there are hints of personification that make Mammon into a demon. That the same word is used in many European languages, for example, Danish, Finnish and Polish, is due entirely to the Bible's influence on vernacular vocabulary.

Mana *P*. A supernatural power or force believed to dwell in a person or sacred object or which any object may accrue by practical or ritual means. Mana in people is said to derive from divine and actual ancestors and the closer one is in relationship to this source the more powerful the mana will be. It is a feature central to **Polynesian religion**, where mana is also a form of respect, whether it be for another person or for nature. On this is hung other notions such as authority, power and prestige. Mana may accrue to an object such as a spear or a bow if it has been consistently successfully in hunting. To lend such a spear to another would be to transfer its mana. A fetish object or charm may be endowed with mana by ritual means, but the association of mana with magic, once well supported, is now generally discarded by anthropologists and sociologists of religion. More broadly, mana resides within anything that calls out a sense of awe and respect and some scholars have plausibly suggested that this may be a form of proto-religion, a precursor of all religions. (See **Numinous**) The concept has associations of luck with which the West is familiar in terms of protective crucifixes, Stars of David, charms, lucky coins and mascots, but here there is a definite link with **superstition**. Mana has become (or has always been) a universal archetype of a life force, the underlying element that makes up the universe and everything in it. The idea of life-energy is present in most ancient religions, but the concept is too defuse to define clearly, the religious traditions in question each having their own perception of it.

FINAL WORD: 'Mana is life force, the power that enables us to live. So many people go throughout life without even using mana; they walk through life like they are in a fog. With mana you perceive what life really means and what it's saying to you.' (Lanakila Brandt)

Mandaeans *I*. A small 'Gnostic' Islamic sect found in Iran and southern Iraq. See **Gnosticism**, **Sabians**.

Mandala *H. B.* Skt. 'Circle' or 'arch'. In **Hinduism**, a term used for the considerable collection of stanzas that make up the **Rig-Veda**, which is divided into mandalas or song-cycles. Also a symbolic drawing or diagram, the basic traditional form of which is a square enclosing a circle.

In **Buddhism**, mandalas are symbolic representations of cosmic forces but are revered as sacred images. In Tibetan Tantric Buddhism (see **Tantra**) they are of particular significance, being used to evoke the mystical cosmic forces that are the focus of meditation and to support a meditation practice that requires visualization. The images themselves are frequently a complex synthesis of disparate elements that find unity of meaning in the design that brings them together. In **Vajrayana**, the mandala may function as a shrine on which ritual objects are placed. The meditator can 'read' into the mandala the phenomenal world, his own body and consciousness. In general, there are three kinds of mandalas, the Body Mandala, embodying a specific deity; Speech Mandalas, which represent the sound aspect of a seed syllable placed at their centre and Mind Mandalas, that represent various aspects of mind with symbolic images such as the lotus or the wheels. In Tibetan Buddhism the human body itself can be used as a mandala, when it is perceived as the support for or abode of, the divine presence. The body then becomes a sacred vessel which when used according to the correct rituals, can lead to nirvana. In some practices the mandala remains completely abstract; it does not need to be drawn but can be memorized and visually recalled in meditation; it does not have to be a permanent image, but having,

Figure 6 C. G. Jung found in the mandala one of the great primordial images of mankind.

for example, been drawn on the ground, it is then destroyed once the practice is concluded. It may also be traced in the air, then imagined and visualized by the meditator or it may danced, as is sometimes done by the **Bon**. C. G. Jung saw in the mandala an archetypal image representing the deepest aspects of mind, even the soul itself.

FINAL WORD: 'The mandala serves a constructive purpose – namely, to restore a previously existing order. But it also serves the creative purpose of giving expression and form to something that does not yet exist, something new and unique.' (Jung [1978])

'When, then, the Indian or Tibetan artist designs a mandala he is not obeying the arbitrary command of caprice. He is following a definite tradition which teaches him how to represent, in a particular manner, the very drama of his soul.' (Giuseppe Tucci)

Manes *R*. In **Roman Religion** the name for the spirits of the dead. *Di Manes* referred originally to the dead collectively, as a group of divine beings, but came to be used for the spirit of a dead individual. There was a February festival of the dead, when it was believed they returned from the underworld to haunt the living.

Manicheanism *X*. An extreme form of Persian dualism taught by Mani, Latin, Manichaeus (215–275 CE). He held to most **Zoroastrian** beliefs but deviated from them in teaching that all forms of matter were evil, the response to which was rigorous asceticism and celibacy. Manichean mythologies of creation and redemption and its ethical system are similar to those of **Gnosticism**. St **Augustine** was a Manichean during the years leading to his conversion to Christianity. See **Bogomils**, **Docetism**

Manifest Sons of God See **Latter Rain Movement**

Manitou *Ami*. The Algonquin Indian name for spirit beings and the super-natural power found permeating the whole of Nature as, 'the secret life of every created thing'. It was the **shamans**' function to make contact with these spirit-powers. The **Midewiwin**, the shamanic secret society, was believed to have been founded by the *manitous*. Almost everything, animate and inanimate, could be classed as a *manitou*; it might also be the guardian spirit of an individual, perhaps in the form of an animal (see **Daemon**) that revealed itself in a dream. There is the concept of Great Manitou, a supreme being, virtually a name for God, a concept probably influenced by the Indian's encounter with Christianity. The Indians seemed to have little contact with Great Manitou, he was of less concern to them than the more immediate pluralistic manifestations. The term may also refer to a quality in animals or birds, like 'excellence'; in people, *manitou* is a kind of disposition or ambience rather than the actual presence of a supernatural power.

Mankind United A socio-religious utopian cult founded by the Christian Scientist and entrepreneur, Arthur Bell, in the early 1930s. His published text, *Mankind United*, sought to address the old questions as to why the world was tyrannized by war, poverty, greed and hate. He believed a conspiracy of the rich was the root of the world's evils, obstructing the material and spiritual plenty that all could enjoy. The movement appealed to many disenchanted with traditional religion. Their Golden Rule was the one prescribed in Matt. 7:12, 'Always treat others as you would like them to treat you'. Bell based his cult on an earlier group, The International Institute of Universal Research and Administration, referring to them as 'the Sponsors'. In 1919 they formed 'The International Legion of Vigilantes', to which Bell claims to have been recruited. The Legion launched the '30 Days of Proof', an intensive broadcasting of irrefutable evidence as to how the conspiracy of the rich and the money changers worked and of their alternative Utopia. The ensuing depression was fertile ground for every manner of Salvationist schemes, on which Bell sowed the seeds of Mankind United. 30,000 were recruited with the target to sign-up 200 million 'educated and religious people'. By 1939, the Federal Government had infiltrated the movement and as support for Government policy burgeoned, so Mankind United dwindled. From then on the Movement's manifesto and activities become confused; in the face of Government opposition Bell persuaded his followers to surrender their fortunes to his newly formed, 'Christ's Church of the Golden Rule', and by 1945 he had accumulated property worth $3 million in California, but his membership was down to about 850. The Movement then drifted away from its original mandate and driven by what he believed was the ultimate selfishness of mankind he proposed colonizing other planets, to which those who remained faithful would be transported 'during the brief instant immediately preceding one's so-called death'. Bell, at least, seemed to disappear from view. Despite rumours, there is no evidence to suggest that the cult has re-emerged in the north of England, as Man United.

Mansion of Ka *E*. Mansion of Ka is an alternative name for **Mansion of the Gods**, the 'Ka' being a person's life-force, one of the five constituent parts of the soul.

Mansion of the Gods *E*. In ancient **Egyptian Religion** a general term for the temples, solar temples, **Aten** temples and the New Kingdom cult with its mortuary temples. The latter were developed from crude reed shrines that were representations of the mythological '**Island of Creation**'. See also **Akhenaton**

Manthras *Zo*. 'Holy Word'. The term refers to particular sections of the **Avesta**, the Zoroastrian scriptures that are poetic in character and endowed with spiritual qualities. Zoroaster believed himself to be a *man-thram*, someone specially gifted with the art of composing **mantras**, words or phrases embodying powerful spiritual significance.

Mantike *G*. A form of ancient Greek divination the purpose of which was not necessarily to predict the future, but to seek advice concerning an action about to be undertaken. The enquirers might be either individuals or the state. The basic method was the interpretation of omens by a *mantis*, a diviner or an *exegete*, an official interpreter. The most familiar Mantike were offered by **oracles** such as the famous installation at Delphi. See also **Anthropomancy, Auspicia, Bibliomancy**

Mantra *H. B*. Skt. *Mantram*. In Hinduism, a term for the canon of sacred Sanskrit literature. More significantly, a mantra can be the name of a god given by a guru to his pupil as part of his initiation into the spiritual path. The mantra, sometimes in the form of seed syllables, is synonymous with the god and contains, in a compressed form, the essence of the guru's teachings. Disciplined repetition of the mantra can lead to enlightenment. In **Buddhism** a mantra is a syllable or series of syllables invested with cosmic force and energy, sometimes thought of as the Buddha mind. It is continuously repeated as a form of meditation. In **Vajrayana**, mantra chanting shields the mind against the vibrations of thought and speech and is an accompaniment to detailed visualizations and specific body postures. A distinction is made between the written form of the mantra and its sound. The written form can be visualized, either in the space before the meditator or within his own mind and body. 'Sound concentration' can mean either murmuring the mantra or holding its sound within the mind. See **Om**

FINAL WORD: 'Unlimited powers are said to reside in the shorter mantras, especially the mystic syllables known as *bijakshara* (monosyllabic) mantras and great benefits accrue from their repetition. The most powerful of all is the sound *Om*.' (Benjamin Walker [1968])

Manu *H*. In Indo-European mythology Manu is depicted as the first man, semi-legendary, but possibly based on an actual king. For Hinduism, Manu is the primordial father of the human race. Lord of the earth, he instituted all religion, its ceremonies and laws. The *Laws of Manu* are set out to consolidate the high **caste** position of the Brahmans. (See **Brahmanism**) Manu had ten sons who devoted themselves to the study of the Vedas. The story is told in the **Mahabharata**. See **Puranas**

Maoism From the early 1950s millions of people in China were enthralled with the 'Little Red Book', the *Quotations from Chairman Mao Zedong*. The book was an alternative bible and the Chairman an alternative god. Maoism is both the 'thoughts' of Mao Tse-Tung and a political revolutionary ideology that transformed China. It was, in effect, Marxist-Leninism adapted to the needs of China, a kind of Sino-communist manifesto. Mao's unique contribution was to move the revolutionary focus from the town to the county, from urban workers to peasants. Radical agricultural reform led to Collectivization and this led to the Cultural Revolution and 'the Great Leap forward', an enforced industrialization. The Cultural Revolution which took China between 1966–76, led by the Red Guards, was not only a putsch against the existing power structure, but a force designed to change the attitudes, motivations and behaviour patterns of the Chinese people. It was a utopian vision the aim of which was radical egalitarianism ironically subsumed to Mao's personality cult. Religion of every kind was vigorously persecuted and countless places of worship were destroyed along with the artefacts of thousands of years of Chinese art and architecture. The revolution and its inner caucus, the Gang of Four, was finally overthrown in 1976 by Mao's death and a coalition of political, police and military leaders. See **Communism**

FINAL WORD: 'A revolution is not a dinner party or writing an essay or painting a picture or doing embroidery.' (Mao Tse-Tung)

'Communism is not love. Communism is a hammer which we use to crush the enemy.' (Mao Tse-Tung)

Maori *P*. A Polynesian people whose ancestral migrations to New Zealand started in the 9th century CE. 'Maori', in Austronesian means, 'normal', or 'ordinary', and was used to distinguish themselves from the gods, as mortals. Their religion is a form of nature and ancestor worship based on the belief that everything is endowed with *mauri*, a life force or spiritual essence. Their pantheon includes **Tangaora**, the ocean god and creator of fish, **Tane**, god of the forest and creator of birds and Rongo, a god of peace and agriculture. *Tapu*, is anything sacred and implies spiritual restrictions or prohibitions in the general sense being '**taboo**'. It is applied to many objects and places such as the house of the *Te Puni*, the Chief and to the clothing of high-ranking people. The Maoris welcomed Christianity and adapted its concepts to their own beliefs and culture, but retained the ritual of *tapu* for anything associated with sickness, death and burial. The practice of *Ta Moko*, tattooing, is a vestige of their Polynesian ancestry. The *hei-tiki* neck pendants carved from greenstone and worn by many, are symbols of fertility. There are several modern syncretistic cults such as **Ringatu** (Upraised Hand) founded in 1833 by Te Kooti. It is based on an oral liturgy derived from the Hebrew scriptures and they observe Saturday as the Sabbath and practise faith-healing. The **Ratana Church** founded in 1918 by Wiremu Ratana, a healer during the influenza epidemic, is the largest of the newer sects. It rejects the received traditional religion, looking to angels and Ratana as mediators with the gods. Its 25,000 members are thought to wield significant political influence. The celebrated Haka, danced by the All Blacks, the New Zealand rugby team, is just one of many such ritual dances and is performed not so much to intimidate the 'enemy', but to fire themselves up in the face opposition they believe to be impressive. Thus, the performance of the Haka should not be understood by England's rugby XV as a threat or provocation, but as a compliment to their reputation as warriors.

Mara *B*. The evil demon who tried to seduce the meditating Buddha with visions of beautiful women who in some of the legends were thought to be his daughters. In Buddhist mythology he is the personification of 'unskillfulness', causing the death of the spiritual life. For human beings, Mara is the tempter who makes the material world alluring and the negative seem positive. 'Buddha defying Mara' is a frequently used pose of sculptures of the Buddha, using the **mudra** of the right hand on the right knee and the left hand, palm upwards, in the lap.

Marcionism *X*. A dualistic and heretical understanding of the roots of Christianity put forward by Marcion, a Christian from Asia Minor who came to Rome c.144 CE. He claimed Christianity to be a unique revelation totally independent of the **Old Testament**. Since the most persistent persecution of early Christians came from Jewish sources, Marcion denied the Jewish roots of Christianity claiming that the world was created by an evil demiurge totally incompatible with the love revealed in Jesus Christ. Although there is evidence that they were widely distributed, Marcion's writings are lost. In modern theological debate, 'Marcionism' refers to any interpretation of Christianity that does not give due weight to the Old Testament. Rudolph **Bultmann**, for example, suggested that 'for the Christian faith the Old Testament is not in the true sense God's Word.' **Atheists**, **agnostics** and **secular humanists** share Marcion's disregard for the Old Testament because of its record of genocide and other atrocities which, they contend, discredits belief in God. Marcionism was strongly attacked by the African Church Father **Tertullian**. The heresy faded away during the 5th century.

Mardi Gras The celebration of Shrove Tuesday, the last day of the carnival preceding **Lent**, a merry-making precursor to the following period of abstinence. The carnival season figures largely in Roman Catholic countries and in some of the USA southern states. The carnivals have attracted many non-Christian associations which organize parades and street festivals. In New Orleans, for example, there is a parade of the Mystic **Krewes**, one of a large group of carnival clubs, such as the Babylon Krewe and Bacchus Krewe and the women's Cleopatra Krewe. But the standard for all carnivals is Rio de Janeiro.

Marduk *AME*. In Sumerian the name means 'bull calf of the sun'. He was a Babylonian god that became supreme in the pantheon centred on the city of Babylon. See **Mesopotamian Religion**

Marga Guru Shri Anandamurti See **Sarka, Prabhat, Ranjan**

Maria Legio *X*. A breakaway Kenyan Catholic sect. Thought to have some 250,000 members, it is the largest independent African Church. It was founded in 1963, by two Luo catechists, Simeon Ondeto and Guadencia Aoko, who named the sect after the **Legio Maria**. It is a syncretism of the Latin Roman Mass and forms of **Pentecostal** healing and exorcism, bound by a strict ethic. It gives great prominence to the role of women with an emphasis on devotion to Mary, the mother of Jesus. See **Mary and Mariology**

Mars *G. R.* Identified with the Greek god **Ares**, he was the legendary father of Romulus and adopted as the Roman god of war. Probably derived from the **Etruscan** god Maris, he was originally a god of fertility, vegetation and cattle and only later became associated with battle. As god of Spring, the season of his major festivals, he presided over agriculture. Wearing his war-lord hat, he was offered sacrifices before battle, appearing on the field with his wife-sister-daughter-cousin, Bellona, sometimes called Nerio. His principal temple, shared with **Jupiter** and Quirinus, was on the Capitoline Hill. There were other temples where he enjoyed unique dedication such as Mars Ultor, 'the avenger' in the Forum Augustus and Mars Gradivus, 'he who precedes the army in battle'. The field where soldiers and athletes trained was called the Field of Mars. The blood-red planet and the third month of the year were named for him.

Martinism An occult school founded in Grenoble during the 18th century, by Louis-Claude de Saint-Martin, based on the writings of Martinez de Pasqually. Pasqually's ideas were influenced by **Gnosticism**, the **Kabbalah**, **Hermetica** and the early Christian theologian Origen. Martinist Christianity is unorthodox; their 'saviour' Jehoshua, known as the last of the Guides, is not necessarily identified with Jesus. Subsequently there have been lesser or temporary Guides, the Elus-Cohen or Elected Priests of the Universe who as masters of spiritual doctrines achieved the Réaux-Croix, the highest degree of the Order of Knight-Masons. Initiation to the Order included the calling down of an angelic eminence that became the permanent partner or guardian of the novice. The magical rites of the lower orders were designed to enable the 'operator' to establish contact with the Invisible World. As recently as 2002, a new Martinist Order of the Réaux-Croix (O.R.C) was founded '*to work the traditions and orders of Martinez de Pasqually, Louis Claude de St Martin and Jean B. Willermoz in one organization, where each of the affiliations keeps its unique light*' (website mission statement).

Martyr Those who suffer for a cause. Familiar examples include the mass suicide of the **Essenes** at **Masada**, and the early Christians who died rather than renounce their faith. Christianity has seen a steady succession of martyrs, some of whom were elevated to the status of saint, but most of whom are unsung heroes, enjoying their reward in heaven. Famous martyrs include St Catherine who died on the wheel that gave us a blazing firework and St Sebastian whose body was riddled with arrows. Saints like these have become the centres of popular devotional cults. Religion does not have a monopoly of martyrs. Suffragettes martyred themselves to win the vote for women; Japanese Kamikaze pilots flew their planes into their targets; Ghandi was assassinated working for the socio-political freedom of India's Hindus and Martin Luther King, for the cause of civil rights. Islamic suicide bombers are held to be martyrs by the cause they serve. Today, the term is loosely used for anyone who suffers for a cause.

Marxism Karl Marx (1818–83) together with Frederick **Engels** (1820–95) developed an atheistic philosophy of communism based on the 'class struggle' and the theory of socio-economic evolution derived from **dialectic materialism**. It has sometimes been confused with or rationalized by, a biblically inspired socialism that 'cares for the poor' or with the voluntary sharing of production and resources practised by both religious and secular communities. Marx was greatly influenced by the **idealist** philosophy of **Hegel**, but termed his own form of it, '**materialism**'. From this, he advocated the establishment of a classless, stateless society to be established by revolutionary force. Such a society has never been achieved, since in practice a form of totalitarian 'statism' emerged, born of the need for political orthodoxy. Having said that, the *bourgeoisie*, the middle class were virtually eradicated, but the proletarian masses were left in poverty. Marxism's social doctrine apart, its vehement, almost military atheism has had profound effects on religion worldwide. Marx wrote, 'The criticism of religion ends with the teaching that man is the highest being for man ... he looked for a superhuman being in the fantastic reality of heaven and found there nothing but the reflection of himself.' Engels was even more vitriolic, '... we have once and for all declared war on religion and religious ideas and care little whether we are called atheists or anything else.' In 1913 **Lenin**'s hostility approached hysteria, 'Every religious idea, every idea of God, even flirting with the idea of God, is unutterable vileness ... of the most dangerous kind.' Since the end of the First World War there have been many forms of Marxism, most of these are not philosophies but social theories. The genuine philosophies include, for example, the work of George Lukacs (1885–1971) and Ernst **Bloch** (1885–1977), who also developed aspects of Hegelian philosophy. Many have seen Marxism as a **secular** religion, regarding Marx's writings as sacred texts; some who have become Marxists have used terms like 'conversion', and 'faith' to describe their adoption of the communist creed. See **Leninism**, **Secularism**, **Trotskyism**

Mary and Mariology X. Referring to Mary, the mother of Christ and the cults, sects and various religious traditions formed around her worship, as well as to the orthodox Roman Catholic doctrines concerning her life and her virtues. These are founded on 'the **immaculate conception**', the doctrine that despite conceiving Jesus, she was a virgin and, based on the tradition that she had no further children after Jesus, she remained virginal and without any form of sin. In Catholicism, Anglo-Catholicism and the Orthodox Churches, she is placed above the saints and worshipped as the Mother of God and the Mother of the Church. She is particularly revered for her power of intercession with Christ and the rosary cycle of prayers is based on this belief as are other special forms of devotion. The image of the Sacred Heart, Christ displaying his heart as a symbol of his love for humanity, is an iconography also accorded to Mary. Traditionally she has appeared to people in visions and the places where this has occurred have become the object of pilgrimages, such as

Lourdes. In a Bull of 1950, Pope Pius XII defined her Assumption: 'The immaculate Mother of God, Mary ever virgin, the course of her earthly life having finished, was taken up, body and soul, into the glory of heaven' (*Munificentissimus Deus*, 1st November, 1950). The Bull merely gave dogmatic status to a tradition which was established before the 6th century. The Feast of the Assumption is celebrated on the 15th August. In countries such as Italy, Latin America, Spain and Portugal, Mariology has become syncretistic, absorbing pre-Christian cults. Ever suspicious of idolatry, Protestantism has endeavoured to undermine Mariology by referring to it as, 'Mariolatry'.

The Virgin Mary is much revered in Islam (see **Mihrab**) and she is the only woman to be named in the Koran which describes her, for example, as an *Ayat Allah*, a Sign of God to mankind. She is 'a purified one … exalted above all women of the Worlds' (Surah 3.42). It is of interest to note that the account of the annunciation given in Luke's Gospel is almost identical with that of Surah 19. Hajja Muhibba has said that for Muslims, 'there are as many paths to God as the children of God have breaths, but of all the paths to God the Way of Mary is the sweetest and gentlest of all.'

Masada *J.* Heb. 'fortress'. The infamous site overlooking the Dead Sea, where the **Zealots**, making the final stand of their 'Great Rebellion' against Roman occupation, committed mass ritual suicide rather than surrender. The only written source of the events is in **Josephus**' histories. FINAL WORD: 'And so they [the Romans] met with the multitude of the slain, but could take no pleasure in the fact, though it were done to their enemies. Nor could they do other than wonder at the courage of their resolution and at the immovable contempt of death which so great a number of them had shown, when they went through with such an action as that was.' (Josephus)

Masks The 'false face' has been worn since antiquity for example, by actors in Greek and Roman drama, both to identify character and to amplify the voice. They are the most important man-made religious artefacts and their secular use also has considerable significance. In primitive societies masks were a link with the world of the spirits, providing a new persona by which means the wearer can connect with supernatural forces. Important to the male cult rites of the Melanesians (see **Male Cults**), masks dramatize the presence of ancestors, gods and spirits on whom the wellbeing of the tribe depends. Ritual masks are housed in shrines and their display, often with full costume, takes the form of elaborate dances such as a fire or hunting dance and ritual fighting. In many cultures masks may have the form of animals or birds or combine these with human features. In Sri Lanka healing masks are worn that were grotesquely distorted imitations of the effects of diseases that caused spots, skin rashes and infections of the eyes or ears. Examples may be cited from just about every religious culture, but what they have in common is that they are heavily tabooed and believed to have their own independent powers and existence. Masks, it is said, are not made but discovered. While masks are widely used in a religious context, they are also used in the celebration of folklore festivals, such as the Tyrolean Devil mask. Strange and ugly masks designed to terrify, are sported by children for parties or to celebrate festivals such as Halloween. In secular usage, masks are worn for amusement at, for example, fancy-dress balls and carnivals. They are also used in various traditions of theatre, such as the commedia dell 'Arte and Japanese No theatre. But as well as the face, an atavistic belief lurks behind the wearing of a mask; disguise has a liberating effect, allowing the wearer to play a role otherwise never assumed. By means of the mask a thoroughly secular person may become 'open' to the sacred and the mundane may be seen to be magical.

FINAL WORD: 'It was the mask engaged your mind,
And after set your heart to beat,
Not what's behind.'
W. B. Yeats, 'The Mask'
'Man is least himself when he talks in his own person. Give him a mask and he will tell you the truth.' (Oscar Wilde)

Maslow, Abraham (1908–70) Humanist psychologist. See **Human Potential Movement, Transpersonal Psychology**

Masonic Knights Templar The Knights Templar can be encountered in a number of different manifestations, some being splinter groups of the original medieval Order of Knights Templar founded to protect crusading travellers. The modern Masonic order is a branch of **Freemasonry**, working the highest degree of the Masonic York Rite, but there is no direct historical link with the original medieval foundation. It exists today as one of the most active American philanthropic organizations and is the largest of the world's Templar orders. It differs from Freemasonry in requiring its members to take an oath to defend Christianity, an echo, presumably of the original Crusading Order, whereas Freemasonry is fully ecumenical in offering fraternity regardless of religious affiliation, based on a general affirmation of belief in an ultimate power. See **Knights Templar**

Masonry See **Freemasonry**

Mass X. L. *Missa*. A name for the **Eucharist** adopted principally by **Roman Catholicism**. Its root is *mittere*, 'to send' or 'dismiss' and probably applied to the sacraments from which the laity were excluded or, who having celebrated the Mass were dismissed by the deacon, *Ite, missa est* ('Go, you are dismissed'). Cranmer, in his Prayer Book of 1549 retained 'Mass' as an alternative to the 'Supper of the Lord' and 'Holy Communion'.

Materialism A term used in philosophy for the theory that whatever exists is either matter or dependent on matter for its existence, including material causes. A consequence of this view is that such notions as 'mind', 'spirit' and 'God' must be eliminated from a metaphysical scheme. Everything depends on how 'matter' is defined. Is it, for example, anything that is palpable or anything that can be extended in time and space? If the latter, then rainbows and shadows are examples of matter as well as trees and stones. The range of possible answers shows that materialism is far from being a water-tight thesis, philosophically it remains ill-defined. Even if it was made clear, it does not have to be true, since there is no analytic or observational method that could establish it as true. For this reason, materialism has more the feeling of an attitude or a policy, than a philosophy; it is a point of view assumed so the world may be examined in a particular way, in order to see what might be the result. See **Dialectic Materialism**, **Empiricism**, **Rationalism**

Matrimandir *H*. A sacred building on the Sri **Aurobindo** Ghose Ashram, at Auroville on the Bay of Bengal, north of Pondicherry. It is intended to be a model 'universal township' that is still to be completed. The Matrimandir is spherical and contains in its inner chamber the largest, optically perfect glass globe made. The gardens or Peace Area, can be visited and permission obtained to enter the Matrimandir to meditate for a period of time.

Mawali *I*. Arab. Singular, *mawla*. Originally a term used of a slave, freedman or client, but under the **Umayyads** it was used to designate non-Arab converts to Islam. By a contract, called, *wala'*, non-Arab Muslims were accorded the rights and privileges of the Arabs, but they had to pay an additional tax. Under the **Abbasids** the distinction was eroded, but the Mawali continued to be used to form troops in the service of a **caliph**. See **Mamluks**

Maya *H. B.* Skt. 'illusion'. In Hinduism originally a magical power for creating illusion or deceit. It became the basic concept in *Advaita Vedanta* philosophy in which the term is used to describe the multifaceted 'appearance' of the world, which in reality is a non-dualistic whole, known as **Brahman**. Maya and Brahman are as inseperable as fire and heat and in combination are known as **Ishvara**. *Avidya*, 'ignorance', is the cause of our identifying ego as a separately existing self (see **Self-realization**) an entity among countless others in the illusory world of multiplicity when, in fact, what we think of as an independent existing self is part of what Ramesh Balsekar [2002] calls 'the Divine hypnosis'. Ignorance leads us away from God-realization.

For Buddhism the emphasis of *maya* is also on illusion or deception that causes us to assume that the world of forms and appearance is the only reality. However, *maya* is also the opposite of the immutable, the unchanging absolute Buddha essence. In **Zen**, to regard the phenomenal world as real is not necessarily an illusion, the deception being the assumption that it is the *only* reality, thus veiling what is essential.

Enlightenment, or 'awakening', is the experience of the non-duality of the relative and the absolute. See **Atman, Dualism**

Maya *B*. The name of the mother of **Gotama**, the historical Buddha. She is traditionally supposed to have all the necessary qualities to bear a Buddha. While she conceived in the normal way, on the day she conceived she dreamt that a Bodhisattva came to her in the form of an elephant carrying in its trunk a white lotus and entered her right side. The myth is frequently depicted in temple murals.

Mayan Religion *CA*. The Mayas were Mesoamerican Indians who spoke Mayan languages across the greater part of the Mexican states of Yucatan and Chiapas and the Central American isthmus. They were the only pre-Columbian civilization to develop a written language. Mayan culture peaked during what is termed the Classic period c.300–900 CE, but it had a long evolution and their mythology indicates an extensive polytheism built on earlier beliefs that probably predate 1000 BCE. The Mayan religious drama is complex and multilayered with a cast of hundreds of gods. They acknowledged five cardinal directions, four of which were associated with colours: north, white; south, yellow; east, red; and west, black. The fifth cardinal point is the centre occupied by the huge ceiba tree, the Tree of Life, the axis of the cosmos. The five cardinal directions have their associated gods, together with the natural seasonal and astronomical cycles. The mythology tells of 13 heavens, each with their own god, together with nine gods of the underworld. The earthly plane lies between the heavens and the underworld and in Mayan art is frequently shown as a two-headed turtle or caiman floating in a great lake. All natural, observable elements had their own gods, their associations changing according to the Mayan calendar and the positions of the planets, sun and moon. The *Popol Vuh*, the Quiché Mayan book of creation, tells how the two principal creator gods, Tepeu and Gucumatz decided to consolidate their divine legacy by creating a race of beings who would worship them. Huracan, *The Heart of Heaven*, less personified and more like a natural element such as a storm (hurricane, perhaps), did most of the creating, while his associates looked on, advised and guided the process. He began by creating Earth, then animals. Huracan had problems with creating humanity, making several false starts with mud before finally creating people out of *masa*, corn dough. Thus, maize was not simply the foundation of the Mayan diet but the substance from which human beings were made. This somewhat pictorial cosmology belies its concrete expression in the magnificent cities the Mayans built, together with huge stone temples and pyramids. These architectural wonders were constructed despite their having no knowledge of the wheel or metal tools. Anthropologists have no real idea of the source of the sophisticated system of mathematics and astronomy the Mayans developed. Together they formed the basis of several calendars, including the *Tzolkin*, the Day Count calendar and the Long Count calendar, the accuracy of which is greater than the Gregorian calendar. The Long Count calendar was calculated from 3114 BCE and ends at the Winter Equinox, 2012 CE. Considerable interest is being generated by prophecies based on this calendar that hint of a global catastrophe, possibly ecological, an Armageddon-type conflict or of a great spiritual awakening and the start of a 'new age' (see Gilbert). After the Spanish conquest of Mexico in the 16th century, the Mayans were gradually moved back from one city stronghold to another until early in the 18th century, seemingly in accord with one of the prophecies of one of the few surviving books, the *Book of Chilan Balam*, the Spaniards made an expedition against the last city only to find it deserted, the population having vanished into the jungle. Today, although a few communities survive in the forests of Peten, Mayans, mostly Catholics, live as citizens of Mexico, Guatemala and other Central American countries. There is evidence, however, of a revival of the 'old religion', the re-establishment of the class of the 'Elders' and the continued observance of the calendar rites. See **Mexican Religion**

Mazda Ahura *Zo*. The transcendent god of **Zoroastrianism**. See **Ahura Mazda, Parthians**

Mazdaism *Zo*. See **Zoroastrianism**

Mazdayasni Zarathushtri *Zo*. See **Zoroastrianism, Traditional**

Mazdayasnian *Zo*. A worshipper of the true god, Mazda (see **Ahura Mazda**). The obverse were the evil **Daevayasnians**, who worshipped the evil spirit manifested as **Daevas**. See **Angra Mainyu, Zoroastrianism**

Mbona *A*. The god or spirit of a central African territorial cult. The territory is usually marked out with shrines, for example the principal shrine of Mbona is at Khulubvi among the Mang'anja people of Malawi. Membership of the cult is by virtue of living within a defined geographical region. The cult's main purpose was rainmaking, but Mbona is also invoked against plagues of locusts, epidemics and floods, indeed against anything that might threaten the fertility of the land or the people. The cult, which is at least 500 years old, has resisted or adapted to political and social change. Whatever the circumstances Mbona enjoyed spiritual and moral independence. The cult maintains a 'spirit wife' for Mbona, a woman whose life was consecrated to the cause and who received, by visions and dreams, revelations from the deity. On ceremonial occasions the role of spirit wife is assumed by a local woman, but apart from the spiritual wife, the cult is served by priests and mediums. The status of Mbona seems to symbolize the status and wellbeing of the kingdoms and States. When all is well the cult diminishes, where there are problems or a crisis the cult flourishes. What is reflected here is the extent of the subjection of the common people to an established or imposed aristocracy. Under Portuguese missionary influence in the 17th century, Mbona took on Christ-like qualities and it was this association that led to its greatest territorial expansion and to it becoming one of the most influential religious organizations in Africa.

Mecca *I*. The holiest of Islamic cities and the birthplace of **Muhammad**. It is also the site of the **Ka'bah**, the 'point' which Muslims all over the world face while in prayer. It was from Mecca that Muhammad made his formative *hijrah* or 'emigration' to **Medina** in 622. Mecca is now in Saudi Arabia. See **Islam**, **Islamic Dynasties**
FINAL WORD: 'Mecca admits no non-Muslim foot within its portals. But within that exclusiveness … there is an overwhelming inclusiveness of race and speech and culture.' (Cragg)

Medes The 'cities of the Medes' are referred to in the **Old Testament** (2 Kings, 17:6). Originally thought to have been a branch of the **Indus valley Aryans**, they eventually established an empire in northern and western Iran whose future civilization and empire was derived from the unification of the Medes and the Persians. Their religion, **Zurvanism**, was a heretical branch of **Zoroastrianism**, and associated with the most familiar Median priestly tribe, the **Magi**.

Medicine Bundles *Ami*. The sacred bag or pouch that is the talismanic sign of a visionary's supernatural power. They contain items of significance to the owner such as an eagle's feather, taken from the nest of the bird, shells, parts of dried animals, tobacco, together with the calumet, the reed pipe, herbs and porcupine quills. Its conferment is usually part of the **vision quest**, and a tangible sign given by the subject's guardian spirit. The Bundle was presented together with instructions on its care and use and an orally transmitted medicine song. See **Shamanism**, **Volva**

Medicine Man A controversial English term loosely applied to **Amerindian** religious personages, such as the shaman (see **Shamanism**). Their function is to win the help of the spirit world and **Manitou**, the Great Spirit, for the general benefit of the community. Medicine Men are not always male. The term has also been used for the Witch Doctors or Juju Men of African tribal religions. There is a feeling among some scholars that the term is slightly disrespectful, if not pejorative.

Medina *I*. Arab. *Medinat al-Nabi*, 'City of the Prophets' in Saudi Arabia. Islam's second holiest city after **Mecca**. It was to Medina that **Muhammad** made his consequential **hijrah** from the persecuting Meccans in 622 and where he began to give **Islam** its religious and social cohesion. See **Islamic Dynasties**

Meditation *H. B. Z.* A general term referring to a wide variety of religious disciplines designed to bring the meditator to an experience of **enlightenment**, liberation or awakening. The many techniques used vary considerably, but it is claimed they all lead to this same goal. In **Hinduism** techniques of **yoga** (Skt. yoke) are used to harness or link oneself to God and include practices akin to meditation. A brief survey of some of the terms used will give an idea of the range of meaning and practice represented by the term 'meditation'.

Bhavana (Skt. Pal.) 'cultivation', as of the mind. A general term for any type of meditation requiring unbroken focus of the mind on a chosen object.

Samadhi (Skt.) 'establish' or 'make firm'. In Hinduism, a state of deep meditation trance in which all normal aspects of mental activity cease. There are various stages proceeding to Samadhi; the highest, unmoving or changeless point leads to the realization of union with the divine. 'I am Brahman,' remains just an idea in the mind until the subject-object relationship is transcended in the experience of non-duality (see **Dualism**). In **Buddhism** the goal of meditation is the same. **Mahayana** identifies a great number of *samadhis* designed to achieve different results. The term 'one-pointedness', refers to concentration on a single object using a process that quietens the constant passage of discursive thought in the mind (see *Samatha*). In the **Eightfold Path**, *samadhi* is the general term used for the last three of the eight components, Right Effort, Right mindfulness and Right Meditation.

Sadhana (Skt. from *sadh*) 'to arrive at a goal' so as to perfect something. In Hinduism, *Sadhana* are practices that enable the meditator to master a particular path of yoga. In **Vajrayana** Buddhism, it is a central form of **Tantric** meditation based on a liturgical text that describes in detail the specific deities with which the meditator may be brought into union. To achieve this, a technique of intense visualization is used which brings about the elimination of the subject/object duality. The practice has to be followed under the guidance of a master who will transmit to the pupil the **mantra** associated with the deity. Similar texts and practices are found in Chinese and Japanese traditions of meditation.

For two other important forms of meditation practice, see *Zazen* and *Shikantaza*.

Buddhism offers various meditation techniques, among the principal forms of which are *Samatha* (Skt. Pal.) 'calming' or 'tranquillity' and *Vipassana* (Pal.), 'insight'. *Samatha* is concerned to bring the mind to a state of total tranquillity and stillness by relieving the tensions caused by the conflict between attraction and repulsion. This is achieved by reaching for the state of mental absorption known as 'one-pointedness of mind', where the mind remains totally focused on its meditation subject. Once achieved, the meditator will progress through various levels of *dhyana* or trance. Probably the most familiar technique is to concentrate on the breath as it enters and leaves the nostrils. In some traditions, such as Zen, the pupil is asked to count the combined inward and outward breath as a cycle, usually to ten, then resuming the count. Alternatively, the practitioner can focus on a *kasina* (Pal.) an external object of his choice or on one of the 40 traditional meditation subjects. The result is a physiological change within the body and an altered state of consciousness that enables spiritual development. *Vipassana*, with its goal of 'special insight', uses techniques to bring about direct personal apprehension and verification of the truths of Buddhism. Such insight leads to **enlightenment** and **nirvana**, by means of the intellect. Usually, since they compliment each other, it is recommended that *Vipassana* and *Samatha* techniques are use together.

It is not appropriate here to go into the details of meditation postures and techniques. There is a considerable literature available and there are numerous institutions that offer training in their traditions of meditation. But mention must be made of one of the classical texts on the subject, the yoga sutras of **Patanjali** (2nd century BCE). He set out eight stages in the practice of meditation: i) External ethics; the practitioner's life must be ethically beyond reproach so at to ensure, for example, that he causes no harm or injury to anyone. ii) Internal ethics; this requires the elimination of negative emotions like anger, acquisitiveness, lust, greed and so on. Only on this unimpeachable moral ground, can a meditative practice be established. iii) Bodily posture; some of these, like the lotus position, are extremely difficult to achieve. iv) Breath (*prana*) control; breath is one of the great potencies of the universe. v) Sense control; reducing to a minimum, the distractions of sense experience. The awareness of the both the body and the emotions must be controlled. vi) *Dharana*, concentration, holding the mind firm and steady by using an object on which to meditate. Concentration should not be confused with meditation. Meditation is not an exercise of the will, nor is it the form of practice. It is rather, a state of being that emerges from the cessation of thought. vii) Contemplation, *dhyana*, a turning within of the consciousness. viii) *Samadhi*, superconsciousness, the supreme goal of meditation.

Hinduism and Buddhism are not alone in having meditation traditions, as the following brief survey illustrates.

Taoism exemplifies ancient Chinese practices and teachings which can appear to be paradoxical in that they suggest there should be no conscious intention to meditate or to achieve any goal. The meditator should let go the effort to try or to aspire, abandoning all teachings, doctrines and liturgy, so as to arrive at the state of *wu wei*, 'non striving'. The point is to do nothing and keep still, then the mental sediment will settle.

In **Sufism**, the mystical tradition of Islam, meditation falls into two main groups, *maqam*, based on individual effort and *hal*, based on God's grace. It is said that '*Maqam* is earned, *hal* is gifted'. The individual needs to draw on every form of ritual observance, charity, fasting and pilgrimage. Gradually these external necessities fall away to the point where all veils covering the face of God are raised, leading to an experience of ecstasy. 'Everything perishes except his Face.'

The practice of meditation in **Kabbalah**, a Jewish mystical tradition, focuses on the ten *sefiroth*, divine emanations diagrammatically represented in the form of a tree. In this image, the sefiroth span the great distance between our present finite world, the foot or root of the tree and the infinity of God, the top of the tree. The practitioner is trained in meditative exercises called, 'rising on the planes'. Consciousness is carried along a path formed by links made between the sefiroth, each being a gateway to an alternative world or level. Under the guidance of a

Kabbalist the student will progress along this ascending path through each of these worlds until, at the top, God is encountered. In this journey, the student is always conscious of the experience.

Christianity developed its own meditation traditions based on ancient Greek and Jewish sources. Desert-dwelling monks in Egypt and Syria developed forms of practice as early as the 3rd century CE. In the Middle Ages a form of contemplative practice known as **Hesychasm** was developed by monks of the monastic orders of the Orthodox Church (see **Orthodoxy**). Many Christian mystics, for example St Francis of Assisi (c.1181–1226), St Ignatius of **Loyola** (1491–1556) and St **Teresa** (1515–82) record having been transported into the presence of the divine through their meditative and contemplative disciplines. St Ignatius' *Spiritual Exercises* is effectively a manual of spiritual practice. Accounts of these experiences tell of the dangers of such transportations. St John of the Cross (1542–91) in his intense, mystical poem, *Noche oscura*, described the journey to union with the Beloved as the 'Dark Night of Faith'. St Teresa wrote of 'the great dereliction' and others of a kind of mystical death or a descent into hell. These are, however, the practices of recluses, men and women who have withdrawn and renounced the world. There seems to be no general Christian meditative practice for the lay person except, perhaps, for those able to join a religious retreat. More contemplative orders such as the **Society of Friends** and the **Quietists** bring people together to share a 'sitting in silence' which may give rise to the group being charged with new spiritual dynamism. See **Anapanasati, Discursive Meditation, Satipathana**
FINAL WORD: 'Methods of meditation all have value in helping to develop mindfulness. The point is to use this mindfulness to see the underlying truth. With this mindfulness, we watch all desires, likes and dislikes, pleasures and pains that arise in the mind. Realizing they are impermanent, suffering and empty of self, we let go of them. In this way, wisdom replaces ignorance, knowledge replaces doubt.' (Achaan Chah [2001(b)])

Meditation for Children Historically the practice of meditation lies at the heart of all the great religions. More recently meditation has been extracted from these religious roots and used as a secular practice. There is convincing evidence from scientific research confirming the positive physiological and psychological effects ensuing from the practice of meditation for both adults and more recently for children. These benefits, briefly summarized are:

Physiological: a lowered heart rate; reduced blood pressure; reduced anxiety; reduced stress; relaxed muscles; improved motor skills; alleviated pain; reversed heart disease; alleviation of drug dependency, heightened perception; heightened auditory acuity; increased synchronicity of the two hemispheres of the brain; a new sense of centeredness and wellbeing, among many other things.

Psychological: increased concentration and attention; improved cognitive functioning, increased clarity of thought; increased intelligence;

improved memory; increased creativity; increased empathy; improved self-confidence and self-discipline among many other side effects.

Meditation therefore promotes a unique physiological state which is both deeply relaxed, yet highly alert. This has been shown to be the optimum state for effective learning and performance at any age. Education is beginning to understand the physical, cognitive and emotional benefits of meditation for children. For a variety of reasons, children only take in a small percentage of the material that is presented to them, which renders much learning that is done in schools and elsewhere highly inefficient. Certain prerequisites must be in place before meaningful learning can occur. However exciting the contents of a lesson and however dynamic the teacher is at presenting the material (although these help), little will be learned unless the pupil is fully present, not just physically, but both mentally and emotionally.

The research calls for a new paradigm for education, replacing the over-emphasis on the acquisition of knowledge with an understanding of the paramount importance of mental and emotional states. At its most essential, meditation is the art of learning to pay attention. Being able to concentrate and focus is a highly prized skill which is at the heart of peak performance in all areas of life.

FINAL WORD: 'It never occurs to most people to try to control their minds and unfortunately this basic training is left out of contemporary education, not being part of what is called the acquisition of knowledge. Yet without it what we learn is difficult to retain because we learn it improperly, wasting much energy in the process. Indeed we are virtually crippled unless we know how to restrain our thoughts and concentrate our minds.' (Philip Kapleau)

Medium A person who claims to be able to receive messages, visions or revelations from spirits or ghosts or more specifically, that they can 'channel' not simply the message, but the spirit or non-corporeal being. In the first case the medium will be simply a mouthpiece, in the latter the person will be possessed by the communicating spirit. In both cases the medium may be taken with a form of trance known as mediumistic automatism, when the message may be communicated in the form of writing or drawing without the medium having conscious control. The ouija board, the 'medium's medium', is an example of automatism. The most familiar mediumistic session is the séance, where the medium will be a channel by which a dead friend or relative can communicate with someone present. Sceptics believe such people are deluding themselves or that the mediums are charlatans trading on the needs and susceptibilities of sensitive people. But 'results' in controlled conditions suggest that the processes involved merit serious research for what insights may be gained into the subconscious levels of the mind. See **Extra-Sensory Perception, Spiritualism**

FINAL WORD: 'The hypothesis of surviving intelligence and personality – not only surviving but anxious and able with difficulty to communicate

– is the simplest and most straightforward and the only one that fits all the facts.' (Oliver J. Lodge)

Medmenham Club A notorious club that met at Medmenham Abbey, on the river Thames. See **Hellfire Club**

Medmenham Monks The Cistercian abbey of Medmenhem, founded in the 12th century, fell into ruins at the dissolution of the monasteries in 1547, when all that was left of a community that had never prospered was one, solitary monk. In 1755, it became the location of the **Hell Fire Club** whose former, somewhat ironic name was the 'Medmenham Monks'. Hogarth's portrait of its founder, Sir Francis Dashwood, shows him wearing the monk's habit and kneeling before a statue of **Venus**.

Medusa *G*. A female gorgon-like character whose glance could turn people to stone. Some of the mythologies placed her with Stheno and Euryale, as one of the three gorgon sisters, who had fangs, brass hands and hair of venomous snakes. In what is probably the best known account, Medusa was once a beautiful woman who was raped by **Poseidon** in Athena's temple. As punishment for the desecration of her temple, **Athena** changed Medusa's body to match that of her sisters. While pregnant with Poseidon's child she was beheaded by the hero Perseus, the legendary founder of Mycenae.

Meher Baba (1894–1969) An Indian spiritual **guru** and teacher who claimed to be an **avatar**, or incarnation of God. For most of his life he remained silent, but his teachings spread through his extensive travels and publications, one of which, *Don't Worry, Be Happy*, became well known through Bobby McFerrin's song. It reflects Meher Baba's ultimate optimism that in the end we will all be united with God. He became famous, among other things, for his work with 'Masts' or the 'Mast-Allah', those 'intoxicated with God' who appeared to be mentally disabled but who were, in fact, spiritually disabled because of their 'higher plane' experiences. Meher Baba visited thousands of them, sometimes setting up ashrams where they could be cared for. His cosmology is a combination of **Vedanta** philosophy (see **Vedas**), **Sufism** and Christian mysticism. His teachings are available in numerous publications from which he singled out *God Speaks* (1954) which he said was the most important for this age. His tomb-shrine at Meherabad in India, is a place of pilgrimage.

Melanesian Religion *P*. The vast oceanic area and innumerable archipelagos of the Pacific known as Melanesia includes Fiji, New Caledonia, the Solomon Islands, Papua New Guinea, Papua and Vanuatu. The region offers an equally extensive range of religion. Most Christian denominations are represented together with primitive, almost stone-age animism, scarcely touched by the modern world. Behind the headhunting, cannibalism and human sacrifice, for which these religions are infamous, is a belief in a multiplicity of supernatural powers generally focused in the concept of **mana**. Other general characteristics include oral traditions of stories of **dema-deities** the *Tumbuna*, or tribal ancestors, the initiatory **male cults** that are associated with the **Haus Tambaran**, and the complex trading relationships which have ritual bond-making significance which, in some places, have developed into prophet-led renewal movements called **Cargo Cults**. Many Melanesian traditions also share extravagant festivals of ritual and dance called **Singsing**, and the universal practice of *poisen*, secret techniques of healing, magic and sorcery. Sadly, traditional indigenous practice has declined as a result of Christian mission, but the old beliefs still lie beneath what in many places is a thin veneer of 'civilized' religion and emerge from time to time in new syncretistic forms like the Cargo Cults. See **Polynesian Religion**

Melchizedek *J. X.* King of Salem and 'Priest of the Most High God' (Gen.14:18). He blessed Abraham and gave him hospitality. Some traditions understand the bread and wine offered to Abraham was a proto-Eucharist. More importantly is the establishment of Melchizedek as the origin of a succession of idealized priests, which Heb. 6.20 and 7.1ff, affirms was continued with Jesus. For some Christian denominations the priesthood of the 'order of Melchizedek' is taken as the authority for anticlericalism and the 'priesthood of all believers'. Numerous cults and sects have been built around the concept of Melchizedek's succession for example, the **Gnostic Order of Christ** and the **Holy Order of MANS**. These and other sects believe that priests of every tradition of the Western world are ordained into the priesthood of Melchizedek.

Mencius (371–289 BCE) *C.* A Latinization the Chinese name, Meng-tzu, 'Master Meng', a Chinese philosopher who spent his life trying to persuade the constantly warring central states to base their government on Confucian morality. Mencius' influence has survived in his basic thesis that 'human nature is good', and that people have a predisposition to lead morally responsible lives. A good ruler would win the unqualified support of the people if he governed on this basis. Confucian morality, however, does not just happen and while the seed of it resides in every human heart, it needs cultivation. His many conversations with rulers were recorded in the *Meng-tzu*, itself an expansion of Confucian philosophy. See **Confucianism**, **Confucius**

Mende Religion *A.* The Mende are a large ethnic group of about 700,000 people, whose tribal lands are in Sierra Leone, Liberia and Guinea. Their mythology suggests that from the 2nd century onwards they migrated from Southern Sudan. The Mende are an agricultural community, cultivators of rice and other crops and practise crop rotation. The supreme creator god, Ngewo, rules the universe, assisted by other spirits and the ancestors. The earth is sometimes thought to be his wife. Ngewo and the other spirits are invoked for protection, to sustain the wellbeing of individuals and the community and to ensure fertility. They are usually appealed to through the ancestors, but may be approached directly in time of crisis. Close ancestors are called Kekeni and the more remote, Ndebla. Ancestor worship is the basic religious ritual involving post-funeral grave rites and sacrifices offered to ancestors at a time of misfortune. Much of Mende religion is centred on secret societies which control the rites of passage. The Poro oversees male initiation, education and political progress through the tribal hierarchy; the Sande supervises female initiation, including **circumcision**, childbirth, virtue, the laws of marriage and sexual relations. Carved **masks** believed to be the manifestation of the spirit Nga-fa, are used in religious ceremonies. It is one of the features of Mende religious culture that it is the women who, through the Sande Society, control the commissioning, carving and wearing of the Sowo mask or Bundu helmet. Throughout Africa women often act as intermediaries between the spirit world and the earthly world, but there are no other known African examples of them having the exclusive use of ritual masks. The dancer wears a long grass dress, so that only the mask is evident in the dance, enhancing the impression of the presence of a spirit rather than a human being. It is expected that the spirit of Sowo, will be embodied in the dancer during the ceremony. In the 19th century large numbers of the Mende were sold into slavery; in the 1930s an American linguist found a family in coastal Georgia that sang an ancient song in the Mende language which had been passed down over a period of 200 years. In the 1990s, in a Mende village in Sierra Leone, the same song was still being sung. The story is told in a 1998 documentary film, *The Language You Cry In*.

Mendelssohn, Moses (1729–86) *J.* A philosopher at the centre of the German Enlightenment. His wide-ranging interests covered, for example, Homer, Aesop, Pope, Burke and **Rousseau**. He was nicknamed the 'Jewish Luther', working for Jewish civil rites and translating the **Pentateuch** and Psalms into German. His eclecticism and broad vision brought him into conflict with both Jewish and Christian orthodoxy involving him in long-running arguments about Pietist theology (see **Pietism**) pantheism and his assertion that Judaism was founded on reason. His philosophy, which addressed such matters as the immortality of the soul and the existence of God, is known for its lucidity. He had a close association with the playwright G. F. Lessing. See **Scientific Society of the Study of Judaism**

Mendicants *B. Z. X.* L. *mendicare*, 'to beg'. Sometimes known in Christianity as 'Holy beggars'. Certain orders of friars, the 'Begging Friars', lived entirely on alms. These orders include Franciscans, Augustinians, Carmelites and Dominicans. Their commitment to begging is based on the vow of total poverty, of not having any personal possessions and refusing to handle money. In Buddhism the mendicant tradition is followed by **bhikkus**, the fully-ordained male members of the **sangha**, or community. The same vows of poverty and renunciation also apply to the *bhiksuni*, the nuns.

Mennonites *X*. Followers of Menno Simons (1496–1561) a priest from Dutch Friesland who absconded from the Roman Catholic Church. In 1536 aged 40, he joined the **Anabaptists** to become a pacifist leader among them and eventually to establish the Mennonites, an Anabaptist splinter-group. With several other sects they came to form part of the **Radical Reformation**. Their theology and beliefs are fundamentalist, salvation is by faith alone through conversion and confirmed by **baptism**. Practice includes rigorous nonviolence and total separation from the 'abomination', the **Roman Catholic Church**. In April 1632 the Dutch Mennonites adopted the Dordrecht Confession of Faith, other groups adopting it in the following years. Wherever they travelled they found themselves in conflict with the established churches and forced to flee. One of the monarchs that gave the group sanctuary was Elizabeth I and while in England they made contact with the **Baptist** John Smythe. Eventually Smythe led his Pilgrims, first to Holland and then to America. Mennonite teaching influenced the Baptists and the **Quakers**, thus contributing to the religious freedom characteristic of modern America. In 1768, Catherine the Great of Russia gained land from the Turks in the area of the Black Sea, the present-day Ukraine. She invited Prussian Mennonites to farm the land of the Steppes in exchange for religious freedom and military exemption. The group thus settled in the Ukraine are known as the Russian Mennonites. In 1870, many of them emigrated to the Plains States of the USA and the western Canada and others followed after the First World War and the Russian Revolution. There are also Mennonite orders in India. See **Amish, Hutterian Brethren, Old Order of Mennonites**

Menorah *J*. 'You shall make a lamp stand of pure gold …' (Ex. 25:31) The opening words of the instructions given by God to **Moses** for making a seven-branched lamp that would provide perpetual light in the sanctuary, later the Temple. It gradually became the universal symbolic ornament of Judaism, later to be supplanted by the *Mogen David*, the Star of David. The Menorah used for the feast of **Chanukah** has eight lights and an additional one, the *Shammash*, from which the others are lit. Menorahs are usually made of silver or brass, embossed or moulded and with a wide variety of ornamentation.

Mercury *R*. Mercury is the Roman takeover of the Greek **Hermes** and most of the old god's functions were assimilated into the cult. He was the god of trade, commerce and profit. As messenger-boy of the gods he is depicted wearing winged sandals and helmet. The caduceus he carried, a staff with two entwined snakes, was a gift from **Apollo**. His temple was built in 495 BCE, on the Circus Maximus, a racetrack and major trading centre, so a suitable place for his temple to be. It stood between the plebeian Aventine and the patrician Palatine, heightening Mercury's function as mediator. The cult was very popular among the colonized nations of the Empire and became identified with the **Celtic** god Lugus and the Germanic god Wotan.

Merkabah Mysticism *J*. Heb. *Merkabah*, 'a chariot'. An earlier, long phase of Jewish mysticism before it crystallized into the medieval **Kabbalah**. A form of Jewish Gnosticism, its literary sources can be traced from the 1st century BCE. Although the tradition of Jewish mysticism was mostly carried by Kabbalah, Merkabah had its own, unique, doctrines, the central one being 'throne', or 'chariot' mysticism, drawn from Ezekiel's vision in the opening chapter of his prophecy. God's 'throne' or dwelling place, is seen to be moving like a chariot; it is something that has always existed, thus, not created, symbolizing all aspects of creation. This throne-world is similar to the Greek *pleroma*, meaning the totality or fullness of God's power. It is the mystical centre of the Divinity, the region of light occupied by aeons, eternal spiritual beings. The quest is to recover the lost knowledge of the divine origins of human beings, which is why Merkabah mysticism takes its place within **Gnosticism** and **Hermetica**. The Jewish mystic's vision is expressed in the somewhat esoteric language of his own religion. To recover this lost knowledge the adept must pass into a state of mystical meditation and will journey through seven *heikhaltot*, 'halls', each guarded by an angel who will demand the mystical password. The passwords are formed from secret combinations of letters of the Hebrew alphabet and could only be transmitted to a student already endowed with mystical experience and understanding.

Meru, Mt *H*. The name of the legendary mountain of Hindu cosmology, sometimes known as Mt Sumeru. It is somewhat like the Mt **Olympus** of Greek mythology, being the place where Brahma and other deities live. Tradition has it that the mountain is 480,000km high and is to be found on Jambudvipa, one of Hinduism's mythological continents. The main temple at the famous complex of Angkor in Cambodia, is a symbolic representation of Mt Meru.

Mesmerism An 18th-century phenomena introduced in France by the Austrian doctor, Franz Mesmer, who believed **astrological** influences were brought to bear on people through an energy similar to magnetism. He began to treat his patients with magnets or magnetically charged fluids, before deciding that the medium of the cure was an energy or a magnetic fluid actually within the practitioner. It was thought to be similar to electromagnetism, dubbed 'Animal Magnetism'. The movement became famous for Mesmer's ability to induce sleep or a trance state in his pupils, a process which became known as 'mesmerizing'. Eventually it became synonymous with hypnotism and as such had a considerable influence on **spiritualism**, **mind science** religions and any belief system requiring an altered state of consciousness. See **New Thought Movement**

Meso-Paganism A form of paganism which has been significantly influenced by monotheistic or nontheistic world-views but which has been able to maintain an independent religious presence in, for example,

Amerindian religion and **Australian Aboriginal religion**. See **Neo-Paganism, Paganism, Paleo-Paganism**

Mesopotamian Religion *AME*. Mesopotamia (modern Iraq) was the ancient region in southwest Asia, between the rivers Tigris and Euphrates. Settled from c.5000 BCE it spawned several civilizations, including those of the **Sumerians, Assyrians, Akkadians**, Babylonians (see **Babylon**) and **Harranians**. They figure significantly in the Old Testament's history of Israel, each having their own religious traditions. The reign of Hammurabi, recorded by an uncertain chronology as from c.1728 BCE until his death in c.1686 BCE, marked the beginning of a new period in Mesopotamian politics and religion. Prior to Hammurabi, each of the many religious centres had their own chief deity, with a group of minor deities clustered around them together with their female consorts. In general, what emerged was a clearer definition of this pantheon and the growing supremacy of the god **Marduk** in accord with the wishes of secular rulers. It was a move towards centralization and political cohesion, with the local gods of the smaller communities having less significance, but enabling local rulers to maintain the prestige of their satellite cults. Despite subsequent progress towards **monotheism**, for reasons of expediency the cult of Marduk was sustained alongside those of other gods and their consorts. The establishment of Marduk was a thoroughgoing enterprise, with all the original incantations, prayers and lamentations being edited and the polytheistic mythology rewritten in favour of Marduk's supremacy. The cult of **Anu**, originating in Sumeria, ran like a subplot through Babylonian-Assyrian religion. He was a sky god, lord of constellations, the king god of heaven and of spirits and demons. Priests recognized the cult by making him the first of a triad, with Enlil and Ea, symbolizing the heavens, earth and water. A second triad, Shamash, Sin and Ishtar, represented the sun, moon and the life-giving power. Never far in the background was the rivalry between **Assur**, the head of the **Assyrian** pantheon and Marduk, champion of the Babylonians. The rivalry of the gods reflected the military and political rivalry of the two states. In 689 BCE, Sennacherib destroyed Babylon, removing the statue of Marduk to Nineveh. Other than this substitution and that some of the gods had different attributes, the Assyrian pantheon was virtually the same as that of the Babylonians, as were their religions. See **Parthians**

Messiah *J* and *X*. Heb. *mashiach*, 'anointed one'. A term originally associated with Judaism, designating a person set aside and invested by God with a special role. The Greek word for anointed, *christos*, is translated as 'Christ'. In the Old Testament priests were anointed (Lev. 4:3) and more specifically, the king, 'the Lord's anointed', whose person was sacrosanct (1 Samuel 24:6) and in whom theocracy was invested. Judaism teaches that the Messianic concept existed in God's mind before the creation of the world and that the Messiah will be a perfect man, but still entirely human and without any of the associations of divinity ascribed to the concept in Christianity. The anointed Messiah will lead the world towards the fulfilment of prophecy and is not thought to be a personal saviour. Malachi established the prophet Elijah as the forerunner of the Messiah, 'Lo, I will send the prophet Elijah to you before the coming of the awesome, fearful day of the Lord' (Mal. 3: 23). For this reason the Messiah is potentially present in every **circumcision**, he is anticipated at the conclusion of every Sabbath and a place is set for him at the celebration of every **Passover**, which is not only a remembrance of Israel's flight from Egypt, but also as a celebration of hope in the Passover of the Future.

Inevitably, throughout post-biblical Jewish history, there has been a succession of false messiahs. Perhaps the most famous were Shabbethai Zevi who proclaimed himself messiah in 1648 and Jacob Frank (1726–91) For a short while these pretenders gathered around them 'prophets' and a small but enthusiastic following. These glittering but ephemeral lights remind the Jewish people that the true Messiah has to be earned, that he will come only when Israel has achieved sanctification through humility and the complete acceptance of the will of God. Rabbinic tradition has it that the Messiah will come when Israel fulfils the conditions encapsulated in such phrases as, 'O, that today you would hearken to his voice' (Ps. 95:7); 'If Israel would keep a single Sabbath in the proper way, forthwith the son of David will come' (Babylonian Talmud); and 'if Israel repents for one day, forthwith the son of David will come'(ibid). Running parallel to the hope of a spiritual Messiah, is a secular and political interpretation of the messianic concept. Simeon Bar Kokhba (Son of the Star) the Jewish general who led the rebellion against Rome, 132–135 CE, was heralded as Israel's deliverer who would establish a new age in which the Jews would be independent and free of the tyranny and occupation of the Romans. Bar Kokhba and his followers were annihilated by the Roman general, Julius Severus. The Jewish people have had to wait until 1947 before such an independent Jewish state was constituted and there are those who see in this political 'miracle' the fulfilment of the Messianic prophecy. Messianic hope has strengthened Jews throughout their centuries of **diaspora** and persecution and has lent a certain mystery and energy to Jewish legend and folklore. This concept of an expected, anointed, deliverer 'of the house of David', was carried through into the New Testament (see Matt. 2:4–6) and the title 'Christ' was accorded to Jesus at the time of his birth on the authority of angels, 'Today in the city of David a deliverer has been born to you – the Messiah, the Lord' (Luke 2:11). At his trial Jesus was asked 'Art thou the Christ?' to which he answered affirmatively (Mark 14:61ff) a reply confirmed after his resurrection when he identified himself with the Messiah of the Old Testament (Luke 24:26). Belief in the coming Messiah and the Messianic Age is still prevalent among orthodox Jews. Presumably, for Christians, this event will be the second coming. See **False Prophets, Salvation**

FINAL WORD: 'Our Christian conviction is that Christ is also the messiah of Israel. Certainly it is in the hands of God how and when the unification of Jews and Christians into the people of God will take place.' (Joseph Ratzinger, Pope Benedict XVI)

Messianic Movements Generally, movements that have sprung up around individuals who proclaimed themselves messiah, or who have been hailed as such by their devotees. It is not always easy to make a distinction between prophets (false or otherwise) and visionaries. Many so-called visionaries speak of impending doom and the way to avoid it and some of them have had messiaship thrust on them. Usually it is a claim to divinity that marks out the founders of messianic movements. A somewhat spectacular modern movement in Britain, was that of the **Agapemonites** (1846–1956) another appeared in Holland in the 1950s when Louwrens van Voorthuizen, a fisherman, declared himself to be God. Happily, he preferred to be called, Lou, who as God incarnate taught that the Bible, the churches and the clergy were superseded by him. He had a passion for cigars and when asked about this, replied, 'Why shouldn't God smoke?' Many of his tracts, explaining that the end of time was imminent, were sold around the streets of Amsterdam by his women followers. When he died in 1968, it seemed his claim to immortality failed the final challenge. Other, so-called, messiahs include Haile Selassie, the Abyssinian Emperor whose cult was established by the **Ras Tafari** movement; Mohammed Ahmed, the Mardi, who stirred up rebellion in the Sudan in the 1880s and Hsui-Chuan who, influenced by American missionaries in the mid-19th century, believed himself to be the younger brother of Jesus. His followers became a Chinese version of the children of Israel, whose Promised Land was the *Ta'-p'ing t'ien kuo*, the heavenly kingdom of great peace. This was to be gained by overthrowing the Manchu government and his movement, probably exploited by political and military leaders, inspired the Taiping rebellion which began in China in 1851 and lasted until 1864. There are innumerable messianic movements and claimants can be found throughout history and from within most religious cultures, but modern examples have usually appeared in non-Christian and underdeveloped countries. See **Messiah**

Metaphysics Some scholars have suggested the word was first used when an untitled manuscript was found among **Aristotle**'s effects. It followed the work titled, *Physics*, thus it was simply called Metaphysics, *meta* being the Greek word for 'after'. But 'after physics' has come to have a philosophical meaning. The Greek philosophers were much concerned with *Phusis* or *Physis* – that is 'nature', and with the protogenos, the primeval god of the origin and ordering of nature. Such philosophies were interested in what today are called the physical sciences but they also speculated about the origin, meaning and nature of the universe, matters that were beyond their actual knowledge. Such metaphysical theories, for example **monism** and **pluralism**, eventually examined the physical, mental and spiritual characteristics of the universe until the discipline became identified with three specific subjects: i) ontology, the study of 'being'; ii) theology, the study of God or gods; and iii) universal science, which we know as logic. In the modern curriculum these have become reordered as the philosophies of religion, mind and perception. Metaphysics has been attacked as being a futile and vague enquiry by, for example, **Hume, Kant, Heidegger, Russell** and **Ayer**. See **Logical Positivism**

Metempsychosis The transmigration of souls or the passage after death of a human or animal soul into a new body, which may be of the same or a different species. In ancient Greece and in India, notably in **Hinduism**, it was believed that the **soul** would take a new physical form on a higher or lower plane, depending of the quality of the life lived. The idea is also basic to most schools of Buddhism. See **Karma, Reincarnation**

Methodism *X*. Originally a nickname for the 'Holy Club', an 18th-century religious society in Oxford to which both John and Charles Wesley belonged. On 24th May 1738, John Wesley experienced an evangelical conversion, 'I felt my heart strangely warmed,' he wrote. Influenced by Calvinism, Wesley taught that only faith was need for salvation and the realization of Christian perfection. Together with his brother Charles (who wrote the hymns for which he became well known) and George Whitefield, John Wesley established a chain of societies linked by Christian commitment and fellowship, eventually separating from **Anglicanism** to form the Methodist Church. They have suffered many subsequent divisions but were mostly reunited in 1932. Church government is similar to **Presbyterianism**, and its supreme authority is the Methodist Conference consisting of equal numbers of lay and ordained members. Its worship makes use both of a prayer book drawn from Methodism's earlier Anglican roots and of informal extemporary prayer and hymn singing. In 1794, Methodism was carried to north America where it spread rapidly to become a major presence; in 1968 it joined with the Evangelical Brethren to form the United Methodist Church. There are Methodist Churches throughout the world, many with their own independent Conferences.

Mevlevi *I*. Or, Mawlawi Tariqah. A Turkish **Sufi** Dervish order, well known as 'the whirling dervishes' for their celebrated dance tradition. (See **Sema Ceremony**) Apart from their dancing, the order is distinguished by its form of initiation which requires a long period of *khalwah*, 'seclusion' and the practice of group chanting as a form of meditation. It traces its origin to the 13th century and to the great **Rumi**, since when the order is known for its liberalism and religion of love, offering spiritual refuge and enlightenment to anyone wanting to develop their humanity to the highest level. See **Dervish, Dervish Groups, Murid, Tariqah**

Mexican Religions The indigenous religions have developed through the successive civilizations of the Olmec, from c.2300 BCE, the Teotihuacan (c.300 BCE–c.650 CE), Maya (c.250–c.900 CE), Toltec, from c.700 CE and Aztec, at its height from the 14th–16th century. The Spanish conquest from the middle of the 16th century, began the process of Christianization. **Aztec** and **Mayan** religion and mythology have left a legacy that suggests the ancient mythologies still reside beneath the cultic practices of the predominantly Catholic faith which, in some regions, is syncretized with elements of the ancient religions. For example, the Virgin of Guadalupe, a Roman Catholic icon in the Basilica of Guadalupe, is a symbol of Mexican nationalism, Zapata's followers having worn the image on their hats during the Revolution. More profoundly and enduringly, perhaps, the Virgin is taken to be a mystical link between Catholicism and the indigenous religions, a syncretic manifestation of the indigenous goddess Tonantzin and the Virgin, thus combining cultural pluralism with a kind of spiritual *mestizaje* or fusion.

FINAL WORD: 'The Mexican people, after more than two centuries of experiments, have faith only in the Virgin of Guadalupe and the National Lottery.' (Octavio Paz, 1976, Nobel laureate)

Mezuzah *J*. Heb. 'doorpost'. A cylinder usually made of metal containing the first two paragraphs of the *Shema*, which is attached to the doorposts of Jewish houses. See **Phylacteries**

Micronesia *P*. A region of small islands in the western area of the North Pacific, together with its people, culture and religions. The Federated States of Micronesia are made up of Guam, the Marshall Islands and other island nations in the Pacific. Melanesia includes Fiji, New Caledonia, the Solomon Islands, Papua New Guinea, Papua and Vanuatu. The region, which both overlaps and is sandwiched between Polynesia and Melanesia, comprises people with language groups that differ from the other regions. Their original, indigenous religions are similar in character to Polynesia and Melanesia but form a less distinctive pattern. A scant mythology suggests that many Micronesian cultures believed the world to have always existed, an article of faith that simplifies matters considerably. Within the ever-existing world, the earth separated from the water, the islands emerging from the sea with the sky ever apart as a celestial observer of these events. Fire may have been stolen from the sun. Stories tell of the origins of food and tobacco, otherwise the religious culture is familiar, with ancestral and sacrificial cults, but with the rituals and the priesthood comparatively less developed. Mana is given through personal relationships rather than by a spirit. See **Melanesian Religion, Polynesian Religion**

Midewiwin *Ami*. A secret society of Ojibwa and Chippewa shamans known also as 'The Grand Medicine Society' or 'Lodge', but some scholars believe this association to be erroneous (see Eliade [1989]). The process of initiation into the Midewiwin rehearses a return to the mythical times of the beginning of the world when the Great Spirit revealed the mysteries of the first 'great doctors'. It includes a ritual death and rebirth. There are four levels of initiation and it is the higher level initiates who are regarded as **medicine men**. An extended period of instruction is necessary to acquire the herbal knowledge and philosophy transmitted by elders. For admission to the first level, the novice must fast and undertake a **vision quest**. The philosophy stresses the importance of a balanced personal life and respect for plants and animals, so as to achieve social harmony. The Midewiwin today has a significant membership in the upper Great Lakes region and has spread from the Ojibwas to neighbouring Indian people.

Midrash *J.* Heb. 'investigation', 'study' or 'exegesis'. The term is used of Rabbinic literature to denote, i) a method of interpretation and ii) the name of a collection of exegetical texts or of a single verse subjected to the midrashic method. The method is one of eliciting meaning from a biblical text that goes beyond the literal, thus Midrash is always an interpretation usually relevant to the moment or period in question. There are two kinds of Midrash, halakhic Midrash (see **Halakhah**) which interprets law and haggadic Midrash (see **Haggadah**) with interprets non-legal texts. The writing and compilation of Midrash occurred over a long period, roughly from 400 CE to the 13th century and are grouped in families or series according to their dates. Another level of Midrash involves making comparisons between interpretations made at different periods.

Mihrab *I.* Arab. An ornamented arch containing a 'niche', situated at the eastern end of a **mosque**, to signify the direction of **Mecca**. All Muslims must face Mecca when praying or prostrating. The *Mihrab* is the architectural and institutionalized symbol of the central Islamic concept of a common orientation or focus for all Muslims; the orientation is itself a symbol of the unity of the one and only God. God is one, humanity is one and the two are bound together in the one true religion. The *Mihrab* focuses all of this in the one mosque, just as all mosques through the *Mihrab* are focused on the *Ka'bah*.

An entire chapter of the Koran is given to the Virgin Mary (see **Mary and Mariology**). Her cult in Islam is figured in the *Mihrab* itself, which is sometimes inscribed with a quotation from the Koran that honours her. If a burning lamp is a feature of the *Mihrab*, the presence of Mary is believed to be symbolized by its blue flame.

Milarepa (1052–1136) *B.* Tib. *Mila*, 'one who wears the cotton cloth of an ascetic'. Buddhist teacher and philosopher to whom were transmitted by his own teacher, Marpa, the complete teachings of the **Mahamudra**. His teaching and application of the philosophy brought about the founding of the **Kagyupa** School.

Mill, James (1773–1836) Scottish philosopher, historian and economist, a follower of Jeremy **Bentham**. He was a passionate protagonist of education and one of the founders of University College, London. His work was developed by his son, John Stuart **Mill**. As a utilitarian, Mill argued that religion did not advance human happiness but beset people with anxiety and conflict, encouraging painful practices such as celibacy, fasting and other forms of voluntary self-torture. His son records that he remained in a state of troubled perplexity until he accepted the truth that, 'concerning the origin of things, nothing whatsoever can be known'. The account continues, 'He found it impossible to believe that a world as full of evil was the work of an Author combining infinite power with perfect goodness and righteousness. His intellect spurned the subtleties by which men attempt to blind themselves to this open contradiction.' See **Utilitarianism**

Mill, John Stuart (1806–73) English empiricist philosopher and social reformer, who was educated by his father, James **Mill**, and introduced by him to **Bentham** and other utilitarians. He supported Auguste **Comte**, but not his social theories which he believed impeded individual freedom. He contributed to the philosophy of religion, arguing that monotheism was a more scientific form of theism than polytheism. He contrasted the notion of God ruling the world through variable, inconsistent acts of will, with that of ruling by invariable law, the latter being more scientific and therefore, capable of investigation. Probably his most influential work was in the field of logic which influenced Frege and **Russell**. See **Utilitarianism**

Millenarianism A belief in an imminent radical change in the social, political or religious order. Usually the change is expected for negative reasons such as the rulers, government or social organization being corrupt, exploitive and unjust. Some form of powerful force will put the matter to rights. Medieval millenarianism understood the world to be ruled my maleficent demons and until the 19th century the Chinese entertained a similar idea, the demons having a somewhat different connotation, being associated with ancestral spirits and worship. For millenarians in the modern world, the need for change is exacerbated by the worldwide consortiums, commercial and industrial globalization and the spoliation of the planet. In response some religious groups have committed mass suicide as their way of effecting a radical change based on a belief in a transportation to another, 'better place'. To effect change, others have resorted to terrorism or have simply withdrawn to await the intervention of God or the second coming of Christ. See **Messianic Movements**, **Millennialism**, **Mormons**

Millennial Church of *X*. See **Shakers**

Millennialism *X*. An eschatological concept affirmed by some Christian denominations, that the Second Coming of Jesus Christ will usher in 1,000 years of justice and peace on earth. The idea has been the inspiration behind various millennial movements, including those of the **Shakers** and **Mormons**. Some Millennialists believe in an imminent apocalypse and many attempts have been made to put a date to Christ's reappearance as have, for example, the Millerites, the New York and New England followers of William Miller, in the mid-19th century. (See **Millerite Movement**) Amillennialism or Non-Millennialism is an opposing view, holding that the Kingdom of God is already present in human society as the Church or the 'fellowship of believers'.

Millerite Movement *X*. Founded by the **Deist** William Miller (1782–1849), who by means of the 'day for a year' equivalence in biblical time, calculated from the **Old Testament** book of Daniel and the **New Testament** book of Revelation, that Christ's second coming was imminent. He began to preach his advent message in 1831, beginning the revivalist fervour of what is known as the 'great second advent awakening'. In 1836 he published his *Evidences from Scripture and History of the Second Coming of Christ about the Year 1843*. His followers called themselves Adventists. As usually happens, the event did not take place and many left the movement in what was dubbed 'the great disappointment'. See **Advent**, **Adventism**, **Seventh Day Adventists**

Mimamsa *H*. Skt. 'investigation'. One of two branches of Vedic philosophy, the **Purva Mimamsa**, the oldest and the Uttara Mimamsa, also known as **Vedanta**. See **Darshana**

Mindfulness *B*. Skt. *Smrti*, Pal. *Sati*. A central concept of Buddhism and of the various techniques of **meditation** designed to bring about **enlightenment**. See **Anapanasati**, **Samatha**, **Satipathana**, **Vipassana**

Mind Only School of Buddhism Skt. *Cittamatra*, 'consciousness only' or 'mere mind'. The tradition is officially known as the **Yogachara** School of **Mahayana** Buddhism, 'the School that Teaches Knowing'. See **Vijnana**

Mind Science Cults Also known as Mind Therapy Cults, they use methods of mind control and indoctrination. The techniques are based on psychology and neurology mixed with occult practices designed to evoke the latent divinity believed to reside within every individual. Examples include **Heaven's Gate** and **Scientology**. Similar mind-control practices are associated with ideologies maintained by political tyranny, as happened in Stalinist Russia and Nazi Germany. See **Gurdjieff**, **Marxism**, **Stalinism**

Minerva *R*. The Roman goddess of wisdom and crafts whose mythology was heavily influenced by the Greek **Athena**. In early Roman cultic practice she was known as the daughter of **Jupiter** and Methis. Her name may be derived from the Indo-European root *men*, from which the English words 'mental' and 'mind' are derived. The **Etruscans** also had a goddess called Minerva, from which there may have been a secondary influence. As with many of the gods and goddesses she had a busy agenda (Ovid called her 'the goddess of a thousand works'), being identified with warriors, poetry, medicine, commerce and as the inventor of music. Athenian mythology has her sprung directly from the head of her father. She was worshipped throughout Italy but in her warlike function only in Rome where, on the Capitoline Hill, she was one of the Triad with Jupiter and **Juno**.

Minotaur *G*. The Greek mythological creature with a human body and a bull's head, hidden by Daedalus in the **labyrinth** of Knossos, Crete. Every nine years, seven young men and seven maidens were sent from Athens to be its prey. He was killed by Theseus.

Miracle It has never been an easy term to define. There are miracles attributed to God, gods, unspecified and unidentified powers and to humans. One possible definition is, any effect caused by an interruption of or suspension of, natural law, which is therefore ascribed to a supernatural power, but the usefulness of this is relative to time and culture. Such a happening would have been perceived as a miracle in biblical times, as for example, the parting of the Red Sea to give the Israelites safe passage or Jesus' feeding 5,000 people with two loaves of bread and five fish. Typical of miracles are those claiming to bring the dead back to life or working less dramatic but equally extraordinary, healings. Traditionally, therefore, a miracle is observable 'happening' that transcends the powers of nature, because it is caused by divine intervention. Miracles are not providential acts, such as the calm sea at the time of the Dunkirk evacuation, since the purpose of a miracle lies beyond its effects, namely to prove God's existence or the power of the cult's spirit. It can be argued that the incidence of miracles has decreased with time to the point where the philosopher, Thomas **Hobbes** (1588–1679) asserted that since miracles have ceased, revelation of God was given entirely by the Bible. **Spinoza** was ahead of his time in denying all miracles, while **Hume** asserted that experience confirmed the 'uniformity of Nature' to be true and that he could not imagine any evidence that could convince him of a miracle. For Christians the gospel miracles are the main focus of attention, together with other events down the years such as the weeping statues of the Virgin Mary or the shrines of saints that are believed to have the power to heal the sick and the shrine at Trecastagni in Sicily, which can prevent the eruption of Etna.

FINAL WORD: 'Miracles are not contrary to nature, but only contrary to what we know about nature.' (St Augustine)

Mishnah *J*. Heb. 'teaching'. A philosophical code of law compiled c.200 CE by Rabbi Judah ha-Nasi. It formed the basis of later Talmudic and Rabbinic literature and represents the views and opinions of dozens of scholars, often conflicting and presented without comment by the editor. It was carefully arranged into six parts, each subdivided into 63 treatises and each treatise into chapters totalling 525, themselves divided into 4,187 paragraphs, each one a *Mishnah*. The range is comprehensive, covering agriculture and the levying of taxes, prescriptions concerning religious festivals, marriage and divorce, civil and criminal law, the practices of the Temple and its cult and matters of impurity, diet and sexual relations. The language is post-biblical Hebrew but words from

Aramaic, Latin and Greek are used. Further commentaries have been added, most importantly those of Moses **Maimonides** in the 12th century. It has been translated into several languages, including Latin, German and English.

Mitanni *AME.* An influential Hurrian Kingdom. See **Hurrian Religion**

Mithraism *R.* An ancient Persian mystery religion, prominent from 1st century BCE to 5th century CE. Mithras is a syncretism of the Persian-Indic god Mithra and other **Zoroastrian** deities. Known to have flourished for at least 2,000 years, the cult also absorbed **Babylonian** concepts. The religion first came to light in the Eastern Mediterranean and was practised in the Roman Empire, to become popular with Roman soldiers. When in 391 CE Theodosius' decree finally banned all pagan cults, it took the form of an initiatory **mystery religion**. As with other mysteries there were no scriptures and little is known about it. We know that the cultic centre was the *mithraeum*, either a natural cavern or a construction resembling one. It was equipped with raised benches along the side walls where a ritual meal could be eaten, and a sanctuary before which stood a pedestal-like altar. Most temples would have had room for only 30 or 40 individuals. There are many *mithraeum* scattered across the Empire in places where the legions were stationed. Some have survived as crypts beneath Christian churches. The place of honour was accorded to a *tauroctony*, a representation of Mithras slaying a bull and for this reason there is an association with Perseus whose constellation is above that of the bull. The members of the *mithraeum* were divided into seven ranks through which they could progress by successive initiations until the fourth rank, with only a select few proceeding beyond that level. The cult, which was austere, required rigorous ordeals submitted to in underground chambers and became hugely influential in the Roman Empire. Five temples to Mithras have been found in Britain alone. See **Mitra**

FINAL WORD: 'If Christianity had been arrested in its growth ... the world would have been Mithraist.' (Ernest Renan)

Mitra *AME.* A version of the sun-god and an important Iranian deity, first appearing c.1400 BCE inscribed in a **Hittite** treaty made with the Mitanni, a Hurrian kingdom in northern Syria. In this context he is a **Vedic** deity along with Varuna (see **Devas**) and **Indra**. As a proto-Indian-Iranian deity reconstructed as Mitra, he became a major deity of **Zoroastrianism**, with his name rendered as Mithra, the son of god or **Ahura Mazda**. It was as Mithras that, after the conquests of Alexander the Great, the cult was carried to the Roman Empire. See **Hurrian Religion**, **Mithraism**

Mi-tsung or **Chen-Yen** *B.* The Tantric Buddhist 'School of Secrets'. Like some traditions of **Taoism** emphasis is placed on sexual ritual based on the belief that, 'Buddheity is in the female generative organs'. In China,

Mi-tsung flourished during the Yuan Dynasty under the emperor Kublai Khan (1216–94). Most Buddhist schools have denied sexual desire as a means for spiritual advancement and monks and nuns are enjoined to observe celibacy. The literal translation of Mi-tsung is 'Lost Track', a term interpreted by Mi-tsung **Kung-fu** as a means of deceiving the enemy or opponent by concealing one's movements or by deceptive movements. In effect, Mi-tsung is the Chinese form of **Tibetan Buddhism** which introduced **Mandalas** to China and through the agency of the monk Amoghavajra, is said to have converted three Chinese emperors. Practice included drawing mandalas, magic, the casting of spells and elaborate secret rituals probably of the sexual nature referred to above. The Mi-tsung school was eventually replaced by Lamaism and its influence may be seen in Tantrism. See **Lama**, **Shingon School**, **Tantra**

Mitzvah *J*. Heb. 'commandment' or 'precept'. The term refers both to biblical and Rabbinic law and by reference to the total ethical system directing Jewish religious and social life. The Rabbis computed 613 *mitzvoth*, 248 of which are said to correspond to the number of organs in the body and considered to be positive duties; the remaining 365, corresponding to the number of days in the year, are prohibitions. In general terms, *mitzvoth* are any religious or pious obligation. See **Halakhah**

Modalism *X*. A 2nd- and 3rd-century Christian heresy that denies the doctrine of the Trinity, teaching that there is only one person in the **Godhead**. That one person is God, who has manifested himself at different times under different names or modes. Thus Father, Son and Holy ghost, are three different names for the same person, rather than three different persons. The heresy was taught in various forms by Noetus, Praxeas and Sabellius. Modern, modified forms of Modalism are to be found in the teaching of William Branham. See **Branhamism**, **Sabellianism**

Modernism A cultural movement that has had a profound influence on religious philosophy and practice as well as on the process of secularization. Generally associated with an explosion in the arts and architecture, 1910–30, the term has become a critical idiom setting up something of a watershed, first in European culture then, subsequently, more widely. It was in effect a rebellion against the received traditions of the 19th century and a search for new forms or a new language, be it literary, musical or artistic, in which to express new perceptions. First called the 'avant-garde', it set itself against the status quo and was controversial in its advocacy of freedom of thought and expression, radicalism, experimentation and an evocation of primitivism. Typical of the movement was the psychology of **Freud** and **Jung**, the philosophy of **Nietzsche** and Bergson, the Futurist and Communist manifestos, the music of Stravinsky and Diaghilev, the painting of Picasso and Matisse and the writing of Apollinaire, Ezra Pound, Conrad, Proust and James Joyce. Thinkers across most major religious traditions identified with these huge energies in an endeavour to produce a religion without myth, expressed in concepts and a language that was relevant. See **Bonhoeffer, Bultmann, Deconstructionism, Demythologizing, Derrida, Lyotard, Postmodernism, Tillich**

Mohammedanism *I*. Considered offensive by many Muslims, it is an English term for Islam, the religion of **Muhammad**. The objection is based on the assertion that it implies the worship of Muhammad in the same way that Christianity implies the worship of Christ. However, among followers of the orthodox '**Koran Alone**' tradition, the term Mohammedanism is used of the rest of Islam which is seen to use authorities other than the Koran such as the *Hadith* and the *Sunnah*, the sayings and established traditions of Muhammad.

Moirae Gk. The three Fates of Greek mythology, Clotho, Lachesis and Atropos. They were first named in Hesiod's *Theogony*. *Moira* meant a person's 'lot' or 'allotted portion in life', which in general terms was something that was fixed, in much the same way as Hindus and Buddhists understand karma. The Fates, it was believed, are present at birth because at that moment the individual's destiny is decided. See **Fate**

Moksha or **Mukti** *H*. Skt. 'liberation'. The final release from all worldly conditioning and ties, that is, from the cycle of *samsara*. It is the highest of the four goals to which human beings can aspire, the others being wealth, pleasure and duty. For those concerned with the development of their spiritual life and potential, *moksha* should be the sole aim. See **Enlightenment, Nirvana**

Molech or **Moloch** *AME*. Both a pagan god and, arguably a technical term for child sacrifice. An example of this usage is noted in 2 Kings 23:10, where as part of his sweeping anti-Baal reforms King Josiah destroyed ('defiled') the Tapheth, the special altar or pyre where his son, daughter or any child might be offered to Molech. As a god he was worshipped by the **Phoenicians**, but he may also have been the god Baal-Ammon, of Carthage. Old Testament references do suggest that children where sacrificed to Yahweh. We have a clue as to the motive from Micah 6:7, 'Shall I give my first-born for my transgression, the fruit of my body for the sin of my soul?' The prophets disapproved, arguing that such a practice was not a part of Israel's indigenous ritual, but imported as an imitation of the heathen cults by which the Israelites were surrounded. Modern research suggests that use of the name 'Molech' has been misunderstood and that the term refers only to the practice of child sacrifice and not to a god. Moloch is derived from a re-pointing (changing the vowels) of the Hebrew *Melech*, 'King', intended to be a derisory and ironic comment by the prophets on the dangers of syncretism. The jury is still out. See **Male Cults**

Monastery A community of persons bound by vows to live a religious life often in full or partial seclusion. Also, the buildings in which such a community is housed. The monastic tradition is observed in several major religions, such as Buddhism and Christianity. See **Monasticism**

Monasticism Its origin are to be found in 4th-century Egypt, when small groups of hermits took to the desert in search of solitude so as to develop spiritual perfection. The monk's quest for personal salvation became a service to others leading ordinary lives who, it was believed, derived benefit from the withdrawn communities' concentrated spirituality. A monk's main occupations are prayer and manual labour, exemplified by the **Benedictine** motto *Pax ora et labora*, 'Pray and work'. Each monastic community has its own 'rules' which support the individual and help sustain the community's vows of poverty, chastity and obedience. Western monasticism has been primarily influenced by the rule of St Benedict. From the 12th century, orders of friars emerged who, although living by the rule of their order, engaged the world through preaching and teaching. Female orders of nuns were originally more strictly enclosed in their convents but like the friars, they have become visible as nurses, teachers and charity workers. The tradition of monasticism has always posed problematic questions for Christianity. Does the monk's asceticism have lasting and general value for the Christian Church? Is the tradition of withdrawal a necessary balance to outgoing evangelism and the Church's presence in the world? Does the emphasis on celibacy suggest that the married relationship is inferior and does marriage put the higher spiritual experience beyond reach? The monasticism of the **Orthodox Church** constitutes one spiritual body to which all monks and nuns belong. There are no separate orders and the 'rule' focuses on prayer, contemplation or **Hesychasm**, and self-discipline. The **Hindu** tradition varies between the sects, but in general the monks or Sadhus, may form communities. **Buddhism** has its own monastic tradition, the Sangha, divided between the *bhikku* and *bhikkhuni*, the male and female communities. The tradition is coenobitic, the emphasis put on the importance of community life. Islam does not support either monasticism or celibacy, however there are today, initiatives that move towards a form of monasticism such as brotherhoods of dervish monks who live in a monastic style.

Mongols Broadly, the nomadic people of Mongolia, anthropologically, the people of the Mongoloid race. Some time in the 13th century they erupted from Mongolia and through a series of conquests established the greatest contiguous land empire in the history of the world. There are various theories put forward for these invasions most of which focus on the Mongol leader, Genghis Khan. The polytheistic Mongol religion centred on shamanism and Genghis is known to have had committed shamanic beliefs. The legend tells of how the sky god, Tenggeri, called him to bring the entire word into unity under one sword which, in effect, gave Genghis what amounted to a mission to make shamanism a universal religion. The whole story is vast and complex, bound up with the Mongol army's reputation for terror tactics effected by the 'Three All' policy: 'Plunder all', 'Destroy all', 'Kill all'. Because of the fragility and rivalry of their tribal relationships, they were eventually defeated in 1517 by the **Ottoman** Turks. See **Islamic Dynasties**

Monism A philosophical view of **metaphysics** that has its origin in the Greek enquiry into the meaning and nature of the universe. The monist view is that there is just one essence, principle, substance or energy, from which everything else is derived. It is to be distinguished from **dualism**, which asserts there are just two substances, matter and spirit and from **pluralism**, which holds that there are many substances. Monism is associated with pantheism and panentheism, the belief that there is one, absolute God that either is or indwells, everything. The philosophical school of **idealism** is a monism, in that it argues that the one substance underlying everything is, mind. This is sometimes referred to as absolute monism. As a perception of 'man' monism rejects any dualism of body and mind or flesh and spirit. A neutral monism suggests that both the mental and the physical can be reduced to one basic substance, energy. Physical monism holds the view that only the physical is real and that the mental can be reduced to the physical. There are numerous other shades of meaning that adjust, combine or qualify these basic monistic ideas and each of the major religions have developed their own forms of it. The philosophers **Spinoza** and **Hegel**, are among those who have proposed a theory of monism. Neutral monism my be found in the philosophy of William **James** and Bertrand **Russell**.

Monkey A sacred animal in India, probably because of its resemblance to man. The most famous of the monkey chieftains is **Hanuman**. Some **African religions** hold that apes can speak but they refrain from doing so in case they are made to work. In Egypt, the baboon was sacred to the god **Thoth**.

Monolatry The worship of one god only, where it is believed others exist. It is a qualified polytheism, where the existence of other gods is acknowledged but only one of which is worshipped. The practice is to be distinguished from **henotheism**, the worship of many gods one of which is elevated to supremacy. See also **Kanthenotheism, Monotheism**

Monotheism A belief in a single, all-encompassing God, usually given the attributes of omnipotence, omnipresence and omniscience. Traditionally only those religions derived from biblical sources are thought to be thoroughly monotheistic, although Islam sees the Christian **trinity** as seriously undermining this. Pre-biblical religion has its monotheism for example, the cult of Aten during the reign of the pharaoh Akhenaten. Polytheistic religion may have a core of monotheism, as does Hinduism with the concept of Brahman with which all strive to be unified. The *Trimurti*, the Hindu trinity of **Braham**, **Vishnu** and **Shiva**, are believed to be aspects of the one God, in much the same way as are the members of the Christian trinity. The Sikh scripture, the **Guru Granth Sahib**, opens with 'One Universal Creator God. The Name is Truth,' and although there are many names for God they all refer to the same, one, supreme being as do the **Beautiful Names** of Islam. Taoism, perhaps, offers the most abstract monotheism, since the Tao has no personal attributes or qualities. Thus Taoism is free of all the problems of theodicy. Zoroastrianism, one of the earliest monotheisms to be established, has had a major influence on Middle Eastern monotheisms that have taken and adapted to their needs such concepts as, heaven and hell, judgement and the notion of messianic mediation. Monotheism has always been associated with established authority such as Imperialism and the State, since the relative nature of the latter, has needed the absolute sanction of the former. See **Deism**, **Polytheism**, **Theism**, **Unitarianism**

Montanism X. An early Christian sect that appeared in Phrygia c.156 CE, founded by Montanus, a convert to Christianity. He practised and encouraged ecstatic prophecy, based on the authority of 1 Cor. 14: 3, 5. '... when a man prophesies, he is talking to men and his words have power to build; they stimulate and they encourage. ... The prophet is worth more than the man of ecstatic speech.' Montanus was joined by two prophetesses, Prisca and Maximilla and at a time when Christianity was more tolerated, the movement spread rapidly to other regions of the Roman Empire. Probably the most famous Montanist was **Tertullian** (c.160–225 CE), a leader of the Church and a prolific author, who before his defection to Montanism was called the 'Father of the Latin Church'. It has to be remembered that with all early Christian schismatics, there was the faith-hedging belief in the imminent return of Jesus Christ. The Montanists drew on this apocalyptic energy and together with their rigorous asceticism and doctrine of voluntary martyrdom, they found themselves in conflict with the leaders of the Church. Constantine's conversion to Christianity and the beginnings of a Christian empire made Montanism illegal. It was, in any case, accused of harbouring pagan elements and dubious practices that included dyeing the hair and painting their faces, sacred dances performed by virgins, gambling and lending money on interest. By the end of the 3rd century they no longer looked for the New Jerusalem in Phrygia expecting it to be established Palestine, a view supported by Tertullian. In 550 CE, the bishop of Ephesus dug up the corpses of Montanus and the prophetesses and had them burned. Under Justinian (483–565 CE) a sizeable group committed suicide. When it became clear that the end of the age was not imminent, the Montanists had outlived their purpose, but persevered as a protest against the worldliness of the Catholic and Byzantine Church. **Pentecostalism** is sometimes known as neo-Montanism.

'Moonies' The somewhat pejorative nickname of the followers of Sun Myung Moon, founder of the **Unification Church**.

Morality For Christianity, the combined and balanced love of God and man is the foundation of morality. It came to be accepted as the main theological virtue, together with faith and hope, alongside the cardinal virtues of prudence, temperance, fortitude and justice which were derived from classical ethics. In Catholicism the principle of morality was developed into a complex casuistry involving ideas of penance, with fine distinctions made between moral precepts to which, in the 17th century, the Jesuits added the concept of 'probabilism'. This was applied to cases of conscience when certainty was not possible. It implied moral relativism and leniency, rather than absolutism, a position rigorously opposed by the Jansenists (see **Jansenism**), who on the authority of St Augustine, emphasized human depravity, original sin and the indispensability of both divine grace and **predestination**. Post-Reformation Protestantism reacted against Jesuit casuistry, proposing that salvation could be won by the 'good works' of the individual, rather than by faith alone. The creation of an ethical code which is a standard of social and individual behaviour is notoriously difficult to lay down and in the modern age impossible to achieve, either on religious or secular principles. The issues have been debated since Greek philosophers searched for a rational foundation for a just and egalitarian society. By and large, Western society has come to focus on the **Golden Rule**, which generally applied means that people should treat others as they would wish to be treated. Eastern ethical philosophy, for example, that of Hinduism and Buddhism is more holistic, in that it calls for total respect for all nature, specifically for all sentient beings. In some traditions of Buddhism, virtue allied to wisdom, is thought to be more important than *samadhi*. See **Yi**

Moral Re-armament or **MRA** Known in its early days as the Oxford Movement or the Oxford Group, it was founded in the 1920s by an American Christian evangelist, Frank Buchman and a group of Oxford undergraduates. The Oxford Movement created controversy at the outset when the University authorities challenged their right to make the affiliation official. The political context of the Movement's foundation was the tension following the re-militarization of Germany after the First World War, against which they put forward the argument that what was needed was moral, not military rearmament'. They pressed their point by founding what became, Alcoholics Anonymous. In Germany in 1938, Buchman renamed and reconstituted the Oxford Movement, Moral Rearmament, basing it on the 'Four Absolutes', honesty, purity, unselfishness and love and encouraging its members to be politically and socially active. MRA is the source of the idea that changing the world begins with changing oneself. Originally with Christian roots, it has become a movement that draws all kinds of people from both religious and secular backgrounds, staunchly advocating that divine authority and sanction is not necessary for a moral agenda for society. The power of the mind knows and judges what is right and wrong and determines morality accordingly.

FINAL WORD: 'Tom Driberg, in his The Mystery of Moral Re-Armament, quotes a story that was found in the Nazi secret police records that an ex-AA member might find amusing. A Swedish woman who had been angrily denouncing the Nazis, after attending an Oxford Group meeting, felt guilty and proceeded to "make amends", writing a letter of apology to the Nazi leader.' (From a review of Tom Driberg's book *The Mystery of Moral Re-Armament*)

Note: The MRA is not to be confused with the High Church Anglican **Oxford Movement** of the mid-19th century.

Moravian Brothers X. Called also the Bohemian Brethren or Hussites, the commoner names for the *Unitas Fratrum* founded in Bohemia (Czechoslovakia) in 1457 by Jan Hus. The movement was identified with Bohemian nationalism which weakened Catholic influence and, eventually, the Hussites linked up with the Reformation in Eastern Europe. In 1722 the Brethren were 'renewed' by the Lutheran Count Zinzendorf as the Moravian Brethren. Its own statement of intent declared that the Moravian Church seeks 'to exemplify the living Church of Christ constituted of regenerated men and women, while it affords a common meeting point for Christians who apprehend dogmas variously'. The basis of Moravian belief is personal faith in the crucified Saviour, with the scriptures as the only rule of faith, the love of God manifest in Christ and justification by faith alone. To this is added a traditional Christian eschatology, a belief in resurrection, judgement, heaven and hell, with **Baptism** and the **Lord's Supper** the only sacraments. It developed self-sufficient communities and overseas missions. Its devotional forms and liturgy influenced the **Methodists**. See also **Pietism**

Mormonism X. The better known name the 'Church of Jesus Christ of Latter-Day Saints'. The sect was founded in Manchester, New York in 1830 by Joseph Smith (1805–44). Smith claimed to have been given a revelation which enabled him to 'discover' the Book of Mormon, which has become the sect's bible. Under the leadership of Brigham Young, the group moved to Salt Lake City, Utah in 1847. At first their practice of polygamy brought them into conflict with the Federal Government and in 1890 the group was advised to give up the practice. Mormonism has it that Jesus Christ revealed himself to early American settlers who were told that America was the location of his life on earth and where the New Jerusalem will be established. It is an American form of **millenarianism**, the belief that Jesus Christ will usher in a thousand-year period of just rule. Pre-millenarianism teaches that this rule will follow Christ's second coming, post-millenarians that it will prepare for the second coming.

Note: There has never been a religion or institution with the name 'Mormon Church', and its use is potentially offensive. Members are known as 'Latter-day Saints'. 'Mormon' is an ethnic reference and there are Mormons who are not members of the Church.

Morrigan *Cel.* The Celtic 'Great Queen', goddess of Sovereignty. See **Celtic Religion**

Mortal Sin See **Sin, Venial Sin**

Moses *J.* Judaism's most important prophet, teacher and lawgiver. He brought them out of slavery in Egypt, led them through wilderness of the Moab plains and the Sinai desert, towards the Promised Land, where they would settle. Moses was not allowed by God to enter the Promised Land himself, not as is popularly believed because he broke the tablets on which the Law had been carved, but because in enacting the miracle of bringing water out a rock (Num.20) he did not give 'sanctity' and credit to God. Moses was able to see the Promised Land in the distance from the summit of Mt Nebo, where he died and was buried. The turning point in his life was encountering God in a bush that was burning but not consumed. In this form God commissioned Moses to return Egypt where he had been born and raised, and demand Pharaoh to free the Israelites. The **Talmud** identifies Moses as *Moshe Rabbenu*, 'Moses our Rabbi', a sage who studied **Torah** and who was God's first disciple.

Mosque *I.* Arab. *masjid*, 'a place of [ritual] prostration'. In many ways the mosque is similar in form and function to other traditional places of worship such as the synagogue and some churches. In place of an **altar** or **Ark** is the *Mihrab*, an architecturally arched niche set in the *qiblah*, or wall, indicating the way Muslims must face for worship, namely towards the **Ka'bah**, in Mecca. The *minbar*, the steps from which the sermon is preached, is situated next to the *Mihrab*. Mosques have to have a court and at least one fountain, since ablutions before worshipping are obligatory. 'When ye rise up to prayer, wash your faces and your hands to the elbows and wipe your heads and your feet to the ankles' (Koran 5:9). A typical feature of a mosque are the minarets from which the call to worship is made. Muslim worship is a calm and wholly absorbed practice, marked by a certain natural humility that derives from the sense of awe and wonder with which Allah, the creator is held. In accordance with the **Pillars of Islam**, devout Muslims will pray five times a day wherever they are, but ideally congregational worship is preferred. Worship is led by an *imam*, 'one who stands in front', to direct the timing of the ritual movements of prayer. Everyone faces the *Qiblah*, the required direction towards Mecca and both men and women attend. Women, however, are segregated in an area of the Mosque prescribed for them, in much the same way as are women in an orthodox synagogue. Mosques, as with other places of worship, are also centres of religious education, charity, mission and theological debate.

Mother Goddess She is a figure older than history that features in many worldwide religions. Her areas of influence include human love and fertility, the energy that drives people to war, the giver and depriver of life. The Mother Goddess is invariably associated with the earth on which human community has always been entirely dependent. It being inextricably connected with survival, humans since prehistory, have personified the earth and worshipped it together with the elements that have formed and nourished it. Small statues with exaggerated features have been found among man's earliest artefacts across the world, representing the fertility on which human survival is dependent. Perhaps one of the most unfortunate consequences of secularism is that in Western society the earth has become desacralized; the ancient awe and reverence has given way to exploitation from which all the current ecological problems derive. An associated theme throughout more recent religious history is the dominance given to God as male. It was not always like that. Time was when gods and goddesses vied with each other for cult supremacy. Undoubtedly the image drawn from the biblical religions, of God as Father is one of the causes of this imbalance, but the implied question should be faced: If God is Father, who is mother? Historically, even though that history is ancient, the answer would be 'The earth on which we live is the Mother'. The personifications of this notion all bear the attributes of female sexuality and motherhood, but also of virginity, of generosity and grace, while at the same time manifesting violence, destruction and the urge to war. The parallels with Eastern religion are unmistakable. The mother goddess of India is a deity with several qualities, both beneficent and maleficent. **Parvati**, **Siva**'s consort is the 'good wife' in her manifestation as **Sati**. But Parvati, as Bhairavi, is 'the terrible', and as Ambika, she is the source of life. It is characteristic of Mother goddess cults that they combine these opposites, as if mirroring the potential for creation and destruction that resides in every individual. Powerful and influential cults of Semitic goddess are found in the mythologies such as Inanna in Sumeria, **Ishtar** in Babylon and **Astarte**, or Anat among the Canaanites. Identified with **Venus**, they are both the Queens of Heaven and the 'lady of the world'. In ancient mythology the mother goddess cults were numerous and included those of **Cybele**, **Diana** and the cult of the **Eleusian Mysteries**, and in **Norse** mythology, Freya. Christianity has added to these mythologies a worldwide Great Mother cult in the form of Mariology (see **Mary and Mariology**). It has to be pointed out that the cult of Mary the Virgin, the mother of God, is based far more on popular religious practice than on theology or doctrine. Unlike her son Jesus, she was unquestionably and historically human, although her cult has endowed her with attributes that are virtually divine. In worshipping Mary, in revering her image and by asking her to intercede with God, whether it is to forgive sin or to cure a disease, she is being asked to do what the Mother Goddess has done from the before the beginning of history. The Changing Woman of the **Navajo** Indians is one of the most enduring and beautiful expressions of the Mother Goddess cult. There are modern revivals of the Mother Goddess' original cult to be found in Wicca, in Druidism and secularly in Green Peace. See **Divine Mother**, **Earth Mother**

FINAL WORD: 'Concerning Earth, the mother of all, shall I sing, firm earth, eldest of gods, that nourishes all things in the world … Thine it is to give or take life from mortal men.' (Homeric Hymn to Earth)

Mudra *H. B.* Skt. 'seal' or 'sign'. A symbolic bodily posture or hand gesture conveying specific meaning. In Hinduism, the mudras are used in ritual worship to connect actions to spiritual concepts. They can be thought of as outward and visible signs of inward and invisible meanings. They are also used as aids for concentrating the mind on the object of worship, rather like the Christian and Islamic posture of kneeling or placing the palms of the hands together in prayer. In Buddhism the characteristic and extensive repertoire of the Buddha's mudras are shown in paintings and sculptures. They represent a wide range of meaning associated with protection, teaching, touching the earth, granting wishes and supreme enlightenment or wisdom. For example, the *anjali* mudra, showing the hands placed together, is a mudra of greeting and veneration which in Zen is called **Gassho**. In **Vajrayana** a Mudra is any image that is used in meditation to imprint certain qualities on the mind, in the same way as a camera will record an external image on the film or sensor within it.

Muezzin *I.* The **mosque** official who calls the faithful to **Salat** five times a day, from the minaret. He is a professional chosen for his good character and the skills needed. The office goes back to the time of Muhammad, but sadly, an increasing number of mosques are now calling by means of recordings transmitted through loudspeakers.

Mufti *I.* Arab. A lawyer of canon law. His opinion is called a *fatwa*. Usually a man with absolute knowledge of the law and legal tradition, he will be asked for an opinion on a point of law, but his opinion is not binding. Some Muftis are appointed by the State to serve as advisors. See **Ijma**

Muganda *A.* The singular form of Baganda, a large ethnic tribal group of Uganda. See **Ganda Religion**

Mughal Empire (1526–1857) *I.* The Empire centred on the Indian subcontinent, was concurrent with the **Safavid** dynasty of Persia (1501–1736) and the **Ottoman Empire** of the Turkish Sultans (1517–1924). The Mughal founder, **Zahir al-Din Muhammad Babur**, was succeeded by four emperors who ruled the whole of India with exception of the deep south. Akbar (1556–1605) whose reign was characterized for its religious tolerance, established the administrative structure of an Empire that successfully combined the talents of Persians, Indian Muslims and Hindu Rajputs, whose princes had subsequently been the principal defenders of India against the Muslims. Akbar married a Rajput princess himself. His policy of tolerance included efforts to reconcile Hindu and Muslim beliefs (see **Sikhism**). The Emperor Aurangzeb

Alamgir, who ruled from 1658–1707, reversed Akbar's policies in the face of Hindu and Sikh opposition. In 1857 the Mughal Empire, weakened by Hindu revolt, gave way to the British. It achieved, together with the Ottomans and the **Safavids**, an outstanding expression of Islamic religion and culture. Most of the subjects of the Mongol Empire were Hindus, the ruling classes, Muslim. Akbar attempted a radical syncretism of Hinduism, Sufi mysticism, Zoroastrianism and Christianity. He called this the Dim-i-llahi, the 'Faith of God', and it was made a kind of State religion. It was vehemently opposed by Muslim clerics but if fell to Aurangzeb to restore Muslim orthodoxy in India. See **Islamic Dynasties**

Muhammad (c.570–632 CE) *I*. The founding prophet of Islam. The Koran offers some insight into his life, otherwise information is dependent on traditional biographies. He was an orphan of the tribe of Hashim and placed under the guardianship of his uncle Abu Talib. Married to a wealthy widow, Khadija, he had four daughters and three sons. One of his daughters, **Fatima** has taken her place in the Islamic hierarchy. After Khadija's death, he married for a second time, another widow, Sawdah. After the *hijrah*, the emigration to Medina, he took several wives all for reasons of political expediency. In mid-life he turned towards religion and was 39 when, in the face of prevalent polytheism and idol-worship, he received his calling to proclaim Allah as the only true God. Islam, like **Christianity**, draws on the **Old Testament** for its understanding of God, but for a complete concept of God it rests on Muhammed's revelation as recorded in the Koran. Muhammed is God's principal prophet, he is a **Nabi** in the Hebraic tradition and there are strong parallels between his visions and those of the Old Testament prophets. Like his predecessors, Muhammed seems to have enjoyed a close personal relationship with Allah. He believed he was God's messenger, sent to confirm the revelations of previous scriptures. Unlike Jesus of Nazareth, he made no claim to divinity and repudiated any power to perform miracles. For all Muslims Muhammad is a model of piety and spiritual perfection; for scholars he is the great jurist who defined and codified the ritual observance of both religion and **Shari'a**, the sacred law and for mystics, he is a paradigm of the devout and sincere seeker of the truth. His authority is revered by Muslims in much the same way as is Moses by Jews. His cousin **Ali**, also his son-in-law by virtue of marriage to his daughter Fatima, was the first male convert to Islam and the fourth Caliph of the **Sunni** Muslims.

Muhammad, Elijah (1897–1975) See **Nation of Islam**

Mukti *H*. Skt. 'liberation'. See **Moksha**

Mullah Sadra *I*. A Persian philosopher-mystic of the Illuminationist or Ishraghi school, who provided a synthesis of earlier schools of Islamic philosophy, through an enquiry into the concept of *falsafah*, that is philosophy itself. His thought is regarded as Transcendent Theosophy, one of the two major philosophical forms. His most famous work is the *Asfar*, Journeys, in which he established his central theme, that nature is the core of all existences and movements. Much of his work revolves around the concept of **hikma**, 'wisdom' or 'truth' which developed the character of Islamic theology towards mysticism and theosophy. He moved Islamic thinking from theory to experience, in which process his mysticism sought the way in which the human soul could become detached from the defilement of its material, worldly context. This emphasis in Islamic philosophy, which combines the 'truth' about the nature of reality, with intellectual knowledge and the perfecting of one's being has continued as a running theme to present times.

Mulungu *A*. A name given to God in many African religions. For example, for the Nyamwezi of Tanzania, he is the creator god and guardian of the earth who remains aloof and has no personal contact with human beings. He is also worshipped as a sky god. 'Mulungu' is in the vocabulary of many different tribal languages, but may be translated as 'God' in all of them. See **African Religions, Shona Religions**

Mummification *E*. The term is derived from the Latin *mumia*, bitumen. A method of embalming the human corpse by chemical means. It was used in Egypt from the time of the Old Kingdom c.2686–c.2181 BCE. Belief in an afterlife, in which the spirit had need of a body, led Egyptians to adopt mummification to prevent the decomposition of the body; it was believed that the body was the home of a person's Ka, one the five constituent elements of the soul (see **Soul, Egyptian**).The bodies were covered with natron (a mineral salt) to speed the process of dehydration and to prevent decomposition. Originally the dead were buried in reed bindings in trench graves in the sand, the warmth of which dried up the corpse. The practice was carried over to animals, especially to sacred animals identified with **animal cults** such as ibises, hawks and cats. See **Funerary Practices, Summum**

Murid *I* A. 'Would be' or 'a seeker'. In Sufi Islam a disciple or aspirant who submits to the direction, authority and guidance of the murshid, the Sufi master. The surrender of the will is a condition of an initiation in which the aspirant passes through a series of increasingly difficult tasks which will prepare him for the path of mystical development. Afterwards, the initiate is invested with the cloak of the order. See **Dervish, Dervish Groups, Tariqah**

Murjiis *I*. Arab. 'Postponers'. An 8th-century theological school that opposed the puritan extremism of the **Kharijites**. The Murjiis were political conformists, doctrinally liberal and thought to be ethically lax and thus opposed to Kharijite puritanism. They taught that faith was sufficient of itself, irrespective of 'works'. That being so, the fundamental view of judgement and the eternal punishment of sin, was mitigated by the quality of a person's faith. It was rationalization of the doctrine of predestination, a denial of fatalism that disavowed the possibility of eternal punishment. Whether or not a person was a believer is a judgement that should be left to God. Thus, the Murjiis centred their hopes on the mercy and goodness of God, on universal love and tolerance and on the equality of all believers regardless of sect. Many of their doctrines were taken up by the Umayyad Caliphs. See **Mu'tazila**

Muru'ah *I*. A term denoting the manliness of the Muslim which combines various qualities such as bravery, generosity, honour and practical wisdom.

Muslim *I*. Arab. 'one who submits to the will of Allah'. In popular use, Muslim is an alternative form of the word *Islam*, but this usage is too loose. The plural term, in English, is used to refer to the entire body of those who adhere to the Islamic faith, that is to say, it designates religious criteria. Islam or Islamic, however, connote a much broader spectrum of meaning than the religious and includes the rich and varied culture to include architecture, fine arts, decorative arts, music and literature.

Muslim Brotherhood *I*. Also known as the Society of the Muslim Brothers, it was founded in Egypt in 1928, by Hassan al-Banna and six colleagues from the Suez Canal Company. Originally it had a pacifist political, social and religious agenda with the manifesto, 'God is our objective; the Koran is our constitution, the Prophet is our leader; Struggle is our way; and death for the sake of God is the highest of our aspirations.' It has been taken over by terrorist organizations banned in Egypt then reinstated when the State of Israel was created. Gradually, the Brotherhood has become the Middle East power broker for Islamic interests, influential in Saudi Arabia, Egypt, Jordan and the Sudan, Syria, Iraq, Iran and Palestine where it has reorganized and revitalized the terrorist group Hamas. See **Nation of Islam, Wahhabis**

Mut *E*. The divine mother of all living things, queen of all gods and the goddess member of the **Theban** Triad. During the 18th dynasty, c.1539–c.1292, she became the consort of the god **Amun** and the mother of Khonsu. The marriage of Mut and Amun was one of the great Theban annual celebrations. Originally, Mut was the name of the primordial waters of the cosmos, but eventually a distinction developed between the concept of motherhood and the cosmic waters and Mut took on aspects of a creator goddess. She is depicted as a woman with the wings of a vulture, holding an ankh, the looped cross, a hieroglyph for life and wearing the united crown of Upper and Lower Egypt.

Mu'tazila *I*. An Islamic school of philosophical-theology in evidence towards the end of the 1st century CE, but emerging strongly in the 8th. It was mainly concerned with the implications of monotheism, that is, with the unity and uniqueness of the one God. Theirs was an ethical reaction to the fanaticism of the **Kharijites** on the one hand and the ethical and doctrinal liberalism of the **Murjiis** on the other. They strongly opposed both the Kharijite doctrine of 'works' as the only proper criterion of faith and the Murjiis assertion that faith was all that counted, irrespective of the way a person lived. The Mu'tazila taught that there should be a balance between works and faith and thus held the middle ground. In some ways they were an embarrassment to Islamic orthodoxy in believing the Koran to have been created rather than eternally existing; they promoted the notion of free will as a rational means of both defining and choosing between good and evil and sought to find a balance between human reason and divine revelation. For these and other reasons, they did not conform to the standard of orthodoxy set by **Ashari** (c.873–935 CE). It was their application of logic, rational argument and the philosophy of **materialism**, that contributed to the development of a rational presentation of Islamic theology. See **Islam**

Mykultura Self-deification. See **Egotheism**

Mysteries *X*. In Christianity the sacraments are held to be mysteries. For example, the doctrine of **transubstantiation** teaches the actual presence of the body and blood of Christ in the Eucharistic elements (see **Eucharist**) but how this actually takes place remains a 'mystery'. The Eastern **Orthodox** Church acknowledges seven principal mysteries: **baptism**, chrismation (the reception of the Holy Spirit from having the body anointed), **confession**, Eucharist, marriage, *euchelaion* (anointing the sick) and **ordination**. There are several other lesser mysteries such as monastic confession, the blessing of water at **Epiphany**, and the grapes at the festival of the **Transfiguration**. See **Mystery Religions**

Mysterium Tremendum Rudolph **Otto**'s reference to the **numinous**. The 'Mysterium Tremendum' is a numinous power revealed in a moment of 'awe' and 'religious dread'. See **Merkabah**, **Mysticism**, **Throne Mysticism**

Mystery Religions Generally any religion with an Arcanum, a core of secret teaching. Their beliefs and practices are only revealed to those who have been initiated and must not be divulged or profaned. There are therefore, no scriptures that describe the beliefs of the Mysteries. Usually they are esoteric and ineffable and as with **Gnosticism**, truth is discovered experientially. Adherents make use of sacred symbols, forms of initiation, purification and asceticism. The object was to experience and thus to understand, the life-death-rebirth cycle of nature, perhaps leading to an afterlife. It is probable that the Mystery cults had their origins in Egypt. The cults of **Isis** and **Osiris**, for example, were Hellenized after Alexander the Great's conquest. In the **Eleusian Mysteries**, a part of the cult of **Demeter**, initiation was a preliminary to further rites of passage awaiting the adherent. The Mysteries were widespread and it is thought that in Athens alone there were 600 forms of the Eleusian Mysteries, but initiations were held only at Eleusis and Alexandria. From an early period there had been **Dionysian** mysteries which were more universal, the initiations being held in all Greek towns. These spread from Greece to Italy where, because of the orgiastic character of the rite, it was prohibited by the Senate. The Mysteries re-emerged during the Roman Empire, the best known being **Mithraism**; other Roman Mysteries centred around Attis and the Great Mother **Cybele**. The Mysteries were so mutually syncretistic that despite varying practices, their theologies were much the same. Christianity is certainly influenced by the Mystery Religions and Gnosticism, and it has been suggested that it may have begun as a Jewish adaptation of a Greek initiatory mystery religion, drawn by St Paul towards a Hellenism that was more acceptable to Roman culture.

Mysticism Derived from the Greek *mueo*, meaning to 'initiate' into a secret cult or 'mystery'. The word has become a loosely used term for a huge variety of beliefs, practices, experiences and literature that focuses on the individual's direct and conscious awareness of union with God or the 'absolute', by means of 'cosmic consciousness'. It has been suggested that mystical experience is the one place where all religions meet, but this is quite untrue. There are significant differences between the mystic's experience within similar religious traditions and even greater differences between the mystical traditions of Western and Eastern religions. In addition there are experiences of a similar kind that owe nothing to a received religion. Mysticism has always been associated with Gnosticism in that it is based on a belief that some forms of knowledge are unattainable through sense experience and inaccessible to the human mind, save for specialized disciplined practices that in some way heighten the intuition and alter the state of consciousness. Several mystical traditions offer **meditation** or **yoga** as a means of achieving mystical experience through techniques of breathing; others are based on extreme physical aestheticism or long periods of solitary, intensive prayer and contemplation. The literature, for example the Yoga Sutras of **Patanjali**, provides instruction in the techniques and, although described as ineffable, they include long and detailed descriptions of the experiences themselves. In some traditions drugs are used to stimulate mystical illumination by inducing trance-like states; meditating Dervishes smoke *ganja or* drink *bhang*, both derived from hemp. Other drugs include peyote (see **Peyote Cults**), mescaline, marijuana and LSD. The experience of union with the absolute can happen in the unexpected instant, stimulated by the most mundane of causes such as sweeping leaves or watching the street from the top of a London bus. The sudden fleeting glimpse can become the beatific vision. See **Kabbalah**, **Sufism**, **Trance**

FINAL WORD: 'All at once, as it were out of the intensity of the consciousness of the individual, individuality itself seemed to dissolve and fade away into boundless being and this is not a confused state but the clearest, the surest of the sure, utterly beyond words – where death was an almost laughable impossibility – the loss of personality (if so it were) seeming no extinction, but the only true life.' (Tennyson, in a letter quoted by William James)

Myth A story, in narrative or poetic form, that is ingrained in a culture's tradition, describing the activities and deeds of God, gods, heroes and superhuman beings. Such stories will serve as a type or model of the world-view and cosmology of the people of whose culture they are a part. They will also give insight into the meaning and nature of the universe and life and explain aspects of the natural world by outlining the psychology, customs, mores and ideals of that society. Such myths will include explanations of origins and events in both nature and history, that cannot be attributed to the current state of scientific knowledge. Subsequent advances in all branches of knowledge have shown these myths to be false, unfounded explanations, fables made popular by tradition. However, the use of the term in English is relatively recent, entering the vocabulary in the early 19th century, since when it has become a technical term used by social-anthropologists, historians, literary critics, theologians and **Religionsweissenschaft**. It has been understood, that what is important about myth is not the historical veracity of the story it tells, but its symbolic significance in conveying profound truth about the development of a society's culture and religion. Within all myths are truths that were more clearly discernible to the people they originally served, but which have to be disclosed for modern society. In this process, for example, the late 19th century saw the emergence of a greatly influential movement that set out to **demythologize** biblical literature with the intention of interpreting for the modern scientific age the truths the myths contained. See **Folklore, Legend**

N

Nabi *J. I.* Arab. & Heb. 'a prophet'. A person of either sex whom God has selected as a messenger. The **Old Testament** canon includes a collection of literature comprising seven major prophets and 12 minor prophets. In Hebrew tradition there were several ways God used to communicate with his people, whether or not they listened was a different matter. He spoke to people through dreams as in the story of Joseph recorded in Genesis. In the Israelite cult, there was the casting of sacred dice, the *Urim* and *Thummim*, that enabled a priest to determine God's will. By far the most important medium used by God was **prophecy**, and it established an enduring tradition. Prophets were not unique to Israel, but only in Israelite history did prophecy play such a considerable role in shaping the politics and future of a people, with the added result of producing a body of ideas and literature that have had a profound effect on the development of religion as a whole. *Nabi*, is used as a synonym for a man of God, a seer. They have in common their fervency, their conviction, their sense of mission and their ability to communicate the message entrusted with them. Such is the power and commitment of the prophetic movement that it is described by Robert Seltzer as 'an upsurge in Israelite religious-national feeling'. King Saul encountered a band of prophets 'speaking in ecstasy', and was told that, 'the spirit of the Lord will grip you and you will speak in ecstasy along with them' (I Samuel 10:5–6). Ecstasy was understood as a kind of prophetic madness and it evoked fear, awe and respect. It was not the excess of fervency or strange signs and visions that made the Israelite prophetic tradition so notable, but the clarity, relevance and directness of the message. The Old Testament records that Israelites and others were left with something irresistible, rational and indispensable. What is misleading is the translation of the word *nabi* as 'prophet', since it was not the future that was foretold, but God's judgement on the present delivered. Many of the major and minor prophets were poets and their written accounts are in the form of poetry and prose-poems. Improvising poetry before an audience in ancient Israel was common practice, it was a way of telling stories or reporting events, of carrying messages between widely spread communities. Once recorded it became abiding literature. The Psalms are also evidence of this.

Islam assumed this tradition in its entirety, absorbing the Old Testament into its own religious literature and recognizing the divine inspiration of the prophets. **Muhammad** stands at the head of this line; he is the last Prophet, whose message, recorded in the Koran, is the final revelation of the will of God. For Islam the authenticity of the message is to be seen in the quality of the messenger's life; by this means alone, a Muslim may know that a man is sent by God. The Koran uses two words that are translated as 'prophet, one being, *nabi*, the other *rasul*. Some Islamic scholars define a *rasul* as one who has delivered a written revelation or scripture. The Koran identifies an unbroken chain of prophets that include **Adam**, Noah, **Abraham** and **David** (traditionally the author of most of the Psalms). Moses who received the Torah, Jesus who is recorded in the Gospels and Muhammad who brought the Koran. Islamic tradition holds that a *rasul* has been sent to every **umma**, community, and that their message is consistent and coherent, calling people everywhere to turn from evil to the worship of the one God. Muslims are enjoined to believe in the message of all the *rasul*, without differentiating between them.

Nagarjuna *B*. A major philosopher of **Mahayana** Buddhism and accredited with founding the **Madhyamaka** school. The dates for his life are uncertain but probably 2nd to 3rd century CE. He is thought to have received many scriptures from the **nagas**, most importantly the *Prajna-paramita-sutra*, the philosophy of which he systematized and extended. His main contribution to Buddhism was a philosophy of 'emptiness', developed in his principal authentic work, *Memorial Verses on the Middle Teachings*. His premise that everything exists only in relation to its opposite, implies that all existing things are relative, void of essence and thus empty. If this is followed through, it will be seen that there is no difference for Nagarjuna between phenomena and **nirvana**, since they are only different aspects of the same reality and therefore identical. Thus, nirvana can be attained only by the realization of the true nature of phenomena. His was the first philosophical system to have been developed in Buddhism and he is sometimes known as, 'the second Buddha'.

Nagas *H. B*. Skt. 'snake'. A semi-divine human being with the tail of a snake, a human face, but with the cobra's expanded neck. In some traditions, the snake may also be a python. In Indian mythology they were a race, thought to be a thousand in number, who populated regions below the surface of the earth or sea. However, **Varuna**, the Vedic god of storm is considered to be the King of the Nagas. There are numerous Naga traditions in Buddhism which uses the image of single or multi-headed cobra that serve as temple guardians. In Tibetan Buddhism the *nagas* are water sprites or deities who guard the Buddhist scriptures until humanity is mature enough to receive them, a mythology that might have been put at the service of other religions, with advantage. The association of *nagas* with water survives among Lao and Thai people living near the Mekong river, who believe the *naga* rules in it. In China, *nagas* are identified with *l'ong*, the dragon. The term *Mahanaga*, the great dragon, is sometimes used as an epithet for the Buddha. Snake-cults still thrive in modern India. See **Snakes**

Nam simran or **Nam japan** *S*. Pun. 'God remembrance', a technique used in forms of prayer and meditation. *Simran* is the practice of the presence of God, the Sikh notion of holding God continually in mind. The ideal is for the individual to be filled with *Nam*. 'If the mind is defiled by impurity it is cleansed with love of Nam.' Known also as, 'the practice of the Name' it is an essential religious duty. The guru seeks 'the dust of the feet' of those who remember the Name and who make others remember it. As we think, so we become. It is by meditation that we attain to the glory and greatness of the Almighty.

Names The Hebrew name of God is so sacred that it is not written directly and only rarely pronounced. (See **Tetragrammaton**) The goddess **Isis** took the power of the sun god by discovering his real name. Founded on primitive belief that the name of a thing *is* the thing, belief in the magic of names has survived in our superstitions and behaviour and in the names of people and places. Children are frequently named in such a way as to elicit the significance of the association, thus some boys are called Jesus, many girls, Mary. Derived names are similarly used, Nathaniel means 'God has given', Christopher 'Christ-bearing', the Indian name Devadatta means 'God-given'. Old Testament names are in constant use for Jewish children. Without recourse to religion, parents call their children after kings and queens, princes and princesses, famous film stars, singers and actors. Richard Cavendish records that Aleister Crowley named his first daughter, Nuit Ma Ahathoor Hecate Sappho Jezebel Lilith; sadly, the child did not live long and it has been suggested she died of acute nomenclature. The 'name' continues to be significant in the modern practice of magic, be it white or black. See **Anthropomorphism**, **Beautiful Names**

Names of God See **Anthropomorphism**, **Beautiful Names**, **God**

Nanak *S.* Sikhism's first **Guru**. See **Guru Nanak**

Nastika *H.* Skt. 'atheistic'. The term is not used personally, but to identify the unorthodox schools of Hinduism which do not rest on the authority of the **Vedas**. They are mostly schools of the materialist and sceptical philosopher, Charvaka (c.600 BCE) who was primarily concerned with realizing perfection in the present life. They are no longer part of Hindu literature but are quoted in 8th-century **Jain** and Buddhist texts. See **Astika**

Natal Nazarite Church Zulu, *ama-Nazaretha*. Founded in 1911 among the Zulus of Natal, by Isaiah **Shembe**. The Church is named after the Old Testament community of Nazarites who took certain vows, one of which was never to cut their hair. Samson was its most famous member. The Church's principal festivals are **Sukkoth** (Tabernacles) in July and **Rosh Ha-Shanah** (New Year) in January. They have a sacred shrine called Ekuphakameni, close to the holy mountain Nhlangakazi, near Durban. The Church practises mass baptism and holy dances, both expressing the Zulu belief that the proper worship of God can only be effected congregationally and that solitary practice is purposeless. The Church is the largest Zulu independent religious group.

Nath Tradition *H. B.* An Indian ascetic movement that combines a number of yogic sects all of which descend from Gorakhnath, a legendary guru who lived sometime between the 9th and 12th centuries. His teachings are linked to **Vajrayana**, the Diamond Vehicle of **Tibetan Buddhism**. As a means of spiritual liberation, he taught **Hatha Yoga**, the form traditionally practised by Nath. It is a rigorous psychophysical process by which means the spirit ascends to bliss. The movement had a significant influence on **Sikhism** as its founder, **Guru Nanak**, was a representative of the **Santa** movement which drew on Nath principles. The Nath tradition has declined, but still has its adherents.

Nationalism It is usually taken to mean the sharp independence of a nation state which acts entirely in its own interests, emphasizing the achievement of national rather than international goals. It takes what are sometimes extremely violent forms when a country under foreign political, economic or military dominance, seeks to assert its independence. There has always been a close relationship between religion and nationalism, for both positive and negative reasons. Religion was used to maintain the internal cohesion of Greek city-states; the terms of God's covenant with Israel were based on a promise that they will achieve a nationhood established and maintained through his purposes in history; religion was used politically by Constantine in 391 CE, when he made Christianity a lawful cult of the Roman Empire, with Theodosius outlawing all other cults. Throughout history, kings and queens as heads of State, have derived their authority from being anointed as God's rulers. The obverse occurred in Communist Russia, which set itself against religious belief and practice (some churches becoming museums of religion) because it was strongly held that religion in all its forms was incompatible with the application of the Communist Manifesto (see **Communism**). Islamic doctrine includes a mandate for **theocracy**, the establishment of a State ruled by God through his emissaries; Islamic fundamentalism believes it has a divine mandate to make the entire world such a theocracy. See **Islam**

FINAL WORD: 'Nationalism is an infantile disease, the measles of mankind.' (Einstein)

'People no longer believe in God. The new religion is nationalism. Nations no longer go to church. They go to national associations.' (Joseph Roth, *The Radetzky March*, 1932)

National Socialism The most extreme form of nationalism to be established in the modern period, it was the political ideology of the German Nazi Party, of the 1930s and 1940s. The official title was the National Socialist German Workers Party. The party was actually formed by a Munich locksmith, Anton Drexler, and Corporal Hitler became a member in 1919, taking charge of its propaganda and eventually becoming its leader. Since the end of the Second World War, the term has always referred to German Nazism and its derivative groups, such as Neo-Nazism. Before the 1930s the concept had been used by **Trotsky** to describe Stalin's and Bukharin's theories of socialism within one country (see **Stalinism**) and was not in any way associated with its Nazi form. In

its formative period National Socialism fed on influences from occult groups, particularly **theosophy** and **anthroposophy**, which were flourishing more in Germany than in any other European country. Despite rumours to the contrary, Hitler had little use for the occult and astrology but his Deputy Fuehrer, Rudolph Hess, had an appetite for 'fringe' ideas and Himmler was later to rely on astrological advice. Goebbels became greatly interested in the 16th-century prophet Nostradamus, whose quatrains were used by Karl Krafft for purposes of propaganda and psychological warfare and to demonstrate that Hitler's victory was inevitable. It is likely, therefore, that a core of Nazi leaders were associated with the Order of **Germanen**. At its inception, Nazism was given a mystical impetus, but as it became established occult societies were officially harassed. National Socialism, donning its Nazi uniform, became identified with vehement **nationalism**, eugenics, **totalitarianism**, anti-Semitism (see **Semitic**) and anti-communism. (see **Communism**)
FINAL WORD: 'What good fortune for those in power that people do not think.' (Attributed: Hitler)
'But the Third Reich has passed into history.' (Shirer)

Nation of Islam *I*. An American, religious and political movement, founded in the 1930s by Wallace Fard Muhammad, believed by many to be the last great prophet Messiah of **Sunni** Muslims. and the **Mahdi** of the Shiite (see **Shi'ism**) Muslims. Its manifesto pledged to advance the political and social status of black Muslims. and to deepen their spiritual experience and commitment. One of Fard's principle followers was Elijah Poole, renamed by him as Elijah Muhammad (1897–1975). He led the movement from 1934, carrying his discipleship to the point of teaching that Fard was God incarnate. From 1964, **Malcolm X** led a break-away movement committed to Afro-American unity, and familiarly known as **Black Muslims**. The present leader of the Nation of Islam is Louis Farrakhan; the movement's HQ is in Chicago, centred on No. 2 Mosque named Maryam, after Mary, the mother of Jesus. Under Farrakhan's leadership there has been a huge surge in the movement's popularity, which was demonstrated in October 1995 by the 'Million Man March', when upwards of 400,000 black men converged on Washington DC. The Nation of Islam thus holds the record for the biggest Civil Rights demonstration ever to be seen in America. The label 'Black Muslims' was resisted by the Nation of Islam and they have denounced the title. But in the mind of the general public, the two movements are aspects of the same politico-religious energy. See **Black Muslims, Nation of Yahweh**

Nation of Yahweh *I*. Founded in the late 1970s by **Yahweh ben Yahweh**, 'God son of God', born Hulon Mitchell. The movement represented black racial supremacy and radical separatism. God was black and would make blacks powerful. The Nation teaches that Jesus of Nazareth never existed; it demands a strict vegetarian diet and the wearing of white tunics and turbans together with a Tetragrammaton pendant on holy days, many of which are similar to those of Judaism. Blacks are the true Jews and the movement has something in common with the **Black Jews**. The movement deteriorated into violent crime and Mitchell is now out on parole having served a long prison sentence.

Native American Church *Ami.* Gathering momentum around the turn of the 19th–20th centuries, the Church was formally constituted in 1918, as a syncretism of native Indian practice and Christianity. It had two founders. Quanah Parker began the Half Moon peyote ceremony, in which Christianity forms a background; the Big Moon or Cross Fire tradition was started by John Wilson, with Christianity as a clearer presence. It is believed to have recruited in excess of a quarter of a million adherents from over 50 Indian tribes. It is only a loose association, however, focused on the ingestion of the hallucinogenic buds of the peyote plant. (See **Peyote Cults**) The all-night peyote ceremony is usually held monthly, on Saturdays, with the people gathered around an earth altar and sacred fire. Originally banned by both white and Indian authorities, it has won religious freedom, claiming to be a form of Indian Christianity. The Church is open to those from other religious persuasions and anyone who is a member of it is free to worship elsewhere, in whatever tradition they please.

Native American Religion See **Amerindian Religion**

Naturalism A philosophical theory claiming that all physical phenomena can be explained and accounted for in natural or experiential terms. It denies the need for any explanation that goes beyond the observable, physical phenomena. It is thus contrary to **metaphysics**. What is to be studied and understood by social and physical sciences is all that exists, the natural world constitutes the whole of reality and requires no supernatural cause. Thus, the universe is self-existent, self-explanatory and self-operating according to natural law. Its processes are without purpose and humanity's existence is a byproduct of the whole. One of the greatest exponents of the concept was **Darwin** and subsequently all such philosophies fall back on the theory of evolution. Naturalism is also applied to ethics which calls on the neutrality of language in making moral law or judgement. Thus any secular and this-worldly account of value, quality or standard will score as naturalistic. **Hume** [1999] made the point that in such discussions arguments proceed imperceptibly from 'what is' and 'what is not', to 'what ought to be', and 'what ought not to be', the 'ought' expressing a new relation, standard or affirmation that implies a value judgement without good reason being given for it. Ethical naturalism has contributed to the ethical systems of **humanism**. See **Supernaturalism**

Natural Religion A completely spontaneous religious response derived from the contemplation of or sudden encounter with natural phenomena of the kind that evokes awe and wonder. (See **Mysterium Tremendum**)

Such a response may call upon already formed religious beliefs, but the doctrines and practices of the received traditions are not required to explain or sustain the experience other than by their own theologies. Natural Religion may take the form of **pantheism** or **panenthiesm**, or be derived simply from an untutored openness to the miracle of the mundane. One of the principal philosophers of natural religion was David **Hume**, 1711–1776. See **Grail Religion**, **Natural Theology**
FINAL WORD: 'God is not the voice in the whirlwind, God is the whirlwind.' (Margaret Atwood)

'Yes, [I believe in God] if by God is meant the laws of the universe.' (Stephen Hawking, on *Larry King Live* December, 1999)

Natural Theology A term sometimes cast with '**Natural Religion**' and referring to a sense of awe and wonder as a response to the created, visible world. It is claimed that rational reflection on the visible world can give rise to a faith in God either independently of or as an integral part of the doctrines and traditions of religion. St **Paul** assured the Roman Christians that God's 'invisible attributes, that is to say his everlasting power and deity, have been visible, ever since the world began, to the eye of reason, in the things he has made' (Romans 1:20). Such faith-giving perception is contrasted with revelation, a contrast that has given rise to theological conflict between those who hold that divine revelation is indispensable to salvation (see **Barth**) and those who believe that inward reason and reflection can open the eyes of faith (see **Aquinas**). Since John **Locke** (1632–1704) many theologians have accepted that natural theology is the only foundation for theological understanding. In his *Dialogues*, David **Hume** (1711–76) set out the beliefs attainable by reason that were presumed to be common to all humanity. Natural Theology is now the accepted term for such beliefs. See **Arguments for the Existence of God**, **Deism**, **Grail Religion**, **Neo-Orthodoxy**

Navajo *Ami*. Originally Canadian members of the Athapascan linguistic group of Amerindians. Sometime before 1300 CE they migrated to the southwest of the USA, settling to a sheep-raising and agricultural economy that displaced their hunting culture (see **Amerindian Religion**). Their way of life and religion was formed from an interrelationship with the spectacular, harsh beauty of the landscape around them and the extent to which they were attuned to nature. Navajo religion contains much of beauty in the form of poetry, music, ritual chant and sand-painting that mirrors the environment. All of this is focused in their chief deity, an **Earth Mother** called Changing Woman (see **Mother Goddess**). Her name reflects the belief that her eternal beauty is renewable, that she changes through the seasons, growing old in winter, but being restored to girlhood each spring. With the sun, she produced Twins, mythological heroes, archetypes of brave, virile warriors. Changing Woman is the creator of life and the first man and woman. She taught them all the lore, magic and wisdom she used to create the universe and mankind, the Earth Surface People. 'Earth Surface' is a reference to the mythology of the present age

as the last of five, the first four being subterranean. Wrapped around these core beliefs is a
large pantheon of spirits, the 'Holy People'. As is
typical of animistic traditions, some spirits are
personifications of natural forces, such as thunder
and wind. The gods, like life itself, are unpredictable, at times accessible through prayer, ritual
and shamanistic intervention, but at other times
wilfully negligent and destructive. The Navajo

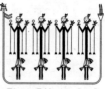

*Figure 7 Navajo Sand
Painting*

have only a vague notion of life after death, there is no 'happy hunting
ground' in the sky, just a kind of ill-defined limbo. Their religion is wholly
concerned with life, its struggles and its wonders. The dominant rituals are
healing ceremonies expressing the belief that illness and injury are caused
by displeasing one of the Holy People or by witchcraft. There are also ceremonies called 'Blessing Way', that celebrate the good things of life. The
whole tribe assembles for these rituals, in which magic and dreams make
a significant contribution, as does a divination technique called, 'hand-
trembling'. Both the rituals and everyday life are wrapped around with an
extensive system of taboos.

The Navajo draw their myths in beautiful, intricate sand paintings, the
creation of which is accompanied by sacred chanting that links the medicine man with the spirits. The abiding quality of Navajo religion is the
extent of its integration with ordinary, worldly life, a unity so complete
as to eliminate the dualism of the sacred and the secular. For this reason,
perhaps, Navajo Indians are, themselves, fully integrated into modern
American life without having compromised their tribal identity.

Navjote or **Naujote** *Zo*. A Parsee name for the **Zoroastrian** rite of initiation meaning, 'new prayer', thus a new initiate who will offer up prayers.
Irani Zoroastrians call it *sedreh-pushi*, 'putting on the shirt'. Parsees,
Indian Zoroastrians, should be offered for initiation between the ages of
7 and 15; among the Irani age is of no consequence. The rite is in four
parts starting with the *Nahn*, a ritual purification bath, followed by
prayers and repentance. The child is then invested with the *sudre*, the
sacred shirt and the *kusti*, the sacred thread, the latter reminiscent of the
sacred thread of the twice-born Hindu. (See **Sacred Thread Ceremony**)
Relatives and friends are invited to be present, they bear witness to the
candidates declaration of commitment to the faith made during the
investiture of the *sudre* and *kusti*. The rite of passage is comparable to the
Jewish **bar mitzvah** or Christian **confirmation** and as with these ceremonies, it is an occasion for rejoicing.

Nazism See **National Socialism**

Near-Death Experience (**NDE**) Usually any paranormal or supernatural
experience a person might have when near to death. They include the
kind of experiences reported when someone 'thinks', or is aware of
having died and is then resuscitated. Over the past half-century, records

of such experiences have become more frequent as a result of medical science enabling people to be revived from comas, brain damage and other critical conditions. There have been numerous accounts from patients of out-of-body experiences, the sense of 'themselves' separate and distinct from their bodies, indeed of seeing their bodies lying unconscious. Other recorded experiences include: altered states of feeling, of peace and well-being, of heightened bodily sensation and fear; there may be the sounds of bells, music or a buzzing, rushing noise, the awareness of another reality, of coloured lights, deep peace, of passing through a corridor or tunnel, of meeting other beings such as the saints or Jesus Christ or an angel and the more familiar review of one's life. Some have recorded a world of preternatural beauty and of reaching a barrier or boundary beyond which they cannot proceed. In almost all cases, the experiences result in a life change, in altered attitudes and relationships. **Tibetan Buddhism** has systematized near- and post-death experiences in the **bardos**, six intermediate states, three of which can occur, periodically, during our lifetime and three of which are deemed to occur during the 49-day period between death and rebirth. It is these last three bardos that form the subject matter of the **Tibetan Book of the Dead**. By being trained in special techniques to recognize what is happening, it is possible to determine one's passage through these post-death experiences. See **Out-of-Body Experience**

FINAL WORD: 'If you would indeed behold the spirit of death, open your heart wide unto the body of life. For life and death are one, even as the river and the sea are one.' (Kahlil Gibran)

'I knew with total certainty that everything was evolving exactly the way it should and that the ultimate destiny for every living being is to return to the Source, The Light, Pure Love.' (Juliet Nightingale, on her near-death experience)

Necromancy A form of **divination** which attempts to discover the future or obtain other information through communication with the dead, usually by **occult** methods. It is thought to be the 'blackest of black arts' since one aspect of it is the use of corpses and not just the spirits if the dead. The magical techniques, which are known only to the most advanced magicians, are intended to harness the will of the dead to the will of the living. The site of the practice had to be chosen with care, frequent use being made of cross-roads, vaults, old ruins, isolated forests, copses and heaths. Sometimes a form of identification was used, such as a portrait of the dead or a personal object that belonged to them. Churchyard necromancy was a more specialized practice, with the rites climaxing on the strike of midnight. Officially, most religions banned such practices and they are prohibited in the Bible, despite the account of Saul summoning the dead Samuel through the services of the witch of Endor (1 Sam. 28). The common medieval attitude to summoning the dead was one of dread and horror, thus Hamlet demanded to know of his father's ghost, 'Be thou a spirit of health or a goblin damned? Bring with thee airs from heaven or blasts from hell?' Modern occult practice has moved on a pace, believing that the deceased leaves behind an astral corpse with vestiges of life that can be invoked in the physical world. This is the belief behind séances and the work of **mediums**.

Nectar In Greek mythology nectar was a sweet liquid produced by certain plants and the favourite drink of the gods. It was believed that any human that drank it would become immortal. In Homer's poems the drink nectar and the food **ambrosia** are distinguished, but they may be just different forms of the same substance possibly, honey. In some accounts they are reversed, with Ambrosia being the drink and Nectar the food. Nectar is mentioned in Hindu mythology, specifically in the **Upanishads**, and in the epic poems of the **Puranas** that celebrate the power and works of the gods. See **Fountain of Youth**

Neo-Confucianism *Con.* A syncretism of Taoist cosmology, Buddhist spirituality and Confucian concern for the principles of good government and an equitable society. See **Buddhism**, **Chinese Religions**, **Confucianism**, **Taoism**

Neo-humanism A holistic philosophy developed by Prabhat Ranjan **Sarkar** (1921–90) that was concerned with development of individual potential in spiritual, economic and political terms. The fullness of mind or mental expansion, was linked with ecology and personal spirituality, the latter advanced through the teaching of **Tantra** and the practice of **Yoga**. It refined and extended **Humanism** by including all sentient beings, considering them to be worthy of the same respect as one would show to another person. See **Ananda Marga**, **Progressive Utilization Theory**

Neo-orthodoxy A term referring to a Protestant theological school which has been greatly influential in the modern period. The theological agenda for neo-orthodoxy was set out by Emil Brunner (1889–1966) and by Karl **Barth** (1886–1968) in his *Church Dogmatics*. It was a reaction against what they believed to be a watered-down and barren Christian liberalism of the 20th-century inter-war period. They believed that the 'word' of God, as revealed, enshrined and communicated by scripture, was the infallible means of salvation. Although the Bible was created by flawed (sinful) and fallible human beings it became inspired when, in the process of it being read, the Holy Spirit enlivened the faith and obedience of the readers or hearers. It is a neo-orthodox movement, in that it returns to the pre-Reformation orthodoxy of the Bible being the infallible word of God and the sole authority in matters of faith and the only standard in matters of doctrine. The term is also derived from a broader movement that reinterpreted the classical Protestant theology of the **Reformation**. Other terms associated with neo-orthodoxy are 'kerygmatic theology' from the Greek *kerygma*, that is, God's revelation through Christ and his salvatory role; 'dialectical theology', that emphasizes the inexpressibility of God and his work; **'crisis theology'** which stresses the divine Word as a judgement (Greek, *krisis*) on the world. Barth opposed **natural theology** because he believed human reason had been corrupted by the **Fall**, and was therefore incapable of achieving, on its own, a saving knowledge of God. Neo-orthodoxy however, like the liberalism it set out to mitigate, is subjective and based on an 'existential' encounter with the 'Word', thus denying any absolute propositional truth in revelation. See **Logos**

Neo-paganism A term generally descriptive of religious movements drawing on pre-Christian or pre-Judaic religions. As the name implies, such religions are 'pagan', although the nature and origins of the paganism is frequently disputed. Because the sources are the vast and ancient, neo-paganism is based on the beliefs and practices that are diffuse and unclassified. Many of the new cults are syncretistic, melding together bits and pieces from disparate sources. Some forms of neo-paganism, such as those associated with **New Age** religions, practise modern forms of spirituality that would be unrecognizable and incomprehensible to their original adherents. The character of neo-pagan religions may be summarized as: a reverence for nature, a belief in **animism** and **pantheism**, sometimes expressed in ecological activism such as organic farming, animal rites and permaculture; the use of ancient mythologies, such as those of the Celts, Norse, Greek, Roman, Sumerian and Egyptian; a reinvention of **polytheism** and the adoption and adaptation of ancient cults. There is frequently an attachment to living traditions such as Kabbalah, Christian spiritualism, Tibetan **Tantra**, and in some instances to political philosophies like neo-Nazism. Many neo-pagan practices overlap with occultism and witchcraft, for example, **Wicca**, probably the largest neo-pagan religion. See **Caer Avalon**

Neoplatonism Actually, not so very 'neo', Neoplatonism is a mystical interpretation of **Plato**, first offered by **Plotinus** (c.205–270 CE). What Plotinus did, in effect, was to combine Platonic thought with that of Pythagoras, **Aristotle** and **Stoicism**. He proposed three elemental substances or levels of reality, the Soul or Psyche, the Nous or Intellect, the One or the Good. They could be regarded as metaphysical entities in their own right or as something to be experienced by the philosopher through contemplation and reflection. Such 'meditation' would enable a thinker to see that the Soul is the mind and as such is the medium of memory and sense perception. It is the eternal, surviving element in man, which at death, if lacking the necessary qualities to warrant a better state, is reincarnated into a new body. The Intellect is the timeless dwelling place of the (Platonic) 'forms'; experiencing these the philosopher might arrive at the truth, both intuitively and directly, as immediate perception. The 'One' is God the absolute, the ultimate transcendent reality, the experience of which is the philosopher's goal, realizable by contemplation. These three elements formed the basis of Plotinus' recasting of Plato, but the Greek-speaking world found that his system was too vague and intellectual to provide the looked for rival to Christianity. His successors, such as Porphyry (c.232–305 CE) and Iamblichus (c.250–325 CE), developed the three hypostases into a more complex hierarchy, replacing contemplation with *theurgy*, a form of ritual magic. Two schools of Neoplatonism emerged, one was the **Athens Academy**, which because of its magical and pagan character was finally closed down in 529 CE. The other school was based in Alexandria, where becoming Christianized, it had a formative and rational influence on the development of Christian doctrine. See **Philo**

FINAL WORD: 'The only way to God is through philosophy,' and the only way to union with the divine is, 'by living the philosophical life and thinking philosophy through to the end.' (Plotinus)

Nephesh *J*. Heb. *naphesh*, 'vital breath'. The word occurs over 750 times in the Old Testament. In Gen. 2:7, which tells of the creation of Adam, *nephesh* is translated 'breath of life', but usually in Christian versions of the Bible it is translated as 'soul'. There is also an association with 'spirit', the 'Spirit of God', suggesting the creative force or energy with which God created. In Kabbalistic mysticism, *nephesh* is one of three parts of the human soul, being the vital principle of life manifest in animal instincts, passions and the 'serpent brain'. See **Kabbalah**, **Ruach**

Nephthys *E*. 'The Lady of the House'. Within the **Ennead** her family relationships included being sister to **Osiris** and **Isis**, and unwilling wife of **Seth**. 'House' refers to the portion of the sky inhabited by **Horus** as sun god. Disguising herself as Isis, she seduced Osiris but Seth found out and planned to kill his wife's lover. She sustained her role as the faithful sister of Isis and helped her to regain the scattered parts of Osiris' body when he was murdered and dismembered by Seth. Nephthys was also present at the birth-bed to give aid to the birth of new children. Although thought to be barren **Anubis** was assumed to be the union of her liaison with Osiris. She is depicted wearing horns and a sun disc surmounted by the symbol of her name, a house topped by a basket. Her role as supporter of Isis has kept her in the background of Egyptian mythology and she never became a major cult. See **Egyptian Religion**

Neptune *R*. In Etruscan and Roman mythology the equivalent of the Greek god **Poseidon**. He was worshipped in Rome as Neptune Equester, patron of horse-racing. A temple was built for Neptune in 25 BCE, near the Circus Flaminius racecourse in Rome and a second on the Campus Martius, the Field of Mars. Because of their association with fresh as well as salted water, Neptune/Poseidon became figured as fountains.

Nestorianism *X*. A Christian doctrine that Jesus existed as two persons, Jesus the man and Jesus the divine son of God. Although he denied holding the view, it is associated with Nestorius, 386–451 CE, the Patriarch of Constantinople. The association is further confused by Nestorianism's adoption by the **Assyrian Church of the East**, which refused to denounce Nestorius for heresy. In fact, the Assyrian Church did not teach Nestorianism, but a similar view offered by Babai the Great, the unofficial head of the Church. He taught that Christ had two *gnomes* or essences, that are separate but eternally united in the one personality. Nestorianism is, in effect, a Christological heresy, an attempt to find a rational explanation for the two persons, the incarnation of the divine **logos**, and Jesus the man, the second person of the **Trinity**. The heresy lies in its implication of the dual nature of Jesus as being both man and divine logos. A further implication is that Nestorians must then reject such statements as 'God died' or 'God suffered', since they believe that the victim was the 'man' Jesus and not the divine Christ. For the same reason they reject the Greek title *Theotokos*, Giver of birth to God, for the Virgin Mary, since she only gave birth to the *man* and is thus only, *Anthropotokos*, Giver of birth to Man. The Assyrian Church of the East and the Nestorian Church of the East, are still with us. That Mary is merely the mother of Christ's humanity is a doctrine ghosted by some Protestant and Reformed Churches. In 431 CE, the Council of Ephesius denounced Nestorius' teachings.

New Age Religion The 'New Age' describes a broad, heterogeneous 20th-century movement in Western culture. It has its own spiritual leaders but is far too diverse to be, of itself, a new religious movement, although it may comprise of several. The movement is characterized by a holistic approach to medicine and the environment, by an interest in UFOs, earth mysteries and crop circles and by practices such as channelling, meditation and crystology. Their beliefs and practices are associated with **astrology**, **spiritualism**, **theosophy**, **magic**, **alchemy** and the **Kabbalah**. Many of its adherents believe in previous existences and reincarnations. As a **counterculture**, the New Age is mostly in evidence in shops specializing in herbs, aromatherapy and books on relevant themes and at trade fairs, folk festivals and ceremonies associated with the solstices. Other distinct energies such as **neo-paganism**, **transpersonal psychology**, altered states of consciousness and **Harmonic Convergence** overlap with New Age interests. It offers a huge curriculum that enables freedom of choice, freedom of association and belief and freedom of expression. It also fosters the kinds of qualities that engender a strong sense of community and belonging, such as those established at Auroville in Indian (see **Aurobindo**), **Christiania** in Copenhagen, Findhorn Foundation near Forres, Scotland and Glastonbury in Somerset. See **Transcendental Meditation**, **White Magic**

New Church of the New Jerusalem *X*. A part-Christian movement founded on the work of Emanuel **Swedenborg** (1688–1772), a Swedish scientist, philosopher and mystic. The Church has other names such as Neo-Christianity, New Christians and The New Church. It was founded on the belief that Swedenborg witnessed or had a vision of the **Last Judgement**, and the second coming of Christ. His vision included the inauguration of the New Church and an explanation of the literal meaning of the scriptures. His followers in the New Church believe his teaching, collected as *The Writings* are, with the Old and New Testament, the third part of the Bible. His philosophy and the belief system stemming from it gave rise to the establishment of churches in America, Australia and Canada. But they have also had a much wider, non-affiliated influence on such people as widely divergent as William Blake, Coleridge, Jung, Helen Keller and Walt Whitman.

New Fire Ceremony A form of the ceremony is to be found in various cultures, for example, Cherokee Indians number the Fire Ceremony among their seven sacred rituals. The fire, which burns continuously, is 'put to sleep' then resuscitated as a welcome to the returning sun after the winter. The Aztecs also performed the ceremony to encourage the return of the solar orb, thus to ensure the survival of human civilization. The festival was calendric and celebrated as an intercalation for 12 days every 52 years, thus maintaining perfect synchronicity with the cycles of the earth and sun. See **Goma Fire Ritual**

New Jerusalem A biblical image that has two associations, one being the final resting place of the souls redeemed in Jesus Christ, the other being an ideal community on earth which may or may not be established in time. The notion is founded on the importance given in the Old Testament to Jerusalem as the city of David, Israel's first king, with its Temple as the cultic centre of the God-covenanted religion of Israel. It was the centre of a **theocracy** intended to be a prototype of the ideal future community on earth when everything would be renewed: 'Then I saw a new heaven and a new earth, for the first heaven and the first earth had vanished and there was no longer any sea. I saw the holy city, new Jerusalem, coming down out of heaven from God, made ready like a bride adorned for her husband' (Rev. 21:1). See **Elysian Fields**

New Lotus School A Japanese Buddhist cult. See **Nichiren**

New Religious Movements Since the 1960s there has been a mushrooming of new religions and cults across the Western world. It has happened before, for example in Rome during the 1st and 2nd centuries CE, in Europe in the mid-16th century, in England in the mid-17th century and in the USA with the Great Awakening of the 1730s and the second phase of revivalism in the mid-19th century. The modern proliferation, however, is entirely different in that the new movements are eclectic, drawing on every major world religion, mythology and paganism. (See **Neo-paganism, New Age Religion**) There are several causes suggested, the first being what was called the '**counter-culture**' of the 1960s. More substantial philosophically- or theologically-based movements gathered momentum a decade later, flourishing across Europe and America and in a variety of forms in most parts of the world, although in some regions, like Scandinavia and Eastern Europe, they were less in evidence. Many of these movements, by definition disillusioned with traditional religion, have looked to humanism as a way of making relevant religious commitment. (See **Humanism** and, for example, **Buddhist**, **Christian** and **Jewish Humanism** and **Religious Humanism**.) New religious energies are associated, for example, with **Falun Gong**, **ISKCON** and **Kabbalah**. They are all part of a quest for new meaning, a reaction to materialism and to what some regard as the barrenness of **secularism**. They have also been supported by people that were already sincerely religious, but who had come to believe that their received tradition somehow impeded the realization of their own, unique, spiritual potential. In this process some have exchanged one form of orthodoxy or authoritarianism for another, surrendering to techniques of brainwashing, mind control and transpersonal **psychology**. Others have been carried by an apocalyptic energy, a belief in the dawning of a new age or a more defined form of **millenarianism**, often fronted by charismatic leaders with revivalist tendencies. Not all of the new movements were powered by religious energy some such as humanism, **Scientology** and the **Human Potential Movement** are secular systems. This spiritual gold rush, while centred on Europe and America, has its parallels in Japan and Africa and in more primitive cultures such as **Melanesia**.

New Testament The collection of books that constitute the second major biblical collection, being the canonical writings of Christianity. The first collection is the **Old Testament**. See **Bible**

New Thought Movement With its origins dating back over a century, the movement is not to be confused with the **New Age**. The founding of the movement is generally accredited to Phineas P Quimby, a clock maker, born in New Hampshire in 1802. His life was changed when, having suffered a 'shock' from bringing a bolting horse under control, he found himself dramatically cured from the weakening and disabling disease that threatened his life. Concerned to understand exactly what had happened he was drawn to **mesmerism**, and became an able mesmerist and hypnotist. He began to study the Bible, in particular the methods Jesus used to heal the sick. From these studies he made the connection between the mechanism of suggestion and the activity of faith. What developed were theories of what he called a 'spiritual science'. Quimby died in 1866, but his work was not lost. One of his pupils, Mary Baker Eddy, who had been healed of a crippling disease, founded her own Church, the **Christian Scientists**. Since the early 1920s many New Thought schools have sprung up. See also **Divine Science**, **Religious Science**
FINAL WORD: 'My theory: the trouble is in the mind, for the body is only the house for the mind to dwell in ...' (Quimby)

Nibbana or **Nirvana** *B*. Pal. The goal of spiritual practice in all branches of **Buddhism**. See **Nirvana**

Nichiren *B*. A school of Japanese Buddhism known as the 'The School of the Lotus of the Sun' or 'The New Lotus School'. It was founded by Nichiren (1222–82 CE) who was born on the south coast of Japan, the son of a fisherman. He set out to search for the true teaching of the Buddha, a quest that brought him firstly to Kamakura and then to Mt Hiei, the centre of the **Tendai** school of Buddhism. There he came to believe that the *Lotus Sutra* enshrined the essence of what the Buddha taught. Convinced that in Tendai practice the Sutra was not accorded its proper place, Nichiren returned to his own monastery and founded his independent movement. In contradistinction to some other Buddhist schools, he believed that enlightenment can be experienced within a person's present lifetime. He maintained that this could be achieved by repeating, mantra-like, but with true devotion, the full title of the Sutra, 'Veneration to the Sutra of the Lotus of the Good Law' (Jap. *Nam-Myoho-Renge-Kyo*). Almost from the outset, Nichiren Buddhism spawned other schools and sub-schools. Some of these maintained **Shinto** shrines and allowed the worship of ancient and indigenous Japanese deities. In modern Japan, new schools have developed with their roots in Nichiren, for example, Nichiren-shoshu, 'The True School of Nichiren', Shoshinkai, Kenshokai and **Soka Gakkai**. The latter has active and powerful political affiliations which stretch to Japanese communities world wide under the auspices of Soka Gakki International. See **Japanese Religions**

Niebuhr, Reinhold (1892–1971) An American Protestant theologian influential in the second quarter of the 20th century. He held the post of Professor of Applied Christianity at the Union Theological Seminary in New York, from which base he developed a theology firmly within the tradition of biblical revelation. He believed that liberal theology and metaphysics did not take fully into consideration human sinfulness and that Marxist views of human nature and history lacked insight into the real nature of the human predicament caught in the tension of nobility and suffering. This is perfectly expressed in the suffering of divine love exemplified by Christ's death. Suffering love is the reconciling link between God and man and in all inter-human relationships and sets the agenda both for ethical judgements and responsible Christian involvement. The ethical implications of Niebuhr's philosophy touch on the concepts of democracy, justice, equality and welfare capitalism. Appearing at a critical time in world history, his thought influenced both the recovery of America's national identity and the philosophy of Martin Luther King. He was awarded the Presidential Medal of Freedom in 1964.

Nietzsche, Friedrich Wilhelm (1844–1900) A German philosopher, writer and something of prodigy, being appointed professor of classics at the University of Basel when he was only 24. Richard and Cosima Wagner lived nearby and became his friends. From an enquiry into what was the basis of human values and morality, Nietzsche set about a criticism of culture, religion and philosophy. The key subjects of his philosophy are: **nihilism** and the 'death' of God (see **Death of God Theology**); the idea of eternal recurrence (see **Eternal Return**); his concept of the *Übermench* (Superman or Overman); master and slave morality; Christianity as an institution over against Jesus the 'Overman';

and the will to power. The addition of these wide-ranging and complex themes represent one of the most individual philosophical perceptions to have occurred and its influence, while not much felt in Nietzsche's lifetime, has grown hugely through the 20th century, being misunderstood, misused and politically exploited. His thought, courted by both the German left and right wings, was at one time (1894/95) threatened with charges of subversion and at another time thought to be the inspiration of German First World War militantism. The Nazis, who promoted Nietzsche as one of their founding fathers, used his ideas to popularize concepts of German culture and **nationalism** and to encourage the cult of dominant personality and individualism. Nietzsche's appeal to the **Nazis** was, to some extent due to his sister, Elizabeth, who had edited his work and was a Nazi sympathizer. Nietzsche, however, had disapproved of her anti-Semitism. It is thought his sister amended some of his work, cutting re-ordering and re-titling it, to create what is known as the 'fake Will to Power'. Nietzsche's famous assertion that 'God is dead' is a prime example of how he can be misinterpreted and misused. Inevitably taken up by atheistic groups and anti-religious political regimes, they conveniently forgot Nietzsche's main argument, that the death of God was at the hands of religious institutionalism and that God is not only alive, but 'free' to live within any individual that has faith. During the late 1880s Nietzsche's health began to fail and he suffered a mental breakdown which developed into insanity. He contracted pneumonia and died on 25th August, 1900. Among the first to acknowledge Nietzsche's importance were the philosopher **Heidegger** and the novelist Thomas Mann. He has continued to have far-reaching influence through the 20th century on **existentialism**, **phenomenology** and postmodern philosophers such as Foucault, Lyotard and Derrida and on poets, novelists, dramatists and artists far too numerous to list.

FINAL WORD: Freud said of Nietzsche that he had 'more penetrating knowledge of himself than any man who ever lived or was likely to live.' (Ernest Jones)

Niflheim *Nor*. In Norse mythology, a name for the underworld. See **Hel**

Nihilism A philosophic perception that life and the universe is without any point or meaning. If there is a nihilistic creed it would say that God does not exist, all forms of morality are false and that a secular ethic is also impossible. All values are baseless, nothing can be known, thus nothing can be communicated. It is akin to anarchy and absurdity as critical idioms and as such is sometimes associated with **Dadaism** and **Deconstructionism**. The philosophies of **Heidegger** and **Nietzsche** have nihilistic elements. It is said that nihilism and religion cannot coexist, since the former considers religion to hold a monopoly of truth, while religion will not admit to nihilistic values in society. Nietzsche, with almost prophetic vision, anticipated the themes of postmodernism. He suggested that if we survive our destruction of all received interpretations of the world, mankind might then find its proper way. See **Anarchism**

FINAL WORD: 'Life's … a tale told by an idiot, full of sound and fury, signifying nothing.' (Shakespeare, *Macbeth*)

Nihilistic Movement An 1860s Russian cultural movement that questioned all received and traditional social, ethical, political and religious ideas. It was a form of **anarchism**. Championing the freedom of the individual, the group opposed the Russian serf system, demanding freedom, equality and democracy. Its activists were associated with bombs and terrorism and were responsible for the assassination of government officials and in 1881, of the Tsar Alexander II.

Nikayas Skt. Pali. 'corpus' or 'assembly', being the five collections of sutras of the Pali canon, known as the **Tripitaka**, the 'Three Baskets'. *Nikaya* is virtually synonymous with the Skt. *Agama*, 'source of the teachings' and is also used for a group of monks or a monastic community

Nilotic Religion *A*. A group of several culturally and linguistically related tribes that inhabit regions of the Upper Nile, the best known of which are perhaps, the **Dinka** and the **Nuer**. The common characteristics of the religion stem from a pastoral way of life and a form of democratic monotheism. The central Divinity or High Spirit, is believed to be the creator to whom lesser spirits are subject; it is associated with the sky and heavenly phenomena and is responsible for the daily and ongoing circumstances and quality of life. In Nilotic ritual, cattle are sacrificed to God, the ashes from a ritual fire being rubbed onto the back of the cows, symbolizing the transference of the owner's sin to the animal. Subsistence depends on the herds and the cattle economy is the foundation of family and community life, with cows used as marriage dowries. The cattle shed is holy, both a kind of shrine and a meeting place. A person's prestige is measured by the size of his family's or village's herds, the owner of a large number being called an 'Ox'. Both men and spirits are given ox names representing their characteristic traits. Allowing for local variations other common themes include, the reverence accorded to ancestors; the activation of natural forces by their associated spirits, especially rain; the lack of any distinction between natural and supernatural; the extraordinary powers shown by certain men and women for healing, divination and for the ritual manipulation of people. While sorcery is present among the Nilotes, it is far less in evidence than, for example, among West African tribal religions. Another sharp contrast with West African culture is the almost complete lack of any form of religious art. This may be because their religious perceptions remain remarkably abstract, their interpretation of the universe drawing on invisible spiritual, nonmaterial forces that are rarely given concrete form.

Nirodha *H*. *B*. Skt. 'destruction', 'dissolution'. In Hinduism it refers to an intense state of meditative concentration that 'destroys' all forms of subject-object relations. In Buddhism it may describe the dissolution of *dukkha*, suffering, as in the third of the **Four Noble Truths**, or as the termination of *samsara*, the birth-death-rebirth cycle. *Nirodha* is sometimes used as the equivalent of **nirvana**, but emphasizes the means of eliminating the causes of suffering rather than the state to which that elimination will lead.

Nirvana or **Nibbana** *H*. *B*. *Z*. Skt. and Pal. 'extinction'. In Hinduism the term refers to the extinction of the subject-object relationship and the merging of **atman** with **Brahman**. The result is nirvana, freedom from suffering. It is described in the **Bhagavad-Gita** as *brahman-nirvana* and in the **yoga** disciplines as *nirbija-samadi*. In all forms of Buddhism, nirvana is the goal of the **Eightfold Path**. On achieving the state of nirvana the adherent will experience a radically different sense of being. The root of the word nirvana, *va* 'to blow', gives rise to the familiar image of a candle being blown out, which suggests some kind of termination. Usually, this is thought to be the termination of life, an annihilation, especially in the West; but what is terminated is 'suffering' or 'illusion', not life itself. The 'flame' is not extinguished, it is simply no longer visible, by virtue of having another mode of being. Attaining nirvana may well be something the adherent achieves during life. The experience itself, however, usually comes gradually rather than as a sudden event and for this reason the canonical texts do not support the idea of the extinction of a light. The Buddhist **Mahayana** tradition introduces the notion of 'bliss', the peace and tranquillity that is the result of realizing one's unity with the absolute. Another misunderstanding arises from thinking of nirvana in nihilistic terms. Nirvana is not nothing and what we are faced with is the inadequacy of language in attempting to describe something that is beyond words, concept or logic. For precisely this reason, the Buddha declined to speak about the nature of nirvana. Throughout the various Buddhist schools there are doctrinal difference which amount to differences of emphasis. For example in **Hinayana**, nirvana achieved during one's lifetime is less than perfect in that it retains a certain degree of conditionality; in Mahayana, because of the **bodhisattva** ideal of remaining in service to all sentient beings, complete nirvana is postponed and an intermediate form of it willingly accepted. Zen also sees nirvana as something that is not, necessarily, separate from this world or from life. It is the realization of the true nature of mind, which is our inborn buddha-nature. It is achieved by wisdom, *prajna*, which having been attained is the same as nirvana.
FINAL WORD: 'That which comes and goes is dependent and changing, That, when it is not dependent and changing, is taught to be nirvana.' (Nagarjuna, *Mulamadhyamikakarika*, Ch. 25 verse 9: Garfield trans)

Nirvana School *B*. A 5th-century branch of Chinese Buddhism established by a succession of monks who followed the teachings of the *Nirvana Sutra*. As so often happens, the school emerged out of controversy concerning a mistranslation of the sutra that implied there was a class of beings, the *icchantika*, who lacked buddha-nature and were thus excluded from the possibility of enlightenment. One of the monks, Tao-sheng, claimed that such a teaching contradicted the spirit of **Mahayana**; by questioning a sacred text he was excommunicated, but later, when the fault in translation was verified, he was reinstated. The school extrapolated from the Nirvana Sutra what it believed to be the central teachings of Buddhism: i) that nirvana was not annihilation; ii) that all sentient beings have buddha-nature and thus carry the potential of realization; iii) that the potential is the same as the ultimate nature of reality; iv) that since this ultimate reality is without qualities and cannot be systematized or grasped, it must be comprehended in its entirety, by means of sudden enlightenment; v) that the doctrine of **anatman**, of no-self, does not mean there is no self to realize nirvana. In fact, wisdom, *prajna*, reveals the buddha-nature to be the real self, beyond all forms of illusion and transitoriness. To call this movement a school is probably wrong. It never sought or achieved institutional structure or an independent identity, with scriptures of its own. It is more in the way of being a doctrinal lineage followed by students and teachers alike. In 581 CE, under the Sui dynasty, when the **T'ien-t'ai** school was founded, the Nirvana Sutra and its followers were absorbed. The Sutra together, with the Lotus Sutra, came to be considered Buddhism's most sublime records of truth.

Noetus *X*. Noetus was a presbyter of the Church in Asia Minor c.230 CE, possibly at Ephesus. He became a notable spokesman for a form of Christology known as **modalism**, or **patripassianism**, the heretical belief that God the Father and God the Son are simply different names or aspects of the one God. Noetus was excommunicated for his heresy. See **Sabellius**

Nominalism The view in philosophy that universal concepts have no existence beyond the names that designate them. The argument is contrary to **Plato**'s theory of Forms or Ideas. One of the leading Nominalists was William of Ockham (1285–1349), an English Franciscan who proposed anti-realist theories of universals. In modern philosophy, Nominalism proposes that the meaning of a universal term is to be found by characteristics particular things have in common. Thus 'blueness' can only be understood by the way it denotes the common property of anything that is blue. The concept has continued through Western philosophy from **Hobbes** to the **logical positivists**. See **Particularism**

Nonconformism The refusal to accept common rules, customs or beliefs. In Christian usage, nonconformists or dissenters, are members of the Protestant churches (see **Protestantism**) who have refused to accept the received tradition of theological orthodoxy. Examples include **Presbyterians**, **Congregationalists**, **Baptists**, **Methodists** and **Quakers**. Following the Act of Uniformity in 1662, the term was used to refer to any English person who was not a member of the Anglican Church or to identify adherents of non-Christian religions.

Non-Dualism See **Dualism**

Nontheism The absence of belief in both the existence and nonexistence of God or of a deity. It is distinct from **agnosticism** which holds a more open mind on the basis of there not being sufficient evidence on which a decision as to the existence or nonexistence of God can be made. The implication for agnosticism is that irrefutable proof would warrant a change of mind. Nontheism seeks to heighten the total irrelevance of such questions or possibilities. Questions as to the existence of God, gods or spirits are simply meaningless, they have no more relevance than debates about the existence of fairies or Father Christmas. The view is held philosophically by the **logical positivists'** concern for the integrity of language and is developed in the philosophies of, for example, **Russell** and **Wittgenstein**. The difference between Nontheism and **Atheism** is slight, but significant. In a broad sense, Atheism is an absence of belief in God, that might in some contexts be something to be debated, as for example in the reasons put forward to oppose the classical arguments for God's existence. Nontheism would not take up the debate, dismissing the whole exercise as pointless.

Norse Mythology The pre-Christian beliefs and legends of the Scandinavian and Icelandic people. They represent the best-preserved accounts of the earlier Germanic mythologies, which were interconnected with Anglo-Saxon mythology, itself evolved from Indo-European mythology. See **Anglo-Saxon Religion**, **Edda**, **Germanic Religion**

Noumenon A term coined by **Kant** to refer to the 'thing-in-itself'. It is the opposite of phenomenon, in that it exists independently of the mind. Noumena are realities behind sense experience and, therefore, remain unknowable; we may assume their existence since moral decisions and the scientific method cannot proceed without them. They are part of our intellectual intuition residing in the mind as concepts.

Noyes, John Humphrey (1811–86) An American **utopian** and founder, in 1848, of the **Oneida Movement**.

Nubian Nation of Moors See **Ancient Mystical Order of Melchizedek**

Nuer A. 'What small black ants are to man, so is man to God' (Nuer proverb). One of the Nilotic people of southern Sudan and western Ethiopia. They form one of the largest ethnic groups in East Africa, whose beliefs are said to be among the most intelligent and sensitive of primitive religions. (Evans-Pritchard [1957]) Pastoral people, they rely entirely on a cattle economy, the cows being used as a form or currency. Their animistic religion is focused on a father-figure, Kwoth, the creator God or Spirit, who is both distant and immanent and some claim to establish a personal relationship with him. In other respects Nuer religion supports the general characteristics of Nilotic tribes for example, cattle figure significantly in their rituals and no important ceremony is complete without the sacrifice of cattle. Cows are dedicated to the ghosts of the owner's lineages and to whatever personal spirits will have possessed them. By means of such sacrifice the Nuer pray for health and the general wellbeing of the family and tribe. There is no concept of an afterlife location for the deceased's spirit, the emphasis clearly being on the demands of this life. Ancestral spirits, however, can have a marked effect on the quality of the present life. The more recent a relative's death, the more powerful will be the spirit's influence. See **Nilotic Religion**

Numerology Theories based on the assumed magical and esoteric relationships between numbers and the characteristics, qualities and actions of both living things and physical objects. As early as Pythagoras (580–500 BCE) numerology was practised as a form of **divination**, but today it is considered to be pseudomathematics and is associated with **astrology** and similar practices. Its relationship to pure mathematics is the same as that between astronomy and astrology or alchemy and chemistry. The esoteric significance of numbers may be illustrated by an example: One: The initial number when counting, it is therefore considered to have great power. Without 'One' there would be no numbering system as we know it. It symbolizes the origin of all things, representing perfection, the Absolute or the deity in **monotheistic** faiths. A numerological reading would suggest that 'One' can be happy, loving, selfish, individualistic, romantic, dynamic and charismatic; on the downside it can be egotistical, self-absorbed, melodramatic, obstinate and alone. 'One' is often associated with male or masculine energy. 'One' is the origin, the beginning. **Gaia**, the Word or **Logos**.
FINAL WORD: 'Numbers are the sources of form and energy in the world. They are dynamic and active even among themselves …
almost human in their capacity for mutual influence.' (Attributed: Theon of Smyrna)

Numinous An important and much-used term coined by the German theologian Rudolph **Otto** (1869–1937). It is a concept similar to awe and what inspires it, such as the mysterious, the uncanny or the supernatural. However, the numinous can just as well be a response to something that is not supernatural or transcendent, but to a natural object, be it a lake or mountain, the call of a bird or a flower. Conversely, the numinous may be the feeling of awe that is close to dread, a response to the **Mysterium Tremendum**, 'the overpowering mystery'. Otto believed such a response or state of mind to be the origin of religion, in that it determined a quality of experience that defined man's relationship with the landscape and all natural forces and phenomena. The numinous, in some ways, is close to the Polynesian concept of *mana*. See **Scientific Pantheism**
FINAL WORD: 'Awe is the best of man: howe'er the world's
Misprizing of the feeling would prevent us.
Deeply we feel, once gripped, the weird Portentous.'
(Goethe, *Faust*)

Nun *E*. A member of the **Ennead** of Heliopolis, the God of the primeval ocean and the one god all the Egyptian creation myths have in common. After the world was created, the limitless and motionless waters of Nun lay at its edges, ready to return to destroy everything and so begin the cycle over again. He was responsible for the protection of the gods **Shu** (air) and **Tefnut** (moisture) at their birth and for keeping the powers of chaos under control. He is portrayed as a bearded man with a blue or green body, the symbolic colours of water and fertility. He is sometimes shown with female breasts and carried a palm frond in his hand and hair, a symbol of long life. See **Egyptian Religion**

Nut *E*. The goddess daughter of **Shu** and **Tefnut**, and as wife to **Geb**, the earth god, she is the mother of **Osiris**, **Isis**, **Seth** and **Nephthys**. She was worshipped as the goddess of the daytime sky and the region where clouds are formed. In later mythology she became the overall goddess of the sky. Mythology tells of her renewing the sun daily by swallowing it at night and giving birth to it the next morning. She is depicted with her blue body covered in stars and carrying a vase of water on her head; sometimes her body is arched so that both her hands and feet touch the ground. In this image she represents the heavens, her arms and legs the pillars supporting the sky, but also separating cosmic chaos from the order of the world. See **Egyptian Religion**

Nyaya *H*. Skt. 'correctness' or 'propriety'. One of the six orthodox schools of Hinduism, founded by **Gautama** Gotama who is thought to have lived between the 6th and 3rd centuries BCE. Nyaya is based on a system of logical proof and analysis that arrives at a 'fitting' conclusion about the true nature of phenomena and the purpose of human existence. More than the other five schools (see **Darshana**), it allows for the appropriation of knowledge by the senses and takes into account natural law. Such knowledge, however, is brought under the scrutiny of critical examination. See **Purva Mimamsa**, **Sankhya**, **Vaiseshika**, **Vedanta**, **Yoga**

Nyingmapa School *B*. Tib. One of the four principal schools of **Tibetan Buddhism,** being the 'Old School' stemming from **Padmasambhava** who brought Buddhism to Tibet in the 8th century. Their supreme doctrine is **Dzogchen**, 'The Great Completion', which was systematized by **Longchenpa**. The first Nyingmapas, laymen as well as monks, established three lineages, the historical, direct and visionary. The historical or, *kama* lineage is based on the transmission of teachings from teacher to disciple; the direct or *terma* lineage refers to Padmasambhava's secret or hidden texts that would be revealed at the right time; the *dag-snang*, the visionary lineage is that of direct spiritual contact with previous teachers, that gives rise to empowerments. It was in this lineage that Longchenpa received the teaching of Padmasambhava. The head of the Nyingmapa School is called the Karmapa, currently his Holiness Gyalwang Karmapa who, like the Dalai Lama, is now in exile from Tibet.

He lives near Dharamsala but will eventually take up residence in the Rumtek Monastery, the traditional Indian seat of the Karmapa. See **Gelugpa, Kagyupa, Sakyapa**

Nymphs *G*. In Greek mythology a nymph was a personification of feminine youth, charm and beauty and their origin lies in the most ancient traditions of popular Greek folk-religion. Some nymphs were associated with the sea, others with trees or mountains. The nymphs of streams, rivers and lakes were the divine emanations of the young girls that came there to purify themselves. They were also connected to other more abstract aspects of nature, such as dazzling light, reflections, sun and moon beams and their names were derived from whatever association they had with natural phenomena. As representatives of the throbbing life within all of Nature, they were the companions of the lustful **satyrs**. The mythologies frequently set them in the company of the more superior divinities, such as the huntress **Artemis**, the prophetic **Apollo**, the reveller **Dionysus** and with **Pan** and **Hermes**.

O

Obeahs *A*. A form of religious belief of African origin, practised in some parts of the West Indies, Jamaica and nearby tropical America, involving sorcery. An object, charm or fetish is used in the rituals involved. See **Voodoo**

Occasionalism A philosophy of causation arguing that neither matter (see **Materialism**) nor mind (see **Idealism**) can be the true cause of events. Every effect is caused by God. The relationship between cause and effect only occurs because God wills it to occur. For example if we are hungry, a mental event, and the hunger causes us to eat, a physical event, we do so only because it is God's will that we should. Similarly if we fall down, a physical event and by consequence suffer pain, a mental event, it is because God has caused the conjunction. The theory is based on the notion of the dualism of mind and matter that asserts they are fundamentally two separate entities and as such they cannot affect each other. If this is true then my mind is not the cause of my fingers typing these words, the cause is God and what I write is truly inspired! A short step further takes us to the position that the physical world has no actual existence beyond the one given to it by our senses. The philosopher George **Berkley** went even further in claiming there was no such thing as matter and that even our perception of it was caused by God. One of the earliest people to develop Occasionalism was the 11th-century Islamic philosopher al-Ghazali.
FINAL WORD: 'What is mind? No matter. What is matter? Never mind' (Thomas Hewitt Key, *Punch* 29.19, 1855)

Occult From the Latin *occulere*, 'to conceal'. The Occult is a system of belief or practice that is secret or mysterious, remaining hidden behind the mere appearances of things. Access to the secrets and knowledge thus concealed is usually by initiation of some kind or by the use of magical rites or esoteric mystical practices. Most occultists would claim however, that occultism is the study or quest for a spiritual reality the lies beyond reason and the material sciences. In this sense most of the established religions have occult elements, while distinct occult systems stand outside them. Examples are numerous and include **voodoo**, **magic**, **witchcraft**, **spiritualism**, **ESP**, **astrology** and **numerology**. Occultism was brought to public attention by **Aleister Crowley** (1875–1947), who in his younger days was a member of the **Hermetic Order of the Golden Dawn**. See **Gnosticism**, **Hermetica**, **New Age**, **Neo-paganism**

Odin *AE*. The chief or supreme God of Scandinavian mythology and the leader of the **Aesir**, one of the principal pantheons. The Norse god of wisdom, war, art, culture and the dead, the supreme deity and creator of the cosmos and humans. He was known as Wodan to the Germanic people and identified by the Romans as **Mercury**. The mythology has him as 'shapechanger', able to take any form he wished and as the leader of the Wild Hunt and the God who welcomes to **Valhalla** the heroes who will later help him at **Ragnarok**, the end of the world battle. See **Germanic Religion, Norse Mythology**

Odinism *AE*. A reference to any movement or cult concerned with a return to the gods of **Norse mythology**, Odin being the chief of those gods. It is formalized in the modern cult, the Odinic Rite, a German pagan reconstructivist society whose aims are to promote all aspects of German paganism. The movement is organized in Chapters, but most adherents seem to remain solitary or meet in small groups in units called 'Hearth' to perform Blots or Blotar, ceremonies at which the ancient gods are honoured. Professed members take an oath of fealty to the gods and to the society and receive the *tork*, a small shield. They are enjoined to live their lives in accordance with the 'Nine Noble Virtues' and the 'Nine Changes'. Odinism continues to have a presence in Great Britain, Australia and the USA. See **Neo-paganism**

Ogdoad *E*. Gk. *ogdoas*, 'eight'. The eight Egyptian deities worshipped at Hermopolis in Upper Egypt. The gods, the primal forces of chaos, were arranged in four male-female pairs, in which the males were associated with frogs and the females with snakes. The pairings were, Nut-Naunet, Amun-Amaunet, Kuk-Kauket and Huh-Hauhet. Each pair represents the male-female aspect of, respectively, water, air, darkness and eternity, the primal state of things before creation. In the original form of the myth, a mound of earth rose from the water on which an egg was laid by a cosmic goose. **Ra** was hatched from the egg. The egg was said to be laid by Ibis and eventually when the cult was centred around **Thoth** it was presented to him as a gift. After the assimilation of **Atum**, as Ra-Atum, the lotus variation of the myth developed and Atum was believed to have issued from a blue lotus.

Figure 8 Lemniscate symbol

Eight is the constant characteristic of the Ogdoad, linked with the lemniscate symbol of infinity, 8 placed horizontally. See **Egyptian Religion**

Ohrmazd *Z*. A combination of the two words 'Mazda' and 'Ahura'. They form an alternative Pahlavi name for the supreme being of **Zoroastrianism, Ahura Mazda**.

Old Believers *X*. A sect of the Russian **Orthodox Church** whose origins lie in a 17th-century attempt by Nikon (1605–81) Patriarch of Moscow, to reform the liturgy by bringing it into conformity with Greek practice. The reforms were supported by Tsar Alexis I but opposed by Archpriest Avvakum who rightly claimed that the traditional liturgy was older. Avvakum was burnt, his followers persecuted and excommunicated, splitting into numerous groups. The *Popovtsy* tried to establish their own priesthood and in 1846 a deposed bishop joined them and recreated the apostolic priestly hierarchy. The *Bezpopovtsy* ('priestless people') disavowed the necessity of a priesthood, claiming that the true Church of Christ has ceased to exist on earth. As well as the priesthood they disavowed all the sacraments except **baptism**. In their various forms, the Old Believers maintain the original liturgical forms of Russian Orthodoxy that existed before the reforms were implemented. There are probably still a million Old Believers maintaining a tradition that differs from the Orthodox Churches in practice, but not in doctrine.

Old British Church *X*. See **Celtic Christianity**

Old Catholics *X*. A group of various national Churches that broke with Roman Catholicism. They include the Church of Utrecht which separated from Rome in 1724, the German, Austrian and Swiss Old Catholics who refused to accept dogmas such as the infallibility of the pope as defined by the 1870 Vatican Council. They established their own episcopal succession from the Utrecht Church. The third group, of Slavic origin, include national Church movements among Poles in the USA (1897) and among the Croats (1924). In 1889, the Declaration of Utrecht established the doctrinal basis of the Old Catholic Churches.

Old Order of Mennonites *X*. A branch of the Mennonite Church, but the name is generally used of **Mennonite** communities that endeavour to live without recourse to modern technology. They do not believe technology is 'evil' and its avoidance is more concerned with the nature of the community they have formed. If it will not benefit the community, it is abandoned, thus its ban is not absolute. An Old Mennonite would not own a car, but would be prepared to use one in an emergency. Similarly, they would not use electricity in the house, but so as to conform with regulations it would be installed in the milking barn. See **Amish**, **Hutterian Brethren**

Old Testament *J*. Traditionally, the first of two major divisions of the official canon of the Christian **Bible**. Judaism refutes the term 'old' since it implies recognition of the 'New' Testament, the second major division of the Bible. In the Christian canon the Old Testament is made up of 39 'books', beginning with Genesis and closing with Malachi. The equivalent Jewish canon is called the **Tanakh**, an acronym from the Hebrew words for **Torah** (Pentateuch), **Nebi'm** (Prophets) and **Ketubim** (Sacred Writings). These three sections also form the structure of the Tanakh which arranges the 39 books in a different order to that of the Christian canon. See **New Testament**

Olympus *G*. In Greek mythology, the home of the pantheon of 12 Gods, being the highest mountain (10,000ft) of the Greek peninsula, between Thessaly and Macedonia. See **Pantheon, Greek**

Om or **Aum** *H. B.* Skt. An ancient sacred syllable or **mantra**, carrying several complex explanations in the sacred literatures. In Hinduism it is a symbol of spiritual knowledge which when sounded, is so sacred that no one should hear it. It is frequently used to open a prayer or ritual and is to be found preceding the opening line of a book. In the **Upanishads**, where *Om* first appears, it has mystical power and is regarded as the object of the most advanced forms of **meditation**. In its three-letter form *Aum*, it came to symbolize the unified Hindu triad, *a* representing Vishnu, *u* Siva and *m*, Brahma. It is not considered to be a word, but a presentation of spiritual knowledge and power that affirms the presence of the absolute in all forms of *maya*, illusion.

Figure 9 Aum

The three curves of the Sanskrit form of the syllable (1,2,3) represent the physical, mental and unconscious worlds; a point with a semi-circle (4) stands alone and above the three curves and represents supreme consciousness. It is thought that the *Aum* of the **Vedas** is the *Hum* of **Tibetan Buddhism**, the *Amin* of Islam and the *Amen* of the biblical religions and possibly a synonym for the Logos, the 'Word'.

Om Mani Padme Hum *H. B.* Skt. The oldest and most significant mantra of **Tibetan Buddhism**, thought to be linked with the bodhisattva **Avalokitesvara**. It is variously translated as 'Praise to the jewel in the lotus, hail' or just 'jewel in the lotus', leaving 'Om' and 'Hum' as seed-syllables. The mantra is also variously interpreted. It can be taken as an invocation to Manipadmi, a female deity, but the problem is that the deity is unknown. Another form of interpretation is to read the six syllables of the mantra as being symbolic of the six possible realms of rebirth in the **samsara** cycle. The **bodhisattva** tradition seems, however, to encourage Tibetan Buddhists to use the six syllables to express both the attitudes of compassion and the mind's yearning for liberation, not only for oneself, but for all sentient beings. What seems to be agreed by scholars is that the mantra must be interpreted and used within the symbolic system of the magical and psychological practices of Tibetan **Vajrayana**. Probably the most popular use of the mantra is to see the imagery of the jewel as a symbol of the awakened mind, Skt. *bodhicitta*, a flowering of the lotus of human consciousness.

Oneida Movement Founded in 1848 in Oneida, near New York, by John Noyes, the movement was an expression of American **utopianism**.

Noyes called his developed philosophy and social theories 'perfectionism'. It was, at root, a Christian sect with strong socialist overtones that radically challenged accepted structures of family life. Noyes required that all members of the Oneida Community should be married to each member of the opposite sex, with housing, finance and work communally shared and governed. The complex and problem-fraught communality of marriage was maintained by male continence and training in the control of ejaculation similar to **Tantric** sexual ritual. Until the skill was mastered, boys were only allowed to have sex with women of post-menstrual age. Every member was subject to criticism by any of the numerous committees, by the community as a whole or by an individual. The object was to eliminate bad character traits. A form of hierarchy, called Ascending Fellowship, conferred certain privileges on the more senior members of the community. Mostly this amounted to who had the privilege of first marriage to a virgin, for which the attendant responsibility for both spiritual and sexual indoctrination had to be accepted. By 1878 the community had over 300 members, with smaller communities in several other cities. The community began to decline when Noyes attempted to hand the leadership over to his son who lacked his father's talent for leadership and who was not a Christian. Complex marriage was abandoned in 1879. Surprisingly, the community's joint stock corporation is still in existence and they are a major producer of cutlery under the brand name, Oneida Limited.

Oneness Pentecostalism X. Regarded by Christian orthodoxy to be heretical (see **Heresy**), the movement denies the **Trinity**, stating that there is only one person in the Godhead and that in order to be saved you have to be baptized. **Speaking in tongues** is an indispensable sign of having received that salvation. In believing in the one God, the sect affirmed the deity of Jesus and a strict monotheism. Their teaching is also referred to as 'Jesus-Only doctrine' or **Sabellianism**, a 3rd-century movement that believed the three persons of the Trinity were just different modes or aspects of the one God. There are many Oneness Pentecostal organizations, The Apostolic Assembly of the Faith in Christ Jesus and The Assemblies of the Lord Jesus Christ, being among the largest of them. See **World Faith Movement**

Ontological Argument X. One of the classical arguments for the existence of God, which begins by examining the concept of God. It demonstrates that the 'being' to which the concept would apply, exists necessarily. The argument was first developed by **Anselm** (1033–1109). He conceived of God as *En Realissimum*, 'something than which nothing greater can be conceived'. From this premise he argued that something existing in reality must be greater than the something that exists in the mind, because if I can understand the definition then, on its own terms, God must really exist since that existence must be greater than my conception of him. Anselm took this a step further; he argued that it is greater to exist both as an idea *and* as real thing, then merely to exist as an idea, therefore God must exist both in reality and as idea. The point is, that if God does not exist in reality, then something greater than him could be conceived. This, by definition, is impossible. The argument has been addressed by all metaphysical philosophers, some refuting it, others developing it, but most wanting to maintain a distinction between what exists in reality and what exists only in thought. See **First Cause**, **Teleology**

Ontology A branch of **metaphysics** concerned with the study of existence itself. A 'Being' is anything that is said to exist, sentient or otherwise and as well as having the characteristics of immanence or transcendence, innumerable other characteristics may apply, each one known as a 'category of being'. The categories are a way of classifying beings to the point where they become a 'thing'; that point is reached when the subject cannot be reduced to anything else or moved to any other category. **Aristotle** arrived at ten categories, one of which was 'substance'. **Kant**, however, in the *Critique of Pure Reason*, developed a large and complex list of categories that were grouped together under headings or 'classes', such as Quantity, Quality, Relation and Modality (see **Modalism**). Naturally, philosophers have very different views on what are the fundamental categories of 'Being'. Some confine them to physical objects which may be subdivided according to their concreteness, a tree and a cloud, for example, would fall into different physical categories; others, such as Descartes, included those 'parts' of us that think and perceive, giving rise to fundamental divisions between mind and body or body and spirit, leading to **dualism** and **functionalism**. Cutting across this and in terms of religion, ontology has a long history and, as any study of the nature of 'Being' must, it has made considerable contributions to the discussion of God's existence, to the relationship between faith and knowledge and to the quest for a workable ethical theory. **Aquinas**, Aristotle and **Plato** figured significantly among the classical ontologists; prominent modern ontologists include **Spinoza**, **Heidegger**, **Sartre** and **Wittgenstein**. See **Existentialism**, **Ontological Argument**, **Religious Existentialism**

Opus Dei X. Full name, 'Prelature of the Holy Cross and Opus Dei' was founded in 1928 by a Spanish Roman Catholic priest, St Josemaria Escriva de Balaguer. The Prelature, established by the **Roman Catholic Church**, comprised of a prelate, secular priests and lay people, whose mission it is to spread the Catholic message that everyone is called to become a saint and an apostle in the normal, everyday context of their lives. In effect the result is that work is sanctified and made holy, no matter how humble or exalted it is. The principle was first stated by St Josemaria, 'Work is the way to contribute to the progress of society; even more, it is a way to holiness.' Opus Dei has had the support of popes and Catholic leaders. But as is well known, the Prelature has been accused of secrecy, ultra fundamentalism and conservatism, of having a right-wing political agenda and cult-like practices. Recently, scholars like John

Allen have done much to contradict these accusations; Dr Massimo Introvigne, the Director of the Centre for Studies on New Religions, has pointed out that Opus Dei has become the target of secularists who cannot tolerate the secularized society's 'return to religion'. Many Catholics believe Opus Dei to be a 'Sign of Contradiction', that is a person or organization the holiness of which is to be judged by the extent of the opposition it attracts. Despite recent world best-selling fiction, the jury is still out.

Oracle A person or agency that is believed to have the ability to offer prophecies, advice and wise counsel to anyone seeking it. The information given is thought to be infallible and of a spiritual nature. The advice can be in the form of a prediction of the future, given by the gods, sometimes spoken through an object. In classical antiquity there were many places with a reputation for offering oracular wisdom and these were known as oracles. The questions taken to an oracle ranged in importance from wanting to know the best time to go to war or to contract a marriage, to how to settle the strike of workmen or solve a paternity dispute. Oracles in various forms, were to be found in many of the world's religious cultures. The most important for the Greeks was that of Apollo at **Delphi** which was widely used throughout the Greek world. Other important oracles were at Dodona, Crete and the Temple of Ammon in Egypt. China had ancient oracular traditions. The famous *I Ching*, the 'Book of Changes' (2852–2738 BCE) is still consulted by people across the world and oracular bones were used by the Shang Dynasty (1600–1046 BCE). **Norse mythology** describes how **Odin** conferred with the severed head of the god, Mimir; the Aztecs consulted a 'mummy-bundle' or human effigy; Tibetans use the term 'oracle' for the spirits that enter human beings acting as **mediums**; the Dalai Lama describes consulting the *Nechung Oracle*, the state oracle of the government of Tibet. In Dahomey, drummers summon the dead who being free from the world's time-scale, are able to see the future and offer prophetic oracles; the **Yoruba** Ifa oracle is probably the most complex oracular system to be found in Africa. Originating in the city of Ifa, it has spread to other West African countries. The constant need for information and guidance, ensures that the modern world has its own oracular sources such as **astrology**, **Tarot** and **palmistry**.

Order of Knights Templar The original military medieval Order of **Knights Templar** was established after the first Crusade and lasted from 1118–1312, founded by two French knights, Hugh de Payens and Geoffrey de St Omer. 'In this same year, [1118] certain noble men of knightly rank, religious men, devoted to God and fearing him, bound themselves to Christ's service in the hands of the Lord Patriarch. They promised to live in perpetuity as regular canons, without possessions, under vows of chastity and obedience. Since they had no church nor any fixed abode, the king, gave them for a time a dwelling place in the south wing of the palace, near the Lord's Temple' (William of Tyre). Bernard of Clairvaux drew up the Order's first rule and Pope Honorius II recognized the Templar as an independent and virtually autonomous Order, answerable to the pope and to no secular authority. They were organized into a hierarchy under the direction of a Grand Master and council, developing a specialist military force distinguished by their white robe and the red eight-pointed star on the left shoulder. After the crusading ended, the Templars become money-lenders and accumulated vast wealth and land-holdings, then gradually fell into disrepute. Their wealth was eventually dispersed among other groups such as the Knights Hospitallers and secular rulers. Traditions exist suggesting the Templar formed the **Freemasons** and the **Rosicrucians**.

Order of Melchizedek *J. X.* Some rabbinical authorities identify Melchizedek with Shem, the son of Noah, others that he instructed Abraham in **Torah**, and that he called Jerusalem, Salem. The traditions seem to come together in associating him with a line of priests who ordained the Kings of Israel, a succession finally realized in Jesus Christ based on the authority of Psalm 110:4 which asserts the Messiah will be, 'a priest for ever in the order of Melchizedek'. The typology of priest-hood in the Order of Melchizedek has been drawn on by several societies and orders founded down the years. See **Gnostic Order of Christ**

Order of the Holy Cross See **Gnostic Order of Christ**

Order of the Rosy Cross See **Rosicrucians**

Order of the Solar Temple One of several names of a secret society founded on a **New Age** myth that the **Knights Templar** continue to exist. Tradition has it that the order was founded in Geneva in 1984, by Joseph di Mambro and Luc Jouret as, *l'Ordre International Chevaleresque de Tradition Solaire* (OICTS) and renamed *Ordre du Temple Solaire*. Other members or founders who may have been involved remain unknown to the public. What can be said about the Order has not been verified, but as to its aims, one of its members, Robert Chabrier, in his book, *Pourquoi la Résurgence de l'Ordre du Temple?* declares that it is to establish 'correct notions of authority and power in the world', to affirm the primacy of the spiritual over the temporal, to assist humanity through a great 'transition' and to prepare for the second coming of Jesus as Solar God-King and advance the unification of all of Christendom with Islam. An ambitious agenda! Although founded relatively recently the Order's family tree shows a complex genealogy that connect it to Solar Lodges in Canada, Australia, Switzerland, Martinique and many other countries. Present members, including its founders, believe themselves to have been members of a 14th-century order in a previous existence, when di Mambro's daughter, Emmanuelle was the 'cosmic child' born of a virgin. After death they were to be led to a planet revolving around the star, Sirius. The order is one of several groups claiming either descent from or to be a reincarnation of the original Knights Templar, warrior monks authorized by the pope to assist with the Crusades and to protect pilgrims to the Holy Land. They are thought to have amassed huge wealth and treasure, which includes the **Holy Grail**. In 1986, Jouret and di Mambro moved to the Canadian province of Quebec, establishing a chapter of the Order of the Solar Temple, near Montreal. Despite controversial practices that has brought the Order into conflict with the law, they continue to exist, one group owning an organic bread bakery near Quebec.

Ordination A ceremony of consecration or initiation into sacred office, sometimes referred to as 'Holy Orders'. It is by this process clergy are authorized to lead and superintend the rites of their denominations. Normally, these would be the sacraments which take different forms in **Catholicism**, **Protestantism** and **Orthodoxy**, but would generally include **baptism**, the **Eucharist**, marriage and, in some traditions, Supreme Unction for the dying. In churches based on Apostolic succession the sacrament of Ordination can only be administered by a bishop. In Protestant traditions that hold to the **'priesthood of all believers'**, ordination is simply a public ceremony presided over by a minister, who together with elders or deacons of the church consecrate the candidate by 'the laying on of hands'. Most other major religious traditions have equivalent ceremonies that set apart men and women to be leaders of their communities. See **Priest**

Origin of Religion The perennially debated theme to which the different disciplines of historians, sociologists, anthropologists, theologians, philosophers and psychologists have contributed, but about which no consensus has been reached. The problem for researchers is to find a society or context, in which there were no religious perceptions or terms of reference. To argue that religion begins with **'revelation'** or **'realization'** or with scripture, mythology, ritual or custom, is to miss the point, since each of these are evidence of a religious culture that already exists. Many scholars today are inclined to the view that religion began in the simplest of ways, in man's intuitive and natural response to his environment. It is in the nature and quality of that response that the origin of religion is, perhaps, to be found. One significant energy in that response is what Rudolph **Otto** termed the **'numinous'**, that special sense of awe generated by a person's perception of a natural event or object. As the need for explanations arose, together with the drive to account for the origin of both the universe and the tribe, so did the mythologies begin. (See for example, **Australian Aboriginal Religion**). An answer in this form will not, of course, satisfy many of the established religious traditions, especially the Abrahamic religions of the Bible. These traditions explain the origin of their religion as an integral part of their belief systems, which unambiguously assert that all things began with the ever-existing, uncreated creator God, of whom human beings have knowledge only by grace of his self-revelation. Eastern traditions may be nearer the primal cause, in that their observation of a world in constant flux, the changing seasons, the movements of the stars, the journey from birth to death and the vicissitudes of human feelings and emotions, set them on the way to looking for the one, unchangeable, immutable essence of all things, for what T. S. Eliot termed, 'the still point of the turning world' ('Burnt Norton', *Four Quartets*). Most psychologists would agree that human beings have what may be termed a 'religious instinct', or an inborn 'sense' of the other. This does not mean that because the instinct or sense is there, so is the 'religion' or the 'other'. Either might be a symptom of our feeling of deep insecurity, *angxe or* dread, in response to our place in the enormity of the universe, the infinity of space and time and the fact that we live with the knowledge of our own mortality. See **Religion**

FINAL WORD: 'Among all my patients in the second half of life …there has not been one whose problem in the last resort was not that of finding a religious outlook on life.' (Jung [1933])

'Every dogma, every philosophic or theological creed, was at its inception a statement in terms of the intellect of a certain inner experience.' (Adler)

Original Sin *X.* In Christian theology, the state of sin that human beings are heir to since the **Fall**. The doctrine has its origin in the causal connection between Adam's sin of disobedience in eating the forbidden fruit in the Garden of Eden and our sin and takes its authority from Paul's Letter to the Romans, 'It was through one man that sin entered the world and through sin death and thus death pervaded the whole human race, in as much as all men have sinned' (Romans 5:12ff). Since infants have not (yet) sinned, the propensity to do so must be inherited (Romans 9:10–12) thus infants must be **baptized**, so that the sacrament can mitigate the blood-inherited state of separation from God. How this sin is transmitted is unclear, but **Augustine** clearly associates it with the sexual act in that in its performance the organs are not within the control of the will. In arguing that the problem is one of lack of control, Augustine takes no account of other involuntary bodily functions, such as breathing and swallowing. **Aquinas** makes a distinction between the pre-Fall Adam who had 'pure nature' and the post-Fall Adam who was deprived of the supernatural gifts and privileges that would otherwise have enabled him to perfect his nature. What became established was the notion that original sin meant a lack of Original Righteousness without the overtones of concupiscence. Confronted by rationalism and natural science, both Catholicism (see **Roman Catholicism**) and **neo-orthodox** Protestantism have reaffirmed the dogma of Original Sin. What the doctrine represents is a truth that runs through each generation in turn, that 'evil' can neither be eradicated, nor entirely controlled socially or politically. See **Traducianism**

Orpheus *G.* The Greek god of song and inventor of the lyre. Borrowed from Thracian Orphic Mysteries, he is of considerable importance to the religious history of Greece. Acknowledged as one of the pioneers of civilization, he taught mankind the art of agriculture, medicine and writing.

No one cult monopolized him and the Orphic hymns can't be systematized, but in the Roman Empire a particular poem assumed canonical status and subsequent literature took account of it. Otherwise, he was generally revered as an auger and seer, gifted in magical arts and astrology. His legend is the foundation of several cults, such as that of **Apollo** and **Dionysus**, and the mainspring for private and public mystic rites based on initiatory and purifying practices. The poetry associated with him forms a considerable body of literature that tells of his exploits. With his musical talents Orpheus could charm wild beasts, make trees and rocks dance and stop or change the flow of a river; he saved Jason and the Argonauts by singing in competition with the bidding Sirens; he descended into Hades to recover his wife Eurydice, but the celebrated account has him failing because he turned to look at her before they reached safety. He died on Mt Pangaion, where he was torn to death by the Maenads (the **Bacchantes**) for not honouring Dionysus. Orpheus was adopted as the founder of the **Eleusinian** and **Dionysus** mysteries and linked with cults on the island of Aegina and in Sparta and Phrygia. His followers practised vegetarianism, not even eating eggs and refrained from sex, a manner of living known as the 'Orphic way of life'.

Orthodox Church *X*. A communion of Churches mostly of Eastern Europe. They are also known as 'Eastern', 'Greek' or 'Greco-Russian'. Each group is independent originating in the ancient patriarchies of Alexandria, Antioch, Constantinople and Jerusalem and all share the same faith. Historically, they developed from the Church of the **Byzantine Empire**, with the gradual process of division between Constantinople and Rome conventionally completed in 1054. The main doctrinal differences concerned the authority and infallibility of the pope and the Western Churches' inclusion in the Nicene **creed** of the phrase 'and the Son', which implies that the Holy Spirit proceeds both from the Father 'and the Son', a doctrine known as the 'Double Procession'. The doctrines of the Orthodox Churches were based on the dogmatic definitions of the seven Ecumenical Councils held from 325 to 787 CE. The Roman Catholic Church recognizes 14 further councils as having Ecumenical authority. In Orthodox practice **baptism** is by immersion and children are taken into **Communion** from infancy. Services are mostly conducted in the natural language of the congregation and the veneration of **icons** is an important aspect of public and private worship. Orthodoxy has always supported a monastic tradition and since the 10th century the principal monastic centre has been Mount Athos. Parish priests are usually married, the bishops drawn from the monastic clergy. The distribution of the Orthodox tradition is now present, in one or more of its forms, in most parts of the world.

Osho-Rajneesh Movement *H*. A new religious movement founded in India by **Bhagwan Shree Rajneesh** (1931–90). Its religious base is syncretistic, combining with Hinduism, elements of Western philosophy and the teaching of other religions. The adherents are sometimes dubbed, the

'Orange People', a reference to the colour of their robes and are some-times known as neo-Sannyasins (see **Sannyasin**). Centres of the Movement exist throughout the world. See **Rajneesh Meditation**

Osiris *E*. An important deity of the **Ennead** of Heliopolis and one of the four children of **Geb** and **Nut**, the earth and sky gods. He was murdered by his brother **Seth**, who dismembered and scattered his body. It was reassembled by his wife **Isis**, who was then able to conceive their son, **Horus**. Horus sought revenge for his father's death and after Seth was banished to the desert, he succeeded as king. Osiris became the symbol of immortality and the divine judge in the Underworld. Usually he is depicted as a mummified man with a beard and as judge with the symbols of kingship, the crown, flail and crosier, the stylized staff of office. The reassembling of Osiris' body provided the basis for Egyptian belief in resurrection and the afterlife, from which the tradition of **mum-mification** and all the **funerary practices** developed. Like all other Egyptian myths, it has evolved with every political change of power. See **Egyptian Religion**

Osirian Triad *E*. An association of three Egyptian gods, Osiris, Isis and Horus who were bound by their interrelated mythologies. **Osiris**, mur-dered by his brother **Seth**, had his dismembered body reassembled by his wife **Isis**, who was then able to conceive their son, **Horus**.

Otto, Rudolph X. (1869–1937) An eminent German Protestant theologian and scholar of comparative religion. He is known for his book, *The Idea of the Holy*, which since its publication in 1917 has never been out of print and is currently translated into more than 20 languages. He defines the concept of 'holy' as something that is '**numinous**', which he defines as 'a non-rational, non-sensory experience or feeling whose primary and immediate object is outside of oneself' (ibid). The concept has had far-ranging influence on philosophical theologians such as Paul **Tillich**, and anthropologists such as Mircea Eliade. It also has philosophical signifi-cance in arguing that the numinous and/or the religious, is non-reducible and thus an original 'category' in its own right. See **Ontology**

Ottoman Empire *I*. Islam barely recovered from the devastating effects of the Mongol invasions under the leadership of Genghis Khan, suffered in the 13th and 14th centuries. When the Mamluk Sultan, Baybars ousted the Mongols, they replaced them with a succession of **Abbasid** Caliphs, who themselves became subjected to the **Mamluks**. This regime lasted until 1517, when Ottoman Turks established an Empire centred on Constantinople that lasted until 1923. From 1204 CE, Constantinople had been under regular attack and was virtually destroyed and depopulated by the Crusaders; it was rebuilt by Sultan Mehmed II. He welcomed thou-sands of Jews fleeing from persecution in Christian Europe who provided support to the massive task of rebuilding the city. The Ottoman Empire reached its peak under the reign of Suleiman the Magnificent (1520–66)

What was achieved was an unprecedented and extraordinary syncretism that combined the energies of Islam's major sects, the **Sunnis** and the **Sufis**, with groups of Christians, Jews and Muslims, each responsible for the religious and secular duties of their respective communities. From the early 19th century and until 1922, the Empire implemented a range of reforms and from 1909–18, enjoyed a brief democracy. From 1918, Mustafa Kemal Ataturk led the Turks in their war of independence and in 1923 the Turkish Republic was established as the first secular state of the Islamic world. See **Islamic Dynasties**

Out-of-Body Experience (OBEs) Any experience in which a person believes that his or her spirit has temporarily left the physical body and then returned to that same body. Some OBEs are related to 'near-death experiences', others are associated with the **occult**, and mystical practices resulting in what are called Astral Projections. See **Near-Death Experience**

Ox Herding Pictures *B*. A well-known series of pictures that emerged in the **Ch'an** Buddhist tradition in China, illustrating the meditational path that would lead to enlightenment. 'Herding an Ox' (see *Figure 10*) is a literary metaphor for controlling the mind or the unruly thoughts passing through the mind, that have to be herded and controlled. It dates back to the T'ang dynasty (618–907 CE) The series of ten pictures show the practitioner as the herdsman and the ox as the mind or the unruly thoughts; the ox originally black, gradually becomes whiter until, finally, it has completely disappeared. It is an image of both the end of discursive thinking and the mind as a separate entity clinging to concepts.

Figure 10 Ox Herding

'The whip and rope are necessary,
Else he might stray off down some dusty road.
Being well trained, he becomes naturally gentle.
Then, unfettered, he obeys his master.'

In the 12th century the sequence of images was fixed at ten by the master Kuo-an Shih-yuan and these pictures have become the received version used both in training and as objects of meditation for Ch'an and **Zen** practitioners.

Oxford Movement *X*. A loose association of High Church Anglicans or Anglo-Catholics, most of them members of Oxford University. They set out to demonstrate that the Church of England was in direct descent of the early Christian Church established by the Apostles. It was also known as, the Tractarian Movement, because of its series of publications, *Tracts for Our Times* (1833–41). Among the eminent Tractarians were, Edward Pusey, Regius Professor of Hebrew at Christ Church, John Henry Newman, fellow of Oriel College and Vicar of the University Church of St Mary the Virgin and Archdeacon Edward Manning. In the final, 19th tract, Newman argued that the doctrines of the Roman Catholic Church, established by the Council of Trent (1545–63) were compatible with 16th-century 39 Articles of Faith of the Church of England. As well as wanting to re-establish the Apostolic succession, the Oxford Movement was concerned to restore the Church of England to true spirituality in the face of what they believed to be its increasing secularization. Newman converted to Roman Catholicism in 1845, followed by Manning in 1851. Anglo-Catholicism has had a massive influence on worldwide Anglicanism and continues to do so.

Note: This 'Oxford Movement' is not to be confused with the **Moral Re-Armament** (MRA) founded in Oxford in the 1920s by Frank Buchan.

P

Pacific Northwest Indians *Ami.* See **Amerindian Religion**

Pacific Religion See **Melanesian Religion**

Padmasambhava *B*. Skt. 'The Lotus-born', from the legend that he was born in a lotus flower on the banks of the river Indus. Known as 'Guru Rinpoche', he is revered by his followers as the 'second Buddha'. During the 8th century CE he travelled from India to Tibet, taking with him *Dzogchen*, a teaching known as 'the Great Perfection', considered to be the definitive yet most secret teaching of **Shakyamuni Buddha**. Padmasambhava became one of the founders of **Tibetan Buddhism** and when under his direction, *Dzogchen* was adopted as the philosophy of the **Nyingmapa school**, he became identified with the tradition of *mahasid-dhas*, 'master of the great perfection'. In around 767 he supervised the construction of a monastery at Samye, the oldest monastery and transla-tion centre in Tibet. Given the task of subduing nature gods and spirits who opposed the introduction of Buddhism, he made use of ritual instru-ments such as the *phurba*, a three-edged dagger for subduing demons. Such manifestations of magical powers were evidence of his enlighten-ment, for which reason he has become something of a legendary figure.

Padmasana *H. B.* Skt. 'the lotus position'. The classical body-posture for **Hatha-yoga meditation** that is considered particularly suitable. It is said the posture removes all evil influences from the practitioner. It is also known as the 'locked position'.

Pagan *L. peganus.* 'countryman', 'rural' or 'rustic'. Originally the term was used in reference to someone who believed in nature gods, a **pantheistic** form of **natural religion** frequently associated with the poly-theism of Greece and Rome. 'Pagan' was also used of someone who was neither Jew, Christian nor Muslim. Christianity was first centred in the towns and cities and therefore a sharp distinction was made between the new, emergent religion and the old religion of the country dwellers or peasants – a cognate word from pagan. In modern usage it has pejorative implications used to define someone who is an atheist, thus having no religious beliefs at all. In this sense the term is interchangeable with 'heathen'.

Paganism Originally, from L. *paganus*, a civilian as opposed to *militus*, a soldier. Early Christians called themselves 'soldiers of Christ', hence a pagan was someone who was not a Christian. The term has come to be used generally to deprecate belief systems that disavow the biblical reli-gions and more broadly to cultures that are thought to lack religion and which are therefore assumed to be atheistic or **heathen**. The religions of Greece and Rome were described as paganisms by emergent Christianity, not just for their polytheism but because of their ritual use of shrines and images which were evidence of biblically condemned idolatry. Since the advent of **romanticism**, 'paganism' has been used positively in admiration of what was seen to be a more 'natural' and vital system of belief. By implication Victorian Christianity and other biblical religions were criticized as lifeless, authoritarian and increasingly secularized. The established religions reacted by dubbing 'pagan' any religion or movement that appeared to be sensual, materialistic and self-indulgent. See **Atheism**

Pahlavi Dynasty *I*. The Dynasty that ruled in Iran from 1925 to 1979. Disillusioned with the foreign influence of Britain and Russia and with the government of Ahmad Shah, the last of the Qajar Dynasty, Reza Khan, a military officer, led a successful coup and as the new Shah he adopted as his name, Pahlavi which is synonymous with 'Middle Persian'. In doing so he drew on the ancient cultural heritage of the Pahlavi language in literature. (See **Pahlavi Literature**) He had ambitious plans to modernize every aspect of Iranian life and hundreds of Iranians were sent to Europe for training. In 1941 he was succeeded by his son, Muhammed Reza Shah. Among further reforms he replaced the lunar Islamic calendar with a solar Imperial calendar and was strongly opposed by Islamic clerics. The religious unrest led to the 1979 revolution the return to the Iran of the exiled Ayatollah Ruhollah Khomeini.

Pahlavi Literature *Zo*. From c.300 BCE to c.950 CE, Pahlavi was the Middle Persian language in which the Zoroastrian texts, previously transmitted orally, were written and preserved and Pahlavi literature is the main source for modern studies of **Zoroastrianism**. The traditional redactions of many of these texts were completed in the 9th century by the **Magi**, Zoroastrian priests vehemently defensive of their faith. See **Avesta**

Paleo-paganism The term is used to refer to the original polytheistic forces of **paganism**. Also, to indigenous belief-systems that have not been disturbed or disrupted by other cultures, for example, **Hinduism** before Islam, **Shintoism** and **Taoism**. See **Meso-Paganism, Neo-paganism, Paganism**

Palestine Originally the name given by the Romans to the region of **Canaan** after they defeated the revolt of Bar Kokhba, 132–135 CE. The country is known to Jews as *Eretz Yisrael* (Heb.), the 'Land of Israel' and as the 'Holy Land'. It is the territory referred to in Genesis, promised by God to Abraham for the people of Israel on the condition they kept the **covenant**. Then, the land was called Canaan. Throughout the history of Israel the borders have always been contested, but for the Jewish religion, of greater importance was the holiness of the country which is inextricably associated with its occupancy by the 'Holy People'. The 'Land' *and* the 'People' were intended by God to constitute the new Eden, but because of Israel's sin this was indefinitely postponed and the Jewish people dispersed (see **Diaspora**). The Jewish expectation of the Messiah is dependent on Israel's atonement for that sin and its reconciliation with God. In that event, Palestine, the 'Land' and the Jews, the 'People', will be restored to each other. For this reason the founding of the independent State of Israel was interpreted by some Jewish groups as a socio-political fulfilment of the Messianic promise. See **Israel, State of Israel, Zionism**

Pali *B*. Language of the text of the **Tripitaka**, the canon of **Theravada** Buddhism. Views vary as to the origins of the language. The tradition suggests that the original language was a variation or dialect of Magadhi, the Buddha's own language. It is more likely, however, that Pali was a central Indian dialect in more generally use.

Pali Canon *B*. See **Tripitaka**

Palm Sunday *X*. The Sunday prior to Easter, celebrated by Christians to commemorate Jesus' arrival at Jerusalem on the back of an ass. Some of the people shouted 'Hosanna' and strew palm fronds across his path. Since ancient antiquity the palm frond has been a symbol of victory and triumph (see Rev.7:9) and in some Christian traditions miniature crosses are made from palm leaves and distributed in church.

Palmistry The popular term for Chiromancy, the belief that a person's destiny is imprinted on the palms of the hands. It is a form of **divination**, a means of foretelling a person's future by interpreting the lines of the left and right palms. Palmistry is practised worldwide with variations according to the culture. It has an ancient history with perhaps origins in India where it was highly developed; it was practised in China, Tibet, Persia, Mesopotamia and Egypt. Palmistry as we know it stems from Greece. Anaxagoras, a Greek philosopher (500–428 BCE) believed that 'The superiority of a man is owing to his hands.' **Aristotle** (384–322 BCE) affirmed that 'The hand is the organ of organs, the active agent of the passive powers of the whole system.' The dominant hand is the one used for writing and the technique of 'reading the palm' involves an interpretation of the lines (creases) according to certain qualities such as their length and how they intersect. The heart, head and life lines are the most significant. In some traditions the reading includes the fingers, fingernails, fingerprints, skin patterns and the general shape and flexibility of the hand. Eastern practice believes that a person's past-life, karmic information and hereditary qualities are also contained in the palm's markings. Although palmistry is widely practised and a popular feature at fairs and festivals, many regard it as a pseudoscience. In some Buddhist traditions bringing the palms together in a form of greeting symbolizes the union of opposites; in **Zen** Buddhism the gesture is called *Gassho*. See **Karma**

Pan *G*. In Greek mythology, the god of woods, fields and flocks. He is depicted with a human torso and head or with a goat's legs, torso and horns. In popular usage and in literature Pan is the god of animals. The mythology tells of him pursuing the **nymph** Syrinx, who to avoid him was changed by her sisters into reeds which Pan cut and from them fashioned the instrument known as Pan Pipes. He became associated with the Greek **Dionysus** and the Roman Faunus.

Pan African Orthodox Christian Church *X*. Or the Shrine of the Black Madonna, the denomination was founded in 1953 in Detroit, USA, by Albert B. Cleage known also as, Jaramogi Abebe Agyeman. There is no relationship whatsoever with the canonical Eastern Orthodox Churches. The group teach that Jesus is the Black Messiah who was sent to reconstitute the Black Nation Israel and 'to liberate black people from all forms of oppression and exploitation of the white gentile world' (from the Black Nationalist Creed). Their mission statement includes working to bring the black Church back to its historical roots, sharing the faith of Jesus of Nazareth and the revolutionary power of God that is incarnate in his followers and obedience to the covenant God established with Abraham. See **Black Muslims**, **British Israelites**, **Nation of Islam**, **Nation of Yahweh**

Panchen Lama *B*. After the **Dalai Lama**, the second highest ranking lama of the **Gelugpa** sect of **Tibetan Buddhism**.

Panentheism The belief that God is immanent, not just present, but actually *within* all creation. It does not mean that God *is* everything, that is, synonymous with the universe (see Pantheism) but that while God is *in* (en) the material universe, he is more than the material universe. He is both immanent and transcendent, both the creator and the source of universal morality. Most religions hold to a form of Panentheism, believing that God is both immanent and transcendent. Examples include some **Amerindian** tribes, Eastern and Oriental Christian **Orthodoxy**, liberal forms of **Judaism** and some traditions of **Hinduism**. See **Logos**, **Neoplatonism**, **Process Theology**

Panja kakke *Sik*. Pun. See **Five Ks**, the distinguishing marks of Sikhs of the **Khalsa**.

Panlogism A concept suggested by **Hegel**, [1988] 'the real is rational, the rational is real', in effect a paean for the rational basis of everything that exists and that the world is an actualization of pure Mind or **Logos**. The idea has been taken up by rationalists to demonstrate that reason is the universal foundation of knowledge and that it should be promoted, encouraged and nurtured wherever it is found. Panlogist beliefs do not fall into any clear categories, more importantly, whatever a Panlogist does believe will be entirely supported by rational argument. See **Rationalism**

Panna *B*. Pal. 'cognitive wisdom' founded on an understanding of **Dependent Origination** and the concept of 'not-self'. See **Prajna**

Panth *H*. *S*. Skt. 'path' or 'way'. A term used generally in India for groups following a particular teaching or path. For example, the **Sikh** community was first known as the Nanak-panth, the followers of Nanak (see **Guru Nanak**).

Pantheism The belief that everything is God and God is everything. The apparent diversity of the universe obscures the unity that is God or the Absolute. This includes everything that is abstract in terms of human emotion and feeling, all forms of change, all concepts and experiences of evil and suffering, all forms of limitation and infinity, everything that is good, immutable, eternal, the sum of all these *is* God. Pantheism may also be acosmic, that is world-denying, to include those traditions that hold all sense-experience to be illusory, leaving only the Divine as real. See **Macrocosm and Microcosm**, **Process Theology**, **Panentheism**, **Scientific Pantheism**, **Theism**

Pantheon, Greek *G*. Twelve supreme gods formed the Olympian pantheon, with their home on Mt **Olympus**, between Thessaly and Macedonia, which at 10,000ft is the highest mountain on the Greek peninsula. The divine dozen were: **Zeus**, **Hera**, **Poseidon**, **Demeter**, **Apollo**, **Artemis**, **Ares**, **Aphrodite**, **Hermes**, **Athena**, **Hephaestus** and **Hestia**. 'By the Twelve!' was a popular oath. See **Greek Religion**

Pantheon, Roman *R*. The Romans assimilated their own deities to those of the Greeks and it is by these names that they have become most familiar. The 12 gods were **Apollo**, **Ceres**, **Diana**, **Juno**, **Jupiter**, **Mars**, **Mercury**, **Neptune**, **Venus**, **Vesta** and **Vulcan**. See **Roman Religion**

Pantocrator *X*. From the Greek meaning 'Lord' or 'Master' of the Universe. It is one of the names given to Christ by the Greek Orthodox Church and a painted or mosaic image that figures magnificently in church decoration. In Byzantine churches the icon occupies the ceiling of the central dome or the nave of the church. It was the Council of Nicaea (convoked in 325 CE) that decided Christ would be given the title Pantocrator, 'master of everything'.

Papa *H*. Skt. 'sin' or 'evil', 'baseness'. The term is used with *Purusha*, as *papa-purusha* to mean a man or a human being, in effect, personified wickedness. It is the opposite of *punya*, merit or virtue.

Papacy *X*. Originally the term pope, 'Father', was used of any bishop of the Church who was deemed to merit the title, but is now restricted to the Bishop of Rome as head of the **Roman Catholic** Church. The pope is also known as 'the Vicar of Christ'. The pope's authority is derived directly from Jesus Christ through the Apostle Peter who was the first

Bishop of Rome, but the universality of the pope's power developed gradually, reaching its zenith with Boniface VIII (1294–1303). In his Bull *Unam Sanctam* of 1302, he declared that both temporal and spiritual power were within the authority of the Church and that, to ensure salvation, every human being should be subject to the pontiff. The pope's temporal power was finally eroded, but his universal spiritual authority has been maintained. To many non-Catholic Christians the nature of the papacy with its centre in the Vatican, seems hard to reconcile with Christian humility. The pontificate of John XXIII (1958–63), who was respected as a spokesman of Christian opinion, did much to restore the public image of the papacy, as did the Second Vatican Council which emphasized the collegiality of all the bishops with the pope, as a way of limiting his absolute authority.

Parable A simple narrative in prose or verse, intended to illustrate what otherwise might be the hidden meaning of a religious, philosophical or moral idea. Well-known examples are the parables of Jesus and Aesop's Fables. George Townsend, in a foreword to his translation of these wrote, 'The Parable is the designed use of language purposely intended to convey a hidden and secret meaning other than that contained in the words themselves and which may or may not bear a special reference to the hearer or reader.' In the sense that a parable is a story with a meaning, usually religious, what is presented is a religious subject in a secular form. Whether the secular form colours the religious meaning or whether the religious dimension infuses the secular form, is a moot point casuistically debated.

Paracelsus (1493–1591) A man of many parts, he was a philosopher, alchemist, physician and occultist. Born Theophrast von Hohenheim in Switzerland, he assumed the name Paracelsus, 'superior to Celsus', who was a Roman physician. He travelled widely, visiting Egypt, the Holy Land, Arabia and Constantinople. He did not think of himself as a magician, but he was a practising astrologer, as were most physicians of his day. He is famous for pioneering the use of chemical and minerals in medicine, for propounding the then ridiculous notion that a wound would heal itself if kept clean and left to drain and that cauterization or amputation were not inevitable. He also introduced the now axiomatic theory that illness is caused by a disease, something extraneous to the body, thus introduced to it and that the amount (dose) of a medicine was of equal importance as the medicine prescribed. Today, in German-speaking countries there remains a place for what is called Paracelsian medicine, which is loosely associated with homoeopathy.

Paradise The term is most familiarly associated with the Garden of Eden, the utopia from which in biblical tradition, the first man and woman were expelled because of their disobedience to God's will. The theme of biblical religions has been how Paradise might be regained as a post-death location or condition where the '**soul**' will live in blissful communion with its creator-God. The concept of paradise is not confined to the biblical religions, nor does it originate within them. The mythologies of most religions have a similar concept, for example, the Avalon of Arthurian legend, the Greek **Elysian** Fields and the Norse **Valhalla**. **Mahayana** Buddhism has a series of graded paradises, but these are not the adherent's ultimate goal. See **Fall of Man**, **New Jerusalem**, **Nirvana**, **Pure Land**, **Utopianism**

Paramita *B*. Skt. 'that which has reached the other shore' or 'crossed over', usually translated as 'the perfections'. In **Mahayana** Buddhism, Paramitas are qualities 'perfected' by a **bodhisattva** in the course of his own spiritual development. Traditionally there are six qualities, generosity, discipline, patience, energy or vitality, **meditation** and wisdom. Later, to bring the virtues in line with the ten stages or levels of a bodhisattva's evolution, four more qualities were added, skilful means, vows, power and knowledge.

Parapsychology A branch of psychology that deals with supernatural phenomena such as **extra sensory perception**, **possession**, haunting and the like. The study of such phenomena was put on a formal basis with the founding of the English Society of Psychical Research in 1882, since when university departments have been set up to promote serious research in Britain, the USA and Australia. Research aims to give scientific validity for the occult and paranormal activities and to the alleged psychic abilities of **mediums** and **clairvoyants**.

Parinivana *B*. Skt. Pal. 'final' or 'highest' form of **nirvana**. Sometimes translated as 'total extinction'. More usually, *parinivana* refers to the nirvana entered at death, when the subject is finally free of the birth-death-rebirth cycle. But in the earlier literature it is also used of *nirvana* realized during life. The term is sometimes used to speak of the death of a monk or nun.

Parousia *X*. Gk. 'Appearance' or 'subsequent presence with'. In Christianity, the term refers to the **second coming** of Christ. For the ancient Greeks and Romans a parousia was an official visit by an important person or royalty. Christ's return was interpreted by Matthew and Mark as something that will happen in the foreseeable future, linked with Jesus' prediction of the destruction of the Jerusalem Temple in 70 CE. Some Christian traditions, notably the **Jehovah's Witnesses**, believe the Parousia has already happened, interpreted as Christ's unseen presence, the visible effect of which will be manifested at a later time.

Parsees *Z*. A **Zoroastrian**-based religion whose adherents are descendents of those who moved to India to avoid conversion to Islam. They settled in Gujarat in northwest India c.936 CE where they lived in peace until Muslim armies invaded in the 13th and 14th centuries, following which they were persecuted. They have been able to maintain their beliefs, customs and identity. Indian law gave the Parsees special consideration in that they have Indian nationality, in recognition of which Parsees have contributed significantly to the Indian Independence Movement. But they are non-Indians in terms of their ethnicity and traditions. A Parsee is someone who is directly descended from the original Persian settlers or someone who has been formally admitted to the faith. There are, however, Zoroastrians in India known as *Iranis* who are not, by this definition, Parsees; the matter is confused more because *Irani* is also a Parsee surname. In the case of mixed marriage it is the father who has to be a Parsee to allow the children to be admitted to the **Navjote** ceremony that admits a child to the faith. In practice the matter is more fluid since the gender equality of the Indian Constitution renders the patrilineal distinction void. The main Parsee communities today are to be found in Bombay, Iran, Pakistan, Britain, the USA and Canada, with a small diaspora throughout the world. In 2002 the worldwide Zoroastrian community, including both Parsees and Iranis, was estimated at between 180,000 and 250,000. But according to www.adherents.com the number is now thought to be 2.6 million. Inter-religious marriage and proselytizing are discouraged, although an increasing number of Westerners are converting to the faith. See **Zoroastrianism, Traditional**

Parthians *AME*. The second, native dynasty of Iran and archenemy of Rome, that ruled the Iranian plateau from the late 3rd century BCE and Mesopotamia intermittently from c.224–c.150 BCE. It was the most enduring empire of the ancient Near East, achieving a remarkable fusion of religious beliefs drawn from Iranian, Semitic and Greek traditions. The rise of this Iranian dynasty did much to protect **Zoroastrianism** from the Hellenizing policies of Alexandra the Great (see **Hellenism**). The Parthians themselves were **Mazda** and fire-worshippers, governed by the **Magi**, the ancient Persian priestly cast. The syncretism of their religion is graphically present at two sites; the huge statues of the tomb of Antiochus I (69–34 BCE) of Commagene are identified as, Zeus-Ohrmazd, Apollo-Mithras, Helios-Hermes, Artagnes (a god of war) and Heracles-Ares. The second is the carved slab from Hatrah, showing a bearded, male deity whose body is entwined with serpents, his head surmounted by an eagle with outstretched wings, reminiscent of Egyptian iconography and his right hand grasping an axe, a typical symbol of Semitic and Hittite weather gods. To his left, is a three-headed dog, representative of **Cerberus**, the Greek god of the underworld. In eastern Parthia there were convivial contacts with Hindu and Buddhist sects and in the west Jewish communities flourished, along with early Christian communities. See **Mesopotamian Religion**

Particularism A term used by some philosophers to heighten an aspect of **epistemology**. Particulars are 'things', universals are their qualities. Particularism is the view that only particulars exist and more specifically that their characteristics and the relations between them are themselves particular and not universals. The enquiry begins with the question,

'What do we know?' or more usually, 'How do we know?' In developing the answer the discussion moves to how can we be sure that what we know is 'real', or 'right', or 'true'. The point is that whenever we ask such questions as, 'How do we know?' the assumption is already made that there is something to be known. Particularism makes no such assumptions and may come to the conclusion that we know nothing, thus making the second question, 'how?' irrelevant. In the philosophy of religion the enquiry about what we can really know is applied to metaphysics, at which point Particularism would ask that any claims made be validated, so that the ground for moving from the 'what do we know?' to the 'how do we know?' is secure. Particularism is also used by cultural sociologists to refer to an exclusive, even obsessive, devotion to the interests of one's party, sect or nation. See **Nominalism**, **Pluralism**, **Singularism**

Parvati *H.* The mountain-goddess consort of **Siva** who is associated with the Himalayas. Her cult is especially revered by married women who seek the longevity of their husbands. In some Hindu mythologies she is regarded as a manifestation of **Shakti** or **Durga**.

Pascal, **Blaise (1623–62)** A French mathematician, physicist and philosopher. In 1654 he had what he described as a mystical experience after which he devoted himself to philosophy and theology, producing two famous books, *Provincial Letters* and the *Pensées*. From 1648 to 1654 he lived through what he called his 'worldly period' and when his father died in 1651, leaving him a fortune, his worldliness became excessive. His fascination with gambling was to contribute to his work on probability theory, the nature of choices made under uncertainty, which made a significant contribution to mathematics. During this period his sister Jacqueline entered the convent of Port-Royal. In 1654 Pascal suffered an accident and remained unconscious for 15 days; on recovering consciousness during the night of 23rd November, he had an intense religious vision later recorded specifically between 22.30 and 00.30. He made a brief note. 'Fire. God of Abraham, God of Isaac, God of Jacob, not of the God of the philosophers and the scholars ...' which he concluded with Psalm 119:16, 'I will not forget thy word. Amen.' The document, which was sewn into his coat and transferred when he changed, was discovered after his death by a servant. Pascal is famous for what is known as, 'Pascal's Wager', a name ironically associated with his excessive gambling. There are three wagers in the *Pensées* which are an application of his probability theory to a belief in God. Pascal's God was the Christian God of the Bible, but the Bible only provided information *about* God, not proof of his existence. The main argument of his wager suggests that it is always a better 'bet' to believe in God, because the expected value to be gained from believing in God is always greater than the expected value resulting from non-belief. This is not an argument for the existence of God, but simply a claim that it is more advantageous to believe than not to believe. Similar applications of decision theory are to be found in **Hinduism** and **Buddhism**. The Buddha suggested in the Kalama Sutra, that even though the concepts of **rebirth** and **karma** are complicated, acting *as if* they are valid brings positive results now. Pascal was of the same mind. See **Jansenism**

FINAL WORD: 'If He [God] doesn't exist you will lose very little. But suppose you don't believe in His existence and don't lead a Christian life? If he does exist, then you will suffer eternal damnation! So it is rational and prudent to believe in God's existence and to live Christian life.' (Pascal)

Passion The suffering of Jesus following the Last Supper, to the time of his crucifixion, as described in the New Testament. Passion week is the week leading up to Easter, with Passion Sunday being the Sunday before Easter. In the Church calendar this is **Palm Sunday**.

Passionists *X*. The common name for members of the congregation of 'Discalced Clerks of the Most Holy Cross and Passion of our Lord Jesus Christ'. The order was founded by St Paul of the Cross (1694–1775) born in Ovada, Italy, who became a famous preacher and miracle worker. In addition to the three customary vows of poverty, chastity and obedience, the Passionists took a fourth vow to honour the Passion of Christ and to promote it by word and deed.

Passover *J*. Heb. 'Pesach'. One of the most important festivals of the Jewish liturgical year, celebrating the emancipation of the Hebrews from slavery in Egypt. It is observed from 15th of Nissan (March-April) and lasts for eight days. Sometimes it is referred to as the Feast of Unleavened bread, as the Hebrews had no leaven with which to bake. In the celebration of the Passover Jews may not eat bread, replacing it with matzos (*matzah*). So stringent is this law that even today in an orthodox Jewish home, the house is thoroughly searched lest any traces of leaven remain and what is found must be given or sold to gentiles. Crockery and cutlery kept just for the Passover, replaces what is usually used. The first two nights of the Passover festival are called *Seder* ('order') nights which are celebrated in the home and centred around a banquet, the eating of which is an integral part of the liturgy of the *Haggadah*. The Passover Haggadah narrates the story of the Exodus in the form of questions usually asked by a young boy or girl, the first being, 'Wherefore is this night different from all other nights?' The Passover service is a response to these questions. The Passover Haggadah is a detailed interpretation of Deut. 26: 5–9, directing the family through a banquet ritual that includes symbolic foods, the nature of which vary according to different Jewish traditions. These food-symbols include the roasted shank-bone of a lamb, to represent the original Paschal sacrifice, the *maror* or bitter herbs (horseradish, etc.), representing the bitterness of the Hebrews' suffering in Egypt, the *charoset* (a mixture of apples, nuts, spices and wine) to symbolize the mortar used in the forced-labour building and a roasted egg, reminiscent of the Temple-based ritual offering. Wine is another important feature and at a certain point in the liturgy a drop is spilt to represent each of the plagues sent by God to persuade Pharaoh to free the Hebrew slaves. A goblet is set aside for the prophet Elijah who is believed to be the precursor of the coming Messiah, thus the Passover meal does not only look back to a formative event in Jewish history, but also forward, in hope of the Messianic age and final emancipation.

Patanjali *H*. A yogic philosopher who lived in c.2nd century BCE, although some authorities suggest he might have lived in the first century CE. He was not the originator of the yoga system, but recast and organized methods that had long existed. These were based on one of the six orthodox Hindu philosophical Schools (see **Darshana**) the School of *Sankhya*, concerned with the union of consciousness with nature. Patanjali revised *Sankhya* philosophy, putting the emphasis on theism, meditation and human nature, thus directing his yoga system to a mastery of both the physical and the psychic elements of consciousness. The two aspects, the physical body and the observing mind, have to be controlled and unified. It was expected that his yoga discipline would have numerous effects; the body would cease to be restless, the inward power of life enhanced, the length of life increased, the mind calm and at peace. All these effects, once realized, are put at the service of the quest for spiritual emancipation. Patanjali's theories are not other-worldly or metaphysical, he is entirely concerned with a practical method to achieve enlightenment through a system of physical discipline based on the power of will. His system, together with his commentaries on it, are to be found in his Yoga-sutras.

Paterfamilias *R*. L. The paterfamilias, the head of a household or father of a family, was also the high priest of his home's religious cult. Honour was given to the gods of his father and to the spirits of his ancestors and he would have expected his sons to continue the tradition. The cult was based on the notion that it was the father who formed and maintained the link with tutelary gods and spirits. Among the gods were the Penates, usually associated with the profession or craft of the paterfamilias. If he happened to be a craftsman, **Minerva** would have been among the household pantheon; if a merchant, then Mercury would be honoured. The household also observed domestic religious rites from birth to death. Taboos associated with the cult of the paterfamilias made his home and property sacred, protecting it in much the same way as civil law.

Path Symbolism The path or road, together with the crossroads, is a familiar image for the journey through life. Paths may be peaceful or stormy, steep or level, narrow or broad, stony or strewn with primroses. The journey is usually spiritual and in the form of a quest, as with Pilgrim's search for the Celestial City, in Bunyan's *Pilgrim's Progress*. Psalm 23 is the best-known poetic description, 'He leads me to still waters; ... He guides me in right paths ... Though I walk through a valley of the shadow of death … I will not fear.' In John ch.14, Jesus makes the Christian's path clear, 'I am the way and the truth and life; no one comes to the Father but by me.' Other traditions offer, for example, the 22 paths of the astral otherworld, each one corresponding to a letter in the Hebrew alphabet or the 22 major trumps of the **tarot** and the Milky Way was thought to be the path (or river) along which the souls of the dead travelled on their journey to the other world. Right- and left-hand paths refer to a

Figure 11 The Celtic Knot

choice in types of religion, the former associated with the worship of one or more deities and an observance of a clear moral code, the latter to the advancement of the 'self', frequently associated with **Satanism** and **Black Magic**. In **Taoism**, two paths are gender-distinguished in concepts of **Yin and Yang**.

The compelling knotwork or interlace, is symbolic of the way the spiritual and physical paths of our life constantly crisscross. See **Labyrinth**, **Landscape Symbolism**, **Sacred Geometry**

Patriarch *J. X.* The term has various usages. Generally it refers to the 'father' or ruler of a tribe, familiar examples of which are the **Old Testament** ancestors of Israel: **Abraham**, **Isaac** and **Jacob**, together with their extended families. Originally, these patriarchs came from **Mesopotamia**, then lived in **Canaan** before Jacob and his family settled in Egypt. There is some debate about whether these patriarchs were actual historical individuals and the progenitors of tribes or names representing tribes. In this latter case, the journeys of the individuals would represent the migrations of the tribes and their biographies the experiences and histories of the people. Christian sources include **David** among the patriarchs and rabbinical sources exclude the sons of Jacob. Judah ha-Nasi (see *Mishnah*) was given the title Patriarch in the 2nd century CE, as leader or governor of the Jews of the Land of Israel by Roman and Christian administrations. His son and grandson, the last of a distinguished line, also succeeded to the title. In Christian usage the title was accorded to the bishops of Rome, Constantinople, Jerusalem, Antioch and Alexandria and in **Roman Catholicism** to the bishop who held the highest rank after the pope. Eastern Orthodoxy's Patriarchs (see **Orthodox Church**) are the bishops of the senior sees who have authority over other bishops.

Patripassionism X. A 3rd-century Christian heresy which holds that instead of the Trinity, the Godhead comprises only the Father who reveals himself in three ways or modes. A problem arises from the gospel accounts of the Crucifixion that record Jesus the son, speaking to God the Father while he was on the cross. The heresy argues that the Father was born of the Virgin Mary, lived and co-suffered with the human Jesus on the cross. The son was the Father in a different mode and that everything that happened to the Son happened also, to the Father. The heresy is also known as **Sabellianism** which is a refinement of Patripassionism. See **Modalism, Oneness Pentecostalism**

Paul, St X. d. c.65 CE. Known as the 'Apostle to the Gentiles'. Born a Jew in Tarsus, in Cilicia and called, Saul, he was brought up a Pharisee receiving a rabbinical education under Gameliel I in Jerusalem, and accorded Roman citizenship. First a vehement opponent of the early Church he was converted (c.33 CE) and became the leading Apostle of the Church he endeavoured to exterminate. He travelled widely, establishing churches in the provinces of Syria, Cilicia, Cyprus, Galatia, Macedonia, Greece and Ephesus. Most of his converts were gentiles, but the conversion of Jews required a reappraisal of Jewish Law which created problems with the more conservative Jewish Christians who held that without **circumcision** gentiles could not be saved. He returned regularly to Jerusalem and on his last visit was charged with violating the sanctity of the Temple and teaching transgression of the Jewish Law. As a Roman citizen he appealed to have his case transferred to the tribunal in Rome and he was sent there in 59 CE. Tradition has it that he was either executed on the Ostian Way, near Rome or martyred during the Neronian persecution. The **New Testament** includes 13 letters Paul wrote to the churches he established, some of which were probably written while he was imprisoned.

Peace Mission Movement Founded by Father Divine (c.1880–1965). His syncretistic teaching combined **New Thought**, **asceticism**, **perfectionism**, utopian communalism (see **Utopia**), a denial of race and discrimination. All members of the movement were required to hand over all their property and income and to sever their ties with everything except the Mission. Room, board and a small allowance were given in exchange for what was otherwise unpaid work in the Mission's businesses and projects. Father Divine never claimed to be God, but fostered such a belief in his followers, who understood all biblical messianic Jewish prophecies to have been realized in him. Father Divine certainly expected the loyalty and obedience that might be due to God. The Mission considered itself to embody the essence of all religions, accepting both the Ten Commandments and the Sermon on the Mount. America is the chosen location for the coming of the Kingdom of God which will be built on the principles of Americanism, Brotherhood, Democracy and the combination of all true religions. As of 2005, Edna Rose Ritchings (Mother Divine) still conducted services to a dwindling congregation. The Mission still holds various properties and chapters exist in California, Pennsylvania and New York.

Peculiar People *X*. A branch of the Wesleyan denomination founded in England in 1838, by John Banyard. Their name is taken from an alternative translation of the Old Testament epithet, 'Chosen People', a name for Hebrews covenanted to God (see for example Deut. 14:2 KJV and I Peter 2:9). The word 'Peculiar' in this context does not mean 'odd' but 'special' or 'select' and is translated this way in modern versions of the Bible. In 1956 the denomination merged with several others to form the Union of Evangelical Churches. Their practice and worship is puritan by character and only the King James version of the Bible is used. They practise faith-healing, refusing medical care, a policy that has brought them into conflict with the social services when children have died.

Pelagianism *X*. A heretical theological doctrine asserting that people can take the first step to achieving salvation without recourse to divine grace. The doctrine was developed by Pelagius (370–440) a British monk who taught in Rome. He argued that because people have free will, the sinful state is not inherited (see **Original Sin**). God's grace is therefore an aid to human righteousness and not its only source. For the same reason Pelagius denied the doctrine of **predestination**. St Augustine preached and wrote against Pelagius' doctrine (see **Augustinianism**).

Pentateuch *J*. The Greek term for 'The **Torah**', the five books of **Moses** being, Genesis, Exodus, Leviticus, Numbers and Deuteronomy. According to Jewish tradition the Pentateuch is of Mosaic origin, except for the last chapter of Deuteronomy, which recounts the death of Moses and was written and appended later. However, the Mosaic authorship cannot be supported. Biblical criticism has shown that the Pentateuch draws on four different original sources known as 'J' (9th century BCE), 'E' (8th century BCE), 'D' (7th century BCE) and 'P' (post-exilic 6th century). These sources were compiled by a later, unknown editor. The Pentateuch is the basis of Jewish religion and education and at least one copy of it, in the form of a hand-written scroll, is placed in the **Ark** of every synagogue.

Pentecost *X*. The Greek name for the Feast of Weeks, a Jewish festival (Heb. *Shavuot*) celebrating the harvest 50 days after the **Passover**. In Christian tradition the Apostles received the Holy Spirit during this festival (Acts 2:1) to which the name Pentecost is given, being calculated as 50 days after Easter. Its annual celebration is familiarly called Whitsunday.

Pentecostalism *X*. The Pentecostal Movement lies within Protestant Christianity placing special emphasis on what are called the 'gifts' of the Holy Spirit. The Holy Spirit is itself, thought to be the most important gift the receiving of which is described in the New Testament account of

Pentecost in the Act of the Apostles. Pentecostalism has much in common with Charismatic Christians (see **Charismatic Movement**), representations of which are to be found throughout the denominations of the Church. The movement is aligned with Evangelicalism (see Evangelism) and holds to a fundamentalist view of the inerrancy of the Bible. There are numerous forms of Pentecostalism to be found throughout the world. See **Oneness Pentecostalism**, **Vineyard Churches**, **World-Faith Movement**

People's Temple A cult that became a worldwide news item because of a mass suicide in Jonestown, Guyana, November 18th, 1978. The Temple cult was founded Indianapolis, USA in 1953, by Rev Jim Jones. He opened new branches in Ukiah, San Francisco and Los Angeles, where the cult earned a reputation for helping the poor, racial minorities, drug addicts and the homeless. They opened soup kitchens, day-care centres and medical clinics with counselling programmes for any who wanted to turn their lives round. The cult declined because of reports of financial scandals, sodomy, members being put under duress if they wanted to leave and Jones proclaiming himself to be the Messiah. When the law enforcement agencies and politicians began asking questions, Jones countered with charges of persecution. Ostensibly to escape this, Jones moved his 800 followers to Guyana where instead of the promised peaceful paradise, they were made to build Jonestown. In November, 1978, Congressman Ryan and three journalists were killed when, having visited the town, they tried to leave. Later the same day, the mass suicide took place.

FINAL WORD: 'Don't give up your education, your hopes and ambitions to follow a rainbow.' (Jeannie Mills, an early defector. She, her husband and daughter were murdered in 1980)

Perfect Liberty Kyodan A Japanese religious cult formed by Tokumitsu Kanada (1863–1919), known also as Kakuri-oya, 'Spiritual Father'. As the law in Japan requires a new religious group to be registered under an already established organization, P. L. Kyodan is recorded as a branch of **Shintoism**. Tokumitsu's teachings are, however, based on those of Kobodaishi, a Buddhist monk who died around 838 CE. The purpose of life is 'joyful self-expression'. Suffering, in all its forms, is the consequence of forgetting God. The believer prays for his problems to be transferred to the Spiritual Father. The sect is centred on Habikino, near Osaka and is thought to have 2.5 million adherents worldwide. See **Japanese Religions**

Perfectionism Generally, a meticulous, perhaps obsessive pursuit to reach excellence. In philosophy, it is the idea that the promotion of individual and social excellence should be the standards by which the worth of a society should be judged. Perfectionism is a modern application of the principle of the greatest good for the greatest number. In the philosophy of religion, the concept is applied to the realization of full spiritual maturity, of the form suggested by **Thomas à Kempis** (1380–1471) in his book *The Imitation of Christ*. See **Egotheism, Human Potential Movement, Transhumanism**

Persephone *G*. In Greek mythology the young daughter of **Zeus** and **Demeter** who was carried off by her uncle **Hades** (or **Pluto**) to be his bride. The myth of Persephone is the story of sowing and harvesting corn. Demeter was the seed corn stored underground until it is sown in the autumn to produce its crop. The sprouting is the return of Persephone, the maiden. Demeter and Persephone are sometimes understood to be one concept, the growing corn that vanishes, then returns. The myth has fed the rituals that celebrate the sowing and reaping of corn in several pagan cults.

Persia Persia was the official international name for Iran. The name is derived, firstly from *Pars*, a region within Cyrus the Great's Achaemenid Empire, then from *Persis*, the name given by the Greeks. 'Iran', from ancient Persian words, means 'the Land of the Aryans'. In 1935 Shah Reza Pahlavi asked all the Western countries to use the word 'Iran' as their languages' name for Persia. Early Elamite and Jiroft civilizations settled the region from 3200–c.539 BCE, followed by the Mannai and the Medes which during the period, c.648 BCE–c.650 CE (see **Zoroaster**) gave way to a succession of empires, such as the new Empire 255–641 CE, and the period of Persian **Hellenism**. From that time onwards various forms of Islam controlled the country, including both **Umayyad** and **Abbasid** Caliphates (see **Caliph**) and a period of Turkic rule followed by the Safavids (see **Safavid Dynasty**). Caught between Afghanistan, the Ottomans, the Russians and a British presence to protect their oil-field interests, Persia was drawn into the First World War. In 1925 Reza Pahlavi ousted the Qajars (established 1794 CE) and founded the Pahlavi Dynasty. It was the last Persian monarchy before the establishment of the Islamic Republic in 1979. Iran has recovered slowly from Iraqi attempts at genocide, thought to have been perpetrated by the use of chemical weapons. The government and politics of the Islamic Republic is based on the 1979 Constitution, the *Qanun-e Asasi*, the 'Fundamental Law'. The country is a founding member of the United Nations and a member of the Organization of the Islamic Conference. See **Persian Religion**

Persian Religion From the 7th century, Persia/Iran has been Islamic. Prior to that during the Achaemenid Empire (c.549–311 BCE) the southwest of the country was taken by Zoroastrianism. Herodotus offers this summary: '[the Perses] have no images of the gods, no temples nor altars and consider the use of them a sign of folly. This comes, I think, from their not believing the gods to have the same nature with men, as the Greeks imagine.' Herodotus tells us of a cult that made sacrifice to, 'the sun and moon, to the earth, to fire, to water and to the winds. These are the only gods whose worship has come down to them from ancient times. At a later period they began the worship of Urania, which they borrowed from the Arabians and Assyrians. Mylitta is the name by which the Assyrians know this goddess, whom the Arabians call Alitta and the Persians [Anahita].' Anahita was later identified with Mithras. (For the religion of the successive empires see **Parthian** and **Sassanian**.) The majority of Iranians are now Shiite Muslims (see **Shi'ism**) with a strong **Sunni** representation and Islam is a virtual **theocracy** as the State religion. A Christian presence is represented by Assyrian and Armenian orthodoxy (see **Orthodox Churches**) who enjoy parliamentary representation, together with **Roman Catholicism** and a smattering of Adventists and Protestants. See **Persia**

Pesach *J*. Heb. See **Passover**

Peyote Cults *Ami*. Their origin is pre-Columbian, re-emerging in the 19th century in fully developed forms among the Amerindians of the southern plains. The cults are centred on the ingestion of the hallucinatory substance, mescal, made from the peyote, the bud of a cactus plant. Originally the drug was used as a medicine, as preparation for warfare and for divination. The peyote is believed to have healing qualities and to help control alcoholism. If taking the peyote bud results in vomiting, the body and the mind is being cleansed of impurities. The drug enhances the quality of thought and behaviour, for which reason it is regarded as a 'teacher', healer or saviour of the tribe, thus only someone who is morally sound can take the peyote. The drug induces profound introspection which may be accompanied by visual and auditory experiences believed to be spiritual in nature. The period of hallucination can last from 10 to 12 hours. The practice should be supervised by someone with experience, like a **shaman**, otherwise the user should be in the company of a 'Trip-sitter'. The modern cult is a syncretism of indigenous practices such as drumming, chanting, the use of the sacred pipe or **Calumet**, Christian practices of healing and prayer. See **Native American Church**, **Native American Religion**

Pharaoh *E*. From the Egyptian *Pr-Ah*, meaning 'Great House' or 'palace'. The term was used as the title for an Egyptian king and is overlaid with mythologies that claim the Pharaoh to be the emanation of the chief state-god. In keeping with this parentage, he was given a fivefold titulary, the standard naming convention which symbolized worldly and divine power. The first name was the Pharaoh's birth name, the other four given when he assumed the throne. As well as expressing the distinct personality of the Pharaoh, the combined names offered a kind of manifesto or agenda for a Pharaoh's rule. The Pharaoh wore the double crown, comprising the white crown of Upper Egypt and red crown Lower Egypt, decorated with an *uraeus*, a stylized, upright cobra or serpent, the symbol of sovereignty, royalty and deity. Under the 25th Dynasty this was doubled. When **Akhenaton** moved Egypt towards a true **monotheism**, the relationship was made between the one all-powerful and absolute god and the Pharaoh (King), thus setting the precedent for the association between divinity and monarchy, that influenced the concept of the Roman Emperor, the **Papacy** and subsequent rulers. See **Divine Kingship**

Pharisee *J*. Heb. *Perushim*, 'separatists' or 'scrupulous'. Thought sometimes to denote a Jewish political party, but this is mistaken. From c.160 BCE the Pharisees represented a sect or group within Judaism claiming that 'tradition' as well as **Torah** was revealed by God to Moses at Sinai, thus they are the custodians of a specific kind of Jewish orthodoxy. Believing themselves to be the real heirs of biblical religion, they preserved orally transmitted traditions. Pharisees believe in: the immortality of the soul, the existence of angels, divine destiny or fate, the freedom of individual will, messianic redemption through the intervention of a personal Messiah and the resurrection of the dead. These aspects of Talmudic Judaism were underwritten by an orthopraxy based on laws of purity and sanctification rituals designed to maintain the Temple cults. The Pharisees were mainly laymen and together with the **Sadducees**, who were priests, they are recorded in the New Testament as opponents of Jesus; inevitably, both groups were subjected to Christian polemics that have given them a negative reputation that is undeserved. See **Essenes, Zealots**

Phenomenology of Religion An objective study of religious phenomena ('that which appears') without any consideration as to the truth or falsity of religious beliefs and claims. Such a study will draw on the findings of disciplines such as the history, sociology and psychology of religion, so as to interpret the different ways the sacred 'appears' to people. All presuppositions, together with the assumptions of theology and philosophy, must be put aside so the phenomena can 'speak for themselves'. The result will be a classification of religious ideas, actions, paraphernalia, scriptures and symbols. However, both 'phenomenology' and 'objectivity' are terms that lack a certain precision. See also **Religionswissenschaft**

Philippines Religion The Philippines has the distinction of being the only Christian country in Asia; over 90 per cent of the population register a Christian affiliation, 83 per cent of which are Catholic. The minority are made up of Taoists, Buddhists, Protestants and **Muslims**, among which survive vestiges of the indigenous tribal animism. Inevitable syncretism has spawned numerous cults, many with a revivalist mandate (see **Revivalism**) and a millenarian objective (see **Millenarianism**). Thousands of Filipinos have been drawn to religious cults that are anti-modernist and charismatic. Processional flagellation and re-enactments of the Crucifixion are reminiscent of medieval Europe but which, in context, show the need for a cohesive energy that engenders fraternity and community spirit. The authoritative dominance of Catholicism is being challenged by fundamentalist groups such as the **Jehovah's Witnesses**, **Seventh Day Adventists** and **Iglesia Ni Kristo** in the 'war for souls'; it is these smaller sects that are showing the greatest growth rate.

Philistines *AME*. A people who inhabited the southern coast of Canaan and who were present at the time of the Israelite migration to that territory (c.1200 BCE) which was also known as Philistia. They are one of what were called the 'Sea Peoples', a confederacy of ship-faring raiders and traders recorded in an Egyptian reference of c.1213 BCE. Their cities were ruled by *seranim*, 'lords' who acted together in what was virtually a perpetual war between them and the Hebrews, by whom they were finally defeated during the reign of King **David**. The account of these conflicts is recorded in the Old Testament stories of Samson, Samuel, Saul and David. They were skilled at iron smithing and the biblical description of Goliath's armour confirms this technology (I Sam. 14:4–8). There is a biblically-based tradition founded on texts in the Books of Amos and Jeremiah, that the Philistines originated from Cyprus, Crete and other eastern Mediterranean locations. It ties in with them being one of the 'Sea Peoples'.

Philo (c.20BCE–c.40CE) *J*. The most famous and influential philosopher of Hellenistic Judaism, known to the early Christian Fathers as, Philo Judaeus. He lived in Alexandria as a member of an important Jewish family, his brother being the head of the Egyptian Jewish community. Among his main writings were a presentation of Judaism to the Greek-speaking world which took the form of a philosophy of religion. He also wrote religious philosophy for Hellenistic Jews who were interested in the concepts of Greek philosophy. It is to Philo we owe the concept of the **Logos**, the Word, as the instrument of God's activity and the form of his immanence in the universe. His philosophy had a formative influence on the development of Christian doctrine and on **Neoplatonism**. See **Hellenism**

Philosopher's Stone A mythical substance believed to be able to turn ordinary metals into gold or produce an elixir that delayed aging and thus prolonged life. It was the much sought-after 'grail' of medieval alchemy. In alchemy's mystical tradition, creating the philosopher's stone led to enlightenment. It is in the sense of it being a spiritual metaphor that the term has had most currency, with the chemical processes of alchemy being symbolic of spiritual, rather than physical processes. The stone itself was a metaphor for inner spiritual potential and the transmutation of base human imperfections into the pure gold of mystical realization. With the modern revival of interest in mysticism, the metaphysical and philosophical conception of the stone has become central, particularly with some of the New Age cults.

Philosophy of Religion The objective methods of philosophy critically applied to religious beliefs, practices and claims to knowledge, in relation to other disciplines such as science, history, psychology and sociology. Since Aristotle, the subject has been regarded as part of **metaphysics**, for the rationalists of the 17th and 18th century this was '**Natural Religion**', 'Philosophy of Religion' being a more modern term. Its prime consideration is the nature of God and religious belief – not, as might be thought, the nature of religion itself. Thus, it asks two basic questions: 'What is God?' and 'Are there any good reasons to think that God does or does not exist?' From that base it goes on to ask the same questions of miracles, of the efficacy of petitionary prayer, then to examine the relationship between faith and reason and between morality and religion. More fundamentally perhaps, it applies analytic logic to ascertain the status of religious language. Philosophy of Religion is not confined to Western, biblically-based religions and the major religious traditions of the East have ancient, profound and extended philosophies. See **Buddhism, Confucianism, Hinduism, Islam, Shintoism, Zen**

Phoenicians *AME*. The people of an ancient civilization settled along the coast of what is now Lebanon and Syria, 1200–900 BCE. They were enterprising traders and colonizers, open to the adoption of foreign cultures and their gods. The Greek name for them, *Phoiniki*, was synonymous with a purple dye which was a major part of the Phoenician textile trade and they became known as the 'Purple People'. They were probably Semitic, speaking a language the Romans called *Punic* (*puniceus* L. 'purple'). In the **Old Testament** the Phoenicians are not mentioned as a people, but by their cities of origin for example, the citizens of Sidon are referred to as Sidonians (see for example Judges 3:3 and 1 Kings 5:20). The Phoenician, Hiram of Tyre, provided architects, cedar timber and workmen for the Temple of Solomon. Jezebel, a princess from Tyre, became the consort of King Ahab and brought her gods with her, thus inviting Ezekiel's angry criticism. The Phoenicians worshipped a variety of fertility goddesses as well as the famous **Ba'al**, a weather and war god; **El** was worshipped as the father of both Ba'al and mankind; **Astarte** was his sister. Ba'al also became one of the leading deities of Carthage, a satellite city of Tyre. Sidon had its own city-god protector called Eshmun, later to be adopted by the Greeks as **Asclepius**. There was an important temple culture together with shrines, somewhat like standing stones and rites that include animal sacrifice, a practice that was probably adopted by the Jews together with some of the Phoenician festivals. The mythology mostly explains the annual death and revival of vegetation. Little is known about their eschatology; graves were equipped with goods and family vaults were furnished and provisioned, suggesting the onward journey of a soul that needed sustenance, as in the **Egyptian** tradition. There is also evidence of sacred prostitution and child sacrifice, the latter from excavations at Punic **Carthage**.

Phylacteries *J*. Heb. *Tephillin*. They comprise of two small black boxes made originally from the skin of ritually clean animals, together with the leather straps (*rezuoth*) for binding them on the head and left arm. They are used by male Jews over the age of 13, that is, post-**bar mitzvah**. The black boxes contain pieces of parchment on which are written the first two portions of the *Shema*, and other verses from scripture. One is bound on the left arm nearest to the heart, the other on the hairline of the forehead. Phylacteries are worn as a literal and ritual affirmation of Exodus 13 which institutes the Festival of the **Passover**. Verse 16 concludes, 'And so it shall be a sign upon your hand and as a symbol on your forehead that with a mighty hand the Lord freed us from Egypt.' The command is also found in Deut. 6:8 and 11:18. The texts include the injunction to inscribe the verses on the doorposts and gates of houses. The parchments used for this purpose are rolled and placed in cylinders called *mezuzah*.

Pietism *X*. A tendency originating in the German Lutheran Church ascribed to P. J. Spener (1635–1705) and A. H. Francke (1663–1727). The object was to inject new life into Protestantism. Spener set out his programme in his *Pia Desideria* (1675) and sought to apply it through prayer circles and Bible study groups. The movement believed in the priesthood of all believers but although it had no intention of separating from the Church, a clash with the establishment became inevitable when Francke criticized the Leipzig theologians for their philosophy and intellectualism, demanding that all lectures should be turned into devotional meetings. For a while the university of Halle, founded in 1694, was the movement's centre. Pietism influenced the **Moravian Brethren** and the Evangelical Revival which gathered momentum from 1720s. See also **Revivalism**

Pieve *AE*. The sun god of the Lapps. See **Lapp Religion**

Pilgrimage A journey undertaken to visit a sacred place, shrine or person. During the medieval period, Christian pilgrimages included, the Holy Land, Santiago de Compostela and the shrine of Thomas Becket in Canterbury. Jews travel to Mt **Sinai**, where **Moses** received the Law from God; Buddhists travel to Bodh Gaya, the place of the Buddha's enlightenment and the fifth of the **Pillars of Islam**, requires Muslims to make a pilgrimage to Mecca at least once in their lives (see **Hajj**). There are many secular equivalents in which devotees participate with the same commitment, sincerity and passion. Examples include pilgrimages to Elvis Presley's home Graceland (see **First Preslyterian Church of Elvis the Divine**), the war cemeteries of northern Europe, and the Lenin Mausoleum in Moscow.

Pillar Saints *X*. See **Stylites**

Pillars of Islam *I*. Arab. *Arkan al-Islam*. The *Dar al-Islam* (Arab. 'the Household of Islam') has Five Pillars that support and sustain the faith. They represent the five official and obligatory acts required by all devout Muslims:

  i) *Shahadah* or *Kalima* refers specifically to the liturgical Word of Witness (or Confession) with which a Muslim opens all forms of worship: 'There is no God but the one God, Muhammad is the Apostle of God.' The first phrase represents the absolute heart of Islamic faith, repudiating all aspects of polytheism and establishing the sin of making any association between any other creature, actual or mythological, with the creative and sustaining power of Allah. (See *Shirk*) The second phrase affirms the sequence of prophets, the line of which ends definitively, with Muhammad, who gave the final revelation in the Koran to which the repetition of the *Shahadah* bears witness. Anyone who does this, even an infidel, cannot be excluded from the *umma*, the Community of Muslims.

ii) *Salat*. Arab. 'connection' or 'contact' in the form of prayer or worship. The ritual prayers Muslims are required to make five times a day, by which means the faithful bare witness to their commitment to the *umma*, the Islamic community. Also, the means by which they remain 'connected' to God. The prayers proceed through a series of *rakahs*, specific movements, prayer positions and prostrations. The five set times for prayer are; daybreak, with two *rakahs*, noon and mid-afternoon, with four *rakahs*, after sunset, with three *rakahs* and, in the early part of the night, with four *rakahs*. Ideally these will be performed congregationally, directed by the prayer-leader, the *imam*. The worshippers form rows facing the *Qiblah*, which points the direction of Mecca. The hours of prayer are heralded by the *muezzin*, calling traditionally from the minaret of the **mosque**. Before entering the prayer hall or participating in any kind of worship, the adherent is required to undergo a ritual ablution.

iii) *Zakat*. Arab. 'alms'. In the Koran the obligation to give alms is joined with the obligation to observe the ritual prayers. Being an obligation, *zakat*, is differentiated from *Sadaqa*, voluntary almsgiving and in the early period of Islam, *zakat* was imposed as a tax on the possessions of Muslims. Even today, a Muslim is required to give annually 2.5 per cent of what they earn. Thus *zakat* signifies that a Muslim has a proper sense of the place of material things, of profit and of responsibility to others less fortunate. Such observance, even though obligatory, is a sign of spiritual maturity and of the purity of one's values. The revenue derived from *zakat* is used to advance the faith and for charitable purposes such as helping those in debt, freeing slaves, assistance to travellers and to pay for the administration of *zakat* itself. Muslims do not think of *zakat* as a tax, but as a loan made to God for the advancement of the faith. So far as *sadaqa* is concerned, the extent of voluntary giving is left to individual conscience.

iv) *Swam or siyyam*. Fasting is the fourth obligation imposed on a Muslim. This is focused in the fast observed for the whole of *Ramadan*, the ninth month of the Islamic lunar calendar and as with many fasts observed by all religions, it ends with a feast. Other than *Ramadan*, various Islamic traditions encourage voluntary fasts of which there are several throughout the year as, for example, the fast of Asura observed on the tenth day of the month of Muharram or, in general practice, fasting on Mondays and Thursdays. Expiatory fasts can be undertaken for certain kinds of sin or to make up for a failure in one's duty to observe the Five Pillars. Some Muslims, such as the Sufis, will use a self-imposed fast as a from of spiritual exercise and discipline.

v) *Hajj*. Arab. 'pilgrimage'. The Islamic calendar fixes the first ten days of the month of *Dhu al-Hijjah* (January) as the period for an annual religious pilgrimage of Muslims to Mecca. Something like two million Muslims take part. As with all the Pillars, *hajj* is an obligatory duty to be performed at least once in a person's lifetime. The pilgrim is aware that he is not just coming to the birthplace of Muhammad, but to a geographical point (*Qiblah*) symbolic of divine revelation, where he will fulfil an intensive form of **dhikr**, the devotional practice of remembering or reminding oneself of God. At what is believed to be the naval of the earth, the Muslim recalls the divine revelation of Allah, through Muhammad and the Koran. In this place Abraham, a true man of faith who opposed to all forms of idolatry, was believed to have built the first house at Bakkah (Mecca). Here the pilgrims passionately greet the **Ka'bah**, proclaiming the **Labbaika**, 'Here I am, here I am, present before you.' The *hajj*, properly performed, absolves the pilgrim from sin and is sometimes used as a rite of passage for new converts to Islam or to coincide with life-events such as the onset of adulthood, marriage, the birth of a child, a career change, retirement, illness or near death.

In the Koran the Pillars of Islam are described as the framework of worship and the indispensable signs of a Muslim's commitment to the faith. Across the different sects of Islam there is a broad consensus as to how these should be carried out and the Sunnis and Shiites agree in essential detail. The Sufi, however, consistent with their forms of piety, internalize the five pillars as acts of devotion and spiritual practice in much the same way as, for example, a Buddhist might use the **Five Precepts** as a focus for meditation, as well as a framework for living. Also, with their mystical orientation, the Sufi will turn *Shahadah*, their witness, into a from of *dhikr*, a devotional act of remembrance, making life a process of constant prayer and meditation.

Pittsburgh Platform *J*. The name given to a meeting of reform Jewish rabbis who met in Pittsburgh in 1855 to set down principles for guiding the thought and practice of Reform Judaism (see **Judaism, Reform**). The statements were revised in 1937, by the Columbus Platform and again by the Centenary Platform in 1976, it having been the centenary of the Union of American Hebrew Congregations and the Hebrew Union College-Jewish Institute of Religion. The principal subjects on which statements were issued were God, the Torah and Israel. The first statement of the original Platform is typical in expressing both religious tolerance and a fierce pride in the Jewish religious heritage: 'We recognize in every religion an attempt to grasp the Infinite and in every mode, source or book of revelation held sacred in any religious system, the consciousness of the indwelling of God in man. We hold that Judaism presents the highest conception of the God-idea as taught in our Holy Scriptures and developed and spiritualized by the Jewish teachers, in accordance with the moral and philosophical progress of their respective ages.'

Plainchant or **Plainsong** See **Gregorian Chant**

Plants, sacred Such plants figure profusely throughout the history of religion, mythology and folklore. They have been considered sacred for many reasons; some are believed to have properties that can prolong life indefinitely, others have medical or magical qualities. Plants that can produce hallucinatory states like the peyote and 'sacred' mushroom or are associated with formative events in the history of a particular religion, like the Buddha's Bodhi tree, are also considered sacred. It is odd that many useful plants known to herbalists have no mention in the mythologies, while somewhat ordinary plants like verbena, are significant. Among the food plants corn is the most familiar symbol of the annual cycle of death and recovery. Many plants with healing qualities have attracted rites, some of them associated with magic, designed to exploit their power. Among plants used in magic is the infamous mandrake, whose root vaguely resembles a human being; laurel became a favourite among the Greek **oracles** because when chewed or smoked, it provoked a state of agitation. See **Ambrosia**, **Elixir of Life**, **Nectar**, **Peyote Cults**

Plato (c.428–c.348BCE) *G*. A student of **Socrates** and an immensely influential Greek philosopher. Writing in the form of dialogues in which Socrates is a frequent voice, Plato's style was light, humorous, ironic, as full of good characters as a well-made play and crammed with almost anecdotal, mundane detail. Among the philosophers Plato has to be a 'good read'. Every aspect of his biography and thought is copiously covered in an immense literature, but a brief overview of his themes includes, forms of government, the conflict between nature and convention, the influence of heredity and the environment on human intelligence and personality and a kind of proto 'nature versus nurture' debate. Other fundamental dichotomies Plato examined were, knowledge and opinion with their confederate, objective and subjective evaluations. It is an indication of Plato's formative influence and staying power that all these themes are perennially debated in the history of Western philosophy, taken up and developed by, for example, **Aristotle**, and through him to the theological philosophies of **Scholasticism** and thence to **Hobbes**, **Locke**, **Hume** and **Kant**, and on through the postmodernists and their opponents. Plato's philosophy is cast in the form a radical metaphysical dualism which he presents as two worlds, one being that of 'Forms', the other that of what we actually see around us. The world of Forms is intelligible, comprised of fixed, unchangeable and unchanging perfect ideas which are models or templates of the ideal. The perceptible is the second world, being the imperfect or flawed copies of the Forms of the intelligible world. The intelligible form of the 'Good', is usually taken to be Plato's God and therefore, also the ultimate object of knowledge. How then is the mind capable of conceiving the intelligible world? Plato tells us that it is possible only by dint of reason, intellect and understanding, a function of the 'mind' that is not dependent on sense-perception, much less on imagination. In Books VI and VII of *The Republic*, Plato uses

numerous metaphors to illustrate these concepts, most famously his analogies of the cave, the sun and the divided line. In combination these metaphors express a complex and, in parts, difficult epistemological theory of how we know what we know and when having decided what we know, how we decide what that knowledge is about. Plato's influence cuts across several disciplines and is to found as much in those who agree with him, as disagree; Nietzsche attacked his moral and political theories and Heidegger argued against what he felt to be his confused and vague notion of 'being'. Einstein drew on Plato's concept of the immutable reality that lies behind the flux of appearance, while Karl **Popper** believed Plato's concept of government outlined in *The Republic*, was a proto-totalitarianism. Love him or hate him, Plato will continue to inspire philosophical argument and aesthetic and religious sensibility. In the *Phaedrus*, Plato has Socrates tell the tale of Theuth, the Egyptian **Thoth**, god of language, writing and wisdom. In so doing he celebrates the watershed in culture that the development of writing represents, although he makes the point the writing will never help in the search for truth – unlike dialectic it does not answer questions! See **Neoplatonism**
FINAL WORD: 'The safest general characterization of the European philosophical tradition is that it consists of a series of footnotes to Plato.' (Alfred North Whitehead)

Pleroma Gk. 'fullness'. A **Gnostic** term referring to the power or complete being of God. In Christianity it is used generally for the wholeness of God, as in Col. 2:9 'For it is in Christ that the complete being of the Godhead dwells embodied.' This reference is used by theologians to argue that Paul was a Gnostic. In Gnostic belief the world is ruled by evil archons, among which is the deity of the **Old Testament** that imprisoned the human spirit. The heavenly pleroma is the centre of divine life, an effulgent light in which spiritual beings like **aeons** live. Jesus is a mediating aeon sent by the pleroma to assist human beings in recovering the lost knowledge or *gnosis*, of their origin.

Plotinus (205–270CE) A Greek philosopher who we know about mostly from Porphyry's preface to his edition of Plotinus' *Enneads*. He began to study philosophy in his mid-twenties, travelling to Alexandria to do so and where he remained for 11 years, before proceeding on a great adventure to study the philosophies of the Indians and Persians. To this end, he joined the army of Gordian III and marched to Persia where, in the aftermath of military failure he found himself in an alien land. Only with much difficulty was he able get to Antioch and safety, eventually settling in Rome where he gathered about him a group of eminent students, including, Porphyry. His philosophy is founded on the concept of a supreme, transcendent 'One' without qualities that can be distinguished and beyond human categories of being and non-being. This 'One' is the source of all existence, not as creator, since that implies qualities, but as the source from which everything emanates in succeeding stages of lesser and lesser perfection. Thus, he offered an alternative to the Christian concept of creation, *ex nihilo*, that God created 'out of nothing'. Instead, Plotinus suggested that everything emanates, *ex deo*, 'out of God' thus establishing the absolute transcendence of the 'One', who is without mind, actions or the quality to create. The cosmos is a consequence of its existence. Plotinus' philosophy is a re-casting of Plato and he is usually thought of as the father of **Neoplatonism**. See **Creationism**

FINAL WORD: 'There have been few great philosophers whose life was as completely integrated with their thought as that of Plotinus ... He made no fuss about religion ... nor did he, as a rule make much fuss about morality ... To his circle he was not only a philosophical teacher but a spiritual and moral guide and a kindly and practical friend.' (A. H. Armstrong.)

Pluralism In the area of philosophy of mind, the view that the world as perceived, comprises many substances which cannot be reduced to one (see **Monism**) or two (see **Dualism**). Pluralism is a philosophical examination of diversity and its implication. Its conclusion is that there is no single explanation possible for the multifarious phenomena of our world. Some philosophers make a distinction between the idea that there are, on the one hand, many substances and on the other, many *kinds* of substance. Leibnitz, for example, argued that there were many substances, but since he believed them all to be of one kind, namely 'monads', he was a monist. Bertrand Russell's '**logical atomism**', which attempted to identify the atoms of thought that cannot be divided into smaller units of thought, is probably the most complete pluralism in philosophy. William James, both pragmatist (see **Pragmatism**) and pluralist, summed up Pluralism's perception neatly: 'Things are with one another in many ways, but nothing includes everything or dominates over everything' (James [1977]).

Pluto *R*. The Roman name for the Greek god **Hades**, identified in Roman mythology as the god of the underworld. The myth tells of him abducting **Persephone** to be his bride and of her mother's grief, so acute, that it caused winter. Originally the god of wealth, the Romans revered him for the gift of gold, silver and other precious metals. Because these had to be mined he became associated with subterranean regions and eventually by reference as the god of the spiritual underworld and thus death. In such a manner, do the myths evolve.

Plymouth Brethren *X*. A sect, so named because its first centre was founded in Plymouth in 1838, by J. N. Darby a former Anglican priest. It is a fundamentalist movement combining elements of **Calvinism**, **Pietism** and **Millenarianism**. They denounced all secular occupations that did not conform with a way of life defined by **New Testament** values. They have no ordained ministry, their worship being centred around the 'Breaking of Bread', a simplified Eucharistic ritual intended to be a memorial to Christ's Last Supper. Arguments about the human nature of Christ and about Church government led to a split in 1849, between the 'Open Brethren' and the 'Exclusive Brethren'. The latter had severe standards, prohibiting many aspects of modern life such as the use of radio or television, the wearing of make-up by women and the avoidance of all forms of entertainment. Social contact is limited to their membership, even at the cost of not seeing their own families.

Poisen *P*. **Melanesian** technique of healing, magic and sorcery; a form of black magic directed against a chosen victim with the intention of causing illness or death. The familiar imitative magic may be used, that of burning or injuring an effigy of the intended target. It is believed many sorcerers can change their form, enabling them to fly or even to become invisible. In Melanesian religion, techniques of **divination** or the use of **mediums** enables sorcerers and witches to be detected and dealt with. The victims themselves, by confessing antisocial behaviour, such as theft or adultery, might enable the sorcerer to be found. Poisen, therefore, maybe a means of ordering society and regulating its morality. In Melanesian culture, sorcerers are not seen to be people serving the community in a positive way; despite the fact that their skills are employed for rain-making, for charms that can protect against evil, for ensuring the success of a hunt or a courtship, they are viewed as outcasts, rogue elephants to be avoided.

Polynesian Religion *P*. Polynesia is a vast triangular area of the Pacific Ocean, pointed by three groups of islands, New Zealand in the south, Hawaii in the north and Rapu Nui (Easter Island) in the east. The region includes the Cook Islands, Easter Island, French Polynesia, Samoa, Tonga, Hawaii and other archipelagos. The indigenous peoples of Taiwan are also included in this section, as they speak Austronesian tongues related to Polynesian languages. These widely dispersed groups represent eight main Polynesian cultures and the people are thought to share a common origin with the **Melanesians**. The cultures share a polytheistic and animistic form of religion with inevitable regional variations. An example is Easter Island's unique, huge monolithic statues that were set up in burial places and are believed to represent ancestors or tribal progenitors. Figure-carving on a smaller scale is a common feature, the images representing gods and spirits such as the creator god or the sea god or dancers in a state of trance celebrating a festival. Their mythologies relate how the cosmos came into existence, usually from a primordial nothing or emptiness, with the darkness gradually giving way to the light of the sun and the moon. Polynesia shares with Melanesia the concept of **mana**, the spiritual power that flows through everything and channelled by ancestors to the chief and to the priests and prophets whose skills of healing and divination serve the community. Daily life is a round of rituals and ceremonials associated with subsistence focused on the rites of passage and practical occupations such as tree-felling and canoe making. A well-populated polytheism gathers around the concept of a supreme god whose name varies according to the region; they are usually personifications of nature or of forms of work and cultural activities.

Tangaroa is probably the most dominant, being a personification of the origin of fish; unsurprisingly his cult is popular among fishermen and sailors. Among the **Maori** he is known as Tangaroa-whakamautai. Many of the gods are male, but the female principle is strongly represented in Papa, the **Earth Mother**, and in Ina (also Hina or Sina) the first woman, a personification of the moon. In some regions the god Kane (or Tane) is thought to be the originator of human life. Sacrifices of first fruits and fish are made to the gods who are worshipped at feasts with chants, dances and kava-drinking. The eschatology is simple, the rites of burial direct the spirit of the deceased to the underworld and then to **Hawaiki**, their mythological home. From the late 17th century the indigenous religions began to encounter Christian missionaries, resulting in the inevitable displacement of the indigenous culture and the establishment of various form of Christianity as well as new religions like the **Cargo Cults**. In French Polynesia, in sharp contrast to the secularism of the colonizing country, politics became closely linked to religion, primarily Christianity.

FINAL WORD: 'All these strange people live close to each other, with different languages and different thoughts; they believe in different gods and they have different values; two passions alone they share, love and hunger. And somehow as you watch them you have an impression of extraordinary vitality. Though the air is so soft and the sky so blue, you have, I know not why, a feeling of something hotly passionate that beats like a throbbing pulse through the crowds. (W. Somerset Maugham)

Polytheism A belief in many gods. They may be associated with different aspects of nature such as the earth, the sky and the sea or with fire and the elements, storms, rain and wind. In some traditions there are gods of the underworld, Hades or hell or gods specializing in fertility, motherhood, death and with the rites of passage. The religions of ancient Greece and Rome are examples of established polytheisms with their pantheons organized in a hierarchy. Most **animistic** traditions are polytheistic, while **pantheism** and **panentheism** may be monotheistic. See also **Henotheism**, **Kathenotheism** and **Monolatry**

Pontifex Maximus *R*. The high priest of the **Pontifical College**, the most senior and most prestigious position in Roman polytheistic religion. It was a state cult and originally only a patrician, a member of the Roman elite could occupy the post. In 254 BCE the first plebeian assumed the role. Under the early Roman Republic it was a distinguished religious office, but gradually and inevitably, it became more involved in politics and under Augustus the post became part of the Imperial office. The pontiffs served for life but it was never a full-time job and holding the office did not preclude the pontifex from being a magistrate or serving with the army. Their duties included keeping the minutes of elected magistrates, together with the public diaries which collected and collated are a valuable source of information for Roman religion. The pontifex was in charge of the Roman calendar, determining what intercalary days needed to be added so as to synchronize with the seasons. This function was open to abuse since magistrates were elected for a year and the pontifex could, if he so chose, lengthen the year to increase the term of office for a friend. One of the legacies of the office is that the Pontifex Maximus is now one of the titles of the pope, in English rendered Supreme Pontiff, to distinguish it from what was a high office in a pagan religion.

Pontifical College *R*. The Pontifical College was responsible for the administration of the state-sponsored religion of Rome and under the leadership of the **Pontifex Maximus**. Fifteen **flamens** or sacred priests formed part of the college membership.

Pope *X*. See **Papacy**

Popol Vuh *CA*. A sacred scripture of the Quiché, a Mayan state of Guatemala, known as the 'Council Book' or the 'Book of the Community'. The scripture contains creation mythologies and stories of the twin hero gods, Hunahpu and Xbalanque who played *Juego de Pelota* (see **Ball Court**) against the gods of the underworld. The scripture also records the history of the foundation of the Quiché civilization. See **Mayan Religion**

Popper, Sir Karl (1902–94) A hugely influential philosopher of natural and social science. One of his major contributions was the notion that scientific generalizations offer only a restricted view of a truth, that can never be certain since, as with Newtonian physics, they were constantly under review. The implication is that science and scientists can only have faith that some kind of uniformity of nature exists and that even if it does, it is probably impossible to define or prove. His philosophy of history ran parallel to his philosophy of science in that he questioned the historicism of **Plato**, **Hegel** and **Marx**, who assume history to have immutable laws or principles. Thus, Popper asserted, it was impossible to make predictions about the future of society or predetermine its nature, since among the factors contributing to society's development were individual and collective decisions that would respond to the situation as it would be. For Popper, the world was held in the tension between what we know and the uncertainty of that knowledge. This 'open mindedness', which admitted the notion of faith and trust, did not amount to a religious perception, it did not imply a metaphysic, only the possibility that such a dimension might exist. To live as though it was there, in order to prove that it was, would have been perfectly acceptable to Sir Karl.
FINAL WORD: 'Whenever a theory appears to you as the only possible one, take this as a sign that you have neither understood the theory nor the problem which it was intended to solve.' (Popper)

Poseidon *G*. The brother of **Zeus** and the second most important male deity in the Greek pantheon. He was the god of the sea, earthquakes and horses and in Homer the major initiator of events. As god of the sea,

Poseidon has a golden palace deep below the ocean where the sea creatures danced for him. The sea is known as the 'earth-carrier', and it
followed that when Poseidon made the sea turbulent, the earth would also
heave and toss. By the time of Homer, his cult was celebrated every two
years at a national sports meeting held on the Isthmus of Corinth, but his
status had been reduced and he was honoured like a god in retirement,
sharing the fête with others. Poseidon's association with horses is probably derived from an aristocratic horse god, assimilated when Greeks
became more dependent on the sea than the land. He was also the major
god of cities such as Athens and Corinth and several cities of Magna
Graecia, the southern Italian region colonized by the Greeks. In Etruscan
and Roman mythology, Poseidon was known as Neptune.

Positivism A term used in philosophy to refer to the view that the only real
knowledge of the world we can acquire, is derived from the natural
sciences. It was first propounded by Saint-Simon (1760–1825), the
American founder of the Saint-Simonian, a mystical Christian socio-
scientific movement. It was Auguste Comte (1798–1857) whose
development of the theory made it influential. The term 'positive' designates that which is established or laid down, something to be accepted
because it is found to be like that and may be comprehended without
further explanation. Comte, who believed the scientific method would
replace **metaphysics**, pursued the reciprocal relationship between observation and experiment, using the phrase 'order and progress', later to be
adopted by Brazil as its national motto. Philosophy may still perform a
useful function in defining the scope of science and in applying the findings of science to life. Outside of that, it must surrender its claim to
knowledge, accepting that metaphysics addresses questions which, for all
practical purposes, are unanswerable and therefore, irrelevant. Positivism
was carried on a wave of optimism in the achievements and benefits of
science and Comte tried to develop it into an alternative religion, providing the philosophical foundation for **humanism**. In many countries
positivist societies were formed in which reverence for humanity
replaced the worship of God. The **utilitarianism** of **Bentham**, and James
and John Stuart **Mill** drew on the new positivism, while rejecting some of
Comte's more extravagant claims.
FINAL WORD: 'From the study of the development of human intelligence,
in all directions and through all times, the discovery arises of a great
fundamental law ... that each of our leading conceptions – each branch
of our knowledge – passes successively through three different
theoretical conditions: the theological or fictitious; the metaphysical or
abstract; and the scientific or positive.' (Comte)

Possession The condition of being indwelt by a spirit which is usually
demonic. There is a difference between possession and the inducement of
trance states so as to bring about intense religious experience of the kind
associated with **peyote cults**. Possession in its various forms is a feature
of many religions, ranging from the major established religions to

shamanism and African tribal religions such as the Orisha of the **Yoruba**, and derivative cults in North and South America. The possession of both human and animal corpses is also recorded, but usually the spirit or spirits, enter a living body. Opinions are divided as to whether the possession is actual or a symptom of mental illness. In Christianity and other religions, possession by a demon may be 'cured' by exorcism. The earliest records are found in **Sumerian**, **Arcadian** and Chaldean cuneiform inscriptions that may be as early as the 4th millennium BCE. Each of the synoptic Gospels record Christ curing a demon-possessed man, whose superhuman strength enabled him to break his restraining chains. In the Middle Ages the Church drew up a list of symptoms that had to be observed before demon-possession was confirmed. Animals were not exempt and cats, dogs and goats were killed because it was believed they were possessed by a demon. Spiritual, as opposed to demon possession is associated with **spiritualism**, popularized in the West by Helena **Blavatsky**. Generally the biblical religions do not seek or encourage spiritual possession, but there is a strong charismatic tradition in Christianity of individuals being possessed by the Holy Spirit, manifesting their possession by speaking in tongues (see **Glossolalia**) or other signs. See **Energumen**, **Kardecism**, **Pentecostalism**, **Spiritism**, **Vineyard Churches**

FINAL WORD: '… the demonical strategy is to create fear in order to begin breaking the human will, the entrenched spirit tends to either launch a bombardment of incredible phenomena or embark on a surreptitious psychological attack, dedicated to the complete domination of the victim's will. ' (Gerald Brittle)

Possibilism See **Actualism**

Posthumanism An emergent European philosophy that sets aside the ideas and perceptions of Renaissance **humanism** so as to take into account 21st-century scientific **rationalism**. It denies the assumption made by Western religio-culture that human beings are set above other natural species, as a kind of superior being, not as the 'Overman' of Nietzsche, but the as the 'Overbeing' in nature. An application of this would assert that human beings have no natural right or *a priori* ethical basis to destroy or exploit nature. Although the term **transhumanism** is usually thought to be synonymous with posthumanism, current debate suggests that they are 'no longer informed by the same literature, nor are they speaking with the same intentions' (Andy Miah on the posthumanisms.blogspot.com). The posthumanist position is allied to secular humanist philosophy which, withdrawn from the subjective 'authority' of metaphysical control, leaves the human being with a certain kind of limitation or better, an objective acceptance of the limitation of human intelligence and the tools it uses to advance knowledge, such as the sciences. Interestingly, posthumanism is the energy behind new arts such as Shannon Bell's performance philosophy which aims 'to develop through enactment new understandings of the self, the other, essence, consciousness, intelligence, reason, agency, intimacy, life, embodiment, identity and the body'. See **Democratic Transhumanism**

Postmodernism Postmodernism is a sceptical philosophy that calls into question what other discourses claim to be certain. Its central thesis, based on extreme scepticism, asserts that a correct description of reality is impossible. Put briefly, postmodernism constantly questioned the assumption that there are valid grounds for basic beliefs about anything. The related term, 'postmodernity', is understood to be the culmination of the early 20th-century modernist movement, a kind of cultural buffer state between that and postmodernism. **Modernism**, having found new perceptions and new languages with which to express them, became the new status quo, the strikingly original having become the customary, to the point where the best of what was being produced was simply a re-enactment or reinterpretation of modernist culture. The themes that recur in discussions about postmodernism include, globalization and consumerism, the fragmentation of authority and knowledge as a commodity. 'Globalization' means far more than the global monopoly of businesses or industrial consortia, it means any concept, philosophy, religion, narrative, economic or gender issue that sets itself up as a paradigm with universal validity and application. The implication or result, is that in postmodernist culture there are no absolutes either in terms of law or morality, there are no critical criteria that enable any one discourse to disavow another and that any standard or paradigm, whether it be for a form of government, the aesthetics of architecture, literary or artistic criticism or the rightness or wrongness of any action, only holds good for the current issue and the evidence then available. Every idea, as logicians would claim, is 'partially interpreted', thus the theoretical concepts remain 'open' and it is the responsibility of research to 'close' them, although they will never be closed completely. The matter is confounded further because the term is used pejoratively when certain critical theories and idioms are ascribed to postmodernism, such as relativist, nihilistic, counter-Enlightenment, science, rationalism and foundationalism. **Lyotard**, one of postmodernism's leading theorists, was an antifoundationalist (see **Antifoundationalism**). Postmodernism rejects the universalizing tendencies of religion and philosophy, together with most of the 'isms' associated with them. The positive face of postmodernism is its emphasis on power relationships, on personalization and on 'discourse' on the construction of truth. In this emphasis equal place is given to the rational and irrational, for which postmodern thinkers are criticized. Postmodernism is but an adolescent and any assessment is premature. See **Deconstructionism**, **Derrida**
FINAL WORD: 'The quest for certainty has played a considerable part in the history of philosophy: it has been assumed that without a basis of certainty all our claims to knowledge must be suspect.' (A. J. Ayer)

Pragmatism A philosophical 'school' too diverse to be neatly defined, but generally taking their mandate from **Protagoras**, that 'man is measure of all things'. Most pragmatists would claim a vital component of their system is the practical consequences and real effects of applying their philosophy. It is a way of saying that the belief, theory or point of view is itself the reality it represents, a claim some pragmatists would refute. Instead they would say that in place of the belief, etc. is a disposition, a habit or tendency to act in a particular way, its truth or falsity decided on the extent to which the intended goals are realized. In the effort to make something true, the belief gathers meaning; if in its application the belief or theory is successful, its truth is proved. In general, pragmatists are not interested in short-term solutions or successes, most arguing that only what contributes to the greatest good in the longest term is true. For pragmatists theories have to be applied and tested in order to validate them and it is the needs of society that should write the agenda for philosophical enquiry. Among American pragmatists are Charles Peirce, John Dewey and William **James**, who was the first to use the term in writing. Each of these philosophers agree that what is important for pragmatism is how the practical effects of philosophy impact on life. One of the better-known, frequently caricatured pragmatist summaries is 'truth is what works', which is to say that any idea that is of practical use, is true. The theory is a great deal more subtle when put in William James' [1995] own words, 'Ideas become true just so far as they help to get into satisfactory relations with other parts of our experience.' Thus, for James, our theories are the instruments we use in order to solve problems in our experience and should be judged on the extent to which they actually do solve the problems. James applied his pragmatism to religion and religious experience by examining what he termed their 'cash-value'. By trying out dogma dispassionately, not worrying about whether it is true or false, we can see if it has currency for us, thus removing questions of moral and religious belief from theological controversy and scientific analysis. The **Buddha** cautioned his followers from believing what he taught them simply on the strength of his word, encouraging them to go out and practise what he taught *so as to see* if his philosophy was true. (See Introduction, **Kalama Sutra**) In that sense, **Buddhism** is pragmatic. See **Functionalism, Utilitarianism**

FINAL WORD: 'Pragmatism asks its usual question. "Grant an idea or belief to be true, it says, 'what concrete difference will its being true make in anyone's actual life? How will truth be realized? What experiences will be different from those which would obtain if the belief were false? What, in short, is the truth's cash-value in experimental terms?" (William James [1995])

Prajna *H. B. Z.* Skt. In H. 'Consciousness' or 'Wisdom'. The highest soul which has no object outside of itself. In Buddhism and Zen, it is usually translated 'wisdom', but is better understood as 'insight', the kind of knowledge and experience that enables discrimination. In this form, the term expresses a central idea of Mahayana, an immediate experience of intuitive wisdom that cannot be communicated by conceptual or intellectual terms. All humans are born with *prajna*, but most fall short of its true potential. *Vipassana* meditation techniques train the mind in the development of the kind of special insight *prajna* represents.

Prana *H*. Skt. 'breath' or 'breath of life'. A cosmic energy that can enter the body and is believed to sustain it. *Prana* is evident in every sentient being as breath. It is the basic energy drawn on in the yoga system of **Patanjali**. Hinduism identifies five different kinds of *prana*: i) the basic life-force or energy, ii) the energy that determines the circulation of the blood, iii) that which controls our metabolism, the intake and digesting of food, iv) the aspect that effects the elimination of waste material and v) the energy that moves through the upper torso and forms an inner bridge between the physical and spiritual aspects of human nature, thus furthering spiritual development.

Pranayama *H*. Skt. 'control of the *Prana*' or 'breath'. A yoga discipline which is the fourth step in **Patanjali**'s system, known also as Raja Yoga. The control techniques are a combination of inhalation, exhalation and breath retention and can be used with **mantra** practice.

Prayer A communication addressed verbally or in silence, to God, a god or supernatural power. It may be offered privately or congregationally or with a small group, like a family. Praying is something anthropologists believe has been in existence since pre-history; the earliest attested prayers are dated c.3000 BCE. Sometimes prayer is accompanied by a ringing bell, burning incense, lighted candles, telling a rosary or by gestures such as making the sign of the cross; prayer may require facing a specific direction as Muslims do, towards the **Qiblah** of the **mosque**, which indicates the direction of Mecca. Various postures are assumed, including kneeling, crouching, standing, genuflexing or prostrating. The different religions have their customary habits, Christians put their hands together, Native Americans dance, Sufis whirl, Hindus offer sacrifice, Jews rock and bob their heads, Buddhists meditate or chant, Quakers sit in silence. Several traditions have their liturgical books, such as the Anglican 'Book of Common Prayer', the Catholic Missal and the Jewish *Siddur* or 'Authorized Daily Prayer Book'. Prayers are offered as praise, thanksgiving, lamentation, confession and as intercessions and petitions. The central liturgical prayer for Jews is the *Shema*, for Christians the **Lord's Prayer**, for Muslims the *Salah* and *Shahadah* (see **Pillars of Islam**). In **neo-pagan** cults prayers are mostly offered to the gods of pre-Christian Europe and in some case, like **Wicca**, may be associated with ritual magic. In ancient Greek and Roman religion prayer was highly formalized, ritualized and accompanied by sacrifice. Frequently it was proffered in the form of a bargain to be struck, using the formula, *do ut des*, 'I give so that you may give in return.' Prayer has always posed problems for the philosophers of religion, central to which are questions like, why pray to an all-knowing, omniscient God, who will already be aware of your intentions, gratitude and needs? So, why ask God a favour, why ask him to cure an illness or to alter an aspect of creation or to control a natural element or force? Each of the biblical religions have produced copious literature, especially from the Middle Ages, endeavouring to address these problems. See **Prayer Wheel**

FINAL WORD: 'When we pray to God we must be seeking nothing – nothing.' (St Francis of Assisi)

'Prayer does not change God, but it changes him who prays.' (Kierkegaard)

Prayer Wheel *B*. As used in Tibetan Buddhism, it takes the form of a rotating cylinder pivoted around a handle and filled with printed sheets of **mantras**, and sometimes images of gods. Rotating the prayer wheel activates the mantras, conferring merit and protection on the user. Prayer wheels can be attached to walls or poles and operated by the wind or placed in a stream to be driven by water. Prayer flags function in much the same way.

Precepts *B*. Condensed forms of Buddhist ethics. In the basic form there are five precepts: i) Do not kill; ii) Do not steal; iii) Avoid misconduct in sensual matters; iv) Do not lie; v) Do not drink intoxicants. They have their origins in early Buddhism and form the foundation of Buddhist morality. All schools of Buddhism subscribe to them. Monks and nuns follow a moral code of ten precepts which include the five set out for lay people. To these are added, abstention from solid food after noon, avoiding entertainment, giving up the use of cosmetics and perfume, sleeping only on a low, hard bed and renouncing all contact with money. There is also a group of eight precepts which expand the last of the basic five, to include refraining from sexual activity and adding three that are supportive of meditation. See **Ten Good Deeds**

Predestination *X*. A doctrine derived from **New Testament** texts asserting that human free will and co-operation with God have no part in gaining salvation, because God has already decreed who should be saved and who should not. The main sources are Matthew 20:23, where Jesus explains that those who will sit on his right or left side have already been chosen by the Father and St Paul's letter to the Romans 8: 28–30, where he explains that those who are called according to the purpose of God were known to him even before they were born. Paul refers to the 'chosen' as the 'fore-ordained'. The doctrine was developed and established by St Augustine (see **Augustinianism**) who cast it as a mystery inaccessible to human reason but which is, nevertheless, perfectly just. Predestination was a cornerstone of **Calvinism**, which rejected the universalism of salvation – Christ did not die for the whole world but only for the 'chosen'. Another term used for the same doctrine is 'election'. Some Christian sects such as the **Jehovah's Witnesses** and the **Mormons** are founded on the notion that only a certain number of people will be saved to share the bliss of heaven in an afterlife. See **Providence**

Prediction See **Anthropomancy, Astrology, Auspicia, Bibliomancy, Divination, Mantike, Palmistry**

Prehistoric Religion What we know can only be conjectured from arte-facts made before recorded history – bones, tools, weaponry and works of art such as cave paintings. Some field anthropologists have suggested that a reconstruction can be made from a socio-historical comparison with extant tribes believed to be close to the way of life and culture of say, stone-age man. Tribes have been contacted in Papua New Guinea and the Amazonian forests, but such comparisons are uncertain because even though there may be seeming parallels, all cultures change, modify and adapt through time and it is impossible to conclude how close the present primitive societies are to those from which they developed over many thousands of years. Other conclusions have been drawn from the unsupported assumption that all of mankind share the same psychic or intuitive responses to the environment and its natural forces and to what **Otto** calls the '**numinous**'. But social conditioning and perceptions of the way the world is seen vary so considerably that it is impossible to draw all but very general conclusions. Dominated by knowledge of their mortality, early communities developed complicated funerary practices and rituals associated with the last rite of passage. Important insights into prehistoric religion have been gained from excavations at, for example, Ternifine in Algeria, Maur near Heidelberg and Choukoutien near Peking. These suggest there may have been skull cults that showed concern for, reverence and awe of the dead and it is likely that some forms of ancestor-related cults existed. *Homo sapiens*, appearing 30,000 to 10,000 BCE, had elaborate burial rituals in which corpses were dusted with red ochre. All of these suggest that a belief in some kind of after-world existed, was part of the earliest religious perceptions. As hunting communities began to settle to a primitive form of agriculture and stock-breeding, fertility became the central concern of the beliefs and rituals that ensured survival. Cave paintings are very revealing in this respect; a painting in the cave of the Trois Frères, in France, of a man dressed in animal skin, playing what seems to be a musical instrument and dancing, appears to illustrate hunting rituals and imitative magic. The discovery of carved figures of women, clearly pregnant, with grotesquely enlarged breast and genitals, mark the emergence of a Great Mother or **Earth Mother** cult. The Earth Mother cult is not, of itself, evidence of Palaeolithic belief in a supreme deity, but of a belief that survival both in this and any future life involves forces over which humans have no control. It follows, plausibly, that they began to wonder what or who did have control, especially as the cycle of the seasons seemed to be ordered by some great power, such as the sun. This cycle of life and death, matched to the waning and waxing of their own lives and the conjecture that human life might well continue after its own winter, will have inspired the earliest beginnings of animism. See **Mother Goddess, New Age Religion, Wicca**

FINAL WORD: 'If prehistory is a time of which we do, in fact, know very little, then the more imaginative reconstructions which we possess of how things might have been, the better. To be of real value, such reconstructions need to be based upon the latest archaeological data and to make clear precisely where the data end and speculation begins.' (Hutton)

Pre-Nicene Gnostic Catholic Church See **Ecclesia Gnostica**

Presbyterianism *X.* A post-Reformation form of Church government derived originally from **Calvinism** which set a board of presbyters or 'elders' at the head of Church administration. The purpose of the movement was to restore the government of the Church to its New Testament model. Acts 14:23, referring to the churches founded by St Paul points out that, 'They also appointed elders for them in each congregation', a pattern Jewish members of the early Church would have found familiar, since synagogues had the same hierarchy. Presbyterian churches are now governed by a hierarchy of Kirk-Session, Presbytery, Synod and General Assembly, comprising elected ministers and elders. The standard of doctrine and faith is the **creed** of the Westminster Confession and the catechisms issued in 1647, which are traditionally Calvinistic. Presbyterianism is now established throughout the world, with Scotland having the only established Presbyterian State Church. Other large groups are to be found in the USA, Hungary, Holland, Northern Ireland, Switzerland and France. In 1970 the Church became part of the World Alliance of Reformed Churches.

Priest Priests or priestesses, whether by their actual power or their assumption of office, fulfil the role of mediator between human beings and the divine. In some religions men and women become priests by vocation and training, followed by **ordination** or **anointing**; others, like shamans and medicine-men, are set apart by their societies to serve a similar function, by virtue of their special gifts. The office of priesthood is to be found in pagan and primitive religions such as **Egypt**, the **Maya** and the **Druids**, and in ancient **Greek** and **Roman** religion. Most of the major religious traditions have a form of priesthood. In biblical Judaism the function was served by the *Kohanim*, members of the tribe of Levi, the direct descendents of Aaron. (See **Priest, High**) In modern Judaism the Kohen still exists, but the more important office is that of the **rabbi**. In Shiite Islam the **Imam** is thought to be a descendent of Muhammad, with divine authority to provide spiritual leadership. In Hinduism, the Brahmins form a priestly cast and Tibetan Buddhism is served by the **Lama**. See **Flamen, Priesthood of All Believers**

Priest, High *J.* Heb. *Kohen.* In biblical Judaism the supreme spiritual authority who represented Israel before God. Aaron, the first high priest, was appointed after the founding of the Hebrew theocracy at Mt Sinai and the construction of the tabernacle in the wilderness. The office was hereditary, the succession determined by primogeniture. In post-exilic Israel, when there were no kings or princess, the high priest was virtually head of state, combining religious and political responsibility, aided by a council. In most religions with an established priestly hierarchy, there will be the equivalent of a high priestly office, such as that of pope or archbishop.

Priesthood of All Believers *X*. A doctrine in Protestant Christianity based on an interpretation of 1 Peter 2:9, 'But you are a chosen race, a royal priesthood ...' It is argued that because the entire body of believers is likened to a priesthood, the notion of a separate ordained, hierarchical priesthood is unwarranted. Its most radical form was to be found among the **Lollards**, and the concept is strongly held by **Methodists**. However, they and other non-conformist denominations, do have an ordained clergy regarded as 'professionally' necessary not just in terms of spiritual authority, but also to ensure stable Church government and a 'spiritual' democracy.

Process Theology *X*. A modern theological construction which emphasizes the evolutionary nature of man and the world, which are in process of constant change and development. Because of his relationship with a changing world, God is also in the process of development. The main movers of process theology were A. N. Whitehead (1861–1947) and Charles Hartshorne (1897–2000). The principal notions state that to be real is to be in process, to be responding to the environment and thus to have a temporal dimension. God also has a temporal dimension. Whitehead developed a unified perception of reality by means of reflection on its constituent parts. Hartshorne based his thought on *a priori* arguments as a means of perceiving the nature and reality of God; he developed St **Anselm**'s ontology, the argument from 'being', but was concerned not to prove *that* God exists, but '*how*' God exists. Process theology stands in contradistinction to **theism**, which makes a clear distinction between the world and a timeless and impassable God and to **pantheism**, which identifies God with the world. Process theology suggests a **panentheism**, the assertion that God is *in* everything and embraces everything in the process of drawing all things to an ultimate aesthetic potential.

Profane Generally, an attitude of irreverence towards sacred and religious subjects or as profanity, close to blasphemy. Originally, the term was applied to those not initiated into the mysteries or in ecclesiastical usage, to those who were not baptized. This meaning is retained by, for example, the Freemasons for those who are not yet initiated. More broadly, the profane is identified with a pejorative description of the **secular**.

Professional Sport See **Sport**

Progressive Utilization Theory (PROUT) An American Hindu-based programme, the theories of which were propounded in 1959 by Prabhat Ranjan **Sarkar** as an alternative to capitalism and communism. It built on the ideas of the **Ananda Marga** Society, founded in India in 1955 by Shri Anandamurti. Sarkar's aim is to establish a unified world government, Proutist Universal. Its main tenet combines spiritual wisdom with a universal outlook and perseverance towards self-reliance. PROUTist adherents are creating an alternative civilizational discourse, by calling on spiritual and neo-humanist values. The movement believes that economic democracy is just as important as political democracy and that the two should co-operate to form a decentralized economy that will not exploit ecological systems. Political and economic leadership requires a commitment to these principles and complete ethical integrity. The organization publishes *Prout Journal* and *Global Times*.

FINAL WORD: 'Alternative visions are crucial at this moment in history. PROUT's co-operative model of economic democracy, based on cardinal human values and sharing of the planet for the welfare of everyone, deserves our serious consideration.' (Noam Chomsky)

Projection Religion *X*. The thesis that God does not exist independently of the mind's conception of him. Thus, the reality of God is no greater than the reality of our mental projection of him, even if this is unconscious. The idea is similar to **Hume**'s suggestion that God was a personification of the forces of nature encountered by primitive man (see **Prehistoric Religion**). The concept was taken up by Feuerbach (1804–72), who argued that God was an illusion that represented to humanity their own ideal qualities. Theories of projection influenced **Marx**'s hostility to religion, **Nietzsche**'s criticism of religious institutionalism, **Durkeim**'s reading of religion as a mythological interpretation of social structures and **Freud**'s notion of God as an ideal image of the child's father. See also **Anthropomorphism**

Prometheus *G*. In Greek mythology, the Titan mostly renowned for steeling fire from the gods so as to make a gift of it to mortals, for which purpose he used a stalk of fennel. Unsurprisingly, he was the god of fire, burning and craft, for which latter function he had a shrine in the potter's quarter of Athens. Because he is the source of fire and the inventor of sacrifice he is considered to be the father of civilization and was worshipped in ancient Rome, although the sources for this are uncertain. Aeschylus' play *Prometheus Bound* and Shelley's poem 'Prometheus Unbound' have made the mythology well known. For opposing **Zeus**' despotism, Prometheus was bound to a rock and an eagle came each day to feed on his liver which regenerated during the night.

'Nailed to this wall of eagle-baffling mountain,
Black, wintry, dead, unmeasured; without herb,
Insect or beast or shape or sound of life,
Ah, me! Alas, pain, pain ever, for ever!'
(Percy Bysshe Shelley, 'Prometheus Unbound')

He was supported in his suffering by the sea-nymphs. A c.4th-century allegorical interpretation of the Promethean myth had 'fire' as philosophy, understood by the Stoics as divine 'Forethought', the original man-forming concept (see **Logos**). Prometheus' punishment was understood to represent debilitating worry.

Promise Keepers A Canadian movement founded on the 'new commandment' given by Jesus to his disciples: 'love one another as I have loved you' (John 13:34). It is layman-inspired movement that gathered momentum from 1990, designed to help men to live biblically-based lives. Why men only? The information given tells us that, 'Men as a whole communicate, learn and relate in substantially different ways than women. A male-only context of safety and familiarity such as a hockey arena – a familiar setting for so many men in Canada – helps men to achieve that level of intimacy that, in turn, facilitates spiritual growth.'

Promised Land *J. X.* The biblical Israel or *Eretz Israel*, being the territory 'promised' to the descendents of the Hebrew patriarchs **Abraham, Isaac** and **Jacob**. The territory was finally delivered to them by Joshua, successor to Moses. Originally, the Promised Land was **Canaan**, but the whole region was designated **Palestine**, by the Romans in 135 CE following the failed Bar Kokhba rebellion. Christianity uses the term as metaphor for heaven, while for the early pilgrims America was their 'promised land'.

Proofs for God's Existence See **Arguments for the Existence of God**

Prophecy *J.* and *X.* An aspect of biblical revelation, prophecy, in this context, is the inspired message of God delivered by chosen individuals. Both the content and the style of delivery differ according to the personality of the prophet and the spiritual, social and political needs of the time. The erroneous notion frequently attached to prophecy, is that it foretold the future; this was only one of its minor and implied functions. More importantly, the prophet was a teacher who charged with God's message, endeavoured to maintain a high standard of ritual spirituality and to warn against what might happen if this was compromised. Talmudic tradition (see **Talmud**) believes the age of prophecy to have ended with the post-Exile messengers, Haggai, Zechariah and Malachi. After the Exile, the rabbinical teacher took the place of the prophet. Christianity reads some of the **Old Testament** prophetic texts as foretelling the Messianic message of the **New Testament**. For example, Isaiah 7:14 speaks of 'A young woman with child' who will give birth to a son called Immanuel. There is evidence in the New Testament (1 Cor 12:28 and Eph. 4:11) that prophecy existed in the primitive Church as a separate ministry. See **False Prophecy, Nabi, Prophet**

Prophet Generally, a human spokesman for a god or God, called to **prophecy** by virtue of his special relationship with the Divine who empowered him to act. His calling may be validated by the performance of miracles. In the **Old Testament** the Hebrew *Nabi* is translated 'proclaimer', someone who is given an unequivocal divine mandate: 'I will raise up a prophet for them … I will put my words in his mouth and he will speak to them all that I commanded him' (Deut. 18:18). Such was the prophet's authority that anyone not taking his message seriously was answerable to God. Thus, the Old Testament prophets were not seer-priests or diviners of the future, but the mouthpieces for God. Prophets are found in many religions. The indigenous, sacred sites of Greece were the forerunners of **oracles**, which exercised both a prophetic and consultative mandate; Muslims understand Muhammad to be the last and greatest of Allah's prophets; the **Mormons** hold Joseph Smith to have been a prophet and the Baha'i, Baha'ullah. What is important, is that the original concept of a prophet was of someone called by God to carry his message; only in the sense of the message including a warning of what might happen if an individual or nation did not change its direction, can prophecy be thought of as foretelling the future. However, a looser use of the word has led to people being designated 'prophet' because telling the future was what they claimed to do. The most beguiling of these was Merlin the Wizard, the most distinguished Nostradamus, the most appealing Mother Shipton. See **Nabi**

Proselyte *J. X.* From the Koine Greek *proselytos*, used in the **Septuagint** to translate the word 'stranger'. In biblical times a proselyte was a non-Jew who lived in Israel, a 'sojourner'. In the New Testament they were converts to **Judaism** from **paganism**. The 'righteous' proselyte was someone who desired to be converted to Judaism without compromise or ulterior motive. If male, he would be circumcized and required to fulfil the entire Law of the Torah and once admitted would, in every way, be considered Jewish. The 'gate' or half-proselytes, were not considered to be sincere or were believed to have ulterior motives for becoming Jewish and were not required to be circumcized or to comply fully with the Law. Frequently they would revert. The issue of whether or not gentile converts to Christianity should be circumcised was debated in the New Testament Pauline epistles, is a marker of the extent to which the Early Church believed itself to be a Jewish sect.

Protagoras (c.481–c.420BCE) One of the most interesting of the pre-Socratic Greek philosophers known to us through Plato and by epigrams that have become very familiar. For example, 'Man is the measure of all things: of things which are, that they are, and of things which are not, that they are not.' This is quoted in Plato's *Theaetetus*. Protagoras was an agnostic (see **Agnosticism**). 'Concerning the gods, I have no means of knowing whether they exist or not or what sort they may be, because of the obscurity of the subject and brevity of human life.' Protagoras was a **sophist** and his views are probably fairly represented in an early dialogue of Plato's *Protagoras*, which debates whether virtue can be taught.

Protection Theology A term usually found in discussions about the relationship between science, religion and faith. Religious adherents look to their faith to protect them from what they feel are the dehumanizing effects of science, which nevertheless provided essential knowledge beyond the scope of '**revelation**'. Protection theology is therefore concerned to examine the relationship between revealed and empirical knowledge, understanding that science is itself, a protection against faith as mere mystery. Protection theology can take the form of a theology of science, an acknowledgement that true theology cannot confine itself to its traditional subjects, God and Man. A scientific analysis of faith can only result in a deeper understanding of the symbiotic relationship between religion and science.

FINAL WORD: 'Neither science nor technology can or should tell us who the human being ultimately is. For this one must turn to a different authority. The relationship between science and faith can be dynamic and healthy, because truth is a dynamic relationship.' (Kresimir Cerovac)

Protestantism *X*. Those Christian denominations, together with their doctrines and forms of administration that are based on the principles of the **Reformation**. The term derives from the Latin *Protestatio*, specifically the protest of members of the Diet of Speyer (1529) and the German princes against what they judged to be the errors of Roman Catholicism. The main original branches of Protestantism are **Lutheranism**, **Calvinism** and **Zwinglianism**. Anglicanism contains both Protestant and 'reformed' Catholic elements, but in common usage English Protestantism includes both the Church of England and most Nonconformist Churches. Common to all is the use of the **Bible** as the exclusive source of revealed truth, the doctrine of justification by faith and the '**priesthood of all believers**'. Generally it can be said that Protestantism is less sacramental than Catholicism, less subjected to the priesthood, more democratic in terms of the laity but also more susceptible to outside influences such as **secularism**, and more exposed to and involved in the world. For these reasons it embraces the extremes of fundamentalism and liberal theology. The acceptance of human free will and the freedom to exercise choice based on one's own judgement on everything from the interpretation of scripture to morality, accounts for the proliferation of denominations and sects that gather to the Protestant flag.

Proudhon, Pierre-Joseph (1809–65) A French socialist-anarchist and philosopher and the first to call himself an anarchist (see **Anarchism**). He advocated a radical restructuring of society that dispensed with money and the concept of the 'State' and a form of communism called 'communitarianism'. Somewhat naively, he believed that once the new structure was established the natural good will of people would make it work. Unsurprisingly, he corresponded with Karl **Marx**. See **Bakunin**

FINAL WORD: 'Property is theft! Anarchy is order.' (Proudhon)

Providence A vaguely defined influence or power that is believed to determine the course of both universal events and of an individual's life. It is not to be confused with 'fate' since providence is felt to be mostly benevolent, whereas fate may be fortunate or unfortunate. In Christianity, the term is sometimes used for God's will and foreknowledge. The extent to which any concept of providence implies a limitation of human free will has been long debated and will continue to be so. See **Predestination**

Psyche *G*. The Greek word for 'breath' and may mean 'life', 'soul', 'spirit' or 'mind', and in this latter sense is similar to the Platonic *Nous* (see **Neoplatonism**). In Greek mythology, Psyche was a beautiful girl and lover of Cupid. Their union is taken to be a parable of the union of the human soul and divine love.

Psychical Research The establishment of the English Society of Psychical Research in 1882 and several modern institutions, has done much to shift the whole question of psychic or paranormal phenomena from the realm of superstitious fantasy towards an educated open-mindedness to the subject. Its modern history begins with the an interest in **mediums**, **séances**, **mesmerism** and the growth of movements like **spiritualism** and **theosophy**, and with the work of a number of eminent people including Helena **Blavatsky** and Sir Oliver Lodge (1851–1940). Among the contemporary research institutes is the Committee for the Scientific Investigation of Claims of the Paranormal, whose objectives are 'to encourage the investigation of paranormal and fringe-science claims from a responsible, scientific point of view and disseminate factual information about the results of such enquiries to the scientific community and the public.' See **Near-Death Experiences**, **Out-of-Body Experiences**, **Parapsychology**, **Spiritism**

Psychology of Religion An examination of religious experience and beliefs, so as to arrive at a psychological understanding of their causes and functions. It has been suggested that if these can be explained in psychological terms, then the truth or falsity of the subject matter is irrelevant. Clearly, to understand the natural causes of religious behaviour, does not indicate that the beliefs are groundless. Conversely, those who study the psychological causes of religious commitment will not necessarily be persuaded by the belief system in question. What perhaps, is more fundamental, is the light psychology can throw on why certain types of religion appeal to certain types of personality. Frequently conversion from one religion to another shows an exchange of traditions that have features in common regardless of their theologies and doctrines. Thus, a person in need of a strong, clearly defined belief-system, contained perhaps by a creed may, in the process of conversion, exchange one form of authority for another. Similar perception may be made by examining why those without any religious background may be drawn to a particular religion. A plausible case had been made by many psychologists that psychology and psychiatry are, themselves, a valid alternative

to religion. See **Anthropomorphism, Freud, James, Jung,** Otto, **Projection Religion**
FINAL WORD: 'When educated man lost faith in formal religion, he required a substitute belief that would be as reputable in the last half of the 20th century as Christianity was in the first. Psychology and psychiatry have now assumed that role.' (Martin Gross. Not sourced)

Ptah *E*. Ptah was the deification of the primordial mound of the **Ennead** creation mythology (see **Ogdoad**). One version of the myth has Ptah creating the world by dreaming it up. **Atum** was said to have been created by Ptah to rule over creation from the primordial mound that emerged from the waters of chaos. Since Ptah was the primordial mound and called creation into being, he is known as the god of craftsmen, especially stone-based crafts, whose destinies he controlled. As the first among craftsmen Ptah eventually became the god of reincarnation (re-creation) following on his personification of the sun in its night journey, during which it was being reincarnated. The centre of the cult was at Memphis, where Ptah was worshipped in his own right as the most ancient and pre-eminent of all the gods. His consort was Sekhmet, who gave birth to their son, Nefertum, an early form of Atum. Another god of craftsmen was Seker, who was eventually assimilated with Ptah to become Ptah-Seker.

Pueblo Indians See **Amerindian Religion**

Puja *H. B*. Skt. 'worship', 'ceremony', 'religious service', offering reverence. In Hinduism, a ritual ceremony using Ganges water, flowers, bells, incense and **mantras. Mudras,** symbolic gestures, are used to draw a mystical circle around the worshipper, thus creating a barrier between him and the impermanent aspect of the world. In **Theravada** Buddhism, *Puja is* a ceremony in which flowers, food, incense and water are offered, with the recitation of refuge formulas and a meditation practice. The Tibetan forms of *puja*, can be very complex. *Pujas* are performed on special occasions such as the fasts observed on the moon's quarter-days. In **Vajrayana,** *pujas* may include the recitation of texts and the use of mantras, mudras and ritual offerings for the evocation of deities.

Punya *B*. Skt. Spiritual karmic merit gained by the giving of alms and the reciting of **sutras.** The Buddhist layperson places great importance on the accumulation of positive **karma,** since it will offset whatever negative karma has been accrued through this or a previous lives. This emphasis is more typical of **Hinayana** traditions; **Mahayana** sees the accumulation of *punya* to be more meritorious when it is transferred to others, thus contributing to the enlightenment of all beings in accord with the **bodhisattva** vow.

Puranas *H*. Skt. 'old'. Ancient, Hindu epic poems that tell of the power and work of the gods. They have five distinguishing subjects: i) the creation of the universe; ii) its destruction and restoration; iii) the genealogy of the gods; iv) the reigns of the **Manus** that form periods called, Manwantaras; and v) the history of the solar and lunar races of kings. The 18 poems vary in length and date, the longest having 81,000 couplets, the oldest probably originating in the 13th or even 16th century BCE.

Pure Land Buddhism *B*. A major school of Chinese and Japanese Buddhism founded in 402 CE by a Chinese monk called, Hui-yuan and brought to Japan by Honen. The objective of the School is to ensure rebirth in the pure land of the Buddha **Amida**, or Amitabha. The School is in some ways uncharacteristic of Buddhism, since it gives to the Amida Buddha active and unlimited compassion which invokes a response of faith. The Pure Land School is, therefore, regarded as the 'way of faith'. It represents an innovation sprung from the idea that enlightenment or nirvana does not, necessarily, mean extinction but allows for the possibility of remaining in the world to help others. 'Pure Land' gives a perception of the Buddha who, having set aside the delusions under which we all live, sees the world as it *really* is, in all its purity.

Purgatory *X*. A Roman Catholic doctrine of a place or state of temporal existence and punishment, where those who have died in a state of grace expiate their unforgiven (venial) **sins** before being admitted to the beatific vision. Without the concept of purgatory, the custom of offering prayers and Mass for the dead has little point. The doctrine of purgatory was developed to account for the state of souls between death and the Final Judgement. Aquinas taught that the guilt of venial sin is expiated immediately by an act of perfect charity, but the punishment remains to be borne. The reformers rejected the notion of purgatory, asserting that people are set free of sin and its consequences by faith in Christ alone and that if 'saved' they go immediately to heaven after dying.

Purim *J*. Heb. A Jewish festival that is social rather than religious, commemorating the deliverance of Persian Jews from the threat of persecution and destruction during the reign of the Persian King, Ahasuerus (5th century BCE). The event is recorded in the book of Esther which is read in its entirety during the course of the festival. It is celebrated on the 14th of the Jewish month of Adar (usually March) and is a 'fun' occasion when both children and adults wear costumes and synagogues take on a carnival atmosphere. Behind enjoyment, however, is the brooding message about the dangers always lurking to threaten Jews of the **diaspora**.

Puritanism *X*. An English movement intended to purify the Church in the face of the religious settlements of Elizabeth I, which were supposedly unscriptural and corrupt. The settlement concerned such matters as church ornaments, vestments, organs, surplices, the sign of the cross and ecclesiastical courts. From the 1570s the institution of episcopacy was attacked by extreme Puritans. The Great Rebellion, from 1642, sometimes called the Puritan Revolution, led to the brief triumph of **Presbyterianism** and the proliferation of sects. Puritans were among the first settlers of the North American colonies, famously the Pilgrim Fathers, the vanguard of what seemed like a Puritan exodus from the homeland. They have left a lasting influence on American religion and society. The term is now loosely used for a form of biblical fundamentalism and for severe, narrow views mostly concerned with sexual morality.

Purna or **Integral Yoga** *H*. See **Aurobindo, Yoga**

Purva-Mimamsa *H*. Skt. 'earliest investigation'. Mimamsa, one of the six orthodox schools of Hindu philosophy established by Jaimini. Its date is uncertain, but the earliest work of the School is traditionally placed in the 3rd century BCE. The Purva system was based on the notion of ritual, especially its purifying action as a preliminary to achieving higher or enlightened knowledge. The performance of ritual always preceded the search for knowledge, but the correct practice is dependent on the way in which the Vedic texts are interpreted. Maharshi Jaimini (c.4th century BCE) systematized and codified the instructions in an attempt to ensure right practice. Modern Hinduism still gives a central place to Purva-Mimamsa since correct procedure is thought to satisfy every spiritual and material desire. It has been suggested that the rhythms and style of the poetry of the Purva-Mimamsa texts influenced the Greek mystery religions practised by the **Orphic** and **Eleusian** cults, which themselves influenced the philosophies of Pythagoras and Plato. See **Darshana, Nyaya, Sankhya, Vaiseshika, Vedenta, Yoga**

Pyramid Texts *E*. A collection of ancient texts compiled at the time of the Old Kingdom c.2686–c.2181 BCE. They are mostly found as inscriptions on the wall of tombs and pyramids and describe Egyptian eschatology and the afterlife and the means by which the soul of the deceased can ascend to the sky. Written some 5,000 years ago, they are some of the oldest forms of writing known to us. At the end of the Old Kingdom, the Coffin Texts, comprising magical funerary spells, superseded them and are the characteristic inscriptions of the Middle Kingdom, c.2055–c.1650 BCE. The texts democratize the afterlife, making it accessible to everyone. A common name for other funerary texts is 'The Book of the Dead', a collection of spells, charms and passwords. It was not a book in the usual sense, but texts carved on the outside of the sarcophagus only later to be written on papyrus to form scrolls which were placed in the sarcophagus with the deceased as a portable post-death urvival manual. See **Funerary Practices**

Pyramidology A study of the **pyramids** of Egypt and the **Maya** which are believed to enshrine a meaning beyond their function as tombs, concerning mystical knowledge and a special power for endowing spiritual understanding. The theories involved are pseudo-scientific combining, architecture, astronomy, history, mathematics and numerology and were put together in the 19th century by Charles Taze Russell, based on the earlier work of John Taylor who attributed the construction of the Great Pyramid to Noah and Charles Smyth who claimed it was built by the Hebrews. It is also held that the architecture of the pyramids is God's plan for world, a solid mandala, constructed in stone. In this latter sense pyramidology is seen to be an aspect of **sacred geometry**. See **Divine Plan of the Ages**

Pyramids *E*. The Egyptian word for these constructions was *mer*, meaning perhaps, 'the place of ascension'. The familiar name is derived from the Greek *pyramis*. They were royal tombs built for the rulers of the Old and Middle Kingdoms, c.2686–c.1650 BCE. The first pyramid, the Step Pyramid at Saqqara, was built by the architect **Imhotep** for King Djoser who reigned c.2630–c.2611. The constructions are built up from *mastabas* (from the Arabic for 'bench') flat-roofed, rectangular buildings with sloping walls that were the first, more primitive burial places of an earlier period. It was probably Imhotep's idea to stack a number of *mastabas* on top of each other. The shape of the pyramid is thought to symbolize the primordial mound (**Island of Creation**) on which the world was created. The sloping walls represent the rays of the sun and some pyramids were faced with polished limestone to provide a reflective surface. Their names sometimes indicated this intention such as the pyramid at Dahshur known as 'The Southern Shining Pyramid'. Opinions differ as to the theological principles that gave rise to the constructions, but it seems to be generally accepted that they were a form of stairway to heaven by which means the soul of the deceased could ascend. The gateway, sometimes called, Star Gate, was said to be the dark area of night sky around which the stars were thought to revolve and, perhaps coincidentally, the main shaft of the Great Pyramid passes directly towards the centre of this area of sky. All the pyramids were built on the west bank of the Nile, being the location of the setting sun, a realm associated in Egyptian mythology with the dead.

Q

Qaddish *J*. A blessing for the Sabbath and other festivals. See **Kiddush**

Qadi *I*. An Islamic judge presiding in the **Shari'a** courts originally a judicial representative of the **caliph**.

Qiblah *I*. The architectural feature in a **mosque** indicating the direction Muslims face during prayer. It takes the form of a wall (prayer wall) which holds the *mihrab*, the niche, which marks the direction of Mecca and the *Ka'bah*. *Qiblah* also has an abstract or symbolic significance, being the direction in which those who travel the Islamic Way are 'pointed'. They are orientated towards the **Pillars of Islam**, the focal point for all Muslims, of all religion, devotions and actions. For this reason they regard themselves as the People of the Point.

Qiyama *I*. The Islamic concept of **resurrection**. It is the bringing back to life of a human being so as to face the final Judgement. The Koran is clear about the 'Last Hour', the end of the world preceded by the appearance of the Antichrist. The angel Israfil, will raise people from their graves, the first being Muhammad. Orthodox Islam has never contested the doctrine of Qiyama, but modern interpreters suggest that the resurrection and subsequent judgement may be of a more spiritual than physical nature.

Qliphoth *J*. Heb. plural (singular *Qliphah*), 'shells', 'husks'. The Kabbalistic concept of evil forces. *Qliphoth* are figured as the dark, evil tree. They are the mere husks of the positive energies, the shadowy side of the **sephiroth**, the divine emanations of the **Tree of Life**. *Qliphah* is also known as the realm of 'demons'.

Quakers See **Society of Friends**

Quetzalcoatl *CM*. Meaning 'feathered snake' or 'plumed serpent'. The Feathered-Serpent was an ancient deity of Mesoamerica, a god of Mexican and north-central American religion. The name was also used as a title for the rulers of the Toltec, a pre-Columbian native American people c.10th–12th centuries CE. The cult practised animal sacrifice, but is believed to have opposed human sacrifice. The tradition tells how Quetzalcoatl gave his rights and powers to one man to perform his religious duties, he also gave his name as authority, but it was pronounced differently to indicate that the holder of the title was mortal. The system was dualistic, Quetzalcoatl having an opposite or opponent, Tezcatlipoca; when the **Aztecs** adopted the cult, the two gods became twins, opposites but equals. Quetzalcoatl had another name among the Aztecs, 'Ipalnemohuani', meaning 'by whom we live'. Its singular form, suggests that the cult has become monotheistic. The tradition that the Aztec

Emperor Moctezuma II, believed the landing of Cortés in 1519 was Quetzalcoatl's return, is a matter of controversy among scholars in the field. See **Mayan Religion**

Quietism X. A term with several applications. As a Christian philosophy, it rested on the practice of intellectual stillness and inner peace as the way to spiritual perfection. In this respect it is not dissimilar to *Samatha*, the concept of 'tranquillity' in Hindu and Buddhist **meditation** techniques. Its origins are found in the earliest period of Christianity with the **Stoics**, Epicureans and the Emperor Marcus Aurelius (121–180 CE) whose philosophy included the practice of *ataraxia*, complete serenity. In the 17th century the philosophy spread rapidly through France, Italy and Spain, but since the possibility of achieving a sinless state of union with the **Godhead** was denied, it was pronounced a heresy by the Roman Catholic Church. Quietism is also to be found in the mystical traditions of Islam for example, in Iraqi **Shi'ism**. Because Shi'ism endeavours to keep politics out of religion, it is vehemently opposed by the Sh'ia government, which after assuming power in 1979 persecuted Muslim Quietists. The philosopher, Schopenhauer, understood Quietism to be a state of selflessness that would lead to freedom from suffering. The term is also generally used to denote tranquillity, dispassion, inaction, even indifference.

Quimbanda The name is from the Kimbundu language of Angola and means 'Healer' or 'Diviner'. It is a traditional Afro-American religion practised in the larger urban areas of Brazil. Historically associated with the syncretistic **Umbanda** cult, Quimbanda is now asserting its independence and attracting more young, middle-class people. Its beliefs, which are a form of ancestor worship, focus on the spirits of old slaves. Its practices include divination and the preparation of amulets and potions, together with anything else that might invoke the help of spirits to cope with the brutishness of modern life. It has become recognized as an official religion, but this has caused controversy and conflict as the evangelical Christian sects show less tolerance to religions derived from the African origins of Brazilians. See **Candomblé, Macumba**

Quimby, Phineas P. (1802–66) An American New Englander accredited with founding the **New Thought movement**. His reflections on the experience of being suddenly cured from a critical illness led him to **mesmerism**, and to the study of mind over matter and the mechanisms of suggestion combined with faith.

Quintessence L. *quinta essentia*, the pure fifth element of Aristotelian physics. It was believed to be an element from which heavenly bodies were made. In medieval philosophy, quintessence was distinguished from the other four elements – earth, air, fire and water – but understood to be inherent in them. For alchemists the *quinta essentia* was synonymous with the *prima materia* or first matter, from which they believed the world was made and they tried to distil it from the other elements. The term has been used to refer to the base, foundation or essential nature of anything, including gods or God. For example there is a tradition in Hinduism that affirms the 'quintessence' of a god is a particular sound, sometimes the sound of the god's name and known as its seed syllable. They are sometimes represented at the pivotal centre of **mandalas**.

Qumran Community An ascetic Jewish community settled in a region northwest of the Dead Sea, 130 BCE–70 CE. See **Dead Sea Scrolls**, **Essenes**

Qur'an I. See **Koran**

Qur'an Alone Muslims See **Koran Alone Muslims**

Quraish I. An eminent Muslim tribe which, during the lifetime of Muhammad, was united by its leader Quasayy after whom it was named. They were centred on Mecca and were mostly successful merchants who controlled the region's trade routes. Muhammad was born into the Hashemite clan of the Quraish tribe. They have an entire chapter of the **Koran** (Surah 106) given over to them and today they are the honorary holders of the keys of the **Ka'bah**.

R

Ra or **Re** *E*. A sun-god cult centred on Heliopolis, the gods of which make up the **Ennead**. Ra was the creator god, with the sun either as his whole body or just his eye. The cult was at its most popular during the Old Kingdom (c.2686–c.2181) when Ra was elevated to the status of a national deity and universally worshipped as the king of the gods and father of all creation. Eventually the god **Atum**, the primordial creative force, became an aspect of Ra and combined to form the cult Ra-Atum. Solar beliefs continued throughout Egyptian history. Meaning 'mouth' in Egyptian, Ra, by the power of his speech, was believed to be the creator of the **Ogdoad** pantheon. He is depicted as a Pharaoh wearing the sun disc on his head. See **Egyptian Religion**

Rabbi *J*. Heb. In Judaism the term means 'teacher' or 'great one', 'great' referring to the extent of his knowledge. Thus originally, the title was given to those distinguished by their learning, specialists in the Law appointed to be the spiritual leaders of their community. A similar function is given to them today, the synagogue rabbis being know as 'pulpit rabbis' who represent their communities and offer guidance on all matters of Jewish religion. They are also involved in the rites of passage such as **bar mitzvahs**, marriages, etc., but are not essential for the observance of synagogue liturgy and congregations can flourish without a rabbi. In some **Chasidic** traditions the rabbi may not have been ordained, gaining their position by lineage or the reputation of their learning in **Halakah** and **Torah**. Within the Orthodox tradition only men may be rabbis, but Reform and Reconstructionist Judaism ordain women, although there is no formal requirement that either men or women should have *semicha* (ordination) in order to be accepted as a rabbi by the community. Most countries with an established Jewish community have Chief Rabbis as administrative heads of the Orthodox community.

Radha-Krishna *H*. The love story between Radha and Krishna permeates Hinduism as both a physical and transcendent ideal. Physically, their love is a figure of unity, the overcoming of all forms of duality; spiritually, it is a figure of the eternal play between the soul and God, which eventually leads to unity. The quest for unity is the theme of **Vaishnavism** and Bhakti-Yoga (see **Yoga**). Hinduism is consistent in affirming the spiritual heights achievable by the path of devotion and love. See **Krishna**

Radical Feminism A more radical form of the feminist movement that seeks complete emancipation from what they believe is exploitation by the male community. Some lesbian proponents represent an activist anti-male position. It has its place in various contemporary religious movements such as liberal Christianity, liberation **theology**, **Wicca**, goddess worship, New Age cults and **neo-paganism**. The range and diversity of these movements has resulted in widespread recruitment.

Radical Reformation The 16th-century reaction to the perceived corruption of both the Roman Catholic Church and the rapidly expanding **Protestant** movement. It was a grass-roots energy rising among the peasant classes of Germany and the Low Countries, which spawned denominations like the **Anabaptist**. These groups were frequently millenarian, holding to the imminent return of Christ and the end of the current age. Other groups that sprung up included the **Mennonites**, the **Amish** and **Hutterites**. See **Reformation**

Raelianism A UFO cult that offers its own doctrine of creation. Named from Rael, otherwise known as Claude Vorilhon (b.1946) a French journalist who believed that scientifically sophisticated aliens called Elohim created life on earth through genetic engineering. Earth was chosen, along with two other worlds, as a laboratory for their experiments with DNA. 'Elohim' was translated by Rael as, 'those who came from the sky', but there is no etymological support for this. Rael claimed to have been contacted by extra-terrestrials in the crater of an old volcano near Clermont-Ferrand in France. The **cult** believes that through a process of cloning, human beings can attain immortality through science. The process is based on the concept of continued evolution dramatically speeded-up by having human memory and personality backed up on silicon, then processed. The development and application of the technique is conditional on humanity outgrowing its tendency for aggression and violence. To assist with this there is an Order of Angels, an international group of women who are evangelists of femininity and refinement. Raelianism is classified by some as a religion, by others as a cult or UFO religion. It promotes doctrines of sexual self-discovery (sensual meditation) and the spirit of sharing and responsible living based on humanitarian values. Their main beliefs include the existence of infinite levels of life and an immaterial God, that humanity has entered the Age of the Apocalypse, that God and the DNA are the sources of life, that the Elohim will return and that an embassy must be built to welcome them. World government is to be based on humanitarianism and the leadership of geniuses, for which the term 'geniocracy' is used. It is thought that there are about 55,000 members across many countries with concentrations in France, Japan, Quebec and at various locations in the USA. See **Atherius Society, Chen Tao, Heaven's Gate, UFO Cults**

Ragnarok *AE.* 'The doom or twilight of the Gods'. In **Icelandic** and **Norse** mythology the occasion for this is the final battle at the end of the world, to be fought between the **Aesir**, the Norse pantheon led by **Odin**, and their traditional opponents the Jotuns or **Fire Giants**, together with various monsters led by **Loki**. Surt, one of the Fire Giants, sets the world (the land) alight and it sinks beneath sea, but rises again, fresh and rejuvenated with the tree, **Yggdrasil**. It is likely that this image of death and resurrection was influenced by early contact with Christian teaching. The source of the mythology is the Prose **Edda**.

Rainmaking The rituals of some primitive societies to induce rainfall by dances and forms of magic. The tradition is ancient and has its origins in the beginnings of human settlement, especially in those regions where rain was seasonal and life depended on its annual fall. The developing mythologies all had rain gods or sky gods, whose union with an earth goddess resulted in the rain that penetrated and fertilized the earth. In ancient Rome small figures or images were dropped into the Tiber to bring rain. Witches, medicine men and shamans have their own rain-making rituals. In countries where the rain is copious, for example, Java, ceremonies exist to prevent it and the medicine man may be asked to 'prop up the clouds that are lowering'. Rainmaking ceremonies are still practised. At a time of drought in Greece, children process around all the springs and wells of the region. In Romania, the Paparuda rain ritual is observed by a young girl wearing a skirt of vines, who dances through the village, stopping at each house where water is poured on her.

Rajah-Yoga *H*. Skt. 'the royal yoga'. One of the four principal yogic paths. See **Yoga**

Rajas *H*. Skt. 'striving' or 'restlessness'. One of the three *gunas*, or fundamental qualities of all objects in the manifest world of Hinduism. See **Sattva, Tamas**

Rajneesh Meditation A meditation technique based on the teachings of the Indian guru, Shree Rajneesh, established in the early 1970s. By means of 'dynamic meditation', a combination of breathing exercises and violent physical movement, individuals can harness 'bio-energy', something Rajneesh believed to be a basic to the life force of the cosmos. See **Bhagwan Shree Rajneesh**

Rakahs *I*. The various prostrations, postures or cycles used by Muslims when observing ritual prayer, combining the words with actions. The practice is particularly associated with the **Sufis**. The custom will vary according to the tradition, but in general a *rakahs* begins with the supplicant facing the **Qiblah** of the **mosque** which indicates the East, the direction of Mecca. He will then kneel and lean forward so the forehead touches the ground while he recites the prayers or verses from the **Koran**. He will then return to the kneeling position. Depending on the hour, two or four rakahs are required five times a day. See **Pillars of Islam, Salat**

Rama or **Ramachandra** *H*. or. Skt. An **avatar** and the seventh incarnation of Vishnu. His story appears briefly in the Mahabharata, but is fully told in the **Ramayana**. The mythology tells of Vishnu's manifestation as a response to an appeal for help from the gods who were in terror of the extraordinary powers of Rakshasa, king of Lanka. Rama and his wife **Sita** are worshipped by Hindus as the ideal husband and wife. The way Rama won Sita is familiar from legends and fairy stories of a suitor having to prove himself when courting a princess. Visiting King Janaka, he learned that whoever could string his bow which had belonged to Siva, would win his daughter. Rama strung the bow and broke it. The tale that follows is long and involved. The name Rama, is used in India as a common form of greeting, 'Ram! Ram!'

Ramadan *I*. The ninth month of the Islamic calendar year, during which Muslims have to abstain from food or drink of any kind during the hours of daylight. Exceptions are made for children and the sick. In the latter case, they would be expected to fast at a later date. The lunar calendar month is 11 or 12 days shorter than the solar year; for this reason, over approximately 33 years the fast is cycled through all the seasons. *Swam* (or *siyyam*), a fast, is the fourth obligation imposed on a Muslim by the **Pillars of Islam**.

Ramakrishna Paramahamsa (1836–86) *H*. One of the most significant and revered Hindu teachers. He taught that each individual's goal in life was God-realization, religion consists of this and has no other point or purpose. His meditation technique is known to Hindus as *nirvikalpa samadhi*, 'constant meditation' and absorption in the all-encompassing consciousness. The different religions simply represent the various ways to reach the Absolute and believing this, Ramakrishna spent a part of his life practising his own understanding of Christianity, Islam, Yogic and Tantric sects. He believed that wherever there was a living being there was **Siva**, and he taught his followers to practise 'not kindness to living beings, but serving the living being as Siva himself'. His key concepts were i) the oneness of existence; ii) the divinity of all living beings; iii) the unity of God and the harmony of all religions; iv) the main mental bondage in human life is lust and greed. His life and teaching did much to inspire the 19th-century Hindu renaissance in India.

Ramana Maharshi, Sri *H*. (1879–1950) A Hindu mystic who taught the method *Atma-Vishara*, self-enquiry, as the path to liberation. Other than for his teachings Ramana is celebrated for what he described as a life-changing experience that happened when he was 16. Alone in a room he had an intense and frightening experience of his imminent death which he attempted to examine objectively. His response is recorded by Sri Sadhu Om; 'Yes, death has come. Let it come. What is death? To whom does it come. To me. Who am I? What is it that is dying? Yes, it is the body that is dying. Let it die.' At which point he lay down on the floor and continued to examine what he believed to be the experience of dying. In this state he realized that he was other than the 'perishable body' and that what he was essentially was indestructible. His teachings are within the philosophical tradition of ***Advaita*** (non-duality. See **Dualism and Non-Dualism**) which seeks to free the mind of every perception that is 'not self', an enquiry that results in only the 'self' remaining. The self is hidden within five sheaths or *skandhas* (see **Five Aggregates**). The enquiry focuses on an intense consideration of the single question, 'Who am I?' Ramana, renowned for the completeness of his realization and the for the quality of his devout life, was one of India's most respected Indian masters. His teachings have gradually achieved worldwide recognition and as a result of the numbers seeking his guidance, an ashram developed around him at the holy hill of Arunchala.

Ramanuja. *H.* (1055–1137 CE) The renowned Tamil Brahmin, the philosopher of qualified non-dualism (see **Dualism and Non-Dualism**). He was concerned to draw Hindu philosophy away from the absolute and somewhat impersonal non-dualism (**Advaita-Vedenta**) of **Shankara** (788–820 CE) that was based on the 'way of knowledge'. Ramanuja promoted the alternative 'way of devotion'. Ramanuja perceived creation as a manifestation of the Absolute's personality and, as such, it expressed the need to love and to be loved. The implication of Ramanuja's philosophy is that our individual essence, **atman** or soul, once enlightened, is one with God, but also separate in its individuality. It is a qualified non-duality and it leaves open the possibility of relationship, thus giving to Hinduism attributes such as grace and devotion. See **Dvaita-Vedanta, Madhva**

Ramayana *H.* Skt. 'The Life Story of Rama' or 'The Adventures of Rama', an epic poem beginning with his boyhood and continuing until his reunion with his abducted wife, her death and his arrival in heaven. Written about four or five centuries BCE by the sage Valmiki, it is the oldest of the Sanskrit epic poems. There were several Bengalese revisions before the poem assumed its final form in the 2nd century BCE. It comprises 24,000 couplets arranged in 7 chapters. Next to the Mahabharata, it is the most important and influential poem in Indian literature and is much venerated. An introductory verse assures the reader that, 'He who reads and repeats this holy life-giving Ramayana is liberated from all his sins and exalted with all posterity in the highest heaven'.

Rastafari Movement A new religious movement that emerged in Jamaica in the 1930s amongst peasants and the working class. Its title is taken from the pre-coronation name of Haile Selassie, Ras Tafari. The movement is founded on the belief that Haile Selassie I, the former emperor of Ethiopia, is *Jah*, the Jehovah of the Old Testament and the promised messiah. The inspiration arises from a prophecy of the conquering Lion of Judah (Rev. 5.5) and the emperor having been the only African king. The energy behind the movement was Marcus Garvey's prophetic vision of black social and political advancement that gave the oppressed and underprivileged a new and optimistic world-view. Its doctrines include the promotion of pride in being black, the return to the primitive naturalism of their original African religious roots, to be seen in the dreadlocks, the use of marijuana and in eating *ital or* 'vital', meaning natural, pure, clean foods. Haile Selassie will one day call the Day of Judgement when the righteous will return to Mt Zion, located in Africa. The scene is confused, because of groups observing practices very similar to those of the Jews, a cultural anomaly accounted for by slaves who converted to

Judaism (see **Black Jews, Nation of Yahweh**). Rastas believe in a post-death physical survival through the reconstitution of the body; their bodies are thus the 'temple of the living Lord' and the Movement has no need of church buildings. The term 'ever living' is used in preference to 'ever lasting'. A famous cultural flowering of Rastafari is its reggae music, notably that of Bob Marley. Most Rastas are vegetarian and those eating meat do so in strict accordance with the 'kosher' dietary laws of Leviticus and Deuteronomy. In principle they are against homosexuality, but attitudes to this vary. Some authorities cite the Rastafari movement as an example of **emperor worship**.

Rasul *l*. Arab. 'a prophet'. See **Nabi**

Ratana Church Thought to be the largest syncretistic **Maori** cult, it was founded in 1918 by Wiremu Ratana (1873–1939) who was known as 'Mangai', the mouthpiece of God. Ratana rejected some old Maori traditions, such as carving, tribalism and the practices of the shamanistic Tohunga priest and their use of magic. After the First World War Ratana became known as a faith-healer and spiritual leader and in 1925 his followers formed the new Church, breaking from the established Churches. In 1930 Ratana allied itself to the New Zealand labour party and their combined membership dominated the Maori seats in parliament until the 1990s. Ratana remains active both as a religion and as a significant political force that has its headquarters at Ratana, near Wanganui.

Rationalism Theories of knowledge such as those of **Plato**, **Descartes**, **Spinoza** and **Leibnitz** are classed as 'rationalist' because they assert that by applying 'reason alone', we can acquire reliable knowledge of the nature of what exists. Rationalism thus stands over against experience (see **Empiricism**) especially when associated to religion, for which reason it has always been linked with the 'scientific method' and the comforting notion that everything is explicable. Reason builds on '**innate ideas**', the pool of knowledge with which, some assert, we are born; this, together with what we learn rationally, amounts to the real world. Generally, rationalism is the rejection of religious beliefs simply because they are held to be irrational and the debate is therefore frequently cast as being between reason and faith. Other presumed sources of knowledge, such as custom and superstition are also abandoned. Rationalism challenges religious belief, not the least because it encourages people to think for themselves (see **Free Thinkers**). It follows that most rationalists are atheists or agnostics, who may be adherents of rationalism's sister movement, **humanism**. Nevertheless, Descartes managed to use reason to prove (for himself) the existence of God and according to Blaise **Pascal** (1596–1650), God enabled human beings to know truth by means of reason. See **Enlightenment, The**; **Freethinkers**
FINAL WORD: 'Surely you don't believe in gods? Where are your arguments? What is your proof?' (Aristophanes)

Re c.2480 BCE, at the time of the Egyptian Old Kingdom, the cult of Re, the sun god, reached its zenith at Heliopolis, being in partnership with the Pharaoh king. While Re, the sun ruled the heavens, the Pharaoh ruled the earth. The cult influenced the liturgies of the temples (see **Mansions of the Gods**). When the Old Kingdom collapsed and the cult lost its royal patronage, solar-related beliefs continued with, for example, the cult of **Amun**, which eventually combined with Re to form Amun-Re, which became so powerful that Egypt was, effectively, **theocracy**. See **Akhenaton, Egyptian Religion**

Realization A term much used in some religions to refer to the discovery of a truth which, when experienced, transforms a mental concept or ideal, into an enduring conviction, however 'inner' or subjective this may be. Such realization is usually gained by means of inward contemplation and meditation since the truth to be realized is itself, indwelling and inherent in human spiritual potential. Frequently the general concept is more clearly focused as **self-realization**, in the sense that the truth sought is the **quintessence** of the person seeking it. This is not the same as the ego, which is the receptor of constantly changing impressions that associate every sense experience with the 'I' or 'me'. Because these impressions are in a constant state of flux, they are unreliable and insecure. In the religions of realization, what is to be ascertained is the *unchanging* self or the 'true' self. In **Hinduism** this is called '**Atman**', while the unchanging essence of the universe is **Brahman**. What is to be realized through practices of **yoga** and **meditation**, is the union of the two which affords, for the individual, the experience of being perfectly in union with the whole cosmos. A similar concept is to be found in other Eastern religions such as **Buddhism** and **Taoism**. Religions of 'realization' are to be distinguished from the biblically-based religions of the West, which are religions of '**revelation**', in which the truth or message is revealed by God. Without the revelation the truth remains inaccessible. Unfortunately, the concept of realization has virtually been made a commodity in the West, spawning a huge number of societies that offer forms yoga, tai chi, chi kung and various types of meditation, supported by a massive market and its associated literature. Among these there are, undoubtedly, genuine and properly authorized teachers, but the seeker must tread very warily in search of them.

Rebirthing A New Age term for practices that enable the participant to rid themselves of negative **karma**, trauma, anxieties and problems by being taken back to the womb and re-enacting the drama of their birth experience or previous births in former reincarnations. Techniques include hypnosis, '**transpersonal psychology**', the use of warm baths, forms of psychoanalysis and dream analysis.

Recusancy X. A refusal by English Catholics to attend the services of the Church of England. In 1558, Queen Elizabeth I succeeded her Catholic sister Mary and immediately re-established the Protestant Anglican

Church, making attendance compulsory by the 1559 Act of Uniformity. The Laws defined recusancy (from the Latin *recusare*, 'to refuse') as a refusal to submit to authority. From 1570 to 1791, the laws were aimed at English Catholics. In 1580, the arrival of the Jesuits from the continent gave the recusants a powerful impetus. Recusancy was considered to be a potentially dangerous problem because of its roots in the social structure of certain regions for example, in the north of England and heavy fines were imposed. Following the Catholic Relief Act of 1791, the refusal to attend Anglican services ceased to be a crime, but Roman Catholics continued to suffer restrictions and prejudice.

Redaction Criticism An important new branch of biblical literary criticism that attempts to understand the purposes of the 'redactors', the anonymous editors, compilers and revisers of the texts. The original editors shaped the form and emphasis of books of the Bible, particularly the Gospels. Whereas **form criticism** tries to discern the literary styles, forms and origins of specific passage, redaction criticism is concerned to understand what the uses and intentions of those passages were, so as to convey the meaning of the book as a whole. If the editor of the book in question used different sources, why was one source used or emphasized more than another? Presumably, the answer is that the editor wanted to emphasize certain events and theological concepts over against others; his selection was guided by his intention. Redaction criticism creates a problem for evangelical scholars who may feel that redaction criticism might undermine the spiritual inerrancy of the text. See **Higher Criticism**, **Source Criticism**, **Textual Criticism**

Redemption Deliverance from sin and its consequences. Redemption is a concept associated with monotheistic religions that support a doctrine of a Redeemer or Messiah. In Judaism, redemption is associated with the **covenant** that established a special relationship between God and his 'Chosen People', Israel. Given Israel's faithfulness to the covenant, a historical redemption will be initiated by the coming of the Messiah, the consequences of which will be the return of the Jews of the Diaspora to the Land of Israel, the restoration of the Temple, the resurrection of the dead and the Final Judgement. The actual nature and sequence of these events varies according to the different traditions of, for example, **Chasidism**, **Kabbalah**, the 16th-century revivalism of Safed Messianism and Rabbinic thought. The intensity of the Jewish messianic longing is, without doubt, based in Judaism's history of exile, diaspora and the sufferings brought about by persecution. Redemption in Christianity is by faith in Jesus Christ who effected **atonement** for his followers by the vicarious sacrifice of his life. The absolution for past sins is available to anyone who is 'justified by faith'. It is synonymous with salvation and on the basis of the doctrine of original sin, everyone stands in need of redemption. There is no clear concept of redemption in Islamic **eschatology**. The Koran does not offer a doctrine of original sin as a barrier between humanity and Allah. There is a concept of sin but Allah, who is supremely merciful will forgive any sin, large or small, so long as the sinner repents. More importantly for the Muslim is obedience to the **Pillars of Islam**, that is the measure of a man's righteous standing before Allah. Repentance as Judaism and Christianity understand it, seems of less importance in Islam, except for the sin of unbelief. For Allah to forgive that a person must repent.

Redemptorists *X*. The common name for the 'Congregation of the Most High Holy Redeemer', founded by St Alphonsus Liguori in 1732. He lived in period marked by **scepticism**, and believed the rigours of the confessional discouraged rather than encourage sinners. He set out his moral theology in his famous *Theologia Moralis*. The Congregation's mission was to work among the poor and heathen of Europe.

Red Power Movement *Ami*. Gathering momentum during the heydays of the 1960s, Red Power was an Amerindian political movement concerned to recover territories lost to the colonizing Westerners. It became associated with a civil rights quest similar to that of Black Power. Many of the protagonists, however, came from urban ghettos and not from the traditional Indian reservations. The Movement first gathered momentum in the State of Minneapolis in 1968, from where it developed into a pan-American force. The civil rights campaign carried with it a revival of Indian culture and indigenous religion. See **Amerindian Religion, Peyote Cults, Sweat Lodge, Vision Quest**

Reductionism In general a method of explaining a complex concept or series of facts by an alternative simpler idea or set. In science, it is a way of understanding the complexity of the whole by examining smaller parts of it. Richard Dawkin's *The Selfish Gene*, offers the example of reductionist science by arguing that all of life and human behaviour can be understood from a study of genetics. In philosophy it requires that certain **rationalist** or **empiricist** conditions must be met if an assertion is to be meaningful. Reductionism presupposes that these conditions have not been met by traditional accounts of religion. However, the reductionist is quite happy to put the matter right by analysing and re-writing rationally incomprehensible texts in such a way as to satisfy the conditions required by either rationalism or empiricism. Reductionism has had its greatest influence on philosophical theologians whose concern has been to extrapolate what is essential to a religion. Thus, for example, did **Feuerbach** and **Buber**'s reductionism 'reduce' theology to anthropology. In Christian theology this led to the radical programme of demythologizing. See **Bonhoeffer, Demythology, Tillich**

Reformation *X*. A term loosely covering far-reaching changes in Western Christendom during the 16th and 17th centuries. It is usually thought to have begun with Martin **Luther**'s attack on the corruption of Rome and abuses associated with the selling of indulgences in 1517. In fact Luther was not really breaking new ground, since the Great Schism and the

conciliar movement had already weakened the authority of the **papacy**. The energy for the Reformation did not come from innovation, but from a desire to return to the original model of the early Church in which faith, rather than works, was the measure of a person's spirituality. Such reforming thought raised doubts about papal authority and supremacy and brought about attacks on doctrines such as transubstantiation (see **Eucharist**) and the celibacy of the clergy. There was a demand in Germany for the abolition of papal power and for a reform of the religious order. By 1530, the princes of Saxony, Hesse, Brandenburg and Brunswick, as well as the Kings of Denmark and Sweden were won over to the reformers cause and they assumed responsibility for the administration of their own Churches on Lutheran principles. In Switzerland, the prime mover was **Zwingli** in Zurich, followed by John Calvin in Geneva. **Calvinism** became the main reforming energy in Western Germany, France, Holland and Scotland. All the Reformation's doctrinal, clerical and ecclesiastical principles were linked with political controversy and social upheaval, leading to a permanent split in Western Christendom. The English Reformation was insular and apart from the main movement, at least to begin with. The papal power was overthrown by Henry VIII and one of its more visible results was the dissolution of the monasteries. Henry's clear objective was the extension of monarchical sovereignty over every aspect of English life. In the 16th century there were further movements to reform termed the '**Radical Reformation**' based on **millenarianism**, **fundamentalism** and a rigorous morality. The post-Reformation revival of the **Roman Catholic Church** was progressed by the **Counter-Reformation**, and led by the **Jesuits**. See **Wycliffe**

Refrigerium L. 'refreshment'. A rather odd use of the word by Latin-speaking Christians, to describe the wonder and everlasting happiness that awaits the faithful in heaven. 'Refreshing coolness' was something to be desired, perhaps in contradistinction to the 'fires of hell'. The need of the dead for cool water is recorded in the Egyptian Pyramid and Coffin Texts compiled c.2500BC (see **Funerary Practices**). The Epic of **Gilgamesh** describes the dead feeding on dust and clay and in urgent need of water. In excessively hot countries it was believed thirst and heat were as unpleasant and undesirable in death, as in life. Thirst has been used as a metaphor for being spiritually parched and Jesus offered 'water' which if drunk, would quench thirst for ever (John 4:13–14). Images of rivers, cool streams and fountains abound in the eschatological writings of many religions, perhaps the most impressive of which occurs in the **New Testament**, at the end of the vision in Revelation, 'Then he showed me the river of the water of life, sparkling like crystal, flowing from the throne of God and of the Lamb ...Come forward, you who are thirsty; accept the water of life, a free gift to all who desire it' (Rev. 20:1–2, 17).

Refuges, Three *B*. The **Buddha**, the **Dharma** and the **Sangha**. See **Three Jewels**

Reincarnation Literally, 'to be made flesh again'. The belief in some religions that the individual **quintessence**, the **soul** or **divine spark** will, after physical death, be reborn in a new body. The eschatology of biblical religions includes the hope of physical resurrection on the day of Final Judgement. Some traditions speak of a new body, presumably because of the demise of the original one, thus implying a form of reincarnation. In Eastern thought the personal survival of 'self' does not carry the same sense of substance, it being part of the greater illusion that clouds our perception of the truth of things as they really are. The goal is to break out of the suffering cycle of *samsara*, a process which for both Hinduism and Buddhism may take innumerable reincarnations. The cycle of rebirth continues until, by means of **enlightenment**, there is a final death after which reincarnation no longer occurs. It is likely that the concept came to ancient Greece from Egypt or by contact with Hindus; either way, in the 6th century BCE, reincarnation featured in Orphism and Pythagoras was its most famous philosophical exponent. The Old Testament and Rabbinic writings are silent on the subject, but it is a feature of Jewish mysticism (see **Chasidism**, **Kabbalah**, **Zohar**). Except in fringe denominations like the Liberal Catholic Church and the Rosicrucian Fellowship, Christianity staunchly rejects reincarnation and other than some Sufi groups so does mainstream Islam. Yet in this respect Islam seems to be ambivalent, since the Koran assures us that 'God generates beings and sends them back over and over again, till they return to Him'. See **Immortality**, **Metempsychosis**
FINAL WORD: 'I died as a mineral and became a plant, I died as a plant and rose to animal, I died as an animal and I was man. Why should I fear? When was I less by dying?' (Rumi, 13th-century Islamic poet)

Relativism An important, but somewhat general term in philosophy that recognizes that any statement about truth or a moral value, is not absolute, but will vary according to circumstances, historical and social tradition and the laws, customs and mores of a society. Its application is usually in conjunction with other disciplines like anthropology and the sociology of knowledge. Thus, in trying to understand the beliefs, functions and social meaning of a religion, the relativist will consider its use of language and the way its meaning may have changed within an evolving culture, since the original use of a word or phrase. What may have been accepted as a literal truth at an earlier stage of that culture's development, might, at a later stage be understood to have been a myth, now interpreted for its spiritual, rather than literal content. Relativism, therefore, both recognizes and qualifies the subjectivism of belief. The most general criticism of relativism is that it leads to a form of 'believe what you like, anything goes' religion and in society to anarchy, since a relativist view of rules or laws makes it impossible for them to be universally implemented. On the other hand, it is argued that for 'man to come of age', relativism is needed since only an 'immature' religion will rely on inviolable creeds and dogmas and only an immature society will require a rigid framework of extensive law to ensure its stability. Relativism, both in religion and life, assumes that people are sufficiently mature to accept responsibility for their beliefs and their actions and sufficiently tolerant to live with what may be radical differences of opinion. See **Spinoza**

Religion A notoriously difficult term to define with any kind of precision. It has an obscure etymology with a range of suggested meanings that include 'reverence', 'to bind', 'reconnect', 'to link', 'to gather together' or to 'give careful consideration to'. **Wittgenstein** advised that the meaning of a word is best discovered by asking how it is used, thus for 'religion' we can say:

It is used to refer to the teachings and philosophy of a movement that asserts there is a God, gods or other spiritual beings responsible for creating and sustaining the multifarious forms of life and the universe.

It is used to imply a system of God-given destiny or fate, revealed or realized, that controls the course and purpose of human life.

It is used to refer to doctrines and creeds that are statements of belief which initiate or invite a spiritual quest leading from a defined starting point and continuing to an ultimate goal or destiny to be attained in an afterlife.

It is used to refer to the belief systems of institutions that aid the adherent in reaching the desired development, achievement or consummation, such as salvation or enlightenment and which are held to be indispensable to the fulfilment of their declared goals.

It is used of institutions who hold to a Divine authority intended to be administered through a hierarchy, which has special powers, responsibilities and disciplines that govern or influence society.

Religion is not satisfactorily defined by any one of these usages and, probably, not even by an addition of them, since exceptions can always be found and qualifications made. What is apparent, is that religion fulfils certain functions which may be summarized as: i) a way of accounting for the origins of the universe; ii) a means of understanding the purpose of human life and destiny; iii) the need to account for and come to terms with evil and suffering; iv) the ground for a hope of life beyond death; v) an authority for a pattern of life or ethical code; vi) a focus or cohesive force which binds groups of people together; and vii) a means by which the individual can connect with the 'ground of his being' and thus feel part of a reality that is not transient but transcendent.

In practice these usages or functions may take the precise form which at one extreme is of a life bound by monastic rule or at the other, a broad pattern of faithfulness and devotion to some undefined ultimate principle. Each religion offers goals to be achieved by means peculiar to its tradition and provides answers to perennial questions such as the meaning of life and the way to ascertain its purpose. By far the most significant preoccupation of religion is the fear or mystery of death and what lies beyond it. The 'path' implies a journey or quest, a progression from whatever perception the religion has of the meaning of life, to an ideal conception of that life which may include a doctrine of **reincarnation**, or of life continuing after death in some ultimately perfect place (see **Heaven**). All religions offer copious guidance on how to walk the path so as to arrive at the desired destination. The conditions for achieving this vary hugely; they may be stated precisely as in a **creed**, or take the form of vague inner principles based on subjective experience. Within these wide terms of reference a bewildering variety of religions have appeared represented by the major traditions and the countless denominations, sects and cults spawned by them, together with their **secular** alternatives. See **Existentialism, Origin of Religion, Secularism**

FINAL WORD: 'This is my simple religion. There is no need for temples; no need for complicated philosophy. Our own brain, our own heart is our temple; the philosophy is kindness.' (H. H. The Dalai Lama)

'Religious discourse is a distinct language game or use of language which neither has nor needs any justification outside of itself.' (Wittgenstein)

Religion of the Light and Sound of God See **Eckankar**

Religion, Philosophy of See **Philosophy of Religion**

Religion, Psychology of See **Psychology of Religion**

Religion, Sociology of See **Sociology of Religion**

Religionswissenschaft An addition of disciplines concerned to examine scientifically the history of religion and comparative religion. (See for example, **Scientific Study of Judaism**.) What is important for the objective study of religion, is that to understand the function of religion within society and its determining effect on the development of culture, the techniques of several complementary disciplines are needed. These will include history, the sociology of religion, anthropology, linguistics and philosophy. See **Phenomenology of Religion, Science of Religion**

Religious Existentialism Existentialism or the philosophy of existence, concerned as it is with meaning *in* existence, is customarily inclined to a non-religious interpretation. Religion traditionally defines God as being both eternal and unchanging, but the standard proofs of the existence of such a Being (see **Arguments for the Existence of God**) succeed only in establishing the logic of the argument, not the reality of God's existence. Alternatively the claim is made that God exists because people have experienced Him (see **Empiricism**), but the problem here is that the experiences we have are within time and constantly changing, thus we are not experiencing an eternal and unchanging Being. Further to this, if God is to be experienced here and now, He would have to be part of our history which again is in time and in flux. Thus, 'If one believed that God existed in time, that God was able to act in human historical situations, one would be believing something that is logically absurd' (Popkin and Stroll). **Existentialism** has become associated with themes such as anxiety, dread, our knowledge of our mortality and with concepts of freedom. The existentialist perception of 'being' is similar to that of Buddhism's *dukkha*, suffering, the difference being that existentialism offers no solution to an existence of anxiety, whereas Buddhism moves its adherents towards nirvana (see **Four Noble Truths**). In the modern period, Kierkegaard set the pace for an existentialist understanding of religion, by conceding that the universe was paradoxical and that the free choices we are responsible for making are the condition of individual transcendence; it is by such choices that individuals make up the 'structure' of their existence. **Kierkegaard**'s 'leap of faith' was later followed by Paul **Tillich** whose 'ground of being' was a definition of God, and Dietrich **Bonhoeffer** whose search for a new religious language gave rise to religionless Christianity and the concept of a 'world come of age', which can dispense with much of the religion's mythological impedimenta.

Religious Humanism A form of **humanism** which while disavowing traditional and institutional forms of religion remains **theistic** or **deistic**, or which holds, in some way, to there being a supernatural dimension to human experience. The term may also apply to those who believe the essence of a religion is it ethics and that while this ethical system forms a framework for their lives and that of their society, they see no reason to presume that it has a divine source. Thus religious humanism allows a philosophy of self-fulfilment within, for example, the framework of Jewish or Christian principles. It makes religion a personal affair and a personal responsibility. See **Buddhism, Humanistic, Judaism, Humanistic, Secular Humanism**

Religious Science See **Science of Mind**

Reliquary A container such as a glass case or coffer, for displaying and keeping relics. In Christian usage, the contents are sometimes claimed to be pieces of the original Cross or relics of the actual body parts of saints or sacred objects associated with them. They are traditionally heavily decorated with jewels, set in gold or silver and engraved. Martin **Luther** opposed their use, claiming it to be idolatrous. Most of the world's religions have reliquaries. They have secular counterparts such as the mausoleum housing the embalmed body of **Lenin**. In general use, memorial portraits or sculptures serve to make a connection between the viewer and the person represented and hair cut from the head of a deceased person might be a 'keep-safe' reminder. See **Shrine**
FINAL WORD: 'Reliquaries are commonly of metal and provided with a lock to prevent the contents from coming out and performing miracles at unseasonable times' (Ambrose Bierce)

Ren *E*. One of the five constituents of the Egyptian concept of the soul. See **Soul, Egyptian**

Renaissance Humanism An intellectual attitude that coloured the philosophy of Renaissance Europe and which has had a lingering effect. Renaissance man inhabited a kind of cultural no-man's land between a medieval world-view and the coming of scientific rationalism. Here he lived in the tension between faith and reason where secular and humanistic concepts could be freely developed and where Providence as predestined fate, gave way to Fortune as chance and unpredictable future. What emerged was a burgeoning confidence in human potential inspired by the recovery of Classical philosophy and culture. Although the emphasis was on what man as man could achieve, the movement was not incompatible with religious belief but his was construed as partnership with, rather than servitude to the Divine (see **Humanism**).

Resurgent Atavism The reversion of people in the modern era to the beliefs and practices of ancient religion. Decline of traditional religions has resulted in the search for alternatives among ancient practices and beliefs such as nature religions, magic, the occult and Wicca. Aspects of these are thought to be original, the first intuitive response of humanity to the environment and the cycles of nature and human life. See **Atavism, Germanic Religion, New Age Religion**

Resurrection The belief that after death, a physical resurrection of the body will take place prior to a Final Judgement. In Christianity the precedent is the resurrection of Jesus and the various texts and references that offer the hope of a similar resurrection for his followers. Resurrection accounts feature in many religions including for example, the Greek cult of Adonis and the Egyptian cult of Osiris. Islam holds to the doctrine of *Qiyama*, which orthodoxy understand in physical terms, but which modern interpreters suggest is a spiritual concept. There are also accounts of actual resurrection occurrences; Paramahansa **Yogananda** tells how the guru Lahiri Mahasaya brought Rama back to life after he had died from cholera. Resurrection should not be confused with either **immortality** or **reincarnation**.

Revelation The communication of a message, instructions or information by a god or God to human beings. The biblically-based religions have knowledge of God only because it has been disclosed to human beings by him. Orthodox and fundamentalist adherents claim that revelation is the only way to get access to ultimate truth and that once it is received it is inviolable. God's revelation is recorded in the Bible, the 'Word' of God, which becomes the ultimate standard and authority in all matters of faith. There have been numerous claims made by people to have been the recipient of special, divine revelation, for example Joseph Smith, who on the strength of the revelation given, founded the Church of the Latter Day Saints (see **Mormons**). 'Revelation', the last book in the New Testament, is an account of the revelation God received by Jesus, communicated to John by an angel so that it could be recorded. The perennial debate is about whether or not revelation is fixed, in the sense that it was disclosed in a final form or whether it can be added to or modified by subsequent revelations. Many contemporary theologians, among them the Jewish philosopher Martin **Buber**, believe revelation to be evolutionary, with a life of its own and something that grows and continues. Those that hold to the latter view have distanced themselves from a fixed received tradition, interpreting revelation simply as the response of certain people of a particular time, to certain kinds of experience. Islam holds to the notion of an immutable revelation received by Muhammad and recorded in the Koran. Eastern religions do not give much importance to the concept of revelation, since there is no concept of a 'revealer'. Rather, truth is disclosed by special insight or **realization**.

Revitalization Movement *Ami*. A modern energy in **Amerindian religion** that seeks to throw off the influences of contemporary life, **secularism** and assimilation so as to recover the original, indigenous beliefs and cultic practices of the various tribes. Some of the forms these cults take are heavily syncretistic, due probably to the intermingling an inter-marriage of tribal groups. See **Peyote Cults**, **Red Power Movement**, **Sweat Lodge**, **Vision Quest**

Revivalism *X*. A type of intense, often ecstatic form of worship caused by evangelical fervour supported by intense preaching and prayer. The international Evangelical Revival, which began in the 1720s, involved the **German Moravians**, the **English Methodists**, **Anglicans** and Evangelicals. In America the 'Great Awakening' was led by Jonathan Edwards (1705–58) who combined **Calvinism** with the **natural theology** of John **Locke**. Revivalism is characterized by inward religion with an emphasis made on the subjective experience of being 'born again' in Jesus Christ. In England, intense inward religious excitement has usually been associated with the artisan and working class, but also touched the upperclass with groups such as the 'Clapham sect' led by William Wilberforce who campaigned against slavery. In 19th-century America revivalism was led by Moody and Sanky, followed in the 20th century by evangelists such as Billy Graham, who travelled the world. Revivalism has had more influence and success in America, claiming to have brought about social reforms. In England it has been more muted, due mainly to the established Anglican Church, being somewhat unresponsive. See **Pietism**

Rhea In Greek mythology, Rhea was the mother of the gods, the daughter of **Uranus** and **Gaia**. She is identified with the mother goddess, **Cybele**, from Asia Minor, known also as Magna Mater, the 'Great Mother'. Her worship sometimes included orgiastic rites. See **Earth Mother**, **Environmentalism**

Rifa'is *I*. An order of **Sufi dervishes**, mostly of the Arab Middle East, but found also in Turkey and the Balkans. They trace their origin to the 12th-century pious Sheik Amid al-Rifa'i, a descendent of **Muhammad**. Known as the 'howling' dervishes, they cut and pierce themselves with needles and knives. Their practice is based on a story of al-Rifa'i being touched by the hand of Muhammad while make the hajj, in response to which people who had witnessed this wounded themselves in ecstasy, only to be healed by the sheik. Thus, the Rifa'is *tariqah or* path, has always been associated with healing. See **Dervish, Murid, Tariqah**

Right-handed Path An identification of any religious 'way' that elevates the spiritual above the carnal, in contradistinction to left-handed religions that glorify self and personal power. In some accounts the right-handed path is associated with white magic and the left-handed with black magic, this demarcation is, however, thought to be far too narrow. Both paths have their origin in Western occultism, the names having been introduced either by the **theosophists, shamanism** or **Satanism**, or through influences from each of these. Rudolph **Steiner**, (see **Anthroposophy**) affirmed that the right-handed path is a manifestation of the Christ-impulse, 'based upon very demanding and time-consuming moral purification of body, soul and spirit and the cultivation of total harmlessness and unconditional selfless love toward all living creatures'. See **Left-Handed Path**

Rig-Veda *H*. Skt. 'The Divine Knowledge'. Thought to be the most ancient of the four Vedic anthologies (see **Vedas**) probably compiled between the 12th and 8th centuries BCE. As such, it takes its place among the oldest Indian literature. It is a vast composition of 1,028 hymns arranged in ten song cycles or **mandalas**, some of which take their names from the **rishi** thought to be its author. Originally they were sung or recited by a chief priest at sacrificial rites, as an invitation to the gods to accept the sacrifice. One complete cycle of verses of the Rig-Veda is concerned entirely with **soma** and soma sacrifice.

Ringatu *P*. The 'Upraised Hand'. A syncretistic **Maori** cult founded in 1833 by Te Kooti Rikirangi. While in prison he studied the Bible, concentrating on the Psalms and the books of Joshua and Judges. He converted other prisoners and, like Moses, led them to freedom, escaping by commandeering the schooner *Rifleman*. Eventually the community settled near Poverty Bay. Ringatu is a calm, dignified religion, the services of which are based on the Old Testament. Originally a protest against European colonialism, Ringatu is now an indigenous Christian Church.

Rinzai Zen *Z*. One of the most significant schools of **Zen** Buddhism (Chinese, Ch'an). It was founded in Japan during the Kamakura period in the 11th century CE by a Chinese master with the Japanese name, Rinzai Gigen. Early in its development the school split into two lineages, Rinzai Oryo which has not survived and Rinzai Yogi which still functions in

Japan. Rinzai places particular importance on **koan** practice as an intense, fast-track to **enlightenment**, Jap. *kensho* or *satori*. See **Soto School**

Rishi *H.* Skt. A broad term referring to seers or inspired poets. More specifically the term is used of the seven *rishis* inspired to write the **Vedas**. A Thai form of the word means an ascetic hermit.

Rish'o Koseikai *B.* Jap. A modern Buddhist folk movement of Japan. See **Japanese Religion**

Rita *H.* Skt. 'truth', 'divine order'. The Hindu conception of the living truth that emanates from the divine. Also, Vedic term for the principle of cosmic-ethical interdependence. See **Vedas**

Rite A solemn procedure or observance, that may or may not be religious. Religious rites have almost certainly been practised since human beings made their first wondering response to the environment and the forces of nature (see **Numinous**). Examples include the Christian rite of **baptism**, the fertility and initiatory rites of ancient nature religions and those of Masonic lodges, such as the York or Scottish rite. See **Ritual**

Rites of Passage The religious ceremonies associated with the formative moments of life, usually birth, initiation, puberty, marriage and death. The rites were first distinguished by van Gennep, a Flemish anthropologist whose book *Les Rites des Passages* was published in 1909. The forms and practices associated with these rites vary according to the religions and cults performing them and the variety is endless. Perhaps the most familiar are the rites that initiate a person into a religion or into adulthood, such as the baptism of Christians, the bar mitzvah of the Jews, the **Navjote** of the Zoroastrians and the **Amritsankar** of the Sikhs. African tribal religions observe rites of initiation which for both sexes may require circumcision; boys with be put through trials of pain and strength to prove their manhood, girls will be prepared for marriage and domestic duty.

Ritual The prescribed order or method for the performance of **rites**, whether religious or not. In religion, ritual amounts to the set forms of worship or liturgies officially prescribed by the Book of Common Prayer, for the Anglican Church or the Missal of Catholicism which gives the *Ordo Missae*. Ritual is also an integral part of secular life to be seen in the proceedings of Parliament and various military and civic routines. The term has become confused with 'ceremonial', and someone may be dubbed a 'ritualist' for being pedantically concerned with ceremonial procedure. In everyday use we make rituals out of anything that becomes a habit, something repeatedly done at regular intervals. See **Ritual Magic**

Ritual Magic Usually very precise and complicated sequences of the words, objects and actions used to summon up powerful spirits or a spiritual force so as to harness and direct it. The **grimoire**, the manuals of ritual magic available to practitioners, give exact instructions for making love potions, **charms**, **talismans** and the like, but their main concern is to give instruction into the complicated and lengthy rituals for invoking spirits. The complicated detail of magical rituals is, perhaps, their most striking feature and almost certainly a means of making it virtually impossible for the uninitiated to practise the art. The instructions 'are certainly calculated to deal the death-blow to any notions harboured by intended practitioners that magic is a short cut to their desires' (E. M. Butler).

Roman Catholicism X. A Christian denomination denoting the faith and practice of those who are in communion with the Pope. The term has been used of Catholics since the **Reformation** so as to distinguish them from the Protestant churches. The Roman Church takes its authority from Jesus Christ through the Apostle Peter who was the first bishop of Rome (see **Papacy**). With **Orthodoxy** and **Protestantism**, Catholicism represents one of three major Christian traditions. Sine the Reformation and the **Council of Trent** (1545–63), Catholic theologians have concentrated on the structure and authority of the Church, the role of the Virgin **Mary** in the process of salvation and the function of the papacy. The Church's religious life was enriched by the **Counter-Reformation** and the establishment of new orders such as the **Jesuits**, who spearheaded a missionary initiative that carried the faith to every part of the world. In more recent time the Church has shown increasing interest in the **Ecumenical Movement**, but has stopped short of full participation.

Roman Religion The Romans did not have a narrative mythology until their poets began to borrow from Greek models during the 1st century BCE, the later years of the Republic. The basis for ancient Roman religion was a complex, interlocking pattern of relationships between the gods and human beings held together by a highly organized system of rituals, priestly colleges and a hierarchical grouping of the gods. Originally, religion was based on rural, animistic traditions, the belief that individual spirits or gods called *numina*, were responsible for aspects of the cosmos as well as for ordinary human occupations such as ploughing. This practical interest is exemplified by the god **Janus** and **Vesta** guarding the door and hearth, respectively. In addition the Romans worshipped the *Lares Familiares*, family guardian spirits or ancestors, each family honouring its own gods and observing their own rites (see **Paterfamilias**). Two types of god were distinguished, the original gods of the Roman State (*Des Indigetes*) and the later divinities (*novensides*) whose cults were introduced when the need for them arose. Thus what we have is not a pantheism, but a polydemonism in which the gods were invoked by name, calling them to perform certain functions. These were practical, serviceable gods, not emanations to which one could relate personally. The early pantheon was headed by the triad **Jupiter**, **Mars** and Quirinus, whose priests were called *flamens*. This triad was eventually replaced by the Capitoline Triad Jupiter, **Juno** and **Minerva**, which assumed the supreme place in Roman religion. To this pattern can be added the worship of **Diana** on the Aventine Hill and the introduction of the **Sibylline books**, prophecies of world history. During the period of the Roman Republic (c.510–c.27 BCE) the fixed hierarchy of priests was headed by the **Pontifex Maximus**, with the *flamens* supervising the cults and augers responsible for the omens.

It was during the late Republic and early Empire that many of the Greek gods and their cults were assimilated into Roman practice and given Roman names (see **Pantheon, Greek** and **Pantheon, Roman**). This assimilation of foreign gods resulted in a decline of the priesthood and the old rites, but offered a new, anthropomorphic perception of the gods. There was a shift to Imperial centralization of religion due to the deification of the emperor and in **emperor worship**, which amounted to a State religion. It was celebrated, for example, on Roman coinage showing the emperor sporting a halo. Inevitably, with the expansion of empire, more and more foreign religions were assimilated and grew in popularity such as Egypt's **Isis** and Persia's **Mithras**. Especially in the vicinity of Rome, the ancient cults and their traditions of worship continued to thrive, together with old festivals such as **Lupercalia** and **Saturnalia**. Christianity, which despite heavy persecution, gained converts and was finally officially supported by Constantine. In 391 CE the edict of the Emperor Theodosius I, prohibited all the cults except Christianity.

Romanticism An overwhelming energy which overran Europe at the end of the 18th and the beginning of the 19th century. It was a reaction to the established influences of neoclassicism and rationalism. The movement, which touched, irrevocably, every aspect of European culture, had its beginnings in France with **Rousseau** and in Germany with the *Sturm und Drang* literature of the late 18th century and with **Kant**'s idealism. It was a breaking out of the restraints of classical formalism, a freeing of the imagination so that it could explore and express man's relationship to nature, in which it revelled. It had its over-written and excessive edge that gave expression to fantasy, myth and the picturesque. Although the movement ran through the Western world, in different countries it took different forms, such as renewed interest in folklore and local history and the revival of minority languages, leading in some cases to a passionate nationalism. It was both carried by and contributed to the huge social and political upheavals caused by the American, French and Industrial revolutions and it provided the confidence for enormous expansions in trade and colonialism. Its effects on religion were as widespread as its effects on the arts and political idealism. The period saw the spread of Protestant denominations such as **Congregationalism**, **Methodism** and **Presbyterianism**. It stimulated the **Oxford Movement** and the High Anglican revival. More importantly, it recovered nature for religion and forms of **pantheism** and **natural religion** were to be found across the different religious groupings. An integral part of romanticism was the huge cultural sweep of the **Enlightenment**, driven by new science and **empiricist**, **naturalist** and **materialist** theories.

FINAL WORD: 'To say the word "Romanticism" is to say modern art … that is, intimacy, spirituality, colour, aspiration, towards the infinite, expressed by every means available to the arts.' (Charles Baudelaire. Quoted in Mayne.)

Roma Religion Also known as 'gypsies' or the Romany people, with their Western European language Romani. Believed to have originated in northwest India, they first migrated to Persia (c.200–c.600 CE) and then to the Middle East (c.600–c.900). They are thought to have come to Europe during the Middle Ages. Today most Roma have settled communities and only about 5 per cent are thought to be nomadic. Throughout their history they have suffered extreme persecution, particularly in Europe where in the 1930s, they were victims of Nazi genocide. Their belief system is inevitably syncretistic, adopting aspects of the religions of their host countries. Originally, during their first migrations from the Indian subcontinent, they would have carried with them elements of Hinduism; eventually, in Europe, the Roma were the last of the Goddess worshippers, the cult having clear similarities with **Wicca**. At the outset of the 21st century there is no one Roma culture or religion, the dispersed Romani groups following various beliefs, traditions and customs. Most are converted to the religion of the countries in which they have settled, thus adopting forms of Christianity or Islam. However, these established traditions are mingled with aspects of the vestigial beliefs that are engrained in family lore, mores and tradition. These revolve around *Del* (God), *beng* (Satan), *bibaxt* (ill luck), *mulo* (spirits and ghosts) and in the power of charms, amulets, talismans, curses, healing rituals and a whole network of taboos designed to guard against *marimé*, impurity. It is thought that with the enlargement of the European community, there are now some four million Roma who are citizens of the EU.

Rongo The **Maori** god of peace and agriculture.

Rosary A string of beads used to count or tell, the prayers in personal devotions. In the West it is familiarly associated with Catholicism and the string has 150 beads, 15 of which are large and set in to divide the rosary into sections of ten. There are various schemes of prayer, for example the *Paternoster*, the Lord's Prayer, is recited on the large beads, while the smaller ones are used for *Ave Maria*, the Hail Mary. The sequence of *Aves* is followed by the recitation of the *Gloria*, with each group of ten beads being associated with one of the 'mysteries' of Christ's or the Virgin's life, such as the Annunciation or **Resurrection**. The use of the rosary was established in Eastern religions long before the emergence of Christianity. The *japa-mala* (Skt. 'muttering chaplet) is a means of counting the number of prayers made and in Hinduism its construction varies according to the sect. Buddhist use of a rosary varies according to the tradition, as does number of beads. The Muslim rosary has 99 beads, with a terminal bead making up 100. These refer to the '**Beautiful Names**' of Allah. In Judaism the use of a rosary is rare, but they have no religious significance and are rather like 'worry beads', something with which to keep the hands busy on the Sabbath, when work is prohibited.

Rosetta Stone *E*. A dark-grey granite stone on which texts were carved in Egyptian and Greek, in three scripts: **hieroglyphic**, demotic Egyptian and Greek. Because Greek was well known, the stone became a key to the eventual deciphering of hieroglyphics. It was discovered by Captain Pierre-Françoise Bouchard (1772–1832) in the port of Rosetta, near the town of el-Rashid. It was eventually brought to Britain and has been housed in the British Museum since 1802. Jean-Françoise Champollion, building on the work of Thomas Young, is credited with being the principal translator of the stone's text. Its contents concern decrees (judicial decisions or orders) issued by the priests of Ptolemy as a means of establishing the legitimacy of the ruler and to create a royal cult. These decrees were inscribed on stones and erected throughout Egypt. The Rosetta stone, which is number three in a series of three, is a copy of the decree issued in Memphis and opens with, 'The new king, having received the kingship from his father ...' Texts describe various taxes repealed by Ptolemy V and issue instructions to erect statues in temples.

Rosh Ha-Shanah *J*. Heb. 'the Head of the Year'. The name for the Jewish New Year, celebrated on the 1st and 2nd of the Jewish month of *Tishri* (September-October). It is sometimes called *Yom Teruah*, the Day of the Trumpet, a reference to the blowing of the *Shofar*, the ram's horn during the synagogue liturgy, which symbolically awakens the congregation to their need of God's atonement for their sins. It is the most theological of all the Jewish festivals, its multi-layered meaning combining the themes of God's creation of the world, his sovereignty, his memory and judgement, his revelation and **redemption**, and the reciting of *Selichot*, prayers of repentance and the singing of hymns celebrating God's mercy and forgiveness. Traditionally Rosh Ha-Shanah marks the anniversary of God's creation of the world and the Jew is called to reflect logically on the creation of his own brief life, 'I live, I die'. A Jew will contemplate the salient truth, that as God made his purpose known, people can be in no doubt as to what is required of them and will be judged accordingly. These themes are carried in daily liturgies, from the Saturday night before Rosh Ha-Shanah to **Yom Kippur**, the Day of Atonement.

Rosicrucians The name represents a tangled reference to different mystical fraternities that may or may not stem from the same medieval source. It is thought to have originated in Kassel, Germany, in the early 17th century. Three anonymous documents, reputedly recorded the life of a 14th-century alchemist, Christian Rosenkreutz (1378–1474), who travelled to the East, returning with scientific and alchemical information. On his return, he founded the Order of the Rosy Cross. The published documents excited considerable interest, but enquirers could find no trace of the Rosicrucians as such and it is suggested they were fictitious. There are various theories, some claiming that the manifestos were written by a German Lutheran Pastor, Johann Andrae (1586–1654) who had proposed forming an order for the transformation of social life, but because of his office wished to remain anonymous. There are other scholars who believe that Rosicrucianism was a hoax, still others who understand the Order to have been made deliberately obscure and inaccessible so as to guard its secrets. In all events, the order combined the intention to transform society, to study alchemy, the Kabbalah and other forms of mysticism, together with Christian theology. Thus, on this one front, it blended into the Christian Pietism characteristic of Germany at the time. Eventually the movement spread across Europe, only to decline during the 18th century. Through a 19th-century revival of interest in the occult, the Rosicrucians saw the light of day again, forming a close relationship with the **Freemasons**. Being an occult group, the Rosicrucians make their teaching known only to initiated members, which makes it difficult to make any objective assessment of their beliefs and practices. There are many established but fragmented Rosicrucian orders, that may or may not be in 'fellowship' with one another. Their strongest presence is probably in the USA. See **Ancient Mystical Order Rosae Crucis**, **Gnostic Order of Christ**

Rousseau, Jean-Jacques (1712–78) A political philosopher, born in Geneva who, from 1741 lived mostly in Paris. He was one of the principal proponents of **romanticism**. The theme for which he is best known is what amounts to a celebration of nature carried in his two most influential later works, *Emile*, a philosophy of education, and *The Social Contract*, both published in 1762. They were so controversial that Rousseau was forced to leave France. His argument was that there was a conflict between society and human nature, that man was essentially and naturally good, but that society was an arbitrary and artificial structure which frustrated and stilted everything that was best in human kind. The ideal was the way men lived as animals before the beginning of civilization. In that condition, the individual voluntarily submitted to the group so as to ensure the survival of the whole. In doing this he was fulfilled, he was the 'noble savage'. In phrases that became part of romanticism's manifesto, Rousseau asserted that, 'Man was born free, but is everywhere in chains'. If the individual is coerced to submit to the 'general will', he will be 'forced to be free', thus he cast society in the tension between liberal individualism and voluntary conformity. The philosophy had huge appeal to anyone who wanted to tap into the natural energies of life, who wished to have one finger on nature's pulse and another on society's pulse thus being, as it were, at the centre of things, forming, leading and developing new ideas. Rousseau's influence is considerable, it is reflected by Kantian ethics, it carried to the principle of democracy and is the foundation a child-centred philosophy of education. In terms of religion, people need to break free of dogma and institutional forms and respond openly to nature, allowing their imagination and intuition to inform them metaphysically and spiritually. The idea that man should be liberated from the conditioning forces of society, so that he is 'free' to discover who he really is, is the basis of romanticism, but because of the place he gave to reason, Rousseau is also thought of as a philosopher of the **Enlightenment**.

FINAL WORD: 'Nature never deceives us; it is we who deceive ourselves.' (Rousseau)

Rta *AME*. In **Indo-Iranian** religion, *Rta* is the central doctrine of the balance and harmony of the moral and physical order of the universe. It was associated with the elements of water and fire, both of which were used in the rituals. There are indications that *Rta* was sometimes regarded as a divinity, as was the consuming fire of a sacrifice. It foreshadows **Ahura Mazda**, the creator god of **Zoroastrianism**, who held *Rta*, the world order, in balance with *Asha*, an empowering cohesive force. *Antra*, chaos, is the opposing concept.

Ruach *J*. Heb. 'spirit', 'wind', 'breath' and 'mind'. It is the actual breath of all living creatures and the breath or 'spirit' of God. Job testified that, 'the ruach of God is in my nostrils' (Job 27:3). It is God's *ruach* that imparts the image in which man was created, together with the attributes of reason, will and conscience. Applied to God, *ruach* is the energy both of original and continuing creation, the latter in the sense of providence, the fulfilment of God's purposes. When applied to people, it is the animating principle within each human being, the soul or *nephesh*.

Rumi, Jalal al-Din al (c.1207–73) One of the great mystics and poets of Islam. So fine is his poetry that he has been claimed as one of mankind's poetic geniuses, transcending religious and national boundaries. Born in what, today, is Afghanistan, he lived in Anatolia. (Turkey) In 1244 Rumi's meeting with a wandering **dervish**, Shams Tabriz, began his spiritual transformation; Shams' death initiated in Rumi ecstatic grief and an emotional mysticism expressed in an outpouring of poetry, music and teaching. After Rumi's death his teaching led to the formation of the Sufi *tariqah*, the **Mevlevi**, popularly known as the 'whirling dervishes'. His poetry amounted to more than 70,000 verses that describe experiencing God's presence in creation. The frequent image is of the anguish of separation from the Beloved and the ineffable joy of reunion. His most famous sequence of poems, *Mathnawi*, are thought to express the innermost meaning of the Koran and is sometimes referred to as 'the Koran of the Persian tongue'.

FINAL WORD: 'Why should I seek? I am the same as
He. His essence speaks through me.
I have been looking for myself!' (Rumi)

Runes *AE*. Characters of primitive Teutonic alphabets in use from the 3rd to 17th centuries CE. In old English the word *rün*, from a more ancient form, *round*, meant to whisper or talk in secret. Rune words, believed to have magical properties, were used in many forms of spells and to construct calendars or encode secrets. They were, thus, a developed form of cipher, symbols of sounds written or carved, each rune with its own name. The first six runic signs were, f, u, th, o (a), r, c (k), hence the name *futhark* given to the alphabet of which there were two, one of 16 characters, another of 24, the latter simply being the original alphabet with 8 added characters. They were used to write numerous languages including Gothic, German, English, Swedish and Norwegian, Icelandic and Russian and even Semitic languages such as Hebrew. The most well-known *futharks*, are the Elder, Anglo-Saxon and the Younger. A rune is also a Finnish or Old Norse poem.

Rupa *H. B.* Skt. Pal. 'Matter' or ' Form', anything that takes shape or is apparent as substance. In the context of the five *skandhas*, *rupa* represents the material form or the human body.

Russell, Bertrand (1872–1970) A British mathematician and philosopher who was awarded the Nobel Prize for Literature, the citation referring to his *History of Western Philosophy*. The range of Russell's philosophy is considerable and much of it is accessible to the general reader. His greatest contribution is probably, *The Principles of Mathematics*, in which he posited a world full of imperceptible realities. He adapted this theory to what he called 'logical constructions' and in so doing became a pioneer of **logical positivism**, a philosophy developed by members of the Vienna Circle such as **Wittgenstein**. In *A Free Man's Worship*, Russell criticized religious belief as irrational and throughout his life held that the existence of God might be proved logically, but there was not enough evidence to believe that he existed. Al Seckel records that on Russell's 90th birthday, one of his guests suggested to him that he may have been wrong about God's non-existence: 'What will you do, Bertie, if it turns out you were wrong?' Russell was delighted with the question. He pointed a finger upward and cried, 'Why, I should say, "God you gave us insufficient evidence."'
FINAL WORD: 'Three passions, simple but overwhelmingly strong, have governed my life; the longing for love, the search for knowledge and unbearable pity for the suffering of mankind.' (Russell [1967–9])

Russian Mennonites Mennonites who were invited by Catherine the Great to settle in the Ukraine in the 18th century. See **Mennonites**

S

Sabbatarianism *X.* Any rigorous observation of the **Sabbath**. The view that the **Old Testament** Sabbath should be literally observed by the church is typically a feature of the English and Scottish **Reformation**, being unknown in Europe even among the **Calvinists**. Its first impetus came from the publication of Bound's *True Doctrine of the Sabbath* (1595), an argument for the Old Testament standard of observation which required keeping the day holy (Exod. 20:8). In its extreme form, membership of the Church, even salvation, is conditional on the strict observation of the Sabbath. It is both a form of legalism and a denial of salvation by grace. In the 17th century, Sabbath observance became politically controversial when James I published his *Book of Sports* (1618) which prohibited work on Sundays but allowed 'lawful recreation'. Despite Acts of Parliament implementing the Puritan Sabbath, it was the thin edge of the secular wedge and sabbatarians, through the Lord's Day Observance Society, have since fought a rearguard action.

Sabbath *I.J.X.* The etymology of the Hebrew word *Shabbat* is uncertain but it is not derived from the usages usually ascribed to it such as 'rest', 'seven', 'seventh' and 'sit'. Some authorities have suggested, unconvincingly, that the Jewish weekly Sabbath is derived from the Babylonian 9th 'Day of Rest'. For Jews the observation of the Sabbath is one of the holiest prescriptions and the day is wrapped around with every kind of law, prohibition and taboo. It begins before sunset on a Friday evening, marked by blessing the Sabbath over lighted candles and ends after sundown on the Saturday night with the *Habdalah*, a liturgy of thanksgiving for God's beneficence to Israel. The Sabbath is also observed as a sign of the covenant (Exod. 31:16–17). Celebrated on Saturday, the seventh day of the Jewish week, it was inaugurated to serve two purposes, the worship of God (Exod. 31:13–17) and recreation both for people and cattle (Deut. 5:14). Jewish law (see **Halakhah**) detailed the regulations against work, which was why the **Pharisees** complained of Jesus' healing on the Sabbath (Matt. 12:10–14). Both Christian and Muslim Sabbaths are derived from the same sources. The Christian Sabbath is observed on Sunday, the first day of the week, since traditionally it was on this day that the resurrection took place and the term 'Sabbath' was displaced by 'the Lord's Day' (see **Lord's Day Observance Society** and **Sabbatarianism**). The Muslim Sabbath is celebrated on Fridays. 'O ye who believe! When the call is proclaimed to prayer on Friday (the Day of Assembly), hasten earnestly to the Remembrance of Allah and leave off business (and traffic): That is best for you if ye but knew!' (Koran, 62:09)

FINAL WORD: 'Some keep the Sabbath going to Church,
      I keep it staying at home,
      With a bobolink for a Chorister
      And an orchard for a Dome.' (Emily Dickinson)

Sabellianism *X*. A Christian heresy named after Sabellius, thought to have been a theologian in Rome during the 3rd century. He claimed the **Trinity** was merely three modes, aspects or names for the one God and not three distinct persons. In place of the Trinity, Sabellianism understands God to be just one interchangeable essence, Father, Son and Holy Spirit, each manifested at different times, but not together. See **Modalism, Oneness Pentecostalism, Patripassionism**

Sabians *I*. A syncretistic Islamic sect found in Iran and southern Iraq, that combines elements similar to Gnosticism with Parsee beliefs and an astrological system similar to those of **Babylon** and the **Magi**. The sect survives today and is mentioned in the Koran as one of those 'allowed' to exist. See also **Harranian Religion**

Sacerdotalism Lat. *sacerdos*, 'priest'. What pertains to a priest or priest-hood. The character and methods of the priesthood, a kind of 'priestcraft' or a passion for priestly things.

Sacrament *X*. Sacraments have been defined as an outward and visible sign of an inward and invisible commitment. Originally the Latin *sacramentum* meant a soldier's oath of allegiance, but came to assume the meaning of the Greek *musterion*, a mystery (see **Greek Religion**). In Christian theology the sacraments are a means of endowing the subject with spiritual grace ordained by Christ. As many as 30 sacraments have been listed by theologians, but the number was settled at seven by the **Council of Trent: baptism, confirmation**, the **Eucharist**, penance, extreme unction (see **Anointing**), orders (see **Ordination**) and matrimony. They are observed by both the **Orthodox** churches and the Church of England, where a distinction is made between the two sacraments ordained by Christ and the other five. See **Salvationism**

Sacred Set apart or anointed for religious use. Something worthy of religious veneration, such as the **Koran** and the **Guru Granth Sahib** of the Sikhs, or places consecrated for worship like cathedrals, synagogues and mosques or the sacred groves of ancient Greece. Also, the accoutrements of religious practice, such as the bread and wine of the Christian **Eucharist**, the vestments of priests, the **medicine bundles** of shamans, the **totems** of Amerindians or **charms** and **amulets**. Certain religious rites are deemed to be sacred such as the **sacraments** of the Christian Church, the Jewish practice of **circumcision** and the use of skulls in African ancestor worship. See **Holy, Profane**

Sacred Cow *H*. For Hindus the cow is *aghanya*, an animal that is not to be slaughtered. The cow is not, nor has it ever been worshipped by Hindus and its being 'sacred' is a European misconception. However the cow is taboo, but not for reasons of vegetarianism, since in the Vedic age beef was eaten after the animal had been sacrificed. In the **Vedas** the cow is associated with 'light' or 'radiance', a theme taken up by Sri

Aurobindo. Indian culture understands the cow to be symbolic of abundance and through its supply of milk, like that of the human mother, gives a great deal without asking for recompense.

Sacred Fire See **Fire, Sacred**

Sacred Geometry The attribution of religious values to the representation of mathematical relationships and the design of man-made objects that symbolize these relationships. In Greek and Roman architecture the **golden ratio** was the rationale of the design; something similar is true, for example, of **yantras** and **mandalas** (see *Figure 12*), and of the architecture of **pyramids**, **synagogues**, churches, cathedrals and **mosques**. The golden ratio (mean or section) was based on a ratio between two dimensions of a plane figure or two divisions of a line such that the smaller is to the large, as the large is to the sum both. That represents a ratio of roughly three to five. These are sometimes indicated by the Greek letters 'Phi' or 'Tau', or the irrational number 1:618, which was believed to represent significant properties. The Pythagoreans held that the ratio represented an underlying truth about the meaning of existence. By means of sacred geometry a connection is made between the concrete forms and designs and abstract thought.

The golden mean is sometimes applied to all forms of moderation, as with the Buddhist 'Middle Way' (see **Madhyamaka**). It implies the perfect balance of thought and behaviour that avoids excess. The philosophy of **Summum** argues that the golden mean should be applied also to the human **psyche**, since it is our mental disposition that dictates how we respond to harmony or disharmony. Such responses form our perceptions and attitudes and we remain captive to them. This 'sacred' proportion is also applied to the human form, ratios being found, for example, in the structure and conformation of the face and in the ratio of the hand to the arm. The human body is represented in **Hinduism** and **Tantric Buddhism** as a living mandala with the **chakras** disposed significantly within it.
FINAL WORD: 'Mighty are numbers; joined with art, resistless.' (Euripides)

Figure 12 'The Sri Yantra: Drawn from nine triangles, four pointed downward and five pointed upward, thus forming 42 (6 × 7) triangular fragments around the central triangle. There is probably no other set of triangles which interlock with such integrational perfection.' (Robert Lawlor)

Sacred Heart *X.* A form of devotion originating in the Middle Ages with Bernard of Clairvaux (1090–1153) and focused on the sacred heart of Jesus. It was inspired by a reverence for Christ's humanity and represented a departure from earlier forms of piety, it being more subjective and individualistic. The heart, as a symbol of love, calls for openness to the loving heart of Christ and to 'giving' one's heart to him. The subjective passion of this kind of piety carried through the Reformation to influence Protestant forms of devotion, inspiring the hymns of Isaac Watts (1674–1748) 'When I survey the wondrous Cross' and John Newton (1725–1807) 'How sweet the name of Jesus sounds …'

Sacred Mushroom Also known as the magic or psychedelic mushroom. Rock paintings such as those of the Tassili plateau in Algeria show their use dating back at least 5,000 years, and Mesoamerican societies of Mexico and Guatemala built mushroom temples and carved stone sculptures in the form of mushrooms. The Spanish priest Bernardino Sahagun records in the Florentine Codex that when **Aztecs** ate the mushroom they called *noncatl*, that it caused drunkenness, hallucinations and lechery and induced visions. Although the identification of the actual mushroom is debated, the possibility exists that the Vedic **soma** was derived from it. The subject became one of controversial debate when J. M. Allegro suggested that the name 'Jesus' was a New Testament code word for a mushroom that was used as a sacramental inducement of altered states of consciousness. See **Sacred Mushroom Church of Switzerland**

Sacred Mushroom Church of Switzerland Founded recently, the Church does not claim that the mushroom, Teonanacatl, is a god, but that it does have the capacity to 'heal' the soul. Its members claim that by ingestion (symbiosis) of the mushroom, religion in various forms is practised. The 'Church' is not a physical entity but a spiritual community and all that is needed for 'worship' and true religious experience is the Sacred Mushroom itself. The group's website states: 'As Europe has long been home to many Sacred Mushrooms, we see ourselves as spiritual successors of the Celtic druids (murdered by the Romans), the witches (murdered by the Roman Catholics) as well as the Sacred Mushroom-based civilization of the Inca (murdered by the Spanish Roman Catholics).'

Sacred Name Movement *J.* Orthodox Judaism holds that the actual name of God is too sacred to be spoken or written, hence the use of the **Tetragrammaton** symbol. Nevertheless the movement, which began in the late 1920s and early 1930s, claims that God must be addressed by one of the divine names in the Old Testament, such as Yahweh, **Jehovah** or **Elohim**. Some assert that the name must be used in its Hebrew form. Whatever name is chosen, it relegates all others as references to false deities. The movement further holds that salvation is dependent on knowing the correct name of God.

Sacred Path of the Warrior *B*. A Tibetan Buddhist concept the literature of which uses military metaphors showing that surmounting the challenges of the spiritual life is like the mastering of martial skills. The terms 'warrior' or 'warriorship' do not designate violence but are from the Tibetan *pawo*, 'one who is brave' or 'fearless'. The spiritual life is every bit as arduous and demanding as that of a soldier's, but on the inner battlefield the spiritual warrior works with gentleness, courage and self-knowledge. This tradition of the Tibetan warrior is shared by the Japanese **samurai**, and by some **Amerindian** tribes. A similar idea figures in both the legend of King Arthur and the code of medieval European knights. The concept has continued in Christianity as 'soldiers of Christ'. See **Salvation Army, Shambhala**

Sacred Thread Ceremony *H*. Skt. (*Upanayana*. 'taking up', 'initiation' or 'sitting close by'). An initiation ceremony undertaken by the upper three **castes** of Hinduism. The ceremony marks a boy's acceptance into his *varna*, caste, at which point he becomes 'twice born'. His **guru**, to whom he will 'sit close', becomes his spiritual father and the **Vedas** become his spiritual mother. He is given the *jenoi or* sacred thread which he will wear for the remainder of his life. If it gets soiled or shabby it is replaced, but the old thread is never taken off until the new thread has been put on. The ceremony involves shaving the head, ritual bathing and dressing in new clothes. The **Gayatri Mantra**, one of the most sacred verses of the **Rig-Veda**, is read to the initiate who will then be expected to recite it three times a day, at dawn, noon and dusk. His guru may give him a spiritual name to identify his 'second birth'. The ceremony concludes with the boy offering a traditional gift to his guru. In modern practice, *Upanayana* may be offered to girls, but they will not be given the sacred thread. See **Four Stages of Life, Initiation, Varnasramadharma**

Sacrifice The Greeks sacrificed 500 goats in thanksgiving for their victory at Marathon; the Aztecs sacrificed considerable numbers of their fellow human beings to the sun to ensure the fertility of the fields; Abraham was brought to the point of sacrificing his son **Isaac** as a test of his faith in God; the most sacred Jewish sacrifices were the sin and guilt offerings (Lev. 4:7) which re-established the severed relationship between man and God. This sacrificial practice reached its climax in the festival of **Yom Kippur**, the Day of Atonement. Christianity teaches that there was no one to 'stay' God's hand when he sacrificed his son, Jesus, as a propitiation for humanity's sin. Muslims are obliged to sacrifice a lamb during their **hajj**, and may do also for the *Aqiqah*, a sacrifice offered at the time of a birth. The practice of sacrifice has been a running theme throughout the history of religion and is the most graphic expression of human dependence on a higher power. Blood is a universal symbol of life, thus a 'blood sacrifice' is understood to be the offering of life to the deity; it is also a symbol of the preservation of life, as when the Hebrews sacrificed lambs using the blood to mark the door posts, so the Angel of Death would recognize the houses that belonged to a Hebrew family and 'pass over' it on his way to killing the first born of each Egyptian household. In Christian theology, Christ is understood as the Passover Lamb – a 'fitting' sacrifice rehearsed every time the **Mass, Eucharist** or **Lord's Supper** is observed. In many cultures the sacrifice was burned, the smoke carrying the scent of food to the gods as in the *Epic of Gilgamesh* and the story in Genesis 8, telling of when the flood abated: Noah offered burnt offerings to God, 'and when the Lord smelled the pleasing odour ...' he vowed never again to destroy the earth and humanity. The process of secularization has virtually eradicated the world view in which sacrifice was believed to be efficacious; secularism regards such practices and the beliefs that sustain them as pagan or primitive. And yet, in both Western and Eastern religious traditions the anti-sacrifice lobby has always been present. 'For I desire goodness, not sacrifice; obedience to God, rather than burned offerings' (Hos. 6:6). Nevertheless, we live at a time when self-sacrifice is synonymous with martyrdom, suicide-bombers being the most ominous weapon of terrorism. See **Anthropomancy**

Saddha *B*. In all traditions of Buddhism, *saddha* is 'faith' in the **Buddha**. It is not blind faith and in the **Kalama Sutra** the Buddha encourages his followers to use their reason and personal experience as the measure of whether or not anything taught is true – 'After observation and analysis, when you find that anything agrees with reason and is conducive to the good and the benefit of one and all, then accept it and live up to it.' In **Theravada** 'Faith is the seed, practice the rain and wisdom is my yoke and plough.' For **Mahayana** it is the be all and end all of enlightenment, the Buddha assuring us 'that unsurpassed Awakening [**Bodhi**] has faith as its cause. The causes of Awakening are innumerable, but if stated as faith, this covers everything.'

Sadducee *J*. Heb. Despite etymological problems, the name Sadducee is thought to have derived either from Zadok, Solomon's high priest, or from Ezekiel's ideal high priest. They existed from the 1st century BCE through the 1st century CE and were frequently in opposition to the **Pharisees**. They were either priests or supportive of the priestly class as the supreme authority in Jewish religious matters. Drawn from aristocratic Judeans, the Sadducees were wealthy and doctrinally conservative to the point of interpreting scripture literally. They did not believe in the received oral tradition of ancient Israel, their authority being the written tradition which was fixed and sacrosanct. The Pharisees' emphasis on oral tradition enabled them greater flexibility in the interpretation of both doctrine and ritual. The Sadducees rejected belief in the resurrection of the dead and the immortality of the soul, in angels and divine intervention. Their literalism and inflexibility was partly the reason why they did not survive the destruction of the Temple and its cults in 70 CE.

Sadhana *H. B*. Skt. from *sadh*, 'to arrive at a goal', to complete or perfect something. In Hinduism it refers to the practices leading to the mastery of a yogic path (see **Yoga**). In **Vajrayana** Buddhism, a *sadhana* is a liturgical text with meditation techniques usually associated with visualization. 'To arrive at the goal', empowerment and consecration by a **guru** is required. See **Meditation**

Sadhu *H*. Skt. *sadh*, 'to guide towards fulfilment'. A holy person or monk. An Indian ascetic credited with supernatural powers. The *sadhu's* principal characteristic is his renunciation of the world.

Safavid Dynasty *I*. The ruling caliphs of Persia (Iran) from 1501–1736. Together with the **Ottoman** and **Mughal** Empires, the dynasty achieved the highest expression of Islamic culture. Its origins are to be found in the *Safaviyeh*, a long established order of Sufi Islam (see **Sufism**) which had flourished in Azerbaijan since early in the 14th century. The order was named after Sheikh Safi Al-Din (1252–1334). Significant for the faith and history of Islam was Ismail I, being made Shah of Iran in 1502. He embraced Shiite Islam (see **Shi'ism**) making it mandatory for the whole nation on pain of death. The existing religious authority, the Sunni **Ulema**, were either killed or exiled. From that point onwards Iran became a feudal theocracy based on Shiite assumptions, beliefs and values. Constant conflict with the Ottomans drove the site of the capital from Tabriz to Qazvin in 1548 and later under the greatest of the Safavid rulers, Shah Abbas I, the capital was moved deeper into Iranian territory, to Isfahan, where a new city was built next to the ancient Persian town. From then onwards the Safavids began to establish a new Iranian culture and monarchy. The continuing story is one of never-ending war and conflict, of changing national boundaries, of the vacillating occupation of cities, especially that of Baghdad. A treaty between Iran and Turkey in 1639, established the frontier between northwest Iran and southeast Turkey, a demarcation which still stands. War was extended to the Kurds (see **Kurdish Religion**), the consequences of which are still very much in evidence in the community of 1.7 million people now living in northeast Iran who are descendents of deportees from Kurdistan to Khurasan. Despite this history of constant conflict, there developed the high culture for which Persia is renowned. It influenced architecture, fine and decorative arts, poetry, manuscript illustration, calligraphy and the carpet weaving for which it has a worldwide reputation. Not least, is the influence of **Mullah Sadra**, one of the most famous of Muslim philosophers, who achieved a synthesis of Sufi mysticism and Shiite theology he called 'metaphilosophy'. The Safavid cultural achievement amounted to an Islamic renaissance of the arts, literature and philosophy and in terms of religious orthodoxy and administration, set down the foundation for modern Iran. See **Safarid Dynasty**

Sagas *AE*. Icelandic legends originally transmitted orally, then preserved (c.1120–1400 CE) as collections of prose narratives. They tell of the families that first settled in Iceland, of their descendents, of the history of the kings of Norway and of the legends of early **Germanic** gods. Usually, they have mythological and supernatural themes that give insight to original Icelandic life and culture. The term is also used for any kind of epic story.

Sahaja *H*. Skt. 'natural' or 'innate'. The actual presence within us of the enlightenment that lies behind all illusion and obscuration created by the unenlightened mind. Thus, it is the state of mind or consciousness the practitioner endeavours to achieve. Put differently, it is our real self in the state of *samadhi*, as it experiences the bliss of ultimate union with the absolute.

Sahaja Yoga *H*. A meditation discipline founded in India in 1970, by Shri Mataji Nirmala Devi. The method leads to **self-realization** or *moksha*. The system which is promoted as being accessible to anyone, is understood as the next stage in human evolution, which is spiritual rather than physical and the 'birthright of every individual'. Practice focuses on the **chakras** and *kundalini* yoga. See **Yoga**

Sai Baba b. 1926 in Andhra Pradesh in South India. In 1940 he declared he was an **avatar**, an incarnation of divinity, explaining that, 'I am God. And you too are God. The only difference between you and me is that while I am aware of it, you are completely unaware.' He took upon himself the task of uniting mankind as one family and 'to reveal the Divine on which the cosmos rests'. The Sri Sathya Sai Seva Organization was founded in the 1960s to promote Sai Baba's teachings and mission.

Saint-Martin, Louis-Claude de (1743–1803) Founder of the **Martinist** occult school based on the writing of Martinez de Pasqually.

Saints Generally holy men and women of all religions who are known to have performed miracles and to have lived lives of unblemished service and purity. Most commonly they are associated with **Roman Catholicism**, probably because saints are still being canonized. Mother Teresa, for example, is in the process of being beatified, the first stage of being made a saint. During the first centuries of Christianity, some of those martyred, such as St Celia, were made saints while others became associated with places or countries to become their patron saint, like St George, also one of the early martyrs. No complete hagiography, giving a definitive list of saints, has ever been made. See **Martyrs**, **Mysticism**, **Visions**

Sakina *I*. In Islam, the presence or peace of God. The Koran (48.4) mentions that Allah has placed God's peace and presence in the hearts of the faithful. It signifies an interior, spiritual illumination in much the same was as does the Hebrew concept of **Shekinah**. The signs of *Sakina* are 'spiritual breaths or divine breezes', which can only be discerned with care or, miraculously, they may be so clear that they manifest in a form everyone can see. They are a confirmation, for struggling and troubled believers, of God's presence, strength and mercy.

Sakti *H*. Skt. 'force', 'power', 'energy'. The goddess consort of **Siva**.

Sakyapa *B*. Tib. One of the four major schools of Tibetan Buddhism, named after the Sakya 'Grey Earth' monastery founded in 1073 in southern Tibet. The community devoted itself to the transmission of **Vajrayana** teaching. A philosophical and academic school, it was occupied with a systematic codifying of Tantric writings and Buddhist logic. In the 13th and 14th centuries they exerted considerable political influence in Tibet and subsequently on the spiritual life of the country. See **Gelugpa**, **Kagyupa**, **Nyingmapa**, **Tantra**, **Tibetan Buddhism**

Salaam or **Selam** *I*. Arab. A Muslim form of salutation meaning 'peace'. The word spoken with a deep bow forms a ceremonial greeting. *Al-salaam alaykum*, 'peace be upon you.' The use of the term as a greeting predates Islam and was employed in much the same way as the Hebrew '**Shalom Aleichem**'. In prayer *salaam* is offered to the Prophet as preparation for the confession of faith. *As-Salam* is one of the 99 names for God. See **Beautiful Names**

Salat *I*. Arab. 'connection' or 'contact', in the form of prayer or worship. The ritual prayers Muslims are required to make five times a day. See **Pillars of Islam**

Salik *I*. The wayfarer or journeyer and in this sense, also the student or disciple. The first step on the way of the Salik is repentance; from there the *Tariqah*, the basic principle of the mystical path of **Sufi** Muslims, guides the Salik to the *haqiqah*, 'truth' or 'reality'. Once the Salik has found the right teacher he is expected to stay with him until end of the Path is reached. Some initiates lack *sabr*, 'perseverance', become impatient and unable to sustain the necessary effort, and leave their teacher. Those that do persevere renounce the world and put themselves entirely in the hands of God, a true *Islam*, 'submission'.

Salvation Meaning 'deliverance', it is a term applicable to a root theme in Western religions. The entire **Old Testament** is an account of how God effected the deliverance of his 'Chosen People' from their enemies and from their own spiritual shortcomings. Prefigured within this history is the salvatory work of Christ on behalf of humankind. Concomitant with salvation is forgiveness, the two perfectly balanced by the human-divine partnership established in the covenants God made, firstly with Israel and then with all who profess faith in Jesus Christ, the instigator of the 'new covenant', offering atonement and reconciliation. Salvation is conditional both on people acknowledging their need for it by seeking forgiveness and God's mercy and grace to forgive. Judaism, Christianity and Islam are classed as 'salvation' religions, offering a diagnosis of humanity's spiritual maladies and the path that must be taken to regain spiritual health. Salvation implies the need for a saviour, which in biblical terms is associated with the notion of a **messiah**. Islam relies on the unmediated grace and mercy of Allah as revealed by Muhammad. Religions of salvation are usually religions of revelation, with the means of deliverance communicated either by God as direct revelation or through a succession of elected people such as prophets, as progressive revelation. See **Salvation by Grace, Salvation by Works, Soteriology**

Salvation Army *X*. A 19th-century **revivalist** movement founded in 1878 by W. Booth, a former **Methodist**. Organized on a military model with a 'general' at its head, it is known for its red shield emblem and its motto, 'Doing the Most Good'. The Salvation Army developed into an international evangelistic sect strongly engaged in social work, concentrating on the provision of hostels for the homeless and canteens for the hungry. It is famous for its hymn-singing and the brass bands that accompany it. The S. A. rejects both the **sacraments** and an ordained ministry. Today, with a worldwide presence, it provides on-the-spot relief for victims of war, famine and natural disasters.

FINAL WORD: 'The Army's doctrine follows the mainstream of Christian belief and its articles of faith emphasise God's saving purposes. Its objects are "the advancement of the Christian religion ... of education, the relief of poverty and other charitable objects beneficial to society or the community of mankind as a whole."' (Salvation Army Act, 1980)

Salvation by Grace *X*. A **New Testament** emphasis that teaches eternal life is not achieved by 'good works' alone, nor is it conditional on them, but is an unmerited gift of God. Once endowed with the gift of God's grace, eternal life is dependent on one's faith in the efficacy of his **salvation** made available through his Son. The authority is St Paul's letter to the Ephesians (2:8–9). 'For it is by his grace you are saved, through trusting him; it is not your own doing. It is God's gift, not a reward for work done.' See **Grace, Salvation by Works**

Salvation by Works *X*. A Christian doctrine that denies **salvation by grace** *alone*. It affirms that salvation is merited and earned through human effort, religious ritual, financial support of the Church and by obedience to the laws of the Church. The doctrine does not deny the need to be aware of one's sin, but it does deny that such awareness is not, of itself, sufficient to warrant eternal life. Faith in the efficacy of God's work of salvation through his Son must be in evidence in the quality of one's life. 'My brothers, what use is it for a man to say he has faith when he does nothing to show it? Can that faith save him?' (Jam. 2:14).

Salvationism Any religious doctrine that stresses the salvation of the soul as the goal of the religious life. Usually, the emphasis is presented along with the terms and conditions by which such salvation can be achieved. In Christian history, Salvationism has been divided into to two opposing views, the one placing all authority in the efficacy of the Church's sacraments so that, for example, **baptism** ensures the adherent of eternal life, regardless of the quality of the life lived. The alternative is based on the notion that salvation has to be earned and that the adherent will be judged by the moral and ethical quality of his life (see **Salvation by Grace** and **Salvation by Works**). The emphasis on salvation has been the impetus behind all forms of evangelical (see **Evangelism**) practice and the 'saving of souls' which, together with manifesting the gifts of the Holy Spirit, has been the energy behind **Pentecostal** traditions.

Samadhi *B. Z.* Skt. to 'establish' or to 'make firm'. A state of consciousness that lies beyond waking, dreaming and deep sleep and in which mental activity ceases. It is reached by the practice of **meditation**, and implies a deep level of concentration and absorption in the object of meditation. Whether that object is the absolute, the breath, the infinite spirit of the universe, a flower or candle flame, the result for the practitioner is union with that object. There are many stages of *samadhi*, of which the highest is *nirvikalpa-samadhi*, 'changeless *samadhi*'. In this state, the duality of subject-object relationship slips away and a state of 'no-mind' achieved. It is the ultimate, non-dual union with the absolute.

S*ammai* or *zammai* is the Japanese form of *samadhi*. In Zen Buddhism, it is the wakeful, total absorption of the mind in itself and carries the feeling of abstraction or refinement and of heightened and expanded awareness. It is also a non-dualistic state of consciousness, where the experiencing subject becomes one with the experienced object. It is sometimes referred to as 'one-pointedness of mind'. This is not to be understood as concentration on the one point to which the mind is directed, since this would retain the underlying dualism of subject and object. Rather the one-pointedness refers to the absorbed or 'realized' union with the object. See **Sahaja**

FINAL WORD: 'Some people see that the breath has disappeared and get a fright; they are afraid they'll die. We simply notice that there's no breath and take that as our object of awareness. This is the firmest type of *samadhi*: an unmoving state of mind. Firmly establish your mind like this.' (Ajahn Chah)

Samaritans *J.* Originally Israelites of central Palestine at the time of the Second Temple (c.516 BCE) The mountainous region known as Samaria lay between Judah in the south and Galilee in the north. After the fall of the northern Israelite kingdom (c.721 BCE) there occurred an amalgamation of the native Israelites and settlers from Assyria who 'took possession of Samaria and dwelt in its towns' (2 Kgs 17:24). This new community gradually adopted a form of Judaism with its own Samaritan Pentateuch. Their offer of help to rebuild the Temple was rejected by Zerubbabel and for this reason they formed their own community centred on Mt Gerizim, where in 332 BCE, with the permission of Alexander the Great, they built their own temple. The Jews called the Samaritans

Cutheans, Cutha being one of the places where the first settlers had come from. Their Judaism was based entirely on the Pentateuch, rejecting both the rabbinic tradition and the prophetic writings. The political existence of the Samaritans was virtually ended in 529 CE by Justinian. The sect revived in the 14th century under their high priest Phineas (b. Joseph), with colonies in Damascus, Gaza, Cairo and elsewhere. It has now declined with but a handful of around 500 followers in Nablus, which was captured by the Israelis in the 1967 Six Day War, reuniting communities divided by national boundaries. They are held in Western consciousness by Jesus' familiar parable of the Good Samaritan and by the eponymous telephone call-in service that offers 24/7 assistance to anyone who is distressed and contemplating suicide.

Samatha *H. B*. Skt. 'dwelling in tranquillity' by calming or tranquilizing the mind. In the **Gelugpa** school of Tibetan Buddhism, *Samatha* is a precondition of the concentrated mind that leads to *samadhi*. It is one of two conditions for enlightenment, the other being *vipassana*, 'special insight'. The image used for *Samatha* is of a clear, still lake in which the 'fish of special insight' swim. The concept of *Samatha* has been developed by the literature of the *Yogachara* school, as a structured form of meditation in nine stages. See **Anapanasati, Mahamudra, Meditation, Mindfulness, Satipathana, Smriti**

Samaveda *H*. Skt. The second of the four **Vedas**, comprising a collection of hymns or songs written to be chanted during the rite of *soma* sacrifice. They were chanted by the *udgatri* (singer) who would have been one of the four priests officiating at the ritual.

Sami *AE*. The Lapps' preferred name for themselves. 'Lapps', originally introduced into the Norse languages, was used pejoratively. See **Lapp Religion**

Sammai *B.Z.*. See **Samadhi**

Samsara *H. B. Z*. Skt. 'journeying'. In Hinduism the birth-death-rebirth cycle to which we are all subjected until we overcome our ignorance and achieve unity with **Brahman**. In Buddhism the term also refers to the cycles of birth and death, but also to modes of existence that may be good or bad with innumerable intermediary states. In what mode we are reborn is determined by one's personal **karma**. Hatred, craving and delusion bind us to *samsara* until, by consequence of enlightenment, we gain liberation. Somewhat confusingly, **Mahayana** identifies *samsara* with *nirvana* by dint of understanding everything to be a mental construction, thus, these terms for seemingly opposed states, are mere labels and have no real substance. The point is, that if while bound up with *samsara*, we see the 'true' nature of the world, of all phenomena, it would not be different from nirvana. Some insight into the way the cycles of rebirth are maintained is offered by the doctrine of **Dependent Origination**. See **Wheel of Life**

Samskara *H. B.* Skt. 'impression', 'formation' or 'consequence'. In Hinduism the complex process of imprints formed on an individual's psyche by thought and action in this and previous lives. The running total of *samskara* creates a person's character or disposition. The imprints are particularly in evidence if the thought or action, whether good or bad, is habitual. The term is also used for the 40 purifying sacraments or rituals an orthodox Hindu should perform or have performed for him. Buddhism shares the notion of the formational function of *samskara*, both in reference to the act of constructing character and to the actual form a person's character will take. The Buddhist concept of *samskara* is developed further. As 'mental formation' it is the fourth of the *skandhas* or **Five Aggregates** that make up an individual's personality. It is also the second link in the chain of cause and effect in the doctrine of **Dependent Origination**, where it assumes the notion of volition and consciousness.

Samudaya *B.* Skt. The truth of the origin of suffering, being the second of the **Four Noble Truths** of **Buddhism**.

Samurai *Jap.* A member of the medieval Japanese warrior class, recruited by local land-owning lords, to form the Kamakura Shogunate in 1192. A code of conduct, the *bushido*, based on honour, heroism and loyalty, controlled the relationship between the samurai and his lord. The samurai were in the process of being established when Buddhism was brought to Japan from China, to develop as **Zen**. There was much in the philosophy and practice of Zen that appealed to the samurai class, who found it cultivated the mental/physical control and calm detachment required by their form of martial art.

Sanatana Dharma *H.* Skt. *Sanatana*, 'imperishable', 'eternal'. The eternal religion or truth of **Hinduism**. The religion is not derived from a human founder, as with Christianity or Buddhism, thus Hindus believe the truth to be eternal, revealed to the *rishis* and recorded in the **Shruti**, the holy scriptures of Hinduism.

Sanctification The practice, followed by many religions, of making someone or something holy. In Roman Catholic theology the soul is sanctified by grace, through baptism. The sanctified state is neither definitive nor permanent; it can be lost as a result of sin and it can be restored and developed, usually by means of the **sacraments** and **prayer**. Hinduism has numerous personal sanctification rituals (see **Samskara**) others include, for example, sanctifying the ground on which a temple is to be built and imparting holiness to a particular colour. Buddhist monks pass through eight stages of sanctification and Sikhs, in obedience to the **Khalsa** code, observe the sanctification of religious symbols, such as the turban. Judaism practises various forms of sanctification. These include

Kiddush, a prayer sanctifying the Sabbath wine and the first of the two-part ceremony of Jewish marriage which sanctifies the marriage state. Because of the nature of Jewish history, God's name is traditionally sanctified through any death that brings honour to him, such as martyrdom. Today, however, Jews 'sanctify the Name' not by dying as Jews, but by living as Jews.

Sanctity Holiness, the state of having been sanctified. In reference to God, sanctity implies moral perfection of God's nature; applied to people, it means that degree of personal union with God that leads to moral perfection. Sanctity belongs to God by definition, to people by association; thus, as applied to a society or institution such as a monastery, it refers to its ability to promote the holiness of its members. When addressed to abstract notions such as 'marriage' or 'life', sanctity imparts an ultimate value that places taboos around them so as to preserve them in their ideal form.

Sangha *H. B. Z.* Skt. 'crowd'. In Hinduism a community gathered around a master so as to learn from him and receive guidance in attaining the highest spiritual knowledge. In Buddhism, the sangha is made up of monks, nuns and novices usually associated with a settled monastic community. More broadly, the sangha includes all lay Buddhists. It is one of the **Three Jewels** of Buddhism, the other two being the **Buddha** and the **dharma**.

Sankhya *H.* Skt. 'number'. One of Hinduism's six orthodox philosophies and probably its oldest. It was founded by the **rishi** Kapila (dates unknown), who offered the beguiling teaching that the universe has its origin in the union of nature and consciousness. The philosophy of *Sankhya* enumerates ('numbers') the 25 principles of the universe. It developed an evolutionary theory that every effect lies dormant in its cause and is a potential of it, requiring a liberating influence to realize that potential. Thus, the cause alone is the undeveloped state, the effect the developed. However, it works both ways, since while generation is development, destruction is return, a reversion to the cause. Evolution is but one side of the coin, the other being involution. See **Darshana, Nyaya, Purva-Mimamsa, Vaiseshika, Vedanta, Yoga**

Sanna *B.* Pal. Perception. See **Five Aggregates**

Sannyasa *H.* Skt. 'Renunciation'. For Hindus the fourth and final stage of life, the time when a Hindu severs his worldly attachments, both material and mental. See **Ashrama, Four Stages of Life**

Sanskrit *H.* Skt. 'perfect' or 'complete' or 'made final'. The refined language of people migrating from the northwest into India (see **Aryan**), in which the mystical truths revealed to the *rishis* were written. The record is found in the **Vedas, Upanishads** and the **Bhagavad-Gita**. Sanskrit is capable of expressing considerable philosophical and religious nuances, providing a vast, specialist vocabulary for which there are no adequate parallels in the West. Today it is a dead language, like Latin, but continues to be the sacred vernacular of Hindus. The language has no similarity with our own, the vowels precede the consonants, the silent ones preceding those that are sounded. There has been no general agreement in the West about the best way to transliterate Sanskrit words and names and this lack in standardization has resulted in numerous and sometimes confusing variants even when diacritical markings are used.

Santeria A syncretistic Caribbean religion with various names that include Regla de Ocha and Lukumi. Its origins go back to the time of the slave trade. The ironic and pejorative name Santeria (the Way of the Saints) was given by the Spanish to the religion of the so-called savages. It combines the worship of the orishas or head guardians of their indigenous African religion, with the beliefs of the **Yoruba** and **Bantu** of southern Nigeria and aspects of Roman Catholicism, especially an excessive worship of the **saints** who are equated with the orishas. Their ritual includes animal sacrifice, which has brought the Santerians into conflict with animal rights activists.

Sant Tradition of North India *H*. The Sants (from the Skt. *Sat*, 'truth', 'reality') grew to prominence as a school or group of **gurus** in North India during the 13th century. Drawing on the tradition of *bhakti*, they promoted an inner, devotional way of relating to God, reflected in their social egalitarianism that contrasted sharply with the **caste** system. The Sants threw up a tradition of devotional poets such as Kabir (d.1518) and **Guru Nanak**, who became the founder of **Sikhism**. Sant poetry is said to have influenced the medieval poetry of the **Sufis**, for example that of the great poet **Rumi**. The Sant emphasis is on devotion as the means to liberation, *moksha*. Their concept of God is reminiscent of Gnosticism, God is without form and has no human attributes – that is, anthropomorphized qualities; he cannot be incarnated or represented in images. True contemplation of God can only be inward.

FINAL WORD: Kabir says: 'Student, tell me, what is God? He is the breath inside the breath.'

Saraswati *H*. Skt. The Hindu goddess of knowledge, music and the creative arts. She is known as the Mother of the **Vedas**, the consort of Brahma and guardian of his creative intelligence. She is also known as Vak Devi, the goddess of speech, representing consciousness and wisdom and is revered as the dispeller of chaos and confusion.

Sarkar, **Prabhat Ranjan (1921–90)** Something of a 20th-century renaissance man, his philosophy contributed to social theories, art, linguistics, agriculture, history, medicine and cosmology. He was also revered for being one of the foremost teachers of **Tantra** and **Yoga**. He assumed the name Marga Guru Shri Anandamurti, describing his philosophy as **Neo-**

Humanism, an energy that was behind his foundation of **Ananda Marga**. See **Progressive Utilization Theory**

Sarn Phapoom A Thai shrine for animist spirits. See **Animism**, **Spirit House**

Sartre, Jean-Paul (1905–80) Novelist, dramatist and French **existentialist** philosopher. His principal interest was to examine the nature of human existence and the problem of free will within it. His first statement was in the form of a novel, *Nausea* (1938), which was partly autobiographical. Following the war, during which he worked with the French resistance, he wrote *Existentialism and Humanism* (1946) in which he asserted that we are condemned to be free in the choices we make, but this imposes on us an almost intolerable burden of responsibility. His principal work, *Being and Nothingness* (1943), is an examination of the nature of our existence, of what we term the 'self' and the part played by our emotions and imagination. Sartre concluded that our 'being' is greater than the sum of its various manifestations, that is, what we are 'in essence' is more than the categories and labels we use in our attempt to define 'being'. He distinguished between being *en-soi*, 'being in itself', which is characteristic of an inanimate object such as a stone or a planet and being *pour-soi*, 'being for itself', which implies consciousness, energy, power, a degree of determinism and openness to life. His concept of 'freedom' is entirely concerned with the mind's imaginative power, its own self-awareness, its ability to be reflective and to deny 'received tradition'. His philosophy combines various ideas or movements, such as post-Hegelian phenomenology, **Marxism** and existentialism. Sartre's thinking is grounded in atheism, although in later life he expressed interest in Messianic Judaism. In 1964 he refused the Nobel Prize for Literature.

FINAL WORD: 'To understand Jean-Paul Sartre is to understand something important about the present time.' (Iris Murdoch)

'There is no ultimate meaning or purpose inherent in human life; in this sense, life is absurd.' (Sartre [1974])

Sarvastivada *B*. Skt. 'the teaching that says that everything *is*'. Originally, a school of **Hinayana** Buddhism that broke away from the **Theravada**, c.3rd century BCE during the reign of King **Asoka**. Its philosophy was based on the notion of the simultaneous existence of everything, regardless of past, present and future time. An extreme **pluralism**, it nevertheless contained a form of proto-**Mahayana** that was to become significant for the concept of the 'future' Buddha, the **Maitreya**. Geographically, the school became established and influential in northwest India, Kashmir and Gandhara and in the development of Buddhism was a bridge between Hinayana and Mahayana. The Sarvastivada canon is preserved in Chinese and Tibetan translations.

Sassanian Empire *Zo*. A Persian empire founded in 226 CE by Ardashir who had conquered Parthia (see **Parthians**). The empire, which derived its name from his grandson, Sasan, is also known to history as the second Persian Empire. The period is important for the apogee of Persian culture, which had considerable influence on Rome, western Europe, Africa, China and India. Its religion was a **Zoroastrianism** that varied from the orthodox Avestan (see **Avesta**) religion as a result of reforms designed to mould the faith to its own social and political purposes. The most significant differences were those developed by Mani (see **Manicheanism**) and Mazdak, a philosopher and social reformer, who shared the dualistic principles of Manicheanism. The 'reformed' Zoroastrianism created conflict and Mazdak was hanged (c.529) and his followers massacred. The empire was destroyed in 651 CE by Muslim invasion.

Satan *J.X*. The name is from a Hebrew or Aramaic root, meaning 'accuser' or 'adversary'. In the long-running saga of the biblical religions, Satan is the agent of evil and the enemy of God, typically representing the dualistic conflict. He has his equivalent in all dualistic forms of religion, for example the *shaytan* of **Islam**, and **Angra Mainyu** of **Zoroastrianism**. See **Angel**, **Devil**, **Lucifer**

Satananda *H*. founder of the **Nyaya** school of Hindu philosophy. See **Darshana**, **Gautama Gotama**

Satanic Verses *I*. Not, as is popularly believed, a term coined by Salman Rushdie for his eponymous novel, but by Sir William Muir in his *Life of Mahomet* (1858). Muir recounts a report by al-Tabari (d.923) that Satan interjected words into the Koran at Surah 53:19–20, that empowered the mediatory influences of Arabian pre-Islamic pagan deities. According to al-Tabari's report the corrupted verses were annulled. The Koran offers its own reassurance: 'We sent not ever any Messenger or Prophet before thee, but that Satan cast into his fancy, when he was fancying; but God annuls what Satan cast ...' (Surah 22:51–52)

Satanism In various forms a movement which throughout history has been in opposition to Christianity, worshipping **Satan**, rather than God. It is a graphic expression of a religion cast as an absolute dualism, presenting the spiritual quest as one of radical choice between good and evil and their respective champions. Anton Szandor LaVey (1930–97) founder of San Francisco's Church of Satan, wrote the Satanic Bible in which he summarized Satanism by turning the Golden Rule on its head, 'Do unto others as they do unto you.' This inversion is an integral part of the **Black Mass**. Satanists are lovers of darkness rather than light, worshippers of the Prince of Darkness, despite his alternative name, Lucifer, meaning 'light bearer'. There is no record of these practices before the 19th century; from the Middle Ages, devil-worship was believed to be practised by witches. However the roots of Satanism are far older than its more recent manifestations and can be traced to the earliest Gnostic sects;

these were not Satanist, but they did believe the world to be absolutely evil and life a living hell. It followed that the power which created it must be the power that rules. Such ideas passed through history by means of the **Bogomils** and **Cathars**, who identified the God of the Old Testament as the Devil, with the true God withdrawn, remote from the horrors of the world created by **Yahweh**, and accessible only by means of special knowledge.

Satanism, in its more familiar form, also appeared in the 15th century as a reaction to the **Inquisition**. As with traditional religious forms, Satanism has its secularists who do not believe in Satan as a literal or personal devil. Rather is he an archetype or a symbol of the Satanic philosophy. For Satanic secularists (see **Secularism**) ideals include rational self-interest, self-indulgence and anti-social values associated with **anarchism**. Modern Satanism emerged with the **Occult** revival of the late 1800s and was made familiar by the novels of Dennis Wheatley and films such as Roman Polanski's 1968 *Rosemary's Baby*. See also **Succubus**)

FINAL WORD: 'Since Satanism is essentially a religion of the self, it holds that the individual and his personal needs come first. If that means playing with trains or spiked-heeled shoes or singing in the bathtub, those are its sacraments and devotions.' (Anton Szandor LaVey)

Sati *B*. Pal. (Skt. Smriti) A term related to the Buddhist notion of 'mindfulness'. The term is rarely used on its own, thus, *samma sati*, 'right mindfulness' and *anapanasati*, 'mindfulness with breathing'. See **Mindfulness, Smriti**

Sati *H*. Skt. 'a virtuous woman'. The wife of **Siva**, daughter of Daksha. The Vishnu Purana tells us that, 'she abandoned her body in consequence of Daksha's anger', which is generally taken to be that when her father insulted and quarrelled with her husband, she committed suicide. The myth became tragically familiar through the practice of *suttee*, 'widowburning', which has scriptural authority, 'It is proper for a woman after her husband's death, to burn herself in the fire with his corpse', and the Atharva-Veda (see **Veda**) indicated that this practice was quite common. Although many widows observed *suttee*, it is believed they were not coerced. The practice is now abandoned.

Satipathana *B*. Pal. (Skt. Smriti) 'The Four Awakenings of Mindfulness'. The mind's ability to recall, to know and to contemplate itself. It is one of the basic **meditation** practices of **Hinayana** developing **mindfulness** of i) the body, ii) the feelings, iii) the mind and iv) of mental objects. The technique is outlined in the Satipathana Sutra which explains that it can be practised either formally in sitting meditation or during all the ordinary activities of life. See **Anapanasati, Samatha, Vipassana**

Satori *Z*. Jap. The Zen term for the experience of **enlightenment** or 'awakening'.

Sattva *H*. Skt. 'harmonious' or 'composed'. One of the three *guna* or basic qualities in Hinduism's understanding of reality and human consciousness. See **Rajas, Tamas**

Saturn and **Saturnalia** *R*. The Saturnalia was a festival celebrating the Roman god Saturn, who was identified with **Cronus** of Greek mythology. It was originally held on 17 December, lasting just for the day, but eventually the celebrations and rites lasted a week. It was a kind of free-for-all, when the roles of masters and slaves were reversed, moral restrictions lifted and the rules of social etiquette ignored. It is said that the festivals of Saturnalia and **Lupercalia** are the origins of what today is the carnival season. Saturn's temple was the Forum Romanum which held the Imperial Treasury. **Ceres, Jupiter** and Veritas each claimed to be his children, his wife was Ops (see **Rhea**) and he is associated with the Norse god **Loki**. One account has Saturn's son Jupiter killing him so as to prevent him eating his children; Jupiter then castrated him and threw the genitals into the ocean where **Venus** was spawned from the god's parts.

Satyagraha *H*. Skt. 'holding (*graha*) to the truth (*satya*)'. **Mahatma Gandhi** gave the term to the world when in the 1920s and 30s he established in India his movement of non-violent disobedience. When Lord Hunter asked him to explain the *satyagraha* movement, Gandhi replied, 'It is a movement intended to replace methods of violence and a movement based entirely on truth.'

Satyr *G*. In Greek mythology the satyrs were traditionally the companions of **Dionysus**. They were believed to be part human, part beast, somewhere between a lesser god and a demon. As nature spirits they were depicted rather like dwarfs, small, with sprouting hair, upturned noses, pointed Spock-like ears and with small horns. They might be dressed in animal skins or wrapped in ivy or vines. Some combine a human torso with goat-like haunches. They play musical instruments, romp around, cause mischief, behave in a lewd, pleasure-loving way, as might be assumed of anyone in the retinue of Dionysus. They have clearly become a role-model for the behaviour of some sectors of contemporary society. Silenus was a kind of prototype satyr, described by E. R. Dodds as 'that ancient Falstaff, bald, jovial and rotund' and in company with his wine bag.

Savoy Declaration *X*. A 1658 modification of the Westminster Confession (see **Creeds, Presbyterianism**), that gave tentative structure to Congregationalist principles of faith and church government. See **Congregationalism**

Sawm or **siyyam** *I*. Arab. 'fasting'. The fourth obligation of the Five **Pillars of Islam**. See **Ramadan**

Scandinavian Religion *AE*. See **Germanic Religion, Norse Mythology**

Scapegoat *J. X.* The concept is based on the reference in Lev. 16:22 which records how High Priest Aaron transferred 'all the iniquities and transgression of the Israelites', to the goat's head, '… the goat shall carry on it all their iniquities to an inaccessible region; and the goat shall be set free in the wilderness.' Thus, the goat 'escapes' with a burden of sins that are not its own. The ritual was performed on the Day of Atonement (see **Yom Kippur**) and has become a 'type' or model for Jesus Christ by whose death atonement was made for the sins of humanity. Frazer, in *The Golden Bough*, gives an account of human sacrifice being made in Nigeria of a young girl purchased from a distant tribe. While still alive she was dragged along the ground from the village to a place beyond it. All members of the community were expected to make a contribution to the cost of buying the 'scapegoat'. Although the goat was not sacrificed and got off lightly, it was a substitute victim and the concept set the pattern for biblical religions of a salvation achieved by vicarious sacrifice, the innocent being substituted for the guilty. See **Sin Eater**

Scepticism Pyrrho (c.360–c.270 BCE) systematized arguments for the 'suspension of belief' to form the basis for a complete attitude to life. He asked and gave answers to three questions, which have always had current value. i) What are things really like? Answer: Unknowable. ii) What should our attitude be towards them? Answer: Non-committal. iii) What will we gain from this attitude? Answer: Peace of mind. The **Academy** continued to develop the doctrine of Scepticism through **Socrates** and the **Stoics** until 80 BCE, when it began to fall away before its antithesis, Dogmatism. See **Agnosticism, Dogmatics, Hellenism**

Scholasticism *X.* Lat. *schola*, from the Greek *shcole*, 'leisure', 'debate', 'school'. The term refers to the medieval Christian traditions of philosophy and theology that were grouped into schools around their principal protagonists. The agenda for Scholasticism was set by St **Augustine**, who pioneered the link between belief and understanding and by Boethius, who introduced medieval thought to logic through his translations of **Aristotle** and Porphyry. The role of human reason, in contradistinction to God's revelation in scripture, was a central issue which has continued to be debated into modern times (see for example **Barth**). Much energy was spent debating and commentating on the philosophical systems of previous thinkers and the term 'scholastic' became pejorative, as representing something unoriginal and irrelevant. In general this is a misreading, since thinkers like **Aquinas**, John Scotus Erigena, Duns Scotus, **Anselm** and Abelard, were all concerned to further a deeper understanding of faith and life as a living theology.

Schoolmen See **Scholasticism**

Schopenhauer (1788–1860) A German philosopher considered by some to represent a pessimistic world view, understanding the normal experience of life to be one of suffering, in world that is evil. Against this seemingly doom-laden background, his thinking is a form of **Voluntarism**, in that his description of reality combines a world that exists simultaneously, as both will and representation. Interestingly his perception has similarities with aspects of both Hindu and Buddhist philosophy, claiming an influence from the **Upanishads**. Schopenhauer shares their perception of deliverance from suffering being achieved by compassion, aesthetics and asceticism. His influence is far-reaching, having touched, for example, **Nietzsche**, **Darwin**, **Wagner**, **Freud**, **Jung**, **Wittgenstein**, Dylan Thomas, Thomas Mann, Tolstoy and many other writers, artists and musicians.

FINAL WORD: 'Kant and Berkley always seemed to be very deep thinkers, but with Schopenhauer you seem to be looking at the bottom straight away.' (Wittgenstein)

Science of Man See Holy Order of MANS

Scientific Pantheism A modern form of **pantheism** that reveres the universe, both the macrocosm and microcosm accessed by all forms of modern science. It is also known as 'natural pantheism'. The movement does not believe in deities or supernatural powers or a creator God. Its energy is an aesthetic and emotional response to the **numinous** power of the universe with which the adherent 'feels' total unity.

FINAL WORD: 'A religion old or new, that stressed the magnificence of the universe as revealed by modern science, might be able to draw forth reserves of reverence and awe hardly tapped by the conventional faiths. Sooner or later, such a religion will emerge.' (Carl Sagan)

Scientific Society for the Creation of Values *B*. Jap. See *Soka Gakkai* and Japanese Religions

Scientific Study of Judaism *J*. (Ger. *Wissenschaft des Judentums)* is a spin-off from the **Enlightenment** which has had considerable influence on modern Jewish thought and culture. The 'scientific' method of study implied a scrupulous objectivity, specifically in the search for an understanding of Judaism through a methodical analysis of its history. The subject of study was brought under the scholastic scrutiny of a number of disciplines, principally philosophy, philology and history. It has its origin in 19th-century Germany, the prime mover being Nachman Krochmal (1785–1840) who was influenced by Moses **Mendelssohn's** (1729–86) liberal philosophy of tolerance, universal religion and education. Krochmal's main interest was in the philosophy of history and he believed a theological understanding of Judaism was best found through an understanding of its historical energy derived from an interventionist God. Judaism and history were indissoluble, because God was a God of history who used individuals, communities and nations to further his purpose for humankind. Inevitably, the methods implied by *Wissenschaft des Judentums* involved **secular** ideas and methods of study that were not confined to the study of Judaism. The academic disciplines of

Wissenschaft became the greatest challenge to all religious systems, because it undermined the principle of unchanging precepts and doctrines, of fixed revelation and absolute truth and demanded answers to questions about the nature of authority. The academic inter-disciplinary study of religion that became established in European and American universities has its origin in the *Haskalah*, the Jewish Enlightenment. See **Judaism and Secularism**

Scientism A movement or attitude of scientific fundamentalism, believing that science affords absolute and exclusive access to the truth. As such it takes precedence over other disciplines such as religion, ethics and **humanism**. It asserts that only what is knowable through the natural sciences is valid and that consequently it is necessary to disregard, even to eradicate, the claims made by metaphysical and philosophical speculation. Popular during the 19th and early 20th century, it came to owe a great deal to the methods of inductive logic, **logical positivism** and the philosophy of Bertrand **Russell**. It stands in opposition to the conclusions of explanatory dualism which accepts, for example, that while movements of the human body can be explained scientifically, not all forms of human behaviour can. This form of dualism allows for the irrational and for explanations that are drawn from other sources than the natural sciences. One of Scientism's staunchest advocates was Herbert **Spencer**. See **Darwinism**, **Dualism**, **Positivism**
FINAL WORD: 'The maps produced by modern materialistic scientism leave all the questions that really matter unanswered. More than that, they do not even show a way to a possible answer; they deny the validity of the questions.' (E. F. Schumacher)

Scientology Originally a secular philosophy propounded by L. Ron Hubbard in 1952, then redefined as an 'applied religious philosophy' with 'Scientology' as a 'study of knowledge'. The Church of Scientology was established in New Jersey in 1954. Its wide-ranging beliefs included the realization of human potential, reincarnation, salvation as freedom from the limitations of matter, energy and space and the existence of *engrams*, a form of mental record of pain and unconsciousness that may have been laid down in a previous life. *Engrams* have to be 'audited', a process that costs hundreds of thousands of dollars. Its agenda was varied, comprising drug treatment centres, criminal rehabilitation, mental health and educational programmes, a 'moral' values campaign, business management and consultancy, publishing and lobby groups aimed at political leaders to implement 'The Universal Declaration of Human Rights'. The Church attracted considerable controversy and was accused of having a pseudoscientific basis and of being a cynical and unscrupulous commercial institution which harassed and exploited its members. Hubbard left over 500,000 pages of writings and over 2,000 tapes that constitute the Church's scriptures. It has attracted celebrity practitioners such as John Travolta and Tom Cruise.

Scriptures Lat. *scruptura*, literally, anything written. The term is familiarly associated with the official canons of religious literature, but not
exclusively with the Old and New Testaments of the Bible and the Koran.
Although 'sacred books' or 'sacred texts' is used of the Hindu Vedas, the
Buddhist Sutras and for the equivalents of other religions with a written
tradition and authority, the term 'scripture' is sometimes loosely applied.
The officially accepted forms of sacred literatures are the authority of its
orthodoxy and in some instances the physical volumes are themselves
held to be sacred, such as Judaism's *Sefer Torahs* (see **Torah**), housed in
the Ark of the synagogue. Scripture is held to be the definitive record of
revelation and commentary, the canon of which is usually fixed at a given
point in history by the councils governing the religions in question. After
these dates, nothing can be added or withdrawn from the canon.

Séance From the French meaning 'a sitting'. Used of a meeting of people
who are gathered to receive messages from the dead or to study whatever
the **mediums** are able to disclose. Sometimes such messages are not
given through the medium, but through the automatic writing of, for
example, the ouija board or planchette or by an interpretation of table-
turning. Those attending séances usually sit around a table holding hands,
thus creating a unified field of 'force' through which the spirit can manifest itself. See **Spiritism**, **Spiritualism**

Second Coming X. The *Parousia* (Gk. 'presence' or 'arrival'). A term
referring to the return of Christ in glory at some future time. The tradition of Christian eschatology affirms that when this takes place both the
living and the dead will be judged and the present world order will be
replaced by one of justice and peace over which Christ will reign (see
also **Millenarianism**). The early Church believed that the return of Christ
was imminent but as the years have rolled by without this taking place,
Christianity has discouraged speculation about the precise time and
manner of the event. Nevertheless, Adventist groups have emerged interpreting current events as signalling the expected return of Christ. See
Advent, **Adventism**, **Millerite Movement**, **Seventh Day Adventists**,
Shakers

Secret Societies From the earliest of Egyptian and Greek **mystery religions** to the modern **Freemasons**, secret societies have been a familiar
scene throughout the history of religions. Usually the need for secrecy is
the desire to keep certain forms of knowledge inaccessible except to
those initiated. The reasons for this are various; in some cases, the knowledge sought was thought to be esoteric and would risk corruption in the
hands of the wrong people. Some societies, at risk politically, used
secrecy as a form of protection, others established loosely within a
broader structure, like the **Knights Templar**, guarded their exclusivity in
order to fulfil the function for which they were founded. More simply, as
with the Freemasons, the 'secrets' were originally designed to protect the
guild practices and standards of the medieval operative masons. More

interesting today is the question as to why anyone should wish to join a secret society. The social and psychological needs are not hard to discern, but whatever these may be there is something to be said for preserving groups that have a long and rich history and which, as such, are a part of our cultural heritage.

FINAL WORD: 'The very word "secrecy" is repugnant in a free and open society; and we are as a people inherently and historically opposed to secret societies, to secret oaths and to secret proceedings.' (John Fitzgerald Kennedy)

'Do nothing secretly; for Time sees and hears all things and discloses all.' (Sophocles)

Sect Literally, a 'cutting' or 'scion'. The word is usually applied to a group broken away from its original association and standing apart from both society and its own roots. The term is frequently used pejoratively in a Christian context, as for example, of heretical groups. The sociology of religion (see **Religion, Sociology**) uses the term neutrally to refer to breakaway groups that emphasize a particular aspect or doctrine, of their original religious affiliation at the expense of others, to the point of developing as distinct religions. In time, these are accommodated into the general religious culture. Examples include **Christian Scientists**, **Jehovah's Witnesses** and the **Mormons**; in China the **Yellow Turbans**; in **Sikhism** the *Sahaj-dhari* Sikhs. See **Sectarianism**

Sectarianism In general a narrow-minded attitude confined to the limited dogmas and terms of reference of a particular point of view, which is usually a bigoted commitment to a factional opinion. It has its origins in post-Reformation **Protestantism**, where splinter-groups were pejoratively termed 'sects', but today sectarianism is used in reference to inter-religious and inter-ideological conflict as, for example, between Protestants and Roman Catholics in Northern Ireland or between Shiite and Sunni Muslims. **Marxism** understands sectarianism to be the attitude of those who put their own philosophies and needs above those of the proletariat. Further examples were evident in the Balkan civil war as Croats, Slovenes, Serbs, Macedonians, Bosniaks and Albanians fought to establish their religious, cultural and linguistic identities. Sociologists of the Indian subcontinent use the term 'communalism', in reference to the conflicts between Hindu and Muslim (see **Islam**), Hindu-Sikh or Hindu-Christian communities.

FINAL WORD: 'Sectarianism is a perverse form of worldliness in the disguise of religion; it breeds a narrowness of heart in greater measure than the cult of the world based upon material interest can ever do...' (Rabindranath Tagore)

Secular Alternatives to Religion Most secular alternatives to religion address a psychological need for the characteristic features of religion such as **idealism**, the security of a dogmatic uniformity offered, for example, by **Communism**. Some movements offering a secular alternative focus on a personality, for example the Cuban Marxist revolutionary, Che Guevara, who in the late 1960s became an icon symbolizing a left-wing political ideology for young people throughout the world. A further example is the cult wrapped around Elvis Presley now constituted, not too seriously, as the **First Preslyterian Church of Elvis the Divine**. Secular alternatives are broadly cast in two groups, the first of which, 'hard secularism', rigorously denies any form of metaphysical terms of reference. The second group, 'soft secularism', allows the possibility of a reinterpretation of religious concepts in secular forms, such as the 'religionless' Christianity of Dietrich **Bonhoeffer**. What lies at the heart of a secular alternative to religion is the nature and intensity of an individual's commitment. There need be no actual equivalent to a belief in God or to any metaphysical resource; what constitutes the alternative is whatever it is that serves the same function as religion in the life of the secular individual. The commitment and the ideology to which it is made, will provide all the resources necessary to enable the individual to understand the meaning and purpose of life and to realize his personal potential for creative fulfilment. Philosophies such as **Positivism**, **Utopianism**, **Utilitarianism**, together with ideologies like **Environmentalism**, **Gaia**, **Life Spring**, **Humanism** and **Marxism** provide a context for secular 'faith'. Texts such as More's *Utopia* and **Rousseau**'s *Social Contract*, and others such as *The Sayings of Chairman Mao*, *The Origin of Species*, the *Communist Manifesto* and *Mein Kampf* have had for many, the authority of scripture. The proliferation of sects in Japan (see **Japanese Religions**) reflects a general movement away from religion to the complete secularization the religious quest.

Secular Humanism A term coined during the 20th century to distinguish its philosophy from **Religious Humanism**. While the latter allows for the possibility of a spiritual, secular humanism disavows the existence of any form of metaphysics. However, it does seem to offer itself as a thoroughgoing alternative to religion, in that it addresses ultimate concerns even though 'ultimate' is relative to this one life and to those who will succeed us. Secular Humanists are concerned to test beliefs by scientific methods; they are committed to the realization of human potential, to growth and creativity; their inner quest is for objective truth and their dominant concern is for a better world based on viable personal and social morality, tolerance and the acceptance of personal responsibility for the choices we make. Such preoccupations and goals may well serve, for the secularist, the same functions and fulfil the same needs as religious belief and commitment. See **Humanism**, **Human Potential Movement**, **Secularism**

FINAL WORD: 'Secular humanists reject supernatural and authoritarian beliefs. They affirm that we must take responsibility for our own lives and the communities and world in which we live. Secular humanism emphasizes reason and scientific inquiry, individual freedom and responsibility, human values and compassion and the need for tolerance and co-operation.' (From the website of The Council for Secular Humanism)

Secularism A philosophy affirming that all forms of belief, morality, thought and institutions, should be withdrawn from religious and metaphysical control and influence. Every aspect of life and culture should be determined by what is best for society in purely existentialist terms (see **Existentialism**). The word 'secular' has a very long history and originally meant, from the Latin *saeculum*, a period of time, roughly that of the life-span of a human being, that is, of a generation. The term came to be used for 'this present world' or 'the present age'. This classical meaning changed during the medieval period, when *saeculum* was used by the Church to refer to the clergy who lived in 'the world' rather than in a religious order. Today the term is used generally in contradistinction to the term 'sacred'. 'Secularism' is the philosophy of the secular. It is the development of ideas and concepts that describe and define life and society without recourse to religious perceptions, values and terms of reference. 'Secularization' is the long process that has freed the human mind, 'first from religious and then from metaphysical control of his reason and his language' (van Peursen); it is a process which necessitates radical change.

In place of received religious authority, traditions and values, secularism makes a rational appraisal of society's needs which focuses on the *saeclum*, the 'here and now' in terms of its uniqueness. In practice this would include, for example, the withdrawal of State sponsorship of religious groups; the end of religious teaching in State-funded education; the exclusion of religious criteria in appointments to public office or in the application of civil rights; the repeal of legislation designed to protect religiously defined values, as for example, in all forms of censorship or to safeguard the religion itself. In effect, secularism allows people the freedom to deviate from values and practices held to be sacrosanct for generations, to abandon tradition and to think for themselves. A truly secular culture is not anti-religious, but creates the free space in which religions of every kind can benefit from the free choice people make, uninfluenced by established and official policy. A truly secular society is an 'open' and pluralistic society.

Secularism has had a formative influence on modern history and present culture. It has to be understood as a consequence of the philosophies of the **Enlightenment** such as John Stuart **Mill**'s **utilitarianism**, Auguste Comte's positivist humanism (see **Positivism**), **Rousseau**'s *Social Contract* and Ludwig **Feuerbach**'s reduction of theology to anthropology. To these energies must be added, Darwin's perception of the 'created' world (see **Darwinism**); Marx's radical revision of the nature of society (see **Marxism**) and Lenin's **dialectic materialism** (see **Leninism**). It would seem inevitable that all religions and mysticisms would either gradually evaporate in the clean air of secular **rationalism** or remain as vestigial and rather quaint folk customs, perhaps subjects for a museum of religion. Not only has this not happened, but new forms of traditional religions have faced the challenge of secularism and by consequence have gathered strength. In an attempt to speak to the present age in terms that are relevant and sustain meaning, most religions have gone through a process of **demythologizing** and 'dereligionizing'. One example is **Bonhoeffer**'s attempt to restate Christianity in secular terms, placing the theological emphasis on this world, rather than on any expectation of a world to come, on behaviour rather than belief, on creative thinking rather than on a slavish adherence to **fundamentalism**. A further example is the 19th-century Jewish enlightenment (see *Haskalah* and the **Scientific Study of Judaism**) which gave rise to a new **Jewish Humanism** that searched for a modern expression of Judaism that holds to its ancient roots. In their Western forms, both Buddhism and Hinduism try to address the modern secular mind, reinterpreting central doctrines such as **karma** and **reincarnation** in terms of a psychology and sociology of **religion**, and of a more rational understanding of human life and the universe.

The process of secularization is so much part of Western culture that 'secular' is no longer thought of as an antonym of 'sacred'. Happily, this dualism has mostly fallen away to be replaced by an existentialist perception of the miracle of the mundane. See **Evolutionary Humanism, Human Potential Movement, Pluralism, Pragmatism, Religious Humanism, Secular Humanism**

FINAL WORD: 'Not even the visionary or mystical experience ever lasts very long. It is for art to capture that experience, to offer it to, in the cause of literature, its readers; to be, for secular, materialistic culture, some sort of replacement for what the love of God offers in the world of faith.' (Salman Rushdie)

'The fundamental mistake of Indian secularism is that Hinduism is put in the same category as Islam and Christianity. Islam and Christianity's intrinsic irrationality and hostility to independent critical thought warranted secularism as a kind of containment policy. By contrast, Hinduism recognises freedom of thought and does not need to be contained by secularism.' (Koenraad Elst)

Sefer Torahs See **Torah**

Sefiroth See **Sephiroth**

Seicho-No-le *J*. Jap. 'Truth of Life'. The movement was founded in Japan in 1930 by Dr Masaharu Taniguchi. After years of intensive study and meditation he received divine inspiration, intuitively hearing the voice of God speaking to him. The Truth of Life Movement teaches that all evil stems from the deluded mind of human beings and that everything in the environment is a reflection of that mind. Phenomena do not exist, only God and his manifestations are real and eternal. All religions are derived from the one God and all human beings are his children. Everyone has a divine nature and carries the potential of God's creative powers. 'Jesus Christ's crucifixion means the perfect negation of flesh. If and only when

man crucifies his flesh in this sense, can he acquire eternal life.'
Taniguchi carried out a healing ministry, many being cured of their illnesses and infirmities simply by listening to his talks.

Seiyu Kiriyama *B*. the founder of **Agon Shu Buddhism**.

Sekem *E*. One of the seven constituent parts of the Egyptian concept
of the soul, being the divine inner light or life-force of the person. See
Soul, Egyptian

Seku *E*. The mortal remains of a deceased person or the house of the soul.
See **Soul, Egyptian**

Selah *J*. The term used in or to conclude a Psalm. Its meaning is doubtful
and some authorities believe it to be a remnant of musical pointing for
chanting the verses, indicating a breath, a pause or the finale. In the
Talmud the term is taken to mean, 'for ever and to all eternity', a
meaning which in most instances fits the text.

Selam *I*. A form of salutation. See **Salaam**

Self-realization From being a 'noble' concept in Eastern religion, 'self-
realization' has become something of a vogue term in the West.
Numerous religious and secular groups exist offering ways and means to
the realization of one's 'true self' (See **Human Potential Movement**,
Self-Realization Fellowship). Such movements offer a sharp contrast to
salvatory religions like Christianity that teach the need for the self to die
or the surrendering of the self to God as a condition of salvation. The
person we 'imagine' ourselves to be is conditioned by genetics, environment, culture and education. Self-realization movements are focused on
the notion that we have an original unconditioned self, the discovery of
which constitutes a form of **enlightenment**. The experience or realization
of this self radically changes our perceptions so that we begin to see
things 'as they are' and not through a gauze of illusion. The consequences
of self-realization depend upon the tradition in which this is achieved.
See **Atman**, **Life Spring**, **Maya**, **Nirvana**, **Sahaya Yoga**

Self-Realization Fellowship (**SRF**) Formally, the Yogoda Satsanga
Society of India, the SRF was founded in the USA in 1920 by
Paramahansa **Yogananda**. Its principal aim is the worldwide dissemina-
tion of the techniques of kriya **yoga**, for the spiritual benefit of all
humanity. The Fellowship's headquarters is in Los Angeles, California.
Yogananda defined the aims of SRF to be 'fellowship with God through
Self-Realization and friendship with all truth-seeking souls'.

Seljuk *I*. An Islamic Turkish dynasty that dominated central and western
Asia from the 11th–14th century. Tradition provides an historical
founder, Kynyk Seljuqs, the *bey* or chieftain of a Turkish clan c.1000 CE.

Having defeated the Byzantines at Manzikert in 1017, the Seljuks defended the Holy Land against the **Crusades**. They eventually established a considerable empire that made possible the settlement of Turkic-speaking people in Anatolia, an event that led, by way of the Ottomans, to the founding of the Turkish Republic in the 20th century. Seljuk methods of government and education prevailed in Iran until the 19th century. See **Islamic Dynasties, Sultanate**

Sema Ceremonies *l*. A central ritual of the **Mevlevi Tariqah**, based on the whirling dance for which they are renowned. The *semahane* is the circular hall where this takes place under the supervision of the *semazenbashi*, the dance master. The ceremony is highly ritualistic and the combined choreography of the dervishes' movements are complicated, while those of the individual's dance is relatively simple. Both are symbolic. The dance is intended to induce a state of meditation on the love of God; each dervish whirls smoothly and effortlessly around his own axis, one foot always firmly on the ground, the other passing over and around it in a kind of pirouette. It is a figure of the movements of the planets. Their right hand is carried high to receive God's mercy which passes, by way of the heart, through the body to be transmitted to earth by means of the lowered left hand. The music to which they dance has elements of classical Eastern forms, but cannot be written down. See **Dervish Groups, Sufism**

Semiotics The theory of signs and symbols or more generally the study of the patterns of communication systems, including language. Also called 'semiology'. The term was first used by the 17th-century philosopher John **Locke**, who from the Greek *semeion*, 'mark' or 'sign', coined the word 'semeiotike'. The system, first developed by the American philosopher C. S. Peirce (1839–1914) (see **Pragmatism**) and the Swiss linguist Ferdinand de Saussure (1857–1913) aims to understand how meaning becomes attached to signs and how they are interpreted by both individuals and groups. Semiotics understands language to be a complex relationship of signs which should, itself, be subjected to analysis so as to understand how words have meaning ascribed to them and how that meaning is interpreted. The system has had far-reaching influence on, for example **Structuralism** and Post-Structuralism, on new perceptions and theories of theology, theosophy, Western and Eastern mysticism and biblical hermeneutics. See **Atomism, Logical Positivism, Logical Atomism, Symbolism**

Semitic Generally of or concerning Semites, their language and culture. The languages include Arabic, Hebrew, Amharic and Aramaic. The noun 'Semite', customarily refers to Jews and Arabs. As an adjective the word is derived from 'Shem' or its Greek form in the **Septuagint**, 'Sem', one of the three sons of Noah (see Genesis 5:31, 6:10). The term is most familiar in its negative form, anti-Semitic, which designates the political ideas, attitudes and superstitions associated with the persecution of Jews. See **National Socialism, Ugaritic**

Seneca *Ami*. The Iroquoian term meaning 'people of the standing stone' or 'projecting rock'. One of the Six Nations or original tribes of the Iroquois League. See **Handsome Lake Religion**

Senussi *I*. Or *Sanusi*. A religio-political organization founded in 1837 in the Sudan and Libya, by Muhammad bin Ali al-Sanusi (1791–1859). He was known as the 'Grand Sanusi'. His movement was, in effect, a religious revival for which Sanusi drew on the teachings of the various Sufi orders, adapting them for life in the desert. Concerned about the general weakening of Islam, he called for overt political activism of the kind associated with the **Wahhabis** in Arabia. They unsuccessfully resisted French and Italian colonial ambitions in the Sahara and Libya. Most of their *zawaya*, places of worship and welfare centres, were destroyed by the Italians and the Senussi never really recovered. However, both in Libya and the Sudan there remain groups affiliated to the Senussi.

Sephardim *J*. Heb. 'Spanish'. The Sephardim are Jews who migrated from the Middle East to the Iberian Peninsula in the 8th–9th centuries. In 1492 they fled Spain because of the **Inquisition**, and five years later were expelled from Portugal. They spread through North Africa, southeastern Europe, then back to the Near and Middle East and eventually to America. Despite the **diaspora**, Sephardic traditions and culture has thrived. The Sephardim also include Jews from Islamic Mediterranean countries, together with those settled in northern Spain's Christian kingdoms. In Spain under Islamic rule, Jews were free to work in most areas of trade, industry and agriculture and they were also landowners. Culturally, the Sephardim held secularism and religion in a creative balance with the result that by the middle of the 11th century Judaism emerged from its religious and cultural isolation to established an intellectual independence (see **Maimonides**). This assimilation did not undermine their Judaism and Sephardic Jews were responsible for notable compilations of Talmudic commentaries, for *Halakhah*, and for establishing centres for the Kabbalah. The Sephardim are one of two major Jewish traditions, the other being the **Ashkenazim**.

Sephiroth or **Sefiroth** *J*. A central concept in the teaching of the **Zohar** and the practice of Kabbalah. They are the ten attributes, manifestations or radiances of God as the *Ein Sof*, the Crown being the highest of them. The other nine manifestations are: wisdom, intelligence or knowledge, mercy or loving-kindness, judgement or might, beauty, victory, glory or splendour, foundation and kingdom. The names of the manifestations are arbitrary and traditional and their deeper 'hidden' significances are wrapped around by Kabbalistic mysticism. The opposite of the Sephiroth are the *Sitra Achra*, the 'other side' or the forces of evil that underlie all reality and which derive mostly from human sin. The ten Sephiroth form a channel of divine energy, a path which if followed overcomes all dualities, making an immediate connection between male and female, light and darkness, sin and righteousness, good and evil, spirit and matter. Thus, the Sephirothic path leads the adherent from duality to non-duality, to the soul's true 'at-one-ment' with the divine. See **Dualism**

Septuagint *J. X.* The pre-Christian Greek translation of the Jewish scriptures sometimes designated LXX, accomplished in Alexandria, Egypt, between 300 and 200 BCE. It was to be used extensively by Hellenistic Jews (see **Hellenism**) who being less than fluent in Hebrew needed a Greek translation so as to access their scriptures. The Septuagint also allowed non-Jews an insight into the Jewish faith. During the reign of Ptolemy Philadelphus, 70 scholars (hence LXX) were commissioned to work on the translation. The Septuagint had a considerable influence on developing Christian thought since it provided insight to the Old Testament not previously available. The Eastern Orthodox Church (see **Orthodox Church**) still uses the Septuagint for its teaching on the Old Testament and modern translations of the Bible continue to rely on it. See **Tanakh**

Serapis *G.* A Hellenistic-Egyptian god whose earlier Greek cult, Osiris-Apis, became Serapis. In the accounts of the death of Alexander the Great, there is mention of Serapis' temple in Babylon where he was consulted on the King's behalf. It was held that Serapis was a god of healing, who through dreams and visions cured those who slept in his temple. This association with Alexander's death may be the reason for Osiris-Apis becoming the chief cult of Ptolemy. In 385 CE, Christians destroyed the Serapeum (Serapis' temple) in Alexandria and Theodosius banned the cult by decree. See **Healing**

Sermon on the Mount *X.* The familiar name given to Jesus' discourse to his disciples and assembled crowd as recorded in Matt. 5–7. The title is assumed from Matt. 5:1, 'When he saw the crowds he went up the hill.' The sermon set out the main precepts of Christian ethics and includes the **Beatitudes** and the **Lord's Prayer**.

Serpent See **Snakes and Snake Deities**

Serpent Seed A tradition based on the belief that Eve's sin (see **Fall of Man**) in the Garden of Eden (Gen. 3) was of a sexual nature. Having had intercourse with the Serpent (see **Satan**), she gave birth to Cain, Adam not being his true father. The descendents of Cain survived the flood through Noah's son Ham, whose descendents are associated with various ethnic and social groups. For example, the **Christian Identity Movement** believe Ham's descendents are the Jews, the **Unification Church** say they are atheists and communists; the Nation of **Yahweh** have them as the whites, and **Branhamism** as the lost and eternally damned. See **Snakes and Snake Deities**

Set *E*. A member of the Great **Ennead**, one of the children of **Seth** and **Tefnut**. Although listed separately as a child of Seth, it is likely that Set and Seth are manifestations of the same god, however over the periods of the different dynasties the relationship became confused. See **Church of Set**

Seth *E*. The god of wind and storms and a member of the Osirian Triad in the **Ennead** of Heliopolis. He murdered his brother **Osiris**, whose son Horus took revenge and, with the support of the council of gods, banished him to the deserts. The myth has it that Seth was evil from birth, having torn his way out of his mother's body by ripping a hole in her side. He became the embodiment of evil but was never all bad, being the protector of the barge of **Ra**, the sun god, during his nightly journey through the underworld. He is depicted as a man with the head of an unknown animal or takes the form of a crocodile. In his conflict with Horus he is sometimes represented as a hippopotamus or a black pig.

Seveners *I*. A familiar term for Shiite Isma'ilis. The name is derived from Ismail, the son of the sixth **Imam** Jafar al-Sadiq (d. 765) who is believed by the sect to have founded the legitimate succession with Ismail as the seventh Imam. See **Isma'ilis**, **Shi'ism**, **Twelvers**

Seventh Day Adventists *X*. An Adventist group that grew out of the prophetic **Millerite movement** during the 19th century 'Great Awakening' in the USA. Expecting the return of Christ around 1843, they began to observe the **Sabbath** on the seventh day of the week, although the name itself was not assumed until 1861. The group was formed in England in a Southampton mission in 1878. They are vehemently **Protestant**, practising adult baptism and the observation of the Sabbath in accordance with Jewish tradition, from sunset on Fridays to sunset on Saturday. See **Advent**, **Adventism**, **Second Coming**

Sexual Symbolism Sex, as passion, ecstasy, love and intimate union, has provided religion with one of its most powerful analogies. The intimate joining of two separate beings is a poignant image of the soul's or 'true' self's union, with the divine. 'The mutual attraction of the sexes is the craving of an incomplete being to be made complete' (Benjamin Walker). **Aphrodite** and **Venus** are examples of deities that had hugely successful cults devoted to sexual love. A medieval Kabbalistic (see **Kabbalah**) sect taught that the universe was sustained by human sexual activity, which if stopped would see the gradual disintegration of the created world. The Rabbinical interpretation of the Old Testament's *Song of Solomon*, a love story, is of God's love for his wife, Israel; in the New Testament the Church or the 'new' Israel is 'the Bride of Christ'. In one of his poems, St **John of the Cross** describes mystical union as the:
'night that joined the lover,
To the beloved bride,

Transfiguring them each into the other.'
(Trans. Roy Campbell)

Many of the actual or simulated rituals of sexual intercourse were associated with fertility rites, enacted to ensure a good harvest and increased
flocks and herds. The Tutelos, a **Sioux** nation absorbed into the **Iroquois**,
performed the naked dance, known also as 'shaking the bush'. During the
dance a man and woman copulated to act out a ritual symbolizing the
ploughing of fertile fields. The explicit sexual nature of some Hindu and
Buddhist art is associated with traditions such as **Shaktism** and
Tantrism, that use sex as a means of 'awakening' or **enlightenment**;
each god has his female consort and the focus is on the act of creation and
on the energies involved in bringing the universe into existence. In
Tantric sexual practice the participants are trained to hold back at the
point of orgasm and to redirect the energy through the **chakras**. This
moment of intense restraint, together with techniques of breath control,
are said to bring about hallucinations and an ecstasy that is metaphysical.
See **Vajrayana**

FINAL WORD: 'The whole question of sexual symbolism within religion is
a vast and complicated one, but it is worth remembering (especially for
those whose cultural environment is that of European Protestantism) that
sexual forces are too real and powerful simply to be dismissed as having
no part in religion.' (Trevor Ling)

Shahadah or **Kalimah** *I*. Arab. 'witness'. The first obligation of the
Pillars of Islam.

Shaivism *H*. The devotional cult associated with **Siva**, who with **Brahma**
and **Vishnu** makes up the Hindu trinity. The cult's name varies in
different regions of India. Shaivists devote themselves exclusively to
the veneration of Shiva, whose worship is one of the three established
traditions of Hindu devotion, the other two being **Vaishnavism** and
Shaktism.

Shakers *X*. Under the leadership of James Wardely, who was influenced
by the French millennial prophets the *Convulsionaires* (1720–70), the
sect broke away from a Manchester Quaker group (see **Society of
Friends**). They are also known as 'The United Society of Believers in
Christ's Second Coming' or 'The Millennial Church'. The origin of the
name 'Shakers' is pejorative being a description of their physical movements during ecstatic experiences when they danced, shouted, trembled
and spoke in tongues (see **Glossolalia**). In 1772, the leadership of the
Shakers was assumed by Ann Lee, known as Mother Ann who, as a result
of a vision whilst in prison, believed herself to be 'the female principle
in Christ' and the fulfilment of his **Second Coming**. In 1774 she took a
group of Shakers to the USA; they settled in Albany, NY, where they
became known for their celibacy and for the simplicity of their way of
life (cf. the **Amish**) as they sought to establish on earth their vision of
heaven. The celibacy is reflected in their calling each other 'sister' and

'brother', and even married couples who converted were expected to abstain from sexual practice. Their considerable growth in number was due entirely to adoption and conversion. Known for their honesty and hard work, their farms and businesses brought them considerable prosperity and the quality of their designs and products are to be seen, for example, in their furniture. At their height, 1830–40, they numbered around 6,000. In 1997 it was thought the Shakers consisted of only seven or eight women. See **Camisards**

Shakti or **Sakti** *H*. Skt. 'force', 'power' or 'energy'. The goddess wife or the female energy of a deity, but especially of Siva. She is worshipped throughout India under a variety of names. As the female energy of **Siva** she is associated with creativity, the force that sustains the universe and makes all life possible. By her power Siva creates, maintains and destroys the world. In Tantra, each *chakra* is controlled by a Shakti.

Shaktism *H*. Also called Tantrism. The devotional cult associated with the worship of Shakti as the primal force or energy, most commonly identified with the sexual vitality that resolves male and female duality, resulting in the creation of life. Unsurprisingly, the symbols of Shaktism are explicitly sexual in nature and Hindu iconography graphically portrays the act of sexual intercourse (see **Sexual Symbolism**). Devotees of Shaktism make use of sexual ritual of the kind described in the *Karma Sutra* and practised in *kundalini* yoga. Many Shaktism cults now use sexual rites as symbols of meditation techniques designed to achieve spiritual, rather than physical union (see **Sexual Symbolism**, **Tantra**). See **Shaivism**, **Vaishnavism**

Shakyamuni Buddha *B*. An epithet for the historical **Buddha**, the wise one of the Shakya clan, of which his father was chief.

Shalom Aleichem *J*. Heb. 'May peace be upon you.' The traditional greeting used when two Jews meet; also the name of the song that begins the Friday-night Sabbath meal. At the simplest level God is asked to bless the house with peace, to ensure there are no conflicts between members of the assembled family and their friends. At a deeper level, the Hebrew root *shalem* means 'complete' and the song asks God to bless the home, indeed the whole world with 'completeness', so that it should lack nothing essential. The Sabbath, being a celebration of creation, the perfection and completeness of God's original work, is to be reflected in the quality of individual and collective lives. See **Salaam**

Shamanism A spiritual world view characteristic of Siberian, Central Asian and Native American people. It is not a religion in itself, but a tradition not dissimilar to mysticism, that is found within or as part of various religions. Shamanism is 'one of the archaic techniques of ecstasy – at once mysticism, magic and "religion", in the broadest sense of the term' (Mircea Eliade). The shaman's role is vocational and sometimes hereditary; he stands apart from the community which he serves, separated by the intensity of his own spiritual experience and his unique communion with the spirits of another world. The shaman is both a witch doctor and spiritual leader who can provide healing, guidance through divination and wisdom through **spiritism** and altered states of consciousness. The shaman must pass through a form of initiation that comprises both traditional and ecstatic instruction, the one involving tutorship in shamanic techniques and esoteric knowledge, the other derived from dreams and their interpretation and from visions received in a state of trance. Indispensable to the shaman's ritual is his drum, a vehicle of the sound and beat which conveys him into the other world. Part of his baggage will include hallucinogenic plants like **peyote** (see **Peyore Cults**) and the psilocybe mushrooms or *Rivea corymbosa*, the Morning Glory, which are not addictive. Such plants may be carried by the shaman in **medicine bundles** together with tobacco, bits of bone, stones or crystals that have magical properties and talismanic associations. While enacting his rituals the shaman may wear the skin of a specific animal or be disguised as a particular bird, so as to experience a form of metamorphosis or better perhaps, metemsomatosis, which enables a level of unity between the shaman and the spirit of the creature in question. During his ecstatic trance he may descend into the underworld or be carried off to heaven, 'ecstasy' here meaning the soul's release, at least temporarily, from its physical confinement. In this process he will encounter gods, demons and the spirits of the dead and, thus, being better able to communicate with them, he can plead for the cure of a life-threatening disease or for the passage of a soul he accompanies to its final resting place.

FINAL WORD: 'Shamanism is an ecstatic religious complex of particular and fixed elements, with a specified ideology that has persisted through millennia and is found in many different cultural settings. They [the shamans] can be found ... wherever hunting-gathering peoples still exist and wherever this ancient sacred tradition has maintained its shape in spite of the shifting of cultural ground.' (Joan Halifax)

Shamash *AME*. The Babylonian sun god of **Harranian Religion**, and since he could see everything on earth, he was also worshipped as the god of justice. His consort was Aya. See **Mesopotamian Religion**

Shammash in Judaism *J*. It has two meanings. It is the name given to the central stand of the **Menorah**, the traditional candelabra, which some scholars believe to be a reference to the Harranian sun god (see **Shamash**), an influence stemming from the Babylonian exile. But the linguistic evidence for this is doubtful. Secondly, a shamash was the beadle of a synagogue or the attendant of a rabbi or other notable person. The synagogue shamash was also the secretary, but the function has now deteriorated.

Shambhala *B*. A legendary, northern Tibetan kingdom that was the source of wisdom and culture for all Eastern religions and societies. The *Kalacakra Tantra*, the core scripture of this kingdom, is said to be the record of advanced Tantric teaching given by Shakyamuni Buddha to Dawa Sangpo, the first king of Shambhala. The legend is similar to that of Shangri-La and some Tibetans believe the land can still be found, hidden in a remote Himalayan valley. An alternative belief is that Shambhala disappeared with the rise of Islam in India and will not reappear until a new king emerges to lead his army against Islam. The legend has it that all the people of Shambhala, through the teachings of the Buddha and the practice of meditation, were spiritually advanced and that this was reflected in the order of their society and the unbroken peace they enjoyed. In this respect, the mythical kingdom is an expression of a basic human need for a fully realized life and culture. Some interpreters understand Shambhala to be the potential for 'awakening' that resides in all of us, individually and collectively, making for a truly balanced existence in an enlightened society. The spiritual tradition of Shambhala is also known as the **Sacred Path of the Warrior**.

FINAL WORD: 'Ultimately, that is the definition of bravery: not being afraid of yourself. Shambhala vision teaches that, in the face of the world's great problems, we can be heroic and kind at the same time.' (Chogyam Trungpa)

Shambhala International A community founded by Chogyam Trungpa centred on meditation centres across the world that 'welcomes anyone interested in the practice of meditation and anyone who aspires to expand the experience of gentleness and nonaggression into all areas of life' (from the S. I. website).

Shankara (788–820 CE) *H*. The renowned Indian philosopher. His name means 'he who brings blessing'. He developed Hinduism's definitive philosophy of **Advaita-Vedenta**, non-dualism (see **Dualism**), seeing creation as a kind of game, *lila* of illusions played by the Absolute. He is the author of numerous influential works including commentaries on the **Bhagavad-Gita**, on some of the **Upanishads**, the *Atmabodha* (Skt.) 'knowledge of self' which contains the most important principles of non-dualism and the *Upadesha-Sahasri* (Skt.), 'the thousand-fold instruction' or 'teaching', written in both prose and poetry. The prose section spells out for the student the need to realize the non-dual self, while the poems tell of the nature of consciousness. He was born on the coast of Malabar, at Kaladi and died at the age of 32 in Kedarnath in the Himalayas. See **Dvaita-Vedenta, Madhva, Ramanuja**

Shao-Lin *C. Z*. Westerners associate Shao-Lin with **kung fu**, itself a form of *Chi-kung*. These ought not to be understood simply as a combat sports, but as highly evolved systems of spiritual training designed to develop insight and power, centred on *chi*, or energy. Shao-Lin concentrates on techniques that cultivate strength of 'mind over matter'. It can produce extraordinary feats of strength and agility made familiar from the kung fu film genre. It is based on the teachings of **Bodhidharma**, who as well being credited with bringing Ch'an to Japan, where it became known as Zen, is also considered to be the first patriarch of Shao-Lin kung fu. Shao-Lin is actually a Chinese Buddhist monastery built in 477 CE on the sacred mountain of Sung-shan, by the Emperor Hsiao-wen. Bodhidharma stayed at Shao-Lin when he realized the time was not right for China to accept his dharma teachings. Tradition records that he remained there for nine years, during which time he taught the Shao-Lin monks two sets of physical exercises, the Eighteen Lohan Hands and the classic of Sinew Metamorphosis. These together formed the basics of Shao-Lin kung fu and Chi Kung.

FINAL WORD: 'If you want to soar to the heights and reach the depths of kung fu, you must practise Chi Kung; if you want to soar to the heights and reach the depths of Chi Kung, you must practise meditation.' (Ho Fatt Nam, a Shao-Lin grandmaster)

Shari'a *I*. Arab. 'law'. For Muslims, the immutable will of God and the sacred law. Called by H. A. R. Gibb 'the Highway of divine command and guidance', the Shari'a has retained a remarkable consistency through the centuries. Its sources lie in the Koran and in Muhammad's *Sunnah*, his example, and is considered binding on all believers, it being the way to maintain the highest quality of spiritual life for the *umma*, the community of Islam. Only about 90 verses of the Koran are expressly concerned with law, but the Islamic legal system has developed them into extensive codes that embody a whole range of social, economic, civil, criminal, personal and communal law that touches every area of life. It co-exists in the administration of law with normal jurisprudence and has absorbed the *urf* or customary law of the territories it has conquered. The authority and sanction of Shari'a for Muslims is quite simply the immutable will of God. See **Fiqh**, **Ijma**

Shavuot *J*. Heb. 'weeks', Greek name '**Pentecost**'. A Jewish festival also known as 'the Season for the Giving of the **Torah**'. It is observed 50 days or seven weeks after the **Passover**, on the 6th and 7th of the Jewish month of Sivan (May–June). The festival celebrates God giving the Torah to Moses at Sinai and Israel's reception of it. There is also a pastoral and agricultural association since in the Holy Land, the festival usually coincided with the end of the barley harvest and the beginning of the ripening of wheat, for which reason it is sometimes referred to as the Festival of First Fruits. It is primarily a synagogue-based celebration and orthodox Jews keep vigil throughout the first night, reciting and studying the Torah. The synagogue is sometimes decorated with plants and flowers. Since the Torah is compared to milk and honey, dairy produce is eaten. *Akdamut*, rhymed hymns, are sung in Aramaic as part of the liturgy and the Book of Ruth is read as a reminder of Ruth's acceptance of Torah. This is highly significant, since it defines **Israel** in other than ethnic and genealogical terms; Ruth, a woman of dubious racial origin, not born a Jewess, becomes by choice a member of the Chosen People by accepting the Torah. She also becomes an ancestor of the coming Messiah. Israel is thus confirmed as Israel by reason of the giving of and acceptance of Torah.

Shaytan *I*. 'Satan', the Islamic devil, consistent with biblical tradition as the rebellious angel who was ejected by God from heaven. The Koran also tells of Iblis (from the Gk. *diabolos*) who is thought to be a particular Satan or devil.

Sheikh *I*. Arab. The title covers a fairly wide range of meanings that include 'patriarch', 'elder' and 'chief'. The **dervishes** used it as an honorific title of respect. Various official posts bear the title of sheikh, whether they be heads of religious orders, Koranic scholars, jurists or those who direct worship in the mosque. It is generally required of a sheikh that he has considerable knowledge of *urf*, customary law, that he can offer hospitality on a large scale and, originally, was able to lead his men in times of war. The office of sheikh is not hereditary and can be gained or lost.

Shekinah *J*. Heb. 'dwelling' or 'dwells'. The most important rabbinic designation for God's presence in the world, based on the much-repeated biblical assurance that God dwells (Heb. *shakhen*) in the midst of his people, specifically in the tabernacle (see **Ark of the Covenant**) during the years of wilderness wandering and in his Temple on Mt Zion. The term, however, has a much wider application, closer in some ways to the **Logos** or **Holy Spirit** of Christian theology. Shekinah is, in a sense, 'Emanuel', 'God with us', both collectively and as an indwelling presence in each spiritually aware individual (similar to the Islamic concept of **Sakina**). The rabbinical tradition associates this presence with moments and places of intense holiness, as when men study Torah or esoteric lore, thus gaining special insight. The Shekinah is also sensitive to everyday, mundane acts of kindness, charity and hospitality; on the other hand, the presence can be driven away by the opposites of these virtues. The significance of this for the Jew, is that the interdependence of the Shekinah and the individual carries with it the potential for hallowing the world. There are passages where God is represented talking to the Shekinah whose presence in the world is in the form of light and the familiar association with radiance and glory. This tradition, combining both the transcendence and immanence of God, is talked about in terms of 'as it might be' or 'as if it could be', thus sustaining the notion of its potential. There are additional and esoteric levels of meaning given to the Shekinah by **Kabbalistic** mysticism.

FINAL WORD: 'Enoch was a cobbler and with every stitch of his awl that drew together the top and bottom of the leather, he joined God and the Shekinah ... Man exerts influence on the eternal and this is not done by any special works, but by the intention with which he does all his works. This is the teaching of the hallowing of the everyday. This issue is not to attain to a new type of acting which, owing to its object, would be sacred or mystical; the issue is to do the one appointed task, the common, obvious tasks of daily life, according to their truth and according to their meaning.' (Buber [1946])

Shema *J*. Heb. 'hear'. The *Shema* is central prayer of Jewish liturgy which opens with the imperative command, 'Hear, O, Israel, the Lord thy God, the Lord is One,' an affirmation of Judaism's inviolable monotheism. See **Mezuzah, Phylacteries**

Shembe, Isaiah (1870–1935) Founder of the **Natal Nazarite Church**. He had no formal education, but developed to become one of the most prominent Zulu figures of his time. During his youth he became famous as a visionary prophet and healer. He was baptized into the African National Baptist Church (1906), but later broke away to found the Nazarite Baptist Church (1911). Five years later, having announced he had been the recipient of revelations, he established a holy village near Durban. On his death in 1935 he was revered as a black messiah. His son Johannes Galilee Shembe inherited leadership of his Church. Johannes, a Fort Hare College graduate, lacked his father's charisma and had trouble maintaining the leadership. Nevertheless, in 1970, he still had 80,000 adherents.

She'ol *Heb*. 'unseen'. The abode of the dead or the underworld. See also **Hades**.

Sheut *E*. A person's shadow and the one of the five constituent parts of the Egyptian concept of the soul. See **Soul, Egyptian**

Shi'ism *I*. Arab. Shiite Muslims were originally the followers of Ali, the cousin and son-in-law of Muhammad. Shiite passion has its source in the defining event of their history, the Umayyads' assassination in 681 of Husayn, the third Shiite Imam who was the son of Ali (also murdered by the Umayyads) and **Fatimah**, Ali's wife and Muhammad's daughter. Martyred with them were the male members of his family and several companions. Husayn's tragedy is, for Shiites, the quintessence of sorrow; it blends together the accounts of Jacob mourning for the lost Joseph, Rachel weeping for her children (Genesis 37) and the personification of all the victims of tyranny. This early history, together with the Old Testament tradition, shaped the Shiite's consciousness of suffering and martyrdom. Husayn's death is annually commemorated and pilgrimage to his tomb in Karbala is, for Shiites, second only to the *hajj*. Tradition has it that the **Mahdi**, the expected messiah, will return to avenge his blood, thus to the passion for resistance and revolution is added an eschatological hope. In essence, Shiite energy is mystically drawn from the suffering of innocents. Believing themselves to be the true inheritors of Koranic truth and the Prophet's authority, they mystically interpret heredity as the guarantor of authenticity. In contradistinction to the

Sunnis' reliance on community, Shiites rest their faith on the **imams**. So central is this, both theologically and politically, that the Shiites elevated belief in the Imam to the Sixth Pillar of Islam (see **Pillars of Islam**). But even among themselves the line of inheritance was contested. From c.680 to the Imamate of Ja'far in 765 CE, there was a continuity of six Imams, at which point the succession was contested. Those who supported Ja'far's son, Ismail, as the seventh successive Imam, have become known as the Seveners or **Isma'ilis**; their opponents, known as the Twelvers or **Imamis**, believed in another line from Ja'far. These two, together with the **Zaydis**, form the main branches of Shiite Islam. Its modern expression was formulated in the late 1960s and 1970s by Ali Shariati, who combined Islam with a revolutionary political idealism that turned the passive suffering of the Shiite into the radical activism that inspired the Iranian **Ayatollah** Khomeini and the Lebanese Imam, Musa al-Sadr. There followed the Islamic revolution of 1979 and the establishing of the Islamic Republic of Iran. See **Caliph**, **Islamic Dynasties**, **Sunni**

Shiite See **Shi'ism**

Shikantaza Z. Jap. 'nothing but sitting'. A particular form of *zazen* meditation practice. Here all supportive techniques of the kind given to the novice are withdrawn. The practitioner hopes to maintain an alert state of focused attention on nothing, free from the process of discursive or specific thought, directed to nothing in particular. It is considered to be the purest form of meditation practice and for the Western adherent, wanting freedom from every kind of thought and distraction, it has considerable attraction. But because it is totally abstract, it is probably one of the most difficult forms of meditation to establish. See **Soto**
FINAL WORD: 'You must sit with a mind which is alert and at the same time unhurried and composed. This mind must be like a well-tuned piano string: taut, but not over tight.' (Roshi Philip Kapleau)

Shila *B*. Skt. Pal. 'Obligations', 'precepts'. Buddhist ethical guide. See **Sila**

Shilluk *A*. A Nilotic, West Bank people whose religion offers an established example of divine kingship centred on the mythological King Nyikang who led them in a migration 'across the river' to where they now live. The king stands as symbol of the people, their rites, customs and well-being. Nyikang is descended from the god Juok and although he is a man, his mother, Nyakaya, was some kind of river animal, perhaps a crocodile. There are shrines to Nyikang throughout Shilluk territory together with his life-size image. Communities are made up of several hamlets, each with a council that elects a headman. Nyikang lives on in the *Reth*, the ruler, believed to be divine and who was originally chosen from the previous king's sons. His well-being conditions the state of affairs in the kingdom. When the king was contented and in good health the kingdom prospered when he was angry and ill, the kingdom would suffer a similar effect. Shilluk society is organized into a hierarchy of commoners, royal retainers and slaves. Many Shilluk have converted to Christianity, but some still observe the traditional religion. In 2004, they were overrun by the civil war in the Sudan.

Shingon School *B*. Jap. 'School of the True Word'. An esoteric tradition of Japanese Buddhism founded 774–835 CE by Kukai and based on the **Mi-tsung** (School of Secrets) of Tantric (see **Tantra**) Chinese Buddhism. It is based on the three functional attributes we all share: body, speech and mind. However, each of these conceals secrets which, when discovered, can lead to buddhahood, the inborn true nature that resides within us all. Practices involve rituals that are not generally accessible such as the **Goma fire ritual**. Because the secrets cannot be disclosed verbally, the use of images such as mandalas is obligatory. The school is not world-denying and balances esoteric practice with an eye on material benefit. The origin of the teachings is accredited to Vairochana, a cosmic Buddha understood as the universe itself, without limit, beginning or end. Access is only available by means of initiatory rites.

Shinreikyo *Jap*. A new religious movement founded in Japan in 1947 by Kanichi Otsuka (Kyososama) and his co-founder Kunie Otsuka (Kyobosama). While the movement offers certain original ideas, it is also syncretistic, the founders being influenced by **Buddhism**, **Taoism** and **Shintoism**, with a clear parallel established between Kyososama and Jesus Christ. The sect thrives on the idea of miracles and of powers that can transform the mediocre in any business, profession or sport into outstanding successes and which can reinvigorate the lives of older, fading talents. Belief in such 'miracles' pivots around the notion of divine power which emanates from ultimate truth. 'This Truth or fundamental principle,' taught Kyososama, 'cannot be expressed using words or written characters. It is easiest to understand by coming into contact with its power and personally experience it.' In Christian theology, Jesus Christ was the 'Word' made flesh (see **Logos**). In much the same way Shinreikyo believes Kyososama is 'at one' with God. One of the original doctrines is that the skulls of believers expand to accommodate the rapid growth of new brain cells by which means the individual improves both mentally and spiritually. This is part of the continuous presence of miracles that happen all the time, but we are so used to their occurrence that we cease to notice or marvel. Shinreikyo is said to have around 100,000 adherents. FINAL WORD: 'A flower blooms. A larva becomes a mosquito. An egg hatches into a chick with a beak and feathers and the chick walks. No one can explain the principle that works behind these things, but people are so familiar with the normal course of events that they lose sight of how miraculous these events are.' (Kyososama)

Shintoism *Shin*. Jap. Shinto is a Chinese word translated into Japanese as *Karmi no Michi*, 'The Way of the Gods'. 'The Way' is a reference to a possible influence from **Taoism**. The plural 'Gods' alludes to the original polytheistic nature religion of Japan which can be traced back 2,000 years to the beginnings of the Common Era. In one sense, Shinto is a syncretism. It started out as a nature religion that worshipped nature deities to such an all-inclusive extent as to be a true pantheism dominated by Father Heaven and Mother Earth who were the creators of the Japanese archipelago and all the other deities. During the 5th and 6th centuries it was greatly influenced by Chinese Confucianism from which it drew one of its major characteristics, **ancestor worship**, and by Buddhism, from which it borrowed both ritual and philosophy. At this point, it became a complex system, but always in the shadow of Buddhism. Despite attempts to develop metaphysical doctrines and a clear ethical or moral code, Shintoism lacks both of these and although it retains the veneration of ancestors, it has no eschatology and little to say to its adherents about the inevitability of death. Strange it is then that, in 1868, it was given the status of a state religion in which the emperor was worshipped as the direct descendent of the sun goddess. In 1945, the state religion was disestablished and the Emperor denounced his divine lineage. Shintoism is now subsumed in Japanese Buddhism, especially within the **Tendai** and **Shingon** schools. Even so, today the Japanese are often married according to Shinto rites and buried according to Buddhist rites. It is rather like having both a vicar and a rabbi sharing the rites of passage of inhabitants of an English village. Probably a key word for understanding Shinto is *karmi*. Holton says that 'No other word in the entire range of the Japanese vocabulary has a richer or more varied content and no other has presented greater difficulties to the philologist. Yet to attempt to understand the meaning of this concept is essential if one wishes to reach an understanding of Shinto itself.' The word brings together numerous notions that include 'upper' or 'above', 'awesome', 'numinous' or 'dreadful'. Some linguists associate *karmi* with *mana*, a word always current throughout the Pacific, used to refer to a mysterious sense of power or wonder, something experienced or perceived. *Karmi* might well represent anything that is strange or unusual that has mysterious power and inspires awe.

FINAL WORD: 'One remarkable fact deserving notice … is that Shintoism, which is regarded as the official embodiment of the national spirit of Japan, did not assert itself as doctrinally independent of either Confucianism or Buddhism. The most probable reason for this is that Shintoism has no philosophy of its own to stand on; it is awakened to its own consciousness and existence only when it comes into contact with one of the others and thereby learns how to express itself.' (Suzuki)

Shirk *l*. Arab. 'association'. The sin of representing the divine in human form or image or of associating any kind of creature, actual or mythological with Allah, the true creator and sustainer of all life. In Islam this is an unforgivable sin, since it aims to compromise the pure and absolute monotheism that is the foundation of the faith.

Shiva *H.* 'The kind one' or 'the friendly one'. The third member of the Hindu trinity with **Brahma** and **Vishnu**. See **Siva**

Shona Religion *A.* The Shona are a dispersed people spread across Zimbabwe and southern and western Mozambique. Originally their religion was monotheistic, centred on the one god, Mulungu, whose cult is wrapped around with a belief in two kinds of spirits, one being the *vadzimu* (or *midzimu*), the ancestor spirits, the other *shave* or wandering spirits. These are thought to roam outside Shona territory and may be associated with other people, migrating animals or even Europeans. Among the *shave* are bad and good spirits, the former associated with witchcraft, while the good spirits are manifest as individual talents and healing. The ancestors being the custodians of abiding values and morally impeccable traditions, the *vadzimu* carry into the present everything that is best about Shona life. It is their function to protect Shona culture and fortunes, but this service may be withdrawn if the community becomes morally lax. A broader reference identifies 'Shona' with people of southern Africa and the **Bantu** language. Many Shona have converted to Christianity, but the traditional ancestor-spirit religion is still widely practised.

Shrine The term carries various meanings across the world's religions. It may refer to the location of sacred relics and their container or the tomb of a famous person such as a saint. Also any site that is hallowed, venerated or made sacred because of its associations with a person or an event or with folk or cultic beliefs in the presence of spirits, gods or oracles. The term is also used in a secular sense, thus Independence Hall, on Chestnut Street, Pennsylvania, is the shrine of American liberty. See **Reliquary**, **Stupa**

Shruti or Sruti Skt. 'hearing'. The holy scriptures of Hinduism. Divided into *Shruti* and **Smriti**. The former are derived entirely from revelation (see **Sanatana Dharam**) and hold absolute authority. These include the **Vedas**, **Samhitas**, **Brahmanas** and **Upanishads**. Smrti are texts derived from ongoing tradition, but validated by *Shruti*.

Shu *E.* Created by **Atum**'s masturbation, he is one of the primordial gods of Egypt and a member of the **Ennead** of Heliopolis. Known as the god of air, he was presumed to be a cooling and calming influence, eventually to be associated with Maat, daughter of **Ra** and goddess of truth and justice. Much later, at the end of the Old Kingdom (c.2181 BCE) Shu represented terrible weather conditions. As an air-sky god he is said to hold up the firmament, separating it from the earth. See **Egyptian Religion**, **Geb**, **Nut**, **Tefnut**

Shunyata or Sunyata *B. Z.* Skt. Pal. 'emptiness', 'void' or 'nothingness'. A central and very important concept in Buddhist philosophy. It has various nuances of meaning across the different Buddhist schools. In

Hinayana, emptiness is applied specifically to the right understanding of the individual, whereas in **Mahayana**, *everything* that exists, including the individual, is regarded as being 'empty', that is, without essence. There is no clear parallel in Western philosophy and it is not an easy concept for Westerners to grasp, since, for us, the concept of *shunyata* seems to be founded on a paradox. We assume phenomena exist because they have substance, shape and various other qualities such as texture, colour, smell, weight and so on, that we appropriate by sense experience. Buddhists would say that such apprehension is based only on what phenomena 'appear' to be and that mere appearance is a poor measure of things as they really are. When rightly perceived 'things' lack essence, that is they are empty because they lack the quality that makes them permanent or unchanging. The Western mind slips into thinking that the Buddhist claim that phenomena do not exist is a form of nihilism. This would be to misunderstand. *Shunyata* affirms that phenomena exist without doubt, but *only* as appearances and as such are illusory. They have no contribution to make to our perception of a permanent, unchanging reality. For the school of the middle way, the **Madhyamaka**, this philosophy is associated with the doctrine of **dependent origination**; the linked chain of cause and effect demonstrates that because everything arises conditionally, it lacks essence. We are, of course, in the realm of high abstraction even at the point of *Maha sunyata*, the 'Great Emptiness', requiring us to abandon even the concept of emptiness. The philosopher **Nagarjuna** established for Buddhism the notion of two truths, i) apparent truth (relative or conventional truth) where most of us are most of the time and ii) the absolute truth (ultimate or supreme truth) of *shunyata*, the 'emptiness' of everything which cannot be explained or expressed in words and which is accessible only by direct experience. In the Mahamudra tradition of Tibetan Buddhism the concept of *shunyata* as supreme reality takes on the notion of 'openness', meaning openness of mind that allows the kind of clarity that leads to **enlightenment**.

Sibylline Books *R*. Romans could ascertain the will of the gods by consulting the Sibylline Books, a collection of oracular statements set out in Greek hexameters. Sibyls were priestesses of Apollo and in Greece were associated with prophecy. An early Roman legend recorded that a Sibyl who lived in Cumae, informed Tarquin Superbus (the mythological last king of Rome) that she had nine books describing the destiny of Rome. She offered to sell them to him for a set price which Tarquin declined. She promptly burned three of them then renewed her offer which again, Tarquin refused. She burned three more and he bought the remaining three at the original price. The Sibylline Books do not appear to have contained prophecies so much as *remedia* – advice on what to do when the gods were clearly annoyed. The Books were heavily consulted when Rome chose to innovate its religious practices, as happened when they adopted many of the Greek cults. A major cultural and religious consequence of the Books was the application of Greek cultic practice and the influence of Greek conceptions of the deities on indigenous Roman religion, which was already deeply influenced by Etruscan tradition. Eventually the Books were placed in the custody of 15 men, plebeians and patricians, who housed them in the Temple of Jupiter on the Capital. At the command of the Senate, they consulted the books to discover what religious rites could be used to avert disaster. See **Auspicia, Cybele**

Sibyls *R*. See **Sibylline Books**

Siddhartha Gautama *B*. The traditional name given at birth to the historical **Buddha**.

Sikhism Sik. Pun. *sikhna*, 'to learn', sometimes translated as 'disciple'. Sikhs are followers of **Guru Nanak** and of the nine successive gurus. The movement emerged in the early 16th century, a time when northern India was ruled by the **Mughals**. The Muslims opposed much of what was essential to Hinduism, especially the use and worship of images. Nanak was influenced by the poetic mysticism of Kabir (1440–1518) a modest weaver who became one of India's greatest religious poets. In what is reminiscent of prophetic style, Kabir aimed to convince Hindus and Muslims that they were all one in the one God and thus of the same family. His hymns, or poems, concentrated on the divisive aspects of both religions, caste, idol-worship, pilgrimage, reverence for sacred buildings, legalism and ritual. Kabir's philosophy was a form of ecumenism or universalism, undogmatic in style and broadly cast so that no one believing in God could object to his message of devotion and brotherly love.

'O, servant, where dost thou seek me? Lo! I am beside thee.
I am neither in temple nor in mosque: I am neither in **Ka'bah** nor in Kailash:
Neither am I in rites or ceremonies, Nor in yoga and renunciation.
If thou art a true seeker, thou shalt at once meet me in a moment of time.
Kabir says, "O, Sadhu, God is the breath of all breath."
(Trans. Rabindranath Tagore, *The One Hundred Poems of Kabir*)

It is generally accepted that Kabir's message made a deep impression on Nanak. Tradition records that following his morning bath in the Ravi, the local river, Nanak disappeared for three days. When he returned he remained silent, for how long we do not know, but when he finally spoke he said, 'There is neither Hindu nor Muslim so whose path shall I follow? I shall follow God's path. God is neither Hindu nor Muslim and the path which I follow is God's.' Around 1521, having settled in Kartarpur, Nanak founded the first Sikh *panth* or community. The core of his message was similar to that of Kabir: 'One God, the True, the Creator'. He also affirmed that everyone, regardless of caste, religion or sex, had the potential to experience God and to realize *Jivan mukti*, liberation during the present lifetime (see **Moksha**). More controversially and influentially, Nanak made the dissolution of the *varnasramadharma*, the traditional fourfold caste system of Hinduism, a condition of spiritual emancipation. He put the emphasis on *grihastha* (Skt), the 'householder', which was one of the Hindu traditional **four stages of life**. The married couple, Nanak insisted, is the basic social unit through which a family may enjoy, in moderation, all the good things life has to offer. It would seem in this respect, that Guru Nanak's message has timeless and universal relevance.

Nanak's doctrine of God is a monotheism. God is one, eternal, ineffable. The divine is transcendent, but everywhere present and compassionate to the point of ensuring people have access to the means of salvation. This access is given by revelation through the succession of the ten inspired gurus. The Sikh doctrine of man is consistent with a revelatory religion. People are wilful, blindly seeking salvation through inappropriate means such as the rituals of worship in temples and mosques, misguidedly placing their faith in the efficacy of the outward signs of religious practice. They are the victims of *haumai*, self-will and thus heedless of *hukam*, the will or order of God by which their lives should be directed. The means of salvation is provided by the message of the gurus and it is important to understand the Sikh concept of **guru**, which is developed under its separate entry. It can be summarized by saying that God is the original Guru imparted his message to his chosen servant Nanak, who then became the Guru himself, that is, the physical manifestation of the inwardly spoken voice of God. The hymns of Guru Nanak were compiled and collected first by Guru Angad (guru 1539–52). Following the death in 1708 of the last guru, Gobind Sing, the final canon of sacred scriptures was established and given the name **Guru Granth Sahib**. In 1577 work began on the **Darbar Sahib** (*Pun.* 'Divine Court'), more familiarly known as the Golden Temple located in Amritsar. It was completed in 1601.

In the face of increasing Muslim hostility, Guru Gobind Sing transformed the Sikh community into the quasi-military sect that has became so celebrated. He formed the **Khalsa** community in 1699, membership of which was by *amritsankar*, a ceremony of initiation that included a form of baptism; the new community was structured by the Khalsa Code, which amounted to a series of prohibitions some of which, because of the prevailing political situation, were distinctly anti-Muslim. The *amritdhari*, the initiated members of the community, were made clearly distinguishable by the enforcement of the *panja kakke* or **Five Ks**, the most familiar of which is the Sikh's uncut hair covered by the characteristic turban. Sikhs have always believed that to die fighting in the Sikh cause is to gain Paradise. This is one of the beliefs Sikhism culled from Islam and it gave rise to the doctrine of *Dharam Yudh*, the concept of the 'just war', which in the light of Sikhism's troubled history has been a much-needed source of courage and inspiration.

It is unlikely that Guru Nanak set out to create a new religion or even a new sect. His vision was that people might experience the abiding truth which could not be encapsulated or monopolized by any one religion, the dogmas and practices of which obscured the truth they claimed to enshrine. Various reform movements have sprung up amongst Sikh communities, notably in the late 19th century, the **Singh Sabha** movement noted for reclaiming Sikhism from 'a state of utter ossification and inertia and articulated the inner urge of Sikhism for reform and gave it decisive direction' (Sangat Singh). Sikhs in India are now mostly centred in the Punjab, but substantial communities are also to be found throughout the world. See **Akal Purakh, Waheguru**

FINAL WORD: 'One of the central points of Sikh faith is the ideal of service to one's fellow men, no matter to what religion, race, political group, sex or sect they belong.' (*Sikh Courier*, London, Spring, 1967)

Sikhism and Secularism *S*. Sikhism as a way of life is not incompatible with secularism and does not feel the need to oppose its philosophy or the process of secularization. The secular society is understood as the context in which the Sikh continues to search for truth while living fully and responsibly in the world. The Sikh life is an active life in no way withdrawn from society; there is no place for asceticism. What is important is finding the right way to make a living, that is, right 'living-dharma'. Whatever the Sikh does should be exemplary, he should endeavour to be a better teacher, doctor, farmer, soldier, labourer or banker. The **Adi Granth** says that, 'salvation is not incompatible with laughing, eating, playing and dressing well.' The secular (Indian) state is accepted as the proper context for religious freedom and for the realization of both individual and collective religious potential. See **Secularism**

Sila *B*. Skt. Pal. The Buddhist term for morality or a moral precept. Its purpose is to provide a standard or model for behaviour and the cultivation of virtue. Sila are not commandments or rules enforced by a religious authority, such as in Buddhist or Christian monasticism. Rather they are a reflection of the behaviour of the Buddha and represent the kind of life that might be led by those enlightened (see **Enlightenment**). The term is also used to refer to the first of the three divisions of the **Eightfold Path**. See **Precepts**

Silsilah *I*. Arab. 'chain'. A term used in **Sufism** for the lineage of past masters, down which the spiritual teachings have been transmitted. Many of the original masters traditionally trace their own origin to **Muhammad** or **Ali**. An individual becomes a link in the chain when he is initiated into the **tariqah** of his choice, which involves taking an oath of loyalty to the original past master and his current representative. See **Dervish, Dervish Groups, Islamic Dynasties**

Sin A concept characteristic of biblical religions identified as disobedience to the will of God or the infringement of a moral code or the mores and customs of the society, group or established authority. Christianity interprets the 'fall of man' in the Genesis story as the inception of original **sin**, being the state in which everyone is born. The salvatory function of Jesus Christ is concerned to restore humanity to its sinless state and to the union with God that this allows. The Roman Catholic Catechism understands sin to be '… an offence against reason, truth and right conscience;

it is a failure in genuine love for God and neighbour.' A distinction is made between moral and venial sin, the former 'destroying charity in the heart of man', the latter 'allows charity to subsist, event though it offends and wounds it' (from 'The Catechism of the Catholic Church'). In Judaism the prevailing standard is the **Law**, the *Halakah*, contravention of which is confessed on Yom Kippur, the Day of Atonement. Observance of *Halakah* is so important that Judaism is more clearly understood as a religion of orthopraxy and not just orthodoxy. Islam holds to two forms of sin, inadvertent and intentional, for which there are prescribed forms of repentance (see **Dhanb**). For Hinduism and Buddhism there is no parallel to the biblical concept of sin. The determining consequences of the **karma** of previous lives means that an individual cannot be held responsible for what transpired in a former existence. In broad terms, all positive forms of living will contribute to good karma and reduce the bad karma already accrued, while for negative forms of living, the converse is true. Responsibility is focused on the conscious effort made to uphold the highest moral standards which are not derived from divine authority or revelation as, for example, are the Ten Commandments, but from the precepts and ethics inherent in the teachings of the religion (see **Five Precepts**). In the process of observing what Buddhist term *sila*, virtue, the individual will be living out his karma. This is not just a question of observing rules or laws; true virtue is generated by wisdom so that the life lived will be a seamless joining of precept and compassion.

FINAL WORD: 'It ain't no sin if you crack a few laws now and again, just so long as you don't break any.' (Mae West)

'Sin is sweet in the beginning and bitter in the end.' (Talmud)

'No one saves us but ourselves. No one can and no one may. We ourselves must walk the path.' (Buddha)

Sin *AME*. The moon god of **Harranian** Religion. See also **Mesopotamian Religion**

Sinai, Mt *J*. Judaism's holy mountain where God delivered the Ten Commandments to **Moses** (Exod. 19). There is some confusion as to which mountain in the Sinai peninsula it is, but tradition identified it as Gebel Musa. The incident of the burning bush in which God appeared to Moses (Exod. 3) was also presumed to have taken place there. The monastery of St Catherine, built at the foot of the mountain, is a place of pilgrimage. See **Decalogue**

Sin Eater *X*. A person who assumes the role of **scapegoat** for someone who has just died. Bread with milk, beer or wine are placed on the corpse and then the sin eater will consume them, thus taking into himself the sins of the departed. The sin eater was paid and for as long as it was believed that anyone dying risked hell, he would never be out of work. As the drink was believed to represent the blood and the bread the flesh of the dead person, sin eating was a form of referred **Eucharist**, in the sense that the ritual carried the sins to the sin eater. By taking the bread and wine of the Eucharist, as the body and blood of Christ, the participant's sins are forgiven and he will be in a 'state of grace'. There is no actual or apparent forgiveness in the sin eater's role, he simply carries the sins away from the dead person.

Singh Sabha *S*. Pun. A 19th- and early 20th-century Sikh reform movement, concerned to rejuvenate the faith and to distinguish Sikhism from Hinduism and prevent conversion to Islam. The movement generated new cultural, educational and political initiatives. The celebrated Khalsa college (see **Khalsa Code**) at Amritsar was founded and numerous Khalsa schools were established throughout the Punjab. A new, confident Sikh self-image led to emigration and communities settled in Canada, the USA, the UK, Africa and Malaysia. See **Sikhism**

Singsing *P*. Melanesian festivals of ritual feasts and dance, particularly associated with **male cults**. A singsing involves the whole community who prepare the ceremonial dance 'floor', the sacred **masks**, the shrines and the **haus tambaran** (the **Spirit House**). The festival invokes the spirits of the dead (see **Tumbuna**) to whom offerings of food and ritually slaughtered pigs are made, together with objects considered to be valuable or especially endowed with **mana**. The important singsings will occur with the changing seasons. Tamed and toned down by Christian influence, singsings are still a feature of community life in the highlands of Papua New Guinea.

Singularism A term used by sociologists of religion (see **Sociology of Religion**) to describe the exclusive focus on one creed or doctrine in contradistinction to others and also of a society that admits of one religion to the detriment of others. It is, in effect, a declaration that the religion in question holds the monopoly of truth. It has, of course, a secular application as an obsessive devotion to the interests of one's own party, sect or nation. This has the more ominous implications of ethnocracy and the centralization of power by members of a particular group, for example in the South African policy of apartheid. See **Particularism**, **Pluralism**, **Universalism**

Sion, Mt See **Zionism**

Sioux *Ami*. An important Amerindian group, identified by the Hokam-Siouan language. They also call themselves Dakota, Nakota or Lakota. As a result of the influence of European colonizers their religious traditions have changed radically over the years. Central to Sioux religion; and retained by it, is the acceptance of the universe as incomprehensible, but believed to be sustained by an animating force, **Wakan Tanka** or Wakonda, the omnipotent ruler of the cosmos. Like the buffalo, human beings were conceived by and formed within the womb of Mother Earth. Consistent with nature religions generally, subordinate beings or spirits are identified with the sun, moon, thunder and the elements, earth and water. There are also spirits associated with the lodge. The world of the spirits is contacted by means of **vision quests**, for which rigorous preparation must be made in the **sweat lodge**. All rituals are believed to have a cohesive power and practising them is designed to express and increase the sense of the unity of the tribe and the tribe with nature. Central to these rites is the acquisition of a guardian spirit, usually given by the stars at the birth-rite in the form of a life-breath or personal **daemon**, which at death returns to its source. Both the **sun dance** and the **ghost dance** feature among Sioux rituals, together with the use of the **calumet**, the sacred pipe. Today, about half the Sioux are converted to Christianity. FINAL WORD: 'You have noticed that everything an Indian does is in a circle and that is because the power of the world always works in circles and everything tries to be round ... The sky is round and I have heard that the earth is round like a ball and so are all the stars. The wind, in its greatest power, whirls. Birds make their nest in circles, for theirs is the same religion as ours ... Even the seasons form a great circle in their changing and always come back again to where they were. The life of a man is a circle from childhood to childhood and so it is in everything where power moves.' (Black Elk Oglala, Sioux Holy Man)

Sirah *I*. Arab, A genre of Islamic literature based on the biographical tradition of Muhammad's life. The Sirah record the life and work of the Prophet as the fulfilment of divine will and revelation. Because of the Islamic concept of history as the drama within which God acts, Sirah includes the lives of Muhammad's confederates and of the saints. They are used as authoritative guides or models for social interaction, conversion and the standard against which reform and innovation is measured. See **Sunnah**

Sita *H*. Skt The wife of **Rama** and one of the main characters of the **Ramayana** epic. She is a model of womanhood and of wifely virtues. Hindu mythology tells of Sita being an avatar of **Lakshmi**, the consort of **Vishnu** who; wanting to reincarnate herself; did so as Sita. This reincarnation into the troubled world of human beings so as to serve as an example of all the virtues is taken to be an example of selfless giving.

Siva or **Shiva** *H*. Skt. 'the kind one', 'the friendly one'. The third member of the Hindu trinity, with **Brahma** and **Vishnu**. He represents the destroying principle, especially with reference to the destruction of *avidya*, ignorance, but his powers and qualities are far wider and it must be remembered that in Hinduism, to destroy has reproductive implications and Siva is continuously restoring what has been dissolved. It is for this reason that in Hindu iconography he is represented by a linga or phallus in conjunction with a yoni, the female organ, the symbol of his consort or female energy, **Shakti**. It is in this form that Siva is most frequently worshipped. A further aspect of Siva is as the *Maha-yogi*, the great yogi, the model of asceticism, of penance and of transcendental meditation, that endows him with absolute power and the highest spiritual knowledge. In this form he is shown as a naked fakir, his body covered with ashes, his head weighed down with a mass of matted hair. See **Shaivism**

FINAL WORD: 'Shiva and Shakti are so intimately unified that they swallow each other all the time in order to prevent any breach in their unity; they are separate themselves only to enjoy each other their reciprocal love.' (Amritanubhava, Jnaneshwar, quoted by Alan Jacobs)

Sitra Achra See **Sephiroth**

Skandha *B. Z.* Skt. 'group' or 'aggregate'. See **Five Aggregates**

Skilful Means *B.* (Skt. *upaya*, 'skill in method or means'). Of central importance to **Buddhism**, the term has two applications: i) the skill of a **bodhisattva** to guide people to enlightenment. These skills can be straightforward or entail devices and ruses or the use of miracles. It is an ability the bodhisattva perfects in the seventh stage of his development. ii) A core concept of **Mahayana** Buddhism, referring to the skills of teaching so as to transmit the **dharma** to the pupil as directly as possible. 'Skilful Means' is both a tool for transmitting the teachings and a form of implied wisdom. Mahayana holds the view that Buddha employed *upaya* by adapting his teaching to the capabilities of his pupils. It is suggested that he taught **Hinayana**, the 'small vehicle' first and later the Mahayana, specifically the Lotus Sutra, towards the end of his life. Tradition records that in taking into consideration the individual needs of each of his pupils, their temperament, stage of development and their natural abilities, the Buddha left over 84,000 skilful means. The implication follows that a Buddhist, in applying the teachings to life, will also live by 'skilful means'.

Skoptsy *X.* A Russian Christian sect. The name, from the Russian, means 'eunuch' and the sect were self-castrators. They were first discovered by the civil authorities in 1771, when a charge was brought against a peasant; Andrei Ivanov, for persuading 13 men to castrate themselves. The sect was a reaction against the Khlysty, an orgiastic flagellant sect who believed in overcoming sin with sin, primarily through group sex. Kondraty Selivanov, the founder of the Skoptsy, preached the total subjugation of lust which could only be achieved through the 'baptism of fire' and the sacrifice of the penis. His authority is Jesus Christ's pronouncement about eunuchs given in Matt. 19:12, in which he said, 'There are some eunuchs which were so born from their mother's womb; and there were some made eunuchs by men. And then there are eunuchs which have made themselves eunuchs for the Kingdom of Heaven's sake. He that is able to receive it, let him receive it' (RSV). The men were castrated by the use of a hot iron, hence the 'baptism of fire'. The abhorrent practice included women. There was no coercion and all such castrations were accepted voluntarily. It became usual practice for male adherents of the sect to start a family before becoming a full member, but gradually the sect began to speak of 'spiritual castration'. In the second half of the 19th century Skoptsy was believed to number over a million members, but although the last recorded castration was in 1951, it is thought that only a small group still exist, their descendents having hidden in the reed wilderness of the Danube delta.

Sky Father A recurring theme recorded from the earliest periods of religious history and one found throughout nature religions. Sometimes the deity is associated with the sky in general and sometimes specifically with the sun, always in association with the elements. Because of his elevated position the sky-father is frequently the supreme god, an omniscient omnipresence from which no part of the earth can hide. For this reason, heaven is traditionally located in or above the sky and biblical religions refer to the one God as the 'Heavenly Father'. In primitive religion he is the complement of the **earth mother** and in many traditions his union with her, which is the theme of a creation myth, results in all forms of fertility. There are inevitable variations of the established traditions. For example Egyptian mythology offers a sky mother, but the earthly counterpart is a dying and regenerating, god of vegetation. This god is further associated with the seasons of sowing and reaping, together with the irrigation effects of the Nile floods. **Shintoism** gives precedence to a sun goddess, while the more common Japanese association of the solar disk is with a deity who is born each morning and dies each evening, passing through the underworld during the night. While belief in sky gods remains a living component of several religious traditions such as **African** tribal and **Amerindian** religion, its interest has been revived in the West by **neo-paganism** and **New Age** cults. See **Prehistoric Religion**

Slavic Religion *AE*. Prior to their conversion to Christianity in the 12th century, Slavic religion was based on nature worship. There is little original evidence available outside the 11th- and 12th-century accounts of early Christian missionaries and what can be gleaned from folklore and archaeology. As is characteristic of all nature religions the gods were personifications of the Slavs' experience of nature, associated with specific landscape features such as lakes, springs, ravines and specific objects like oak trees and boulders. Philologists have found a relationship between the names of some of the gods and those of **Indo-European** religions. Those that have come down to us include Perun, a thunder god, Svarog, a sun and fire god, Volos or Veles, the god of herds and flocks. More significant is 'The Holy Mother Earth' known as 'Mokosh', meaning 'moist', her worship being linked with a water cult. Subsisting with theses major gods was a larger pantheon of local deities, with their cults established around simple temples like the one at Arcona on the isle of Rugen, destroyed in 1168. There were several animal cults allied to the worship of the bear, the deer, the cock and sacred horses were related to divination cults. A mythological god, Volkh, was able to assume many forms, most popularly that of a hawk. More unusually, the Slavs believed in domestic spirits, particularly that of the Domovoy, a hirsute, human-like creature that acted as a kind of family guardian and guide. There is evidence that Slavic religion had a significant shamanic element (see **Shamanism**) which was strongly dualistic and practised human sacrifice.

Smriti *H*. Skt. (*B*. Pali. *Sati*.) For **Hinduism**, one of the two types of holy scripture, the other being *Shruti* (revealed scriptures). Smrti includes texts based on tradition, but thought of as valid only if they are derived from *Shruti*. In Buddhism the term has the markedly different meaning of '**mindfulness**' or 'reflective awareness' (see **Sati**). A central concept, it is the mind's ability to recall, to know and to contemplate itself. It goes beyond meditation, performing consciously the activities of ordinary life, including autonomic functions like, breathing, walking, eating, etc. Perfect mindfulness is detailed in the **Eightfold Path**. The purpose is to bring the mind under complete control and into a state of rest. *Smrti-upasthana*, the 'cultivation of mindfulness', is the seventh of the Eightfold Path and the foundation of Buddhist practices leading to insight and wisdom. See **Anapanasati**, **Meditation**, **Samatha**, **Vipassana**

Snake-handling Cults The Gospel of Mark 16:18 lists as one of the miraculous signs of a believer the ability to handle snakes without risk. This is the authority behind the numerous Christian snake-handling cults such as those of Tennessee, Kentucky and Virginia in the USA. The cults are a part of the **Holiness Movement**, the adherents of which claim sanctification through the blessing of the **Holy Spirit**, and who witness to this by handling and fondling snakes, as well as by other 'signs' such as speaking in tongues (see **Glossolalia**) and faith-healing (see **Pentecostalism**). The authorities in some states have banned the cults and insurance companies refuse to insure against the snake bites inflicted during church services. Snake-handling also occurs among the shamans (see **Shamanism**) of the Hopi Indians and Comanche, some of whom encourage rattlesnakes to bite them so as to demonstrate their resistance and protective medicines.

Snakes and Snake Deities The snake is a creature constantly present in the myths and folklore of most religions. In the Bible, it is familiarly associated with Satan who, as the tempter of Eve in the Garden of Eden, took the form of a serpent. The **Nagas** of Hindu mythology have the body of a serpent and **Krishna** is depicted dancing on the head of Kaliya, the king of serpents so as to subdue him. Because it lurks under stones and dark places, the snake was thought to be chthonic, an underworld being, and many depictions of the Last Judgement and of hell show the damned being tortured by snakes. This theme is well illustrated in Greek mythology in the battle between sky and earth represented by the glittering new Hellenistic sky god, Apollo and his fight with Python, the serpent monster he destroyed at Mt Parnassus. The Dahomey or the Fon of Benin in West Africa, have a serpent deity called Dan or Da, who contributed to the creation of the cosmos which he supports with his coils,

3,500 of which are above and 3,500 of which are below the universe. Here, as elsewhere, the snake takes the form of a rainbow as an intermediary between sky and earth. Dan is represented with his tail in his mouth and reappears in Haitian Voodoo as Damballah. But snakes do not always represent evil. Because it casts its skin as it grows, it can symbolize rejuvenation, longevity and wisdom, as well as being associated with sexuality, due its phallic shape. In many mythologies there are close links between snakes, dragons and sea-serpents. See **Nagas**

Social Darwinism. See **Spencer, Herbert**

Socialism The concept has various meanings, but is generally associated with political labour movements based on the principle of common ownership of the means of production and distribution of all forms of goods and services. Thus, what is usually characteristic of societies led by a socialist government is the public ownership and administration of services such as health, education, transport, the 'social services', and the infrastructure. In general it differs fundamentally from **communism** in its avowal of ethical and democratic values and in making a distinction between common and State ownership. Its origins are to be found in the Enlightenment and as socialist philosophies developed they assumed a distinct utopian character which was a secular reaction to the Salvationist (see **Salvationism**) theories of society and its ideal of the Kingdom of God on earth. Thus, many socialist theories were atheistic, particularly **Marxism**, which moved socialism from its idealistic roots to something like a scientific theory. In broad terms the Christian-based Salvationist theories of society were unable to tolerate or accommodate opposition and were consequently authoritarian. The **utopianism** of scientific socialism was ideologically more democratic, claiming to engender a more open society but, ironically, as the history of communism shows, its ideology became the new orthodoxy, every bit as authoritarian as the dogma and doctrines of the established churches. Protestantism, however, showed a distinct socialist face with its 'salvation by works' ethic and the zeal for addressing the worst inequalities and abuses of society, actively reforming education, prisons, medical services and promoting the principle of universal suffrage. These are the clearer parameters of religious and secular socialism, but the history is more confused. In Germany, Lutherans (see **Luther**) and **Roman Catholics** worked with Bismarck to suppress Social Democracy; in the turmoil of 1917, the Russian Orthodox Church was the close confederate of the Tsar; on the grounds that it was unethical and unchristian to question private ownership, the Vatican consistently opposed socialism; Italy and Austria attempted the 'Christian Socialism' pact, but leaders in Italy held back from genuine socialist principles. Socialism has always been associated with the Left in politics and with an emphasis on the State's control of the market and economic growth. The question most current is whether socialism can preserve its unique and original identity. Throughout Europe, other than in extreme statements, the political differences between Left and Right are becoming less clear and the battle that is being fought is for the 'middle ground'. It can be argued that this centre-ground secularism of socialist politics has become a paradigm for the ecumenical and liberal theologies of all the religions participating in European society. See **National Socialism**

FINAL WORD: 'Onward Christian workers,
    Marching on to peace,
    By the love of Jesus,
    Making strife to cease.'
    (Chorus from Bishop Spalding's parody of 'Onward
    Christian Soldiers')
    'This is the final struggle,
    Let us gather and tomorrow
    The Internationale
    Will be mankind!'
    (Chorus from 'The Internationale')

Society for the Advancement of Judaism *J*. Founded in 1922 by Mordecai Kaplan. See **Judaism, Reconstructionist**

Society of Dependents *X*. A strict Puritanical sect founded in 1850, in London, by a shoemaker, John Sirgood. See **Cokelers**

Society of Friends X. A Christian sect familiarly known as the 'Quakers' which first emerged in the mid-17th century. George Fox (1624-91), credited with being their founder, recorded in his journal that when he was arraigned before the justices on a charge of blasphemy, the judge called them Quakers because 'we bid them tremble at the word of God.' The full name is 'The Religious Society of Friends', which started life as a Nonconformist breakaway from English **Puritanism** (see **Nonconformism**). The Quakers based their teaching on the belief that Christ's message was immediately available to anyone and that no consecrated building or ordained ministry was necessary. Worship is unprogrammed and mostly silent, but this is modified in some American practices; it is focused on the Quaker doctrine of the 'Inner Light', a sense of the divine and of the presence of Christ in the soul. They were viciously persecuted and from 1698–1833, were banned from sitting in the Westminster Parliament. Having gradually established themselves in Europe, in 1681 William Penn founded Pennsylvania on Quaker principles. There is a strong emphasis on social work exemplified by John Woolman's anti-slavery reforms and Elizabeth Fry's work to improve prisons. Since the turn of the 20th century they have been active in international relief. See **Shakers**

FINAL WORD: 'Keep within. And when they say, "lo here" or "lo there" is Christ; go not forth; for Christ is within you. And they are seducers and antichrists, which draw your minds out from the teachings within you.' (George Fox)

'Silence is Wisdom, where Speaking is Folly; and always safe … For the more mental our Worship, the more adequate to the nature of God:

the more silent, the more suitable for the Language of the Spirit.'
(William Penn)

Society of Jesus *X*. See **Jesuits, Loyola**

Sociology of Religion The discipline aims to study the functional role of
religion in society in terms of its practices, history, belief structures and
institutions and the dialectical relationship between religion and society
itself. Religions are classified according to types, for example, ecclesia,
denominations, **cults** and **sects**. Sociologists are not only descriptive in
their accounts of the role of religion, but also predictive; for example a
rise in religious commitment was anticipated following the 'God is dead'
culture of the 1950s and 1960s; the religious aspect of the 'culture wars'
of the late 20th century were predicted by Peter Berger who, however,
was wrong in his prediction of global secularization. Others predicted the
rise of Islamic fundamentalism and its connection with terrorism.
Building on the work of, for example, Émile Durkheim (1858–1917) and
Max Weber (1864–1920), the subject is hugely documented and offers an
extensive literature. See modern treatments by Martin, Robertson, Weber.

Socrates (c.470–399 BCE) *G*. An Athenian philosopher who, although he
wrote nothing, has exercised a formative influence on Western philosophy. So marked is this influence that what was developed in philosophy
before his time is designated as 'Pre-Socratic'. We owe mostly to **Plato**
the dissemination of Socrates' ideas, a task he took up when Socrates,
aged 70, was condemned to death by the Athenian Assembly for supposedly corrupting the youth. He died by drinking hemlock, an event Plato
recorded in *Phaedo*. While the Socratic influence on Plato's own philosophy is considerable, we see Socrates through Plato's representation of
him, with the addition of insights from Xenophon and Aristophanes. It is
not always possible to extrapolate from these accounts the ideas that were
originally Socrates'. Traditionally, Plato's earlier ideas and methods are
believed to be Socratic, but as his philosophy developed in later years, it
is unlikely that Plato was simply playing the role of recorder and historian and that what emerged were Plato's own ideas. Socrates claimed not
to be concerned with 'things beneath the earth and in the skies', that is,
his philosophy was not focused on nature. Rather, his interest was in
values as applied the problems of God and to the concepts of 'good' and
'beautiful'. The relationship between good and beauty was the basis of
his ethics which grew naturally from aesthetics. He also addressed the
questions that became a running theme in philosophical theology,
namely, is 'religion' a matter of faith or knowledge? Is the claim of a
knowledge of God's existence based simply on belief, that is, faith? From
the point of view of such knowledge how is one to regard other religions
and their gods? How does the believer 'know' that his religion is true
over and against other religions that may be false or heretical? Socrates
was, above all, a rationalist (see **Rationalism**) and yet a deeply religious
man who believed in gods that were, in every way, superior to human

beings. His religion was all one with his philosophy in that his enquiry into morality was the basis of it. His rationalism led to a sensitive but critical examination of the religious tradition of his time and of the newer cults always emerging and it was these criticisms that brought him into conflict with the Athenian authorities. See **Scepticism, Socrantic, Stoics** FINAL WORD: 'The unexamined life is not worth living.' (Socrates)

'I do nothing but go about persuading you all, young and old alike, not to take thought for your persons or your properties, but and chiefly to care about the greatest improvement of the soul. I tell you that virtue is not given by money, but that from virtue comes money and every other good of man, public as well as private. This is my teaching and if this is the doctrine that corrupts the youth, I am a mischievous person.' (Socrates, quoted by Plato in *The Death of Socrates*)

Socratic Method *G*. Known also as *elenchos*, Gk. 'cross-examination'. Originally, a cross-examination of a statement or concept usually of a moral nature, for the purpose of refuting it. The method is traditionally illustrated in Plato's *Socratic Dialogues*, which are a 'model' of the dialectic method of teaching. Put simply, the teacher assumes the role of questioner and by posing the right questions in the right order stimulates a discussion in a question-and-answer format that enables the teacher to lead his pupil to the correct conclusion without ever actually stating that it is true. For example, taking up a theme like the nature of justice or virtue, Socrates would ask his pupils what they understood by these concepts. Rather than contradict their replies, he would pose further questions and so on to each of their subsequent responses, thus leading them to the conclusions he had in mind. Should Socrates agree with a pupil's response he would, of course, say so. We have to remember that Plato was able to record both the questions and the answers. Anyone reading Plato's earlier dialogues can, as it were, play along (without cheating!) by forming their own responses to Socrates' questions.

Sodom and Gomorrah *J*. The infamous 'cities of the plain' (Gen. 19) believed to have been located at the southern end of the Dead Sea. They were destroyed by God because of the sexual profligacy and corruption practised by its inhabitants. The story has contributed the word 'sodomy' to our vocabulary. It is likely that the cities were ruined by some natural disaster.

Soka Gakkai *B*. 'Scientific Society for the Creation of Values'. A mystical form of Buddhism based on the teachings of the 13th-century Japanese fisherman Nichiren Daishonin, who taught that the true interpretation of the Buddha's teachings were recorded in the Lotus Sutra. See **Japanese Religions, Tenry-Kyo**

Soka Gakkai International An American cult of **Soka Gakkai** Buddhism (See **Japanese Religions**). The cult offers *gongyo* as an enlightenment practice. This requires kneeling before a *gohonzon*, a black wooden box containing passages from the Lotus Sutra, reciting verses from this and chanting the mantra, *nam-myoho-renge-kyo*. The cult proselytises aggressively and is alleged to be politically ambitious and authoritarian, practising mind-control techniques.

Solomon *J*. b. c.1000 BCE. King of Israel, 970–928 BCE and the younger son of David and Bathsheba. He was renowned for building his eponymous and magnificent Temple on Mt Moriah. Political expediency led him into marriages with foreign women, which meant assimilating aspects of their religions and the practice of pagan rituals, at the expense of the cult of Yahweh. To develop and maintain his extravagance, he used forced labour and the people turned against him, so that his empire lasted for only two generations. The tradition presents Solomon as being hugely wealthy and endowed with divine wisdom. Mythology has him as a master magician who, with a magic ring, could control demons and talk to animals. It is believed he used demons in the building of the Temple. An ancient text book of magic, *The Key of Solomon*, is attributed to him, together with other texts. Solomon is also counted among the prophets of **Islam** and there are numerous references both to him and his writings in the Koran. See **Grimoire**

Soma *H*. *Zo*. Skt. There are numerous candidates for the hallucinogenic plant used by the Aryans, Indo-Iranians and others. Richard Rudgley lists cannabis, Ephedra, Syrian rue (*Peganum harmala*), rhubarb, ginseng, opium and wild chicory. The fly-agaric mushroom *Amanita muscaria* and the climbing plant *Asclepias acida*, a species of milkweed, have also been suggested. Rudgley suggests the arguments for Syrian rue are convincing but not definitive and that the mystery is never likely to be solved. Whatever soma might have been, it was sacred in ancient India and featured in the earliest Vedic literature, the **Rig-Veda**, that has one cycle (**mandala**) of 114 verses entirely concerned with praising its uses. Here, Soma is personified as a god, all-powerful, all-healing, the giver of riches. The drink was made from the juice pressed out of the stalks of the plant which was then fermented, filtered and mixed with milk or other beverages. It was imbibed by the **brahmans** officiating at the sacrificial rituals and it seemed to observers that as a result, they were endowed with supernatural power. For this reason, Soma itself was given the status of an all-powerful deity, a personification of which was worshipped and sometimes identified with the Supreme Being. It was believed to have the power to heal any kind of disease and to impart wealth; not surprisingly, the Hindus called soma 'the wine of immortality'. The effect of drinking soma is not alcoholic intoxication, but more like the experience of a hallucinatory drug which brings on a state of ecstasy in which the worshipper becomes capable of deeds beyond normal human power. **Indra**, the god who personifies the atmosphere, was said to be particularly fond of the drink. Daniélou says that *soma* was the food of ritual fire (see **Fire, Sacred**), the offering itself; it is also semen and semen was sometimes offered in sacrifice as an alternative to a human being. See **Sacred Mushroom**, **Samaveda**

FINAL WORD: 'The food of the ritual fire is soma, the ritual offering. Every substance thrown in the sacrificial fire is a form of soma but the name is more particularly that of the sacrificial liquor through which the flames can be kindled. This is the "elixir of life", the ambrosia which stimulates the fire and intoxicates its priests … He who drinks this ambrosia partakes of divinity.' (Daniel Daniélou)

Son of God *J. X.* In the Old Testament 'sons of God' were generally the people of the **covenant**, but more specifically men known to have a special relationship to God, the Father. The **Logos** of intertestamental mysticism had the connotation of 'son of God' and was adopted as an epithet for Jesus, used throughout the New Testament to heighten the divinity of Jesus Christ as against his humanity, expressed by the title 'Son of Man'.

Son of Man *X.* A **New Testament** title Jesus Christ used for himself. Apart from one reference in the Acts of the Apostles, the title is found only in the Gospels. Its actual meaning has always been debated and is variously interpreted by theologians. In the **Old Testament** the term is used, for example, in Dan. 7:13, which is traditionally translated 'son of man' but modern translations, including the **Tanakh**, render the term 'like a human being'. Generally it is taken that when Jesus used the title of himself, it was to heighten his humanity and humility in contradistinction to his divinity, which is denoted by the term '**Son of God**'. As a fulfilment of Old Testament prophecy and typology, a phrase like 'Son of David', pointing to Jesus' genealogical line to the King of Israel, was thought to interpret his mission nationalistically; thus, 'son of man' is also understood to express the universalism of his message.

Sophists Gk. 'expert'. A group of professional and usually itinerant teachers who were influential in Greece during the 5th–4th centuries BCE. They were required to provide a higher education and wisdom (*sophia*) together with instruction in the arts of public debate, a specifically political skill. There was much use of the techniques of rhetoric and 'sophistry', but casuistic misuse of logic has coloured their reputation. Despite this, their influence encouraged independent thinking and experiment with new ideas free of the received philosophical traditions. Between them they covered a very broad curriculum, so we have, for example **Protagoras** (c.485–c.421) propounding his thesis that 'man is the measure of all things,' while Gorgias (c.483–c376) taught aesthetic theory. If there was a common theme it was the debate about the antithesis of nature and convention as the basis of morality. By and large the Sophists were sceptics; had Huxley's term '**agnostic**' been coined at the time, they would certainly have used it of themselves.

Soteriology The doctrine of **salvation** and its study.

Soto *Z*. Jap. One of the two major schools of **Zen** Buddhism, the other being **Rinzai**. It was founded by Dogen Zenji 1200–53 CE who brought the tradition from China to Japan. The two schools broadly share the same goal, but the techniques of attaining them differ. Soto puts its emphasis on *mokusho* or silent practice and on *zazen*, a meditation technique that is not dependent on supports like the **koan**. Its characteristic meditation form is *Shikantaza*, and its main concern is the **realization** of our inborn buddha nature.

Soul Derived from the **dualism** of Greek philosophy, especially that of Plato, man was understood to comprise of two parts, body and soul. The same concept is carried into the Genesis myth of the creation of Adam who was endowed, by divine breath, with an immortal soul. **Aquinas** established the Christian view that the soul is an independent spiritual substance, the 'form' (in the Platonic sense) of the body. The Greek *psyche* carries the notion of the soul of the inner, essential self, similar to the Hindu concept of **atman**. The soul may be separate from the body and exist independently as happens after death and there has been speculation about the soul's pre-existence. There are two views of the soul's origin, one being **Creationism** – that it is created by God in every human being – the other **Traducianism**, the belief that the soul is transmitted to the unborn child by the parents. This latter theory has been used to explain original **sin**. Creationism was the vogue during the Middle Ages, but both **Lutheranism** and **Calvinism** favoured Traducianism as being consistent with the Reformation's belief in the depravity of human nature. The question of the physical **resurrection** of the body and the soul's existence within it has been a contentious issue throughout Christian history. This same dualism has dogged Western philosophy (see **Descartes**, for example) where the notion of 'mind' displaced that of the soul.

Soul, Egyptian *E*. The Egyptians believed that the **soul** was made up of seven parts: the *Ka, Ba, Akh, Sheut, Ren, Sekem* and *Seku*. The *Ka* is a kind of alter ego, created at the conception of the person it doubles. It represents a vital force so real that arrangements had to be made for it when the person died. The tomb is thus called *het Ka*, 'the house of *Ka*'. The *Ba* is an independent aspect of the person which at death flies free of its physical cage but remains near. Perhaps, for this reason the *Ba* is represented in Egyptian art as a bird with a male or female human head depending on the sex of the deceased. *Akh* is perhaps the nearest we get to a Western understanding of 'soul', being the eternal aspect of a human being that survives death, passing into the heavens to circle the stars. *Sheut* is the person's shadow, something essential and thought to be always present in a mythology where the sun figures so dominantly. It was believed that a person could not exist without a shadow. *Ren* is a person's name and was believed to carry with it mystical and sacred associations uniquely concerned with the individual. The *Ren* lived longer than the person, indeed for as long as the person was remembered and spoken about. For the name to survive was a kind of insurance of the individual's survival in another world. For this reason monuments and memorials were of central importance to the Egyptians, who placed the names of the deceased in cartouches or 'magical rope' so as to protect them. Conversely, the recorded names of enemies or those whose reputations became questionable were erased. The *Sekem* or 'radiance of the sun' is associated with the life-power or energy of the deceased. The *Seku* are the remains of a person's physical body, the house or container of the other six parts of the soul.

Source Criticism A literary and critical examination of the texts of sacred literature so as to ascertain the sources used by authors and compilers. See **Form Criticism**, **Higher Criticism**, **Redaction Criticism**, **Textual Criticism**

Speaking in Tongues *X*. A characteristic practice of the Pentecostal Movement. See **Glossolalia**, **Pentecostalism**, **Xenoglossolalia**

Spencer, Herbert (1820–1903) Philosopher and sociologist and one of the principal proponents of the Darwinian theory of evolution which Spencer applied to sociology and philosophy. His argument was that if nature works on the principle of natural selection, then so does society; those that survive and flourish do so because of the natural evolutionary process of social institutions. Both Spencer and Social **Darwinism** have been accused of **anarchism**, a point possibly substantiated by Spencer's belief that, 'If every man has freedom to do all that he wills, provided he infringes not the equal freedom of any other man, then he is free to drop connection with the state – to relinquish its protection and to refuse paying for its support.' See **National Socialism**, **Scientism**

Sphinx *E*. The name 'sphinx', which means 'strangler', was first given by the Greeks to a fabulous creature that had the body of a woman, the head of a lion and the wings of a bird. In Egypt the sphinx usually has the body of a lion with the head of a man wearing the head-dress of a king. There are also sphinxes with rams' heads associated with the creator deity **Amun**. The Great Sphinx in Giza near Cairo, constructed c.2500 BCE, is believed to be the guardian of those buried in the tombs of the Great Pyramid built by the Pharaoh **Khafre**. It is considered to be the greatest monumental structure ever made by man. There is no agreement as to whether the face of the sphinx was intended to be a sculpture of Khafre, but some believe the face resembles his brother, the pharaoh, Djedefre-Radjedef.

Spinoza, Baruch de (1632–1677) A Dutch **rationalist** philosopher. He was born in Amsterdam of Jewish parents who had fled the Portuguese **Inquisition**. But even in the more tolerant ambience of Holland he was expelled from the Jewish community on the ground of heresy and his 1670 *Treatise on Theology and Politics* was attacked by the Christian establishment and finally banned in 1674. The notorious difficulty of his philosophy is compounded by his use of an idiosyncratic vocabulary, itself an indication of its free-thinking innovator, who believed that matters such as ethics should be examined independently of any official doctrine, be it Jewish or Christian. What then, is there about Spinoza's philosophy that caused such controversy? First, there is the question of his denial of man's free will: 'All things which come to pass, come to pass accordingly to the eternal order and fixed laws of Nature.' He is therefore a determinist in the same tradition as the **Stoics** and **Descartes**. This of itself is not radical, but in application to ethics it is difficult to argue, on the one hand, that man is not free to act as he chooses, while on the other hand arguing that he is capable of necessary responsibility. Secondly, Spinoza is a **relativist**. He argues that nothing, of itself, is good or bad but can only be judged as being either in relationship to someone or something else. Again it is the implications of this that ran Spinoza into such trouble, for we cannot both argue that ethics are relative while at the same time holding that there are absolute standards of right and wrong as the established authorities did and must do. Spinoza, however, tells us that nothing has 'goodness' or 'badness' as an inherent quality; anything, a medicine or a charitable act, may only be judged to have one or another of these qualities according to the effect it has on a particular person at a particular time. It has also to be considered that the same 'thing' might have a different effect on the same person at another time or a different effect altogether on another person at any time. Against this double premise, in what does the good life consist for Spinoza? He argues that it resides in an attitude towards life and the world, an attitude that is both rational and emotional. This conjunction is hugely important for the history of both religious and secular ethics and is sometimes called 'the concept of positive freedom', in as much as freedom resides in the extent to which we control our passions and emotions. Happiness for both individual and society resides in the ability of the individual to accept things as they are, for example to accept that there are limits to human power, talent and knowledge and to accept that human beings die and that such an event is both natural and inevitable and there is no point in kicking against it or indulging in self-pitying grief. To the degree a person 'accepts' so will his struggles against everything cease and his peace of mind increase. The final sticking point for the authorities was that Spinoza argued that God's freedom is as limited as man's. All freedom is relative, in as much as both God and man act out of necessity, since how they act is determined by their natures. Nevertheless, there is a relative freedom to be responsibly exercised, namely that what both God and man do is self-determined. Regardless of his reception by his contemporaries, Spinoza has emerged as one of the most influential figures in the history of ethics.

FINAL WORD: 'It has been resolved, the Councillors assenting thereto, to anathematize the said Espinoza and to cut him off from the people of Israel … with the following malediction … "Let him by cursed by the mouths of the Seven Angels … Let God never forgive him for his sins … And we warn you that none may speak with him by word of mouth

nor by writing, nor show any favour to him ..."' (From the
Excommunicating document of the Council of the Jewish Community of
Amsterdam)

'All happiness or unhappiness solely depends on the quality of the
object to which we are attached by love.' (Spinoza)

'I do not know how to teach philosophy without becoming a disturber
of established religion.' (Spinoza)

Spirit Lat. *spirare*, 'to breathe'. Understood to be the animating energy of
all living things, in distinction from the physical or matter. Also a form
of being that exists without a body or a sensible manifestation or is separated from it. Examples include angels, fairies, ghosts, **demons**, etc. The
term 'spirit' is frequently used as a synonym for the **soul**. Animistic traditions hold that inanimate objects such as rocks, stones, mountains, the
earth and sky, rivers, lakes and pools may have an indwelling spirit or
spirits. See **Animism, Holy Spirit, Spiritism**

Spirit House They come in a variety of forms. In **Melanesian** religion, the
Haus Tambaran serves the spirits of ancestors (see **ancestor worship**).
In Thailand, the Sarn Phapoon is a miniature temple mounted on a plinth
and devoted to animist spirits; offerings are left to so as to appease the
spirits that might otherwise prove troublesome. Based on the assumption
that all such spirits must live somewhere, a 'dwelling' is constructed for
them, especially if their natural habit at has been destroyed or disturbed
by, for example, the felling of trees or diverting a stream or the removal
of stones and rocks in the process of cultivating land. Thailand preserves
the tradition as part of their cultural inheritance and the spirit house may
be placed in the vestibules of businesses, in the concourse of shopping
malls and other public places.

Spiritism The belief found in many primitive cultures that inanimate
objects, together with plants and animals, are possessed by spirits, which
may be good or evil. Either way their appeasement and favours must be
sought through **occult** practices. The term has come to be used more generally for any contact with spirits through occult techniques. See
Amerindian Religion, Kardecism, Spiritualism, Swedenborg

Spirit Possession Mark 5 tells the story of a deranged man living in a
cemetery, who when asked his name by Jesus replied, 'My name is
Legion for we are many.' Jesus then cast out the demons possessing the
man, sending them into a herd of swine. Such stories of spirit or demon
possession are characteristic of many religions; some believe the possessing spirits are evil and resort to exorcism, while others go so far as to
encourage people to be spirit-possessed. The biblical religions hold to
both forms of possession. The Holy Spirit figures importantly throughout
Christianity, but is especially significant in its ecstatic forms such as
Pentecostalism, which actively seeks to be possessed by the 'Paraclete',
the 'comforter' or 'advocate'. In several religions dancing to the accom-

paniment of drumming is used to induce the state of spirit-possession; examples include the Southern African **Bushmen**, the **Yoruba** and the **voodoo** practices in Haiti, the principal function of which is to for a worshipper to be possessed by a *loa*, a spirit that rides the subject like a horse. Mircea Eliade [1989] gives numerous examples of how the shaman (see **Shamanism**) is possessed by spirits, yet offers the ordinary person protection from spirit or demon possession. However, care must be taken to distinguish between rituals designed to induce spirit possession and those intended to induce a state of trance. They are by no means the same but both may occur, for example, at revivalist (see **Revivalism**) meetings as John Wesley's *Journal* records. It has become apparent that the descriptions and symptoms of spirit possession show a marked resemblance to the case-histories of modern psychiatry and its methods of treatment.
FINAL WORD: 'Especially important is the warning to avoid conversations with the demon. We may ask what is relevant but anything beyond that is dangerous. He is a liar. The demon is a liar. He will lie to confuse us. But he will also mix lies with the truth to attack us. The attack is psychological, Damien and powerful. So don't listen to him. Remember that – do not listen.' (Father Merrin, in *The Exorcist*)

Spiritual Eye See **Third Eye**

Spiritualism The website of the Christian Spiritualist Church states that 'Spirit Communion or Spirit Communication has always existed and it is given by God for the furtherance of mankind and his spiritual progression.' The Spiritualist Movement is said to have begun in 1848 with the 'raps' of the Fox sisters, Kate and Margaret in Hydesville, USA, during what became familiarly known as a séance. The sisters were taken with the ancient belief that the spirits of the dead can make contact with the living and they claimed to have discovered a way of communicating with the dead, specifically, in this case, with a dead man. Because communication with the spirits of the deceased was taken as irrefutable evidence of personal survival, Spiritualism was heralded as a new religion, particularly by non-Christians, while others suggested that spiritualist beliefs were the original energy behind all religions. Practice is focused on the medium, a person especially gifted and with a heightened sensitivity to the spirit world, through whom the dead communicate, usually by a form of spirit possession; the medium will also interpret the alternative means of communication, such as table-rapping or the movements of the ouija board. The Spiritualist Movement was brought to Britain in 1852 and gradually developed into the Spiritualist National Union Ltd, constituted in 1902. Despite the association with Spiritualism of such eminent people as Sir Oliver Lodge and Sir Arthur Conan Doyle, the movement was subjected to fierce criticism by both the Church and secular scientific groups and several law suits were filed against it. As recently as 1951, Parliament passed the Fraudulent Mediums Act and while it is inevitable that such practices will be exploited by charlatans, there are undoubtedly genuine mediums who, with their equally genuine followers, testify to the human being's survival of death. Spiritualism is also a concept in philosophy arguing that 'spirit', as opposed to matter or reason, is the ultimate reality; this includes the religious belief that some kind of 'essence' or **soul**, within the human make-up, survives death and is eternal. See **Spiritism**

Splanchomancy Divination by examining the entrails of sacrificial victims. See **Anthropomancy**

Sport The publication in 1618 by James I of his *Book of Sports*, republished by Charles I in 1633 with a brief addendum, wonderfully illustrates that passion for sport and the need for recreation are no new things. As well as masques and theatre, the sports included archery, horse racing, cricket, croquet, football and golf. The context for the publication of the books was the observance of the Sabbath, a contentious issue even in the 17th century, since recreation of any kind on Sundays compromised the rigors of Puritan Sabbath observance. More significantly, the royal declaration of the right to take recreation on Sundays was believed to be an invidious attempt by the King to appease the people and to mitigate their discontent. Not only was this the thin edge of the wedge of Sunday observance, but it undoubtedly began the process of offering sport, not simply as an alternative to Church, but as an alternative to religion. Who can doubt that the commitment and passion generated by professional sport is not akin to the same zealous sentiments given to religious faith and its observance? There are probably millions of people who would affirm that for them sport is a secular alternative to religion. Football, it would seem, has gained the universalism of which the established religions have only dreamed. Bill Shankly, one of Britain's most successful and famous football managers, a high priest of his cause, put the matter succinctly: 'Some people believe football is a matter of life and death ... I can assure you it is much, much more serious than that.' See **Sabbatarianism**
FINAL WORD: 'I tend to believe that cricket is the greatest thing God ever created on earth ... certainly greater than sex, although sex isn't too bad either.' (Harold Pinter, unsourced)

Sri Aurobindo *H*. See **Aurobindo**

Sri Sathya Sai Seva Organization See **Sai Baba**

Sruti *H*. Hindu holy scriptures, see *Shruti*.

Stalinism The political ideology and methods of Joseph Stalin (1879–1953). His theories were a reaction to the Bolshevik (see **Bolshevism**) principle that the survival of the Russian revolution depended on similar proletarian revolutions taking place throughout Europe. Russia, as an isolated state of 'workers', developed unprecedented problems of development and government that the Bolsheviks believed could never be solved while it remained a socialist island in a

capitalist sea. Stalin disagreed. He came to power as a result of his struggle to succeed Lenin and used his power to establish a one-country socialism. This could only be achieved by means of remorseless tyranny which imposed the collectivization of both agriculture and industry. To ensure the progress of his policies, he established a notorious police control and effected ruthless purges. Leon Trotsky (see **Trotskyism**), in *The Third International After Lenin*, dubbed the Stalinist concept of one-country socialism 'a reactionary theory'. The worst purges were inflicted between September 1936 and December 1938, a period known as *Yezhovshchina*, 'Yezhov Time', when Nikolai Yezhov was People's Commissar for Internal Affairs, that is, the head of the secret police, the KGB and MVD. There followed the Stalinist personality cult when every aspect of Russian culture was used to promote Stalin as the caring father-figure of a happy and prosperous people. Russian success in the Second World War and its post-war expansion did much to establish the notion that Russian socialism was destined to overrun the world. In effect, by putting the economic development of Russia above everything else, Stalinism betrayed the working-class struggle; the people had simply exchanged one kind of imperialism for another. His 'stages' policy, that of completing national democratic revolution *before* the worldwide socialist revolution, created the new imperialism within the socialist state and by reference a new bourgeoisie with a revolutionary function. The whole concept was contrary to **Marxism**. Only in recent years has Russia effectively completed the process of de-Stalinization and disassociating Marxist-Leninism from Stalinism by acknowledging what Khrushchev called 'the errors of the personality cult'. See **Communism**, **Leninism**
FINAL WORD: 'The experience of Stalinism does not refute the teaching of Marxism but confirms it by inversion. The revolutionary doctrine which teaches the proletariat to orient itself correctly in situations and to profit actively by them, contains of course no automatic guarantee of victory. But victory is possible only through the application of this doctrine.' (Trotsky)

State of Israel *J*. In November 1947 the United Nations voted to partition **Palestine**, according to the Jews their own territory. When the British withdrew in May 1948 the leaders of the Jewish State assembled in Tel Aviv to announce the independence of the State of Israel. This Jewish hegemony in what had been Arabic Palestine, had been the focus of Jewish hopes since the destruction of the **Temple** in 70 CE, indeed some would say since Israel's flight from Egypt and the establishment of the Sinai covenant. The constitutional residency of Jews in Israel has always been linked with the concept of the **messiah**, and with their messianic hopes. In modern politics, the movement achieving this has been led by **Zionism** which has always had an extreme nationalist element inde-pendent of Israel's religious heritage. See **Israel**

Stella Matutina See **Hermetic Order of the Golden Dawn**

Stigmata *X*. Lat Usually marks and or bleeding appearing on a person's body that simulate the wounds inflicted on Jesus Christ as a result of his crucifixion. Throughout Christian history numerous cases of stigmata have been recorded, most of them being women. The first known case was St Francis of Assisi (see **Franciscans**). In the 20th century, Therese Neumann and the Capuchin Padre Pio have exhibited stigmata and were examined by medical authorities. It is significant that all the cases deserving study are from within the Roman Catholic Church, which although thoroughly investigating them, has offered no explanation for the occurrences. Hinduism and Buddhism have histories of paranormal phenomena but, as with Islam and Judaism, outside the tradition of miracles, there is little evidence of bodily manifestations of heightened religious experience. Medical explanations of stigmata account for them as cataleptic or hysterical reactions.

Stoics *G*. A Greek school of philosophy founded by Zeno c.308 BCE. It was named after the *Stoa Poikile*, a meeting place in Athens where Zeno first introduced his ideas. He taught that God designed and ordered everything for the best and that human happiness can be assured by living virtuously. Its definitive and systematic form was given by Chrysippus (280–207 BCE) who combined logic, ethics and physics with the concept of the **logos**. He advocated living a life consistent with nature and reason, since to live this way was, ethically, the one supreme good. The Stoics were materialist in that they denied that anything could exist without a physical form. The Roman form of the philosophy advocated a calm acceptance of one's place in life and of everything that might happen, since everything is the unavoidable consequence of divine will. It is this form that has put 'stoicism' into our vocabulary in reference to an attitude of impassivity, accepting uncomplainingly pleasure or pain, good or bad fortune. Stoicism is probably the most influential philosophical school of the Roman Empire and our knowledge of Stoic principles has determined the views and popular mythologies about Romans. See **Materialism**, **Spinoza**

Structuralism The study of the hidden agenda both of texts and of social structures, to the end of disclosing hidden meanings or patterns. It is thought that these underlying structures carry a deeper and more diverse meaning that is not apparent by what is actually presented. The method has been applied to both linguistics and the social sciences. It holds that language is best understood in terms of its irreducible units, such as inflexion and word-formation in grammar and the language's sound-system or phonology. The methods of structuralism have made a considerable contribution to the social sciences and to anthropology, by interpreting the patterns of living and behaviour in terms of the underlying structures of a society's organization. The method is closely related to **semiotics**. Both methods have led to a greater understanding of many aspects of religious belief and practice, for example in their application to the study of myths, to the examination of texts, to the way religious language works and to the underlying meaning of religious symbolism. See **Atomism, Logical Atomism, Logical Positivism, Symbolism**

Stupa *B*. Skt. 'hair knot'. This odd image is the characteristic form of Buddhist architecture, the obvious top-knot feature of many Buddhist temples and monasteries. The architecture will vary according to the country and some have the familiar pagoda-like form. Originally, stupas were rather grandiose gravestones, memorials erected over, or to house the remains of eminent spiritual leaders, including the Buddha. They were also built on specific sites to commemorate historical events such as Lumbini, thought to be the birth-place of Shakyamuni Buddha or Bodhgaya, the location where the Buddha achieved **enlightenment**. By the 3rd century CE and the reign of King Asoka, such memorial venera-tion of holy men had become the custom. There are stupas that do not enshrine human remains but sacred scriptures and others that are just symbolic, like the three-dimensional mandalas of Tibet, representing the body, speech and mind of the Buddha. Forms of worship or *puja*, take place at the stupas, the most characteristic being to walk round them fol-lowing the course of the sun. Whatever their location and whatever they enshrine, they are seen as symbols of the enlightened mind and as a support for meditation. Small replicas of stupas are often used by fami-lies as **reliquaries** of deceased relatives. In the *Mahaparinibbana Sutra*, the Buddha left instructions that a stupa should be built over his remains, thus giving authority to their construction.

Stylites *X*. Also known as pillar saints, they were a group of recluses that practised extreme asceticism. Founded by Simeon the Elder in 423 CE, stylites retired to the Syrian desert and perched on top of pillars (*stylos*) believing that by extreme self-mortification the salvation of their souls would be ensured. Simeon lived for 70 years, 42 of which were spent on top of his pillar, accessed by a rope ladder 50 to 60 feet off the ground. He endured the daytime desert sun and the cold of the night wearing only a simple leather tunic. The platform was not large enough for him to lie down and he spent most of the time standing upright. It is said he preached two sermons every day, praying all night with his hands raised. He ministered to the crowds who came to hear him, healing, settling dis-putes and maintaining a correspondence with Church officials. His funeral was attended by thousands. He became an example for many pillar saints and the base of Simeon's original column is still to be seen standing at Qalaat Samaan, in Syria. The practice, which never became established in the West, continued until the 12th century. See **Hermit**

Subud A Javanese spiritual movement founded by R. M. Mohammed Subuh Sumohadiwidjojo (1901–87). *Subud* is an acronym for *Susila*, *Budhi*, *dharma*. *Susila* means to be able to live according to the will of God; *Budhi* means that in every created being, including human beings, there is divine power working both within and outside them; dharma refers to the possibility of every created being submitting to the will of

God. The central spiritual exercise of *Subud* is *latihan*, a trance-like state that can give rise to ecstatic experiences or total calm, by which means submission to God's will may be achieved.

FINAL WORD: 'Only by surrendering himself completely to God, not making use of his mind, his heart or desire, is it possible for man to come into contact with the Power of God ... and what really happens in latihan is that you will be introduced to your real inner self – to the real I' (from the *Subud* official website, www.subud.org). '*Subud* is not a religion, it has no rituals or teachers. It is an association of people who wish to be in contact with the Great Life Force.'

Succubus The female counterpart of the **incubus**, which traditionally takes the form of a demon that makes love to men while they sleep. In the mythologies of **Satanism**, the Devil, as an incubus or succubus, fathered progeny that exhibited the signs of their Satanic parent by being deformed and demonic. The origin of the succubus may be the images seen in dreams and nightmares which have been made familiar through the paintings of artists like the Swiss romantic, Johann Heinrich Fuseli's, *The Nightmare*, painted in 1781.

Suchness See **Tathata**.

Sufism *I*. Arab. *suf*, 'a woollen garment'. Known generally as the tradition of Islamic mysticism, Sufism represents what many feel to be the most attractive face of Islam. However, as with other notable forms of mysticism, when it tends to self-indulgence or is popularized to the point of being fashionable, it deteriorates into decedent superstition, even obscurantism. Then, in the place of true and pious mystics, arrive the charlatans and the pretenders, the personality cults. All mystical movements are centrally important to the religions in which they develop, but since by definition they enshrine the purest forms of religious experience, they are peculiarly difficult to treat or analyse systematically. What we can say with certainty about Sufism is that it was influenced by the traditions of the monastic asceticism of Egypt and western Asia. The influence was, however, secondary and the main-spring for Islamic mysticism was the Koran itself, especially its **eschatology**, and the superstitious but frenetic fear of punishment and hell it contained. Inevitably there arose a positive quest for God, based not on fear, but on devotion and for the mystical experience that would ensure a person's unity with God. The closeness of God and the expectancy of personal union with him is asserted by the Koran, 'I am near to answer the call of the caller when he calls me' (2:182). Like most mystics, Sufis tended to disregard conformity to both traditional practice and theology, nor is Sufism an exception to the theosophical extravagances that can be found in most mystical practice. But alongside such fringe traditions were Sufi groups faithful to the orthodoxy of the Koran. In its various forms, Sufi mysticism spread through all sects of Islam and across all its territories. But it was never an independent or identifiable group. Sufis were and are to be found within

Sunni and **Shiite** Islam as an emphasis, a pattern of spirituality etched into the whole Islamic community, always challenging and vitalizing the faith of Muslims, even when controversial. As well as ascetic practices disciplining all forms of bodily appetite, Sufi ritual typically involves the recitation of passages from the Koran, prayers, poems and the rhythmic repetition of divine names (see **Beautiful Names**). Some traditions such as the **Mevlevi** dervishes (see also **Dervishes**) use dance to induce meditative focus on the divine. A community may develop around a master that might be either temporary or if given an institutional structure, permanent. In all its forms, Sufi mysticism has left a vast literature, as poetry, hagiographies, commentaries on the progress of the spirit as it ascends the path to God and notes on the psychological transformations experienced. The style is frequently characterized by *sukr*, 'intoxication' by ecstasy and by joy. Modern Islam is inclined to blame Sufism for Islamic backwardness, arguing that mystical experience is incompatible with the new revolutionary and revivalist expressions of the Islamic faith. History denies this, showing Sufism to be a strongly cohesive force in a society increasingly challenged and on the edge of crisis. But its tradition has two sides, the one shows true piety, wit and discipline and an openness to the world; the other side tends to decadence, superstition and perhaps like all mysticisms at some point, to obscurantism. At its best Sufism relies on orthodox Islamic faith, the truths of which, as Idries Shah put it, 'are recorded by the mind and experienced by the heart'. See **Bektashis, Chishti, Fakir, Murid, Rifa'is, Rumi, Silsilah, Tariqah, Wali, Zuhd**

FINAL WORD: 'Question: What is common to all forms of Sufism?

'Answer: The being of the teacher, the capacity of the disciples, the peculiarities of individuals, the interaction between the members of a community, the Reality behind forms.' (Idries Shah)

Sukkoth *J*. Heb. 'booth' or 'tabernacle'. A religious festival held on the 15th of the Jewish month of Tishri (Sept/Oct) and lasting seven days. It commemorates God's protection of Israel during the years of wilderness wandering and also the 'ingathering', the harvest of fruit in Palestine. The festival is celebrated as 'The Season of our Rejoicing' and is the climax of the autumnal season of holy days which begins with the festivals of **Rosh Ha-Shanah** (New Year) and **Yom Kippur** (Day of Atonement). The festival is an observation of the prescription given in Lev. 23:33–44, where the Lord instructed Moses to tell the people of Israel to 'Mark, on the fifteenth day of the seventh month, when you have gathered in the yield of your land, you shall observe the festival of the Lord [to last] seven days; … You shall live in booths, in order that future generations may know that I made the Israelite people live in booths when I brought them out of the land of Egypt.' Families sometimes build booths in the garden, covering them with branches from trees and decorating them with fruit and other harvest produce. The booth is an image, not only of Israel's insecurity in the desert, but also, because of its impermanence, of the fragility of its existence in the 'desert' of Diaspora. The seasonal fruit is a reminder that throughout the ongoing experience, God will provide for his people even as he did in the wilderness.

Sultanate *I*. An office of real political power introduced by the **Seljuks** (1038–1194), a unified Turkish military force, the immediate forebear of the Ottomans (see **Ottoman Empire**). The sultan was responsible to the **Abbasid** caliphs for government and legal adjudication. It was not necessarily a territorial title and after the termination of the Abbasids in 1258 and under Ottoman administration sultans were appointed over the courts and as rulers of countries. The sultanate was a symbol of the unity of Sunni Islam in the face of the political claims of the Shiites (see Shi'ism), but some of the Deccan (Indian) sultanates were Shiite in principle. The rise of the Islamic nation state saw the demise of the sultanate, which now exists only in Oman, Brunei and Dar el Salam. See **Islamic Dynasties**

Suma Ching Hai The founder of the eponymous association founded in Taiwan in 1982. Her actual name is Hue Dnag Trihn and there are various stories as to how she discovered she was a reincarnation of the Buddha and Jesus Christ. She teaches that all religions are concerned with the same truth, the divine presence within, realized by prayer and meditation on the Inner Light and the inner sound. Her method uses the Chinese characters '*Quan Yin*' pointing to the contemplation of sound vibration. 'The Word' or Logos is the Inner Sound which Master Ching Hai says, 'vibrates within all life and sustains the whole universe. This inner melody can heal all wounds, fulfil all desires and quench all worldly thirst.' During the rite of initiation, the Master offers 'spiritual transmissions' or 'sudden enlightenment', and the subject has to make a lifetime commitment to vegetarianism.

Sumerian Religion *AME*. Sumerian mythology has it that the world emerged out of an ancient sea in the form of the universe, gods and people. They believed that the universe was ruled by these gods, who were anthropomorphic (they had human features and personalities) and who represented various natural phenomenon. Each Sumerian city-state had its own patron deity to whom the citizens paid homage. Temples, known as **ziggurats**, were often erected in the cities to honour and house each city's god. For example, the city of **Ur** constructed a ziggurat for Nanna, the god of the moon. The key gods of the Sumerians were Enki (god of water), Ki (god of earth), Enlil (god of air) and An (god of heaven). These main gods were believed to have created the rules of Sumerian society to which all people were expected to adhere, since the reason for human existence was to serve and delight the gods. The observance of certain rituals and animal sacrifices were considered necessary in order to satisfy these often capricious deities. The Sumerians of lower Mesopotamia share the great distinction with the early Egyptians of being the first, some 5,000 years ago, to create 'visible speech', that is a form of writing that was able to express everything said and thought. See **Egyptian Religion, Mesopotamian Religion**

Summum A modern form of mummification which follows the ancient Egyptian process but which uses modern liquids and chemicals, for the preservation of the body, some of which are also used for genetic engineering. The body is totally immersed or 'baptised' in the liquids, then wrapped in modern materials such as cotton gauze, polyurethane, fibreglass and resin. Following rites within a form of pyramid, the body is placed in a bronze or stainless-steel coffin, which itself is filled with amber resin. The mummy may then be placed in a special sanctuary or buried traditionally in a cemetery. A similar service is offered for pets. The rationale behind Summum is the belief that some form of individual essence survives death; the 'spirit' will be in unfamiliar surroundings and in risk of being dislocated. Its mummified form serves as a reference point, a location or place of attachment that enables the spirit of the deceased to receive guidance to its new destination. A secondary, but important purpose of Summum is that by preserving DNA material, the individual might be perfectly recreated so as to serve, once more, as a 'house' for the spirit. See **Mummification, Soul**

Summum Bonum Lat 'The Highest Good'. In general use, the ultimate standard from which all moral values are derived. One source of the concept is **Zoroastrianism**'s supreme god, **Ahura Mazda**, 'The Ultimate Good'. In the West, *summum bonum* is a Neoplatonic notion (see **Neoplatonism**) that St **Augustine** attributed to the Christian God. This was the point of his U-turn from **Manicheanism**; he denied the existence of absolute evil in favour of a world view with God, the supreme good, at the centre. In ancient Greek political philosophy, the *summum bonum* was *agathon*, a transcendent standard of the highest justice.

Sun Dance *Ami.* Many North American Indian groups practise a form of sun dance, but most have certain features in common such as dancing to the rhythm of drums and singing, fasting, the experience of visions and, in some cases, self-mortification. For the Plains Indians the dance is a central ceremony practised at the time of the summer solstice and lasting upwards of a week, starting and ending with the sunset. The dance has numerous symbolic layers all associated with the continuity of life after death thus, with regeneration, a cycle of life, death and rebirth. The dance also figures the interdependency and equality of everything in nature. The entire ceremony is run by a priest or shaman (see **Shamanism**) who, as the sun dance Lodge maker, oversees the ceremony of cutting a carefully selected forked tree which serves as the sun-pole. The lodge is constructed around the Sun-pole by the principal 'dance maker' and his tribesmen, who place a buffalo's head on top of the pole so that it faces the setting sun. The vertical line of the pole makes a connection between heaven and earth. The fork represents the nest of an eagle, a central sacred image and symbol of the Plains Indians: 'In an eagle there is all the wisdom of the world.' It flies high, it is the closest being to the sun, carrying messages to the god **Wakan Tanka**. During the ceremony the principal dancer sometimes cuts himself with a knife, the wounds being symbolic of death; dancing through this mutilation is a figure of resurrection. After the dance is completed the pole and other sacred items, together with the lodge, are left for nature to deal with as she pleases. The whole ceremony is an affirmation of balance and renewal and of humanity's place in nature.

Sunnah *1*. Arab. 'established custom', 'precedent', 'tradition'. The term usually refers to the personal practice and example of the Prophet Muhammad. Its written record is known as *Hadith*. They are held to be an extension of the revelation in the Koran which establish an ethical standard and a source for Islamic law. In legal practice, *Sunnah* is a fine-tuning of the more general precepts and principles of the Koran. In another sense, *Sunnah* is an attempt to give historical verification to as much detail of Muhammad's life as possible and in this context stands together with sirah, the biographical tradition of the Prophet. In both senses, *Sunnah* is used as a template against which personal morality can be judged and legal debate adjudicated. The **Sunni** branch of Islam is named from the concept of *Sunnah*. The opposite of *Sunnah* is *bid'a*, 'innovation', which implies divergence from established law and custom and thus a divergence from orthodoxy.

Sunni *1*. Arab. *sunnah*, 'tradition'. Sunni Islam is the largest Muslim school or community and it is on the concept of community that they base their faith, in contradistinction to the Shiite (see **Shi'ism**), whose belief system is based on the concept of **Imam**. The name 'Sunni' is derived from *Sunnah*, the codes of public law and personal conduct based on the practice and example of Muhammad. Thus the name came to be applied to the community of orthodox Muslims who followed the 'customary' practices of the community. The School is founded on allegiance to the first four legitimate successors to Muhammad who are known as 'the Rightly Guided' or 'the Orthodox' Caliphs of Medina. The Sunni assert that, following them (see **Islamic Dynasties**), bitter conflicts over the succession carried Islam away from the original orthodoxy. The head of the Sunni community is a **caliph**, responsible for the administration of justice through the application of the *Sharia'*, the law which is as an expression of the immutability of God's will. The caliph is not, like the imams of Shi'ism, divinely appointed and sinless, but is either elected by the community or nominated by his predecessor.

The **Seljuk** Dynasty that ruled much of the eastern Islamic world (c.1038–1300) marked a revival of the Sunni after a period in which the Shiite dominated in **Fatimid** Egypt, Iraq and Iran. An 18th-century reforming zeal has carried through to the present day in the form of a revival of Koranic studies and Islamic law. In general, the Sunnis disavow rationalism or intellectualism and instead take their energy from the dynamic spirit of the Koran. Based on this intense Koranic focus, questions with far-reaching implications have been asked concerning the relationship between religion and the State, some concluding that they should be separate institutions, while others like the Islamic Brotherhood (see **Muslim Brotherhood**) hold more traditionally to the view that an Islamic state is the only structure that can realize the potential of Islamic faith. New movements have given rise to proposing a Universal Declaration of Human Rights, that would stand alongside that of the United Nations. Other reforms are proposed for religious freedom and tolerance and for the rights of women and minority groups. There are four schools or *Fiqh* of Sunni Islam, the most dominant being the Hanafi, founded by Abu Hanifa (699–767) and known for being open to reform and modern ideas and the Shafi'i who are more orthodox.

Sunyata *B. Z.* Skt. Pal. See **Shunyata**

Supernaturalism The belief that a force or power is in existence that is greater than that to be found in nature and which may be the creator of it. This supernatural force in biblical religions is taken to be God, a doctrine substantiated by a creationist theology. A variant, which may owe nothing to religion, is the belief that man is above everything in nature and that all of nature's resources, inanimate and animate, are at human disposal. In Eastern religious philosophy, there is no place for the kind of theism found in biblical religions and creationist doctrine. Humans are only transcended by their 'true' or 'real' selves, a mode of being to be realized. Once realized all dualities are overcome since the true self is identical to 'ultimate reality' or consciousness, a concept Buddhism knows as 'Buddha nature'. See **Naturalism**

Superstition A belief or perception that is without any explicable ground or rational basis. Not all superstitions are associated with religion, but most religions have established superstitions. Examples of secular superstition, taken seriously by many, include the conviction that to walk under a ladder or to open an umbrella in the house is bad luck and that to cross one's fingers or to be splattered with bird droppings might elicit good luck. An example of religious superstition is the belief that the conjunction between the number '13' with a Friday is prescient of misfortune. As an unlucky number, 13 is derived from Judas being the 13th to be seated at the **Last Supper**; Friday, by tradition, as the day of Jesus Christ's crucifixion. Many superstitions can be understood as evidence of humanity's deep-seated anxieties; they are two-edged, being used both to avoid unwanted events and to encourage favourable ones, usually in the sense of good and bad luck. There is scarcely a corner of life without its superstitions and for many of them there are **charms** or **amulets** available for controlling or avoiding their consequences; every occupation, trade and profession, every sport, every location has its lucky objects and numbers, its lucky days and dates. Similarly, there is not a period of life untouched by superstition, the rites of passage being particularly cluttered with them. It has been suggested that at the root of every superstition is a belief in or a vestige of magic, based on what might once have been an actual experience or the observation of particular causes and their effects. See **Folklore**, **Symbolism**

FINAL WORD: 'Superstition is to religion what astrology is to astronomy, the mad daughter of a wise mother.' (Voltaire [1994])

Surya *H*. A Hindu god of the sun. See **Devas**

Sutra *H. B. Z.* Skt. Pal. 'a thread'. In Hinduism, a summary or digest of the Brahmanas, set out in short, pithy statements that require commentary for real understanding. They are intended to be applied to practical situations such as the performance of sacrifice, the direction of household affairs, the rites of passage and social duties. From these developed books of law. The Buddhist sutras are records of the teachings and discourse of the Buddha arranged as the Basket of Teachings, the second part of the **Tripitaka**, the Buddhist canon. Each text is introduced with the words, 'Thus have I heard,' the speaker being Ananda, a pupil of the Buddha. The tradition records that following the death of the Buddha c.483 BCE, Ananda transmitted the discourses verbally, from memory, at the first Council of Rajagriha, called in the same year. The sutras have been preserved in both Pali and Sanskrit and there are Chinese and Tibetan versions.

Suttee *H*. The self-immolation of a Hindu widow on her husband's funeral pyre. See **Sati**

Swam *I*. Arab. 'fasting'. The fourth of the Five **Pillars of Islam**. See **Fast**

Swami *H*. A Hindu holy man who might also be a teacher. The title is given to someone who has reached a high spiritual state by virtue of ascetic practices and renunciation of the world.

Sweat Lodge *Ami*. An Amerindian purification rite held in a form of sauna and practised widely among central and southwestern tribes. It serves various purposes such as reinvigorating an individual's spirituality or reviving them physically as a preparation for contact with the spirit world. The sweat lodge is usually created out of willow saplings to a pattern symbolic of a creation myth and covered with skins or blankets. The participants sit around a pile of heated stones over which water is poured; they are supervised by a priest or shaman (see **shamanism**), who leads them in prayers and songs to invoke the presence of the spirits. Those taking part will also share the **calumet**. A major side-effect is the cleansing of toxins from the body, since bacteria and viruses cannot survive in a temperature much more than 98.6°F. It is thought that the rise in temperature stimulates the endocrine glands, inducing physical relaxation with mental alertness. The origins of the ritual are ancient and not confined to Amerindians. Hippocrates (460–377 BCE) wrote, 'Give me the power to create a fever and I shall cure every illness.' Finnish saunas, Russian *bania* and the Islamic *hamman* all serve a similar purpose. See **Sioux**, **Vision Quest**

Swedenborg, Emanuel (1688–1772) A Swedish scientist and mystical thinker, accredited with being the founder of crystallography. His earlier, scientific publications held seeds of his later religious perception. In 1743, he had a vision in which he became conscious of direct contact with the spiritual world, 'such dizziness or deliquium [swooning] overcame me that I felt close to death.' He records that a hand clutched his and that he saw Christ, vicious dogs and his dead father who praised his religious insight. He continued to have ecstatic experiences during which he claimed to have visited heaven and hell and he developed a capacity for prophecy and clairvoyance (see **Spiritism**). On one occasion whilst away from home, he wrote about a fire raging in Stockholm that threatened his own home. The following day his account of the blaze was fully confirmed. **Jung** (1973) wrote of this, 'We must assume there was a lowering of the threshold of consciousness, which gave him access to absolute knowledge. The fire in Stockholm was, in a sense, burning in him too.' Having published in 1744 *On the Infinite and Final Cause of Creation*, and in 1745 *Worship and the Love of God*, religion became his one, driving concern. He believed God had created humanity to live simultaneously in both the physical and spiritual world. The spiritual world has its own separate place within our memory, which is what survives after death. There is no Satan and heaven is where our spirits continue to live in much the same way as they did on earth. Jesus' death did not atone for our sins, since we make our own heaven and our own hell depending on how we use our freedom and accept our spiritual responsibility. Eternal life is something we already have, it is an inner condition that cohabits with our earthly existence. Our redemption is personal and worked out according to the extent we express love in all of our relationships. Swedenborg believed he had received a mandate to share these ideas with the world. The method was to be a new Church, not in contradiction or opposition to other churches, but to encourage fellowship with all who shared his vision which was a combination of pantheism and philosophy. He spent most of his later years in England, paving the way for the Romantic movement and influencing the writings of William Blake. **Kant**, however, criticized him and wanted him consigned to an asylum.

FINAL WORD: 'There are two worlds, a spiritual world where angels and spirits are and a natural world where men are.' (Swedenborg)

Symbolism Jung (1978) suggested that 'it is the role of religious symbols to give a meaning to the life of man.' The same may be said of secular symbols. It seems that for the human mind the abstract idea or the written concept is not sufficient or sufficiently secure and that some visible and tangible representation is indispensable. The world's religions, together with its secular ideologies, have amassed an inestimable range of symbols to the point where almost everything of which the human mind is aware has symbolic reference. So unconsciously entrenched is our symbolic language, that psychologists applying the Rorschach test (for which people are asked to interpret the shapes and scenes of ink-blots by

association with whatever comes to mind) claim to be able to gain insight into the subject's personality. What is embedded in the personal and collective unconscious is, according to Jung, a massive library of archetypes. These images and signs work at many different levels; they may be an encouraging or comforting support of faith and an aid to worship; they may engender a sense of belonging to the group or movement identified by the symbol; they may, through their identification with otherwise disparate groups, bring about unity of purpose and commitment; or they may be intensely personal, endowed with talismanic power to lend courage when distressed, to evoke love, single-mindedness or a sense of responsibility and loyalty. Symbols are frequently associated with **superstitions**. It is by an understanding of symbols that dreams are interpreted and religious creeds understood; it is symbols that provide the means of relating to spirits, to any one of a pantheon of gods or to God or to a sacred object or place. Symbols are mediators between the abstract and the concrete, they are the clearly apparent communicators of otherwise mysterious and subtle concepts. See **Semiotics, Structuralism**
FINAL WORD: 'There is hopeful symbolism in the fact that flags do not wave in a vacuum.' (Arthur C. Clark, unsourced)

'There isn't any symbolism. The sea is the sea. The old man is an old man. The boy is a boy and the fish is fish. The sharks are all sharks no better and no worse. All symbolism that people say is shit. What goes beyond is what you see beyond when you know.' (Ernest Hemingway, 1952, unsourced)

Sympathetic Magic The term was coined by Sir James Fraser, who defined it as things 'acting on each other at a distance through a secret sympathy'. It is based on the principle of mimicry, 'that like produces like or that an effect resembles its cause'. See **Imitative Magic, Magic**

Synagogue *J*. From the Greek meaning 'meeting' or 'assembly'. The foremost institution in Judaism. Although sometimes called a '**temple**', especially by modern Reform Judaism (see **Judaism, Reform**), it is not meant to be a representation of Solomon's building, which was considered God's residence and was administered by a strict hierarchy of priests. The synagogue is a centre for Jewish community life and offers a range of facilities and not just a sanctuary for worship. Aside from public prayer it is, at its best, a centre of study which will include a *chadah*, a school for teaching children the Hebrew language and Jewish history. There will also be rooms available for social activities such as the celebration of **circumcision, bar mitzvahs** and weddings. In the history of the **diaspora**, the existence of a synagogue indicated not just of the size of the community, but the extent to which the Jews felt securely settled. The orthodox sanctuary is frequently round, with separate accommodation for men and women. In the older, more traditional synagogues, women sometimes sat in a gallery behind fretted screens that enabled them to observe and take part in the services without being seen themselves. The architecture of the sanctuary is designed to focus on the ark (see **Ark of the Covenant**) where the sacred scrolls of the Torah and other writings are housed. These are usually secluded behind doors or curtains, the opening of which is an impressive moment in the liturgy. The architecture, however, has no centralized model and usually reflects the aesthetic interests of the community that builds it. The synagogue staff includes a *chazzan*, the cantor, who leads the worship, a *shamash*, the attendant or caretaker responsible for the maintenance of the building, and – only since the 19th century – a rabbi, employed by the synagogue authorities to lead the worship and to assume pastoral duties and general administration. A *minyan* is a quorum of ten or more males over the age of bar mitzvah usually convened for communal prayer. If there is *minyan*, wherever they meet serves the same function as a synagogue but the location will not be as holy as a consecrated building.

Syncretism The mingling of the different beliefs and practices of various religions so as to form a new religious group or the absorption by one religion of the beliefs and ideas of another. It is a process that predates history and syncretistic elements are to be found within the development of every religion. During its expansion, the religions of the Roman Empire (see **Roman Religion**) absorbed elements of Eastern religions, for example, Mithraism (see **Mithras**). **Gnosticism** absorbed elements from Egyptian, Greek and Christian religion, even as Christianity absorbed Jewish and Gnostic concepts. Many Eastern and Western elements have combined to form new religious groups, see for example **New Age religion**, Neo-paganism and modern occult sects.

Synod of Whitby *X*. Held in 664 CE, this effected a crucial step in the Christianization of Britain, begun by **Augustine of Canterbury** in 597. Tension existed between Celtic Christianity and that of England which followed Rome, the variant practices running side by side. Sometimes the conflict was within a single family, as with the household of King Oswy of Northumberland. Bede offers a full account of the Synod which brought together the various parties that included, King Oswy, with Bishops Colman and Chad representing the Celtic tradition and Alchfrid, son of Oswy, and Bishops Wilfrid and Agilbert representing Rome. It was King Oswy who determined the outcome of the debate by deciding for St Peter: 'I dare not longer', he said, 'contradict the decrees of him who keeps the doors of the Kingdom of Heaven, lest he should refuse me admission.' Thus, did Britain, once more, become Romanized. See **Roman Catholicism**

Syrian Religion, Ancient *AME*. The famous Ras Shamra texts from Ugarit, written in alphabetic cuneiform, are the fullest contemporary accounts we have of religion in early Syria. The ugaritic texts include lists of offerings made to gods, rituals, legends and the mythologies of a fertility cult, all current in the 14th century BCE. The senior god of the Syrian pantheon was El, whose procreative talents were represented by the epithet 'the bull'. His confederate was **Baal**, or Baal Raman, 'the

Thunderer'. In various adopted forms several Syrian gods travelled with their myths to **Mesopotamia** and **Canaan**, to be known under other names. Thus, for example, Baal became the Mesopotamian **Tammuz**, and the 'Virgin Anat' of the Ras Shamra texts became **Astarte**, whose fertility cult flourished throughout the Middle East as **Aphrodite**, **Demeter** and **Osiris**. Other gods listed in the texts include Dagan, the Canaanite corn god Reshef, a warrior and war god who became assimilated with **Apollo**, and Eshmun, a healing god later to be identified with **Asclepius**. The will of god was sought through oracles, divined (see **Divination**) through the study of auspices (see **Auspicia**) and the examination of the entrails of sacrificed animals, by the interpretation of dreams and the visions of ecstatics that seem to prefigure the Islamic dervishes. Archaeology shows that temples covered a large area and were made up of various sanctuaries with central shrines similar to the **Holy of Holies** of Solomon's Temple. Under the king, who was the chief priest, the temples were well-staffed with a hierarchy of male and female priests, temple prostitutes, chanters, seamstresses who made vestments, sculptors and other craftsmen. Sacrifice was a central rite in which offerings of blood and entrails were made to the gods; the priests ate the sacrificial flesh in what seemed to be a form of communion feast shared with the community. Some sacrifices were entirely burned on the altar, others served as offerings for purification and in redemption for firstborn sons. Stone jars full of the bones of infants confirm the practice of child sacrifice, probably that of the firstborn, being a 'first fruits' offering to a fertility goddess. Several of the gods and some forms of sacrificial practices have clear references in the **Old Testament**, recorded as part of the history of Israel's occupation of the '**Promised Land**'. Canaan being one of the countries in which the Syrian gods were assimilated, Israel's prophets and priests considered them to be pagan, setting the worship of Yahweh, the God of their radical monotheism, against them. See **Assyrian Religion**

T

Tabernacles *J*. A religious festival held on the 15th of the Jewish month of Tishri (Sept/Oct) and lasting seven days. See **Sukkoth**

Table-turning Also known as table-titling or rapping, it is a feature of **séances** in spiritualist practice (see **Spiritualism**). Through a **medium**, the communicating spirit may tilt the table and rap the legs on the floor in response to simple questions which may be answered, for example, by one tap for 'no' and two taps for 'yes'. The participants rest their fingers on the table so as to be sensitive to its movements.

Taboo *P*. Also 'tabu'. From the Polynesian *tapu*, 'forbidden'. In Oceania to mark or set aside a person, object or location as sacred or impure, so as to prohibit contact or their use. Fraser records that the men of Logea, an island near Papua New Guinea, who have 'killed or assisted in killing enemies shut themselves up for about a week in their houses. They must avoid all intercourse with their wives and friends and they must not touch food with their hands.' They may only eat specially prepared vegetables since 'the intention of these restrictions is to guard the men against the smell of the blood of the slain; for it is believed that if they smelt the blood they would fall ill and die.' In general use it can mean to ostracize. Taboos are part of the culture that has created them, they are not isolated restrictions or prohibitions, but features of a complete system of order and classification and their use can only be understood in their cultural and social context. Examples include the taboo against men and women sitting together in orthodox **synagogues**, the prohibition, in some counties, on Islamic women appearing outside unveiled and the ban on wearing shoes on holy ground, such as a **mosque** or Buddhist meditation hall. Sometimes special shoes or sandals are provided. The term 'taboo' also carries with it the notion of danger, impurity or something strange and mysterious, together with the 'feeling' that if the taboo is broken the culprit will be subjected to punishment. Other than for people, places and objects, many established taboos apply to diet, as in the **kosher** and *halal* restrictions of Jews and Muslims, to sexual relations such as incest, sodomy, adult with child, humans with animals and to nudity and bad language.

T'ai Chi Ch'uan *T*. Chin. 'the fist-fighting method of the supreme ultimate' or 'Boundless Fist'. T'ai Chi can be translated as 'the grand ultimate', a figure of the cosmos. Familiar in the West as a progression of balletic movements done in slow motion, of the kind the Chinese, for example, practice in parks on their way to and from work. Across the Western world there are innumerable societies and classes offering T'ai Chi Ch'uan given by teachers of various grades of expertise. Somewhat like **yoga**, it is thought the practice will ensure good health and personal well-being. While to some extent this is true, T'ai Chi is rarely taught with respect to its original purpose. As the English translation suggests, it began as a martial art concerned not with aggression, but self-defence. Moreover, the succession of physical movements were intended as a support for a technique of meditation. The Western mind is conditioned by the traditional and fundamental dualism of the physical and spiritual; the Chinese recognize this seeming opposition to be part of a reality greater than both. The sequence of movements, when properly taught and mindfully performed, is an acted parable of aspects of **Taoist** philosophy with their origins in the *I Ching*. Movements, slowly executed in a flowing, seamless sequence are difficult to sustain, it requires mental-muscular control, a concentrated and well-focused mind, with both mind and body free of tension and each held in perfect balance. What is brought into balance are the polarities of **yin and yang**. Taoist philosophy makes it clear that even though the foundation of T'ai Chi Ch'uan is a martial art, the ritualized forms are not primarily concerned with ensuring good health through gentle exercise, but with spiritual fulfilment.

The earliest reference to Tai Chi Ch'uan was recorded during the Tang Dynasty (c.618–c.907 CE) since when, six classical forms have developed of which the following serve as examples. Wudang Tai Chi Ch'uan is accredited to Zhan San Feng (b.1247), who is thought to be the founder of the form as we know it today. Its goal was for the practitioner to realize the truth of the cosmos. The yang-style of Tai Chi Ch'uan was developed by Yang Lu Chan (1799–1872) and is probably the form 'most widely practised, to the extent that many people have the mistaken impression that it is the only form of Tai Chi Ch'uan' (Wong Kiew Kit [1996]). The form follows the characteristic 'soft' and graceful movements that engender good health. Sun-style Tai-chi Chuan was formed by Grandmaster Sun Lu Tang (1861–1932). His style uses high patterns and rapid movements and was influenced by his mastery of three forms of internal **kung fu**, and is designed to harness the power of the will rather than physical strength. In all forms, the movements of Tai Chi Ch'uan should flow like water. This is more than just an apt simile, since it relates the movements to the philosophy of Taoism.

FINAL WORD: 'The best thing is water,
        Water benefits all things yet does not struggle.
        The softest thing in the world
        Overcomes the hardest thing in the world.
        Nowhere can the soft not enter the hard.'
        (*Tao-te Ching* 8, 43)

Talisman An object that is believed to have the power to attract good fortune. Unlike an amulet, which is personal and protective, a talisman's power can attract good fortune regardless of ownership and is therefore much sought after. Talismans may be made out of materials, such as jade, metal, gemstones, parchment or wood, and are likely to have figures or characters carved on them, which invoke planetary influences (see **astrology**) or are believed to have occult powers. They are associated with healing, as illustrated by the handkerchiefs and scarves that had been touched by St Paul, which when taken to the sick healed them and cast out the evil spirits possessing (see **possession**) them (Acts 19: 11–12). The astrologer Sepharial, born Walter Richard Old (1864–1929), in his *Book of Charms and Talismans* (1923) encourages all travellers to carry a talisman: 'Train drivers and guards should certainly wear it and signalmen too. All those who hold any position on board ship … should wear it as it will assist from the safety standpoint, will help to prevent seasickness …' See **Amulet**, **Charms**, **Mana**

Tallit *J*. Heb. A rectangular prayer shawl in which male worshippers wrap themselves, usually at morning prayer. Made of either wool or silk, it is decorated at the ends with broad black or blue stripes and a knotted fringe hangs from the four corners. This is a literal interpretation of Num. 15:37ff and Deut. 22:12. The purpose of the fringe is symbolic, the worshipper may, 'look at it and recall all the commandments of the of the Lord and observe them' (Num. Ibid).

Talmud *J*. Heb. 'study' or 'teaching'. There are two Talmuds both of which are lengthy amplifications and interpretations of the *Mishnah*, the philosophical code of law compiled c.200 CE by Rabbi Judah ha-Nasi. The earlier Talmud is known as the Jerusalem or Palestinian Talmud and is the result of discussions in the rabbinic academies of Galilee and probably redacted by c.400 CE. The other is the Babylonian Talmud which records the debates of the academies of Sassanian Persia and was probably completed by c.500 CE. Because of the influence and pressures caused by the Christianization of the Roman Empire, the editing of the Jerusalem Talmud is thought to have been hasty and incomplete. For this reason the Babylonian Talmud is accepted as being a more sophisticated and comprehensive work and is the edition most studied and used by Jewish communities throughout their history. Frequently, the discussions of the Talmud are in the form of a dialogue, as if echoing the actual debates of the various academies. The form of dialectic reasoning is called *pilpul* (Heb. 'pepper') and doubtless there were times, when opinions differed and the discussion got hot on points of law, for example, the new insights and arguments lending spice to the subject matter. This form of argumentative discussion set the tone for Jewish debate on absolutely everything! The resulting Talmudic compilations are a balanced record of abiding and immutable Law, showing the justice and inner harmony of *Halakah*, which successfully binds the different traditions of the oral and written Torahs.

Tamas *H*. Skt. 'darkness' or 'blindness'. One of the three *gunas* or basic qualities of manifest phenomena in Hinduism. See **Rajas**, **Sattva**

Tammuz *J*. Derived from the Sumerian–Babylonian god, Dumuzi, who with the shortening days towards the end of the year was afforded a six-day funeral, a ritual period of mourning for the 'killing' of the summer's heat. Ezekiel (8:14–15) was taken 'to the entrance of the north gate of the

House of the Lord; and there sat the women bewailing Tammuz'. What the prophet witnessed was the lamentation for the waning year and the drying up of the vegetation because of the summer heat. It is a striking example of the widespread influence of the cult of the **Mesopotamian** god. The name has slipped into Jewish usage as the 4th month of the year, being June-July. On the 17th of the month, Jews celebrate the Fast of Tammuz which commemorates the breach made in the walls of Jerusalem by Nebuchadnezzar after a two-year siege. Tradition records that on that same infamous date, **Moses** descended from **Sinai** to find the Israelites worshipping the Golden Calf and smashed the tablets of the law in anger and that the Greek, Apostomos, burned the **Torah** and placed an idol in the Holy of Holies during the Maccabean rebellion. With such dire associations, little wonder the date ushers in three weeks of national, ritual mourning when the orthodox refrain from every kind of pleasure, when meat may not be eaten, marriages may not be celebrated and when some go to the extreme of refraining from drinking wine.

Tanakh *J*. An acronym for the Hebrew scriptures of the **Old Testament**. The word is made up from the initial letters of i) **T**orah, the **Pentateuch**, ii) the Nebi'im, Prophets and iii) **K**etubim, Sacred Writings. The Jewish Bible is made up of 24 books, where the first and second volumes of a work are counted as one (e.g. 1 and 2 Kings) and where all 12 books of the 12 prophets are counted as one. The canon is the same as that of the 39 books of the Protestant Bible, but the order is different. See **Septuagint**

Tane *P*. The **Maori** creator god of man, forests and birds. In Maori creation mythology, Tane took clay from a place called Kurawaka and formed a woman, breathing life into her and calling her Hine-ahu-one, the 'maiden formed from earth'. They had a daughter with whom Tane had an incestuous relationship; when she discovered who the father of her children was, she fled and became Hine-nui-te-po, the 'goddess of the night'.

Tangaroa *P*. The **Maori** and **Polynesian** ocean god, who separated the earth from the sky. He is sometimes shown as a huge fish, giving birth to all the sea creatures, including mermen and mermaids from whom sprung human beings. He may change into a green lizard, symbolic of good weather in which form he only needs to breathe once every 24 hours. It is his breathing that is responsible for the sea's tidal movements. To ensure successful and safe fishing, Polynesian and Micronesian fishermen are said to keep a piece of brain coral in their boats which is symbol of Tangaroa.

Tantra *H. B*. Skt. 'weft', 'context' or 'continuum'. One of the most important elements in the 'eternal religion' of Hinduism. It focuses on the energy or creative power of the female aspect of the gods, known as *devi*, or goddesses. Usually these are represented as the wives of the god in question notably, for example, **Shakti**, the wife of **Shiva** who can take many forms. Hindu Tantrism is based on the belief that the generative power of male and female sexual organs is a symbol of higher, magical spiritual potencies. Tantrics, while seeking revelation or salvation through sex, are not concerned with the transitory nature of sensual pleasure; the energies involved are sublimated in the quest for higher and lasting union. The type or model for this practice is the relationship between Shiva and Shakti and the sexual interplay between them is a figure of the composition and activity of the universe. So central is this, that Tantrism is frequently known as **Shaktism**. Tantra refers also to a collection of texts and esoteric practices that without guidance and spiritual discipline are considered to be dangerous. Most of the literature emerged during the 10th century CE, earlier records having been destroyed by Hindu fundamentalists. There are two schools of Tantra, the left-handed path, which practises forms of sexually-orientated yoga, and the right-handed path of purification rituals requiring total submission to one of the various forms of the Divine Mother. In **Tibetan Buddhism** a variety of Tantric texts deal with wide-ranging subjects such as astrology, medicine, gods and the appropriate forms of worship, the creation and dissolution of the world, the forces of nature, magical rites and so on. The practices generally follow the meditation techniques of **Vajrayana**. Tantrism and magic are inextricably combined and many of its features are familiar in Western forms of magical rites that use, candles, bells, incense, wands, circles and other geometric figures, chants and auspicious numbers. The Tantric practitioner has to undergo long periods of training to master respiratory techniques, the stimulation of the body by the sun, the control of certain autonomic functions such as heart and pulse rate, body temperature and the muscular reflexes responsible for ejaculation. Perhaps the most mysterious aspect of Tantra and thus the most beguiling is the practice of *kundalini* (Skt. 'snake'), focusing on the lowest **chakra** or 'root centre' of the human body which lies at the base of the spine. Here a tiny snake is coiled, symbolic of our unawakened spiritual potential. *Kundalini* yoga is used to rouse the 'snake', which then rises to the highest chakra to be manifest, through visions, as spiritual knowledge. All Tantric traditions use the familiar mandala for ritual and meditation. The Buddha **Shakyamuni** is credited with forms of Tantra known as 'continuum', a system centred on the potential of our spiritual experience developed by means of ground, path and fruition. The ground is the practitioner, the path is meditation and the fruition is the state resulting from Tantric practice. See **Sexual Symbolism**

Tantrism See **Shaktism** and **Tantra**

Tanzil *1.* Arab. 'transmission' or 'downward flow' of the **Koran** as the final revelation and guidance from God. It is sent down at intervals: 'With the truth, We have sent it down and with the truth it has come down; ... and a Koran We have divided, for thee to recite to mankind at intervals and We have sent it down successively' (Koran 17:106).

Because reason alone is an inadequate source of truth, humanity needs revelatory truth concerning the mysteries of creation and existence. For Muslims, revelation is a unique and immutable form of absolute knowledge.

Taoism *T.* A general Western term for two different aspects of Chinese philosophy and religion, the one being philosophical Taoism, principally that of **Lao-Tzu** (c.6th century BCE) and **Chuang-tzu** (c.369–286 BCE), the other being religious Taoism made up of several schools. Philosophical Taoism is a form of mysticism that elucidates the Tao or the 'Way'. The religious schools were concerned with how to achieve immortality, the teachings and practices often resorting to magical and alchemical techniques. Preserving and prolonging human life is basic to all Taoist beliefs and practices; there are obvious implications for medicine, the art of self-defence, charity and general concern for human welfare. It follows that the Tao, while it is familiarly known as 'the Way', also refers to the 'Teaching', specifically with respect to human behaviour and ethics. This is the emphasis in the texts of **Confucianism**. It was Lao-Tzu who, in the *Tao-te Ching*, first ascribed to the Tao a mystical interpretation which he called 'the nameless unnameable', something 'complete and nebulous which existed before the Heaven and the Earth, silent, invisible, unchanging, standing as one'. The Tao is thus an all-embracing first cause from which everything arises and to which everything returns. It is beyond the grasp of the intellect and as such is paradoxical. Chuang-tzu says of the Tao, 'it may be known by no thoughts, no reflections. It may be approached by resting in nothingness, by following nothing, pursing nothing.' The Tao resides in silence and stillness and various practices were developed to help realize it by means of meditative absorption. The most important techniques evolved by the School of the Inner Elixir, are based on breathing. The *Tao Tsang*, the Taoist canon, in the form in which we know it, was compiled in 1436 CE, during the Ming Dynasty. It comprises 1,120 volumes, all that survived of a larger collection burned in 1281 by Kublai Khan. The earliest sections date from the 5th century CE.

Taoism was gradually replaced by **Confucianism**, but has by no means disappeared in China where it continues to appeal to the Chinese love of nature and landscape. In 1957 the China Taoist Association was founded in Beijing and in 1997 Min Zhiting assumed its chairmanship. See **Wu-wei**

FINAL WORD: 'Return is the movement of the Way; yielding is the function of the Way. All things in the world are born of being; being is born of non-being.' (Lao-Tzu)

Tao-te Ching *T.* Chin. 'The Book of the Way and Its Power'. The famous and influential Taoist text attributed to **Lao-Tzu**, a contemporary of **Confucius** (551–479 BCE). Tradition tells of the text being given to Lao-tzu, The Guardian of the Mountain Pass, before he continued his journey to the West. The authorship is, however, more a matter of tradition than of historical record and the book is thought to have been written somewhere between 500 and 300 BCE. The oldest existing copy dates from 206 to 195 CE. The book was almost certainly not written by a single author, but is a redaction of much earlier writings and oral traditions. Taoists believe the book contains the wisdom of the universe and a huge number of subsidiary texts grew from commentaries on the original work, which is made up of two parts, *The Book of the Way* and the *Book of the Te* comprising 37 and 44 brief chapters respectively. By the 7th century the library of books dependent on the *Tao-te Ching* is said to have amounted to 4,500 volumes. Lao-Tzu was elevated to the status of a god, temples were built in his name and the capital of every Chinese state had the original book carved into stone. The teachings of the book are cryptic, paradoxical and irrational. There are two dominant themes, the first being the 'Way' which is not clear, there is no explicit goal or discernible path to it since 'the Tao that can be put into words is not the eternal Tao.' The second theme is *Te*, virtue or power or the power of virtue; other themes concern *wu-wei*, non-doing or unmotivated action and *fu*, the notion that everything returns to its source. These concepts form the basic philosophy of **Taoism**.

Tapas *H*. Skt. 'glow', 'heat', 'fervour', ' austerity'. The intensity of spiritual exercises practised out of a 'burning' desire to realize **Brahman**. In Indian culture, heat is a symbol of struggle and self-discipline. Tapas is one of the five virtues required in the second stage of raja yoga practice (see **Yoga**). The other four are cleanliness or purity, contentment, the study of holy scripture and surrender to the divine.

Tapu *P*. The **Maori** concept of the sacred. It also implies spiritual restriction or **taboo**.

Taqiyya *I*. 'dissimulation', 'concealment'. An Islamic provision which allows a Muslim to deny religious belief in the face of possible persecution. It was a device first used by Shiites (see **Shi'ism**), who throughout Islamic history have been subjected to opposition by the Sunni majority. Against the charge of hypocrisy it is argued that Taqiyya is 'with the tongue' only, never with the heart or mind. The practice is authorized by the **Koran**, for example at 3:28 and by a **Hadith**.

Tariki *B. Z*. Jap. 'power of the other'. A reference to liberation by means of help and guidance from the power of **Amida**, or Amitabha, a Buddha of the **Pure Land School**. The adherent is required to recite the name of the Buddha sincerely and fervently, as an expression of absolute trust. In reward, he will be reborn in the Pure Land. The term is the opposite of **Jiriki**, 'one's own power', characteristic of **Zen** Buddhism.

Tariqah *I*. Arab. 'Path' or 'Way'. The regime or specific guidance of a master in the **Sufi** order. They can be **Shiite**, **Sunni**, both or neither. The order is made up of *murid*, a 'would be' or 'a seeker', one committed to knowing and loving God. The master will offer both teaching and practice, the latter including devotions, recitations and study of the literature of piety. For Sufis, Tariqah is identified with the 'truth' as given by a particular teacher and the devotional literature associated with him. It also refers to the community developed around a particular master which may be temporary or, if given an institutional structure, permanent. In their more mystical forms, a Tariqah may be a secret order. See **Dervish, Tasawwuf**

Tarot Generally thought to be a set of fortune-telling cards, but this is considered by serious practitioners to be a debased use of the symbolic system the cards represent. In Western use, the symbolism is heavily syncretistic, having an association with Kabbalah, Egyptology and Indian theosophy. They are used as aids for reflection on one's personal life and for meditation. The origin and history of the cards is obscure, their first appearance dated between the 12th and 14th centuries, probably in northern India. Occult tradition holds that the cards came first from Chaldea, then Alexandria, then Fez in Morocco. The pack consists of 78 cards, 56 of them making up four suits, the remaining 22 'trump' cards, the Major Arcana. The four suits are Wands, Cups, Swords and Pentacles, each with a range of interconnected meaning using symbols of, for example, fire, water, air and earth. Each suit has a 'court' card, the King being the 'essential self' or spirit; the Queen, the 'soul' or the unique aspects of a person's character; the Knight, energies and self-awareness; the Page, the body, the physical aspect of a person. Each of these four cards corresponds to a letter that makes up the sacred name for God in Hebrew, thus, Ya-h-w-eh (see **Tetragrammaton**). The 22 Major Arcana represent the 22 paths or *sephiroth* of the Kabbalahist Tree of Life. The Tarot has many different designs and ranges of symbols, but the themes they represent are generally the same. As with the hexagrams of the *I Ching*, the interpretation of the symbols is subjective, depending on their juxtaposition the contemplation and meditation of the way the cards 'fall', and on the experience and understanding of the reader. See **Kabbalah, Egyptian Religion**

Tasawwuf *I*. The path followed by Sufis to reach God, the truth. The term stresses the theoretical or philosophical aspect of the search for truth, but in practical terms, Tasawwuf is understood simply as 'being a dervish'. The path implies the annihilation of the ego by God, then being directed by God's will to the point of permanently being in his presence. Another meaning puts the stress on seeing through the outward appearance of things, so as to see all things and events in relation to God Almighty. See **Dervish, Sufism, Tariqah**

Tathagata *B. Z.* Skt. Pal. An epithet for the Buddha as the 'thus-gone, the thus-come, the thus-perfected one'. One of the ten titles of the Buddha, which he used of himself after his enlightenment. See **Buddhism**

Tathata *B*. Skt. 'Suchness', a central notion of **Mahayana** philosophy referring to the absolute, unconditioned nature of all things. *Tathata* is the quid-
dity of phenomena that are beyond the grasp of intellect, something that is
immutable, formless, unmade and without consciousness. It stands in contradistinction to everything that is apparent, distinguishable and capable
of being named and classified. *Tathata* is the hallmark of non-duality
(see **Dualism**), the state achieved when the subject-object relationship
is transcended.

Tatloc *Az*. The rain and fertility god of **Aztec** religion.

Taurobolium *G. R*. A rite enacted as part of the initiatory ritual of the
mysteries of **Cybele** and Attis. A large pit was dug into which the
candidate stood while a bull was sacrificed over him, soaking him in the
blood. The initiate was thought to have been 'reborn'. In effect, the
Taurobolium was a form of **baptism**.

Tawantin Suyu *CA*. The Four United Regions, the name of the **Inca**
Empire.

Tawhid *I*. Arab. The core doctrine of Islam that affirms an absolute
monotheism rigorously applied to the establishment and government of
the *umma*, the Muslim community. In Islamic philosophy, especially in
its mystical aspect, *Tawhid* is identified with God's essence and attributes. (see **Beautiful Names**). *Tawhid* also provided the authority and
rationale for the **Caliphate**. In the 18th century it was used as an ideal
standard or criterion against which the religious rigour of the *Umma* was
measured and to protect Islam from spiritual atrophy and foreign influence. In this form *Tawhid* became the principal underlying the foundation
of the modern state of Saudi Arabia, setting the pattern for radical,
absolute monotheism as the basis for the social structure and government
of Islamic states. During the Iranian Islamic revolution, Ali Shariati
(d.1977) and Ayatollah Ruhollah Khomeini (d.1989) developed *Tawhid*
into a passionate and modern movement concerned to promote activism
and revolution. Islamic nationalism has thus become an expression of the
unity, majesty and authority of Allah, in socio-political terms.

Tawiscara *Ami*. The 'evil' twin of **Iroquois** Indian cosmology, being the
principle of evil in their dualistic creation myth. See **Dualism**, **Ioskeha**

Tefnut *E*. One of the pantheon of the **Ennead** of Heliopolis and, with her
brother **Shu**, the first deity to be created by **Atum**. In a country where
very little rain fell, Tefnut was the lunar goddess of moisture, linked with
warm air in the neighbourhood of the Nile and with fertility. Made pregnant by her brother Shu, she became the mother of **Geb** and **Nut**. The
myth has her quarrelling with father Atum and leaving to inhabit Nubia
where she changed into a cat, the symbol of war. Only **Thoth** was able to
persuade her to return. The separation is said to have caused the terrible

weather that brought the Old Kingdom to an end. Tefnut is sometimes depicted as a cat or as a woman with a lion's head. See **Egyptian Religion**

Teleological Argument One of the classical arguments for the existence of God based on the concept that there is a perceived order and design in the universe (see **Teleology**), thus implying a 'Designer' or a cosmic intelligence that planned and organized the whole creation. The argument was used by Thomas Aquinas as one of five ways of knowing that God exists. William Paley (1743–1805) made the teleological argument familiar by comparing the universe to a watch which has many independent parts working together in a kind of complex harmony. Modern supporters of the argument are inclined to focus on what they call the 'fine tuning' of nature, physics, chemistry and so on, which suggests that everything is exactly as it needs to be in order to maintain life. Opponents of the argument are inclined to dispute whether the complexity and interrelatedness of nature constitutes a design. See **Arguments for the Existence of God**, **First Cause**, **Natural Theology**, **Ontological Argument**

Teleology From the Gk. *telos* meaning 'the end' or 'intrinsic aim of existence' or 'ultimate concern'. The 'aim' or 'ultimate concern' usually refers to that of nature, implying that the whole cosmos was designed to realize a specific end. However science has shown that there is much that is random in nature and that the notion of design no longer bears scrutiny. The concept of nature being designed or ordered so as to achieve a specific end is the basis of the **teleological argument** for the existence of God.

Temenos *Gk.* A sacred place, particularly those associated with deities. The Latin *templum*, a temple, is derived from it. Examples of Temenos include the Temples of Apollo or Aphrodite, but the term is not confined just to the **temple** but to the whole area of land containing it, together with an atrium holding a cult image of the deity, statues and an altar where votive offerings were given to the gods. The term is also used of sacred groves, trees, springs and the sites of **oracles**. Similarly, in Egyptian architecture, a sacred enclosure.

Templar Originally, a knight of a religious military order, established in 1118 CE after the first Crusade to provide protection for pilgrims and for the Holy Sepulchre in Jerusalem. See **Knights Templar**, **Masonic Knights Templar**, **Order of Knights Templar**

Temple of Set See **Church of Set**

Temple of Solomon *J.* L. *templum*, Hebrew *Beit Adonai*, the 'House of God'. Since April, 70 CE, when the Romans under Titus destroyed Solomon's Temple in Jerusalem as a reprisal for Israel's revolt (see **Essenes**), it has been a potent symbol of Jewish religion and aspiration.

There is a tradition that the Jews, themselves, set fire to the Temple to avoid its desecration.

Ten Commandments *J*. The basic law as given to **Moses** on Mt **Sinai**. See **Decalogue**

Ten Good Deeds *B*. Skt. *Das-kusala-karmapatha*. Also known as the Ten Good Paths of Action, they form a moral formula of particular importance to Mahayana **Buddhism**. They are i) do not kill, ii) do not steal, iii) do not indulge in sexual misconduct, iv) do not lie, v) do not slander, vi) do not use harsh words, vii) do not gossip or speak idly, viii) do not be greedy, ix) do not hate, x) hold right views. They are not commandments or rules with ultimate or divine authority, but directions based on pragmatic principles designed to ensure social well-being generally, as well as that of the monastic community. At a higher level when practised by 'skilful means' and 'insight', they may lead to liberation. See **Precepts**

Tendai *B*. The Japanese form of the Chinese **T'ien-t'ai** school which was brought to Japan in the 8th century by the monk Saicho (also known in Japanese as Dengyo Daishi). The teachings of the school are fundamentally the same as those of T'ien-t'ai, while new esoteric rituals were introduced to the practice. Its centre was the temple of Enryakuji on Mt Hiei, near Kyoto, where it became an extremely wealthy land-owning foundation that influenced the ruling and aristocratic classes. The eclectic teachings of Tendai complement the more focused and narrow doctrines of its rival school, **Shingon**. So wide-ranging were those teachings that during the Kamakura period (1185–1392 CE) they fuelled new forms of 'breakaway' Buddhism such as **Zen**, **Pure Land** and **Nichiren**, introduced by monks trained in the Tendai tradition. Intolerant of opposition, the school used the *sohei*, a corps of so-called warrior monks, in reality armed gangsters, to intimidate the new schools. Tendai became a military threat event to those in power and in 1571 its centre on Mt Hiei was destroyed, together with 3,000 of its adherents. Tendai gradually recovered only to be eclipsed by the popularity of the new Buddhist schools its teachings spawned. Tendai is now an insignificant part of modern Japanese Buddhism.

Tenry-Kyo *B*. Jap. A syncretistic Japanese Buddhist sect. The teachings combine elements from Buddhism, Christianity and other religions, bound by a hierarchical system where the main or original 'church' stands at the apex of a number of subordinate churches. The obligations of belonging to Tenry-Kyo are very demanding and even in a quasi-religious context, it is typical of the Japanese ethic that a relationship should be maintained at all costs. See **Japanese Religions**, **Soka Gakkai**, **Shintorism**

Tephillin See **Phylacteries**

Teresa, St (1515–82) *X*. Born in Avila, Spain, she became a Carmelite nun, a Doctor of the Church and one of the foremost saints and mystics of the Roman Catholic tradition. In 1555 she experienced a second conversion and mystical visions, one of which was of creating a reformed Carmelite House of discalced nuns living in strict observance of the rule. In 1562 she founded the Convent of St Joseph in Avila and subsequently established other foundations, including convents of friars. Her great collaborator was St **John of the Cross**. Eventually, St Teresa established 17 convents, bringing about a remarkable reawakening of faith in Spain. After her death, her movement spread across the Christian world to become a leading influence in the Counter-Reformation. See **Mysticism**

Territorial Cults Cults whose members live within specific geographical boundaries. Its identity is entirely territorial and not at all tribal, ethnic or kinship related. Many of the cults are found in Africa, centred around rituals intended to protect against drought and flood, blights and pests and diseases that might threaten cattle or humans. They are concerned with the well-being and economic viability of the community and it has been suggested that such cults support a ritually protected ecosystem. A typical example is the **Mbona**, the god or spirit of a central African territorial cult that marks out its boundaries with shrines. Other examples are found in Japan where villages mark out their territory with cult signs.

Tertullian (c.160–225 CE) A lawyer from Carthage who converted to Christianity to become an African Church Father and the author of a number of books on such subjects as apologetics, theology and ascetics. He appealed for Christianity to be tolerated and attacked paganism, from which Christians must distance themselves. He was an advocate of the true Church, pleading it alone had the right to interpret scripture. On this authority his treatise *Against Praxeas* attacked heresies such as **Marcionism** and **Modalism**, and developed a positive theology of the **Trinity**. Tertullian eventually became a Montanist (see **Montanism**).

Tetragrammaton *J*. Heb. A name for God represented by four Hebrew letters (*see* Figure 13).

The word thus produced is transliterated in English as YWEH (Yahweh), but misunderstood as **Jehovah**. It was usually translated as 'Lord' and pronounced only by the high priest in the Holy of Holies of the **Temple** on **Yom Kippur**. Because of its holiness, when the term is encountered in the reading of the **Torah**, the name *Adonai* or *Elohim* is used. See **El Shaddai**, **Sacred Name Movement**

Figure 13 Hebrew letters of the Tetragrammaton

Teutonic Order See **Germanen, Order of**

Textual Criticism Also called 'Lower Criticism', this involves a literary and critical examination of the primary language sources of sacred literature so as to recover, as closely as possible, what the authors actually wrote. See **Form Criticism**, **Higher Criticism**, **Redaction Criticism**, **Source Criticism**

Theism A belief in a single divine being, that is, in God rather than in a god. Usually theism understands God to be the creator, personal and salvatory, omnipresent, but distinct from other aspects of the creation. For these reasons theism is held in the tension of immanence and transcendence. See **Deism**, **Monotheism**, **Pantheism**
FINAL WORD: 'The only theism worthy of our respect believes in God not because of the way the world is made but in spite of that. The only theism that is no less profound than the Buddha's atheism is that represented in the Bible by Job and Jeremiah.' (Walter Kaufmann)

Theocracy In general any government taking the form of an established religious authority or which is ruled by one. In some forms, the leaders are themselves members of the clergy and the State's laws are based on religious law. Several early civilizations were governed in this way, for example, Israel with its divine mandate of the Abrahamic and Mosaic covenant; Egypt, under the pharaohs who were regarded as gods. (see **Amun**) In the modern world, Saudi Arabia, Iran and the Vatican are examples of theocratic states. See **Islam**, **New Jerusalem**

Theodicy A concept within philosophical theology that aims to defend the goodness and compassion of God in the light of the suffering and evil in the world. The term was coined by the German philosopher **Leibnitz** in 1710. In the essay in which he first developed the idea, Leibnitz argued that evil in the world does not conflict with a kind and merciful God, that even with all the suffering and anxiety to which life is susceptible, we live in the best of all possible worlds. The arguments of theodicy examine both the absolute attributes of God, infinity, omnipresence, eternity, etc. and the relative attributes of God, being his knowledge, volition and works. Among the conclusions reached by different religions are i) suffering and evil do not have real existence but are illusory; ii) that evil is part of a divine plan that is wholly good, but which our limited vision prevents us understanding; iii) that God, being perfect lacks nothing, so is both good and evil, since if evil were not one of God's attributes, something would be lacking; iv) evil is the price we pray for the inestimable privilege of having free will. Suffering is a test of our humanity and our faith, since without the potential for both good and evil, we would be little more than automata. Those arguing against theodicy do so mainly on the grounds that it is impossible for humanity to establish criteria by which God can be analysed and judged. The Holocaust has focused the thinking of Jewish philosophers on the problem of the existence of both God and evil. Braiterman, coined the term 'antitheodicy', suggesting the pointlessness of trying to justify whatever might be the relationship between God and evil. He assures us that antitheodicy does not mean 'atheism', and that if a Jew 'blames' God for what happened in the Holocaust, then continues to pray, it is a valid form of human-divine discourse in the context of theodicy. The debate, both between people and between people and God, continues.

Theogony The accounts given in the mythologies of the origins of the gods, in the form of a divine genealogy which shows their line of descent. Because many of these gods practised incest and other irregular sexual relationships and because they were sufficiently versatile to change their form and sex, theogenies can become very complicated. In addition, when their mythologies travel to other countries, the gods usually become known by other names, confusing the genealogies even more. 'Theogony' is the title of Hesiod's poem describing the genealogy of the Greek gods. See **Creation Myths**

Theology In general use, discourse about God. Christianity has perhaps, one of the most developed theologies. Two kinds of theology are recognized: **natural theology**, to which human reason has access, and revealed theology (see **Revelation**) based on God's revelation, the authority of which is generally assumed by to be absolute. However, Protestant theologians have argued that all theology is 'revealed', but that its authority is relative to the means by which it was given. Eastern religions, for example Hinduism, allow the possibility that some texts and oral traditions have other than a human source, but since there is no parallel to the Western doctrine of monotheism, discourses on the texts are not best described as 'theology'. Attempts continue to be made to establish an ecumenical theology through the **Ecumenical Movement** and inter-religious dialogue.

Theomorphism The notion that human beings may have or can assume the form of God. The idea is inherent in the biblical doctrine of creation which affirms that 'God created man in his own image' (Gen. 1:27). **Anthropomorphism** suggests the opposite, that humankind created God in its image. Some traditions, notably the Mormons, believe in a God who is a literal physical entity and that we are actually made in that image. See **Thnetoi**

Theosis *X.* A term used by 2nd-century **Church Fathers** to refer to the goal and purpose of the Christian life. It is similar to the Sanskrit *yoga*, meaning 'yoked' to God. Theosis is not an event, but a process by which the individual draws closer to God and thus develops a deeper spirituality. The concept is more developed in the tradition of Eastern **Orthodoxy**, which seeks deification through liturgy and ritual.
FINAL WORD: 'The son of God became man that we might become God.' (St Athanasius of Alexandria)

Theosophical Society Founded in New York in 1857 by H. P. **Blavatsky**, and others, to promote the doctrines and way of life of theosophists. See **Theosophy**

Theosophy and Theosophists X. Generally, any system of thought concerned with an intuitive knowledge of God's relationship with the creation, which leads to a direct experience of the divine. Theosophy combines forms of pantheism with natural mysticism and has been applied to **Kabbalah**, **Neoplatonism** and the philosophy of Jakob **Bohme**. More specifically, theosophy is now identified with the Theosophical Society founded in New York in 1857, by Helena Blavatsky and Col. H. C. Olcott. Its mandate had three objectives: to promote brotherhood, to study comparative religion and to investigate the 'unexplained laws of nature and the powers latent in man'. All religions are understood to be expressions of the one esoteric truth, the 'theosophy'. The Society's influence has diminished, but remains active across the world, especially in India with its headquarters in Madras. It has been instrumental in promoting Eastern religions in the West.
FINAL WORD: 'There is no religion but truth.' (Helena Blavatsky)

Theravada B. Pal. 'teaching of the elders of the order'. The only school of the early **Hinayana** ('small vehicle') tradition to have survived. It is claimed that its teachings are closest to the original teachings of the Buddha and that its canon constitutes the record of the early discourses. Missionary initiative by Mahinda, the son of **Asoka**, carried the school to Sri Lanka c.250 BCE, where monks established the Mahavihara monastery. Schisms developed which spread Theravada throughout South East Asia, including Thailand, Burma, Kampuchea and Laos. The teachings, which are founded on the **Four Noble Truths** and the **Eightfold Path**, are shared with all other Buddhist traditions. Central to Theravadan teaching is an emphasis on the individual's attainment of liberation, which is mostly achieved by personal effort with a meditation practice developed on the sure foundation of impeccable morality and the disciplines of monastic life. The ideal role-model for Theravada is the **Arahant**, the 'worthy one' who has attained the highest level of spiritual life. While there are indications that monks are challenging the tradition, Theravada remains conservative, maintaining the characteristic analytical approach of **Abhidharma**.

Theseus G. The mythological king of Athens, famous through a variety of literature recording his exploits and adventures and which have provided the subject for images on countless vases. Among the most famous of these was his killing of the Minotaur. His adventures feature in Plutarch's *Lives* and are described in the standard Greek mythologies, (see Grant and Graves). They have also been made entertainingly accessible in Mary Renault's novels.

Theurgy Divine or supernatural intervention in human affairs or the assistance of beneficent spirits by means of miracles or magic, as affirmed by some **Neoplatonists**. In practice, magical rites will be observed to invoke the presence of the gods or spirits whose help is sought. Neoplatonism regarded the whole universe as an interplay of emanations of the godhead. Matter was the basest of these, but retained the attribute of divinity. The Kabbalah is an example of theurgy, as is the Roman Catholic Mass (see **Eucharist**), which invokes the power of Christ through the 'Host', and thus to the communicant.

Third Eye *H*. Also known as the eye of the spirit or the spiritual eye. The common term for the highest of the body's **chakras** (the *ajna chakra*), the centres of energy. It is located between the eyebrows in the centre of the forehead. It is also known as the 'mind centre' and associated with the colour indigo. The concept of the third eye is found in many religious cultures but is probably drawn from its Indian, Hindu origin. In more popular use, it is a term for 'second sight' or intuitive perception. The 'intuitive' eye does not, therefore, have the limitations of the physical eye with respect to either time or space. With the third eye it is possible to see something happening in another country or at another time, be it past or future. Mostly it is used to survey and monitor one's own patterns of energy during a **meditation** practice in which it is the gateway to the highest states of spiritual and divine awareness. It is thought that it was the third eye Jesus referred to in Luke 11:34–36, 'The lamp of your body is the eye. When your eyes are sound, you have light for your whole body … it will be as bright as when a lamp flashes its rays upon you.'

Thnetoi, Athanetoi *G*. Gk. 'immortal' and 'human beings' respectively. Terms used in Greek mythology to maintain a distinction between gods and men or immortals and mortals. Thnetoi is the Greek term for 'mortal' and, by implication, 'men'. Athanetoi is the Greek term for 'immortal' and by reference for 'god' and 'divinity'. For the Greeks to believe the soul was immortal was to believe that it was divine, thus if a man hoped to be immortal, he must become a god. Both the Greeks and Romans believed man was capable of divinization and was thus, potentially immortal. The early Church, much influenced by Greek philosophy and mythology (see **Hellenism, Philo**) faced the charge that the central doctrine of its faith, incarnation, was a natural continuation of pagan mythology. The **Church Fathers**, as apologists, addressed this problem assiduously. See **Greek Fathers, Latin Fathers, Theomorphism**

Thomas à Kempis (1380–1471) *X*. A priest, monk and writer, known almost entirely through his book, *The Imitation of Christ*, which is a manual of personal spirituality. Kempis encourages the believer to bring every aspect of his life into conformity with the will of Christ. See **Perfectionism**

Thomasine Church *X*. Centred on the Malabar coast in Southern India, the Church is made up of the followers of Syriac Christianity, a community distinguished linguistically and culturally. Their origin goes back to 1st-century Christianity and to the seven churches founded by St Thomas the Apostle. The various communities within the Thomasine Church form the Nasrani people, an ethnic group who identify themselves as *Mar Thoma Khritianis*, the Saint Thomas Christians. Tradition has it that St Thomas preached the gospel to the Jewish communities settled along the Malabar coast, but that his first converts were brahmans. It seems that the converted Jews, the Jewish-Christians, formed one of the denominations of the Church known as the Knanaya and the brahmans the other. Today, the Knanaya are not an independent Christian denomination, but look either to Rome or to Syrian Orthodoxy for their ecclesiastical authority. Their churches were modelled on the style of the synagogue. The Thomasine Church offers an interesting example of both cultural and religious syncretism, having the culture of south Indian, Christian doctrine and a Syriac-Judaeo form of worship.

Thomism *X*. A theological school that distinguished between the natural and the supernatural, human reason and revelation, the created and the divine. The ideas were developed from the teachings of Thomas **Aquinas**, whose *Summa Theologia* is the dominant influence on Roman Catholic theology.

Thor *AE*. Germanic god of thunder, developed as Donar, the red-bearded god, who by killing trolls and giants with his hammer became something of a role-model for the **Vikings** of western Scandinavia. He was also the ruler of winds and showers, clement weather and good crops, in short a divine meteorologist. His wife, Sif, was known for her brilliant hair, probably golden in colour to associate her with ripe corn and a dominant fertility cult. Thor's mother was the Earth, herself. His hammer was a magic implement and a powerful weapon, which when flung at giants shattered rocks and boulders. Many accounts have survived of Thor's struggle with the World Serpent, which he caught with the bait of a bull's head attached to a huge fishing line. The giant Hymir, rowing the boat, cut the line and the World Serpent fell back into the ocean. In some versions Thor slays the serpent, in others the story is set in the battle of **Ragnarok**, the world's final battle. Thor was highly revered by Icelandic farmers and fishermen. See **Germanic Religion**

Thoth *E*. The lunar god of wisdom, language and writing. In the **Ogdoad** system the moon was seen as the eye of **Horus**, the sky god, in his semi-blinded one-eyed manifestation, but gradually the cult became a lunar deity in its own right. The crescent moon resembled the curved beak of the ibis and Thoth was sometimes known as Djehuty, meaning ibis. The night light of the moon enables the continuation of the measurement of time, but its phases contributed significantly to early astrology and astronomy. The moon's cycles also governed the civil and religious rituals of Egyptian society which led to Thoth being associated with wisdom and magic, in which capacity he was the secretary and councillor of Ra, the sun god. As the inventor of writing, Thoth became the scribe of the Underworld and the object of worship for Egyptian scribes. In the later period of Egyptian history, Thoth's cult gained prominence in Hermopolis Magna, where thousands of dead ibises were mummified in his honour; the Ogdoad cosmogony was rewritten to show that it was Thoth who gave birth to **Ra**, by laying an ibis egg, from which he hatched. A later adjustment turned the ibis into a goose, which may be the precedent for a goose laying a golden egg. The baboon was sacred to Thoth. See **Tefnut**

Thracian Rider God *AE*. A demigod of ancient Thrace (now Bulgaria) recorded in sculptures and inscriptions from c.4th century BCE to c.4th century CE. Greek and Latin inscriptions call the 'Thracian Rider', 'the Hero'. He carried the epithet 'healer' and is thus associated with **Asclepios**, as well as other gods such as **Apollo** and **Dionysus**. He is thought to have significance for survival after death, but the problem of the god's original identity remains puzzling and little is known about the cult itself which seems to have declined during the early part of the 4th century CE.

The 3HO *S*. The 'Healthy Happy Holy Organization' with the official name the 'Sikh Dharma of the Western Hemisphere'. A modern sub-sect of **Sikhism**, it was founded in 1969 by Harbhajan Singh Puri, known later as the *kundalini* Yoga Master Yogi Bhajan. The stated object of the Society is to 'share the lifestyle, yoga and meditation practices of kundalini yoga … as a method of helping people to live, healthy, happy and holy lives' (from the Society's website). The Society, uniquely, has an ordained ministry and members adopt Khalsa (see **Khalsa Code**) as their surname. It was the Akal Takhat, the spiritual authority of Sikhism that authorized Yogi Bhajan to teach the faith in the western hemisphere. That it should combine with orthodox Sikh doctrine the mysteries of Hindu *kundalini* yoga may seem odd, until it is remembered that originally, Sikhism set out to dissolve the differences between Hinduism and Islam. Of the 250,000 Sikhs in North America, something like 10,000 are 3HO Sikh Dharma members.

Three Jewels *B*. Skt. *Triratna*, the three fundamental components of Buddhism: the **Buddha**, the **dharma** and the **sangha**. In the process of becoming a Buddhist, the adherent will take the vow of seeking refuge in each of these, using the formula, 'I take refuge in the Buddha, I take refuge in the dharma, I take refuge in the Sangha.' They can also be used as an aid to meditation by repeating them as a **mantra**: 'Buddha, dharma, sangha'. They are three of the ten *anussati* (contemplations or reflections).

Three Marks of Existence *B*. The *Trilaksana*. The three characteristics of all conditioned phenomena. The three marks, although distinguishable, are inter-related. They are *anatman*, egolessness or the absence of a real self, *anitya*, impermanence, and *dukkha*, suffering. The implications of the *Trilaksana* are the subject of the first two of the **Four Noble Truths**.

Throne Mysticism *J*. Derived from Old Testament prophetic visions of the glory and majesty of God seated on a high throne in heaven. 'In the year that King Uzziah died I saw the Lord sitting upon a throne, high and lifted up ...' (Isaiah 6:1ff and see Ezekiel 1:1–26) The visions were an important influence on the development of both Kabbalistic (see **Kabbalah**) and **Merkabah** mysticism, which interpreted the visions as the *Mysterium Tremendum*, the soul's experience of communion or even union with God. Because of Ezekiel's vision, the throne is sometimes referred to as a 'chariot', Heb. *Merkabah*. See **Mysticism**

Tibetan Book of the Dead *B*. (Tib. *Bardo thodol*, 'in-between state'). Based on a concept found in both **Hinayana** and **Mahayana** Buddhism, that there are intermediate states that link the process of dying with the process of rebirth. The idea, which stems from **Padmasambhava**'s **Vajrayana** teachings were developed and systematized in the 14th century; the result has become well known in the West as the *Tibetan Book of the Dead*. The book gives instructions that help a dying person to become liberated while passing through the *bardos*, the intermediate phases of dying, the death itself and rebirth. In this process the subject will encounter visions that have to be understood as false projections of the mind that conceal the true nature of reality. The visions all involve light; the *bardo* of the actual moment of death emanates as dazzling white light; the *bardo* of supreme reality has lights of five colours in the form of **mandalas**; and the *bardo* of becoming, a light of lesser intensity. Each of these three forms of light are also manifestations of the *trikaya*, the three types of the Buddha's body, the five types of wisdom and the six modes of existence. The teachings associated with the *Tibetan Book of the Dead* have been made accessible in Sogyal Rinpoche's book *The Tibetan Book of Living and Dying*.

Tibetan Buddhism Marco Polo tells a story of being present at the Mongol Court with some lamas from Tibet. They were able to raise the Khan's cup from the ground to his lips, seemingly without any physical contact. It was a demonstration sufficient to convince the Khan of Tibetan Buddhism's superiority to Christianity. Certainly, Tibetan Buddhism, especially **Tantrism**, is associated with developed forms of magic. Also called Lamaism (see **Lama**), the tradition developed in Tibet from the 8th century CE, later spreading through the Himalayan region to the neighbouring countries of Bhutan, Nepal and Sikkim. The Tibetan tradition developed four major schools: **Nyingmapa**, **Kagyupa**, **Sakyapa** and **Gelugpa**. Pre-Buddhist Tibetan religion was called **Bon**, the indigenous religious tradition of the region and the source of many of the characteristic features of Tibetan culture. Buddhism was first brought to Tibet by **Padmasambhava** in the 8th century CE. Known as Nyingmapa, the 'Old School', it took the form of **Vajrayana**, a Mahayana school that combined elements of ancient Indian nature religion, magical ritual and yoga. The non-celibate monks who followed Padmasambhava became known as the 'red hats'. During this early period of Tibetan Buddhism, the Nyingmapa school was founded on the doctrines and traditions stemming from Padmasambhava, most importantly, the **Dzogchen** teachings. It remains one of the four main schools. During this same period, 9th–10th century CE, the Tibetan Buddhist canon was compiled. Tibetan monks travelled to India and Nepal collecting and translating into Tibetan the greater part of Indian Buddhist writings. Tibetan religious life came to be modelled on 10th- to 12th-century Indian Buddhism with its organized monastic rule, a systematized religious philosophy, complex liturgies and disciplined meditation practices, all enclosed by characteristic vernacular architecture and the detailed and highly symbolic painting and iconography.

Padmasambhava's death was followed by an unsettled period of conflict during which Buddhism virtually disappeared. It was definitively re-established in the 11th century by Buddhist missionaries, most notably Dipankara Srijnana or Atisha, the Venerable Lord, whose followers were known as 'yellow hats'. This Buddhist revival led to the development of the four major schools referred to above. The fourth, the Gelugpa School, is also known as **Madhyamika**, the 'Middle Way' school, which became determinative of Tibetan Buddhism and from which the succession of Dalai Lamas has evolved. Tenzin Gyatso, the 14th Dalai Lama, is its current leader.

The most important features of Tibetan Buddhism are: i) its vast and rich literature, which include the **Tantra** texts. Each of the schools compiled its own canon, manuals of rituals, histories and biographies of the important founders and revered teachers such as **Milarepa** and Gampopa; ii) the emphasis on the master-disciple relationship for the transmission of teachings, scholarship and meditation, together with the tradition of guru **yoga**; iii) the recognition of a huge pantheon of buddhas, bodhisattvas, saints, demons and deities; iv) the independence of the schools and sects, derived not so much from doctrinal disputes as from the secular powers of rival monastic foundations; v) the joyful and resilient piety of both the monks and the lay Tibetan community, with their prayer wheels, pilgrimages, the circumambulations of holy sites, prostrations, offerings, the recitation of texts and the chanting of mantras, typical of which is the familiar invocation of Avalokitesvara, *Om Mani Padme Hum*; vi) probably the most sublime theme of Tibetan Buddhism is the ideal of the **bodhisattva**, which is of great importance to Buddhism. It has a particular application in Tibetan schools. The path is intended to lead to the perfection of compassion and the bodhisattva ideal is of one who, having achieved enlightenment, chooses to remain in the cycle of **samsara** and rebirth thus continuing to be of service to others.

Since 1959, when Tibet was invaded by China, the Buddhist community

has been in exile and has its centre at **Dharamsala** in northwest India. The communist Chinese authorities have persecuted and suppressed Buddhism. Tibetan sources record that something like 1.2 million people were killed, that 150,000 have become refugees in India and the West and that most of the 6,000 monasteries have been destroyed. See **Tibetan Book of the Dead**, **Wheel of Life**
FINAL WORD: 'Becoming a refugee is acknowledging we are groundless and it is acknowledging that there is really no need for home or ground. Taking refuge is an expression of freedom, because as refugees we are no longer bounded by the need for security. We are suspended in a no-man's land in which the only thing to do is to relate with the teachings and ourselves.' (Chogyam Trungpa [1991])

Tidewater Anglicanism *X*. 'Tidewater' refers to an area of Virginia, associated with **Bible Belt** Christianity. Tidewater Anglicanism is derived from the Church of England, through the colonial foundations of **Protestantism**. See **Appalachia Presbyterianism**

T'ien-t'ai *B*. Chin. 'School of the Celestial Platform'. A Chinese Buddhist school based founded on the Lotus Sutra and given its definitive form by the scholar Chih-i (538–597 CE). It is better known as the Lotus School, of which **Nagarjuna** was the first patriarch. Put briefly, the school teaches that all phenomena are an expression of the absolute, of *Tathagata*, 'suchness'. Even **dharmas** are empty but interpenetrate, thus the whole and its parts are one. Emptiness, phenomenology and the middle state being a combination of the two, are all aspects of a single existence. The masters of T'ien-t'ai say that, 'One thought is the 3,000 worlds,' meaning that one thought embodies the universality of everything. The school synthesized the existing extremes and was thought to be Universalist (see **Universalism**) in teaching that all beings are endowed with Buddha nature. The school was brought to Japan in the 8th century by the monk Dengyo Daishi, where it is known as **Tendai**. See **Nirvana School**

Tillich, Paul (1886–1965) A German philosophical theologian who taught theology and philosophy at several major universities. Because of opposition to the Nazis (See **National Socialism**) he was dismissed from his post at Frankfurt in 1933 and was obliged to leave Germany. He was appointed Professor of Philosophical Theology at Union Theological Seminary in New York and became a USA citizen in 1944. His highly systematic work was strongly influenced by **existentialism** from which base he developed a theology of culture so that, 'faith need not be unacceptable to contemporary culture and contemporary culture need not be unacceptable to faith.' His existentialism focused on the nature of being and the fears derived from our existence. The 'ground of being' was Tillich's definition of God, who is being-itself and not one being among others. Christ is the 'New Being'. To speak of the 'ultimate' in terms other than that of 'being' is to speak symbolically and the entire language of the Bible is to be symbolically understood as is all spiritual and theo-logical knowledge. Tillich's perceptions of faith, culture and God, are a rigorous challenge to religious **fundamentalism**. See **Symbolism**

Tirtha *H. J*a Skt. 'a ford' or 'sacred water'. In practice a place of pil-grimage where one can easily cross from this world to the bliss of nirvana. While *tirtha* are traditionally physical locations for both Hindus and **Jains**, the *Santi Parva* of the Mahabharata speaks of *tirtha* of the mind, of bathing the mind in the sacred water of purity. 'That man, whose limbs only are wet with water, is not regarded as one that is washed. He, on the other hand, is regarded as washed who has washed himself by self-denial. Even such a person is said to be pure both inwardly and outwardly.' See **Pilgrimage**, **Pillars of Islam**

Tonpa Shenrab Miwoche *B*. The founder of the **Bon** religion of Tibet. Shenrab was one of three brothers, who given the teachings in heaven, were commissioned to carry them to earth and to be guides for man-kind. Of the brothers it is said Dagpa came in the past world age, Shepa will come in the future world age and Shenrab is here for the present world age.

Torah *J*. Heb. 'instruction', 'teaching' or 'revelation'. The term has various uses. It can refer to the complete revelation of God or to the entire body of Jewish religious teaching, the detailed laws governing practical day-to-day living and to interpersonal and community relationships. It has its origins in both oral and written forms, the latter including the books of the **Tanakh**, the Hebrew Bible. The oral forms, believed to have been transmitted by God to Moses, were eventually written in order to preserve them; they form the body of literature known as the **Talmud**. Used with the definite article 'the', Torah' refers exclusively to the **Pentateuch**, traditionally ascribed to the authorship of Moses and in a handwritten form is housed as a scroll in the **ark** (see Ark of the Covenant) of all **synagogues**. They are referred to as the *Sefer Torahs*, the Books of the Law.

Totalitarianism A theoretical account of an extreme authoritarian, unde-mocratic social philosophy such as Nazism (see **National Socialism**), **Fascism** and some periods of Russian communism (see **Stalinism**). It is usually based on a single-party ideology under which all forms of oppo-sition or descent are suppressed by, characteristically, secret police ter-rorism. Under such a regime, dissidents are either executed, placed in political concentration camps or 're-educated'. Totalitarianism implies the absolute control of the media, education, the professions, the labour market and the suppression of freedom of speech, the press, worship and unauthorized public meetings. Religious extremism and fundamentalism have sometimes come close to creating a totalitarian society such as **Calvin**'s Geneva and in some fundamentalist Islamic states. In their more modern forms, totalitarian states have been, in principle, secular.

Totem Usually an animal or, according to Freud, 'more rarely a plant or a natural phenomenon (such as rain or water) which stands in peculiar relation to the whole clan.' Either way, the totemic object is understood as being the clan ancestor and guardian spirit; the relationship is reciprocal in that the clan will undertake not to kill, destroy or damage the animal, plant or object in question. The clan's totem can be inherited through either the male or female line and its relationship with the totem is more significant than that of blood or tribal membership. In many groups such as the **Australian Aboriginals** and the **Amerindians**, ritual dances mimic the movements of the totem animal. For Amerindians the totem may be either a personal guardian spirit or that of the whole clan, with images of, for example, animals and birds carved into the familiar totem pole. In general, the image is a symbol of the intimate relationship between human beings and nature, a relationship determinative of the very earliest forms of religious response and, perennially, of most religions since.

Towers of Silence (*Zo.* '*Dakhma*' or '*Dokhma*') **Zoroastrian** funerary towers. Those belonging to the dislocated **Parsee** community were situated around Mumbai, in India; the ones used by the Iranian Zoroastrians were located at Yazd and Kerman. Zoroastrianism, being a religion passionately concerned with purity, regarded the human corpse as unclean. For this reason they were unable either to bury or to cremate the dead for fear of the corpse polluting the elements of earth and fire. The dead were placed on top of the Towers of Silence, left there to be consumed by vultures and other carrion birds. Eventually, only the bones remain, gradually to become sun-dried and bleached clean, at which time they were thrown into the ossuary, a pit dug in the centre of the tower. In Iran, the towers were situated on the tops of hills or in the desert and away from human settlements. Modern Zoroastrians now bury their dead in cemeteries and even though it is forbidden by the **Gathas**, cremation is practised by a few. In Parsee tradition, the towers are low buildings frequently set among forest or gardens. Access to them is limited to the official pallbearers. The bodies are laid out in three circles, the men on the outside, women next, with the children in the centre. This practice is at risk because of the declining vulture population.

Tractarian Movement See **Oxford Movement**

Traducianism *X*. The theory that the human soul is transmitted by the parents to their children. The idea was proposed as a way of explaining the doctrine of original **sin**, which through St Augustine had become one of the dominant concerns of Latin theology. Traducianism was eventually displaced by **Creationism**. See **Immacualate Conception**, **Virgin Birth**

Trance A hypnotic or ecstatic state used to bring about various forms of religious experience which, by definition, transcend consciousness. Trance may be induced by drugs such as the peyote (see **Peyote Cults**) or by a belief in spirit possession (see **Pentecostalism**), Communication with the spirit world is characteristically undertaken by **mediums**, themselves in a trance state in which they become spirit-possessed. A trancelike state is also associated with the intense religious experiences of the kind recorded by mystics. See **Mysticism, Possession, Séance, Visions**

Transcendent Various nuances of meaning are suggested. A transcendent idea or concept is one that goes beyond rationalist comprehension. As an attribute of God, it describes his being beyond and other than the material world, in contradistinction to his immanence. It is one of the pivotal terms in the philosophy of religion's debate about 'reality' and what is 'knowable'. Secular philosophers argue that there is no empirically discernible reality beyond thought and the proper subject of philosophical investigation is thought itself. In the biblical religions and Neoplatonic philosophy (see **Neoplatonism**), transcendence is the attribute of God which refers to the purity and perfection of his total 'otherness', to the point of his being beyond all of our concepts and categories. See **Immanent, Transcendentalism**

Transcendentalism In philosophy, the notion of there being events and concepts that pass beyond everyday, mundane experience. It is an integral part of **Kant**'s philosophy, but found also in most forms of philosophical **idealism**. Kant uses the term 'transcendent' to refer to the **noumenon** – intellectually intuitive data that is beyond the realm of possible experience. The religious implications of transcendentalism had considerable influence on 19th-century American literature, for example on Ralph Waldo Emerson, Henry David Thoreau and Margaret Fuller. It was their reaction to the theological and restrictive orthodoxy of **Calvinism** and to the rationalism of the **Unitarian** Church. The group first called themselves the 'Hedge Club', later to be renamed the 'Transcendental Club'. Their ideas were published in a magazine, *The Dial*, which sought to develop a new spiritual energy and ideal; in their turn, their influence touched such writers as Hawthorne, Melville, Whitman, Samuel Taylor Coleridge, Henry James and D. H. Lawrence.

Transcendental Meditation A form of **yoga** that became familiar through Maharishi Mahesh Yogi. During the 1960s with the rise of the 'hippy' movement, TM became a vogue **New Age** practice focused on altered states of consciousness. Yoga and TM promise to expand creativity, personal awareness and world peace. The movement is centred on the Maharishi University of Management at Fairfield, Iowa, USA, through which the **meditation** technique can be learned.

Transhumanism The current use of the word is somewhat different from its literal suggestion of a super-human state or existence. Put simply, it is used to identify an energy in modern culture that aspires to the ethical uses of science and technology so as to expand human ability and capacities. It has to do with biopolitics, the combination of politics and radical bio-sensitivity. The proper use of science is a form of continuing, natural evolution, that will lengthen human life, human mental, psychic and noetic abilities. This will enable 'everyone to enjoy better minds, better bodies and better lives' and to be 'better people' (website of the World Transhumanist Association). See **Democratic Transhumanism**, **Posthumanism**

Transhumanists Members of an international and cultural social movement known as **Transhumanism**, concerned to support new sciences and technologies so as to develop human cognitive ability and overcome such problems as disease and ageing. See **Democratic Transhumanism**

Transmigration See **Metempsychosis**

Transpersonal Psychology The term 'transpersonal' was coined by Jung, 'transpersonal consciousness' being a synonym for the 'collective unconscious'. The term is currently used for the point of meeting between the disciplines of psychology and spirituality. The subject was developed by Abraham H. Maslow (1908–70) from his research into self-actualizing individuals. 'TP' is an adjunct of the psychology of religion, attempting to understand in scientific terms what actually happens during mystical experience (see **mysticism**), **meditation**, shamanic practices (see **Shamanism**) and religious rituals such as the Catholic **Mass** or **baptism**. The enquiry is also interested to examine the relationship between religious experience, depression and psychosis. The practice is based on the principle of non-duality (see **Dualiom**), that each separated individual is part of the cosmos; self-transcendence enables people to experience a broader identity with the whole. 'TP' is not a religion, it has no creed or beliefs, but its interests are represented by various organizations and societies, such as the Institute for Transpersonal Psychology at Palo Alto in California, USA. Techniques used include meditation and phenomenological analysis. See **Human Potential Movement**

Trans-polytheistic Theism *H*. An important concept for the understanding of Hinduism, which regards its polytheism to be varied reflections of the one reality. The concept rests, for example, on a well-known verse in the **Rig-Veda**, 'They call it **Indra**, **Mitra**, **Varuna** and **Agni**, and also heavenly delightful Garutman; The Real is one, though sages name it variously.'

Transubstantiation *X*. In the Roman Catholic **Mass**, the real and actual change of the substances of the elements bread and wine, into the body and blood of Jesus Christ. The outward appearance, known as the 'species' or 'accidents' of the elements, remains unaltered. The 'real and actual' change in the substances is known as the 'real presence'. The concept is denied by Protestants who believe in a 'spiritual presence', and that the bread and wine are entirely symbolic. See **Eucharist**

Tree A familiar religious symbol with many associations, the most familiar, perhaps, being the Tree of Knowledge bearing the forbidden fruit in the Genesis story of Eden (see **Fall of Man**). The tree provides a structure for genealogies such as the Tree of Jesse showing the line of Jesus' descent to David, frequently illustrated in the stained glass of cathedrals and churches. Trees have been oracular sources like that of 'the tree of the diviners', at Shechem (Judges 9:37). The bo tree sheltered the meditating Buddha, oaks formed the sacred groves of **Zeus** at Dodona, laurel was associated with the Delphic oracle and the **Maya** have Yaxche, the Tree of Life. The fig tree is India's tree of knowledge, the Koran has the multi-fruited Tooba tree. Several religious cultures have worshipped trees, their roots deep in the earth, their branches reaching yearningly for heaven. In comparison to man's brief life, a tree, especially the evergreen, was an obvious image of immortality, symbolized by the planting of yew trees in graveyards. Perhaps the most enduring symbolism is that of the Tree of Life, a concept shared by such diverse traditions as **Kabbalah** in which the tree is a figure of the structure of the universe and the Scandinavian ash, the **Yggdrasil** or 'world tree'.

FINAL WORD: 'Keep a green tree in your heart and perhaps a singing bird will come.' (Chinese proverb)

Trikaya *B*. Skt. 'three bodies'. The **Mahayana** tradition of Buddhism teaches that the Buddha has three bodies, that is, modes or dimensions. They are: i) *Dharmakaya*, the true nature of the Buddha, the essence of the universe, thus the unity of the Buddha with everything existing (see **Won Buddhism**). It also represents the **dharma**, the expounded teachings of the Buddha; ii) *Sambhogakaya*, 'the body of delight' the buddhas who, in the buddha-paradise, 'enjoy' the truth they embody. iii) *Nirmanakaya*, 'the body of transformation', being the Buddha and other buddhas and **bodhisattvas**, who with a human body, appeared to teach and to guide people to enlightenment. The symbolism of the Trikaya is interpreted differently by the various Buddhist schools. In **Zen** the three bodies represent three levels of reality in reciprocal relationship to each other. Respectively, they are: i) the cosmic body or cosmic consciousness; ii) the experience of the ecstasy of enlightenment, of sharing the dharma-mind of the Buddha; iii) the radiant, transformed buddha-body as represented by the historical, Buddha Shakyamuni. To illustrate the reciprocal relationship Zen uses the metaphor of medicine, respectively, i) medical knowledge, ii) the education of the doctor and iii) the application of the knowledge in restoring a patient's health. In **Vajrayana**, the three bodies express different experiences of enlightenment: i) the fundamental truth of emptiness, ii) the supreme reality or the experience of enlightenment itself, iii) the 'form-bodies', being the means of communicating the experience of the absolute.

Trilaksana *B*. Skt. 'three marks'. The three characteristics of all conditionally arisen phenomena. See **Three Marks of Existence**

Trimurti *H*. Skt. 'three-form'. The Hindu trinity, comprising **Brahma**, **Vishnu** and **Shiva**. They represent, respectively, the principles of creation, maintenance and destruction.

Trinity *X*. The foundational Christian doctrine that one God exists as on substance in three persons, Father, Son (see **Son of God**) and Holy Spirit. It is accepted as a mystery in that the notion of Trinity is perceived only by revelation and not by reason, neither can its truth be explained by reason, once revealed. There is no clear formulation of the Trinitarian concept in the New Testament and it has been deduced from salvation-history, with the Father incarnated in the Son, crucified and resurrected, then bestowing the Holy Spirit, the Paraclete or comforter as God's empowering agency in the world (see **Pentecost**). The doctrine has continuously posed major problems for Christian apologists, especially with regard to Christianity's avowed claim to be monotheistic (see **Monotheism**). Exegesis of the Trinity has called on most philosophical systems and has given rise, at times, to extraordinary theological casuistry. Attempts to define the Trinity in doxologies and creeds have been made in the face of heresies which have abandoned the Trinitarian notion altogether or which in the process of making it intelligible, have undermined its doctrinal strength. By and large, arguments about the Trinity have been concerned with the nature of the relationships between its three members; do the three persons differ in *origin*, in that the Father is ungenerated, the Son generated, with the Holy Spirit 'proceeding' from the Father through the Son? Are they entirely *different* persons combined in much the same way as members of the same family or are they in fact, just three facets of the one person, differing according to their *functions*? Are they thus, of one substance, similar substances or of separate substances? Many answers have been devised to which the various Christian denominations have attached themselves according to their theological inclinations, with some, like the **Unitarians** and **Christadelphians**, abandoning the doctrine altogether. No other doctrine in Christian history has been so divisive and in the end the Church has had to admit that 'all things issue in mystery.' Kipling was baffled: 'Three in One, the One in Three? Not so! To my own Gods I go. It may be they shall give me greater ease, then your cold Christ and tangled Trinities' (Lispeth). Trinities of various kinds are to be found in other religions such as the Greek and Roman triads, Hinduism's **Brahma**, **Siva** and **Vishnu**, and the conceptual trinities of Buddhism, such as the **Three Jewels**. See **Sabellianism**

Tripitaka *B*. Skt. 'Triple Baskets' of the Pali Canon, the canon of Buddhist scriptures arranged in three parts: i) the *Vinaya-pitaka*, containing some of the oldest records of the Buddha's discourses, compiled in the decades following his death. It provides an account of the beginning of the Buddhist **sangha**, and the rules ordering monastic life; ii) the *Sutra-pitaka* contains the original discourses of the Buddha or his disciples and is arranged in five parts; iii) the *Abhidharma-pitaka* is an analysis of and commentaries on psychology and philosophy of the texts. Each school of Buddhism has its own canon, but the differences are slight. Only the Pali **Canon** has been preserved in its entirety, so-called because of the language in which it was written. Tradition has it that the canon was agreed at the Council of Rajagrha held a year after the Buddha's death in c.483 BCE. Because of the internal evidence of changes and the development of doctrines, this early date is unlikely. Despite the definitive canon, **Mahayana** considered the collection was still open to additional texts and for over a thousand years new material was added, especially to the Tibetan and Chinese versions. Because of these additions, the threefold division is not maintained in these collections. See **Sutra**

Triratna *B*. Skt. 'three precious ones'. See **Three Jewels**

Troth, The An organization with members throughout America, Europe and Australia, that practise Norse and Germanic heathenry. See **Asatru**, **Germanic Religion**, **Norse Mythology**

Trotskyism A form of **communism** identified with Leon Trotsky (1879–1940). After Lenin's death he contested the leadership of the Party with Stalin but was defeated and banished from Russia. Their opposing views were irreconcilable. Stalin's political philosophy (see **Stalinism**) was concerned to make Russian socialism impregnable to counter-revolution. Trotsky, on the other hand, promoted the thesis of permanent revolution, wanting to use Russian communism as the basis for world revolution. Trotsky thought of himself as an orthodox Marxist (see **Marxism**) and as such rejected the thesis of 'Socialism in One Country'. He and many other Fourth Internationalist groups opposed Stalin's **totalitarianism** believing that true socialism could not succeed without democracy. Having continued to criticize Stalin from afar, Trotsky was finally assassinated in his home in Mexico by a Stalinist agent. He died of a wound inflicted to his head by an ice-pick, an unusual weapon to be found in such a hot country.

Truth of Life Movement *J*. See **Seicho-No-Ie**

Tumbuna *P*. Melanesian clan ancestors (see **Ancestor Worship**) who, while living in a spirit realm, are constantly in contact with their living descendents and who are believed to be the means by which tribal rites and customs are endowed with **mana**. They are honoured in various ways, such as by the rituals of the **male cult**. The actual presence of *tumbuna* is confirmed through dreams, **mediums** and diviners (see **Divination**) and by association with sacred stones or places. They are visually represented by participants wearing **masks**. The obligation of Polynesian religions to honour the *tumbuna* is their dominant religious observance.

Twelve Tribes of Israel *J*. The progenitors of the traditional 12 tribes were the patriarch **Jacob**, his wives Leah and Rachel and his concubines. After **Canaan** was conquered by Joshua, the emergent Land of Israel was divided between the tribes (see Gen. 49). The 12 are Reuben, Simeon, Levi, Judah, Zebulon, Issachar, Dan, Gad, Asher, Naphtali, Joseph and Benjamin. After the death of Solomon, all but Judah and Benjamin separated to form the Kingdom of Northern Israel. In 721 BCE, they were conquered by the Assyrians and exiled. What happened to them and who their descendents are remains something of a mystery (see **Lost Tribes**). The tribes of Benjamin and Judah that formed the southern Kingdom of Judah are the ancestors of present world Jewry. See **Judaism, Ethnic Divisions of**

Twelvers *I*. Common name for the largest Islamic subdivision, the **Imamis**, whose lineage comprises a succession of 12 imams starting with **Ali Ibn Abi Talib**, whom Shiites believe to have been appointed by Muhammad. See **Bektashis, Hidden Iman, Isma'lis, Shi'ism**

Two-by-Twos *X*. A Christian sect founded in 1863 by William Irvine of Kilsyth, Scotland. Members of the sect were sent out to preach and teach in pairs, hence the name. They are known by other names including the No-name Church and the Coonyites from Edward Cooney, a co-worker. Irvine introduced the 'Living Witness' doctrine, claiming that salvation is gained only by hearing a Two-by-two worker. Irvine's message and mission was based on Mat.10:8 – 'Heal the sick, raise the dead, cleanse lepers, cast out devils.' His workers were required to accept the terms of the following verses, that is, to have no money, no provisions, no second coat or shoes and to earn their own keep. Although the movement was beset by controversy and Irvine's progressive extremism, the movement spread abroad, to the USA, Australia and elsewhere. Attempts to estimate their numbers indicate 50,000 to 150,000 members.

Types of Buddhas *B*. Buddhist tradition identifies three types of Buddhas. Firstly, the 'fully awakened one' (Pal. *Samyak-sambuddha*). This is a **Buddha** who has, without any kind of outside aid assistance or tradition, attained complete and perfect **enlightenment** or *samyak-sambodhi*, the 'enlightenment of a perfect Buddha'. The historical Buddha, **Shakyamuni**, is considered a Buddha of this type. Secondly, the 'solitary awakened one' (Pal. *Pratyeka-buddha*). This type of Buddha has also attained perfect enlightenment but does not form a *sangha* to carry his teaching, preferring to remaining solitary. They are sometimes known as 'silent Buddhas'. Thirdly, the 'hearer' or 'a Buddha who has heard' (Pal. *Shravakabuddhas*). This is a Buddha who has attained enlightenment from having heard the teachings of the first kind of Buddha, after which they may lead others to enlightenment. Their own enlightenment is therefore dependent on the tradition and lineage of the teachings of a *Samyak-sambuddha*. See **Arahant, Buddhism**

Typology The interpretation of sacred literature based on characters and events of an earlier period, thus prefiguring, prophesying or foreshadowing what is written. A typical example is the interpretation of the **New Testament** according to the 'types' or models of the **Old Testament**. On this pattern, the suffering servant of Isaiah is interpreted as a prefiguring of the Messiahship of Jesus Christ. Other specific examples include Christ as the second Adam, the lamb of God as the **scapegoat**, and St Paul's use of the Israelites crossing the Red Sea as a type of baptism.

Tyr The one-handed Scandinavian sky god, worshipped as Tiw by the Anglo-Saxons and as Tiwaz in **Germanic religion**. 'Tuesday' is derived from his name. He is also identified as the Greek **Zeus** and the Roman **Jupiter**. See **Anglo-Saxon Religion, Scandinavian Religion**

Tzadik *J*. Heb. 'righteous one'. A person who is a redemptive spiritual presence in the world or a religious leader considered to be especially spiritual, such as an inspired **rabbi**. The tradition is particularly associated with **Chasidism**. See **Zaddik**

Tzimtzum *J*. Heb. 'contraction', or, 'concealment'. A concept developed by the Kabbalist philosopher, Isaac Luria (1534–72) as an answer to the problem of how God could create a world 'outside' of himself, since he was himself, everything. Another way of forming the problem is to ask how the infinite could ever be involved with, communicate with or create the finite, since any involvement would be a limitation of the attribute of infiniteness. The doctrine of God's self-contraction is based on the idea of God concealing himself or his Light, so as to be able to reveal himself. In short, what we have is the concept of the refraction and concealment of God's radiating emanations which takes place in a number of progressive stages, so that by degrees the infinite becomes finite and physical substances become present gradually. In **Chasidism** the concept was used of the teacher who concealed the level of his knowledge in order to relate naturally to a student who had absolutely no background or perception of the subject in which he was engaging.

U

UFO Cults Movements associated with Unidentified Flying Objects and the mythologies that have been attached to them. For many years sightings of unidentified flying objects have been reported from all over the world and speculation has been rife about them being flying-saucers and other forms of alien space craft. Enquiries into the sightings has mostly shown them to be natural phenomena such as a comet, a shooting-star and the planet Venus or man-made objects like weather-balloons and satellites. Various forms of UFO cult assert that the Earth was visited by extraterrestrials many thousands of years ago, their appearance being the origin of the concept of a supreme being that became the subject of mythologies. Some affirm that aliens have always been amongst us, but in a non-physical form. Communication with them is by means of telepathy or psychic phenomena. See **Atherius Society, Chen Tao, Heaven's Gate, Raelianism**

Ugaritic *AME*. An extinct Semitic language of ancient northern Syria, identified with the city of Ugarit (destroyed 1180–1170 BCE). It was written in cuneiform adapted as an alphabet. Ugaritic is only known from archaeological findings and inscriptions, such as those of the tablets found in the village of Ras Shamra. Its principal importance has been to the research of texts such as the Old Testament, enabling the verification of the meaning of Hebrew words and phrases, especially those culled or borrowed from the languages of the pagan cultures that surrounded them. Ugaritic was used predominantly by the Canaanites (see **Canaan**), whose territory the Israelites conquered under the leadership of Joshua. See **Syria**

Ulema *I*. Arab. 'the learned' or 'the one possessing knowledge'. Sunni muslims regard the Ulema as the defenders of orthodoxy against **secularism** and modernism and as the arbiters of Shari'a, the sacred law. The term is also used a general term for the Islamic clergy. See **Fiqh, Ijtihad**

Umayyad Caliphate *I*. The dynastic Mecca-based clan that ruled Islam from 661–750 CE. The founder was Muawiyah Ibn Abi Sufyan, who by the time of his death in 680 CE, had established Damascus as the capital of the rapidly expanding Islamic Empire. Successive caliphs strengthened the administration and gave to the Arab world its own coinage. Under the Umayyads, Islam spread westwards through North Africa and into Spain, then penetrated France as far as Tours and Poitiers. Eastwards, the Islamic Empire spread to Iran, Central Asia and northern India. More concerned with military and political expansion than with the spread of Islamic faith, the Umayyads were accused of building an Arabic rather than an Islamic empire. Perhaps for this reason they were judged to be secular, both in their moral character and administration. In the ensuing revolt of 750 CE, the Umayyads were displaced by the **Abbasids**. However, it is important for an understanding of Islam, to keep in mind that in 756, the Umayyads developed a rival empire in Spain and much later, in 929, a rival caliphate. They were supported by the **Kharijites** of North Africa and by the **Berbers** who had arrived in Spain earlier. The Umayyad Caliphate thrived for the next three centuries and established a sophisticated Islamic culture, the Moorish culture, which was radically different from that of the Iranian-Semitic culture of the Abbasid Caliphate. See **Ali Ibn Abi Talib**, **Caliphate**, **Islamic Dynasties**, **Shi'ism**

Umbanda A religious movement that emerged in Brazil in the 19th century. Heavily syncretistic, the religion melds together **Yoruban** ancestor worship and deity beliefs, with the Catholic tradition of patron saints and a complex hierarchy of spirits and **spirit possession**. Gathering in a *terreiro* or enclosure, rituals are performed both publicly and privately. The meeting might open with a hymn, followed by trance sessions, ceremonies of possession, consecration and baptism. See **Despachos**

Umma *1*. Arab. 'community'. A basic and important concept in Islam which regards the worldwide fellowship of Muslims as equal despite national, racial and cultural differences. In the Koran the term is used to refer to a people who are the subject of the divine plan and to whom God has sent a prophet to reveal it. *Umma* is also associated with the concept of *Dar al-Islam* or 'Household of Islam', geographical territories defined by the sovereign rule of Islamic law. *Umma* is similar in concept to the Hebrew *Eretz Israel*, the 'People of the Earth', in this instance 'earth' being the Promised Land; it is also analogous to the Christian concept of the addition of believers constituting the 'body' of Christ.

Unction See **Anointing**

Unification Church A modern millenarian (see **Millenarism**) movement founded in Korea by Sun M. Moon. He claimed that in the late 1940s and early 1950s he had received visions and messages from God that recognized him as the returned Christ (see **Second Coming**). The 'Divine Principles' was the esoteric knowledge imparted to him, comprising laws by which God governed man, explanations of the causes of suffering and God's purpose in human history. It taught that death and suffering have no reality and that God's eternal kingdom would be established on Earth. The Church's concept of God is interpreted as the intangible essence of Life. God the Father is the Principle, of whom Jesus is the complete manifestation. A reconstruction of the Genesis myth has Eve contracting a spiritual union with Satan before her physical union with Adam (see **Serpent Seed**). It is an account of the origin of the 'original sin' with which all human beings are born. As the returned Christ, Moon by his own marriage began the steady process of redemption by repopulation. His famous mass weddings of believing couples were intended to generate children who would be born uncorrupted. Moon quickly gathered a following based in Seoul, Korea, which in the early 1960s spread rapidly outside of Korea. In 1967 they became the focus of attention in the USA when groups of parents, whose children had 'deserted' them for the cult, formed a national organization aimed at recovering their families.

Unitarianism *X*. An affirmation of Christian monotheism that rejects the doctrine of the **Trinity**. God, being one person, the divinity of Christ and the Holy Spirit is denied. Its critics claim that Unitarianism leaves Christianity without its core message of a God who loved the world to the point of sacrificing his son in the process of saving it. The movement, which has no formal creed or confession, has its origins in the **Reformation**, and in the 16th–17th centuries established organized communities. It was taken up by English Dissenters such as the **Presbyterians**, and since 1925 Unitarianism has been a separately organized, but increasingly rationalist denomination. In America, Unitarian ethics contributed to New England's distinctive culture. In 1961 the American Unitarian Association merged with the Universalist Church to form the **Unitarian-Universalist** Association. The Jehovah's Witnesses, Christadelphians and some traditions of the Quakers are among Christian denominations that do not hold to the doctrine of the Trinity.

Unitarian-Universalists *X*. Although acknowledging Jewish roots, the Unitarian-Universalists are a Christian religious movement that has no official creed. God is believed to be non-dual, that is, one person and salvation will be gifted to the whole human race. A combination of conscience and reason is the basis from which beliefs are nurtured and practised, in the process of keeping an open mind about many of the doctrines with which Christianity has struggled throughout its history. What governs religious belief is personal experience allied to reason and conscience. Congregations are self-governing. See **Unitarianism**

United Church of God See **Armstrongism**

United Reform Church *X*. Formed in 1972 by the amalgamation of the **Congregational** Churches of England and Wales and the **Presbyterian** Church of England.

United Society of Believers in Christ's Second Coming See **Shakers**

Unity School of Christianity A New Age cult with a Christian persona. Its central doctrines include **pantheism** and an assortment of other New Age interests. It was actually founded in 1889, by Charles and Myrtle Fillmore, to be incorporated as a Church in 1903 as the Unity Society of Practical Christianity. Originally intended as a society for physical healing it became increasingly syncretistic, absorbing elements of many forms of metaphysics. Its co-founder admitted that 'We have borrowed the best from all religions, that is the reason we are called Unity ... Unity is not a sect, not a separation of people into an exclusive group of know-it-alls. Unity is the Truth that is taught in all religions, simplified ... so that anyone can understand and apply it.' (Charles Fillmore)

Universalism Originally an Old Testament view held by anti-nationalist prophets such as the Second Isaiah and Jonah, that God's intervention in history was not exclusively for the 'Chosen People', but for all nations. Universalism, however, does not reject the Particularism of Israel's covenant relationship with God, which is to be understood not as a special favour but as a special mission, the responsibility to present God's message to the whole world. A Christian formulation of universalism, *Apocatastasis*, first developed by the more liberal Greek Fathers (e.g. Clement of Alexandria and Origen) asserts that hell is temporal and temporary and that finally all human beings will be saved, even the Devil himself. St **Augustine** refuted the doctrine which was condemned by the Council of Constantinople in 543 CE and since the Reformation it has had no place in either **Catholicism** or **Protestantism**. The doctrine survives, however, in liberal theology, affirmed by denominations such as the **Anabaptists**, **Christadelphians** and **Moravians**. The universalist concept may be applied to any view or doctrine the aim of which is the salvation or enlightenment of all human beings. The Buddhist response to universalism, is represented by **Mahayana** which includes in its all-embracing vision, not only human beings, but all sentient beings.

Universal Life Church The sect has no official doctrines and seems to be a movement that believes simply in, 'love God and do as you like.' Its adherents are free to work out and to practise what seems right to them, the only restriction being that one must not infringe the rights of others. Its website declares, 'We are advocates of the good life! We want to be competent, to be proficient, to be co-operative, to love our fellow man, to appreciate, to be humble, to be honest, to be moral, to live positively, to be what we profess.' On the basis of this comprehensive mission statement, the sect sets out its refreshingly simple agenda, i) to do that which is right, ii) to work for a fuller life for everyone, iii) to reach for eternal progression, an iv) to live and help live. Allowing for the need to qualify some of these terms, it seems almost everyone is a member by default.

Universal Man A concept based on the idea that the universe or macro-cosm, is like an immense human body perceived as the primal universal man. One of its established expressions is found in **Kabbalah** as **Adam Kadmon** whose body is made up of the ten **Sephiroth** of the **Tree** of Life. It is based on the idea that we are made in the image of God, thus every human being is a miniature of the universal man. Kabbalists understand Adam Kadmon to be the whole universe as currently understood. The universal mind of the universal man is similar to **Jung**'s concept of the collective unconscious.

Universals Universals are the qualities of 'things'. Things are particulars. Blueness, for example, is the universal property predicted of all blue things. There are philosophers who argue that universals exist independently of the properties they instance. Plato and Platonists believe the world we see is but a reflection of the real world, thus Plato's Forms are something like universals. See **Particularism**

Untouchables *H*. Literally 'outcasts'. The lowest group of the Hindu **caste** system that amounted to about 24 per cent of the population. They were regarded as being untouchable because they were ritually polluting. An even lower subsection of this caste, the 'unseeables', were considered so ritually impure that they had to keep out of sight and do their work at night. In 1949, the Indian Government banned the use of the term 'Untouchable', granting them special educational and political privileges. **Gandhi**'s reforming work lead to the Untouchables being called the Harijans, the 'Children of God'.

Upanayana *H*. Skt. 'Sitting close to' or 'initiation'. A Hindu boy's rite of passage into becoming a 'twice born'. See **Four Stages of Life**, **Sacred Thread Ceremony**

Upanishads *H*. Skt. 'to sit down near to'. This means at the feet of a guru who will transmit the secret teaching. In effect, the collection of texts known as the Upanishads form the final section of the **Vedas**. The more ancient Upanishads, among which are some of the most important, were originally textbooks of the various Vedic schools and sometimes take the form of question-and-answer dialogues between sages and the king whose courts they were visiting. They are philosophical in nature and vary in the way they discuss the relationship of the 'soul', or essential self, to absolute reality. Some Upanishads represent this in impersonal and abstract terms, illustrated by analogy. One of the most familiar of these is an account of a father asking his son to put salt in a glass of water, then tasting it at various levels. The salt can be tasted, but not seen. 'You don't perceive the one Reality exists in your own body, my son, but it is truly there. Everything that is has its being in that subtle essence. That is Reality! That is the Soul! And you are that, Svetaketu!' (Chandogya Upanishad, vi. 13). In the later Upanishads, the ultimate is perceived as something approaching a personal God. 'He encircles all things, radiant and bodiless, unharmed and untouched by evil. All-seeing, all-wise, all-present, self-existent, he has made all things well for ever and ever' (Isa Upanishad, 8). This description of the Absolute will be familiar to most theists. The movement between an impersonal cosmic entity and a personal God, set the agenda for the later development of Hinduism and, indeed, some traditions of Buddhism such as **Amidism**. See **Vedanta**

Upaya *B*. Skt. 'skill in means or methods'. A concept of central importance to **Mahayana** Buddhism. See **Skilful Means**

Uposatha *B*. The sacred days before the four stages of the moon's waxing. The days are used for reciting the monastic rules and by laymen for taking the uposatha vows, the Eight **Precepts**, a condensed form of Buddhist ethics.

Urantia, The A book that has its origins in Chicago of the 1920s and 1930s, in a case study of psychiatrist, Dr W S Sadler (1875–1965). His patient was found to be talking lucidly in his sleep and had no memory of this on awakening. Sadler claimed that this was not a case of possession, channelling or automatic writing, but of a spirit dictating a text through the voice of the sleeping man. The outcome over the period 1934–35 was the *Urantia* book, 'Urantia' being an ancient name for the planet Earth. The book was published by the Urantia Foundation formed in 1950 and the English version appeared in 1955. A brief survey cannot do justice to its complex cosmology that claims the universe to be far older than any scientific hypothesis suggests and that its existence is owed to a creative intelligence. The book does not represent a complete religion and there is no creed or clergy. Its teachings include the nature of the Deity and Paradise, the organization of various levels of the universe and the significance of evolutionary models. Jesus is the incarnation of Michael of Nebadon, one of hundreds of thousands of 'Creator Sons of God'. The Foundation and its adherents regard the book as scripture.

FINAL WORD: 'Its ultimate mission is to increase and enhance the comfort, happiness and well being of man, as an individual and as a member of society, through the fostering of a religion, a philosophy and a cosmology which is in line with man's current intellectual and cultural development' (Mission Statement from the Urantia Foundation website).

Uranus *G*. In Greek mythology Uranus was the god of the sky and his wife **Gaia**, goddess of the earth. Their union resulted in **Cronos** and his fellow Titans, the one-eyed Cyclops and the Hecatoncheires, monsters with 50 heads and 100 hands. Uranus was castrated by Cronos and when his blood fell on the earth, semi-divine beings emerged. See **Rhea**

Urf *I*. The common name for unwritten, customary law in most Islamic countries, but known differently elsewhere. In the east, for example in Indonesia, the term *adat* is used. Generally *urf* refers those laws that relate to the way people conduct their social relationships and how they administer their businesses in the markets or order ceremonies such as marriage. *Urf* also directs local law administered by the ruler and governs the practice of common courts. There is no consensus as to whether *urf* or *adat* are sources of law. See **Fiqh, Ijma, Ijtihad, Shari'a**

Utilitarianism A thoroughly practical philosophy advancing the simple idea that the value of anything is to be judged by its usefulness. In short, whatever is useful is good. The ideas were developed by Jeremy **Bentham** (1748–1832) and his student and secretary, James **Mill**

(1773–1836) into a comprehensive political, ethical and aesthetic system. The philosophy was carried forward by James Mill's son, John Stuart **Mill** (1806–73). Bentham argued that the ultimate aim of social and political doctrine should be to ensure the greatest happiness of the greatest number. Mill argued that ethically, virtue is to be found in the attitudes and tendencies concerned to establish the highest degree of happiness possible and that utility should be the only criterion of morality. Bentham was the prime mover, through his students, in making Utilitarianism influential around the world. One of the principle advocates was Robert Owen (1771–1858) a committed socialist and founder of the Co-operative movement. John Stuart Mill carried Utilitarianism into the concept of social liberty, arguing that 'the only purpose for which power can be rightfully exercised over any member of a civilized community, against his will, is to prevent harm to others. His own good, either physical or moral, is not sufficient warrant.' Utilitarianism can be read as a secularist manifesto; the rightness of any action being judged by its usefulness to the individual and society, frees both ethical and political theory from metaphysical terms of reference. Even though Bentham asserted that 'No power of government ought to be employed in the endeavour to establish any system or article of belief on the subject of religion', Utilitarianism would not stand against religious practice, since by the same criterion of usefulness, religion might well promote the desired end of happiness. See **Positivism, Secularism, Voluntarism**
FINAL WORD: 'The greatest happiness of the greatest number is the foundation of morals and legislation.' (Bentham)

Utopianism The political doctrine that holds to the unachievable scheme of realizing human perfection and a perfect society. Utopian vision combines the idealism of economics, politics and religion. The quest has sometimes been driven by an atavistic yearning for a previous perfect state, such as the Eden of Genesis, the Krita Yuga of the **Mahabharata**, or the Golden Age of Ovid's *Metamorphosis*. More realistically, the quest has been for a simpler, more honest way of life, in tune with nature. The term 'Utopia' was coined by Thomas More (1478–1535) as a name for an imaginary island nation, the subject of his book *Utopia*, written in 1515. More contrasts the warring European Christian states with the peaceful non-Christian society of his Utopia, where all things are held in common, there being no private property and total religious toleration. It has been noted that **Marx**'s vision of ideal communist socialism resembles More's society. See also **Mankind United, Oneida Movement**
FINAL WORD: 'The golden age was first; when Man, yet new,
No rule but uncorrupted reason knew:
And, with a native bent, did good pursue.
Unforc'd by punishment, un-aw'd by fear.' (Ovid)

Uttara-Mimamsa *H*. Skt. 'later discussion'. One of the six classical schools of Hindu philosophy that was instrumental in establishing the

Vedas and an alternative name for **Vedanta**. It succeeded the **Purva-Mimamsa** both chronologically and philosophically, being concerned with the attainment of knowledge conditional on purification effected by the rituals of the former Mimamsa. See *Darshana*, **Mimamsa**

V

Vaikuntha *H*. In **Vaishnavism**, the divine realm of **Vishnu** or his **paradise**. Its location is believed to be either on Mt **Meru** or in the northern ocean. Both Vishnu and **Indra** are sometimes called Vaikuntha.

Vaiseshika *H*. Skt. 'referring to distinctions'. It is thought to be the oldest of the six orthodox schools of Hindu philosophy. Vaiseshika was established by Kanada, between the 6th and 3rd centuries BCE. The interest is in science more than philosophy and the school is considered complementary to **Nyaya**, dividing the multiplicity of the natural world into six categories, matter, properties, karma, ubiquity, distinctiveness and intrinsicality. Sometimes referred to as the Atomic School (see **Atomism**), it proposed the existence of an impermanent world composed of agglomerations of eternal atoms. See **Darshana**, **Purva-Mimamsa**, **Sankhya**, **Vedanta**, **Yoga**

Vaishnavism or **Vishnuism** *H*. The cult associated with the god **Vishnu** and one of the three principal forms of worship in Hinduism together with **Shaivism** and **Shaktism**. Vishnu is recognized as the supreme being and the originator of everything, revered in the **Mahabharata** as Prajapati, the creator god. His followers worship him in all of his many incarnations, but primarily as **Rama** and his wife **Sita**.

Vajrayana *B*. Skt. 'diamond vehicle'. A **Mahayana** school of Buddhism that developed in northern India from around the 7th century CE. It was concerned to extend the magical and psychological world view of Buddhism and its associated magical practices. It began with small groups who studied the **Tantras** under the guidance of a guru, which were gradually assimilated by monastic communities. Because of the use of sacred syllables and **mantras**, the movement is sometimes known as the Mantrayana. See **Mahamudra**, **Sakyapa**, **Trikaya**, **Tibetan Buddhism**

Vak Devi *H*. See Saraswati

Valhalla *Nor*. In **Norse mythology**, the 'Hall of the Slain' presided over by Odin. The Hall, a kind of military fortress, is symbolic of battle. M. F. Lindemans tells us 'The rafters are spears, the hall is roofed with shields and breast-plates litter the benches. A wolf guards the western door and an eagle hovers over it.' The slain heroes brought to Valhalla will assist Odin at **Ragnarok**, the final battle between the gods and the giants. Every day they leave the 'shining citadel' to occupy themselves with training and mock battles on the great plain of Asgard; at night they return to feast on roasted boar and to drink mead. See **Germanic Religion**

Valkyries *AE*. In Germanic mythology, the warrior-maidens of **Odin**. They presided over battles, choosing those who should be slain, then killing and devouring them, thus they are associated with crows and ravens, the scavengers of the battle-field. They brought the souls of the dead back to **Valhalla**. Their famous chief was Brunhild who led her warriors on horseback across the sky, wearing helmets and carrying spears. They have been given a certain notoriety by Wagner, who features them in his opera *Die Walküre*. They may be compared to Morrigan and Badb, the Celtic war-goddesses. See **Celtic Religion, Germanic Religion**

Vanaprastha *H*. Skt. 'forest abode'. For a Hindu the third of the **Four Stages of Life**. See **Ashrama, Sacred Thread Ceremony**

Vanir *Nor*. One of two groups of gods in **Norse mythology**. They are wild nature and fertility gods and goddesses and the vehement opponents of the other group, the **Aesir** who are warrior gods. Some gods or goddesses appear to be members of both, a feature that illustrates they way the Aesir and Vanir interact, for example, by taking hostages and counting them among their own pantheon. The Vanir include **Freyr, Freyja** and **Frigg**. See **Anglo-Saxon Religion, Germanic Religion**

Varna *H*. Skt. See **Caste**

Varnasramadharma *H*. Skt. The term is made up of *varna*, 'caste', *asrama*, 'stage of life' and dharma, 'upholding the balance'. The teaching combines the traditional Hindu fourfold caste system with the **four stages of life**, outlining principles that must be observed by the twice-born Hindu (see **Sacred Thread Ceremony**). It sets out a social structure categorizing the duties of the castes through the four stages of life. The purpose is to find and maintain the balance between material necessity and spiritual development.

Varuna *H*. A Hindu god of the sky and at one time the most important god of the Hindu pantheon. He is related to the Greek Ouranos and the Latin **Uranus** ('Heaven'). As a sky god Varuna supported cosmic order and its human counterpart, the morality that ensured social stability. His cult was eventually eclipsed by the emergent greater gods **Vishnu** and **Siva**. See **Devas, Trans-polytheistic Theism**

Vedana *B*. Skt. Pal. 'sensation' or 'feeling'. The combination of the physical and psychological faculty of feeling. The range of feelings are usually subdivided as, pleasant, unpleasant or neutral. To the five senses Buddhism adds 'mental impressions', this latter category enabling discrimination between sensations to be made. Vedana is the second of the *skandhas* or **Five Aggregates** and the seventh of the 12 links of the chain in **Dependent Origination**.

Vedanta *H*. Skt. Veda + *anta*, 'the end of the Vedas' which conclude with the **Upanishads**. Vedanta is one of the six classical schools of Hindu philosophy and the foundational philosophical system of Hinduism. It is primarily concerned with the relationship between **Brahman** and **Atman** and the techniques available to realize the unity of the two. There are three principal sections of Vedanta philosophy: i) **Advaita**-Vedanta, concerned with non-**dualism**; ii) Vidyaranya-Vedanta or qualified non-dualism; and iii) **Dvaita-Vedanta**, dualistic Vedanta. See **Brahmana Darshana**, **Nyaya**, **Purva-Mimamsa**, **Sankhya**, **Vaiseshika**, **Yoga**
FINAL WORD: 'Of all the Hindu systems of thought, the Vedantic philosophy is the most closely connected to Indian religion and in one or another form it influences the world view of every Hindu thinker or the present time.' (Radhakrishnan)

Vedas *H*. Skt. *Vid* 'to know'. Thus, 'knowledge, sacred teaching'. A collection of texts thought to be the oldest in Indian literature. Traditional Hinduism rests on the divine origin and authority of the Vedas and their having being revealed to the **rishis** while in a state of profound meditative absorption. Thus they are sometimes called the *shruti*, 'that which was revealed'. Approximately six times the length of the **Bible**, the Vedas are divided into four sections: i) the **Rig-Veda**, in the form of poetry; ii) the **Samaveda**, in the form of songs; iii) the **Yajurveda**, a group of texts concerned with the rituals of sacrifice; iv) **Atharvaveda**, credited to Atharvan, a priest of the mysteries of the fire ceremony (see **Fire, Sacred**). Each of the Vedas are subdivided by content, form and date of origin and each has supplementary texts, the **Aranyakas** and the **Brahmanas**. The Vedas were tantamount to manuals used by the chief priests presiding over what was a sacrificial cult. As with so many ancient sacred texts, the Vedas were transmitted orally and while no definite date can be given for the composition, most authorities would agree that they were compiled from around c.1500 to 1200 BCE. It is possible that some of the compositions might predate the Aryan migration into India, which would push the above dates back a thousand years. The **Upanishads**, the final, supreme development of the Vedas, form their last section.

Veneration of Ancestors See Ancestor Worship

Venial Sin *X*. Lat. *venialis*, 'forgiveness', 'pardon'. In **Roman Catholic** doctrine a form of sin that does not deprive the sinner of sanctifying grace. The distinction between venial and 'mortal' sin is based on 1 John 5:16, 'There is such a sin as deadly sin ... but although all wrongdoing is sin, not all sin is deadly sin.' Thus, venial sin does not concern a 'grave' matter, is committed in ignorance and without deliberate or complete consent. However, such sins are to be taken seriously. St **Teresa** of Avila said, 'For the love of God, take care never to grow careless about venial sin, however small ... There is nothing small if it goes against so great a sovereign.' See **Sin**

Venus *R*. The Roman goddess of love, broadly associated with the Greek goddess **Aphrodite**. Her cult had a specific start on 18 August 293 BCE when her original temple was dedicated at Ardea, south of Rome. Venus Genetrix was instituted by Julius Caesar as goddess of motherhood and domesticity and she was often referred to with the epithet *Venus Erycina*, 'of the heather'. During the Renaissance, Venus became a popular subject for sculpture and painting and because of her 'classical' status, her nudity was acceptable, even with the hint of eroticism derived from her association with sexual healing. Venus was, perhaps, the queen of Mother **goddesses**, the giver of vegetation, the creator of animals, goddess of sexual love, marriage and maternity, whose cult was sometimes associated with sacred prostitution. See **Sexual Symbolism**

Vesta *R*. Lat. Analogous to the Greek goddess, Hestia, the Roman goddess was the personification of the public hearth. Her cult was centred on the ever-burning fire, a symbol of the unity of all Romans as a kind of extended family. The fire was not allowed to go out unless it was ritually extinguished and ritually re-lit, requiring rites of purification and renewal. There are similarities with the concept of the 'eternal flame', and the ever-burning lamps of religious sanctuaries. By extension the goddess was linked with the private hearth and with domesticity and the right ordering of family life. She was a native Roman deity, the daughter of **Saturn** and **Ops**, and sister to other members of the extended family that included **Jupiter** and Neptune. Vesta seems devoid of personality and has no developed mythology, which may be why the cult was understood as an abstraction, the sacred flame symbolizing her numinous presence. It was this fire that was guarded by her priestesses, the **Vestal Virgins**, who ritually renewed it every 1 March. It burned until 391 CE when Theodosius' edict prohibited public pagan worship. See **Fire, Sacred**

Vestalia *R*. Lat. The festival of **Vesta**, goddess of the hearth, celebrated from 7–15 June. On the first day the inner sanctum of the temple was opened for women to make offerings, usually of plain food. The **Vestal Virgins** prepared the *mola salsa*, the holy cake, using grain harvested during the previous month, water drawn from a sacred spring and salt made from brine. The festival was also celebrated by bakers and millers.

Vestal Virgins *R*. Known also as the Vestals, they were the only full-time clergy in Roman religion. To be a Vestal, the girl had to be between the ages of six and ten, a patrician, a virgin and to take a vow to be chaste for 30 years. The Vestals lived together in a house near the Forum, under the supervision of the **Pontifex Maximus**. If a Vestal broke her vow she was condemned to be buried alive in the 'Field of Wickedness'. They wore a *tunica*, a simple dress used both in the temple and for everyday wear.

Vijnana *H. B*. Skt. 'consciousness' or 'knowledge'. A faculty of perception that goes beyond the mental or intellectual awareness. In Hinduism, it is the supreme spiritual perception of Brahman, not intuited in the state of *samadhi*, but in the here and now of the actual world which is a manifestation of Brahman. Buddhism associates a different form of consciousness with each of the five senses, thus eye-consciousness, ear-consciousness, etc. To these five is added a sixth 'sense', mental awareness. *Vijnana* is an awareness that is both conscious and unconscious, a difficult notion for the Western mind to grasp. It is the fifth of the **Five Aggregates** and a concept fundamental to the important Vijnanavada (the 'Way of Consciousness') School of Buddhist philosophy, better known as **Yogachara**.

Vikings *AE*. The inhabitants of the Scandinavian peninsula whose raids and occupation of Britain (8th–11th century), as pagan plunderers, is fully documented (see for example, Jones, Wilson). Their religion and its supporting mythology was polytheistic, the gods (see **Aesir**, **Vanir**) occupying the realm of Asgard. Their raiding brought them into contact with Christianity in Ireland, Britain and Normandy and in the process of settlement they were quick to adopt it, carrying the faith back to the Scandinavian peninsula, thus Christianizing their homelands. See **Anglo-Saxon Religion**, **Germanic Religion**, **Norse Mythology**

Vineyard Churches *X*. A new religious movement found by Ken and Joanie Gulliksen and John Wimber, in 1974 as an off-shoot of the Calvary Chapel Movement. Their beliefs focus sharply on the gifts of the spirit and great importance is given to public healing, **glossolalia**, **possession** (see **Demonology**) and **prophecy**. With these priorities, the Church holds to an orthodox theology on matters such as the **Trinity**, the deity of Christ, **salvation by grace** and the divine inspiration of the scripture. See **Pentecostalism**

Vipassana *B*. Pal. 'insight', 'clear seeing'. An important concept in **Mahayana** Buddhist practice which develops a critical examination of the nature of things 'as they are', so as to develop insight into the true nature of the world as *shunyata*, emptiness. It is one of the two essential conditions for **enlightenment**, the other being *Samatha*, calming the mind. See **Anapanasati**, **Mahamudra**, **Meditation**, **Mindfulness**, **Satipathana**, **Smriti**

Virgin Birth *X*. A central Christian doctrine that **Mary**, the mother of **Jesus**, was a virgin before and after the conception and birth of her son. It is axiomatic to Christianity that its founder was not 'sent down' from heaven or created from the earth, like Adam, but incarnated in a body that was 'supplied' by Mary. Christian doctrine declares Jesus to be sinless and the virgin birth as the device used to ensure he was not tainted by 'original sin', a condition transmitted through conception. Thus are human beings born in a state of separation from God that only **atonement** can rectify. The doctrine is confused with that of the 'immaculate conception', since although Jesus was born of a virgin, Mary herself was born as a result of the normal processes. However, her conception by a human mother and father was 'overshadowed' by the Holy Spirit, so that she was, in fact, 'born without taint of original sin'. See **Traducianism**

Virgin Mary See **Mary**

Vishnu *H*. Skt. from root *vish*, 'to pervade' or 'to work'. The second god of the Hindu trinity, the first being **Brahma** and the third **Siva**. Wrapped in a complex mythology, Vishnu is represented in the **Rig-Veda** as the 'worker', a sun god who strides the sky in three steps, the rising, the apex and the setting. As his cult developed, other gods, such as Hari (see **Hari-Hara**) and Narayana become epithets for him until, finally, he is interchangeable with Brahma and Siva as the supreme deity. In a way, somewhat similar to the Christian Trinity, each aspect has its own function, thus Vishnu sustains the universe, Brahma created it and Siva destroys it. Vishnu is also the custodian of **dharma**, a function integral to his role as sustainer, since whenever there is need he incarnates as an **avatar** to inspire and encourage people. He has a specific geographical location in the region of the Ganges and Himalayas, but his followers are to be found throughout India. As they developed Vishnu's cult **Vaishnavism** or Vishnuism became one of the three great forms of devotional worship in modern Hinduism, the other two being **Shaivism** and **Shaktism**. See **Vaikuntha**

Vishvakaram *H*. Skt. 'all-creating'. The personified activity of creation, celebrated in hymns of the **Rig-Veda**, as the creative urge or energy and as the architect of the universe. Reminiscent of the Christian concept of the **Pantocrator**, Vishvakaram transmutes into the world without recourse to any substance or urge beyond himself, thus being a self-sufficient generator of all things. In an extended mythology he is the source of architecture and the mechanical sciences and becomes an advisor to the gods, their builder and armourer.

Vision Quest *Ami*. An Amerindian spiritual ceremony involving **out-of-body experiences** and astral projection, sometimes referred to as the 'Way of Inner Journey'. It is usually a personal quest, by which means the subject will endeavour to communicate with the Creator or spiritual beings, in order to get the answer to specific questions. It is unlikely that any form of drug or hallucinogenic is used, since the quester knows that the vision is something given in response to the clarity and sincerity of the quest. Vision quest can be thought of as an acted prayer and as with all prayer, it is reciprocal, something is given and something received. See **Sioux**, **Sweat Lodge**
FINAL WORD: 'Believe none of what you've heard second-hand and believe half of what you see. Get true vision from the eye of your heart.' (Dhyani Ywahoo)

Visions Visual perceptions experienced by something other than natural sight. They are usually associated with mystical experiences and a sense of 'seeing' divine events or beings, as with the eye. In some forms of meditation, a vision may be a mental image created by the imagination as a focus for the mind (see **Visualization**). Visions may be inspirational and revelatory. For example the **New Testament** book, the Revelation of John, is thought to have been inspired by a vision. Frequently, records of such visions begin with the word, 'Behold ...' as of something seen. John testifies to having been 'caught up the Spirit' and to hearing 'a loud voice, like the sound of a trumpet, which said to me, "Write down what you see ..."' (1:10–11). Visions have been recorded by saints and mystics of all religions and are the energies behind the founding of new sects and cults by the person to whom the vision was given. Visions differ from dreams, in that they can occur at anytime, the recipient being fully conscious of the experience. See **Dreams, Mysticism, Trance**

Vispered *Zo*. Or *Vispe Ratavo*, 'All the Chiefs'. A Zoroastrian scripture that is a supplement to the **Yasna** both being used in the liturgies of worship. It is structured in 24 chapters and contains invocations and words of homage to 'all the Lords'. See **Avesta, Yashts**

Visualization *B*. A form of **meditation** used in different Buddhist schools, in which the pupil is instructed to visualize the Buddha or another divine manifestation. In **Mahayana** the process is interior and does not, in these practices, utilize an external object on which the meditator gazes. The subject is creatively imagined for purposes of devotion or spiritual transcendence. In the earlier Theravada tradition, use was made of the ten *kasinas* listed in the Pali Canon (see **Tripitaka**) and these objects were externally observed until the practitioner captured a mental image. Visualization is also one of the central techniques of **Tantric** Buddhism. In this tradition the purpose is to self-identify with the image of the Buddha or another deity. See **Visions**

Visualization for Children Techniques of visualization currently used with children and adults, are an inward use of the imagination, for secular rather than, religious or spiritual ends. Visualization is here understood to be the language of the subconscious mind and may be used to dissolve emotional learning blocks, to enhance memory, introduce learning themes and tap into creativity, thus setting effective goals such as the increase of positive self esteem. Guided visualizations are exercises in structured imagination. These are distinct from, but linked to, meditation practices (see **Meditation for Children**). Visualizations have in common with most meditation practices the turning of the attention inwards. Unlike concentration meditation, which aims to focus the attention on a specific stimulus to the exclusion of others, visualizations are a conscious structured use of imaginative thought towards a particular goal. Individuals are usually, but not always, guided or led through the exercises which can take the form of going on a journey in the imagination.

It is now known from scientific research that the mind does not know the difference between what we imagine and reality. Mentally rehearsing an activity in the imagination has the effect of strengthening the neural pathways associated with that activity – as if one had actually carried out the action in reality.

FINAL WORD: 'When I examine myself and my methods of thought, I come to the conclusion that the gift of fantasy has meant more to me than my talent for absorbing knowledge'. (Einstein, cited in Neville)

Vodoun See **Vodun, Voodoo**

Vodun A. Recognized in 1996 as the official religion of **Benin**, vodun is thought to be the original form of what is better known as **voodoo**. From a word meaning 'spirit', the religion is traceable to the **Yoruba** who populated Dahomey (the earlier name for Benin) in the 18th and 19th centuries. However, the spirit practices of vodun are very ancient and are believed to have existed for 6,000 years. See **African Tribal Religions**

Voltaire (1694–1778) The pen name for François Marie Arouet, French philosopher, essayist and historian, who became one of the leading lights of the **Enlightenment**. During a three-year exile visit to England (1726–29) he was influenced by the liberalism of the political institutions, the philosophy of **Locke** and the mathematics of Newton. Returning to Paris his writings in favour of English institutions were taken to be a criticism of France; he contrasted English liberalism and tolerance with the despotism of the French authorities and the extravagant privileges of the aristocracy, which he advocated should be balanced by the rise of the merchant class, equitable taxation and state sponsorship of the arts and sciences. A deist (see **Deism**), he was nevertheless anti-Christian and critical of the clergy. From 1717–18 and again in 1726, he was imprisoned in the Bastille for criticizing the Regency. Despite his plea for tolerance he was hostile to Jews and Muslims. His political and social philosophy is presented in his major work, *Dictionnaire Philosophique* and famously satirized in his novel *Candide*, where he questions **Leibnitz**'s optimism ('God must have created the best of all possible worlds') insisting that the world God had created harboured great evil. His ideas were more sceptical than those of **Rousseau**, whom he did not like, but the thinking of both men contributed to the political energy that led to the French Revolution. See **Fideism**

FINAL WORD: 'In general, the art of government consists in taking as much money as possible from one class of citizens to give to the other.' (Voltaire)

Voluntarism A theory or doctrine that emphasizes the centrality of will in mental and spiritual life. In some applications God or ultimate reality is conceived as some form of will. It is an emphasis intended to correct the presumed role of the intellect or reason. It is a theme running through the history of philosophy and in its medieval form was championed by Duns

Scotus and William of Ockham. Its modern forms have their origin in **Kant**'s plea [1988] for the 'the primacy of the practical over pure reason.' From this basis, **Pragmatism** and **Utilitarianism** can be read as forms of Voluntarism, since in these systems it is the will that applies the basic principle, 'whatever is useful is good.' **Schopenhauer**'s philosophy is, in effect, a philosophy of Voluntarism in that while he regards the will as irrational, he makes it the basis of ultimate reality. Much in Buddhism is given over to the nature of mind and its training through meditational techniques and practice, that rests on an advanced degree of the will's control on processes of thought. A secular view of historical, social and political processes assumes the ability of the will and of personal choice to determine the right decisions without recourse to other agencies. **Determinism**, on the other hand, assumes that everything we do is predetermined by, for example, genetics and environment and that there is no place for Voluntarism.

Volva *AE*. In Norse mythology a 'cunning woman', or shaman. Their function was regarded as *ergi*, unmanly, nevertheless, there were male *volva*, but fewer in number. They worked as itinerant magicians, carrying their magical items in a pouch (see **Medicine Bundles**). Typically, the *volva* would enter a trance state, communicating with spirits so as to discern answers to questions. See **Anglo-Saxon Religion**, **Germanic Religion**, **Shamanism**

Voodoo A religious tradition originating in Africa, possibly thousands years ago, where it was known as **vodun**. It has become known only since the slave trade carried it to the west, where it is now one of the most familiar syncretisms. The essence of voodoo is the belief that nothing whatsoever in life happens by chance or accident. This basic tenant is captured in the term itself, voodoo, vous deux, 'you two', 'you too', implying the interconnectedness of the entire creation. Followed through, this means that not only does everything we do affect others, but it also affects oneself because we *are* the other. This is true not just of life, but of death, there being a sacred cycle and relationship between the living and the dead. Voodoo is a form of spiritualism and its practices include rituals, dance, prayers, drumming, singing, the consultation of **oracles**, and animal sacrifice. Priests and priestesses are consulted for advice about both material and spiritual problems, the adherents looking to them to ease or end their suffering. In some aspects, the religion is akin to witchcraft and there are spells for just about every contingency. Its public image has suffered as a result of books and films that associate its practices with sexual frenzy and or 'black' **magic**. John Cussans suggests that voodoo is constructed around certain central themes, the voodoo doll, the zombie, the witch doctor and the notion of possession. The fetish-doll figures as a symbol of the relationship between the animate and inanimate, the living and the dead and the anxieties Freud claimed were caused by these tensions. The zombie is a resurrected figure with no will or mind of its own, directed by someone else to perform certain acts. The zombie is another icon that explores the relationship between the living and the dead. The witch doctor is the controller of zombies and as such is believed to exercise huge power and to be able to call up that power by means of ancient occult practices. Possession is just one step away from the control exercised over a zombie. It is having one's will taken over without being conscious of it and thus being under the direction of another's will. This is usually understood to be **spirit possession**. This also points to unconventional relationships, in this case between the 'soul', conscious will, the body and, in the state of possession, the nature of the relationship between the possessed and the possessor.

FINAL WORD: 'What is unquestionably true and at the same time most remarkable in Voodoo, is that sort of magnetism which prompts those who are assembled to dance to insensibility. The prepossession in this regard is so strong that even the Whites found spying on the mysteries of this sect and touched by one of the members who have discovered them, are sometimes set to dancing and have agreed to pay the Queen Voodoo, to put an end to this punishment.' (Joseph J. Williams)

Votive Offering Specifically dedicated or consecrated offerings left, for example, by Celtic and Germanic people in sacred places or dropped into water. Such offerings are usually in the form of personal property such as jewellery, agricultural implements and items of clothing. They might also include booty gathered during a war and offered as a thanksgiving for victory, carved figures or animals sacrificed to fertility gods. The offerings are made as an affirmation of the subject's religious vows.

Vourukasa *Zo.* 'with wide bays'. Originally an epithet for a lake in the region of northwest India occupied by the **Aryans**; the name was carried to the Middle East, but only a vague location has been suggested in Iran. In the mythology, it is the cosmic or celestial ocean of **Indo-Iranian** religion. There are references in the **Yashts** of the name being given to water gods.

Vrata *H. Ja.* Skt. 'religious vow', a term found throughout Hindu mythology, liturgies and practice. The etymology (from the root *vrn*, 'to choose') implies that the vow is taken freely without any sense of duress and in some instances practised for a specific period of time. In the West, giving up meat for Lent would be considered a *vrata*. Usually, *vrata* are taken in reference to a particular deity from whom the adherent wants some form of service; the *vrata* has to be totally sincere and taken with true devotion. The taking of *vrata* was originally fenced about by stringent rules, but in modern times these have become more relaxed. The rules concern cleanliness, chastity, truthfulness and a vegetarian diet. The *Mahalakshmi Vrata*, is a sacred day celebrated annually and centred on a ceremony performed by married women. For Jains, vratas are any of the vows that govern the way of life of monks and laypeople. All Jains take a vow not to injure any sentient being; the *Mahavratas* or 'Great Vows', which include chastity and renunciation of all possessions are taken by monks. See **Jainism**

Vritra *H*. Skt. 'storm cloud' or 'enveloper'. A demon overcome by **Indra**, the dark cloud being an image of indolence and ignorance obscuring the light of knowledge, exactly the conditions that oppose **enlightenment**. In the **Vedas** he is known as Ahi, 'snake', a three-headed serpent cognitively associated with **Azhi Dahaka**, the serpent or dragon of **Zoroastrian** mythology.

Vulcan *R*. The Roman form of the Greek god **Hephaestus**, who as the divine smith of Greek mythology reappears in Latin literature as Vulcan in much the same form as his Greek antecedent. The origin of the name 'Volcanus' is obscure and may be based on the Etruscan deity Velchanos, itself of eastern origin. Vulcan was the god of fire, but in a more menacing manifestation than associated with Hephaestus, he is also the eponymous god of volcanoes.

W

Waheguru *S*. Pun. 'Wonderful Lord'. The more personal, devotional name for God in **Sikhism**, which has many such names. The other principal name is **Akal Purakh**.

Wahhabis *I*. A **fundamentalist** Islamic movement named after Muhammad Ibn Abd al-Wahhab (1703–92). It is currently the dominant form of Islam in Saudi Arabia and has spread to other parts of the world. The name is not used by members of the group today, it being thought that its use by Westerners is pejorative and insulting. In its place Wahhabis use the term *muwahiddun*, 'Unitarians', or *Salafiyyun*, from the root *salafi*, 'to follow', a reference to the early companions of Muhammad. Their 18th-century founder, al-Wahhab, was disillusioned by what he judged to be the moral decline of Islamic society. He believed that **Sunni** Islam had been corrupted by *bid' a*, innovations, such as **Sufism**. He identified popular belief and practices as forms of idolatry and urged a return to the original and fundamentalist practices of Islam. To this end, he formed a coalition with Muhammad bin Saud (the founder of the modern Saudi dynasty) to unify the disparate tribes of the Arabian Peninsula. Their beliefs are fundamentalist to the point of using their own methods to interpret the **Koran** and *Hadith*-based texts, using the traditional methods only as a point of reference. As a result, their theology has become puritanical and legalistic in all matters of faith and religion. Since 1932, when the state of Saudi Arabia was constituted, there has been a close relationship between the ruling family and the Wahhabis' religious establishment.

Modern adherents are not a unified movement or sect, so much as a radical emphasis that is found among various Islamic groups worldwide, in Africa, Asia, North America and throughout the Middle East. Their passionate support of *jihad*, holy war, is relatively recent and some date its adoption to the 1980s resistance to the Soviet occupation of Afghanistan. Since then other groups, like the Taliban, have taken up *jihad* and the Jihadist Salafi regimes now include Al Qaeda and its leader, Osama bin Laden. American Wahhabis have used the events of 11 September 2001 to further their own fundamentalist political agenda against American national interests. The principal allegations against the Wahhabis seem obvious, that they represent terrorism and intolerance, but it must be noted that a 'reformist' trend represents the view that violence should be used only as a last resort. The reformers claim to argue their case for opposing violence on the Prophet Muhammad's own practice and example. However, in this respect, the early history of Islam is not very reassuring. FINAL WORD: 'Wahhabism exalts and promotes death in every element of its existence: the suicide of its adherents, mass murder as a weapon against civilization and above all the suffocation of the mercy embodied in Islam.' (Stephen Schwartz)

Wahy *I*. Arab. 'Revelation'. The term has a number of meanings in the Koran linked by the underlying concept of inspiration, guidance and psychic possession. The term is used, for example, of the divine inspiration of the Koran, the implication being that *wahy* is not just concerned with general ideas, but also with the direct transmission of the specific words given through a prophet. The concept, therefore, is Islam's authority for scriptural fundamentalism.

Wakan Tanka or **Wakonda** *Ami*. For the **Sioux**, the supreme god of the cosmos. *Wakan* means spirits or beings, with *Tanka* as a kind of collective noun implying all the many gods and spirits are, in fact, one. The term can also mean the 'Great Spirit' or the 'Great Mystery'. See **Amerindian Religion**

Waldenses *X*. Histories of the Church of Piedmont have references to this Christian breakaway group, existing at the beginning of the 12th century; their name is derived from their founder, Peter Waldo. Despite persistent and cruel persecution, the Church's survival to this day is due, almost certainly, to their being tucked away in the isolated and inhospitable mountain valleys of the Cottian Alps, located on the Franco-Italian border. Originally mendicant preachers, they have been regarded as the forerunners of **St Francis of Assisi** (1181–1226) and, because of their teaching concerning infant **baptism**, as anticipating the **Baptists**. Their 1120 Confession affirms belief in the 12 articles of the Apostles' Creed (see **Creeds**) and the recognition of books of the canonical scripture. The point of divergence with **Roman Catholicism** begins with the **Bible**, which while regarded as authoritative should not be subjected to the traditions of the established Church of Rome or to the interpretations of 'popish scholars'. Their confession states, unequivocally, that 'Moreover, we have ever regarded all the inventions of men (in the affairs of religion) as an unspeakable abomination before God; such as the festival days and vigils of saints and what is called holy-water, the abstaining from flesh on certain days and such like things, but above all, the Masses.'

Wali *I*. Arab. 'protector', 'guardian' or 'friend'. Commonly the representative of a woman seeking marriage. A woman who has previously been married may represent herself. More broadly, in the spiritual tradition of Islam a Wali is a friend of God, typically members of the **Sufi** mystical orders. In the **Ottoman** Empire, Wali was a title for a Turkish governor.

Walloons *X*. American **Huguenots** originally from Wallonia in southern Belgium.

Walworth Jumpers *X*. See **Girlingites**

Waqf *I*. A religious endowment intended to provide revenue for supporting **mosques** and other religious institutions, such as schools. Waqf was indispensable before the establishment of the modern Islamic states and gifts could take the form of arable land, farms and oases under the direction of a manager, who ensured the revenue actually went to the right place. The origin of 'Waqf' is obscure, but is likely to have existed in pre-Islamic culture.

WASP The familiar American acronym for 'White Anglo-Saxon Protestants', used in a slightly pejorative sense of the **Protestant** upper-middle-class establishment and its culture. The acronym is thought to have been first used by early Irish Catholic (see **Roman Catholicism**) immigrants, but was popularized by the sociologist E. Digby Baltzell in his book *The Protestant Establishment: Aristocracy & Caste in America.*

Watchtower Bible and Tract Society A publishing company founded by Charles Taze Russell in 1879, responsible for the publication of the **Jehovah's Witnesses'** magazines *The Watchtower* and *Awake!* The society also publishes doctrinal books.

Way of the Saints See **Santeria**

Wheel of Life *B.* Skt. The 'Bhava-chakra', 'the wheel of becoming'. An iconographic representation of *samsara*, the cycle of birth-death-rebirth. Widely used in **Tibetan Buddhism**, the imagery is usually very elaborate and intricate, drawn and painted in the style of **mandalas**. The wheel is divided into six segments representing the types and qualities of experience to be had in this life; the upper half of the wheel is inhabited by gods, titans and human beings, the lower half by animals, hungry ghosts and those that dwell in hell. The common message is of death, suffering and their causes. The detailed symbolism represents central Tibetan Buddhist teaching on whatever it is that binds us to the wheel of *samsara* such as craving, ignorance, aggression. Also symbolized are the 12 sequences of the doctrine of **Dependent Origination**. The whole wheel is sometimes represented as being held in the claws of **Yama**, the god of death and the underworld. Some interpretations suggest that the wheel represents a mirror held up for the dying so they can see the different levels at which they might be reborn. The outcome is determined by the kind of **karma** accumulated through the long cycles of successive lives.

Whit Sunday See **Pentecost**

White Eagle Lodge The Lodge was founded in 1936. White Eagle is the spokesperson for a spiritual brotherhood who adopted Grace Cook, an advanced **medium**, as the means of communicating his message. The purpose of the White Eagle Lodge is to aid humanity in discovering its true nature. This is done through retreats during which healing and meditation practices are followed. The way of realizing human potential is by means of the radiating light of Christ; love is the power and wisdom behind everything and it is the aim of the Lodge to enable people to apply this to ordinary, everyday life. The Lodge is non-profit making and non-proselytising and teaches tolerance of all religions and spiritual paths. The term 'Christ' is therefore not used exclusively in its Christian context, but to refer to the light as the divine essence, a mystical entity similar to the **Logos**. The Lodge exists throughout the world and has a Mother centre in England. See **New Age**

FINAL WORD: 'There is no restriction on a person's soul other than that which it places upon itself … Therefore think of having a pair of wings on your shoulders, of a winged disc, the latter being the symbol of the sun; and the sun, of course, being the Christ Spirit; the wings, indicating the power of the soul to fly – to rise above your limitations.' (White Eagle, through the mediumship of Grace Cook)

White Friars X. By reason of their white habits and scapulars, a common name for the order of **Carmelite** Friars.

White Magic A form of **magic** practised for good and positive purposes such as healing and as a protection against **black magic**. Its ultimate goal is union with the divine or effecting a realization of or contact with your 'real' self and your personal spirit guide or guardian angel. In some popular forms there are clear associations with **Egyptian** religion and mythology, with practices concerned to evoke such gods as **Osiris**, **Thoth**, **Ra** and **Isis**. White magic is concerned with gaining wisdom and with cultivating cosmic consciousness and a non-dual relationship to nature and the universe. For these reasons, white magic is frequently associated with **Wicca**, fringe conservationist groups and **New Age** religion. See **Dualism Left-Handed Path**, **Right-handed Path**, **Witchcraft**

Whole Earth Catalogue See **Counterculture**

Wicca Witchcraft practice that focuses on nature worship and on invoking pagan and neo-pagan gods and goddesses, mostly pre-Christian. Its leitmotif creed is 'Do what you will and harm none.' The various Wicca groups share a reverence for nature and concern for the ecology. They recourse to ancient mythologies and to practising magic. Some groups believe in **reincarnation**. See **Grimoires**, **New Age Religion**, **Witchcraft**

Wisdom Literature A tradition of sacred literature concerned both with rules of conduct and philosophical wisdom. It is a critical idiom of the **Old Testament**, its 'wisdom literature' including Job, Proverbs and Ecclesiastes. In the **Apocrypha** wisdom books include the Wisdom of Solomon and Ecclesiasticus. Wisdom is sometimes personified as the female aspect of God and is celebrated as such in Prov. 3:15–18.

'She is more precious than rubies,
All of your goods cannot equal her.
In her right hand is length of days;
In her left, riches and honour.
Her ways are pleasant ways,
And all her paths, peaceful.
She is a tree of life to those who grasp her,
And whoever holds on to her is happy.'

Wissenschaft des Judentums See **Scientific Study of Judaism**

Witchcraft Behind the extreme cruelty of the Church-perpetrated witch hunts of medieval and 16th- and 17th-century Europe, there is more than a superstition that witches practised powerful forms of magic. The Church's opposition was based on the belief that only the Devil can be the source of such power, therefore the practices were, by definition, maleficent. It is likely that many of those burned at the stake were not witches at all, but simply the luckless targets of personal jealousies and superstitions. Of those who did practise a form of witchcraft, the majority would have been harmless, using their skills to heal or to ensure safe childbirth and the fecundity of crops and animals. Doubtless there were those who were 'in league' with the Devil and their burnings would have been in the same category as the execution of heretics. It is doubtful that any distinction would have been made between black and white witchcraft (see **Black Magic**, **White Magic**). Throughout the world, some of the beliefs and practices associated with ancient witchcraft are still in use today. One of the familiar icons is the use of a doll to inflict injury or worse, by imitative magic such as fire or the insertion of pins (see **Voodoo**, **Fetish**). This form of practice was well known in ancient Greece and Rome. Another, is the witch's 'familiar', in the form of animals, insects and birds, typically in Europe a cat, goat or crow, while in Africa hyenas, owls and red ants serve the purpose. Modern European culture might have suspended belief in witchcraft, but secularized attitudes associated with it have not been abandoned. Lives may be threatened, careers and reputations destroyed because of 'witch-hunts' against those accused of political and social deviance and non-conformity, as was brilliantly illustrated by Arthur Miller's 1953 play, *The Crucible*. Using the conceit of the 17th-century Salem witch trials, the play opened on Broadway at the height of McCarthyism's anti-communist 'witch-hunt'. The play was an unequivocal attack on Salem's modern parallel but, of course, the message was rationalized. See **Grimoires**, **Wicca**

Witch Doctor A. A general and commonly used term for a sorcerer, prophet or shamanist healer, usually referring to African religious practices. Only rarely would a witch doctor be malevolent, his skills most frequently being used for healing. In fact there is a basic misunderstanding that a witch doctor uses witchcraft to cure maladies; the opposite is true, that he will use his powers to treat illnesses *caused* by witchcraft. He is therefore, in one sense, a specialist doctor of witch-induced suffering. In England the term is associated with folk magic, but to the same end of turning back onto the perpetrator the effects of spells cast to cause harm.

Wittgenstein, Ludwig (1889–1951) Considered by some to be the most significant philosopher of the 20th century, whose main concern was with the scope and limitations of language. His search for a perfect language began with his contribution to his teacher Bertrand **Russell**'s **logical atomism**, offered as something called Picture Theory. Briefly put, the perfect language would serve and mirror the world accurately, in much the same way as a map, setting up interconnected co-ordinates and conventional signs so as to allow us to know where we are in the picture of reality. Thus, as an explorer of the 'territory' of language Wittgenstein set out to chart its everyday features by means of what he called, 'the method of language games'. Moving away from his mentor's method of 'analysis', he examined how language was used by ordinary people. The emphasis on how a word or phrase is used is the origin of Wittgenstein's famous advice, 'Don't ask for the meaning, ask for the use.' His principle of examining the correct use of key terms is without regard to their context, thus the theories he developed are applicable to the language used to describe both religious and secular concepts. He is not primarily concerned with whether a word or statement is valid in terms of what is *believed* about its meaning – that is, he is not here concerned with the verification of truth. Wittgenstein reasoned that once the use of the language is apparent, the meaning the user intends to convey will be clear. Only when the use of a word or phrase is unambiguously understood, can the matter of the validity of its meaning be considered.

FINAL WORD: 'An unknown German appeared ... obstinate and perverse, but I think not stupid ... I shall certainly encourage him. Perhaps he will do great things ... I love him and feel he will solve the problems I am too old to solve.' (Bertrand Russell, quoted in Monk)

'Tell them I've had a wonderful life.' (reputedly, Wittgenstein's last words)

Won Buddhism *B*. Also, Wonbulgyo or Wonbuddhism. A South Korean modern religious movement founded in 1916 by Soe-tae San (1891–1943). It focuses on two aspects of Buddhism, the realization of one's Buddha-nature and 'timeless and placeless Zen'. Adherents endeavour to see the unity *of* all things and the Buddha *in* all things and to follow a way of life in accordance with these perceptions. Meditation is not confined to a specific time, like early morning or late evening or to a specific place such as a meditation hall. The practice is timeless and placeless, one lives, always and everywhere, in the meditation mode. The only meditation object is a black circle on a white ground which symbolizes the cosmic body, the *dharmakaya* of the Buddha. See **Trikaya**

World Council of Churches *X*. Constituted in Amsterdam in 1948. Its mandate defines it as a 'fellowship of Churches which accept our Lord Jesus Christ as God and Saviour'. It was formed from an amalgamation of earlier movements 'Life and Work' and 'Faith and Order'. The organization has its headquarter in Geneva. Apart from the **Roman Catholics** and **Unitarians**, the WCC's membership includes all the major Western denominations, most of the Eastern **Orthodox** churches and numerous Asian and African churches. The Catholic churches are, however, represented by observers and are full members of the WCC's Faith and Order Commission. The function of the Council is advisory and educational, but is committed to inter-Church and international aid and to the refugee services.

World-Faith Movement *X.* Founded by E. W. Kenyon (1867–1948) but established as an effective organization by Kenneth Hagin (1917–2003), a **Pentecostal** faith-healing evangelist. It holds the belief that man is a being created in God's image and that therefore, human beings are 'little gods'. Sin, caused by the 'fall' of Adam (see **Fall of Man**) resulted in us all having Satan's nature, thus the incarnation of God in Jesus is the 'way' for human beings to become 'renewed' incarnations. Jesus died both physically and spiritually on the cross and his descent into hell followed by the resurrection is a figure of 'being born again'. Belief in Jesus empowers the adherent to 'speak words of faith' so as to obtain bodily health and material prosperity. Most followers of World-Faith are Pentecostalists or other evangelical Christians. See **Charismatic Movement, Oneness Pentecostalism**

World Soul (Lat. *anima mundi.*) The term is used in philosophy, to denote a universal spirit or soul that functions as an organizing or unifying principle. The early Greek philosophers were inclined to understand the visible world as a paradigm of one universal principle. Plato was the first to suggest that this concept stood in the same relation to the world as the human soul did to the body. Friedrich Wilhelm Josef von Schelling (1775–1854) a German Idealist (see **Idealism**) used the term as a unifying life principle, coordinating the organic and inorganic. The concept of the world soul is absent in biblical religions but prominent in Asian philosophy. Hinduism has a concept similar to the 'world soul', called **Brahman**, a critical insight developed in the **Vedanta** and **Upanishads**.

Worldwide Church of God See **Armstrongism**

Worship The sincere love and devotion accorded a deity, an idol (see idolatry) or a sacred object, together with the ceremonies, prayers, religious rituals and liturgies by means of which this expressed. The character of worship varies hugely. Many forms of Western worship are conducted through a fixed **liturgy** such as that of the Catholic Mass, the Anglican Book of Common Prayer or the Jewish Authorized Daily Prayer Book. Muslim worship is founded on the repetitious use of prayers combined with actions, offered five times a day (see **Salat**). In contrast, Protestant and Reform Jewish liturgies are less structured and allow for a degree of serendipity. Other forms of worship, such as those practised by **Pentecostal** churches, Islamic dervishes (see **Dervish**), **Amerindians** and some New Age cults are spontaneous and ecstatic or, as with the Quakers, mostly silent. Eastern forms of worship are equally varied. They take the form of simple domestic rituals as with the household gods of Hinduism or of colourful and noisy public ceremony as in some Hindu festivals (see **Hindu Festivals and Feasts**). Tibetan Buddhism worships through complicated rituals and the use of instruments, chants and **mandalas**. Other forms of Buddhism also use chanting, the repetition of mantras and prostrations or focus on meditative silence as, for example in Zen Buddhism. See **Puja**

Wudu *I*. Arab. 'ablution'. Purifying rituals followed by both sexes, usually undertaken prior to prayer. The ritual requires washing the mouth and face, the hands and arms to the elbows and the feet to the ankles. Sometimes a worshipper will also pour water over the head. In the absence of water, clay or sand can be used. Certain form of defilement are unavoidable, such as sleep, sexual intercourse, menstruation, childbirth and using the toilet. In some of these cases a *ghusl*, a ritual bath, is prescribed.

Wu-hsing *T*. Chin. 'five-movers' or 'five virtues' or 'elements'. In **Taoism** the doctrine of the phases of transformation of natural phenomena. The elements, water, fire, wood, metal and earth, are not used literally but as symbols for their abstract characteristics; water flows and makes wet, fire heats and rises, wood is supple, it bends and straightens, metal is malleable and can be cast into any form and earth is fertile. These qualities are inter-lined and may affect each other, for example, water can extinguish fire, fire can melt metal, metal can destroy wood. These correspondences have been applied to Chinese medicine, to the seasons of the year and to numerous other groupings. In the 3rd century BCE the elements formed the basis of an independent school, The Five Elements School, which during the Hang Dynasty was amalgamated with the **yin and yang** school.

Wu-wei *T*. Chin. 'non striving'. A central philosophy of **Taoism** developed in the *Tao-te Ching*. It is a philosophy of non-action, not in a negative sense but in a passive sense, in that the proper response to the ever-varying natural course of events is non-intervention. This does not mean that the life is spent doing nothing, but that with the right sense of what is appropriate and fitting what we do is unpremeditated and spontaneous. It will be the totally correct and 'natural' thing to do in whatever the situation demands. In the *Tao-te Ching*, **Lao-Tzu** is credited with saying, 'The world is ruled by letting things take their course. It cannot be ruled by interfering.'

Wycliffe, John (c.1320–84) *X*. Scholar and reforming theologian who, although born 200 years before the **Reformation**, anticipated the ideas and theology of **Luther** and Calvin, earning him the somewhat poetic name, 'the Morning star of the Reformation'. His concept of Church government and priesthood prefigured the 17th-century **Congregationalist** dissent. He is probably most famous for his translation into English of the Latin **Bible**, the first translation into any language undertaken for over a thousand years. He also instigated the **Lollard** movement, a group of itinerate preachers, but the movement was violently suppressed and short-lived. He was finally expelled from his teaching post at Oxford and decades after his death the Pope ordered his bones to be exhumed and burned.

X

Xaman Ek *CA*. A **Mayan** god of the North Star, therefore, the guide and protector of all who travel, especially merchants. Offerings, such as burning incense, are made to him at wayside shrines while travelling. Images show him to be snub-nosed. The North Star is part of a Mayan constellation called Ah Chimal Ek, believed to offer protection because of its geometric or regular positioning around the polar star. The constellation appeared to Mayans as guardians and was used as a kind of night clock.

Xavier, Francis (1506–52) *X*. Priest and pioneering missionary who, with Ignatius **Loyola** and others, took the vow of poverty and chastity and founded the Society of Jesus, well known as the **Jesuits**. The greater part of his life was spent in foreign missionary work, involving long voyages that took him to Mozambique, India, Ceylon, Goa, Indonesia, Japan and China, where he died on the island of Shangchuan. The **Roman Catholic** Church believe him to have converted more people to Christianity than anyone since St **Paul**.

Xenoglossolalia The phenomenon of speaking in a language unknown to the speaker, but recognized by the listener. See **Glossolalia**

Xenophanes (c.570–475 BCE) Of Colophon in Ionia. After the **Persians** conquered his homeland, he became a peripatetic poet and philosopher, using this art form to attack the immorality and crude **anthropomorphism** of the Homeric religion (see **Greek Religion**). Interestingly, tucked away in his negative criticism is a glimmer of monotheism. Xenophanes was fascinated by fossils and argued from his findings that the entire earth had been subjected to a series of floods. He believed that 'the gods have not revealed all things to men from the beginning' and that by continuously (re)searching, everything will be revealed to them at the right time. His epistemology was founded on scepticism, in the sense that our increasing knowledge simply exposes our errors; what we claim as truth is, at best, only 'opined as resembling the truth'. Some aspects of Xenophanes' methods were admired by Karl **Popper**.

Xenophon (420–355 BCE) Greek historian, most notable for being a disciple of **Socrates**. After the Greeks were defeated by Persia, Xenophon became one of the leaders of the heroic retreat. His most famous work, the *Anabasis*, tells this story. His *Apology and Symposium*, offer an objective and practical interpretation of Socrates and are an indespensible alternative view to **Plato**'s more philosophical treatment.

Xizang The Chinese name for the autonomous region of Tibet. See **Tibetan Buddhism**

Xmucane and **Xpiayoc** *CA*. The oldest of the gods of the **Mayan** pantheon, being the mother and father gods who, according to the **Popol Vuh**, a Quiché sacred text, created the first human beings. They were called Grandmother of Day and Grandmother of Light and Bearer twice over, Begetter twice over and given the pleasing epithets of midwife and matchmaker.

Y

Yahweh *J*. Heb. See **Tetragrammaton**

Yahweh ben Yahweh *I*. Heb. The leader of the **Nation of Yahweh**, a black supremacist cult founded in the late 1970s. Born Hulon Mitchell Jr, the first of 15 children, in Kingfisher, Oklahoma, his father was a Pentecostal minister. Drawn to black movements, he studied the **Nation of Islam** before assuming the title 'God son of God'.

Yajurveda *H*. Skt. The third of the four **Vedas** consisting of formulas chanted during the observation of the sacrificial rites; it is a form of ritual handbook. The chanting was lead by one of the *adhvaryu*, the four chief priests responsible for the ritual. Two redactions or versions of the Veda have to be distinguished; the earlier *Krishna* or *Black Yajurveda*, thought to have been compiled c.1000 BCE, consisting of five books which are a mixture of prose and mantras and the later *White Yajurveda* being a collection of mantras. The *Shukla* or *White Veda* is clearer and more structured, containing texts that are not found in the alternative Black version. It may have come into existence as the result of a schism led by its compiler, Yajnawalkya. It certainly gave rise to schism and the adherents of the two *Samhitas*, the primary collections, were antagonistic. The combined texts indicate the character of Vedic religion at the time they were written. See **Hinduism, Vedanta**

Yama *H. B*. Skt. 'self control'. It has various meanings for Hinduism: i) the first of the eight stages of raja-**yoga** and is based on the observance of five ethical tenets, avoiding physical injury to others, not lying, not stealing, chastity and controlling acquisitiveness. These five must be observed in thought, speech and deed; ii) Yama as the author of a law book, the Dharma-Shastra, but the term refers to the whole body of Hindu law; iii) Yama as the 'restrainer', the god of the dead, with whom the spirits of the deceased live.

Yang See **Yin and Yang**

Yantra *H. B*. Skt. 'to sustain' or 'an instrument'. Geometrical diagrams, usually of interlocking triangles which are iconographic representations of divinities or aspects of the divine. In **Hinduism** they are used to fix the concentration in meditation, pointing to a higher level of consciousness. Adherents are able to worship the divine element in the yantra by identifying themselves with it. They are microcosmic images of the macrocosm. The design is intended to draw the eye to the centre or innermost triangle which may contain a seed syllable, the sound of which is believed to be the essence of the deity the yantra represents. They were not used in early **Buddhism**, but in the development of **Tibetan Buddhism** yantras were used as the basis of **mandala** design, in which the geometry is a representation of a particular form of energy, together with the force patterns of **mantras** and their seed syllables. In Buddhist use, the yantra diagrams are usually enclosed in a pattern of concentric circles, the whole image sometimes being referred to as a Yantra mandala. One of the best-known Indian yantras is the Sri Yantra, a symbol of the entire cosmos that serves to remind the practitioner of non-duality, that there is no difference between subject and object. (see **Dualism and Non-Dualism**). The yantra shown here illus-trates the use of the seed syllable. The syllable at the centre is the seed of illusion. See **Sacred Geometry**

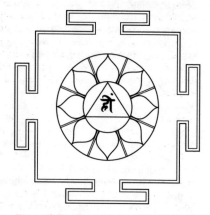

Figure 14 The Yantra Raja or King Yantra

Yardanism 'Cult of Angels'. See **Kurdish Religion**.

Yashts *Zo*. A collection of 24 **Zoroastrian** hymns in honour of various divinities, some of which have days in the month named after them in the Zoroastrian calendar. They are a primary source of **Persian** mythology. The divinities include Ardvi Sura, goddess of water, Mithra (see **Mithraism**), god of light and truth, Verethragna, god of victory, and the god Kavaya Hvarenah, 'kingly glory'. Some of the hymns contain fine poetry and have a metric form. See **Avesta**, **Vispered**, **Yasna**

Yasna *Zo*. 'worship'. *Yasna* refers both to worship generally and to one of the books of the Zoroastrian scriptures, the **Avesta**. Perhaps, most impor-tantly, it is the name of a complex ritual service in Zoroastrian liturgy at which the text of the *Yasna* is recited. There are distinct parallels with the rituals and sacrificial practices of the early **Vedas**, and it is probable that the originally rite was pre-Zoroastrian with its roots in **Indo-Iranian** reli-gion, when the practice required animal sacrifice, a feature no longer a part of the modern Parsee **rite**. Essentially, the *Yasna* is a rite of purifica-tion and consecration of a variety of items. These include water, pomegranate twigs, representing the plant world but now replaced by metal strips, milk, bread and most importantly, *haoma* or **soma** juice, which is strained through a ring (the *varas*) made of hairs from a sacred bull. Two priests, one of whom maintains the sacred fire (see **Fire, Sacred**), preside over the ceremony which is performed on behalf of the believing community. The *Yasna* amounts to a ritual drama, an enactment of the ultimate struggle between **Ahura Mazda** and **Angra Mainyu**, the good and evil spirits. The participants themselves become ritually involved in the conflict between the Lord of Wisdom and the *druj* or lie and by using ritual action and the consecrated items, they demonstrate their choice for truth. A separate and specially consecrated room of the temple is used for the *Yasna* rite. Lay men and women attend, but congregational worship is not a feature of Zoroastrianism. The main function of the *Yasna* rite is to offer reverence to the **Bounteous Immortals**, to sanctify the present, immediate world and to harmonize its material and spiritual aspects. The whole is a prefigurement of the final *frashokereti* the renovation or restoration of the universe. See **Vispered**, **Yashts**, **Zoroastrianism**

Yggdrasil *Nor*. 'The Terrible One's Horse', also referred to as 'The World **Tree** of the **Aesir**', the collective name for the pantheon of Norse gods. The allusion to horse is thought to come from *Ygg*, an epithet for **Odin**, and *drasil*, steed or horse. Hence, Odin's Horse. Odin is thought to have spent nine nights hanging from the tree looking for the **runes**. As the giant ash tree, it became the guardian tree that links and shelters all the worlds. Three realms are located beneath its roots and three wells at its base, the Well of Wisdom, the Well of Fate and *Hvergelmir* or 'Roaring Kettle', the source of several rivers. The four deer that run among its branches represent the four winds and the tree is host to other animals, such as Ratatosk, the squirrel; and a golden cock that surmounts the tree. On the day of **Ragnarok**, the last battle, Surt, the leader of the **Fire Giants**, will set the World Tree on fire. See **Anglo-Saxon Religion**, **Germanic Religion**, **Norse Mythology**

Yi *Con*. 'Righteousness'. In effect the moral disposition (see **morality**) or the inclination to do good. It works as a kind of intuition, an inner guide or sense which directs the conscience in situations demanding a decision between various courses of action. The value of the rightness of the act lies entirely in it being 'right' regardless of the consequences. Anything is best done because it is good in itself and not as a means to an end. In this sense the ethic is similar to that of **Kant**'s. See **Jen**

Yiddish *J*. The vernacular language of the Jews of central Eastern Europe. It originated among German Jews in the Middle Ages and is thus derived, like modern German, from Middle High German to which are added Hebrew elements. It is written with Hebrew cursive characters. Since the Middle Ages, due to Jewish migration, Yiddish has absorbed Slavic and other elements. The language developed its own distinctive literature and culture and became the vehicle for proverbs, folk tales and songs, legends and allegories, especially of the **Chasidic** rabbis, an example being the wonder stories of Rabbi Nachman of Bratzlav (1770–1811) which have become well known through the translations of Martin **Buber**. Mendele Mocher Seforim (1835–1917) is known as the grandfather of Yiddish literature, followed by humorist Sholem Aleichem, the novelist Sholem Asch and a long string of others including Isaac Beshevis Singer, who won the Nobel Prize for literature in 1978. Yiddish theatre, with its origins in the amateur theatricals of the Jewish festival of **Purim**, supports a rich tradition of drama which thrives in America, Poland, Romania and Israel. The Yiddish Scientific Institute, founded in Vilna, Poland, 1925, collects material related to Jewish life from all parts of the world. Its headquarters have been in New York since 1940. It houses a vast multi-media archive and serves as a research and adult education centre, offering Yiddish language classes. There are societies of Friends of the Institute in many countries.

Yin and Yang *T*. Chin. In Taoist philosophy yin and yang represent two opposed energies, the interaction of which is said to be the creative cause of the universe. The supreme absolute in **Taoism** is the unified, non-dual **Tai Chi Ch'uan**, the yin and yang being its polar expressions. Physically, these are expressed as earth and sky. There follows a whole series of correspondences, yin being associated with the northern slope of a mountain, sunless, cold, swollen waters, the sky hidden by clouds, the feminine energy or principle, passivity, receptivity, dark, soft and symbolized by the moon, water, clouds, the tiger, the turtle, the colour black and all even numbers. Yang was associated with the southern slopes of a mountain, brightness, warmth, the masculine energy or principle, active, creative, hard and symbolized by the sun, fire, the dragon, the colour red, the south and all odd numbers. The two in balance are represented by the familiar symbol (*see* Figure 15).

What we see is the universe made up of yin and yang in perfect harmony. Only by the two aspects being together is the whole formed. The two spots represent the respective energies of yin and yang, the one in the other, each an incipient seed potentially capable of being transformed into its polar opposite. The yin and yang are important to Chinese medicine, which understands their imbalance to be the cause of illness. Too much yang results in the hyper-activity of the organs, too much yin makes them function badly.

FINAL WORD: 'These two energies … transform themselves, one rising upwards, the other descending downwards; they merge again and give rise to forms. They separate and merge again …That is the never-ending course of Heaven and Earth. Each end is followed by a beginning; each extreme by transformation into its opposite. All things are attuned to each other.' (Wilhelm [1975])

Figure 15 Yin and Yang

Yoga *H. B.* Skt. 'yoke' or 'link'. Yoga is one of the six **darshanas**, the classical schools of Hindu orthodoxy. In Hinduism, the 'link' is to be made with a god with whom unity is sought. Any of the paths effecting this link can be called yoga, with the result that there are numerous types of yoga according to the god being sought. In the West, the term usually conjures up a series of contortionist body movements frequently associated with toning up the muscles and keeping fit. As with **Tai -chi**, yoga is not always taught with reference to its original mystical or spiritual purpose. Put simply, all ascetic techniques for attaining **nirvana** are properly called either yoga or **meditation**. In Hinduism, the classic system of yoga was developed by **Patanjali** and recorded in his Yoga Sutras. He was not the inventor of the system, but someone who recast and organized methods that had long existed, based on the philosophy of the School of *Sankhya*. What was important to Patanjali and to our subsequent understanding of yoga, was the emphasis he placed on theism and the practice of meditation. We need to understand that in India, physical yoga is considered to be only a preparation for the 'real' thing. To realize the spiritual aims of yoga, it has to be combined with meditation and indispensable techniques of breath (*prana*) control. We should also understand that yoga, in its broadest sense, is not confined to India. The literal translation of the word as 'yoke' or 'link' implies that anyone seeking union with the divine, whether they are Christian, Kabbalist, Sufi, Tantric, Shamanic or secular lay mystics, is a yogi.

As there are numerous forms of yoga, a brief survey of some of the most familiar will illustrate the range. They are outlined here for convenience, rather than under their separate entries:

Bhakti Yoga: The yoga of devotion, the first of the four primary Hindu systems. It leads to the elimination of the ego by the expulsive power love for the divine or ultimate Being and to the realization that everything is a manifestation of the divine. Devotion is frequently given to a divine incarnation with which the ego of the worshipper is merged. It is considered to be the most direct method of experiencing the divine since devotion is the root of faith. This form of yoga finds expression in the majority of the world's religious traditions.

Dhyana yoga: The yoga of intensely focused meditation, usually on a single object, leading to lucid awareness. The yogi follows a scheme of eight stages leading to the suspension of all the senses. **Dhyana** yoga is associated with both **Ch'an** and **Zen**.

Hatha yoga: Another form of yoga with its origins in Patanjali's system. It is concerned with activating the **chakras**, the centres of psychic energy dispersed through the body from the base of the spine to the space immediately above the crown of the head. It uses similar techniques to those found in *kriya yoga*, especially the methods of breath control. In the West, most hatha yoga classes focus on its physical aspects so as to increase the body's flexibility, but in its original form it was a yoga designed to achieve self-realization or **enlightenment**. It involves one of the most esoteric forms of yoga, in that its aim is to rouse the sleeping 'force' that lies dormant in the lowest chakra at the base of the spine. This force or 'serpent power', is known as **Kundalini**, and is represented in iconography as a serpent. The awakened force rises through the chakras to manifest itself as spiritual knowledge and the experience of ultimate reality. This form of practice is also known as *kundalini yoga*.

Jnana yoga: The yoga of knowledge, the second of the four primary Hindu yogas. It leads to union with God through knowledge and intellectual analysis. It is the way of seeing through the multifarious manifest world, to the single, unchanging reality, **Brahman**, to the point of 'knowing' that this is all that exists. In this process all forms of ignorance have to be dissolved. See **Jnana**

Karma yoga: The way of selfless conduct. Arising from the doctrine of **karma**, the ineluctable effects in this life of acts performed in a previous existence, the yogi practice offers every act, together with their consequences, to God as a form of sacrifice. It is necessary for the aspirant to reach the point where he is the observer of the action rather than the one who effects the action. Of equal importance, is to cultivate non-attachment, where one acts without any thought of the results of one's actions.

Kriya yoga: The Sanskrit word '*kriya*' literally means 'cleansing'. As a form of yoga the term carries associations of 'deed', 'action' or 'effort', and generally, it is any practice undertaken to achieve higher knowledge. Kriya yoga combines various other forms of yoga and is distinguished by techniques of kriya **pranayamas**, breath or 'life-force' control, that form the fourth of the eight steps in Patanjali's system. It is designed to purify and cleanse the energy channels in the body and may also be combined with a **mantra** practice. The yoga form was brought to wider public notice through the publication of Paramahansa **Yogananda**'s *Autobiography of a Yogi*, which presented kriya as the most effective method of gaining union with the divine.

Mantra yoga: A discipline that leads to union with God by techniques of mantra repetition. The mantra can be repeated aloud or in the mind or whispered with a slight movement of the lips. Such repetition 'yokes' the mind, so that it ceases to be restless, the resulting concentration leading to pure awareness. Mantra yoga is sometimes offered to those who find other forms of yoga too physically or mentally strenuous.

Purna or integral yoga: A form of yoga made familiar through Sri **Aurobindo**, who is the founder of this system. He called it 'integral yoga' because it is not just concerned with the subject's total union with the divine, but also with integrating the divine into the entire world or matter and into everyday life.

Raja yoga: The 'royal yoga'. This is the yoga system set out in the Yoga Sutras of Patanjali. The practice is developed through eight sequences: the first two establish a moral code by which we should live, as the foundation for the rest; the third concerns bodily posture, the fourth breath control, the fifth the quietening of all sense experience, the sixth concentrating the mind on an object to the exclusion of everything else and without distraction, the seventh true meditation where the dualism of the subject-object relationship is entirely dissolved, and the eighth is *samadhi*, a transcendent state where the entire manifest world ceases to exist.

Other forms of yoga are to be found in pre-Hindu **Tantra**, in **Shaivism** and **Shaktism**, in the pre-Buddhist **Bon** religion of Tibet and its neighbouring countries, in the yantra yoga of Tantric Buddhism of Tibet, in **guru yoga** and in the practices of Taoist sexual alchemy. In general terms, as with meditation, yoga as a 'link' to the divine has its parallels in the mysticisms of all major religions. See **Nyaya**, **Purva-Sadhana**, **Mimamsa**, **Sankhya**, **Sahaja Yoga**, **Transcendental Meditation Vaiseshika**, **Vedanta**

FINAL WORD: 'The ideal of Yoga, Jivan mukta, one liberated while still alive, is to live in an "eternal present", outside of time.' (Mircea Eliade)

'The active performance of yoga involves ascetic practice, study of sacred lore and dedication to the Lord of Yoga. Its purpose is to cultivate pure contemplation and attenuate the forces of corruption. The forces of corruption are ignorance, egoism, passion, hatred and the will to live.' (Patanjali)

Yogachara *B*. Skt. 'application of yoga'. An important school of **Mahayana** Buddhist philosophy that emerged in the 4th century CE. Its alternative name is the School of Vijnanavada, 'the Way of Consciousness' or the Mind Only School (see **Vijnana**). This form of philosophy is understood in the West as the philosophy of mind. The contribution to this from both Hindu and Buddhist schools of philosophy is considerable, but takes us into concepts not developed in Western traditions. Essentially, Yogachara argues that everything we experience is 'mind only', that is, other than in the process of knowing, nothing actually exists as an object. As nothing exists as an object, so also there is no subject to experience it. In one sense, Yogachara can be seen as the most abstract of the philosophies developed to dissolve duality, the subject-object relationship (see **Dualism**). It is the most complex and sophisticated of Buddhist philosophies. The yoga reference tells us that the philosophy is derived from meditational experiences that bring together the nature of mind and the nature of experience. Briefly put, all our knowledge is derived from previous experience (which may include that of previous existences) stored in our 'consciousness', and which bears seeds that grow into mental phenomena. These seeds inter-react, ripen and develop as the deception that everything actually exists. We thus have the seeds of sense consciousness and we have the mind which, being corrupt, produces the illusion of a personal 'I' or ego and thus gives rise to subjectivity. The school, which became fully established in the 6th century, was centred on the monastic university of Nalanda in northern India with branches in Kashmir and Tibet. Several sub-schools developed offering different philosophical emphases. The School of **Madhyamika** were staunch opponents of Yogachara. See **Samatha**

Yogananda, Paramahansa (1893–1952) *H*. A notable Indian Hindu mystic, he become one of the pioneers of yoga in the West, emphasizing the underlying unity of the world's religions. His method centred on what

he termed 'scientific' practices of meditation and yoga, known as **kriya yoga**, which requires a form of initiation. 'Scientific' should not be understood in the sense of rational **empiricism**, and the teachings and techniques of practice are highly esoteric. Yogananda himself uses the term 'esoteric meditation'. *Kriya* yoga was brought to wider public notice through the publication in 1946 of his *Autobiography of a Yogi*, which remains one of the best-selling books of its kind. In 1920, Yogananda founded the **Self-Realization Fellowship**, known in India as the Yogoda Satsanga Society of India. See **Self-Realization**
FINAL WORD: 'May thy love shine forever on the sanctuary of my devotion and may I be able to awaken thy love in all souls.' (Yogananda Paramahansa)

Yogoda Satsanga Society of India See **Self-Relization Fellowship**

Yom Kippur *J*. Heb. 'The Day of Atonement'. Sometimes called the Sabbath of Sabbaths, is the most sacred and solemn festival of the Jewish liturgical year. It is marked by 24 hours of fasting and continuous prayer and shares with **Rosh Ha-Shanah**, the distinction of being one of the only two festivals that have an entirely religious character. It is a day of repentance, but not of gloom. The biblical requirement (Lev. 23:33) is explicit: 'It shall be a sabbath of complete rest for you and you shall practice self-denial; on the ninth day of the month at evening, from evening to evening, you shall observe this your sabbath.' The self-denial is taken to mean total abstention from labour, food and drink. The observance of Yom Kippur has gone beyond the prescriptions of biblical times. Rabbinic tradition has enriched the theology and the **Talmud** now gives it *imprimatur* to the annual regeneration of a purified and righteous Jewish life, since on that same day God pardoned Israel for the sin of worshipping the Golden Calf. On the Day of Atonement, the Jew becomes 'at one' with his Maker. One of the most sacred moments occurs in the opening service the night before Yom Kippur, when the congregation make the Kol Nidre, 'All vows', declaration; 'All vows, bonds, devotions, promises, obligations, penalties and oaths wherewith we have vowed, sworn, devoted and bound ourselves from this Day of Atonement unto the next Day of Atonement, may it come unto us for good: Lo, all these we repent us in them.' The Talmud, thus discourages all vows, for one should not need a special vow, either to live the right life or to bind oneself to God. But human psychology is such that on the Day of Atonement it might seem natural to make vows and promises to live a better life during the next year. Such vows would be rash, thus the Kol Nidre warns against them. While God will forgive transgressions made against himself, he will not forgive those transgressions made against other people until the wrongful act has been rectified and pardoned. Thus, to the extent to which a person seeks forgiveness and is forgiving, will he be forgiven. See **Scapegoat**

Yoni *H*. Skt. 'womb', 'origin or 'source'. Used to refer to the primal source of all life and phenomena. Its symbol is the downward-pointing triangle representing the female sexual organ, which itself denotes the mystery of the cosmos. In conjunction with the **linga**, the male organ, it is venerated in **Shakti** worship.

Yoruba Religion *A*. The Yoruba are widely dispersed across Western Nigeria and **Benin**. Their ancient beliefs are founded on **ancestor worship** and reverence for nature. From this broad base, the variations in the belief system and the wide variety of practices suggest that the Yoruba do not have a single, unifying religion. The two principal gods are called Olodumare, meaning 'the One who has the fullness of everything' and Olorun, 'the One who lives in heaven'. These supreme beings brought everything else into existence, including a crowded pantheon of deities. The polytheism is focused in the worship of 'orishas', deities who are personifications of various aspects of nature, such as wind, rain, trees, rivers, sea, mountains, etc. Orishas are associated with specific function, such as Babalu Aye with illness, Ogun with war, work and iron and Orunmila with divination. Historical figures, such as kings, cult heroes and the founders of cities, are also deified. Through the slave trade orisha worship spread to the west to be widely established as new syncretistic (see syncrehism) cults in the orisha movements for example of Brazil, Cuba, the USA, Mexico and Trinidad and Tobago. Lineages are also found in Asia and Europe. There is an established and renowned tradition of divination centred on the Ifa Oracle (see **Oracles**), the consultation of which requires the babalawo, a priest, to interpret the patterns of palm nuts and cowrie-shells randomly cast as a way of assessing the influence of the supernatural powers on the individual consulting the oracle. The Yoruba established an enlightened and progressive culture, with their own cities, army, priesthood and political system. The nation of Benin has become world famous for its lost-wax technique of bronze sculpture and mask making. Islam has been present in Nigeria since the 17th century, Christianity since the middle of the 19th and many of the Yoruba have converted from the traditional religion to one or the other of these. See **Santeria, Vodun, Voodoo**

Young Hegelians Also known as the 'Left Hegelians' (see **Hegel**). A group of philosophers inspired by European romanticism and revolutionary ideals, whose influence and energy was felt, in the main, from 1830–48. As an identifiable philosophical movement, they were first noted in an early treatise of one of their more enduring members, Ludwig **Feuerbach**. Using Hegel's dialectic method and philosophy of history, they set out to undermine the established alliance between the State, Christianity and philosophy. They opposed the Old or Right Hegelians who ran the academic establishment and maintained the *status quo* with the authority of the Christianity in its Lutheran form. They published treatises designed to undermine the theological and historical authenticity of the Church. David Strauss, for example, in his *The Life of Jesus*, argued that the Jesus' teachings were perverted in the cause of politics; Ferdinand Bauer claimed the entire New Testament story was a myth that rested tenuously on two extra-biblical references, one by Tacitus, the other **Josephus**. Feuerbach, in Th*e Essence of Christianity*, suggested that religion merely encouraged the projection of fantasies on the real world. When the group suffered censorship and reprisals and were expelled from their posts in university faculties, they became pamphleteers, journalist and independent scholars. Members of the group were all young men and they included Karl **Marx** and Friedrich **Engels**, whose thought and work would survive beyond 1848, as communists. See **Communism**

Yule An **occult** holiday celebrated originally by Germanic pagans on 21 December, it being the winter solstice, the shortest day of the year. The holiday is now popularly known as Yuletide and traditionally extends from 24 December to 6 January. Its conjunction with Christmas has resulted in Yuletide being an alternative name for the holiday. There are numerous references to Yule in the Icelandic sagas, but no detailed account as to how the ancient festival was celebrated. Nevertheless, the pagan festival has left evidence of its influence on the Christian celebration through the use, for example, of Christmas trees, Yule logs, holly and mistletoe. These vestiges are what survive of the measures used by the first Christian missionaries to convert the northern heathen. It was accepted that the task would be made easier if they were allowed to keep some aspects of their traditional practice. For this reason these features were not suppressed or replaced, but given a Christian interpretation. The measure was sanctioned by Pope Gregory I (c.540–604 CE) to the end that, 'whilst some gratifications are outwardly permitted them, they may the more easily consent to the inward consolations of the grace of God.' In the southern hemisphere, Christmas occurs in the heat of summer and some Australians, for example, celebrate a second, secular, festival called Yulefest. 'Christmas in July' celebrations remove the festival from all religious association and people enjoy it as a secular event. The terms Yule and Yuletide, are today used by many as secular names for 25 December, Christmas Day.

Z

Zaddik *J*. Heb. 'righteous one'. The Jewish philosopher, **Maimonides**, defined the Zaddik as 'one whose merit surpasses his iniquity'. A mystical tradition of the **Kabbalah** and **Talmud** has it that, if at any time there are 36 anonymous *tzadikim nistarim* ('concealed saints') or zaddiks forming a 'pool' of absolute righteousness, for their sakes the world is not destroyed. Their identity is not known even to each other, but their collective influence justifies mankind in the eyes of God. The tradition is based on Prov. 10:25, 'But the righteous man is an everlasting foundation [of the world].' As well as of a righteous presence in the world, 'zaddik' can be used of any righteous person, but is more usually associated with **Chasidism** where the zaddik is a spiritual leader. He is a person of unusual gifts, a supreme example of *devekut*, 'devotion', the cleaving of the soul to God. His special task is to lead the souls of his followers towards the divine light. To do this he must step down from his own spiritual elevation to 'sit where they sit', a principle known as 'descent for the sake of ascent'. The Chasidic tradition of the zaddik was entirely innovatory and requires the follower's absolute devotion. Never before in rabbinic Judaism had unquestioning loyalty to the person of the religious leader been a prerequisite for salvation. In some ways, devotion to the Zaddik is similar to the guru–pupil relationship in **Tibetan Buddhism** and the practice of **guru yoga**.

Zakat *I*. Arab. 'almsgiving' or 'payment'. The third of the five **Pillars of Islam**.

Zammai *B*. *Z*. See **Samadhi**

Zande *A*. Also Azande, the people of the Zande. Dispersed across southwest Sudan, northeast Zaire, the Democratic Republic of Congo (Kinshasa) and the Central African Republic, the Zande are a widely distributed cultural group rather than an ethnic tribal entity. They subsist through hunting and agriculture based in homesteads and farms, forming a highly secular but traditional society, valuing courtesy, good judgement, humour, hospitality and scepticism. Mbori is the supreme being and creator of all things, but there is no standard cult. Witchcraft, magic and divination are central features of social life. The society is hierarchical across several kingdoms, each king ruling his province either directly or through his brothers and sons. The kings are, however, subject to the rituals of the Mani of the secret society, that protect against witchcraft or encourage good fortune. The Zande are well known for their art, especially figurative sculptures in wood or terracotta, pottery and bowed musical instruments. See **African Religions**

Zarathustra *Zo*. See **Zoroaster**

Zaydis *I*. A more moderate branch of Shiite Islam that emerged during the conflict over the Imamate succession in the 7th and 8th centuries. They proposed Zayd ibn Ali, the grandson of Husayn, the murdered third Shiite Imam and the son of **Ali**, as the rightful successor and in so doing they opposed the **Isma'ilis** and **Imamis**. The first Zaydis state was founded in 864 in northern Iran and continued until 1126. A second state was established in the Yemen in 893, lasting until 1962. See **Shi'ism**

Zazen *Z*. Jap. 'Sitting with absorption'. An intensely focused meditation practice of **Zen** Buddhism, considered to be the most direct, unhindered way to **enlightenment**. Because *zazen* is designed to free the mind entirely, so that, being empty, it achieves the condition of 'no mind', the practice abandons the usual terms of meditation. In standard practice, at least to begin with the meditator will focus on an either an external object like a flower or **mandala**, or an internal abstract notion, such as the idea of impermanence. All such aids are dispensed with in *zazen*, including **koan** practice. Diligently pursued, the sitter will develop a mind free of the distractions of thought, but wakeful and alert to receive sudden enlightenment, the realization of his own buddha-nature as being identical to that of the universe. See **Shikantaza, Soto**

Zealots *J*. (Heb. *Kannaim*, 'the jealous ones' [on behalf of God]). The term refers to a 1st-century CE Jewish political movement whose religious fervency approached fanaticism. Sparked off by tax reforms imposed by Quirinius in the newly created province of Judea, the Zealots provoked an uprising against the occupation. It is probable they were joined by the **Essenes**, many of whom believed they were engaging in the final battle, the Armageddon that would usher in the messianic age (see **Messiah**). In Jewish history the uprising is known as the **Great Rebellion** (66–70 CE). Opposed to Roman rule, the Zealots aimed to overcome it by violence and as well as inciting Jews to fight, they eliminated Jewish collaborators. These assassinations were perpetrated by an extreme group known in Latin as *sicari*, 'dagger men'. Today they would be called freedom fighters or, dependent on one's point of view, terrorists. Josephus describes the Zealots as the 'fourth sect' or 'philosophy', the others being the **Pharisees**, **Sadducees**, and Essenes. He records that the Zealots 'agree in all other things with the Pharisaic notions; but they have an inviolable attachment to liberty and say that God is to be their only Ruler and Lord.' The **Talmud** condemned the Zealots, calling them *baryonim*, 'boorish' or 'wild' for refusing to compromise in order to save the survivors of the Romans' siege of Jerusalem. Their fanatical militarism resulted in reprisals throughout Judea and in the ruin of Jerusalem and the destruction of the Temple in 70 CE. The insurrection came to a climax at the desert fortress of Masada which the Zealots had stormed and taken, killing all of its Roman occupants. The Romans recaptured the fortress in 74 CE, to find that, rather than submit to Roman rule, the community had committed mass suicide.

It is possible that Jesus of Nazareth recruited two Zealots, Judas Iscariot and Simon the Canaanite, who is referred to by Luke as Simon the Zealot (Luke 6:15). The name 'Iscariot' is derived from *sicarius*, a corruption of the plural form *sicari*. Paul of Tarsus is also thought to have been a Zealot before his conversion to Christianity (Gal. 1:13–14).

Zen *B*. *Z*. Jap. An abbreviation of *zenna* or *zeeno*, the Japanese form of the Chinese *ch'an-na*, shortened to **Ch'an**. This itself is the Chinese translation of ***dhyana***, the deep state of meditation that dissolves all forms of duality. Zen is the most familiar school of Buddhism in the West, caught up in the 1960s with the hippy and 'flower-power' cults, with being 'cool' and spaced out. In France the phrase *reste Zen*, is still current. There are now numerous Zen centres and monasteries throughout America and Europe, indeed throughout the world, some strictly adhering to original Japanese monastic way life, others using Zen as a base from which to offer therapy, counselling and guidance to anyone needing it.

What is Zen? It is a Chinese–Japanese school of **Mahayana** Buddhism. There is no requirement to express faith in a personal creator-God, independent of and other than the universe. There is no collection of scriptural texts that evoke the same reverence as does, for example, the **Torah** for Jews, the Bible for Christians, the **Vedas** for Hindus. Nevertheless, Zen is regarded by its followers and by the world at large as a religion because it focuses on ultimate matters concerning the nature of this world, the human individual and the purpose of life in a way that transcends the mundane. If Zen had a creed it would be the one, brief, injunction of the Buddha, 'Look within, *thou* art the Buddha.' This seemingly simple command was echoed by one of Zen's most important masters, Hui-Neng (638–713 CE) known in Japanese as Eno, who said the practices were designed 'to see into one's own nature', where ultimate truth is to be discovered and experienced. D. T. Suzuki (1970) believed this to be 'the most significant phrase to be coined in the development of Zen'. Something of this quest for self-knowledge is recognized by modern Western psychology and psychoanalysis, although not all practitioners would agree that in the process of **self-realization**, one realizes or becomes unified with the absolute. There are themes in Buddhist tradition that would see self-realization as a contradiction in terms, since truth is be found only when the 'self' is let-go and forgotten. In summary, Zen affirms that by means of concentrated, disciplined, introspective effort, we are each capable of attaining the Buddha's enlightenment, known to Zen as *satori*.

What are the origins of Zen? Its inception in a Chinese school of Buddhism, Ch'an, founded by an Indian, **Bodhidharma**, who arrived in Canton c.520 CE. The Chinese sources, however, have a legendary feel about them and it is possible that Bodhidharma's teachings were not Buddhist at all, but rooted in Indian **Vedanta**. Ch'an's main thrust came during the Tang dynasty (619–906 CE) as a reaction to imposing on monks endless hours of study, pedantic scholasticism and the overstructuring and systemizing of meditation techniques. In addition, there was the growing conviction that **enlightenment** (Chin. *wu*, awareness) could be achieved in this one life, without an endless succession of rebirths. As a result and under the direction of Hui-Neng and Po-Chang (720–814 CE) the Ch'an School began to take on some of the characteristics that were later to be associated with Zen. During this process, Ch'an combined elements of *dhyana* Buddhism and **Taoism**. Underlying the changes that took place over a long period of time was the consistent emphasis on moral discipline considered to be the indispensable foundation of enlightenment. Two other characteristics were to be carried to what eventually, in Japan, developed as Zen, the significance of the master–pupil relationship and the individual's own spiritual initiatives and efforts both before and after enlightenment. It was this evolved form of Ch'an that was carried to Japan c.9th century CE, but it did not begin to gather momentum until the monk Eisai Zenji (1141–1215 CE) returned from his second journey to China in 1187 CE. He then founded the first **Rinzai** Zen monastery, Shofuku-ji. Later he moved to Kamakura which became, together with Kyoto, a principal centre of Zen in Japan. The **Soto** school was founded by Dogen Zenji.

How does Zen work? **Meditation** techniques are formed around the basics of place, various postures and methods of concentration focused on the process of breathing. The student is given training in quietening the mind so as to arrive at the point of eliminating all discursive thought. The two major schools of Zen Buddhism, Rinzai and Soto, employ different techniques; Rinzai works with **koans**, Soto with *mokusho* or silent practice and with *zazen*. However, these techniques overlap and the differences are more a matter of emphasis.

A few misconceptions need to be pointed out. Neither *zazen* nor *shikantaza* is meditation. In Zen, meditation has an object, it may be an actual image or an image visualized or a sacred word spoken or held in the mind or the mind working with a koan. These are techniques, just that, ways and means of arriving at a specific goal, they are not in themselves meditation, but a scaffolding supporting the mind in training. *Zazen* stands alone in meditation practice in that it aims to free the mind from all such thought-forms so as to achieve complete emptiness. There are those who believe *zazen* to be just a kind of reverie or a vacant, idle inactivity, while others, even reputable Western teachers, see little point in sitting still when it becomes both physically and mentally difficult to do so. The first group will abandon the practice because it is felt to be boring or pointless, the second rationalizes the practice on the grounds that it is not an obligatory part of Zen. Both points of view are misguided. It is sometimes held that monks in Zen monasteries do little more than meditate day and night and that to be a Zen monk means endless hours of *shikantaza*, 'just sitting'. Roshi Philip Kapleau records that at the monastery of Hosshin-ji, which is fairly typical, the monks will sit for an hour and a half in the morning and two to three hours in the evening. They will sleep for six to seven hours, so the remaining 12 or 13 hours is occupied with practical work of all kinds. They also have to spend some time visiting the villages in order to beg their food. Po-Chang, who founded the rules for ordering monastic life said, 'A day of no work, is a day of no eating.' Thus, whether they are busy in the gardens or maintaining and cleaning the buildings, tending graves, cooking or getting water, they are occupied in what is termed 'mobile *zazen*'. The point is to carry the focused mindfulness of meditation into the humdrum round of daily life. See **Monasticism**, **Trikaya**, **Yoga**

FINAL WORD: 'At a time when "things are in the saddle and riding mankind" as never before, when tensions of fear, anxiety and estrangement are devastating the minds of modern man, the fact that ordinary people through enlightenment can discover meaning and joy in life, as well as a sense of their own uniqueness and solidarity with all mankind, surely spells hope for human beings everywhere.' (Roshi Philip Kapleau)

Zendo *Z.* Jap. 'Zen Hall'. Usually a large hall in monasteries or other buildings where Zen Buddhists practise meditation. It is specially designed to allow an arrangement of *zafus*, the sitting cushions used by the practitioners, normally facing a wall to limit distractions. Zen masters, however, stress that Zen meditation does not necessarily require a special room in a quiet place, even though these might be helpful to beginners. Dogen Zenji said, 'Your own heart, that is the practice hall.'

Zeus *G.* Top god in Greek mythology, his name means 'divine king'. He is the leader of the gods and himself the god of sky and thunder. His origins are eclectic, being associated with Indo-European religion, German and Norse mythology and the **Vedic** god Dyaus Pitar. His role in the **pantheon** is huge and he fathered generations of heroes and heroines and featured in their mythologies. So wide was his influence that he is the embodiment of Greek religion and the archetypal Greek god. His pan-Hellenic cult (see **Hellenism**) had its major centre at Olympia, the home of the pantheon, where he was celebrated in the famous quadrennial games. Under his various titles he was also to be found in temples from Asia Minor to Sicily. Some of the rites were universal, such as the sacrifice of a white animal over a raised altar, while other more local cults had very different forms of practice. In Crete, for example, he was worshipped in caves at Knossos as an athletic youth who presided over military-athletic training; in the backwoods of **Arcadia**, the cult of the Lykaios Zeus took on lupine features, whose primitive cannibalism had its own bizarre rites. Contradicting his sky-god origins, forms of a subterranean Zeus were worshipped by Athenians, Sicilians and others, who sacrificed black animals in sunken pits and some oracular sites were also dedicated to him. Zeus was assimilated into the Roman cult as **Jupiter** (from *Jovis Pater*, 'Father Jove'). Syncretism also identified him with the Egyptian Amun and the Etruscan Tinia and in Rome, as Sabazius, an assimilation of the Phrygian god, Sabazios. The numerous legends and mythologies are exhaustively researched and described. See for example, Graves, Rose and Grant.

Ziggurat Temple towers of the ancient Mesopotamia, the terraced pyramid style probably originating in Assyria, Babylonia and Sumeria. They were not used as places of public worship, but as dwelling places for the gods who were patrons of the local city; only priests could enter a ziggurat to attend to the gods' needs. In this way the gods could be close to the people whose religion was centred on city cults. The ziggurat was usually the dominant building and the focus of civic pride. Among the earliest ziggurats were those built by Ur-Nammu (2112–2095 BCE), a late Sumerian king of Ur. The sizes varied from three to as many as seven levels.

Mesopotamia was not the only region in which ziggurats were built. They were also found in Central America, built by the **Aztecs**, but these were constructed some 3,000 years after the early Mesopotamian ziggurats. See **Babylonian Religion**, **Mesopotamian Religion Sumerian Religion**

Zion, Mt See Zionism

Zionism *J*. From, Zion or Sion, thought to have referred to the hill in Jerusalem on which the **Temple** was built, then to identify the Temple itself. Thus, Zion came to symbolize the Jews' covenant relationship with God, the **Promised Land**, the hope of Israel's return there at some future date, the messianic hope and heaven. In modern history, Zionism is a Jewish political movement that from the 19th century focused the yearning of Jews for the establishment of their own state in Palestine. The term derives from Mt Zion, the highest of the hills on which Jerusalem was built. David's 'conquest' of the Jebusite city of Jerusalem is usually dated c.1000 BCE, since when the ideas of Zion and Zionism have carried various levels of meaning, all of which are emotive for the Jewish people. The biblical tradition of Deutero-Isaiah (the unnamed prophet of the exile thought to have written the second half of the Book of Isaiah) personified Zion as a symbol of both the redemption of Israel and of universal salvation. The figure is of Zion (the City of God) as the mother abandoned by her children, but who are about to return to her from exile or as contemporarily understood, from the **diaspora** to the State of Israel. 'Zion says, "The Lord has forsaken me, My Lord has forgotten me." Can a woman forget her baby or disown the child of her womb?' (Isaiah 49:14–15). Other personifications of Zion, as a widow or refuted bride, illustrate the strong passions and yearnings characteristic of Zionism. Zionists are divided over the extent to which this perennial theme is to be understood in religious or secular terms. Political Zionists argue that the religion and practices of Judaism were necessary for preserving Jewish identity during the long period of homelessness in the diaspora and that with the establishment of the State of Israel, the religious heritage of the Jews has been made irrelevant. If there is a lingering belief in the coming messiah, this can now be triumphantly proclaimed in terms of its secular fulfilment in the State. In opposition to this, religious Zionists believe that Judaism has only been observed in a weakened and compromised way in the diaspora and that while that was part of the divine plan for a perfect balance of orthodoxy and orthopraxy, Israel as a state is indispensable, since the coming of the messiah is conditional on it. It is argued further that a state is necessary to Judaism since its social and political structure is intended, by **covenant**, to be a **theocracy**. For these reasons a Jewish State is necessary for Judaism to flourish as it should. Typical of this view is the *Neturei Karta*, a Chasidic sect centred in Jerusalem, who argue that only a Jewish state can make possible the full observation of Torah, *Halakhah* and *mitzvo*th (see **Mitzvoth**), and thus realize the potential for righteousness that will usher in the messianic age. The eventual establishment of the State of Israel was achieved by a confederacy of both political and religious Zionists triggered by the Russian pogroms of 1881–82. Zionism, as a movement, was founded by Leon Pinsker (1821–91) and Theodore Herzl (1860–1904). In 1897 Herzl organized the First Zionist Congress in Basel, Switzerland, which founded the World Zionist Organization and elected Herzl as its first president. After Herzl's death, Chaim Weizmann (1874–1952) became leader of the movement. A professor at a British university, Weizmann used his extensive contacts to lobby the British government for a statement in support of Zionist aspirations. In this he was successful and in 1917, the British foreign secretary, Lord Balfour, made his famous Declaration: 'His Majesty's Government view with favour the establishment in Palestine of a national home for the Jewish people and will use their best endeavours to facilitate this objective, it being clearly understood that nothing shall be done which may prejudice the civil and religious rights of existing non-Jewish communities in Palestine ...' (Foreign Office, 2 November 1917). Before this could be implemented the Second World War had to be won and Jews had to come to terms with the **Holocaust**. Zionist history is exhaustively documented and excellent accounts have been written by, for example, Cohen, Halpern, Laqueur and Weizmann. See **State of Israel**

Zohar *J*. 'The book of Splendour, Radiance, Enlightenment'. The principal text on which **Kabbalah** mysticism is based. It is traditionally attributed to Rabbi Simon ben Yohai who is thought to have lived towards the end of the 1st century CE. Modern scholarship, however, now regards the Zohar to be a compilation put together in Spain during the 13th and 14th centuries CE by Moses de Leon and others. A completed edition was not achieved until the 16th century when the manuscripts were being prepared for publication by Kabbalists. Essentially the book is a commentary on the mystical aspects of **Torah**, that is, the **Pentateuch**, the five books of Moses, together with the 'Five Scrolls', the books of Esther, Ruth, Song of Songs, Ecclesiastes and Lamentations. It was written in Hebrew and medieval Aramaic, not as a single book but as a group of books. The commentary addresses the nature of God, the origin of the universe, the soul, sin and redemption, the problem of good and evil, all forming a mystical perspective which unfolds from the godhead or ultimate infinity, known as the *Ein Sof*.

Zoroaster *Zo.* The Greek form of the Persian name Zarathustra. Other than knowing he was the founder of **Zoroastrianism**, his biography remains uncertain and scholars continue to dispute his dates. Parsee tradition suggests a period c.6000 BCE, but few would agree with this very early date. The language of the **Avesta**, the Zoroastrian scriptures, is contemporary with that of the Hindu **Vedas**, which would suggest a time during the period 9–10th century BCE. This date would make him the first recorded religious prophet. Tradition has it that Zoroaster was born smiling and that his head shook to the point where his parents had difficulty in holding him. This was taken to be a sign of coming wisdom. The **Parsee** tradition records that from the age of six, approximately the age when future Zoroastrian children were initiated in the **Navjote** rites, he was placed under the tutelage of a 'wise teacher'. Having survived an assassination attempt, he decided to devote himself to religion and, aged 20, left the home of his tutor-guardian to spend the next seven years meditating in a cave. There, he contemplated such problems as man's relationship to the universe and the meaning of life. His meditations are recorded in the **Gathas**, the section of the Avesta it is believed he composed himself.

'This I ask Thee, tell me truly, Ahura. Who upholds the earth beneath and the firmament from falling? Who the waters and the plants? Who yoked swiftness to winds and clouds? Who is, O Mazda, creator of Good Thoughts? This I ask Thee, tell me truly, Ahura. What artist made light and darkness? What artist made sleep and waking? Who made morning, noon and night, that call understanding man to his duty?' (Gathas 44.4–5).

Zoroaster had visions of **Ahura Mazda** who called him to preach the new message of salvation, very much in the style of Old Testament **prophecy**. At first there were many failures and disappointments, but after mysteriously curing the paralysis of the favourite horse of Vishaspa, King of Chorasmia (approximately the region of the Turkmen Republic) both the King and his wife accepted the prophet's message. Many others in the kingdom followed and gradually the movement assumed huge importance and influence, becoming the established faith of successive Iranian empires, first the Achaemenid (c.549–311 BCE), followed by the **Parthian** (2nd century BCE–224 CE), and lastly the **Sassanian** (226–651 CE) a period spanning over 1,000 years. The tradition records that Zoroaster was 77 when he was murdered while at prayer. Even though Zoroastrianism gave way to the repression and persecution of **Islam**, the religion survived in small groups settled in the remoter areas of Iran. Muslims called them *Zardushti*, the *gabr* or 'infidel'.

Zoroastrianism or **Mazdaism** *Zo.* One of the world's oldest monotheistic religions. Its origins are attributed to the prophet Zarathustra, more familiarly known in the West as **Zoroaster**. The religion is sometimes known as Mazdaism or by its adherents as Mazdayasnas, the Mazda Worshippers. The names are derived from **Ahura Mazda**, the Zoroastrian name for God or the Supreme Being. An understanding of ancient Zoroastrianism is obscured because the available sources are contradictory. The **Avesta**, the scripture, is not consistent either with itself or with the Greek accounts of Persian (Iranian) religion, of which there are few contemporary records. Herodotus' account of Persian religion refers to features that are obviously Zoroastrian, such as the exposure of the dead on the **Towers of Silence**, the concern not to pollute nature, especially the earth and water, the 'sacrifices to the Sun, Moon, Earth, Fire, Water and Wind'and the interest taken in the education of children. Inscriptions from the Achaemenid dynasty (c.549–311 BCE) record the worship of Ahura Mazda, but because Babylonian and Egyptian rituals were also used during this period of the religion's development, the scene is confused.

Zoroaster's principal message started with a denial of the **daevas**, the 'false gods' of **Indo-Iranian** religions. These are displaced by Ahura Mazda, who is One, holy, righteous and the creator of everything both seen and unseen. This monotheism expresses a unity in diversity, since Ahura Mazda is manifested as the holy spirit or *Fravashi*, the creative urge, the Good Mind, Righteousness and as **Asa**, the empowering force of Truth. However, Ahura Mazda is himself opposed by **Angra Mainyu**, the 'Hostile Spirit'. The **Gathas** state that the opposing spirits are twins, with the implication that they must have one progenitor that is higher than Ahura Mazda. For this reason a Zoroastrian sect proposed an absolute first cause, *Zurvan i Akanarak* or 'infinite time' (see **Zurvanism**). The early history of Zoroastrianism seems to have alternated between the idea of a first cause or principle and the absolute dualism of Ahura Mazda and Angra Mainyu until, towards the end of the **Sassanian** Empire (226–651 CE), the dualistic view was finally made the official tradition. Ultimately, Angra Mainyu would be defeated by Ahura Mazda by means of the *Frashokereti*, the total renovation of creation. The principal Zoroastrian beliefs are to be found in the *Fravarane* (the creed).

Zoroastrianism is primarily a religion of ethical monotheism, although, as explained above, that monotheism needs to be qualified. A characteristic feature of the religion is its **dualism**, clearly cast in the opposition of a wholly good God, Ahura Mazda, known alternatively as Ohrmazd and a wholly evil spirit, Angra Mainyu, also known as Ahriman. Zoroastrians would suggest, however, that this dichotomy is false since their doctrine of creation, *Bundahishn*, affirms that the one God created both the material and the spiritual world in all their aspects. It is more probable, however, that the dualism-non-dualism argument represents the different ways the religion developed and was interpreted by the three empires during which it held sway. Hinnells neatly suggests that monotheism might have been characteristic of the Zoroastrianism of the first phase, a qualified dualism characteristic of the second phase and dualism the dominant doctrine of the third phase, for which orthodoxy finally settled. It is the ethical doctrines that emerge as the most important, in that to bring about the ultimate triumph of the *Frashokereti*, Ahura Mazda remains dependent on human will and people's predisposition for the 'Truth'. In this process he is aided by his retinue, the Amesha Spentas or '**Bounteous Immortals**', mythological beings close in concept to biblical angels, archangels or guardian angels. To help humans choose the righteous way, Ahura Mazda gave them *Asa*, an empowerment for the Truth, thus making every individual responsible for their choices between good and evil. There is no place here for a doctrine of reincarnation, **predestination** or **karma**, since nothing created has the power to impose either good or evil on a person. Reward and punishment, joy and sorrow, depend entirely on how an individual lives his life. Ultimate blessing will accrue to those whose lives are based on the 'Good Thoughts, Good Words, Good Deeds', that constitute the Holy Way, the *daena*, the law or order of the universe. Human beings choosing to live in this manner can bring about the impotence of Angra Mainyu and the omnipotence of Ahura Mazda. On this basis they will be finally judged when, after death, they cross the **Chinvat Bridge**, which fixes the gulf between this world and paradise. The gulf is hell, into which the unrighteous will fall when, as their deeds are weighed in the balance, they are found to be evil. The righteous soul will be invited to cross.

It is worth noting that it is this combination of will and morality that interested Frederick **Nietzsche** in Zarathustra. In his introduction to Nietzsche's [1964] *Thus Spoke Zarathustra*, R. J. Hollingdale wrote; 'Zarathustra was the first to see in the struggle between good and evil the essential wheel in the working of things. The translation of morality into the realm of metaphysics, as force, cause, end-in-itself, is his work.' In his book Nietzsche, of course, puts his own words into Zarathustra's mouth and in so doing makes an application of the original philosophy to his own period.

Traditionally, Zoroastrian children begin their education around the age of five and this includes preparation for the **Navjote**, the ritual of initiation which usually takes place at the age of seven. Worship is focused on the temple where the central ritual is *Yasna*, a rite of purification which includes the *haoma* (**soma**) sacrifice. *Yasna* is officiated by a priest, with an assistant who tends the sacred fire. Together with the sun, fire is a symbol of creative energy; they are enduring, radiant, pure and life-sustaining. Zoroastrians usually pray either before a fire or a source of light, which are used only as symbols and not as objects of worship.

Zoroastrianism has unique historical importance in that Iran stood on the trade routes spanning east and west. Its ideas and concepts travelled, creating formative links with the biblically-based Western religions. Most markedly this is seen in the Judeo-Christian notions of good and evil and the conflict waged between them in cosmic dualistic terms, in the doctrines of God and the Devil, heaven and hell, the resurrection of the dead, the final judgement and reward and punishment. It has been suggested that an influence is also to be seen in the concept of a coming saviour, the *avatar* of Hinduism, the **Maitreya** of Buddhism and the **messiah** of Judaism and Christianity.

The conquest of Alexander the Great and the spread of Islam resulted in the virtual eradication of Zoroastrianism in Iran. In search of religious freedom, groups migrated to northwest India, settling there in the 10th century CE . It is these migrating groups that formed the nucleus of the modern **Parsees**. See **Karapans, Kavis**

FINAL WORD: 'Is it necessary to elaborate that a god prefers to stay beyond everything bourgeois and rational? and, between ourselves, also beyond good and evil? His prospect is free – in Goethe's words. – And to call upon the inestimable authority of Zarathustra in this instance: Zarathustra goes so far as to confess: "I would believe only in a God who could dance."' (Friedrich Nietzsche [1964])

Zoroastrianism, Traditional *Zo. Mazdayasni Zarathushtri*, old or traditional **Zoroastrianism**, is maintained by **Parsees** and Iranian and Indian Zoroastrians. They uphold the main tenets of the ancient religion, the sacredness of the **Gathas**, fire temples (see **Sacred Fire**) and the *Yasna* rituals. Ethnic identity and religion are synonymous, thus, marriage is encouraged within the faith. Compromises have had to be found with the *Dakhma-nashini* method of disposal of the dead when corpses are placed on towers to be consumed by birds. See **Towers of Silence**

Zuhd *I.* Abstinence or asceticism. In the traditional sense of self-discipline, *zuhd* is the avoidance of material comfort so as to devote oneself to religious devotion and study. The practice is particularly associated with some **Sufi** orders of Islam, where a form of dress marks the piety of the wearer.

Zulu A people of the Natal Province of South Africa, who originated from a 16th-century migration from the Congo. They incorporated many of the customs of the San, a neighbouring group of northern South Africa, including the well-known clicking sound of their khoisa speech patterns. In the 19th century, under King Shaka, they became a renowned military force and hugely expanded their territory. Zulu belief is founded on its creator god, Nkulunkulu, a withdrawn god, not interacting with ordinary human life. Individuals may contact the spirit world by appealing to the *Ama Dlozi*, the ancestors through a processes of divination, in which the diviner is usually a woman who plays a central part in the everyday life of the Zulu. Every misfortune, including death, is the result of sorcery or the influence of spirits that have been offended, thus, misfortune is never accepted as the consequence of natural causes. Cleanliness is an important practice amounting to a religious prescription and requires the use of different utensils and plates for different foods. Frequently, a person might bathe three times a day. Christianity only managed to influence the Zulus through a form of syncretism, that allowed them to retain aspects of their traditional religion, within a Zionist-Pentecostal context such as the **Natal Nazarite Church** of Isaiah **Shembe**. See **African Religions**

Zurvanism *Zo.* Zoroastrian heresy founded on time being understood as the first cause, a concept possibly derived from a Babylonian influence. In the mythology, Zurvan was the father of the 'twin spirits' **Ahura**

Mazda and **Angra Mainyu**, representations respectively of the basic **dualism** of good and evil. To the first was given the office of high priest, the rulership of the spiritual world and final victory; to the latter Zurvan gave the kingdom. What the myth offers is the attempt to identify Zurvan, from whom the twins, the manifold, were derived as the undifferentiated, the one behind the many. The heresy lies, by implication, in the attribution of an inherent weakness or evil in Zurvan as time or the absolute, since the evil and destructive Angra Mainyu is derived from him. The heresy is compounded by the belief that this negative tendency rules the world as the embodiment of relative time. A further implication is that the heresy contains a fatalism which is far from being in accordance with Zoroastra's emphasis on free will. Fate might pervert the mind and actions of a good man, while honouring the mind and actions of the weak and evil. Zurvanism shows time to be remorseless and pitiless, again a concept that contradicts Zoroastrianism's most dearly held belief, that we are free to choose our path and may enjoy success by our own efforts. See **Magi, Medes, Zoroastranism**

Zwingli, Ulrich (1484–1531) *X.* The prime mover of the Swiss Reformation and an ordained priest who was elected People's Preacher at the Old Minster in Zurich in 1518. His first reforming thrust came from his lectures on the **New Testament** given in 1519; these were followed by criticisms of the doctrine of **purgatory**, the invocation of the saints and of **monasticism**. He wrote his first Reformation tract in 1522 which presaged a radical denunciation of **Roman Catholicism** based on the notion that the Gospels were the only source of truth and that the authority of the **papacy**, the sacrifice of the Mass, fasts and clerical celibacy were untenable. His teachings on the **Eucharist** denied the corporeal presence in the elements, arguing that Christ's body remained in heaven (see **Transubstantiation**). This brought him into deep conflict with Luther, which the Colloquy of Marburg (1529) failed to resolve and the division put paid to any hope of unity among the emergent Protestant groups. In 1531, the three Forest Cantons of the Old Swiss Confederacy attacked Zurich and Zwingli was killed.

Chronology

DATE	EVENT
BCE	
40th–21st century	
40,000–35,000	The possible period during which the Aborigines migrated from SE Asia to settle in Australia. See **Australian Aboriginal Religion**.
6000	The **Parsee** date for **Zoroaster**. But see 1700 BCE.
c.5000	The beginning of settlement of Mesopotamia. **Dravidians** begin to settle the Indus Valley.
c.4000	**Dravidians** thought to have begun their migration to India. The beginnings of **Mesopotamian** civilization.
c.3500	An early date for the beginning of the **Aryan** migrations from the Indus Valley into India. See **Hinduism**.
c.3200	Maharshi Jaimini codifies the Vedic texts. See **Purva-Mimamsa**, **Vedas**.
c.3200–c.2780	Egyptian Thinite Period. See **Egyptian Religion**.
c.2852–2738	Traditional dates of the *I Ching*.
2750–c.2500	The *Epic of Gilgamesh* is set during this period.
2700–c.540	Period of the **Elamite** Dynasties.
c.2686–c.2181	Old Kingdom of Egypt. The period of writing of the **Pyramid Texts**. See **Egyptian Religion**.
c.2630–c.2611	King Djoser of Egypt. See **Imhotep**, **Pyramids**.
c.2520–2494	The rule of **Khafre**, the Egyptian king who built the Great **Pyramid**.
c.2500–c.1050	Minoan-Mycenaean Age. See **Greek Religion**.
c.2500	The construction of the Great **Sphinx** at Giza, Egypt. The beginning of **Hurrian** influence in **Mesopotamia**. An early date for the beginnings of **Indus Valley Civilization**. See 1500 BCE. The traditional date for the Egyptian Coffin Texts. See **Funerary Practices**, **Pyramid Texts**.
c.2480	The ascendance of the sun god **Re** in Egypt.
c.2400	Beginning of the period of Sumerian expansion. See **Sumerian Religion**.
2340	**Akkadians** conquer Sumer and begin to establish their empire.

DATE	EVENT
c.2300	Beginnings of the Olmec civilization in Mexico. See **Mexican Religions**.
c.2125	Collapse of the **Akkadian** Empire.
2112–2095	Ur-Nammu, Sumerian king and builder of **ziggurats**.
c.2055–c.1650	Middle Kingdom of Egypt. See **Egyptian Religion**.
20th century	
c.2000–c.1500	**Abraham**'s migration from Ur in **Chaldea**.
c.1900 – c.612	The Assyrian civilization of northern Mesopotamia. See 1120 BCE and **Assyrian Religion**, and c.8th–6th centuries.
18th century	
c.1728–c.1686	**Hammurabi** king of **Babylon**. See **Mesopotamian Religion**.
c.1700–c.1400	The likely period for **Zoroaster**.
17th century	
1600–1046	Shang Dynasty in China. See **Oracle**.
16th century	
c.1550–c.1069	New Kingdom of Ancient Egypt. See **Egyptian Religion**.
c.1550	The Egyptian god **Amun** elevated to king of gods.
c.1539–c.1292	18th **Egyptian** Dynasty. See **Mut**.
1500–1200	The period during which the **Vedas** were written. See **Hinduism**.
c.1500	Believed to be the date of the beginning of the **Aryan** migration to the Indus valley.
15th century	
c.1460–1190	The **Hittite Empire**.
c.1400	The appearance of the Iranian deity, **Mitra**.
14th century	
c.1352– c.1336	The reign of **Akhenaten** (or Amenhotep IV). See **Egyptian Religion**.
c.1300	The Exodus of the Jews from Egypt. See **Passover**.
13th century	
1200–1025	The long period of the Judges and the Hebrew conquest of/migration to **Canaan**.
1200–900	The **Phoenician** civilization.
c.1200	Ancestors of the Celts settle in northern Europe. See **Celtic Religion**.

DATE	EVENT
12th century	
1180–1170	Period during which the city of Ugarit was destroyed. See **Ugaritic**.
c.1120	Tiglath-Pilesar I founds the **Assyrian** Empire which flourishes 11th–6th centuries.
11th century	
c.1005–c.965	The reign of **David**, King of Israel.
c.1000	The suggested date for the writing of the **Black Yajurveda**. **Solomon** is born.
10th century	
970–928	The reign of King **Solomon** of Israel. See **Temple**.
c.933–721	The Kingdom of **Israel**.
c.933–568	The Kingdom of **Judea**.
c.911–612	The **Assyrian** Empire at its height. See **Assyrian Religion**. **Assyrian Empire**.
900–700	The period of the composition of the **Brahmanas**.
9th century	
c.814	The **Phoenicans** found **Carthage**.
800–400	The writing of the **Upanishads**.
8th century	
c.750	The start of the prophetic tradition of the **Old Testament**, with Amos, Hosea and Isaiah. See **Prophecy**. Foundation of the Greek city-states. See **Greek Religion**.
722	Samaria overrun by the **Assyrians**. See **Samaritans**.
721	The **Assyrians** conquer the northern Kingdom of Israel. See **Twelve Tribes of Israel**.
c.700–500	The period of the composition of the first **Upanishads**.
c.700	**Etruscans** settle in Italy.
7th century	
689	Sennacherib destroyed **Babylon**. See **Mesopotamian Religion**.
c.612	The collapse of the **Assyrian** Empire. See **Assyrian Religion**. **Babylon** becomes the seat of the Neo-Babylonian Empire.
605–562	Nebuchadnezzar II. See **Babylon**.

DATE	EVENT
c.600	Charvaka, Hindu sceptical philosopher. See **Nastika**.
6th century	
6th–5th century	**Gautama** Gotama, or Satananda, founder of the **Nyaya** school of Hindu philosophy, is placed during this long period. The period during which Siddhartha Gautama, the historical **Buddha** lived. **Jainism** founded during this period by Mahavira Tirthanakara.
6th–3rd century	**Vaiseshika** School of Hindu Philosophy. See **Atomism**. **Nyaya** school of Hindu philosophy. See **Gautama Gotama**.
599–572 or 549–477	Mahavira, the 24th and last of the Jain 'Ford-Makers'. See **Jainism**.
586	The fall of Jerusalem and the destruction of **Solomon's Temple**. The end of Israel's southern Kingdom of **Judea**, and the beginning of the Babylonian exile of the Jews. See **Lost Tribes**.
580–500	Pythagoras. See **Numerology**.
c.570–475	**Xenophanes**, Greek poet.
c.563–c.483	The dates generally accepted for the **Buddha**.
c.555 BCE–330 CE	Gradual migration of the **Magi** to Greece and Italy.
c.551–c.479	**Confucius**, traditional but approximately correct dates. See also 136 BCE. **Lao-Tzu**, contemporary with **Confucius**. But see 4th century and **Confucianism**.
c.549–311	The Achaemenid Empire. See **Zoroastrianism**.
c.546–c.334	The Persian Empire. See **Persia**.
539	Cyrus defeats the Babylonian army and frees the Israelites. The Jews begin to return to Israel from Babylon. The beginning of the **Persian** period in the Near East. See **Babylon**.
c.530	**Buddha** preaches his first sermon at Benares. See **Buddhism**.
515	Dedication of the rebuilt **Temple** in Jerusalem.
c.510–c.27	The Roman Republic. See **Roman Religion**.
500–428	Anaxagoras, Greek Philosopher. See **Palmistry**

DATE	EVENT
500–300	*Tao-te Ching*, traditionally ascribed to **Lao-tzu**, probably written during this period.
5th century	
c.5th–4th century	The beginnings of the influence of **Confucianism** on Far Eastern countries. See also 551–479. The **Sophists** active and influential in **Greece**.
c.5th–3rd century	The writing of the **Mahabharata**.
496	The Romans adopt the goddess **Ceres**.
495	The temple of **Mercury** built on the Circus Maximus.
c.485–c.421	Protagoras, Greek Sophist philosopher. See **Sophists**.
c.483	d. of the **Buddha** and the first council of Rajagriha at which Ananda transmitted the teachings of the Buddha. See **Buddhism**.
480	The battle of Salamis – aided by **Eleusian** deities. See **Eleusian Mysteries**.
c.470–399	**Socrates**, Greek philosopher.
468–465	The reign of the Persian king, Ahasuerus. See **Persia**, **Purim**.
460–377	**Hippocrates**, Greek physician (said to be the descendant of **Asclepius**, the Greek god of medicine).
431	The Council of Epheseus. See **Nestorianism**.
c.428–c.348	**Plato**, Greek philosopher and student of **Socrates**.
420–355	**Xenophon**, Greek historian and disciple of **Socrates**.
c.400	The prophet Ezra preaching in **Judea**.
400–200	The **Brahma-Sutra** written during this period. Canonical status of the **Old Testament** books established.
c.400–100CE	The **Intertestimental Period**.
4th century	**Lao-Tzu** given as living early in the century by some authorities. But see 551. The earliest writings of the Mimamsa school of Hindu philosophy. See **Purva-Mimamsa**.
395	The sanctuary of Eleusis destroyed by Alaric. See **Eleusian Mysteries**.
c.385	**Plato** founds the Hellenistic Academy. See **Academy of Athens**.
385	Christians destroy the Serapeum. See **Serapis**.
384–322	**Aristotle**, philosopher, student of **Plato** and tutor to Alexander the Great.

DATE	EVENT
371–289	**Mencius**, Chinese philosopher. See also **Chih**.
c.369–286	**Chuang-tzu. See Taoism.**
c.360–c.270	Pyrrho, Greek philosopher accredited with being the first sceptic. See **Scepticism**.
c.356–323	**Alexander the Great.**
335	**Aristotle** founds the Lyceum, his school of philosophy.
334	**Alexander the Great** invades Asia.
332	The **Samaritans** build their own temple at Mt Gerizim. **Alexander the Great** conquers the Persians. See **Persia**.
331	**Palestine** conquered by **Alexander the Great**.
323–c.31	The Hellenistic period. See **Hellenism**.
317	Theophrastus founds the Peripatetic School. See **Academy of Athens**.
c.308	Zeno establishes the **Stoics**, a Greek school of philosophy.
300–200	The translation of the Jewish scriptures into Greek, called the **Septuagint**.
300 BCE–650 CE	The Teotihuacan civilization in Mexico. See **Mexican Religions**.
300–c.950 CE	The period of **Pahlavi literature**. See **Zoroastrianism**.
3rd century	**Sanna**, the 'Five Elements School' of **Taoism**. The **Buddhist** philosophical school **Sarvastivada** breaks away from the **Theravada**.
18 August 293	The dedication of **Venus's** original temple of Ardea, Rome.
280–207	Chrysippus, Greek philosopher and developer of Stoicism. See **Stoics**.
c.270–232	**Asoka**, the Magadhan emperor, patron of **Buddhism**.
264–241	1st Punic War. See **Carthage**.
c.250	**Theravada** Buddhism carried to Sri Lanka by Mahinda, son of **Asoka**.
c.224–c.150	**Parthians** rule Iran from late 3rd century and Mesopotamia intermittently during this period.
218–201	2nd Punic Wars. See **Carthage**.
3rd–2nd centuries	The traditional date for **Lao-Tzu's** *Historical Records*.

DATE	EVENT
2nd century	**Patanjali**, author of the **Yoga** Sutras.
186	Rome bans the **Bacchanalia**.
168	The revolt of Judas Maccabeus against the Syrians. See **Chanukah**.
136	**Confucianism** made the official State cult in China.
2nd century–224 CE	The Parthian Empire. See **Parthians**, **Zoroaster**.
1st century	
1st century BCE–5th century CE	**Mithraism** prominent.
145 BCE–c.85 CE	Sima Qian, court historian to the Han dynasty. See **Confucius**.
130 BCE–70 CE	The **Qumran Community**. See **Dead Sea Scrolls**, **Essenes**.
100 BCE–100 CE	The period of the **Sadducees**.
44	The cult of **emperor worship** started by Julius Caesar.
c.30	The end of the Hellenistic period. See **Greek Religion**, **Hellenism**.
c.20 BCE–c.40 CE	**Philo**, a Hellenized Jewish philosopher born in Alexandria. See **Hellenism**.
5	The generally accepted year of the birth of **Jesus** of Nazareth.
c.5 BCE–0 CE	The period during which **Jesus** of Nazareth was thought to be born.

DATE	EVENT
CE	
1st century	The beginnings of **Grail Religion**, **Mahayana**. Buddhism and **Shintoism** in Japan. The **Zealots**, a politically fervent Jewish sect. See **Essenes**, **Great Rebellion**.
c.29–33	The period in which the date of **Jesus** of Nazareth's crucifixion is traditionally placed. See **Christianity**.
371 BCE– c.100 CE	Flavius **Josephus**, Jewish historian and apologist lived in this period.
c.42	The Apostle Mark establishes **Coptic** Orthodox Christianity in Egypt.
c.46–127	Plutarch, Greek historian and biographer. See **Carthage**.
c.50–c.135	Rabbi Akiba systematizes the *Halakhah*.
c.61–68	The Catechetical School of Mark the Evangelist in Alexandria. See **Catechism**.
64–65	The burning of Rome under Nero's emperorship and the persecution of Christians. See **Christian Expansion**.
65	The traditional year for the death of St **Paul**.
66–70	The 'Great Rebellion'. See **Essenes**, **Zealots**.
70	The Romans' destruction of Jerusalem, together with the **Temple** of Solomon. See **Israel**, **Judaism**.
70–132	The council of Yavneh reforms early **Judaism**.
85–160	Marcion, Gnostic writer. See **Gnosticism**.
2nd century	**Christianity** reaches Britain by late in the century. **Modalism**, a Christian **heresy**.
2nd–3rd century	Traditional period for **Nagarjuna**, Buddhist philosopher. The compilation of the **Hermetica**.
c.100–c.153	Valentius, Gnostic philosopher and teacher. See **Gnosticism**.
132–135	The Bar Kokhba revolt defeated by the Romans. See **Palestine**.
140	The Jewish council of Usha. See **Judaism**.
c.144	The dualistic heresy of **Marcionism** introduced in Rome by Marcion.
c.156	Montanus founds the Montanists. See **Montanism**.
c.160–225	**Tertullian**, church leader and author. See **Montanism**.
185–c.254	Origen, **Dogmatic** theologian. See **Greek Fathers**.

DATE	EVENT
3rd century	**Sabellianism**, a Christian heresy.
c.200–c. 600	The **Roma** migrations to Persia from the Indian subcontinent.
c.200	Rabbi Judah ha-Nasi begins to compile the **Mishnah**. See **Halakhah**, **Talmud**.
205–221	Varius Avitus Bassanius, Roman emperor and practitioner of **Anthropomancy**.
205–270	**Plotinus**, **Neoplatonist** Greek philosopher.
211–217	Caracalla's reign as emperor of Rome. See **Harranian Religion**.
215–275	Manichaeus. See **Manicheanism**.
226–651	**Sassanian** Empire and the likely period of the writing of the **Gathas**. See **Avesta**, **Zoroaster**.
c.230	**Noetus**, a presbyter of the Church in Asia Minor. See **Modalism**.
c.232–305	Porphyry, Greek philosopher, see **Neoplatonism**.
c.250–325	Iamblichus, Assyrian **Neoplatonist** philosopher.
c.250–c.336	Arius of Alexandria, whose doctrines gave rise to the heresy of **Arianism**.
c.250–c.900	Classical period of the Maya civilization. See **Mexican Religion**.
255–641	The new Persian empires. See **Persia**.
c.292	b. of Pachomius, thought to be the founder of **Coenobitic monasticism**.
296–373	Athanasius, early theologian. bishop of Alexandria. See **Arianism**, **Greek Fathers**.
3rd–4th century	**Kumarajiva**, important translator of Buddhist texts from Sanskrit to Chinese.
4th century	**Monasticism** has its beginnings in Egypt. **Yogachara**, an important school of **Mahayana** Buddhist philosophy, appeared during this century.
4th–5th century	**Donatist** schism.
c.650	End of Teotihuacan civilization in Mexico. See **Mexican Religions**.
313	Constantine's Edict of Milan legitimizes the existence of Christianity as a recognized religion. See **Christian Expansion**.
316–321	Rome suppresses the **Donatists**.
323	Pachomius founds his first monastery at Tabennae. See **Coenobitic**.

DATE	EVENT
325	Council of Nicaea. See **Creeds**, **Pantocrator**.
325–787	The Ecumenical councils of the **Orthodox** Church.
330–379	St Basil. See **Greek Fathers**.
331–363	Julian the Apostate, the last pagan Roman emperor, who practised **Anthropomancy**. See also **Harranian Religion**.
340–397	St Ambrose. See **Latin Fathers**.
347–c.420	St Jerome. See **Latin Fathers**.
354–430	St **Augustine** of Hippo, the first significant Christian philosopher. See **Latin Fathers**.
370–440	Pelagius, instigator of the Pelagian heresy. See **Pelagianism**.
379–395	Reign of the Emperor Theodosius. See **Byzantine Empire**.
381	Council of Constantinople, see **Creeds**.
382	Jerome's translation of the **Bible** into Latin commissioned by Pope Damasus. See **Septuagint**.
386–451	Nestorius, patriarch of Constantinople. See **Nestorianism**.
389	Theodosius makes Christianity the state religion of the Roman Empire. See **Christian Expansion**.
391	Theodosius' decree bans all pagan cults in favour of Christianity. See **Mithraism**.
5th century	
c.400	The Palestinian **Talmud** probably redacted by this date. The beginnings of feudal Japan. See **Japanese Religion**.
402	**Pure Land Buddhism** founded by Hui-yuan.
410	St **Augustine** begins his *City of God*.
420–1453	**Byzantine** Empire.
423	Simeon the Elder founds the **Stylites**.
431	Council of Ephesus condemns **Nestorianism**.
440–528 or	**Bodhidharma**, founder of the **Ch'an** School of Buddhism in China. See 470–543 and **Zen**.
c.450	Angles, Saxons and Jutes come to England from northeastern Europe, to form the Anglo-Saxons.
451	Council of **Chalcedon**.

DATE	EVENT
470–543	Alternative dates for Bodhidharma. See 440–528 and **Ch'an** and **Zen**.
476	Western Roman Empire overrun by barbarian invaders. See **Christian Expansion**.
477–495	The building of the **Shao-Lin** monastery at Sung-Shan in China by Emperor Hsiao-wen. See **Bodhidharma Kung-fu**.
c.480–c.550	St Benedict, founder of the **Benedictines**.
483–565	Justinian, the Eastern Emperor, known as the 'Last Emperor'.
5th–6th century	**Ch'an** Buddhism brought to China by **Bodhidharma**.
6th century	
500–428	Anaxagoras, a Greek philosopher of Asia Minor. See **Palmistry**
500–800	The **Alvar Saints**, a group of 12 mystic teachers born during this period.
c.500	The date by which the Babylonian **Talmud** had been redacted. The date of the earliest texts of the Sankhya school of Hindu philosophy.
c.520	**Bodhidharma** arrives in Canton from India. See **Zen**.
529	d. Mazdak. See **Sassanian** Empire.
538–597	**T'ien-t'ai** school of Chinese Buddhism.
c.540–604	Pope Gregory I. See **Anglo-Saxon Religion**, **Yule**.
543	The Council of Constantinople. See **Universalism**.
551–628	Babai the Great, head of the **Assyrian Church of the East**.
c.570–632	**Muhammad**, the founding prophet of **Islam**.
581	**Nirvana School** of Chinese Buddhism absorbed into **T'ien-t'ai**.
594	**Mahayana Buddhism** a state religion in Japan.
597	**Augustine of Canterbury** begins to evangelize England.
7th century	
7th–8th century	The **Zaydis** develop as a moderate branch of **Islam**.
c.600–c.900	The **Roma** migrations to the Middle East.
606 or 614–632	**Fatimah** Zahra, the daughter of **Muhammad** and his first wife, Khadija.
610	The beginning of the 'sending down' of the **Koran**.

DATE	EVENT
c.618–c.907	The Tang Dynasty in China. See **T'ai-chi**.
622	Muhammad 'emigrates' from Mecca to Medina. See ***Hijrah***, **Islam**.
624	Buddhism becomes a state religion in China.
638–713	**Zen** master Hui-Neng.
641	The Arabic conquest of Egypt. See **Coptic Church**, **Islamic Dynasties**.
652	Caliph Uthman puts together the definitive **Koran**.
656	The assassination of Caliph Uthman ibn Affan. See **Fitnah**, **Kharijites**.
656–661	First Islamic civil war. See **Fitnah**.
660	The murder of **Ali Ibn Abi Talib**, the central figure in Shiite Islam. See **Kharijites**, **Shi'ism**.
661–750	The **Umayyad Caliphate**. See **Caliphs**, **Islam**, **Islamic Dynasties**.
664	The **Synod of Whitby** that decided for **Roman Catholicism** over **Celtic Christianity**.
c.672–735	The Venerable Bede. See **Easter**.
681	Assassination of Husayn, 3rd Shiite Imam. See **Shi'ism**.
683–685	Second Islamic civil war. See **Fitnah**.
690–730	Basra made a centre of Islamic theology by the **Kharijites**.
8th century	**Padmasambhava** travels from India to Tibet, taking the philosophy of **Dzogchen**. See **Nyingmapa** School.
8th–9th century	Jews migrate from the Middle East to Spain, to become the **Sephardim**.
711	Muslim invasion of Spain. See **Islamic Dynasties**.
c.720–814	Po-Chang, **Ch'an** master. See **Zen**.
c.742–814	Charlemagne, founder of the **Holy Roman Empire**. See **800 CE**.
750–1258	The **Abbasid Caliphate**. See **Caliphs**, **Islam**, **Islamic Dynasties**.
750	**Abbasid Caliphate**, the **Sunni** dynastic house, overthrows the **Umayyads**.
765	d. of Shiite Imam Ja'far al-Sadiq. See **Seveners**, **Shi'ism**.
c.767	The construction of the Tibetan monastery at Samye. See **Padmasambhava**.
774–835	The **Shingon** School of Buddhism founded in Japan.

DATE	EVENT
788–820	**Shankara** Hindu philosopher of non-dualism.
788–985	**Idrisid** dynasty rules in the Maghreb. See **Abbasid Caliphate**.
790–11th century	**Vikings** plunder and occupy Britain.
9th century	Ancestors of the **Maori** migrate to New Zealand. **Zen Buddhism** brought to Japan. See **Japanese Religion**, **T'ien-t'ai Zen**. **Mamluk** army first recruited in Baghdad by Abbasid Caliphs.
9th–10th century	Compilation and redaction of the Tibetan Buddhist canon. See **Tibetan Buddhism**.
9th–11th century	The **Byzantine Empire**'s 'golden age'.
9th–11th century	Toltec civilization in Mexico. See **Mexican Religions**.
9th–12th century	Broad range for the life Gorakhnath, a Hindu **guru**. See **Nath Tradition**.
800–1000	The development of **Gregorian Chant**.
800	**Shankara** begins to develop for **Hinduism** his philosophy of non-Dualism. (See **Dualism**). The coronation of Charlemagne and the establishment of the **Holy Roman Empire**.
c.838	d. of the Japanese Buddhist monk, Kobodaishi. See **Perfect Liberty Kyodan**.
864–1126	The first **Zaydis** state established in northern Iran. See 893.
c.873–935	Abu-Al-Hasan **Ashari**, Isma'li philosopher and theologian whose works are the standard for Islamic orthodoxy. See **Mu'tazila**.
893–1962	The second **Zaydis** state, established in the Yemen. See 864.
10th century	The *Bhagavad-Purana*, the myths, legends and stories of **Krishna**.
909	**Fatimid Caliphate** founded.
923	Death of al-Tabari. See **Satanic Verses**.
936	Zoroastrians move from Iran to Gujarat, India, to form the first **Parsee** community.
950–1396	The **Bogomils**, a **Gnostic** sect in Bulgaria.
960–1279	The Sung Dynasty in China and the formation of **Confucianism** as we know it today.
969–1171	**Fatimid Caliphate** rules Egypt. See **Caliphs, Fatima, Islam, Islamic Dynasties**.

DATE	EVENT
969	Shiites conquer the Abbasids in Egypt. See **Fatimid Caliphate**.
998	Orthodoxy becomes the state religion of Russia. See **Orthodox Church**.
11th century	The appearance of the 'Four Branches', the earliest part of the Celtic **Mabinogion**. The emergence of the **Druzes**, an off-shoot of **Isma'li** Shi'ism. **Ramanuja**, Hindu philosopher, born mid-11th century. See **Dualism and Non-Dualism**. **Madhyamaka** school of Buddhist philosophy carried from India to Tibet. See **Nagarjuna**. Rinzai **Zen** founded in Japan.
11th–14th centuries	The **Seljuk** Dynasty, the forerunners of the Ottomans. See **Islamic Dynasties**, **Sultanate**, **Sunni**.
11th–13th centuries	The period of the **Crusades**.
11th–12th centuries	The compilation of *The Blue Cliff Record*. See **Koan**.
1009	Al-Hakim destroys the Church of the Holy Sepulchre in Jerusalem. See **Druzes**.
1021	d. of al-Hakim. See **Druzes**.
1033–1109	St Anselm, medieval philosopher and theologian and Archbishop of Canterbury from 1093. See **Ontological Argument**.
1052–1136	**Milarepa**, a famous yogi and poet of Tibet, formatively associated with the Kagyupa School.
1054	The conventional date for the division between Constantinople and Rome. See **Orthodox Church**.
1055–1137	**Ramanuja**, Tamil Brahmin philosopher of non-dualism. See **Dualism** and **Non-Dualism**.
1066	The Norman conquest of England.
1073	The Sakya monastery founded in Tibet. See **Sakyapa**.
1090–1153	Bernard of Clairvaux. See **Sacred Heart**.
1096–1099	The first Crusade. See **Hospitallers**, **Crusades**.
12th century	Kabbalism develops in southern France. Compilation of the *Gateless Gate*. See **Koan** and 1229.
12th–13th centuries	The **Cathars** or **Albigensian** heretics flourish in southern France.
12th–14th centuries	The traditional period during which the cards of the **Tarot** first appeared.

DATE	EVENT
1118–1312	The period of the **Order of Knights Templar**.
1120–1400	Period of recording and preserving the Icelandic **sagas**.
1135–1204	Moses **Maimonides**, Jewish philosopher and physician. See **Judaism**.
1141–1215	Eisai Zenji, **Zen** monk, founder of the first Rinzai Zen monastery.
1154	Foundation of the **Carmelite** order in Palestine by St Berthold.
1168	The Slavic Arcona temple destroyed. See **Slavic Religion**.
1171	Sulah ad-Din (Saladin) returns the Fatimid territories to Sunni rule. See **Fatimid Caliphate**.
1178–1241	Snorri Sturluson, compiler of the Younger **Edda**.
c.1181–1226	St **Francis** of Assisi, founder of the **Franciscan** order or 'Friars Minor'.
1184	The first inquisition set against the **Cathars**. See **Inquisition**.
1185–1392	Kamakura period in Japan. See **Tendai**.
1187	The Rinzai **Zen** monastery founded by Eisai Zenji. See **Buddhism, Japanese Religions**.
1192	The founding of the Kamakura Shogunate in Japan. See **Samurai**.
1199–1278	**Madhva**, a Hindu dualistic philosopher.
13th century	The Sants form a school in north India. See **Sant Tradition**. **Inca** Dynasty founded in Peru.
13th–14th centuries	The period of the Mongol invasions. See **Islamic Dynasties, Mongols, Ottoman Empire**.
1200–1253	**Soto** school of Zen Buddhism founded by Dogen.
1200–1280	Albertus Magnus or Albert the Great, theologian. See **Dominicans**.
1202–1204	The **crusade** against Constantinople. See **Byzantine Empire**.
1206	Genghis Khan begins conquest of Asia. See **Mongols**.
c.1207–1273	**Rumi**, Islamic mystic and poet.
1209	**Carmelite** rule laid down. **Franciscan** order founded by St Francis. The Albigensian **Crusade** against the **Cathars**.
1216–1294	Kublai Khan, Chinese Emperor. See **Mi-tsung**.

DATE	EVENT
1220–1221	The Councils of Bologna where St Dominic founded the **Dominicans**.
1220–1225	Genghis Khan's Mongols make incursions into the northern and eastern provinces of the Islamic Empire. See **Islamic Dynasties**.
1221	St Francis founds the Tertiaries. See **Franciscans**.
1222–1282	**Nichiren**, founder of a Japanese Buddhist school.
1223–1277	Baybars, the **Mamluk** sultan of Syria and Egypt.
1225–1274	Thomas **Aquinas**, Catholic philosopher and theologian.
1229	Publication of *The Gateless Gate*. See **Koan**.
1230	The second inquisition set against the **Cathars**. See **Inquisition**.
1252–1334	Sheikh Safi Al-Din. See **Safavid Dynasty**.
1254	The **Mamluks** seize power in Egypt, undermining the **Fatimid Caliphs**.
1258	The **Mongols** overthrow the **Abbasid Caliphate**.
1260–1277	The Mamluk sultan, Baybars, fights against the crusaders in Syria-Palestine.
1280s	Moses de Lyon writes the *The Book of Splendour, Radiance, Enlightenment* – the Zohar. See **Kabbalah**.
1285–1349	William of Ockham. See **Nominalism**.
1294–1303	Pope Boniface VIII. See **Papacy**.
1297	Muslim invasion of India. See **Islamic Dynasties**.
14th century	
14th–15th century	**Conciliar Movement** of the **Roman Catholic Church**.
14th–16th century	Aztec civilization at its zenith. See **Aztecs** and **Mexican Religions**. The compilation of the **Iroquois**' 'The Great Law of Peace'.
c.1300–1923	**The Ottoman Empire**.
c.1300	The 'Upsala Codex'. See **Edda**. Aztecs settle in Tenochtitlan.
1302	Pope Boniface VIII's Bull *Unam Sanctum*. See **Papacy**.
1308–1364	**Longchenpa**, philosopher-teacher of the **Nyingmapa** school of **Tibetan Buddhism**. See **Dzogchen**.
1317	Pope John XXII orders the consolidation of the Franciscan 'Observant'. See **Franciscans**.

DATE	EVENT
c.1320–1384	John **Wycliffe**, English theologian and Bible translator. See **Lollards**, **Congregationalism**.
1378–1474	Christian Rosenkreutz, founder of the Order of the Rosy Cross. See **Rosicrucians**.
1380–1471	**Thomas à Kempis**.
15th century	The start of the **Renaissance** in Italy.
1414–1418	The Council of Constance. See **Conciliar Movement**.
1436	The final compilation of the Taoist canon. See **Taoism**.
c.1438–c.1533	The empire of the **Incas**.
1440–1518	Kabir, an Indian mystic poet. See **Sikhism**, **Guru Nanak**.
1452	The order of **Carmelite** Sisters founded.
1453	Islam displaces the **Byzantine Empire**. See **Christian Expansion**.
1457	Jan Hus founds the **Moravian Brethren** in Czechoslovakia.
1463–1494	Giovanni Pico della Mirandola, Italian Renaissance philosopher. See **Christian Kabbalah**.
1469–1536	Desiderius **Erasmus**, Humanist philosophy. See **Humanism**.
1469–1539	**Guru Nanak**, founder of **Sikhism**.
1478–1535	Thomas More. See **Utopianism**.
1478–1834	The Spanish Inquisition. See **Illuminati**, **Inquisition**.
1483–1530	Zahir al-Din Muhammad **Babur**, first Mughal ruler of India.
1483–1546	Martin **Luther**.
1484–1531	Ulrich **Zwingli**, prime mover of the Swiss **Reformation**.
1486	b. **Gouranga**, founding father of the **Hare Krishna** Movement.
1487	The *Malleus Maleficarum*, of Heinrich Kramer. See **Demonology**.
1491–1556	Ignatius **Loyola**, founder of the **Jesuits**.
1492	The **Sephardim** expelled from Spain as a result of the **Inquisition**.
1493–1591	**Paracelsus**, philosopher, alchemist, physician and occultist.
1496–1561	Menno Simons, founder of the **Mennonites**.

DATE	EVENT
16th century	The beginnings of **Sikhism** early in the century. The **Reformation** and **Counter-Reformation**. The beginnings of English **Puritanism** during the reign of Elizabeth I. See 1533.
16th–17th century	The emergence of the **Doukhobors** in Russia. See 1899 and **Unitarianism**.
1501–1736	**Safavid Dynasty** of caliphs, Persia (Iran). See **Islamic Dynasties**, **Mughal Empire**.
1502	Ismail I made Shah of Iran. See **Safavid Dynasty**.
1506–1552	Francis **Xavier**, Jesuit priest.
1509–1564	John Calvin. See **Calvinism**.
1512–1517	5th Lateran Council finally condemns the **Conciliar Movement**.
1515–1582	St **Teresa** of Avila founder of the order of **Carmelite** nuns.
1517–1924	Period of the **Ottoman Empire** of the Turkish Sultans.
1517	The Ottoman Turks overrun the **Mongols** and conquer Egypt. See **Islamic Dynasties**.
1520s	Emergence of the **Hutterian Brethren**.
c.1521	**Guru Nanak** founds the first Sikh *panth*, community. See **Sikhism**.
1520–1566	Suleiman the Magnificent. See **Ottoman Empire**.
1522	**Zwingli** writes his first **Reformation** tract.
1526–1857	The **Mughal Empire** in India. See **Islamic Dynasties**.
1529	The Rule established for the Order of **Capuchins**. See also **Franciscans**. The Diet of Speyer. See **Protestantism**. The Colloquy of Marburg. See **Zwingli**.
1530	The Augsburg Confession. See **Luther** and **Lutheranism**.
1533–1603	Elizabeth I.
1534	Society of Jesus founded by **Loyola**. See **Jesuits** Henry VIII breaks with Rome.
1534–1549	Pope Paul III introduces the Index of prohibited books. See **Counter-Reformation**.
1534–1572	Isaac Luria, Kabbalistic mystic. See **Kabbalah**, **Tzimtzum**.
1536	The Portuguese Inquisition set up in parallel to the Spanish **Inquisition**.
1538–1541	The dissolution of the monasteries in England, Wales and Ireland. See **Reformation**.

DATE	EVENT
1539–1552	Guru Angad, the first compiler of the **Guru Nanak's** hymns. See **Guru Granth Sahib**, **Sikhism**.
1542–1591	St **John of the Cross**, Spanish mystic and poet and reformer of the **Carmelite** order.
1542	Establishment of the permanent Roman **Inquisition**, the Congregation of the Holy Office.
1545–1563	Council of Trent. See **Counter-Reformation** and **Roman Catholicism**.
1549	Thomas Cranmer publishes his prayer book. See **Mass**.
1550	Calvin establishes his Reformed Church. See **Calvinism**, **Huguenots**. Pope Paul III ratifies the **Jesuits**. See **Loyola**.
1552	d. Matteo dei Bassi. See **Capuchins**.
1554–1612	John Smyth, instigator of the **baptism** of believers. See **Baptisms**.
1556–1605	Akbar, Mughal emperor. See **Mughal Empire**.
1557	The first band of **Covenanters** formed.
1558	Elizabeth I assumes the throne of England. See **Recusancy**.
1559	The Act of Uniformity set the liturgy of the Book of Common Prayer for **Anglicanism**. See **Recusancy**.
1560–1609	Jacobus Arminius, whose modification of **Calvinist** doctrine became known as **Arminianism**.
1561–1626	Francis **Bacon**. See also **Empiricism**, **Idols of the Mind**.
1562	The start of the French Wars of Religion and the massacre of **Huguenots** at Vassy (1 March) and Paris (23/24 August) France.
1564–1642	**Galileo Galilei**, Italian scientist and philosopher.
1564	Cardinal Borromeo's Catechism of Trent. See **Counter-Reformation**.
1571–1640	**Mulla Sadra**, Illuminationist Islamic philosopher.
1571	The destruction of the Temple of Enryakuji on Mt Hiei, Japan. See **Tendai**.
1574–1637	Robert Fludd, Paracelsian physicist, astrologer and mystic. See **Macrocosm and Microcosm**, **Paracelsus**.
1575–1624	Jakob **Bohme**, German Lutheran mystic.
1577–1601	The building of the Sikh 'Golden Temple' at Amritsar. See also **Darbar Sahib**, **Sikhism**.

DATE	EVENT
1578	Altan Khan bestows the title **Dalai Lama** for the first time.
1581–1606	Guru Arjan who first compiled the **Adi Granth**, the Sikh scriptures. See **Guru Granth Sahib**.
1581	John Craig establishes the anti-Catholic National Covenant in Scotland. See **Covenanters**.
1585–1638	Cornelius Otto Jansen, See **Jansenism**.
1588–1679	Thomas **Hobbes**, English rationalist philosopher.
1592	Robert Browne publishes his theories of union. See **Congregationalism**.
1595	Bound's *True Doctrine of the Sabbath*. See **Sabbatarianism**.
1596–1650	**Descartes**, French philosopher.
1598	Henry IV's Edict of Nantes brings to an end the War of Religions. See **Huguenots**.
17th century	
1605–1681	Nikon, Patriarch of Moscow, liturgical reformer. See **Old Believers**.
1607	The first Anglican church founded in America at Jamestown, Virginia. See **Episcopalians**.
1611	The King James Version of the **Bible** appears.
1612	Thomas Helwys founds the General **Baptists**.
1618	James I publishes his *Book of Sports*. See **Sabbatarianism**.
1618–1619	The Council of Dordrecht, Holland, ratifies Calvin's doctrines (see **Calvinism**) and condemns **Arminianism**.
1618–1648	The Thirty Years War. See **Counter-Reformation**.
1620	Francis **Bacon** publishes his *Novum Organum Book 1*. See **Idols of the Mind**. Pilgrim Fathers leave England in the *Mayflower* to arrive in New England.
1623–1662	**Pascal**, French mathematician, physicist and philosopher.
1624–1691	George Fox, founder of the Religious **Society of Friends**.
1629	La Rochelle, the last free city of the **Huguenots**, falls to Richelieu.

DATE	EVENT
1632	**Galileo**'s *Dialogue on the Two Chief Systems of the World.* The **Mennonite** Dordrecht Confession of Faith.
1632–1677	Baruch de **Spinoza**, Dutch rationalist philosopher.
1632–1704	John **Locke**, philosopher.
1635–1705	P. J. Spencer, Lutheran minister and preacher. See **Pietism**.
1638–1715	Louis XIV. See **Divine Kingship**.
1638	Final ratification of the National Covenant in Scotland. See **Covenanters**.
1642	The Great Rebellion in England. See **Puritanism**.
1643	The Codex Regius found in Iceland. See **Edda**.
1644–1718	William Penn, Quaker founder of Pennsylvania. See **Society of Friends**.
1647	Westminster Confession and Catechism. See **Presbyterianism**.
1648	George Fox founds the Religious **Society of Friends**, known as the 'Quakers'. Shabbethai Zevi proclaims himself **Messiah**.
1650–1750	The Age of Reason: The English **Enlightenment**. See also **Illuminism**, **Hobbes**, **Locke**.
1658	The **Savoy Declaration** provides preliminary guidance on **Congregationalism**'s principles of church government.
1658–1707	The Emperor Aurangzeb Alamgir. See **Mughal Empire**.
1662	The Book of Common Prayer and the Act of Uniformity. See **Free Churches**, **Nonconformism**, **Liturgy**, **Recusancy**.
1663–1727	A. H. Francke, German Protestant churchman and instigator of **Pietism**.
1674–1737	John Hutchinson. See **Hutchinsonism**.
1674–1748	Isaac Watts, Christian **hymn** writer. See **Sacred Heart**.
1681	William Penn founds Pennsylvania on Quaker principles. See **Society of Friends**.
1685	Louis XIV revokes the Edict of Nantes. See **Camisards**.
1685–1753	Bishop George Berkley, Irish idealist philosopher. See **Idealism**.

DATE	EVENT
1688–1772	Emanuel **Swedenborg**, Swedish scientist and mystic. See **New Church of the New Jerusalem**.
1690	William of Orange assumes the English throne. See **Covenanters**.
1694–1775	St Paul of the Cross. See **Passionists**.
1694–1778	**Voltaire**, French philosopher, essayist and historian. See **Fideism**.
1698–1833	**Quakers** banned from the English Parliament.
1699	The **Khalsa** community founded by Guru Gobind Singh. See **Sikhism**.
18th century	The **Dunkers** emigrate from Germany to Pennsylvania. Martinist occult school founded in Grenoble. See **Martinism**. **Mesmerism** introduced into France from Austria by Franz Mesmer.
1700–1760	Israel ben Eliezer, the Baal Shem Tov, founder of **Chasidism**.
1703–1792	Muhammad ibn Abd al-Wahhab. See **Wahhabis**.
1705–1758	Jonathan Edwards leads the Great Awakening in America. See **Revivalism**.
1707	Act of Union between England and Scotland. See **Covenanters**.
1708	The death of Gobind Sing, the last of the Sikh gurus. See **Guru Granth Sahib**, **Sikhism**.
1711–1776	David **Hume**, Scottish empiricist philosopher.
1712–1778	**Rousseau**, Jean-Jacques, philosopher of **Romanticism**.
1717	Formation of the Grand Lodge of England. See **Freemasonry**.
1720s	The beginnings of the international Evangelical Revival. See **Pietism**, **Revivalism**.
1720–1770	The Convulsionnaires, French millennial prophets. See **Shakers**.
1723	The 'Anderson Constitutions' published. See **Freemasonry**. Jansenists consecrate their own bishop in Utrecht. See **Jansenism**, **Old Catholics**.
1724	The Church of Utrecht breaks with Rome. See **Old Catholics**.
1724–1804	Emanuel **Kant**, German philosopher.

DATE	EVENT
1725–1807	John Newton, Christian **hymn** writer. See **Sacred Heart**.
1726–1791	Jacob Frank, who proclaimed himself **Messiah**.
1729–1786	Moses **Mendelssohn**, German-Jewish philosopher who is attributed with starting the 'renaissance' of European Jewry. See **Scientific Study of Judaism**.
1732	St Alphonsus Liguori founds the **Redemptorists**.
1735–1815	Ganioda'yo, founder of the **Handsome Lake Religion**.
1738	John Wesley, one of the founders of **Methodism**, experiences an evangelical conversion to Christianity.
1741–1825	Johann Heinrich Fuseli, Swiss romantic painter. See **Succubus**.
1743–1803	Louise-Claude de **Saint-Martin**, founder of the Martinist Occult school. See **Martinism**.
1743–1805	William Paley, natural theologian. See **Teleological Argument**.
1745–1812	Rabbi Shneur Zalman, founder of the **Lubavitch**.
1746–1763	The **Hell Fire Club** located at Medmenham Abbey during this period. See **Medmenham Monks**.
1748–1832	Jeremy **Bentham**, one of the founders of **Utilitarianism**.
1760–1825	Henri de Saint-Simon. See **Positivism**.
1763–1825	Jean Paul Richter. See **Death of God Theology**.
1768	**Mennonites** offered land in Russia (Ukraine) and form the Russian Mennonites.
1770–1811	Rabbi Nachman of Bratzlav. See **Yiddish**.
1770–1831	George **Hegel**, German idealist philosopher.
1771	**Skoptsy** castration sect discovered by the Russian civil authorities.
1771–1858	Robert Owen, socialist activist. See **Utilitarianism**.
1772	The English Quaker revival in England. See **Society of Friends**.
1772–1832	Pierre-François Bouchard, the discoverer of the **Rosetta Stone**.
1773–1836	James **Mill**, Scottish philosopher, historian and economist. See **Utilitarianism**.
1774	Ann Lee takes a group of **Shakers** to Albany, USA.
1775–1854	Von Schelling, German Idealist philosopher. See **World Soul**.

DATE	EVENT
1776	The founding of the Order of **Illuminati**.
1782–1849	William Miller, instigator of the **Millerite Movement** in the USA.
1785–1840	Nachman Krochmal, prime mover of the **Scientific Study of Judaism**.
1787	Edict of Toleration establishes some civil and religious rights to **Huguenots**.
1788–1860	**Schopenhauer**, German philosopher. See **Voluntarism**.
1789–1799	The French Revolution.
1791	The Catholic Relief Act in England. See **Recusancy**.
1791–1859	Muhammad bin Ali al-Sanusi, founder of the Islamic Tariqah, **Senussi**.
1794	**Methodism** carried to North America. The start of the Qajar Dynasty in **Persia**.
1798–1857	Auguste Comte. See **Positivism**.
1798	Napoleon invades Egypt and defeats the **Mamluks**.
Late 18th century	The founding of the **Lubavitch** Movement. The beginnings of **Romanticism**.
19th century	**Kardecism** developed by Allen Kardec.
1802–1866	Phineas P. **Quimby**. See **New Thought Movement**.
1804–1872	Ludwig **Feuerbach**, philosopher and theologian. See **Projection Religion**.
1804–1888	Rabbi Hirsch promotes neo-orthodox Judaism. See **Judaism, Orthodox**.
1805–1844	Joseph Smith, founder of the **Mormons**. See 1830.
1806–1873	John Stuart **Mill**, English empiricist and social reformer. See **Utilitarianism**.
1806–1881	Louis Auguste Blanqui, French political activist. See **Anarchism**.
1809–1865	**Proudhon**, French social philosopher, thought to be the first anarchist thinker.
1810–1888	Philip Henry Gosse, English naturalist. See **Creationism**.
1811	**Mamluk** massacred in Egypt by Muhammad Ali.
1811–1836	John Humphrey **Noyes**, founder of the **Oneida Movement**.
1813–1855	Soren **Kierkegaard**, Danish philosopher and theologian.

DATE	EVENT
1814–1876	Mikhail **Bakunin**, one of the founding fathers of **Anarchism**.
1815–1930	Adolf Harnack, Protestant theologian. See **Liberal Protestantism**.
1817–1892	**Baha'ullah** (Mirza Husayn Ali Nuri), founder of the **Baha'i** faith.
1818–1883	Karl Marx. See **Marxism**.
1819–1850	Sayyid Ali Muhammad. See **Babism**.
1820–1895	Frederick **Engels**.
1820–1903	Herbert **Spencer**, English philosopher and political theorist. See **Darwinism**.
1821–1891	Leon Pinsker, founder, with Theodore Herzl, of the Zionist Movement. See **Zionism**.
1821–1910	Mary Baker Eddy, founder of the **Christian Scientists**.
1822–1889	Albrecht Ritschl, Protestant theologian. See **Liberal Protestantism**.
1823–1900	Max Muller, orientalist. See **Kathenotheism**.
1827–1886	Mary Anne Girling. See **Girlingites**.
1830–1848	**Young Hegelians**.
1830	**Mormonism** founded by Joseph Smith.
1831–1891	Helena Blavatsky, spiritualist. See **Psychical Research**, **Spiritualism**, **Theosophy**.
1831	**Lord's Day Observance Society** founded in the UK.
1833	**Ringatu**, a **Maori** cult, founded by Te Kooti Rikirangi.
1833–1841	Series of publications, *Tracts for our Times*. See **Oxford Movement**.
1836–1886	**Ramakrishna** Paramahamsa, revered Hindu teacher.
1838	**Plymouth Brethren** founded by J. N. Darby **Peculiar People** founded by John Banyard.
1839–1908	Mirza Ghulam Ahmad, founder of the **Ahmadiyyah Movement**.
1839–1914	C. S. Peirce. American polymath and philosopher. See **Pragmatism**, **Semiotics**.
1842–1910	William **James**, American psychologist and philosopher.
1843	William Miller's predicted date of Christ's second coming. See **Adventism**.
1844–1900	Friedrich **Nietzsche**, philosopher.

DATE	EVENT
1846	The **Agapemonites** founded by Rev. Henry Price. The community lasted until 1956.
1847	Brigham Young moves the Mormons to Salt Lake City. See **Mormonism**.
1848	The Fox sisters of Hydesville start the Spiritualist Movement. See **Spiritualism**. The Communist Manifesto. See **Marx, Engels, Communism**. **Oneida Movement** founded in Oneida, New York, by Noyes.
1848–1849	John Thomas writes the *Elpis Israel*. See **Christadelphians**.
1849–1905	Muhammad Abduh, reformer of the curriculum of Al-Azhar. See **Islamic Modernism**.
1850–1929	William Wade Harris, founder of the **Harris Movement**.
1850	**Cokelers**, or Society of Dependents, founded by John Sirgood.
1851–1864	The Taiping rebellion in China. See **Messianic Movements**.
1851–1940	Sir Oliver Lodge, physicist and writer. See **Psychical Research**.
1852	The Spiritualist Movement brought to Britain. See 1902 and **Spiritualism**.
1852–1917	Charles Taze Russell, founder of the **Jehovah's Witnesses**.
1854	The **Immaculate Conception** made an article of faith by Papal Bull.
1854–1918	S. L. MacGregor Mathers. He became leader of the **Hermetic Order of the Golden Dawn**.
1855	The **Pittsburgh Platform**. See **Judaism, Reform**.
1856–1939	Sigmund **Freud**, Austrian neurologist and psychoanalyst.
1857–1913	Ferdinand de Saussure. See **Semiotics**.
1858–1917	Emile **Durkheim**, French sociologist of religion.
1859	**Konkokyo**, Shinto sect, founded by Bunjiro Kawate.
1860s	The **Nihilistic Movement** in Russia.
1860–1904	Theodore Herzl, co-founder of the Zionist Movement with Leon Pinker. See **Zionism**.
1861–1925	Rudolph Steiner, founder of **Anthroposophy**.

DATE	EVENT
1861–1947	A. N. Whitehead, theologian and philosopher. See **Process Theology**.
1863	**Two-by-twos** founded by William Irvine.
1863–1919	Tokumitsu Kanada, founder of **Perfect Liberty Kyodan**.
1864–1929	Walter Richard Old, astrologer, known as 'Sepharial'. See **Talisman**.
1865–1927	**Sri Haranath**, Hindu mystic and teacher.
1865–1935	Rashid Rida. His journal influenced the founding of the **Muslim Brotherhood**. See **Islamic Modernism**.
1867–1948	E. W. Kenyon, founder of the **World-Faith Movement**.
1868	**Shintoism** adopted as the official State religion of Japan. See **Japanese Religion**.
1869–1937	Rudolph **Otto**, German protestant theologian. See **Numinous**.
1869–1948	Mahatma **Ghandi**.
1870–1935	Isaiah Shembe, founder of the **Natal Nazarite Church**.
1870–1924	Vladimir **Lenin**, Communist revolutionary leader.
1870	First Vatican Council establishes Papal infallibility. See **Conciliar Movement**.
1872–1950	Sri **Aurobindo** Ghose, Indian spiritual leader and philosopher.
1872–1970	Bertrand **Russell**, philosopher and mathematician. See **Logical Atomism**, **Logical Positivism**, **Wittgenstein**.
1873–1939	Wiremu Ratana, founder of the Maori **Ratana Church**.
1874–1952	Chaim Weizmann, President of the World Zionist Organization. See **Zionism**.
1875–1961	Carl Gustav **Jung**, psychiatrist and philosopher.
1875–1965	W. S. Sadler, psychiatrist. See **Urantia**.
1875	Theosophical Society founded by Helena Blavatsky and Col. Olcott. See **Theosophy**, **Spiritualism**.
1877–1945	Edward Cayce. See **Association for Research and Enlightenment**.
1878–1973	Mira Alfassa, the 'Mother', the companion of Sri **Aurobindo** Ghose and founder of the **Matrimandir**, the Auroville ashram.
1878–1965	Martin **Buber**, Jewish philosopher.

DATE	EVENT
1878	The **Salvation Army** founded by William Booth. The **Seventh Day Adventists** formed in Southampton.
1879–1940	Leon Trotsky. See **Trotskyism**.
1879–1950	Ramana **Maharshi**, Hindu mystic and teacher.
1879–1953	Joseph Stalin. See **Stalinism**.
1879	The Church of Christ the Scientist founded in Boston. See **Christian Scientists**. **Watchtower Bible and Tract Society** founded by C. T. Russell. See **Jehovah's Witnesses**.
1880–1965	Father Divine. See **Peace Mission Movement**.
1880s	The start of **Ghost Dance** religion. The beginnings of the **Cargo Cults**.
1881–1882	The Russian pogroms trigger political **Zionism**.
1881–1983	Mordecai Kaplan. See **Judaism, Reconstructionist**.
1881	**Indian Shaker Church** founded by John Slocum.
1882–1973	Jacques Maritain, proponent of **Christian Humanism**.
1882	The founding of the English Society of **Psychical Research**. See **Parapsychology**. Father McGivney founds the **Knights of Columbus** in the USA.
1884–1976	Rudolph **Bultmann**, German theologian. See **Demythology**.
1885–1971	Georges Lukacs, Hungarian Marxist philosopher. See **Marxism**.
1885–1977	Ernst Bloch, German Marxist philosopher and atheist theologian. See **Marxism**.
1886–1929	Franz Rosenzweig, philosopher and Jewish reformist. See **Judaism, Reform**.
1886–1965	Paul **Tillich**, German philosophical theologian.
1886–1968	Karl **Barth**, Swiss Protestant theologian. See **Crisis Theology, Neo-Orthodoxy**.
1886	William Saunders Crowdy's preaching leads to the establishment of the **Black Jews**.
1887	**Divine Science** founded by Nora Brooks and Fannie James. Founding of the **Hermetic Order of the Golden Dawn**.
1888	**Knights Hospitallers** revived.
1889–1951	Ludwig **Wittgenstein**, philosopher. See **Logical Atomism, Logical Positivism, Russell**.

DATE	EVENT
1889–1966	Emil Brunner, Protestant theologian. See **Neo-Orthodoxy**.
1889–1976	Martin **Heidegger**, philosopher of 'authentic living'.
1889	Declaration of Utrecht agrees the doctrinal basis of the **Old Catholics**. **Unity School of Christianity** founded by Charles and Myrtle Fillmore.
1890	The Massacre of Hunkpapa Indians at Wounded Knee. See **Ghost Dance**.
1891	Founding of the Baptist Union of Great Britain and Ireland. See **Baptists**.
1891–1943	Soe-tae San founder of **Won Buddhism**. See 1916.
1892–1971	Reinhold **Niebuhr**, Protestant theologian.
1892–1986	Herbert Armstrong, who established **Armstrongism**, or the World Wide Church of God.
1893–1952	Paramahansa **Yogananda**, Hindu mystic and teacher.
1893–1976	Mao Tse-Tung. See **Maoism**.
1894–1969	**Meher Baba**, Indian spiritual guru.
1895	The foundation of the **Church of the Nazarene** in Los Angeles.
1897–1975	Elijah **Muhammad**, founder and leader of the **Nation of Islam**. See **Black Muslims**.
1897–2000	Charles Hartshorne, philosopher. See **Process Theology**.
1897	The reunification of disparate groups of **Franciscans**, etc. The first Zionist Congress which founded the World Zionist Organization. See **Zionism**.
1899	**Gideons** International founded. The first group of Russian **Doukhobors** allowed to emigrate to Canada.
19th–20th century	The emergence of **Singh Sabha**, the Sikh reform movement. See **Sikhism**.
20th century	The beginnings of the **Liturgical Movement**.
1900–1989	Ayatollah Ruhollah Khomeini. See **Hidden Imam**.
1901–1987	Mohammad Subuh Sumohadiwidjojo, founder of **Subud**.
1901	American Revised Standard Version (RSV) of the **Bible**.

DATE	EVENT
1902	The founding of the Spiritualist National Union Ltd. See 1951 and **Spiritualism**.
1902–1975	Josemaria Escriva, founder of **Opus Dei**.
1902–1994	The Chief Rabbinate of Menachem Schneerson. See **Lubavitch**. Sir Karl **Popper**, philosopher of science, sociology and politics.
1903–1917	The period of **Bolshevism** in Russia.
1905	Baptist World Alliance founded. See **Baptists**.
1905–1980	Jean-Paul **Sartre**, French novelist, dramatist and existentialist philosopher. See **Existentialism**.
1906–1945	Dietrich **Bonhoeffer**, pastor and theologian of the German Confessional Church.
1908	**Tenry-Kyo** given government recognition in Japan. See **Japanese Religions**.
1908–1997	Dr Emanuel Bronner, founder of the **All-One-God Faith**.
1908–1970	Abraham M. Maslow, who developed Transpersonal Psychology. See **Human Potential Movement**.
1909	*The Fundamentals*, Christian tracts distributed in the USA. See **Fundamentalism**. Marinetti publishes *The Futurist Manifesto*. See **Futurism**.
1909–1965	William Branham. See **Branhamism, Holy Rollers**.
1910	International Missionary Conference, Edinburgh. See **Ecumenical Movement**.
1910–1930	**Modernism**, the formative European cultural movement.
1910–1989	A. J. **Ayer**, British atheist and philosopher of **logical positivism**.
1911	**Natal Nazarite Church** founded by Isaiah **Shembe**.
1912	The collapse of the Ch'ing dynasty in China and the demise of **Confucianism** as the State cult. See **Chinese Religions**. Founding of the Order of **Germanen**. Steiner founds the Anthroposophical Society. See **Anthroposophy**.
1914	**Iglesia Ni Cristo** founded by Felix Manalo.
1914–1918	First World War.
1916	**Won Buddhism** founded in South Korea by Soe-tae San.

DATE	EVENT
1917	The Balfour Declaration. See **Zionism**.
1917–1918	Date from which the **Liberal Catholic Church** existed independently.
1917–2003	Kenneth Hagin, a Pentecostal evangelist who developed the **World-Faith Movement**.
1918	**Ratana Church** founded by Wiremu Ratana. See **Maori**. **Native American Church** incorporated in the USA.
1919	The Fascist Movement formed by Mussolini in Italy. See **Fascism**. The massacre of Sikhs at the **Golden Temple** in Amritsar. The International League of Vigilantes formed. See **Mankind United**.
1919–1997	George King, founder of the **Aetherius Society**.
1920s and 1930s	**Gandhi's** *satyagraha*, the movement of non-violent disobedience. The founding of the **Moral Rearmament** movement by Frank Buchman, out of the Oxford Movement. The Vienna Circle of Philosophers. See **Logical Positivism**. **Local Church** founded by Ni To-Sheng (Watchman Nee) in China. See 1962.
1920	Paramahansa **Yogananda** founds the **Self-Realization Fellowship** in the USA.
1921–1990	Prabhat Ranjan **Sarkar**, Indian philosopher, social revolutionary, poet and linguist. See **Neo-Humanism**.
1921	Kimbangu founds **Kimbanguist Church**. **Legio Maria** founded in Dublin. A Church of England order of **Franciscans** is established at Cerne Abbey.
1922	Kemal Atatürk displaces the Ottoman Sultans. See **Caliph**. **Gurdjieff** founds the **Institute for the Harmonious Development of Man**. Founding of The Society for the Advancement of Judaism. See **Judaism, Reconstructionist**.
1922–1945	Mussolini prime minister of Italy. See **Fascism**.
1924–1981	Karmapa Rangjung Rigpe Dorje. See **Mahamudra**.
1924–1998	Jean-François **Lyotard**, French postmodernist philosopher.

DATE	EVENT
1924	End of Qajar Dynasty. See **Persia**. Stalin succeeds Lenin. See **Stalinism, Communism, Marxism, Leninism**.
1925–1965	**Malcolm X**, black nationalist leader.
1925–1979	The **Pahlavi** dynasty rules Iran. See **Pahlavi literature, Persia**.
1926	**Cao Dai** established in Vietnam. b. **Sai Baba**, founder of the SAI Organization.
1928	**Muslim Brotherhood** founded by Hassan al-Banna. **Opus Dei** founded by St Josemaria Escriva.
Late 1920s	The beginnings of the **Sacred Name Movement**.
1930s	The **Rastafari** movement emerges in Jamaica.
1930s–1940s	The Nazi Party rises to power in Germany See **National Socialism**.
1930	**Seicho No-Le** founded in Japan by Dr Masaharu Taniguchi. **Nation of Islam** founded by Wali Farad.
1930–1997	Anton Szandor Lavey, founder of San Francisco's **Church of Satan** and author of *The Satanic Bible*. See **Satanism**.
1930–2004	Jacques **Derrida**, French philosopher. See **Deconstructionism**.
1931	The founding of the **Association for Research and Enlightenment**.
1931–1990	**Bhagwan Shree Rajneesh**, founder of the **Osho-Rajneesh Movement**.
1932	Saudi Arabia constituted as a state. See **Wahhabis**.
1933–1945	The period of the **Holocaust**, the Nazi anti-**Semitic** extermination policy. See **National Socialism**.
1934	Arthur Bell publishes his *Mankind United*, to launch the cult.
1936	The **Divine Life Society** founded by Swami Sivananda Saraswati. **White Eagle Lodge** founded by Grace Cook.
1936–1938	The period of Stalin's intensive purges. See **Stalinism**.
1938	Rish'o Koseikai founded in Japan. See **Japanese Religions**.
1939	The founding of **Adidam** by Adi Da Samraj.
1939–1945	Second World War.
1941	Eli Siegel founds the **Aesthetic Realism Foundation**.

DATE	EVENT
1942	Maurice Glendenning founds the **Aaronic Order**.
1945	Shintoism disestablished as the State Religion of Japan. See **Japanese Religions**. Dietrich **Bonhoeffer** executed by the Nazis.
1946	The **Church of Set** founded by Michael Aquino Emperor Hirohito of Japan renounces his claim to divinity. See **Emperor Worship**. b. Claude Vorilhon. See **Raelianism**.
1947	**Shinreikyo** founded in Japan by Kanichi and Kunie Otsuka. The United Nations votes to partition **Palestine** to provide a homeland for the Jews. See **State of Israel** and 1948.
1947–1956	**Dead Sea Scrolls** discovered and excavated.
1947–1960s	**Latter Rain Movement**.
1948	The **State of Israel** constituted and its independence declared. See **Israel**. The **World Council of Churches** formed. See **Ecumenical Movement**. **Gandhi** assassinated.
1949	The establishment of the People's Republic of China. See **Chinese Religions**. d. George Gurdjieff.
1950s	The emergence of **Discordianism**. The beginnings of the **Counterculture** movement. The emergence of *Juche* in Korea.
1951	British Parliament passes the Fraudulent Mediums Act. See **Spiritualism**.
1953	**Pan African Orthodox Christian Church** founded by Albert Cleage. The **People's Temple** founded by Rev. Jim Jones. See 1978.
1954	L. Ron Hubbard founds the Church of **Scientology** in New Jersey, USA. The **Aetherius Society** founded by Sir George King.
1955	**Ananda Marga**, an Indian yoga and relief society, founded by Shri Anandamurti. The creation of the Latin American Episcopal Conference. See **Liberation Theology**.
1956	The Union of Evangelical Churches formed from the **Peculiar People** and other groups.
1958–1963	Pontificate of John XXIII. See **Papacy**.

DATE	EVENT
1959	Tibet invaded by China. See **Tibetan Buddhism** **Ecclesia Gnostica** founded in USA. **Kimbanguist Church** formally recognized in Zaire.
1960s	The emergence of **Asatru**, neo-Norse paganism **Alliance for Jewish Renewal** founded by Rabbi Schachter-Shalomi. The beginnings of the **Freak Scene**. Beginnings of the **Red Power Movement** in America. The Kingdom of God (Black Jewish community) founded in Chicago by Ben Ammi Carter. See **Black** **Jews**.
1960	The **Divine Life Mission** founded by Sri Hans Ji Maharaji.
1961–1970	The New English **Bible**.
1962–1965	2nd Vatican Council. See **Liberation Theology**.
1962	Witness Lee founds the Living Stream Ministry in the USA. See **Local Church**.
1963	**Maria Legio** founded by Ondeto and Aoko. Bishop John Robertson publishes *Honest to God*. See **Demythology**.
1964	Daisaku Ikeda establishes the Komeito party in Japan. See **Japanese Religions**, **Soka Gakkai**.
1965	The creation of the **Ananda Marga** Universal Relief Team.
1966	LaVey founds the **Church of Satan**. The Jerusalem **Bible** is published in English. The founding of **ISKCON**.
1966–1968	The Cultural Revolution in China. See **Maoism**.
1967	The 'Six Day War'. See **Holocaust**. The **Ibo** secede from Nigeria to form the State of Biafra. See 1970.
1968	**Ananda Church of Self-Realization** founded by Swami Kriyananda. Founding of the **Holy Order of MANS**. **Methodism** joins with the Evangelical Brethren to form the United Methodist Church.
1968–1972	Twice-yearly publication of *The Whole Earth* *Catalogue*. See **Counterculture**.
1969	Paul Shockley founds the **Aquarian Church of** **Universal Science** in the USA. **3H0** founded by Harbhajan Singh Puri.

DATE	EVENT
1970s	**Nation of Yahweh** founded by Hulon Mitchell. **Bhagwan Shree Rajneesh** introduces Rajneesh Meditation.
1970	The Nigerian civil war brings to an end the State of Biafra. See **Ibo**. **Sahaja Yoga** founded by Shri Mataji Nirmala Devi in Indian.
1971	**E.S.T.** founded in the USA by Wemer Erhard. **Divine Life Mission** taken to the USA by Prem Rawat. The start of the **Emin** association.
1972	**United Reformed Church** formed from the merger of the **Congregationalists** and **Presbyterians**. See **Ecumenical Movement**. Gustavo Gutiérrez publishes *A Theology of Liberation*. See **Liberation Theology**.
1974	**Life Spring** founded by John Hanley. **Vineyard Churches** founded by Gulliksen and Wimber.
1975	**Falashas** begin to emigrate to Israel from Ethiopia.
1976	**Fellowship of Isis** founded at Clonegal Castle.
1978	**Agon Shu Buddhism** established in Japan by Kiriyama Kancho. The mass suicide of members of the **People's Temple**.
1979	The Islamic revolution and establishment of the Republic of Iran. See **Persia, Shi'ism**.
1980	**Lion and Lamb Ministries** founded by Monte Judah.
1980s	**Harmonic Convergence** founded by Jose Arguelles The beginning of the demise of East European **Communism**.
1982	The founding of the **Suma Ching Hai** Association in Taiwan.
1984	**Order of the Solar Temple** founded in Geneva by Mambro and Jouret. Philip Berg founds his Los Angeles **Kabbalah** Centre.
1986	Asahara Shoko founds **Aum Shinri Kyo**, the Japanese doomsday sect.
1988	Founding of the **Gnostic Order of Christ**. The **First Preslyterian Church of Elvis the Divine** founded in Bethlehem, USA.
1990s	**Branch Dravidians** founded by David Koresh.
1990	**Promise Keepers** founded in Canada.

DATE	EVENT
1991	The fracturing of the Soviet 'Block'. See **Communism**.
1992	**Falun Gong** founded by Li Hongzhi.
1993	The **Ancient Mystic Order of Melchizedek** founded by Dwight York. **Chen Tao**, the **UFO cult**, founded by Hon-Ming Cheng in the USA.
1996	**Vodun** made the official religion of Benin. Osama bin Laden issues a *fatwa* against the USA.
1997	**Jesus Revolution Army** founded by Stephen and Anne Christiansen. The **Heaven's Gate** mass suicide.
1998	Osama bin Laden issues a second *fatwa* against the USA.
21st century	
2001	11th September attack on the World Trade Center, USA, believed to be in response to bin Laden's 1998 *fatwa*.
2002	James Hughes coins the phrase '**Democratic Transhumanism**'.
2004	Civil war in the Sudan. See **Shilluk**.
2012	The conclusion of the **Mayan** Calendar and the prophecy of the end of time. See **Maya Religion**.

Bibliography

The Canonical Biblical Scriptures
Tanakh, The Holy Scriptures (The Jewish Publication Society, Philadephia, PA, 1985)
The Jerusalem Bible, The Holy Scriptures in Hebrew and English (Koren Publishers, 1988)
The King James Version of the Bible (numerous publishers at numerous dates)
Holy Bible, Revised Standard Version (Holman Press Text Edition, Eyre and Spottiswoode, 1952)
The Greek New Testament, the text translated in the New English Bible (ed. R. V. G. Tasker; Oxford University Press and Cambridge University Press, 1964)
The New English Bible, Old Testament (Oxford University Press and Cambridge University Press, 1970)
The New English Bible, New Testament (Oxford University Press and Cambridge University Press, 1961)
The Non-canonical Scriptures
The New English Bible, The Apocrypha (Oxford University Press and Cambridge University Press, 1970)
The Gnostic Gospels (Alan Jacobs; Watkins, London, 2005)
The Gospel of Thomas (trans. Hugh McGregor Ross; Watkins, London, 2006)
Baha'i
Baha'ullah, *Tablets of Baha'ullah Revealed after the Kitab-i-Aqdas* (Baha'i Publishing Trust, Rutland, 1995)
Baha'ullah, *The Book of Certitude* (3rd edn; Baha'i Publishing Trust, Rutland, 1982)
Buddhist
The Dhammapada (trans. Thomas Byron, Shambhala Publications, Boston and London, 1994)
Buddhist Scriptures (trans. Edward Conze; Penguin, London, 1968)
Buddhist Texts Through the Ages (trans. Edward Conze; Horner, Snellgrove & Waley, Oneworld, Oxford, 1995)
In The Buddha's Words, An Anthology of Discourses from the Pali Canon (ed. Bhikkhu Bodhi; Wisdom Publications, Somerville, MA, 2005)
Confucian
The Analects of Confucius (trans. Raymond Dawson; Oxford University Press, 2000)
Hindu
The Bhagavad Gita (trans. Juan Mascaro; Penguin, London, 1962)
The Upanishads (trans. Juan Mascaro; Penguin, London, 1965)
Rig-Veda (ed. Wendy Doniger; Penguin, London, 1981)
Hindu Scriptures (ed. and trans. Dominic Goodall; Phoenix Press, Orion, London, 2005)
The Yoga Sutras of Patanjali (trans. Barbara Stoler Miller; Bantam Books, 1998)
Islamic
The Koran (trans. and introduced by Arthur J. Auberry; Oxford University Press, 1998)
The Koran (trans. N. J. Dawood; Penguin, London, 1966)
Jewish
The Talmud, Selections (trans. H. Polano; Shapiro Valentine & Co., London, Tamuz 5636)
Everyman's Talmud (ed. and trans. Abraham Cohen; Schocken, 1975)
Forms of Prayer for Jewish Worship (The Reform Synagogues of Great Britain, London, 1977)
Authorised Daily Prayer Book of the United Hebrew Congregation (Eyre and Spottiswoode, 1935)
The Kabbalah, The Essential Texts from the Zohar (trans. S. L. MacGregor Mathers; Watkins, London, 2005)
Sikh
Adi Granth or *Guru Granth Sahib* (Munshiram Manoharlal Publishers Pvt Ltd, New Delhi, 1978)

Taoist
Chuang Tzu, Basic Writings (trans. Burton Watson; Columbia University Press, 1996)
The Book of the Heart (Loy Ching-Yuen; trans. Trevor Carolan and Bella Chen; Shambhala, Boston and London, 1990)
Back to Beginnings, Reflections on the Tao (Huanchu Daoren; trans. Thomas Cleary; Shambhala, Boston and London, 1990)
Zoroastrian
Avesta: Visperad (trans. L. H. Mills; Kessinger Publishing, Whitefish, MT, 2004)
General
Abul-Fadl, Mona, *Introducing Islam from Within* (The Islamic Foundation, 1991)
Acaster, John, 'What is Freemasonry?' (Address given at the Cornerstone Society annual conference, 9 November 2002)
Adler, Alfred, *Understanding Human Nature* (Oneworld, London, 1992)
Allegro, John, *The Sacred Mushroom and the Cross* (Hodder and Stoughton, London, 1970)
Allen, John, *Opus Dei: The First Objective Look Behind the Myths and Reality of the Most Controversial Force in the Catholic Church* (Doubleday, 2005)
Altmann, Alexander, *Essays in Jewish Intellectual History* (Brandeis University Press, 1981)
Anselm, *Proslogian or Discourse on the Existence of God*, 1077–78 Williams Norris. Trans. (Hacket Publishing 1996)
Apple, Gersion, *A Philosophy of Mitzvoth* (Ktav, NJ, 1975)
Aristotle, *Nichomachean Ethics* (Penguin, London, 1963)
Armstrong, A. H., *The Architecture of the Intelligible Universe in the Philosophy of Plotinus* (Cambridge University Press, 1940)
Augustine, Bishop of Hippo, *A Treatise on Nature and Grace, Against Pelagius, 415 CE* in Selected Writings, Jones, T K [Ed] (Upper Room Books, 1997)
Aurelius, Marcus, *The Meditations* (Dover, 1997)
Aurobindo Ghose, Sri, *The Secret of the Veda* (Lotus Press, 1971)
Ayer, A. J. *Language, Truth and Logic* (Pelican, 1971)
Babb, L. A., *The Divine Hierarchy* (Columbia University Press, 1975)
Bainton, R. L., *Here I Stand: A Life of Martin Luther* (Mentor, 1950)
Balsekar, Sri Ramesh, *Experiencing the Teaching* (Advaita Press, 1998)
———, *The Ultimate Understanding* (Watkins, London, 2002)
Barth, Karl, *Church Dogmatics & The Epistle to the Romans* (T & T Clark, 1961)
Baudelaire, Charles, *The Mirror of Art, Critical Studies* (ed. and trans. Jonathan Mayne) (Phaidon, 1995)
Becker, R. de, *The Meaning of Dreams* (Allen & Unwin, 1968)
Bede, The Venerable, *Ecclesiastical History of the English People*, completed 731 CE (Penguin Books, 1990)
Bell, Shannon, *Reading, Writing and Rewriting the Prostitute Body* (Indiana University Press, 1994)
Bellows, H. A. *The Poetic Edda* (Dover, 2004)
Bentham, Jeremy, *Commonplace Book* in Works, vol. X (Clarendon Press, 1996)
Berdyaev, Nikolai, *The Meaning of History* (Obettsk, Berlin, 1923)
———, *Freedom and the Spirit* (NY, 1935)
Berger, Rabbi Dr, David, *The Rebbe, The Messiah and the Scandal of Orthodox Indifference* (The Littman Library of Jewish Civilization, Oxford, 2001)
Berger, Peter, *Heretical Imperative: Contemporary Possibilities of Religious Affirmation* (Doubleday, 1980)
———, *Other Side of God* (Anchor, 1981)
Berkeley, George, *An Essay Towards a New Theory of Vision* (Echo Library, 2005)
Berkovits, Eliezer, *Faith After the Holocaust* (Ktav, NJ, 1973)
Bierce, Ambrose, *The Devil's Dictionary* (Bloomsbury, London, 2003)
Black Elk Oglala, *Black Elk Speaks* (University of Nebraska Press, 2004)
Blake, William, *Auguries of Innocence* (Cygnet Press, 1975)

Bloch, Ernst, *The Principle of Hope* vols 1–3 (MIT Press, Cambridge, MA, 1986)

Blofeld, John, *The Book of Changes* (Allen Unwin, London, 1968)

Bonhoeffer, Dietrich, *Letters and Papers from Prison* (Fontana, 1960)

Braiterman, Zachary, *(God) After Auschwitz: Tradition and Change in post-Holocaust Jewish Thought* (Princeton University Press, 1998)

Brandt, Lanakila, quoted in M. J. Harden's *The Voices of Wisdom – The Elders Speak* (Aka Press, 1999)

Bright, John, *A History of Israel* (The Westminster Press, 1981)

Brittle, Gerald, *The Demonologist* (Berkley Books, 1980)

Brunner, Emil, *The Divine Imperative* (Lutterworth Press, Cambridge, 1961)

Buber, Martin, *Mamre, Essay on Religion* (Melbourne University Press, 1946)

———, *The Eclipse of God* (Harper & Row, 1957)

———, *I and Thou* (T & T Clark, 1959)

———, *The Knowledge of Man* (George Allen & Unwin, London, 1965)

———, *Tales of the Hasidim, Early Master* (Schocken, 1975)

Bultmann, Rudolph, *Theology of the New Testament* (English translations 1952 and 1955) (SCM Press, 1952)

Butler, E. M., *Ritual Magic* (Cambridge University Press, 1949)

Butler, Samuel, *Rebelliousness, Notebooks* (Jonathan Cape, London, 1951)

Buren, Van, Paul, *The Secular Meaning of the Gospel* (Penguin, London, 1968)

Byron, Robert, *The Byzantine Achievement* (Routledge & Kegan Paul, 1986)

Campbell, Joseph, and Moyers, Bill (eds), *Betty Flowers* (Doubleday, London, 1988)

Camus, Albert, *The Fall* (trans. Justin O'Brien; Penguin, London, 1958)

Cartledge, Paul, *The Greeks, A Portrait of Self and Others* (Oxford University Press, 1993)

Carus, Paul, and Suzuki, Teitaro (trans.), *Tai Shang Kan Yin P'ien* (Open Court Publishing, Chicago, 1906)

Cavendish, Richard, *The Black Arts* (Routledge, 1967)

Cerovac, Kresimir, 'Complementarity of Faith and Science' (a paper prepared for *Continuity + Change: Perspective on Science and Religion*, 3–7 June 2006, Philadelphia, PA, USA)

Chah, Ajahn, *Being Dharma* (Shambhala, Boston and London, 2001)

———, *A Still Forest Pool, The Insight Meditation of Ajahn Chah* (compiled by Jack Kornfield and Paul Breiter; Quest, Wheaton, Il, 2001)

Chesterton, G. K., *What's Wrong with the World* (Dodo Press, 2006)

Chogyam Trungpa, *Shambhala, The Sacred Path of the Warrior* (Shambhala, Boston and London, 1984)

———, *The Heart of the Buddha* (Shambhala, Boston and London, 1991)

Chomsky, Noam, in his Preface to *After Capitalism, Prout's Vision of a New World* (Dada Maheshvarananda, Proutist Universal Publications, 2003)

Churchill, Winston, *A History of the English-Speaking Peoples, 1: The Birth of Britain* (Cassell, 1974)

Clark, Peter, *Zoroastrianism, An Introduction to an Ancient Faith* (Sussex Academic Press, 1998)

Cohen, Israel, *The Zionist Movement* (Fredrick Muller, 1945)

Comte, Auguste, *Course of Positive Philosophy* (Londra, 1905)

Conzelmann, Hans, *History of Primitive Christianity* (DLT, 1973)

Cook, Grace, *Meditation* (University Printing House, 1965)

Cox, Harvey, *The Secular City* (SCM Press Ltd, 1966)

Cragg, Kenneth, *Man's Religious Quest, Course AD208 Units 20–21: Islam and the Muslim* (The Open University Press, 1978)

Creel, H.G., *Confucius, The Man and the Myth* (Routledge & Kegan Paul, 1951)

Crichton, Michael, 'Environmentalism as Religion' (a talk given to the Commonwealth Club, San Francisco, September 2003)

Cussans, John, 'Voodoo Terror: (Mis)representations of voodoo and western cultural anxieties' (a talk given at The October Gallery, London, 14 October 2000)

Dalai Lama, *Freedom in Exile* (Orbit, 1991)

Daniélou, Daniel, *Hindu Polytheism* (Routledge & Kegan Paul, London, 1964)

Day, Jennifer, *Creative Visualisation with Children* (Element Books, Shaftesbury, 1994)

Debo, Angie, *A History of the Indians of the United States* (Random House, 1995)

Dennett, Daniel, *Freedom Evolves* (Viking, London, 2003)

Descartes, Rene, *Discourse and Method* (Phoenix Press, 1994)

Diderot, Denis, in correspondence sparked by Voltaire's letter commenting on *Letter to the Blind*, quoted in Jim Herrick, *Against the Faith* (Glover and Blair, London, 1985)

Dodds, E. R. *The Bacchae* (Oxford University Press, 1960)

Dowson, John, *A Classical Dictionary of Hindu Mythology* (Routledge and Kegan Paul, London, 1986)

Dungen, van den, W; 'Words of Wisdom' in webpublications of www.sofiatopia.org (Antwerp, 2004, http://www.maat.sofiatopia.org/saa.htm)

Durkheim, Emile, *The Elementary Forms of the Religious Life* (trans. Joseph Swain; Free Press, 1965)

Einstein, Albert, *The World as I See It* (Filiquarian Publishing, 2006)

Eliade, Mircea, *Rites and Symbols of Initiation* (Harper Torchbooks, 1958)

———, *Yoga, Immortality and Freedom* (trans Willard D. Trask; Pantheon and Bollingen Foundation Inc., New York, 1958)

———, *Shamanism, Archaic techniques of Ecstasy* (Arkana, London, 1989)

Elst, Koenraad, *Bharatiya Janata Party, vis-à-vis 'Hindu Resurgence'*, (Voice of India, 1997)

Engels, Frederick, in his review of Thomas Carlyle's '*Past and Present*' 1843 (online version)

Evans-Pritchard, E. E., *Nuer Religion* (Clarendon Press, London, 1957)

———, *Theories of Primitive Religion* (Clarendon Press, London, 1965)

Fadhlalla Haeri, Sheikh, *The Journey of the Self* (Element Books, Shaftesbury, 1989)

Foucault, Michel, *The History of Sexuality* (Vintage, London, 1990)

Fox, George, *The Epistles of George Fox* (Kessinger Publishing, 2007)

Fraser, Sir James, *The Golden Bough* (Macmillan, 1959)

Freud, Sigmund, *Civilisation and its Discontents* (trans. James Strachey; W. W. Norton, NY, 1961)

———, *New Introductory Lectures on Psychoanalysis* (W. W. Norton, NY, 1965)

———, *The Future of an Illusion* (W. W. Norton, NY, 1989)

Friedman, Maurice, *Martin Buber, The Life of Dialogue* (University of Chicago Press, 1976)

Galbraith, J. K., *The Affluent Society* (Penguin, London, 1965)

Gandhi, M. K., *Harijan* (8 July, 1933)

———, *Hindu Dharma* (Narajivan Publishing House, Ahmedabad, 1950)

———, *The Story of My Experiments with Truth* (Penguin, 1983)

Ghose, Shri Aurobindo, *Letters on Yoga* (Sri Aurobindo Ashram, Pondicherry, India, 1979)

Gibb, H. A. R., *Islam* (Opus Books, 1969)

Gibran, Kahlil, *The Prophet* (Pan, 1980)

Gilbert, Adrian and Cotterell, Maurice, *The Mayan Prophecies* (Element, Shaftesbury, 1995)

Gimbutas, Marija, *The Gods and Goddesses of Old Europe, 7000–3500 BCE* (University of California Press, 1974)

Govinda, Anagarika Brahmacari, *Foundations of Tibetan Mysticism* (Rider, Allahabad, 1959)

Grant, Michael, *Myths of the Greeks and Romans* (Weidenfeld and Nicolson, London, 1962)

Graves, Robert, Joshua and Podro, *The Nazarene Gospel Restored* (Cassell, London, 1953)

———, *The Greek Myths* vols 1 & 2 (Pelican, London, 1955)

Green, V. H. H., *Luther and the Reformation* (New English Library, London, 1974)

Groves, C. P., *The Planting of Christianity in Africa* vol. IV 1914–1954 (Lutterworth Press, Cambridge, 1958)

Guiley, Rosemary Ellen, *The Encyclopedia of Witches and Witchcraft* (Facts On File, 1989)

Guillaume, Alfred, *Islam* (Penguin, London, 1983)

Habersetzer, Roland, *Tai Ji Quan* (Editions Amphora S. A., Paris, 1996)

Haeri, Sheik Fadhlalla, *The Journey of the Self* (Element, Shaftesbury, 1989)

Halifax, Joan, *Shamanic Voices* (Arkana, London, 1979)

Halpern, Ben, *The Idea of a Jewish State* (revd edn; Cambridge University Press, 1969)

Harnack, Adolf, *What is Christianity?* (Augsburg Fortress Press, Minneapolis, MN, 1987)

Hawking, Stephen, *A Brief History of Time* (Guild Publishing, 1990)

Hegel, G. W. F., *The Philosophy of Right* (Dover, NY, 2005)

———, *Introduction to the Philosophy of History* (trans. Leo Rauch; Hackett, Indianapolis, IN, 1988)

Heidegger, Martin, *An Introduction to Metaphysics* (Anchor Doubleday, 1961)

———, *Being and Time* (Harper Brothers, 1962)

Hein, Steven and Prebish, Charles (eds.), *Buddhism in the Modern World* (Oxford University Press, 2003)

Herodotus, *The Histories* (trans. Aubrey de Sélincourt; Penguin, London, 1954)

Hillerbrand, Hans J. *The Reformation in its Own Words* (SCM Press, London, 1964)

Hinnells, John, *The Zoroastrian Quest*, in *Man's Religious Quest* Units 26, 27, 28 (Open University, 1978)

Hobbes, Thomas, *Leviathan* (J. M. Dent, London, 1983)

Hoekendijk, Hands, Strasbourg, 1960, quoted in *Student World*, 'Secularisation' (World Student Christian Federation. vol. 1, no. 1, 1963)

Hoffman, Helmut, *The Religions of Tibet* (Allen & Unwin, 1961)

Holt, P. M, Lambton, A. and Beckingham C. F. (eds), *Cambridge History of Islam* (2 vols; Cambridge University Press, 1970)

Holton, D. C., *The National Faith of Japan* (Routledge, 1938)

Horowitz, George, *The Spirit of Jewish Law* (Central Book Company, 1973)

Hume, David, *On Miracles* (Thoemmes Press, 1996)

———, *The Natural History of Religion* (Oxford University Press, 1999)

———, *Enquiry Concerning Human Understanding* (Dover, NY, 2004)

Hutton, Ronald, *The Pagan Religions of the Ancient British Isles; Their Nature and Legacy* (Blackwell, 1991)

Huxley, Aldous, *The Perennial Philosophy* (Chatto & Windus, London, 1946)

———, *The Doors of Perception* (HarperCollins, 1977)

Huxley, T. H., *Science and Christian Tradition* (Macmillan, 1894)

———, *Collected Essays* (Macmillan, 1910)

Isaacs, Jennifer, *Australian Dreaming, 40,000 Years of Aboriginal History* (Lansdowne Press, 1980)

Jacobs, Alan (ed.), *The Wisdom of Balsekar* (Watkins, 2004)

James, E. O. *The Ancient Gods* (Castle, 2004)

James, William, *Pluralistic Universe* (Harvard University Press, 1977)

———, *Pragmatism* (Dover Publications, 1995)

———, *The Varieties of Religious Experiences* (Signet Classics, 2003)

Jones, Ernest, *The Life and Work of Sigmund Freud* (Penguin, London, 1974)

Jones, Gwyn, *A History of the Vikings* (Book Club Associates for Oxford University Press, 1963)

Josephus, *The Works of Flavius Josephus* (trans. William Whiston, ed. D. S. Margoliouth; Routledge, 1906)

Jung, C. G., *The Archetypes and the Collective Unconscious* (trans. R. F. C. Hull; Princeton University Press, 1969)

———, Foreword to Richard Wilhelm's translation of the *I Ching* (Arkana, London, 1989)

————, *Man and His Symbols* (Picador, Pan, 1978)

————, *Modern Man in Search of a Soul* (Kegan Paul, London, 1933)

————, *Psychology and Religion: West and East*, vol. 11 (Routledge and Kegan Paul, London, 1958)

————, *Psychology of the Unconscious* (Dover, 2003)

————, *Synchronicity* (Bollingen, 1973)

Kaltenmark, Max, *Lao Tzu and Taoism* (Stanford University Press, 1969)

Kant, Emmanuel, *Critique of Pure Reason* (trans. J. M. D. Meiklejohn; J. M. Dent, 1988)

————, *Groundwork of the Metaphysics of Morals* (Cambridge University Press, 1998)

————, *Prolegomena to Any Future Metaphysics* (trans. Carus, Paul; Hackett Publishing Co. 1987)

Kaplan, Mordecai, *The Meaning of God in Modern Jewish Religion* (Reconstructionist Press, 1962)

Kapleau, Philip Roshi, *The Three Pillars of Wisdom. Teaching Practice and Enlightenment* (John Weatherill Inc., 1965)

Kapleau, Philip Roshi, *The Three Pillars of Zen* (Anchor Doubleday, 1989)

Kaster, Joseph, *The Literature and Mythology of Ancient Egypt* (A. Lane, Penguin Press, 1970)

Katz, Steven T., *Post-Holocaust Dialogues, Critical Studies in Modern Jewish Thought* (New York University Press, 1983)

Kaufmann, Walter, *Religion in Four Dimensions* (Reader's Digest Press, 1976)

Keller, Helen, *Optimism* (Kessinger Publishing, 2003)

Keller, Werner, *The Bible as History* (trans. W. Neil; The Reprint Society, 1961)

Kempis, Thomas à, *The Imitation of Christ* (Penguin, London, 1952)

Kierkegaard, Soren, *Journals* (ed. and trans. Ronald Gregor Smith; Collins, 1965)

Köler, Ludwig, *Hebrew Man* (SCM Press, 1956)

Korbani, Agnes G., *The Political Dictionary of Modern Middle East* (University Press of America, 1995)

Kyososama, *Divine Teachings*, selected readings available on the Shinreikyo home page website

Lam Kam Chuen, Master, *The Way of Energy* (Simon and Schuster, 1991)

Lane Fox, Robin, *The Search for Alexander* (Little Brown & Co., 1980)

Lao-Tzu, *Tao-te Ching* (trans. Thomas Cleary; Shambhala, 1993)

Laqueur, Walter, *A History of Zionism* (Schocken, 1976)

Latourette, Kenneth Scott, *Christianity in a Revolutionary Age*, vol. III, *The Nineteenth Century Outside Europe. 1815–1914* (Eyre Spottiswoode, 1961)

Lawlor, Robert, *Sacred Geometry* (Thames and Hudson, 1982)

Lazzarato, Maurizio, 'From Biopower to Biopolitics', *Pli, The Warwick Journal of Philosophy* Vol. 13, 2002, pp. 99–113 (University of Warwick, 2006)

Leibniz, G. W., *The Monadology* (Prentice Hall, 1965)

Lenin, Vladimir, letter written 13 November, 1913 in V. I. Lenin, *Collected Works* (Progress Publishers, Moscow, 1978, vol. 35, p. 122. Online Version)

Léon-Portilla, Miguel, *Native Mesoamerican Spirituality* (trans. Léon-Portilla, J. O., Anderson, A., Dibble, C. E., Edmonson, M. S.; SPCK, 1980)

Levi, Eliphas, *Transcendental Magic* (Rider, 1986)

Lienhardt. R. G., *Divinity and Experience, The Religion of the Dinka* (Clarendon Press, Oxford, 1961)

Lindemans M. F., *Encyclopedia Mythica Online* www.pantheon-org

Ling, Trevor, *Buddha, Marx and God* (The Macmillan Press, 1979)

————, *A History of Religion East and West* (The Macmillan Press, 1982)

Linsky, Bernard, 'The Metaphysics of Logical Atomism', in Nicholas Griffin (ed.), *The Cambridge Companion to Bertrand Russell* (Cambridge University Press, 2003)

Lissner, Ivar, *The Living Past* (trans. Brownjohn, J. M.; The Reprint Society, 1961)

Lovelock, James, *Gaia: A New Look at Life on Earth* (3rd edn; Oxford University Press, 2000)

Loy, David, *Nonduality, A Study in Comparative Philosophy* (Yale University Press, 1988)
——, *Lack and Transcendence* (Humanities Press, New Jersey, 1996)
Lyotard, Jean-François, *The Postmodern Condition: A Report on Knowledge* (Manchester University Press, 1984)
——, *Presentations*, an essay in Alan Montefiore (ed.), *Philosophy in France Today* (Cambridge University Press, 1983)
Maccoby, Hyam, *The Myth Maker, Paul and the Invention of Christianity* (Weidenfeld and Nicolson, 1986)
Mansukhani, Gobind Sing, *The Quintessence of Sikhism* (Shiromani Gurdwara Parbhandak Committee, Amritsar, 1965)
Margulis, Lynn, *Symbiotic Planet : A New Look at Evolution* (Basic Books, 1998)
Maringer, Johannes, *The Gods of Prehistoric Man* (Phoenix Press, 1960)
Maritain, Jacques, *Introduction to Philosophy* (Sheed and Ward, 1956)
Marmur, Dow, *Beyond Survival, Reflections on the Future of Judaism* (Darton Longman & Todd, 1982)
Marriot, McKim, *Village India* (American Anthropological Association Memoir, no. 83. Menasha, Wisconsin, 1955)
Martin, David, *A Sociology of English Religion* (Heinemann, 1967)
Marx, Karl, *Contribution to the Critic of Hegel's Philosophy of Rite* (DeutschFranzösisch Jahrbücher, 1844; online version)
——, *The German Ideology* (written with Engels, 1845–46, Prometheus Books, 1998)
Mascaro, Juan, Translator, *The Bhagavad Gita* (Penguin, London, 1962)
Maslow, Abraham, 'A Theory of Human Motivation' (*Psychological Review* 50, 1943, pp. 370–96)
Maugham, W. Somerset, *A Trembling Leaf* (Macmillan ELT, 1992)
Mawdudi, Sayyid Abul A'la, *Let Us Be Muslims* (The Islamic Foundation, 1982)
Melville, Herman, *Moby Dick* (Wordsworth, 1992)
Merton, Thomas, *The Way of Chuang-tzu* (Shambhala, Boston and London, 1992)
Mona Abul-Fadl, *Introducing Islam from Within* (The Islamic Foundation, 1991)
Monk, Ray, *Bertrand Russell, 1921–1970, The Ghost of Madness* (Jonathan Cape, London, 2000)
Moule, C. F. D., *The Phenomenon of the New Testament* (SCM Press, 1967)
Muhibba, Hajja, in *Mary's Vineyard*, Harvey, Andrew and Hanut, Eryk (Quest Books, Wheaton, IL, 1996)
Muller, F. Max, *Biographies of Words and the Home of the Aryas* (Kessinger Publishing, 2004)
Murdoch, Iris, *Sartre, Romantic Rationalist* (Fontana/Collins, 1953)
Nakane, Chie, *Japanese Society* (University of California Press, 1970)
Nasr, Seyyed Hossein, *The Heart of Islam* (HarperCollins, NY, 2002)
Neville, Bernie, *Educating Psyche. Emotions, Imagination and the Unconscious in Learning* (Collins Dove, NY, 1992)
Niebuhr, Reinhold, *The Nature and Destiny of Man* (Nisbet & Co., 1946)
Nietzsche, Friedrich, *Thus Spoke Zarathustra* (trans. Hollingdale, R. J., Penguin, 1964)
——, *The Will to Power* (trans. Walter Kaufmann; Vintage, NY, 1968)
——, *The Gay Science* (Vintage, 1974)
——, *Beyond Good and Evil* (trans. Hollingdale; Penguin, 1988)
——, *The Antichrist* (Dover, NY, 2004)
Norbeck, Edward, *Changing Japan* (Holt, Rinehart and Winston, Case Studies in Cultural Anthropology, 1965)
Otto, Rudolph, *The Idea of the Holy* (Pelican, 1959)
Ouspensky, P. D., *In Search of the Miraculous: Fragments of an Unknown Teaching* (Harcourt, Brace & World, 1949)
Padmasambhava, *The Light of Wisdom* (Shambhala, Boston & London, 1995)
Padwick, Constance, *Muslim Devotions* (Oneworld, Oxford, 1996)

Paley, William, *Natural Theology: or, Evidences of the Existence and Attributes of the Deity, Collected from the Appearances of Nature*, 1802 (Oxford University Press, 2006)

Paramahansa Yogananda, *Autobiography of a Yogi* (Rider, 1994)

———, *Man's Eternal Quest* (Self-Realization Fellowship, LA, 2000)

Parrinder, Geoffrey, *Religion in Africa* (Penguin, London, 1969)

Pascal, Blaise, *Pensées* (Penguin, London, 1970)

Patanjali, *The Yoga Sutra* (trans. Muller, Barbara Stoler; Bantam Books, 1998)

Paton, H. J., *The Modern Predicament* (Muirhead Library of Philosophy, George Allen & Unwin, 1958)

Payne, Richard K., *The Tantric Ritual of Japan: Feeding the Gods – the Shingon Fire Ritual* (Aditya Prakashan, 1991)

Penn, William, *Some Fruits of Solitude* (Kessinger Publishing, 2004)

Peursen, van W. T., from the author's notes taken during a conference on Secularism at the Ecumenical Institute of Bosey, Switzerland, September 1959

Piggott, Stuart, *Prehistoric India* (Penguin, London, 1950)

Pinch, Geraldine, *Egyptian Myth, A Very Short Introduction* (Oxford University Press, 2004)

Pindar, *Odes* (trans. G. S. Conway; J. M. Dent, 1972)

Pope Jean-Paul II, *'The Church and the Scientific Communities: A Common Quest for Understanding* (1987)

Popkin, Richard and Avrum Stroll, *Philosophy Made Simple* (ed. Kelly, A. V.; Heinemann, 1982)

Popper, Sir Karl, *Objective Knowledge: An Evolutionary Approach* (Oxford University Press, 1972)

Proudhon, Pierre Joseph, *What is Property?* (Cambridge University Press, 1994)

Quimby, Phineas P., *The Complete Writings* (DeVorss and Company, 1988)

Radhakrishnan, S., *Eastern Religions and Western Thought* (Clarendon Press, Oxford, 1939)

———, *Indian Philosophy* (Muirhead Library of Philosophy, George Allen & Unwin, 1962)

Rael, Joseph E., *Beautiful Painted Arrow* (Element, Shaftesbury, 1992)

Raphael, Chaim, *The Springs of Jewish Life* (Chatto & Windus, The Hogarth Press, 1983)

Ratzinger, Cardinal Joseph (in 2006 he became Pope Benedict XVI), *Liberation Theology* (December 2004)

Renan, Ernest, quoted in Manfred Clauss, *The Roman Cult of Mithras, The God and his Mysteries* (Edinburgh University Press, 2000)

Renault, Mary, *The King Must Die* (Pantheon Books, NY, 1958)

———, *The Bull from the Sea* (Pantheon Books, NY, 1962)

Rinpoche, Sogyal, *The Tibetan Book of Living and Dying* (Rider, 1992)

Ritsema and Sabbadini, *The Original I Ching Oracle* (Watkins, 2005)

Robertson, Roland (ed.), *Sociology of Religion* (Penguin, London, 1969)

Robinson, J. A. T., *Honest to God* (SCM Press, 1963)

Robinson, J. M., *A New Quest for the Historical Jesus* (1959)

Robinson, Roland, *Wondjina, Children of the Dreamtime: Aboriginal Myths and Legends* (Jacaranda Press, 1968)

Roisman Joseph (ed.), *Brill's Companion to Alexander the Great* (Brill Academic Publishers, 2003)

Rose, H. J., *Ancient Roman Religion* (Hutchinson's University Library, 1948)

———, *A Handbook of Greek Mythology* (Methuen, 1985)

Rousseau, Jean-Jacques, *Emile or, On Education* (J. M. Dent, 1974)

Rubenstein, Richard, *After Auschwitz: Radical Theology and Contemporary Judaism* (Bobbs-Merrill, Indianapolis, 1966)

Rudgley, Richard, *The Encyclopaedia of Psychoactive Substances* (Little Brown and Co., 1998)

Rumi, Jalal al-Din, *Rumi, Selected Poems* (trans. Coleman Banks; Penguin, London, 1995)

Russell, Bertrand, *Our Knowledge of the External World as a Field for Scientific Method in Philosophy* (Open Court Publishing, Chicago and London, 1914)

————, *Logic and Knowledge: Essays 1901–1950* (ed. Robert C. Marsh; George Allen & Unwin, 1956)

————, *The Autobiography of Bertrand Russell* vol. III *1967–1969* (Allen & Unwin)

Russell, Charles Taze, *Thy Kingdom Come*, vol. 3. *Millennial Dawn* (copyright 1891, The Watch Tower Bible and Tract Society; 1904 edition)

Rutherford, Adam, *Pyramidology* (4 volumes released between 1957 and 1972; Harpenden)

Safid, Omid, *Newsletter* (International Institute for the Study of Islam in the Modern World, December 2003)

Sagan, Carl, *Pale Blue Dot* (Ballantine Books, 1997)

Santayana, George, Introduction to *Spinoza's Ethics* (Gregory, T. S.; J.M. Dent, 1955)

Sartre, Jean-Paul, *Existentialism and Humanism* (Methuen, 1974)

————, *Being and Nothingness* (Routledge, 1990)

Schmidt, Karl Ludwig, *The Place of the Gospels in the General History of Literature* (University of South Carolina Press, 2002)

Scholem, Gershom G., *Major Trends in Jewish Mysticism* (Schocken, NY, 1941)

Schonfield, Hugh, J., *The Passover Plot* (Hutchinson, 1966)

Schumacher, E. F., *A Guide for the Perplexed* (Abacus, Sphere Books, 1978)

Schwartz, Stephen, *The Two Faces of Islam: The House of Saud From Tradition to Terror* (Anchor, 2003)

Schweitzer, Albert, *The Quest of the Historical Jesus* (English trans. 1954; Adam and Charles Black, 1948)

Seckel, Al (ed.), *Bertrand Russell on God and Religion (Great Books in Philosophy)* (Prometheus Books, 1986)

Seltzer, Robert M., *Jewish People, Jewish Thought, The Jewish Experience in History* (Macmillan, 1980)

Shah, Idries, *The Way of the Sufi* (Arkana, 1990)

Shantideva, *A Guide to the Bodhisattva's Way of Life* (trans. Batchelor, Stephen; Library of Tibetan Works and Archives, Dharamsala, 1979)

Sharpe, Clifford, in the *New Statesman*, 3 and 17 March 1923

Shirer, William L., *The Rise and Fall of the Third Reich* (Secker and Warburg, 1959)

Singh, Sangat, *The Sikhs in History* (Uncommon Books, New Delhi, 2001)

Slater, Gilbert, *The Dravidian Element in Indian Culture* (Asian Educational Services, New Delhi, 1924)

Smith, Edwin W. (ed.), *African Ideas of God* (Edinburgh House Press, 1966)

Soloveitchik, Rabbi Joseph B., *Halakhic Man* (trans. Lawrence Kaplan; The Jewish Publication Society of America, Philadelphia, 1983)

Spencer, Herbert, *The Right to Ignore the State* (TMC Press, 1977)

Sri Sadhu Om, *The Path of Sri Ramana, Part 1* (Varkala, Kerala, 1981)

Steiner, Rudolph, *An Outline of Occult Science* (trans. Monges, Maud and Henry B.; Anthroposophic Press, 1910)

————, *Anthroposophy and the Inner Life* (also published as *Anthroposophy, an Introduction*; lectures from 1924 or 1925; Rudolf Steiner Press, 1994)

————, *Anthroposophical Leading Thoughts* (Rudolf Steiner Press, 1973)

Suzuki, D. T., *Essays in Zen Buddhism* (first series Grove Press, NY: 1961; second series NY: Weiser, 1970; third series NY: Weiser, 1970)

————, *Zen and Japanese Culture*, Bollingen Series LXIV, Pantheon Books, 1965.

Swedenborg, Emmanuel, *True Christian Religion* (Swedenborg Foundation, 1965)

Szandor Lavey, Anton, *The Most Powerful Religion* (*The Cloven Hoof* 127, 1931)

Szasz, Thomas, *The Myth of Psychotherapy* (Doubleday/Anchor Press, Garden City, 1978)

Thomson, Hunter S., *Fear and Loathing in Las Vegas* (Picador, Pan, 1971)

Tillich, Paul, 'Martin Buber and Christian Thought' (*Commentary* 5 & 6, June 1948)

Toynbee, Arnold, *A Study in History, 1934–1961* (Oxford University Press, 1948)

———, *War and Civilisation* (Oxford University Press, 1951)

Trilling, Lionel, *The Liberal Imagination* (Peregrine Books, London, 1970)

Trotsky, Leon, *Stalinism and Bolshevism* (New Park Publications, 1974)

Tucci, Giuseppe, *The Theory and Practice of Mandala* (trans. Alan Houghton Brodrick; Rider, 1961)

Twain, Mark, *Letters from the Earth* (HarperCollins, 2004)

Underhill, Evelyn, *Mysticism, The Nature and Development of Spiritual Consciousness* (Oneworld, Oxford, 1993)

Unterman, Alan, *Jews, Their Religious Beliefs and Practices* (Routledge & Kegan Paul, 1981)

Van Buren, Paul, *The Secular Meaning of the Gospel* (Penguin, London, 1968)

Voltaire, *Dictionnaire Philosophique* (Garnier Flammarion, Paris, 1964)

———, *A Treatise on Toleration* (Prometheus Books, NY, 1994)

Walker, Benjamin, *Hindu World: An Encyclopaedic Survey of Hinduism* (George Allen & Unwin, 1968)

———, *Sex and the Supernatural* (Macdonald, 1970)

Watson, Burton (trans), *Chuang-Tzu, Basic Writings* (Columbia University Press, NY, 1996)

Weber, Max, *The Protestant Ethic and the Spirit of Capitalism* (Dover Publications, 2003)

———, *The Sociology of Religion* (Methuen, 1965)

Weizmann, Chaim, *Trial and Error* (Hamish Hamilton, 1949)

Wheeler, Sir Mortimer, *Civilisations of The Indus Valley and Beyond* (Thames and Hudson, 1966)

Whitehead, Alfred North, *Process and Reality* (Free Press, 1979)

Wilde, Oscar, *The Critic as Artist, Critical Writings of Oscar Wilde* (ed. Ellman, Richard, University of Chicago Press, 1968)

Wilhelm, Hellmut, *The Book of Changes* (trans. Baynes, Cary F., Forward, Jung, C. G., Routledge, 1951)

———, *Change: Eight Lectures on the I Ching* (Routledge & Kegan Paul, 1975)

William of Tyre, *Historia rerum in partibus transmarinis gestarum*, XII, 7, *Patrologia Latina* 201 (trans. James Brundage as *The Crusades: A Documentary History*; Marquette University Press, Milwaukee, WI, 1962)

Williams, Joseph J. S. J., *From Voodoos and Obeahs: Phases of West India Witchcraft* (Dial Press, 1932)

Wilson, David, M. and Campbell-James, Graham, *The Viking World* (Ticknor & Fields, New Haven, CT and NY: Ticknor & Fields, 1980)

Wittgenstein, Ludwig, *On Certainty* (ed. Anscombe, G. E. M. and von Wright, G. H.; trans. Paul, Denis and Anscombe, G. E. M.; Blackwell, Oxford, 1975)

———, *Philosophical Investigations* (trans. G.E.M. Anscombe; Blackwell, Oxford, 1976)

Wong Kiew Kit, *The Art of Chi Kung* (Element, 1996)

———, *The Complete Book of Tai Chi Chuan* (Element, Shaftesbury, 1996)

Woodroffe, Sir J. G. (Arthur Avalon), *The Serpent Power* (Dover, NY, 1975)

Young, Arthur, *The Geometry of Meaning* (Wildwood House, London, 1977)

Ywahoo, Dhyani, *Voices of Our Ancestors* (Shambhala, Boston and London, 1987)

Zaehner, R. C., *Hinduism* (Oxford University Press, 1962)

———, (ed), *The Concise Encyclopaedia of Living Faiths* (Hutchinson, 1983)

———, *Hindu & Muslim Mysticism* (Oneworld, Oxford, 1994)